ENCYCLOPEDIA OF CHRISTIAN EDUCATION

ENCYCLOPEDIA OF CHRISTIAN EDUCATION

Edited by
George Thomas Kurian
and Mark A. Lamport

ROWMAN & LITTLEFIELD
Lanham • Boulder • New York • London

Published by Rowman & Littlefield
A wholly owned subsidary of The Rowman & Littlefield Publishing Group, Inc.
4501 Forbes Boulevard, Suite 200, Lanham, Maryland 20706
www.rowman.com

Unit A, Whitacre Mews, 26-34 Stannary Street, London SE11 4AB

British Library Cataloguing in Publication Information Available

Library of Congress Cataloging-in-Publication Data

Encyclopedia of Christian education / edited by George Thomas Kurian, Mark A. Lamport.
    pages cm
  Includes bibliographical references and index.
  ISBN 978-0-8108-8492-2 (cloth : alk. paper) — ISBN 978-0-8108-8493-9 (ebook)
  1. Christian education—Encyclopedias. I. Kurian, George Thomas, editor. II. Lamport,
Mark A., editor.
  BV1471.3.E53 2015
  268.03—dc23
                                                                2014021410

∞™ The paper used in this publication meets the minimum requirements of American
National Standard for Information Sciences—Permanence of Paper for Printed Library
Materials, ANSI/NISO Z39.48-1992.

Printed in the United States of America

Contents

S

Sabbatarianism as Christian Practice

Sabbatarianism is a movement that views the fourth commandment of the Decalogue as a perpetual moral law, not restricted to the ceremonial law of the Jews, but having originated in the creation account, having been practiced by Jesus in the Gospels, and therefore binding on Christians. Its distinguishing feature is setting aside an entire day each week to rest, with abstinence from secular employment and all activity that distracts from both private and public worship of God. Despite some ambiguity in the term sabbatarianism, according to John H. Primus (1989): "It has always had at its heart the issue of the appropriate *day* of worship." However, church history bears witness that it is possible to observe the Sabbath on either Saturday or Sunday and still be considered a sabbatarian.

Early History
Though some scholars conceive of sabbatarianism as a Puritan invention originating in 16th-century England, Kenneth L. Parker (1988) convincingly argues that it is impossible to separate Elizabethan sabbatarianism from its medieval origins. Leslie Hardinge (1995) meticulously documents how seventh-day Sabbath keeping can be dated back to the ancient Celts. Possibly one of the most influential first-day sabbatarian documents, "The Lord's Epistle on Sunday," was a sixth-century apocryphal letter of Christ. It fed medieval fears with portrayals of sulphurous fire, flying serpents, invading pagans, and ultimately the threat of eternal damnation for all who dared violate the sanctity of Sunday, often referred to as "The Lord's Day."

Such fantastical accounts bring into question the origin of such thinking. Sabbath keeping has been a constituent practice and teaching for Christians since the New Testament. Over time the church interpreted the scriptures regarding the Sabbath in a variety of ways. The church, during its first few centuries, interpreted the Sabbath allegorically as rest from sin. This gave way to an analogical explanation whereby Old Testament Sabbath laws were applied to the Christian Sunday. But it was the Scholastics, most eminently represented by Thomas Aquinas, who made the distinction between the moral and ceremonial parts of the Sabbath. Nearly all subsequent sabbatarian writers accepted this Thomistic distinction.

Sabbath interpretation became more nuanced with the magisterial reformers. Luther reacted strongly against the legalistic sabbatarianism of the medieval church and dismissed the Sabbath as a Jewish institution. Calvin, on the other hand, favored an analogical interpretation and defended Sunday as a legitimate Christian replacement for the Sabbath. It was Calvin's view that would win the day and later laid the foundation for a significant movement within the Reformed tradition: Puritanism.

The Puritan Legacy
Once English Christians in the 16th and 17th centuries rejected the Church's authority to interpret the Bible, the Decalogue acquired new meaning and took center stage. Coupled with the social changes of industrialization beginning in the 18th century, the fourth commandment came to be viewed as one significant solution for the need to regularize rhythms of work and rest. This was the Elizabethan era of Puritanism—a movement that distinguished itself from the Anglican Church by emphasizing implacable fidelity to scripture and inward sanctity. It was in this milieu that the Puritans developed the idea of a Sabbath Sunday with new thoroughness and precision, thus inculcating it with more importance than it previously held during the Reformation.

The sabbatarian fervency continued with the publication of numerous books and pamphlets, most notably Nicholas Bownde's *True Doctrine of the Sabbath*, the epitome of sabbatarian doctrine. At the beginning of the 19th century, the great sabbatarian crusades began, with sabbatarian organizations cropping up in both Great Britain and the United States. In the United States, the mission of these organizations included protecting Sunday from the running of trains, selling of merchandise, delivering of mail, and opening of public libraries, as well as a variety of other activities. Sabbatarianism was one of the leading topics of the day. However, as the American economy became more diversified, sabbatarianism as a movement eventually disappeared; the weight of the competing economy was too much to bear. This, along with an accretive culture of leisure in the United States, led to Sunday becoming more of a holiday than a holy day.

Existing Traditions

Though sabbatarianism has nearly disappeared across the American landscape, with the few remnant blue laws largely being disregarded, there are still sabbatarian expressions in the 21st century. The most prominent includes the Seventh-day Adventists, the Seventh Day Baptists, and the Church of God (Seventh Day). Of these, the Seventh-day Adventists are the most numerically significant seventh-day sabbatarians. With more than 17 million members worldwide (as of 2011), there are more Seventh-day Adventists observing the seventh-day Sabbath than there are Jews. As for first-day sabbatarians, they are few and far between and not particularly organized along denominational lines, except for some conservative denominations within the Baptist and Reformed traditions. Amid the recent array of texts on the Sabbath, individual authors may have specific affiliations but do not necessarily write as representatives of their particular denomination. For most Protestant Christians, as Alexis McCrossen posits, Sunday Sabbath has become a day for "a little church, a little revelry or sport, and some shopping."

Relevance to Christian Education

Why observe the Sabbath today? Considering the rapid global changes and increased loss of existential meaning, Sigve K. Tonstad (2009) notes that the Sabbath as an idea and practice speaks to a "missing zone of quietude and community, as time protected from commerce and commotion, and even time set apart for worship." More than just a day of worship distinguishing one religion or Christian denomination from another, the Sabbath embodies a portfolio of meaning and possesses pedagogical value for interreligious understanding, ecumenical con-

versation, psychological health, and physical well-being. In short, the biblical precedent of ceasing work and resting one day in seven, as exemplified by sabbatarians past and present, reminds us of our need for belonging, the necessity of rest, and most important, God's faithfulness and presence in our lives.

References and Resources

Hardinge, Leslie. 1995. *The Celtic Church in Britain*. Brushton, NY: TEACH Services, Inc.

McCrossen, Alexis. 2000. *Holy Day, Holiday: The American Sunday*. Ithaca, NY: Cornell University Press.

Parker, Kenneth L. 1988. *The English Sabbath: A Study of Doctrine and Discipline from the Reformation to the Civil War*. New York: Cambridge University Press.

Primus, John H. 1989. *Holy Time: Moderate Puritanism and the Sabbath*. Macon, GA: Mercer University Press.

Tonstad, Sigve K. 2009. *The Lost Meaning of the Seventh Day*. Berrien Springs, MI: Andrews University Press.

—ERIK C. CARTER

SABBATH AS CHRISTIAN PRACTICE

A good place to begin understanding the Sabbath is with the Gospels, where the ministry of Jesus is brought into direct encounter and conflict with the Sabbath observance of Israel. However, the coming of God's reign in Jesus Christ is preached as the "Day of the Messiah," which extends and moves beyond the Sabbath to the morning of the first day of the week. The Sabbath, however, is not negated but rather is reinterpreted and elevated in its Christological and messianic significance. It is the day, according to the biblical depiction, when creation was brought to completion. According to Genesis 2:2–3, the seventh day was blessed by God and God rested on that day from "all the work he had done" in creating. The Sabbath is a day of fulfillment in just this sense, when the goal of creation is made visible by God. For Israel, it is a day of covenant fulfillment, when people and relationships are made whole, when they enjoy rest in God and recover the harmony and good order of life in and with God and in relation to all other creatures. The Sabbath then merges for Christians into the Lord's Day, the Day of Resurrection and the new creation, and is immediately filled with the life and salvation incarnate in Christ.

One of the most instructive characteristics of the teaching of Genesis on the Sabbath is that God celebrates His delight in creative work with human creatures. The work of human beings is then set within and in relation to God's prior action; the completion of creation is found only within the movement of God's generous self-giving.

Although the man and woman created by God had done no prior work, God still shared His freedom, rest, delight, and enjoyment with them. The Old Testament traditions continue to understand Sabbath remembrance as primarily God's work. For Christians, moreover, the Sabbath is also an intimation of the incarnation and the central place of worship for God's people. While God indeed always rests in Himself, on the Sabbath God rests in time to share His rest with creatures, to give them time to delight and participate in the divine work. For this reason, the Sabbath commandment has serious implications for the other commandments, in that God is merciful to human creatures, so that the other commandments point back to the God who is for humanity and will be faithful to humanity. This means human creatures are not self-sufficient or able to complete their own lives; even creation is itself a work of grace.

The New Testament portrays the life of the church in relation to Jesus Christ in Sabbath terms. He is the One in whom believers find true rest, the fulfillment of the Sabbath, resting with Him and with the communion of saints. The Christian celebration of Easter remembers the covenant of grace and God's rest with creation in Genesis 2. The Sabbath command of the Decalogue, seen in light of Christ, is both a promise of Easter and a summons to a great and final Lord's Day, which will be an eternal Sabbath in communion with the Triune God. The Sabbath, then, is about time, particularly about the way God works in and through time and is not detached or removed from creation. The Sabbath also calls attention to the cosmic scope of salvation, in that the whole creation—things visible and invisible—has been embraced by God's love. At the same time, the Sabbath is directly linked to ordinary, everyday, concrete realities; the places, tasks, relationships and responsibilities of life are put into perspective as gifts of a gracious God and thus acts and offerings of praise and thanksgiving to God.

References and Resources

Danielou, Jean. 2002. *The Bible and the Liturgy*. Notre Dame, IN: University of Notre Dame Press.

Heschel, Abraham Joshua, and Susan Heschel. 2005. *The Sabbath*. New York: Farrar, Straus & Giroux.

Wirzba, Norman. 2002. *Living the Sabbath: Discovering the Rhythms of Rest and Delight*. Grand Rapids, MI: Brazos Press, 2002.

—Michael Pasquarello III

SABBATH SCHOOLS

Sabbath schools, or Sunday schools, are the direct forerunners of the modern public education system in English lands. Sunday schools also closely correlate to the Industrial Revolution in England, having developed as an attempt to alleviate many of the poor conditions found there among the working classes, especially children. Somewhat confusingly, Sunday schools are sometimes called "Sabbath schools" because not all faiths or denominations view Sunday as the Lord's Day.

Background

During the late 18th century, on the eve of the Industrial Revolution, there was a growing emphasis on more mass education. Since at least the Renaissance, children of the aristocracy had generally received decent educations, albeit to varying degrees. Similarly, the "bourgeois" class that had arisen during the years of capitalist development also generally had become educated. Still, on the eve of the Industrial Revolution, the vast majority of common children—in both the rural areas and the ever-growing urban slums—lacked decent primary education.

Historians generally agree that literacy was more widespread in Protestant countries than in Catholic ones, arguably due to the Protestant emphasis on scripture reading. Nevertheless, the overall access of young children to decent education and training was sorely lacking, on a mass scale.

Perhaps understandably, the growing concern about the education of children came first from religion. Methodism in particular is often equated with the 18th century's increasing concern with education of poor children, both in England and North America. The famous British historian E. P. Thompson emphasized this link between Methodism and the Sunday school movement in his still essential work *The Making of the English Working Class* (1963). Areas like Wales and Cornwall were heavily, predominantly Methodist. Methodism also flourished in the inner cities and in less affluent rural environments.

The Sunday school movement also corresponded to the use of child labor. Some concerned religious groups established charity schools, designed to teach basic literacy and some trade skills to working- and lower-class children. Perhaps ironically, many lower-class families relied on income from their children's labor on weekdays, making them hesitant to enroll their offspring in the charity schools. For this reason, schooling was often held on the Sabbath, the only day usually available for schooling. In the coming decades, "Sunday schools" spread throughout much of England, Scotland, Wales, and other lands of the British Empire. The movement also grew rapidly in North America.

Sunday school featured a wide variety of ages and levels of preparedness, making overly rigorous instruction practically impossible. Adults freely mingled with children. By the mid-19th century, many Sunday schools barely taught writing, as was revealed by the *Child Labor Inquiry* of 1842. Nonetheless, for many decades Sunday school was the primary exposure many working-class people in the English-speaking world had to education and literacy.

The Rise of Public Education in England

By 1850, probably more than a third of the English population was functionally illiterate. In 1870 Parliament passed The Education Reform Act, signaling the dawn of a new and more secular age in English education. In theory, the state extended sponsorship to parish and Sunday schools, but in truth the state had begun to assert its primacy over the education of children. In the coming years, secular, compulsory public education inexorably became the norm in England, as in much of the rest of the Western world.

During the mid-19th century, England began to ban child labor. The first of these laws—passed in 1833—only outlawed the hiring of children under the age of nine. Initially it was irregularly enforced, but subsequent legislation continued to reform the abuses of child labor. By 1870—when the Education Reform Act was passed—child labor had largely been reformed out of existence. Somewhat ironically, the banning of child labor created a need for children to be occupied during the long weekdays that were now free from work.

Sunday School after 1870

Despite having lost their important social roles to state-sponsored education, Sabbath/Sunday schools left their mark. The Christian urgency about aiding poor children in urban slums continued, perhaps best characterized by the efforts of William Booth (1829–1912), founder of The Salvation Army, especially his work in London's notorious East End.

Today, the habits of Sunday school continue to flourish in church communities across the English-speaking world. Often reserved for the hour just prior to weekly worship, its democratic approach, with lay teachers and students of all ages and backgrounds, continues to play a vital role in many Protestant denominations. However limited its efforts might be, Sunday school is the primary exposure many Protestant people have to Christian teachings, history, and scripture.

References and Resources

Checkland, S. G. 1985. *British Public Policy, 1776–1939*. Cambridge, UK: Cambridge University Press.

Mingay, G. E. 1986. *The Transformation of Britain, 1830–1939*. London, UK: Routledge & Kegan Paul.

Rule, John. 1986. *The Laboring Classes in Early Industrial England, 1750–1850*. London, UK: Longman.

Thompson, E. P. 1963. *The Making of the English Working Class*. New York: Vintage Books.

—David Walter Leinweber

SACRAMENTAL THEOLOGY

In a narrow sense, *sacramental theology* refers to sacred rites or actions called sacraments within certain Christian churches. Broadly speaking, sacramental theology can also refer to the way God is mediated in creation, particularly through visible or physical acts. In both instances the gift of Godself, which is the saving action of Christ, is given to humanity by way of grace. Sacraments are mediated encounters with God through Christ that are both personal and transformative through the work of the Holy Spirit.

Sacraments are signs that effect what they signify; namely, they convey the grace that is signified by each sacrament. They are visible acts that mediate Christ in the life of the church. In the Roman Catholic Church, the sacraments are signs of grace made possible by the work of Christ. These visible acts are entrusted to the church to be given to the church community. Catholics and Protestants differ about the role of faith in the reception of the sacrament. Catholics identify the faith of the church as preceding the faith of the believer. Protestants typically hold that sacraments must be received by faith. Across both traditions, however, there is the shared conviction that there must be a response of faith in order for sacraments to be transformative. What is considered a sacrament and the official number of sacraments has been a point of disagreement among Christians for centuries. Protestants only subscribe to two—baptism and communion—while Roman Catholics and those of the Eastern Orthodox faith list five more: confirmation, penance, holy orders, matrimony, and anointing of the sick.

Broadly, sacramental theology is a way of expressing God's saving activity in the world. The sacraments are the visible representation of God's self-communication to the world. Therefore the basic or fundamental sacrament is as Karl Rahner (1978, 412) states: "God's victorious offer of [Godself] to the world and to individuals." The sacrament is above all God's unique and transformative offer of Godself manifested in a physical and visible way to the world. According to Rahner (1978, 412), whenever God's offer "becomes manifest in the concrete in the life of the individual through the church which is the basic sacrament of salvation, we call this a Christian sacrament." Sacraments are communicated in the contemporary situation and remind believers of God's activity in the past and continued presence in the present and the future to come. Sacraments are not ways of compelling God to act; rather, they are recognition of God's free gift that has been given to humanity. Even the reception of the sacrament is made possible by God's redemptive power.

Sacraments are not things, but rather personal saving encounters of God through Jesus Christ. Edward Schillebeeckx (1963, 54) notes that "a sacrament is the saving action of Christ in the visible form of an ecclesial action." These visible rites remind believers that all of God's activity in the world is sacramental. What takes place in a sacrament, writes Schillebeeckx (1963, 62), "is the immediate encounter in mutual availability between the living *Kyrios* and ourselves." Michael Lawler (1987, 61) states that sacraments "inform believers that God is Creator, life-giver, source of every blessing, and invite them to believe and trust and hope and be grateful in a life patterned after the life of Jesus."

Sacraments are a form of symbolic communication that both reminds and transforms believers of God's continuing presence and activity in the world in cooperation with God's church. The sacraments are encounters with the living Christ that communicate Christ and the Kingdom of God on earth. The sacrament involves human action. Human action functions symbolically, and the Holy Spirit uses these actions to make Jesus Christ, according to Herbert Vorgrimler (1992, 71), "memorially, really, and actually present." Human action is essential in sacramental action, but human beings do not act alone. God works through the event and supports and strengthens the symbolic activity (Vorgrimler 1992, 71).

Sacraments are experienced by and take place in church communities. Brad Harper and Paul Metzger (2009, 123) suggest that "the sacraments are community events whereby we participate in God's story and God's family life." Veli-Matti Karkkainen (2002, 31) echoes the need for community in stating that for Roman Catholics, "sacraments are at the starting point of the church as a communion." Sacraments are best understood in the context of a community where relationships are built. The celebration of the sacraments allows for the possibility of sacramental worship where Christ's redemptive presence is celebrated and shared among the church community. Harper and Metzger (2009, 135) describe this as "a kind of community theater in which the church experiences the grace of God through reenacting the gospel drama in space and time." The sacraments shape communities and remind believers of God's continued eternal presence in the here and now. David Powers (1999, 147) states that "[s]acrament signifies and celebrates the presence of the divine and the presence of Word and Spirit in the daily wisdom of practical living and the common table." Sacraments are meant to be practical reminders of God's presence in ordinary life.

They are personal encounters of dialogue and communication between God and humanity. God's gift of love should invoke a human response. Chauvet (2001, 124) argues that sacraments require the "*return-gift* of faith, love, conversion, of heart, witness by one's life. . . . In other words, the 'validity' of the sacrament depends on God, its 'fecundity' depends on the believing subject." Sacraments are gifts that are meant to be used.

Implications for Christian Education

Sacramental theology has important implications for Christian education. As mediators of Christ, the sacraments affirm that God is actively involved in the daily practices of human activity. While not recognized as an official sacrament, education nonetheless should be sacramental in its outlook. Sacramental theology reminds educators that God is involved in the molding and shaping of Christians through the sacraments. In a similar way, Christian educators help to shape young men and women into the people God has called them to be. Educators share, teach, and remind students of God's activity in history, particularly God's redeeming action in Christ. Education is therefore a way of mediating and making present the free gift of Jesus Christ in the lives of students. In this way, Christian education shares with sacramental theology the goals of transforming individuals and building healthy Christian communities.

References and Resources

Catholic, C. 1997. *Catechism of the Catholic Church: Revised in Accordance with the Official Latin Text Promulgated by Pope John Paul II.* New York: Doubleday.

Chauvet, L. M. 2001. *The Sacraments: The Word of God at the Mercy of the Body.* Collegeville, MN: The Liturgical Press.

Harper, B., and P. L. Metzger. 2009. *Exploring Ecclesiology: An Evangelical and Ecumenical Introduction.* Grand Rapids, MI: Brazos Press.

Karkkainen, V. M. 2002. *An Introduction to Ecclesiology: Ecumenical, Historical & Global Perspectives.* Downers Grove, IL: InterVarsity Press.

Lawler, M. G. 1987. *Symbol and Sacrament: A Contemporary Sacramental Theology.* Mahwah, NJ: Paulist Press.

Powers, D. N. 1999. *The Sacraments: The Language of God's Giving.* New York: Crossroad Publishing.

Rahner, K. 1978. *Foundations of Christian Faith: An Introduction to the Idea of Christianity.* New York: The Seabury Press.

Schillebeeckx, E. 1963. *Christ the Sacrament of the Encounter with God.* Kansas City, MO: Sheed & Ward.

Schmemann, A. 1973. *For the Life of the World: Sacraments and Orthodoxy.* Crestwood, NY: St. Vladimir's Seminary Press.

Vorgrimler, H. 1992. *Sacramental Theology.* Collegeville, MN: The Liturgical Press.

—Jonathan L. Best

SACRAMENTS

What is the manner and degree of Christ's presence/absence in the sacraments? What is the relationship between sacramental grace and believers' responses of faith? How many sacraments should the church practice? Who is worthy to offer or receive the sacraments? These questions point to the need for Christian educators to be well-versed in the sacramental theologies and practices of their own traditions. This entry focuses instead on three possible relationships between or approaches to sacraments and Christian education.

Sacramental Participation *Is* Education

Historian Thomas Finn artfully suggests that the "theology of the church of antiquity was the result of symbols deeply lived."[1] This claim is supported through awareness of "anamnesis" and "prolepsis" in relation to liturgical action. *Anamnesis* is usually translated "remembrance" in English—as in Jesus's Eucharistic bidding: "Do this in remembrance of me"(1 Cor. 11:24). But it intends more active force than the English conveys. To do Jesus's *anamnesis* summons all His past saving actions into the present sacramental moment and seeks to bind worshippers into them. Similarly, characterizing sacraments as proleptic is to acquire through them a "foretaste" of God's realm, the future shalom made present. To participate in the sacraments is educative, therefore, because it incorporates worshippers into all of God's storied past, present, and future salvation.

Esteem for sacraments as educational in their own right is also finding renewed support in relation to theology, for anthropological and epistemological reasons. Sensing the church's long captivity to the rationalism, empiricism, and materialism born out of the Enlightenment and the consequent portrayals of human beings as disembodied "minds," Christian educational scholars are reemphasizing humanity's embodied, affective, storied, and even ritualizing nature. Hence sacramental participation gains credibility as education for inviting Christians to *perform* their identities by way of embodied language uniquely available through liturgical action, for enacting worshippers in God's *story* of salvation, or for the ways liturgy engages human affectivity and imagination to shape the *heart* in virtue.[2]

Sacramental Participation *Prompts* Education

In this approach, most commonly identified with catechesis, the emphasis is on sacraments as objects of study in relation to the life of the believer. Assisting people in reflecting on the implications of sacramentally enacted stories and theologies is one common educational means of faithful discipleship. To that end, catechetical instruction often utilizes action/reflection pedagogies to prepare people for sacramental participation and then to invite their reflections on their experiences. Beyond linking scripture and theology to sacraments and faith, educators may also facilitate learners' linkage of sacramental practice with justice-seeking practices of everyday life. Hence hunger sated at the Eucharist table propels believers outward to meet and fill the many hungers of the world.[3]

Sacramental Participation *Shapes* Education

Here, assumptions about epistemic and theological dimensions of sacramentality shape educators' curricular, pedagogic, and teaching practices, whether these practices are expressly oriented to the sacraments or not. Sacramentally related concerns about eliciting or cultivating persons in aesthetic capacities for surprise, wonder, creativity, playfulness, and dwelling in the mystery of paradox are primary in this approach. In addition, sacramentally shaped education invites learners to imaginatively tap into the surplus of meaning resounding within metaphor and ritual symbols such as water, bread, and wine. This form of education taps into human creativity to support engagement with a God who is at once immanent and transcendent.[4]

Obviously, Christian education shaped by sacramentality is not merely aesthetic, nor is that its end. Consistent with the sacraments themselves, it is fundamentally Christological. Its aesthetic bent, however, along with its openness to linking the spiritual with the material, and because it fosters associative and expansive modes of knowing, inclines it to see Christ's saving work broadly within the historical, material, and social practices of the world.

—FRED P. EDIE

1. Thomas Finn, *Early Christian Baptism and the Catechumenate: West and East Syria*, vol. 5 of *Message of the Fathers of the Church* (Collegeville, MN: The Liturgical Press, 1992), 5.

2. To explore these themes, see E. Byron Anderson, *Worship and Christian Identity: Practicing Ourselves* (Collegeville, MN: The Liturgical Press, 2003); Fred P. Edie, *Book, Bath, Table and Time: Christian Worship as Source and Resource for Youth Ministry* (Cleveland, OH: Pilgrim Press, 2007); Don Saliers, *The Soul in Paraphrase: Prayer and the Christian Affections* (New York: Seabury Press, 1980); and James K. A. Smith, *Desiring the Kingdom: Worship, Worldview, and Cultural Formation* (Grand Rapids, MI: Baker Academic, 2009).

3. Two examples of this approach are Thomas H. Morris, *The RCIA: Transforming the Church: A Resource for Pastoral Implementation* (New York: Paulist Press, 1997); and Bryan Hardesty-Crouch, ed., *Holy Things for Youth Ministry: 13 Practical Lessons* (Cleveland, OH: Pilgrim Press, 2010).

4. Examples of sacramentally shaped education are Maria Harris, *Teaching and the Religious Imagination: An Essay in the Theology of Teaching* (San Francisco: HarperSanFrancisco, 1991); Jerome Berryman, *Godly Play: A Way of Religious Education* (San Francisco: Harper, 1991); and Mary Elizabeth Moore, *Teaching as a Sacramental Act* (Cleveland, OH: Pilgrim Press, 2004).

SAINT JOHN'S BIBLE, THE

The Saint John's Bible is the first completely handwritten and illuminated Bible commissioned by a Benedictine abbey since the invention of the printing press.

At the end of 1990s, a document outlining the vision and values behind The Saint John's Bible was written. These goals and principles guided the artists and scholars involved and included the following principles of Christian engagement: (1) ignite imagination, (2) glorify God's word, (3) revive tradition, (4) discover history, (5) foster the arts, and (6) give voice to those who are now unprivileged.

These principles are embodied in a striking diversity of illuminations in the Bible, which include abstract renderings of color and movement alongside beautifully detailed pictures of flora and fauna native to the land in which the abbey is located (Minnesota). Several of the illuminations can be viewed online at The Saint John's Bible website (http://www.saintjohnsbible.org/see/).

Donald Jackson, senior scribe to Her Majesty Queen Elizabeth's Crown Office at the House of Lords, headed up a group of calligraphers in Monmouth, Wales, who collaborated directly with a team of theologians and scholars at Saint John's University in Collegeville, Minnesota, to produce the handwritten text and illuminations. Fr. Michael Patella, chair of the Committee on Illumination and the Text, has noted about the process: "The illuminations are not illustrations. They are spiritual meditations on a text. It is a very Benedictine approach to Scriptures."

The teams relied on both ancient and contemporary practices in their collaboration. The calligraphers used the ancient tools of vellum, hand-carved quills, and hand-mixed inks combined with computer mapping of the text to plan and write the pages. The scholars used the ancient form of *lectio divina* as well as other forms of scripture study to engage the texts, and then offered their insights to the calligraphers on possible illuminations, using e-mail and other digital media to communicate.

Gospels and Acts was the first volume of The Saint John's Bible to be written, completed in May 2002. Pentateuch was completed in August 2003, and the Book of Psalms in April 2004. Next to be completed was Prophets, in April 2005, and Wisdom Books in July 2006. Historical Books was completed in March 2010 and Letters and Revelation in May 2011. Binding into seven volumes will not take place for several years, thus allowing widespread exhibition of the pages to the public. The Bible in seven volumes will be large for liturgical and exhibition purposes (each page measures 15¾ inches wide by 23½ inches tall, making the book almost three feet wide when opened).

In addition to exhibiting various pages at art museums and galleries around the world, Saint John's University is making available a limited edition, full-size fine art reproduction known as "the Heritage edition," which has been purchased by a number of universities and other institutions. Smaller trade editions of each volume have been published and are available through The Liturgical Press.

Following the completion of the Bible, faculty and staff from the School of Theology and Seminary at Saint John's University, in collaboration with The Liturgical Press and The Saint John's Bible project, developed a practice of *visio divina*, which uses the illuminations from the Bible as the centerpiece of a form of praying with visual images. This practice is adapted from the sixth-century Benedictine practice of Bible reading, called *lectio divina*. The Seeing The Word project provides curriculum resources for all those engaged in scripture study, catechesis, and homiletics and for all other servants of the Word of God.

References and Resources

http://www.saintjohnsbible.org/news/faqs.htm
http://www.saintjohnsbible.org/
http://www.seeingtheword.org/
www.litpress.org

—MARY E. HESS

SALVATION

Salvation is one of the most central concepts in Christianity and in Christian education today. The term *salvation* in the New Testament is directly associated with the verb *save* and also with the noun *savior*. Salvation has been widely used in Christian theology to express the provision of God for salvation from sin, deliverance from God's wrath in the future, and incorporation into God's kingdom. In the New Testament the title "savior" is applied to both God and Jesus, in that God acted in Jesus to bring salvation.

When the Hebrew verb *save* is used in the Old Testament, it is an acknowledgment of the lordship and dominion of the one invoked for assistance in a situation of conflict or peril (2 Kings 6:26; 2 Sam. 14:40). Yahweh intervenes on behalf of Israel and brings divine victories over its foes (Exod. 15:2; Ps. 74:12). The Hebrew verb *save* is also used as a term for deliverance, assistance, and salvation in a future time (Isa. 49:8f.).

The New Testament takes over these basic meanings and applies them to the manner in which God acted in Jesus Christ. Matthew announces that the Messiah is to be called "Jesus" (literally "Yahweh is salvation" or "Yahweh saves/has saved") in Matthew 1:21 because "he will *save* his people from their sins." Throughout His life

Jesus states that He has come with a mission to sinful people (Matt. 9:10–13, 11:19). This coincides with the stated purpose of His death at the Lord's Supper, where He declares that His blood is to be poured out for the forgiveness of sins (Matt. 26:28). In Luke 13:23 Jesus is asked, "Lord, *will* only a few *be saved*?" Luke's understanding of salvation is summed up in 19:10, where the Son of Man's mission is to seek and save the lost. To be lost means to have a life apart from Jesus and ultimately death. To be saved means to possess life right from the moment when Jesus's teaching transforms a human being to the point of repentance. In the Gospel of John, salvation is associated with the mission of the Son of God. To be saved is the same as to gain eternal life and be delivered from judgment and condemnation. For example, John 3:16–17 reads, "For God so loved the world that he gave his only Son, so that everyone who believes in him may not perish but may have eternal life. . . . God did not send the Son into the world to condemn the world, but in order that the world might *be saved* through him" (see also John 12:47).

The apostle Paul uses the term *salvation*, the verb *save*, the noun *savior*, and other derivatives (*salvation* and *bringing salvation*) in a restrictive sense to describe what Christ has done in His great saving act for sinners. God acted in Christ to reconcile humanity with Himself: "For God has destined us not for wrath but for obtaining *salvation* through the Lord Jesus Christ" (1 Thess. 5:9). Paul develops this thought in his later letter to the Romans when he claims that sinners are God's enemies, but now they have been reconciled through the death of the Son and, having been reconciled, "*will be saved* in his life" (Rom. 5:9). For Paul salvation is a comprehensive term having past, present, and future aspects. Paul can say, "For in hope *we were saved*" (Rom. 8:24), meaning that salvation is something already accomplished when someone receives the Spirit and becomes adopted as a child of God at the initial point of conversion (Rom. 8:15). At the same time, Paul can speak of an ongoing saving activity. This is a progressive salvation, otherwise called sanctification. "For the message about the cross is foolishness to those who are perishing, but to us *who are being saved* it is the power of God" (1 Cor. 1:18). Salvation for Paul is primarily a future occurrence as well. In Paul's earliest written letter in the New Testament, he states, "But since we belong to the day, let us be sober and put on the breastplate of faith and love, and for a helmet the hope of *salvation*. For God has destined us not for wrath but for obtaining *salvation* through our Lord Jesus Christ" (1 Thess. 5:8–9). In this passage, salvation refers to the Last Judgment and the Christian's deliverance from the wrath of God (see also Rom. 5:9; 1 Cor. 3:15, 5:5; cf. 1 Thess. 1:10).

References and Resources

Foerster, W., and G. Fohrer. 1971. "Save, Salvation, Saviour." In *Theological Dictionary of the New Testament*, edited by Gerhard Kittel, VII:965–1024. Grand Rapids, MI. Eerdmans.

Green, E. M. B. 1965. *The Meaning of Salvation*. London: Hodder and Stoughton.

Marshall, I. H., L. Morris, and P. W. Barnett. 2004. "Salvation I: Gospels, Salvation II: Paul, Salvation III: Acts, Hebrews, General Epistles, Revelation." In *The IVP Dictionary of the New Testament*, edited by Daniel G. Reid, 998–1010. Downers Grove, IL: InterVarsity Press.

O'Collins, Gerald G. 1992. "Salvation." In *The Anchor Bible Dictionary*, edited by D. N. Freedman, V:907–914. New York: Doubleday.

Reumann, J. 2003. "Save, Salvation, Savior, Deliver, Deliverance, Deliverer, Rescue." In *The Westminster Theological Workbook of the Bible*, edited by Donald E. Gowan, 449–455. Louisville, KY: Westminster John Knox Press.

—JOHN A. BERTONE

SANCTIFICATION

The Old and New Testaments make clear that humanity is called to be holy, to reflect fully the character of God. In the Old Testament, God commands, "You shall be holy to me; for I the Lord am holy, and I have separated you from the other people to be mine" (Lev. 20:26). Paul picks up this theme in the New Testament: "Since we have these promises, beloved, let us cleanse ourselves from every defilement of body and of spirit, making holiness perfect in the fear of God" (2 Cor. 7:1). Jesus describes holiness as an outward conformity of action to the will and character of God, as well as an inward alignment of the heart (Matt. 5:22–48), summarized in the two greatest commandments: to love God with all one's heart, soul, mind, and strength and to love one's neighbor as oneself (Mark 12:28–31).

However, humanity exists under the guilt, power, and nature of sin, unable to fulfill God's call to holiness. Because humanity has broken God's commandments personally and corporately, we carry sin's guilt: alienated from God, unable to enter the presence of a holy God, and justly standing under divine condemnation (Col. 1:21; John 16:8; Rom. 6:23). Humanity is also under the power of sin, a slave to it. Even when they desire freedom from it, people are unable to walk in ultimate obedience to God (Rom. 7:14–25). Finally, because of Adam and Eve's sin in the Garden, humanity is born in a state of depravity with a sinful nature, a perpetual "bent" toward rebellion, disobedience, and selfishness (Mark 7:21–23; Gal. 5:17). Holiness is contrary to the natural orientation of the human heart.

Therefore, if holiness is to be a human possibility, only God's grace can bring it about. Sanctification is the process by which God addresses the problem of sin and makes humanity holy. The Christian experience of sanctification in this life begins in three intimately connected divine acts: justification, whereby Christians are forgiven their sins and the righteousness of Christ is imputed to them (Rom. 3:24; 1 Cor. 1:30; Heb. 13:12); adoption, through which they are reconciled to God and become the children of God, joint heirs with Christ to the Kingdom of God (Rom. 8:15–17); and regeneration, whereby the Holy Spirit imparts the righteousness of God to them and begins to make them actually holy (Rom. 6:18; Titus 3:5). Justification and adoption resolve the problem of sin's guilt, while regeneration blunts the power and nature of sin in humanity.

After the experience of regeneration, the Holy Spirit carries on the work of sanctification by transforming humanity's attitudes, interests, and actions over time to bring greater conformity to the likeness of Christ and ultimate holiness (Eph. 4:21–24). As a part of progressive sanctification, the Spirit continues to weaken the power of sin inwardly and deliver humanity increasingly from the nature of sin, enabling Christians to love God more fully with their entire being and their neighbors as themselves (Rom. 8:1–8; Gal. 5:17–23; 1 John 2:1–4). Finally, in death the Spirit completes whatever is left in sanctification and through glorification gives humanity holiness in incorruptible fullness (Rom. 8:28–30; 1 John 3:1–3).

Although there are differences among Christian denominations and theological traditions in their understandings of sanctification, centering on the degree to which humanity can be sanctified in this life and the level of responsible participation God expects in the process of sanctification, all believe that sanctification brings about real change in Christians. Some views reflect great optimism in God's grace; Wesleyans believe the Spirit can perfect Christians in this life by freeing them from the power and nature of sin, and Keswicks teach that Christians can be liberated from sin's power, if not its nature. Other perspectives reflect more pessimism; Calvinists believe humanity can never be completely free from the power and nature of sin, but only make increased strides in overcoming them. Still, similarities exist: all agree that sanctification requires and empowers Christians to reflect God's holy love in their personal lives and that the Bible promises success through the power of the Spirit in the struggle against sin.

Christian education plays an intimate role in the experience of sanctification. First, it is responsible for teaching Christians across generations about the divine call to, content of, and means to holiness. Second, it plays a major role in spiritual formation, introducing believers to the means of grace and Christian practices the Spirit uses to transform people into the likeness of Christ, and demonstrating how to incorporate these disciplines into life. Finally, it provides different opportunities to practice these disciplines that lead to the holy life.

References and Resources

Alexander, Donald, ed. 1989. *Christian Spirituality: Five Views of Sanctification.* Downers Grove, IL: InterVarsity Press.

Dieter, Melvin, et al. 1987. *Five Views on Sanctification.* Grand Rapids, MI: Zondervan.

Oswalt, John. 1999. *Called to Be Holy.* Nappanee, IN: Evangel Publishing House.

Willard, Dallas. 1998. *The Divine Conspiracy: Rediscovering Our Hidden Life in God.* San Francisco: HarperCollins.

—CHRISTOPHER T. BOUNDS

SANCTIFICATION AND LEARNING

Sanctification is God's will for us (1 Thess. 4:3). It is a progressive and unending task of integration toward holiness and assimilation into the life of Christ. In the economy of salvation, it follows conversion to and acceptance of the Gospel. It occurs subsequent to the initial, "entry steps" of Christian faith—conviction of sin, repentance, election, and justification—being an application of these as shown in the changes brought about in us by our obedient attachment to Christ and in response to the empowering guidance of the Holy Spirit. Sanctification brings us to spiritual maturity (Eph. 3:16) and gives us the power to become children of God (John 1:12); it is being indwelt by the Spirit (1 Cor. 6:19), who makes us "partakers of the divine nature" (2 Pet. 1:4). It is displayed in a life marked by faith, hope, and love and in which there is ever more profound openness to God's will.

Sanctification comes from directing our minds toward God. However, it is more than a goal, fruit, or destination of a spiritual life; it is also the route, the path to be followed. Unless sanctification is already under way, we will have no taste for, will not even recognize, God's will and ways. Thus we need sanctification if learning of the divine is to be possible; at the same time we need to learn about the processes, elements, and pathways of sanctification in order to follow them and allow ourselves to be transformed by them. Here illumination and perfection are integrally connected and mutually conditioning; spiritual learning and perception are dependent on living a God-shaped, Christ-informed, Spirit-empowered, and moral life. Such a life depends on some degree of knowledge and appreciation of the nature and implications of God's offer of salvation in Christ. There is a recurring cycle of spiritual learning and spiritual growth in sanctification; only the pure in heart can see God. The knowledge of

God is simultaneously the beginning, in the midst of, and the end of sanctification. God provides the initial prompt, without which we could not get started. His ways lay down the path, with God's Son the pattern of virtue and the antidote for vice, and God's Spirit supplies the power for the journey of transformation. Full communion with God is the ultimate goal. Augustine's personal journey of salvation, as described in his *Confessions*, is an extended example of how sanctification and learning are linked.

Sanctifying knowledge, knowledge that is salvific, transforms us by the way that it challenges, purifies, heals, frees, and elevates us; all of this is God's work in us (Phil. 2:12–13) through guidance, discipline, protection, encouragement, consolation, forgiveness, and loving presence. It is linked, on our side, to humility, obedience, fidelity, repentance, prayer, and moral living, and it issues in the fruit of the Spirit: love, joy, peace, patience, kindness, goodness, faith, gentleness, and self-control (Gal. 5:22–3). In the relation between sanctification and learning, there is a beneficial interaction among growth in virtues, the development of understanding, and the movement (always incomplete) toward holiness. Participation in the divine light and willing acceptance of the divine life go together.

For Christian educators, a focus on sanctification is a reminder that a primary aim should be formation in holiness. This will entail, for all disciples, dying to sin; that is, letting go corrosive bad habits, misdirected emotions, areas of brokenness, self-destructive obsessions, and the temptation to set up idols. In this way, sanctification will release and enhance our capacity for spiritual perception. It should also lead to caring for creation, loving neighbors, and responding in gratitude to God by living generously and with deepening spiritual discernment and wisdom about the will and ways of God. In the holistic learning that accompanies sanctification, teachers in churches and seminaries, and those working in Christian schools, colleges, and universities, should ensure that the following verbs are engaged by disciples and students: listen, pay attention, be prepared to learn, commit to memory, put into practice, think about, seek understanding, question, decide, evaluate, reflect on, pray. The learning that should accompany sanctification needs to be cognitive, affective, and active. In their concern for understanding, Christian educators facilitate thinking like a Christian; in their concern for valuing, they make possible experiencing life as a Christian; in their concern for performance, they foster living and serving in a Christian manner.

References and Resources

Augustine. 1962 *Confessions*. Translated by R. S. Pine-Coffin. Harmondsworth, UK: Penguin.

Castelo, Daniel, ed. 2012. *Holiness as a Liberal Art*. Eugene, OR: Pickwick.

Healy, Mary, and Robin Parry. 2007. *The Bible and Epistemology*. Milton Keynes, UK: Paternoster.

Orsuto, Donna. 2006. *Holiness*. London & New York: Continuum.

Parrett, Gary A., and S. Steve Kang. 2009 *Teaching the Faith, Forming the Faithful*. Downers Grove, IL: IVP Academic.

—JOHN SULLIVAN

SAYERS, DOROTHY L.

Dorothy Leigh Sayers was an English author perhaps best known for her highly regarded Lord Peter Wimsey detective novels, but she was also an accomplished scholar and Christian lay theologian. As an influential though reluctant spokesperson for the Christian church, Sayers used her skills as a creative writer to clarify the orthodox creedal teachings of the faith. In so doing, she underscored the importance of God as maker and the way in which all of creation, including humanity, reflects this attribute. As a High Church Anglican, she held a sacramental view of life. Key concepts in her religious writings include the essential relationship of faith and intellect as well as the critical importance of understanding Christian doctrine. Her 12 radio dramas on the life of Christ—*The Man Born to Be King*—and her translation of Dante's *The Divine Comedy* were both significant literary and theological achievements.

Early Background and Education

Born 13 June 1893 in Oxford, England, Sayers spent the majority of her early years in the fen country of Cambridgeshire, where her father was an Anglican rector. An only child, Sayers was raised in an artistically creative and intellectually stimulating home. Her education began at an early age with her mother's instruction in reading and her father's teaching of Latin. She continued to be taught at home, eventually with the tutelage of a governess, until age 15, when she enrolled at Godolphin School in Salisbury, England. From there Sayers earned a scholarship to Somerville College, Oxford University, where she graduated in 1915 with first-class honors in modern languages. At the time, women were not eligible for a formal degree from Oxford University. Five years later, Oxford passed a statute that officially received women into membership, and on 14 October 1920, Sayers was in the historic first group of women who received their bachelor's and master's degrees from the university.

Significant Contributions to Christian Education

Always a strong proponent of the value of a liberal arts education, Dorothy Sayers's most significant contribution remains her 1947 lecture "The Lost Tools of Learning," given to the faculty and students of an Oxford University summer course. Sayers voiced her concern that education was failing in its true object: to prepare individuals to develop the skills to enable them to think critically and thereby acquire trained habits of the mind that apply successfully to the requirements of daily life. Her solution to this scholastic failure was to suggest a return to the medieval method of education, in which a pupil spent his or her early years learning the three subjects known as the *trivium* (grammar, logic, and rhetoric), which would later be used as "tools" to master and analyze subsequent subjects. In the medieval system, the four content subjects to be learned (arithmetic, geometry, music, and astronomy) were known as the *quadrivium*. Today, the classical education curriculum has greatly broadened beyond these original four, but the approach remains the same: having acquired the ability to understand language (read and write with comprehension); having developed the skill to apply logic with discernment; and having learned how to argue effectively, both verbally and in writing, the pupil is now prepared to employ these tools in the study and mastery of other subjects. Thus, Sayers considered that education was only successful when it taught students *how to teach themselves*.

As she firmly believed:

> For the tools of learning are the same, in any and every subject; and the person who knows how to use them will, at any age, get the mastery of a new subject in half the time and with a quarter of the effort expended by the person who has not the tools at his command. To learn six subjects without remembering how they were learnt does nothing to ease the approach to a seventh; to have learnt and remembered the art of learning makes the approach to every subject an open door.[5]

For those who are interested in the practical application of Sayers's theory, Douglas Wilson's *Recovering the Lost Tools of Learning* (1991) describes his successful efforts using these principles in his Logos School, which has become a model for the classical Christian education movement in the United States.

Most Notable Publications

Sayers, Dorothy L. 1941. *The Mind of the Maker*. London: Metheun.

———. 1947. *Creed or Chaos?* London: Metheun.

———. 1963. "The Lost Tools of Learning." In *The Poetry of Search and the Poetry of Statement*. 23–48. London: Victor Gollancz.

—MARJORIE LAMP MEAD

---

5. Dorothy L. Sayers, "The Lost Tools of Learning," in *The Poetry of Search and the Poetry of Statement* (London: Victor Gollancz Ltd., 1963), 174.

SCANDINAVIA AND CHRISTIAN EDUCATION

Scandinavian countries have a reputation for being high among the most secular countries in the world, yet they seem to be among the best countries in which to live. They place near the top of the Human Development Index and have high life expectancy, low child mortality and crime rates, gender equity, and some of the best health care on the planet, available to all citizens (Lejon 2011). Scandinavian countries have low scores on most measurements of religiosity, and most Scandinavians simply do not care much about religion. Americans have a tendency to exaggerate their religiosity, while Europeans tend to underestimate theirs.

One of Sweden's most respected morning newspapers, *Svenska Dagbladet* (2010), ran a series on the theme that religion is back in Sweden. Scandinavians seem to be rediscovering their theological language. Scandinavian conversations about spirituality and Christian faith have become more open. There also seems to have been an increase between 1994 and 2007 in Scandinavians' curiosity about Christianity and its belief system (Lejon 2011). This shift is a significant opportunity and challenge to those committed to Christian education in Scandinavian countries.

Though a majority of Scandinavians deny most of the traditional teachings of Christianity, they call themselves Christian and are content to remain within the traditional national churches (branches of Lutheranism). Scandinavians resist the label "atheists." Many have been baptized, confirmed, or married in a church. Yet they either decline or are hesitant to talk about religion. Phil Zuckerman, in *Society without God*, uses phrases such as "benign indifference" and "utter obliviousness" to define the relationship Scandinavians have with religion. There is a sense of unconscious incompetence when it comes to Christian education. Scandinavians seem unaware of what it is they do not know about Christianity and unconcerned with what they do know. They appeared to be entertained by the novelty of Zuckerman's questions during his interviews. Conversations about God and religion are rare and not part of mainstream intraction. After more than a year living among Scandinavians, Zuckerman concluded that religion wasn't really so much a private, personal issue as a nonissue. According to Zuckerman, the word "God" was one of the most embarrassing words a Scandinavian could say (Steinfels 2009). Among Zuckerman's interview subjects was a 68-year-old Scandinavian man who stated, "We are Lutherans in our souls—I'm an atheist, but still have the Lutheran perceptions of many: to help your neighbor. Yeah. It's an old, good, moral thought" (Zuckerman 2008). This statement typifies the Scandinavians' relationship with religion in general and Christian education in particular. They may embrace and see value in morals it affords, but they seem to disregard the moral giver.

On the other hand, in her 2009 dissertation "I'm a Believer—but I'll Be Damned if I'm Religious," Ina Rose discusses the fact that how religiosity is defined will skew the statistics about the Scandinavian people. Using her definition of "unpacked" religion, she found that two-thirds of Danes claim to be believers (Lejon 2011).

Although Zuckerman's research into the apparent prosperity of a society without religion sheds some vicarious light on the Scandinavian attitudes and practices regarding Christian education, his work is weak in historical context. For example, although he states that the secular countries of Sweden and Demark were among the first nations to push for widespread literacy, he fails to link this to the historical, religious educational efforts of Lutheranism! In fact, most of the characteristics associated with the Scandinavian welfare state can be traced back to Scandinavia's Lutheran roots (Lejon 2011).

Scandinavian culture and history are connected with religion, and Scandinavia has a strong Lutheran ethos that has informed societal norms and values. In fact, religious education is a part of the core curriculum in public education in Sweden, Norway, Denmark, and Finland. However, religious education as taught in the public school system is irreligious, or perhaps transreligious. One of the principal aims of these courses is to teach the pupils to approach religion in a transreligious and secular way (Jensen 2008). As recently as 2009, the Swedish National Agency for Higher Education required that state-supported schools favor religious studies over theological education. The nuance may seem slight, but the ramification is that if the shift is not accommodated, accreditation is threatened (Hansen 2009). In Scandinavian public religious education, spirituality and spiritual intelligence is becoming a more acceptable focus than subjective theological interpretations (Sagberg 2008).

References and Resources

"Guds aterkomst" newspaper [The return of god], in *Svenska Dagbladet*, February 23–25, 2010 and March 2–4, 2010.

Hansen, Collin. 2009. "Seminaries in Peril: Government Evaluation Threatens Training of Swedish Pastors." *Christianity Today*. Accessed, March 1, 2013. http://www.christianity today.com/ct/2009/julyweb-only/130-11.0.html

Lejon, Kjell and Marcus Agnafors. 2011. "Less Religion, Better Society? On Religion, Secularity, and Prosperity in Scandinavia." *Dialog: A Journal of Theology*. Vol 50, No. 3, 297–307.

Sagberg, Sturla. 2008. "Children's Spirituality with Particular Reference to a Norwegian Context: Some Hermeneutical Reflections." *International Journal of Children's Spirituality*. Vol. 13, No. 4, 355–370.

Zuckerman, Phil. 2008. *Society without God: What the Least Religious Nations Can Tell Us about Contentment*. New York: New York University Press.

—LARRY H. LINDQUIST

SCHMEMANN, ALEXANDER

Alexander Schmemann (1921–1983), an émigré from Estonia who grew up in Paris and moved to the United States, was an Orthodox protopresbyter, leader in the Orthodox Church in America, and dean of St. Vladimir's Orthodox Theological Seminary from 1962 to 1983. He gave direction to Orthodox education and also influenced other branches of Christianity through his writings on liturgy, especially the sacraments. In his many writings and lectures, he showed how worship redefines reality, and in particular critiques secular society. As an educator, he taught the Orthodox about their tradition and the West about Orthodoxy.

Biography

His family was one of many that left Russia after the 1917 revolution. The Russian enclave in Paris maintained separate schools, and young Alexander (or Sasha, as his friends knew him) went first to a Russian military school in Versailles, then to a Russian *gimnazii* (high school). He continued his education by studying at a French lycée, then at the University of Paris. From his teenage years, he also became drawn to the Orthodox Church. He served first as an altar boy and then as a subdeacon.

From 1940 to 1945, during the Nazi occupation of France, Schmemann studied at the Theological Institute of St. Sergius in Paris. He was influenced by Georges Florovsky, who taught historical theology, and Nicholas Afanassiev, whose ideas on sacraments and ecclesiology he incorporated into his own thinking. Schmemann eventually obtained his doctorate from St. Sergius in 1959.

In 1943, at age 22, he married Juliana Ossorguine, who came from a church-oriented Russian family. She was studying classics at the Sorbonne. After the couple moved to the United States, she became headmistress of the Spence School in New York City. They had three children: Serge, who became a Moscow correspondent for the *New York Times*; Anne, a *matushka* (literally, "little mother," or wife of an Orthodox priest) and homemaker; and Mary (Masha), who was active in women's ministry and education in the Orthodox Church of America.

In the United States, Schmemann immediately joined the faculty of St. Vladimir's and soon became widely recognized as a leading authority on liturgical theology. A number of institutions invited him to speak and teach, including Columbia University, New York University, and Union Theological Seminary in New York. In 1962, he accepted the post of dean of St. Vladimir's, which he held until his death in 1983.

Significant Contributions to Christian Education

Schmemann's writings showed how the church's liturgy offered a vision of reality that critiqued modern secular thinking. His approach can be seen, for example, in his discussions of chrismation, the service of anointing conjoined to Orthodox baptism. He explained how this anointing restores people to their true vocation as prophets, priests, and kings. The prophet is able to relate what is human and temporal to what is divine and eternal. This prophetic ability is undervalued by modern educational approaches that strive to know the world apart from God. Nonprophetic knowledge is called "objective" and seen as superior, but in fact, says Schmemann, this objective knowledge and its techniques have not prevented Western civilization from becoming "one all-embracing crisis—social, political, ecological, energetic, etc." Purporting to liberate us, this knowledge has led instead to feelings of enslavement and loneliness. A "horrible feeling of a total vacuum permeates the very air we breathe and cannot be dispelled by the superficial euphoria of our 'consumerist society.'" Prophetic knowledge, by contrast, holds together physical and spiritual dimensions. The prophet is distinguished not by being esoteric, but by a "sobriety" that seeks to understand "reality in its totality."[6] The preceding example illustrates a procedure Schmemann often followed: introduce a Christian term, show how it critiques a secular worldview, then explain the term in a way that also critiques popular Christian understandings.

Schmemann was among the first and most compelling voices to point out how consumerism and individualism have affected the church in the 20th century. He proposed that the physical world should be seen not just as the raw material for producing commodities, but also as a means of communion with God—starting with the physical element of water in baptism.

Overall, Schmemann urged the church to provide more Christian education to help people understand the meaning and power of its worship, so that worship could in turn teach people how to think and live. Faith and theology, he contended, should grow out of worship, and worship should grow into everyday patterns of living.

Most Notable Publications

Schmemann, Alexander. 1965. *Sacraments and Orthodoxy.* New York: Herder & Herder.

——. 1966. *The World as Sacrament.* London: Darton, Longman & Todd.

———. 1973. *For the Life of the World: Sacraments and Orthodoxy.* Crestwood, NY: St. Vladimir's Seminary Press.

———. 1974. *Of Water and the Spirit: A Liturgical Study of Baptism.* Crestwood, NY: St. Vladimir's Seminary Press.

———. 1979. *Church, World, Mission: Reflections on Orthodoxy in the West.* Crestwood, NY: St. Vladimir's Seminary Press.

—RUSSELL HAITCH

SCHOLASTICISM AND THE HUMANIST RESPONSE

In the High Middle Ages (c. 1000–1300), "Scholasticism" represented the apex of medieval thought. It tried to synthesize Christian truths with the approaches and insights of the classical philosophers and scientists gaining influence at the time, especially Aristotle. Scholasticism evolved from years of controversy and division about the relationship among reason, faith, and knowledge. In the mid-13th century it produced its most definitive genius, the towering figure of St. Thomas Aquinas, and the philosophy sometimes called Thomism. Though a figure more equated with literature than with systematic philosophy or theology, the Florentine writer Dante can also be considered a kind of Scholastic, since his outlook and his attempt to unify knowledge and faith reflect impulses similar to those of the Scholastics.

During the Renaissance, Scholasticism was subjected to much criticism from the humanist movement originating in Italy. To the humanists of the Renaissance, Scholastic learning seemed impractical. It appeared ill-suited to the educational needs of a dynamic and increasingly wealthy society. At worst, it fostered insular, remote, and largely irrelevant debates among the relatively few "Schoolmen" who represented Scholastic thinking in the great universities. Nonetheless, the significance of Scholastic learning is hard to overemphasize. The great debates from which Scholastics like Aquinas emerged reflect issues that remain central in both academic as well as spiritual life. For its part, the humanist criticism of Scholasticism also embodies some of the key issues in the purpose of education, past and present.

Together, Scholasticism and humanism reflect some of the most important tensions in the long history of Western education. Though the underlying assumptions and the vocabulary that accompanies them have obviously changed over the past several centuries, the great issues that Scholasticism and humanism raised have remained crucial considerations for students of the history of education and of the philosophy of education.

The High Middle Ages

The High Middle Ages are usually said to have begun around 1000—with the convenient, easy-to-remember

---

6. Alexander Schmemann, *Of Water and the Spirit* (Crestwood, NY: St. Vladimir's Seminary Press, 1974), 101–102.

"new millennium" date of AD 1000 separating the later medieval centuries from the "Dark Ages" of the early period. Between 1000 and 1300, Europe emerged from its unsettled period of tribal migrations and political chaos. What developed in its wake was a medieval Europe that ranks as one of the world's great civilizations.

The High Middle Ages saw the development and maturation of some of medieval society's most iconic achievements. This was the period that saw the rise of Gothic architecture, for example. The Gothic buildings of this period still rank among the world's most famous and recognizable structures. Cathedrals rightly rank alongside Greek temples, Roman amphitheaters, Egyptian pyramids, and Sumerian ziggurats as some of the world's most splendid specimens of architectural prowess. Politically, the High Middle Ages saw the stabilization of countries and the beginnings of ethnic and linguistic consolidation of the various European peoples. By 1000, several major states had finally emerged: England, France, and the Holy Roman Empire of Central Europe. They provided a relatively stabilized geopolitical situation in many areas of Western Europe. Similarly, the papacy by 1000 had emerged as the most important international office in Western Europe, making the Catholic Church a vital component of medieval society. The church gave a Latin overlay to all of Occidental Christendom, as well as a coherent international administration. Ecclesiastical and linguistic ties in the Catholic West connected medieval people across many diverse regions and vernacular languages.

The Medieval Universities

While the growth of large governments and a church no doubt created as many problems as they solved, they also aided the rise of increasingly wealthy and sophisticated institutions that supported education. Chief among these were the great universities that arose in Western Europe during the High Middle Ages—especially the University of Bologna in Italy, as well as the University of Paris in France and Oxford University in England. Developing from the cathedral schools of earlier medieval centuries, universities provided some of the most focused support for intellectual life that had existed since the classical period. Today, virtually all Western universities are patterned more or less along the lines of these mother schools. Traditional academic offices and titles such as deans, provosts, and chancellors all harken back to the medieval institutions of higher learning. The universities also provided a livelihood for the quarrelsome faculties, who earned their tenure-like status in an apprentice system patterned after chartered guilds.

The rise of Scholasticism in the 12th and 13th centuries is inextricably interwoven with this larger context of the growth and development of the medieval universities. This is true for several reasons. First of all, having grown out of both the monastic tradition and the cathedral schools, universities reflected a common base of Christian assumptions and culture. Education was the domain of the church, and all scholars within the universities were actually some type of priest. Indeed, it was out of this priestly capacity of university education that the image of the "robed professions" emerged. This common base of Christian teaching and purpose gave university scholarship a singular focus. Whether the focus was theology, law, or medicine—the main areas of advanced university study—all forms of learning needed to harmonize with the larger truths of the Christian faith.

Modern academia is arguably more comfortable with "loose ends" than medieval scholars would have been. Today, verified facts can be accepted as such, without having to meet the impossible requirement that they also correspond to some larger, universal framework of belief. In medieval scholarship, each minute detail of any given system was some small part of a microcosm that mirrored some larger macrocosm. God had created everything. It was considered essential that each specific detail fit into the larger framework of belief in a divine order of things.

Not only did the need to harmonize Christian beliefs with all knowledge exist generally as part of the generally Catholic Christian culture of medieval Europe, but it was also enforced by the formal policies and expectations of the university governing structure. In the most extreme cases, theses or studies that undermined faith or decreed truths could be labeled heresy, a crime punishable by death. This meant that it behooved each and every medieval scholar to relate his particular areas of focus to the big picture, as determined by ecclesiastical authorities or established Christian scholarship. This impulse to make each and every detail fit smoothly into a larger framework lent Scholastic learning its massive, compendium-like quality. All the particular pieces needed to be considered and cataloged, but they also needed to relate clearly to the larger framework of the medieval worldview.

Another reason that the university system helped foster Scholasticism is that it generally adhered to a common core curriculum. This meant that medieval scholars all studied a relatively connected body of knowledge. While proponents of a core body of knowledge still exist in education today, it arguably seems that the modern university has predicated itself more on specialization and niche areas of expertise, a trend that became especially powerful during the late 19th century. In the Middle Ages, the famous seven liberal arts drove the university curriculum. Broken into two distinct units, the *trivium* and the *quadrivium*, these core branches of knowledge formed the basis of virtually all medieval learning. The *trivium* somewhat foreshadowed modern undergraduate education, featuring the three primary disciplines of grammar, rhetoric, and logic. The *quadrivium*, for more advanced students, included arithmetic, astronomy, geometry, and music.

The seven liberal arts collectively manifested a very solid education. The *trivium* and the *quadrivium* were highly complementary, with the *quadrivium* building on the foundation taught in the *trivium*. In particular, the *trivium* ensured a general level of literacy, both in terms of reading and writing, particularly in Latin, the language of instruction. The texts and commentaries studied as part of the *trivium* also provided general familiarity with history and classic literature—or at least what passed for those things in the Middle Ages. The *quadrivium* featured applied, specific branches of learning: arithmetic, astronomy, geometry, and music. Faculty each taught from within one of their designated specialty disciplines, but students generally were expected to demonstrate competency in all the major areas. Advanced degrees—something comparable to graduate degrees, enabling students to become teachers themselves—were given in one of three areas: theology, law, or medicine. But even given these professional degrees, the seven liberal arts at their base provided a kind of comprehensive education.

All the forms of knowledge had to harmonize with one another. All forms of knowledge had to support what medieval people believed to be God's truth as revealed in the Bible or in church teachings and traditions. In this sense, all forms of medieval learning were, in effect, a branch of theology. Even doctors and lawyers studied their specific disciplines from within the assumptions of theology, which was the ultimate discipline and focus of each and every university intellectual endeavor. All learning pointed to God, being predicated on Christian and Roman Catholic truths. This meant that all intellectual activity—no matter how ostensibly secular or technical by today's standards—was subject to theological scrutiny. The Scholastic controversies of the 13th and 14th centuries derived from this notion that all learning should ultimately fall under the larger macro rubric of theological training. Theology was the queen of the sciences.

The universities also benefited from having Latin as the lingua franca of Western European learning. Study of the *trivium*, in particular, guaranteed proficiency in the ancient tongue, now in its medieval phases. Lectures were given in Latin, an important point since nothing like the modern textbook or campus bookstore existed in the days of calligraphy and illuminated manuscripts. In many cases, students paid tuition for the privilege of hearing a professor read to them from books.

The Latin tongue had created a sense of a shared intellectual community that was truly vast in geographical scope. Latin already connected disparate churches all over Western Europe—from Ireland and Iceland and Scandinavia down to Sicily and Malta. Common prayers, liturgies, and texts unified Christians all over the Catholic Occident. In education, Latin proved equally utilitarian. While important vernacular works appeared throughout the Middle Ages, with increasing frequency by the Renaissance and the Reformation, Latin would remain the essential language of virtually all Western scholarship until well into the 17th century. When important works in a vernacular did appear, their translations into other vernaculars were generally unavailable. Even famous vernacular authors such as Chaucer or Dante were largely products of their regional settings. While this gave such works their powerful local charm, personality, and human insight, it also limited their audience.

Western Europe's common Latin enabled the great debates and fissures of the Scholastic scholars. It created a common linguistic infrastructure in which debates (and even quarrels) could flourish. Since the fifth century, even the Bible—originally written in Hebrew and Greek—had had an officially sanctified version in Latin, the Vulgate. By the High Middle Ages, other types of writings also flourished in Latin. This common linguistic framework made possible the precision in language and reasoning that the best scholarship always entails. Scholastic writings and debates frequently featured excruciatingly careful discussions of terminology and the underlying assumptions of words and phrases. Scholasticism therefore benefited from the common linguistic framework of medieval universities, which not only fostered intellectual communication across a more widespread area in the mundane sense, but also provided a common base of language that could be assumed of all Western scholars.

In short, something like "academia" existed in Western Christendom. A relatively common purpose, curriculum, and language connected the universities of Western Europe. Faculty ranks and procedures were recognized collectively in the various schools. Scholars could move from one institution to another, with the larger patterns of academic and intellectual life uniting faculty across countries and regions.

The Importance of Plato and Aristotle

In this medieval "academia," Scholasticism developed from the great debates that inevitably occur in virtually any vibrant university setting. Especially important in this regard was the medieval Christian relationship to pagan, classical philosophy, especially the writings of Plato (427–347 BC) and Aristotle (384–322 BC). Indeed, the Scholastic debates—which took place in medieval settings far removed in time and place from the ancient Athenian settings of Plato's academy or Aristotle's lyceum—show exactly why the philosophical schools of the fourth century BC have proven to be so central to Western thought, in all periods.

For most of the Middle Ages, the writings of Aristotle were forgotten. Some of this was no doubt due to the natural passage of time. But it was also because orthodox Christians had found the writings of Aristotle problematic in terms of Christian teachings. His analytical approach to any philosophical inquiry generally sought to break down common assertions, practices, or beliefs into their singular, constituent parts. Only examining singular details of a larger problem or item could achieve a valid, verifiable knowledge of a phenomenon or problem. This emphasis on doubting and verifying each component of a belief or assertion often seemed problematic when applied to such matters as faith or the power of established authorities.

Actually, Aristotle espoused something comparable to modern naturalism—with all nature governed by natural laws and patterns that existed apart from divine intervention. While he did believe in a creator deity, he largely rejected the popular Greek dichotomy between the physical and spiritual worlds. Aristotle's naturalistic and analytical approach to inquiry had distinguished him somewhat from his colleague and one-time mentor Plato. Plato's writings often invoked a metaphysical realm that transcended the physical one. Plato's famous cave analogy—in which a man chained facing the interior of a cave must glean information about the greater world outside from fleeting clues like shadows and bits of fleeting conversation—highlighted a larger pattern in Plato's work in which truth and ideas occupied a higher plane than human experience, a plane that transcended nature. Another example would be shapes and forms, such as a perfect circle. For Plato, perfect shapes such as circles and rectangles and triangles existed as mathematical concepts and therefore were "real" in the literal sense. At the same time, mathematically perfect shapes like circles or squares did not exist in nature itself. This belief in a larger reality—"realism"—transcending the human senses, or even time and space, constituted the somewhat confusing metaphysical beliefs Plato's writings often encouraged.

Along with his ideas in a transcendent realm beyond the observable, physical universe, Plato's writings also seemed to envision the human soul or "psyche" as distinct from the body—a forerunner of what later philosophers would call the "mind-body problem." This notion of an immortal soul that existed separately from the physical body—though often presented in simplified or even childlike terms—was another key feature of Plato's thought. Plato's abstract distinction between the mind and the body as two separate entities—which had many antecedents in numerous ancient religions—rank among Western thought's most powerful and sophisticated notions of the human spirit, an essential part of each person that ultimately transcends the physical bounds of the body, and even death.

With the rise of Christianity, Plato's ideas had been loosely absorbed into Christian teachings. This is not to say that early Christians were self-consciously Platonists, per se (though some were). Rather, Plato's proto-Christian feel had diffused into many aspects of intellectual life in later antiquity. His notion of a transcendent reality beyond the natural cosmos seemed compatible with Christian emphasis on faith. Indeed, Platonic language and concepts would prove helpful to Christians in the classical world as they attempted to explain complex Christian teachings to the sophisticated elites of the Hellenistic and Roman worlds. Conversely, Aristotle's writings proved less popular with Christian theologians. Even in the early fifth century, Augustine of Hippo, writing in his *Confessions*, had expressed his relative contempt for Aristotle. While a student at Carthage, Augustine reported reading Aristotle's *Ten Categories* (no longer extant). He was disgusted by what he regarded as the presumptuous arrogance of Aristotle, who argued that all existing matter could be reduced to 10 categories (Augustine, *Confessions*, IV. 16). Conversely, Augustine lauded the Platonist "academics" he encountered, who believed that nothing could be known for certain. Augustine saw their views as wiser and humbler—more compatible with faith than the haughty scholars he normally encountered (Augustine, *Confessions*, V. 10).

Augustine's distaste for Aristotle seems prescient. In the centuries following the fall of the Roman Empire in the West, Aristotle was largely forgotten. Platonism, however, indirectly corresponded to much Catholic teaching. Even if the writings of Plato were not necessarily specifically referenced with frequency, his Christian thinking and teaching echoed many of Plato's most famous ideas. At the same time, in the Arab and Byzantine worlds Aristotle remained a powerful intellectual figure. When the Arabs passed into Spain in 711, they brought Aristotle with them. In the Moorish universities established during the years of Islamic control of the Iberian peninsula, Aristotle's writings were core texts read by virtually all students. The important Spanish Muslim Averroës (1126–1198) is one of the Middle Ages' most important figures in terms of medicine, but he also was a learned and influential scholar on the writings of Aristotle. His works would prove especially significant as the Arabs moved across the Pyrenees into France.

Realism and Nominalism

In the Middle Ages, Platonist "realism" was the dominant mode of Catholic medieval theology. As some medieval theologians grew more confident, however, they began to question key aspects of realist teachings. The challenges to realist suppositions are sometimes labeled "nominalism." Nominalism argued that the larger, "real" universals envisioned by realist thinkers were only names—merely functions of language. In the 11th and 12th centuries, debates between the two approaches to knowledge and inquiry began to form two camps, the realists and the nominalists.

Most thoughtful medieval thinkers reflected a mix of the two approaches. Nonetheless, there were real differences between the two groups. Realist philosophy of the day ascribed a transcendent or "universal" reality to any given item or term in a way reminiscent of the teachings of Plato. The implications for medieval thinkers were explosive. In realism, each noun and verb had an overarching universal meaning. Particular things were mere singular parts of these universal qualities. For example, the idea of a tree connoted a universal quality of tree, of which each individual tree was only a component. Some larger "real" tree also existed, embodying the universal, whole qualities of trees.

The idea of larger, universal realities corresponding to particular things grew particularly divisive when the terms in question involved items of vital concern for Christians and the church. One of the most important early figures in this regard was Peter Abelard, remembered as one of Western civilization's finest teachers. At the cathedral school in Paris, Peter Abelard (1079–1142) questioned the metaphysical "real" or universal qualities that medieval theologians attributed to words such as "The Church" or "The Papacy." In celebrated "disputations" with his teacher at the cathedral school in Paris, William Champeau (1070–1121), Abelard attacked the popular idea that each particular thing (noun) was essentially part of a larger universal thing—that each individual thing was identical in quality to the universal thing of which it was a part. For Abelard, such words were merely words and only represented singular manifestations of individual entities. Pushed to an extreme, such reasoning could deny the holy nature of essential Christian teachings, as well as the idea of a transcendent soul or supernatural reality beyond the physical cosmos.

In his reasoning, Abelard pushed Christian thinkers to challenge their core assumptions, promoting new methods of inquiry. Above all, Abelard argued that the assumptions underlying a given argument or point of inquiry should be verifiable and defensible in terms of rigor and reason. Thus the nature of the dispute between realists and nominalists arguably entailed more of a struggle over methods of inquiry than it did a debate over any particular belief or item of faith. Indeed, pushed to an extreme, raw philosophical nominalism implied a

naturalism that few medieval scholars would have dared to espouse. But above all, Abelard's disputations with his teachers, and his later writings about them in his famous work *My Calamities*, established him for all time as one of the most important early voices in the debate between realists and nominalists and laid the foundation for the Scholastic movement that arose in later years.

In later years, many scholars found inspiration in Abelard's writings. Peter Lombard (1100–1160) was one of the most famous scholars inspired by Abelard. His book *The Sentences* further honed the approaches to knowledge espoused by Abelard, which influenced Thomas Aquinas in the 13th century. Martin Luther was also an expert on *The Sentences* of Peter Lombard, having earned a degree in theology at the University of Wittenberg in 1509 with his writings on Lombard. While Luther is generally regarded as a humanist who, even in his period as a monk, railed against the influence of Aristotle in Christian theology, it can also be said that his writings reflected deep exposure to the Scholastic theology still popular in medieval universities in the early 16th century. His use of the "thesis" statement as a call to discourse, and his biblically based challenges to traditional authorities, owed at least something to the theological debates and approaches of earlier times. Luther had also trained for the law, prior to his decision to become a monk. Legal training at that time was also quite Scholastic in its approach. Therefore, although Luther would later chafe at many aspects of his medieval education, at least some elements of it seem to have stood him in good stead. His reasoned and coherent attacks on church doctrines such as the sale of indulgences or papal supremacy owed at least something to his upbringing as a law and theology student in late medieval Germany.

Calvin was another Protestant reformer with a legal background, and his systematic and logical theological works would prove very influential during the years of the Reformation. His notion of predestination, articulated so forcefully in his famous work *The Institutes of the Christian Religion* (1536), flowed logically and coherently from his starting presuppositions regarding an omnipotent, omniscient, and omnipresent God. This kind of reasoning was the product of good legal training. And in the 16th century, good legal training was still heavily influenced by the Scholastic universities, where law had emerged as such an important degree.

In addition to genuine issues of intellectual import, the nominalist challenge to medieval realism reflected a struggle over authority. The call of scholars like Abelard or Peter Lombard to question everything, while perhaps popular as a literary motif in ancient Athenian philosophy, was much more problematic as a genuine habit in modern-day discourse. Indeed, a little reflection will show that while the habit of questioning all assertions—of subjecting each statement to doubt and scrutiny—may find favor in an academic classroom setting, such insubordination would likely fare less favorably in any kind of actual workplace environment, like a business or a military hierarchy. This was no less true in medieval times. Faith in the Middle Ages was no mere psychological exercise or personal choice. It was interwoven with worldly power. Wealthy and powerful institutions like the papacy promoted faith not only as an article of Christian living. Faith in God closely intersected with the authority possessed by rich institutions like the papacy, the episcopate, guild, and the lay feudal order. Therefore, seeming to question matters of faith or church dictates was quite explosive, whatever the motivation.

At its purest, medieval realism contained a beautiful holiness. Two of the most important realistic thinkers of the High Middle Ages were Bernard of Clairvaux (1090–1153) and Bonaventura (1221–1274). They epitomized realism's defense against nominalist queries. In response to nominalism's challenge to account rationally for each and every Christian belief—an impossible task, by any reckoning—scholars like Bernard and Bonaventura emphasized the ultimately unknowable and unfathomable truths of God. Following the lead of Saint Augustine of Hippo, they railed against overly intellectual attempts to reconcile faith and reason. Excessive intellectualism resulted from sinful human pride and arrogance, as well as a chimerical folly. Only error and confusion could result. How arrogant of puny intellectuals to question truths that had been handed down via divine inspiration in the Bible or in centuries of church tradition. Such mysteries should be welcome as the gifts of faith that they were, not debated with false pride and inflated pseudo-intellectual reasoning. Christians should focus instead on worship—on the beauty of the Mass and the mystery of Christ's salvation for humanity.

Aristotle in the West

Challenges to the church's most cherished values grew more urgent in the mid-12th century. Some time around the year 1150, Aristotle's writing were translated into Latin and appeared in France at the University of Paris. They would have a profound impact. Aristotle's approach strengthened the critical approaches of reason and doubt already favored by the nominalists.

Aristotle's writings raised many issues of a religious nature, as well as in terms of philosophical approach. First, Aristotle was a pagan. His powerful intellect and persuasive writings came from a world before Christ had even been born. And unlike the Hebrew prophets of the Old Testament or certain classical writers such as Virgil or Plato, who were often deemed somehow proto-Christian, Aristotle's writings seemed self-sufficient and complete on their own terms. Plato's writings could seem to point medieval Christians to God—if one so desired. God was harder to reconcile with Aristotle. What need for God or Christ was there in such a powerful intellect as this?

On a related note, Aristotle's writings came to France by way of Islamic Spain—during the height of the Crusades, no less. Borrowing their name from one of Islamic Spain's most important Moorish compilers of the Aristotle texts, Averroës (1126–1198), the Averroists, as they came to be called, seemed to venerate Aristotle in an almost unsettling fashion. As his works became more readily available in Western Europe, his adherents began to treat the texts in almost canonical fashion. On the other side were those, like Bonaventura, who seemed to reject almost out of hand any systematic theology, especially one that eschewed Christian presuppositions. As one might imagine, the debates that ensued also generated a fair amount of all-too-human academic politics, which apparently dominated universities, then as now. At the University of Paris and the other great schools, factions from the two camps almost resembled political parties.

Theology: The Queen of the Sciences

In response to the challenge from Aristotle, medieval theologians began to work toward a unified body of Christian belief that was rigorously presented and defended. Their approach sought to assume nothing, in keeping with Aristotelian (or even nominalist) ideas of doubt, evidence, logic, and when possible, observation. The new approach demanded a response. Though attractive at an emotional and rhetorical level, Bonaventura's or Bernard's simple focus on faith and the beauty of worship seemed inadequate to answer the Averroists' challenge. Taking on the challenge, theologians in the late 12th and early 13th centuries began to work toward a more systematic and logically rigorous approach to knowledge—one that, for better or worse, reflected the deep influence of Greek philosophers.

The approach that emerged from this endeavor is commonly called Scholasticism. In the 13th century, Scholasticism emerged as the greatest form of science in the Middle Ages. While theology and science may seem like oil and water to most modern students—at least in Western universities—the medieval Scholastic approach can rightly be seen as a crucial stage in human cultural and intellectual activity—one that ultimately resulted in the scientific revolution of the Renaissance. Key in this regard was the Scholastic embrace of the language of "proof." Assertions or hypotheses were canvassed and discussed. Invalid assertions were discarded. Assertions that could withstand logical scrutiny moved ahead in the discourse, where they were weighed against related assertions, subjecting them to further logical scrutiny.

The systematic approach to Scholastic theology borrowed heavily from the meticulous dialectical approaches of the Hellenic philosophers. But it also foreshadowed the scientific method, later espoused more directly by thinkers like René Descartes, famous for *Cogito Ergo Sum*—I think, therefore I am. Only by reducing any given supposition to its most unassailable, truest components could a scholar begin to construct a larger argument based on reason and logic. With this approach, Scholars hoped to prove the existence of God: to demonstrate the truth of God's creation with unassailable, impeccable rational rigor.

Even today, the notion that God's existence can be proved—at least as a logical supposition—stands at the heart of much theological discourse. It is often linked to the branch of philosophy known as ontology (the study of being), which argues that the philosopher's task involves determining which things can be categorically said to exist. Derived from Plato, ontology constitutes an important link between philosophy and theology. Today it remains an important area of study in both disciplines. The first Christian thinker equated with ontology is usually Saint Anselm (1033–1099), the archbishop of Canterbury. His work *Cur Deus Homo (Why Did God Become Man?)* sought to cite arguments for God's existence, based on supposedly irrefutable logic. Though early, his work foreshadowed later Scholastic writers and heavily influenced figures such as Thomas Aquinas.

Thomism and the Apex of Medieval Learning

The Scholastic movement reached its apogee in the writings of Thomas Aquinas (1226–1274). A Dominican scholar based at the University of Paris for much of his career, Aquinas was perhaps the most successful of all the Schoolmen in his attempts to resolve the tension between Aristotelian methods of inquiry and Christian teachings. His writings emphasized that faith and reason could co-exist, ostensibly bringing together the disputing factions of the Averroists and the Bonaventurists. His branch of philosophy came to be called Thomism, probably the quintessential specimen of medieval thought. His primary work was the *Summa Theologica*, one of the most classic texts in the Middle Ages. In it, Aquinas argued that the existence of God could be proved. Moreover, in arguing his case using careful dialectical approaches, he consistently used observable and natural phenomena, largely silencing the Averroists.

The *Summa Theologica* included some of the most famous arguments for the existence of God ever penned. It included famous assertions that the movements of natural bodies such as planets and stars lacked intelligence, yet moved with an observable design. For Aquinas, whatever lacked intelligence could not move purposely to a given end. It followed that such movements came from an intelligent designer being, which humans call God. Another related argument in the *Summa* was that since the heavenly bodies are set in motion, something must have been the "first cause" of this motion, since inert motionlessness cannot initiate its own movement. Therefore, it followed that there was a First Mover, whom humans call God.

The arguments in Thomism had many manifestations, but they are often remembered as core ingredients in the Ptolemaic (earth-centered) conception of the cosmos that prevailed in the Middle Ages. God existed beyond the starry firmament, apart from the created natural order He had fashioned. He was the great "Unmoved Mover," a concept borrowed from Aristotle and popularized by Aquinas. In a world predating Newton's Law of Gravity, arguments like those espoused by Aquinas provided powerful reasoning that helped fortify traditional Christian teachings against the period's most rigorous standards of scrutiny.

Even after the scientific revolution, Thomism's notions of an intelligent design of the cosmos remained significant. They often corresponded to Enlightenment deist ideas, with their Watchmaker God who created the matter of the cosmos and set it in motion, thereby establishing the natural laws of physics that governed the universe. Even today, such notions can seem vaguely reminiscent of intelligent design, often presented as an ostensibly plausible theistic alternative to a strictly materialist view of evolution and the origins of the universe. In general, despite his medieval trappings and the limited parameters of the known cosmos as it was understood in the 13th century, Aquinas has remained one of Christianity's most towering intellectual figures. He remains a doctor of the church—the "Angelic Doctor." His ideas about harmonizing faith and reason and the extent to which observable patterns in nature can point human intellects to a belief in God still sway millions.

The Importance of Scholasticism and Its Decline

It would be hard to overemphasize how important Scholasticism was in terms of the development of intellectual life in the Middle Ages. It had an enormous influence on later periods. The study of law and medicine, for example, which came to represent major areas of professional training in medieval universities, was deeply shaped by the systematic approaches and high standards of intellectual rigor achieved by the Scholastics. Indeed, the influence of Scholastics on law and medicine arguably equaled its impact on Christian theology and teaching.

Overall, Scholasticism represented the apex of medieval learning. Thinkers such as Aquinas shaped discourse for many centuries to come. Indeed, Scholastic ideas remain important, not only in terms of the history of Western thought in the Middle Ages, but also in and of themselves. Thomism represents one of the most powerful achievements of theistic intellectual endeavor—perhaps the closest human thinking has come to reconciling the warring camps of faith and reason. The arguments canvassed by Aquinas and the other Schoolmen contemporaries remain significant fixtures of education and learning. Today, echoes of Thomism are frequently found in a number of contemporary guises, notably the notion of an "intelligent designer" God. For many, the various proofs espoused by Aquinas remain important and thoughtful defenses against the excessive materialism that drives much of modern academic and intellectual life.

Finally, Scholastic science and systematic theology are part of a larger package featuring medieval civilization at its most brilliant, confident, and attractive. Scholastic thought corresponds almost uncannily with Gothic architecture, for example. Gothic cathedrals, with their explosive minutiae of details all unified around a singular focus and a steeple pointing to God, are in many ways a physical embodiment of the medieval Scholastic ideal—of the ultimate unity between all created things, great and small, universal and particular.

Scholasticism also corresponds with some of the finest literature of the High Middle Ages. Dante (1265–1321), in particular, is a Scholastic figure. Though he wrote in earthy Italian vernacular as opposed to the universal tongue of Latin, his *Divine Comedy* reflected Scholastic outlooks. His journey from hell, through purgatory, and on into heaven was very Scholastic in the sense that it sought to categorize and systematically account for all knowledge, harmonizing a welter of seemingly divergent details into a coherent, Roman Catholic worldview.

Scholasticism's undoubted intellectual achievements reflected the high water mark of medieval thought. In the 14th century, Europe began to undergo wrenching change, culturally as well as institutionally. Sometimes called "The Calamitous Fourteenth Century," due to the bubonic plague that shocked Europe in the late 1340s, as well as the crisis in the papacy that resulted in the popes moving to Avignon, Europe began to change precipitously and inexorably after 1300. These years are still, by virtually any definition, part of the Middle Ages per se. Yet they also seem to exhibit a failure of the confidence and strength that medieval culture and institutions had demonstrated during the preceding centuries.

In the centuries after 1300, Europe would undergo a series of challenges that transformed medieval institutions and in some cases eradicated them altogether. Po-litically, the rise of powerful national monarchies in nations like France or England threatened both the "feudal" order, as well as the unrivaled international status of the popes. Economically, the rise of capitalism, banking, and trade slowly but surely undermined medieval economic arrangements, notably the institution of manorialism. In terms of learning and education, a richer and more diverse Europe, on the eve of the Renaissance, inevitably demanded a broader and more down-to-earth education. This new approach to learning, which borrowed heavily from the classical world, is usually called humanism. Humanism would soon eclipse Scholasticism as Europe's most powerful and important mode of education.

The Humanist Response to Scholasticism

However powerful Scholasticism had been, it had always had its critics. One particular problem was its excessively academic nature. Scholasticism was strictly academic, in both the best and worst senses of the term. In the best sense, it reflected rigorous academic standards. Scholasticism necessarily involved subjecting one's ideas to rigorous doubt. And as it arose largely in the context of intellectual debates and disagreements, Scholasticism also entailed public discourse and peer-based scrutiny, another hallmark of academic life, then and now.

Scholasticism was also "academic" in that it hinted at the notion of objectivity, a feature of scientific reasoning that would emerge in later centuries. Admittedly, virtually all formally sanctioned medieval scholarship had to uphold Christian teachings at some basic level. But Scholasticism reflected an early version of the notion of the "disinterested" pursuit of knowledge. Scholars must go where truth and inquiry lead, not fearing the possible outcomes. This proto-scientific quality was one of Scholasticism's most lasting legacies—one far surpassing the religious issues and terms that prevailed during its heyday.

On the other hand, Scholasticism could seem strictly academic in the more pejorative sense of the term: that it was seemingly divorced from any practical application to the individual human's life. It could seem to value a clever intellectual over a contrite heart and a sincere faith. After all, an issue that is "just an academic issue" is literally meaningless in terms of practical application. Participation in some academic disputation with collegial adversaries over some point of theology did not in any way ensure that the participants were in any way actually living their lives in accordance with the humble examples found in the Gospel or the early church. The best theologian was not necessarily the best Christian.

Over time, criticism of Scholasticism grew. It increasingly seemed an overly intellectual exercise—a wordy contest to see who could be cleverest in constructing verbal arguments that often seemed arcane or even silly to the uninitiated. Also, most of Scholasticism's debates had thrived in a relatively small, insular world of university members. The quarrelling realists, nominalists, and their various subgroups seemed like a cadre of obscure, petty faculty maestros. In their great debates, they seemingly formed an invisible circle in which they all faced each other, keeping their backs to the outside world. Such criticisms gained strength during the Renaissance, finally resulting in the rise of the humanist movement.

Background to Renaissance Humanism

Humanism—a move toward an intellectual and cultural life that was more embracing of human experiences and needs—is one of the most defining characteristics of the Renaissance. The Renaissance, commonly equated with the 15th and 16th centuries, is one of Western Europe's most important periods. Along with the fine arts, music, literature, and other culturally brilliant aspects of the period, the humanist movement deeply shaped mentalities during this period.

Scholasticism, though it never disappeared, gradually ceded its place of dominance in universities. Part of the reason for this was the natural evolution of human ideas, which have always tended to move from one fashion to another. But humanism's rise was also the by-product of profound intellectual changes shaping Europe as the West moved into the Renaissance. These social and economic changes are crucial considerations when discussing the development of humanism and the movement away from medieval modes of learning.

During the Renaissance, Europe underwent wrenching economic changes. The rise of trade and commerce that began in Italy resulted in the ascendancy of a new class of entrepreneurs and professionals: lawyers, bankers, merchants, and doctors. Trading for precious commodities in the East created enormous private fortunes, transforming urban life. Many families, like the famous Medici in Florence, rose from relative obscurity to great prominence in the new economic climate.

With the rise of private wealth, the demand for a newer form of education emerged—one that was less focused on eternal heaven and Almighty God and more focused on earthly things. During the heyday of the Scholastic movement, the greatest intellectual figures in Europe had largely been monks, hardly the role model desired by the worldly, pleasure-loving, nouveau riche now on the rise. In the wealthy cities of Renaissance Italy, education would need to be less monastic, and less theological, if it was to appeal to the new economic elites.

The new economy also required new legal education. Medieval law, to the extent it existed at all, largely focused on canon, or church, law. There was precious little in

medieval law to deal with complex situations regarding private property. Some of the thorniest problems in this regard involved how risk should be shared by business partners. Division of property in such matters as inheritance and divorce also raised new questions. Given the dearth of medieval commentary on such matters, during the Renaissance people began to turn to ancient Roman laws, which contained many forms of contract law. Rome also had a broad and solid range of laws involving such general economic matters as the possession and sale of private property. It was therefore in the Renaissance that the revival of interest in classical texts emerged. Originally considered a last resort to answer thorny problems in terms of contracts or property disputes, the rediscovery of ancient Roman laws soon led to a larger rebirth of interest in classical writings as a whole.

This revival of interest in antiquity played an important role in the revival of humanism during the Renaissance, a mind-set often equated with the classical world. The proud, grounded intellectual culture of the Greeks and Romans seemed a perfect antidote to the monkish spirituality and arcane theology that increasingly dominated Scholastic debates in Europe's leading universities.

Instead of the medieval world's archetypal scholar monk, sworn to poverty and laboring over ancient texts in a humble cell, the Renaissance required new educational models. Along with the new "bourgeois" elites coming from businesses like trade and banking, there were also more and more nobles seeking education. This was a profound change from the "warrior age" of the earlier Middle Ages, when aristocrats often left extensive formal learning to monks and priests. The rise of royal power in the later Middle Ages created new positions and opportunities in palace courts. The growing civil service in governments, which were increasingly bureaucratized during this period, required a basic level of decorum and civility.

Aside from economic, legal, and political pursuits, humanist influences also began to shape Christian values and mores in the later Middle Ages. As was the case with the rise of more secular-minded educational goals in Renaissance Italy, Christian humanism arose from dissatisfaction with the obscure nature of Scholastic discourse. Criticism of the Scholastics persisted on the older realist grounds that only inspiration, intuition, and faith could ever truly lead the mind and heart to Christ. Some things were just beyond the realm of human reason, especially reason basing itself on the observation of nature or physical things. Duns Scotus (1266–1308) and William Occkam (1300–1349) both continued to fault the Scholastic doctrines of Aquinas on these grounds, arguing against an excessive intellectualism in matters of faith. Movements like the

Lollard movement, begun by John Wycliffe (1320–1384) in England, which attacked corruption in the church, as well as superstitious elements in Christian medieval culture raised urgent questions for which Scholasticism seemed to offer relatively few answers.

The Renaissance Man or Woman

In this new climate, both nobles and the newly moneyed elites—the bourgeoisie—began to seek positions in the universities. But they naturally eschewed the intensely ecclesiastical nature of most education there. They instead sought to cultivate themselves for lives beyond the university—unlike most of the Scholastics, who were professional teachers and scholars. In so doing, they stimulated the rise of a new educational model based on the idea of the broadly, generally educated person. This educational model, which was closely related to humanism, would stand for many centuries to come as one of the chief goals of a liberal arts education in a university or college setting. Over the years, a person possessing such an education was often referred to as a "Renaissance man."

The proverbial "Renaissance man" was a "jack of all trades, master of several." Today the term has arguably lost some of its panache. Modern-day expectations of specialization and career focus have diminished the old Renaissance ideals of a broadly educated person, at least in many Western schools. The term is also gender exclusive. Nonetheless, during the Renaissance, this well-rounded, well-versed humanist education became the most fashionable and prestigious academic background. Many members of the English Tudor court, for example, were famous for their refined humanist education, including Thomas More and, notably, well-educated "Renaissance women" such as Jane Grey, Catherine Parr, and Queen Elizabeth I. All these women were fine writers, fluent in both French and Latin, and well-read in the important books of the day, as well as in Greek and Roman literature. Queen Elizabeth was also a fine musician, though she often declined to perform in public once she became queen.

One of the books most closely linked to the historical model of the Renaissance person is *The Book of the Courtier*, by Balldasare Castiglione (1478–1529). It was designed as a kind of handbook for future "courtiers": aristocrats destined to inhabit the courts of the rich and powerful, where they would occupy sophisticated and fancy fields such as diplomacy and secretarial positions. Castiglione's book emphasized that proper gentlemen should not only have generally sound backgrounds in literature and languages (including the classical texts), but also have sound physical training and good manners. *The Book of the Courtier* is probably one of the most influential books ever written on the subject of education

and training, at least on an indirect level. Machiavelli's (1469–1527) famous book *The Prince* (c. 1513) also purported to provide lessons and training for aspiring public officials. Machiavelli, though, provided decidedly different perspectives and admonitions than did Castiglione. Machiavelli's "the end justifies the means" approach to public service and political life stands in stark contrast to the genteel ideals in *The Book of the Courtier*. Nonetheless, both books reflect the ideals of broad and public-minded humanistic training, each in its own fashion.

Humanism was also reflected in the wonderful art of the Renaissance. While much earlier medieval art often appeared more exclusively in sacred settings, art in the Renaissance moved into private homes, public squares, and municipal buildings. Reflecting the focus on all things human, portraits of private citizens came into vogue, a trend epitomized by Leonardo da Vinci's (1452–1519) famous *Mona Lisa* and many other fine examples. Such works not only sought to capture the subject's humanity; they also reflected broadly secular themes. Renaissance portraits are generally set in private, nonreligious environments. Fine clothing and comfortably furnished rooms in the background recall a brilliant culture that welcomed wealth and prosperity. Artists even reduced the prominence of such religious iconography as halos, which in medieval art had been very heavily used as a device to connote larger than life religious people such as saints and the Virgin Mary. Renaissance artists more generally chose to focus on the human details of facial expressions and movements. Even when depicting saints and heroes of the Bible, the subject's humanity was a paramount concern of the artist.

Renaissance art also embraced the physical beauty of men and women, arguably contrasting with the emphasis on depravity and original sin that colored many sacred paintings of saints and sinners in earlier Christian art. Celebrating humanity, Renaissance artists strove to depict anatomical features with the attention and skill they deserved. The nude sculptures of Renaissance masters, like Michelangelo's *David* (1504), are virtually studies in human anatomy, as well as being tributes to larger than life, idealized human forms. *David* is as much an uncircumcised Greek god—with a perfect idealized Hellenic physique—as it is a humble Hebrew shepherd. In this regard, the classical nude, which reappeared during the Renaissance after a thousand-year absence, celebrated the pure aesthetic of the human body and generally reflected a much more optimistic view of the human condition. The magnificent *Creation of Adam*, the centerpiece of Michelangelo's complex of paintings in the Vatican's Sistine Chapel, has a similarly optimistic view of the basic human condition: man, created in the image of God. In the crowning moment of the Genesis creation, God touches Adam's outstretched hand, imbuing him with the divine spirit of love and creativity. The message, drawing from scripture, is clear. Of all the wondrous things in God's creation, man is the most blessed and wondrous of all. This reflects the bright, quintessential spirit of Christian humanism during the heyday of the Renaissance.

Certainly the reemergence of the classical nude during the Renaissance also had to do with humanism's more sympathetic appreciation of sex and reproduction, as well as enhanced artistic techniques. In the Middle Ages, the idea of original sin had informed basic understandings of the human condition, an idea that owed much to influential theologians, including St. Augustine of Hippo and even the apostle Paul. The idea of original sin was also a prevalent fixture in Thomism. Moreover, such beliefs involved sexual intercourse, the means by which innate sinful depravity passed from every mother to every child. Belief in original sin supported many medieval cultural traits, such as modesty and chastity (especially in women), and the discouragement of nonprocreative sex. In the Renaissance, the explosion of skill and artistic genius that emerged coincided with a culture that seemed more welcoming of erotic beauty and pleasure. Venus, the pagan deity of sexual and romantic love, reemerged as one of Western art's most iconic female motifs, rivaling even the Virgin Mary herself. This embrace of paganism, with its beautiful anthropomorphic deities, is also a type of humanism.

Humanism and the Northern Renaissance

As the Renaissance moved into northern Europe, especially rich blends of Christian faith and practice combined with humanistic influences. In the early 15th century, a somewhat murky figure commonly named Thomas à Kempis wrote his famous *The Imitation of Christ*. One of the most popular and widely read books ever written, it reminded Christians of the simple, humble New Testament lives found in the early church. Kempis asserted that God was more pleased with a humble carpenter than a learned astronomer who could name all the stars but did not follow the one who created them. What good does it do to gain praise for a learned discourse on the Trinity, he wondered, if by one's arrogance and intellectual pride, one displeases the Trinity?

Like many humanist authors of the period, Thomas à Kempis wrote in an accessible style for a widespread audience, another important distinction pitting him against the Scholastics. His couched his brilliant reasoning, inspiring devotional gems, and thoughtful points in a simple and inspiring style (in Latin) that seemed to move all, from the learned faculty sitting at the great universities down to the common laborer. Some elements of his writings emphasized personal introspection and mysticism, which always worried some church officials because of its potential for undermining established church authorities. Other elements of his arguments and reasoning presaged Protestant thinking that emerged in the 16th century, including some of the more austere movements such as Anabaptism. Nonetheless, he was ultimately embraced by both Catholics and Protestants. And unlike many Scholastics, his writings continue to appeal today not only to scholars, theologians, and historians, but also to common laypeople. Millions today continue to find the writings of Thomas à Kempis enormously valuable for personal devotion and encouragement—for wise insights into the nature of God and the Christian life.

Other humanists of the Northern Renaissance also wrote in the accessible, plain language of Kempis, echoing his call for a humbler, less hierarchical, and less superstitious faith. Some, however, added humorous commentary and even polemics to their work. Especially notable in this regard was Erasmus (1466–1536). His *Praise of Folly* lambasted many aspects of medieval Catholicism, including the veneration of relics, witch hunts, and pilgrimages. But he reserved special vitriol for the university Schoolmen, with their maze of complex categories, their shameless name-dropping, and their seemingly intentional obfuscation. For Erasmus, the universities seemed to encourage an "Emperor's new clothes" world of intellectual phonies and group-think. Asserting that many listeners are the more impressed the less they understand, he lampooned an academic culture that seemed to favor gibberish and jargon. Erasmus's arguments denouncing medieval theology, popular religion, and even ecclesiastical offices can be seen as Protestant in many senses. But though he was a contemporary of Luther, he remained a nominal Catholic throughout his life.

Erasmus corresponded to the humanist educational model in that he was a very finely educated person, with a strong background in the Greek and Roman classics. He wrote brilliantly, yet in a clear and accessible manner. He was often funny to the point of being hilarious, a quality that seldom seemed to find its way into the learned discourses of the Scholastics. Moreover, Erasmus's humanist tendencies appeared not only in his philosophy and beliefs, but also in the sort of education he had himself and espoused for others.

In many parts of Europe—especially in the North—an education well-versed in languages, literature, the Bible, mathematics, and often music found its way into many homes, in increasingly broad cross-sections of society. In many geographical areas, especially after the Reformation, literacy and education were emphasized, if for no other reason than to encourage the reading of scripture. More generally, humanist learning gained popularity at precisely a time when much of Europe was literally learning to read. Literacy levels were rapidly rising in many areas of Europe, unlike the largely illiterate demographics of the earlier Middle Ages. Founded in 1502, the University of Wittenberg, where Martin Luther taught, typified these new schools. In general, the rise of new universities helped expand learning not only geographically, but also in terms of new approaches and people. This spread of humanist education was not only reflected in religion, but also in important developments such as the scientific revolution and the consolidation of vernacular languages.

References and Resources

Colish, M. L. 1997. *Medieval Foundations of the Western Intellectual Tradition.* New Haven, CT: Yale University Press.

Haren, Michael. 1985. *Medieval Thought: The Western Intellectual Tradition from Antiquity to the Thirteenth Century.* London, England: Macmillan.

Haskins, Charles Homes. 1957. *The Rise of Universities.* Ithaca, NY: Great Seal Books.

Kristeller, Paul Oskar. 1961. *Renaissance Thought: The Classic, Scholastic, and Humanistic Strain.* New York: Harper & Brothers.

Panofsky, Erwin. 1951. *Gothic Architecture and Scholasticism.* Latrobe, PA: Archabbey Press.

—DAVID WALTER LEINWEBER

SCHOLASTICISM, REFORMED

Defining Reformed Scholasticism

Discussion of Reformed Scholasticism has often suffered for want of a proper definition. *Reformed* here means that stream of Protestant Reformation thought and church life that was distinguished from about the 1540s onward from the Lutheran branch of the international movement. The defining issues revolved around the sacraments and Christology, for example, the Reformed being unhappy with the theory of Christ's physical ubiquity developed by the Lutherans as part of their commitment to consubstantiation. Reformed is a better term than the overused "Calvinist," since it identifies a movement consisting of a number of major theologians (such as Bucer, Bullinger, Vermigli, and Zanchi) as formative and significant rather than a single man who, though important, was never the sole arbiter of what counts as confessionally orthodox even in his own day.

Scholasticism in this context refers to an academic method used by those in the Reformed tradition particularly during the late 16th to 18th centuries. Indeed, it was a method and style of disputation and writing they shared with Lutherans and Roman Catholics who also worked in university settings. Richard Muller (2003b) outlines the basic core of the scholastic approach as the *quaestio* method: presentation of a thesis or *quaestio*; discussion of the related issues, or *status quaestionis*; careful treatment of arguments against the adopted positions, or *objectiones*; and formulation of an answer or *responsio* to the question, along with answers to the previous objections. Such structure can be found very clearly in earlier scholastic texts, such as Thomas Aquinas's *Summa Theologiae*, as well as in Reformed Scholasticism, and is the heart of the academic method.

Seen in this light, it is clear that scholastic or "classroom" method is not intrinsically or necessarily linked with any particular dogmatic *content*. To refer to someone as scholastic would not identify his actual doctrinal beliefs any more than calling someone "educated" or "learned" would today. "Scholastic" is, however, closely related to the university or school setting. One would not expect a Reformed Scholastic, or indeed any kind of scholastic, to write or speak in such a fashion outside of that academic context. Reformed Scholasticism is therefore a particular strain of Reformed thought and writing that was designed for use in that specific environment.

Preconceptions about the Scholastic Method

Older scholarship on this subject tended to assume or assert that scholasticism led to particular commitments in terms of content, such as overplaying the role of reason in theology or importing alien Aristotelian concepts and distinctions into the discipline. There was, as Willem van Asselt and Eef Dekker (2001) put it, "the presupposition that post-Reformation scholasticism was not much more than a rigid and inflexible complex of dogmas involving regression to outdated medieval patterns of thought." The lively Gospel message of the early reformers was supposedly replaced by a Gospel-obscuring scholastic dead letter, the personal by the propositional and the dynamic by the static. Luther had attacked Thomists and scholastics, and Calvin's *Institutes* contains many negative references to *scholastici*; therefore to revert to scholasticism and scholastic authors was to abandon the Gospel.

This idea has now been exploded in the scholarly literature, though the general perception at the popular level of a distinction between, for example, "Calvin and the Calvinists" may well persist, with the latter being seen as dry rationalists and forcible systematizers because of their supposedly fatal scholasticism. Apart from the problematic nature of identifying a "golden age" of Reformation thought, or elevating John Calvin into the sole standard against which later developments are to be definitively measured, this fails to take account of the differing contexts and time periods in which early and later Reformed theology was written.

As attacks on Reformed doctrine became more and more sophisticated, from both Lutherans and Roman Catholics, it was quite natural for Reformed academics to counter them with a comparable level of academic sophistication. This was done quite deliberately to demonstrate the biblical defensibility and intellectual credibility of Reformed doctrine among the educated, but was also increasingly necessary as the Reformation movement began to settle and build institutions. Reformed Scholasticism therefore developed as a way of institutionalizing, propagating, and protecting the doctrines of grace and the Gospel, which had been preached so powerfully at the Reformation, for the educational benefit of the next generation.

When the reformers' polemic against scholastics is reexamined in this light, it appears less as an all-encompassing rejection of academic method per se. What Luther and Calvin, for instance, were opposing was often simply the semi-Pelagianism and speculative nature of late medieval nominalism, a particular brand of scholastic deviation from orthodoxy. When Luther opposed "Aristotle" he took this to stand for any synergistic conception of salvation; and Calvin's own French translation of the *Institutes* renders his most negative uses of *scholastici* (and not all references to such people *are* negative) as *theologiens Sorbonniques* (theologians of the Sorbonne)—a very specific contemporary reference to certain Parisians rather than a wholesale dismissal of academic culture in general.

Phases and Leading Lights
It is common to identify various phases through which Reformed Scholasticism moved over time. "Early Orthodoxy" (roughly 1560–1640) saw the development of early confessions and catechisms, with the international Synod of Dort (1618–1619) often seen as particularly important. Theodore Beza was the leading Reformed theologian, while Roman Catholic polemicist Robert Bellarmine was a key figure, since his elaborate scholastic attacks on Protestant faith elicited hundreds of responses from Reformed theologians, such as William Whitaker and William Ames.

In "High Orthodoxy" (roughly 1640–1725), the orthodoxy of the confessions was developed and expanded in some detail before the onset of de-confessionalization at the beginning of the 18th century. Anti-Trinitarian Socinianism became a major theological threat and was countered by Reformed Scholastics such as John Owen and Francis Turretin. Herman Witsius and Johannes Cocceius developed Reformed interest in covenant theology, and in Britain the Westminster Confession and Catechisms were produced.

"Late Orthodoxy" (1725–1790) saw the decline and stagnation of the movement of Reformed Scholasticism as the Enlightenment took hold. Deism, hyper-Calvinism, and antinomianism were major threats. Evangelical revival preachers such as Augustus Toplady (who translated Zanchi's work on predestination from Latin) and Jonathan Edwards were enthusiastic appropriators of the previous tradition against the deviant theologies of their day.

References and Resources
Muller, R. A. 2003a. *After Calvin: Studies in the Development of a Theological Tradition.* Oxford: Oxford University Press.
———. 2003b. *Post-Reformation Reformed Dogmatics: The Rise and Development of Reformed Orthodoxy, ca. 1520–ca. 1725.* 4 vols. Grand Rapids, MI: Baker.
Van Asselt, W., ed. 2011. *Introduction to Reformed Scholasticism.* Grand Rapids, MI: Reformation Heritage Books.
Van Asselt, W., and E. Dekker, eds. 2001. *Reformation and Scholasticism: An Ecumenical Enterprise.* Grand Rapids, MI: Baker.

—LEE GATISS

SCHOOL CHOICE LEGISLATION'S IMPACT ON CHRISTIAN SCHOOLS

School choice initiatives have been at the forefront of American educational policy debates since the 1980s (Ajuwon and Bradshaw 2009). Studies of the effects of school choice on participating students and families have been under way since the late 1990s (Wolf 2008). School choice legislation, including state-funded tuition vouchers that enable students to attend private Christian schools, has had an impact on the trajectory of Christian education and the Christian school movement for the past 30 years.

Expansion of Private Education
Private schools are generally thought to provide an "expensive education for the rich and elite" while "excluding those without the financial resources available to pay" (Boerema 2009 34). School choice programs, however, include state-funded vouchers or subsidies for low-income families, few of whom may have been able to pay private school tuition (Maranto, Milliman, and Stevens 2000). At a minimum, such vouchers reduce a portion of the cost of tuition for private Christian schools and in many cases provide sufficient funding for tuition altogether (Goldhaber 1997, 143). The number of parents who choose schools other than neighborhood public schools has "grown substantially" in recent years (Berends et al. 2009, xiii). The number of religiously af-

filiated private schools in the United States has increased, from 7.5 percent in 1993 to 8.7 percent in 2007 (USDE, NCES 2009). Such increases in enrollment have been fueled in part by school choice initiatives that have created new opportunities for Christian schools and the families they seek to serve (Reichard 2012).

School choice has been deemed a "revolutionary approach" to the privatization of education and "in its ideal form, parents would be able to use a state-provided education voucher to send their children to any public or private school of their choice" (Simon and Lovrich 1996, 670). The intention of school choice programs is to expand the range of educational options available to parents beyond public schools (Andersen and Serritzlew 2007, 343). In effect, school choice programs allow families to choose Christian schools for their children without the financial barriers of tuition. Social issues such as racial segregation and socioeconomic disparity can thereby be addressed by Christian schools that participate in school choice programs.

Constitutionality and Legality

From a constitutional perspective, proponents of private vouchers have contended that voucher programs do not "change the relationship between the state and the schools," because the voucher funds are distributed directly to parents, not to private schools (Menashi 2002, 40). Parents receive the subsidization directly from the state and choose where to direct it on behalf of their children. The intention of such programs is to expand the range of possible schooling opportunities for students, especially for those whose public schools are underperforming. Thus, proponents of school choice argue that because vouchers are not provided directly to Christian schools, there is no violation of the establishment clause or blurring of the roles of church and state. Opponents argue that school choice programs indirectly lead to state funding of religious institutions.

State and National Contexts

At present, private voucher programs are available in more than 50 cities in the United States (Berends et al. 2009, xvii). School choice programs range from universal voucher programs, to failing school voucher programs, to special needs scholarships; these programs are diverse in their legislative details, but widely available in more than a dozen states in the United States (Nemeth 2011). Universal vouchers are available in some countries, including Sweden, The Netherlands, and Belgium, and in some Canadian provinces; such programs permit students to attend qualified private Christian schools without restrictions (Wolf 2008). The impact of widespread school choice legislation has been to open the door for the expansion of Christian education into new missions and markets in the 21st century.

References and Resources

Ajuwon, P. M., and B. K. Bradshaw. 2009. "An Empirical Study on Factors Influencing Parents' School Choice." *Religion & Education* 36 (3): 39–53. doi:10.1080/15507394.2009.10012456.

Andersen, S. C., and S. Serritzlew. 2007. "The Unintended Effects of Private School Competition." *Journal of Public Administration Research and Theory* 17 (2): 335–356. doi:10.1093/jopart/mul019.

Berends, M. 2009. *Handbook of Research on School Choice.* New York: Routledge.

Berends, M., Springer, M., Ballou, D., and Walberg, H. 2009. *Handbook of Research on School Choice.* New York: Taylor & Francis

Boerema, A. J. 2009. "Does Mission Matter? An Analysis of Private School Achievement Differences." *Journal of School Choice* 3 (2): 112–137. doi:10.1080/15582150902996708.

Goldhaber, D. D. 1997. "School Choice as Education Reform." *Phi Delta Kappan* 78 (2): 143+. Accessed 6 July 2012. http://www.questia.com/PM.qst?a=o&d=5000516357.

Maranto, R., S. Milliman, and S. Stevens. 2000. "Does Private School Competition Harm Public Schools? Revisiting Smith and Meier's *The Case Against School Choice.*" *Political Research Quarterly* 53 (1): 177–192. doi:10.1177/106591290005300109.

Menashi, S. 2002. "The Church-State Tangle: School Choice and Religious Autonomy." *Policy Review* 114:37+. Accessed 6 July 2012. http://www.hoover.org/publications/policy-review/article/6217.

Nemeth, C. 2011. "School Choice: The Civil Rights Issue of the 21st Century, the Nature of the Problem: Freedom, Choice and the Right to Educate." *Law & Policy Monitor.* Institute of Law and Policy at California University of Pennsylvania. Spring 2011, 1–6.

Reichard, J. 2012. "Religious Values and Tuition Vouchers: An Empirical Case Study of Parent Religiosity as a Factor of School Choice." *Journal of School Choice* 6 (4): 465–482.

Simon, C. A., and N. P. Lovrich. 1996. "Private School Enrollment and Public School Performance: Assessing the Effects of Competition upon Public School Student Achievement in Washington State." *Policy Studies Journal* 24 (4): 666–675. doi:10.1111/j.1541-0072.1996.tb01655.x.

U.S. Department of Education, National Center for Education Statistics. 2009. *The Condition of Education 2009*, Table A-32-1. NCES 2009-081. Accessed 6 July 2012. http://nces.ed.gov/pubsearch/pubsinfo.asp?pubid=2009081.

Wolf, P. J. (2008). "School Voucher Programs: What the Research Says about Parental School Choice." *Brigham Young University Law Review*, 415–446.

—Joshua D. Reichard

SCHOOL CHOICE MOVEMENT, THE

For more than 20 years, Christian schools have been leaders in the school choice movement. School choice provides parents with educational options for their children and can provide government funds for private educational institutions. In 2002 the U.S. Supreme Court found in *Zelman v. Simmons-Harris* that school choice is not a breach of the first amendment (Garnett 2010), allowing individual states to offer school choice without significant legal complications. Christian schools utilize school choice in two major ways, charter schools and voucher programs.

Charter Schools

Charter schools began in St. Paul, Minnesota, and are currently found in 42 states plus the District of Columbia. They are privately run schools that are owned by the government. Being government owned, they must respect the separation of church and state and cannot allow religious beliefs to influence student selection, hiring practices, curriculum, or even the display of religious pictures or Bible verses. They can teach the value of their religion and are usually more integrated within their community because they are "tailored to the needs of the community they serve" (Bailey and Cooper 2009, 274).

Voucher Schools

Voucher schools have more religious freedom. They are privately owned; the government has a financial arrangement with the parents through vouchers given to the private school the parent selects. Because the financial arrangement is with the parents, not the school, the school has greater freedom and faces fewer government regulations. However, Coulsen (2011) notes that school choice will always include government regulation. With vouchers, these regulations are decided by each state. In Wisconsin, the first state to use vouchers, Christian schools accepting vouchers can use Christian standards in hiring, curriculum, and décor, but cannot refuse to accept a student based on religion or force a student to attend religious classes (Bible or chapel). However, Reichard (2012) states that a primary reason school choice parents select a religious school is that they want religion taught to their children, and Cohen-Zada and Sander (2007) note that religious parents will choose religious voucher schools. Most voucher schools are required to have state-approved accreditation and yearly testing for the voucher students who attend them. Often, vouchers are tied to a financial means test, whereby only families below the poverty line (or a multiple of the poverty line established by the state) may receive vouchers.

Some Christian voucher schools were established before school choice and will only accept a predetermined percentage of voucher students. Other Christian schools began as a response to the opportunity vouchers create, and they enroll primarily voucher students. These schools are generally urban schools, with the majority of their students' families being at or below the poverty line. Often these students will also come from failing public schools.

Benefits of School Choice

Research demonstrates several benefits of school choice, including greater parent involvement and satisfaction (Reichert 2012). There is also a positive correlation between student test scores and length of time spent at a choice school. In addition, attending a choice school positively impacts school attendance, high school graduation, college attendance, and even college graduation (Cowen et al. 2013). An increase in college graduation of black students using vouchers has been especially significant (Chingos and Peterson 2012). In addition, school choice students are less likely to be involved in crime (Dills, Hernandez, and Julian 2011) and are given an option other than the failing schools in their neighborhood (Rabovsky 2011). The Christian school experiences increased growth and the enrichment of greater student diversity.

Negative Concerns Regarding School Choice

There are, however, possible negative consequences of school choice. With greater regulations there is an increased cost. Barb Weir, director of admissions at Heritage Christian School in Brookfield, Wisconsin, notes that costs include a yearly audit, additional testing, and additional administrative support due to government forms and increased regulation (personal communication, 30 May 2013). David Bramlett, principal at Hope Fortis School in Milwaukee, Wisconsin, adds that many voucher students have attended failing schools and need additional assistance to reach grade level, requiring schools to hire tutors (personal communication, 30 May 2013). One report also found that when school choice is brought to a community, some private Christian schools close (Ewert 2013).

Impact on School Culture

Character and moral development remain a foundational goal in Christian education, and character is formed not by curriculum, but by culture. Critics of school choice question the impact on a school's moral culture when all students, regardless of their beliefs, moral standards, or past disciplinary infractions, must be admitted to the school. However, David Bramlett states that success can be achieved when schools give "students a vision of success, a purpose to their lives and an expectation of their achievement." Garnett (2010) argues that Christian schools, as advocates of "pluralism, diversity, opportunity, and basic justice" (97), must promote school choice. Jamie Luehrins, executive director at Hope, points out: "Our cities are in trouble. We need to impact all children with the educational difference great schools and Christ can make" (personal communication, 30 May 2013).

References and Resources

Butcher, J. 2013. "School Choice Marches Forward." *Education Next* 13 (1): Retrieved May 28, 2013, from http://education next.org/school-choice-marches-forward-2/.

Chingos, M., and P. Peterson. 2012. *The Effects of School Vouchers on College Enrollment: Experimental Evidence from New York City.* Washington, DC: The Brookings Institution. Retrieved May 28, 2013, from http://www.brookings .edu/research/papers/2012/08/23-school-vouchers-harvard -chingos.

Cohen-Zada, D., and W. Sander. 2007. "Private School Choice: The Effects of Religious Affiliation and Participation." *Journal of Urban Economics* 64: 1–45.

Coulson, A. J. 2011. "Do Vouchers and Tax Credits Increase Private School Regulation? A Statistical Analysis." *Journal of School Choice,* 5: 224–251. doi: 10.1080/15582159.2011.576577.

Cowen, J. M., D. J. Fleming, J. F. Witte, P. J. Wolf, and B. Kisida. 2013. "School Vouchers and Student Attainment: Evidence from a State-Mandated Study of Milwaukee Parental Choice Program." *Policies Studies Journal* 41 (1): 147–168.

Dills, A. K., and R. Hernandez-Julian. 2011. "More Choice, More Crime." *Education Finance and Policy,* 6(2), 246–266. DOI: 10.2139/ssrn.1078906

Ewert, S. 2013. "The Decline in Private School Enrollment." SEHSD Working Paper Number FY12–117. U.S. Census Bureau, Social, Economic and Housing Statistics Division.

Garnett, R. W. 2010. "School Choice and the Challenges That Remain: A Comment on Richard D. Komer's 'School Choice and State Constitutions' Religion Clauses'." *Journal of School Choice* 4: 93–99. DOI:10.1080/15582151003626459.

Harr Bailey, M. J., and B. S. Cooper. 2009. "The Introduction of Religious Charter Schools: A Cultural Movement in the Private School Sector." *Journal of Research on Christian Education* 18: 272–289. DOI: 10.1080/10656210903345255

Rabovsky, T. 2011. "Deconstructing School Choice: Problem Schools or Problem Students?" *Public Administration Review* 71 (1): 87–95.

Reichard, J. D. 2012. "Religious Values and Tuition Vouchers: An Empirical Case Study of Parent Religiosity as a Factor of School Choice." *Journal of School Choice: International Research and Reform* 6 (4): 465–482.

—Wendy Lundberg

School Finances

Close to the core of every successful Christian ministry is a well-thought-out philosophy for how the administrator and board approach the establishment of the price tag placed on the services they provide. In a presentation to Christian school leaders attending an Association of Christian Schools regional meeting in Greensboro, North Carolina, Brian Carpenter (1998) described the decision-making process. Carpenter, who has served as an administrator at Gastonia Christian School, argued that there are three simple ways of thinking about managing and leading a Christian school: education, ministry, and business. If you have the business and education legs only, you will have a *private school.* If you have the business and ministry legs only, you will have a well-funded *youth group.* If you have the education and ministry legs only, you will have *no school.*

Carpenter strongly urges leaders not to minimize the importance of the *business* dimension of the school. He believes that *tuition should be set at a rate that is needed to appropriately fund the entire operating budget of the school.* In addition, a primary factor in determining this rate is teachers' salaries, which should be near the salaries of their public-school counterparts. He encourages schools to provide adequate benefits for employees and to establish procedures to monitor the efficient collection of tuition payments. On the other hand, Carpenter strongly discourages the use of fund-raising as a means of keeping tuition rates low. For families needing assistance with tuition payments, he recommends an endowment program to help with the annual expenses of the school (1998).

Few spokespersons on the topic of tuition rates for Christian schools articulate these issues as clearly as D. Bruce Lockerbie, chairman of Paideia, Inc., in Stony Brook, New York. In ACSI's *Leadership Academy 2004 Report* (Ross, 2004), Lockerbie describes the preceding approach as a "cost-based" philosophy. Supporting the idea of funding the operating budget with tuition income, he notes: "In order for the *ministry* of Christian schooling to exist at all, it must be funded by some means adequate to fulfill the promise made by our mission statement" (2004, 92). He charges administrators and board members with the responsibility to consider carefully the average "cost-to-educate" as they set their school's tuition rates. Another significant point he wants school administrators to consider is the perception the community has about a particular school when its tuition rate is artificially suppressed so "everyone can afford it" (92–93). He makes a powerful philosophical statement about whether or not a Christian school should raise its tuition to a level that is closer to its cost-to-educate: "A Christian school should raise its tuition if the board recognizes that the *mission/budget* test reveals a disparity between missions claims and available funding to fulfill those claims" (94).

There are opponents of this approach to establishing the tuition rate. Randy Ross, the director of the ACSI Ohio River Valley Region, arues that a higher "cost-based" tuition does not lend itself to achieving the goal of helping as many parents as possible to obey the mandate of providing a Christ-centered education for their children. Ross is concerned that ever-increasing tuition rates create the perception that Christian schools are elitist and exclusive, as opposed to inclusive. He fears that many families will refuse to take even the first step in the application process. He and others prefer the faith-based approach, which encourages parents of more modest incomes to seriously consider Christian education. This model requires each participant to have faith that God will meet the needs of the school as all members of the community are made aware of the school's financial needs (Ross, 2004).

Calculating Tuition Rates: The Philosophical Framework

1. You must *determine* your mission. *If you want people to invest in children through your school and expect to charge them appropriately, you must to be able to communicate to them what you are about!*
2. *Honestly* evaluate how well you are fulfilling your mission statement from one year to the next.
3. Communicate the fulfillment of the mission to your constituents.
4. *Realize* that approximately 75 percent of any school's operating budget is usually appropriated for salaries and benefits. Thus, the following is an irrefutable rule: As tuition goes, so go salaries. (And as salaries go, so goes the program.) Generally speaking,

    low tuition = poor staff retention = poor quality program

    appropriate tuition = better staff retention = high quality program

In *From Candy Sales to Committed Donors*, Lockerbie (1996, 47) presents some weaknesses of product sales:

- Fund-raising by product sales demeans the very idea of mission.
- Fund-raising by product sales enables the school's board and administration to avoid asking anyone to give.
- Fund-raising by product sales relies on the public's desire for a tangible exchange of goods in return for money, rather than the intangible benefits of good work to the glory of God.

Christian school leaders need to help their donors recognize how their gifts support personnel and programs essential to a school.

Does Your Tuition Cover Your Operating Expenses?

Your goal should be that tuition covers 100 percent of your school's operating expenses (depending on your board's response to the issue of tuition-based budgeting versus faith-based budgeting). If your school's tuition is not covering 100 percent of its operating expenses, consider increasing the percentage it does cover by a little more each year. I have seen a school's budget depend on fund-raising to supplement over 10 percent of the annual budget. This plan included the expectation that the school would earn over $10,000 at the annual sale of Christmas trees. What if it rained for two weeks in December, and no one bought a tree? The leaders of the school would have to go through an entire budget year uncertain of whether they could meet their obligations for the *fixed* costs they had taken on. Serious and prayerful consideration should be given to planning a budget that is tuition-based and to communicating to parents the importance of their support.

What Percent of the Total Budget Covers Salaries and Benefits?

Your goal should be that salaries and benefits make up 66 percent of the budget. David Roth advises: "Salaries and fringe benefits are important variables in the budgeting process. Compensation may comprise up to 75 percent of the costs on the expense side of the ledgers, a major factor to be reckoned with when creating a budget. Expect annual tension between appropriate teacher compensation and affordable student tuition. Every administrator deals with this challenge" (2002, 251).

Are There Portions of the Budget, Such as Cafeteria or Athletics Expenses, That Should Be Close to Self-Sustaining but Demand More from Tuition Income?

Your goal should be that expenses and income are a wash. Do the cafeteria expenses exceed the income from the cash collected from those who buy their lunches? Are noneaters paying for this service? Extra expenses such as paper goods supplied for class parties add up quickly. Another issue is the benefit of allowing teachers to eat at no charge. Does the athletic program require a disproportionate amount of the operating fund when compared to the number of students who participate? Should booster club activities or participation fees be expected to offset these expenses? Are bus transportation expenses covered by the students who ride the buses, or are other students who are nonriders subsidizing the cost with their tuition?

Budget Management

You need to develop a procedure to manage the budget (capital and expenses) changes that occur each year. Since budgets are developed prior to the beginning of the year and certain items may change during the year, the administration needs to be able to manage "between the banks." This procedure allows administrators to re-allocate dollars from one account to another as part of their daily management process. It also allows them to reallocate funds on the basis of a certain percentage- or dollar-change maximum without returning to the board for approval. An example is the need to hire new teachers each year. If the school loses a teacher who has two years of experience and hires a teacher who has 10 years of experience to fill the vacant slot, there is no change in head count, but there will be an impact on the salary budget. Managing the budget "between the banks" provides a way for the administration to handle this process within a board-designated percentage or dollar amount each year (e.g., 3 percent or $100,000).

Financial Integrity

Few events will sidetrack or even bring a ministry to its end faster than the failure of its leaders to provide careful procedures for handling money. People demand careful accountability in handling money, and the law requires it. Most important, we owe it to the Lord as stewards of the money that people have given to this work. The apostle Paul understood this concept when he gave instructions in 2 Corinthians 8. In verses 1–4, he discusses the collection that was being taken throughout the region, including the generous offering made by financially struggling churches of Macedonia. In preparation for this collection, Paul sent Titus (v. 6) and another believer "whose fame in the things of the gospel has spread through all the churches" (v. 18, NASB). Paul describes the companion of Titus: "And not only this, but he has also been appointed by the churches to travel with us in this gracious work" (v. 19, NASB). In this passage, Paul establishes at least two concepts required of every ministry, including your school. First, he presents a form of recommendation and a type of background check for the person being considered for hiring. Today, the administration should require these for anyone handling money. The presence of a sizable amount of debt or a bankruptcy in the applicant's past may be cause for serious reservations. Second, Paul addresses a major concept that today is found in procedures known as generally accepted accounting principles (GAAP). According to these principles, whenever money is collected, counted, and recorded, a minimum of two adults who are not related should be present. I refer to this concept as the rule of two. Paul spoke very powerfully about making sure that these people are trustworthy and that they will perform their duties with integrity. Paul explains that these precautions are necessary so that no one can discredit how a gift is administered: "For we have regard for what is honorable, not only in the sight of the Lord, but also in the sight of men" (2 Cor. 8:21, NASB). Do you need a justification for spending money on an annual audit? Look no further than 2 Corinthians 8. Establishing the strongest internal controls places the administrator in the best position to approach a possible donor and discuss the school's stewardship.

References and Resources

Carpenter, Brian. 1998. "Managing and Leading a Christian School." Presentation at the ACSI Convention in Greensboro, NC, February.

Coley, Kenneth S. 2010. *The Helmsman: Leading with Courage and Wisdom.* Colorado Springs, CO: Purposeful Design.

Lockerbie, D. Bruce. 1996. *From Candy Sales to Committed Donors: A Guide to Financing Christian Schools.* Milwaukee, WI: Christian Stewardship Association.

Ross, Randy. 2004. "Should Tuition Be Cost Based or Ministry Based? Counterpoint." In ACSI's *Leadership Academy 2004 Report,* 95–98. Colorado Springs, CO: Association of Christian Schools International.

Roth, David L. 2002. "Turning Vision Into Reality: Managing School Budgets." In *Called to Lead: Understanding and Fulfilling Your Role as an Educational Leader,* edited by Kenneth O. Gangel, 243–255. Colorado Springs, CO: Purposeful Design Publications.

—KENNETH S. COLEY

SCHOOL LAW

In modern Western democracies, the education of the young is of legitimate interest to both parents and the state. However, in the light of various United Nations declarations and conventions, the prime responsibility for the education of their children rests with parents, thus offering some protection from secularizing pressures for those who want their children to receive a Christian education.

The International Convention on the Rights of the Child grew out of the Declaration of Human Rights and was adopted by the UN General Assembly in 1989. It sets out the fundamental rights and freedoms of all people under the age of 18 (the age set by the UN as the end of childhood unless, under a particular nation's laws, the age of majority is earlier) and, while not conferring legally enforceable rights, it does impose minimum obligations on signatory nations. Articles 2(1), 14, and 18 are particularly relevant when considering the respective rights and duties of states and parents and confirm the primacy of parents in the upbringing and development of their children.

It has been argued that minorities to whom the convention applies are afforded the benefits of a degree of special protection, and any individual seeking the protection of Article 27 may do so solely on the basis of membership in an identifiable group. The convention rights apply whether or not a minority group is recognized by the state and are protected in this way to ensure the survival and continued development of the cultural, religious, and social identity of the minority concerned. The state's compliance with Article 27 will be tested primarily through meeting objective criteria, such as providing or allowing schools for minority populations and possibly the means by which members of such groups can obtain access to them.

Members of the Council of Europe signed the European Convention on Human Rights on 4 November 1950. For the purposes of this article, the relevant sections of the convention are Articles 9, 14, and 2 of the First Protocol. Article 9 gives qualified rights to religious minorities. It provides protection against persecution and requires the state to respect the religious beliefs of its citizens, subject to certain controls. Article 14 is concerned, in a general way, with preventing unfair discrimination in relation to the other convention rights.

When developing a legal framework of parental and children's rights in education, the prime concern of the post–World War II international agencies was to protect children from indoctrination by political extremists. This applied particularly to state-run schools. One way of achieving freedom from possible state indoctrination was to give parents rights over their children so that those rights would prevail over the wishes of (possibly malevolent) governments.

The right to an education in conformity with the religious and philosophical convictions of the parents is the subject of Article 2 of the First Protocol of the European Convention. It has been interpreted in various ways and been subject to caveats in a number of countries. For example, some jurisdictions, such as the United Kingdom, while adopting a broad interpretation, do so only insofar as it is compatible with the provision of efficient instruction and training and the avoidance of unreasonable public expenditure. Though the education of children is compulsory in the United Kingdom, to ensure that it conforms to their religious convictions, parents there may decide to educate their children at home, providing the education provided is suitable and of an appropriate standard. In other countries, for example Germany, homeschooling is not allowed.

The child's right to a suitable education places an obligation on the state, in the exercise of any functions that it assumes in relation to education and teaching, to respect the right of parents to ensure such education and teaching in conformity with their own religious and philosophical convictions. However, no mention is made of any rights accruing to children. Their religious and philosophical convictions carry only subsidiary weight (if any). Some critics have argued that this is an inappropriate state of affairs and that greater consideration should be given to the rights of children.

The idea that children enjoy rights is not new, but there are difficulties when decisions are made, especially if the child's wishes conflict with the parents'. The immaturity and inherent powerlessness, particularly of young children, means that their rights are only enforceable as obligations on adults who can, legitimately, only be either their parents (or guardians) or the state. In Western democracies, it would require unusual circumstances for the state to usurp the normal functions of parents, though in cases of, for example, real or alleged child neglect or abuse, it may well do so, irrespective of the expressed wishes of the child. On the other hand, it is argued that older and more mature children should at least have their views taken into account when decisions are made on their behalf. Of course, when they attain adulthood, they can legally make their own decisions, entirely independently of the views of their parents, if they so wish.

Legal cases brought under various jurisdictions have failed to resolve unequivocally the question of what rights children may have under international law if they disagree with the religious or philosophical views of their parents. The dilemma is that if parents must be given the right to intervene on behalf of their children, in order to assert and protect their children's rights, then the children themselves cannot be given a right to litigate separately and/or in disagreement with their own protecting parents.

However, it has been argued that children of an appropriate age and maturity should have their own views respected and taken into account. In England, some have argued that the principle of Gillick Competence—that is, the gradual transfer of rights from parent to child according to their age and maturity—fits easily with the Article 9 sphere of freedom of thought, conscience, and religion and with the right to education in Article 2 of the First Protocol. While this may be the case above the age of compulsory education, it is difficult to see any application before that age where the state places the duty solely on parents to ensure their children are educated.

References and Resources

Van Buren, Geraldine. 1998. *The International Law on the Rights of the Child.* The Hague/Boston/London: Martinus Nijhoff.

Whitbourn, Simon. 2003. *Education and the Human Rights Act 1998*. Austin, TX: National Foundation for Educational Research.

—Andrew B. Morris

Schools for Missionary Children

Since the 1850s, when the first missionary families were sent overseas, there has been discussion about how to best educate missionary kids. Until the 21st century, there were limited options for missionaries living abroad. From the onset, missionaries such as J. Hudson Taylor with the China Inland Mission advocated for educating missionary kids in mission schools located near their parents' ministry. As early as 1854, the first boarding school, the Woodstock School, was established in India for children of foreign missionaries. In 1880 the China Inland Mission followed suit, founding the Chefoo School, or Protestant Collegiate School, in China. From their establishment, mission-run boarding schools have primarily employed foreign missionaries as teachers, taught Western curriculum, incorporated Christian education, and focused on preparing students for entrance into Western universities.

Since the 19th century, international schools for missionary kids have gained prominence. Educational options are still limited, however, for missionaries located in restricted countries or isolated locations. Many parents in these situations choose to either homeschool their children or send their children to local schools until adolescence. After elementary school is completed locally, missionary kids often return to their country of origin to complete their secondary and tertiary education.

Notable Academic Institutions
In the 21st century, there are multiple options for educating missionary children, including national schools, international schools, mission-affiliated schools (boarding and nonboarding), government-affiliated schools, and homeschooling. There are hundreds of accredited international schools, among which the foremost institutions are Faith Academy in the Philippines, Ukarumpa International School in Papua New Guinea, Black Forest Academy in Germany, Morrison Christian Academy in Taiwan, Rift Valley Academy in Kenya, Dakar Academy in Senegal, and Alliance Academy International in Ecuador.

Various academic and social factors influence parents' decisions about their children's education while overseas. Research has shown that parents are often torn between two goals: the desire for their children to integrate into the local culture and language and the desire for their children to be able to reintegrate back into the educational system of their country of origin. These priorities often lead parents to choose Western-style institutions over national schools even when local institutions provide English language and multicultural curriculum. Preparing children for academic success in their home collegiate system has been noted as another high priority for parents.

Christian Philosophy and Mission of Education
The Association of Christian Schools International (ACSI) is one of the principal organizations serving international schools, with almost 24,000 member schools in more than 100 countries. In articulating its vision, the ACSI notes its commitment to promoting Christian education and providing training and resources for Christian educators. The ASCI encourages curriculum that is biblically sound, academically challenging, focused on social justice issues, and culturally relevant. In recent years, international schools have incorporated Christian education into their formal and informal curriculum in a variety of ways. Many Christian institutions require students to take Bible classes and attend on-campus chapel services. Prayer, Bible study, community service projects, and short-term mission opportunities are also encouraged.

References and Resources
Danielson, Edward E. 1984. *Missionary Kid, MK*. Pasadena, CA: William Carey Library.

Hill, Frances M. 1954. *Missionary Education of Children*. Philadelphia: Judson Press.

Lockerbie, D. Bruce. 1975. *Education of Missionaries' Children: The Neglected Dimension of World Mission*. Pasadena, CA: William Carey Library.

Pollock, D. C., and R. Van Reken. 2001. *Third Culture Kids*. Yarmouth, ME: Nicholas Brealey Publishing/Intercultural Press.

—Sarita D. Gallagher

Schweitzer, Friedrich

Friedrich Schweitzer (1954–) was born in Germany into a family with a long history of engaging in the pastoral profession. He was a good student in school and a candidate for an elite-type scholarship.

He entered university in 1974, where he studied theology and education, including psychology and sociology as minor subjects, and pursued a degree in both of the former subjects. His dissertation, partly written at Harvard University in the early 1980s (Schweitzer 2001) was about the formation and development of personal identity and reflected his growing interest in the social sciences. As a postgraduate student in the United States, his attempt to internationalize his own work shaped his understanding of religious education. Schweitzer wrote a number of books strongly influenced by Piagetian development psychology, including its religious varieties, set forth in the theories of James W. Fowler and Fritz Oser, who became his friends.

Since the early 1990s, Schweitzer has been interested in practical theology, which in the German-speaking world is considered the umbrella or "mother" discipline to which the subdiscipline of religious education belongs. He completed a habilitation in practical theology at Tübingen. He is a trained minister and ordained. After working as a minister and teacher of religion, he was appointed full professor at the University of Mainz and later at the University of Tübingen as professor of religious education and practical theology.

Schweitzer is one of the leading figures in Christian education in Germany. He is director of the Institute of Religious Education in the Context of Vocational Schools and chair of the board of the Comenius-Institut, a Protestant center for research and development in education. His research includes major projects in the fields of

- education and religion: general education and religion, religion in kindergartens, and moral education (2001);
- religious education in schools: research on teaching religion (2007, 2009, 2012a);
- confirmation work (national and international study) (with Wolfgang Ilg and Henrik Simojoki 2010);
- history of religious education; and
- international comparative studies (2001, 2004; Osmer and Schweitzer 2003; Schweitzer, Riegel, and Ziebertz 2009).

Schweitzer brings together theology, education, and social sciences. As he notes: "The bible remains a decisive basis for my personal faith as well as for my understanding of theology or my understanding of what the church should be. Moreover, the justification never through my achievements but by 'faith alone,' obviously is one of my deepest convictions" (2012b, 167).

Most Notable Publications

Osmer, Richard Robert, and Friedrich Schweitzer. 2003. *Religious Education between Modernization and Globalization: New Perspectives on the United States and Germany*. Grand Rapids, MI: Eerdmans.

Schweitzer, Friedrich. 2001. "Religious Education Beyond the Nation State: The Challenge of Supranational and Global Developments." In *The Fourth R for the Third Millennium. Education in Religion and Values for the Global Future*, edited by Leslie J. Francis, Jeff Astley, and Mandy Robbins, 159–176. Dublin: LIndisfarne Books.

———. 2004. "Comparative Research in Religious Education: International-Interdenominational-Interreligious." In *Towards a European Perspective on Religious Education: The RE Research Conference, March 11–14, 2004, University of Lund*, edited by Rune Larsson und Halldis Breidlid, 191–200. Bibliotheca theologiae practicae, 74. Skellefteå: Artos & Norma.

———. 2007. "Religious Individualization: New Challenges to Education for Tolerance." *British Journal of Religious Education* 29 (1): 89–100.

———. 2009. "Religious Education's Contribution to Social Cohesion: General Perspectives and the Need for Research." *Journal of Religious Education* 57 (3): 38–45.

———. 2012a. "Principled Pluralism and Theology's Contribution to Religious Education: A Protestant Perspective." In *Teaching Religion, Teaching Truth. Theoretical and Empirical Perspectives*, edited by Jeff Astley, Leslie J. Francis, Mandy Robbins, and Mualla Selcuk, 31–46. Religion, Education and Values no. 1. Oxford: Lang .

———. 2012b. "Religious Education, Identity and Faith in (Post-)Modernity: More Than a Biographical Approach? A Personal Attempt at Finding the Red Thread in My Academic Work on Religious Education." In *On the Edge: (Auto)biography and Pedagogical Theories on Religious Education*, edited by Ina ter Avest, 163–174. Rotterdam: Sense Publishers.

Schweitzer, Friedrich, Wolfgang Ilg, and Henrik Simojoki, eds. 2010. *Confirmation Work in Europe: Empirical Results, Experiences and Challenges; A Comparative Study in Seven Countries*. 1st ed. Konfirmandenarbeit erforschen und gestalten no. 4. Gütersloh: Gütersloher Verl.-Haus.

Schweitzer, Friedrich, Ulrich Riegel, and Hans-Georg Ziebertz. 2009. "Europe in a Comparative Perspective—Religious Pluralism and Mono-religious Claims." In *How Teachers in Europe Teach Religion: An International Empirical Study in 16 Countries*, edited by Hans-Georg Ziebertz und Ulrich Riegel, 241–255. Berlin, Münster: Lit.

—Peter Schreiner

SCIENCE

Science is a word with many meanings. The acquisition of new knowledge is properly called science, as is the systematizing of that information into some kind of fundamental compilation of ideas. The methodology by which one obtains knowledge is also science, and yet the practical usage of such knowledge is science. The word *science* is multifaceted in meaning and usage. It is the organization of knowledge and the method by which that information is acquired and employed. It involves discovery, methodology, organization, and application; in order to accomplish these tasks, distinctions must be made to demarcate the varieties of scientific endeavor.

In today's world, it is necessary to distinguish between the study of nature and other studies that primarily focus on individuals and groups of people. The term *science* can be applied to both studies. *Social science* is the study of people, and includes studies such as economics, humanities, psychology, and sociology. *Natural science* is the study of nature and involves objectively observable phenomena that pertain to the relationships and transformations of energy and matter.

Within the context of a Christian education, natural science is learning more with regard to the Creator, as one engages in study of His handiwork. The study of science is conducive to the spiritual maturity of a Christian. God decreed to create a physical world, yet it was not necessary for Him to do so because He was not lacking in any regard (cf. Gen. 1–2; John 1:1–3; Heb. 1:2). God chose to create the world, then declared that the creation was very good (Gen. 1:4, 10, 12, 18, 21, 25, 31). God created for his own purposes (Col. 1:16–17). Unfortunately, the creation was affected by the fall of humanity (Gen. 3) and is not perfect as it once was. Nevertheless, the dignity of God's creation is evident in that—in the person of Jesus Christ—the Lord God became a part of His creation (John 1:14). Science can thus be described as "thinking God's thoughts after Him" (in the words of Johannes Kepler), which is the meaning of natural revelation. For example, to examine a musical composition is to learn something regarding the mind of the composer. Similarly, natural science reveals the mind of the Creator (cf. Ps. 19: Rom. 1:18–20). Humanity alone has been given responsibility for the stewardship of God's creation (Gen. 1:28–30); thus one must understand how the creation works.

Natural science may be divided into two primary categories: biological science (the study of living things) and physical science (the study of nonliving things). Biological science can be subdivided into two broad and primary categories: botany (the study of plant life) and zoology (the study of animal life). Physical science is represented by many disciplines, such as astronomy (the study of celestial bodies), chemistry (the study of the composition, properties, and structure of matter), geology (the study of the earth), meteorology (the study of the atmosphere and its phenomena), and physics (the study of energy and matter in expressions of force and motion). The broad categories of natural science can be subdivided into smaller disciplines of study. For example, a biologist who focuses on microscopic organisms is called a microbiologist. A chemist who is focused on determining substance compositions is called an analytical chemist. Biology and chemistry may even coincide, as in the study called biochemistry.

If one is to acquire a general education, science has always been regarded as a necessary component. The first scientists were educated with a general knowledge of and demonstrated a particular interest in the earth and the heavens surrounding it. The first true scientific discipline was probably astronomy. Within the Greco-Roman culture, the course of study for students included grammar, logic, and rhetoric (the *trivium*), which was considered preparatory for the *quadrivium* (arithmetic, astronomy, geometry, and music). Whereas music and rhetoric are regarded as arts, the disciplines of arithmetic, geometry, and grammar are the tools of art and science. An understanding of the sciences is an essential component of a general education, and anyone who is entirely uninformed with regard to science must be regarded as having a deficient education.

References and Resources

Bigalke, Ron J., Jr., comp. and ed. 2008. *The Genesis Factor: Myths and Realities.* Green Forest, AR: Master Books.

Denton, Michael. 1986. *Evolution: A Theory in Crisis.* Bethesda, MD: Adler & Adler.

Johnson, Phillip E. 1995. *Reason in the Balance.* Downers Grove, IL: InterVarsity Press.

Morris, Henry M., and Gary E. Parker. 1982. *What Is Christian Science?* El Cajon, CA: Master Books.

Ramm, Bernard. 1955. *The Christian View of Science and Scripture.* Grand Rapids, MI: Eerdmans.

Whitcomb, John C., Jr., and Henry M. Morris. 1967. *The Genesis Flood: The Biblical Record and Its Scientific Implications.* Philadelphia: Presbyterian and Reformed.

Wiker, Benjamin, and Jonathan Witt. 2006. *A Meaningful World.* Downers Grove, IL: InterVarsity Press.

—Ron J. Bigalke

Scientific Discoveries, Impact of

Introduction

The presence of science, as a study of the natural world and the nature of humans, has presented many challenges to Christian faith and life. While Christian educators may receive and adapt a number of scientific judgments and their accompanying technologies, some require redefinition and radical change in either theological understanding or pedagogical practice. Often these insights challenge issues concerning the nature of being (ontology) and the nature of truth (epistemology), and even the nature of God or God's ultimate ends (metaphysics). Undergirding these differences might be competing philosophical claims concerning terms such as "mind," "knowledge," and even "justification," terms that prove crucial to a discussion in the philosophy of science and religion.[7] Singular theories, or discoveries, have at times yielded radical changes for Christian education.

Historical Accounts

At least three shifts in science have presented radical points of departure in Christian teaching. Two shifts are well known and extensively documented, with one remaining an area of deep contestation. The third shift (which occurred between the other two) remains significant for current Christian education and points to future studies as well.

The first notable discovery might best be captured in the work of Nicholas Copernicus (1473–1543) and particularly Galileo Galilei (1564–1642), which revealed that the earth was not the center of the universe. This discovery shifted a generally accepted Christian geocentric (earth at the center) view to a heliocentric view of a rotating earth, revolving with heavenly planets around the sun. Copernicus actually updated an idea advanced in ancient Greece, but one dismissed by the church. His publication of *On the Revolutions of Heavenly Spheres* (1543) really did develop the argument for the sun's true influence on the earth's rotation, though he lacked complete empirical proof (supplied later by astronomers and physicians, including the Christian astronomer Johannes Kepler).[8]

Galileo Galilei advanced Copernicus's argument based on his refinements of the telescope and subsequent stellar and planetary observations. While his major work, *Dialogue on the Two Chief World Systems, Ptolemaic and Copernican*, was not published until 1632, Galileo experienced difficulties with Catholic Church authorities (the Inquisition) beginning with his letters in 1615 supporting Copernicus. Galileo's highly controversial trial and condemnation (not excommunication) set the stage for a continuing controversy into the 20th century on his status as a Catholic.[9] Overall, the overturning of the geocentric view of the world did more than unseat the notion that humanity stood at the center of the universe. The controversy challenged the church's particular way of reading scripture and teaching of history, including Genesis 1–11. In addition, this shift in natural sciences opened the way to future discoveries, including evolutionary views of geological change that eventually supported the second major shift.[10]

Another major controversy, still contested today, revolves around the research and writing of Charles Darwin (1809–1882) and his publications *On the Origin of Species* (1859) and *The Descent of Man and Selection in Relation to Sex* (1871). Christian educators should note that Darwin continued to revise his evolutionary theory through subsequent revisions of *Origin*. However, the idea of natural selection, and Darwin's attendant ideas concerning human evolution, invited both adaptation by liberal Christianity and outright rejection by both conservative Christians (including the fundamentalists) and the Roman Catholic Church of that era. Even Catholic scientist and layman George Jackson Mivart, who originally refuted some of Darwin's presuppositions, was ultimately excommunicated for holding an alternative theory that still embraced elements of evolutionary theory.[11] In addition, the subsequent trial of John T. Scopes in 1925 for teaching evolutionary theory in Tennessee divided committed Christians in the United States along specific lines governed by particular readings of scripture as well as differences in theology. Reflections on theistic evolution, intelligent design, and more contemporary instances of theistic "fine tuning" arise in response to either evolutionary thinking or the more nuanced rejection of natural selection as the mechanism within evolutionary thought.[12]

Whereas Copernicus and Galileo shifted the cosmological center of the universe, Darwin shifted the anthropological center of the universe by challenging human uniqueness. These shifts created several conceptual disagreements around interpreting basic theological categories, such as the nature of the image of God, the nature of sin, and the scope and process of salvation.[13] Entire educational ventures rose to promote either creationist or evolutionary thought.[14] To date the controversy still remains open to debate.[15]

---

7. Nancey Murphy, "The Role of Philosophy in the Science/Religion Dialogue," in *A Science and Religion Primer*, ed. Heidi A. Campbell and Heather Looy (Grand Rapids, MI: Baker Academic, 2009), 23–27; Michael Stenmark, "How to Relate Christian Faith and Science," in *The Blackwell Companion to Science and Christianity*, ed. J. B. Stump and Alan G. Padgett (Oxford: Blackwell Publishers, 2012), 63–73; Nicholas Rescher, "Authority," in *Blackwell Companion to Science and Christianity*, ed. Stump and Padgett, 74–81.

8. Maurice A. Finocchairo, "The Copernican Revolution and the Galileo Affair," in *Blackwell Companion to Science and Christianity*, ed. Stump and Padgett, 14–16.

9. Ibid., 16–25; Don O'Leary, *Roman Catholicism and Modern Science: A History* (New York: Continuum, 2007), 1–6.

10. O'Leary, *Roman Catholicism and Modern Science*, 9–16.

11. Ibid., 78–112.

12. P. J. Bowler, "Christian Reponses to Darwinism in the Late Nineteenth Century," in *Blackwell Companion to Science and Christianity*, ed. Stump and Padgett 37–47; Edward J. Larson, *Summer for the Gods: The Scopes Trial and America's Continuing Debate over Science and Religion* (New York: Basic Books, 1997); Adam A. Shapiro, "The Scopes Trial Beyond Science and Religion," in *Science and Religion: New Historical Perspectives*, ed. Thomas Dixon, Geoffrey Cantor, and Stephen Pumfrey (Cambridge, UK: Cambridge University Press, 2010), 198–220.

13. Bowler, "Christian Reponses to Darwinism," 42.

14. Bronislaw Szerzynski, "Understanding Creationism and Evolution in America and Europe," in *Science and Religion*, ed. Dixon, Cantor, and Pumfrey, 153–174.

15. Jon H. Roberts, "Religious Reactions to Darwin," in *The Cambridge Companion to Science and Religion*, ed. Peter Harrison (Cambridge, UK: Cambridge University Press, 2010), 80–102.

Between the previous two historical events stands one other discovery that warrants attention by Christian educators. Rather than focusing on the planet in general, or the origins of humanity, this revolution began with the shift from heart to mind. Sir Thomas Willis (1621–1675) was an Oxford physician, minister, and one of the forerunners of the Royal Medical Society in England.[16] Though Willis's formal education proved obsolete at best,[17] he built up a small medical practice surrounded by a group of young scientists, known as the *Virtuosi*. Physicians, pharmacists, surgeons, technicians, and artists inhabited his circle, including William Petty and Robert Boyle, members of the original Royal Society for Promoting Natural Knowledge, and Sir Christopher Wren, the architect of Saint Paul's cathedral in London.[18] Willis's publication of *Cerebri Antome*, or *The Anatomy of the Brain*,[19] established him as a leading neuroanatomist, psychiatrist, and even nascent philosopher-theologian.[20] Most of all, the discoveries of Willis and the *Virtuosi* ushered in what historian Carl Zimmer calls the "neurocentric" age, in which "the brain is central not only to our body but to our conception of ourselves."[21] This view would extend to the rise of future psychologists and educational theorists, including Sigmund Freud, Jean Piaget, and Erik Erikson, all of whom took the workings of the mind as a crucial beginning point of their varying psychological theories.

Willis's contribution is evident today in contemporary investigations in neuroscience through computational studies using noninvasive technology like functional magnetic resonance imaging (fMRI) or electroencephalography (EEG), which yield new insights into brain functioning and learning.[22] As a result of this continuing study, researchers are able to recommend current pedagogical methods that appear "neuro-logical" in encouraging learning based on brain changes.[23]

Future research may yield even greater insights as educational methods correspond to the research. In addition, neuroscience research offers a fresh approach to dealing with issues of holistic learning and divine causation.[24] Ultimately, discoveries in this field may produce new insights for theology and pedagogy that will shape the future of Christian education.

References and Resources

Diamond, Solomon. 1971. Introduction to *In Two Discourses Concerning the Souls of Brutes Which is That of the Vital and Sensitive Man*, by Thomas Willis, translated by S. Pordage, in 1683, v–x. Gainesville, FL: Scholars' Facsimiles and Reprints.

Dixon, Thomas, Geoffrey Cantor, and Stephen Pumfrey. 2010. *Science and Religion: New Historical Perspectives*. Cambridge, UK: Cambridge University Press.

Finger, Stanley. 2000. *Minds Behind the Brain: A History of the Pioneers and Their Discoveries*. New York: Oxford University Press.

Green, Joel. 2003. "Science, Religion and the Mind-Brain Problem—The Case of Thomas Willis (1621–1675)." *Science & Christian Belief* 15 (2): 165–185.

———. 2008. *Body, Soul, and Human Life: The Nature of Humanity in the Bible*. Grand Rapids, MI: Baker Academic.

Hughes, J., and Trevor Thomas. 1991. *Willis 1621–1675: His Life and Work*. London: Royal Society of Medicine Services Limited.

Jeeves, Malcolm, and Warren Brown. 2009. *Neuroscience, Psychology and Religion: Illusions, Delusions and Realities about Human Nature*. West Conshohocken, PA: Templeton Foundation Press.

Larson, Edward J. 1997. *Summer for the Gods: The Scopes Trial and America's Continuing Debate over Science and Religion*. New York: Basic Books.

Murphy, Nancey. 2009. "The Role of Philosophy in the Science/Religion Dialogue." In *A Science and Religion Primer*, edited by Heidi A. Campbell and Heather Looy, 23–27. Grand Rapids, MI: Baker Academic.

Sousa, David A., ed. 2010. *Mind, Brain, & Education: Neuroscience Implications for the Classroom*. Bloomington, IN: Solution Tree Press.

Stump, J. B., and Alan G. Padgett, eds. 2012. *The Blackwell Companion to Science and Christianity*. Oxford: Blackwell Publishers.

Willis, Tomas. (1664/1681) 1971. *The Anatomy of the Brain: The 1681 Edition, Reset and Reprinted with the Original Illustrations by Sir Christopher Wren*. Taukahoe, NY: USV Pharmaceutical Corp.

16. Stanley Finger, *Minds Behind the Brain: A History of the Pioneers and their Discoveries* (New York: Oxford University Press, 2000), 85–99.

17. Ibid., 86–87; J. Trevor Hughes, *Thomas Willis 1621–1675: His Life and Work* (London: Royal Society of Medicine Services Limited, 1991), 15–17.

18. Carl Zimmer, *The Soul Made Flesh: The Discovery of the Brain—And How It Changed the World* (New York: Free Press, 2004), 117–145, 185–187.

19. Tomas Willis, *The Anatomy of the Brain, The 1681 Edition, Reset and Reprinted with the Original Illustrations by Sir Christopher Wren* (Taukahoe, NY: USV Pharmaceutical Corp., 1664/1681/1971).

20. Solomon Diamond, introduction to *Two Discourses Concerning the Souls of Brutes Which Is That of the Vital and Sensitive Man*, by Thomas Willis, translated by S. Pordage in 1683 (Gainesville, FL: Scholars' Facsimiles and Reprints, 1971), ix; Joel Green, "Science, Religion and the Mind-brain Problem—The Case of Thomas Willis (1621–1675)," *Science & Christian Belief* 15, no. 2, 2003, 165–185.

21. Zimmer, *Soul Made Flesh*, 7.

22. David A Sousa, ed. *Mind, Brain, & Education: Neuroscience Implications for the Classroom* (Bloomington, IN: Solution Tree Press, 2010).

23. Judy Willis, "The Current Impact of Neuroscience on Teaching and Learning," in *Mind, Brain, & Education*, ed. Sousa, 46.

24. Joel Green, *Body, Soul, and Human Life: The Nature of Humanity in the Bible* (Grand Rapids, MI: Baker Academic, 2008); Malcom Jeeves and Warren Brown, *Neuroscience, Psychology and Religion: Illusions, Delusions and Realities about Human Nature* (West Conshohocken, PA: Templeton Foundation Press, 2009).

Zimmer, Carl. 2004. *The Soul Made Flesh: The Discovery of the Brain—And How It Changed the World.* New York: Free Press.

—DEAN BLEVINS

SCOTLAND AND CHRISTIAN EDUCATION

Religious education is a compulsory curriculum subject in Scotland, as it is in the rest of the United Kingdom. The modern history of education in Scotland can be traced back to the 19th century and the initiative of the Christian churches to provide schools for the rapidly expanding urban population; understandably, "religious instruction" was an essential subject in the curriculum. The 1918 Education (Scotland) Act established two types of schools: denominational and nondenominational. At that time the majority of schools, which were originally Presbyterian, transferred into the state nondenominational system, whereas Roman Catholic schools continued with denominational status. The focus in both types of schools was on providing Christian nurture, in a broad nondenominational form in the former case and a doctrinally Catholic form in the latter.

The Millar Report of 1972 into the nature and provision of nondenominational religious education recommended that schools abandon Christian nurture and embrace nonconfessional religious education, that the subject should be inspected, and that teachers of religious education should have specialist training and certification. Over the next decade these measures were implemented and adopted; while the influence of Christianity in Scotland continued to be acknowledged, so too was the presence and importance of "other" religions. In the early 1990s, national "5–14 Guidelines" for all subjects were produced, including "religious and moral education" (Bryce, 2008); these introduced a common structure and organizing concepts for subject areas and represented a move toward a national curriculum for Scotland. The three main areas of focus within religious education were Christianity, other world religions, and personal search. The guidelines also allowed for the study of other worldviews, philosophies, and stances on living. It was originally envisaged that the guidelines would be adopted by the Roman Catholic sector, but this did not happen, and after discussion and debate, a separate set of guidelines, entitled *5–14 Religious Education (Roman Catholic Schools)*, was produced. These guidelines, though adapted from the parallel nondenominational document, were set within a vision of Catholic faith formation, with an emphasis on Christianity and on sacraments and liturgy; some teaching on world religions; and the concept of "personal search" interpreted from the perspective of

Catholic Christianity. The 1990s also saw the emergence of formal, external examinations in religious education, which enhanced the academic credibility of the subject.

A "national debate" on education was conducted in 2002, and the consequent recommendation for a "Curriculum for Excellence" was accepted by the Scottish Executive in 2004; it is now in the process of implementation. The curriculum areas and subjects include religious education, construed as before with two parallel sets of guidelines that pursue two different sets of experiences and outcomes.

References and Resources

Bryce, T. G. K., and W. M. Humes, eds. 2008. *Scottish Education.* Edinburgh: Edinburgh University Press.

McKinney, S. J., and J. C. Conroy. 2007. "Religious Education in Scotland." In *Religious Education in Europe: Situation and Current Trends in Europe*, edited by E. Kuyk, R. Jenson, D. Lankshear, E. L. Manna, and P. Schreiner, 149–171. Oslo: Iko Publishing House.

—L. PHILIP BARNES

SCOTTISH COMMON SENSE REALISM

Scottish common sense realism (SCSR) was a product of 18th- and 19th-century Scotland that pitted Thomas Reid's (1710–1796) commonsense philosophy of sensation against the skepticism of David Hume (1711–1776), which questioned the reliability of cause and effect, and George Berkeley's (1685–1753) idealism and the way of ideas devoid of external reality. The leading proponents of SCSR included Francis Hutcheson (1694–1746), who held the chair of philosophy at the University of Glasgow beginning in 1729; Reid, who held teaching credentials in moral philosophy at Glasgow; and Dugald Stewart (1753–1828), who held the chair of moral philosophy at the University of Edinburgh beginning in 1785. John Witherspoon brought SCSR with him to the College of New Jersey (later Princeton University), serving as its sixth president (1768–1794).

Key Concepts

Thomas Reid, "the principal formulator of the Scottish Common Sense philosophy" (Marsden 1982), believed the skepticism that characterized his age was the result of philosophical speculation, especially that of German philosophers like Hegel and Kant. Commonsense realism believed and assumed that God endowed every human being with mental faculties that allowed humans to construct meaning and an organized system of thought. Reid and other commonsense realists would argue that underlying such thought "is a core of shared basic common sense beliefs found in all ages and cultures" (Hatch and Noll 1982). According to Reid (1827), "Common sense is that degree of judgment which is common to men with whom we can converse and transact business" (421). Common sense led one to believe that experienced sensations were trustworthy and constitutive of reality. According to Ahlstrom (1955), Reid taught that "philosophy depends on scientific observation" (261). Francis Bacon's inductive scientific method was an attractive synthesis for many who held commonsense beliefs, because they believed that one could discover truth by empirical observation and the application of inductive reasoning. A conclusion drawn from this aspect of beliefs associated with SCSR was that such a process of observation and reasoning, common to all humans, was the intuition of moral absolutes that governed the universe God had created.

Adherents to SCSR reacted against the rampant skepticism, idealism, and revolutionary fervor of the French Enlightenment. It provided a sense-based system of thought that allowed its disciples to affirm with confidence belief in moral, spiritual, religious, biblical, and theological absolutes.

Commenting on Reid's version of SCSR, Wolterstorff (2001) demonstrates that Reid held two contradictory and ultimately unresolvable first principles (shared first principles and taken for granted first principles). Wolterstorff's conclusion from his analysis of Reid's writings is that rather than functioning as first principles, they sit behind the first principles as "background and substratum for our beliefs, not basis" (226). He argues that all philosophers take for granted commonsense principles as "the background of his reflections—not the premises from which he draws his conclusions but the ever-present substratum of his philosophical activity" (246). Paradoxically, Reid was "one of the great antirationalists of the philosophical tradition" (260), who accepted with humility the inability of human reason to explain everything to our human satisfaction. Reid's piety ultimately compelled him to conclude that human reason "is entirely dependent upon God, and upon the laws of nature which he has established" (cited in Wolterstorff 2001, 261).

Influence

It seems to be the consensus among scholars that SCSR was the dominant intellectual tradition between the early 1700s and the end of the American Civil War. Speaking to this issue, Ahlstrom (1955) notes:

> The Scottish Philosophy achieved a wider influence by far than any other school. It also broke down denominational barriers with amazing facility, becoming very popular in Great Britain . . . and a strong influence at the Roman Catholic University of Louvain. In America it would rise to dominance for longer or shorter periods among Unitarians, Congregationalists, Presbyterians, American Lutherans and Episcopalians . . . During the first two-thirds of the nineteenth century, at least, it was to become among American Protestants the chief philosophical support to theological and apologetical enterprises. (356)

In regard to its influence among Presbyterians, many believe that the so-called Old Princeton theologians like Charles Hodge (1797–1868) and B. B. Warfield (1851–1921) were deeply indebted to SCSR tenets (overt rationalism with no way to account for subjective elements of human knowing), and many believe that they compromised their Calvinistic theology accordingly (Hatch and Noll 1982; Hoffecker 1990). Those who hold this view believe that Old Princeton theologians applied the inductive reasoning process of SCSR to the formulation of theology. During this theological task, "theologians garner facts from the Bible as scientists investigate facts of nature" (Hoffecker 1990). Smith (2011) has countered these claims, particularly concerning B. B. Warfield, noting that Warfield eschewed both rationalism and mysticism but followed a more Calvinistic appreciation for the work of the Holy Spirit to illuminate the mind of the redeemed and to convict the mind of the not-yet-redeemed. Marsden (1982) indicates that the SCSR hegemony emanating from Princeton began to wane "between the Civil War and World War I" (115), because of its adherents' inability to "account for the wide prevalence of error" (114).

Common sense realism's influence on American evangelical Christian educators was indirect but significant. The Scottish philosophy, combined with Baconian theological induction, provided the fertile soil for Princeton theologians like Hodge and Warfield to formulate their doctrine of biblical inerrancy and authority, provided a philosophical defense against German higher criticism, and emphasized the superiority of the inductive study of scripture (Hatch and Noll 1982; Marsden 1982, 1991). Reid (1788) argued that our commonsense endowment to make rationale judgments through sense perception was "one of the noblest gifts of God to man" (57). Evangelical Christian educators generally understand this as part of the creational endowment of the image of God that makes possible the pursuit of teaching and learning accompanied by the empowerment of the Holy Spirit.

References and Resources

Ahlstrom, S. 1955. "The Scottish Philosophy and American Theology." *Church History* 24 (3): 257–272.

———. 1972. *A Religious History of the American People*. New Haven, CT: Yale University Press.

Hatch, N., and M. Noll. 1982. *The Bible in America: Essays in Cultural History.* New York: Oxford University Press.

Hoffecker, W. A. 1990. "Princeton Theology." In *Dictionary of Christianity in America.* Downers Grove, IL: InterVarsity Press.

Marsden, G. 1982. *Fundamentalism and American Culture: The Shaping of Twentieth-Century Evangelicalism 1870–1925.* New York: Oxford University Press.

———. 1991. *Understanding Fundamentalism and Evangelicalism.* Grand Rapids, MI: Eerdmans.

Noll, M. 1985. "Common Sense Traditions and American Evangelical Thought." *American Quarterly* 37 (2): 216–238.

Reid, T. 1764. *Inquiry into the Human Mind on the Principles of Common Sense.* London: T. Cadell in the Strand.

———. 1788. *Essays on the Active Powers of Man.* Edinburgh: John Bell.

———. 1827. *Essays on the Powers of the Human Mind.* London: R. Griffin.

Smith, D. 2011. *B.B. Warfield's Scientifically Constructive Theological Scholarship.* Eugene, OR : Pickwick Publications.

Wolterstorff, Nicholas. 2001. *Thomas Reid and the Story of Epistemology.* Cambridge, UK: Cambridge University Press.

—STEPHEN D. LOWE

SCOTTISH UNIVERSITIES

The original four Scottish universities are University of St. Andrews (established 1413), University of Glasgow (established 1451), University of Aberdeen (established 1495), and University of Edinburgh (established 1583). The first three were founded during the rule of the Roman Catholic Church in an era when the roles of the church and state were unified. The fourth institution (Edinburgh) was founded as a seminary during the Reformation. These universities pride themselves on their research and global influence. All four are considered ancient institutions, as no more such institutions were added in Scotland until 1964. Currently there are 15 universities in Scotland.

Noteworthy among the original four Scottish universities was the establishment of the University of Aberdeen. Originally there were two colleges in the city of Aberdeen: King's College, founded in 1495, and Marischal College, founded in 1593. Through an act of Parliament in 1858, the two colleges merged to form the University of Aberdeen.

The ancient Scottish universities underwent significant transitions, from being founded as Roman Catholic institutions during the pre-Reformation era to being removed from Catholic authority during the Reformation. The turbulent times led to an absorption of significant protestant and Calvinistic tendencies after the Reformation. Under the strong influence of Calvinist thinking in Scotland, a unique dynamic developed showcasing a political, intellectual, social, and theological struggle in "a land of one religion ruled by a monarch of another" (Shelley 1995, 262). This transition to Calvinistic thought permeated the halls of the Scottish universities to various degrees, with reform efforts in the university with its new "protestant identity" (Reid 2008, 191). Presbyterian minister and educator Andrew Melville tried to bring about major reforms that resulted in some modest influence on the Scottish universities. Following Melville, Robert Howie was credited with playing a larger role by adapting to the middle ground perspective of the Episcopalian movement in England. During this time, the pedagogical commitment to the liberal arts continued while institutional identity questions were processed. The result was four institutions with a Protestant identity.

Part of the significance of the ancient Scottish universities was the development of the concept known as Scottish realism, "which attempted to overcome the epistemological, metaphysical, and moral skepticism of the Enlightenment philosophy of David Hume (1711–76) with a philosophy of common sense and natural realism" (Kelly 2001, 1079). The founder of Scottish realism was a Presbyterian minister, Thomas Reid (1710–1796), who studied at Marischal College and became a professor of King's College. Reid's ideas were picked up by other scholars in the four Scottish universities and continued to be refined until "empiricism in Britain and idealism in Germany drove realism from the field" (1079). However, Scottish realism had a significant influence on French and American philosophers during the 19th century. Kelly notes that, "while it has long been recognized that conservative Calvinist theologians of Princeton adopted Scottish Realist epistemology wholesale, Ahlstrom demonstrates a less noted fact: moderate Calvinists of Andover and liberals of Yale, and Unitarians of Harvard were also deeply indebted to the same common sense realism" (2001, 1079). Kelly goes on to state that Scottish realism "provided the epistemological structure utilized by both 'liberals' and 'conservatives' in nineteenth-century America" (2001, 1079).

Another effect was the development of student missionary societies, which were founded at all four of the ancient Scottish universities during the 1820s (Roxborogh 2000, 861). There was a strong Calvinistic influence and missionary theme within the four universities. These Scottish student missionary societies were significant because they were a form of Christian education internally and also provided opportunities abroad. They provided models for Protestant student missionary societies in the United States.

The ancient Scottish universities are an extraordinary group of institutions worthy of further study purely on their own merits. Their longevity, commitment to the liberal arts, global influence, and Protestant identity provide an example for other institutions. The high value placed on education by the Scottish was carried across the Atlantic Ocean and influenced the development of Protestant Reformed institutions of higher learning in the United States. The student missionary societies also provided a model for Protestant mission clubs and organizations in the United States, which have had a lasting influence on many college campuses around the world from a Christian education perspective.

References and Resources

Kelly, D. F. 2001. "Scottish Realism." In *Evangelical Dictionary of Theology*, edited by W. A. Elwell, 1079. Grand Rapids, MI: Baker.

Reid, S. J. 2008. "Education in Post-Reformation Scotland: Andrew Melville and the University of St. Andrews." PhD diss., University of St. Andrews. http://research-repository. st-andrews.ac.uk/bitstream/10023/849/3/StevenJReidPhD Thesis.pdf.

Roxborogh, J. 2000. "Scottish Mission Boards and Societies." In *Evangelical Dictionary of World* Missions, edited by A. Scott Moreau, 860–861. Grand Rapids, MI: Baker.

Shelley, B. L. 1995. *Church History in Plain Language*. Dallas, TX: Word Publishing.

—Daniel Bennett

Secular Literature and Christian Education

To what extent does secular literature contribute to or comprise Christian education's goal of cultivating virtues that would prepare the soul for the fullest realization and fulfillment of the *logos* given in Jesus Christ? Modern notions of the secular as being in contradistinction to the religious are in many ways incapable of acknowledging the sinewy connections that define their relationship. Equivocation regarding the proper relationship between secular literature and Christian education can easily be traced back to the influence of Roman and Greek ideas and cultures on the burgeoning Christian religion. The philosophies, myths, and poems of the ancients were far from secular, but the extent to which they were non-Christian is uncertain.

"What Has Athens to Do with Jerusalem?"

On the one hand, there were those, including Jerome, Augustine, and Tertullian, who insisted on the dangers Greek and Roman thought posed for Christianity. In the same text in which Tertullian (AD 160–225) famously asks, "What has Athens to do with Jerusalem, or the Academy with the Church?," he also writes that heresy denotes a "self-willed choice" to privilege non-Christian influences over what he sees as Christian truth or "Rule." Tertullian warns: "Valentinus is indebted to Plato, Marcion to the Stoics, Lucanus to Epicurus, Hermogenes to Zeno, Apelles to Hereclitus, while the Gnostic denial of the Resurrection is common to all philosophers" (VII).[25] Tertullian indicts his contemporaries as heretical based on guilt by association with their non-Christian philosophical influences. He therefore presents a division between secular and Christian ways of knowing in which "there is an irreconcileable antagonism" (ibid).

If Tertullian's distrust of philosophical literature meant that the church should have little to do with Greece, Clement of Alexandria presented an altogether different view of Christian education. Clement viewed philosophy and the literature of the ancients as a seed that served to bring the Greek world to Christ. As director of the catechetical institution in Alexandria, Clement expanded Christian education to include the sciences and literature of the Greeks.[26] The strongest argument for incorporating the works of, for example, Homer, centered around the extent to which these works promoted virtue and moral development. For Clement, the process of discerning a hierarchy of heavenly versus earthly knowledge was essential to spiritual growth.

Secular and Religious

It is through this debate about the value of secular thought and education that one can begin to explore a definition of secular literature more specifically. What we call secular literature today, in early Christianity would not only have included philosophy in its strictest sense, but also the philosophical writings of the poets and historians of ancient Greece and Rome. This literature was secular in the Christian sense of *secularis*, meaning that it belonged to the non-Christian world. But secular did not mean it was empty of content that one could call religious or even Christian. Whether philosophical, scientific, or artistic in design, in the West these discourses were rarely if ever developed in complete isolation from Christendom.

During the Middle Ages, the line between secular and religious was entirely blurred as theologians read "secular" literature as religious prophecy. Literary biblical scholar Stephen Prickett notes, "Thus Virgil's fourth *Eclogue*, with its prophecy of a coming ruler, was understood as a paral-

---

25. Tertullian, *Quinti Septimii Florentis Tertulliani: De Praescriptione Haerticorum Ad Martyras; Ad Scapulam*, trans. T. Herbert Bindley (Oxford: Clarendon Press, 1893).

26. Michael J. Anthony and Warren Benson, *Exploring the History & Philosophy of Christian Education: Principles for the 21st Century* (Grand Rapids, MI: Kregel, 2003).

lel to Isaiah and a foretelling of Christ."[27] Medieval interest in the multiple layers of meaning meant that all literature gestured toward a greater truth. Courtly love poetry, for instance, was often incorporated in devotional writing.

During the Reformation and Counter-Reformation, many Catholic and Protestant reformers developed a heightened interest in humanism's textual study, including attention to translations accompanied by careful analyses of texts in their original languages. Perhaps the most famous Christian humanist, Erasmus, read the Greeks as a means to delve more deeply into the biblical text. Whether these techniques would provide greater access to the meaning of the text or obfuscate the truth given in divine revelation remained equivocal.

The most notable shift delineating the boundary between secular and religious arose during the Enlightenment. The Enlightenment's focus on science and its criteria of rational scrutiny engendered antagonism from traditional views regarding the divine revelation and inspiration of biblical and theological Christian literature. Those who wanted to subject Christian thought and writing to developments in the study of secular literature applied techniques that despiritualized the biblical text; however, these same critics often found artistic inspiration in the forms, language, and style of the biblical text. For these latter critics associated with 18th- and 19th-century romanticism, the result was a blossoming of secular literature with religious themes of transcendence, the supernatural, universal truths, and so forth. Writers such as Milton and later Coleridge are often said to have benefited from these developments in literary studies.

The centuries-old debate regarding the proper role of secular literature in Christian education has more recently become a question not of the inevitable relationship between secular culture and religious life, but rather of how to approach this interaction. Can there be a Christian discourse that locates common values in a post-Christian world in which diversity actively undermines universal concepts and ideals? In her essay on secular children's literature and Christian education, Sheryl O'Sullivan (2006) takes a page from the medieval world, suggesting that regardless of explicit Christian commitments, literature that promotes virtue and spiritual development evidences God's presence. To suggest otherwise would be to limit God's acting presence in the world.

References and Resources

Anthony, Michael J., and Warren Benson. 2003. *Exploring the History & Philosophy of Christian Education: Principles for the 21st Century.* Grand Rapids, MI: Kregel.

O'Sullivan, Sheryl. 2006. "The Invisible Being: Finding Images of God in Secular Children's Literature." *Christian Education Journal*, Series 3, 3 (1): 43–57.

Prickett, Stephen. 1999. "Biblical and Literary Criticism: A History of Interaction." In *Literature and the Bible: A Reader*, edited by David Jasper, Stephen Prickett, and Andrew Haas, 12–43. Malden, MA: Blackwell.

Tertullian. 1893. *Quinti Septimii Florentis Tertulliani: De Praescriptione Haerticorum Ad Martyras: Ad Scapulam.* Translated by T. Herbert Bindley. Oxford: Clarendon Press.

—WESLEY NAN BARKER

SECULARISM, THE CHALLENGE OF

The word *secular*, from the Latin word *sēculāris*, means "worldly, temporal." However, there is an absence of consensus among scholars about the definition of secularism. In general, secularism is a humanistic-oriented philosophy based on arguments concerning political, cultural, and social values without reference to religion or religious values. According to George Jacob Holyake (1817–1906), who coined the term *secularism*, it seeks "the development of the physical, moral, and intellectual nature of man to the highest possible point."[28] Secularism promotes the advancement of humanity by upholding human reason and needs, advocating the material importance of life and the human capacity to achieve. The postmodern world calls this *humanism* or *secular humanism*.

The challenge of secularism for Christianity is like two sides of a coin: it has both threatened Christian ideals and provoked the formation of Christian identity. Robert Bellah (1969, *Beyond Belief*), a sociologist, considers that the introduction of Greek philosophy represents an influence of secularism, which pursues a clear, definitive knowledge based on human reason. Defending ecclesiology and exploring a proper relationship between secular authority and the church, St. Augustine (354–430), bishop of the city of Hippo, wrote *The City of God* in the early fifth century. Martin Luther (1483–1546), who led the Protestant Reformation, defended the spiritual independence of individuals by advocating salvation by faith alone through his writings about the doctrine of the two kingdoms, which became a foundation for the idea of the separation of church and state in the modern world. During the Enlightenment, John Locke (1632–1704), an English philosopher, through his work on social contract theory, delineated the legitimacy of the government and the church as he attempted to protect individual liberty

---

27. Stephen Prickett, "Biblical and Literary Criticism: A History of Interaction," in *Literature and the Bible: A Reader*, ed. David Jasper, Stephen Prickett, and Andrew Haas (Malden, MA: Blackwell, 1999).

28. George Jacob Holyake, *The Principles of Secularism* (London: Book Store, 1871), 282; http://www.gutenberg.org/files/36797/36797-h/36797-h.htm.

from the absolutism and despotism of 17th-century Europe. He suggested that human souls should be guarded by the church without the interference of a secular government that promotes the general welfare by focusing on external human interests. Locke's idea was influential in the formation of the constitutional amendment that defines separation of church and state in the United States of America.

The challenges of so-called secular force throughout history—science, philosophy, the pursuit of definite knowledge, and the defining of civil authority—have actually reinforced the church in clarifying and identifying basic Christian beliefs, which enabled the church to form ecclesiology. Harvey Cox, a well-known American theologian, wrote *The Secular City* in 1965, which inspired sensational discussions about the church as a faith community rather than an institution. Cox presented an idea that the revelation of God is found in both the secular and faith communities (both-and) rather than the traditional dualistic understanding (either-or) of secular life and Christian belief. In *The Future of Faith*, Cox further explicated that "Faith is about deep-seated confidence . . . it is about the 'heart.' . . . Belief is more like opinion. They are more propositional than existential."[29] This raises the question: "Is Christian education about teaching subjects based on Christian belief or about cultivating a soul based on Christian faith?" And this leads to the question: "How should Christian education interact with secularism in the postdenominational 21st century?"

The uniqueness of Christian education is that it nurtures students in wisdom and virtue based on Christian values rather than requiring knowledge-based skills as its main object. Christian education is about forming an individual based not only on Christian belief but also through faith, making it a life-forming discipleship process. Formation nurtures individuals who are conscientious about justice and the well-being of humanity. Christian education both cultivates the soul and increases knowledge and skills by integrating human experiences, the result of a God-given human ability to question and explore nature. When Christian education is able to balance these two tasks well, it contributes to humanity as a pathway to God's revelation in spite of challenges concerning secular education as the only "real education."

One of the critical challenges facing Christian education is keeping a clear vision of its unique role in developing the implicit and explicit needs of an individual. Another challenge is financing educational institutions in the midst of an economic downturn and the scarcity of funding sources for private schools.

---

29. Harvey Cox, *The Future of Faith*, Kindle ed. (HarperCollins, 2009), 3.

References and Resources

Bellah, Robert. 1969. *Beyond Belief: Essays on Religion in a Post-Traditionalist World.* Berkeley, CA: University of California Press.

Cox, Harvey. 1965. *The Secular City.* New York: Macmillan.

—HiRho Y. Park

SECULARIZATION OF CHRISTIAN COLLEGES

In recent years, there have been many accounts of the secularization of Christian colleges, perhaps the most important and comprehensive being James Burtchaell's *The Dying of the Light* (1998). Secularization seems to have two distinct meanings. The first denotes the loss or giving up of direct ownership and formal control of the college or university by its sponsoring religious body. This is a widespread phenomenon lamented by Burtchaell, but in fact it does not necessarily lead to the second meaning of the word: the waning of the public relevance of the sponsoring religious body's vision (intellectual tradition) and ethos (way of life, especially the role of chapel) and the diminishing presence of people from that religious body. As this second type of secularization proceeds, it is no longer important to the college to have the sponsoring body's intellectual tradition passed on, its way of life strongly represented in the shared life of the school, and its adherents constituting a critical mass among the personnel of the college. The college no longer privileges these elements in any serious way, because they have become irrelevant to its life and mission.

There are many reasons that secularization, especially of the second sort, has happened to the vast majority of colleges that were once begun, owned, controlled, and pervasively influenced by a specific Christian denomination. There are a number of external factors. First is the struggle for survival in a competitive educational market. There are many schools offering education in the United States, and Christian schools have to compete with them for students and faculty. If the religious tradition is not producing enough prospective students or faculty for its college, the college will often redefine itself to appeal to a larger base of students and faculty. In that redefinition, more specific religious characteristics of the college are often the first to be eliminated. The college assumes prospective students and faculty will be put off by a "sectarian" presentation, so it softens or eliminates those elements of its identity. It slowly secularizes itself in order to be competitive.

The second external cause of secularization has been the dominance in elite circles of what could be called the Enlightenment paradigm, the conviction that the only reliable knowledge originates in science and reason. Religious sources for claims to truth—revelation, religious tradition, theology—are viewed by the Enlightenment paradigm as historically contingent, narrow, and irrational—mere opinion or unfounded belief. This paradigm, promulgated with great success by German and then American research universities, convinced many faculties that theology should be banished from higher education in favor of the "universal truth" of science and reason. The colleges of the Protestant mainstream were particularly vulnerable to this dismissal of theology, because they gathered and honored faculties trained in graduate schools dominated by the Enlightenment paradigm. But all Christian schools have to deal with faculty who have been trained to marginalize religious claims or dimensions in the fields in which they have been trained.

In recent years, postmodern thinking has challenged and in many instances has undercut the Enlightenment approach. Postmodernism emphasizes the social conditioning of all knowledge, thus leading to perspectivalism. In some public universities, that has opened the door to Christian perspectives in many fields, but in Christian colleges postmodernism can work as a secularizing force. Its suspicion of meta-narratives and comprehensive schemes of meaning can lead to the demotion of Christian claims based on the biblical drama of redemption and the Christian intellectual tradition. Christian doctrine comes under heavy suspicion and cannot be trusted to guide the life of the college or to provide trustworthy intellectual claims.

But external pressures are not the only factors in the widespread secularization of Christian colleges and universities. One major internal factor has been the inability of the academic leadership to articulate and embody a clear theological vision of the mission of the college to meet external challenges. Even clergy presidents were not educated well enough to define the mission of the college in a winsome way that avoided sectarianism on the one hand and a thinning out of the religious character of the college on the other. Further, few in administrative or faculty leadership were sophisticated enough to counter the claims of the Enlightenment paradigm. Because they had no clear vision of the role of theology in the mission of the college, they hired faculty who were only too eager to follow the Enlightenment imperative to marginalize the intellectual and moral claims of the school's Christian tradition.

Some religious traditions were pietistic. They were religions of the heart and not the mind. They had weak intellectual traditions and therefore entrusted the religious character of the college to its extracurricular activities. Meanwhile, the central educational functions of the college have been dominated by Enlightenment or postmodern assumptions, both of which have led to the public irrelevance of Christian intellectual claims. This has led to what is called the "two spheres" approach to Christian higher education. Only the extracurricular environment is recognizably Christian. Education itself is thoroughly secular.

Finally, the secularization of the colleges has been precipitated by a gradual loss of faith in the intellectual and moral relevance of the Christian faith itself. As faith receded, other sources of inspiration, knowledge, and moral guidance took its place. Soon the influence of the faith became dispensable, sometimes an object of hostility.

References and Resources

Benne, R. 2001. *Quality with Soul: How Six Premier Colleges and Universities Keep Faith with Their Religious Traditions.* Grand Rapids, MI: Eerdmans.

Burtchaell, J. 1998. *The Dying of the Light: The Disengagement of Colleges and Universities from Their Christian Churches.* Grand Rapids, MI: Eerdmans.

Gleason, P. 1996. *Contending with Modernity: Catholic Higher Education in the Twentieth Century.* New York: Oxford University Press.

Longfield, B., and G. Marsden, eds. 1992. *The Secularization of the Academy.* New York: Oxford University Press.

Marsden, G. 1994. *The Soul of the American University: From Protestant Establishment to Established Nonbelief.* New York: Oxford University Press.

Schwehn, M. 1993. *Exiles from Eden: Religion and the Academic Vocation in America.* New York: Oxford University Press.

Sloan, D. 1994. *Faith and Knowledge: Mainline Protestantism and American Higher Education.* Louisville, KY: Westminster John Knox Press.

—Robert Benne

SEEKER COURSES

A seeker course is an evangelistic, small group course that introduces participants to basic elements of the Gospel. The targeted participants are "seekers" who are searching for meaning, truth, or "divine" experience. These courses serve as an evangelistic teaching tool in a post-Christian world where a simple Gospel witness is no longer sufficient to communicate the Gospel to the unchurched. Thus, teaching the Gospel does not occur *after* evangelism as a transition to discipleship, but becomes a mode of discipleship even *before* people come to faith in Christ. The term "seeker' refers to the church growth movement of the late 20th century, notably to the Willow Creek Community and Saddleback churches as nationally known seeker-oriented churches.

With the breakdown of traditional forms of Christianity and Christian formation in the second half of the 20th century, few unchurched people had any recollection of church or the Gospel, so the need arose to reorient evangelistic ministries, often inspired by the ancient catechumenate, resulting in a large variety of seeker courses.

Available Materials

Materials from the 1970s from the Navigators and Campus Crusade focused on basic Gospel elements (creation, sin, forgiveness, and new life) in a series of booklets with fill-in blanks. In the 1990s the Alpha course was developed, focusing on knowing Jesus, the nature of faith, prayer and the Bible, resisting evil, and experiencing the Spirit's power (Gumbel 2003). *Purpose-Driven Life* focuses on discovering God's purpose for one's life (Warren 2012). *Christianity Explored* asks who Jesus was and what He came to do, based on readings only from Mark's gospel (Tice and Cooper 2002). The course *From Creation to Christ*, developed in tribal settings, is now used in the Western world, describing the history of salvation from the beginning in 52 lessons (McIlwain and Everson 1993; for an adaptation, see Cross 1996), while other courses generally offer 8–12 sessions. Most courses contain apologetic elements for the existence of God, Christ's divine nature, scriptural authority, and sometimes creation, while more recently experiences of Christ's presence or the Spirit's power have received attention. In addition, dozens of locally produced materials are available, usually to tailor these courses to the desires and needs of particular leaders and denominations.

Seeker course offerings have expanded in two ways. First, new courses target new audiences, such as *Celebrate Recovery* (coping with addictive habits), *Alpha Marriage*, and *Emmaus Youth*. Second, follow-up courses aim to overcome the frequent complaint that participants find it difficult to transition into regular congregational life. The Emmaus course is a prime example, with its three stages to be covered in five course books, two versions of *Emmaus Youth*, and several *Emmaus Bible Resources* for further Bible study (Cottrell, Croft, and Finney 2012). With the increasing use of Internet-based evangelism, such courses are often accompanied by websites. A recent development is the *New City Catechism* by Keller and Shammas, formatted as an app for the iPad and smart phones (http://www.newcitycatechism.com/).

Common characteristics of seeker courses are a small group setting, participant and leader handbooks, and video material on DVD, sometimes with a preceding meal following the Alpha course format.

Effectiveness

Seeker courses function best in the context of an overall strategy for evangelism and enfolding new members into the church fellowship (Lawless 2005; Searcy and Henson 2008). Although their effectiveness is significantly influenced by pastoral support, overall strategy, and leader training, a crucial factor is that the entire membership needs to attract new participants from their own social networks; where contacts from such networks "dry up," these courses generally falter. In addition, regional and cultural factors may enhance or inhibit response, so training and consultation services are offered regionally and locally.

References and Resources

Cottrell, S., S. Croft, and J. Finney. 2012. *Emmaus the Way of Faith: Introduction*. London: Church House Publishing.

Cross, J. R. 1996. *The Stranger on the Road to Emmaus: A Clear and Simple Explanation of the World's Best Seller*. Sanford, FL: Goodseed.

Gumbel, N. 2003. *Questions of Life*. Eastbourne, UK: Kingsway.

Lawless, C. E. 2005. *Membership Matters: Insights from Effective Churches on New Member Classes and Assimilation*. Grand Rapids, MI: Zondervan.

McIlwain, T., and N. Everson. 1993. *Firm Foundations: Creation to Christ*. Sanford, FL: New Tribes Mission.

Searcy, N., and J. D. Henson. 2008. *Turning First-Time Guests into Fully Engaged Members of Your Church*. Ventura, CA: Regal Books.

Tice, R., and B. Cooper. 2002. *Christianity Explored*. Milton Keynes, UK: Authentic.

Warren, R. 2012. *The Purpose Driven Life: What on Earth Am I Here For?* Grand Rapids, MI: Zondervan.

—Jack Barentsen

SEMINARIES IN UNIVERSITY-BASED SCHOOLS, CURRENT STATUS OF

More than 35 percent of the seminaries that are members of the Association of Theological Schools in the United States and Canada are related to larger institutions of higher education, such as a college or university. Some of these theological schools are quite small in enrollment, and others are very large. Some offer only basic professional and academic degree programs, while others offer these basic degree programs as well as advanced academic degrees, including the research doctorate.

Institutions called "universities" can be very different from one another. There are at least four kinds of universities that have theological or divinity schools related to them. (1) Some are small universities that are primarily undergraduate institutions where the seminary is the only graduate or postbaccalaureate professional school. Many of these institutions were previously called colleges but have changed their names to "university" because their degree programs have grown more extensive than traditional liberal arts colleges typically offer. (2) Many seminaries are related to a university that has other professional schools or graduate professional programs in business, education, law, or nursing. These universities are primarily undergraduate institutions, and while they have a variety of graduate professional programs, they typically have limited or no academic graduate degree programs. (3) A third kind of institution is the research-intensive university, the kind of institution that often comes to mind in the context of a university-based seminary or divinity school. These institutions are categorized as "research-intensive" because of the amount of external research grant funding that they attract, the strong research expectations for faculty, and the wide range of research doctorates they offer. The faculty members of divinity schools related to a research-intensive university teach in research doctoral programs (PhD or ThD), which may be offered either by the divinity school or by the university's graduate school. In addition, they teach in the professional and academic master's level degree programs. (4) Another kind of university-based theological seminary is uniquely Canadian. These seminaries function in some ways as freestanding schools but are federated with a university. The federation arrangement results in the theological schools ceding much of the academic control, as well as the awarding of degrees, to the university academic governance structures. These schools are truly university related, but not in the way the first three kinds of schools are.

The governance of all university-related theological schools, with the exception of the uniquely Canadian model, is part of the broader academic and institutional governance structure of the universities to which they are related. Funding of the theological school varies. Some universities provide significant subsidies for the divinity school, and others expect the theological school to generate all of the funds needed for its operation. Because several university-related theological schools offer research doctorates, a significant number of faculty members who teach in North American theological schools have earned their PhD and ThD degrees in these settings. The focus of research-intensive divinity schools also contributes significantly to theological research that is referenced and used throughout North American theological education.

References and Resources

Cherry, Conrad. 1995. *Hurrying Toward Zion: Universities, Divinity Schools and American Protestantism.* Bloomington: Indiana University Press.

Miller, Glenn. 2007. *Piety and Profession: American Protestant Theological Education, 1870–1970.* Grand Rapids, MI: Eerdmans.

—Daniel O. Aleshire

SEMINARIES IN UNIVERSITY-BASED SCHOOLS, DEVELOPMENT OF

The first European universities arose in the late 11th and early 12th centuries to continue the church's efforts to provide a well-rounded education for its clergy. In 1079, Pope Gregory had issued a papal decree mandating that bishops create schools at their cathedrals for this purpose. These "cathedral schools" spread throughout Europe and soon evolved into universities, with the University of Bologna founded in Italy in 1088 and the University of Paris in 1150. Although originally started for the education of clergy, these institutions began to expand their offerings into "secular" fields such as law, mathematics, science, and medicine as Europe transitioned from the "Dark Ages" into the Renaissance.

This secularization of the university's mission led the Catholic Church, in 1563 at the Council of Trent, to mandate "the local creation and maintenance of an institution whose sole purpose was the intellectual and professional formation of clergy" (Comerford 1998, 999). Completely separate from the universities and under total ecclesiastical control, these institutions were to be established in each bishop's see and were to become "perpetual seed-plots for the ministers of God" (Waterworth 1848, 189). The designation "seminary" derived from the Latin word for seed-plot, *seminarium*, and indicated that these institutions would be places where "candidates for the priesthood could be nourished and formed in their sacred calling, apart from distracting 'worldly' influences" (Calian 2002, 1) present in the universities. The segregated seminary soon became the predominant model for clerical education, expanding throughout the Christian world, and has continued into the 21st century.

By the 19th century, however, a few Protestant seminaries began to appear in university contexts in certain parts of Europe. Although these schools were associated with universities, they also maintained their independence through their ties to denominations as well as their commitment to their mission of preparing clergy for the church rather than just theological scholars. Their church ties also provided theological parameters within which each school was to function. Unlike the earlier Catholic model of seminaries that provided all of the potential priests' education in a cloistered environment, these seminaries assumed candidates had a broad, general education before entering the seminary. An English example is St. Stephen's House, which was founded in 1876 and is a part of Oxford University. Although not officially a part of the University of Cambridge, Ridley Hall (Anglican), Wesley House (Methodist), and Westcott House (Anglican) are located in Cambridge and maintain close ties with the university's Faculty of Divinity.

In the United States, two of the first university-embedded seminaries were Harvard Divinity School (1816) and Yale Divinity School (1822). Both were parts of universities (Harvard and Yale) that were founded to provide a broad education to prepare people "for Publik employment both in Church and Civil State" (Yale 1701) and to prevent leaving "an illiterate ministry to the churches, when our present ministers shall lie in the dust" (Harvard 1636). As the universities' educational missions expanded and curricula became secularized, the seminaries were later established as professional schools to provide focused education for clergy, and as such maintained a distinction from the university's religious studies programs.

The 20th century saw the rise of evangelical seminaries in university contexts. This was often the result of the growth and evolution of schools initially founded for ministerial preparation into broader institutions of higher education. Bible institutes and Bible colleges became liberal arts colleges and universities. However, the schools' mission to prepare church leadership continued as seminaries were formed within the larger institution. Examples of this in the United States include Biola University (Talbot School of Theology), Bethel University (Bethel Seminary), Trinity International University (Trinity Evangelical Divinity School), and Cornerstone University (Grand Rapids Theological Seminary). Because of their common heritage, the seminaries and their universities exist within theological parameters determined by a denomination or a well-defined set of constituent churches. As seminaries, these schools have retained their practical focus on the preparation of ministers for the church and are not seen as graduate schools of religion within the university. However, as schools within the university, the seminaries typically function at the graduate level and strive to maintain the university's standards of scholarship and academic excellence. As members of the university's faculty, seminary professors have the opportunity to interact with and be informed by the broader range of disciplines associated with the university at large.

References and Resources

Calian, Samuel. 2002. *The Ideal Seminary: Pursuing Excellence in Theological Education.* Louisville, KY: Westminster John Knox Press.

Comerford, Kathleen. 1998. "Italian Tridentine Diocesan Seminaries: A Historiographical Study." *The Sixteenth Century Journal* 29 (4): 999–1022.

Harvard. 1636. "General Court of Massachusetts Bay Colony." Accessed 3 May 2013. http://www.hds.harvard.edu/about/history-and-mission.

Stackhouse, Reginald. 1977. "The Place of the Theological College in the University." *Theological Education* XIII (2): 101–106.

Waterworth, J., trans. 1848. *The Canons and Decrees of the Sacred and Oecumenical Council of Trent.* XXIII session, ch. XVIII. London: Dolman.

Yale. 1701. "Yale Charter." Accessed 3 May 2013. http://www.yale.edu/about/history.html.

—John Lillis

SEMINARIES, FREESTANDING

Freestanding seminaries in North America are special-purpose institutions of higher education that offer graduate professional degree programs oriented to the practice of ministry in its various forms or graduate level academic study of theological disciplines. They are special-purpose institutions because their educational offerings are generally limited to professional or academic programs in theological disciplines. A freestanding seminary is an independent institution with its own faculty, facilities, administration, governing board, and students, and these kinds of schools constituted the dominant institutional form of theological education in North America in the 20th century. The first freestanding seminaries in the United States included Andover Theological School in Massachusetts and St. Mary's Seminary in Baltimore. These kinds of schools are authorized to grant degrees by the state or province in which they are located, and most are accredited by the Commission on Accrediting of the Association of Theological Schools and/or a U.S. regional accrediting agency. The Association of Theological Schools in the United States and Canada (ATS), which is the primary membership agency for all kinds of seminaries and theological schools, includes among its members about 180 freestanding seminaries in the United States and Canada.

In North America, freestanding seminaries vary significantly in enrollment, ranging from a very small enrollment (fewer than 50 students) to large enrollments (more than 3,000 students). The size of the faculty varies from three to four teachers in the smallest seminaries to more than 100 in the largest. The degree programs offered by freestanding seminaries also vary significantly. The smaller schools offer only a few degrees (usually the master of Divinity [MDiv] and perhaps another professional or academic degree), and the larger seminaries typically offer a wide array of degree programs that would include the MDiv, specialized professional master's programs (such as degrees in counseling, youth ministry, religious education, and missions), academic master's degrees (often in areas like Bible, theology, and church history), and advanced academic research degrees such as the master of theology (ThM) and PhD.

Christianity in North America can be grouped into three large ecclesial families (mainline Protestant, evangelical Protestant, and Roman Catholic/Orthodox), and each of these families has freestanding seminaries related to it. While the majority of freestanding schools are related to a single denomination, many are nondenominational (having no formal relationships with any one denomination) or multidenominational (having formal relationships with more than one denomination). Some freestanding seminaries are owned and operated by the denomination to which they are related; others are not owned by the denomination, but sponsoring denominations exercise some form of control, such as election of members of the board; and still others have self-perpetuating boards, in which the board elects its members without control from a denomination.

References and Resources

Aleshire, Daniel. 2008. *Earthen Vessels: Hopeful Reflections on the Work and Future of Theological Schools.* Grand Rapids, MI: Eerdmans.

Miller, Glenn. 2007. *Piety and Profession: American Protestant Theological Education, 1870–1970.* Grand Rapids, MI: Eerdmans.

White, Joseph. 1989. *The Diocesan Seminary in the United States: A History from the 1780s to the Present.* Notre Dame, IN: University of Notre Dame Press.

www.ats.edu/Resources/PublicationsPresentations/Pages/ArchivedADTs.aspx (This website identifies extensive current and archived data on seminaries that are related to the Association of Theological Schools in the United States and Canada.)

—Daniel O. Aleshire

Seminaries, Theological Schools, and Divinity Schools

The terms "seminary," "theological school," and "divinity school" all refer to special-purpose higher education institutions that provide education for religious leaders and academic study in the theological disciplines. In North America, the schools that use these names operate at the postbaccalaureate level and offer graduate professional or graduate academic degrees. Some schools that use these names are freestanding, independent institutions, and others are related to colleges or universities. The names are generally synonymous and do not distinguish one kind of education or institutional form from another.

There is one exception to this general rule. In Roman Catholic theological education, "seminary" refers to schools that provide the academic and formational education necessary for the ministerial priesthood, and only those schools use the term "seminary." Roman Catholic schools that provide academic theological education for priestly education, but not the formational components, are considered schools of theology.

"Seminary" was used for a range of institutions in 19th-century America. Some focused on specialized areas of study, like teacher education, and others on the liberal and domestic arts. Now "seminary" refers exclusively to schools that educate ministers and other religious leaders. "Divinity school" is often associated with theological schools related to research universities, but there are also freestanding divinity schools and divinity schools related to smaller universities that do not offer research or other academic degrees. "Theological school" is used by a few institutions, and given the range of terms referring to these kinds of schools, it often serves as a generic reference for all of them. The membership organization that these schools have formed, for example, is the Association of *Theological Schools* in the United States and Canada.

By whatever name, these schools all provide education for religious leaders and study in academic disciplines. The predominant degree offered by these schools, whatever name they use, is the master of divinity (MDiv). It consists of the equivalent of three years of full-time study in four primary areas: the texts and traditions of a religious community, the skills necessary for public and religious leadership, the skills necessary to assess the cultural and congregational contexts in which ministry takes place, and the spiritual and personal formation that should characterize religious leaders. These educational areas are served by a variety of academic disciplines. Most of these schools also offer professional master's programs that prepare graduates for specialized areas of ministry such as religious education, counseling, and nonprofit leadership. Many also offer academic degrees that focus on one of the theological disciplines (like biblical studies) or several disciplines (often identified as a degree in theological studies).

Some of these schools are owned and operated by religious denominations; others are independent of any denomination. Some are related to larger higher education institutions, like a college or university; others are freestanding schools.

References and Resources

Carroll, Jackson, Barbara Wheeler, Daniel Aleshire, and Penny Long Marler. 1997. *Being There: Culture and Formation in Two Theological Schools.* New York: Oxford University Press.

Foster, Charles, Lisa Dahill, Lawrence Goleman, and Barbara Tolentino. 2005. *Educating Clergy: Teaching Practices and Pastoral Imagination.* San Francisco: Jossey-Bass.

Miller, Glenn. 2007. *Piety and Profession: American Protestant Theological Education, 1870–1970.* Grand Rapids, MI: Eerdmans.

—DANIEL O. ALESHIRE

SEMINARY CURRICULA

The term "curriculum" comes from the Latin verb *currere*, which means "to run." Thus, a "curriculum" is a running course or race course of learning experiences designed to achieve certain learning objectives based on an institution's mission and purpose.[30] In the broadest terms, curricula include both the materials and the experiences used for teaching and learning. For the seminary setting, according to the General Institutional Standards of the Association of Theological Schools (ATS), curriculum is "a set of practices with a formative aim—the development of intellectual, spiritual, moral, and vocational or professional capacities."[31] Seminary curriculum, therefore, can be viewed as a "blueprint" or plan designed to help students cultivate a lifestyle of theological reflection, practiced and skilled ministry, moral development, spiritual formation, global awareness, and academic theological participation within a community of faith and learning. To accomplish these educational goals, the scope of the curriculum offered by a seminary should seek to provide collaborative learning opportunities both inside and outside of the classroom that facilitate student growth in academics, experiences, and relationships.

The arrangement of the teaching, learning, and research activities afforded by a seminary is primarily embodied in its available degree programs. The principal degree offered by seminaries that is designed to prepare learners for pastoral ministry and leadership is the master of divinity degree (MDiv), considered by most seminaries to be their most comprehensive degree, encompassing the breadth of educational disciplines provided by an institution. Generally, an MDiv degree is broken up into thirds, with one-third being Bible and language, one-third being theology and church history, and one-third being practical ministry and field work.

In addition to the general MDiv degree, many institutions offer more specialized academic degrees, often in the form of a master of arts in an area of expertise (MA, MTS). Generally, academic MA degrees provide more

research opportunities than do practical degrees, with the design of helping students prepare for a PhD in the field. Some seminaries also offer other types of degrees in specialized ministry, affording students an intensive experience in a particular area of ministry. In addition, doctoral degrees in ministerial leadership (DMin) are available in some seminary settings.

References and Resources

Ford, Leroy. 1991. *A Curriculum Design Manual for Theological Education.* Nashville, TN: Broadman Press.

General Institutional Standards. 2012. Bulletin 50, Part 1. Pittsburgh: Association of Theological Schools Commission on Accrediting.

—EDWARD W. WATSON

SERBIA AND CHRISTIAN EDUCATION

Christianity in Serbia started with the first Slav migrations due to Christian missionaries in the fifth, seventh, and ninth centuries. These tribes were baptized successively. However, the turning point of their Christian spiritual reinforcement was marked by the great ecclesiastical figure of St. Sava, archbishop of the Orthodox Church in Serbia, at the beginning of the 13th century, when the Serbian principalities were united in their allegiance to the Ecumenical Patriarchate of Constantinople and the other Orthodox Churches in the East. During the rule of the first tsar, Stefan Dusan (1331—1355), medieval Serbia became an imperial kingdom and the Archbishopric of Pec a Patriarchal See (1346). It was abolished and restored several times, finally in 1920. During World War II, bishops, priests, and 70,000 lay Orthodox Christians were killed by the Moslem and Croatian fascists, and hundreds of churches were destroyed. Under communism, the church was persecuted again and religious education prohibited; it was reintroduced in 2001.

Today, the Theological Faculty in Belgrade, founded in 1920, trains clergy and laypeople to serve the church and teach Christian religion in schools. Besides the major Orthodox faculty in the University of Belgrade, there are also a Catholic faculty in Zagreb, a catechist institute of church music, an institute of theological culture for laypeople, and a Protestant institute. Religious education is confessional.

—ANCA POPESCU

SERMON ON THE MOUNT, THE COMPONENTS OF THE

The Sermon on the Mount is found in Matthew 5:1–7:27. It has been given this title because of its setting. Jesus sees

---

30. Leroy Ford, *A Curriculum Design Manual for Theological Education* (Nashville, TN: Broadman Press, 1991), 34.

31. *General Institutional Standards,* Bulletin 50, Pt. 1 (Pittsburgh: The Association of Theological Schools on Accrediting, 2012), G-5.

the multitudes, goes up onto the mountain (5:1–2), is followed by His disciples, and begins to teach. The word *sermon* can be misleading to Christian educators. It is not a previously crafted homily composed in quiet study and research, to be spoken on Sunday. Rather, it is Matthew's report of an extended teaching segment that Jesus used to encourage and challenge His disciples to apply their faith in a tangible way. A condensed version is also found in Luke 6:17–49, called the Sermon on the Plain because it is said that Jesus "stood on a level place" (6:17). Many believe this extended teaching is part of an earlier collection of the sayings of the historical Jesus, adopted from the Q source (a written collection of the sayings in Jesus predating the Gospels of Matthew and Luke and used by both of them). The structure of the Sermon on the Mount is as follows: The Beatitudes (5:3–12) and Changing the World (5:13–16), the Law and the Prophets (5:17–7:12), the epilogue (7:13–27).

The Beatitudes (Matt. 5:3–12) and Changing the World (Matt. 5:13–16)

The term "beatitude" comes from the Latin "beatus," meaning "blessed," but in some places it is referred to as a "macarism" from the Greek *makarios*, meaning "blessed, fortunate, or happy." In the Gospel of Matthew, the beatitudes are associated with the promise of participation in the Kingdom of Heaven (5:3, 10). The first four beatitudes (5:3–6) emphasize a state of blessedness that is associated with dependence on God. For example, to be "poor in spirit" is an acknowledgment of spiritual bankruptcy before God and is a confession of one's unworthiness and utter dependence upon Him. The next five beatitudes express the outworking of this dependence upon God (5:7–12). For example, people who show mercy to others will themselves be the recipients of mercy. "Mercy" is a comprehensive term that embraces both forgiveness for the guilty and compassion for the suffering and needy. The consequence of these actions is to experience God in full measure in the kingdom: "they will be shown mercy," "they will see God," "they will be called the sons of God," "theirs is the kingdom of heaven," "great is your reward in heaven."

Disciples of Christ can have a profound effect upon the world, as Matthew 5:13–16 indicates. The influence disciples have is directly proportionate to the attitudes they possess, as described in the beatitudes. Jesus uses salt of the earth as a metaphor. Disciples, like salt, penetrate society for good and act as a kind of moral antiseptic. Also, as light dispels darkness, followers of Christ shine forth God's character through their actions.

The Law and the Prophets (5:17–7:12)

In this section of the Sermon on the Mount, Jesus begins to expound on the Old Testament Law and shows that in each case a deeper principle is involved. It was not just the specific Law itself that was important; Jesus was not abrogating the Law, but exposing the limitations in which some provisions in it had been misunderstood. For example, "You shall not murder" makes one liable to the court of justice (5:21). The words following, "but I tell you" do not indicate that Jesus replaces the Law with his own commands, for in no case that follows does He relax a provision of the Law. Rather, Jesus shows that when rightly understood, the Law goes much further than His hearers had understood. Jesus actually goes to the beginning cause of murder and includes anger in the scope of command. In essence, the cause of murder is a failure to acknowledge the worth of the individual who is murdered and who is also a child of God.

Matthew 7:12 states what many call "the Golden Rule": "So in everything, do to others what you have them do to you, for this sums up the Law and the Prophets." This verse has its roots in Leviticus 19:18 ("Do not seek revenge or bear a grudge against one of your people, but love your neighbor as yourself") and Leviticus 19:34 ("The alien living with you must be treated as one of your native-born. Love him as yourself") and also makes an association with the Great Commandment in Matthew 22:39 ("Love your neighbor as yourself"). The passage in Leviticus is a negative prohibition, but the Golden Rule in the Sermon on the Mount emphasizes the need for positive action that brings benefit to another, not simply restraining oneself from actions that would bring harm to another. This is the essence of the Law and the Prophets.

The Epilogue (7:13–27)

The epilogue of this sermon contains a series of contrasts: the wide gate and the broad road versus the small gate and the narrow road, the bad tree versus the good tree, the foolish builder and the wise builder. The general point of all of these contrasts is the distinction between those who hear and obey the words of Jesus and those who do not. Similarly, these two alternatives confront every reader. The challenge is for all who read the sermon to hear the words of Jesus and put them into practice.

References and Resources

Betz, H. D. 1985. *Essays on the Sermon on the Mount.* Philadelphia: Fortress Press.

Blomberg, Craig L. 1992. *Matthew.* Vol. 22 of *New American Commentary.* Nashville, TN: Broadman.

Guelich, R. A. 1982. *The Sermon on the Mount: A Foundation for Understanding.* Waco, TX: Word.

Stanton, G. N. 1992. "Sermon on the Mount/Plain." In *Dictionary of Jesus and the Gospels*, edited by Joel B. Green et al., 735–744. Downers Grove, IL: InterVarsity Press.

Strecker, G. 1988. *The Sermon on the Mount: An Exegetical Commentary.* Nashville, TN: Abingdon Press.

—JOHN A. BERTONE

SERMON ON THE MOUNT, THE MEANING OF THE

The Sermon on the Mount is a discourse of Jesus in the Gospel of Matthew (Chapters 5–7) that took place on a mountainside in Galilee. In Luke's Gospel it is called the Sermon on the Plain, as Jesus is referred to as speaking on a "level place" (Luke 6:17–49). Jesus is portrayed as a teacher and possibly as a second Moses (Deut. 18:15), addressing the crowd and His disciples. He is teaching them the principles and practices of the Kingdom of God (or heaven), which He inaugurated through His person and ministry. In His teaching, the ethics of the kingdom demand a new way of life.

The sermon starts with the beatitudes or statements of blessing (the Greek word, *makarioi*, meaning "blessed ones"), in which the poor in spirit, those who mourn, the meek, those who hunger and thirst for righteousness, the merciful, the pure in heart, the peacemakers, and the persecuted ones on account of their justice are blessed in the kingdom (5:3–12). Jesus wants His followers to be the salt of the earth and the light of the world (5:13–16). They should live a life pertaining to the kingdom principles whereby other people see it and honor their heavenly Father.

Jesus teaches that He came to fulfill the law and the prophets (5:17–48). The introductory formula that He uses to illustrate His teaching is: "You have heard that it was said to people of old . . . but [and] I say to you. . . ." The teaching covers subjects such as murder and anger (5:21–26), adultery and lust (5:27–30), divorce and marriage (5:31–32), oaths (5:33–37), and generosity (5:38–48). In all these, Jesus teaches that doctrine and ethics cannot be separated.

Jesus further teaches that dedication to God is not a performance to be seen by other people but devotion to be carried out in secret. In this respect, He includes the acts of almsgiving (6:2–4), prayer (6:5–15), and fasting (6:16–18) and warns His followers to guard against pharisaic, hypocritical practices. He also encourages His followers to store up treasures in heaven, as earthly treasures are not safe due to decay or theft (6:19–21). In serving God, one has to have single-minded devotion to God and total dependence and trust in God (6:22–33).

The sermon concludes with a further set of warnings and encouragements. The statement, "Do not judge that you may not be judged" opens the prohibition of judging others (7:1–6). God is portrayed as the heavenly Father who answers prayers and provides for His children (7:7–12). In this context, the ethical behavior is summarized as the Golden Rule: "Therefore, whatever you wish people to do to you, do so to them, for this is the Law and the Prophets" (7:12). Jesus then contrasts the metaphors of two roads (broad and narrow) and two gates (wide and narrow) and asks the followers to choose the narrow road and narrow gate, which lead to life and which only a few seek (7:13–14). He warns against false prophets (7:15–20) and asks the audience to test them. He also warns of the false followers who simply call Him their Lord, but do not do the will of the heavenly Father (7:21–23). It is not simply one's lip service and the claim to have charismatic ministry that matters, but one's commitment to God and obedience to the principles and practices of the kingdom. Such committed and obedient people hear and do the teaching of Jesus and are like the wise man who built his house upon the rock (7:24–27). Such people would not fall away in adverse circumstances.

In summary, the Sermon on the Mount teaches us that the followers of Jesus must demonstrate a high moral and ethical standard that exceeds that of the unbelievers. The Kingdom of God demands a life of total dependence on God. Total obedience and commitment are mandatory for life in the kingdom. In Christian education and life, theology and ethics cannot be separated. Jesus's followers should be aware of and keep away from hypocrisy in devotion to God. Likewise, they should be aware of false prophets and false followers. It is not simply charisma or lip service that matters, but kingdom characteristics. Life in the kingdom has sufferings and blessings. The arrival of the Kingdom of God demands a new way of life. The kingdom has present and eschatological implications. Disobedience will have consequences and will meet with final punishment. In Christian education, the Sermon on the Mount should not be treated as an "impossible ethic" but as a radical life and ethic to be lived out.

References and Resources

Blomberg, Craig L. 1992. *Matthew.* Vol. 22 of *The New American Commentary: An Exegetical and Theological Exposition of the Holy Scripture NIV Text.* Nashville, TN: Broadman Press.

Davies, Margaret. 1993. *Matthew.* Sheffield, UK: Sheffield Academic Press.

Davies, W. D., and D. C. Allison. 2004. *The Gospel According to Matthew.* Vol. 1, *Matthew 1–7* International Critical Commentary. London: Continuum.

Garland, David E. 1993. *Reading Matthew: A Literary and Theological Commentary on the First Gospel.* London: SPCK.

Keener, Craig S. 1997. *Matthew.* The IVP New Testament Commentary Series. Downers Grove, IL: InterVarsity Press.

—V. J. SAMKUTTY

SERVANT LEADERSHIP

How organizational leaders develop influence relationships with local church Christian education staff significantly affects not only the ministry, but also the culture of the local church. Organizational leadership studies since the 1970s have spawned numerous new leadership theories, starting with the theory or paradigm of servant leadership. Jesus pointedly discussed the kingdom value and expectation that His followers would lead with the spirit of a servant in both Matthew 20 and Mark 10.

Servant Leadership Theory

Modern servant leadership models or theories began to emerge beginning with Robert Greenleaf's servant leadership theory in the 1970s. Greenleaf (1991) focused on the relationship between the leader and the follower, wherein the leader first seeks to serve the needs of the follower and organization. His central focus posits: "The servant-leader is servant first . . . . The leader-first and the servant-first are two extreme types. . . . The difference manifests itself in the care taken by the servant-first to make sure that other people's highest priority need are being served" (1991, 7). From that mind-set and disposition, Greenleaf believed that such servant leaders would provide direction like other leaders (9). They have drive and determination much like other leaders (3).

Laub (2004) defines (servant) leadership as "an intentional change process through which leaders and followers, joined by a shared purpose, initiate action to pursue a common vision ("). Van Dierendonck (2011), in a meta-analysis of servant leadership theory and research, synthesized six key characteristics of servant leadership behavior as experienced by followers. Servant leaders empower and develop people; they show humility, are authentic, accept people for who they are, provide direction, and are stewards who work for the good of the whole (1232).

Servant Leadership Practice

Numerous servant leadership studies utilizing Laub's (1999) Organizational Leadership Assessment (OLA) indicate that effective servant leadership practice provides significant benefits to many kinds of organizations. The OLA measures six servant leadership indicators, including provision of leadership, sharing leadership, authenticity, building community, developing people, and valuing people. In Rauch's (2007), studying of 28 manufacturing units, he reported that on a five-unit scale of servant leadership, each positive increase of one unit resulted in a reduction of over 41 percent in absenteeism and in attrition of over 22 percent. Drury (2004), in a higher education setting, found a statistically significant

and positive relationship between servant leadership and job satisfaction. Rauch (2007) reported a highly significant correlation between servant leadership and team effectiveness. Witter (2007), in a study of Plymouth Brethren local church leadership practices, demonstrated high levels of organizational health utilizing the OLA.

However, few servant or organizational leadership studies beyond Witter have been done in local churches. Garverick's (2013) research on volunteer satisfaction in the context of a local church and its organizational leadership found evidence of servant leadership indicators. Five implications of leadership effectiveness stood out. First, when local church leadership provided vision, direction, and planning, this energized volunteers and enhanced their experience of satisfaction. The results of this provision helped volunteers follow their organizational leadership and connect their volunteer service to the organization's mission.

Second, where local church leadership invited or welcomed volunteers to exercise liberty to accomplish their ministry or to envision new ministries, these volunteers experienced high levels of satisfaction. Volunteers needed organizational leadership to both provide leadership and share leadership with them. Local churches with empowering cultures developed volunteer trust and willingness to risk new ministry ventures. In an empowering culture of shared leadership, volunteers sensed that they were all partners in God's work alongside organizational leadership.

Third, when local church organizational leadership recognized and applauded a wide variety of volunteer ministries and teamwork across a congregation, cumulative satisfaction occurred. These volunteers saw God at work in many areas of their local church and experienced satisfaction, not only from their individual ministry, but also from the totality of God's work in their local church.

Fourth, when local church organizational leadership highlighted God as central to the life of the church and its volunteer service, volunteers often saw God in the same light. When leadership affirmed that volunteers were accomplishing God's will, following God's lead, and using their gifts and passions as an act of worship, core satisfaction occurred. Volunteers saw this as the highest level of volunteer satisfaction (see Volunteerism, Local Church and Volunteer Satisfaction, Local Church).

The fifth implication for local church organizational leadership practice occurred when volunteers found their leadership open to their new ministry ideas. When leadership sought to sense God's will for those new ministry ideas, these volunteers understood that not only was God leading through their leadership, but He also was leading them as volunteers. This gave rise to a theory of Triune leadership, in which God leads both local church organizational leaders and volunteers within that local church. Stated another way, God leads, leaders lead, and volunteers lead. This kind of leadership can maximize local church potential. At Pentecost (Acts 2, New International Version), God promised he would pour out his Holy Spirit on all people. God seeks to work through both leaders and volunteers in the local church, not just its leadership. Leaders who will not or refuse to share leadership prevent Triune leadership from developing and handicap God's work and his mission through local church volunteers. Conversely, a local church contagious with God's presence and leading among leaders and volunteers finds not only great volunteer satisfaction, but also great potential for kingdom increase.

References and Resources

Boezeman, E. J., and N. Ellemers. 2009. "Intrinsic Need Satisfaction and the Job Attitudes of Volunteers versus Employees Working in a Charitable Volunteer Organization." *Journal of Occupational & Organizational Psychology* 82 (4): 897–914.

Drury, S. 2004. "Servant Leadership and Organizational Commitment: New Findings and Implications." Paper presented at the 2004 Servant Leadership Research Roundtable, Virginia Beach, VA, August.

Garverick, P. 2013. "How Volunteers Experience Ministry Satisfaction in the Context of a Local Church and Its Organizational Leadership: A Case Study." PhD diss., Indiana Wesleyan University, Marion.

Greenleaf, R. K. 1991. *The Servant as Leader*. Indianapolis, IN: The Robert K. Greenleaf Center.

Laub, J. A. 1999. "Assessing the Servant Organization: Development of the Servant Organizational Leadership Assessment (SOLA) Instrument." PhD diss., Florida Atlantic University. Retrieved from DAI-A 60/02, p. 308.

———. 2004. "Defining Servant Leadership: A Recommended Typology for Servant Leadership Studies," Paper presented at the 2004 Servant Leadership Research Roundtable, Virginia Beach, VA, August.

Rauch, K. 2007. "Servant Leadership and Team Effectiveness: A Study of Industrial Manufacturing Correlation." PhD diss., Indiana Wesleyan University, Marion. http://proquest.umi.com/pqdweb?did=1597602261&Fmt=7&clientId=48621&RQT=309&VName=PQD.

Van Dierendonck, D. 2011. "Servant Leadership: A Review and Synthesis." *Journal of Management* 37 (4): 1228–1261. doi:10.1177/0149206310380462.

Witter, S. 2007. "An Analysis of the Leadership Practices of the Churches of the Plymouth Brethren Movement in the United States." PhD diss., Capella University. http://proquest.umi.com/pqdweb?did=1313910181&Fmt=7&clientId=48621&RQT=309&VName=PQD.

—Paul E. Garverick

Servant Leadership and the Christian Teacher

Leadership

Leadership is an enormous and multifaceted topic that has been the focus of a plethora of scholarship. Historically, writing in this area has focused on the functions or tasks of the leader. However, more recent literature has turned to the characteristics of the leader, resulting in the concept of leadership becoming more relationally oriented (Padget 2011). Shane D. Lavery (2009) suggests that there are many different theories of relationally based leadership, including Covey's (1992) principle-centered leadership, Sergiovanni's (1992) moral leadership, Harris's (2008) distributed leadership, and Duignan's (2006) authentic leadership. Within the Christian context, one of the most common approaches is servant leadership.

Definition of Servant Leadership

The term "servant leadership" was coined by Robert Greenleaf in *The Servant as Leader* (1970). In this influential work, Greenleaf developed and explained the idea. His most commonly cited definition was published in 1977 (13):

> The servant-leader is servant first. . . . It begins with the natural feeling that one wants to serve *first*. Then conscious choice brings one to aspire to lead. That person is sharply different from one who is leader first, perhaps because of the need to assuage an unusual power drive or to acquire material positions. For such it will be a later choice to serve—after leadership is established. The leader-first and the servant-first are two extreme types. Between them are shadings and blends that are part of the infinite variety of human nature . . . The difference manifests itself in the care taken by the servant-first to make sure that other people's highest priority needs are being served.

This servant leadership approach is modeled by Jesus, who stresses that leaders are not people of power but rather people of service. Jesus's example of leadership is one "in which the leader is a vulnerable servant who needs the people as much as they need him" (Nouwen 1989, 45). In *Lead Like Jesus: Lessons from the Greatest Role Model of All Time*, Blanchard and Hodges (2005, 195) suggest that servant leadership puts the love of Jesus into action and models Jesus to others.

Biblical/Theological Understanding of Servant Leadership

Jesus's service-based approach to leadership is clearly delineated in the Gospel accounts of His life and teaching ministry. In Matthew 20:28, Jesus says "the Son of Man did not come to be served but to serve, and to give his life as a ransom for many" (NIV). He explains this approach to leadership in several conversations with His disciples; see Mark 10:42–45, Matthew 23:8–12, Luke 22:24–27, and John 13:12–17. Jesus embodies His philosophy of leadership in His gracious interactions with the marginalized of His day: lepers (Mark 1:40–44), tax collectors (Luke 19:1–10), women (Luke 10:38–42), children (Luke 18:15–17), and the visually impaired (Matt. 20:29–34).

Servant Leadership and the Educational Ministry of the Church

Servant leadership is commonly associated with pastoral ministry (see Oden 1987 and Peterson 1980). In Christian education, a great deal has been written on leaders modeling the servant approach of Jesus in the person, content, and curriculum of teaching within the church (Wilhoit 1991; Pazmino 1988; Groome 1980; and Yount 2008).

Servant Leadership and the Christian Teacher

There appears to be much less written specifically addressing the idea of servant leadership and the Christian teacher in an educational context. Lavery (2009, 7) suggests that servant leadership is a fitting model for religious educators in a school setting, since "1) it is the way that Jesus exercised leadership, 2) it provides religious educators with an excellent set of principles and values and 3) it is appropriate to develop in young people." Teachers have a unique opportunity to model Christ in their pedagogical approach and relationship to students.

References and Resources

Blanchard, K., and P. Hodges. 2005. *Lead Like Jesus: Lessons from the Greatest Role Model of All Time.* Nashville, TN: Thomas Nelson.

Covey, S. 1992. *Principle-Centered Leadership.* New York: A Fireside Book.

Duignan, P. 2006. *Educational Leadership: Key Challenges and Ethical Tensions.* Melbourne, Australia: Cambridge University Press.

Greenleaf, R. 1977. *Servant Leadership.* New York: Paulist Press.

Groome, T. 1980. *Christian Religious Education.* San Francisco: Jossey-Bass.

Harris, A. 2008. *Distributed School Leadership.* Oxford: Routledge.

Lavery, S. 2009. "Religious Educators: Promoting Servant Leadership." *Religious Education Journal of Australia* 25(1): 31–36.

Nouwen, H. 1989. *In the Name of Jesus: Reflections on Christian Leadership.* London: Darton, Longman and Todd.

Oden, T. C. 1987. *Pastoral Theology: Essentials of Ministry.* San Francisco: Harper & Row.

Padget, A. G. 2011. *As Christ Submits to the Church: A Biblical Understanding of Leadership and Mutual Submission.* Grand Rapids, MI: Baker Academic.

Pazmino, R. 1988. *Foundational Issues in Christian Education: An Introduction in Evangelical Perspective.* Grand Rapids, MI: Baker.

Peterson, E. 1980. *Five Smooth Stones for Pastoral Work.* Atlanta, GA: John Knox Press.

Sergiovanni, T. 1992. *Moral Leadership.* San Francisco: Jossey-Bass.

Wilhoit, J. 1991. *Christian Education and the Search for Meaning.* Grand Rapids, MI: Baker.

Yoder, J. H. 1994. *The Politics of Jesus.* Grand Rapids, MI: Eerdmans.

Yount, R. 2008. *The Teaching Ministry of the Church.* Nashville, TN: B & H Academic.

—Stacie Reck

SERVICE LEARNING AS CHRISTIAN PRACTICE

"Service-learning is a form of experiential education in which students engage in activities that address human and community needs together with structured opportunities intentionally designed to promote student learning and development" (Jacoby 1996, 5). It has a long and sustained history in the United States, dating from the 1600s to the present. As an effective and transformative pedagogy, service learning balances educational objectives with the needs of the community. As a result, there is much that it can offer to the field of Christian education in terms of service, holistic education, collaboration, and kingdom building.

Democracy, Education, and Service: A Brief History in the United States

In the United States, service learning has a long history dating back at least to Harvard's founding in 1636 with the purpose of preparing "citizens for active involvement in community life" (Jacoby 1996, 10). It includes post–Revolutionary War nation building, abolitionist student movements before the Civil War, and the land grant movement of the 1860s (Jacoby 1996, 10; Stanton, Giles, and Cruz 1999, 13). Later, in the early 1900s, John Dewey conceived of education as being essential for a democratic society; his writings would come to form a central part of the philosophy of this pedagogy (Berman 2006, xxi; Jacoby 1996, 12). There was then increased interest in service learning in the 1960s and early 1970s as faculty, students, and communities became more politically engaged in social activism. "They were community activists and educators who found themselves drawn to the idea that action in communities and structured learning could be combined to provide stronger service and leadership in communities and deeper, more relevant education for students" (Stanton, Giles, and Cruz 1999, 1). In particular, the Peace Corp and VISTA programs, instituted under the Kennedy and Johnson administrations, further gave service learning the strong foundations that continue today as it continues to be utilized in K–12 and higher education institutions (Berman 2006, xxi; Bringle, Phillips, and Hudson 2004, 7; Eyler and Giles 1999, 5; Jacoby 1996, 11).

Service Learning as a Transformative Pedagogy

Service learning is considered to be one of the best practices for educators to use because of the kinds of transformation that it fosters (Bringle, Phillips, and Hudson 2004, 4; Eyler and Giles 1999, 7). More specifically, this pedagogy nurtures student self-esteem, learning from experience, social problem solving, real-world skills, reflective abilities, critical thinking, cultural competency, spiritual growth, civic engagement, and a host of other personal and interpersonal forms of development (Berman 2006, xxiii; Eyler and Giles 1999, chs. 1 and 2). In addition, it benefits the communities in which service-learning projects take place and develops mutual relationships among various organizations within the community (Kaye 2004, 8).

Service learning is essentially a praxis approach to education, embodying in-depth learning, community action, and intentional reflection (Berman 2006, xxiv; Kaye 2004, 10). At its heart, service learning is most effective when it integrates the specific objectives of the educational program with the needs of the community in which the projects are carried out (Berman 2006, xxv; Eyler and Giles 1999, 183–185). Differing from simple volunteer work or community service, it intentionally strives to link what students are learning in the classroom with what they are experiencing in the community through these projects (Eyler and Giles 1999, 4).

Service-learning projects are as diverse as the classrooms and programs in which they are utilized. Examples are after-school programs, environmental research projects, community health screenings, advocacy work on behalf of specific groups, starting and maintaining community gardens, and work with soup kitchens and homeless shelters. They can range in duration from one-day service events to multi-year-long community projects (for detailed examples, see Berman 2006; Kaye 2004). Overall, this effective pedagogy seeks to have an impact not only on the lives and learning of the students themselves but also on the wider communities of which they are a part.

Implications for Christian Education

As a transformative pedagogy, there is much that service learning has to offer to Christian education. Following are some of these possible contributions:

1. *Nurturing the virtue of service.* Service has long been considered to be a virtue in Christianity. Service learning intentionally integrates this virtue directly into educational programs by helping students become aware of and respond to the needs of others, often with the same preference for the poor and marginalized that Jesus had.

2. *Holistic transformation.* As a praxis-oriented transformative pedagogy, service learning impacts the mind, body, heart, and spirit of individuals. In addition, as the examples above illustrate, it strives to respond to and further enhance the assets and needs of one's community politically, socially, and economically. Service learning can therefore both challenge and empower Christian education to pursue such holistic transformation.

3. *Collaborative communal connections.* Service learning fosters collaborative connections because it seeks to partner with other organizations in the community. Institutions of Christian education and ministry can therefore use this pedagogy to further nurture mutual partnerships with these organizations as they work collectively to positively impact our world.

4. *An individual and corporate kingdom.* Service learning, from a Christian perspective, can be asserted to view the Kingdom of God at both individual and communal levels. Theologically, service learning therefore supports the view that God is actively seeking to nurture this kingdom at both of these levels and provides a means of working in partnership with God toward that end.

See also Community-Building as Christian Practice; Holistic Education; Kingdom Education; Kingdom of God; Social Justice; Virtue.

References and Resources

Berman, Sally. 2006. *Service Learning: A Guide to Planning, Implementing, and Assessing Student Projects.* 2nd ed. Thousand Oaks, CA: Corwin Press.

Bringle, Robert G., Mindy A. Phillips, and Michael Hudson. 2004. *The Measure of Service Learning: Research Scales to Assess Student Experiences.* 1st ed. Washington, DC: American Psychological Association.

Eyler, Janet, and Dwight Giles. 1999. *Where's the Learning in Service-Learning?* 1st ed. San Francisco: Jossey-Bass.

Jacoby, Barbara. 1996. "Service-Learning in Today's Higher Education." In *Service-Learning in Higher Education: Concepts and Practices*, edited by Barbara Jacoby, 3–25. San Francisco: Jossey-Bass.

Kaye, Cathryn Berger. 2004. *The Complete Guide to Service Learning: Proven, Practical Ways to Engage Students in Civic Responsibility, Academic Curriculum, & Social Action*. Minneapolis, MN: Free Spirit Publishing.

Stanton, Timothy, Dwight Giles, and Nadinne I. Cruz. 1999. *Service-Learning: A Movement's Pioneers Reflect on its Origins, Practice, and Future*. 1st ed. San Francisco, CA: Jossey-Bass.

—ERIC J. KYLE

SEVENTH-DAY ADVENTIST CHURCH CHRISTIAN EDUCATION

The Seventh-day Adventist Church is a worldwide denomination with more than 17 million church members. The church has a presence in 232 countries. Although initially hesitant to develop an educational system, the denomination has grown into one of the largest private parochial systems in the world. As of 2010, the denomination had 1,673,828 students enrolled in 7,804 schools (including 110 colleges and universities) and employed 84,997 teachers.

Historical Introduction

The Adventist movement revolved around the Millerite revival of the 1840s. The main emphasis was the return of Christ "about the year 1843," but as time drew closer, the date settled on was 22 October 1844. The "Great Disappointment," when Christ did not return as anticipated, was a severe blow, but a small handful of believers sought a new meaning of their interpretation of the "cleansing of the sanctuary" from Daniel 8:14. From 1848 to 1850, through a series of Bible conferences, a small group of Sabbatarian Adventists grew to several hundred individuals and formulated a core set of doctrines that revolved around the priestly ministry of Christ in the heavenly sanctuary, the significance of the seventh-day Sabbath, the last day bestowal of spiritual gifts—as manifested in the prophetic life and ministry of Ellen G. White (1827–1915)—and a view of conditional immortality of the body. They continued to cling to the hope of the Second Advent, although they eschewed any further date setting. By 1863, the group of believers had grown to approximately 3,500 adherents and organized into a formal denomination.

Formal education was the last major institutional development of the Seventh-day Adventist Church. This was partly due to a theological emphasis that viewed long-term plans such as education as a lack of faith in the Second Advent. From 1853 to 1872, there was a series of failed ventures to begin such a school. The first successful attempt was made by Goodloe Harper Bell, a veteran public school educator who had converted while he was a patient at the Health Reform Institute; he opened a classroom in Battle Creek, Michigan, with 12 students in 1872. In this same year, Ellen G. White issued a clarion call for a distinctly Adventist understanding of education in *Testimony 22*, a pamphlet with the subtitle "Proper Education," in which she called for Adventist educators to be "reformers" who combined practical aspects of education with the study of books. This call for change expanded support for the fledgling education work as it expanded into Battle Creek College (1874).

The real revolution in Adventist education occurred during the 1890s. After two decades of experimentation, Ellen G. White urged denominational educators not to copy other schools but to implement a unique Adventist philosophy of education. She believed that Battle Creek College was a faulty pattern. Instead, the Bible needed to be at the center and not the periphery of the curriculum. This "second beginning" was put into action while White served as a missionary in Australia. She helped to found a mission school, Avondale College, which modeled other reform-minded institutions such as Oberlin College. Education expanded significantly after these reforms were broadly implemented.

In 1902, the General Conference adopted a "Department of Education" that was responsible for "all educational matters" for the denomination. The principles enunciated by Ellen G. White, although dimly understood at first, progressively became the foundation of a distinctive philosophy of Seventh-day Adventist education. White's final and perhaps most significant contribution occurred at the end of her life, when she urged denominational leaders to operate their own state-chartered medical school to teach courses required by state medical authorities so that its graduates would qualify for medical licensure. This set in motion a chain of events after her death that ultimately led to the push during the 20th century for all denominational schools to become accredited.

Adventist Philosophy and Mission

Seventh-day Adventists believe in a holistic view of education that sees human beings as playing a significant role in the cosmic conflict between Christ and Satan. Human beings were designed to love and serve God, and next, to care for others. The transgression by Adam and Eve in the Garden of Eden created a barrier between God and humanity; yet it is God's purpose through the plan of salvation as demonstrated in the life, death, and resurrection of Jesus Christ to restore fallen humanity. "To bring man back into harmony with God," wrote Ellen G.

White, "so to elevate and ennoble his moral nature that he may again reflect the image of the Creator, is the great purpose of all the education and discipline of life."[32]

Ellen White's best-known statement on the philosophy of Adventist education elucidates this unique understanding: "True education means more than the pursual of a certain course of study. It means more than a preparation for the life that now is. It has to do with the whole being, and with the whole period of existence possible to man. It is the harmonious development of the physical, the mental, and the spiritual powers. It prepares the student for the joy of service in this world and for the higher joy of wider service in the world to come."[33] Accordingly, the chief objective of Adventist education is to lead young people to a personal relationship with Jesus Christ, to grow their character as productive members of society, and to be ready for Jesus Christ when He comes again.

Accreditation and Academic Programs

After Battle Creek College, other colleges opened: in 1882, Healdsburg College (now Pacific Union College) in California and South Lancaster Academy (later Atlantic Union College, now defunct) in Massachusetts. During the 1890s, after Ellen White's appeals for educational reform, schools multiplied rapidly along with parallel publishing and health-care institutions, which together became signature aspects of Adventist expansion. Thus Adventist schools accompanied evangelistic efforts throughout Latin America, Africa, and China during the early 20th century. In the Lake Titicaca region of Peru, for example, Ana and Ferdinand Stahl established a school at La Plateria about 1911 that multiplied into 26 additional schools by 1918, and still further to 113 more schools by 1951.

As Adventist schools proliferated, local elementary schools were operated by the local church, conferences (regional groups of churches) sponsored secondary schools, and unions (regional groups of conferences) sponsored colleges and universities. A few select schools, most notably seminaries, received additional support and funding from the overarching General Conference of Seventh-day Adventists. These varying levels of constituency created different levels of accountability. New resources were also created to support teachers, such as the *Journal of Adventist Education* (formerly *The True Journal of True Education*, begun in 1939), which continue to provide Adventist educators with a forum for dialogue on pertinent issues.

In 1915 the General Conference, following Ellen White's strong support, voted to pursue accreditation from the American Medical Association (AMA) for the College of Medical Evangelists. In 1922 the institution received an "A" rating from the AMA, but in order to maintain that rating, it had to accept only students from accredited colleges. This started an intense debate within the denomination. In 1928 the church formed the Seventh-day Adventist Board of Regents, and the following year, the Association of Seventh-day Adventist Colleges and Secondary Schools. This organization served as a requisite accrediting agency at first. When this failed to meet AMA specifications, Adventist colleges sought accreditation from regional associations. Pacific Union College became the first Adventist college to do so and in 1932 received senior college accreditation. By 1936, the General Conference had rescinded all restrictions on accreditation. Afterward, Adventist schools shifted from training denominational employees to providing a broad range of programs. In 1970, the General Conference extended its accreditation process overseas, beginning first with Newbold College in England. Two decades later the original Accrediting Association of Seventh-day Adventist Schools, Colleges, and Universities was replaced by the Board of Regents; it complements the work of other government and regional accrediting bodies.

Adventist graduate education began during the 1950s. In 1959, the General Conference moved the newly formed Potomac University to Berrien Springs, Michigan, and combined it with Emmanuel Missionary College (previously Battle Creek College) in order to provide graduate-level training. During the 1970s and 1980s, the combined institution, known as Andrews University, developed doctoral programs in theology, biblical studies, ministry, and education. Adventist graduate education became international after 1987 with the establishment of the Adventist International Institute for Advanced Studies, in the Philippines.

References and Resources

Knight, George R., ed. 1983a. *Early Adventist Educators*. Berrien Springs, MI: Andrews University Press.

———. 1983b. "Oberlin College and Adventist Educational Reforms." *Adventist Heritage* 8 (1): 3–9.

———. 1987. "The Transformation of Education." In *The World of Ellen G. White*, edited by Gary L. Land, 161–175. Washington, DC: Review and Herald.

———. 2006. *Philosophy and Education: An Introduction in Christian Perspective*. Berrien Springs, MI: Andrews University Press.

White, Ellen G. 1903. *Education*. Oakland, CA: Pacific Press Publishing Company.

---

32. Ellen G. White, *Counsels to Parents, Teachers, and Students Regarding Christian Education*, 49.

33. Ibid., 13.

——. 1923. *Fundamentals of Christian Education: Instruction for the Home, the School, and the Church.* Nashville, TN: Southern Publishing Association.

——. 1943. *Counsels to Parents, Teachers, and Students Regarding Christian Education.* Mountain View, CA: Pacific Press Publishing Association.

White, W. G., Jr. 2002. "Accreditation of Seventh-day Adventist Liberal Arts Colleges in the North Central Association Region of the United States, 1922–1939." PhD thesis, The University of Reading.

—Michael W. Campbell

Shared Christian Praxis

Thomas Groome's five-movement shared Christian praxis (SCP) is a methodology of education and ministry that attempts to forge critical self-reflection in and through communal reflection in the lives of the participants for a threefold purpose: education for the reign of God, for Christian faith, and for human freedom. Groome contends that the skeletal process of his praxis method of doing Christian religious education is not merely a teaching-learning method, but an approach to theory and practice that is generative, in that it can be readily adapted to a great variety of pastoral theology and ministry situations and tasks.

The impetus behind SCP was Groome's assessment of the seemingly irreconcilable gap between beliefs and actions among Christians and the church. The goal of religious education for Groome, then, is not to deliver static truths or cultivate certain desired values, but to create a safe and hospitable atmosphere in which participants can critically engage in praxis for the ongoing life and freedom of the Christian community and beyond. In interacting with Aristotle's three categories of knowing—i.e., *theoria, praxis,* and *poiesis*—Groome asserts that praxis is a combination of the *theoria* dimension (reflection) and the *poiesis* dimension (action). Moreover, while crediting Marx for claiming that knowledge is primarily something that is done, and that it is not knowledge until it is done, Groome finds Marx's praxis to be overly materialistic and simplistic, for it propounds that self-consciousness is totally dependent on one's labor.

Upon further reflection, Groome finds in the Frankfurt school of critical theory, especially in the work of Jürgen Habermas, an epistemological framework that permits a deeper grasp of human praxis as a way of understanding. Groome agrees with Habermas in his belief that critical reflection can be emancipatory for individuals by uncovering the interests, assumptions, and ideologies of their own praxes and of their sociocultural contexts. Groome asserts that for this sort of critical reflection to take place

in the lives of religious people, it must incorporate one's religious tradition and community in the process. In *Sharing Faith* (1991), Groome advances this epistemological articulation by introducing a new concept, "epistemic ontology" to describe how "knowing" and "being" should be fused in the philosophical foundations of his shared Christian praxis. Groome sees the process of formulation of such an integrative and liberating epistemology as a crucial task of Christian religious education. He believes that through this kind of Christian religious education, true emancipation of humankind occurs. Following is a description of his five movements of SCP.

At the outset, participants are invited to explore the ways in which a "generative theme" (a lively focus that will engage all participants, chosen for a session of shared learning) is important in their lives; Groome calls this movement "Naming/Expressing Present Action." This movement includes the expression of aspirations, feelings, needs, hopes, and beliefs of those present. The important goal here is to elicit a personal statement on present action rather than a statement of *theoria* based on what "they" say. This is ensured by having participants reflect on their *own* feelings and actions, rather than on what they are supposed to think or on the store of knowledge from their tradition.

The second movement, "Critical Reflection on Present Action," is the beginning of critical reflection proper. It directly addresses the questions, "Why do we do as we do?" and "What do we hope to get out of it?" It involves shared reflection of the theme introduced in the first movement on all the underlying factors, particularly the internal factors that involve deep-seated attitudes, interests, and beliefs of the participants themselves. The focus is particularly on the participants' own social conditioning (answering "Why we do what we do?") and visions of the future (answering "What do we hope to get out of it?").

The third movement, "Making Accessible Christian Story and Vision," brings scripture and religious tradition to bear on the generative theme. Groome calls this the Christian Story/Vision. The participants are invited to explore what is critical to the theme, drawing upon scripture, tradition, and liturgy to present the variety of options that Christianity has presented, rightly or wrongly, on the theme. The Story/Vision must be presented in a way that continues the praxis mentality, in order to ensure that the participants reflect upon, grapple with, question, and personally encounter what is presented.

In movement four, "Dialectical Hermeneutic to Appropriate Story/Vision to Participants' Stories and Visions," participants consider what they have seen of the theme within themselves and in society. Both are interpreted in light of what they now understand as the Christian Story/Vision. The Story is appropriated to their lives in dialectic with their own (personal) stories. They are challenged to ask if their practices are affirmed or challenged by the Christian Story/Vision. They are also encouraged to search for honest ways to fuse their own life stories/visions with the Christian Story/Vision so that both are more faithful to the reign of God. This is the beginning of the decision-making phase.

In the last movement, "Decision/Response for Lived Christian Faith," participants are given the opportunity to decide how to live the truths they have arrived at in the preceding movement, a dialectic between Vision and vision. This is the point at which praxis develops, the practical action that will redress the imbalance and inconsistencies noted and draw closer together the practice and the theory (i.e., the way it is and the way it should be begin to merge). As in all critical education, the assumption is that religious education is not complete until the students possess both the will to and a mechanism for change.

References and Resources

Groome, Thomas H. 1980. *Christian Religious Education: Sharing Our Story and Vision.* San Francisco: Harper & Row.

_____. 1991. *Sharing Faith.* San Francisco: HarperCollins.

_____. 2001. *Educating for Life: A Spiritual Vision for Every Teacher and Parent.* New York: Crossroad.

_____. 2011. *Will There Be Faith? A New Vision for Educating and Growing Disciples.* New York: HarperOne.

—S. STEVE KANG

SHEMA

If one were to summarize the entire Jewish faith, that summary could be found in Deuteronomy 6:4–9, or the *Shema.* The *Shema* can be understood as the lynchpin of Judaism and its most basic truths and duties. The title derives from the imperative biblical Hebrew verb that begins Moses's declaration to the people of Israel prior to their conquest of the Promised Land. The literary structure and language of the *Shema* is similar to that seen in ancient Near Eastern treaties, and the imagery used is comparable to that of a father/child concept, with God as the Father and Israel as the child. Within Deuteronomy, the *Shema* acts as both the book's focal point and as a bridge between the Ten Commandments found in Chapter 5 and the main body of the Law in Chapters 12–26.

Opening with what may possibly be a traditional Israelite tribal summon, Moses gives Israel one of its earliest creeds: a monotheistic confession from its own experi-ences. The likely meaning of the latter half of verse 4, "the Lord is one," focuses on the singleness and uniqueness of the Lord, thereby negating the idea of several different forms or manifestations of the Lord. The Israelites generally understood Moses's command to love (or possibly fear, as in reverence) this one Lord in three ways. The heart was seen as Israel giving its complete and undivided loyalty with both its good and evil inclinations. Loving with the soul meant to be committed to the Lord even unto death and martyrdom, and might was understood as all of one's wealth and property.

The exhortations of verses 6 through 9 demonstrate that the commandments were meant to be all-inclusive of both family and public life. The parents were to diligently instruct the children to prevent resistance to the faith of the adult community, and verse 7 demonstrates how much effort it would take to make sure their faith would be passed on to their future descendants.

Lawson notes that the *Shema* "presents both the goal and process of education. The people were called to acknowledge and love the one true God and teach his Word to their children in the daily activities of life . . . as parents grew in their knowledge of God's law, they were to teach it to their children and reinforce it through their own example and conversation."[34] It can be said that the *Shema* provided the educational framework for faith formation of the Jewish community. *Shema* serves as a deeply formational command, one that would ensure that the Jewish community not only maintained deep knowledge of the Lord, but also was formed inwardly and outwardly, first loving the Lord with all of one's being, and then allowing that love to transform various aspects of people's lives.

The binding on the hands, eyes, doorposts, and gates were taken literally, though Samaritans and medieval Jewish commentators saw these commands as figurative.[35] This literal interpretation led to the development of *Shema*-inscribed amulets worn on the hand and head, and phylacteries similar to those used by modern-day Jews were developed toward the end of the Second Temple period. The rabbis saw these amulets/phylacteries as an outward testimony, and if one did not have them, that person was considered a false witness to the Lord's covenant. The *Shema* was not just a command or demand; it was what made Israelite life possible, through inward appropriation of the heart and the external symbol of the

---

34. Kevin Lawson, "Historical Foundations of Christian Education," in *Introduction to Christian Education: Foundations for the Twenty-first Century,* ed. Michael J. Anthony (Grand Rapids, MI: Baker Academic, 2001), 17.

35. Moshe Weinfeld, *Deuteronomy 1–11: A New Translation with Introduction and Commentary* (New York: Doubleday, 1991), 341–342.

testimony closing together within a covenant community set apart by the Lord.

References and Resources

Anderson, Bernhard W. 1999. *Contours of Old Testament Theology*. Minneapolis, MN: Fortress Press.

Bartholomew, Craig G., and Michael W. Goheen. 2004. *The Drama of Scripture: Finding Our Place in the Biblical Story*. Grand Rapids, MI: Baker Academic.

Brueggemann, Walter. 2005. *Worship in Ancient Israel: An Essential Guide*. Nashville, TN: Abingdon Press.

Craigie, Peter C. 1976. *The Book of Deuteronomy*. Grand Rapids, MI: Eerdmans.

Hahn, Scott W. 2009. *Kinship by Covenant: A Canonical Approach to the Fulfillment of God's Saving Promises*. New Haven, CT: Yale University Press.

Lawson, Kevin. 2001. "Historical Foundations of Christian Education." In *Introducing Christian Education: Foundations for the Twenty-First Century*, edited by Michael J. Anthony, 17–25. Grand Rapids, MI: Baker Academic.

Rad, Gerhard von. 1966. *Deuteronomy*. Philadelphia: Westminster.

Waltke, Bruce K., and Charles Yu. 2007. *An Old Testament Theology: An Exegetical, Canonical, and Thematic Approach*. Grand Rapids, MI: Zondervan.

Weinfeld, Moshe. 1991. *Deuteronomy 1–11: A New Translation with Introduction and Commentary*. New York: Doubleday.

—Benjamin D. Espinoza and J. Chase Franklin

Sherrill, Lewis Joseph

Early Background and Education

Lewis Joseph Sherrill (1892–1957) was born in Haskell, Texas, and graduated from Austin College and Louisville Presbyterian Theological Seminary. He also studied at Northwestern University and graduated from Yale University with a PhD. He pastored a Presbyterian congregation in Tennessee before becoming professor of religious education at Louisville Presbyterian Theological Seminary in 1925. After serving as dean at Louisville, he became Skinner and McAlpin Professor of Practical Theology at Union Theological Seminary in New York.

Sherrill's short, four-year tenure as a pastor greatly influenced his approach to Christian education. He expressed his feelings of inadequacy in responding to the problems parishioners faced after graduating from seminary. He could handle issues of biblical reliability, but was not prepared theologically or psychologically to cope with pastoral care demands. This experience motivated Sherrill to seek a deeper understanding of "the meaning of the Bible, of theology, of man, and of the most effective ways of communicating through preaching and teaching."[36] Sherrill believed the key to responding effectively to these concerns was to take a holistic approach to human persons that emphasized the transformative role of redemptive relationships in a community of faith. This conviction led him to pursue an integrated model of Christian formation, building on depth psychology, correlation of the biblical redemption drama with human concerns, and a dialogical method.

Significant Contributions to Christian Education

Lewis Sherrill's definition of Christian education highlighted the essential theological and psychological underpinnings of his integrationist approach: "Christian education is the attempt, ordinarily by members of the Christian community, to participate in and to guide the changes which take place in persons in their relationships with God, with the church, with other persons, with the physical world, and with oneself."[37]

Sherrill spoke of the limited but significant ability of others to influence the formational changes in persons. He was attracted to psychoanalytic theories of human functioning because he believed they took more seriously the complexity of human beings with their relationships, fears, loves, and anxieties. He steadfastly resisted mechanistic understandings of human behavior that ignored interiority. Christian formation, then, is a cooperative activity with persons capable of agency and enabled to experience God's grace through relationships in the faith community. Sherrill's theology of the "Word as Divine Person" seeking human persons shaped his relational, communal, and holistic understanding of Christian education.

Sherrill's theological, hermeneutical, and psychological perspective anticipated later developments in Christian education and theological studies. He emphasized the personal nature of revelation and the reality of human anxiety in the face of life's uncertainties and human finitude. His dialogical approach to scripture, focusing on two-way communication between the Divine Person and human persons and emphasizing aligning the drama/s of the Bible with human experience—while having affinity with the Tillich method—also looks very much like contemporary narrative hermeneutics. His insight into the need to treat persons as whole and ability to see the impact of social-emotional ills on faith experience anticipated later formation emphases—if not the very use of the word "formation" to describe Christian discipleship. Moreover, his positing a psychological order of the student's mind over the conventional logical order of material was ahead

---

36. Lewis J. Sherrill, *Bulletin of the Pastoral Psychology Book Club*, cited in Roy W. Fairchild, "The Contribution of Lewis J. Sherrill to Christian Education," *Religious Education* 53, no. 5 (1958): 404.

37. Lewis J. Sherrill, *The Gift of Power* (New York: Macmillan, 1955), 82.

of his time. He also anticipated later tensions between age-graded and intergenerational approaches to Christian education. Finally, his priority for personal transformation in the context of graceful relationships in community in relationship with the Word as Person and knowledge *of* God over mere transmission of information *about* God was also a significant contribution.

Most Important Publications

Lewis J. Sherrill's best known published works on Christian education include *The Rise of Christian Education* (1944), a history of Christian education; *The Struggle of the Soul* (1963), dealing with the challenge to grow and the temptation to maintain the status quo; and *The Gift of Power* (1961), his discussion of the potential for Christian education through relationships and community experiences of grace. For many years, Sherrill's history of Christian education was the most authoritative treatment of the subject.

References and Resources

Fairchild, Roy W. 1958. "The Contribution of Lewis J. Sherrill to Christian Education." *Religious Education* 53 (5): 403–411.

Sherrill, Lewis J. 1944. *The Rise of Christian Education.* New York: Macmillan.

———. 1955. *The Gift of Power.* New York: Macmillan.

———. 1961. *The Struggle of the Soul.* New York: Macmillan.

—James P. Bowers

SHOCKLEY, GRANT

Grant Sneed Shockley is one of the most significant voices in Christian religious education of the 20th century and a pioneer in the inclusion of the black religious experience as a source for theological reflection. Grant was born 3 September 1919 in Philadelphia, Pennsylvania. His father, Andrew Caleb Shockley, was a pharmacist as well as a trustee and Sunday school superintendent in their local congregation, Haven Methodist Church. Mattie Blanche Sneed Shockley, his mother, was a public school teacher prior to her marriage and later taught in the Sunday school at Haven Methodist Church. Grant's only sibling, an older brother, died in childhood. In 1946, Grant married Doris Taylor; they had one daughter, Muriel Elizabeth Shockley.

Grant Shockley grew up in Philadelphia and attended local schools. Graduating from Northeast High School, where he received the Gottschalk English Award, Shockley began his undergraduate studies at Lincoln University, Chester County, Pennsylvania, and graduated in 1942. He then attended Drew Theological Seminary, graduating in 1945, and continued his studies at Teachers College-Columbia University, where he received the

master of arts degree in 1946 and the doctor of education degree in 1952. His dissertation, "Improvement of the Status and In-service Education of Negro Methodist Accepted Supply Pastors," foreshadowed his career emphasis on enhancing the quality and availability of professional education for leaders in black congregations.

While pursuing his educational goals, Shockley also provided pastoral leadership in the Methodist Church. He was "ordained a deacon (1943) and an elder (1944) in the Delaware Annual Conference of the all-black Jurisdiction of The Methodist Church by Bishop Alexander P. Shaw."[38] While in college, he served congregations in New Rochelle, New York and Spring Lake, New Jersey, and he was an associate at St. Mark's Methodist church in New York City while in seminary. He later provided pastoral leadership at Whatcoat Memorial Methodist Church in Dover, Delaware (1951–1953) and the Janes Methodist Church in Brooklyn (1953–1959).

The relationship between Shockley's teaching and scholarship and his service to the church was complementary. He began his teaching career at Clark College in Atlanta, Georgia, in 1946 as an instructor in Bible, religion, and philosophy and then taught religious education at Gammon Theological Seminary in Atlanta from 1949 to 1951. Over the next eight years he served in pastoral appointments, returning to academia in 1959 as professor of religious education at Garrett Theological Seminary (1959–1966). Shockley became Garrett's first black tenured professor. "In 1966 he joined the Interboard Committee on Christian Education of the World Division of the Board of Global Ministries of the United Methodist Church as its executive secretary" and traveled internationally for the next four years.[39] Returning again to academia, Shockley punctuated his career with several academic appointments, including as professor of Christian education and the first black faculty member at the Candler School of Theology, Emory University, in Atlanta, Georgia (1970); president of the Interdenominational Theological Center, also in Atlanta (1975); president of Philander Smith College in Little Rock, Arkansas (1979); and professor of Christian education at The Divinity School of Duke University in Durham, North Carolina, where he retired in 1989. He returned to Clark College in Atlanta after retirement and taught a full course load until the time of his death.

Shockley's life's work evinces his commitment to creating "a more adequate Black voice in Christian religious

---

38. Charles R. Foster, "Grant Sneed Shockley," *Christian Educators of the 20th Century,* http://www.talbot.edu/ce20/educators/protestant/grant_shockley/. This website provides a very extensive biography and bibliography of Grant Shockley's scholarship in Christian religious education and his contributions to the life of the Christian church.

39. Ibid.

education" in church and academy.[40] In the academy, he broke the color barrier and enriched the academic conversation by drawing attention to the black religious experience. Similarly, "he actively encouraged the training of pastors and laity for leadership roles in Christian education" at a time when the Methodist Church was both predominantly white and racially segregated.[41] As a teacher and mentor, he made significant contributions to the ministries and careers of numerous clergy persons and educators and walked alongside colleagues who shared his commitment to articulating black perspectives on Christian education. Perusal of his writings from 1974 until his death also reveals his "growing awareness of the influence of the Black religious experience on the church's education and his growing conviction that important insights drawn from the Black religious experience were contributions to the larger discussions on the shape and practices of religious education." His significant writings include *Heritage and Hope: The African American Presence in the United Methodism*; *Working with Black Youth: Opportunities for Christian Ministry*, coauthored with Charles R. Foster; and *Christian Education Journey of Black Americans: Past, Present, and Future*, coauthored by Charles R. Foster and Ethel Johnson.

At the time of his death, Shockley was in the process of creating the book that would have been the culmination of his career-long commitment to "enriching the thinking about religious education out of the Black experience."[42] This project now lives on in the work of his former students and colleagues. Drawing insights from Grant Shockley's scholarship and teaching, Fred Smith and Charles R. Foster reflect on the significance of his work for Christian education in *Christian Education in the Black Religious Experience: Conversations on a Journey through Double Consciousness*. Contributors to *In Search of Wisdom: Faith Formation in the Black Church* (2002; ed. Anne E. Streaty Wimberly and Evelyn L. Parker) reflect on the life and work of Grant Shockley and offer important insights into the role of Christian education in the black church. Grant Sneed Shockley is a pioneering scholar and church leader, upon whose legacy we stand as we welcome new voices into this ever-expanding dialogue.

—VERONICE MILES

SHORT-TERM MISSIONS

A short-term mission is defined as a domestic or international missional experience of an individual or team ranging from a week to two years in duration, with most trips lasting two weeks or less. There has been a phenomenal increase in the number of participants in short-term trips over the last half century. Recent estimates number participants at more than 1.5 million annually at an estimated cost of over $2 billion. The majority of short-term trips are made overseas, but when economic issues of cost or political issues of security arise, the focus shifts to domestic trips. The popularity of and motivation for short-term missions come from a desire to participate in the great commission and the great commandment. The biblical mandate comes from Jesus sending out the 12 (Matt. 12:5–15) and is illustrated in Paul's missionary journeys, wherein evangelism and acts of mercy were extended to people.

Short-term mission trips are organized by churches, mission organizations, parachurch groups, and individuals. While the majority of participants are youth and college students, a wide variety of people are involved in these experiences, including singles, families, senior citizens, and professionals, particularly in the medical field. The activities of short-term mission trips vary from evangelism to service projects and can include prayer walks and exposure trips. The main benefits of short-term missions for the participant are an awareness of God's work in other places, an understanding of other peoples, and the bonding that occurs among team members. For the church, the greatest value is a global awareness of missions. For the mission organizations and parachurch groups, short-term missions can lead individuals to longer-term mission service.

Short-term missions have four key components: the individual or group going, the sending church or agency, the receiving missionary or organization, and the receiving church or nationals. The needs of each group must be recognized and coordinated for a successful short-term mission experience. The challenge of short-term missions is to allow nationals and the national church to determine and control the short-term experience so that it meets the needs of the national church and is done in a culturally appropriate manner.

A second challenge of the short-term mission experience is adequate pre- and post-training for participants. The success of the experience depends on the pre-field education of the short-termers, and the lasting impact of the experience rests on the post-field reflection. Peterson, Aeschliman, and Sneed (2003) suggest five areas for a pre-field curriculum: cross-cultural training, personal preparation, logistics training, intended activities preparation, and financial preparation. The post-trip training gives the participant an opportunity to process the spiritual and cultural learning of the trip. This debriefing also gives the participant an opportu-

---

40. Ibid.
41. Ibid.
42. Ibid.

nity to extend the experience through life change and consideration of longer term mission involvement. This post-trip training is the most neglected aspect of the short-term mission experience.

Until recently, the value and benefits derived from short-term mission experiences have largely been supported by qualitative narratives from participants. After reviewing nine quantitative studies on short-term missions, Priest (2008) concludes that short-term mission trips "create very little lasting positive change in the participants." Other researchers, such as Livermore (2013) and Howell (2012), are concerned about the cultural and sociological impact that these trips have on nationals and the national church. The mixed reviews of short-term missions demonstrate a need for more research, better definitions of the intentions of short-term missions, and more effective education of the participants in the short-term mission process.

References and Resources

Howell, Brian M. 2012. *Short-Term Mission: An Ethnography of Christian Travel Narrative and Experience.* Downers Grove, IL: IVP Academic.

Livermore, David A. 2013. *Serving with Eyes Wide Open: Doing Short-Term Missions with Cultural Intelligence.* updated ed. Grand Rapids, MI: Baker Books.

Offutt, Stephen. 2011. "The Role of Short-Term Mission Teams in the New Centers of Global Christianity." *Journal for The Scientific Study of Religion* 50 (4): 796–811.

Peterson, Robert R., Gordon Aeschliman, and R. Wayne Sneed. 2003. *Maximum Impact Short-Term Mission: The God Commanded, Repetitive Deployment of Swift, Temporary, Non-Professional Missionaries.* Minneapolis, MN: STEMPress.

Priest, Robert J. 2008. *Effective Engagement in Short-Term Missions: Doing It Right.* Evangelical Missiological Society Series. Pasadena, CA: William Carey Library.

—Philip Bustrum

SILENCE AS CHRISTIAN PRACTICE

Silence is the practice of isolating oneself from all noise and distraction for the sake of creating time to listen to God.[43] The concept of silence as a spiritual discipline is closely linked to the practice of solitude. Solitude is the practice of getting away from the demands of society in order to have time separated out for God.[44]

Scripture testifies to Christ's many retreats to lonely places, beginning with his 40-day fast in the wilderness after his baptism (Matt. 4:1–11, 14:23, 17:1–9; Mark 1:35, 6;31; Luke 5:16, 6:12;). Through the Psalms, God calls believers to "be still" before him (Pss. 37:7, 46:10) and wait for him (Pss. 5:3, 27:4, 33:20, 38:15, 40:1, 130:5–6). In the book of Isaiah, the prophet exhorts God's people that their salvation comes through repentance and rest. Their strength comes through quietness and trust. It is through seeking its own solutions from the world to fix its very present troubles that the nation of Israel will bring about its own demise (Isa. 30:15–17).

Removal from society is not the end goal of silence and solitude. In Christian devotional literature, the practice of silence is meant to cultivate the inner world of an individual so that he can remain united and connected with God in spite of outward circumstances. An individual can therefore engage society and relationships with an inner peace as easily as he can spend time alone without experiencing loneliness or despair.[45] Those who cannot bear silence and solitude are in danger of seeking relationships for the sake of filling their inner void or conflict rather than for the sake of loving those they are relating to. Those who isolate themselves with prolonged silence and solitude are in danger of self-absorption. Cultivating an inner world of restful silence and connectedness to God allows one to enter into both realms with a well-constituted, cohesive, peaceful inner self.[46]

This concept of a deeply rooted unity of the self and union with God is key for the discipline of silence. The practices of solitude and silence allow people to come to terms with areas of their lives that are fragmented or where their hearts and minds are disconnected or in conflict. By devoting time and focus to what is happening on the internal level of feelings such as dread, impulses, anger, sorrow, peace, fear, and exhilaration or joy, an individual can come to terms with her true self. She will then be able to present herself, as she really is in her deepest regions, before God. The Holy Spirit is at work through the entire process, bringing to light the things that the Lord wishes to address in His discipleship of His beloved.

At first, pursuing silence can lead to a sense of chaos or restlessness. It can seem to be a waste of time. It can feel helpless because words are often used to control thoughts and feelings and maintain the outer image that people work so hard to create for themselves and others. As one perseveres in silence, it provides the opportunity for the noise to quiet and the deeply internal aspects of the self to emerge. It also gives the Lord the opportunity to take

---

43. Adele Ahlberg Calhoun, *Spiritual Disciplines Handbook* (Downers Grove, IL: IVP Books, 2005), 107–110.

44. Ibid., 111.

45. Richard J. Foster, *Celebration of Discipline* (San Francisco: HarperCollins, 1988), 96–99.

46. Jeremy Hall, *Silence, Solitude, and Simplicity: A Hermits Love Affair with a Noisy, Crowded, and Complicated World* (Collegeville, MN: The Liturgical Press, 2005), 26–28.

control and speak about what is going on within oneself. This is an incredibly vulnerable place that requires trust in the Lord. It allows internal space for Him to bring His grace and transforming work. It is an exercise of genuine discipline to remain quiet long enough to allow this to happen. Yet it produces a greater trust and intimacy with God as one learns to rest in His presence.

This nearness to the Lord is the true craving of the heart and the genuine answer to the questions and conflicts that cause such internal discord. Moreover, the discipline of silence fosters the ability to attend to one's internal and external speech, enabling one to remain silent or speak according to what the moment requires. It enhances discernment about the self as well as the ability to listen well to others. Times of silence help reorient the mind in its responses to the rush of information, demands on time, and overstimulation. They provide a chance for the things that truly matter to rise above the pressures and preoccupations that are all too easy to succumb to. Silence allows one time to consider the deeper implications of the various areas of life against the fast-paced, bullet point summaries with which one might otherwise evaluate the world.[47] This deeper consideration may include the nature of one's communication with those one loves, the theological or personal meaning of biblical texts and sermons, the development of sinful patterns, or the trajectory of one's life and purpose. Silence before the Lord reveals these things, bringing the awareness and internal transformation necessary to address them.

Connected to the disciplines of silence and solitude is the concept of the dark night of the soul. As it was by St. John of the Cross, it is often described as a stage that comes in the process of spiritual growth wherein God draws His beloved into the divine center of His love.[48] This process involves the removal of things that feel essential. The world seems dull or lonely, there is a loss of the sense of His presence, the intellect and imagination are neutralized, and life feels burdensome and the body weary. The theory of the dark night of the soul suggests that in this state, where there is nothing to distract or excite, the Lord is able to do a special kind of transforming work.[49] The soul is drawn into a far deeper intimacy with God and is empowered to live with greater virtue and single-mindedness for Christ.

References and Resources

Calhoun, Adele Ahlberg. 2005. *Spiritual Disciplines Handbook.* Downers Grove, IL: IVP Books.

Foster, Richard. 1988. *Celebration of Discipline: The Path to Spiritual Growth.* San Francisco, CA: HarperCollins.

Hall, Sister Jeremy. 2005. *Silence, Solitude, Simplicty: A Hermits Love Affair with a Noisy, Crowded, and Complicated World.* Downers Grove, IL: IVP Books.

—Jennifer Jagerson

Simplicity as Christian Practice

Simplicity is the spiritual practice of seeking freedom from complexity and thus anxiety, leading to inner experiences that create more space for a relationship with God. It is also the process of setting aside unnecessary possessions, commitments, and relationships in order to promote spiritual growth. Inner realities and outward lifestyles cohere. Often associated with monasticism, simplicity may include the renunciation of wealth, sex, and common social engagements. The spiritual insights gained in the monasteries—even during repeated reforms of monastic communities (Cistercians, Trappists, etc.) made necessary by the wealth that monastic orders gained through their own skills and the generosity of pious laypersons—have influenced circles far beyond the members of the orders in question.

Most Christian reflections on simplicity have taken the life and teachings of Jesus as their starting point. The Gospels depict Him as enjoining His disciples to avoid oaths, bombastic prayer, unnecessary possessions, and excessive attention to appearance or status (e.g., Matt. 5:37, 6:19–21; Mark 10:21; cf. Phil. 4:11–12). Instead, they should "seek first the Kingdom" (Matt. 6:33). In view of the ideals of the Sermon on the Mount and other texts, the second- to third-century Egyptian monk St. Anthony renounced his property, inspiring generations of hermits as well as laypersons. Similarly, later monasticism, beginning with St. Benedict of Nursia, created communities that shared everything, in which all members took vows of poverty, and Celtic prayers and hagiographies are full of experiences with the presence of God made possible by simple living in harmony with creation and consciousness of the ubiquity of the sacred.

Medieval biographies of saints often emphasized their simple lives and sayings, counseling others to share in those lives. St. Francis of Assisi, St. Francis de Sales, and many women mystics fit this category, as do contemporary saints such as Dorothy Day and Teresa of Calcutta, and the ideals of some forms of contemporary Protestant new monasticism.

One of the most influential Catholic thinkers on simplicity was Thomas à Kempis (c. 1380–1471), whose work among the lay movement called the Brethren of the Common Life shaped both contemporary and subsequent

---

47. Ibid., 72–73.
48. Foster, *Celebration of Discipline*, 102–105.
49. Ibid.

generations. His commonsense approach to spiritual discipline, most famously seen in his still popular *Imitation of Christ*, connected simplicity with purity, arguing that the first made room for the second, which in turn allowed a person to experience communion with God. As he puts it in chapter 29 of *Imitation*:

> No good deed will prove an obstacle to you if you are inwardly free from uncontrolled desires. And if you are free from uncontrolled desires, and seek nothing but the Will of God and the good of your neighbor, you will enjoy this inner freedom. If your heart be right, then every created thing will become for you a mirror of life and a book of holy teaching. For there is nothing created so small and mean that it does not reflect the goodness of God.

Such an articulation of the spiritual discipline of simplicity has had a profound effect on a wide range of thinkers, regardless of theological or ecclesial commitment.

On the Protestant side, Anabaptists in the 16th century and Quakers in the 17th became known for plain living and suspicion of power and wealth. They emphasized modest dress and restraint in public display. Quaker approaches to simplicity begin with self-assessment and love of God, moving toward eating simple food, living an uncluttered life, using simple and honest speech, and minimizing possessions. People in other traditions, such as the Shakers and the Amish, have taken similar approaches.

After the societal changes of the 1960s, simplicity as an emphasis reentered Christian thinking from the counterculture. Pursuit of simplicity appeared in works by E. F. Schumacher, Ron Sider, and a range of other thinkers. Contemporary writers on simplicity, such as Thomas Merton, Catherine Whitmire, and Richard Foster, recommend to people living in ordinary circumstances (not monastic communities) such sustainable practices as buying things for their utility, rejecting anything addictive, giving away possessions, enjoying things that belong to others, appreciating creation, avoiding instant gratification, using simple and honest speech, refusing to oppress others, and avoiding all distractions in seeking first the Kingdom of God. Such commitments make room within lives for solitude, silence, prayer, and service. Over time, the practice of simplicity can provide the practitioner with a sense of proportionality that can lead to an uncluttered life free from distractions. Although simplicity is hardly "simple," because it breaks with current trends, it leads to a clarity of life marked by a freedom of attitude and action that opens one up for God's love. Living in a materialistic, technologically focused society makes intentional commitment to simplicity as an individual and communal task both more challenging and more vital,

and thus the resources for such a commitment are more relevant than ever.

References and Resources

Caliguire, M. 2008. *Simplicity*. Downers Grove, IL: InterVarsity Press.

Foster, R. J. 2005. *Freedom of Simplicity: Finding Harmony in a Complex World*. Reprint ed. New York: HarperOne.

Johnson, J. 2011. *Abundant Simplicity: Discovering the Unhurried Rhythms of Grace*. Downers Grove, IL: InterVarsity Press.

Merton, T. 1948. *The Seven Storey Mountain*. New York: Harcourt Brace.

Rohr, R. 2004. *Simplicity: The Freedom of Letting Go*. Fort Collins, CO: Crossroad Press.

Schut, M., ed. 2009. *Simpler Living, Compassionate Life: A Christian Perspective*. Harrisburg, PA: Morehouse.

Whitmire, C. 2001. *Plain Living: A Quaker Path to Simplicity*. Notre Dame, IN: Sorin.

—Samjung Kang-Hamilton

SIMULATION AND DISCUSSION

Discussion allows a shared voice for testing; simulation applies shared research to function. Application of truth to real life is not the pragmatist's dogma. To the pragmatist, something is true because it works. A Christian point of view is premised on the belief that something works because it's true.

Biblical Theology of Simulation and Discussion

Truth claims must be tested. Old Testament teaching begins with a compare-and-contrast methodology. God's point of view versus ancient Near Eastern cultural beliefs is the reason for Genesis 1–11. Assumptions form the basis for belief, belief is sustained by knowledge, knowledge is encouraged through understanding, understanding needs evaluation, and evaluation accepts authority and accountability.

Accountability takes various forms in the Old Testament. All authority comes from God's Word, through prophetical voice, to the people (Deut. 18:15–19). The people were given tests (simulations) to verify true authority (Deut. 13:1–5, 18:20–22). False voices were rejected because their words came out of themselves (Jer. 14:13–14, 23:16; Ezek. 13:2). Hebrews substantiated authority through appointed leaders, elders who had to adjudicate situations (Deut. 21:19; Jos. 20:4; Ruth 4:1) by discussing disputes brought before them. Simulation can be hijacked by idolatry, causing people to believe only what they see (Deut. 4:15–19). Discussion can be contrived by apostates whose sole interest is personal power through persuasion (1 Kings 22:6–23).

In the New Testament, Jesus utilizes discussion regularly with all manner of groups. His use of parables stands as a verbal simulation: "Let me show you how this point of view is true or erroneous" (e.g., Luke 7:36–50). The church was consistently involved in discussion, marked by the need for apostolic replacements (Acts 1:15–26), disagreements about widows (Acts 6:1–7), and the essence of salvation (Acts 15:1–35). False teachers used simulated magic to lead the gullible astray (Acts 8:9–24) or fine-sounding discussions to displace belief in historical truth (2 Tim. 2:16–26). Methods of instruction—simulation and discussion included—can always be usurped for wrong ends. Methods should always be judged based on the theological origins from which they arise, the interpretive influence of the instructor, the exclusion of other points of view, and the outcomes generated from their application. Believers are always susceptible to educational vanities, born along by methods chosen for the task (2 Tim. 3:6–9, 4:3–4).

Biblical Philosophy of Simulation and Discussion

God's law for people is always specific, practical, universal, and dependable (Deut. 4:5–8; Rom. 7:7–12). Whether one reads about the dietary laws of Leviticus, restitution processes in Deuteronomy, animal husbandry practices in Exodus, or parent-child relations in Proverbs, the "Transcendent Source" of knowledge is the basis for biblical life application (Prov. 8). Discussion should be facilitated with love, generosity, grace, and care (Prov. 15:1–2; Eph. 4:25–32). While ideas expressed may be wrong, our way is that of Paul, "speaking the truth in love" (Eph. 4:15). The aims of discussion should be open examination, exploration, exposure, and expression. Simulation is based on God's created order; function and practice require stability. Simulated practice can be found throughout creation, whether one studies math, literature, science, history, or philosophy.

Researched content is essential for any teaching methodology, especially simulation and discussion. Simulation is based on solving problems with real-world examples. Discussion assumes various informed points of view allowing dialogue about the same subject. Flight simulators, for example, would be unnecessary if aerodynamics did not exist. Discussions of medical ethics would be unnecessary were there neither knowledge of human physiology nor concern for right and wrong. Methodology should not usurp the place of study; knowing prompts learning. Methodology helps teachers connect their study to student learning. Students are enlivened by thoughtful questions premised on their own reading.

Christian Practice of Simulation and Discussion

Both discussion and simulation can utilize methods such as Q&A, agree-disagree, circle-response, debate, panels, interviews, projects, peer review, games, and role-playing. But perhaps the best method that exemplifies the two practices is the case study. A case study is a written account of a particular dilemma. It is open-ended and unbiased in reporting the situation, and it leaves the reader with a problem to solve. Group discussion is used to clarify critical issues, acknowledge diverse points of view, and help the individual growth of small group members.

In writing a case study, accuracy and objectivity are important. Opinions should be attributed to characters in the case: a third-person point of view. The following components should be included in a case study:

1. *Introduction*: Arrest attention with an opening statement citing a problem to be resolved.
2. *Background*: Provide context, which is important for the student to understand the situation.
3. *Description*: Give the student a reason to connect with a controversy or concern.
4. *Summary*: Repeat the problem, allowing for open-ended discussion.
5. *Questions*: Help the student focus on the case; at least two to four questions should be devised that establish motivation, conduct, problems, or solutions.

References and Resources

Ellet, William. 2007. *The Case Study Handbook: How to Read, Discuss, and Write Persuasively about Cases.* Boston: Harvard Business Review Press.

Silberman, Mel. 1996. *Active Learning: 101 Strategies to Teach Any Subject.* Needham Heights, MA: Allyn and Bacon.

—MARK ECKEL

SIN

Sin may be defined biblically as any wrongdoing (1 John 5:17) in word, thought, or action against God or God's intentions for humanity and the created order. Sin is a deviation from God's will and character of holy love. It may be committed by an individual (Luke 12:47–8) or group (2 Kings 23:26–7), be one of commission (James 2:11) or omission (James 4:17), and intentional (Luke 12:47–8) or unintentional (Heb. 9:7).

The scriptures use three complementary metaphors to describe the problem of sin and use equivalent descriptions of salvation. First is the legal metaphor (Rom. 4:15), which sees sin as a transgression of the Law of God, leaving humanity under His condemnation. The corresponding idea of salvation is justification (Rom. 5:16–18), conveying forgiveness to humanity and the imputation of Christ's righteousness. The second is the familial or relational metaphor (Jer. 11:10), which portrays sin as a breech in the covenant relationship with God and humanity, leading to alienation and estrangement. In this perspective, salvation is defined in the language of reconciliation (2 Cor. 5:18) and adoption (Rom. 5:18). The final metaphor is cultic, associated with temple worship, and describes sin as making people unclean (Lev. 10:10), leaving humanity unable to come into the presence of God or a holy community. Salvation in this view is sanctification (1 Thess. 4:3–4), whereby humanity is actually made clean or holy.

Theologically, sin has been defined broadly in three ways: as a state, an act, and an infirmity. Sin as a state refers to the problem of original sin, the consequences of Adam and Eve's disobedience in the Garden, resulting in humanity being born depraved, with a perpetual "bent" to commit sin. This propensity is thought to be caused by either a physical or spiritual substance in human nature, an absence of the Holy Spirit's reign in human life, or the corruption of the moral image of God in humanity. Sin as an act refers to any transgression or lack of conformity to a known law of God. Here, people know what the will of God is, through scripture, personal conscience, or ecclesial teaching, and they intentionally or unintentionally break it. This may include sins over which they have control, strongholds of sin over which they have little or no control, and "sins of surprise," springing from people's sinful nature and "seizing them in the moment" without thought. Finally, sin as an infirmity refers to any deviation from the will or character of God because of human ignorance, arising from a lack of knowledge, wisdom, or understanding of God's will.

Biblically and theologically, there are levels and degrees of sin in the eyes of God. In the Roman Catholic tradition, a distinction is made between mortal and venial sins. Mortal sins are crimes of intentional opposition to God, leading to spiritual death. They are blatant offenses freely chosen against God and God's laws. Venial sins are attitudes and actions disagreeable to God, but reflect mitigating circumstances, not committed in direct opposition to the love and will of God. While Protestants generally avoid this type of distinction, they recognize that some sins are worse than others, based on the degree to which a word, thought, or action has been corrupted of God's original purpose, the intentionality of the will behind the offence, the number of other sins tied to it, and whether the sin is directed at God.

The doctrine of sin has been an essential part of Christian education throughout church history. The church has educated Christians and potential believers on humanity's chief problem and its consequences in various ways: through narration, chronicling the fall of Lucifer and humanity's first parents and tracing sin's history; through biblical exegesis, examining key Old and New Testament passages on sin; and through theological studies, systematizing sin into logical categories. This doctrine forms the backdrop for the church's instruction on God's salvation of humanity from sin: justification, adoption, regeneration, sanctification, and glorification.

More specifically, a biblical and theological understanding of sin has provided a standard for Christian training in righteousness, helping to bring lives into conformity with God's will and character. It has identified "mortal sins" Christians must be careful to avoid and has provided the means of evaluating questionable behavior in the church and applying appropriate discipline.

References and Resources

Berkouwer, G. C. 1971. *Sin.* Grand Rapids, MI: Eerdmans.
Erickson, Millard. 1998. "Sin." In *Christian Theology,* 513–602. Grand Rapids, MI: Baker Books.
Wily, H. Orton. 1952. "Hamartiology." In *Christian Theology.* Volume II, 56–89. Kansas City, MO: Beacon Hill.

—Christopher T. Bounds

Singapore and Christian Education

Singapore is a small Southeast Asian island with a multiethnic, multireligious population of 5.31 million people. It occupies a land area of only 714.3 square kilometers but has often been acknowledged as one of the region's economic success stories. Heavy investment in human resources development, excellent information-communications infrastructure, and key engines of economic growth have resulted in the global city's reputation for being vibrant, cosmopolitan, clean, green, and relatively corruption free.

Key societal developments and realities include active global integration, growing affluence and materialism, rising technological pervasiveness and dependence, rapid liberalization of societal mores, escalating income equality, extensive work and school stresses, increase in divorce rates, low fertility rates, a rapidly aging population, substantial transnational movements of people, and adoption of new citizens.

This new emerging context, with its accompanying challenges and opportunities, is shaping identity and the mission of the church in Singapore. Deep-level challenges faced by the church include the increasing attraction of prosperity Gospel, the shaping of values and lifestyles by popular media, growing biblical illiteracy, the draw of the dark side of virtual worlds, ceaseless attention to work demands, stresses on marriages and family, church conflict, and mindless traditionalism.

With rapid societal change, several avenues of ministry and Christian commitment are considered critical: intentional discipling of the church, nurturing new leaders, outreach to children and youth, strengthening marriages and families, bridging generational differences in ministry, promoting reconciliation within congregations, expanding services to the needy and vulnerable in society, relating to different ethnicities and faith commitments, engaging in the affairs of the public square, and mobilizing for home and cross-cultural integral missions.

—Calvin Chong

Single Parents

Single parents are a substantial population worldwide and especially in the United States. The background, context, and realities for single parents are increasingly complex. One may be a single parent by choice or by unwanted, unforeseen circumstances beyond one's control. Single parenthood may be the result of an unexpected teenage pregnancy, a divorce, death of a spouse, or some other cause that led to a broken relationship. The result is a new set of challenges and opportunities for the single parent in serving as the sole primary steward and caregiver for the child or children. The current situation, based on 2012 U.S. Census figures, is that approximately 28 percent of all children live in single-parent homes, approximately 3.5 percent live with another relative or a nonrelative, and 68 percent live with two parents. Current U.S. Census figures also show an increase in the number of single mothers who have never married.

Parenting in general is a God-given calling and responsibility to cultivate the maturation of a child through caring for physical needs, supporting the child's moral and cognitive development, modeling and encouraging healthy management of emotions and character formation, and illuminating awareness for spiritual development to occur (Prov. 4:20–24; Eph. 6:4; 2 Pet. 1:4–7). Faithfully responding to this biblical calling is challenging enough within the construct of a traditional marriage between a man and a woman working together to raise a child (Prov. 22:6); given the range of developmental needs of both the child and the parent, carrying out this biblical mandate as a single parent is far more daunting and challenging. Single parenting demands an extra measure of grace and support, especially from the local church to come alongside and walk with parents and children through difficult times.

In 1960, 1 percent of households with minor children in the United States had single dads. As of the 2010 U.S. Census, a record 8 percent of the total parent population was single dads. Within the single parent population, as of 2011 single fathers comprised 24 percent of the increase in single parents. According to the Pew Center for Research,

> like single mothers, single fathers are typically less educated and less well-off than their married counterparts. They are also younger and less likely to be white. However, single father householders differ from single mother householders on several indicators. Most notably, households headed by single fathers appear to be much better off financially when compared with those headed by single mothers. (Livingston 2013, 3)

There has also been a more modest increase in the number of single parent fathers who have never married. There are also more separated parents among whom the father is parenting the children during the time of separation. Experts are predicting that with the decline in traditional family values, the number of single parent families is going to continue to increase. These statistics point to numerous challenges and stressors that single parents face, including strained family relationships, feelings of rejection, absent parent and role models, fatigue or exhaustion, lack of finances, social anxiety, fear of perception, felt discrimination, lack of trust, and so forth.

Some churches have found ways to have single parents minister to single parents, and this has proven to be an effective ministry tool. Credibility is established by relating to someone with firsthand experience facing a similar challenge. Additional forms of support provided by local churches and parachurch ministries include connecting the single parent to relevant support, such as financial services, health care, education, and employment opportunities. In addition, some local churches have provided child care, after-school programs, and group meetings. Single parents are a growing and unique population to which the local church and parachurch organization must listen and evaluate the their needs within the congregation and the particular cultural context of the local community to determine how to serve and nurture them. Part of the challenge and opportunity for ministries will continue to be discerning to what extent to reach out to this subset of a broader population versus finding appropriate ways to integrate and include single parents in the life of the church. With the changing dynamics of what family looks like and how it is defined, the need for the church to effectively serve as the hands and feet communicating the grace and truth of the Gospel for parents, and particularly single parents, looms large.

The research is clear that youth who succeed and soar from single-parent families or dysfunctional traditional families have had at least one positive, long-term adult mentor who has no hidden agendas, provides consistent emotional support, and loves unconditionally (Devries 2004). Churches and parachurch organizations need to provide opportunities for youth to be able to connect with adults in a natural way to allow such relationships to develop. The church can serve both the single parent and the child as a "lifelong nurturing structure" (Devries 2004, 87) offering hope and the opportunity to experience a healthy Christian family.

References and Resources

Chapman, P. A. 2001. "Single-Parenting." In *Evangelical Dictionary of Christian Education*, edited by M. J. Anthony, 638–640. Grand Rapids, MI: Baker.

Devries, M. 2004. *Family-Based Youth Ministry*. Downers Grove, IL: InterVarsity Press.

Livingston, G. 2013. "The Rise of Single Fathers." 2 July. Pew Research: Social and Demographic Trends. http://www.pewsocialtrends.org/2013/07/02/the-rise-of-single-fathers/.

U.S. Census Bureau. 2012. "America's Families and Living Arrangements: 2012." 13 November. http://www.census.gov/hhes/families/data/cps2012.html.

—Daniel Bennett

Slovakia and Christian Education

The Slovak Republic is located in Central Europe between Poland and Hungary. Its capital, Bratislava, is not far from Vienna, Austria. The population is approximately 5.3 million ("Statistics Table 14" 2011).

Arrival of Christianity

Christians in Slovakia proudly trace their roots to the work of Cyril and Methodius, who arrived in AD 863 from Constantinople. Before that, Christian missionaries from other areas, notably the German-speaking kingdoms and the Eastern churches, sporadically shared the Gospel with the Slavic people. There is some evidence that Mojmír, ruler of Moravia (the region of the modern Czech and Slovak republics), was baptized in 822.

Christianity in Slovakia has been inextricably entwined with its political history. Prompted by the political implications of Germanic influence, Mojmír's successor, Rastislav, asked the Byzantine emperor, Michael III of Constantinople, to send teachers for his people.

Methodius and his brother, Cyril, who was highly educated in Constantinople, were native speakers of a dialect very close to the Slavonic tongue of Moravia. They came as evangelists, teachers, and translators. They established churches with native Slavic clergy, created liturgy for preaching and praying in the local language, and translated the Gospels and Psalms, devising the Glaglitic alphabet (a forerunner of the Cyrillic alphabet) to record the language. Although the Moravian rule ended sometime after 694 and the Magyars took control of the area, Christianity was firmly entrenched (Spinka [1933] 1968).

Christianity in Modern Slovakia

During the 20th century, Slovakia was subject to the waves of political change that engulfed Central Europe. At the end of World War I, when the Austro-Hungarian rule over Slovakia came to an end, the Slovaks were pressed to unite with the Czechs to form Czechoslovakia. During World War II, Hitler invaded the country, and Slovakia became a separate Nazi-controlled state.

Czechoslovakia was reestablished after the war but fell to Communist rule in 1948. Under communism, religion was suppressed; religious properties were confiscated, the training of clergy was severely curtailed, and religious expression was persecuted.

Following the 1989 "Velvet Revolution," a generally nonviolent revolt against Communist rule, Slovakia terminated its union with the Czechs and became an independent state in 1993. The government entered into a treaty with the Vatican, which establishes many of the Roman Catholic organizational rights and responsibilities. The government has similar agreements with other registered religious denominations.

The impression of Communist repression is still strongly felt among Slovak Christians, some of whom became believers through the influence of radio broadcasts and underground evangelistic efforts. Denominational boundaries were blurred as the Communist regime tried to crush all religious expression. Moreover, the secular culture of the period has carried over into the reluctance of some to seek counsel within the church body or to openly evangelize. Religion is considered a private matter.

While Slovakia has a reputation as a "Catholic country," the euphoria that accompanied the fall of communism has long since worn off, and the Slovaks face materialistic influences from Western culture, postmodernism, and European philosophical skepticism.

Denominations and Institutions in Slovakia

According to the census of 2011, 62 percent of Slovaks are Roman Catholic, 6 percent are evangelical Lutheran, 4 percent are Byzantine Catholic, 13 percent declared no religious affiliation, 10 percent did not respond, and the remainder belong to various Christian faiths (including Brethren, Methodist, and Baptist) or other beliefs ("Statistics Table 14" 2011). A study in 2008 indicated that more than 40 percent of the population attends religious services at least once a month, while 25 percent almost never attend (Brislinger 2011).

Christian schools, colleges, and theology departments within secular universities have been established or revitalized since the independence of the Slovak Republic. Comenius University in Bratislava, for example, has a Faculty of Roman Catholic Theology for bachelor's through PhD degrees, as well as a Faculty of Evangelical Theology for bachelor's through master's degrees. Matej Bel University in Banská Bystrica has a Department of Theology and Christian Education, offering degrees up to the PhD level.

Methods of Christian Education

The Slovaks have a long history of support of religious education. Students from ages 10 to 17 in both public and private schools are required to take courses in either religion or ethics. (For children 6 to 10 and 17 to 19, it is optional.) Parents enroll the students, and the religious denominations select the teachers. In most cases, as long as there are enough students for a class, the government subsidizes the teacher's salary. Some schools have faculty members who teach religious education and another subject. Religious content is determined by the denomination. Education about the history and beliefs of other faiths is sometimes taught in history or social studies courses (European Forum for Teachers of Religious Education 2013).

The Catholic Church launched a plan in 2001 to encourage children's and youth groups, children's activities led by laypeople, television programming, sports, community work with parents, mentoring of college students, and other activities, with the goal of crossing generational boundaries and fostering an appreciation for missions (Concordat Watch 2013). There are 189 schools operated by the Catholic Church (European Committee for Catholic Education 2013).

Lutheran churches and Brethren churches have sponsored Christian schools from the preschool level through higher education. An example is the Center for Christian Education in Martin, which was the dream passed down from grandfather, to father, to son during the Communist era, finding its fulfillment in the openness of the new Slovak Republic (see www.cce.sk).

Evangelicals also find that adults are open to inductive Bible studies, traditional teacher/pastor-led studies, small group discipleship, larger group seminars, marriage enrichment seminars, camps, sports, retreats, music ministry, English as a Second Language (ESL) camps, and discussion groups. Some churches have started youth centers, with or without partial government funding, which has accompanying restrictions.

Religious Freedom

Religious freedom is protected by law under the constitution. International observers concur that the people enjoy religious liberty as a practical matter. Slovakia's entry into the European Union in 2004 also brought accountability for maintaining freedom of worship and religious convictions.

References and Resources

Brislinger, Evelyn. 2011. European Values Study 2008: Project and Data Management. Köln: GESIS–Leibniz Inst. for the Social Sciences.

Concordat Watch. 2013. "Pastorisation and Evangelisation Plan of the Catholic Church in Slovakia for 2001–2006." Accessed 25 March 2013. http://www.concordatwatch.eu/showtopic.php?org_id=849&kb_header_id=5411.

European Committee for Catholic Education. 2013. "2009–2010 School Statistics." Accessed 30 April 2013. Statistiques_scolaires_2010, http://www.ceec.be/en_publications.htm.

European Forum for Teachers of Religious Education. 2013. "Religious Education in Slovakia." Accessed 29 April 2013. http://www.eftre.net.

Fletcher, Richard. 1997. The Barbarian Conversion: From Paganism to Christianity. New York: Henry Holt.

International Study of Religion in Eastern and Central Europe Association. 2013. "European Values Study." Accessed 17 April 2013. http://www.isorecea.net/index.php/religion-situation/Slovakia.

Spinka, Matthew. (1933) 1968. A History of Christianity in the Balkans: A Study in the Spread of Byzantine Culture among the Slavs. Hamden, CT: Archon Books.

"Statistics Table 14." 2011. Accessed 30 April 2013. http://portal.statistics.sk/files/tab-14.pdf.

www.euresisnet.eu (detail on religious education in Slovakia)
www.state.gov (International Freedom Reports)
http://portal.statistics.sk/showdoc.do?docid=37770 (public institutions of higher education in Slovakia)

—Carol G. Olsen

SLOVENIA AND CHRISTIAN EDUCATION

The bishops of Salzburg, Virgil (784) and Arno (785–821), sent the first missionaries to the Slovenians in 751. At the time, Carinthia was ruled by Hotimir (r. 752–768), who was baptized at the Monastery of the Holy Saviour on the Awa island on Lake Chiemsee. Another missionary center for the Slovenians was in Aquileia, from where most missionaries were sent by Patriarch Paulinus II (787—802) (Kos 1936). In the sixth and seventh centuries, there was a change in the method by which nations were Christianized: missionary preaching was replaced by a catechumenate. Its objective was not a prolonged and comprehensive preparation for the reception of baptism; a tribe became officially Christian when its leader was baptized. The purpose of missionary preaching was to consolidate the faith and morality of the new Christians, who had been baptized after the example of their elders, so that they could turn from their pagan mentality and actions and live according to the Gospel (Snoj 2003, 22).

According to social surveys for the year 2007, 66.3 percent of the population of Slovenia is Catholic, 1.8 percent evangelical, 1.7 percent Orthodox, and 1.9 percent Muslim. Religious education or denominational activities in schools are not explicitly mentioned in the educational provisions of the Slovenian Constitution. Its Article 7 stipulates that the state and religious communities are separate; religious communities enjoy equal rights and freely pursue their activities. Religious and other beliefs may be freely professed in private and public life (Čepar 2013, 318).

In 1952, the Communist authorities in Slovenia excluded religious education from all schools. The Catholic Church responded by introducing catechism classes in its parishes and training laypeople as catechists. It also drew up curricula and published textbooks for the implementation of the parish catechetical program, intended as a preparation for the reception of the sacraments, the transmission of fundamental Christian doctrines, as well as general religious knowledge. The Catholic Church is intent on preserving this approach to religious education, as it ensures a greater affiliation of children and young people with the parish community and a direct contact with its liturgical life. On the other hand, the more than half-a-century-long exclusion of religious education from schools has strengthened a general conviction that religion has no place in the public domain and schools. After the democratic changes in Slovenia in the early 1990s, the Ministry of Education strongly opposed the reintroduction of religious education in public schools. Instead, a subject of nondenominational religious education, called religions and ethics, was offered to students in the final triennium of elementary school. A decade later it became clear that the subject had failed to generate interest, being read by only a handful of pupils. Thus, Slovenia remains one of the few European countries where religious education is not a part of the regular school program (Stegu 2013).

Under current Slovene legislation, religious education is only allowed in private schools. The subject faith and culture, which aims at developing one's religious view of life in dialogue with other subjects, is taught at four Catholic high schools in Slovenia. Since 2008, religious education is taught at the only private Catholic elementary school (Globokar 2010). The parish catechesis is thus the only available religious education for the vast majority of Catholic children and adolescents, apart from religious education within the family.

References and Resources

Čepar, D. 2013. "Religious Education in the Republic of Slovenia." In *The Routledge International Handbook of Religious Education*, edited by D. H. Davis and E. Miroshnikova, 318–324. London, UK: Routledge.

Globokar, R. 2010. "Verski pouk v Sloveniji—ovrednotenje." In *Religious Education in Slovene Schools: Evaluation and Perspectives*, edited by R. Globokar, 7–11. Ljubljana, Slovenia: Zavod sv. Stanislava.

Grafenauer, I. (1936). *Karolinška kateheza ter izvor brižinskih spomenikov*. Ljubljana, Slovenia: Znanstveno društvo.

Kos, M. 1936. *Conversio Bagoariorum et Carantanorum*. Ljubljana, Slovenia: Znanstveno društvo.

Snoj, A. S. 2003. *Katehetika. Didaktična izhodišča*. Ljubljana, Slovenia: Salve.

Stegu, T. 2013. "The New Evangelization and Adult Religious Education in Slovenia—Challenges and Possibilities." *British Journal of Religious Education* 35: 1–11.

—Tadej Stegu

Small Groups

One of the most prevalent trends in Christian education in recent decades has been the use of small groups. Many churches have restructured their Christian education plans based on the belief that small groups will effectively promote the spiritual growth of adult men and women within the congregation. Small groups are so widespread that they may now be seen as the basic unit of church community. The common assumption in many churches is that the small group educational strategy has greater potential to produce Christian maturity than do large group class formats or even one-on-one mentoring.[50]

Benefits of Small Groups for Christian Education

There are many benefits to utilizing small groups in a Christian educational setting. One is the impact of relational learning on an individual. A widespread emphasis in small group ministry is the importance of establishing close relationships to enhance community among group members. Small group models have the potential for healthy ideals and positive implications. Many people grow best in a community, not in isolation. Education involves real-life issues rather than the mere mastery of facts. In our post-Christian society, where so many have

---

50. Mary Rynsburger and Mark A. Lamport, "All the Rage: How Small Groups Are Really Educating Christian Adults—Part 1: Assessing Small Group Ministry Practice: A Review of the Literature," *Christian Education Journal*, Series 3, 5, no. 1 (2008): 116–117.

experienced brokenness, abuse, and addiction, they often can find love, healing, and acceptance in the body of Christ through small groups.[51]

Johnson and Johnson (1999) list five defining elements of cooperative/relational learning: (a) positive interdependence (a sense of sink or swim together); (b) face-to-face promotive interaction (helping each other learn, applauding success and efforts); (c) individual and group accountability (each of us has to contribute to the group achieving its goals); (d) interpersonal and small group skills (communication, trust, leadership, decision making, and conflict resolution); and (e) group processing (reflecting on how well the team is functioning and how to function even better).[52] Small groups are beneficial in that they provide relational opportunities for learning.

The second benefit is that small groups can function as an instrument for change. Knowles and Knowles assert that six group factors directly correlate to the change that individuals experience through group involvement: (a) those who are to be changed have a strong sense of belonging to a group; (b) the pleasing of the group members is more important than the discomfort of the change; (c) the members of the group share the awareness that change is needed; (d) information relating to the need for change, plans for change, and the positives of change is shared and formulated through the group; (e) the group provides an opportunity for the individual to practice changed behavior without threat or punishment; and (f) the individual is provided with a means for measuring progress toward the change goals as he or she communicates with the group.[53] Small groups are beneficial in that they provide collective aids to produce individual change within the members of the group.

A third benefit is that small groups allow for open discussion. A significant advantage of a learning group is the collective gathering of greater resources than individuals have on their own. Through discussion, the group shares resources. In addition, participants in group discussion are often stimulated to succeed by the presence of others and change their individual attitudes and behavior.[54]

Cautions for Small Groups in Christian Education

It has been observed that group problems arise with some regularity. (1) Groups can occasionally be hurtful. (2) It is possible for a group to be sincere, concerned, and sensi-tive but completely self-centered. (3) A common problem in groups is the existence of a small power clique within the group. (4) Groups often fail when they do not meet the needs of their members. (5) Groups often run into problems with relationships between members. These problems can immobilize the group as a whole.[55]

In a Christian context, when dealing with the teaching of scripture, it is important that a small group be aware and guard against relativism. Often, Bible study within a small group begins with the question, "What does this passage mean to you?" This question is harmful in that it confuses the *meaning* of a passage with the *significance* of the passage. The meaning of a text of scripture never changes, but the significance of that text to the life of a believer is flexible (Russell 2000, 110). E. D. Hirsch argued that "Meaning is that which is represented by a text; it is what the author meant. . . . Significance, on the other hand, names a relationship between that meaning and a person, or a conception, or a situation, or indeed anything imaginable."[56] It is important to safeguard the small group from digressing into potential negative outcomes.

Suggestions for Small Groups in Christian Education

Though caution needs to be observed in a small group educational setting, there are many benefits of a small group teaching model. Leaders of small groups should (1) stress the importance of the task, (2) enhance the esteem of individuals through recognition or by delegating responsibility, (3) emphasize the shared interests of all group members, (4) help members accept the overall group purposes, (5) encourage reflection and inquiry in discussion by affirmation of member discovery, (6) plan programs with meticulous care, and (7) encourage interaction among members.[57]

Small groups are a prevalent style of education in both churches and educational institutions. There are significant advantages to small group education; however, cautions must be observed when developing small groups. With the proper safeguards in place, grouping can have a significant pedagogical impact on individuals in Christian educational settings.

References and Resources

Fest, Thorrel B., Barbara Schindler Jones, and R. Victor Harnack, *Group Discussion: Theory and Technique*. Upper Saddle River, NJ: Prentice-Hall, 1977, 13–18.

51. Robert J. Marzano, Debra J. Pickering, and Jane E. Pollock, *Classroom Instruction That Works Research—Based Strategies for Increasing Student Achievement*, 1st ed. (ASCD, 2001), 85.

52. Rynsburger and Lamport, "All the Rage," 117.

53. David W. Johnson and Roger T. Johnson, *An Overview of Cooperative Learning*, Cooperative Learning Institute and Interaction Book Company, http://www.co-operation.org/?page_id=65 (24 May 2013).

54. Malcolm Shepherd Knowles and Hulda Knowles, *Introduction to Group Dynamics*, rev. ed. (New York: Association Press, 1972), 62.

55. Thorrel B. Fest, Barbara Schindler Jones, and R. Victor Harnack, *Group Discussion: Theory and Technique* (Upper Saddle River, NJ: Prentice-Hall, 1977), 13–18.

56. Clyde Reid, *GROUPS ALIVE—CHURCH ALIVE: The Effective Use of Small Groups in the Local Church*, 4th printing (New York: Harper & Row, 1969), 102–104.

57. E. D. Hirsch, *Validity in Interpretation* (New haven, CT: Yale University Press, 1967), 8.

Hirsch, E. D. 1967. *Validity in Interpretation*. New Haven, CT: Yale University Press.

Johnson, David W., and Roger T. Johnson. 1999. *Learning Together and Alone: Cooperative, Competitive, and Individualistic Learning*. Boston: Allyn and Bacon, 1999.

Russell, Walt. 2000. "What It Means to Me," *Why Small Groups*. Sovereign Grace Ministries.

—ANDREW BURGGRAFF

SMART, JAMES D.

James D. Smart was a Canadian theologian, Christian educator, and Presbyterian pastor. He was born in Alton, Ontario, Canada, on 1 March 1906. His Presbyterian parents provided a Christian, nurturing education that shaped his vocations of ministry and religious scholarship in the disciplines of Christian education and hermeneutics.[58] He received his bachelor of arts degree from the University of Toronto in 1926 and a master of arts degree in 1927. He studied theology at Knox College and graduated in 1929. He studied the Old Testament in Germany at Marburg and Berlin (1929–1930), and in 1931 received his doctorate of philosophy from the University of Toronto.[59]

Curriculum Development

Smart was ordained in the Presbyterian Church in Canada, where he served several congregations from 1931 to 1944. While pastoring St. Paul's Church, Peterborough (1941–1944), he wrote his first book, *What a Man Can Believe* (1943). As a result of publishing this book and his extensive experience in pastoral ministry, he was invited to serve as editor-in-chief of *The Christian Faith and Life Curriculum: A Program for Church and Home* for the United Presbyterian Church, U.S.A. (1944–1950). This curriculum was developed to address the lack of education in the church. Smart advocated that the Presbyterian Church produce a quality theologically and educationally oriented curriculum in order to equip and train denominational leaders and laity. He became a regular *Presbyterian Record* columnist and decided to review the basic principles of Christian education in a pamphlet outlining the new curriculum, *The Church Must Teach, Or Die!* It included four headings: "Why Christian Education?" "Whose Task?" "To What End?" and "What Shall We Teach?" The program followed a three-year cycle: Jesus Christ, Bible, and Church. It included four hallmarks of the curriculum: (1) training for Christian disciple-

ship—emphasis on a Christ-centered curriculum; (2) emphasis on the Bible and doctrine—the Bible as central; (3) honesty about historical-critical scholarship—emphasis on biblical authority and biblical scholarship; and (4) importance of church history—teaching church history to enable people to see they are part of the church.[60] This renewed emphasis led to new energy and numerical growth in Presbyterian congregational education.

Smart returned to the pastorate in Toronto, Canada, and taught Christian education and hermeneutics at Knox College (1951–1957). After serving for several years in the pastorate, he became the Jesup Professor of Biblical Interpretation at Union Theological Seminary, New York (1957–1971). Always a pastor at heart, Smart concluded his ministry where he started, copastoring in Rosemont Presbyterian Church from 1970 to 1974.

Theology and Education

Smart's investment in curriculum development led him to think theologically about church education. His most influential work, *The Teaching Ministry of the Church* (1954), addressed the broader educational concerns of the Presbyterian Church, asserting that Christian education has more roots in secular education than in church tradition. Smart's assertion shook the liberal establishment.[61] He pointed out that the educational curriculum was weak theologically and did not include subject matter related to the Bible and theology. He argued that Christian educators should be responsible theologians and teach a biblical theology of Christian education. Smart's mission was to recover a theological approach to Christian education. He asserted that "The divorce between Christian education and theology was as much the fault of theologians who were educationally blind as it was of educators who were theologically blind. The teacher of the Word requires the same grounding Biblically, systematically, and historically, as the preacher of the Word."[62] He was criticized for his challenge by several of his liberal colleagues. However, as a conservative he was highly influenced by the neoorthodox movement of Karl Barth and Eduard Thurneysen. They helped him connect theology to the church's educational ministries. Smart believed that Christian education was connected to a biblical theology of the church. In keeping with Barthian thinking, he

58. Hartley Atkinson, "James D. Smart," *Christian Educators of the 20th Century*, http://www.talbot.edu/ce20/educators/protestant/james_smart/ (accessed 17 July 2013).

59. Ibid.

60. William Klempa, "The Church Must Teach—or Die! James D. Smart and a Revolutionary Curriculum," *The Free Library*, 1 January 2009, http://www.thefreelibrary.com/The+church+must+teach--or+die!+James+D.+Smart+and+a+revolutionary...-a0192800748 (accessed 17 July 2013).

61. Kenneth O. Gangel and Warren S. Benson, *Christian Education: Its History and Philosophy* (Chicago: Moody Press, 1983), 319.

62. James D. Smart, *The Teaching Ministry of the Church: An Examination of the Basic Principles of Christian Education* (Philadelphia: Westminster, 1954), 41.

rejected the popular liberal theology of optimism that permeated Europe and America. When the two world wars crippled that optimism, he supported H. Shelton Smith's attack against the existential approach of the liberals, but retained a relatively high regard for liberal religious education. He admitted that they might not always ask the right questions theologically, but they did ask the right questions educationally.[63]

Centrality of Scripture

Smart was a biblical theologian, not an educator, but his view of education progressed over the years. He never developed an educational model or approach, but he provided the church with a clarion call to connect theology and education together in the church's educational ministry. Later in his ministry, he lamented the loss of the Bible from the church. This is reflected in *The Rebirth of Ministry* (1960), in which he describes the typical person's encounter with the Bible as fragmented at best. People would receive small portions of the Bible through various programs, but would never deal with the larger themes and concepts of the scriptures. As his convictions developed, Smart asserted the need to involve laypeople in the teaching ministry of the church and to equip them in all aspects of the church's ministry so that the scriptures could be returned to the church.[64] In *The Strange Silence of the Bible in the Church* (1970), he placed blame on biblical scholars who used a scientific approach to interpretation instead of reading the biblical narratives and valuing the theological content of the Bible.

Smart's contribution to the field of education and the church is significant. He authored 19 books, wrote many scholarly publications, and published articles in the *Presbyterian Record*. His most notable contributions to the field of Christian education are *What a Man Can Believe* (1943), *The Recovery of Humanity* (1953), *The Teaching Ministry of the Church* (1954), *The Rebirth of Ministry* (1960), *The Creed in Christian Tradition* (1961), and *The Strange Silence of the Bible in the Church* (1970). His emphasis on grounding Christian education in biblical theology and the church provided a needed corrective to the educational ministry of the Presbyterian Church and the church universal. As he argued, "The teacher and preacher have a common ministry. They serve the same revelation of God which comes to them from the Scriptures and through the total witness of the Church. . . . [T]herefore, both need to be trained to be alert and critical theologians."[65]

---

63. Mark A. Maddix, "The Early Days of Religious Education: 1900–1950's," in *Christian Education: The Heritage of Christian Education*, ed. James R. Estep (Joplin, MO: College Press, 2003), 20–21.
64. Ibid.
65. Smart, *Teaching Ministry*, 41.

References and Resources

Atkinson, Hartley. n.d. "James D. Smart." In *Christian Educators of the 20th Century*. Accessed 17 July 2013. http://www.talbot.edu/ce20/educators/protestant/james_smart/.

Cully, Kendig B. 1940. *The Search for a Christian Education, since 1940*. Philadelphia: Westminster.

Dykstra, Craig. "James Smart's Contribution to the Pastor as Educator." *Quarterly Review* 3 (Fall): 77–84.

Gangel, Kenneth O., and Warren S. Benson. 1983. *Christian Education: Its History and Philosophy*. Chicago: Moody Press.

Klempa, William. 2009. "The Church Must Teach—or Die! James D. Smart and a Revolutionary Curriculum." *The Free Library*, 1 January. Accessed 17 July 2013. http://www.thefreelibrary.com/The church must teach—or die! James D. Smart and a revolutionary . . . -a0192800748.

Little, Sara. 1961. *The Role of the Bible in Contemporary Christian Education*. Richmond, VA: John Know.

Maddix, Mark A. 2003. "The Early Days of Religious Education: 1900–1950's." In *Christian Education: The Heritage of Christian Education*, edited by James R. Estep, 20–21. Joplin, MO: College Press.

Smart, James D. 1943. *What a Man Can Believe*. Philadelphia: Westminster.

———. 1954. *The Teaching Ministry of the Church: An Examination of the Basic Principles of Christian Education*. Philadelphia: Westminster.

—Mark Maddix

SMART, NINIAN

Ninian Smart (1927–2001) was a British scholar who helped establish the academic discipline of the study of religion, while also offering resources for people outside academia who wanted to understand the world's religions in all their complexity.

Early Background and Education

Born to Scottish parents in Cambridge, England, Smart spent time as a member of the British Intelligence Corps, where he was able to study and experience the cultures and religions of Asia. He returned to England to study at Oxford in 1948, concentrating on classics and philosophy and eventually uniting his past experience studying other cultures with his interest in world religions.

Significant Contributions to Christian Education

After several academic appointments in his early career, Smart established the first religious studies department in the United Kingdom at the University of Lancaster in 1967, then went on to further develop the field while at the University of California, Santa Barbara, retiring from there in 1998. Smart was also influential in organizations promoting the study of religion and engaging in interfaith work, and in 2000 he was elected president of the American Academy of Religion.

Smart's influence centered largely in the establishment of understanding other religions alongside Christianity as worthy of study in themselves. Mid-20th-century Western academic institutions considered the study of Christianity and religious studies to be synonymous, and even this study was from a theological perspective. Smart developed a framework of phenomenological inquiry that created a new discipline in which all religious experiences could be understood within their own contexts and from the point of view of the person experiencing that particular expression of religion, whether it was a theistic or nontheistic belief system. His seven categories of inquiry and comparison, or dimensions of religion—doctrinal, mythological, ethical, ritual, experiential, institutional, and material—were critical in providing a way for scholars and laypeople to understand different religions using the same variables. This development not only created space for the interfaith and interreligious movements that continue to develop today, but indirectly created frameworks for Christians seeking to understand their faith in a nontheological framework that was not concerned about matters of orthodoxy.

Notable Publications

Smart's major works include *The Religious Experience*, first published in 1969, *The Philosophy of Religion* (1970), *The Science of Religion and the Sociology of Knowledge* (1973), and *Dimensions of the Sacred: An Anatomy of the World's Beliefs* (1998).

References and Resources

Lamb, Christopher, and Dan Cohn-Sherbok, eds. 1999. *The Future of Religion: Postmodern Perspectives—Essays in Honor of Ninian Smart*. London: Middlesex University Press.

Smart, Ninian. 1997. *Reflections in the Mirror of Religion*. Introduction by John P. Burris. New York: St. Martin's Press.

—KARRI BACKER

SMITH, H. SHELTON

Early Background and Education

H. Shelton Smith (1893–1987) served as a professor at Duke Divinity School from 1931 to 1963. Raised and educated within the early 20th-century liberal religious education tradition, he eventually changed his theological and educational views and became an early leader in the neoorthodox Christian education movement of the

midcentury, influencing many through his teaching and writing, particularly his book *Faith and Nurture* (1941).

Born in Greensboro, North Carolina, he earned his AB degree at Elon College in 1917, and his BD and PhD from Yale in 1923. His studies were interrupted during World War I, during which he served as a chaplain in the U.S. Army in France. Following graduation from his doctoral program, he became director of leadership education for the International Council of Religious Education. He taught briefly at Teachers College, Columbia University (1928–1929) and at Yale Divinity School (1929–1931) before moving to Duke Divinity School. At Duke he began as professor of religious education, then added Christian ethics in 1940, and broadened his focus to American religious thought in 1945. For his last 23 years he served as director of the doctoral program at Duke Graduate School of Arts and Sciences.

Significant Contributions to Christian Education

Influenced by his experiences in ministry during World War I and in the United States during the Great Depression, and by the writings of Karl Barth, Smith began to critique the liberal religious education movement in the mid-1930s, continuing to develop and publish his ideas on the needed theological reconstruction of Christian education through the mid-1940s. *Faith and Nurture* was his most influential publication. Written at least in part in response to Harrison S. Elliot's 1940 book *Can Religious Education Be Christian?*, Smith's book challenged the liberal theological perspective, with its emphasis on the immanence of God, the goodness of human nature, Christ as a moral teacher, scripture as a record of human religious experience, natural developmental processes, and the equating of the Kingdom of God with the pursuit of democratic ideals. He found this perspective to be too optimistic regarding human nature and potentiality, ignoring the impact of sin and human injustice. In contrast, he emphasized the need to focus Christian education on an understanding of God's transcendence, yet incarnation in Jesus Christ, human sin nature and the need for salvation, scripture as a means of God's revelation, and the church's distinctive involvement in the world as the Body of Christ.

Smith continued his theological reflections on human nature and its impact on the church's ministry, publishing *Changing Conceptions of Original Sin: A Study of American Theology Since 1750* in 1955. Another major publication that brought together his interest in church history and Christian education was *Horace Bushnell* (1965), containing many of Bushnell's writings and Smith's assessment of his impact on theology and religious education. Smith also wrote to counter racism within society and the church, publishing several articles that challenged the church's attitudes and practices. His final book, *In His Image, but . . . Racism in Southern Religion, 1780–1910,* discussed the sources of racism in the southern church and countered it with an understanding of all people being created in the image of God and worthy of respect.

Most Notable Publications

Smith, H. S. 1934. "Let Religious Educators Reckon with Barthians." *Religious Education* 29: 45–50.

——. 1941. *Faith and Nurture.* New York: Charles Scribner's Sons.

——. 1955. *Changing Conceptions of Original Sin: A Study in American Theology since 1750.* New York: Charles Scribner's Sons.

——. 1965. *Horace Bushnell.* New York: Oxford University Press.

——. 1972. *In His Image, but . . . Racism in Southern Religion, 1780–1910.* Durham, NC: Duke University Press.

References and Resources

Browning, R. L. n.d. "Smith, H. Shelton." In *Christian Educators of the 20th Century.* http://www.talbot.edu/ce20/educators/protestant/robert_browning/.

Henry, S. C. 1963. *A Miscellany of American Christianity: Essays in Honor of H. Shelton Smith.* Durham, NC: Duke University Press.

Zikmund, B. B. 1990. "H. Shelton Smith: Contagious Christian." *Christian Century* 107F7–14: 151–152.

—Kevin E. Lawson

Social Action as Christian Practice

Social action is the purposeful engagement to transform society. It seeks to change both local and major societal structures, public policies, political institutions, socioeconomic disparities, and all forms of oppression.

There is no doubt that modern social action, especially in Christian education, has origins in the Social Gospel movement at the beginning of the 20th century. Walter Rauschenbusch's *A Theology for the Social Gospel* (1917) provided a look at how to articulate a Christian theology through social action. In light of the Great Depression, the Social Gospel movement and the Roman Catholic Church began looking at a broader range of social issues, such as women's rights, labor relations, nonviolence, and racial and class violence. For example, in 1933 the Catholic Worker movement, led by Dorothy Day, not only addressed social needs such as food, shelter, and clothing, but took social action by publishing the *Catholic Worker,* a paper naming how communities could act for social change. Coinciding with the *Catholic Worker,* the Protestant journal *Social Action,* first published in 1935, advocated for churches to address social issues through civic engagement.

With the threat of World War II on the horizon, Reinhold Niebuhr's *Moral Man and Immoral Society* (1932) claimed that the church should become politically involved in issues of social justice, especially around war. A student of Niebuhr's and arguably the epitome of Christian social action, Martin Luther King Jr. revitalized a national conversation about social action. Dr. King and many who worked alongside him, including Coretta Scott King, Rosa Parks, and James Lawson, embodied social action through nonviolent demonstrations, protests, community organizing, and civil disobedience when needed. Many Christian educators today look to the civil rights movements of the 1960s and 1970s as the essence of social action through Christian communities.

During the 1970s, liberation theology sparked social action from within Christian education. Christian educators began looking to Paulo Freire's *Pedagogy of the Oppressed* (1970) and Gustavo Gutierrez *Teología de la Liberación/ Theology of Liberation* (1971) as influential texts, illustrating how Christians can and need to be social actors. Notably, the Consejo Episcopal Latinoamericano (Latin American Episcopal Conference) meetings at Medellín, Colombia (1968), and Puebla, Mexico (1979), with their emphasis on the preferential option for the poor and oppressed, provided ecclesial support for base communities: local faith communities with an emphasis on socioeconomic liberation achieved through social action.

More recently, social action can be found in such fields as social movement theory and faith-based community organizing. Jennifer Ayers (2011, 11) suggests that with the emergence of social movement theory, religious educators are beginning to ask: "How does religion influence social movements?" and "How does participation in social movements in turn influence religion?" Religion and social movements share one key aspect: social action. Where religion and social movements seek to change the world, social action is the instrument through which both achieve this end.

References and Resources

Ayers, J. 2011. *Waiting for a Glacier to Move: Practicing Social Witness.* Princeton, NJ: Princeton University Press.

Council for Christian Social Action of the United Church of Christ. 1935. *Social Action* 1 (1): 1–4.

Dewey, J. 2000. *Liberalism and Social Action.* New York: Prometheus Books.

Espinosa, G., V. Elizondo, and J. Miranda. 2005. *Latino Religions and Civic Activism in the United States.* Oxford: Oxford University Press.

Freire, P. (1970) 2000. *Pedagogy of the Oppressed*. 30th anniv.
    ed. Translated by Myra Bergman. New York: Continuum.

Gutiérrez, G. 1971. *Teología de la liberación, perspectivas*.
    Lima: CEP.

Niebuhr, R. 1932. *Moral Man and Immoral Society: A Study of
    Ethics and Politics*. New York: Charles Scribner's Sons.

Rauschenbusch, W. 1917. "A Theology for the Social Gospel."
    New York: Macmillan.

—PATRICK BRUNER REYES

SOCIAL JUSTICE

Social justice historically refers to the rights and duties
that arise out of capital and labor, relations between
employer and employee, and the role of the state and
supranational organizations in addressing these questions. It also refers to the duties people owe one another
in virtue of being human. St. Thomas Aquinas asserted
that justice is a virtue; a virtue is a firm disposition, habit,
or tendency to do the good. Virtues, furthermore, are
habits that permit one to perform good acts. The virtuous
person tends toward the good; he pursues the good and
chooses it in specific actions. The virtuous act in the case
of justice is "to render to others their rights." The rights
of others are derived from nature and positive law. And
if something is incompatible with natural justice, positive
law cannot make it just. In other words, nature plays the
primary role in the determination of what is just.

Aquinas distinguished between two types of justice:
commutative and distributive. Commutative justice regulates mutual exchanges between individuals, while distributive justice regulates the part-whole relationship, in
particular of the citizen to the polis:

> This order is directed by commutative justice, which is
> concerned about the mutual dealings between two per-
> sons. . . . [This second] order is directed by distributive
> justice, which distributes common goods proportionately.
> Hence there are two species of justice, distributive and
> commutative. The mean in distributive justice is observed
> according to "geometrical proportion," whereas in com-
> mutative justice it follows "arithmetical proportion.[66]

Subsidiarity and Solidarity

In traditional Christian teaching, there is thought to
be a *via media* between laissez-faire capitalism on the
one hand and the various forms of communism, which
subordinate the individual to the state, on the other. In
achieving this *via media*, it is necessary that government

assume only those activities that surpass the ability of
private persons and groups acting independently. Local
government is preferable to large-scale, central government. Indeed, the family, the state, and the international
order should be in the service of the human person not
some other grouping. Because human individuals are, by
virtue of their nature, social animals, and such institutions as the family, the church, labor unions, and other
voluntary associations are mediating structures that
empower individual action and connect the individual
to society, the subsidiarity principle demands interaction
with the principle of solidarity.

Individual Duties

Christians have duties to the vulnerable and powerless.
On the Day of Judgment, it is taught, God will ask what
each person did to assist them. Christ's words—"Amen, I
say to you, whatever you did for one of these least brothers of mine, you did for me" (Matt. 25:40)—obliges the
Christian to promote social justice and assist the vulnerable. This means showing solidarity with, and compassion for, the poor and the vulnerable. Laws and policies
must ennoble the most vulnerable, not lay them open to
abuse or homicide. Laws must be equitable, not cruel.
There are also corporal and spiritual works of mercy. The
former include the duty to feed the hungry, to give
drink to the thirsty, to clothe the naked, to harbor the
harborless, to visit the sick, to ransom the captive, and to
bury the dead. The spiritual works of mercy include the
duty to instruct the ignorant, to counsel the doubtful, to
admonish sinners, to bear wrongs patiently, to forgive of-
fences willingly, to comfort the afflicted, and to pray for
the living and the dead.

Pope Leo XIII asserted the right of workers to safe and
sustainable working conditions and working hours. Employers are responsible to provide these: "It is neither just
nor humane so to grind men down with excessive labour
as to stupefy their minds and wear out their bodies."
Safety, rest, a living wage sufficient for the support of a
family, and rejection of the use of child labor characterize
his 1891 encyclical, *Rerum Novarum*. It also affirmed the
concept of private property.

Sanctity of Life of the Human Being

Justice is owed by humans to one another. Mainstream
Christianity affirms the sanctity of life, a doctrine over
and above the more general equal dignity principle affirmed in international law. Both doctrines imply the
inherent dignity of the human being and affirm rights
(not to be killed, subjected to degrading and inhuman
treatment, etc.). If human life is sacred, a gift from God,
then there are special duties owing to it and special dangers pertaining to those who deny its true character.

---

66. Thomas Aquinas, *The Summa Theologica of St. Thomas Aquinas
Literally Translated by Fathers of the English Dominican Province* (London:
Burns Oates and Washbourne, 1920), II-II, q. 61, a. 1.

Common Good

The common good was seen by Aquinas as central to the law, so it is a primary purpose of a state to provide for it. All people have equal dignity. Social class is no determinant of dignity, and a good government protects the rights and cares for the needs of all its members, both rich and poor. "As regards the State, the interests of all, whether high or low, are equal. The members of the working classes are citizens by nature and by the same right as the rich; they are real parts, living the life which makes up, through the family, the body of the commonwealth" (*Rerum Novarum* 1891, 33).

Distributism

Distributism is a socioeconomic theory that holds that social and economic structures should promote social justice, including wide ownership of corporations. It is the basis for progressive tax rates, antitrust laws, and economic cooperatives. Among its defenders are such thinkers as Hilaire Belloc, G. K. Chesterton, and Dorothy Day. The Roman Catholic Church's *Rerum Novarum*, *Quadragesimo Anno*, *Centesimus Annus*, and *Caritas in Veritate* are teaching or magisterial documents that support a just distribution of income and wealth and are in contrast to libertarian economics.

In a pluralist society, the Christian laity has the specific responsibility to pursue social justice using reason and natural law. Christian educators have a duty to understand the wealth of reasoning found in their own tradition.

References and Resources

Anscombe, G. E. M. 1958. "Modern Moral Philosophy." *Philosophy* 33: 1–19.

Aquinas, Thomas. 1920. *The Summa Theologica of St. Thomas Aquinas Literally Translated by Fathers of the English Dominican Province*. London: Burns Oates and Washbourne.

Aristotle 1955. *The Ethics of Aristotle: The Nichomacheann Ethics*. rev. ed. Translated by J. K. Thomson. New York: Viking.

Belloc, H. 2009. "An Essay on the Restoration of Property." Norton, VA: HIS Press.

———. 1912. *The Servile State*. London, UK: T. N. Foulis.

———. (1913) 1977. "The Servile Institution Dissolved." In *The Servile State*, 71–83. Indianapolis, IN: Liberty Fund.

Chesterton, G. K. 1910. *What's Wrong with the World*. Glendale, CA: Seven Treasures Publications.

———. 1917. *Utopia of Usurers*. Milwaukee, WI: Wiseblood Books.

———. (1927) 2001. *The Outline of Sanity*. Norfolk, VA: IHS Press.

Foot, Philippa. 1978. *Virtues and Vices*. Oxford: Blackwell.

John Paul II. 1991. Papal Encyclical *Centesimus Annus*.

Laing, Jacqueline A., and Russell Wilcox. 2013. *The Natural Law Reader*. Oxford: Wiley Blackwell.

Leo XIII. 1891. Papal Encyclical *Rerum Novarum*.

MacIntyre, Alasdair. 1985. *After Virtue*. 2nd ed. London: Duckworth.

———. 1999. *Dependent Rational Animals*. Chicago: Open Court.

Pius XI. 1931. Papal Encyclical *Quadragesimo Anno*.

—Jacqueline Laing

Social Media and Christian Education

Social media refers to a rapidly growing movement of Internet and cellular-based technologies wherein participants use networking to share personal information or participate in shared activities such as gaming, information collaboration, and virtual lifestyles. Social media has its roots in the mid-1990s in innovations such as America Online's (AOL) buddy list and the launch of Sixdegrees.com. The movement advanced in 2001 with innovations like Meetup and Wikipedia. Later developments include a plethora of multimedia resources, such as MySpace, Facebook, YouTube, Twitter, Pinterest, and Reddit.[67] Overall, the impact of social media reflects a media culture shift, moving the media audience from primarily a passive mode (e.g., as with television, movies, or radio), to a highly participative engagement with mediated forms.

Social media, often known as Web 2.0, incorporates both interactive, asynchronous (delayed), repositories and synchronous ("real-time") engagement via chat, texting, or video modalities. Overall, the environment of social media seems more closely aligned to younger generations, though the level of adult participation seems to be increasing at a rapid rate.[68]

Christian education's response to social media includes moments of caution, particularly regarding interactions of children and youth. Christian educators may approach social media primarily through the "content" produced and its impact on participants. There is particular concern about content that offends Christian sensibilities and raises larger social/ethical concerns.[69] Christian educators may challenge inappro-

67. Marcia Clemmitt, "Social Media Explosion," *CQ Researcher* 23, no. 4 (January 2013): 83–100, http://library.cqpress.com/cqresearcher/document.php?id=cqresrre2013012500 (accessed 14 June 2013).

68. Michael Hoechsmann, "Updating Your Status: Identity and Learning in Viral Youth Networks," in *Learning the Virtual Life: Public Pedagogy in a Digital World*, ed. Peter Pericles Trifonas (New York: Routledge Press, 2012), 31–42; Maeve Duggan and Joann Brenner, *The Demographics of Social Media Users—2012* (Washington, DC: Pew Research Center's Internet and American Life Project), http://pewinternet.org/Reports/2013/Social-media-users.aspx (accessed 14 June 2013).

69. Gwenn Schurgin O'Keefee, *CyberSafe: Protecting and Empowering Kinds in the digital World of Texting, Gaming, and Social Media* (Elk Grove Village, IL: American Academy of Pediatrics, 2011); Kimberly J. Mitchell, Finkelhor, David Jones, Wolak, and Lisa M. Janis, "Prevalence

priate displays and views through social media, including suggestive portrayals and outright consumption of pornography.[70] However, other theorists note that adult intervention, even in the face of apparent moral misconduct, raises additional issues about adolescent social privacy.[71] Some congregations and ministries, alongside religious researchers, choose to adapt social technology as a means of creative social engagement.[72]

Christian educators should pay particular attention to social media because of its power to create new digital literacies, as well as community practices, that shape future generations. The advent of social media raises a number of key questions concerning literacy (a way of "reading" culture) and the changing epistemological framework that governs young learners.[73] Already social media shapes not only the lexicon of culture but also its delivery. Social media interaction includes the presence of massive open online gaming (MOOG) and multiuser virtual environments (MUVEs). These interactions invite a range of learning practices that include constructivist and situated learning models of learning, as well as group sourcing activities for collaborative engagement.[74]

Mary Hess notes that "we need to keep in mind that digital technologies are cultures we are embedded in, not just tools we use."[75] Young people embedded within globally oriented social media are often labeled "digital natives." The term identifies those who have not only navigated the technologies, but also have adapted personally and grown intellectually through these mediated

cultures.[76] Theorists have challenged this concept based on both practice and quality of learning.[77] Nevertheless, social media engagement does shape learning practices.

Christian educators should note how social media shapes youth practice and their interaction with other social groups and society at large.[78] Dana Boyd notes that social media reverses traditional trends of public and private space. Boyd asserts that often standard social space is primarily "private" (between two people in conversation) so that social engagements must work to make them public (often through media). In contrast, social media space is inherently "public" (via the networked publics among Internet environments), so young people often navigate media to find ways to create more "private" exchanges among friends.[79] This simple shift of the concept of "space" on social media may explain the range of challenges Christian educators face as they explore other basic Christian practices through key themes like ritual, identity, community, authority, authenticity, and religion itself.[80] Sherry Turkel observes that social media and its accompanying technologies may be generating a "new state of self."[81] Christian educators will need to take seriously the embeddedness of social media as it changes not only issues of educational learning but also formative practices and resulting changes in community and conceptions of the self.

References and Resources

Bauerlein, Mark, ed. 2011. *The Digital Divide: Arguments for and Against Facebook, Google, Texting, and the Age of Social Networking.* New York: Jeremy Tarcher/Penguin.

Birdsong, Toni, and Tami Heim. (2010) 2011. *@stickyJesus: How to Live Out Your Faith Online.* Nashville, TN: Abingdon Press/Digital Scribe Press.

Boyd, Danah. 2007. "Why Youth (Heart) Social Network Sites: The Role of Networked Publics in Teenage Social Life." Berk-

and Characteristics of Youth Sexting: A National Study," *Pediatrics* 129, no. 1 (January 2012): 13–20; Walt Mueller, *Youth Culture 101* (Grand Rapids, MI: Zondervan, 2007), 121–136; Dick Thornburgh and Herbert S. Lin, eds., *Youth, Pornography, and the Internet* (Washington, DC: National Academy Press, 2002).

70. R. Stewart Mayers and Mike F. Desiderio, "Not LOL: Legal Issues Encountered During a High School's Response to Sexting," *Brigham Young University Education & Law Journal*, 1 (2013): 1–19.

71. Amy Adele Hasinoff, "Sexting as Media Production: Rethinking Social Media and Sexuality," *New Media & Society* 15 (June 2013): 449–465.

72. Toni Birdsong and Tami Heim, *@stickyJesus: How to Live Out Your Faith Online* (Nashville, TN: Abingdon Press/Digital Scribe Press, 2011/2010); Hanne Eggen Røislien, "Via Facebook to Jerusalem: Social Media as a Toolbox for the Study of Religion," *Fieldwork in Religion* 6, no. 1 (2011): 8–26; Jesse Rice, *The Church of Facebook: How the Hyperconnected Are Redefining Community* (Colorado Springs, CO: David C. Cook, 2009); Mark M. Stephenson, *Web-Empower Your Church: Unleashing the Power of Internet Ministry* (Nashville, TN: Abingdon Press, 2006), 151–202.

73. Chis Dede, "A Seismic Shift in Epistemology," *Educause Review* (May/June 2008): 80–81; Christine Greenhow and Benjamin Gleason, "Twitteracy: Tweeting as a New Literacy Practice," *The Educational Forum* 76 (2012): 463–477; Peter Pericles Trifonas, ed., *Learning the Virtual Life: Public Pedagogy in a Digital World* (New York: Routledge Press, 2012).

74. Chris Dede, "Planning for Neomillennial Learning Styles: Implications for Investments in Technology and Faculty," in *Educating the Net Generation*, ed. Diana G. Oblinger and James L. Oblinger (Educause, 2005), http://www.educause.edu/research-and-publications/books/educating-net-generation (accessed 14 June 2003).

75. Mary Hess, *Engaging Technology in Theological Education: All That We Can't Leave Behind* (Lanham, MD: Rowman & Littlefield, 2005), 90.

76. John Palfrey and Urs Gasser, *Born Digital: Understanding the First Generation of Digital Natives* (New York: Basic Books, 2008).

77. Mark Bauerlein, eds., *The Digital Divide: Arguments for and Against Facebook, Google, Texting, and the Age of Social Networking* (New York: Jeremy Tarcher/Penguin, 2011); Michael Thomas, ed., *Deconstructing Digital Natives: Young People, Technology and the New Literacies* (New York: Routledge, 2011).

78. Mitzuko Ito et al., *Hanging Out, Messing Around, and Geeking Out: Kids Living and Learning with New Media* (Cambridge, MA: MIT Press, 2010).

79. Danah Boyd, "Why Youth (Heart) Social Network Sites: The Role of Networked Publics in Teenage Social Life," Berkman Center for Internet & Society at Harvard University, Research Publication No. 2007-16 (December 2007), http://cyber.law.harvard.edu/publications/2007/Why_Youth_Heart_Social_Network_Sites (accessed 14 June 2013).

80. Heidi A. Campbell, ed., *Digital Religion: Understanding Religious Practice in New Media Worlds* (New York: Routledge, 2013); Rachel Wagner, *Godwired: Religion Ritual and Virtual Reality* (New York: Routledge, 2012).

81. Sherry Turkel, *Alone Together: Why We Expect More from Technology and Less from Each Other* (New York: Basic Books, 2001), 155–168.

man Center for Internet & Society at Harvard University, Research Publication No. 2007–16 (December). Accessed 14 June. http://cyber.law.harvard.edu/publications/2007/Why_Youth_Heart_Social_Network_Sites.

Campbell, Heidi A., ed. 2013. *Digital Religion: Understanding Religious Practice in New Media Worlds.* New York: Routledge.

Clemmitt, Marcia. 2013. "Social Media Explosion." *CQ Researcher* 23 (4): 83–100. Accessed 14 June 2013. http://library.cqpress.com/cqresearcher/document.php?id=cqresrre2013012500.

Dede, Chris. 2005. "Planning for Neomillennial Learning Styles: Impilcations for Investments in Technology and Faculty." In *Educating the Net Generation*, edited by Diana G. Oblinger and James L. Oblinger. Educause. Accessed 14 June 2013. http://www.educause.edu/research-and-publications/books/educating-net-generation.

——. 2008. "A Seismic Shift in Epistemology." *Educause Review* (May/June): 80–81.

Duggan, Maeve, and Joann Brenner. 2013. *The Demographics of Social Media Users—2012.* Washington, DC: Pew Research Center's Internet and American Life Project. Accessed 14 June 2013. http://pewinternet.org/Reports/2013/Social-media-users.aspx.

Greenhow, Christine, and Benjamin Gleason. 2012. "Twitteracy: Tweeting as a New Literacy Practice." *Educational Forum* 76: 463–477.

Hasinoff, Amy Adele. 2013. "Sexting as Media Production: Rethinking Social Media and Sexuality." *New Media & Society* 15 (June): 449–465.

Hess, Mary. 2005. *Engaging Technology in Theological Education: All That We Can't Leave Behind.* Lanham, MD: Rowman & Littlefield.

Ito, Mitzuko, Sonja Baumer, Matteo Bittani, dana boyd, Rachel Cody, Beck Herr-Sptehenson, Heather A. Horst, Patricia G. Lange, Dilan Mahendran, Katynka Z. Martínez, C. J. Pascoe, Dan Perkel, Laura Robinson, Christo Sims, and Lisa Tripp. 2010. *Hanging Out, Messing Around, and Geeking Out: Kids Living and Learning with New Media.* Cambridge, MA: MIT Press.

Mayers, R. Stewart, and Mike F. Desiderio. 2013. "Not LOL: Legal Issues Encountered During High School's Response to Sexting." *Brigham Young University Education & Law Journal* 1: 1–19.

Mitchell, Kimberly J,. David Jones Finkelhor, and Lisa M. Janis Wolak. 2012. "Prevalence and Characteristics of Youth Sexting: A National Study." *Pediatrics* 129 (1): 13–20.

Mueller, Walt. 2007. *Youth Culture 101.* Grand Rapids, MI: Zondervan.

O'Keefee, Gwenn Schurgin. 2011. *CyberSafe: Protecting and Empowering Kinds in the Digital World of Texting, Gaming, and Social Media.* Elk Grove Village, IL: American Academy of Pediatrics.

Palfrey, John, and Urs Gasser. 2008. *Born Digital: Understanding the First Generation of Digital Natives.* New York: Basic Books.

Rice, Jesse. 2009. *The Church of Facebook: How the Hyerconnected Are Redefining Community.* Colorado Springs, CO: David C. Cook.

Røislien, Hanne Eggen. 2011. "Via Facebook to Jerusalem: Social Media as a Toolbox for the Study of Religion." *Fieldwork in Religion* 6 (1): 8–26.

Stephenson, Mark M. 2006. *Web-Empower Your Church: Unleashing the Power of Internet Ministry.* Nashville, TN: Abingdon Press.

Thomas, Michael, ed. 2011. *Deconstructing Digital Natives: Young People, Technology and the New Literacies.* New York: Routledge.

Thornburgh, Dick, and Herbert S. Lin, eds. 2002. *Youth, Pornography, and the Internet.* Washington, DC: National Academy Press.

Turkel, Sherry. 2001. *Alone Together: Why We Expect More from Technology and Less from Each Other.* New York, Basic Books.

Wagner, Rachel. 2012. *Godwired: Religion Ritual and Virtual Reality.* New York: Routledge.

—Dean Blevins

SOCIAL PRACTICES AS CHRISTIAN PRACTICE

Throughout Christian history, as a moral responsibility in light of the call for Christian living, the church has taken forthright positions on social justice concerns.

Christian social practices have been developed on the themes of dignity of the human person, economic justice and options for the poor, rights and responsibilities, the promotion of peace, and global solidarity and development. The social teachings of the church demonstrate the need for integrating theory (biblical and traditional teachings) with practice (deeds) and for connecting personal faith and Christian responsibility in the world—that is, connecting commitment to the common good with concrete action. Pope Leo XIII laid the foundation for social teachings in the Catholic Church in the encyclical *Rerum Novarum* ("On the Condition of Labor") in 1891. The Catholic Church speaks for human rights, capitalism, poverty, and labor. *Gaudium et spes* ("Church in the Modern World"), from the Second Vatican Council in 1965, and *The Compendium of the Social Doctrine of the Church* (2004) are the most comprehensive documents of the Catholic Church related to social teachings and practices.

In the 18th century, John Wesley, the founder of Methodism, advocated for social justice, addressing his concerns about slavery, smuggling, prisoners, and child labor issues during the Industrial Revolution in England. Methodists adopted a social creed in 1908, later called "The Social Principles of the United Methodist Church." John Wesley asserted that "The gospel of Christ knows of no religion, but social; no holiness but social holiness."[82]

In the 1970s, Catholic theologians advocating liberation theology, especially in Latin America, influenced theologies of liberation in other parts of the world, such as MinJung theology in South Korea. Brazilian educator Paulo Freire (1921–1997) developed a teaching method that invokes social practices, outlined in his *Pedagogy of the Oppressed* (1968). The pedagogy of *conscientization* contextualizes students' everyday experiences and the learning subject when everyday experience becomes pedagogical. The term *conscientization* refers to a process of perceiving the political, social, economic, and religious elements that oppress a person (*Freire* 1986).

Juan Luis Segundo (1925–1996), a Jesuit theologian, provides methods of pedagogy using hermeneutics. He asserts that faith and ideology are universal dimensions of human life. Faith provides meaning and value to human existence, and ideology gives structure to that faith. Social practice is a crucial element of faith, a commitment to choose to learn to perceive reality in a new way—a process of learning to learn, a "deuteron-learning." This deuteron-learning requires an ongoing "hermeneutical circle" (*The Liberation of Theology*, 1975), which demands that interpretation of the Bible reflect ongoing changes in individual and social reality. The deuteron-learning process is a dialogical method that empowers teachers and students to think critically and invites them to engage self-determining decision-making processes. Christian education, from Segundo's perspective, should be a liberating act.

Teaching social practice of Christian faith in Christian education is critical, because it contributes to the formation of consciousness. Elisabeth Schüssler Fiorenza, a feminist biblical scholar, uses the process of "conscientization/consciousness-raising" to birth an emancipatory self in Christian education. She believes that learning should evoke a desire for not only personal transformation but also renewal of social and political structures of society. "Conscientization/consciousness-raising" awakens submerged elements that have prevented a person from accessing an emancipatory discovery of self as an independent cultural, social, and religious agent. Learning should enable a person to discover something new with transforming responses, which will gradually construct a new reality. By providing a voice to every student, teaching can engender creativity, enthusiasm, and motivation for living, which Schüssler Fiorenza calls "democratization of teaching" (*Democratizing Biblical Studies*, 2009).

References and Resources

The Book of Discipline. 1965. Nashville, TN: The United Methodist Publishing House, 2012.

Catholic Church. *Pastoral Constitutions on the Church in the Modern World*. Washington: United States Catholic Conference.

The Compendium of the Social Doctrine of the Church. 2004. Strathfield, N.S.W.: St Pauls Publications.

Freire, Paulo. 1986. *Pedagogy of the Oppressed*. New York: Continuum Publishing Corporation.

Pope Leo VIII. 1891. "*On Capital and Labor*." Vatican: the Holy See. Vatican Website. Libreria Editrice Vaticana.

Segundo, Juan L. 1976. *The Liberation of Theology*. Maryknoll, NY: Orbis Books.

Schüssler Fiorenza, Elisabeth 2001. *Wisdom Ways: Introducing Feminist Biblical Interpretation*. Maryknoll, New York: Orbis Book.

———. 2009. *Democratizing Biblical Studies: Toward an Emancipatory Educational Space*. Louisville: Westminster John Knox Press.

—HiRho Y. Park

SOCIALIZATION

Socialization, simply understood, refers to the process of interaction between persons and their social environment that shapes self-identity, values, and worldviews. While the concept, expressed using varying terms, has become quite common in the disciplines of anthropology, sociology, and psychology, it also has deep historical roots and has received much contemporary attention in Christian education.[83] Generally speaking, socialization is understood to involve three major interrelated and simultaneous processes. *Externalization* refers to persons revealing needs, desires, capacities, and possibilities in a social environment. *Objectification* is the reification of our externalizing activity into objective social reality in the form of traditions, laws, political structures, social expectations, roles, and economic systems. *Internalization* is the personal internalizing of the social, cultural, religious, economic, and political possibilities and parameters created by externalization and objectification and shapes self-identity, self-image, and self-consciousness.[84]

---

82. *The Works of John Wesley: The Bicentennial Edition*, vol. 14, *List of Poetical Works* (CD-ROM) (Nashville, TN: Abingdon Press, 2005), 321.

83. See Thomas H. Groome, *Christian Religious Education: Sharing Our Story and Vision* (San Francisco: Harper & Row, 1980), 109–131. Groome has an excellent discussion of socialization theory and traces its influence in the history of Christian education.

84. Groome provides an extensive discussion of these processes and the dialectical interaction between self and social reality (ibid., 110–113).

Religious educator John H. Westerhoff III has provided the most comprehensive definition of socialization: "Socialization is the lifelong formal and informal ways one generation seeks to sustain and transmit its understanding and way of life; seeks to induct its young into and reinforce for its adults a particular set of values and responsible adult roles; and seeks to help persons develop self-identity through participation in the life of a people with their more or less distinctive ways of thinking, feeling, and acting."[85]

Westerhoff also specifically defines religious socialization as "a process consisting of lifelong formal and informal mechanisms, through which persons sustain and transmit their faith (world view, value system) and life-style."[86]

As noted, socialization as an intentional strategy of formation can be traced to early Christian practice—at least to the catechetical work of the early church. Those initiated into the Christian faith were enrolled in a process of discipleship involving an extended period of sponsorship by other believers, limited participation in congregational life, and demonstration of conversion by lifestyle change.[87] Horace Bushnell's understanding of the Christian formation of children through the organic nature of family, church, society, and state represented an anticipation of the modern attention given to socialization in the social sciences and in Christian education. Subsequently, Christian educators from all theological persuasions and traditions have acknowledged the importance of socialization and developed theories and theologies of Christian formation grounded in the idea. George Albert Coe, C. Ellis Nelson, John Westerhoff III, Berard Marthaler, Lawrence O. Richards, Thomas H. Groome, and most recently James K. A. Smith, to name only the most prominent, have all built their understandings of Christian education on some form of socialization theory. Indeed, one cannot talk about the work of Christian education in any context or culture without taking account of the role played by socialization.

References and Resources

Bushnell, Horace. 2000. *Christian Nurture*. Eugene, OR: Wipf and Stock Publishers.

Groome, Thomas H. 1980. *Christian Religious Education: Sharing Our Story and Vision*. San Francisco: Harper & Row.

Mitchell, Leonel L. 1981. "The Development of Catechesis in the Third and Fourth Centuries." In *A Faithful Church: Issues in the History of Catechesis*, edited by John H. Westerhoff III and O. C. Edwards Jr., 37–56. Wilton, CT: Morehouse-Barlow.

Westerhoff, John H., III, and Gwen Kennedy Neville. 1974. *Generation to Generation: Conversations on Religious Education and Culture*. Philadelphia: The United Church Press.

—JAMES P. BOWERS

SOCIETY OF CHRISTIAN ENDEAVOR

At the end of the 19th century, America was going through massive changes. Because of the Industrial Revolution and availability of jobs, more and more people were moving to the cities. Railroads were expanding, the economy was booming, and the middle class was growing. There was optimism in the air.[88] During the 1880s, many church ministers struggled with the "youth problem."[89] Around the turn of the century, parents were concerned about the morality of their children. The church was losing its youth. Due to economic prosperity, there were many appealing activities outside the church. The church services and prayer meetings were boring. The Sunday schools were full of children, but the church was not able to bridge the gap between the Sunday school and the church membership.[90] Ministers were trying to come up with ways to win the youth for Christ.[91] It was in this context that the Society of Christian Endeavor was born.

The Society of Christian Endeavor was founded on 2 February 1881, in Portland, Maine, by Francis Clark, the 25-year-old pastor of Williston congregational church.[92] The pastor and his wife invited more than 60 young people to their house. Clark read the constitution he had prepared and asked the young people to sign it. This agreement demanded a serious commitment to live a Christian life.[93] At first the youth were hesitant, but eventually almost all signed it.[94] The society was originally called Williston Young People's Society of Christian Endeavor.[95] The members pledged to pray and read the Bible every day, attend the weekly prayer

---

85. John H. Westerhoff and Gwen Kennedy Neville, *Generation to Generation: Conversations on Religious Education and Culture* (Philadelphia: The United Church Press, 1974), 39.

86. Ibid., 41.

87. See Leonel L. Mitchell, "The Development of Catechesis in the Third and Fourth Centuries: From Hippolytus to Augustine," in *A Faithful Church: Issues in the History of Catechesis*, ed. John H. Westerhoff III and O. C. Edwards Jr. (Wilton, CT: Morehouse-Barlow Co., 1981), 49–78.

88. Mark H. Senter III, *The Coming Revolution in Youth Ministry and its Radical Impact on the Church* (Wheaton, IL: SP Publications, 1992), 96, 97.

89. Mark H. Senter III, *When God Shows Up: A History of Protestant Youth Ministry in America* (Grand Rapids, MI: Baker Academic, 2010), 58.

90. Ibid., 152, 155.

91. Francis E. Clark, *World Wide Endeavor: The Story of Young People's Society of Christian Endeavor* (Philadelphia: Gillespie, Metzgar & Kelley, 1995), 47.

92. Senter, *When God Shows Up*, 154.

93. Clark, *World Wide Endeavor*, 100.

94. Senter, *When God Shows Up*, 157.

95. Clark, *World Wide Endeavor*, 57.

meetings, and take an active part in them. They also had to attend the monthly meeting, called the "experience meeting" or "consecration meeting."[96] In each month's consecration meeting, the members had to report about their "progress in the Christian life"[97] and renew their loyalty to Christ.[98] If they were absent, each member had to send at least a verse to be read in response to the roll call. Three unexcused and consecutive absences would terminate the membership.[99]

Based on the constitution, there could be two classes of members in the society: "active and associate." Originally the society had a president, vice president, secretary, and five committees: "prayer meeting," "lookout," "social," "missionary," "Sunday school," and "flower."[100] Each member was assigned to one committee and was expected to serve.[101] The main purpose was to help members grow in Christ and in their relationship with each other and to become more useful servants of God.[102]

The responsibility of the prayer meeting committee was to organize the weekly and monthly prayer meetings. The lookout committee had to introduce new members to the society and make sure that before joining the society, they had read and understood the constitution and the prayer meeting pledge. It also had to oversee all the active and associate members and make sure that all were faithful. Roll calling during the monthly consecration meeting was the responsibility of this committee.[103] The social committee had to plan events for fellowship and friendship and organize "sociables." The missionary committee had to do fund-raising for missionary activities and sponsor such meetings.[104] The Sunday school committee had to bring new members to Sunday school and cooperate in any way necessary with those in charge of their church's Sunday school.[105] The flower committee provided flowers for Sunday worship services and for sick members of the society.[106]

On 4 February 1881 the first prayer meeting of the Society of Christian Endeavor was held. Granville Staples, the first president of the society, led the meeting. In that meeting many young men and women spoke up and prayed for the first time.[107] The prayer meeting had a central role in the Society of Christian Endeavor. It was not a lecture by one person.[108] The purpose of the prayer meetings was not instruction, but edification, "*practice . . . inspiration and fellowship.*" Each member had to play an active part in the prayer meeting and confess the Lord in any way he or she wanted: through a simple sentence, a prayer, a song, a testimony, or a verse from the scripture, or in any other way.[109] Eloquence was not expected, but rather simple confession of Christ by every member.[110]

Clark published reports of the success of the Society of Christian Endeavor in various newspapers, and many pastors asked for more information about the society. In reply, the constitution was copied and sent with an explanatory letter.[111] The press played an enormous role in spreading the news about the society. In the spring of 1882, Rev. Clark prepared a 12-page tract about Christian Endeavor. In the summer of the same year, he expanded it and wrote a book entitled *The Children and the Church; and the Young People's Society of Christian Endeavor as a Means of Bringing Them Together.*[112] As a result, the number of societies multiplied, and more societies were formed in different states and countries.[113]

The first convention was held in the Williston Church in June 1882, at which representatives from six societies were present.[114] Representatives from six denominations attended the second convention.[115] At the convention of 1885, the number of represented societies reached 258, with 15,000 members. During this convention, the United Society of Christian Endeavor was formed to be the central organizing body of the society.[116] In September 1887, Clark accepted the full-time presidency of the United Society.[117] During the 14th International Convention at Boston in 1895, the World's Christian Endeavor Union (WCEU) was formed to provide closer fellowship among Christian Endeavor societies. Reverend Clark was elected as president.[118] By 1906 there were 67,000 Christian Endeavor societies in 50 countries, among 80 denominations.[119] *The Golden Rule* was the official organ of Christian Endeavor, which from 1889 to 1898 provided news and curricular and training ideas.[120]

The union of Christian Endeavor societies was not a doctrinal or church governing union, but a fellowship

96. Ibid., 57, 58, 109.
97. Senter, *When God Shows Up*, 157.
98. Clark, *World Wide Endeavor*, 638.
99. Ibid., 58.
100. Ibid., 57.
101. Senter, *When God Shows Up*, 157.
102. Clark, *World Wide Endeavor*, 57.
103. Ibid., 640.
104. Senter, *When God Shows Up*, 163.
105. Clark, *World Wide Endeavor*, 189.
106. Senter, *When God Shows Up*, 163.
107. Clark, *World Wide Endeavor*, 71, 72.

108. Ibid., 58.
109. Ibid., 68, 69.
110. Ibid., 72.
111. Ibid., 91.
112. Ibid., 134, 135.
113. Ibid., 143.
114. Ibid., 98, 99.
115. Senter, *The Coming Revolution*, 99.
116. Clark, *World Wide Endeavor*, 160.
117. Senter, *When God Shows Up*, 165.
118. Clark, *World Wide Endeavor*, 616, 626.
119. Senter, *When God Shows Up*, 167.
120. Ibid., 161.

based on love and service for Christ. It brought together young people from different denominations. While it required loyalty to the church and the denomination to which it belonged, it also provided an opportunity for interdenominational fellowship.[121] Due to some objections, the pledge was revised and a clause was added in which the youth had to pledge to support their church and attend Sunday and midweek services regularly.[122]

The youth were no longer passive observers in the church, but had the opportunity to speak and work for Christ.[123] Important features of the society that helped the youth to be connected with God and the church were accountability, group support, and emphasis on both confessing and serving Christ. Serving on the committees helped them develop leadership skills.[124] Christian Endeavor was an innovation in reaching and keeping the young people, and it shaped the youth ministry.[125]

Today the conventions continue, and the WCEU unites CE unions in 29 countries[126] and has a quarterly newsletter.[127] Nowadays the five basic committees are "devotional," "lookout," "missionary," "recreation," and "church activity."[128] According to Clark, the founder of the society, the "fundamental principles" of Christian Endeavor societies are "devotion to Christ, loyalty to the church to which they belong, outspoken confession of their faith, and earnest, effective service."[129]

References and Resources

Clark, Francis. E. 1895. *World Wide Endeavor: The Story of Young People's Society of Christian Endeavor*. Philadelphia: Gillespie, Metzgar & Kelley.

Robertson, Sara A. 2001. "Christian Endeavor International." In *Evangelical Dictionary of Christian Education*, edited by Michael J. Anthony, 134. Grand Rapids, MI: Baker Academic.

Senter, Mark H., III. 1992. *The Coming Revolution in Youth Ministry and Its Radical Impact on the Church*. Wheaton, IL: SP Publications.

———. 2010. *When God Shows Up: A History of Protestant Youth Ministry in America*. Grand Rapids, MI: Baker Academic.

World's Christian Endeavor Union. 2013a. "About Us." April. http://worldsceunion.org/about_us.

---

121. Clark, *World Wide Endeavor*, 263, 264.
122. Ibid., 185.
123. Ibid., 97.
124. Senter, *When God Shows Up*, 162, 163.
125. Ibid., 144, 167.
126. World's Christian Endeavor Union, "About Us," 2013, http://worldsceunion.org/about_us.
127. World's Christian Endeavor Union, "Service," 2013, http://worldsceunion.org/service.
128. Sara A. Robertson, "Christian Endeavor International," in *Evangelical Dictionary of Christian Education*, ed. Michael J. Anthony (Grand Rapids, MI: Baker Academic, 2001), 134.
129. Clark, *World Wide Endeavor*, 636.

———. 2013b. "Services." April. http://worldsceunion.org/about_us.

—MARIET MIKALELIAN

SOCIOLOGY, CHRISTIAN CONTRIBUTIONS TO

Origins

Sociology is a field of intellectual endeavor both ancient and new. As a formal university recognized discipline, it can be traced to the 19th century. As a study of the nature of society and social life, it goes back to philosophers and thinkers throughout human history, most definitely including religious thinkers.

The term *sociology* originated in a specifically anti-Christian context. Auguste Comte (1798–1857) was a French thinker who sought to replace traditional Christianity with a religion of his own making, one that embraced a claim about the perfectability of society through the sciences. This in turn required the careful study of society, with a view toward its perfection, so he invented the word sociology.

As the scientific study of society increased in the 19th century, leaders in the new field generally took stands either in opposition to Christianity or simply of religious indifference, in the expectation that Christianity would eventually be supplanted by modern science. Borrowing from Comte, the British social evolutionist Herbert Spencer (1820–1903) took a Darwinian perspective, and in Germany, Max Weber (1864–1920) followed a markedly historical comparative perspective. Following French developments, Emile Durkheim (1858–1917) laid claim to sociology as an empirical science of society. Many of these ideas developed from an explicit or implicit engagement with the thought of Karl Marx (1818–1883), whose ideas represented a unique synthesis of French revolutionary thinking, Germanic philosophical and historical consciousness, and British empiricism. Marx's decisive rejection of religion was perhaps more known, but not particularly different from many other founding figures in the new science of society. For this reason, some theologians reject any possibility of dialogue with social science (Millbank 2006).

Sociology of Religion

Though Durkheim's major focus was on religion, and he himself was descended from a long line of rabbis, he saw religion as fundamentally and only social in its origins, as a form of collective consciousness that represented mores and norms of society as a whole. Similarly, Max Weber gave considerable attention to religion, including comparisons of Christianity over time and space, and contributed the theory of the protestant work ethic as embedded in the origins of capitalism. Weber also undertook a great comparative study of world religion. He showed a relatively sensitive understanding of religion. His focus was not on religion for the sake of understanding religion, however, as much as to understand even larger social forces through religion. These scholars, however, paved the way for future studies in the sociology of religion. Drawing on Max Weber's work, the theologian Ernst Troeltsch (1865–1923) crafted his *Social Teaching of the Christian Church* and made important contributions to religious studies. The U.S. social theorist Talcott Parsons (1902–1979) was influenced by his unique synthesis of Durkheimian and Weberian thinking, which grew from a strong grounding in the study of the sociology of religion.

The major theme in the sociology of religion has been secularization. At first, most of the sociology of religion considered elements of the religious field to test and demonstrate trends of secularization. Later, many within the field turned to critiquing and debunking such claims, particularly the more facile and most problematic. Many theorists, including Durkheim, Weber, and Parsons, came from distinctly observant homes and from fathers and families distinguished for religious leadership. Most, however, turned from religion per se to a quasi-religious dedication to the power of sociology and the intellectual life in general. However, the sociology of religion has always had a number of practitioners who were interested in religion for the sake of religion—those who were themselves believers and committed to the future or specific needs of religious persons or organizations. Many brought a particular focus and an insider understanding to the sociology of religion that fueled strong, in-depth studies. This led to the formation of three professional associations in the sociology of religion, aside from the formal sociology of religion section within the American Sociological Association. The Association for the Sociology of Religion is the successor to the Catholic Sociological Society. The Society for the Social Scientific Study of Religion (SSSR) took an approach less informed by Christian confessionalism. The Religious Research Association (RRA) was founded and led primarily by Protestant pastoral researchers.

Pastoral Sociology

An offshoot of the sociology of religion, which is more applied and focused on pastoral needs, descriptions, and plans as ends in themselves, is quite different from the more religiously neutral position common within the sociology of religion. In the United States, such an approach typified much, though by no means all, of the work of Dean Hoge (1937–2008) at Catholic University of America, a Presbyterian who did most of his work in a Catholic context in the late 20th century. Within a Protestant context in the United States, H. Paul Douglass (1871–1953) and others pioneered the adaptation of sociology from community and neighborhood studies to specifically church and congregational studies for planning purposes, a charge taken up by David Roozen and his colleagues at Hartford Seminary for decades. Some of the work also focused on religious education, but it was by no means limited to this field. By the 1960s and 1970s, many Catholics had begun doing the same. Philip Murnion (1938–2003) completed a PhD in sociology from Columbia University so as to advance pastoral planning in a Catholic context, and decades later he helped guide David DeLambo to complete his PhD in sociology from Fordham University with the same goal in mind. The dialogue between sociology and pastoral sociology continues, though in fits and starts (Hegy 2012, 6, 10; Froehle 2007).

Empirical Theology

Throughout this time, theology largely continued as it had been—as a speculative discipline. The need for religious education and pastoral leadership, and countless other church needs, propelled religious leaders, trained more in theology than sociology, to take on the methods of the social sciences in their work, but this was not done as theology per se, though occasionally it was done under the guise of pastoral theology. By the late 20th century, particularly in The Netherlands and German-speaking lands, theologians sought to integrate social science methods into their work, considering themselves scientists conducting true scientific research subject to empirical verification. Johannes van der Ven at Nijmegen was one such pioneer, influenced by the empirical tradition of the University of Chicago. Positioning itself as properly theological, and as more legitimate in its scholarship than pastoral sociology, empirical theology seeks to correlate people's understanding of theological concepts with deeper understanding of those concepts (van der Ven 1998).

Sociological Theory and Method
in Religious Education

Religious education benefits greatly from the insights of sociology, including specifically the sociology of religion. Some work in religious education has been more within pastoral sociology; other work has been more in the areas of empirical theology, including ordinary theology (Astley and Francis 2013) and communicative theology (Scharer and Hilberath 2008); and still other work has been done at the intersection of theology, catechetics, and social science, as is the case for the German practical theologian and religious educator Norbert Mette.

While social science method has nourished the work of pastoral sociology and empirical theology, with the sociology of religion remaining the most cited specialization in these fields, the discipline of sociology is much more than the study of religion. Religious education benefits from wide conversations within sociological theory and method and across a range of sociological fields. Reflections on broader directions within contemporary cultural and society are informed by social theory in general rather than by the sociology of religion alone. Similarly, qualitative-ethnographical, quantitative, and comparative-historical methods all have their use in understanding religious education, whether contextually or programmatically. The possibilities for enriching work within religious education through a dialogue with sociology remain largely untapped.

References and Resources

Asian Social Institute. n.d. "Pastoral Sociology." http://www .asinet-online.org/index.php?option=com_content&view= article&id=33&Itemid=162.

Astley, J., and L. Francis. 2013. *Exploring Ordinary Theology: Everyday Christian Believing and the Church*. Burlington, VT: Ashgate.

Bendyna, M., OP. 2009. "Bridging the Gap Between Research and Pastoral Practice." *Church* (Spring). http://www.church magazine.org/issue/0903/upf_bridging_the_gap.php.

Blasi, T. 2007. *American Sociology of Religion*: Histories. Leuven: Brill.

Froehle, B. 2007. "Catholic Pastoral Sociology in the United States since Vatican II: Making a Path by Walking." *United States Catholic Historian* 25 (4): 85–116.

Graham, G. 2003. "Sociology and Faith: The Witness of Paul Hanly Fufey." *Catholic Social Science Review* vol. 8, http:// catholicsocialscientists.org/CSSR/. http://cssronline.org/ CSSR/Archival/2003/Graham%2520article.pdf

Hegy, P. 2012. *Wake up Lazarus! On Catholic Renewal*. Bloomington, IN: iUniverse.

Houtart, F. 1965. *Sociology and Pastoral Care*. St. Louis, MO: Franciscan Herald Press.

Millbank, J. 2006. *Theology and Social Theory*. London: Wiley-Blackwell.

Nuesse, C. 2001. "The Introduction of Sociology at the Catholic University of America, 1895–1915." *Catholic Historical Review* 87 (4): 643–661.

Scharer, M., and B. Hilberath. 2008. *The Practice of Communicative Theology: Introduction to a New Theological Culture*. New York: Crossroad.

Sullins, P. n.d. "Sociology: A Catholic Critique." http://faculty .cua.edu/sullins/published%20articles/soccath.pdf.

Troeltsch, E. (1912) 1992. *Social Teaching of the Christian Church*. 2 vols. Louisville, KY: Westminster John Knox Press.

Van der Ven, J. 1998. *Practical Theology: An Empirical Approach*. Kampen, Netherlands: Kok Pharos.

Zaccaria, F. 2010. *Participation and Beliefs in Popular Religiosity: An Empirical-Theological Exploration among Italian Catholics*. Leiden: Brill.

Karnataka Pastoral Sociology Institute. http://www.medindia .net/ngos/pastoral-sociology-institute-kolar-karnataka -3460-1.htm

—Bryan T. Froehle

Socrates

Socrates was born in 469 BC in Athens, Greece. His father was a stonemason and his mother was a midwife. Socrates applied his mother's profession to himself, in the sense that he described himself as a midwife who gave birth to truth. Although he never wrote anything, he is one of the philosophers who has exerted the greatest influence on ancient and modern philosophy. Socrates is perhaps the most enigmatic figure in the history of philosophy, although he was frequently mocked in the plays of comic poets (produced in 423 BC, *Clouds* by Aristophanes is the most common example). For the majority of his life, Socrates spent his time in the city marketplaces and squares, talking with the people he met. His life is known primarily through the writings of Plato, who was one of his pupils. Plato's *Dialogues* are dramatized philosophical discussions in which Socrates is the primary character and speaker. Consequently, it is difficult to differentiate the teachings of Socrates from the philosophy of Plato.

Prior to his career as a philosopher, Socrates was enlisted as a hoplite (ancient Greek infantryman) during the war between Athens and Sparta. Plato's *Symposium* recounts how Socrates returned to Athens not to answer questions regarding the war; rather, he was concerned about progress in the search for truth. After his service in the war, Socrates devoted himself to the pursuit of truth. In his writings, Plato depicted the philosopher as always in conversation and continually asking questions. Socrates did not want to instruct anyone in the sense of lecturing, as was the practice of the traditional schoolmaster; his "Socratic Method" was to discuss (to teach by asking questions). Socrates would ask questions as if he did not know the answer (i.e., Socratic irony), all the while using the discussion to lead his opponents to recognize the error of their argumentation. Although he lived at the same time as the Sophists and shared their concern for the purpose of humanity in the world (as opposed to studying the forces of nature), Socrates differed from them significantly in that he did not regard himself as a Sophist, nor did he teach for money.

Socrates's philosophical renown spread throughout Athens and even beyond the city. Even the Oracle of Delphi remarked that Socrates was the wisest man in Athens. Socrates attempted to prove the Oracle wrong by seeking someone who knew what was truly worthwhile in life. When he could not identify such an individual, Socrates admitted that the Oracle must have been correct, because only he was willing to admit his ignorance, as opposed to pretending to know something that he did not.

Socrates insisted that a "divine voice" compelled him to continually demonstrate the erroneous thinking of the Athenians. In 399 BC, he was accused of impiety and corruption of the Athenian youth. He was sentenced to death by poisoning at the age of 70, which he could have appealed, but did not because that would be to deny his conscience and the truth (both of which he valued more than his own life). Plato's *Crito* and *Phaedo* recount the trial and the philosopher's final days. Plato's *Apology of Socrates* is alleged to be Socrates's speech at his trial in response to the accusations brought against him; his persuasive advocacy of the examined life and condemnation of Athenian democracy have made the *Apology* one of the fundamental documents of Western culture and thought. Socrates maintained that the "unexamined life is not worth living," and his insistence that he must obey his conscience demonstrated a new manner of living to the Athenians. Socrates was a man of principle, and he believed that through his death he was demonstrating the true meaning of life, which would resonate not only with the Athenians, but also with all of Western civilization.

References and Resources

Brickhouse, Thomas C., and Nicholas D. Smith. 2000. *The Philosophy of Socrates.* Boulder, CO: Westview Press.

Johnson, David M. 2011. *Socrates and Athens.* Cambridge, UK: Cambridge University Press.

Johnson, Paul. 2011. *Socrates: A Man for Our Times.* New York: Penguin.

Navia, Luis E. 2007. *Socrates: A Life Examined.* Amherst, NY: Prometheus Books.

Rudebusch, George. 2011. *Socrates.* Malden, MA: Wiley-Blackwell.

Scott, Gary Alan, ed. 2002. *Does Socrates Have a Method?* University Park: Pennsylvania State University Press.

Taylor, C. C. W. 2000. *Socrates: A Very Short Introduction.* New York: Oxford University Press.

Vlastos, Gregory. 1991. *Socrates: Ironist and Moral Philosopher.* Ithaca, NY: Cornell University Press.

—RON J. BIGALKE

SOCRATIC METHOD

The Socratic method is a pedagogical strategy designed to lead to deeper critical thinking on the part of participants, through the use of dialogue and questions, resulting in deeper understanding of truths, beliefs, and positions. It is often used in classical education and takes its name from the famous Greek philosopher Socrates. During the fifth century BC, most orators, called Sophists, would present arguments in attempts to entertain or persuade audiences with their skill in rhetoric (Jarratt 1991). Socrates proposed a different method of teaching, which became known as the Socratic method. This method argued by using questions to engage the interlocutor, with the goal of uncovering fatal flaws in the logic of the presenter and thereby disarming the presenter and nullifying his argument. Plato formalized the Socratic dialogue in his works, framing Socrates as the questioner of prominent Athenian rhetoricians, to engage the reader in the linear logic of his position and the apparent flaws in his opponent's.

The Socratic method was employed frequently by Jesus throughout the Gospels. Early in the life of Christ, we see Him responding to His parents' direct question—"Son, why have you treated us like this? Your father and I have been anxiously searching for you" (Luke 2:48)—by asking a question Himself, designed to lead His parents, and us as His readers, into deeper critical thinking: "Why were you searching for me?" he asked. "Didn't you know I had to be in my Father's house?" (Luke 2:49). The following line tells us that they did not understand. Another example is when the authority of Jesus was challenged by the chief priests and the elders, who asked Him: "By what authority are you doing these things?" (Matt. 21:23b). Jesus answered this question with a question of His own: "John's baptism—where did it come from? Was it from heaven or from men?" (Matt. 21:24b). This caused discussion among them, with consideration about how their response might be received and refuted by Jesus, resulting in the response "We don't know" (Matt. 21:27). Other questions that we see Christ asking, in the book of Mark, for the purpose of engaging His audience in deeper reflection and considerations of Truth and their beliefs and positions, include, but are not limited to: "How is it that the teachers of the law say that the Christ is the son of David?" (Mark 12:35); "Why do you call me good?" (Mark 10:18); "Who do people say I am? . . . But what about you? Who do you say I am?" (Mark 27b, 29a); and "Which is lawful on the Sabbath: to do good or to do evil, to save life or to kill?" (Mark 3:4). In each of these examples, the intent is for the audience to consider the question anew and to grow in their understanding of God and His Christ, and their relationship with Him. This method is powerful for Christian educators who want their students to engage fully in the deeper thought process of understanding the content presented (Copeland 2010; Gose 2009).

References and Resources

Copeland, M. 2010. *Socratic Circles: Fostering Critical and Creative Thinking in Middle and High School.* Portland, MN: Stenhouse.

Gose, M. 2009. "When Socratic Dialogue Is Flagging: Questions and Strategies for Engaging Students." *College Teaching* 57 (1): 46.

Jarratt, S. C. 1991. *Rereading the Sophists: Classical Rhetoric Refigured.* Carbondale and Edwardsville: Southern Illinois University Press.

—LAURA BARWEGEN

SOFTWARE, EDUCATIONAL

According to a 2013 report from the Software & Information Industry Association, the market for K–12 educational software and digital products is $7.7 billion.[130] A subsequent study from the Pew Internet & American Life Project revealed that 78 percent of teens own cell phones, 47 percent of which are smart phones, for an overall tally of 37 percent of all teens having smart phones.[131] In the same survey, researchers found that approximately one-quarter of teens have a tablet computer, 93 percent have a computer or access to one at home, and 95 percent of teens use the Internet. With such near ubiquity of computers, including personal computers, laptops, tablets, and smart phones, there is significant interest in using technology to enhance education in Christian and secular communities alike.

Computer Roles

In his landmark work, Robert Taylor defined three roles of computers in education: tutor, tool, and tutee.[132] In the tutor role, the computer software assumes the primary role of instructor, often using tutorials, simulations, and practice drills to educate the student. This can be particularly useful for skill-based subjects that require advanced knowledge, such as learning biblical Greek or Hebrew or advanced mathematics. The second and perhaps most common use of computers, educational or otherwise, is as tools. In such cases the computer isn't being used for direct instruction, but remains an integral part of the learning experience. Using word processing, presentation, photo editing, videoconferencing, or any of a variety of other software in support of learning is using the computer as a tool. The computer as tutee, though it sounds unusual, is when the student actually teaches the computer. This is most common when students learn how to program computers or write their own applications. As Taylor's framework predated the Internet, some have considered the idea of computer as telecommunications device or other roles to expand the framework into the 21st century.

Types of Educational Software

Rather than looking through the lens of computer roles, another approach is to categorize educational software based on how it is used. One classification of educational software divides it into five broad categories: tutorial, discovery, edutainment, authoring, and reference.[133]

Tutorials are the most overtly instructional type of educational software. Whether containing video, audio, graphics, text, quizzes, or other resources, tutorials are designed to serve in the place of a teacher and lead the student through the requisite content. Digital books, flashcards, and quiz programs and apps are common examples of tutorial software.

Discovery programs are also designed to teach students particular content, but rather than delivering the material in the form of computerized or online lessons, students work through the software and learn as a product of their journey. Multimedia virtual tours of ancient Israel, 3D anatomy simulation programs, and other simulations are examples.

Edutainment is a portmanteau of education and entertainment, often in the form of a skill-based game related to a particular subject area. Even a cursory examination of educational software for computers and apps for smart phones reveals the popularity of edutainment, as a majority of such products appear to be games designed for learning.

Authoring software is used for subjects in which students are expected to design or develop content, such as graphic design, computer programming, or musical composition.

Finally, reference software programs are resources such as Bible apps or digital libraries that are valuable

---

130. Sean Cavanagh, "Market for Education Software, Digital Products Has Grown, Analysis Shows," *Education Week*, 17 January 17, http://blogs.edweek.org/edweek/marketplacek12/2013/01/market_for_education_software_digital_products_has_grown_analysis_shows.html.

131. Mary Madden, Amanda Lenhart, Maeve Duggan, Sandra Cortesi, and Urs Gasser, "Teens and Technology 2013," *Pew Research Center*, 13 March 2013, http://www.pewinternet.org/Reports/2013/Teens-and-Tech.aspx.

132. Robert Taylor, *The Computer in the School* (New York: Teachers College Press, 1980).

133. Jason D. Baker, *Parents' Computer Companion* (Grand Rapids, MI: Baker Book House, 1999).

for learning but aren't necessarily written solely for the purpose of education.

Christian Educational Software

The majority of Christian educational software is based on the Bible. There are numerous digital Bibles available, complete with concordances, lexical tools, commentaries, and other theological resources. Such programs, including Logos Bible Software, BibleWorks, and LifeChurch.tv's Bible app for smart phones and tablets, are the most commonly used Christian educational software products. In addition to these searchable Bibles and theological libraries, a number of Bible games are available, including word searches, memory verses, matching, characters, and stories. The homeschooling market has also prompted development of a number of formal K–12 curriculum products for Christian families, such as the *Switched-On Schoolhouse* CD-ROM or the Monarch Christian online homeschool curriculum, both from Alpha Omega Publications.

Educational software can be a powerful resource for the education of children and adults; however, despite the promises of many vendors, such applications shouldn't be used in lieu of engaged teachers and parents. Simply putting children in front of a computer and having them perform endless online drills doesn't promote learning and may even detract from it. To make the most effective use of instructional technology, the software and applications should be carefully selected and integrated into the learning experience and then evaluated to determine their appropriateness and effectiveness.

—Jason D. Baker

Solitude as Christian Practice

In his celebrated book *The Way of the Heart*, Henri Nouwen alerted us to our need for solitude: "[W]e move through life in such a distracted way that we do not even take the time and rest to wonder if any of the things we think, say, or do are *worth* thinking, saying or doing. We simply go along with the many 'musts' and 'oughts' that have been handed on to us, and we live with them as if they were authentic translations to the Gospels of our Lord" (1981, 10). Students experiencing the rigors of the academy, families in the midst of balancing professions and domestic needs, and contextual stressors of events, both globally and locally, often create a compulsive life that feels to many like the proverbial attempt to dance in peanut butter.

Technology has made the contemporary condition all the more insidious. Subtly we become increasingly reliant on the response of others to give us a sense of our validation. Thomas Merton (1960, 3) exposes this tendency, calling it our false self, fabricated by social compulsions that prop up our incessant need for affirmation. Talk becomes the medium we use to ensure that we secure a good name for ourselves in the perceptions of those who surround us.

Against this fabrication, ancient spiritual writers have invited us to a practice of solitude. Solitude is often misunderstood as being equated with being alone, or escaping from the pressures of the world, or being private. However, ancient spiritual mothers and fathers spoke of solitude not primarily as a therapeutic place, but as a place of conversion—where the old self dies and a new self is born (Nouwen 1981, 15). Hence, it remains a critical discipline to be practiced and taught by Christian educators.

Solitude carries us to the place where we surrender all we typically rely on for security and self-importance (Foster 1998, 98). We relinquish the incessant talking that is so typically a veiled attempt at self-justification. We find ourselves helpless and vulnerable, no longer able to cover insecurities through pious conversations whereby we so often seek to manage the impressions we hope we are making on others. Solitude teaches us when to speak and when to refrain from speaking (Foster 1998, 98), helping us recognize how often our speech before others has been a "sacrifice of fools" (Eccles. 5:1). In solitude, we accept the original invitation from God to enjoy with Him the sanctity of a holy rest. Solitude breaks the illusion of our own importance and protects us from being seduced by the urgency of our responsibilities, elevating our own sense that the world somehow depends on us. Through solitude, suggests Wayne Meuller, we learn to "float on the tides of a deeper time" (1999, 89).

Once we understand how transformative solitude can be, it should not be a surprise that Jesus so frequently sought times for solitude. For 40 days before inaugurating His ministry, He went to the wilderness and tangled with the compulsions offered by Satan. Before choosing the 12 to whom He would entrust His mission, He spent the night in prayer. Upon hearing the news of His beloved cousin's death, He withdrew to a lonely place. After long nights of work or following important missional enterprises, He called the 12 to come away with Him to a quiet place. Jesus both lived an inward life of solitude and maintained an outward practice of solitude.

Christian educators support practices of solitude today in a variety of ways. Most commonly, encouragement is given to designate a concrete place and a consistent time to commune alone with the Lord. Longer retreats at a monastery or remote location are advocated to help one quiet internal noise and move beyond the overpopulated self. Short solitudes can be encouraged by pausing in a day to observe awe in nature, to appreciate an unexpected beauty, to recite a Psalm, or to feel the words of a hymn.

Though solitude is most often associated with withdrawing from activity and relationships, it can be deeply missional in its intent. The recentering of our lives in God enables us to reengage with others from an overflowing and grateful heart, free of the subtle ways we manipulate them for our own gratification. As Nouwen writes: "Solitude and silence teach me to love my brothers for what they are, not for what they say" (1981, 15).

References and Resources

Borgman, Paul. 2001. *Genesis: The Story We Haven't Heard.* Downer's Grove, IL: InterVarsity Press.

Foster, Richard J. 1998. *Celebration of Discipline: The Path to Spiritual Growth.* San Francisco: Harper.

Merton, Thomas. 1960. *Thomas Merton: Spiritual Direction and Meditation.* Collegeville, MN: Liturgical Press.

Mueller, Wayne. 1999. *Sabbath: Finding Rest, Renewal, and Delight in Our Busy Lives.* New York: Bantam Books.

Nouwen, Henri. 1981. *The Way of the Heart.* New York: Ballantine Books.

—Chris Kiesling

SOUTH ASIA INSTITUTE OF ADVANCED CHRISTIAN STUDIES

Located in Bangalore, India, the South Asia Institute of Advanced Christian Studies (SAIACS) offers master's and doctoral degrees in theological studies. Increasingly recognized for its pursuit of excellence for the sake of mission, its evangelical ethos, and its training of Christian leaders at the postgraduate level, SAIACS attracts students from across India and other countries. Growing from 12 students in 1983, SAIACS in 2013 had 130 students on or near campus, with another 35 learning at a distance. SAIACS began with a master's program in missions; it now offers five programs and eight disciplines. Celebrating its 30th year of operation in 2012, more than 750 alumni can look back on lives of service dedicated to seminary teaching, church ministry, mission, or the marketplace.

First envisioned in 1981 over a cup of tea between two New Zealand missionaries, Dr. Graham Houghton and Dr. Bruce Nicholls, SAIACS was founded because of concern over the pain of the brain drain. The best people went abroad to study, and about 70 percent never returned. According to Houghton, the Indian evangelical community needed to "demonstrate the desire and resolve to develop theological education of the kind that is a credible alternative to similar courses offered both here and overseas."[134] Houghton, principal for the first 21 years, began with a two-year MTh program in missions in Chennai using the now characteristic modular system: a series of month-long courses, each taught by PhD qualified tutors. Initially operating under the auspices of the Association of Evangelical Theological Education in India (AETEI), the nondenominational program was very successful, and SAIACS grew into its own identity.

Shifting to rented premises in Bangalore in 1983, SAIACS expanded, eventually building a new campus on land purchased in Kothanur village in 1987. Its well-designed buildings, gathered around a "sacred" lawn, communicate a sense of place and encourage academic excellence.

As part of its commitment to evangelical beliefs, SAIACS is accredited through the Asia Theological Association. In academics, an innovative MA in theological studies was introduced for secular graduates to enter, and the MTh degree can now be obtained in seven disciplines. Developed on the strength of the MTh studies, SAIACS' PhD program is now recognized as a leader in South Asia. A practice-based DMin was added in 2003. Further innovations include a context-based learning component, which places students in supervised ministry situations weekly. By 2012, SAIACS had three levels of program recognized by the University of Mysore. SAIACS' strategic significance was underlined by the invitation from the International Council for Evangelical Theological Education (ICETE) to participate in its consultation on doctoral programs in majority world venues, which led to the Beirut Benchmarks.

SAIACS' philosophy of education assumes an integrative epistemology that is hospitable to faith, reason, and action, and this leads to a confessional, rational, and missional approach to education. Aiming to be transformative, SAIACS uses residential mode, evangelical, and PhD-qualified faculty; modular and flexible curricula; and context-based learning to good effect. Its mission is to train Christian leaders to demonstrate Christlikeness and excellence in academics, ministry, and missions, by offering biblical and contextually relevant postgraduate degree programs in a caring and egalitarian community. As of 2013, 232 of SAIACS' alumni were involved in tertiary theological education, 15 of them headed theological institutions, and 4 were heads of indigenous mission organizations. SAIACS has made substantial progress in its aim "to be a world-class post-graduate theological institution in South Asia, greatly serving the mission of the Church of Jesus Christ globally."

---

134. *SAIACS: The First Thirty Years* (Bangalore: SAIACS Press, 2012), 19.

Resource

SAIACS: The First Thirty Years. 2012. Bangalore: SAIACS Press.

—Ian W. Payne

South Korea and Christian Education

Even though Christianity was first introduced to Korea by Catholic missionaries during the Ching dynasty (17th to 19th centuries) in China, the arrival of Protestant missionaries such as Horace Grant Underwood (1859–1916), Samuel Moffett (1861–1925), and H. G. Appenzeller (1858–1902) had remarkable impacts on the growth of Christianity in Korea. While the Yi dynasty allowed the foreigners to build hospitals and modern schools, it set strict rules against religious propagation. However, Christian education and evangelism gained momentum through the works of many faithful Christians after 1885.

Protestants emphasized the spiritual characteristics of evangelicalism and pietistic faith, yet encouraged Christians to abide by the principle of the separation of church and state. This helped to assuage the government's suspicions, and thus allowed Christianity to begin putting down roots in the soil of Korean culture.

The development of Christian education as an academic discipline began at Soongshil University in 1960, and it became recognized as an independent branch from other theological disciplines. The Korean Association of Christian Religious Education was established in 1961, and later the Department of Christian Education and the Research Center for Christian Education were also founded. With the offerings of professional degrees at universities and seminaries, Christian education has experienced continual development through the present, with more than 23 academic departments and 160 scholars participating in the Korean Society for Study of Christian Religious Education (KSCRE).

Over the last 120 years, Christian institutions, Sunday schools, and disciple training have been the most influential means of Christian education for Korean people. While some Christian institutions educated young Koreans for professional training, they also aimed to preach the Gospel, teach the democratic lifestyle, and proclaim gender equality.

References and Resources

Min, Kyung Bae. 2007. *Korean Church History: The History of Formation Process of National Church in Korea.* Seoul: Yonsei University Press.

Oh, In Tak. 2008. *A Comprehensive Bibliography of Korean Christian Education: 1945–2005.* Seoul: The Korean Society for Study of Christian Religious Education.

—Hyun-Sook Kim

South Pacific Association of Evangelical Colleges

As an extension of the Bible college movement in Great Britain and North America, colleges were established in the South Pacific region in the late 19th and early 20th centuries. Angas College, founded in Adelaide in 1893, was the first significant institution in this era, although it closed in the 1920s as a result of the effects World War I. It set the pattern for those that followed. Adelaide Bible Institute (now known as Bible College SA) took its place in 1924.

The movement to train men and women for Christian ministry spread across Australia and New Zealand. New colleges were formed that are still in operation. In New South Wales, Sydney Missionary and Bible College was founded in 1916. In Victoria, the Melbourne Bible Institute (formerly the Bible College of Victoria and now known as Melbourne School of Theology) was founded in 1920. In New Zealand, the Bible Training Institute (formerly the Bible College of New Zealand and now known as Laidlaw College) was founded in 1922. In Western Australia, Perth Bible Institute (now known as Perth Bible College) was founded in 1928.

Other colleges of various types were also founded, mostly under denominational initiatives, but for the most part they operated independently. It was not until the early 1950s that the need to work together arose. A conference for principals was organized in Sydney in 1951, which provided the first opportunity for cooperative discussion. In response to a request from interdenominational mission societies, a conference was convened in Melbourne in 1963. In 1967, another conference was held in Queensland, which provided further opportunities to explore working together.

In Adelaide on 20 May 20 1969, The Association of Bible Institutes and Colleges of Australasia (TABICA) was formed, with nine members. It was managed by a standing committee elected from its members. Only interdenominational colleges with autonomous boards were initially permitted to join, and they were required to offer residential full-time courses with a minimum of two years' duration. Training for Christian ministry at home or overseas was also required. In 1975, the association added an associate member option for colleges that were denominational in nature or managed by a mission organization and that held to the distinctives of the association.

In recognition of colleges from the Pacific region, Christian Leaders Training College (CLTC) in PNG and Talua Ministry Training Centre in Vanuatu, it was decided to change the name to the South Pacific Association of Bible Colleges (SPABC) in 1969. The renamed association then became a full regional member of the International Council for Evangelical Theological Education in 1988, which prompted the development of a new constitution and a revised accreditation process, adopted in 1989. This connected the regional association to the global community of theological education.

SPABC existed to facilitate quality evangelical theological education and ministry training among its members and in the South Pacific region through accrediting its members and their programs. It also promoted mutual fellowship and collaboration among its members through biennial conferences, a regularly published newsletter, and relayed communication among members. In 1996, it added a service of tuition assurance for member colleges that needed this protection to meet state accreditation requirements.

With the opening up of state government accreditation in both Australia and New Zealand during the mid-1990s, member colleges gradually achieved this status, which prompted a rethinking of the role of the association in the new millennium. Its focus shifted from accreditation to fellowship and collaboration, while retaining its concern for the evangelical quality of its members. A practical expression of this was the implementation of a biennial principals' retreat, which met alternately with the biennial conference. A name change to the South Pacific Association of Evangelical Colleges (SPAEC) was adopted in 2009 to reflect the broadening identity of current and potential member colleges.

Regardless of these changes in the association, several features have remained constant from the beginning. Its member colleges provide adult education in which the Bible is central to the curriculum because it is the inspired Word of God, effective in equipping God's people for life and service (2 Tim. 3:16–17). They focus on spiritual formation as integral to the training experience so that students grow in the grace and knowledge of Christ (2 Pet. 3:18), as well as develop a heart for global mission. Finally, all colleges have a concern for practical training to help students become effective in ministering to the real world in which they live or to which they are sent.

—LES CRAWFORD

SOUTH SUDAN AND CHRISTIAN EDUCATION

Christianity arrived in South Sudan in early the 20th century. However, much of rural South Sudan remained untouched by the Gospel until the outbreak of the civil war in 1983, when the church experienced both persecution and growth. The largest church in South Sudan is the Roman Catholic Church, followed by the Anglican Church. Other churches are Presbyterian, Church of Christ, and African Inland. Pentecostal and charismatic churches are the fastest growing churches in South Sudan (Dau 2010).

Most of the clergy who led churches in South Sudan were trained in the diaspora. When they returned to the country, the tasks of reinstalling their families and rebuilding their nation were overwhelming. Today, few local churches have programs to teach Sunday school for children, youth, and other groups. However, many Christian ministry organizations are partnering with local denominations to rebuild churches that were destroyed during the war and to empower the South Sudanese leaders to train believers.

Another problem that the church has faced after the war is that some capable church leaders who were trained in the diaspora have been employed by nongovernmental organizations that needed well-trained local manpower. Consequently, these leaders devote less time to ministry.

South Sudan has a variety of local dialects that have yet to be used in Bible translation. This is a major hindrance to the teaching and training of believers.

Most of the leaders of the South Sudan government are Christians and support freedom of worship. This freedom encourages organizations that want to help South Sudan to go to the country in order to train and empower Sudanese leaders to minister to their own people.

Reference

Dau, I. 2010. "Sudan." In *The Cambridge Dictionary of Christianity (1195–1196)*, edited by D. Patte, 1212–1213. Cambridge, New York: Cambridge University Press.

—FAUSTIN NTAMUSHOBORA

SOUTHERN BAPTIST CONVENTION CHRISTIAN EDUCATION

The Southern Baptist Convention is the largest Protestant denomination in the United States. Southern Baptists reported 16 million members in 2013. They have been involved in church educational ministries since their founding in 1845, as well as establishing a number of institutions of higher education. The Southern Baptist Convention (SBC) promotes Sunday school by publishing educational resources through Lifeway Christian Resources.

Contributions to Education

The SBC has emphasized the primacy of missions and educational ministries from the time it was founded at Augusta, Georgia, in 1845. The delegates who founded the denomination were concerned that opposition to the appointment of slaveholding missionaries by national

Baptist missions organizations would limit such opportunities for people from the South. The SBC provided an alternative means for missions and educational ministries in the South. The Southern Baptist Theological Seminary was established in 1859 as the flagship school for ministerial training. The SBC currently sponsors six seminaries: Southern at Louisville, Kentucky; Southwestern Baptist Theological Seminary at Fort Worth, Texas; New Orleans Baptist Theological Seminary at New Orleans, Louisiana; Midwestern Theological Seminary at Kansas City, Missouri; Golden Gate Seminary at Mill Valley, California; and Southeastern Baptist Theological Seminary at Wake Forest, North Carolina. Mid-America Theological Seminary in Memphis, Tennessee, is an independent seminary that identifies with the SBC, but it is not officially sponsored by it.

The SBC developed a funding mechanism to support its denominational ministries in 1925, called the Cooperative Program. It is a pool of offerings received from member churches and used to fund the denomination's mission and educational ministries. Funds from the Cooperative Program are also given to the six seminaries to supplement their finances.

While the national convention only directly sponsors the six seminaries, Southern Baptists operate a plethora of undergraduate institutions through their state conventions. Most of these are private liberal arts colleges, which are administered by boards of trustees. The trustees are generally appointed by representatives of the state Baptist conventions. In some instances, denominational conflict has resulted in a distancing of state institutions from their denominational sponsors and a renegotiation of the relationship between the academic institutions and the parent denomination. Baylor University in Waco, Texas, and Mercer University in Macon, Georgia, are examples of Southern Baptist entities that successfully changed the structure of their trustee boards to allow more autonomy for the institutions to set the direction of their development and protect academic freedom on campus. Among the undergraduate schools that continue to be closely affiliated with the SBC, Union University in Jackson, Tennessee; Samford University in Birmingham, Alabama; and Houston Baptist University in Houston, Texas, are among the most successful.

Philosophy of Education

Both Southern Baptist undergraduate entities and the six seminaries generally endorse the convention's statement of faith, *The Baptist Faith and Message 2000*. This document, revised for the third time in the year 2000, is conservative theologically, with a high view of scriptural authority and inspiration. It also takes a conservative position on social issues, such as a pro-life stance on abortion and the rejection of homosexual relationships. The document and the SBC schools that endorse it also take a firm position against allowing women to serve in ministerial positions. Southern Baptists were engaged in a traumatic denominational struggle over many of these issues from 1979 to 1992, which culminated in conservative factions gaining control over the educational institutions of the denomination by achieving a critical mass of representation on the trustee boards that governed those institutions. Moderates were ejected from leadership roles, and they eventually separated from the SBC, forming the Cooperative Baptist Fellowship in 1992 as a means of furthering their own missions and educational goals.

References and Resources

Brackney, William H. 2008. *Campus and Congregation: Baptists in Higher Education.* Macon, GA: Mercer University Press.

Hankins, Barry. 2003. *Uneasy in Babylon: Southern Baptist Conservatives and American Culture.* Tuscaloosa: University of Alabama Press.

Leonard, Bill J. 2003. *Baptist Ways: A History.* Valley Forge, PA: Judson Press.

McBeth, H. Leon. 1987. *The Baptist Heritage: Four Centuries of Baptist Witness.* Nashville, TN: Broadman Press.

Sutton, Jerry. 2000. *The Baptist Reformation: The Conservative Resurgence in the Southern Baptist Convention.* Nashville, TN: Broadman & Holman.

Willis, Gregory. 2009. *Southern Baptist Theological Seminary, 1859–2009.* Oxford: Oxford University Press.

—SCOTT CULPEPPER

SOUTHWESTERN BAPTIST THEOLOGICAL SEMINARY

Historical Introduction and Christian Tradition

Southwestern Baptist Theological Seminary is a Christian seminary located in Fort Worth, Texas. It is one of the six seminaries affiliated with the Southern Baptist Convention (SBC). Southwestern was chartered in 1908 by Benajah Harvey (B. H.) Carroll (1843–1914) at Baylor University in Waco, Texas. Previously, the school had incarnations as a religion department as well as a theological seminary with direct ties to Baylor. In 1907, Baylor trustee Carroll suggested that the seminary become an independent entity. After receiving its charter, the seminary remained in Waco and was governed by the Baptist General Convention of Texas.

The school moved to Fort Worth, Texas, in 1910, and was placed under the direction of the SBC in 1925. The seminary currently has two campuses, in Fort Worth and Houston, and extension centers in San Antonio,

El Paso, Plano, and Rosharon, Texas, the latter located within Darrington Prison. Extensions outside Texas are in Shawnee, Oklahoma; Little Rock, Arkansas; and Bonn, Germany.

In its century-long history, Southwestern has had eight presidents: Benajah Harvey Carroll (1908–1914), Lee Rutland Scarborough (1915–1942), E. D. Head (1942–1953), J. Howard Williams (1953–1958), Robert E. Naylor (1958–1978), Russell H. Dilday (1978–1994), Kenneth S. Hemphill (1994–2003), and L. Paige Patterson (2003–present). In 1994, Russell Dilday was dismissed from his duties as president in the midst of conversations and controversies related to the "conservative resurgence" in the SBC, which focused largely on issues related to biblical inerrancy. Dilday remains the only president ever to be removed from service.

As of 2012, the school had over 3,000 enrolled students and 118 full-time faculty members and boasted more than 43,000 graduates. While 94 percent of the student body identifies as Southern Baptist, there are more than 40 Christian denominations represented by the enrolled. In addition to church and denominational service, alumni serve in a broad range of vocations, including journalism, government, politics, teaching, and work with nonprofit and parachurch organizations.

Notable Academic Programs

Southwestern Seminary comprises six schools, each with its own dean, faculty, and programs of study: The College at Southwestern (for undergraduates), The School of Theology, The School of Church and Family Ministries, The Roy Fish School of Evangelism and Missions, The School of Church Music, and the Havard School for Theological Studies (based in Houston). The seminary is accredited to grant bachelor's, master's, and doctoral degrees by the Commission on Colleges of the Southern Association of Colleges and Schools and the Association of Theological Schools in the United States and Canada. In addition, the School of Church Music is accredited by the National Association of Schools of Music.

The school offers the following degree programs: bachelor of arts in humanities and music; bachelor of science in biblical studies; master of divinity; master of arts in theology, archaeology and biblical studies, lay ministry, Islamic studies, missiology, Christian education, biblical counseling, Christian school education, worship, and church music; master of music; master of theology; doctor of musical arts; doctor of educational ministry through the School of Church & Family Ministries; doctor of ministry (DMin) through the Schools of Theology, and Evangelism and Missions; and doctor of philosophy (PhD) through the Schools of Theology,

Evangelism and Missions, Church & Family Ministries, and Church Music.

Christian Philosophy and Mission of Education

The seminary's mission statement reads: "Southwestern Baptist Theological Seminary assists the churches of the Southern Baptist Convention by the biblical education of God-called men and women for their respective ministries, which fulfill the Great Commission and glorify God. The motto 'Preach the Word, Reach the World' captures for a new generation of students the historic pledge of Southwestern Seminary to serve both Southern Baptist churches and a lost world by equipping ministers for their God-ordained task."

Professors at Southwestern affirm the message of the *Baptist Faith and Message 2000*, a confessional statement of the SBC that outlines the denomination's understanding and interpretation of Christian scripture. The statement is used to establish a foundation for Christian faith and practice

Twice each year, in the fall and spring, Southwestern publishes the *Southwestern Journal of Theology*, an academic journal with a Baptist and conservative theological scope.

References and Resources

Baker, Robert A. 1983. *Tell the Generations Following: A History of Southwestern Baptist Theological Seminary, 1908–1983*. Nashville, TN: Broadman Press.

Dilday, Russell. 2004. *Columns: Glimpses of a Seminary Under Assault*. Macon, GA: Smyth & Helwys.

Naylor, Robert. 1995. *A Messenger's Memoirs: 61 Southern Baptist Convention Meetings*. Franklin, TN: Providence House Publishers.

—R. Kevin Johnson

SPAIN AND CHRISTIAN EDUCATION

Spain is a country in the southwest of Europe that for centuries has been considered a bastion of Catholicism. In the 1930s, during the Spanish Civil War, many Catholics were persecuted by the Republican, anarchist, and socialist forces. After the war, Spain once again became a religious state, with a privileged position for the Roman Catholic Church. In the 1970s a constitutional monarchy was restored, and the ideological neutrality of the state was introduced. Strong secularization and liberalization processes began, and the church began to lose its social influence. In 2009, the population of 47 million identified as 73.2 percent Catholic, 2.8 percent Muslim, 0.1 percent Jewish, 1.7 percent followers of other religions, and 22.2

percent nonbelievers. Religious faith does not play a significant role in the lives of many Spanards, the number of spiritual vocations has been decreasing, and moral relativism and family crises are more and more common.

The concordat with the Holy See of 1953 and Article 13 of Ley Organica de Libertad Religiosa of 1980 confirmed parents' right to religious education for their children. Classes in public schools are optional—one to two hours per week—and parents or students older than 16 can choose them. Approximately 63–85 percent of students attend Catholic religion lessons in school. Religious knowledge is evaluated, but outcomes are not. Teachers of religion must have an ecclesiastical (canonical) mission and are paid by religious communities. Religion lessons at school are also available for Protestants, Muslims, and Jews. Parish Catholic catechesis is organized for children and youth. It is facultative and includes preparation for sacraments. Organization of catechesis and preparation of curricula and textbooks are dealt with by the Episcopal Commission on Education and Catechesis (CEEC) and the National Catechetical Secretariat (SNC).

References and Resources

Chalupniak, Radoslaw. 2002. "Wychowanie religijne po hiszpansku." *Katecheta* 46 (4): 55–61.

Kielian, Andrzej. 2010. *Modele nauczania religii rzymskokatolickiej w krajach europejskich.* Kraków: Wydawnictwo UNUM.

Ternero, Antonio A. 2010. "Crisis y esperanzas da la ensenanza religiosa en Espana." In *Wspólczesna katecheza: kryzysy i nadzieja,* edited by Radoslaw Chalupniak, 181–185. Opole: Redakcja Wydawnictw Wydziału Teologicznego Uniwersytetu Opolskiego.

—RADOSLAW CHALUPNIAK

SPECIAL EDUCATION AS CHRISTIAN EDUCATION

From as early as the 17th and 18th centuries, devout Christians have paved the way for today's disability activists. Abbe Charles Michel de l'Epée, an ordained priest, developed sign language for use by the deaf in Paris in 1775. Education for the blind was begun by Louis Braille, a devout Christian. He was a church organist and attended Mass every Sunday. In 1834, he invented the six-dot Braille system, which is still used today.

These men possessed a belief about humanity that was not limited to the societal views of that time, when the handicapped were deemed not educable. Rather, they chose to see individuals with blindness and deafness as children of God, deserving of the specialized education they needed to learn and grow as individuals. It was not good enough for l'Epée or Braille to provide access to worship services for God's children who were deaf or blind; they sought out ways to ensure individuals with disabilities were valuable participants in the congregation who actually worshipped alongside their able-bodied parishioners. They did not pity these individuals, but instead sought to break down the barriers that prevented them from feeling true membership in their communities. These Christian educational innovators exhibited a practice that we define today as inclusionary (Smith et al. 2011).

Today's parents and disability advocates strive to achieve similar goals—to create appropriate and challenging special education programs for students with disabilities—so they may grow up to be valued and contributing members of society (see Smith et al. 2011). As Christian educators, our legal responsibility to our students with disabilities is to provide them with a free appropriate public education (FAPE). All students with disabilities have such rights under both civil law (Section 504 of the Americans with Disabilities Act) and special education law (the Individuals with Disabilities Education Act, Pub. L. No. 94-142) (see Smith et al. 2011). The IDEA provides the procedures for making decisions about student placement, documenting student needs, services, supports, and accommodations, and relates requirements for monitoring student progress. Its latest reauthorization, in 2004 (Pub. L. No. 108-446), has made educators more accountable for ensuring that students with disabilities are meaningfully educated through exposure to grade-level curricula as they sit beside their peers in general education classrooms (Smith et al. 2011). Put simply, offering special education as a viable service delivery option means more than just providing students with disabilities with what is known as a *specialized* education.

As stewards of Christ with the vocation of educating Christ's children today, Christian educators must become more aware of the needs and desires of individuals with disabilities before making educational decisions for them. It is the Christian educator's responsibility to conceptualize special education through the lens of Christ's eyes, just as our forefathers did. Russell (1998) reminds us that such conceptualizing requires us to deconstruct society's long-standing views of individuals with disabilities as victims, deformed or demonic, abnormal, or deserving of our pity, and even as heroic when we view them as overcoming something we interpret as an obstacle in their way. Individuals with disabilities are people first and want to be recognized and celebrated (Russell 1998) because they are children of God, just like their able-bodied counterparts.

Special educators in K–12 who possess this awareness and epistemology will design an individualized educational program (IEP) that ensures the student is placed in the least restrictive environment (LRE) possible, with appropriate supports and services. These teachers will develop their pedagogical skills to ensure all their students are exposed to grade-level academics through challenging and developmentally appropriate curricula, particularly their students with disabilities. They will teach to their students' strengths rather than focusing on a one-size-fits-all curriculum. They will expect more from a special education program than allowing a student to be placed in a general education classroom without appropriate supports. These educators will allow students to express what they know through a range of different media, not just by pencil-paper tests. They will replace terms like *regular classroom* with *general education classroom*, *normal* with *typical*, and *learning deficits* with *different strengths of learning*, because they realize that the original terms send offensive messages about God's children (and *to* God's children).

Christian educators who are responsible for delivering special education should empower the students with whom they work, listen to the individuals who know their students best, and most important, teach their students how to advocate for themselves. Such practices not only allow us to give our students with disabilities the specialized education God intended them to have, but also assist us in empowering them to reach out and share their own God-given gifts as He intended.

References and Resources

Russell, M. 1998. *Beyond Ramps: Disability at the End of the Social Contract*. Monroe, MA: Common Courage Press.

Smith, T., E. Polloway, J. R. Patton, and C. Dowdy. 2011. *Teaching Students with Special Needs in Inclusive Settings*. 6th ed. Boston: Allyn and Bacon.

Nothing about Us without Us. http://www.un.org/esa/socdev/enable/iddp2004.htm

Universal Design for Learning. http://www.cast.org/udl/

Myths. http://www.togetherwerock.com/sites/default/files/Draper_MythsMisc_Nov1.pdf

—Diana D. Abbott

Special Education, The Roots of

The starting point for Christian education is the fact that at the beginning of His ministry, Jesus proclaimed that He had been sent to bring good news to the poor; He predicted and subsequently confirmed with His life that the Kingdom of God is intended for all people, starting with those who are the most disadvantaged.

Many works inspired by the activities and teaching of Jesus subsequently inspired the activity of various people and societies as well as special education as a science. St. John of God (1495–1550) entered into the history of hospitals because he himself suffered brutal treatment methods, which at that time were commonly used with people with mental disorders. He founded a hospital and became the precursor of a modern hospital system. He also took care of the patients' spiritual needs, providing a Holy Mass with a sermon every Sunday or even daily Holy Communion. During the day, he provided the time for common morning and evening prayers. St. Vincent de Paul (1581–1660) should also be mentioned here, because he opened orphanages and shelters for people burdened with various diseases.

Special Education

As a science, special education is referred to in French as *pédagogie spéciale*, in German as *Sonderpädagogik* or *Heilpädagogik*, and in Russian as *spiecyalnaja piedagogika* or *diefiektologia*.

At its inception special education was interested in "handicapped," "disabled," and "socially maladjusted" people. The original theories and practices of education for such people were created on the grounds of medicine. Special schools for deaf-mute people (e.g., Braidwood's Academy for the Deaf and Dumb in Edinburgh, 1760) and for the blind (Institut National des Jeunes Aveugles in Paris, 1784) were established, designed for people with a particular disability. This approach changed as the circle of those who became the subject of special education became broader and broader.

Generally, five categories of people covered by educational exploration were distinguished. The first category includes persons having difficulty with cognition of the world and communication with it because of the lack of or the damage to sensory analyzers. The second category comprises persons whose cognitive processes have an incorrect course, as a result of which they have inadequate cognitive images of reality as well as a limited or below-norm ability to reason and hindered adaptation to life and work. The third category consists of those who because of damage to the locomotor system or some chronic disease have a limited ability to act, to express themselves, and to actively participate in the life of the society. The fourth category embraces all those who require rehabilitation—those socially maladjusted as a result of negligence and upbringing mistakes of their parents and school, leading to a conflict with prevailing social and legal norms and regulations. Finally, the last category covers those who significantly exceed the level of intelligence and ability and need stimulation and targeted education. Specific groups of interest to special education have emerged in some cases independently from these categories.

More recently, the following definition has been adopted: "Special education is a detailed study of pedagogics and its subject is defined as the care, therapy, education and upbringing of people with deviated norms, most frequently individuals less physically able or those disabled ones regardless of the kind, degree and the complexity of the symptoms and the causes and effects of the arisen anomalies, disturbances, difficulties and limitations" (Dykcik 2002, 13).

Special Education versus Christian Education

In recent years, social and ecclesial consciousness has developed, and special education has made undeniable progress, which means that family and other formation places are capable of giving those people appropriate religious education to which they are entitled as the baptized, those called to salvation. Christian education, which primarily occurs within the family but also through catechesis at school or in a center for the disabled, requires methods that are suitable and adapted to particular persons as well as consideration of the findings of educational research, so that it can manifest in a fruitful manner in the context of a person's overall education.

References and Resources

Canevaro, A. 1999. *Pedagogia speciale. La riduzione dell'handicap.* Milano: Mondadori.

Dykcik, W., ed. 2002. *Pedagogika specjalna.* Poznań: UAM.

Kiciński, A. 2011. *Katecheza osób niepełnosprawnością intelektualną w Polsce po Soborze Watykańskim II.* Lublin: KUL.

Speck, O. 2003. *System Heilpädagogik. Ein ökologisch reflexive Grundlegung.* München: Ernst Renhardt Verlage.

Wilmshurst, L., and A. W. Brue. 2010. *The Complete Guide to Special Education.* San Francisco: Jossey-Bass.

—Andrzej Kiciński

SPIRITUAL DIRECTION

The foundation of spiritual direction is the spiritual activity of listening: listening to and responding to the voice of the Spirit as one person (directee) seeks counsel from another person (director) under the presence and inspiration of the Spirit. This relationship among the three participants has been labeled "spiritual friendship," "spiritual guidance," and "discipleship." The purpose of direction is to develop attentiveness to the movement of the Spirit in the life story of the directee and to help the directee live a life of love and Christlikeness. The director, who is further along the spiritual path, acts as a guide in the discernment process of dis-

covering hindrances to the Christian life and suggesting and affirming spiritual practices that develop a deeper awareness of the presence of God. The emphasis, however, is not on technique or methods, but on hearing and responding to the voice of the Spirit. Merton (1960) defines the role of the director as "a trusted friend, who in an atmosphere of sympathetic understanding, help and strengthens us in our groping efforts to correspond with the grace of the Holy Spirit, who alone is the true Director in the fullest sense of the word."

The theological basis of direction is the Spirit speaking into our story and His empowerment to live the Christ life. Direction follows the pattern of listening to God and responding to Him in the presence of another person. Eli directed Samuel in listening to the voice of God (1 Sam. 3:1–18); Barnabas led Paul in discernment of the will of God (Acts 9:27); and Paul counseled Timothy, Titus, and Philemon in responding to the voice of the Spirit. Spiritual direction was practiced by the Desert Fathers and Mothers, and many religious orders and spiritual writers have noted its usefulness through the ages.

Direction differs from psychological or pastoral counseling. While counseling centers on problem solving, direction focuses on listening and responding to the Spirit in a permanent relationship. Barry and Connolly (2009) notes that spiritual direction is in contact with the spiritual realm, which is beyond mere common sense and "strategic problem solving."

Spiritual direction has been a foundational part of the Orthodox and Catholic traditions, where it has been mandatory for clergy and common among the laity. Protestantism in recent years has experienced an increasing awareness and practice of direction. Direction in the Orthodox and Catholic traditions has been more hierarchical, while Protestantism emphasizes the relational or companion aspect of the practice. The communal aspect of direction is emphasized in the group spiritual direction, where, under the supervision of a director, several directees meet to listen to the Spirit and discover where God is moving in their lives.

The educational component of spiritual direction and its close relationship to discipleship cannot be overlooked. In direction, the Holy Spirit is the teacher and guide, leading into all truth as the director facilitates the process. The teaching environment is a safe and transparent place where the director and directee are open to the movement of the Spirit. The director offers accountability and evaluation for the directee in his or her walk with God. With the increasing awareness of the spiritual helps in spiritual direction, particularly in Protestant circles, the challenge for the church is to prepare directors who are trained to offer this ministry to members of the body of Christ.

References and Resources

Bakke, Jeannette A. 2000. *Holy Invitations: Exploring Spiritual Direction*. Grand Rapids, MI: Baker Books.

Barry, William A., and William J. Connolly. 2009. *The Practice of Spiritual Direction*. Rev. and updated ed. New York: HarperOne.

Edwards, Tilden. 2001. *Spiritual Director, Spiritual Companion: Guide to Tending the Soul*. New York: Paulist Press.

Florent, Lucien-Marie. 2012. *Spiritual Direction: Carmelite Studies*. 2nd ed. Wellesley, MA: Christus.

Guenther, Margaret. 1992. *Holy Listening: The Art of Spiritual Direction*. Cambridge, MA: Cowley Publications.

May, Gerald G. 1992. *Care of Mind, Care of Spirit: A Psychiatrist Explores Spiritual Direction*. 1st HarperCollins paperback ed. San Francisco: HarperSanFrancisco.

Merton, Thomas. 1960. *Spiritual Direction and Meditation*. Collegeville, MN: The Liturgical Press.

Vest, Norvene. 2003. *Tending the Holy: Spiritual Direction across Traditions*. Spiritual Directors International Series. Harrisburg, PA: Morehouse Publishing.

—Philip Bustrum

SPIRITUAL DIRECTION, EARLY DEVELOPMENT OF

"Spiritual direction" refers to a relationship in which an individual, gifted by the Holy Spirit, provides private guidance to one or more persons in the pursuit of holiness and the overcoming of internal spiritual obstacles to this pursuit. Such guidance is private in that it is not directly connected with the community's corporate service of worship or with broader institutional practices that aim to impose a homogeneous pattern of behavior on the entire community. Spiritual direction is thus distinguished from catechesis and mystagogy (which prepare initiates to receive baptism and the Eucharist in the public service of worship) and from the instruction of novices in the monastic life (which prepares novices for obedience to monastic superiors in accordance with the rule binding upon the whole community).

The term "spiritual direction" was brought into popular use by Jesuit writers in the 16th century and, strictly speaking, may be anachronistic in dealing with early Christian sources. Patristic and Byzantine authors prefer to speak of the guide as a "spiritual father" (Grk. *pneumatikos patēr*), reflecting the apostle Paul's description of himself as a father to converts and younger partners in ministry (1 Cor. 4:15; Phil. 2:22; 1 Thess. 2:11; Philem. 1:10; cf. 1 John 2:1).

Consultation with a spiritual father became an important practice in the ascetic movement that emerged in Egypt during the fourth century. Those wishing to pursue a life of undistracted prayer and single-minded devotion to God withdrew from cities and towns and settled in less-populated desert areas. There they lived a simple life based on manual labor and the meditative reading and recitation (singing or chanting) of scriptural texts.

When a person pursuing the ascetic life encountered difficulties in prayer or was gripped by a powerful temptation, he or she would seek out the counsel of an experienced spiritual guide (who was often given the honorific title "Abba" or "Amma," i.e., "Father" or "Mother"). The guide was typically an older ascetic who, through experiences of trial and temptation, had come to terms with his or her own weakness, grown in prayer and humility, and received from the Holy Spirit a gift of discernment (cf. 1 Cor. 12:10). The person asking for guidance would explain the hindrance or temptation and describe the inner motions of his or her thoughts and feelings. The guide, listening carefully, would offer a brief, firm counsel (a pithy saying or apothegm). This counsel rested upon an understanding of the underlying dynamic of the temptation, discerning the deceitful thoughts and imaginings (lacking truth) and the disordered desires (lacking love toward God) that gave power to the temptation. The guide's counsel therefore functioned to break the hold of the temptation, inviting the hearer to act immediately to give up the false attachments that impeded spiritual growth. In each case, the form and content of the guide's counsel could be adapted to the specific needs of the individual hearer, for example, relating a short parable to bring insight to the uncomprehending or using indirection and deception to go around the defenses of the stubbornly resistant.

The counsels of renowned ascetic guides were initially transmitted orally by their disciples and then appeared in comprehensive written collections called *Apophthegmata patrum* ("Sayings of the Fathers"). These counsels were given a systematic form in the teachings of Evagrius Ponticus (d. 399), who developed and explained this pattern of practical guidance by reference to an underlying vision of the human person (a theological anthropology and an integrated psychology of action). Evagrius argued that all sinful patterns of thought and action were rooted in eight basic "evil reasonings": pride, vainglory, acedia (diversion and despondency that rejects grace), sinful anger, grieving over the wrong things, avarice, fornication, and gluttony. He described the nature and dynamics of each of these with great acuity and insight, providing a rich repertoire of concepts that could be used in self-examination and the spiritual guidance of others. Evagrius's schema was influential in the Greek East and was transmitted by John Cassian (d. 435) to the Latin West, where it became the basis for the later idea of the "seven deadly sins," which would play an important role in medieval moral and spiritual theology.

From the sixth century onward, spiritual guidance became closely connected with private confession, absolution, and penance (by which sins committed after baptism are absolved). Thus, for example, in early Christian Ireland, the *anamchara* ("soul friend") was a person of holy life (typically an ascetic or monk) who heard confessions and provided spiritual counsel to an individual or family. As the hearing of confessions and pronouncing of absolution became limited to the clergy, there was a tendency for the charismatic role of the spiritual guide to coincide with the institutional role of the priest.

References and Resources

Filoramo, Giovanni, ed. 2002. *Maestro e discepolo: temi e problemi della direzione spirituale tra VI secolo a.C. e VII secolo d.C.* Brescia: Morcelliana.

———, ed. 2006. *Storia della direzione spirituale: I. L'età antica.* Brescia: Morcelliana.

Harmless, William. 2004. *Desert Christians: An Introduction to the Literature of Early Monasticism.* Oxford: Oxford University Press.

Hevelone-Harper, Jennifer Lee. 2005. *Disciples in the Desert: Monks, Laity, and Spiritual Authority in Sixth-Century Gaza.* Baltimore, MD: Johns Hopkins University Press.

Kidder, Annemarie S. 2010. *Making Confession, Hearing Confession: A History of the Cure of Souls.* Collegeville, MN: The Liturgical Press.

Sellner, Edward C. 2002. *The Celtic Soul Friend.* Notre Dame, IN: Ave Maria Press.

Sinkewicz, Robert E. 2003. *Evagrius of Pontus: The Greek Ascetic Corpus.* Oxford: Oxford University Press.

Turner, H. J. M. 1990. *St. Symeon the New Theologian and Spiritual Fatherhood.* Leiden: E.J. Brill.

—Byard Bennett

SPIRITUAL DISCIPLINES

Spiritual disciplines are those activities that lead us into an awareness of God's presence and give God space to transform our souls into Christlikeness (Col. 3:17). God calls us to salvation through repentance and faith in the death, burial, and resurrection of Jesus Christ. Salvation is not the culmination of the Christian faith, but rather the beginning of life in Christ and His call to follow Him in being conformed to His image (Rom. 8:9, 12:1–2; 2 Pet. 1:3–4) and transformed into His likeness. As salvation comes by the work of the Holy Spirit, so this walk in the spiritual life comes through the transforming work of the Spirit. Spiritual disciplines are practices that provide an occasion for spiritual growth and spiritual formation. They are life patterns that direct us to God and disciple

us more fully into the likeness of Jesus Christ. The practices themselves are not the means for attaining spiritual growth. Rather, they give an opportunity for the Spirit to transform our souls in order that He may produce Christian character and spiritual fruit in our lives. "The aim of disciplines in the spiritual life and, specifically, in the following of Christ," declares Willard (1990), "is the transformation of the total state of the soul. It is the renewal of the whole person from the inside."

A Christian is one who is marked and trained by discipline. Several disciplines or practices are mandated in scripture—the sacraments, the Lord's Supper, fellowship, and Sabbath—practices that help us make sense out of life. In addition, Jesus as our teacher modeled for us the disciplines of solitude, simplicity, prayer, the Word, sacrificial living, and fasting. Other spiritual practices handed down to us by the church fathers and mothers include spiritual friendship, spiritual direction, pilgrimage, centering prayer, the divine office, and spiritual reading (*lectio divina*). Various authors have offered classifications of the disciplines. Willard (1990) organized them into disciplines of abstinence and engagement, while Foster (1998) labels them inward, ourward, and corporate disciplines. The educational task of the church is not to number the disciplines but to lead and instruct individuals and groups in the deepening of their faith through the practice of spiritual disciplines, which provide opportunity for the Holy Spirit to transform the heart and soul. Two examples of these disciplines are discussed here.

Silence and solitude is the practice of removing oneself from the distractions of sounds, activity, and people to center one's full attention on God. In silence we make space to hear the voice of God, and in solitude we open ourselves to discovering God as our intimate friend and faithful companion. A biblical basis for this discipline is the Psalmist words, "Be still and know that I am God" (Ps. 46:10). In the practice of silence and solitude we become aware of the divine presence of God in our lives, experience his overwhelming love, and are enabled to love God, ourselves, and others.

Spiritual reading, or *lectio divina*, is reading the text of scripture with the heart. Rather than reading the Bible impersonally or for information, spiritual reading is connecting our spirit with the Spirit-author of scripture. Peterson (2011) says: "In spiritual reading we do not take control of the text, we let the text take control of us." Guigo II, an Italian monk in the 12th century, formalized spiritual reading into the four-step process of *lectio* (reading), *meditatio* (meditation), *oratio* (prayer), and *contemplatio* (contemplation). The purpose of spiritual reading is to allow scripture to permeate our existence so that we live the text in our daily lives.

References and Resources

Foster, Richard J. 1998. *Celebration of Discipline: The Path to Spiritual Growth.* 20th anniversary ed. San Francisco: HarperSanFrancisco.

Howard, Evan. 2012. "Lectio Divina in The Evangelical Tradition." *Journal of Spiritual Formation & Soul Care* 5 (1): 56–77.

Keating, Thomas. 1985. "The Dynamics of lectio divina." *Word and Spirit* 5 (1): 80–89.

Lawrence. 2007. *The Practice of the Presence of God: The Best Rule of Holy Life: Conversations and Letters of Brother Lawrence.* Special journal ed. Shippensburg, PA: Destiny Image Publishers.

Nouwen, Henri J. M. 2004. *Out of Solitude: Three Meditations on the Christian Life.* 1st rev. ed. Notre Dame, IN: Ave Maria Press.

Peterson, Eugene. 2011. *Spiritual Reading (Lectio Divina).* In *Dictionary of Christian Spirituality,* edited by Glen G. Scorgie, 573–579. Grand Rapids, MI. Zondervan.

Willard, Dallas. 1990. *The Spirit of the Disciplines: Understanding How God Changes Lives.* San Francisco: HarperSanFrancisco.

—PHILIP BUSTRUM

SPIRITUAL EXERCISES, IGNATIAN TRADITION OF

Developed as a retreat experience by Ignatius of Loyola (1491–1556), the spiritual exercises are a series of contemplations based primarily on the life of Jesus. Their purpose is to help further dispose a person toward the movements and will of God in his or her life (Barry 1991, 14). With a core principle being to "allow the Creator do deal immediately with the creature" (Modras 2004, 25), the spiritual exercises invite us to rethink Christian education in light of God's presence in the personal lives of our community.

Origins: Ignatius of Loyola

The exercises have their origins in the personal religious experiences of Ignatius of Loyola (Lonsdale 2000, 127). With aspirations of performing heroic deeds for Spain, Ignatius was wounded in a battle with the French. It was during his convalescence that he began to imagine himself instead living a life in service to God. It was out of these daydreams, and the resulting movements of his heart, that the Spiritual Exercises originated (Barry 1991, 12). Ignatius began giving the exercises to others, helping them to deepen their relationship with God through imagination-based contemplations.

An Overview of the Exercises

In Ignatius's own words (1991, 121), spiritual exercises are "a means of preparing and disposing our soul to rid itself of all its disordered affections, and then, after their removal, of seeking and finding God's will in the ordering of our life for the salvation of our soul." The exercises are divided into four weeks, or movements, that may be engaged in a 30-day period or over the course of many months (Modras 2004, 26). After contemplating the love of God for creation, the first week focuses on meditating on the history of sin in one's life and the world (Lonsdale 2000, 131). In the second week, retreatants are invited to imaginatively follow the life of Jesus from His birth through His ministry, culminating in the question of whether they want to follow Him more closely. The third week brings one to an intimate experience of Jesus's suffering and death, thereby intensifying one's identification with Him (Modras 2004, 30). Finally, in the fourth week the joys of the resurrection are pursued (Barry 1991, 13).

Implications for Christian Education

Ignatius founded the Society of Jesus (also known as the Jesuits), for whom the exercises as well as education are central. Beyond this, the exercises have several implications for Christian education in both theory and practice:

1. *Jesus-centered education.* In the exercises, there is an intentional effort made to experience personal encounters with Jesus, and it is these that lead to transformation in one's life. Christian education is therefore called to continually foster the personal encounters of congregants with Jesus as they occur not only in religious education programs and worship services, but also in their daily lives.

2. *A theistic-humanistic orientation.* A fundamental theology of the exercises is the belief that God actively works within and through the imaginations and affections of each individual (Modras 2004, 68). For Christian education, this implies a need to continually listen to the hopes, dreams, and so forth of our communities, for therein may God also be found, according to Ignatius.

3. *Continually discerned adaptations.* In giving the exercises, Ignatius believed that each experience of the retreat would be as unique as each individual making it (Lonsdale 2000, 128–129). This raises the challenge for Christian educators to continually adapt their programs in discerning response to what they are seeing and hearing from their constituents.

4. *Experiential pedagogies.* With imaginative contemplation being a central practice in the exercises, Christian education is invited to include such experiential pedagogies in its repertoire. These may also include narrative approaches, service-learning projects, and mission trips. Overall,

the goal is to foster concrete experiences of God in the lives of Christians.

See also de Sales, Francis; Ignatius of Loyola; Imagination as Christian Practice; Missional Christian Education; Narrative; Service Learning as Christian Practice.

References and Resources

Barry, William A. 1991. *Finding God in All Things: A Companion to the Spiritual Exercises of St. Ignatius*. Notre Dame, IN: Ave Maria Press.

Ignatius of Loyola. 1991. "The Spiritual Exercises." In *Ignatius of Loyola: The Spiritual Exercises and Selected Works*, edited by George E. Ganss, 121–214. New York: Paulist Press.

Lonsdale, David. 2000. *Eyes to See, Ears to Hear: An Introduction to Ignatian Spirituality*. Rev. ed. Traditions of Christian Spirituality Series. Maryknoll, NY: Orbis.

Modras, Ronald E. 2004. *Ignatian Humanism: A Dynamic Spirituality for the 21st Century*. Chicago: Loyola Press.

—ERIC J. KYLE

SPIRITUAL EXPERIENCES

What Are Spiritual Experiences?

For Christians, spiritual experiences relate to the Trinitarian God. They can be natural or supernatural, driven by the Holy Spirit or conversely by contrary forces opposing God's purposes. One need not have faith in Yahweh or Jesus to experience spiritual realities, as the Egyptians learned through the 10 plagues, as the false prophets whom Elijah challenged atop Mount Carmel observed (1 Kings 18:36–39), and as the people of the Gadarenes witnessed when two people who were demon-possessed were delivered (Matt. 8:28–34).

Biblical Examples of Spiritual Experiences

Biblical examples abound of those who directly encountered God through divine provision, miraculous occurrences, or revelation. For example, the Lord appeared and spoke to Moses through a burning bush (Exod. 3:1–22). This spiritual experience changed his life trajectory. Furthermore, the Lord confirmed this guidance through two supernatural occurrences (Exod. 4:1–7). When Moses obediently threw his staff to the ground, it became a snake, and when he picked it back up, it turned back into a staff. When Moses was directed to put his hand inside his cloak, it became leprous, but when he put it back inside, his hand was restored. Through supernatural means, the children of Israel crossed the Red Sea on dry ground through God's mighty act (Exod. 14:21–22), and Joshua led the Israelites across the Jordon River on dry ground. Daniel experienced God's miraculous power when God shut the mouths of lions (Dan. 6:22), while his three friends were not consumed in the fiery furnace (Dan. 3:25–27).

Spiritual experiences through healing and deliverance infused Jesus's ministry. The miraculous feeding of the 5,000 (Matt. 14:13–21) and the 4,000 (Mark 8:1–10), the healing of a demon-possessed man (Mark 5:1–15) and the woman with the issue of blood (Mark 5:25–34), and raising Lazarus from the dead (John 11:41–44) were all spiritual experiences demonstrating God's power. When the Spirit told Philip to join the Ethiopian's chariot, both experienced God's power through revelation and illumination of God's Word. Paul's experience on the Damascus Road further illustrates how God encounters are life-changing (Acts 9:1–19). The Holy Spirit coming at Pentecost likewise validates that God's visitation results in spiritual experiences (Acts 2:1–13).

Historical Examples of Spiritual Experiences

Spiritual experiences do not necessarily involve supernatural encounters. Selected examples of Christian figures throughout history illustrate that spiritual illumination through reading God's Word, meditation, prayer, and encounter with human need results in greater union with Christ. First, Teresa of Ávila (1515–1518), a Spanish Carmelite nun, spoke of spiritual experiences in her best-known book, *Interior Castle*.[135] For Teresa, spiritual experience commences when the soul ascends through six mansions in order to arrive at the seventh, in which union with God is attained through various kinds of prayer, resulting in spiritual transformation through union with Christ. Second, John of the Cross (1542–1591), like contemporary Teresa of Ávila, viewed union with Christ as supreme. His well-known work, *The Dark Night of the Soul*, describes the soul's purification through detaching, purifying, illuminating, and ultimate union with God.[136] Third, Sojourner Truth (1797–1893), an American slave turned abolitionist and women's rights advocate, encountered God prior to her efforts to uphold the rights of the oppressed.[137] Fourth, Sister Teresa of Calcutta, the Albanian-born Roman Catholic nun who established the Missionaries of Charity order, ministered to the poorest of the poor. In one of her letters, she noted visions of a large crowd comprised of the very poor and children, calling: "Come, come, save

---

135. Teresa of Ávila (with commentary by Dennis J. Billy), *Interior Castle: The Classic Text with a Spiritual Commentary* (Notre Dame, IN: Ava Maria Press, 2007). See also Gillian T. W. Ahlgreen, *Entering Teresa of Avila's Interior Castle: A Reader's Companion* (Mahwah, NJ: Paulist Press, 2005).

136. John of the Cross, *Dark Night of the Soul*, trans. E. Allison Peers (Radford, VA: Wilder Publications, 2008).

137. Margaret Washington, *Sojourner Truth's America* (Urbana and Chicago: University of Illinois Press, 2009), 147–148.

us—bring us to Jesus."[138] These spiritual experiences indelibly marked her sense of call.

Desire for Spiritual Experiences

The Christian life invites one to an intimate and life-giving love relationship with God, as depicted in Jesus's metaphor of the vine and the branches (John 15:1–17). Christians draw their life from God as the Spirit makes Christ real to the human heart and designs experiences to deepen that reality. The more one seeks God, the more one will find (Jer. 29:13; Matt. 7:7).

—DIANE J. CHANDLER

SPIRITUAL FORMATION

Defining Spiritual Formation

Christian formation is the lifelong process of development and growth, initiated and maintained by the loving actions of God, which form and mold the believer's understanding, volition, and character to reflect Christlike values and qualities. The process and goal of Christian spiritual formation concerns the believer's growth and maturation in living according to Jesus's commandments: "'Love the Lord your God with all your heart and with all your soul and with all your mind.' This is the first and greatest commandment. And the second is like it: 'Love your neighbor as yourself.' All the Law and the Prophets hang on these two commandments" (Matt. 22:37–40, NASB). St. Paul's Letter to the Galatians is specific in referring to the nature of formative spirituality in the Christian context: "My children, with whom I am again in labor until Christ is formed in you" (Gal. 4:19, NASB). From the process of formation in loving God and neighbor emerges service to God, family, faith community, and the wider contexts of life, ultimately expressing a missional vision that is global in its vision to share God's love with others. Historically, there have been various models of formation, depending on the particular Christian tradition, denomination, or group in which the model was developed. Many models are traditional, having existed for centuries, while others are emergent from contemporary theological views on the nature of Christian formation. The type of spirituality existing in an educational context impacts each student's journey of spiritual formation. The lifelong process of growth and maturity in Christ includes countless daily events, numerous personal challenges, difficulties, and spiritual trials, each of which provides opportunities for the development of Christlike character.

Spiritual formation, as a lifelong process, purposes to support and guide the Christian in maturing the mind, the emotions, and the volition, allowing continuing development in the ability to love and serve God and others. The formational process includes continuing development of one's loving relationship with God through Jesus Christ, development and maturity of Christian character, strengthening of authentic faith, and the expansion of one's knowledge in understanding God. It is important in educational contexts, as in all of life, to understand that one is not formed in Christ by self-effort, but by the action of God, who graciously initiates and continues the process of formation in faith, conformation to Christ's teachings, and transformation of character throughout all seasons of life.

Models of Formation

Numerous models of spiritual formation have emerged throughout Christian history, each developed according to the theology and doctrines of individual traditions and denominations. Involvement with both academy and church influences an individual's formation, conformation, and transformation in Christ. The discipline of worshipping God with the mind results in intellectual development and maturity and is a primary aspect of formation in educational contexts. But the development and maturing of intellectual abilities alone cannot complete the process of formation. The life of the mind does not develop in isolation, but requires the context of an interactive learning community, wherein the development of relationships and the collective practice of spiritual disciplines such as study, prayer, and worship are essential to an integrative experience in Christian formation.

St. Paul: A Trinitarian View of Spiritual Formation

St. Paul the apostle discusses with clarity the Trinitarian nature of formation in his letter to the Ephesians. He confirms that his prayers for the Ephesian Church are with faith "that the God of our Lord Jesus Christ, the Father of glory, may give to you a spirit of wisdom and of revelation in the knowledge of Him . . . that the eyes of your heart may be enlightened, so that you will know what is the hope of His calling, what are the riches of the glory of His inheritance in the saints, and what is the surpassing greatness of His power toward us who believe" (Eph. 1:17–19, NASB). Paul's letter continues this theme of formation in chapter 3, indicating his prayerful desire that God would grant the Ephesian believers "to be strengthened with power through His Spirit in the inner man, so that Christ may dwell in your hearts through faith; and that you, being rooted and grounded in love, may be able to comprehend with all the saints what is the breadth and length and height and depth, and to know the love

---

138. Mother Teresa, *Mother Teresa: Come Be My Light*, ed. Brian Kolodiejchuk (New York: Image, 2007), 99.

of Christ which surpasses knowledge, that you may be filled up to all the fullness of God" (Eph. 3:16–19, NASB). These two passages clearly affirm, in their description of spiritual formation, the Trinitarian nature of the initiation and ongoing action of the Father, the Son Jesus Christ, and the Holy Spirit in the lifelong process of the Christian's spiritual growth and maturity. They express God's gifts to the believer, and the believer's reception of wisdom, revelation, enlightenment, knowledge, hope, inheritance, strength, power, faith, and love as understood in the context of their relevance to the theme of spiritual formation. It is through the gracious actions of the Holy Trinity in the believer's life that he or she is "filled up to all the fullness of God." The two Ephesian passages are especially important in emphasizing the understanding that in all of life, including educational contexts, one is not formed by self-effort, but by the grace of God, who is the initiator of formation.

Formation and Discipleship

These same passages present spiritual formation as the gracious, loving movements and workings of God in an individual life, resulting in one who is formed according to the character of Christ. Discipleship is related to, but distinct from, spiritual formation in that the latter refers to God's actions in forming an individual's character, whereas the former defines one's volitional response to God's actions: the resultant operation and obedience of the human will, in responding to the teachings of scripture and to God's specific activity and guidance in one's life. Several of the gifts included in Paul's description, specifically wisdom, revelation, enlightenment, and knowledge, are values closely associated with education. Paul defines and frames these gifts or value in the context of spiritual formation as it applies to the inner life of the person of authentic faith. These gifts are evidence of an education that transcends the intellectual growth attained by academic study alone; they are God's gracious gifts for the heart and spirit, given by grace, not earned through academic study. However, God's gifts in forming the Christian and a student's efforts in academic study are not mutually exclusive; together, the gifts integrated with discipline of academic study are essential to the student's spiritual well-being and academic achievement. Understood together, they indicate that education in the Christian context requires God's supernatural gifts, received entirely by grace, not by self-effort, and the disciple's willing response to God's gifts, which includes applying oneself to the discipline of study. In a community where faith and learning are integrative, the invisible working of God in each human life supports and enriches the student's disciplined efforts to learn.

The Spiritual Life of the Academy

The life of the academy, at all age levels of learning, provides a context to potentially nurture spiritual formation, not only through students' study of courses and programs but by integrating academic pursuits with classic spiritual disciplines, including prayer and worship, both individual and corporate. Spiritual formation from a biblical perspective includes, among other disciplines, reading, study, memorization, and meditation in scripture. Christian faith-based learning institutions have included in their curricula, both historically and contemporarily, certain courses and/or practices involving various modes and formats for biblical study. In many schools, various spiritual disciplines, including scheduled chapels, or extracurricular activities that support students' formation and continuing growth in faith and character, are an essential part of daily life. This integration of intellectual pursuits and spiritual disciplines is traditional in faith-based academic contexts.

Understanding the Spiritual Needs of Students

In all educational settings, a teacher's spirituality exerts a profound influence on students' formation. The spirituality of the teacher—including his or her character, style of teaching, and ability to integrate course subject matter with spirituality to facilitate students' formation—is among those factors that determine students' spiritual growth. It is important for teachers to understand the stages of spiritual, psychological, relational, and physical growth related to their students' chronological ages. In boarding schools, the teacher's influence on students' formation may be greater due to the students' separation in distance from parents, home environment, and involvement in the family's faith community; therefore, the teacher and the academic community serve in loco parentis for students residing in on-campus housing.

In schools for special education students, including the physically disabled, it is important to realize that the process of spiritual formation must be sensitive in understanding the needs of each student and each special needs group. If a student's intellectual development is limited in some way, or physical or psychological disabilities present hearing, seeing, reading or writing, and relational concerns, teachers' preparation requires understanding the specific developmental needs of all categories of special students. A theology of teaching in special needs educational contexts requires teachers who understand that spiritual formation is not limited by disabilities, but can progress according to the unique personality, spirituality, and giftings of each student, as long as teachers are sensitive to and knowledgeable about the unique formation needs of every student. Judeo-Christian values emphasize respect for the dignity, worth, and potential of each student, no matter what the student's particular educational and formational challenges are. These same values emphasize the reality of God's love for each person, encourage the student's self-respect and sense of personal worth, and support the learner's sense that his or her life has importance and potential: the truth that a divine purpose exists for each life.

Integrating Christian Formation and Academic Goals

The integration of intellectual learning, spiritual discernment, and growth in character is possible when teachers design curriculum with the understanding that an integrative learning process has the potential to develop students in all three areas. Curriculum and methods of teaching that integrate the values of formational spirituality with all course subject matter allow students to understand that all of life, including academic pursuits, is more valuable and meaningful in producing growth and maturity when approached with a worshipful, prayerful attitude in the classroom and during small group and individual times of study. When instructors allow a classroom milieu that encourages openness to a prayerful and worshipful attitude in valuing God's gifts of knowledge, wisdom, discovery, and the whole process of learning, then the disciplines of mathematics, science, social studies, language study, history, philosophy, and other subjects become part of an integrative approach to spirituality in education. Rather than merely pietistic, including prayers that express silent devotion, thanksgiving, dedication of each class session to God; prayers for student needs; and intercessory prayers that unite class members in remembering the needs of the world creates an atmosphere of grace and peace in the classroom or other educational setting. Inclusion of spiritual disciplines appropriate to educational settings assists students in transitioning from other activities so they are fully attentive to the class session, focused on the learning process, and open to the ultimate goal of loving and serving God and neighbor in all areas of life. If appropriate to a school's particular theology of spiritual formation as pertains to educational settings, the pause for a silent or spoken benediction at the conclusion of each class session emphasizes the primacy of God and God's will in students' lives, thus contributing to their formation and continuing growth in Christian character. Glorifying God through the life of the mind is essential to an authentically Christian approach to education, in which the vocation of the learner or the scholar has the goal of loving and serving God and neighbor as actively expressed in academic life and in the eventual vocational service that results from academic study and practical training.

The Formational Goal of Christ-Centered Education

Disciplined responses to God's love may be expressed in educational settings by teachers and students understanding that growth and development in one's intellectual life first begin with spiritual formation. Christian formation in educational contexts includes practical academic disciplines that encourage the process of spiritual formation. The disciplines of classroom attendance, attentiveness to and respect for instructors, reading, individual research and study, completion of course assignments, and sharing in academically related discussions with other students and scholars are essential to academic life. Yet for these disciplines to influence growth in Christian character, they must be integrated with the spiritually formative disciplines of daily individual and corporate prayer and worship, which emerge from a student's commitment to a maturing relationship, in faith, with Jesus Christ.

The ultimate goal of Christian education as it relates to spiritual formation concerns loving God and neighbor to the degree that what is learned educationally will be applied by the learner to areas of vocation and mission with the goal of glorifying God and serving others in meaningful ways. Disciplined responses to God's love result in growth of character, and therefore the reception of knowledge and training achieved in education may be expressed in effective, enriching vocational pursuits that glorify God and positively impact the lives of others. Spiritual formation that has as its goal loving God and loving one's neighbor will lead to expressing that love in missional ways: the active expression of self-sacrificing love for others in meeting the needs of family, faith community, the wider community, and the world. The student who is formed in Christ, whose education is integrated with unconditional love for God and love for neighbor, will possess the motivation and the abilities to translate academic knowledge and skills gained through training to diverse contexts of life, wherein the countless needs of humanity await the compassion and care expressed through authentic Christian ministry and mission.

References and Resources

Ashbrook, Thomas R. 2009. *Mansions of the Heart: Exploring the Seven Stages of Spiritual Growth.* San Francisco: Jossey-Bass.

Balzer, Cary, and Ron Reed. 2012. *Building a Culture of Faith: University-wide Partnerships for Spiritual Formation.* Abilene, TX: Abilene Christian University Press.

Brown, Jeannine K., Carla M. Dahl, and Wendy Corbin Reuschling. 2011. *Becoming Whole and Holy: An Integrative Conversation about Christian Formation.* Grand Rapids, MI: Baker.

Conde-Frazier, Elizabeth, S. Steve Kang, and Gary A. Parrett. 2004. *A Many-Colored Kingdom: Multicultural Dynamics for Spiritual Formation.* Grand Rapids, MI: Baker Academic.

Estep, James R., and Jonathan H. Kim, eds. 2010. *Christian Formation: Integrating Theology and Human Development.* Nashville, TN: B & H Publishing.

Gangel, Kenneth O., and James C. Wilhoit. 1994. *The Christian Educator's Handbook on Spiritual Formation.* Grand Rapids, MI: Baker.

Greenman, Jeffrey P., and George Kalantzis, eds. 2010. *Life in the Spirit: Spiritual Formation in Theological Perspective.* Downers Grove, IL: InterVarsity Press.

Harrison, Nonna Vera. 2010. *God's Many-Splendored Image: Theological Anthropology for Christian Formation.* Grand Rapids, MI: Baker Academic.

Johnson, Suzanne. 1989. *Christian Spiritual Formation in the Church and Classroom.* Nashville, TN: Abingdon Press.

Murphy, Debra Dean. 2004. *Teaching That Transforms: Worship as the Heart of Christian Education.* Grand Rapids, MI: Brazos Press.

Newton, Gary C. 2004. *Growing Toward Spiritual Maturity.* Wheaton, IL: Crossway.

O'Connell, Timothy E. 1998. *Making Disciples: A Handbook of Christian Moral Formation.* New York: Crossroad Publishing.

Parent, Neil A. 2009. *A Concise Guide to Adult Faith Formation.* Notre Dame, IN: Ave Maria Press.

Parker, Palmer J. 1983. *To Know as We are Known: Education as a Spiritual Journey.* San Francisco: Harper & Row.

Thompson, Marjorie J. 1998. *Family the Forming Center: A Vision of the Role of Family in Christian Formation.* Nashville, TN: Upper Room.

Willard, Dallas. 1988. *The Spirit of the Disciplines. Understanding How God Changes Lives.* New York: HarperCollins.

Yust, Karen-Marie, and E. Byron Anderson. 2006. *Taught by God: Teaching and Spiritual Formation.* Atlanta, GA: Chalice Press.

—MARA LIEF CRABTREE

SPIRITUAL FRIENDSHIP AS CHRISTIAN PRACTICE

Background and Definition

Classical Greek philosophers such as Aristotle and Cicero devoted much attention to the role of friendship in creating a virtuous society. "To the Ancients, Friendship seemed the happiest and most fully human of all loves; the crown of life and the school of virtue."[139] Jesus Himself modeled friendship love and spoke of His disciples as "friends."[140] Aelred of Rievaulx highlighted this connection between Greek philosophy and Christianity in a treatise on spiritual friendship in AD 1164, thus providing a rationale for the virtue of friendship in Christian spirituality.[141] This philosophical and inspirational work holds foundational importance for Christian educators and spiritual writers who continue to speak of spirituality in terms of friendship with God.[142] Houston notes that "The flowering of friendship in our lives makes us more fully human. The deepening of love for a friend also shows us the infinitely greater possibilities we see for communion and union with God."[143] The rationale for investing in spiritual friendship is explained by Issler: "If we wish to keep on moving toward a full-orbed friendship with God, we must grow in our relationships with others within the body of Christ in order to stretch our emotional and social capacities for befriending the God who is love."[144]

Spiritual friendship can be defined as a close relationship between two Christians with the purpose of pursuing Christ as they pursue each other. "Ordinary friendships are generally characterized by intimacy, trust and mutual enjoyment of one another. Spiritual friends share those qualities, of course, but are also characterized by another element: spiritual friends actively help us pay attention to God."[145] Spiritual friendship provides a unique perspective on dynamics of intimacy, because it is a mutual relationship, in which love bridges power differentials and both parties maintain the relationship by choice. Therefore, friendship love specializes in mirroring the spiritual concepts of mutual trust and intimacy, the power of choice, and the necessity of safety.

Spiritual Friendship's Contribution to Spiritual Formation

In friendship love, one learns the powerful lesson of mutual trust and intimacy forged through self-disclosure. "Friendship, a reciprocal and mutual love, recognizes this truth about nature: that we need not only to give ourselves in love but also to receive love in return."[146] While charitable love gives with no expectation of return, it does not require mutual self-disclosure. Spiritual friendship is

---

139. C. S. Lewis, *The Four Loves* (New York: Harcourt, Brace & World, 1960), 87.

140. John 15:15.

141. Aelred of Rievaulx, *Spiritual Friendship*, trans. Lawrence C. Braceland (Collegeville, MN: The Liturgical Press, 2010).

142. See Klaus Issler, *Wasting Time with God* (Downers Grove, IL: InterVarsity Press, 2001).

143. James Houston, *The Love of God and Spiritual Friendship* (Portland, OR: Multnomah Press, 1983), xxxii.

144. Issler, *Wasting Time with God*, 39.

145. Mindy Caliguire, *Spiritual Friendship* (Downers Grove, IL: InterVarsity Press, 2007), 17.

146. Gilbert Meilaender, *Friendship: A Study in Theological Ethics* (Notre Dame, IN: University of Notre Dame Press, 1981), 4.

predicated upon mutual intimacy: "A friend is called the guardian of love or, as some prefer, the *guardian of the soul* itself. Why? Because it is proper for my friend to be the guardian of mutual love or of my very soul, that he may in loyal silence protect all the secrets of my spirit and may bear and endure according to his ability anything wicked he sees in my soul. For the friend will rejoice with my soul rejoicing, grieve with it grieving, and feel that everything that belongs to a friend belongs to himself."[147]

Through the special revelation of scripture, we see that God is a self-disclosing God, inviting humans into an intimate relationship.[148] The means of being self-disclosing in return is through spiritual friendship. Badhwar argues that while there are other sources of self-knowledge, "friendship does seem to have features that make it a privileged source of self-knowledge and even, perhaps necessary for *adequate* self-knowledge."[149] For spiritual growth, the investment of oneself in spiritual friendship promotes not only the goal of unity in the body of Christ, but also maturity in the bond of human-divine love.

The second area that spiritual friendship promotes is choice. Friendship, since it is not a legalized institution, requires only the formality of mutual choice.[150] The ontology of spiritual friendship deems that it cannot be forced onto anybody—it must be pursued by two interested and willing parties. The idea of mutual, ongoing volition is the only guarantee of deep friendship. The importance of choice in one's relational dynamic with God is foundational to the sanctification process: "Relationships, if they are valid and authentic ones, are characterized by a sense of partnership and mutuality. So it is also in the Divine-human relationship. In terms of Christian Spirituality, mutuality means that the grace of God, received through faith in Jesus Christ, must be received and acted upon by the human will."[151]

While God's love is freely given to all people (John 3:16), his friendship love is offered only to those who attach themselves to Jesus and are called His disciples.[152] The depth of friendship is predicated upon choice. The less interested party determines the level of intimacy experienced by both. God's desire for friendship with His people is at the mercy of individual choice to respond to Him. Choice in friendship love provides a window on an important spiritual reality, the power of choosing to love and be loved.

The last area that spiritual friendship models is safety. Safety allows for authenticity and a free exchange between two parties. As John says, "Perfect love casts out fear."[153] The experience of spiritual friendship allows earthly realities to mirror heavenly realities that are desired by God and for which humans were originally made. The work of the cross is highlighted in this friendship paradigm. God as the superior has condescended toward the inferior, making a way for love to flow between the two parties. What separated humankind from God—rebellion against God's rule and unrighteousness—is now no longer a barrier. By being in Christ, an individual now has Christ's righteousness imputed to his or her account.[154] The gap of righteous inequality has been bridged by the initiating work of Christ on the cross, and safety has been established. "Therefore, there is now no condemnation for those who are in Christ Jesus."[155] The incarnation, death, and resurrection of Jesus give us hope that God truly desires intimate friendship. "Let us then approach God's throne of grace with confidence, so that we may receive mercy and find grace to help us in our time of need."[156] Safety provides a new motivation behind compliance. Fear of punishment is exchanged for the joy of intimate relationship.

Spiritual friendship on the human level develops mental, emotional, and social paradigms for the dynamics that God enlists in service to greater ends in friendship with Himself, the true nature of progressive sanctification. Spiritual growth is what spiritual leaders and those in Christian education want to promote. In order to understand and encourage spiritual growth, spiritual friendship is seen as a spiritual discipline that promotes and enhances one's relationship with God. Deep, intimate spiritual friendships are an important investment of time and energy, for they can be working models through which God discloses Himself to His people.

—Christine Marie Hill

Spiritual Gifts

Spiritual gifts are sovereignly bestowed by the Holy Spirit "just as He wills" (1 Cor. 12:11) upon all who are born again through faith in Jesus Christ and therefore should play a vital role in all aspects of Christian education. The term "gifts" is a translation of the Greek *charismata*, derived from the root word *charis*, or grace. So spiritual gifts can be defined as gifts of God's special grace, given

---

147. Aelred of Rievaulx, *Spiritual Friendship*, 59.

148. 2 Peter 1:4.

149. N. Badhwar, *Friendship: A Philosophical Reader* (Ithaca, NY: Cornell University Press, 1993), 8.

150. D. Morrison, "Friendships in Religious Life—A Formational Issue," *Pastoral Counseling* 22, no. 1 (1987): 77–86.

151. J. Tyson, *Invitation to Christian Spirituality* (New York: Oxford University Press, 1999), 2.

152. John 15:1–15.

153. 1 John 4:18 (NIV).

154. 2 Corinthians 5:21.

155. Romans 8:1 (NIV).

156. Hebrews 4:16 (NIV).

in order that Christians can complete the tasks God has preordained for all believers (Eph. 2:10). Two Pauline passages provide the primary lists of 16 gifts. In Romans 12:6–8, the listed gifts are prophecy, service, teaching, exhortation, giving, leadership, and mercy. In 1 Corinthians 12:8–10, the list includes word of wisdom, word of knowledge, faith, gifts of healing, working of miracles, prophecy, discerning of spirits, tongues, and interpretation of tongues. Since these lists differ, and other passages indicate that other gifts might exist, they should not necessarily be considered comprehensive.[157] The passage in Corinthians also explains that although there are a variety of spiritual gifts, they are given by the same Spirit, and the same Lord, and the same God "who works all things in all persons" (1 Cor. 12:6) and are given to Christ's church for the common good of all (1 Cor. 12:7).

Sadly, children are all too often neglected when it comes to teaching about, and opportunities to grow in and exercise, spiritual gifts. Yet the understanding, encouragement, and management of these gifts are foundational for Christian teachers and learners. History reveals that children who are filled with the Holy Spirit can operate in spiritual gifts. For example, Sprange[158] describes such behavior during the 1740 Scottish revival. There was considerable evidence of the operation of spiritual gifts and power in many converted children for intensified service. Such impartation, even in children, enables the in-breaking of God's presence, transforms the receivers of it, impacts others bringing about growth in the church, glorifies God, and enhances personal witness to a powerful supernatural dimension. Therefore, Christian educators need to nurture the development of spiritual gifts in believing children. Children need to pursue such gifts from a motivation of love for God. They are to give attention to spiritual gifts and fruit in their lives. These young believers must understand their own particular foundational giftings, which will assist them in identifying the role God requires of them. They should be encouraged to seek infilling by the Spirit so that their foundational capabilities may be extended supernaturally to enable redemptive service. In fact, they must learn how to relate to the Spirit of Christ. They should seek the Holy Spirit's full resources and power for service and ministry.

The gift of teaching is central to much of Christian education, and spiritually gifted teachers greatly enhance the effectiveness of education. The difference between natural teaching ability and supernatural endowment seems to be that the spiritual gift of teaching sanctifies,

enhances, and channels natural abilities into the spiritual realm.[159] While the gift of teaching pertains directly to Christian education, each gift has a place within Christian education. For instance, a Christian public school teacher may or may not possess the spiritual gift of teaching, but may manifest the gift of service or exhortation in her classroom. While the Christian church is divided about which gifts are still dispensed by the Holy Spirit today, certainly all believers can agree that all Christians must learn what gift or gifts they possess and how best to bring glory to God through their use.

References and Resources

Erickson, M. J. 1985. *Christian Theology*. Grand Rapids, MI: Baker Book House.

Sprange, H. 2003. *Children in Revival*. Fearn, UK: Christian Focus Publications.

Zuck, R. 1988. "The Role of the Holy Spirit in Christian Teaching." In *The Christian Educator's Handbook on Teaching*. Kenneth O. Gangel and Howard G. Hendricks (eds.), 32–44. Wheaton, IL: Victor Books.

—James A. Swezey and Thyra Cameron

Spiritual Growth Research

Spiritual growth is a major purpose of Christian education, but it is rarely investigated. Different church traditions have their own understanding of spiritual growth, which encompasses growth in one's relationship to Christ, understanding and communicating one's faith, participation in Christian practices, and Christian service. Sociologically, spiritual growth encompasses the spiritual capital of a religious community, cognitive processes in developing a religious identity, religious messages and their contribution to growth, and the desired goals or outcomes (Gallagher and Newton 2009). As an indication of the breadth of this type of research, three projects are examined here by way of illustration.

Faith Maturity in Mainline Churches

As membership in mainline churches declined rapidly after the 1960s, Roehlkepartain (1993) surveyed more than 11,000 people in 561 such churches to examine the contribution of a church's educational ministry to faith maturity, which was defined along eight dimensions, comprising trust, experiencing the fruits of faith, nurturing faith in community, and advocating social change. This resulted in 36 statements, which respondents rated

---

157. M. J. Erickson, *Christian Theology* (Grand Rapids, MI: Baker Book House, 1985).

158. H. Sprange, *Children in Revival* (Fearn, UK: Christian Focus Publications, 2003).

159. R. Zuck, "The Role of the Holy Spirit in Christian Teaching," in *The Christian Educator's Handbook on Teaching* (Wheaton, IL: Victor Books, 1988), 32–44.

on a continuum from "never true" to "almost always true" about themselves.

The findings suggested how to increase denominational loyalty, how to create a warm and thinking church climate, how to lead an effective educational program, and how to motivate people to social action. The study concluded that an effective Christian education ministry increases loyalty to one's faith tradition and encourages living faith in a stimulating congregational atmosphere, thereby bringing new vitality to mainline churches.

Market-Oriented Research on Spiritual Growth

In 2004, the Willow Creek Community Church initiated "Reveal," a research project to study how well the church made disciples. Spiritual growth was defined as an increasing love for God and for other people. Based on methods of consumer research into brand loyalty and satisfaction, Reveal divided respondents into four segments (exploring Christ, growing in Christ, close to Christ, Christ-centered) and investigated their spiritual beliefs and attitudes, personal spiritual practices, participation in church activities, and Christian service. Participation in church activities was not found to lead to spiritual growth, while reflection on the Bible was always a growth factor. Reveal's online survey (over 50 sets of questions) is available for participating (and paying) churches, which receive several detailed church vitality reports over a five-year period to measure their progress. This contributes to a growing database, with 250,000 participants in more than 1,000 U.S. churches (Hawkins and Parkinson 2011).

Case Study Approach of Three Congregations

Osmer (2005) followed the method of practical theological inquiry to study the educational ministry of three congregations (in the United States, South Africa, and South Korea). He identified catechesis, exhortation, and discernment as Paul's three tasks of the teaching ministry. Then he analyzed each church's educational ministry through the framework of practice, curriculum, leadership, and pilgrimage. The analysis combined in-depth theological reflection with social scientific models, without attempting to be complete in analyzing each church. The study closed with various guidelines for evaluating and strengthening the church's three tasks of the teaching ministry.

Evaluation

The Reveal project offers the most sophisticated analysis of quantitative data, but with minimal theological and biblical reflection; its administration has become a franchise, which limits access to the method. Roehlkepartain's research shows more concern for social action, but its measuring instrument of only 36 questions lacks

sufficient depth for today's complex situations. Osmer's study offers the fullest theological and social scientific reflection on Christian education, providing a rich understanding of the practices involved; while his guidelines require harder work to implement, the theological richness of this study makes it much more than simply an evaluative tool for church leaders.

Conclusion

Research into spiritual growth remains a challenging task, but should be of vital interest to church educators and leaders wanting to understand and enhance the effectiveness of their educational ministry. Approaches vary from a reliance on extensive statistical research that promises scientific accuracy, to the sole reliance on the guidance of the Spirit and the study of scripture. The task of the Christian educator is to achieve a healthy, Spirit-filled balance between biblical and theological reflection and social scientific research, with awareness that "spiritual growth" is defined somewhat differently in each denomination and culture.

References and Resources

Gallagher, S. K., and C. Newton. 2009. "Defining Spiritual Growth: Congregations, Community, and Connectedness." *Sociology of Religion* 70 (3): 232–261.

Hawkins, G. L., and C. Parkinson. 2011. *Move: What 1,000 Churches Reveal about Spiritual Growth*. Grand Rapids, MI: Zondervan.

Osmer, R. R. 2005. *The Teaching Ministry of Congregations*. Louisville, KY: Westminster John Knox Press.

Roehlkepartain, E. C. 1993. *The Teaching Church: Moving Christian Education to Center Stage*. Nashville, TN: Abingdon Press.

—Jack Barentsen

SPIRITUAL LEARNING

Spirituality is often regarded as the heart of religion. It is what makes any religion truly religious. The term may be defined very broadly to cover "those attitudes, beliefs and practices which animate people's lives and help them to reach out towards super-sensible realities."[160] This suggests two functions or dimensions of spirituality: the horizontal and the vertical.

On *the human-horizontal level*, spirituality is a set of attitudes and values, with the beliefs and practices they undergird, that gives rise to and partly constitutes human

---

160. Gordon S. Wakefield, "Spirituality," in *A New Dictionary of Christian Theology*, ed. Alan Richardson and John Bowden (London: SCM Press, 1983), 549.

psychological well-being. This aspect in part maps onto James Fowler's concept of a universal human faith, as a disposition for and activity of creating or finding meaning, and knowing, valuing, and committing oneself to what one takes to be ultimately meaningful. (For Fowler, religious faith differs from other forms of faith only in having specifically religious objects: centers of value and power in which people believe and religious master stories by which they live.)[161] Donald Evans's "attitude-virtues" may be seen as the ideal affective components of this essentially human, yet salvific, spirituality. For Evans, basic trust, humility, self-acceptance, responsibility, self-commitment, friendliness, concern, and contemplation are intrinsically valuable states that are also the main constituents of human fulfillment. As pervasive stances for living, or "modes of being in the world," they are expressed in—and give rise to—both beliefs and worship in religion, and beliefs and conduct in ethics.[162]

Evans also recognizes the *vertical dimension* of spirituality, particularly in his claim that the attitude-virtues are necessary conditions for authentic religious experience, as our trust in God enables us to discern God.[163] John Hick acknowledges this dimension in his reference to a "fifth dimension of our nature which enables us to respond to a fifth dimension of the universe": "the transcendent within us" that answers to "the transcendent without."[164]

It is not unusual for something broadly comparable to the horizontal dimension of spirituality to be explicitly required as an aim of public education. As one might expect, this sometimes leads to controversy, for there is no neutral account of the learning outcomes that are of spiritual value. Christian education focuses on characteristically, if not always uniquely, *Christian* spiritual attitudes, values, beliefs, and practices, so as to help children (and the adults they will become) both to flourish as human beings as they cope with their life experiences and to relate to the Christlike God in religious experience, prayer, meditation, and worship. Inevitably, it is difficult to assess how effective such teaching and learning is in leading to human flourishing, and especially in realizing spirituality's vertical function.

References and Resources

Astin, Alexander W., Helen S. Astin, and Jennifer A. Lindholm. 2011. *Cultivating the Spirit: How College Can Enhance Students' Inner Lives*. San Francisco: John Wiley & Sons.

161. James W. Fowler, *Stages of Faith: The Psychology of Human Development and the Quest for Meaning* (San Francisco: Harper & Row, 1981), 276–277.
162. Donald Evans, *Struggle and Fulfillment: The Inner Dynamics of Religion and Morality* (Cleveland, OH, and New York: Collins, 1979), 1–16.
163. Ibid., 171, 179–184.
164. John Hick, *The Fifth Dimension: An Exploration of the Spiritual Realm* (Oxford: Oneworld, 1999), 2, 8.

Carr, David, and John Haldane, eds. 2003. *Spirituality, Philosophy and Education*. London and New York: RoutledgeFalmer.
Thatcher, Adrian, ed. 1999. *Spirituality and the Curriculum*. London: Geoffrey Chapman.
Wright, Andrew. 2000. *Spirituality and Education*. London and New York: RoutledgeFalmer.

—JEFF ASTLEY

SPIRITUAL STRENGTH

Spiritual strength derives from a relationship with Jesus Christ. By being attached to Christ, the life of God flows through the power of God's Spirit (John 15:1–8) to strengthen the human spirit. Spiritual strength defies external circumstances. For example, after the Amalekites destroyed Ziklag and captured the wives and children of David and his 600 men, David "found strength in the Lord his God" (1 Sam. 30:6b, NIV) to deal with his men's impending rebellion and to recapture all persons and plunder. The apostle Paul identified the spiritual battle between the forces of good and evil by exhorting the Ephesians to be strong in the Lord's power (Eph. 6:10), the source of spiritual strength (Eph. 1:19, 3:7, 17). Both illustrations highlight that spiritual strength comes not from self-assertion but rather from God.

Grace and Spiritual Strength

The Bible clarifies that spiritual strength results from God's grace through the Holy Spirit, given in response to human need, weakness, or request. The apostle Paul noted that the Spirit helps believers in their weakness (Rom. 8:26), in that God chooses the weak things of the world to expose the strong (1 Cor. 1:27), and weakness magnifies God's greatness when acknowledged in humility (2 Cor. 11:30). Paul delighted in weaknesses, knowing that when he was weak, then he was strong (2 Cor. 12:10), and that Christ, who was crucified in weakness, lives in power (2 Cor. 13:4).

Grace, therefore, is extended to those who are humble and dependent rather than proud and independent (James 4:6). Thus, spiritual strength is not based on one's spiritual gifting or ability, but rather on simple dependence upon God. As Paul exhorted Timothy, "Be strong in the grace that is in Christ Jesus" (2 Tim. 2:1). Grace is God's unmerited givingness that enables the believer to accomplish what would otherwise be impossible.

Conduits for Developing Spiritual Strength

God provides many opportunities to receive divine grace and build spiritual muscle. First, the discipleship and sanctification process provides opportunity to deepen attachment to and dependence upon Jesus as one's life source. Second, living within one's family and faith community provides opportunity for building spiritual strength. Believers are not meant to live in isolation, but rather to regularly encourage one other, which builds faith (Heb. 10:25).[165] Third, spiritual strength develops when believers encounter the unexpected, new experiences, and challenges. After enduring a 40-day fast and confrontation with the tempter (Matt. 4:1–11), Jesus demonstrated how testing and temptation fortify spiritual resolve. Spiritual strength develops when believers must change, stretch, get out of their comfort zones, and trust God for personal empowerment.

German theologian Dietrich Bonhoeffer (1906–1945) exemplified how living in authentic community during the Nazi occupation contributed to spiritually strengthening his underground seminary students.[166] Relationality exposes both one's strengths and weaknesses and drives us to seek God's grace, as spiritual writer Henri Nouwen (1932–1996) discovered when he became the pastor of L'Arche Daybreak community outside of Toronto, following a career in higher education.[167]

Fourth, spiritual strength develops through suffering (Heb. 2:10). Suffering stirs a cry for God's grace when available resources are inadequate. Writing on behalf of the Latin poor, Peruvian theologian Gustavo Gutiérrez describes how suffering fosters identification with the Lord Jesus.[168] Finally, engaging in spiritual practices, such as scripture reading, worship, and prayer, bolsters spiritual strength where God's Spirit extends love and grace.[169]

—Diane J. Chandler

Spirituality

Definition of Spirituality

The term *spirituality* conveys various meanings based on context.[170] At its widest lens, spirituality has come to mean what is most important in life, one's values, or connection to the transcendent. For Christians, however, spirituality refers to one's relationship with the Triune God, as informed by the scriptures and as directed by the Holy Spirit. The word *spirituality* derives from the Latin word *spiritualitas* and appears in the New Testament when the apostle Paul used the Greek words *pneuma* (Spirit of God) and *pneumatikos* (spiritual person). According to theologian Philip Sheldrake, *spiritual* connotes "what is under the influence of, or is a manifestation of, the Spirit of God."[171]

Foundations of Christian Spirituality

Christian spirituality is rooted in a relationship with Jesus Christ, who, as the Son of God, reconciles individuals to God the Father through redemption, as demonstrated through the cross.[172] Taking upon Himself the sin of the world, Jesus restores persons into right relationship with God (John 3:16). Being created in the image of God (Gen. 1:26–27), human persons are designed for relationship with God and one another. Early church father Augustine proclaimed, "you have made us and drawn us to yourself, and our heart is unquiet until it rests in you."[173] The Bible instructs believers to follow Jesus (Mark 1:17) and be like him (1 Cor. 4:16) in order to reflect God's divine character in obedience and holiness. The Holy Spirit enables believers to be transformed into Christ's image (2 Cor. 3:18).

At the heart of Christian spirituality is the reception and reciprocity of the love and grace of God that enables believers to reflect God's love and glory to others.[174] This entails a personal and growing relationship with Christ that is fostered through spiritual practices, as described below. Loving God with all one's heart, soul, mind, and strength (Mark 12:30) has holistic ramifications. All facets of life are to be engaged for God's glory, including one's attitudes, behaviors, relationships, and vocation. Through spiritual formation, the Holy Spirit outpours grace into believers' lives, enabling them to understand the scriptures, embrace God's dealings, and display the fruit of the Spirit (Gal. 5:22–23) in "continuous cycles of encounter, change, and action."[175] Engaging in spiritual practices positions believers for divine communion and spiritual transformation through encountering the living God.[176]

---

165. See James C. Wilhoit, *Spiritual Formation as If the Church Mattered: Growing in Christ through Community* (Grand Rapids, MI: Baker Academic, 2008).

166. Dietrich Bonhoeffer, *Life Together*, trans. John W. Doberstein (New York: Harper & Row, 1954).

167. The last 10 years of Henri J. M. Nouwen's life were spent at this L'Arche Daybreak community, where he ministered within a disabled community. Nouwen regularly helped Adam Arnett, one resident with severe disabilities, and found victory over his own severe depression. His book, *Adam God's Beloved* (Maryknoll, NY: Orbis, 1997), describes his own spiritual strengthening.

168. Gustavo Gutiérrez, *On Job: God-talk and the Suffering of the Innocent*, trans. Matthew J. O'Connell (Maryknoll, NY: Orbis, 1987). Also see Gutiérrez's book, *We Drink from Our Own Wells: The Spiritual Journey of a People*, 20th anniv. ed., trans. Matthew J. O'Connell (Maryknoll, NY: Orbis, 2003), esp. 114–121.

169. Several resources on Christian spiritual practices are available. Among the most noteworthy are Richard J. Foster, *Celebration of Discipline: The Path to Spiritual Growth*, 3rd ed. (New York: HarperSanFrancisco, 1988); and Dallas Willard, *The Spirit of the Disciplines: Understanding How God Changes Lives* (New York: HarperCollins, 1990).

170. Lucy Bregman, "Defining Spirituality: Multiple Uses and Murky Meanings of an Incredibly Popular Term," *Journal of Pastoral Care and Counseling* 58, no. 3 (2004): 157–168.

171. Philip Sheldrake, *Spirituality and History: Questions of Interpretation and Method* (Maryknoll, NY: Orbis, 1995), 42.

172. John R. Tyson, "Introduction: Invitation to Christian Spirituality," in *Invitation to Christian Spirituality: An Ecumenical Anthology*, ed. John R. Tyson (New York: Oxford University Press, 1999), 19.

173. Saint Augustine, *The Confessions*, 1.1.1., trans. Maria Boulding (Hyde Park, NY: New City Press, 1997), 39.

174. Bernard of Clairvaux, *On Loving God* (Kalamazoo, MI: Cistercian Publications, 1995).

175. Glen G. Scorgie, "Overview of Christian Spirituality," in *Dictionary of Christian Spirituality*, ed. Glen G. Scorgie (Grand Rapids, MI: Zondervan, 2011), 27–33, esp. 30.

176. See Dorothy C. Bass, ed., *Practicing Our Faith: A Way of Life for a Searching People* (San Francisco: Jossey-Bass, 1997); Richard J. Foster,

Christian Historical Traditions

Christian spirituality emerges not only from the biblical narrative, but also from Christian historical tradition, which provides rich models and resources for spiritual growth.[177] Reading the works of spiritual writers from the early church, the Middle Ages, the Reformation, and our contemporary era provides reflective opportunity to enjoy the diversity within the Christian heritage.[178] Unique expressions are reflected in various spiritualities: Anglican, Eastern Orthodox, Lutheran, Methodist, Presbyterian, Roman Catholic, Wesleyan, Pentecostal, charismatic, or other contemporary expressions.[179] Other factors influencing the expression of spirituality include one's background and culture, personality, and previous experiences.[180]

—DIANE J. CHANDLER

SPIRITUALITY IN CHRISTIAN EDUCATION

Understanding Spirituality

The term *spirituality* is often broadly applied in defining the nature of spiritual life and its related practices concerning numerous obsolete and existing world religions, belief systems, and ideology-based groups or sects. Specifically, the common definition of spirituality refers to one's understanding of God and of the nature and experience of one's relationship with God, during life on Earth and following life after death. In the context of Christian faith and life, spirituality defines the whole of one's spiritual life: its focus, theology, practices, relational nature, and expressions of personal giftings and vocation, as understood within the context of theologically accepted doctrines concerning the primary teachings of both Old and New Testament scriptures.

Education as Essential to Christian Spirituality

Christian education, in all of its diverse historical and contemporary models and contexts, cannot be separated from Christian spirituality. The church, biblically and historically, has viewed education as essential to faith and spiri-

tuality. Each model and context of education expresses a particular emphasis in spirituality, often nuanced in its understanding, due to each model's connection with a specific tradition, denomination, or other Christian religious group. Historically, Orthodox, Roman Catholic, and many Protestant denominations and nondenominational groups have developed educational opportunities for children, youth, and adults, each possessing a distinctive genre of Christian spirituality as expressed through the practices, goals, and processes of academic life.

Modeling Authentic Faith in Educational Contexts

Early leaders in Christian education recognized the need for teachers who were models of sound piety in their devotion to God, whose teaching and character expressed an authentic understanding and practice of the faith. This need for a consistent, enduring commitment to educational mission may explain why, historically and contemporarily, numerous religious orders, among other denominations and groups, have established various types of schools and colleges and developed philosophies and methodologies of education, expressing various aspects of Christian spirituality as connected to each order's particular tradition of worship and life in community. A prominent example of a faith community actively pursuing educational mission is the order of the Society of Jesus (the Jesuits), founded in 1540 by Spaniard Ignatius of Loyola. Members of the order established many schools and colleges, beginning in Europe and over centuries expanding to many regions of the globe. Jesuits are notable for their stringent training and commitment to excellence in the order's continuing ministry of service through education.

Spiritual Distinctives in Faith-Based Education

The primary distinction between secular education and education within a religious context is that in the latter system the student's attainment of spiritual knowledge, growth in faith formation, and development of moral character are of primary concern, and therefore curriculum addresses the knowledge essential to a particular course or program of study, while also integrating this knowledge with the course's relevance to the student's faith and character development. The curriculum, teaching methods, textbooks, assignments, and other necessities of the faith-based educational process are designed to serve the student's spirituality, not merely to impart academic knowledge or train in practical vocational skills.

The spirituality generally common in many Christian traditions, denominations, and groups involved in the ministry of education adheres to a theology of education based on three foci or points of convergence. These foci are primarily based on Jesus's commission to His

---

Celebration of Discipline: The Path to Spiritual Growth, 25th anniv. ed. (San Francisco: HarperSanFrancisco, 1998); James K. A. Smith, *Desiring the Kingdom: Worship, Worldview, and Cultural Formation* (Grand Rapids, MI: Baker Academic, 2009).

177. See Richard J. Foster, *Streams of Living Waters: Celebrating the Great Traditions of the Christian Faith* (New York: HarperOne, 1998).

178. See Richard J. Foster and Emilie Griffin, eds., *Spiritual Classics: Selected Readings for Individuals and Groups on the Twelve Spiritual Disciplines* (San Francisco: HarperSanFrancisco, 2000).

179. Sheldrake, *Spirituality and History*, 45–61.

180. For an African American perspective, see Howard Thurman, *For the Inward Journey: The Writings of Howard Thurman*, ed. Anne Spencer Thurman (San Diego: Harcourt, Brace, Jovanovich, 1984). For a Peruvian perspective, see Gustavo Gutiérrez, *We Drink from Our Own Wells: The Spiritual Journey of a People*, 20th anniv. ed. (Maryknoll, NY: Orbis, 2003).

disciples, but may also include general biblical principles of education and the specific theologies and traditions of each denomination or group. Biblically and historically, the spirituality of Christian education has maintained a perspective strongly supportive of both local and global missions. This sense of mission-centered spirituality in education is based on Jesus's post-resurrection commission to His disciples: "Go therefore and make disciples of all the nations, baptizing them in the name of the Father and the Son and the Holy Spirit, teaching them to observe all that I commanded you" (Matt. 28: 19–20). These three primary converging values of Jesus's commission—which resulted in making disciples and include the mission (1) to go to all nations, (2) to baptize new converts, and (3) to provide catechesis in the faith—are consistent with the unfolding historical development of education in Christian contexts.

Spirituality of the Learner

Both a student's spirituality and the collective spirituality of the institution in which education is received have strong influences on the learner's entire educational experience, including development of worldview, the manner in which curriculum is studied, the style of teaching, and teachers' expectations of learners. For example, if biblical studies, theology, history, philosophy, languages, and the classical mode of education are valued highly, a student's spirituality is shaped by the institution's values, and therefore the student also tends to highly value the importance of classical academic pursuits. If practical studies, including learning to read, write, and attain proficiency in commonly used mathematics, are valued highly, then the learner's spirituality will include a perspective that centers strongly on the importance of education's practicality in preparing the student for productivity in job areas or other life pursuits. Ideally, study in classical subjects should seek to provide the balanced education attained by learning the common subjects needed for proficiency in practical, daily life activities and routines. When this balance is provided, the spirituality of both student and school tends to become holistic in valuing the importance, within Christian faith, of an education designed to enrich every aspect of life, including academic study, missionary endeavors, diverse forms of ministry, and personal vocational pursuits.

References and Resources

Chickering, Arthur W., John C. Dalton, and Liesa Stamm. 2006. *Encouraging Authenticity and Spirituality in Higher Education.* San Francisco: Jossey-Bass.

Cunningham, Lawrence S., and Keith J. Egan. 1996. *Christian Spirituality: Themes from the Traditions.* Mahwah, NJ: Paulist Press.

De La Salle, John Baptist. 2004. *The Spirituality of Christian Education.* Edited by Carl Koch, Jeffrey Calligan, Jeffrey Gros, and Thomas H. Groome. Mahwah, NJ: Paulist Press.

James, Michael, Thomas Masters, and Amy Uelmen. 2010. *Education's Highest Aim: Teaching and Learning through a Spirituality of Communion.* Hyde Park, NY: New City Press.

Jones, Cheslyn, Geoffrey Wainwright, and Edward Arnold, SJ, eds. 1986. *The Study of Spirituality.* New York: Oxford University Press.

Markides, Kyriacos. 2012. *Inner River: A Pilgrimage to the Heart of Christian Spirituality.* New York: Random House.

Mursell, Gordon, gen. ed. 2001. *The Story of Christian Spirituality: Two Thousand Years from East to West.* Minneapolis, MN: Fortress Press.

Peterson, Eugene. 2005. *Christ Plays in Ten Thousand Places: A Conversation in Spiritual Theology.* Grand Rapids, MI: Eerdmans.

Rolheiser, Ronald. 1999. *The Holy Longing: The Search for a Christian Spirituality.* New York: Random House.

Schmidt, Richard. 2008. *God Seekers: Twenty Centuries of Christian Spiritualities.* Grand Rapids, MI: Eerdmans.

Scorgie, Glen G., Simon Chan, Gordon T. Smith, and James T. Smith. 2011. *Dictionary of Christian Spirituality.* Grand Rapids, MI: Zondervan.

Sittser, George L., and Eugene H. Patterson. 2007. *Water from a Deep Well: Christian Spirituality from Early Martyrs to Modern Missionaries.* Downers Grove, IL: InterVarsity Press.

Tisdale, Elizabeth J. 2003. *Exploring Spirituality and Culture in Adult and Higher Education.* San Francisco: Jossey-Bass.

Tyson, John R. 1999. *Invitation to Christian Spirituality: An Ecumenical Anthology.* New York: Oxford University Press.

—Mara Lief Crabtree

Spirituality, Men's

Men's spirituality refers to the way men live and fashion their lives according to their ideas of ultimate value. This shaping consists, in part, of the awakening process a man goes through in hopes of becoming more integrated with what he values most.[181] For a Christian man, spirituality entails patterning his own life to God as witnessed in Christ. Not only does this pursuit transform the individual man and the relationships, structures, and world with which he daily interacts, but the transformation also occurs by way of addressing intrapersonal, interpersonal, and systemic issues that prevent men from becoming more Christlike in thought, will, and action in the first place.

---

181. Sandra M. Schneiders, "The Study of Christian Spirituality: Contours and Dynamics of a Discipline," in *Minding the Spirit: The Study of Christian Spirituality,* ed. Elizabeth Dreyer and Mark S. Burrows (Baltimore, MD: Johns Hopkins University Press, 2005).

The spirituality of men is similar to women's spirituality in that they both consider Christianity's ultimate questions while also contemplating what it means to live *as* sexed bodies. Stemming from women's spirituality and feminist thought, men's spirituality looks holistically at the way a person's life is integrated to Christ. The phrase "we have bodies" carries with it a much different notion than "we are bodies," in that the former allows for a bifurcation of self from body, while the latter integrates the two. Rightly understood, men (and women) can know, and are only known, through the body; thus their spiritual experiences will be different.[182]

If a generalization can be made, men's spirituality differs from women's spirituality largely in the issues it addresses: a man's lived reality is different than a woman's, particularly in the spheres of culture, physiology, and social politics. The question "What does it mean to be a Christian man in today's world?" will yield different answers than the corresponding question posed to women, because a person's lived experience is influenced by the sociopolitically constructed world, which is fraught with deeply embedded meanings regarding the different sexes and gender expressions. Therefore, while contemporary women's spirituality has focused on issues such as power, embodiment, the gender of God, leadership, intersectionality, and human development, various men's spiritual movements have focused on some of these issues (power, integration of the whole self) while addressing others, including, but not limited to, sexuality, intimacy, interdependency, father wounding, and father hunger.

It should be noted that there has been a wide variety of approaches and philosophies along a conservative-progressive spectrum concerning men's spirituality. Kenneth Clatterbaugh describes eight men's movements that have developed since the second wave of feminism.[183] Three of these are important in understanding key foundational differences in men's spirituality, and other approaches to men's spirituality have their bearings in one of these. Groups such as the Promise Keepers comprise the conservative movement and view complementary gender roles as God-ordained and natural. A man's God-given role is to be the head of the household, though this is not meant to place more value on a man than on a woman. Rather, men have different gender roles than do women; men are to lead in selflessness, as Christ did with the church. Furthermore, men have innate traits such as decisiveness and strength, which tend naturally to

leadership. Proponents of this movement seek to reclaim their God-ordained role as servant leaders, and thus, the educating of men includes understanding what it means to be a Godly man, and its equivalent, a Godly woman, in an era that confuses the two. The mythopoetic movement, popular in the 1980s and 1990s and best known for its vision quests, sweat lodges, and drumming circles, is similar to the conservative movement in its essentialist ideology. Each man must re/discover the archetype male in order to come to a place of internal freedom and liberation. Robert Bly's *Iron John* is a foundational text for this movement and relies heavily on the themes of discovery, self-knowledge, and the loosing of the inner man. A third movement, profeminism, while acknowledging with the first two movements contemporary descriptions of masculinity (tough, rugged, powerful), rejects the essentialist underpinnings of the first two and argues that gender is a learned behavior. Therefore, the task for men's spirituality is to look critically at issues of power and gender construction and to address and rectify issues (e.g., violence) that are socially learned. When this occurs, the value of freedom from oppression is made possible for men, women, children, and creation in a patriarchal structure that has overly advantaged men.

References and Resources

Bartkowski, John P. 2004. *The Promise Keepers: Servants, Soldiers, and Godly Men*. New Brunswick, NJ: Rutgers.

Barzan, Robert, ed. 1995. *Sex and Spirit: Exploring Gay Men's Spirituality*. San Francisco: White Crane Press.

Boyd, Stephen B. 1997. *The Men We Long to Be: Beyond Lonely Warriors and Desperate Lovers*. Cleveland, OH: Pilgrim Press.

Boyd, Stephen B., W. Merle Longwood, and Mark W. Muesse, eds. 1996. *Redeeming Men: Religion and Masculinities*. Louisville, Ky: Westminster John Knox Press.

Clatterbaugh, Kenneth C. 1997. *Contemporary Perspectives on Masculinity: Men, Women, and Politics in Modern Society*. 2nd ed. Boulder, CO: Westview Press.

Claussen, Dane S., ed. 1999. *Standing on the Promises: The Promise Keepers and the Revival of Manhood*. Cleveland, OH: Pilgrim Press.

Conn, Joann Wolski, ed. 1986. *Women's Spirituality: Resources for Christian Development*. New York: Paulist Press.

Culbertson, Philip L. 1992. *New Adam: The Future of Masculine Spirituality*. Minneapolis, MN: Fortress Press.

Dittes, James E. 1985. *The Male Predicament: On Being a Man Today*. San Francisco: Harper & Row.

Eldredge, John. 2001. *Wild at Heart: Discovering the Passionate Soul of a Man*. Nashville, TN: Thomas Nelson.

Nelson, James B. 1988. *The Intimate Connection: Male Sexuality, Masculine Spirituality*. Philadelphia: Westminster Press.

---

182. James B. Nelson, *The Intimate Connection: Male Sexuality, Masculine Spirituality* (Philadelphia: Westminster Press, 1988).

183. Kenneth C. Clatterbaugh, *Contemporary Perspectives on Masculinity: Men, Women, and Politics in Modern Society*, 2nd ed. (Boulder, CO: Westview Press, 1997).

Piper, John, and Wayne A. Grudem, eds. 1991. *Recovering Biblical Manhood and Womanhood: A Response to Evangelical Feminism*. Wheaton, IL: Crossway Books.

Rohr, Richard. 2005. *From Wild Man to Wise Man: Reflections on Male Spirituality*. Cincinnati, OH: St. Anthony Messenger Press.

Schneiders, Sandra M. 2005. "The Study of Christian Spirituality: Contours and Dynamics of a Discipline." In *Minding the Spirit: The Study of Christian Spirituality*, edited by Elizabeth Dreyer and Mark S. Burrows, 5–24. Baltimore, MD: Johns Hopkins University Press.

—MARK CHUNG HEARN

SPIRITUALITY, SECULAR

During the 1970s and 1980s, Western culture experienced a significant epistemological shift from the modern era, with its scientific perspective characterized by an objective and rational certainty about truth. A growing sense of unrest and discontent with a world and reality defined solely by empirical, scientific data led to a recognition and acknowledgment that there is more to life than just its material aspects and that humanity also needs to devote attention to the aspects of reality that cannot be quantified. One significant consequence of this shift that exerted considerable influence on contemporary Western culture was an almost universal renewal of interest in spirituality.

Prior to this time, the term *spiritual* was typically reserved for discussions of religions, each defining and promoting a distinct kind of spirituality. However, beginning with the New Age movement in the 1970s and then continuing into a more popularly accepted usage in the general, broader population of Western civilization, the term *spirituality* has taken on a whole new meaning and significance in contemporary culture. In the last few decades of the 20th century, as well as the first decade of the 21st century, one finds a world in which everyone is spiritual in some sense or the other. However, that spirituality is no longer necessarily connected to or derived from a particular religious expression. In today's world, spirituality is not necessarily dependent upon religious participation for its growth and development, but flows from the innate and intrinsic resources of one's own humanity. To be human is to be spiritual.

Although one can find examples of interest in spirituality apart from organized religion long before the latter part of the 20th century (Sharp 2006), the rise of this phenomenon in Western culture, beginning in the 1970s, is unique. In its earlier forms, secular spirituality closely paralleled and was associated with the so-called New Age movement, especially that movement's fascination with the Eastern religions. Early manifestations, in which there was an attempt to gain the credibility that was often absent in New Age writings, included efforts by authors like Capra, Zukav, and de Riencourt to blend the spiritual dimensions of the Eastern religions with the empirical validity associated with the hard sciences. Books such as *The Tao of Physics* (Capra 1975), *The Dancing Wu Li Masters* (Zukav 1979), and *The Eye of Shiva* (de Riencourt 1981) endeavored to show that reality included more than just the empirical materiality and objective epistemology associated with modern science and the accepted metaphysics of the modern era. Whereas life's spiritual components had previously been relegated to a secondary epistemic level of "religious experience," spirituality was now being envisioned as an integral and necessary part of both life and reality.

As the movement grew in the 1980s, it quickly became associated with the rising environmental movement in the West. The movement developed and evolved throughout the next two decades, resulting in a sophisticated support network for those who are interested in developing "green spirituality." For example, the GreenSpirit website (www.greenspirit.org.uk) provides detailed instructions on how one can advertise home study groups, organize meetings, conduct guided meditations focusing on humans' relationship with the planet, invite special "Green" speakers, and even write one's own Green Ten Commandments or devise a Green grace to say before meals. Although akin to and probably influenced by the Christian movement of creation spirituality, the eco-spirituality associated with secular spirituality should not be considered a Christian expression. Nor should it be confused with legitimate Christian efforts to promote and encourage the biblically based ecological responsibilities that Christians have as "earth-keepers" and that also are sometimes identified within Christian contexts as "green spirituality" or "eco-spirituality."

Throughout the last decade of the 20th century and continuing into the first decade of the 21st, various publications have noted this spreading phenomenon and the fact that Western civilization has become a lot more spiritually minded than it had been a few decades earlier. John Naisbitt predicted that society would experience a sweeping revival of interest in spiritual matters that would enable it to be "reaffirming the spiritual in what has become a more balanced quest to better our lives and those of our neighbors" (Naisbitt and Aburdene 1990). In 1994, Eugene Taylor wrote that "an extraordinary amount of evidence suggests that our conception of spirituality is undergoing enormous change" and that this change represents nothing less than "a whole paradigm shift in society with the power to heal the mind-body split that has dominated western thinking for centuries." He observed that the shift represented "a spiritual awakening unprecedented in modern times," and that it was very much a nonreligious, popular phenomenon that "expresses itself in the most innovative, unexpected corners of secular culture" (Taylor 1994). During the 1990s, *Newsweek* magazine published 85 articles in which the word *spirituality* was included in the abstract, compared to only 38 similar articles published from 1975 through 1989. During the first decade of the new century the doubling continued, as 158 articles dealing with *spirituality* were published. These broader discussions included matters such as children's spirituality, pagan spirituality, the newfound alliance between science and spirituality, the spirituality of the Russian language, and the "phantasmagoric" aspects of the spiritual journey.

A common thread through all of these sources is the idea that spirituality is an innate aspect of what it means to be human. All humans, regardless of their religious background or lack thereof, are inherently spiritual. There are many ways to develop that part of one's humanity, and one must find the means that best suits one's own particular proclivities. Since spirituality is a basic human attribute, and there are still many who are not spiritual or who are in need of basic spiritual guidance, the basic human problem with respect to spirituality is ignorance, laziness, or indifference. The various forms of secular spirituality that have become manifest typically offer some self-help plan or program designed to awaken the dormant spiritual potential within.

The challenge for contemporary Christian education is that it can no longer assume a commonly understood definition of the word *spiritual* when discussing spiritual formation, spiritual maturity, and spiritual growth. The church has always faced the syncretistic incorporation of pagan ideas as it confronts the false belief systems of the world with the Gospel of Jesus Christ. So it is with secular spirituality. From a biblical perspective, the portion of humanity that is not spiritual is not seen as merely ignorant, lazy, or indifferent. The basic human problem is not spiritual insensibility; it is spiritual death, as Paul asserts in Ephesians 2:1–3.

References and Resources

Capra, Fritjof. 1975. *The Tao of Physics: An Exploration of the Parallels Between Modern Physics and Eastern Mysticism.* London: Wildwood House.

Cummings, Charles. 1989. "Exploring Eco-Spirituality." *Spirituality Today* 41 (1): 30–41 http://www.spiritualitytoday.org/spir2day/894113cummings.html.

de Riencourt, Amaury. 1981. *The Eye of Shiva: Eastern Mysticism and Science.* New York: Morrow.

Jones, Peter. 2010. *On Global Wizardry: Techniques of Pagan Spirituality and a Christian Response.* Escondido, CA: Main Entry Editions.

Naisbitt, John, and Patricia Aburdene. 1990. *Megatrends 2000: Ten New Directions for the 1990's.* New York: Morrow.

Sharp, Lynn. 2006. *Secular Spirituality: Reincarnation and Spiritism in Nineteenth-Century France.* Lanham, MD: Rowman & Littlefield.

Taylor, Eugene. 1994. "Desperately Seeking Spirituality." *Psychology Today* 27 (6): 54–63.

Zukav, Gary. 1979. *The Dancing Wu Li Masters: An Overview of the New Physics.* London: Rider/Hutchinson.

—John Lillis

SPIRITUALITY, WOMEN'S

Women's spirituality is Christian spirituality that seeks to integrate the "holy" into all of life, to engage God, and to find meaning in life. Yet it is also unique, addressing interests and issues particular to women, seeking to understand the feminine characteristics and nature of God as well as the masculine, ever-present nature of God. *Women's spirituality* can also refer to a larger body of practices that draws on many other historical forms, philosophies, and theologies. This article examines women's spirituality within the biblical, covenant community of believers, then outside the covenant community of believers and beyond the biblical texts, including historical examples for both. Finally, suggestions for developing biblical practices within a Christian education context are provided.

Christian Women's Spirituality

Women's spirituality is first and foremost Christian spirituality, yet the unique difference can be seen in Genesis 1:26, where both male and female are created in the image of God. Women's spirituality arises from the need to discover what it means to be created in God's image as a woman, a female and not a male. Proverbs 31:30 states: "Charm is deceptive, and beauty is fleeting; but a woman who fears the Lord is to be praised." It is set in the context of the "wife of noble character" (Prov. 31:10–31), where the description of a woman who fears the Lord is one who balances care for husband, home, family, the poor, and business investments. Her spirituality results in very practical applications. But for most women, the breadth and perfection of the Proverbs 31 woman seems unattainable and overwhelming when considered as a whole.

Specific practices of a biblical women's spirituality can be seen in some selected, representative biblical examples: (1) the worship of Miriam as she led the women in song and dance to celebrate the Exodus from Egypt

(Exod. 15:20); (2) the prophetesses of the OT, such as Deborah (Judg. 4), Hulda (2 Kings 22:14), and the prophetess of Noadiah (Neh. 6:14); (3) Anna in the New Testament, a prophetess and intercessor (Luke 3:36); (4) Dorcas, a doer of good works and a helper of the poor (Acts 9:36); and (5) Priscilla, who with her husband, Aquila, was a teacher and leader of house churches (Acts 19:18, 26; Rom. 16:3–4).

Women mystics like Hildegard of Bingen, Catherine of Siena, and Teresa of Avila were known as deeply spiritual women who devoted themselves to meditation and worship of God. Julian of Norwich, in some of her reflections, sought to understand and express the feminine nature of God the Father and Jesus the Christ, finding "mother" characteristics and expressions without losing sight of God as "father." Women who served in the community life of convents practiced a spirituality that was often both the hours of prayer and the ministry to the poor. Mother Teresa and her Missionaries of Charity are a modern-day example of this lifestyle.

Women's Spirituality Outside the Covenant Community

Among those beyond the biblical covenant communities, there are examples of women's spirituality in the biblical texts in such practices as fertility cults, witchcraft, and goddess worship. These focus on events in the life cycle of a woman, such as menstruation, pregnancy, birth, menopause, and mother-earth goddess. Witchcraft could be closely associated with any of these life phases, as they were important to a woman's value and survival. Examples can be seen in the Witch of Endor (1 Sam. 28:7), the fertility cults and child sacrifices, and the worship of the goddess Diana/Artemis in Ephesus (Acts 19:23–34).

These same practices appear throughout history in a variety of forms, such as the witches of Salem and various witch covens. Even today, women are seeking spiritual experiences and fulfillment in a wide variety of forms, such as Reiki; goddess spirituality; goddess worship (e.g., Sofia, Ahera, Shakti); sacred feminism; meditation groups; and secular feminism, womanist, feminist/ecofeminist, and mujerista theologies. Any of these practices can also include women from a wide variety of different faiths and practices, such as yoga, Buddhism, Hinduism, and Baha'i. The forms include prayer, silent meditation, meditation in nature, connecting and storytelling with others, 12-step programs, mystical practices, as well as commitments to social action, assisting the poor, and caring for the environment (Mother Earth). Activities can be in groups or as individuals and frequently focus on experiencing and feeling the presence of God or the Divine or seeking the "feminine-face-of-God." (A search of the Internet will produce a long list of opportunities to participate in any number of different experiences.)

Suggestions for Christian Education

The nature and experiences of Christian women as well as non-Christian women's spirituality have some areas of focus that are important for Christian education.

First, as seen in the various forms of women's spirituality, women have a deep inner sense and desire to know who they are in relation to God. While some will seek this knowledge through such experiences as goddess worship, meditation, and nature, Christian women have the opportunity to explore what it means to be created in the image of God along with their male counterparts (Gen. 1:26). A healthy self-image as a woman, created in God's image, is an important foundation. Women need models of godly, spiritual women like Ruth, Esther, Miriam, Deborah, and Priscilla. They can benefit from historical models like Hildegard of Bingen, Catherine of Siena, Teresa of Avila, Gladys Alyward, Amy Carmichael, Catherine Booth, and many other women committed to mission and ministry. Modern examples abound, including, but not limited to, Mother Teresa, Jackie Pullinger, and Heidi Baker.

Second, women's thought patterns often focus on cycles more than on linear progressions. The cycles of menstruation, child-bearing, motherhood, and menopause are all significant elements of women's lives that are in contrast to men's lives. Christian women's spirituality provides the opportunity to embrace these as God-given gifts, understanding changes and needs that vary in a given cycle.

Third, many spiritual practices and disciplines are common to both men and women, though women are frequently drawn to mystic practices, *lectio divina*, centered prayer, intercession, worship, and the prophetic, as well as acts of mercy and ministry. Understanding and practicing these within a safe Christian environment are important learning opportunities and experiences.

References and Resources

Julian of Norwich. 1978. *Showings*. Translated by Edmund Colledge and James Walsy. Edited by Richard J. Payne. The Classics of Western Spirituality. Mahwah, NJ: Paulist Press.

Rakoczy, Susan. 2011. "Trusting Experience: The Foundation of Feminist Spirituality." *Religion and Theology* 10: 32–55. doi: 10.1163/157430111X613656.

Schaaf, Kathe, Kay Lindahl, Kathleen S. Hurty, and Guo Cheen, eds. 2014. *Women, Spirituality and Transformative Leadership*. Woodstock, VT: SkyLight Paths.

Scorgie, Glen G, Simon Chan, Gordon T. Smith, and James D. Smith III, eds. 2011. *Dictionary of Christian Spirituality.* Grand Rapids, MI: Zondervan.

Sheldrake, Philip. 2013. *Spirituality: A Brief History.* 2nd ed. *Blackwell Brief Histories of Religion.* Chichester, UK: Wiley-Blackwell.

—ELIZABETH L. GLANVILLE

SPORTS AND PHYSICAL TRAINING

Christian education that seeks to form people holistically in faith, discipleship, and spiritual vibrancy does so by nurturing a person's intellectual, emotional, social, moral, *and* physical spheres. Tending to the physical sphere can be as simple as participating in leisure ("time free from all non-job duties")[184] and play ("an expressive activity done for its own sake").[185] Sports, however, are organized, competitive activities that encompass more intense physical exertions of the body.[186] Sports offer competition with nature and others, while play exudes communion with them.[187] Unlike play, sports stress focused training of the body toward an internal or external goal, whether the goal is self-discipline and self-awareness, technical mastery, team cohesion, or competitive victory. At other times, the goal is simply to enjoy God and one's self in physical action.[188] In the movie *Chariots of Fire* (1981), Eric Liddell, a Christian Olympic runner, asserts that when he runs, he feels God's pleasure.

These goals appear to protect sports and physical activity from question and criticism. Through Title IX, sports has been a major factor in rectifying gender discrimination. Christian colleges and universities ideologically approach sports as a context for further formation in Christian values.[189] Many contemporary churches even espouse the value of sports in building intracommunity relations and impacting evangelistic efforts, particularly among men.[190] These efforts are not unprecedented, as British and North American Christianity in the mid-1800s worked to make Christianity and the local church experience, on the whole, more muscularized and masculine-friendly, what Thomas Hughes and Charles Kingsley termed "muscular Christianity."[191] Moreover, beefing up the Christian image was an important reason to establish institutions such as the Young Men's Christian Association. Many men felt that Christianity and the church experience had become too effeminate and thus created a gender discrepancy among participants.

Yet in spite of the good that comes from sports, questions remain about the relationship between the Christian and sports. Does the competitiveness that drives people toward physical excellence go too far in extending physical training beyond healthy Christian values and practices? Has contemporary sports, with its valorization of violence, a win-at-all-costs mentality, persistent weekly commitments, and commodification into one of the largest modern industries,[192] become a powerful religion of its own, such that one wonders if Christian education and sports are compatible? The uncritical endorsement of sports by Christians who conflate theological triumphalism with sports and physical training has led Frank Deford to label this phenomenon "Sportianity."[193] Though on the whole, early Christians held favorable views of competitive sport, Tertullian of Carthage warned Christians about gathering at sporting arenas rife with barbarism, prostitution, gambling, and idolatrous worship.[194] In light of Tertullian's warning, the Christian educator and Christian institutions would do well to reconsider why and how they use sports and physical training in their educating and forming of Christian disciples.

References and Resources

Baker, William J. 2007. *Playing with God: Religion and Modern Sport.* Cambridge, MA: Harvard University Press.

Coakley, Jay J. 2007. *Sports in Society: Issues and Controversies.* 9th ed. Boston: McGraw-Hill Higher Education.

Garner, John, ed. 2003. *Recreation and Sports Ministry: Impacting Postmodern Culture.* Nashville, TN: Broadman & Holman.

Higgs, Robert J. 1995. *God in the Stadium: Sports and Religion in America.* Lexington: University Press of Kentucky.

Hoffman, Shirl J. 2010. *Good Game: Christianity and the Culture of Sports.* Waco, TX: Baylor University Press.

Johnston, Robert K. 1983. *The Christian at Play.* Grand Rapids, MI: Eerdmans.

Messner, Michael A. 2002. *Taking the Field: Women, Men, and Sports.* Minneapolis: University of Minnesota Press.

---

184. Robert K. Johnston, *The Christian at Play* (Grand Rapids, MI: Eerdmans, 1983), 12.

185. Jay J. Coakley, *Sports in Society: Issues and Controversies*, 9th ed. (Boston: McGraw-Hill Higher Education, 2007), 7.

186. Ibid., 6.

187. Robert J. Higgs, *God in the Stadium: Sports and Religion in America* (Lexington: University Press of Kentucky, 1995), 3.

188. Thomas Ryan, "Towards a Spirituality for Sports," in *Sport*, ed. Gregory Baum and John Coleman (Edinburgh: T and T Clark, 1989), 110–118.

189. Shirl J. Hoffman, *Good Game: Christianity and the Culture of Sports* (Waco, TX: Baylor University Press, 2010), 196.

190. John Garner, ed., *Recreation and Sports Ministry: Impacting Postmodern Culture* (Nashville, TN: Broadman & Holman, 2003); David Murrow, *Why Men Hate Going to Church* (Nashville, TN: Nelson Books, 2005).

191. Clifford Putney, *Muscular Christianity: Manhood and Sports in Protestant America, 1880–1920* (Cambridge, MA: Harvard University Press, 2003), 1.

192. Michael A Messner, *Taking the Field: Women, Men, and Sports* (Minneapolis: University of Minnesota Press, 2002), 76–90.

193. Hoffman, *Good Game*, 14.

194. William J. Baker, *Playing with God: Religion and Modern Sport* (Cambridge, MA: Harvard University Press, 2007), 11.

Murrow, David. 2005. *Why Men Hate Going to Church.* Nashville, TN: Nelson Books.

Putney, Clifford. 2003. *Muscular Christianity: Manhood and Sports in Protestant America, 1880–1920.* Cambridge, MA: Harvard University Press.

Ryan, Thomas. 1989. "Towards a Spirituality for Sports." In *Sport*, edited by Gregory Baum and John Coleman, 110–118. Edinburgh: T and T Clark.

—MARK CHUNG HEARN

SPURGEON, CHARLES HADDON

Charles Haddon Spurgeon (1834–1892) was a British Baptist pastor, devotional writer, and educator. His grandfather and father, both Independent pastors, influenced his early spiritual life. Converted at the age of 15, Charles became associated with the Baptists, preached his first sermon at 16, and began his first pastorate the following year. Though he was never ordained, his lack of formal theological education was overcome by his voracious reading of the Puritans and 18th-century evangelicals. He acknowledged George Whitefield as the model for his ministry. In 1854, Spurgeon's growing popularity brought him to the once prestigious but now declining New Park Street Chapel in London. Large crowds soon flocked to hear his simple biblical messages, which were known for their humor and vivid illustrations. Growing attendance eventually required the construction of the 6,000-seat Metropolitan Tabernacle. At an early age, Spurgeon suffered from kidney troubles, and he was plagued throughout his life by bouts of depression and gout. Adding to his stress, Susanna, his wife, became an invalid in 1868.

During his second year of ministry, Spurgeon began tutoring a young man in theology and the principles of preaching. This first student, soon joined by another, was the foundation for the Pastors' College (now Spurgeon's College) in 1856. Unlike theological institutions that were becoming more academic and required four years of training for ministry, Spurgeon's was limited initially to two years, though later expanded to three years. The goal was to produce pastors, not scholars, who could effectively preach the Gospel and thereby glorify God. This was not intended to ignore the proper balance of academics, but reflects Spurgeon's conviction that the college was to serve the church and that prayer and spiritual preparation were equally essential for faithful ministry. By the time of Surgeon's death, 863 men had been trained for the ministry. Students were taught a broad curriculum, including Bible, theology, philosophy, history of the church and the world, and English composition and style. Emphasis was placed on mastering Greek and Latin, and

when the student's ability permitted, Hebrew. Finances were never a problem, and tuition was never charged during Spurgeon's time. Students lived in the homes of the congregational members, both reducing costs and providing another dimension of pastoral formation by living with ordinary people. Students were attracted from around the globe, and many returned as missionaries abroad or planted new churches in England. Spurgeon's Friday afternoon lectures to the students reflect his combination of wit and practical application of scripture for daily ministry. These talks, published as *Lectures to My Students*, reveal a range of rich educational principles, including self-examination and the importance of self-knowledge, the nature of preaching and guidance for selecting the proper text, personal and private prayer, dealing with depression, and depending on the Holy Spirit.

Spurgeon's evangelical form of Calvinism was strongly experiential and yet pragmatic and welcomed the Evangelicalism of those from Armininian backgrounds, including John Wesley. Spurgeon had many critics, both of his preaching and his Pastors' College. His amazing success in the pulpit aroused both jealousy and contempt for attracting many from the middle and lower classes, though upper-class listeners were not completely absent. Known as the "people's pastor," Spurgeon was sensitive to the needs of everyday people. His far-ranging interests included founding an orphanage in 1867, outreach and publication ministries, and addressing the social ills of London. He denounced slavery in America and his popularity, especially in the South, suffered greatly as a result.

Spurgeon's legacy continues through his many books of commentaries (*The Treasury of David*, on the Psalms), his *Morning and Evening* devotional, and 63 volumes of sermons. Spurgeon's all-around ministry challenges contemporary educators and preachers to understand their listeners and recognize the importance of spiritual and intellectual needs. His flexible innovation and creative efforts to integrate the heart and mind were always at the service of ordinary people, not some exclusive minority, and directed to the building up of the body of the church.

References and Resources

Bebbington, David W. 1996. "Spurgeon and British Evangelical Theological Education." In *Theological Education in the Evangelical Tradition*, edited by D. G. Hart and R. Albert Mohler Jr., 217–234. Grand Rapids, MI: Baker Books.

Drummond, Lewis. 1992. *Spurgeon: Prince of Preachers.* Grand Rapids, MI: Kregal.

Kruppa, Patricia. 1982. *Charles Haddon Spurgeon: A Preacher's Progress.* New York: Garland.

Morden, Peter J. 2012. *Communion with Christ and His People: The Spirituality of C. H. Spurgeon.* Oxford: Regent Park College.

Randall, Ian M. 2005. *A School of the Prophets: A 150 Years of Spurgeon's College*. London: Spurgeon's College.

Randall, Ian M., and Charles H. Spurgeon. 1977. *Lectures to My Students*. Grand Rapids, MI: Baker Books.

—TOM SCHWANDA

ST. JOHN OF THE CROSS

Early Background and Education

St. John of the Cross was born Juan de Yepes in 1542 in Fontiveros, Spain.[195] He was born into a low-income family, which was made all the more impoverished when his father died when Juan was only seven years old. Juan was educated in a school run by the Jesuits, joined the Carmelite order, and finished his education at the University of Salamanca. At the age of 25, he began teaching and was ordained. Soon after, he and Teresa of Avila became acquainted. This proved to be an influential partnership as they sought to reform the Carmelite order.

The traditional Carmelites rejected the stricter version of the "Discalced" or barefoot Carmelites and put Juan in prison. For nine months, he was whipped and given meager rations of food, but it was in this prison that he wrote some of his most famous pieces of poetry. After escaping, Juan continued to provide leadership for the newly recognized Discalced Carmelites, despite his desire for solitude and contemplation. When conflict arose again, Juan was sent to a small community, as a form of exile, to try to squelch his influence over the order. He died on 14 December 1591.

Significant Contributions to Christian Education

St. John of the Cross articulated a theory of developmental spirituality that normalized disorientation and lack of spiritual passion, called the "dark night" of the soul, which helps spiritual leaders as they disciple others in the journey of faith.[196] He envisioned the spiritual life as a journey involving three movements: purgation, illumination, and union.[197] He saw the dark night of the soul as a sovereignly ordained experience of soul desolation, the absence of the felt presence of God, purging the soul of finite attachments:

> In the first verse, the soul sings of the path she followed as she left behind attachment to herself and to created

things. Through radical humility, she has died to her old self. She tells of living a new life—sweet and delicious—in love with God. The soul calls this going forth a "dark night," which is pure contemplation. The negation of the self and of all things unfolds passively within her.[198]

As a spiritual doctor, he saw a pattern in his "patients," that as people mature in Christ, instead of feeling closer to God in a continuous upward motion, many experience bouts of spiritual dryness and subsequently question God's love. In the dark night, the spiritual activities that used to bring spiritual comfort and consolation no longer bring a sense of relief and closeness. St. John argued that what feels like spiritual backsliding (a dark night of the soul) ends up being part of God's sovereign design for spiritual growth. The new work that God is doing is purgation through desolation. When the soul is in a state of desolation, one has the opportunity to grow in awareness of how much the soul is not attached to God nor has been conformed to Christ. While this is discouraging, and the soul resists painful self-awareness, if one will be open to God in the midst of the desolation, God will illumine the truth and grow the heart to love Him not for the pleasure's sake, which was the underlying motivation, but for the sake of love.

In desolation, one sees the truth of how spiritually impoverished the soul is even as a maturing Christian. Times of spiritual darkness purge the soul of destructive tendencies, known in St. John's tradition as capital vices (pride, gluttony, avarice, wrath, luxury, envy, and sloth). "Of these seven vices, St. John placed special emphasis in addressing the imperfections of spiritual gluttony. . . . As gluttony can be described as a habitual eating to excess, spiritual gluttony can also be described as an excessive seeking and consumption of spiritual consolation."[199] Spiritual gluttony is the use of spiritual activity for pleasure's sake, not for the sake of loving God. Desolation helps expose one's motives and what is really in the heart, for when pleasure is taken away, the soul is faced with the dilemma of continuing forward with love no matter the emotional results or abandoning the journey altogether. "God must purge the believer of these spiritual vices . . . as well as the habit of measuring the presence and favor of God by spiritual feelings or senses."[200] While this is a good work that God is doing, it does not feel good.

Therefore, for Christian educators, who provide varying levels of teaching and soul care to the church, the paradigm of the dark night of the soul provides an interpretive framework for God's activity and the believer's

---

195. Unless otherwise noted, all biographical information is from T. N. R. Rogers, introduction to *The Dark Night of the Soul* by St. John of the Cross (Mineola, NY: Dover Publications, 2003), v.

196. John Coe, "Musing on the Dark Night of the Soul: Insights from St. John of the Cross on a Developmental Spirituality," *Journal of Psychology and Theology* 28 (2000): 293–307.

197. David Wang, "Two Perspectives on Spiritual Dryness: Spiritual Desertion and the Dark Night of the Soul," *Journal of Spiritual Formation and Soul Care* 4 (2011), 27–42.

198. St. John of the Cross, *The Dark Night of the Soul*, trans. Mirabai Starr (New York: Riverhead Books, 2002), 33.

199. David Wang, "Two Perspectives," 33.

200. John Coe, "Musing on the Dark Night," 295.

response. John Coe summarizes the way a believer can cooperate with God in the dark night: (1) consider spiritual dryness a sign that God is at work, not necessarily of God's displeasure; (2) recognize that the role of the spiritual disciplines has changed, from that of being nourishing to that of mirroring what is really in the heart; (3) resist the temptation to fix yourself in the power of the self; (4) learn to expect and want nothing from God except what He wants to give; (5) resist making more of religious experience than what it actually is; (6) continue to faithfully practice the spiritual disciplines despite the lack of pleasure in doing them; and (7) allow God to get your attention to take an inward journey of letting the Spirit teach, attend to, pray for, and love your soul.[201] The dark night of the soul provides an important opportunity to be purged of autonomy and self-effort, which detract from authentic relationship with God. In caring for souls, Christian educators can help believers progress toward maturity by recognizing and embracing this purifying work of God in their lives.

Most Notable Publications

Spiritual Canticle
The Dark Night of the Soul

—CHRISTINE MARIE HILL

ST. MATTHEW, SCHOOL OF

According to the scholarly consensus, the Gospel of Matthew was written at the end of the first century AD by a Jewish-Christian author who belonged to a Christian community located in Syria.

Some scholars further assert that the Gospel of Matthew originated not only in the context of a church but also in the context of a school. The most important presentation of this position is found in Krister Stendahl's seminal study *The School of St. Matthew* (1954; 2nd ed. 1968). Following Ernst von Dobschütz's article "Matthew as Rabbi and Catechist" (German original 1928; English translation 1983), Stendahl considers the author of the Gospel a Jewish rabbi who had become a Christian teacher. The rabbinic/midrashic style of the Gospel of Matthew (cf. Goulder 1974) might indeed support the view that its author was a former rabbi. Whether he was a student of Rabbi Jochanan ben Zakkai (cf. von Dobschütz 1983), however, is less sure.

For Stendahl, the mention of a "scribe (*grammateus*) who has been trained for the kingdom of heaven" (Matt. 13:52) "may be a veiled reference to the author" (1954, 30). On the basis of this identification of the Matthean au-

thor, Stendahl then argues for the existence of a Matthean school: "If we owe the gospel to a converted rabbi, we must suppose that he was not working entirely alone, but that he took an active part in the life of the church where he lived and served. This is tantamount to saying that there was a school at work in the church of Matthew" (30).

Besides Matthew 13:52, the Gospel of Matthew also refers to Christian "scribes" (*grammateis*) in Matthew 23:34. The references to "scribes" (*grammateis*) in Matthew 7:29 and to the titles "rabbi" (*rabbi*) and "teacher" (*kathēgētēs*) in Matthew 23:8–10 might implicitly presuppose Christian scribes/rabbis. Further, the scribe (*grammateus*) mentioned in Matthew 8:19 might be considered a disciple of the Matthean Jesus (cf. Matt. 8:21). In view of the above Matthean material, it is thus possible that the author of the Gospel of Matthew was a scribe and/or that (other) Christian scribes belonged to his community.

However, since something like a formal Matthean school is mentioned in neither the Gospel of Matthew itself nor in any other early Christian document, it remains unclear if the teaching conducted in the Matthean community should be understood in terms of a school. While readily considering the Matthean author a teacher, the majority of scholars are skeptical about Stendahl's school hypothesis (cf. Cope 1976).

References and Resources

Cope, O. Lamar. 1976. *Matthew: A Scribe Trained for the Kingdom of Heaven*. The Catholic Biblical Quarterly Monograph Series 5. Washington, DC: The Catholic Biblical Association of America.

Dobschütz, Ernst von. 1983. "Matthew as Rabbi and Catechist." In *The Interpretation of Matthew*, edited by Graham Stanton, 19–29. Issues in Religion and Theology 3. Philadelphia: Fortress Press.

Goulder, M. D. 1974. *Midrash and Lection in Matthew*. The Speaker's Lectures in Biblical Studies 1969–71. London: SPCK.

Stendahl, Krister. 1954. *The School of St. Matthew and Its Use of the Old Testament*. Acta Seminarii Neotestamentici Upsaliensis 20. Lund: C. W. K. Gleerup.

—BORIS PASCHKE

ST. SERGIUS ORTHODOX INSTITUTE, PARIS

The St. Sergius Institute in Paris, France, is the oldest Orthodox theological school in Western Europe. It was founded by the Russian Metropolitan Eulogius in 1925 and functions under the aegis of the Academy of Paris and under the jurisdiction of the Russian Orthodox Exarchate in Western Europe in the Ecumenical Patriarchate. The church of the institute was founded a year

---

201. Ibid., 304–305.

before, on 18 July 1924, which happened to be the feast day of Saint Sergius of Radonej, so he became the patron saint of the church and the academic school. At first the parish and the school were intended for the education of the future priests who were to serve in the Russian Orthodox Church in Paris, for many Russian people came to France after the Russian Revolution in 1917.

St. Sergius is an institution of private higher education that provides pastoral training and teaching in sacred arts, liturgical singing, and iconography. Its mission is to form educated priests and laypeople to serve in the Orthodox Church and make known the Orthodox theology in the Western world, while contributing to the development of the ecumenical dialogue and to the religious and cultural life of Western and Eastern Christian countries.

Since its foundation, it has had a number of famous professors on the faculty, including Sergius Bulgakov, George Florovsky, Cyprien Kern, Vladimir Lossky, and Nicolas Afanassieff, and it has produced prestigious theologians like Olivier Clement, John Meyendorff, and Alexander Schmemann; bishops and priests; monks; iconographers; musicians; catechetical teachers; and missionaries who have served in the Orthodox Church all over the world. The institute participates in the spirit of international cooperation with other theological schools and in unity and collaboration with other autocephalous Orthodox Churches in France and other parts of Western Europe.

It offers a complete program of licentiate, master's, and doctoral degrees and is also a center of theological education by correspondence, made up of three stages of 12 subjects each. The theological education by correspondence was begun in 1981 and guided by Fr. John Breck. The regular program unfolds in three stages of nine subjects each.

The institute offers theological education for both Orthodox Christians and other people interested in Orthodoxy, as well as a number of scholarships. The educational program includes biblical studies; church history; dogmatic, liturgical, canonical, and pastoral theology; hagiology; iconography; patristic studies; and classical languages, as well as modern Greek, religious philosophy, and bioethics. Teaching is in the French language.

The St. Sergius Institute organizes conferences and colloquies throughout the academic year, as well as annual "Liturgical Week" sessions. It has a library of more than 35,000 books in various languages, journals, and its own journals, *La Pensée orthodoxe* and *Les nouvelles de Saint-Serge*; a printing press; a bookstore; and an Internet network of its own, through which it makes available information on Orthodox Christian theology and education around the world. The parish associated with the institute has the mission of sustaining the liturgical and social life of the faithful, social work, catechetical teaching, and evangelization.

—ANCA POPESCU

ST. VLADIMIR'S ORTHODOX THEOLOGICAL SEMINARY

St. Vladimir's Orthodox Theological Seminary was founded in 1938, resuming the work of Orthodox theological education in the United States that had begun with the school founded by Archbishop Tikhon (later Patriarch of Moscow; d. 1925) in Minneapolis in 1905 and transferred to Tenafly, New Jersey, in 1913 as St. Platon's Orthodox Theological Seminary, but which had closed in 1923 in the aftermath of the Russian Revolution. The establishment of a seminary was discussed at the 1937 "Sobor" (council) of the "Russian Metropolia" (later known as the Orthodox Church in America), and in the following year St. Vladimir's Orthodox Theological Seminary was founded. Initially located in the parish house of Christ the Savior Church on East 121st Street in Manhattan, in 1939 the school took up temporary quarters on the campus of General Theological Seminary and then moved to apartments on West 123rd Street in Manhattan, where it benefited from a connection with Columbia and Union Theological Seminary. Following World War II, a number of renowned scholars emigrated from Europe to join the faculty, most notably Fr. Georges Florovsky (dean 1949–1955) from St. Sergius Institute in Paris. As a result, the seminary was granted a provisional charter by the Board of Regents of the University of the State of New York in 1948. The arrival of further scholars from St. Sergius, especially Fr. Alexander Schmemann (dean 1962–1983) in 1951 and Fr. John Meyendorff (dean 1983–1992) in 1952, enabled the seminary to grow further, and in 1953 it was granted an absolute charter. In 1963, the seminary moved to its current location in Crestwood, New York. The seminary became an associate member of the Association of Theological Schools in 1966 and was fully accredited in 1973. In 1967, the Board of Regents of the University of the State of New York granted the seminary the authority to award the bachelor of divinity (now the master of divinity), and then the master of theology in 1970, master of arts in 1985, and doctor of ministry in 1988. In 2013, the seminary relaunched the doctor of ministry as a "hybrid" course, for the first time using online distance education. After the deanships of Fr. Thomas Hopko (1992–2002), the first American-born dean, and Fr. John Erickson (2002–2007), the first convert to Orthodoxy to become dean, the board of trustees restructured the governance of the school to include a chancellor, Fr. Chad Hatfield (2007–), as well as the dean, Fr. John Behr (2002–), both working alongside the executive chair of the board of trustees. From the beginning, the seminary has understood its mission to be to serve Christ, His church, and the world, by providing theological education of the highest academic, pastoral, and spiritual caliber; by fostering theological research and scholarship able to meet the highest and hardest challenges of the modern world; and by promoting inter-Orthodox cooperation by serving all the various Orthodox communities in the United States, acting as a catalyst for their eventual unification, and worldwide.

—JOHN BEHR

STAGES OF FAITH

Faith was the focus of James Fowler's research and writing for more than three decades, and he is probably best known for identifying the stages of faith development. Fowler (1981) offers Christian educators additional significant insights into the dynamics of faith. Understanding his perspectives on faith aids in understanding the stages of faith.

Understanding Faith

First, Fowler claims that faith is a universal human capacity, present from birth. The environment around the child significantly influences how that faith potential is activated and formed. The child's faith may be formed as religious faith—for example, Christian, Buddhist, or Muslim—or as faith in an ideology, such as communism or materialism. However, the human environment is not the only influence on the faith of the child. The apostle Paul states in Romans 1:20 that "God's invisible qualities . . . have been clearly seen, being understood from what has been made" (TNIV). Young children sense and respond to the transcendent around them in the world, and through grace, God's Spirit seeks the response of the child's heart.

Second, Fowler defines faith as a "dynamic pattern of trust in and loyalty to

1. a center or centers of value;
2. images and realities of power; [and]
3. a shared master story or core story." (1991, 100–101)

By "center of value," Fowler means whatever grasps one's love and devotion and influences all of life. Images of power are the things humans depend on for security. A master story is one a person or group believes to be the true story of how the world works, what is important and powerful. It should provide images of goodness and

God (Fowler 1991, 100–102). Various religions have different centers of value, images of power, and master stories, but these are the focus of trust and loyalty in any faith tradition.

Fowler also sees faith as both maturation and development and recentering and transformation in Christ (1991, 94). Faith matures and develops as a person interacts with the world around him or her, learns and makes changes to handle new life situations. But this responsive maturation is not enough; there is also an essential spiritual element. In the changing seasons, maturing faith needs recentering on God, God's values and ways, allowing Christ to continue inner transformation.

Fowler values the transforming work of God; however, the stages of faith he identified look at the maturing and developing side of faith. They do not tell the whole story, but do provide a helpful picture of the faith process.[202]

Stages of Faith

Over more than 18 years, Fowler and his colleagues interviewed more than 500 children, youth, and adults, listening to them talk about their faith. From the in-depth analysis of those interview transcripts, Fowler identified seven stages of faith, beginning in infancy and continuing throughout life. His understanding was also informed by the research of Erik Erikson, Jean Piaget, and Lawrence Kohlberg and their understandings of psychosocial, cognitive, and moral development.

Stage 1: Primal Faith

Primal faith[203] develops before language and is something the infant "knows" emotionally. From birth the baby begins to discern whether or not the new world and the people in it can be trusted. In relationship with parents and other significant adults, through the normal activities of life, babies learn to trust or to mistrust. Learning to trust parents and others provides the foundation for trust in God. Not developing trust on the human level may hinder the child's ability to trust God later in life (Fowler 1991, 102–103).

Stage 2: Intuitive-Projective Faith

Stage 2 faith[204] begins to develop as the child is acquiring language and the imagination is active. Children use imagination, without the control of logical thought, to help make sense of their world and often have difficulty distinguishing between fact and fantasy. This is the time

---

202. In describing the stages of faith, Fowler initially used language that could apply to faith in any religion or ideology. But in this article the language used describes faith within Christian traditions.

203. *Primal*: first, unconsciously formed.

204. *Intuitive*: knowing or learning something without conscious use of reason. *Projective*: indicative of unconscious traits.

when children begin to construct their first image or intuitive understanding of God. Researchers have found that children, with or without the instruction of adults, begin to form an image of God (Fowler 1981, 129). That image is powerfully influenced by the child's experience with parents and other adults. The characteristics of these adults tend to be attributed to God.

Stories, gestures, symbols, and rituals grasp the imaginations of young children, then combine with their perceptions and feelings to create long-lasting faith images. In stories, young children intuitively grasp elements of deep truth and feelings. The stories they hear and the rituals they experience in the preschool years are important to their faith development. During this period, children are awakening to a sense of what is right or wrong and begin discovering moral standards (Fowler 1991, 103–104).

Stage 3: Mythic-Literal Faith

Children in elementary school usually demonstrate stage 3 faith.[205] They are able to use logical thinking in concrete ways, and they know what is real and what is make-believe. They become aware of the perspectives of others and can begin to consider God's point of view on a situation (Fowler 1981, 136).

Children in the mythic-literal phase love stories, and their faith grows as they enter and experience stories. In the biblical narrative, they see God in action and meet the heroes of the faith. It is in stories that children discover meaning. The meanings they draw from these stories are concrete, and their picture of God is anthropomorphic, but significant to them at this point in the faith journey (Fowler 1981, 136, 139, 147; 1991, 105).

Stage 4: Synthetic-Conventional Faith

The faith of stage 4[206] usually begins to form in early adolescence as young people struggle to form their identity by integrating what they learn about themselves from their many relationships and roles (Fowler 1991, 107–108).

A synthetic-conventional faith requires the forming of a set of beliefs, values, and commitments. These take form when the young person participates in a community that articulates and lives his or her beliefs, values, and commitments in such a way that the adolescent is drawn to embrace them. Adolescents long for relationship with a God who knows, accepts, and confirms them, who is a companion and guide (Fowler 1981, 153, 156). A vital,

deeply felt stage 4 faith is a critical foundation for ongoing faith formation (Fowler 1991, 108).

Stage 5: Individuative-Reflective Faith

The development of stage 5 faith[207] begins when one's faith is seriously questioned. This often occurs when young people move out of the community that nurtured them and are surrounded by people who hold beliefs and values different from theirs (Fowler 1981, 178). This leads to an examination of the values and beliefs they may have embraced without question. The young person may abandon the faith, if no one is there to provide support in this time of questioning. However, serious reflection can lead to deeper understanding and the reclaiming of the values and beliefs that withstand the test of questioning. This examination and reflection leads the young person to choose and commit himself or herself to these values, beliefs, and the way of life that lives them out. Individuated-reflective faith is an "owned faith" (Westerhoff 2000, 95–96; Fowler 1991, 109).

Stage 6: Conjunctive Faith

The move to conjunctive faith[208] begins when one becomes aware of the many sides of issues, when one discovers elements of value in both sides of an argument. It involves looking critically at one's own and other traditions to understand them more fully (Fowler 1981, 185; 1991, 111).

Conjunctive faith is ready to interact with persons from different traditions and expects to discover truth in those traditions that complement or correct its own understanding of truth (1981, 186). Fowler asserts that in conjunctive faith "symbolic power is reunited with conceptual meaning" (1981, 197). After having drawn conceptual meaning from symbols, liturgy, and the biblical text, people want to set conceptualization aside for a time and just experience the symbols and rituals, or spend time in the biblical narrative being open to how God will meet them and transform them. Rather than reading the text, as they have in the past, they allow the text to read them (Fowler 1991, 113).

Stage 7: Universalizing Faith

Universalizing faith[209] is a "completion of a process of decentering from self that began in childhood." People who exemplify stage 7 faith "identify with and participate in the perspective of God so fully that they see and value through God rather than self" (Fowler 1991,

---

205. *Mythic*: coming from the stories of a tradition. *Literal*: taking words at face value.

206. *Synthetic*: synthesized, made by putting things together. *Conventional*: coming from the religious faith of an important community and tradition.

207. *Individuative*: personally owned. *Reflective*: capable of reflecting.

208. *Conjunctive*: joined together, combined.

209. *Universalizing*: caring for all God's children.

113). They yield totally and are open to God. Although they realize they are loved by God, the self is no longer the center of their lives. As they see the world through God's eyes, they are painfully aware of the divisions and injustice in the human family and spend themselves for the transformation of God's desires in the world (Fowler 1981, 199–200).

Fowler says that stage 7 is not something that people set out to attain. He observes that persons of universalizing faith seem to have been "selected by the great Blacksmith of history, heated in the fires of turmoil and trouble and then hammered into usable shape on the hard anvil of conflict and struggle" (Fowler 1981, 202).

References and Resources

Fowler, J. W. 1981. *Stages of Faith: The Psychology of Human Development and the Quest for Meaning.* San Francisco: Harper & Row.

———. 1991. *Weaving the New Creation: Stages of Faith and the Public Church.* San Francisco: Harper.

Holy Bible, The: Today's New International Version (TNIV). 2001. Grand Rapids, MI: Zondervan.

Westerhoff, J. H., III. 2000. *Will Our Children Have Faith?* Rev. ed. New York: Morehouse Publishing.

—Catherine M. Stonehouse

STOKES, OLIVIA PEARL

Olivia Pearl Stokes (1916–2002), an African American, was born on 11 January 1916 in Middlesex, North Carolina. She was the second of four children born to William Harmon and Bessie Thomas Stokes. Her father was a gentleman farmer, and her mother was a schoolteacher. She grew up in a very tight-knit family and community, where the church was the focal point of social life for the black citizens. In fact, Olivia's grandfather donated the land for the building of Stokes Chapel, a Baptist congregation. Today it is a historical landmark.

Stokes began her education in Middlesex, but upon the death of her father, her mother took the family and migrated to New York City. With the move to Harlem, the family affiliated with Abyssinian Baptist Church, where Dr. Adam Clayton Powell was the senior pastor and Dr. Horacio Hill was the director of religious education.

Olivia's education continued in the New York Public School system, and eventually she was admitted to the prestigious Hunter College High School, a public school for gifted students. However, she transferred to Wadleigh High School upon the death of her stepfather. There she pursued secretarial studies. She began her higher education at City College of New York and received her BA degree in education in 1947 from New York University. The following year, she completed a master's degree in religious education. Stokes pursued and finished her doctoral studies in 1952 at Teachers College Columbia University, the first African American female to complete the terminal degree in the field of religious education.

The church had been the center of her life from early childhood and remained a focal point throughout her life. In 1941, she became the associate director of the Baptist Educational Center, which offered training in leadership for 157 black churches. While employed there, she also worked for the New York State Christian Youth Council as well as the United Christian Youth Movement. These experiences contributed to her doctoral studies, and her dissertation was entitled "An Evaluation of the Leadership Training Program Offered by the Baptist Educational Center, Harlem, New York, with Recommendations for Its Improvement."

Immediately after receiving her doctorate, Stokes became the director of religious education for the Massachusetts Council of Churches, in 1953, holding the position for nearly 14 years. She then became the associate director of urban education for the National Council of Churches of Christ in the Department of Educational Development. There she helped to develop the Black Curriculum Resource Center.

In 1973, Stokes accepted a faculty position at Herbert H. Lehmann College of the City University of New York, where she was appointed associate professor of education and chaired the development of the Multiethnic, Multicultural Teacher Education Program. In addition to her professional educational work, she had a strong interest in the African continent. She hoped to change the Africans' image and perception of North Americans through a revision of textbooks. Stokes led many tours to the African continent as well as to Israel. As a result of these trips, she wrote two children's books: *Why the Spider Lives in Corners* and *The Beauty of Being Black.* During this period she developed a graduate teacher education study abroad-ethnic heritage-African program in five Nigerian universities. In regard to Christian education, she wanted to show that African churches were growing and a part of the culture, grooming their own indigenous leaders.

Scholars have noted her contributions to the black church experience, especially in leadership; interpreting the Gospel for addressing everyday problems; education to address the problems and issues of black people and the inculcation of faith in the next generation of black Christians; women's contributions as well as their plight; how Christian education in the African American church (as well as in other churches) can benefit from black theology because it encourages critical thinking; appreciation of blackness; and action for liberation and social change.[210]

Olivia Pearl Stokes died in May 2002.

References and Resources

Stokes, Olivia Pearl. 1953. "An Evaluation of the Leadership Training Program Offered by the Baptist Educational Center, Harlem, New York, with Recommendations for its Improvement." EdD diss., Teachers College Columbia University.

——. 1957. *Sojourner Truth: God's Fighter for Freedom and Justice*. New York: New York Club, National Association of Negro Business and Professional Women's Clubs.

——. 1971a. *The Beauty of Being Black: Folktales, Poems and Art from Africa*. New York: Friendship Press.

——. 1971b. *Emerging Role of African Women*. New York: Friendship Press.

——. 1971c. *Why the Spider Lives in Corners: African Facts and Fun*. New York: Friendship Press.

——. 1973. *The Educational Role of Black Churches in the 70s and 80s*. New Roads to faith: Black Perspectives in Church Education. Philadelphia: United Church Press, Joint Educational Development.

—NELSON T. STROBERT

STONY BROOK SCHOOL

The Stony Brook School in Stony Brook, New York, was founded in 1922 in reaction against the theological "modernism" overtaking American religious institutions at the beginning of the 20th century. In 1909, a group of leading Presbyterian pastors formed the Stony Brook Assembly and began holding summer Bible conferences on Long Island to counter the perceived apostasy at the Northfield Conferences after Dwight L. Moody's death (Lockerbie 2007, 313).

After the end of World War I, the Stony Brook Assembly recruited a Harvard University graduate student named Frank E. Gaebelein (1899–1983) to be founding headmaster of a rigorously academic college-preparatory school for boys, whose curriculum would be centered on the Lordship of Jesus Christ and the truth of scripture—an anomaly then and an even greater rarity now, nearly a century later (Lockerbie 1972, 22–116).

Although small and new, the Stony Brook School sought from the outset to establish itself as a contender among the leading northeastern boarding schools. Frank Gaebelein took advantage of his board members' connections and his own evangelical pedigree as the son

of Arno C. Gaebelein. Stony Brook's first graduate, in 1923, was accepted at Princeton University; since then, Stony Brook has always encouraged its graduates to aspire to the highest level of university education. Stony Brook's reputation was enhanced throughout its first 50 years by its unique place among American boarding and day schools. Unlike most of its peers in American college-preparatory schooling, the Stony Brook School has never wavered from its original commitment to the centrality of biblical authority and the Person of Jesus Christ. While the Stony Brook motto, "Character Before Career," is widely known (Lockerbie 1972, 32), the school's chapel building gives a biblical context to character-building: Over the entry an inscription reads, "Thy Word Is Truth." On the pulpit facing the speaker is this reminder, "Sir, We Would See Jesus."

During his 41 years as headmaster, Gaebelein's school grew to some 200 students from 18 states and 15 foreign countries, and he was influential in helping to form other schools that became members of the thriving Christian day-school movement.

Under his son, Donn Medd Gaebelein, who succeeded him as headmaster (1963–1976), the school recruited in earnest African American students, faculty, and board members; Advanced Placement program courses were introduced; an honor code was implemented; and the teaching of Bible and English literature/composition was combined in grades 11 and 12—not to diminish the significance of textual study of the scriptures, but to heighten the awareness of both students and teachers to issues of worldview and biblical application as portrayed in literary and dramatic texts. The school became coeducational in 1971.

Subsequent headmasters Karl E. Soderstrom, Thad A. Gaebelein, and Robert E. Gustafson Jr. enlarged and improved facilities, expanded the population to include more overseas students, and sustained the mission of the school: "The Stony Brook School is an independent college-preparatory school (grades 7–12) that exists to challenge young men and women to know Jesus Christ as Lord, to love others as themselves, and to grow in knowledge and skill, in order that they may serve the world through their character and leadership" (*Stony Brook School Annual Report 2011–2012*, 3).

While remaining vigilantly and unitedly evangelical in its appointments to the board, administration, and faculty, Stony Brook enrolls students without reference to their own personal religious beliefs; each year students from a variety of backgrounds profess faith in Jesus Christ. Alumni include numerous pastors, evangelists, missionaries, teachers, and lay-leaders in the arts, business, education, entertainment, law, medicine, politics, publishing, and technology.

---

210. Yolanda Y. Smith and Mary Elizabeth Mullino Moore, "Olivia Pearl Stokes: A Living Testimony of Faith" in *Faith of Our Foremothers* (Louisville, KY: Westminster John Knox Press, 1997).

Current enrollment is 320 boarding and day students in grades 7–12, from some 25 states and 20 foreign countries. Joshua Crane is the sixth headmaster as of July 2013 (Stony Brook School Board of Trustees 2013).

References and Resources

Gaebelein, Frank E. 1951. *Christian Education in a Democracy.* New York: Oxford University Press.

———. 1954. *The Pattern of God's Truth: Problems of Integration in Christian Education.* New York: Oxford University Press.

———. 1985. *The Christian, the Arts, and Truth: Regaining the Vision of Greatness.* Edited by D. Bruce Lockerbie. Portland, OR: Multnomah Press.

Heltzel, Peter G. 2009. *Jesus and Justice: Evangelicals, Race, and American Politics.* New Haven, CT: Yale University Press.

Lockerbie, D. Bruce. 1972. *The Way They Should Go.* New York: Oxford University Press.

———. 2007. *A Passion for Learning: A History of Christian Thought on Education.* Colorado Springs, CO: Purposeful Design.

Stony Brook School Annual Report 2011–2012—http://www.stonybrook.edu/commcms/cie/about/CIE%202011-2012%20Annual%20Report.pdf

Stony Brook School Board of Trustees. 2013. "The Stony Brook School Board of Trustees Appoints Joshua Crane as Head of School, Effective July 1, 2013." 3 January. boardoftrustees@stonybrookschool.org.

—D. Bruce Lockerbie

STORYTELLING AS CHRISTIAN PRACTICE

Storytelling is an ancient practice in the Judeo-Christian tradition as a means of education and passing on faith. Narrative is a basic way in which people experience and understand the world. It offers Christian educators an effective means of religious instruction and faith formation (Shaw 1999, ix–x). There is archaeological evidence of drawings on caves and tombs that indicate that storytelling was a means by which early humans shared their beliefs about the cosmos. With the advent of writing about 3000 BC, stories, epics, and myths of creation, cycles of the sun and moon, gods and goddesses were documented on tablets and papyri (Harrell 1990, 616). Ancient Greek and Roman cultures emphasized the art of oral storytelling and written narrative as an educational tool (Shaw 1999, 42–43).

The Bible existed first as oral tradition. According to Hebrew Bible scholar Walter Brueggemann, narrative was "Israel's primal mode of knowing" (1982, 15). With the help of redactors, the oral tradition came to be written down. In Deuteronomy 6:4–9 we find the *Shema*, the central prayer in the Jewish prayer book, which children learn to recite at an early age. It urges God's people to teach the words that God has given, to recite them wherever we go. The biblical stories of creation, the flood, the exodus, and many others were told over and over. Jewish rabbis told stories *about* the stories, known as midrash, which comes from a Hebrew word that means "to go in search of." These stories seek to answer questions that many have about the biblical stories and to fill in the gaps in those stories (Williams 1991, 13, 19).

The early Christian church preserved these stories along with the stories of the life of Jesus and the stories and parables He told. The Gospels are four different accounts of the life, death, and resurrection of Jesus and His teachings. Using oral and written sources such as Q (which refers to *Quelle*, German for source), the Gospel writers told those stories with an evangelistic intent (Shaw 1999, 43). Jesus's parables used objects of everyday life—a lost coin, a grain of wheat, a vineyard—to teach about God and God's coming kingdom. The book of Acts and other New Testament books told the story of the beginnings and struggles of the church and its mission to spread the Christian faith beyond Jerusalem into the Greco-Roman world. Part of the catechumenate of the early church, which was the period of preparation for the baptism of converts, focused on the "hearing of the word."

Beyond the Bible, the church has always told other types of stories as well. Early on, stories of saints, known as hagiography, and martyrs inspired the faith of many. Stories from various cultures have been valued in Christian education. Oral cultures such as Native American, African, and the Pacific Islander have contributed much to the repertoire and art of Christian storytelling. In all times the Christian story has included not only the ancient stories of the tradition, but the faith stories of ordinary people shared as testimony (Buckley 1989, 18–20, 35).

In the mid-20th century, there was an trend against sharing Bible stories with children. The work of British scholar Ronald Goldman, *Readiness for Religion* (1968), claimed that the Bible is an adult book, too intense for children, who were not considered developmentally capable of understanding it properly. However, there was a return to the legacy of storytelling and a resurgence of interest in the art form. Roger Gobbel (Gobbel and Gobbel 1986) and others have countered that Bible stories should be told to people of all ages in a way that relates to their development. Narrative theology, which came to prominence in the late 20th century, claimed that the best way to teach faith was by story rather than propositions. To withhold the stories from children is to deprive them of the dynamic and compelling faith tradition. For a child, story involves human contact and relationship, which becomes as important as the story itself (Buckley 1989, 12).

Storytelling is an interaction between teller and listener. It captures the imagination and helps to form identity. It is fun and entertaining, but it is not merely that. It is educational and connectional as well. One storyteller attests, "When I tell biblical stories, I feel the presence of God in the here and now" (http://www.nbsint.org/). Stories are useful for teaching the content of faith, but that is not the only way they work. Story is closely connected to memory. Christmas pageants, Easter sunrise services, Sunday school, and church camp are just a few of the many places Christian educators tell stories. As people hear stories over and over, those stories become embedded in them, and they know them "by heart."

There is no one right way to tell a Bible story. Each person's telling depends on his or her own life experiences (Williams 1991, 12). Groups like the Network of Biblical Storytellers promote the art of oral performance of the Bible. These are some techniques of storytellers:

1. Read the story aloud and to yourself several times.
2. Reflect on the who, when, where, what, and why of the story.
3. Map out a general order of events. Try visualizing the story. See the scenes in your mind, as clearly as you can. Later, these pictures will help you re-create your story as you tell it—whether or not you consciously call them to mind.
4. Practice telling the story. Do not necessarily aim for word-for-word memorization.
5. Use gestures to bring the story to life. Vary the tone, the pitch, and the volume of your voice; your speed; your rhythm; and your articulation (smooth or sharp). Use silences. Shout a word or phrase, or whisper. Remember, variety catches and holds attention.

References and Resources

Brueggemann, W. 1982. *The Creative Word: Canon as a Model for Biblical Education.* Philadelphia: Fortress Press.

Buckley, R. 1989. *Dancing with Words: Storytelling as Legacy, Culture and Faith.* Nashville, TN: Discipleship Resources.

Gobbel, A. R., and G. G. Gobbel. 1986. *The Bible: A Child's Playground.* Philadelphia: Fortress Press.

Harrell, J. 1990. "Storytelling." In *Harper's Encyclopedia of Religious Education,* edited by I. V. Cully and K. B. Cully, 616–618. San Francisco: Harper & Row.

Shaw, S. 1999. *Storytelling in Religious Education.* Birmingham, AL: Religious Education Press.

Williams, M., ed. 1991. *The Storyteller's Companion to the Bible.* Volume 1. Nashville, TN: Abingdon Press.

Network of Biblical Storytellers. http://www.nbsint.org/

—Susan Willhauck

Stott, John

John Robert Walmsley Stott, CBE (27 April 1921–27 July 2011), was an English Christian leader and *Anglican* cleric who was noted as a leader of the worldwide evangelical movement. He was one of the principal authors of the Lausanne Covenant in 1974. In 2005, *Time* magazine ranked Stott among the 100 most influential people in the world.

Early Background and Education

John Stott was born in London to Sir Arnold and Lady Stott. He was educated at Rugby School, where he became head boy, and Trinity College, Cambridge. At Trinity, he earned a double first in French and theology and was elected a senior scholar.

Stott trained for the pastorate at Ridley Hall, Cambridge. He was later awarded a Lambeth doctorate in divinity (1983) and has honorary doctorates from universities in America, Britain, and Canada.

From the time he was a small boy, Stott attended his local church, All Souls, Langham Place, in London's West End. Following his ordination in 1945, he became assistant curate at All Souls, and then was appointed rector in 1950. He became rector emeritus in 1975, a position he held to the end of his life.

Significant Contributions to Christian Education

Soon after his appointment as rector, Stott began to encourage church members to attend a weekly training course in evangelism. A monthly "guest service" was established, combining regular parochial evangelism with Anglican evening prayer. Follow-up discipleship courses for new Christians were started in people's homes. All Souls also offered midweek lunchtime services, a central weekly prayer meeting, and monthly services of prayer for the sick. "Children's church" and family services were established, a chaplain was appointed to a group of Oxford Street stores, and the All Souls Clubhouse was founded as a Christian community center.

John Stott played important roles in three areas of Christian life in England, serving the church, the university, and the crown. He served as chair of the Church of England Evangelical Council from 1967 to 1984 and as president of two influential Christian organizations: the British Scripture Union, from 1965 to 1974, and the British Evangelical Alliance, from 1973 to 1974. He also served four terms as president of the Universities and Colleges Christian Fellowship, between 1961 and 1982. He was also an honorary chaplain to the queen from 1959 to 1991 and received the rare distinction of being appointed an Extra Chaplain in 1991.

Stott was displeased by the anti-intellectualism of some Christians. In contrast, he stressed the need to relate the ancient Word to the modern world. This conviction led to his founding of The London Institute for Contemporary Christianity in 1982. This Institute "offer[s] courses in the inter-relations between faith, life and mission to thinking Christian lay people." Stott served as its first director and then as president from 1986 onward.

In light of this work, David Edwards has claimed that, apart from William Temple, John Stott was the most influential clergyman in the Church of England during the 20th century. Likewise, Alister McGrath has suggested that the growth of English Evangelicalism after World War II is attributable more to John Stott than to any other person.

Stott's international influence is clear on a number of fronts. First, he was heavily involved in university missions. Between 1952 and 1977, he led some 50 university missions in Britain, North America, Australia, New Zealand, Africa, and Asia. He was vice president of the International Fellowship of Evangelical Students from 1995 to 2003. The extent of his influence on North American Evangelicalism is evident from the fact that he served as the Bible expositor on six occasions at the triennial Urbana Student Mission Convention, arranged by InterVarsity Christian Fellowship.

Second, Stott played prominent roles in drafting important evangelical documents. In 1974, he served as chair of the drafting committee for the Lausanne Covenant at the International Congress on World Evangelization, held in Lausanne, Switzerland. The creation of this covenant, outlining evangelical theology and reinforcing the need for social action, is a significant milestone in 20th-century Evangelicalism. Stott continued to serve as the chair of the Lausanne Theology and Education Group from 1974 to 1981. He was again chair of the drafting committee for the Manila Manifesto, a document produced by the second International Congress in 1989.

Third, Stott helped to strengthen the evangelical voice in established churches. As an Anglican, John Stott was committed to the renewal of Evangelicalism in the worldwide Anglican Church. He founded the Evangelical Fellowship in the Anglican Communion (EFAC) and served as honorary general secretary from 1960 to 1981, and as president from 1986 to 1990. His desire to strengthen ties between evangelical theologians in Europe led to the founding of the Fellowship of European Evangelical Theologians (FEET) in 1977.

The Evangelical Literature Trust and the Langham Trust have now been amalgamated into the Langham Partnership International, directed by Chris Wright. Langham Partnership International includes six national movements (UK & Ireland, USA-John Stott Ministries, Canada, Australia, Hong Kong, and New Zea- land) and some 10 regional councils. These councils allow church leaders from the majority world to give their input, guidance, and direction to Langham's ministry in their countries.

Influential Books

Finally, Stott wrote a number of influential books, which are notable for their clarity, balance, intellectual rigor, and biblical faithfulness. Stott's writing career started in 1954 when he was asked to write the Bishop of London's annual Lent book. Fifty years later, he had written more than 40 books and hundreds of articles.

John Stott's best-known work, *Basic Christianity*, has sold two million copies and been translated into more than 60 languages. Other titles include *The Cross of Christ, Understanding the Bible, The Contemporary Christian, Evangelical Truth, Issues Facing Christians Today, The Incomparable Christ, Why I Am a Christian*, and most recently *Through the Bible through the Year*, a daily devotional. He also wrote eight volumes in *The Bible Speaks Today* series of New Testament expositions.

Two factors enabled Stott to be so productive: strong self-discipline and the unstinting support of Frances Whitehead, his secretary for over 50 years. John Stott never married, though according to his biography he came close to it on two occasions; he acknowledged that with the responsibility of a family, he would not have been able write, travel, and minister in the way that he did.

Books about John Stott

Dudley-Smith, Timothy. 1999. *John Stott: The Making of a Leader*. Vol. 1. Leicester, UK: InterVarsity Press.

———. *John Stott: A Global Ministry*. 2001. Vol. 2. Leicester, UK: InterVarsity Press.

Steer, Roger. 2010. *Basic Christian: The Inside Story of John Stott*. Leicester, UK: InterVarsity Press.

Wright, Chris, ed. 2011a. *John Stott: A Portrait by His Friends*. Leicester, UK: InterVarsity Press.

———. 2011b. *Portraits of a Radical Disciple: Recollections of John Stott's Life and Ministry*. Leicester, UK: InterVarsity Press.

—MARK A. LAMPORT

STREET CHILDREN

Street Children: Numbers, Situation, and Need

The issue of street children is one of the major concerns of the 21st century. However, this phenomenon is not new. The challenge of street children dates back to the Middle Ages and 11th-century Europe. It was not until the 16th century that the first center to deal with such children was established, in England.[211] However, while this institution may have succeeded in getting children off the streets, they were exposed to cruelty and neglect while locked up inside it.[212] Many misguided attempts at dealing with the issue were made in the following centuries.[213]

Both government and nongovernmental organizations (NGOs) have poured extensive resources into alleviating the problem of street children around the world, but the problem persists. And perhaps it will continue until the consummation of the age. However, the case is not hopeless. Jesus Christ placed great value on children (Matt. 19:14, 21:12–16; Mark 9:36–37, 10:14) and does not want anyone to perish. The church has the opportunity to address the challenge of nurturing street children in the Christian faith.

The term "street children" has various definitions from country to country. The United Nations Children's Fund (UNICEF) categorized street children as "children in especially difficult circumstances" (CEDC).[214] Phyllis Kilbourn defines street children as "children who live or spend a significant amount of time on the streets of urban areas to fend for themselves or their families. This also denotes children who are inadequately protected, supervised and cared for by responsible adults."[215] Wherever they are located, street children have one thing in common: they need to be nurtured in the faith.

In 1989, UNICEF estimated that 100 million children were growing up on urban streets around the world. Fourteen years later, UNICEF reported again: "The latest estimates put the numbers of these children as high as 100 million."[216] In 2006, UNICEF reported that "[t]he exact number of street children is impossible to quantify, but the figure almost certainly runs into tens of millions across the world. It is likely that the numbers are increasing."[217] The 100 million figure is still commonly cited, but has no basis in fact.[218] Similarly, it is debatable whether numbers of street children are growing globally

or whether it is the awareness of street children within societies that has grown. While there are understandable pressures for policies to be informed by aggregate numbers, estimates of street child populations, even at city levels, are often hotly disputed and can distract rather than inform policy makers.[219] *Newsweek* magazine has made a perceptive observation regarding the number of street children: "One reason the number of street children is 'impossible to calculate with any degree of confidence,' is partly because of an attempt to hide the real picture. In many countries the government authorities responsible . . . cling to outlandishly low estimates, apparently in an effort to deflect criticism at home and abroad.[220] Given that there are undoubtedly millions of street children, it is impossible to ignore the need for nurturing them in the faith.

How the Church Can Help Street Children Grow in the Faith

UNICEF and the World Health Organization (WHO) have provided the earliest categorization of street children: children *on* the streets (street-working children), *of* the streets (street-living children), and *in* the streets (abandoned children—cut off from all ties with family).[221] All of these children need the love and nurture that God offers. Lawrence Richards asserts: "Wherever a local congregation touches boys and girls, *there* a true and vital expression of faith community must exist."[222] The church is one place where street children may find their way back. Dan Brewster clearly argues: "True holistic development can only be done by a Christian or the church. It is only Christians who have understanding of the nature of sin, God's intention for His people and His creation, and the power of the gospel to bring substantial holistic healing to the whole person."[223]

With street children, the challenge is greater, in the sense that the church is faced with people who require highly specialized training and care. Following are some of the biblical truths that have to be highlighted in ministering with street children. First, children who have been out in the streets need to understand holistically that Jesus loves them. Many of these children have lost what it

---

211. Mohammad Tala't Issa et al., *Social Care for Delinquent Juveniles* (Cairo: The New Library of Cairo, n.d), 326; cited in Defense for Children International, Palestine Section, "Children in the Street: The Palestinian Case," http://www.abudis.net/ChildrenintheStreetEnglish.pdf, 14.

212. Defense for Children International, Palestine Section, "Children in the Street," 14.

213. Ibid.

214. Judith Ennew, "Difficult Circumstances: Some Reflections on 'Street Children' in Africa," *Children, Youth and Environments* 13, no. 1 (Spring 2003): 7.

215. Phyllis Kilbourn, ed., *Children in Crisis: A New Commitment* (Monrovia, CA: MARC Publications, 1996), 10.

216. UNICEF, "State of the World's Children 2003" (2002), 37; also cited in Deborah Meroff, *True Grit: Women Taking on the World, for God's Sake* (Manila: OMF Literature Inc., 2004), 137.

217. UNICEF, "State of the World's Children 2006: Excluded and Invisible," 40–41.

218. For examples, please see J. Ennew et al., *The Next Generation* (London: Zed Books, 1998), and *At Home in the Street* (Cambridge, UK: Cambridge University Press); D. Green, *Hidden Lives* (London: Cassell, 1998).

219. Thomas S. de Benitez, "State of the World's Street Children" (2007), 64, http://www.streetchildren.org.uk/reports/State%20of%20 the%20 World's%20 Street%20Children-Violence.pdf.

220. "Children of the Gutter," *Newsweek*, 1 May 1989, 8.

221. Cited in Shanchobeni Yanthan and Pelekhono Zinyu, "Street Children and Christian Response," in *Children at Risk: Issues and Challenges*, ed. Jesudason Jeyaraj (Bangalore: Cambridge Press, 2009), 268; also cited in Jeff Anderson, "Street Children and Their Families," *Journal of Asian Mission* 13, no. 2 (2012): 38.

222. Lawrence O. Richards, *A Theology of Children's Ministry* (Grand Rapids, MI: Zondervan, 1983), 279.

223. Dan Brewster, *Child, Church, and Mission* (Penang: Compassion International Publishing, 2011), 80.

feels like to be special in the eyes of someone. A research project conducted by sociologist Persida D. Evio at the University of the Philippines found that "street children usually have a poor self-image even before they leave home, but even more so after being on the streets."[224]

Many NGOs have tried programs to bring street children back into normal living by placing them in welfare homes and other shelters, but they have failed because they have neglected to help the street child establish a relationship with Jesus Christ. After almost 35 years of full-time ministry among a variety of people, including street children, Jeff Anderson of ACTION Philippines' Street Impact Team (SIT) testifies, "I am more convinced than ever that the message of Jesus Christ is the only hope for people."[225] Samuel Martin, founder and president of The Arms of Jesus Children's Mission, Inc., says the same: "I am convinced the only hope children have is the gospel of Jesus Christ!"[226] Letting children have a personal encounter with Jesus Christ may come in a slow, painstaking manner, but the effects are lasting. Ministering with street children holistically means providing food, shelter, clothing, alternative livelihood, proper monitoring, and appropriate interventions, all in line with Christian education.

The second issue that needs to be highlighted in ministering with street children is the concept of "family." Without ignoring the roots of economics and social effects of international debt, Italian Senator Susanna Agnelli concluded that "all those on the street, everywhere, can be described as victims of the crisis of the family. The breakdown of family structure and traditional values, massive immigration."[227] James Grant, the late executive director of UNICEF, recognized that family disintegration is a major cause of children being on the street.[228] God has instituted the family in the first place to nurture children. Pope John Paul II celebrates the specifically ecclesial vocation of the family, an "intimate community of life and life," to prepare, nourish, and sustain the "youngest members of the Church in their task of building up the Kingdom of God."[229] However, in the case of street kids, the family is absent, if not negligent of its function. Issues like drugs, sexual abuse, and trafficking arise almost hand in hand when children live in the streets. Many of these children have developed some form of "street addiction." It is almost always a pattern that even when sheltered in homes, street children still go back to street life, for reasons such as distrust of people and a fatalistic approach to life.[230] But Helen Shedd argues that street addiction can be broken by providing a "family setting."[231] Inside a home, there are rules and routine that children who have no experience of "discipline" in love can experience. In this setting, children's participation[232] is needed, and this may give them the "empowerment" that is so crucial for healing. With intentionality, the church can provide a "family setting" for street kids to fulfill their need for love, acceptance, and boundaries.

Who Could Effectively Disciple the Street Child?

Matthew 9:35–36 says, "Jesus went through all the towns and villages, teaching in their synagogues, proclaiming the good news of the kingdom and healing every disease and sickness. When he saw the crowds, he had compassion on them, because they were harassed and helpless, like sheep without a shepherd" (NIV). In one way or another, street children are like "sheep without a shepherd," roaming around the streets—seen, smelled, and heard by almost everyone, but cared for and nurtured by no one in particular. The challenge is for the church to enlist people who have the "calling, motivation and God-given burden to reach street children."[233] Street children have a unique culture, and it takes a strong person to overcome the hurdles of getting through their hardened psyche. The church needs to enlist "holistic" teachers and practitioners. Bryant L. Myers explains, "Holistic practitioners must be committed Christians. They must understand that God's rule extends to all life—their relationship with God, themselves, their neighbors, and their environment."[234] For John Wesley, "masters" or teachers

224. Persida D. Evio, *Perception of Street Children on Themselves, Their Families, Their Street Life and on Agency Programs and Services* (Manila: University of the Philippines, 1991).

225. Jeff Anderson, "Street Children and Their Families," *Journal of Asian Mission* 13, no. 2 (October 2012): 42.

226. Samuel Martin, "The Church and the World's Children," in *Children in Crisis: A New Commitment*, ed. Phyllis Kilbourn (Monrovia, CA: MARC Publications, 1996), 113.

227. Susanna Agnelli, *Street Children: A Growing Urban Tragedy: Report for the Independent Commission on Humanitarian Issues* (London: Weidenfeld and Nicolson, 1986).

228. James Grant, "The State of the World's Children," 23–45. *Esperanza* 5 (Winter/Spring 1993), Childhope Asia.

229. John Paul II, *Familiaris Consortio* (1981), http://www.vatican.va/holy_father/john_paul_ii/apost_exhortations/documents/hf_jp-ii_exh_19811122_familiaris-consortio-en.html par. 17, cited in William

Werpehowski, "Human Dignity and Social Responsibility: Catholic Social Thought on Children," in *Children, Adults, and Shared Responsibilities: Jewish, Christian, and Muslim Perspectives*, ed. Marcia Bunge (New York: Cambridge University Press, 2012), 83.

230. Helen Shedd, "Street Addiction Can Be Broken," in *Street Children: A Guide to Effective Ministry*, ed. Phyllis Kilbourn (Monrovia, CA: World Vision Resources, 1997), 129–132.

231. Ibid., 126–127.

232. Faye G. Balanon, *Making the World Safe for Children: The Experiences of the Center for the Prevention and Treatment of Child Sexual Abuse* (Manila: Center for the Prevention and Treatment of Child Sexual Abuse and Terre des Hommes Netherlands Southeast Asia Office, 2012), 71. In the treatment of sexually abused children, children were consulted and their feedback was considered.

233. Jeff Anderson, "Street Worker Profile," in *Street Children: A Guide to Effective Ministry*, ed. Kilbourn, 119.

234. Bryant L. Myers, *Walking with the Poor: Principles and Practices of Transformational Development* (Philippines: Overseas Mission Fellowship Literature, Inc., 2006), 153.

must be individuals "who were truly devoted to God; who sought nothing on earth, neither pleasure, nor ease, nor profit, nor the praise of men; but simply to glorify God, with their bodies and spirits, in the best manner they were capable of."[235] These are the kinds of individuals who can minister with street children holistically. Jeff Anderson enumerates the tasks of the street worker: (1) know your target audience and their needs, (2) immerse yourself in the children's world, (3) identify with the children, (4) cultivate acceptable relationships, (5) develop an approach, and (6) provide education.[236] These tasks may seem overwhelming, but with intentionality, prayer, and God's grace, street children will be ushered into the kingdom of love and light.

References and Resources

Agnelli, Susanna. 1986. *Street Children: A Growing Urban Tragedy: Report for the Independent Commission on Humanitarian Issues.* London: Weidenfeld and Nicolson.

Anderson, Jeff. 2012. "Street Children and Their Families." *Journal of Asian Mission* 13 (2): 38–54. http://www.action international.org/documents/AndersonStreetChildren-1.pdf

———. 1997. "Street Worker Profile." In *Street Children: A Guide to Effective Ministry*, edited by Phyllis Kilbourn, 59–82. Monrovia, CA: World Vision Resources.

Balanon, Faye G. 2012. *Making the World Safe for Children: The Experiences of the Center for the Prevention and Treatment of Child Sexual Abuse.* Manila: Center for the Prevention and Treatment of Child Sexual Abuse and Terre des Hommes Netherlands Southeast Asia Office.

Brewster, Dan. 2011. *Child, Church, and Mission.* Penang: Compassion International Publishing.

"Children of the Gutter." 1989. *Newsweek,* 1 May, 8.

De Benitez, Thomas S. 2007. "State of the World's Street Children." http://www.streetchildren.org.uk/reports/State%20 of%20the%20World's%20Street%20Children-Violence.pdf.

Defense for Children International. Palestine Section. n.d. "Children in the Street: The Palestinian Case." http://www .abudis. net/ChildionintheStreetEnglish.pdf.

Ennew, Judith. 2003. "Difficult Circumstances: Some Reflections on 'Street Children' in Africa." *Children, Youth and Environments* 13 (1): 7.

Estep, James Riley, Jr. 1997. "John Wesley's Philosophy of Formal Childhood Education." *Christian Education Journal* 1 (2): 50.

Evio, Persida D. 1991. *Perception of Street Children on Themselves, Their Families, Their Street Life and on Agency Programs and Services.* Manila: University of the Philippines.

Grant, James. 1993. *Esperanza* 5 (Winter/Spring): The State of the World's Children, 23-45.

Issa, Mohammad Tala't Issa, et al. n.d. *Social Care for Delinquent Juveniles.* Cairo: The New Library of Cairo.

John Paul II. 1981. *Familiaris Consortio.* http://www.vatican .va/holy_father/john_paul_ii/apost_exhortations/documents/ hf_jp-ii_exh_19811122_familiaris-consortio_en.html par. 17.

Kilbourn, Phyllis, ed. 1996. *Children in Crisis: A New Commitment.* Monrovia, CA: MARC Publications.

Martin, Samuel. 1996. "The Church and the World's Children." In *Children in Crisis: A New Commitment*, edited by Phyllis Kilbourn, 88–101. Monrovia, CA: MARC Publications.

Meroff, Deborah. 2004. *True Grit: Women Taking on the World, for God's Sake.* Manila: OMF Literature.

Myers, Bryant L. 2006. *Walking with the Poor: Principles and Practices of Transformational Development.* Philippines: Overseas Mission Fellowship Literature.

Richards, Lawrence O. 1983. *A Theology of Children's Ministry.* Grand Rapids, MI: Zondervan.

Shedd, Helen. 1997. "Street Addiction Can Be Broken." In *Street Children: A Guide to Effective Ministry*, edited by Phyllis Kilbourn, 189–203. Monrovia, CA: World Vision Resources.

UNICEF. 2003. "State of the World's Children." http://www .unicef.org/sowc03/.

UNICEF. 2006. "State of the World's Children 2006: Excluded and Invisible." http://www.unicef.org/sowc06/.

Werpehowski, William. 2012. "Human Dignity and Social Responsibility: Catholic Social Thought on Children." In *Children, Adults, and Shared Responsibilities: Jewish, Christian, and Muslim Perspectives*, edited by Marcia Bunge, 79–98. New York: Cambridge University Press.

Wesley, John. 1781. *A Plain Account of Kingswood School.* http://archive.org/stream/historykingswoo00schogoog/his torykingswoo00schogoog_djvu.txt.

Yanthan, Shanchobeni, and Pelekhono Zinyu. 2009. "Street Children and Christian Response." In *Children at Risk: Issues and Challenges*, edited by Jesudason Jeyaraj, 29–47. Bangalore: Cambridge University Press.

—NATIVITY A. PETALLAR

STREIB, HEINZ

Early Background and Education

Heinz Streib, PhD, a native of Germany, completed secondary school in 1970. He holds undergraduate degrees in Protestant theology from Tübingen University (1977) and Church of Württemberg, Stuttgart, Germany (1980);

---

235. John Wesley, *A Plain Account of Kingswood School* (1781), 9; see full text at http://archive.org/stream/historykingswoo00schogoog/history kingswoo00schogoog_djvu.txt; also cited in James Riley Estep Jr., "John Wesley's Philosophy of Formal Childhood Education," *Christian Education Journal* 1, no. 2 (Fall 1997): 50.

236. Anderson, "Street Worker Profile," 120–123.

a master of sacred theology from Yale University (1984); a PhD in theology and personality from Emory University (1989); and a habilitation in practical theology from the University of Frankfurt, Germany (1995). He has held a number of professorships since 1977 and is currently professor of religious education and ecumenical theology and director of biographical studies in contemporary religion at the University of Bielefeld, Germany.[237]

Significant Contributions to Christian Education

Streib's most notable work is his religious styles perspective on faith development. Having studied under James Fowler at Emory University, Streib asserts that while Fowler's faith development theory[238] made an important contribution to the understanding of the role of cognition, faith development goes beyond cognition to include a psychodynamic-interpersonal dimension that accounts for experiences and relationships with self, others, traditions, and the social world.[239] Streib argues; "The primacy of the cognitive structures as motor and guideline of religious development should be terminated. . . . Instead, life history and life world . . . should move into the focus of the developmental perspective on religion."[240]

Streib argues that faith does not develop in invariant, sequential, and hierarchical stages that each represent a structural whole, as Fowler asserted,[241] but rather is better understood as a series of religious styles, each style drawing upon and bringing something forward from the previous style(s) that is informed by life-history and life-world and accounts for regression and horizontal movement.[242] Each particular style is depicted by a bell-shaped curve that climaxes in the present style while consolidating and retelling the previous style(s) to some degree.[243]

The "Subjective Religious Style" generally corresponds to intuitive-projective[244] faith; the infant is egocentric and is tasked with developing basic trust (or mistrust if unsuccessfully resolved).[245] It is a period when the earliest conceptions of God emerge based on the child-caregiver relationship.[246]

The "Instrumental-Reciprocal or *Do-ut-des* Style" (I give that you may give) denotes a reciprocal characteristic, wherein the person distinguishes inner and outer self and enters into a reciprocal exchange with his or her own needs and those of others.[247] This reciprocity is carried over into the child's experience of God through aggrandized parental images.[248] Religion is approached from a mythic-literal perspective where religious rules must be followed exactly.[249]

The "Mutual Religious Style" emphasizes the personal and mutual nature of relationships, including one's relationship with God and those in one's religious group. This corresponds somewhat to the synthetic-conventional[250] stage, and the person is unquestionably committed and secure in his or her religious group. "The unquestioned security in one's religious group or the dependence on their judgment reveals that it is difficult to transcend the ideological and institutional group limits, and if one religious home has been left, another will be searched for desperately."[251]

In the "Individuative-Systemic Religious Style," the person understands his or her role in society and the world's system and is able to reflect critically and rationally on religious matters, sometimes at the expense of experiential or symbolic elements of religion. A person may draw upon or reinvent earlier styles in order to incorporate these elements.[252]

In the "Dialogical Religious Style," the person is open to and able to cognitively process differences and tensions in his or her own faith and that of others without threat or exclusivity. This is similar to conjunctive and universalizing stages,[253] characterized by a letting go of self and a new emergence of trust in God despite uncertainties. [254]

Other Contributions to Christian Education

Streib is a proponent of student-centered education and urges teachers to view religious education as a "laboratory for inter-religious dialogue" that emphasizes narrative and discourse among peers as well as with teachers.[255] His recent studies exploring deconversion, atheism, agnosticism, and religious doubt aid in understanding why

237. "Heinz Streib, Ph.D.," Universitat Bielefeld CIRRuS, http://www.uni-bielefeld.de/(en)/theologie/forschung/religionsforschung/personen/streib.html (accessed 22 March 2013).

238. James Fowler, *Stages of Faith* (San Francisco: Harper & Row, 1981).

239. Heinz Streib, "Faith Development Theory Revisited: The Religious Styles Perspective," *International Journal for the Psychology of Religion* 11, no. 3 (2001): 144.

240. Ibid.

241. Fowler, *Stages of Faith*, 57.

242. Streib, *Faith Development Theory*, 143.

243. Ibid., 150.

244. Ibid.

245. As identified by Erik H. Erikson in *Identity, Youth and Crisis* (New York: Norton, 1968).

246. Adapted from Ana-Maria Rizzuto, *The Birth of the Living God: A Psychoanalytic Study* (Chicago: University of Chicago Press, 1979).

247. Streib, *Faith Development Theory*.

248. Ibid.

249. Fowler, *Stages of Faith*.

250. Ibid.

251. Streib, *Faith Development Theory*, 152.

252. Ibid.

253. Fowler, *Stages of Faith*.

254. Streib, *Faith Development Theory*.

255. Heinz Streib, "Inter-Religious Negotiations: Case Studies on Students' Perception of and Dealing with Religious Diversity," in *Towards Religious Competence: Diversity as a Challenge for Education in Europe*, ed. Hans-Günter Heinbrock, Christoph Scheike, and Peter Schreiner (Münster, Germany: Lit Verlag, 2001), 129–149.

people reject or renounce matters of faith, which can inform evangelism and discipleship strategies.

Most Notable Publications

Streib has authored or coauthored more than 90 books, articles, and papers in German and English. Significant works include "Faith Development Theory Revisited: The Religious Styles Perspective,"[256] "Faith Development Research Revisited: Accounting for Diversity in Structure Content and Narrativity of Faith,"[257] *Deconversion: Qualitative and Quantitative Results from Cross-Cultural Research in Germany and the United States of America,*[258] and "More Spiritual Than Religious: Changes in the Religious Field Require New Approaches."[259]

References and Resources

Erikson, Erik H. 1968. *Identity, Youth and Crisis*. New York: Norton.

Fowler, James. 1981. *Stages of Faith*. San Francisco: Harper & Row.

Rizzuto, Ana-Maria. 1979. *The Birth of the Living God: A Psychoanalytic Study*. Chicago: University of Chicago Press.

Streib, Heinz. 2001a. "Faith Development Theory Revisited: The Religious Styles Perspective." *International Journal for the Psychology of Religion* 11 (3): 143–158.

———. 2001b. "Inter-Religious Negotiations: Case Studies on Students' Perception of and Dealing with Religious Diversity." In *Towards Religious Competence: Diversity as a Challenge for Education in Europe*, edited by Hans-Günter Heinbrock, Christoph Scheike and Peter Schreiner, 129–149. Münster, Germany: Lit Verlag.

———. 2005. "Faith Development Research Revisited: Accounting for Diversity in Structure, Content, and Narrativity of Faith." *International Journal for the Psychology of Religion* 15 (2): 99–121.

Streib, Heinz, R. W. Hood, B. Keller, R. M. Csöff, and C. F. Silver, eds. 2009. *Deconversion: Qualitative and Quantitative Results from Cross-cultural Research in Germany and the United States of America*. Göttingen, Germany: Vandenboeck & Ruprecht.

---

256. Streib, *Faith Development Theory*.

257. Heinz Streib, "Faith Development Research Revisited: Accounting for Diversity in Structure, Content, and Narrativity of Faith," *International Journal for the Psychology of Religion* 15, no. 2 (2005): 99–121.

258. Heinz Streib, R. W. Hood, B. Keller, R. M. Csöff, and C. F. Silver, eds., *Deconversion: Qualitative and Quantitative Results from Cross-cultural Research in Germany and the United States of America* (Göttingen, Germany: Vandenboeck & Ruprecht, 2009).

259. Heinz Streib, "More Spiritual Than Religious: Changes in the Religious Field Require New Approaches," in *Lived Religion: Conceptual, Empirical and Practical-Theological Approaches—Essays in Honor of Hans-Günter Heimbrock*, ed. Heinz Streib, Astrid Dinter, and Kerstin Söderblom (Leiden: Brill, 2008), 53–67.

Universitat Bielefeld CIRRuS. n.d. "Heinz Streib, Ph.D." Accessed 22 March 2013. http://www.uni-bielefeld.de/(en)/theologie/forschung/religionsforschung/personen/streib.html.
                                              —Brenda A. Snailum

STUDENT SERVICES

Student services departments have become an essential component of student life on college and university campuses in North America. They typically seek to achieve the integration of three key components of an experience in higher education: (1) formal academics, (2) the life of the student, and (3) learning outside of the classroom.

A prominent goal for the Western university has been to educate students in the liberal arts in order for them to receive adequate training for wise, honorable, and cultivated citizenship in the world. Within classrooms, this task seems clear. Outside of the classroom, however, students are influenced by culture, peers, and the campus ethos as they mature. Student services seek to coordinate this complex environment to serve the mission of the institution by structuring programming in a way that draws students into a cocurricular life that reinforces the messages they receive from professors.

The Christian academy adds to the development of citizens the importance of a unique role of Christian scholars as servants of Christ as Truth (John 14:6). Thus, the campus becomes a microcosm of the life of believers within a culture at large. Preparation for faithful citizenship and truth is engendered and practiced everywhere, from lectures to late night discussions that occur in campus housing. Thus Christian campuses design a safe place to engage truth, and Christ as the Truth, as a precursor to life in the world that involves both the nurture of the Christian community and the challenges of critical thinking and engagement with diversity.

Theologian and veteran educator George Forell notes that the Christian university is distinguished from the public institution by its sense of community. Engendering and nurturing a healthy and appropriate Christian community is the vocation of professionals in student services at a Christian university.

Cultivating a sense of Christian community need not entail promoting an unrealistic environment on a Christian campus. Indeed, such approaches often backfire, as students find they are unable to live up to expectations and hide their self-destructive struggles. Christians, like all other humans, are sinners. Promoting a Christian community thus involves promoting a lively interaction with the non-Christian world and students' personal struggles to live healthy and responsible lives.

Students are the reason campuses exist. Students are not one-dimensional creatures, and Christian campuses need to educate the whole student. For colleges and universities that take this responsibility seriously, the concept of education includes development of students physically, socially, emotionally, morally, spiritually, and intellectually.

For this reason, many student services departments include offices dedicated to recreation, housing, residential education services, wellness and psychiatric health, student conduct, and campus ministry. In addition, the program of cocurricular activities on the average North American Christian campus is quite extensive, including student self-government, religious programming, debates, musical performances, departmental clubs, recreational sports, and intercollegiate athletics.

Christian education gives special attention to integrating many of these programs under the umbrella of campus ministry. In other words, the ministry of the Gospel and Christ as the Truth, and the preparation for life as citizens, happens during counseling sessions, judicial appointments, recreational activities, and choir practice, as well as in roommate conflict meetings. Developing the student's full and balanced Christian maturity is the major objective of cocurricular education.

Christian student services departments often work toward the goal of developing within students a sense of stewardship and the ideal of becoming active, lifelong learners. Cocurricular education makes its most valuable contribution to the life of students in this aspect of their experience. Arguably, Jesus modeled a sense of cocurricular education in His ministry: He not only educated didactically, but through real-life experiences, hardships, mealtime, travels, stories, and examples of real-life people in real-life situations.

Recently a trend of integrating students into living-learning communities has emerged. These communities are small, purposely defined groups of students who are placed together, often within campus housing; they have faculty and student service professionals on site to engage in holistic learning experiences. These communities are distinctive and theme-based residential learning environments that promote Christian faithfulness; encourage student engagement, choice, and design; and promote the mission of an institution.

Within the realm of the university experience, some of the greatest "lessons" a student learns often occur outside of the classroom: in the dorms, lounges, coffee shops, and sports fields, or in a rare moment of quiet while just sitting and reading the scriptures. Christian university student services provide and promote safe and engaging venues for such experiences and lessons to occur. For this to happen, student services and academics seek to work hand in hand to provide coherent educational experiences that combine the values of the institution (educational, behavioral, moral, and theological) with opportunities for students to become engaged in and out of the classroom.

References and Resources

Burtchaell, James T. 1998. *The Dying Light—The Disengagement of Colleges and Universities from Their Christian Churches*. Grand Rapids, MI: Eerdmans.

Holmes, Arthur F. 2002. *The Idea of a Christian College*. Grand Rapids, MI: Eerdmans.

Newman, John Henry Cardinal. 1959. *The Idea of a University*. Garden City, NY: Image Books.

Pelikan, Jaroslav. 1992. *The Idea of a University a Reexamination*. New Haven, CT: Yale University Press.

Simmons, Ernest L. 1998. *Lutheran Higher Education—An Introduction for Faculty*. Minneapolis, MN: Augsburg.

—Scott Leonard Keith

STURM, JOHANN

A German educator who founded and directed the Academy of Strasbourg, Sturm's ideas about curriculum, pedagogy, and educational philosophy, and the way he implemented them in his school, made him the leading educator of the Protestant Reformation.

Early Background and Education

Johann Sturm (also called Johannes, Ioannes, or Jean) was born in Schleiden, a German town near the border with France. Most of his career was spent in the city the Germans called Strassburg and the French called Strasbourg, part of the Alsace region variously held by both countries. Today, Strasbourg is part of France. But Sturm was involved with both the principalities of Germany and the kingdom of France.

Sturm was the son of a court official of the Count of Manderscheid. He attended the University of Louvain in France, where he took his master's degree. Here he embraced the humanist scholarship of the Renaissance. Another resident of Strasbourg was Martin Bucer, who drew him to the Reformation. Sturm became a Lutheran, though like Bucer, he had ecumenical interests and would later veer from Lutheran orthodoxy, particularly regarding the Lord's Supper.

In 1538, Sturm established the Academy of Strasbourg, which he led as rector for 43 years. The institution was modeled after the Gymnasium, a classical liberal arts secondary school designed by Luther's coworker, Philipp Melanchthon. The Strasbourg Academy, however, also included primary instruction, offering a 14-year course of studies, beginning with boys 7 years old and graduating them at the age of 21. The academy offered scholarships to poor students. One of the teachers in this school was John Calvin.

Sturm was also a diplomat, serving as an intermediary between the Protestant states and the king of France. He was active in conferences that attempted to resolve theological disputes among the various Protestant factions. Sturm also worked to make Protestantism acceptable in France, advocating on behalf of the Huguenots.

Significant Contributions to Christian Education

Sturm is credited with inventing grade levels; that is, dividing the curriculum into different age-appropriate stages, which students pass through upon mastering the material and passing an examination at each level. The early grades were organized around the *trivium* of the liberal arts, which entailed the mastery of language: grammar, logic, and rhetoric. In his academy, the first three grades were devoted to grammar, learning to speak, read, and write in Latin. The next six grades were devoted to various combinations of dialectic (that is, logic) and rhetoric. (Greek was introduced in the fourth grade, and Hebrew in the seventh.) After the nine grades were completed, students—now aged 16—attended lectures in various subjects, giving content and a degree of specialization to their education. The subjects of the lectures included, in addition to the liberal arts *quadrivium* of arithmetic, music, geometry, and astronomy (some of which had been introduced in the lower grades), theology, economics, ethics, politics, law, natural philosophy, architecture, medicine, and military science.

Sturm developed specific learning exercises for his students: "psalms, recitations, speeches, written work, declamations, disputations, conversations, demonstrations, dramatic readings, and games."[260] Despite this academically rigorous curriculum, students were in class for only four hours per day. Sturm believed in short lessons, lots of breaks, and time for play.

Throughout the curriculum, Sturm stressed the use of primary sources, the original books by the best authors, rather than commentaries or other secondhand texts, as was the practice in scholastic education. "Schools cannot teach us everything that is useful," he said. "Therefore teachers should select the necessary and best works from the best authors while the rest should be left to private studies."[261] The best authors, he believed, were those of classical antiquity, pagan though they were.

The goal of education, according to Sturm, is to instill a "wise and eloquent piety."[262] Christian piety was the goal, but it was to be joined with wisdom, so that it could function effectively in the world, and eloquence, so that it could be communicated persuasively to others. Formal instruction in the Christian faith took place in the first grade, with study of Luther's *Small Catechism*, and in the ninth, with study of the Gospels and Epistles in the original Greek, as well as church history. In between, the students studied religion by studying everything else. "Religion will be studied," Sturm said, "by teaching and by good speech."[263] Though the Latin and Greek works that made up most of the curriculum were by pagan authors, "they are undertaken for the illustration of religious teaching."[264] That is to say, teachers would continually relate the subjects of the different lessons to Christian truth. And all through the course of their studies, the students' days were organized around prayer, worship, and scripture. They were to sing a psalm, in the words of Sturm, "thrice daily: in the morning when they come into the school; at mid-day when they have returned home, and before the evening meal when the daily work is finished."[265] All of the students attended a church service of prayer twice a day, once in the morning and once in the afternoon. On Sundays, they had to go to two different services. And, in the words of Sturm, "everyone should, before going to sleep, call upon, propitiate, and praise God."[266]

Sturm also believed that schools should help to cultivate virtue. While as a Lutheran he believed that true inner righteousness comes only through faith in Christ, the "civil virtues," which enable us to live in external harmony with others in a sinful world, can indeed be taught and formed in a child. The very process of getting an education, Sturm believed, involves disciplines that instill good character. "First, diligence is essential," he said, "for without it even great talents do not progress very far; then temperance in desires which is the guard of diligence and the preserver of genius and of nature. Then there is constancy in both, so that whatever may be begun will be brought to completion."[267] In addition to these virtues of hard work, self-control, and perseverance, Sturm said that education cultivates specific mental virtues: "The virtues of the mind are ardor in undertaking, zeal in searching, acumen in comprehending, industry in accomplishing, and memory

---

260. Johann Sturm, "For the Lauingen School," in *Johann Sturm on Education*, ed. and trans. Lewis Spitz and Barbara Sher Tinsley (St. Louis, MO: Concordia Publishing House, 1995), 242.

261. "Correct Opening of Elementary Schools of Letters," in *Johann Sturm on Education*, ed. and trans. Spitz and Tinsley, 106.

262. Ibid., 85.

263. Quoted in Spitz and Tinsley, *Johann Sturm on Education*, 50.

264. Ibid.

265. Sturm, "For the Lauingen School," 243.

266. "Laws of the Lauingen School," in *Johann Sturm on Education*, ed. and trans. Spitz and Tinsley, 250–251.

267. "Liberally Educated Nobility," in *Johann Sturm on Education*, ed. and trans. Spitz and Tinsley, 136.

in preserving. For where these exist, there is also that integrity of mind of which Plato speaks—love of truth and hatred of what is false.[268]

Another principle Sturm followed, which may seem surprising in light of the rigor of his teaching, is that education should be made pleasant. A classical, liberal arts education, said Sturm, "delights with pleasantness."[269] "It puts better things ahead of worse things, so that the young person is not only taught in short order, in a brief, easy, and pleasant way, and the teacher himself is not only quickly understood, but is truly very much loved as well."[270] To be sure, a student may not find his or her studies all that pleasant, but this is because he or she does not understand them. "There is nothing bitter in letters," he said, "if they are easily understood."[271] And bringing the student to the point of understanding, of course, is the teacher's job. The good teacher promotes what Sturm called a "playful didactic discipline."[272]

Sturm's academy became a model for many other schools, both Protestant and Catholic, and his educational techniques and philosophy were widely influential. He was a major influence on Roger Ascham, the author of *The Schoolmaster*, a book that would become extremely influential among English-speaking educators. Ascham was the tutor of a young girl, the Princess Elizabeth, who would grow up to become Queen Elizabeth I. Many of Ascham's ideas were taken from his correspondence with Sturm, who also exchanged a series of charming letters with the young princess.

Sturm synthesized humanist learning with Christian piety, not only in theory but in practice. What is more, he institutionalized this approach in a successful school.

Most Notable Publications

Advice on What Organization to Give to the Gymnasium in Strasbourg (1538)

The Correct Opening of Elementary Schools of Letters (1538)

On the Lost Art of Speaking (1538)

Liberally Educated Nobility, for the Werter Brothers (1549)

Concerning the English Nobility, for Roger Ascham (1551)

On the Education of Princes (1551)

Classical Letters (1565)

The Lauingen School (1565)

Academic Letters (1569)

References and Resources

Spitz, Lewis, and Barbara Sher Tinsley, eds. and trans. 1995. *Johann Sturm on Education.* St. Louis, MO: Concordia Pub-

lishing House. (Includes translations of Sturm's major works on education.)

Tinsley, Barbara Sher. 1989. "Johann Sturm's Method for Humanistic Pedagogy." *The Sixteenth Century Journal* 20: 23–40.

—GENE EDWARD VEITH

STYLES OF FAITH

Addressing the question of how an individual experiences faith at different points in life, John H. Westerhoff III (b. 1933), an Episcopal priest and former professor of theology and Christian nurture at Duke University, proposes a four-movement description of faith development. In *Will Our Children Have Faith?* Westerhoff uses the term "styles" to indicate the various ways in which people give expression to their faith, each indicating a somewhat different perspective on the primary resource of faith and on the role of the faith community.

In describing the relationship of the four styles of faith, Westerhoff proposes an analogy of a tree, drawing out four implications for the understanding of faith. First, a one-ring tree and a three-ring tree, though clearly different, are both nonetheless integral trees; each style of faith has its own validity and adequacy, though recognizably distinct from each other. Second, a tree grows most successfully when it is in an environment that supports that growth; likewise, development across the styles of faith is dependent on the nurturing context of the Christian community. Third, the growth of the tree is gradual and successive: it is not possible to go from a one-ring tree to a four-ring tree over night; faith development is also gradual and sequential. Finally, each ring of a tree remains intact as successive rings are added; each style of faith adds depth to faith while incorporating the experiences and dynamics that shape and nurture earlier styles.

Identifying the first style of faith as "Experienced Faith," Westerhoff states that this is the dominate faith style during early childhood. This faith is experienced enactively and is the result of interactions with other people whose lives are shaped by faith, with "faithing selves" (Westerhoff 2000, 91). It is the responsibility of the faith community to provide an environment in which rituals, interactions, and activities foster this style of faith; to do that the members of the community must be people of faith themselves.

The second style of faith is described as "Affiliative Faith." Several characteristics mark this style, which is common during childhood and early adolescence. First and foremost is a sense of belonging: being part of a group in which one's name is known and one's absence would be noted. This group to which one with affiliative faith belongs must have a common and coherent story

---

268. "Correct Opening of Elementary Schools of Letters," 79.

269. Sturm, "For the Lauingen School," 213.

270. Ibid.

271. Ibid.

272. Quoted by Spitz and Tinsley, *Johann Sturm on Education*, 53.

through which meaning is made and identity formed. In addition, this is a faith of the heart and requires attention to fostering religious affections.

"Searching Faith," which can develop during late adolescence, has as a key component the actions of doubting and critical judgment. The faith received in childhood is put under scrutiny and examined intellectually; where affiliative faith is a faith of the heart, searching faith is a faith of the head. With this is an openness to experimenting with various types and expressions of religious beliefs and practices. At the same time, there is a willingness to make commitments to people, beliefs, and movements; some of these commitments are passing, while others can last a lifetime.

The final style of faith, which incorporates the other styles, is designated "Owned Faith." Here the faith that had been experienced as a young child, that had been entered into and joined during childhood, and that had been questioned during late adolescence, becomes personally owned and appropriated in maturity of faith. From within this style one is willing and able to witness to one's faith and to put that faith into action.

As with any developmental schema, care must be taken in how it is used. Westerhoff argues that the most important application of an understanding of these styles is in helping persons understand their own faith and guiding them to find those experiences and interactions that will sustain them in their faith journey, recognizing that this also sustains the faith of others.

References and Resources

Watson, Paul. 2012. "Making Christians: An Interview with John Westerhoff." *Leaven* 4 (3): article 6. http://digitalcom mons.pepperdine.edu/leaven/vol4/iss3/6.

Westerhoff, John H. 1980. *Bringing Up Children in the Christian Faith*. Minneapolis, MN: Winston Press.

———. 2000. *Will Our Children Have Faith?* Rev. ed. Toronto: Morehouse Publishing.

—JANE E. REGAN

SUBMISSION AS CHRISTIAN PRACTICE

Each person in the Trinity fulfills a role, working for a common goal, setting the standard for mutual submission (e.g., in salvation, Eph. 1:3–14). Goals indicate an order; order necessitates authority. Submission assumes an authority. Humans have been given both authority to rule and authorities to rule them.

Biblical Theology of Submission

God made creation with authority; light was given to govern, order, and define time (Gen. 1:14–19). "Subdue and have domination" before sin (Gen. 1:28) indicated ordered, beneficent human conservation and management, production from and protection of creation (Gen. 2:5, 8, 15). By naming the animals (Gen. 2:19), humans were following the Creator's lead (Gen. 1:5, 8, 10). Adam had been given jurisdiction over the creation with a directive to rule. "Naming" required direct, relational rule: time spent to learn the nature of the thing being studied. Naming displayed classification rules: the basis for describing language, art, or science.

Coercion (Num. 32:22, 29) and slavery (Jer. 34:11, 16) corrupted order and rule after sin (Gen. 3:17–19). Pollution and unwise resource usage suggest that at times human selfishness and manipulation of power pervert the intention of creation from "use" into "abuse" (2 Chron. 36:20–21; cf. Hosea 2:8 with 9:16). God's active intervention for redemption is necessary: "He will subdue our iniquities" (Mic. 7:10).

Jesus's submission was required to subdue sin (Phil. 2:5–8; Heb. 9: 26). Jesus's sacrifice was submission to His role (Matt 26:39, 42). Submission is a role taken for ordered benefit: Jesus reinstitutes the original intention for humanity's rule (Gen. 1:28; Ps. 8:5; Eph. 1:22). Because of God's creational order, government is given for human good (Rom. 13:1–7; 1 Pet. 2:13–17), men bear first responsibility at home (Eph. 5:22–25; 1 Pet. 3:1–7), and the younger should be subject to those older (1 Pet. 5:5). Submission was expected to be given to those who had become servants to the church (1 Cor. 16:16). Mutual submission, each person to another, was charged (Eph. 5:21). Ultimately, any person who placed himself under the authority of another was obeying God (1 Pet. 1:2, 14, 22). Proper submission is fulfilled in relationship with others who all live under God's ordained order, albeit in a broken world (1 Pet. 3:8–12).

Biblical Philosophy of Submission

Living under order indicates there is a need for organizational structure in local church polity. Paul left Titus in Crete (1:5) to "straighten out what was left unfinished" by "appointing elders" with clear "direction." The first injunction was to put in order something in addition to what Paul had begun. Elders were to be set down, established, and arranged, not in the sense of ordination but of authoritative election (Acts 14:23) and planned selection (Acts 20:13).

The work of the church should be collaborative, as indicated in the recurrent phrase "fellow worker." Over and over again, the concepts of operating in tandem, partnership, working together, cosubmission, accountability, and shared vision were key in "the work," where status was not the point (1 Cor. 16:3–4, 12, 15–18, 21; 2 Cor. 8:16–24; Eph. 6:21–22; Col. 4:7–17; 1 Thess. 2:17–3:10; 3

John 8). Cooperation was crucial in confederation with fellow mates (the way the term was utilized in the currency of the day). Epaphras, for example, has an undesignated responsibility but is "vouched for" by Paul, who adds that the man "is working hard" for the Colossians (4:12–13). The New Testament suggests clear order with interrelated responsibilities. One should have commitment to the common goals and tasks of doing "everything you can to help," with the general command that "our people must learn to devote themselves to doing what is good" (Titus 3:13–14).

Christian Practice of Submission

Since humans are given jurisdiction over this world by God, exercise of management may require active force. Students will need to memorize spelling words, syntactical rules will be enforced on essays, incomplete assignments will be penalized, clear directions will give latitude and a means of evaluation, mathematical processes will be unqualified, and scientific equations will maintain consistent outcomes. In short, expectations and compliance with order will be mandated throughout the educational process. Teachers and students have responsibility to "subdue" their subjects. "Ruling" instructional disciplines—bringing them under active human control—is God's intention.

Christians should live in submission to authorities God has established. Leaders should be respected (1 Thess. 5:11–12; Heb. 13:17). Others should be honored (1 Cor. 16:15–18; Col. 4:7–15). Since human time is "in God's hands" (Ps. 31:15), time should be stewarded as opportunity (Eph. 5:16) because of its brevity (Ps. 90:12; James 4:14–17) and one's inability to see tomorrow (Prov. 27:1). Since everything belongs to God (Lev. 25:23; Ps. 24:1), property should be used for others' benefit (Acts 2:44, 4:32–37). Christians reclaim the need to prudently manage and conserve everything—time, money, possessions, abilities—because they are responsible to rule. Christians also acknowledge that they obey Heaven's authority and authorities given by Heaven to earth.

References and Resources

Getz, Gene A. 2002. *Building Up One Another.* 3rd ed. Colorado Springs, CO: David C. Cook.

Jones, Thomas S., and Steve Brown. 2008. *Transformational Relationships in the Body of Christ.* Spring Hill, TN: DPI Books.

—MARK ECKEL

SUFFERING AS CHRISTIAN PRACTICE

Human suffering is perceived to be a problem for theology, first because of its sheer extent, second because of its apparently random nature, and third because of the apparent silence of God in the face of it. Suffering must be distinguished from physical pain, although pain may be the cause of some forms of suffering, and while pain may have value, suffering frequently appears to have none.

The Old Testament is primarily concerned with the sufferings of the nation, attributed to a national failure of devotion to Yahweh, exemplified in the Judges cycle and the Captivity. On the individual scale, this same explanation is reflected in Job, whose sufferings are attributed by his friends to Job's sins, an explanation that Job indignantly rejects. There is also Isaiah's recognition of the undeserved and vicarious suffering of the Servant of the Lord.

Jewish belief at the time of Christ was that an individual's suffering was the result of that individual's sinning. This is reflected in the book of Job, but also in the New Testament in the case of the Jews who had been killed by the collapse of an aqueduct tower (Luke 13:1–5). The construction was financed by Temple money, seen by most as an inappropriate use of Temple giving. The death of the workmen was seen as divine retribution. Jesus, however, rejected that idea, but did not offer an alternative explanation of suffering. Similarly, Jesus was challenged to explain the suffering of a man who had been born blind, but while rejecting the current rabbinical explanation, Jesus did not offer anything more than a gloss on the individual case confronting Him.

Suffering, and in particular what is seen as "undeserved" suffering, is a major pastoral concern. Three main arguments have been used to justify suffering in the context of a loving God. The "Greater Good" argument of Richard Swinburne suggests that out of suffering there may come some greater good, outweighing the hurt caused by suffering. The objection here is that while some good may result from suffering, it is not always so, and it is difficult to see how those who suffer are necessarily comforted by a good done to another. Process theology (Charles Hartshorne) places God inside time, so that He does not know the future and cannot be held responsible for the suffering we experience. The problem with this is that God is irresponsible in initiating an event, the creation, without knowing its outcome. A third argument is the free will argument (Alvin Plantinga): since God has given us free will, we must be free to exercise it without reference to God's purposes. This argument deals adequately with suffering imposed by humanity on humanity, but leaves unexplained the suffering caused by natural disasters.

Suffering may often be associated with evil, when it presents theology with a particular problem. It is now generally recognized that no theodicy (the attempt to preserve God's righteousness in the face of evil) can be taken seriously unless it at least takes into account the mass suffering and admitted evil of Auschwitz. Kushner (1982) referred particularly to the practice at Auschwitz of throwing babies into the furnaces alive. The suffering of the mothers and the screams of the babies alike question the silence of God. It must be said that, given belief in an omnipotent and compassionate God, at present no comprehensive explanation of suffering has been formulated.

References and Resources

Cotterell, F. P. 2000. "Suffering." In *New Dictionary of Biblical Theology*, edited by T. D. Alexander and B. S. Rosner, 802–806. Downers Grove, IVP.

Hays, R. 1996. *The Moral Vision of the New Testament*. San Francisco: HarperOne.

Kushner, Harold. 1982. *When Bad Things Happen to Good People*. London: Pan.

Phillips, D. Z. 2004. *The Problem of Evil and the Problem of God*. London: SCM.

Pinnock, Clark, ed. 1994. *The Openness of God*. Downers Grove, IL: IVP.

Surin, Kenneth. 1986. *Theology and the Problem of Evil*. Oxford: Blackwell.

—PETER COTTERELL

SUFFERING, EDUCATIONAL VALUE OF

There is perhaps no other question more poignantly raised among both believers and unbelievers alike than the purpose of human suffering. How are we to make sense of the horrors that confront people every day—the loss of a child, the wreckage and death caused by natural disasters, the death of innocent people caused by the evil actions of a single individual? The scriptures reveal several causes of human suffering.

First, suffering is the result of living in a fallen world where sin and evil thrive in the hearts of all humankind (Gen. 18:21; Jer. 17:9; John 16:33; 2 Tim. 3:1–17; 1 Pet. 5:8; Matt. 15:19; Mark 7:21). Second, suffering is used to demonstrate to Satan that some people serve God because He is God, for His own sake, and not because it simply serves their best interests to do so (Job 6:1–12). Third, suffering is the natural result of wrong living (Num. 14:41–45; Deut. 28–30; 2 Sam. 11:1–5; 1 Kings 11:1–5; Gal. 6:7–10).

Whatever the cause of human suffering may be, the Christian church, from the time of the early church fathers, has taught that suffering serves a purpose for believers, providing an impetus for them to grow in the Christian faith. Saint Augustine believed that although the same affliction, such as the death of a child, affected both a believer and an unbeliever, that did not mean the affliction was the same in both cases. The suffering was the same, but the sufferers were different. Suffering brought low unbelievers, but refined the character and faith of believers.

There are three primary ways we learn through suffering. First, suffering instructs believers, because it alerts us when we are going the wrong way by making poor choices. In ancient Israel, suffering was allowed, through the love and mercy of God, to chastise and discipline the young nation when it turned away from God to worship the false idols of the pagan Gentile nations (Gen. 12:1–3; 1 Kings 14:15; 2 Kings 17:7–8, 18–20; Ps. 78:59–62; Heb. 3:8–11; Rom. 1:26).

Similarly, suffering is instructive for believers today because it gives us the opportunity to repent, to turn away from sin and back toward God. Judges 2:11–19 documents the following cycle: Israel sins, suffers, returns to God, sins again when times are good. In Acts 9:1–16, we read of Saul's suffering, which ultimately led him to repent and become a servant to God. As the writer of Hebrews instructs, "for the Lord disciplines the one he loves, and chastises every son whom he receives. It is for discipline that you have to endure. God is treating you as sons. For what son is there whom his father does not discipline?" (Heb. 12:6–7).

Second, suffering teaches us how to empathize with the suffering of others, and to comfort one another in the same way we have been comforted (2 Cor. 1:3–5). Third, and perhaps most significantly, suffering refines the faith of believers, educating them in the virtues such as endurance and perseverance and providing an opportunity for those virtues to be cultivated (Rom. 5:3–4; James 1:3–4). Coping with suffering wisely not only transforms and strengthens our character, but allows us to learn more about who God is by increasing our understanding of His sovereignty.

References and Resources

Augustine. 1950. *The City of God*. New York: Modern Library.

D'Arcy, M. C. 1935. *Pain and the Providence of God*. Milwaukee, WI: The Bruce Publishing Company.

Farrer, A. 1961. *Love Almighty and Ills Unlimited: An Essay on Providence and Evil, Containing the Nathaniel Taylor Lectures for 1961*. Garden City, NY: Doubleday.

Lewis, C. S. 2001. *The Problem of Pain*. New York: HarperOne.

Talbert, Charles. 1991. *Learning through Suffering: The Educational Value of Suffering in the New Testament and in Its Milieu*. Collegeville, MN: Liturgical Press.

—HALEE GRAY SCOTT

SUNDAY SCHOOL AMONG SLAVES

Historical Introduction

Robert Raikes began a Sunday school to train destitute children who worked in the London factories in moral training.[273] This lay-led movement filled a void in the existing educational structures to teach spiritual truth to children. Raikes believed that by learning basic literacy and the Gospel, the underclass could gain social acceptance and improve their lot in life.[274] Raikes published his work in 1783 in the *Gloucester Journal*, and the response was strong and positive.

Sunday school spread in the antebellum South, as slaveholding women were convinced of their obligation to evangelize slaves; however, this religious instruction by their masters was generally considered a negative by bondmen.[275] Southerners recognized their duty to teach the Gospel to both slave and free, black or white.[276]

Anthony Benezet in Philadelphia established the Quaker "African School" in 1731. He opposed slavery, attempted to educate blacks, and worked to improve conditions for Indians. He also led in providing a school for poor girls.[277] During this time, Baptists in Pawtucket, Rhode Island, provided instruction for poor children, both black and white, through Sunday school. Itinerant Quakers like John Woolman (1720–1772) led the abolitionist movement and advocated schooling for other classes and races. Instruction for blacks was often integrated into the Quaker schools in the 1700s.[278]

In 1824, the Sunday School Union was founded in the United States.[279] American Methodists, interested in teaching poor children, planned an instruction book for both white and black children. Sunday school as implemented in the United States taught rudimentary reading and writing along with the Bible. The common school emerged from the evangelical Sunday school movement.[280]

Sunday School in the South

In the southern colonies/states, education was considered a parental duty and was not relegated to the state or church. Education was approached from two perspectives. Plantation owners employed private tutors or sent children to England to be educated. For those with lesser means, apprenticeship school provided training and trade-related skills.[281]

Sunday school for slaves emphasized basic educational skills such as reading and writing. With the scriptures serving as the text book for Sunday school, basic literacy was needed to teach spiritual truth. Oral instruction was the norm, and a variety of catechisms were used and adapted for illiterate slaves. Building upon the African oral tradition, recitations were used as a primary teaching method. Black Christian education was limited to oral instruction by white ministers or missionaries. A variety of barriers were erected to hinder missionaries from teaching Sunday school unless "approved" topics were used.

Prior to the Civil War, white believers did not teach the "whole Bible" but focused on scriptures, which reinforced hard work and obedience to their masters. Slave owners prohibited teaching of reading, as reading might lead to interest in principles of freedom and equality. A limited education was certain for slaves, since owners failed to teach about freedom in Christ and the value of human beings.

The New England Anti-Slavery Society, established in 1813, taught literacy skills. Levi Coffer, known as the president of the Underground Railroad, began a Sunday school in 1821 for slaves in New Garden, North Carolina, which was later closed due to fear that slave owners might retaliate against the school. As the Sunday school movement expanded in the 1830s, outreach and teaching to slaves met strong opposition by slave owners, who feared educated slaves would no longer obey and be subservient.

First African Church of Savannah, Georgia, started the first black Sunday school in 1825; this was a rarity due to the restrictions placed on black churches. In the North, African American Sunday schools continued and served as a refuge during the Civil War. Postwar Reconstruction brought a golden age of African American Sunday schools that mimicked white curriculum and methodology.

The Nate Turner slave rebellion in 1831 brought Sunday schools for slaves under suspicion, because Turner learned to read in Sunday school. Slave revolts in South Carolina by individuals who attended Sunday school led to a prohibition against teaching reading to slaves. Blacks were forbidden to lead religious services.

In 1835, the abolitionist Frederick Douglass secretly began a Sunday school for Negros with the purpose of teaching slaves, both male and female, to read. Douglass taught 40 people, whose hunger to learn outweighed their fear of punishment.

273. Michael J. Anthony, *Foundations of Ministry* (Wheaton, IL: Victor Books, 1992), 47.

274. D. Bruce Lockerbie, *A Passion for Learning: A History of Christian Thought on Education* (Colorado Springs, CO: Purposeful Design Publications, 2007), 194.

275. Katherine Rohrer, *Black, White, and Sunday School: The Relationship among Religion, the Plantation Mistress, and the Slave in Reality and in Memory* (Athens: University of Georgia, 2007).

276. Judith St. Clair-Hull, *Strategies for Educating African American Children* (Chicago: UMI, 2006), 45.

277. Warren Button and Eugene F. Provenzo Jr., *History of Education and Culture in America*, 2nd ed. (Englewood Cliffs, NJ: Prentice-Hall, 1988), 88.

278. Reed and Prevost, 1983, 296.

279. Ibid., 195.

280. Ibid., 159.

281. James E. Reed and Ronnie Prevost, *A History of Christian Education* (Nashville, TN: Broadman & Holman, 1993), 295.

In 1858, while a professor at Virginia Military Institute in Lexington, Virginia, Thomas "Stonewall" Jackson began a Sunday school for free and slave blacks. Jackson taught both freemen and slaves to read even though it was against the law. Sunday school among blacks, either slave or free, stressed the opportunity to become literate so individuals could read the Bible. The spiritual conviction that all people needed the Savior was an impetus to begin teaching through Sunday schools.

References and Resources

Anthony, Michael. 1992. *Foundations of Ministry*. Wheaton, IL: Victor Books.

Lockerbie, D. Bruce. 2007. *A Passion for Learning: A History of Christian Thought on Education*. Colorado Springs, CO: Purposeful Design Publications.

Reed, James E., and Ronnie Prevost. 1993. *A History of Christian Education*. Nashville, TN: Broadman & Holman.

—STEPHEN K. McCORD

SUNDAY SCHOOL IN THE UNITED KINGDOM

A Sunday school is a church organization designed to teach children about Christianity. Most churches meet on Sunday, which is why it is so named.

Sunday schools were first set up in the United Kingdom in the 1780s to provide education for working-class children on their one day off from the factory or mine. The institution is accredited to Robert Raikes, the editor of the *Gloucester Journal*. His aim was primarily educational (not evangelistic), to teach young people (and sometimes adults) reading, writing, and ciphering. The text for such education was the Bible.

In many ways these, Sunday schools and the ragged schools (for poor children in the cities) were precursors of the free school system started in 1811 by the National Society.

An earlier Sunday school may have been opened in 1751 in St. Mary's Church, Nottingham, but the movement is generally dated to 1781, when Raikes saw the plight of children living in the Gloucester slums. In the home of Mrs. Meredith, he opened the first school on Sunday, the only day these boys and girls living in the slums and working in the factories could attend. Using the Bible as the textbook, he taught them to read and write.

Within four years, more than 250,000 children were attending schools on Sunday throughout England. Many new schools opened in 1784, including the interdenominational Stockport Sunday School, which financed and constructed a school for 5,000 scholars in 1805; in the late 19th century this was recognized as the largest such school in the world.

By 1831, it was reported that attendance at Sunday schools had grown to 1.2 million, approximately 25 percent of the population. They provided basic literacy education alongside religious instruction. By 1895, the Society for the Establishment and Promotion of Sunday Schools had distributed 91,915 spelling books, 24,232 Testaments, and 5,360 Bibles. The Sunday school movement was cross-denominational, and through subscription built large buildings that could host public lectures as well as classrooms. In the early days, adults would attend the same classes as the children, to be instructed in basic reading.

Over time, Sunday schools became known not for their educational but for their nurturing emphasis. After World War II, Sunday schools tended to operate during the main adult service, making them more a form of "children's church" or an age-specific form of teaching.

By the 1960s, the term "Sunday school" could refer to the building and not to any education classes, and by the 1970s, even the largest Sunday school at Stockport had been demolished. From this period, Sunday school became the generic name for many different types of religious education pursued on Sundays by various denominations.

Today many different expressions of Sunday schools exist. They range from traditional methods of teaching, using small groups, Bible-based teaching, familiar songs, and so forth, to the more contemporary. Sunday school is often part of a larger Christian formation program in many churches. Some Roman Catholic churches operate Sunday schools, though Catholics commonly refer to Sunday school as "catechism class."

In 1986 in America, a new kind of Sunday school started out of a ministry of Bill Wilson in the inner city of Brooklyn, New York, called sidewalk Sunday school. This movement is having international influence. Wilson is inadvertently standing on the shoulders of Robert Raikes by focusing on children who are less privileged, and like Raikes his method is to make sure that every child has a home visit in a given period of time. Using delivery trucks that can be converted into stages, he adapts project areas and parks for Sunday school programs. His organization, Metro Ministries, is now in many major cities in the United States and has branches in eight other countries.

References and Resources

Cliff, P. B. 1986. *The Rise and Development of the Sunday School Movement 1780–1980*. Birmingham, AL: National Christian Education Council.

Griffiths, M. 2009. *One Generation from Extinction*. Oxford: Monarch Books.

—HOWARD WORSLEY

SUNDAY SCHOOL MOVEMENT

For almost 200 years, North American Protestant congregations have sponsored a school on Sundays to cultivate the faith of children, youth, and adults. Depending for the most part on volunteer teachers and leaders, these Sunday schools have relied predominantly on curriculum resources produced in denominational or independent publishing houses. Their mission has been extended through a number of allied institutions and organizations. Although both acclaimed and criticized for most of its history, the Sunday school has left its mark on the religious and cultural life of the nation.

Mission

The Sunday school movement in North America has deep roots. Although a few mid-18th-century English Methodists and Quakers taught small groups of children on Sundays, the movement is typically traced back to a Sabbath day school Robert Raikes established in the 1780s for poor working children in Gloucester, England. In the American colonies, the first Sunday schools followed his approach, providing instruction in reading and writing in a religious environment for the children of the poor. By the 1820s, however, Sunday school leaders realized that the poor in a democratic society did not choose to attend schools based on class or caste. A more expansive vision encompassing all children in a community was needed. What began "as an exercise in charity," Robert Lynn and Elliott Wright have noted, was consequently transformed into "a prep school for the whole of evangelical America."[282]

The Sunday and Adult School Union, organized in Philadelphia in 1817, gave the movement focus. Its expansion in 1824 into the American Sunday School Union increased its momentum. Leaders, perceiving dangers to the national character from Catholic immigrants and frontier "barbarism," embraced the mission of establishing "a Sunday school in every destitute place where it is practicable, throughout the Valley of the Mississippi."[283] Enthusiastic advocates included Yale theologian Lyman Beecher, congressional leaders and governors, businessmen, pastors, and members of the laity. Hundreds of Sunday school "missionaries" fanned out across the West, organizing thousands of Sunday schools, leaving behind them libraries of small books, tracts, and pamphlets. Stephen Paxson, perhaps the most famous of these missionaries, is credited with establishing more than 1,200 schools in and around Illinois.

The movement has been shaped by a number of challenges. The need for study books and reading materials provided the impetus to a vast publishing enterprise. Increasing denominational self-consciousness led most to establish their own Sunday school boards and to shift their emphasis from *mission* to *church* schools. Criticism of the "babel" of approaches to Bible study in congregations inspired John Vincent and several Chicago area clergy to develop a curricular format of uniform lessons to order student engagement with the content of the Bible from childhood into adulthood. Adopted in 1872 by the National Sunday School Convention, the Uniform Lesson Series soon dominated Sunday school Bible study. Under the auspices of the National Churches of Christ in the U.S.A., it continues to guide Bible study in many 21st-century congregations.

The confluence of complaints about the lack of time for adequate instruction on Sunday mornings and a growing awareness of the increasing leisure time in middle-class families inspired other related Christian education innovations. The first Chautauqua Assembly in 1874, for example, launched an extensive nondenominational adult education movement of book clubs, lecture circuits, and educational events at Chautauqua Assembly sites around the country. Christian Endeavor, organized in 1881, established a model for most denominational youth, student, and young adult organizations throughout the 20th century and parachurch youth organizations such as Young Life (1941) and Campus Crusade (1951) after World War II. Vacation Bible school (1884), released time (1914) from public school, and child evangelism fellowship (1937) similarly expanded the religious education experience of children.

Supreme Court decisions from the 1960s about the place of prayer and Bible reading in public schools were catalysts to biblically based homeschooling and Christian weekday schools and contributed to the conditions culminating in the restructuring of ecumenical and denominational agencies of Christian education.

Method

A widely shared "union principle" allied the movement with the voluntary efforts of the American Education Society (1815), focused on clergy education; the American Home Missionary Society (1826), committed to clergy support in poor communities; and the American Bible (1816) and American Tract (1825) Societies, which distributed Bibles and religious literature across the nation. It linked the missions of the Sunday school and

---

282. Robert W. Lynn and Elliott Wright, *Big Little School: 200 years of the Sunday School* (Birmingham, AL: Religious Education Press, 1980 [1971]), 36.

283. Ibid., 41.

public school movements in a partnership emphasizing patriotism and Christian piety in forming the national character[284]—a partnership most visible in the daily reading of the King James Bible in public school and its study in Sunday school.

The "union principle" also brought theological coherence, strategic flexibility, and pedagogical clarity to a movement involving different Protestant traditions and several different religious education organizations. Theological coherence was gained by an explicitly nondoctrinal and nondenominational embrace of the central authority of the Bible (especially the King James Version) as source and guide to the Christian life. Since most early Sunday school advocates took the text of the Bible at face value, it provided a unifying vocabulary of faith in matters of personal piety and public discourse. A widely shared commitment to conversion as the change of heart required for a personal relationship with Jesus in this life and in life after death provided a unifying focus for the movement's educational efforts.

The strategic flexibility of the movement may be traced to an emphasis on voluntary consensus as both catalyst to action and its wider acceptance. It took only a few likeminded folk to launch a new initiative—whether a new Sunday school, curriculum resource, or youth ministry strategy—which through publicity and promotion might gain wider acceptance in a community, region, or nation. As a voluntary and entrepreneurial effort, the Sunday school movement encouraged collaboration on shared values while allowing at the same time for denominational differences over such concerns as baptism and standards for the ordination of clergy.

Sunday school leaders also shared a common commitment to a conversion pedagogy. The frequency with which children died contributed a sense of urgency to this pedagogical practice early in the movement. Bible study and songs provided the content for teaching and learning. Through recitation, memorization, and repetition, students confronted the need for conversion, clarified the content of the conversion experience, and after conversion rehearsed guidelines for living the converted life.

Impact

Reinforced by the reading of the Bible in public schools and the popularity of Sunday school songs like "Jesus Loves Me," Sunday schools cultivated a distinctively religious vocabulary for personal and public discourse in national life. Sunday schools energized reform movements in public education and temperance, increased attention to the welfare of children, provided new outlets for the

leadership of women, and gave strong support to local and foreign missions. A reliance on voluntary consensus, however, constrained Sunday schools from addressing challenges posed by slavery, racial and social class discrimination, and the mistreatment of Native Americans and immigrants. New insights from the study of evolution, biblical history, and psychology created tensions in the movement over what to teach and how. Increasingly robust theological and pedagogical critiques led some in the movement to call for reforms, which eventually coalesced in a movement associated with the founding of the Religious Education Association in 1903.

References and Resources

Boylan, Anne. 1988. *Sunday School: The Formation of an American Institution, 1790–1880.* New Haven, CT: Yale University Press.

Kennedy, W. B. 1966. *The Shaping of Protestant Education: An Interpretation of the Sunday School and the Development of Protestant Educational Strategy in the United States 1789–1860.* New York: Association Press, 1966.

Lynn, Robert W. 1964. *Protestant Strategies of Education.* New York: Association Press.

Lynn, Robert W., and Elliott Wright. (1971) 1980. *The Big Little School: 200 Years of the Sunday School.* Birmingham, AL: Religious Education Press.

Seymour, Jack L. 1982. *From Sunday School to Church School: Continuities in Protestant Church Education, 1860–1929.* Washington, DC: University Press of America.

Seymour, Jack L., Robert T. O'Gorman, and Charles R. Foster. 1984. *The Church in the Education of the Public: Refocusing the Task of Religious Education.* Nashville, TN: Abingdon Press.

—Charles R. Foster

SUNDAY SCHOOL, THE

What we know as Sunday school in 21st-century North America has its roots in the British Industrial Revolution in the 18th century. During that time children were forced to work in factories and mines 12 hours a day, six days a week. On Sundays, many of them simply ran wild in the streets. Newspaperman Robert Raikes of Gloucester, England, was concerned about these children and saw education as a means to battle vice and immorality. In 1780, he set up "Sunday schools" for these children to both educate them in reading, writing, and morality, and evangelize them.

As these Sunday schools proliferated, Raikes and William Fox established the interdenominational Sunday School Society (1785). Throughout the first half of the 19th century, both denominational and nondenominational Sunday school societies and unions continued to

---

284. Robert W. Lynn, *Protestant Strategies of Education* (New York: Association Press, 1964).

grow throughout England, promoting the growth of the Sunday school and publishing teaching materials.

Michael Anthony and Warren Benson cite five major contributions of the Sunday school movement in England. It spurred a nationwide religious revival, helped people see the need for public education for everyone, awakened the middle and upper classes to their societal responsibilities for reform, stimulated the publication of religious education materials, and aroused a desire for adult education.

Quickly the Sunday school movement spread to North America, originally developing in the late 18th century as a missionary and philanthropic organization. In 1790, the Sabbath School Society in Philadelphia was established, modeled after Raikes's own Sunday School Society. By the early 19th century, the North American model for the Sunday school began to differentiate itself from the British model. American schools were more inclusive. They were not just for teaching the poor reading and writing; they also became vehicles for missionary activity. The American Sunday School Union was established in 1824 with the goal of planting Sunday schools throughout the Mississippi Valley in two years. While they failed to attain that goal, they did have othersome success with their evangelistic emphasis. This westward expansion was also seen as a way to combat the perceived barbarism of the "Wild West." Sunday schools were seen as a way to Christianize America.

Another contribution of the early Sunday school movement in North America was the establishment of libraries. The American Sunday School Union established libraries with every Sunday school it started. The mark of a bona fide Sunday school was its library. These libraries were always considered to be "public," and by 1959, there were 30,000 in the United States in Sunday schools.

Unfortunately, the largest Sunday school agencies in the United States devoted little attention to the African American population and were for the most part silent on the issues of slavery and abolition.

The North American Sunday School movement experienced a bit of a renaissance at the end of the Civil War (Lynn and Wright 1971, 90). In the Midwest, a group of men, including evangelist D. L. Moody, formed the "Illinois Band," a group, who among other things, were intent on growing and improving the Sunday school. For example, John Vincent established "Sunday School Teacher Institutes" for the training of volunteer Sunday school teachers. These men of the Illinois Band accepted the "mid-nineteenth version of the evangelical faith, complete with literal interpretation of the Bible and the second coming" (Lynn and Wright 1971, 92). By 1832, there were 8,268 Sunday schools affiliated with the American Sunday School Union in 27 states and the District of Columbia.

The revolutionary Uniform Lesson Plan Series was devised in 1872. Under this plan, all teachers taught the same lesson each week, departmentally graded. This uniform plan encouraged denominational teachers' meetings. By 1900, three million Sunday school students were taught using the Uniform Lesson Series.

As the 20th century approached, the Sunday school movement began to encounter some difficulties. As the members of the Illinois Band aged and died off, it was difficult to find successors with the same skill and enthusiasm. The Uniform Lesson Series was coming under criticism, and higher biblical criticism was causing schisms in the North American church, affecting the Sunday school. In addition, the Sunday school movement was coming under fire for its failure to aid African American Sunday schools. Thus, a movement was afoot to reform the Sunday school, to bring it in line with modern culture, and the old timers of the Sunday school were resistant.

In 1903, the Religious Education Association was founded. Its purpose was to reverse the perceived downward trend in church educational ministries and to bring professionalism and biblical scholarship to the world of church-sponsored religious education. Anthony and Benson (2003) note that the Religious Education Association helped transform the Sunday school into a modern institution. However, as the United States experienced the Great Depression and World War II, the Sunday school movement lost some of its momentum and popularity, particularly in the more progressive mainline denominational churches. Evangelical conversion was no longer the goal of these Sunday schools. By 1945, mainline church Sunday schools were in trouble, while Sunday schools of more conservative churches continued to grow. This trend continues through today.

For conservative Sunday schools, much of the growth was fueled by the development of independent curriculum publishers, who offered these churches a more theologically conservative curriculum alternative to what their denominations might be offering. Group Publishing, which burst on the scene in the early 1990s, changed the face of Sunday school curriculum by offering an educational resource (Hands On Bible Curriculum) not dependent on student books, worksheets, or take home papers. Also, the second half of the 20th century was the heyday of the local Sunday school convention. Big cities like Detroit, Chicago, and Los Angeles would draw thousands of volunteer Sunday school teachers to large convention centers, where they attended seminars about every aspect of teaching Sunday school and could wander through an exhibit hall replete with curriculum, book, and resource displays. In the 1970s, large churches began to staff for age level needs. The all-purpose director of Christian education was replaced with the children's pastor, whose largest responsibility was most often the administration and staffing of the Sunday school.

In the 1990s and into the 21st century, many churches stopped calling Sunday school by that name. With a new emphasis on Sunday school being "fun," the idea was that children didn't want to go to school on Sunday. So churches like the mega-church Willow Creek Community Church renamed their Sunday morning children's ministries Promiseland, and many other churches followed suit.

The early 21st century has not been without its challenges for the Sunday school. Consistent volunteer participation in Sunday school has become more difficult to sustain, and teacher training has become more difficult to deliver. Large, well-attended local Sunday school conventions are a thing of the past, with larger national, age-specific training conferences filling the gap for church professionals. Some churches have turned to hiring paid Sunday school teachers for some age levels. Even in conservative churches, families do not attend church as consistently as they once did, presenting challenges for continuity in teaching and relationship building. And some religious educators have even questioned the schooling model of the Sunday school as the best way for churches to spiritually nurture their children. Sunday school curriculum publishers have moved toward publishing several different lines of niche curriculum even as they have suffered because many churches have found it more efficacious to write their own curricula. Yet in the midst of all these issues and changes, most churches continue to offer some form of Sunday school for their children each week.

References and Resources

Anthony, Michael, and Warren Benson. 2003. *Exploring the History and Philosophy of Christian Education: Principles for the 21st Century.* Grand Rapids, MI: Kregel Academic.

Kendig, Ed, and Cully Brubaker, eds. 1963. *Westminster Dictionary of Christian Education.* Philadelphia: The Westminster Press.

Lynn, Robert, and Elliot Wright. 1971. *The Big Little School: 200 Years of the Sunday School.* New York: Harper & Row.

Reed, James E., and Ronnie Prevost. 1993. *A History of Christian Education.* Nashville, TN: Broadman & Holman.

—Ivy Beckwith

SUNDAY SCHOOLS FOR POOR CHILDREN

Across the spectrum of Christian denominations and churches, Sunday schools are the most prevalent and universal institution of Christian education. There were early efforts to start Sunday schools, especially in churches, but the Sunday school movement as it is now known had its genesis outside the context of churches, in schools for impoverished children.

Early Attempts at Sunday Schools

Among the numerous people who attempted to start Sunday school in North America were John Wesley (who in 1737 started a short-lived Sunday school at Christ Church in Savannah, Georgia); Joseph Bellamy (in 1740 in Bethlehem, Connecticut); Eleazar Wheelock (who in 1743 started a Sunday school for Native American children in Lebanon, Connecticut); and James Greeming (in 1744 Philadelphia, Pennsylvania). In England, Theophilus Lindsey (in 1764 in Catterick, England) and Hannah Bell (in 1769 in High Wycombe, England) also started schools to teach scripture to children.

Sunday Schools in the United Kingdom

In the United Kingdom, people outside the Anglican Church were legally banned from sponsoring schools. In 1779, however, Parliament passed the Enabling Act, lifting that prohibition.

During the Industrial Revolution, many poor children worked in factories and mines to help support their families. On Sundays, such children often became involved in vandalism and other criminal activities. They also remained illiterate and otherwise uneducated, thus perpetuating their poverty.

In Gloucester, England, Robert Raikes (1736–1811) was editor of the *Gloucester Journal.* Like his predecessor and father, Raikes championed prison and literacy reform. Due to Raikes's continued social crusading, critics called him "Bobby Wild Goose."

In 1780, Raikes determined to start a school for poor children on Sundays in a Mrs. Meredith's kitchen in her house on Sooty Alley. Raikes paid Mrs. Meredith to teach, but she soon became discouraged, and the school moved closer to Raikes's house on Southgate Street. The main goal was literacy using the Bible as primary text, but the Sunday school also taught the catechism, hygiene, and morals, and the children were taken to church. Raikes eventually wrote his own text, *The Sunday School Scholar's Companion.*

Baptist William Fox, like Raikes, sought more adequate literacy and biblical education for the poor. In 1785, Fox formed a society to fund faculty, purchase and distribute books (especially Bibles), and seek help beyond his own denomination. This was the Society Established in London for the Support and Encouragement of Sunday Schools, or the London Sunday School Society.

Sanction of Sunday schools by the Church of England waxed and waned. At one point, Prime Minster William Pitt wished to ban them as subversive. Some suggested that laity teaching on Sunday violated the fourth commandment. However, the purposes and institutions of the Sunday schools were supported and encouraged by clergy such as John and Charles Wesley and George Whitfield and politicians such as William Wilberforce.

Eventually, the Church of England Sunday-School Institute was formed as other societies sprang up. William Brodie Gurney's Sunday School Union of London focused more on pedagogy and training teachers for Sunday schools. The Society for Superseding the Necessity of Climbing Boys set up Sunday schools for chimney sweeps. In Edinburgh, Scotland, the Gratis Sabbath-School Society was founded, as were two societies especially for Sunday schools in Ireland—the Hibernian Sunday-School Society and the Sabbath-School Society for Ireland—and London's Hibernian Society.

Sunday Schools in the United States

Educational opportunities for poor children were few in the early United States, especially in large cities and in the South. Some Protestant churches did establish Sunday schools for catechetical purposes. However, some nondenominational Sunday schools started in larger cities. Most taught basic literacy and encouraged Bible verse memorization.

In 1790, the ecumenical First Day Society was established in Philadelphia, Pennsylvania, to raise funds to pay teachers and create a "board of visitors" to enhance the Sunday schools it sponsored. In 1816, Joanna Graham Bethune (who with her husband had already begun a Sunday school) founded the Female Union for the Promotion of Sabbath Schools in New York. The American Sunday School Union was founded in 1824.

Virginian William Elliot began a Sunday school in 1785 on his plantation in Virginia to read and teach the Bible to his children, slaves, and neighbor children. Another Virginian, Methodist Francis Asbury, established a Sunday school in 1786, mostly to teach slaves. Such schools became one of the few means by which blacks could be trained in literacy. This was more accepted in the North. In the South, slave education was widely prohibited. After the Civil War and Emancipation, the literacy function of Sunday schools was expanded by various organizations, including missionary societies, freedmen's aid societies, and the American Sunday School Union.

References and Resources

Boylan, Anne M. 1988. *Sunday School: The Formation of an American Institution 1790–1880*. New Haven, CT: Yale University Press.

Lynn, Robert W., and Elliott Wright. 1980. *The Big Little School: 200 Years of the Sunday School*. 2nd ed. Foreword by J. Blaine Foster. Nashville, TN: Abingdon Press.

—Ronnie Prevost

Supreme Court Decisions and Christian Education

The right of parents to perpetuate their faith through Christian education is periodically shaped through decisions handed down by the U.S. Supreme Court. As the court of last resort, the nine justices wield incredible power and can serve as the protectors of religious freedoms or the catalyst through which those freedoms are eroded. The Court is regularly petitioned to address grievances regarding general religious issues, yet on occasion the justices are asked to rule on issues directly impacting Christian education. Three decisions in particular have arguably done the most to shape the practice of Christian education in America: *Pierce v. Society of Sisters* (1925), *Zorach v. Clauson* (1952), and *Good News Club v. Milford Central School* (2001).

Pierce v. Society of Sisters (1925)

On 7 November 1922, the state of Oregon passed the Compulsory Education Act, which was interpreted to deny parents the right to select a Christian education for their children. Specifically, the act required parents to send their children to a public school in the district where the children resided, thus denying them educational control over their children. The lawsuit was brought as a joint effort between The Society of Sisters and Hill Military Academy. The Society of Sisters was a corporation that facilitated care for orphans, educated youths, and established and maintained academies or schools. Hill Military Academy was a corporation engaged in owning, operating, and conducting an elementary, college preparatory, and military training school for boys. The question to be decided was: "Did the act violate the liberty of parents to direct the education of their children?" In a unanimous ruling, all nine justices found that, yes, "the fundamental liberty upon which all governments in this Union repose excludes any general power of the State to standardize its children by forcing them to accept instruction from public teachers only." This landmark ruling affirmed the rights of parents to decide where their children receive an education, thus ensuring their right to choose a Christian education for their children.

Zorach v. Clauson (1952)

Since the early 1900s, organizations have sought means to offer Christian education to public school students. Among the strategies employed are "release time education" (RTE) programs, which provide religious instruction to students who are released from scheduled school activities. After numerous legal challenges, the Supreme Court made its most definitive ruling in *Zorach v. Clauson* (1952). The case was brought by a group of taxpayers who argued that the New York RTE program was illegal, based on a broad interpretation of the Court's earlier decision in *McCollum v. Board of Education* (1948). The program permitted public schools to release students during the school day so they could leave school grounds and go to centers for religious instruction. Students were only released upon the written request of their parents. The Court accepted the case in an effort to decide whether New York had either prohibited the free exercise of religion or had made a law respecting an establishment of religion, in violation of the First Amendment. In its 6–3 decision, the Court found that programs established off-campus and operating with parental consent were legal as long as they were not supported in any manner by taxpayer funds. Reversing its reasoning in *McCollum*, the Court also rejected the argument based on an extensive review of the relationship between the First Amendment and the inculcation of the Jeffersonian phrase "separation of church and state." The *Zorach* decision has opened wide the door for organizations to offer Christian education to today's 50 million public school students.

Good News Club v. Milford Central School (2001)

This case began when a New York state resident applied to use Milford Central School for meetings of a Good News Club. The purpose of the club was to provide children with "a fun time of singing songs, hearing a Bible lesson and memorizing scripture." The district superintendent deemed the request to be equivalent to religious worship and denied the application. The school defended its decision by claiming its community use policy did not allow the use of the facility for religious purposes. The two questions to be decided were: "Did Milford Central School violate the First Amendment free speech rights of the Good News Club when it excluded the club from meeting after hours at the school?" and "If a violation occurred, was it justified by Milford's concern that permitting the club's activities would violate the establishment clause?" The Court's 6–3 ruling found that the school's action was a violation of the free speech clause of the First Amendment and that the school had not raised a valid establishment clause claim. The Court reasoned that because the school allowed other groups to meet at the same time, the school had created a limited public forum. Therefore, the school was not permitted to exclude groups based solely on their content or viewpoints. When a public school allows student and community groups to use its facilities, it must open the doors to all, including groups promoting Christian education.

Conclusion

Christian education plays a vital role in the perpetuation of the Christian faith to future generations. Whether this is accomplished through protecting the right of parents to enroll their children in Christian schools, or to attend RTE Bible programs during the school day, or to attend religious services after school on school grounds, the U.S. Supreme Court stands as the guardian of our right to religious liberty.

—James A. Swezey and Andrea P. Beam

Sweden and Christian Education

Sweden is a secular country. The state church of Sweden is Lutheran, but since 1972 membership has decreased from 95 percent of the population to 68 percent. Fewer and fewer people attend church on a weekly basis, and only about 10 percent of Swedes think religion is important in daily life. However, this does not mean that Sweden has no religious history.

In 1593, a synod of more than 300 Lutheran clergy was gathered in Uppsala. At this gathering, the Evangelical Lutheran Church was declared Sweden's national church. Between the 17th and 19th centuries, religious unity prevailed. All inhabitants were to be Lutheran, and those who were not were denied the privileges of Swedish citizenship. Christian education was public and Lutheran (Alwall 2000). As immigration increased religious diversity in Sweden, the Dissenter Act was passed (1860s), which allowed Swedish citizens to leave the church and organize alternative congregations for the first time. This provided greater freedom in Christian educational endeavors.

Since the 1940s, the predominant policy has been to treat the school subject of religion neutrally and objectively. There is a growing sense of the importance of religion for individual growth and social solidarity. However, since individual religious groups remain dissatisfied with the way public schools handle their religious traditions, Sweden has allowed Free Schools to be created by religious communities and foundations. Swedish law has granted permission for religious groups to arrange religious instruction as an alternative to that found in public schools. However, in 1996 it was decided that pupils in these alternative options should no longer be allowed exemption from the religious instruction required in public schools. Religious instruction by various religious groups should be extracurricular, voluntary, and complementary (Alwall 2000).

Reference

Alwall, Jonas. 2000, January 1. Religious Liberty in Sweden: An Overview. *Journal of Church and State*, np. http://www.highbeam.com/doc/1G1-61586901.html.

—Larry H. Lindquist

SWITZERLAND AND CHRISTIAN EDUCATION

The history of Swiss education is as multifaceted as its political history. Switzerland's unique geography and multiple languages make it impossible to make sweeping generalizations about its forms of Christian education, beyond the fact that it has valued the independence of its schools. Even today, autonomous cantons oversee public school curricula. Since 1874, Switzerland has provided free and compulsory education to all children. Despite periods of provincialism, its approach to teaching the Christian faith has influenced many other parts of Europe, especially early modern England.

The University of Basel—the Swiss Confederacy's oldest university—was established through papal funds in 1460, though it later became an incubator for Protestantism. Though it aligned with the Reformed tradition during the 16th century, its German language facilitated the indirect influence of German-speaking Lutherans. The university trained Reformed pastors who were effective in gradually transforming the theological ideas of Swiss laypeople. Its approach to Christian education usually reflected the broad Evangelicalism of Martin Bucer's (1491–1551) Strasbourg rather than the scrupulously confessional Geneva or the antitraditional Zurich.

Zurich's Christian education drew heavily from the humanist approach to teaching and learning. Hulrich Zwingli (1484–1531), the canton's famous reformer, gleaned many of his ideas from northern humanism and its chief luminary, Erasmus of Rotterdam (1466–1536). Zurich's teachers were typically more interested in textual scholarship and languages than in scholastic sophistication or the fine arts. Granted, Zwingli maintained a personal appreciation for music and visual art, acknowledging their worth in the general culture, but he eliminated congregational singing and instrumentation from Zurich's churches and focused on unadorned biblical teaching. Zurich's most important pedagogue was Heinrich Bullinger (1504–1575); in addition to his church leadership, he was in charge of bringing Reformation education both to future pastors and the urban and regional population. His model of education became a template for other evangelical European schools. By the 19th century, Zurich, with its iconoclastic heritage, was a bastion of classical liberalism and educated many European intellectual refugees.

Geneva's Reformation-era churches emphasized the importance of disseminating anti-Roman Catholic ideas through Protestant teachings and practices in the home, following John Calvin's (1509–1564) theories of child-rearing. Geneva's influential Académie, led by its first rector, Theodore Beza (1519–1605), became the gold standard of theological education for many French Hu-

guenots and English Puritans. In his inaugural address to the Académie, Beza called Geneva a "city, church, and school" and a "scholarly republic." In the institution's theses on theology (*Theses theologicae* 1586), coedited by Beza and Antoine de la Faye (1540–1615), the relationship between theology and other disciplines is clear: theologians interpret the whole of existence through a biblical perspective, but scientists are free to pursue their intellectual vocation with their distinct methodology and objectives. At first, Genevan intellectual freedom had limits. For example, the anti-Trinitarian Michael Servetus (c. 1509–1553), who developed a groundbreaking theory of the circulatory system, came to Geneva as a city of refuge, but he was burned at the stake for heresy. Nonetheless, it was not long before Geneva's independent ethos opened the door to natural theology and the importance of rational inquiry. Reformed orthodoxy followed on the heels of the original Reformation and developed theological expression through increasingly scholastic methodology, as exemplified by polemical theologian Francis Turretin (c. 1623–1687). Once the next generation rose to academic influence, however, intellectuals embraced rationalistic, modernist, and liberalized theology, as exemplified by Francis's son, Jean-Alphonse Turretin (1671–1737), who served as a professor of church history and theology. Jean-Jacques Rousseau (1712–1778) was born in Geneva and signed his books "Citizen of Geneva," despite periods of hostility and exile for his ideas. His innovative perspectives on education, found in *Émile* (1762), laid the foundations for modern public education, including interest in student-centered learning, belief in the innate innocence and rational capacities of children, the cultivation of a natural environment in which the good nature of the child could thrive, reluctance to use corporal punishment, and belief in the importance of tailoring curriculum to the stages of a child's development. Many Christian scholars today are grateful for Geneva's Institut d'Histoire de la Réformation, from which research and critical editions of important texts stream forth.

Today, Swiss Christianity's primary challenge is to establish a place within its secularized and increasingly pluralistic society. Switzerland's Christian educators' organizations tend to group themselves according to linguistic rather than geographical boundaries. These professional associations and institutes are generally interdenominational and evangelical; they include the Association of Protestant and Evangelical Schools in the Francophonie, the Förderverein für christliche Schulen, Initiative für christliche Bildung, and a network of educators called Creduca. They typically subscribe to the Conference of the European Educators' Christian Association (EurECA)'s 1997 Prague Declaration, which articulates the right to free expression of Christian beliefs within a diverse society, the obligation to have a voice within public life and government, the dangers of trusting uncritically in political systems, the responsibility of parents to determine their children's education, and the right to resist statist indoctrination and the false assumption of a universal secular belief system.

References and Resources

Burnett, Amy Nelson. 2006. *Teaching the Reformation: Ministers and Their Message in Basel, 1629–1629.* Oxford Studies in Historical Theology. Oxford: Oxford University Press.

Craig, Gordon. 1988. *The Triumph of Liberalism: Zurich in the Golden Age, 1830–1869.* New York: Charles Scribner's Sons.

Garside, Charles, Jr. 1966. *Zwingli and the Arts.* Yale Historical Publications no. 83. New Haven, CT, and London: Yale University Press.

Good, James. 1913. *History of the Swiss Reformed Church since the Reformation.* Philadelphia: Publication and Sunday School Board of the Reformed Church in the United States.

Gordon, Bruce, and Emidio Campi, eds. 2004. *Architect of Reformation: An Introduction to Heinrich Bullinger, 1504–1575.* Texts and Studies in Reformation and Post-Reformation Thought. Grand Rapids, MI: Baker.

Klauber, Martin. 1994. "Jean-Alphonse Turretini (1671–1737) on Natural Theology: The Triumph of Reason over Revelation at the Academy of Geneva." *Scottish Journal of Theology* 47: 301–325.

———. 1996. *Between Reform Scholasticism and Pan-Protestantism: Jean-Alphonse Turretin (1671–1737) and Enlightened Orthodoxy.* Plainsboro, NJ: Susquehanna University Press.

Maag, Karin. 1996. "Financing Education: The Zurich Approach, 1550–1620." In *Reformations Old and New: Essays on the Socio-economic Impact of religious Change c. 1470–1630,* edited by Beat Kümin, 68–91. London: Scholar Press, 1996.

—Jeff Mallinson

Symbolism

Christian symbolism emerged from Judaism and from the Greek and Roman culture in which it was immersed. The use of symbols in worship emerged from Judaism, in which, for example, the shofar or ram's horn called people to worship and had eschatological meaning as well (Happel 1987, 998). Christian symbols have been teaching devices from the earliest centuries. Catacombs in Rome, some dating back to the second century, tell the story of Christianity in simple line drawings using symbols such as the cross, the fish, the anchor, and the Chi Rho, a monogram formed from the first two letters of the Greek word for Christ.

From the Greek word *symballein,* meaning "to throw together," symbols are defined as words, objects, gestures, sounds, and images that unite the meaning of one thing to another, that induce participation in that to which they refer (Happel 1987, 997). Jesus taught in parables and used symbolism, such as the mustard seed and the vine. In the early church, symbols were used as a primary mode of catechesis and for the rites of initiation (like the imposition of ashes, insufflation, the anointing with oil). Augustine used signs as a way of interpreting scripture. Aquinas described the effectiveness of the sacraments as having signifying power to transform believers participating in them (Happel 1987, 999).

Some reformers distrusted symbols, and the iconoclasts whitewashed church walls and smashed icons because of the fear that these symbols and images were being worshipped in place of God. With the rise of rationalism, symbols lost some of their influence and became suspect, because symbolic meaning was thought to be purely subjective or confessional and parochial. However, the romanticism of the 18th century, as exemplified by poets such as Keats and Coleridge, renewed appreciation for the symbolic (Happel 1987, 1000). Knowing the power of symbols, the church, including ecclesiastics and theologians, has attempted to control symbols in popular piety, but people of faith have made their own use of them, with icons, relics, and altars in the home, sometimes giving the symbols an almost magical power.

Symbols derive their meaning from communal imagination (Musser and Price 1992, 467). The senses are engaged in the process of knowing and lead to the formation of symbols.

Symbols differ from conventional signs such as mathematical symbols, which are unambiguous and give direction. Symbols are polyvalent, such as darkness and light, oil and water. They emerge from human experience and convey a surplus of meaning. Some are universal, and some are culturally contextual. There is not a one-to-one correspondence with the referent, but rather the juxtaposition of unlike elements (Happel 1987, 997).

The discussion of symbolism has ranged through philosophy, literature, the arts, psychology, and theology. Immanuel Kant described symbol as intuitive representation. Symbolism in religion is important because of the literary nature of sacred texts, and because of symbols in worship and the ongoing quest for meaning in the task of linking religious claims to human experience (Musser and Price 1992, 467). There are many books illustrating Christian symbols that are useful for teaching the faith. Because of their power and primordial nature, symbols are important vehicles for religious meaning and Christian education, going beyond propositional doctrines to awaken "an encounter with an ultimate Other at the limits of human existence" (Happel 1987, 998). Paul Tillich (1957) was noted for expressing the theological significance of symbols. He asserted that all language about God is symbolic, so symbolic discourse is the only way we can speak of God. For Tillich, religious symbolism is the exclusive tool for describing the religious dimension of human existence. A symbol participates in the reality it represents, but does not exhaust that reality. A religious symbol uses the categories of ordinary experience, but in such a way as to transcend ordinary experience. To take symbolic language literally, according to Tillich, is to reduce the description of the divine to idolatry (1957, 45–48). Roman Catholic theologians such as Karl Rahner and Bernard Lonergan rehabilitated the notion of symbol in reinterpreting their role in Aquinas in an ontological sense (Happel 1987, 1001). Paul Ricoeur (1967) noted that "the symbol gives rise to thought," and thought then always returns to and is informed by the symbol (348–349).

Today there is continued need for discernment of the difference between symbols that lead toward transformation of society for the good and negative use of symbolism that can absolutize stereotypes. Theologians and educators continue to address questions about the nature of symbolism, in the hope that they can illuminate theology and that Christian theological language can contribute to the understanding and appropriation of the increasing number of symbols in our culture. For example, some postmodern thinkers suggest that the market use of logos, icons, and catchphrases reinforces the power of symbols while at the same time diminishing their ability to communicate religious faith. Christian symbols have been appropriated by and sometimes trivialized in popular culture. Yet the Christian tradition has a wealth of symbols and stories that continue to nourish and heal. David Tracy (1981) has suggested that remaining faithful to that tradition involves allowing new expressions to emerge, especially from those who have been silenced. This includes the willingness to "try on" old symbols to see if they still have their transforming power for good and to try on new symbols as well (Happel 1990, 1244).

References and Resources

Cornwell, J., and H. Cornwell. 2009. *Saints, Signs and Symbols: The Symbolic Language of Christian Art.* Harrisburg, PA: Morehouse Press.

Happel, S. 1987. "Symbol." In *The New Dictionary of Theology*, edited by J.A. Komonchak, M. Collins, and D. A. Lane, 996–1002. Wilmington, DE: Michael Glazier.

———. 1990. "Symbol." In *The New Dictionary of Sacramental Worship*, edited by P. E. Fink, 1237–1245. Collegeville, MN: The Liturgical Press.

Musser, D. W., and J. L. Price, eds. 1992. *A New Handbook of Christian Theology.* Nashville, TN: Abingdon Press.

Rahner, K. 1966. "The Theology of Symbol." In *Theological Investigations.* Baltimore, MD: Helicon Press, IV.

Ricoeur, P. 1967. *The Symbolism of Evil.* Boston: Beacon Press.

Tillich, P. 1957. *The Dynamics of Faith.* New York: Harper & Row.

Tracy, D. 1981. *The Analogical Imagination: Christian Theology and the Culture of Pluralism.* New York: Crossroad.

VanderMeer, H. 2006. *Rings, Kings and Butterflies: Lessons on Christian Symbols for Children.* Minneapolis, MN: Augsburg Press.

—Susan Willhauck

Synagogue

The synagogue, known as the "house of assembly" (*Beth ha Kenesset*) or "house of instruction," was described in the New Testament era by the word *didaskein,* "to teach" (Matt. 4:23; Mark 1:21; Luke 4:15). It was developed after the Babylonian exile in 538 BC for worship, instruction, and education of children and adults, to maintain the teaching of the Torah and the heritage of Jewish culture.

The synagogue was likely a post-exilic institution started by the Jewish communities in Babylonia and Egypt, but not formalized until the Hellenistic exile period (fourth century BC). Many modern scholars attribute the origins of the synagogue to Ezra, perhaps the most recognized post-exilic leader in Judah. By the third century BC, the synagogue spread throughout the Jewish diaspora for community and worship while away from Jerusalem and the Temple.[285] The synagogue became the center of social and religious life, with its chief function being to provide instruction. The synagogue did not rival the Temple, but was an extension of it. The Temple was for worship and the synagogue for instruction. In rabbinical literature, the synagogue is often referred to as the "little Temple."

House of Instruction

While the synagogue had many functions, it was essentially focused on instruction. This included a morning service for preaching and worship and an afternoon service dedicated to teaching. The teaching service provided the reading and interpreting of scripture, as well as group and individual studies. Instruction or teaching was not passive or purely teacher directed, but in the Jewish world it was a blend of articulating the Law with opportunities for interaction, and always in the context of real life. Instruction as the transmission of information,

---

285. James Estep, ed., *Christian Education: The Heritage of Christian Education* (Joplin, MO: College Press, 2003), 5.

conducted in formal schools, where the teacher is revered as the expert and where interaction and questioning are typical and sometimes discouraged, was foreign to Jewish education. The essence of instruction was to distinguish between what is good and evil, and to "fear the Lord is the beginning of wisdom" (Ps. 111:10; Prov. 9:10). Instruction was heavily value laden and related to what the Law actually meant in life. Jewish education was intended to enlighten and inform the mind of every Jew at every stage of life. This was a unique practice among the people of the ancient world, who kept religious knowledge safe with the priest.

When the synagogue appeared as a place of instruction, it was to be a place where people would learn to know in a full and complete sense. The Jew without knowledge could not possibility hope to live the good life. The study of the Torah always leads to action, to practice of the will of God, to doing good. The rabbis saw that the rewards of study led to a deeper and stronger spiritual life. The synagogue was therefore not only a place of prayer; it was a house of instruction. For without the knowledge of the Torah, they would not be a people.

The Jewish leaders wanted to develop a strong educational system to educate the new generation of young Jewish children to ensure a continuance of the Jewish people. The primary curriculum of the synagogue was the Torah.[286] The synagogue school was governed by the *bet hasseper* (house of the book). Students sat on the ground at the teacher's feet. Teaching included memorization and repetition. Students were expected to master the *Shema*, the *Hallel* (a series of psalms), the creation story, and the Levitical law.[287] Jewish families were required to provide Jewish education for their male children beginning at age five. By the fourth century BC, the synagogue was commissioned with instructing boys in Hebrew so they could read and study the Torah. By age 10, they were expected to study the Mishnah, a textbook on oral law, which included instruction about marriage, divorce, and civil and criminal laws.[288] As young boys became men, some of them would become rabbis, teachers of the Torah, to continue the identity and heritage of the Jewish people.

The sermon was one of the most powerful educational tools in the synagogue. The purpose of the sermon was to awaken the mind and cause the adult to think. The sermon was to stimulate the individual not merely to listen to scripture, but to actively mediate upon it and try to derive the deeper meanings inherit in the texts. The

sermon was not passive, but included participation by the hearers. One of the goals of the rabbi was to help students learn the skills of discourse and reasoned thinking. The rabbi, educated in *halakhah* (Jewish law) and tradition, preached to instruct the community to answer questions and disputes raised in the law.

House of Prayer

After the destruction of the second Temple in AD 70, the Jews were determined to maintain their identity and turned to the Torah as the substitute for Temple worship. When a Jew studied the Torah and mediated on its oral interpretations, he was creating a sanctuary where he could offer thanks to God. Many passages of the Torah were inserted in the prayer book, creating a book that harmonized study with prayer. When reading the *Shema* it became a liturgical act and an act of study.

The synagogue was also a "house of prayer" (*beit tefilah*). Worship includes the recitation of prayers, often with instruction and commentary, which are found in siddur, the traditional Jewish prayer book. The *Shema*, which consists of Deuteronomy 6:4–9 and 11:13–21 and Numbers 15:37–41, was recited twice a day, in the morning and evening, based on the first paragraph of the command: "when you retire and when you arise." Jews are expected to recite three prayers daily and more on the Sabbath and Jewish holidays. While solitary prayer is valid, attending synagogue to pray with a minyan (a quorum of 10 adult males) is considered ideal. When 10 or more pray together, the "Divine Presence" (*Shekhina*) is with them. The sages taught that God listens more readily to the prayers of a congregation than He does to those of an individual. Based on Psalm 69:14, it is held that the "favorable time" for prayer (*eit ratzon*), when prayer is most welcomed by God, is when the congregation is praying.[289] Many Jews sway their bodies back and forth during prayer, a practice called *shokeling*. The recitation of prayers is a central component in the synagogue's liturgy.

Conclusion

The synagogue, through instruction and worship, preserved the Jewish identity in the midst of conflicting ideologies and influences. It provided the educational context for the next generation of Jewish leaders and to connect the teaching of the Torah to daily living. The goal was not primarily knowledge, but to develop wisdom and discernment in doing the will of God. As the center of social and religious life, teaching and worship, the synagogue is a powerful example of religious education.

---

286. Michael Anthony, "Synagogue Schools," in *Evangelical Dictionary of Christian Education*, ed. Michael J. Anthony (Grand Rapids, MI: Baker Academic, 2011), 677.

287. Reed and Prevost, *History of Christian Education*, 50.

288. Anthony, "Synagogue Schools," 677.

289. Hayim H. Donin, *To Pray as a Jew: A Guide to the Prayer Book and the Synagogue Service* (New York: Basic Books, 1980), 15.

References and Resources

Anthony, Michael, and Warren S. Benson. 2011. *Exploring the History and Philosophy of Christian Education: Principles for the 21st Century*. Eugene, OR: Wipf & Stock.

Barkley, William. 1959. *Education Ideals in the Ancient World*. Grand Rapids, MI: Baker.

Donin, Hayim H. 1980. *To Pray as a Jew: A Guide to the Prayer Book and the Synagogue Service*. New York: Basic Books.

Drazin, Nathan. 1940. *History of Jewish Education from 515 BCE to 220 CE*. Baltimore, MD: Johns Hopkins University Press.

Eisberg, Azriel. 1974. *The Synagogue through the Ages*. New York: Bloch.

Estep, James, ed. 2003. *Christian Education: The Heritage of Christian Education*. Joplin, MO: College Press.

Gangel, Kenneth O., and Warren S. Benson. 1983. *Christian Education: Its History and Philosophy*. Chicago: Moody Press.

Reed, James E., and Ronnie Prevost. 1983. *A History of Christian Education*. Nashville, TN: Broadman & Holeman.

—MARK MADDIX

T

TAIWAN AND CHRISTIAN EDUCATION

The current evangelical community in Taiwan is largely the result of the work of English and Canadian missionaries who arrived in the 1860s and established the Presbyterian Church, and the influx of missionaries and refugees from the Chinese mainland following the defeat of the Chinese Nationalist regime after the end of World War II. After many years of stagnation, the church has grown rapidly over the past 10 years, and in 2012 Christians made up about 5.5 percent of the population.

Christian Education in Taiwan
All-age Bible classes remain the typical means of educating believers in most churches. However, many have moved from the traditional Sunday school model to one-on-one discipleship and/or small group teaching.

At a national level, leaders meet for monthly prayer meetings, national prayer meetings, and the National Forum of Taiwan Church Leaders. Evangelistic, prayer, and healing rallies and seasonal camps and retreats that focus on worship, congregational prayers, healing, and group sharing have also played a significant role in individual and church renewal. As the Protestant community continues to be a minority in society at large, evangelistic work remains a key ministry in local churches.

In recent years, Taiwanese churches have also reemphasized the importance of believers' daily quiet time, with the publication of journal aids, together with early morning devotional services on week days.

Challenges and Opportunities
Key challenges facing the Taiwanese church in the 21st century include educating for becoming more globally sensitive and kingdom-minded; cultivating intergenerational ministries in a rapidly aging society and church;

strengthening unity among church leaders of different denominations; and developing greater skills in theological reflection.

References and Resources
Cheng, Y. 2008. "A Short Study on Charismatic Movements in Taiwan." *Taiwan Journal of Theology* 30: 95–110.
Chu, J. S. T. 2012. *Taiwan Church Report 2011*. Taichung: Christian Resource Center.
Rubinstein, M. A. 1991. *The Protestant Community of Modern Taiwan: Mission, Seminary, and Church*. New York: M. E. Sharpe.

—LILY K. CHUA

TANZANIA AND CHRISTIAN EDUCATION

Tanzania is a country in East Africa. It has a population of around 48 million (July 2012 estimates) and more than 120 ethnic groups. The population is about 30 percent Christian, although some estimates are as high as 50 percent.

Christian education today has its roots in the coming of missionaries during the late 18th century. Ludwig Krapf of the Church Missionary Society (CMS) and his colleague, Johann Rebman, visited Tanzania in 1848. A mission station was later set up at Bagamoyo to rescue and resettle freed slaves. Religious instruction in mission schools became the primary way Christian education was carried out (Trebon 1980).

After independence (1961), Tanzania's first president, Julius Nyerere, introduced the idea of African socialism known as *Ujamaa*, believed to be the force that saved the country from ethnic tensions common in the region (Mushi 2009). Ujamaa, however, had a downside for the country, as the level of poverty apparently inhibited the establishment of Christian education programs.

A major distinctive in Tanzania is the widespread use of Kiswahili as a language of instruction in schools (Gottneid 1976; Stambach 2010). Hence, more translation and development of curriculum materials in Kiswahili are needed for the growing church, in order to equip believers to understand and defend their faith against the threats of Islamization and syncretism.

References and Resources

Gottneid, J. Allan, ed. 1976. *Church and Education in Tanzania.* Nairobi: East African Publishing House.

Mushi, Philemon Andrew K. 2009. *History and Development of Education in Tanzania.* Daresalaam, TZ: Daresalaam University Press.

Stambach, Amy. 2010. *Faith in Schools, Religion, Education, and American Evangelicals in East Africa.* Stanford, CA: Stanford University Press.

Trebon, Thomas Joseph. 1980. *Development of the Pre-independence Educational System in Tanganyika with Special Emphasis on the Role of the Missionaries.* Denver, CO: University of Denver.

—Rosemary Wahu Mbogo

Taylor, Gardner

Early Background and Education

Gardner Calvin Taylor is an African American, born 18 June 1918, in Baton Rouge, Louisiana, to Washington Monroe and Selina Taylor.[1] Washington Monroe Taylor pastored the historic Mount Zion Baptist Church and also served as vice president at large of the National Baptist Convention, USA, Inc. Though his father passed when Taylor was 13, his standards of academic and moral excellence were strictly upheld by his mother. Taylor developed into an outstanding student under her tutelage and enrolled at Leland College in Baker, Louisiana.

Taylor excelled in academics, athletics, and debate as an undergraduate, mentored by James Alvin Bacoats, the president of Leland College. Taylor did not initially aspire to ministerial service, though influenced by ministers his whole life. He instead endeavored to become a criminal attorney. He was subsequently accepted into the University of Michigan School of Law.

His aspirations to become a lawyer were averted by his involvement in a tragic car accident, in which two whites were killed. The youthful Taylor could easily have been falsely convicted of murder, but a white Southern Baptist minister, Jesse Sharkey, gave eyewitness testimony that he had done no wrong. After this miraculous absolution,

Taylor seriously considered pursuing theological study, attributing the case's dismissal to divine providence. He felt a ministerial calling and enrolled at the Oberlin Graduate School of Theology in 1937.

While at Oberlin, Taylor examined the academic discipline of preaching. There he began his lifelong investigation of the 19th- and 20th-century Australian, Scottish, and American *homiletical colossi*, among them F. W. Robertson, Brooks, Scherer, Maclaren, Norwood, Weatherhead, Macartney, Fosdick, and Spurgeon. These people's lives resonated with Taylor. He shares with them a passionate understanding of the Christian witness. To them he attributes the craftsmanship and artistry that his preaching exudes.

Taylor assumed his first pastorate while still a graduate student at Oberlin. Upon graduating, he took pastorates at two more churches in Louisiana (one of which was his father's former church). At age 29, he was invited to preach at the Concord Baptist Church of Christ in Brooklyn, New York. Taylor became the pastor of Concord soon after the church celebrated the centennial of its founding. Taylor remained there until he retired in 1990.

Contributions to Christian Education

Taylor's most significant contribution to Christian education is the intergenerational legacy of prophetic insight, poetic erudition, palatial eloquence, artistic verve, and unprecedented revelation his preaching exudes and engenders. His acclaim is well documented. *Ebony* magazine asserted that he was "one of the greatest preachers in American history." *Time* magazine dubbed him "the dean of the nation's black preachers." The *Christian Century* described him as "the poet laureate of American Protestantism." *Newsweek* declared that he is one of the 12 greatest preachers in the English-speaking world. He preached at the Baptist World Alliance in Copenhagen, Denmark, before his 30th birthday. He delivered the 1975–1976 Lyman Beecher Lectures at Yale University. His national prominence was further solidified by his invitation to preach at the Presidential Inaugural Prayer Service in 1993. In August 2000, President Clinton awarded him the Presidential Medal of Freedom, the highest honor that can be bestowed on a civilian. Taylor has taught homiletics at Harvard, Yale, Union Graduate School of Theology, New York Theological Seminary, Colgate-Rochester-Crozer Divinity School, and most recently at Shaw University.

Though firmly rooted in the social justice tradition of African American pulpiteers, Taylor has inspired two generations of preachers, globally transcending divides of race, class, and culture. His sermons successfully homogenize 19th-century Victorian sensibility, the African American cultural ethos of solidarity with victims, pathos

---

1. Edward L. Taylor, *The Words of Gardner Taylor*, vol. 1 (Valley Forge, PA: Judson Press, 1999), 1.

for the God of the Bible, and unparalleled oratory. Lischer notes that "Taylor has mastered the inventory of African American pulpit rhetoric—the ponderous ingratiation, the understatement, parallelism, antithesis, the prophetic stutter, the peroration, and the adroit manipulation of thematic set pieces. He manages all this without a hint of artificiality and always in service to the message of the God of the Bible."[2] He further asserts: "'Human' is never restricted to 'black' in Taylor's sermons, but the suffering and triumphs of Africans in America lend to his sermons the poignancy of their example, as well as a point of focus for his mighty perorations."[3] Globally, preachers attest to Taylor's genius for "channeling evangelical doctrine and the great stories of the bible into socially progressive and prophetic utterance."[4]

Taylor's preaching exhorts the Christian responsibility to teach; his practices embody that responsibility. As such, his contributions to Christian education are not merely oratorical. He represents a paradigmatic shift from the normative approach to Christian education. Taylor contextually appropriates educating in faith. Because the Concord Church was situated in central Brooklyn, surrounded by the economic and racial decay common in urban centers, Taylor developed a utilitarian practice of educating in faith. For him, Christian education involves not only the catechizing requisite for discipleship, but also that requisite for citizenship. Gary V. Simpson, his successor at Concord, attests that Taylor believes that America's "divine possibility," provided for in the documents of the nation's founding, is captured in the form of casuistic biblical covenants. That is, if America holds true to the imbedded tenor of its founding documents, which guarantee liberty and justice for all its citizens, then God will hear, heal, and bless its lands. Namely, it is the responsibility of American Christians to prepare God's people to fully enjoy and participate in every attendant right and responsibility the American democratic experiment promises. Taylor thus expands the typical parameters of Christian education to include the Christian responsibility to provide the educated, civic minded, politically engaged citizenry essential to functional American democracy. Taylor is one of a unique generation who, by consensus, interpret the church as a community called to educate at every level, in every venue, by every means.

Most Notable Publications

Proctor, Samuel DeWitt, and Gardner C. Taylor. 1996. *We Have This Ministry: The Heart of the Pastor's Vocation.* Valley Forge, PA: Judson.

Taylor, Edward, ed. 1999. *The Words of Gardner Taylor.* Vols. 1–6. Valley Forge, PA: Judson Press.

Taylor, Gardner C. 1977. *How Shall They Preach?* Elgin, IL: Progressive Baptist Publishing House.

———. 1981. *The Scarlett Thread: Nineteen Sermons.* Elgin, IL: Progressive Baptist Publishing House.

—Wendell H. Paris Jr.

Teacher Character

Teacher character is not defined universally, though it has been described using various lists, which include similar features, attributes, abilities, and traits that describe the nature of a teacher and further distinguish types of teachers. More often than not, the list takes on the form of a judgment[5] of items, indicating a range between extremes or contrasts such as good and bad, honorable and dishonorable, effective and ineffective, or highly qualified and not qualified. Thus, definitions further differentiate and expand the term, with variations in roles and expectations. Yet when describing teacher character, most lists focus on the "effective teacher," about whom Cooper (2010) lists three key determinants: knowledge, skill, and attitudes. Scarpaci (2007, 37) notes that these characteristics "are either inherent in an individual or acquired through experience or training."[6]

Biblically, "the terms [teach, teacher, and teaching] do not so much indicate an office or official function as a service, although both ideas are often expressed or implied."[7] The passage from Matthew 28:16–20 commissions or calls all believers to teach to pass on their faith.[8] The church has a lifelong duty to teach children (Deut. 6:4–7) and all nations (Matt. 28:19–20).[9] Yet scripture also distinguishes this characteristic as a unique gift for some, giving it primacy for Christian teachers.

Knowledge

Teachers characteristically are expected to have three types of knowledge: content knowledge about the subject matter taught, integrated, or modeled; pedagogical knowledge about how to teach; and theoretical knowledge about how

2. William H. Willimon and Richard Lischer, eds., *The Concise Encyclopedia of Preaching* (Louisville, KY: Westminster John Knox, 1995), 465.

3. Ibid., 466.

4. Ibid.

5. David G. Ryans, *Characteristics of Teachers: Their Description, Comparison, and Appraisal: A Research Study* (Washington, DC: American Council on Education, 1960), 343.

6. Richard T. Scarpaci, *A Case Study Approach to Classroom Management* (Boston: Pearson, 2007), 37.

7. Byron H. DeMent, "Teach, Teacher, Teaching," in *The International Standard Bible Encyclopedia*, vol. V, ed. Geoffrey W. Bromiley (Grand Rapids, MI: Eerdmans, 1957), 2921.

8. Frank E. Gaebelein, *The Pattern of God's Truth: The Integration of Faith and Learning* (Colorado Springs, CO: Association of Christian Schools International, 1968), 7.

9. Daryl Eldridge, *The Teaching Ministry of the Church: Integrating Biblical Truth with Contemporary Application* (Nashville, TN: Broadman & Holman, 1995), 89–104.

individuals learn and behave.[10] Graham (2003, 131) asserts: "The Christian life, . . . requires the use of a Christian mind, and teachers who desire to help students develop such a mind must first possess it themselves. This personal characteristic is of utmost importance."[11]

Skills

All teachers need to have a number of identifiable skills or abilities that are important to their success, defined and/or validated in various ways, including, but not limited to, preparation programs, credentialing, and their reputation as judged by the community. It is expected that the Christian teacher's teaching brings life and not death to students (Prov. 13:14). Likewise, teachers model incarnational living, similar to that of Christ, as their lives are evidence of a personal integrity that is not swayed by appearances, opposition, or lack of preparation (Matt. 22:15–16; Acts 4:1–3; Titus 2:7–8). Teachers come alongside their students as guides and companions,[12] in this way mentoring and molding them as they learn. Christian teachers are characteristically seen as those who faithfully teach the truth of the Gospel and who are recognized by all and in high demand (2 Tim. 3:10ff.); gifted by God and likewise guided by him (James 3:1); and given the ability to teach others (Exod. 35:34; Matt. 23:34; Eph. 4:11–12).

Attitudes

Attitudes are sometimes referred to as dispositions, which are often defined by but not limited to "moral or ethical qualities, honesty, courage, integrity and reputation" and further described as tendencies, personal outlook, mood, or choices. For Christian teachers, character is defined by the fruit of the spirit that is evident when they are filled with the Holy Spirit. Teachers will demonstrate what that fruit is, regardless of any particular personality traits they may possess. Scripture defines what the fruit should be as it is played out in character (Gal. 5:22–23, 5:26; Col. 3:12–15; Eph. 4:2).[13] The spiritual gift of teaching is mentioned in several key New Testament passages (Rom. 12:7; 1 Cor. 12:29; Eph. 4:11). The gift of teaching can be described as "a supernatural, spiritually endowed ability to expound (explain and apply) the truth of God."[14]

---

10. Ryan Cooper, *Those Who Can, Teach*, 12th ed. (Boston: Wadsworth Cengage learning, 2010), 163.

11. Donovan L. Graham, *Teaching Redemptively: Bringing Grace and Truth into Your Classroom* (Colorado Springs, CO: Purposeful Design, 2003), 131.

12. Linda Vogel, *Teaching and Learning in Communities of Faith: Empowering Adults through Religious Education* (San Francisco: Jossey-Bass, 1991), 110–124.

13. Graham, *Teaching Redemptively*, 129.

14. Byron Klaus, "Gift of Teaching," in *Evangelical Dictionary of Christian Education*, ed. Michael Anthony (Baker Books; Grand Rapids, MI 2001), 679–680.

References and Resources

Cooper, Ryan. 2010. *Those Who Can, Teach.* 12th ed. Boston: Wadsworth Cengage Learning.

DeMent, Byron H. 1957. "Teach, Teacher, Teaching." In *The International Standard Bible Encyclopedia*, Vol. V, edited by Geoffrey W. Bromiley, 543–547. Grand Rapids, MI: Eerdmans.

Eldridge, Daryl. 1995. *The Teaching Ministry of the Church: Integrating Biblical Truth with Contemporary Application.* Nashville, TN: Broadman & Holman.

Gaebelein, Frank E. 1968. *The Pattern of God's Truth: The Integration of Faith and Learning.* Colorado Springs, CO: Association of Christian Schools International.

Graham, Donovan L. 2003. *Teaching Redemptively: Bringing Grace and Truth into Your Classroom.* Colorado Springs, CO: Purposeful Design.

Ryans, David, G. 1960. *Characteristics of Teachers: Their Description, Comparison, and Appraisal: A Research Study.* Washington, DC: American Council on Education.

Scarpaci, Richard T. 2007. *A Case Study Approach to Classroom Management.* Boston: Pearson.

—Karen L. Estep

Teacher Education

Making purposeful decisions about faith-based education has been on the minds of Christian scholars for centuries (see Palmer 1993). Proponents of faith-based learning consider Christian pedagogy to be integral in transforming both mind and spirit. In its most basic form, the implementation of Christian pedagogy simply means teaching as Jesus would. A process that is "highly devotional" and a curriculum that is continually fulfilling (Ward 1992, 336), the aim of Christian pedagogy in higher education today, continues to mean different things to different people (see Fowler and Pacino 2012; Kelly 2009; Robertson 2008; Ward 1992).

How faith-integration decisions play out in the academy depends on the affiliation, mission, and ethos of the school. Christian institutions of higher education typically require their professors to teach God's Word in the most overt ways, while Christian professors from public, more secular, institutions may choose more covert ways to spread God's Word in their disciplines. Similarly, just how Christian pedagogy shapes teacher education depends greatly on the mission of the institution, as well as on faculty epistemologies that cultivate a specific educational certification program.

Given that the aim of Christian education is to nurture both mind and spirit as one, what, then, would Jesus deem important for disciples of His Word? What are God's intentions for professors of teacher educators?

How might the Christian pedagogy that is implemented in teacher education programs look different than that which is implemented in other college majors?

Robertson (2008) believes that the discipline of teacher education aligns quite effortlessly with the tenets of Christian stewardship. Accordingly, Christian pedagogy can be implemented through a range of teaching methods. Students' spiritual formation and faith journeys can be cultivated by *infusing, sprinkling, spiraling,* or *supplanting* these threads in our course topics, readings, classroom discussions, and assignments (Kelly 2009).

Those who are seeking to better understand faith integration in teacher education can turn to one of the latest collections of work dedicated solely to the field of education, *Faith Integration and Schools of Education* (Fowler and Pacino 2012). This comprehensive text offers valuable contributions about effective faith integration and fostering students' spiritual formation at both the undergraduate and graduate levels, and for students involved in traditional and accelerated programs. It also highlights the most common areas of focus for faith integration: Christ's teaching, servant leadership and stewardship, dedication to social justice, and sharing our God-given gifts with the world.

Expanding on the current work on Christian pedagogy, faculty members in schools of education should consider the following recommendations (see Fowler and Pacino, 2012). First, teacher candidates must acknowledge the inequities and marginalization that exist in the world today; it is with this awareness that they can then be taught to create equitable K–12 learning environments in which all students can master challenging and meaningful standards. Second, teacher candidates must authentically serve their students by setting high expectations through attainable goals and using a range of media. They must realize that it is their God-given responsibility to fully engage all their students. Next, teacher candidates must not just be skilled at creating classroom communities that remove boundaries for their diverse students; they must put this skill into practice. Last, teacher candidates must be taught how to make intentional decisions focused on the students they teach; such student-centered instructional decisions base the assignments they give and materials they use on the needs of their students.

As with all effective instructional decisions, it is important for faculty members to make more intentional decisions about the methods of evaluating student mastery of knowledge and skills (Kelly 2009). Unfortunately, guidelines for effectively assessing the spiritual formation of our students are not as evident in the Christian pedagogy literature. However, following are some questions to consider.

What should we think of as viable tools for assessing our students' mastery of Christian pedagogy? Is it sufficient to expect students to share how they have grown as Christians? How does one put a grade on this? Do we rely on our observation of what students say in class or write in their papers? Should we follow our students into the field to observe their application of theory? The answers to these questions are affected most by one's own relationship with God and one's own spiritual formation.

References and Resources

Fowler, M., and M. Pacino. 2012. *Faith Integration and Schools of Education.* Indianapolis, IN: Precedent Press.

Kelly, A. V. 2009. *The Curriculum: Theory and Practice.* 6th ed. Thousand Oaks, CA: Sage Publications.

Palmer, P. 1993. *To Know as We Are Known: Education as a Spiritual Journey.* San Francisco: HarperCollins.

Robertson, W. 2008. "The Greatest Constructive Educator Ever: The Pedagogy of Jesus Christ in the Gospel of Matthew in the Context of the 5 Es." *Christian Perspective in Education* 1 (2): 1–17. http://digitalcommons.liberty.edu.

Ward, T. 1992. *Facing Educational Issues.* In *E. S. Gibbs' A Reader in Christian Education Foundations and Basic Perspectives.* Ada, Grand Rapids, MI: Baker Publishing Group.

—Diana D. Abbott

TEACHING, EFFECTIVE

Effective Christian teachers employ specific instructional strategies that facilitate the active integration of cognitive, affective, and behavioral dimensions of learning, while promoting the development of Christian thought, life, and practice in the context of authentic Christian care and community. Effective teaching begins with a thorough understanding of the separate elements of teaching and of the interaction and relatedness of the separate elements. The learning outcome's effectiveness depends on the level of active engagement of both sides of the teaching and learning process.

The effective teacher provides expert knowledge and skill within the specific discipline being taught. Students become far more engaged when they perceive the teacher as an authentic and credible source of knowledge and experience, as someone they could hope to emulate. In a Christian context, teachers need to exemplify a deep and sincere faith commitment and passion. Enthusiasm and passion are contagious and have a deep and lasting impact on the quality of learning experience. Effective teachers center lessons on student needs while focusing the content on student engagement, active learning, and student motivation, thereby cultivating interest and receptivity in the area of study. Student motivation, both intrinsic and extrinsic, must be deliberately and systematically attended to by the teacher throughout the course in order to encourage productive academic engagement and progress in learning. Identifying practical principles, applications, and examples of key course concepts helps learners develop a sense of relevance and real-life connection.

Facilitating active learning is one of the most challenging yet rewarding areas of effective teaching. Engaging learning experiences actively involve students in the integration, rethinking, and application of what they are learning in new and reflective ways. This requires thoughtful planning, preparation, and dedication. The typical formula of "lecture and leave" will not suffice. Guided class discussions, small group interactions, in-class presentations, field observations and reporting, and collaborative projects provide students with a variety of ways to actively engage course concepts, theories, and practices. More content, reading and preparation can happen outside the formal teaching setting, allowing class lectures and presentations to dig deeper into selected topics of interest, accompanied by active learning experiences that facilitate the personal interaction and exploration of key course concepts.

Effective teaching also requires excellence in communication. Being able to clearly and articulately engage students in meaningful interaction and discussion is primary to the teaching and learning task. Teachers should remain respectful and approachable, inviting the sharing and exploration of multiple views. Interactivity, connectedness, and building community are high priorities in promoting effective teaching and learning, particularly in the community of faith.

The structure and flow of the course content, assignments, activities, and educational experiences are key to effective teaching and learning outcomes. In addition to providing the appropriate scope of educational content and sequence of course concepts, students need clear, well-defined goals and expectations that provide guideposts along the way. They need to know where they are, where they are going, and how they will get there in the educational journey. Providing an introduction at the beginning and a summary conclusion at the end of each session is a helpful way for students to organize and digest the scheduled topics and concepts. Providing timely and substantive feedback on assignments encourages interaction, connectedness, and motivation, while celebrating excellence and indicating areas for improvement. Along with learning evaluation, this is one of the most important yet underaddresses areas in effective teaching. Students should be guided through course assignments that build knowledge while providing direct evidence of student learning outcomes so that the teacher can offer valuable personalized instruction and encourage-

ment. Including meaningful assignments throughout the course and providing formative instructor feedback and guidance are among the most appreciated practices of the effective teacher.

References and Resources

Barkley, Elizabeth F. 2010. *Student Engagement Techniques: A Handbook for College Faculty*. San Francisco: Jossey-Bass.

Fink, L. Dee. 2003. *Creating Significant Learning Experiences: an Integrated Approach to Designing College Courses*. San Francisco: Jossey-Bass.

Richards, Lawrence O., and Gary J. Bredfeldt. 1998. *Creative Bible Teaching*. Chicago: Moody Publishers.

Yount, William R. 1999. *Called to Teach: An Introduction to the Ministry of Teaching*. Nashville, TN: B&H Academic.

—Gino Pasquariello

TEACHING, HUMAN AND DIVINE

There is ambivalence at the heart of Christianity with regard to teaching. On the one hand, Matthew 28:19 tells Christians to go out and make disciples, teaching being an integral part of this process. On the other hand, in Matthew 23:8, Jesus warns his followers not to let anyone call them teacher, since only God deserves this title. There is both a duty to teach and a reservation about the role and a concern not to attribute learning to the efforts of the teacher.

St. Augustine (354–430) steers a course between promoting (and witnessing to the importance of) the duty while emphasizing the central and indispensable role played by God in all learning related to human salvation. He refers to Christ as the inner teacher, God as the source of light for the intellect, and the Holy Spirit as the effective transformer of our latent, God-given capacities so that they can engage with divine truth. Only divine action can touch the heart from the inside; nevertheless, God wants and enables human teachers to be His instruments. Human agency and divine action are not in competition. An understanding of the relation between human and divine teaching builds on and is an application of an understanding of the relation between nature and grace.

Thomas Aquinas (c. 1225–1270) says that action is shared between God and human beings: "An effect that results from a natural cause and from the divine power is not attributed partly to God and partly to the natural agent, but it is completely from both according to different modes, just as the effect is entirely attributable to an instrument and also entirely to the principal agent (*Summa Contra Gentiles*, III, 70). Prior to this, St. Bernard of Clairvaux (1090–1153), referring to the way that the action of God and our own action should not be considered separate, commented *sed opere individuo totum singuli peragunt* (1988, 106). That is, all of the work is done hand-in-hand, simultaneously, in communion, as a joint enterprise, run together; such cooperation can be called a dancing in tandem of the partners, not a dance by one partner, followed by a dance by another. For Christians in teaching, God makes all the difference; but human teachers also make a vital contribution.

In order to make their contribution, teachers must continue to study sufficiently so as to be knowledgeable about what they teach. They also need to be conversant with the many different ways of learning and to become competent in a range of teaching methods, so that they can engage effectively with students. They must prepare their lessons thoroughly, so that these are accessible to and appropriate for the level of maturity, capacities, and interests of learners. For Christian education, teachers should also be people of prayer, having internalized Christian faith and integrated it into their lives. They should seek to love their pupils and demonstrate understanding of and compassion for them as they construct an environment that is conducive to learning. There should be harmony among the content of what is taught, the modes of communication that are adopted, and the conduct that is both displayed and promoted. In this way, teachers serve as living instruments in God's orchestra, sharing, with other instruments, the task of bringing out the beauty of God's music. It is the duty of each teacher to ensure that he or she is "in tune." They must prepare, not just their lessons, but themselves as persons, if they are to enable learners to be receptive to the work of the Holy Spirit.

Preceding, accompanying, empowering, and bringing to fruition human teaching, divine pedagogy occurs as God reaches down to us in order to lift us up to Godself by engaging and transforming our intelligence, conscience, freedom, and action. As with the best human teaching, divine teaching is progressive, in that it adapts over time to our condition, circumstances, level of maturity, capacities, and questions. Its aim is salvation, both of individual persons and of communities: conversion of heart, liberation from sin, participation in God's life, communion in God's love. The goal and purpose of Christian teaching is to transform lives into greater Christlikeness. Its central content is God's Word: the message of salvation offered in revelation. The principal agents for this are the Holy Spirit and human teachers who work in harmony with this Spirit. Teachers need to be converted and conformed to, dwelling within, familiar with, and invigorated by the truths they seek to convey, if they are to go beyond merely presenting them with clarity and are to portray them with authenticity, conviction, and vitality.

References and Resources

Aquinas, Thomas. 1998. "On the Teacher." In *Thomas Aquinas: Selected Writings*, translated by Ralph McInerny, 193–216. London: Penguin Classics.

Augustine. 1912. *The Catechizing of the Uninstructed*. Translated by E. Phillips Barker. London: Methuen.

———. 1950. *The Teacher*, translated and annotated by Joseph M. Colleran. New York: Newman Press.

Bernard of Clairvaux. 1988. *On Grace and Free Choice*. Translated by Daniel O'Donovan OCSO. Kalamazoo, MI: Cistercian Publications.

Farey, Caroline, Waltraud Linnig Sr., and Johanna Paruch, eds. 2011. *The Pedagogy of God*. Steubenville, OH: Emmaus Road Publishing.

Zuck, Roy B. 1998. *Spirit-Filled Teaching*. Nashville, TN: Thomas Nelson.

—John Sullivan

Teaching in Acts

The book of Acts provides a glimpse of the educational life of the church in its first 35 years. The author, Luke, sets the direction of the book, stating that it is about "all Jesus *began* to do and to teach" (1:1), implying that the church would continue the teaching ministry of Jesus. The Acts' narrative concludes with Paul "teaching about the Lord Jesus Christ with all boldness and without hindrance" (28:30b). From first to last, the book of Acts provides insight into the teaching ministry of the first-century church.

The earliest portrait of communal life for the first believers is found in Acts 2:42: "They devoted themselves to the apostles' teaching and fellowship, to the breaking of bread and the prayers." What characteristics typified the first church? Attention was devoted to doctrine, "apostles' teaching"; ritual observances, that is, communion, "the fellowship"; community formation, "to the breaking of bread," which was often the context of the communal ritual (4:32–37); and finally spiritual disciplines, "the prayers" (three times daily in traditional Judaism).

Paul described his ministry in Ephesus as "teaching you in public and from house to house" (Acts 20:20b). Acts presents a spectrum of teaching venues common to the first-century church. First is public or large group teaching. Acts 3 uses the terms *speaking* and *teaching* together, but not synonymously. Teaching through public speaking is a dominant theme, as in 4:1–2—"teaching the people and preaching in Jesus the resurrection of the dead" (4:1)—but later is simply identified as teaching (4:2). The apostles were frequently seen teaching in the Jerusalem Temple (5:21, 25, 28, 43). Stephen's speech in Acts 7 is indeed a form of teaching. Paul and Barnabas, while in Antioch, taught and preached "the word of the Lord" (15:35). As such, preaching is a specialized form of teaching. Later, Apollos is described as one who "powerfully refuted the Jews in public, showing by the Scriptures that the Christ was Jesus" (v. 28).

Second is teaching in semiformal venues. Paul intentionally participated in synagogues throughout his missionary journeys. This is emphasized in Acts 17:1, in which Paul and Silas "pass through Amphilpolis and Appollonia" *because* they did not have a synagogue, as did Thessalonica. In the synagogues, Paul "reasoned with them [the synagogue] from the Scriptures" (Acts 17:2b). Again, Paul "stayed a year and six months, teaching the word of God among" the Corinthians (18:11). He "entered the synagogue and for three months spoke boldly, reasoning and persuading them about the kingdom of God" (19:8).

However, Paul was not limited to Jewish venues. While in Corinth, he made use of a lecture hall, teaching at "*tā scholā* of Tyrannus"; *tā scholā* has been translated as *school* (KJV, NASB), *lecture hall* (NIV), or just *hall* (RSV, ESV). Actually, the term itself signifies the secondary level of Roman education, a high school. In fact, some Western manuscripts add the phrase, "from the fifth hour to the tenth hour," corresponding to 11:00 a.m. through 4:00 p.m., when most schools were out of session due to the afternoon heat. This is the most likely time for the *schola* to be open for Paul's use.

Third is teaching done individually or in small groups. Apollos (Acts 18:24–28) had received Christian instruction and he taught, as well as further instruction from Aquila and Priscilla. Similarly, Paul taught in a prayer gathering of women in Philippi (Acts 16:14). Testimony too was a form of teaching (Acts 22:1–21; 26:1–23).

What was the early church teaching? Several basic themes can be identified in the content of teaching in Acts: (1) reinterpretation of the Hebrew scriptures in a Christian, Christocentric context, such as reasoning in the synagogues; (2) proclamation of the Gospel and the Kingdom of God, such as the apostolic *kerygma* or preaching, Acts 28:23b; (3) Christian confession of faith, such as baptismal instruction, for exmple, Acts 8:35–37; (4) the life and sayings of Jesus, for example, Acts 1:8, 20:35; and finally (5) ethical teachings, for example of "the Way" (Acts 9:2, 19:9, 23, 24:14, 22) or the Acts 15 letter (cf. Sherrill 1944, 142–153).

Christian education in Acts was not of a formal nature, like its Greco-Roman counterparts. It was regarded as countercultural and irreligious (17:6, 21:28, 26:24). But education in Acts is different than its cultural counterparts. It was for the express aim of personal transformation, including conversion, paralleled by the resulting formation of a distinctive Christian community, the

church. "So the churches were strengthened in the faith, and they increased in number daily" (16:5).

References and Resources

Estep, James. 2008. "Biblical Foundations for a Theology of Education." In *A Theology for Christian Education*, edited by James Estep, Gregg Allison, and Michael Anthony, 44–72. Nashville, TN: Broadman & Holman.

Sherrill, Lewis Joseph. 1944. *The Rise of Christian Education.* New York: Macmillan.

—James Riley Estep Jr.

Teaching in Hebrews

How Hebrews Teaches

Hebrews is a self-styled "word of exhortation" (Heb. 13:22), a title only given elsewhere in the New Testament to the sermon of the apostle Paul in the synagogue at Pisidian Antioch following the reading of the Law and the Prophets (Acts 13:15). This suggests that, like that sermon, Hebrews is intended to be a hortatory exposition of the Gospel from Old Testament scriptures, a sermonic letter. It is structured around a number of major Old Testament texts that are expounded and applied: a catena of quotations in chapter 1, Psalm 8 (Heb. 2), Psalm 95 (Heb. 3–4), Psalm 110 (Heb. 5–7), Jeremiah 31 (Heb. 8–10), and Habakkuk 2 (Heb. 10:37ff.). These texts, as G. B. Caird (1959) has shown, themselves teach the self-attested inadequacy of the old covenant.

The teaching approach of the letter is *paraenetic* as opposed to *protreptic*; that is, it calls on the readers to continue steadfastly in their walk of faith in Christ, complementing and strengthening them where they are already adhering to what is exhorted (e.g., Heb. 6:9), and reminds them of what they supposedly already know (rather than teaching them, as in the alternative rhetorical form of *protrepsis*, to adopt an entirely new way of life). At the same time it is, according to Ben Witherington III (2007), an example of the epideictic rhetoric of praise and blame, an emotional, inspirational, "oral document" seeking to charm on the one hand and cast odium on the other, as a way of moving the listeners to remain in the faith they have embraced.

The essential thesis of the sermon is variously repeated, summarized (e.g., Heb. 8:1), and hammered home from a number of angles in a common didactic manner. The Jewish strategy of arguing from the lesser to the greater (known as *Qal wa-Chomer* or *a minore ad maius*) is a key feature (e.g., Heb. 2:1–3, 9:13–14, 12:25). The intensity of the warnings appears to increase as the letter develops, and the persuasive, encouraging tone is correspondingly strong (e.g., Heb. 12:12). Repetition, particularly in chapter 11, is a notable pedagogical tactic of the letter, which itself calls for constant daily examination and exhortation (Heb. 3:12–13) and commends both obedience to teachers (Heb. 13:7, 17) and learning through suffering (Heb. 5:8).

What Hebrews Teaches

The basic teaching point in Hebrews is that whatever circumstances they find themselves in, believers should stick with Jesus alone, since He is absolutely supreme. The doctrinal, expositional teaching on Christ's supremacy (see the repeated language of "better, greater, superior" in, e.g., Heb. 1:4, 7:19, 8:6, 10:34, and 12:24) serves the pastoral goal of exhorting the hearers not to apostatize from the Gospel but to faithfully endure suffering for it (see the repeated warnings to endure and not slip away in, e.g., 2:1–4, 3:7–18, 6:4–8, 10:26–31, and 12:25–29).

The context is that after enduring some persecution (Heb. 10:32–34), the hearers are perhaps in danger of teetering on the brink of wearily giving up the struggle to follow Christ by paying less attention to His teaching (Heb. 5:11–14), becoming sluggish in discipleship (Heb. 6:12), and ceasing to gather with other Christians (Heb. 10:25). So as John Walters (1996) rightly puts it, in Hebrews, "theology is the handmaiden of paraenesis."

References and Resources

Caird, G. B. 1959. "The Exegetical Method of the Epistle to the Hebrews." *Canadian Journal of Theology* 5: 44–51.

O'Brien, P. T. 2010. *The Letter to the Hebrews.* Nottingham, UK: Apollos.

Walters, J. R. 1996. "The Rhetorical Arrangement of Hebrews." *Asbury Theological Journal* 51 (2): 59–70.

Witherington, B., III. 2007. *Letters and Homilies for Jewish Christians: A Socio-Rhetorical Commentary on Hebrews, James and Jude.* Nottingham, UK: Apollos.

—LEE GATISS

TEACHING IN THE JOHANNINE GOSPEL

Christians have an almost instinctual affection for the Gospel of John. Perhaps the reason is that the teaching in the Johannine Gospel is more explanatory than in the Synoptic Gospels, which do not provide as many chronological notes regarding the duration of Jesus's public ministry as does the Gospel of John. For example, whereas the Gospel of Mark mentions one Passover (14:1), and there is a reference to an earlier spring season (2:23, implying a second Passover), the Gospel of John records three Passovers (2:13, 6:4, 11:55; the number would increase to four, if the unnamed feast of 5:1 is regarded as a Passover). John's chronology of the Lord's ministry is more complete and definitive because it details more structural components (cf. references in 4:35, 7:2, and 10:22 to Jewish festivals or time indications).

The Gospel of John also provides information to better understand the Synoptics, and thus—in its uniqueness—functions in a complementary and supplemental manner. The Synoptics concentrated on Jesus's life in Galilee, but the last section of each of the Gospels focuses on Judea and Jerusalem. Whereas the Synoptics imply that Jesus was involved in ministry prior to Galilee (cf. Matt. 4:12; Mark 1:14), the Gospel of John confirms this truth with information regarding the Lord's earlier work in Judea (ch. 3) and in Samaria (ch. 4). The Johannine Gospel was written primarily from personal (eyewitness) recollection of the events recorded. The eschatology in the Gospel is consistent with the Synoptics, in the sense that the national rejection of Jesus postponed the messianic kingdom. The Gospel does not teach that the kingdom was inaugurated at Jesus's first coming; rather, certain aspects of life in the kingdom are currently enjoyed by Christians as beneficiaries of the new covenant that Jesus ratified by his death (Luke 22:20; 1 Cor. 11:23–24; 2 Cor. 3:6–18).

The teaching in the Johannine Gospel is the most theologically reflective of the four Gospels. The prologue of this Gospel is a unique combination of theological profundity and simplicity; there is an extensive use of monosyllables in contrast to philosophical terms, such as the Word (Greek *logos*), and the symbolism of such contrasting terms as light and darkness. The Gospel is more didactic and discourse oriented rather than narrative (cf. 3:13–17), and it contains the most explicit teaching regarding the Holy Spirit (chs. 14–16).

Throughout the Gospel of John, the reality of sin within the world is emphasized. The gift of God to the world is "His only begotten Son," and the reason God sent His Son into the world was that He "so loved the world" (3:16). Seven signs (miracles) were selected to demonstrate that Jesus is the divine Messiah (2:1–11, 4:46–54, 5:1–9, 6:1–14, 16–21, 9:1–12, 11:1–46). The subsequent discourses explain the significance of the signs. John's Gospel also includes seven emphatic (and unique) "I am" statements that identify Jesus as God and Messiah (6:35, 8:12, 10:7, 9, 11, 14, 11:25, 14:6, 15:1, 5).

According to the Gospel of John, the death of Jesus does indeed benefit the world; however, there is not any actual doctrine of the atonement in that Gospel. John's Gospel simply explains the benefits of Christ's death, never specifying the basis or means by which He "takes away the sin of the world" or "gives life to the world." The majority of the references to the death of Christ within the Gospel of John indicate the benefits of His life for those who trust in Him. For example, Jesus laid "down His life for the sheep" (10:11, 15), who are those who "hear" and "know his voice," and thus "they follow" Him (10:3–4, 27). Jesus laid "down his life for his friends" (15:13), who are those who do what He commands (15:14); however, there is no mention of the benefits for those who are not His friends, that is, those who do not heed His commands. Throughout the Gospel of John, the death of Jesus is "for the glory of God, so that the Son of God may be glorified by it" (11:4; cf. 12:16, 23, 13:31–32, 17:1, 5).

The sacrificial imagery of the Lamb was used for a message of judgment, not to connote the silence, gentleness, or patience of the Lord Jesus, or even the fact that He was not an unwilling victim compelled to be crucified (cf. Isa. 53:2, 7–9); rather, the Lamb metaphor emphasizes the Lord's holiness. The Lamb of God is said to be "the Son of God" (John 1:34); thus the use of the Lamb metaphor conveys the message that the One who "takes away the sin of the world" is Himself pure (cf. Exod. 12:5) (i.e., without sin), and the removal of sins is for the purpose of destroying the works of the devil. Consequently, the metaphorical Lamb of God is similar to the message of Revelation, wherein it is prophesied that the Lamb who was "slain" (5:9) does not administer justice and lordship over the world as a victim, but as He who is enthroned at His Father's right hand (2:21, 7:14–15, 12:11). Unlike the book of Revelation, the Gospel of John does not reference "the blood of the Lamb," nor does it ascribe any unequivocal notion of either atonement or cleansing from sin through the blood of the Lord Jesus.

The purpose of the Gospel of John is to lead unbelievers to faith, confidence, and trust in the Lord Jesus Christ and salvation in His name (20:30–31). The teaching in the Johannine Gospel is thus apologetic and evangelistic. The primary word in the Gospel is the verb "believe" (Greek *pisteuō*), which is used 98 times. The noun form of the verb (Greek *pistis*, "faith") is not used even once, which demonstrates that the evangelistic teaching was designed to emphasize the centrality of active, vital trust in the Lord Jesus. The apologetic teaching is closely related to the evangelistic. The Gospel was composed to provide reasons for belief (trust), and consequently, to provide assurance of the divine gift of "life," which (in Johannine language) is the entirety of all that is imparted by grace through faith in Jesus Christ.

References and Resources

Hill, Charles E. 2004. *The Johannine Corpus in the Early Church*. Oxford: Oxford University Press.

Hill, Charles E., and Frank A. James III, eds. 2004. *The Glory of the Atonement: Biblical, Theological & Practical Perspectives*. Downers Grove, IL: InterVarsity Press.

Hoskins, Paul M. 2009. "Deliverance from Death by the True Passover Lamb: A Significant Aspect of the Fulfillment of the Passover in the Gospel of John." *Journal of the Evangelical Theological Society* 52 (June): 285–299.

Koester, Craig R. 1990. "'The Savior of the World' (John 4:42)." *Journal of Biblical Literature* 109 (Winter): 665–680.

Köstenberger, Andreas J. 2002. "Jesus the Good Shepherd Who Will Also Bring Other Sheep (John 10:16): The Old Testament Background of a Familiar Metaphor." *Bulletin for Biblical Research* 12: 67–96.

Rodriquez, Armando J., Jr. 2008. "Life from on High: The Eschatology of the Gospel of John in Light of Its Vertical Dimension." PhD diss., Loyola University of Chicago.

Tenney, Merrill C. 1985. *New Testament Survey*. Rev. ed. Grand Rapids, MI: Zondervan.

Van der Watt, Jan. 1995. "The Composition of the Prologue of John's Gospel: The Historical Jesus Introducing Divine Grace." *Westminster Theological Journal* 57: 311–332.

—Ron J. Bigalke

Teaching in the Johannine Letters

The Johannine Epistles are frequently categorized with the Gospel of John and the book of Revelation as authored by the apostle John. The five writings would thus comprise the Johannine corpus. However, there is not unanimous agreement about the authorship of the writings. The prologues of First John and the Gospel of John are remarkably similar and indicate eyewitness testimony with regard to the historical Jesus. Furthermore, the purpose of First John and the Gospel of John is consistent: to elicit faith in Christ and to know the certainty of eternal life (cf. John 20:31; 1 John 5:13). Although there is a close relationship between the Gospel of John and the trine Letters, especially with regard to ideas and language, the reasons for writing them differ substantially.

The Johannine Epistles are important because they provide clarity with regard to the circumstances and issues that the church was experiencing by the end of the first century. Even as the church grew numerically, there was also opposition to it. The incipient church depended on traveling evangelists and teachers to communicate the Gospel, which would result in the Lord "adding to their number day by day those who were being saved" (e.g., Acts 2:47). Consequently, there was significant communication among local churches by means of correspondence and personal visitation. As a consequence of these circumstances, the early church members needed to be vigilant in their discernment, because many false teachers sought to present themselves as legitimate leaders.

The Johannine Epistles resume the response to the escalating expressions of false teaching that both Peter (in his second epistle) and Jude addressed. The specific aberrant teaching to which John elicited response in his First

Epistle is not readily apparent. His letter is not entirely polemical, but does provide substantive warning against a Gnosticism that was becoming ever more persuasive. The message of First John is concerned with how the believer may have assurance of fellowship with God and to exhort the Christian to abide in Him. From the beginning of the Epistle, it is evident that John was not content with immaturity by those who assumed such fellowship. Consequently, the message of First John is to provide much hortatory content to assure the believer, who is not perfect and who does sin, yet who tests the spirits and abides in God, and who is able to do so based on the work of Christ as the believer's advocate and propitiation, whom the Father lovingly sent to the world (2:1–2, 4:10). The way to show one's fellowship with God is by walking in righteousness and by heeding the testimony of God.

Second John (vv. 7, 10–11) addresses the same problem of false teaching. The letter is more personal, as it is addressed to "the chosen lady and her children" (either an individual or a figurative reference to a local church). Deceivers are those who deny the true humanity of Jesus Christ; thus the believers are warned against those who do not abide in the truth (v. 4). Biblical love is not a vacuous emotion or sentiment; rather, it is obedience to God's commands (v. 6). Believers are warned not to let false teachers take advantage of their hospitality (vv. 10–11).

Third John is the most personal of the trine Epistles. The sole recipient of the letter is "the beloved Gaius." Hospitality is addressed again, albeit from a different perspective. Second John warns against hospitality toward false teachers, whereas Third John condemns the lack of hospitality toward faithful missionary brethren. Diotrephes was condemned for dictatorial leadership, malicious and slanderous accusations, and excluding anyone who sought to hold him accountable (v. 10).

The epistolary nature of the book of Revelation is evident in that it begins with a prologue (1:1–8) and concludes with an epilogue (22:6–21). The most common date attributed to the book is AD 95. While there is a tendency among conservative scholarship to date all of the New Testament books earlier, some even dating all the books before AD 70, there is no reason not to accept the later date for Revelation, which would correspond with all of the known facts about John's life and the statements that are made within the book itself. The designation of the letter is given clearly in Revelation 1:11. John was told to record the visions he would soon see and to then send his letter to seven specific churches, all of which were located in modern-day Turkey. The occasion for the writing of Revelation is unique among New Testament books. John wrote this letter because he was specifically commanded to do so by the Lord (cf. 1:10–11, 19). While the other books in the New Testament surely came about as a result of the Lord's compulsion to record a certain message, in no other book is so clear a command repeated.

Scholars have debated the purpose for the writing of Revelation for centuries. They have made several suggestions, but three purposes seem to be repeated more often than others. First, the book of Revelation was written to encourage the believers in John's day who were facing terrible suffering at the hands of Rome. The truth of this is evident in chapters 2–3, in which John encouraged the churches to remain faithful. Second, the book of Revelation was written to complete the prophetic truths seen primarily in the Old Testament but also in the New Testament, and thus provides a unity and harmony to God's plans and purposes. Third, the book of Revelation was written to reveal Jesus Christ, which is what the first verse of the book says. Within the pages of Revelation, Jesus Christ is seen in His authority, power, and glory. He is revealed as the One who comes to judge the world and to establish God's righteous kingdom on the earth. Each of these suggested purposes is taught within the book, so perhaps it is best to accept all three as purposes for which Revelation was written and not to exclude any of them. In many ways, Revelation is the final component in the completed revelation that God has given humanity, so many of the themes that were started in earlier books of the Bible find their completion in this book, and thus it is truly a fitting climax to all of scriptural revelation.

References and Resources

Brown, Raymond E. 1982. *The Epistles of John*. Garden City, NY: Doubleday.

Köstenberger, Andreas J. 2009. *A Theology of John's Gospel and Letters*. Grand Rapids, MI: Zondervan.

Kruse, Colin G. 2000. *The Letters of John*. Grand Rapids, MI: Eerdmans.

Longacre, Robert E. 1983. "Exhortation and Mitigation in First John." *Selected Technical Articles Related to Translation* 9: 3–44.

Marshall, I. Howard. 1978. *The Epistles of John*. Grand Rapids, MI: Eerdmans.

Martin, Ralph P., and Peter H. Davids, eds. 1997. *Dictionary of the Later New Testament & Its Developments*. Downers Grove, IL: InterVarsity Press.

Miehle, Helen Louise. 1981. "Theme in Greek Hortatory Discourse: Van Dijk and Beekman-Callow Approaches Applied to I John." PhD diss., The University of Texas at Arlington.

Schnackenburg, Rudolf. 1992. *The Johannine Epistles*. Translated by Reginald Fuller and Ilse Fuller. New York: Crossroad.

Street, Daniel R. 2008. "'They Went Out from Us': The Identity of the Opponents in First John." PhD diss., Southeastern Baptist Theological Seminary.

Thomas, Robert L. 1992–1995. *Revelation*. 2 vols. Chicago: Moody.

Von Wahlde, Urban C. 2010. *The Gospel and Letters of John.* 3 vols. Grand Rapids, MI: Eerdmans.

—Ron J. Bigalke

Teaching in the Pauline Epistles

Epistle is from the Greek word *epistolē*, meaning "letter." When Paul's letter arrived at the proper destination, one would read it aloud as if it were meant for a group of people, unless the letter was specifically addressed to one individual. In the New Testament, 13 of the 27 books are letters claimed to be written by Paul. The apostle Paul's teaching in his Epistles generally falls into the following categories: church administration, ethics, and theology.

Most of the churches with which Paul was associated required advice on church administration. For example, in 1 and 2 Timothy he[15] gives the most extended teaching on church leadership. Three groups of people played special roles in the Christian community: bishops, deacons, and elders (1 Tim. 3:1–13, 5:17–25). Bishops were to display virtues appropriate not only for leadership in the Christian community but also for maintaining a good reputation with nonbelievers. Deacons are described in similar terms. One of the major issues facing some of the Pauline churches was rivalry and divisions. In 1 Corinthians 1:10–17, we learn that there were four rival groups in the Corinthian church. His response to this division was to make the point that "Christ is not divided" and churches should be united around Christ, not various other individuals of influence. The church at Corinth also exhibited certain abuses in public worship based on selfish motives. These concerned the celebration of the Lord's Supper (11:2–34) and the misuse of various spiritual gifts (12:1–14:40). "Love" should be the motivating force in all of these. When people gather for the Lord's Supper in a communal meal, they must make sure all have enough to eat by sharing their food, and when there are expressions of the manifestation of the Spirit (e.g., "tongues"), the motive behind these is the benefit of the church as a whole ("interpretation of tongues").

There were various behavioral standards that Paul expected the churches to meet. Sexual impurity was not to be tolerated. In Corinth, it was discovered that a man was carrying on a sexual relationship with his stepmother (1 Cor. 5:1–13), but the believers in Corinth did nothing about this. Paul instructs them to exercise proper church discipline and use excommunication if necessary, if all other means did not rectify the problem ("Expel the wicked man from among you," 1 Cor. 5:13). Some of the Corinthians were also troubled by the propriety of eating food that had previously been offered in pagan sacrifice ("food offered to idols," 1 Cor. 8:1). Paul says an idol is nothing, eat food freely, but for the sake of the conscience of the "weak," forgo this freedom "not [to] cause one of them to fall" (1 Cor. 8:13).

Paul addressed important theological issues in his letters. Various churches were misinformed regarding the fate of those who did not remain alive at the return of Christ (1 Thess. 4:13–18). Paul assures believers that the believing dead have not been abandoned by God. At the *parousia* ("presence," the Second Coming), the believing dead will be given priority and rise first, and those who are alive will be *caught up* (*harpazō*, "to take by force, take away, carry off, catch up") with the dead to be united with the Lord. Some also believed that the end of time had already come upon them (2 Thess. 2:1–2). Paul warns the congregations not to be deceived, because certain events have to unfold before the end arrives (2 Thess. 2:3–4). For example, an antichrist figure will be revealed before Christ returns, who is ultimately "destined for destruction." This "lawless person" exalts himself above every other, and he will eventually take his seat in God's Temple in Jerusalem "declaring himself to be God." In the end, Christ will triumph ("the Lord Jesus will destroy with the breath of his mouth," 2 Thess. 2:8). Paul also takes up the issue of the future resurrection of those who had died in Christ. Paul reviews the testimony concerning the reality of Christ's bodily resurrection (1 Cor. 15:1–11) and emphasizes that this is the basis of Christian faith. If we believe in the resurrection of Christ, then the future resurrection of believers is a certainty and is part of Christ's complete victory over death (1 Cor. 15:12–28).

In his letter to the Galatians, Paul had uncovered a teaching that insisted believers (Gentiles included) must follow parts of the Jewish Law in order to be fully right before God (e.g., males needed to be circumcised). For Paul, Gentiles who underwent circumcision showed an absolute misunderstanding of the Gospel. This was an affront to God and a rejection of the justification he has provided through Christ. Those who proposed such things perverted the Gospel (Gal. 1:7) and are cursed by God (Gal. 1:8). Paul says that even as a Jew himself, he has come to realize that a person's right standing ("justification") before God does not come through doing the works of the Jewish Law but comes through faith in Christ (Gal. 2:16).

References and Resources

Barnett, Paul. 2008. *Paul: Missionary of Jesus.* Grand Rapids, MI: Eerdmans.

---

15. Some scholars believe that the pastoral epistles were not written by Paul. It was a common practice in Paul's day to have someone write in the name of another, particularly if that person was well known and influential. In that day it was not considered plagiarism, and we should not consider the pastoral letters any less canonical if they were not written by Paul.

Capes, David B., Rodney Reeves, and E. Randolph Richards. 2007. *Rediscovering Paul: An Introduction to His World, Letters and Theology.* Downers Grove, IL: InterVarsity Press.

Dunn, James D. G. 1988. *Romans.* 2 vols. WBC 38A/B. Waco, TX: Word Books.

Fee, Gordon. 1987. *1 Corinthians.* NICNT. Grand Rapids, MI: Eerdmans.

Johnson, Luke Timothy. 1996. *Letters to Paul's Delegates: 1 Timothy, 2 Timothy, Titus.* Valley Forge, PA: Trinity Press International.

—JOHN A. BERTONE

TEACHING, INEFFECTIVE

Research indicates that the percentage of teachers who rate themselves as "above average" is a rather remarkable 94 percent. And the percentage of teachers who rate themselves in the "top quartile" is also bemusing, at 68 percent.[16] Quite revealing indeed, and a clear indication that teachers do not know as much about their efforts and results as they think.

Teaching in Christian Education

Any reflective teacher wonders about his or her effectiveness as an educator: "Why do I do certain kinds of things and not others? What evidence about how people learn drives my teaching choices? How often do I do something because my teachers did it?" Teaching ministry in Christian education contexts—whether they more formal day schools or less formal church or parachurch settings, whether they may be Western or Eastern cultures[17]—is an important endeavor that may benefit from careful observation and close analysis, from revision and refinement, as well as from dialogue with colleagues and the critique of peers.[18]

Ineffective teaching may lead to theological confusion, religious doubt, and misunderstanding of God and His revelation. Being a spokesperson for God must be undertaken with humility and a desire to be faithful, not only in an orthodox content but also in educationally engaging means. To further understand derisory teaching, we also benefit from a careful study of exceptional teaching.[19] It is a grave mistake, even with the best intentions, to believe that little or no preparation for Christian teaching is necessary due to the role of the Holy Spirit as teacher. God asks humans to partner in teaching faith with Christian students.

How is teaching excellence for Christian educators to be defined? Ken Bain asserts that outstanding teachers are those who achieve remarkable success in helping most of their students learn in ways that have a sustained, substantial, and positive influence on how those students think, act, and feel.[20] Based on a study, Bain identifies six recurring themes that describe the most effective teachers.

Six Best Practices for Teaching
Teachers are successful only to the extent that they enable their students to learn. The ultimate goal is for teachers to reconsider their innate and explicit conceptions of education:

1. *The best teachers know their subject extremely well.* They use their knowledge to develop techniques for grasping fundamental principles and organizing concepts that others can use to begin building their own understanding and abilities. They enable learners to construct not only understanding, but also meaning and application.

2. *The best teachers create critical learning environments.* The routine quest is exploring authentic tasks that challenge students to grapple with ideas, rethink their assumptions, and examine their mental models of reality. While teaching methods vary, these conditions are best fostered when learners feel a sense of control, work collaboratively, believe that their work will be considered fairly, and receive feedback.

---

16. Stanford C. Ericksen, *The Essence of Good Teaching: Helping Students Learn and Remember What They Learn* (San Francisco: Jossey Bass, 1984).

17. It is a remarkable phenomenon to observe how prevailing societal customs and educational philosophies in a given region of the world mimic the same stances in Christian schools in those same geographic regions. It is not surprising then—and I have observed it firsthand in Africa, Asia, and much of Eastern Europe—that a teacher-dominated, content-centered, student-dependent, pedagogical model is more common than not in theological education, much like in the more rigid political environments in these regions. Conversely, in many cases theological education, at least in theory, in North America and Western Europe more often leans toward a more egalitarian-based, learner-focused style, much like in the democratic political arenas in these regions.

18. A helpful book guiding teachers in reflection on educational practice is Stephen Brookfield, *Becoming a Critically Reflective Teacher* (San Francisco: Jossey-Bass, 1995); more specific to the task of theological education is Mary Hess and Stephen Brookfield, *Teaching Reflectively in Theological Contexts: Promises and Contradictions* (Malabar, FL: Krieger Publishing, 2008).

19. Some of this is adapted from Mark A. Lamport, "The Most Indispensable Habits of Effective Theological Educators: Recalibrating Educational Philosophy, Psychology, and Practice," *Asbury Journal* (Fall 2010): 36–54.

20. While the book is marketed for college teachers, it has direct relevance for both formal and informal teaching contexts. See Ken Bain, *What the Best College Teachers Do* (Cambridge, MA: Harvard University Press, 2004). The insightful and provocative writings of Neil Postman are relevant here, most notably in *Teaching as a Subversive Activity* (McHenry, IL: Delta, 1971) and *The End of Education: Redefining the Value of School* (New York: Vintage, 1996).

3. *The best teachers prepare to teach as a serious, rigorous endeavor.* Lectures, discussion sections, problem-based sessions, etc., are treated as demanding and important. The best teachers begin with questions about student learning objectives rather than about what the teacher will do. In short, methods are used as a means to the end: student learning.[21]

4. *The best teachers have high expectations for their students.* Simply put, the best teachers expect "more." And more often than not, high expectations yield high learning results. They favor learning objectives that embody the kind of thinking and acting expected for life. They expect but also stimulate high achievement.

5. *The best teachers value their students.* With what can only be called simple decency, the best teachers display openness; reflect a strong trust in students; believe that students want to learn; and assume, until proven otherwise, that they can.

6. *The best teachers evaluate their efforts.* All the studied teachers have some systematic program (some more elaborate than others) to assess their own professional growth and to make appropriate changes. Like most practice-oriented endeavors, those who are most effective for the long haul seem to be able to flex their approaches and orientations for maximum results.[22]

The Uniqueness of Christian Teaching

A unity of sound theological content and relevant principles of educational theory and practice is a necessity for effective teaching, not a luxury. What can Christian educators learn from these best practices? In addition, what obstacles may exist in Christian education that prevent teachers from being as effective in teaching as they might be?

Awareness of several uniquenesses necessarily distinguishes Christian learning from other forms of learning. First, the *subject matter* is the Bible and its instruction on how to live life and view the world. To understand the content of scripture is important, but ultimately subservient to how one interprets and applies these truths to their lives and in the world. Second, the *goal* is transformation,

which affects all aspects of human development, but pursuant of becoming like Jesus in all aspects of one's being. Third, the *dynamics* of Christian education are guided by the Holy Spirit, who is called Teacher, and challenges, convicts, and empowers Christians to be transformed.

In sum, *ineffective* Christian education misunderstands God and His purposes; misuses biblical content merely as historical data; ignores a vital partnership with the home; discounts the scope, sequence, and purpose of the curriculum materials; maintains disproportion between interaction in content, the faith community, and engagement in service to the world; fails to prepare students for life in the real world; shields students from experiences in life involvement; and misunderstands the dynamics of spiritual development. Much is at stake to avoid the ineffectiveness rampant in other contexts of the educational enterprise, and great effort is incumbent upon those who will engage Christians in faith-shaping, reality-testing education.

References and Resources

Blair, Christine Eaton. 2001. *The Art of Teaching the Bible: A Practical Guide for Adults.* Louisville, KY: Geneva Press.

Brookfield, Stephen D. 2006. *The Skillful Teacher: On Technique, Trust, and Responsiveness in the Classroom.* 2nd ed. San Francisco: Jossey-Bass.

Galindo, Israel. 1998. *The Craft of Christian Teaching: Essentials for Becoming a Very Good Teacher.* Elgin, IL: Judson Press.

Palmer, Parker J. 2007. *The Courage to Teach: Exploring the Inner Landscape of a Teacher's Life.* San Francisco: Jossey-Bass.

Smith, David I., and James K. A. Smith, eds. 2011. *Teaching and Christian Practices: Reshaping Faith and Learning.* Grand Rapids, MI: Eerdmans.

—MARK A. LAMPORT

TEACHING METHODS OF JESUS

Jesus is portrayed as a teacher (*didaskalos*) in the Gospels. He is depicted as the one who "sat to teach" after the model of Jewish rabbis (Matt. 5:1). In the feet-washing scene, Jesus refers to the statement of the disciples and confirms their perception of him: "You call me 'Teacher' and 'Lord,' and rightly so, for that is what I am" (John 13:13). Josephus, the Jewish historian of the first century AD, has referred to Jesus as a "teacher." However, Jesus was different from other Jewish teachers, as he taught with authority. His main teaching was centered on the theme of the kingdom of God.

Jesus's pedagogical methods and principles are noteworthy. He taught the disciples and the crowd through

---

21. For more on developing educational methodology, see Stephen Brookfield, *The Skillful Teacher: On Technique, Trust, and Responsiveness in the Classroom* (San Francisco: Jossey-Bass, 2006); Barbara Gross Davis, *Tools for Teaching* (San Francisco: Jossey-Bass, 2009); William McKeachy, *Teaching Tips: Strategies, Research & Theory for College and University Teachers* (Belmont, CA: Wadsworth, 2010); Gary Morrison, Steven Ross, and Jerrold Kemp, *Designing Effective Instruction* (New York: Wiley, 2006).

22. Very helpful resources are Thomas Angelo and Patricia Cross, *Classroom Assessment Techniques: A Handbook for College Teachers* (San Francisco: Jossey Bass, 1993); and Dannelle Stevens and Antonia Levi, *Introduction to Rubrics: An Assessment Tool to Save Grading Time, Convey Effective Feedback and Promote Student Learning* (Herndon, VA: Stylus, 2004).

various methods, including analogies, metaphors, similes, and parables taken from their own familiar context. He used these methods to communicate the truth in a simple and memorable way so that the audience could both understand it easily at times and also think longer to make a lasting and positive response to Him in faith and obedience.

Jesus used his *audiences' knowledge of their own cultural and religious contexts*. He quoted proverbs that were familiar to his hearers: "Physician, heal yourself" (Luke 4:23); "No prophet is accepted in his home town" (Luke 4:24). In his teaching, he alluded to the stories of Old Testament scripture, such as Noah's ark (Matt. 24:37), Lot and Sodom (Luke 17:29), and the people of Nineveh (Matt. 12:42). He also reminded them of their scripture by using the formula, "It is written," or "What is written in the Law?," or "Have you never read?"

Jesus used *demonstration techniques* (the parable of the prodigal son, Luke 15:11–32; the rich man and Lazarus, Luke 16:19–31). He taught the characteristics of the kingdom through his ministry of signs and wonders. He demonstrated great truths of the kingdom, such as faith, humility, and sacrifice, through acted out examples.

He used *modeling* to teach his disciples. It was not simply through words, but through his lifestyle that he communicated the message of humility, sacrifice, and servant leadership. He asked them to emulate what he showed them (John 13:13–15).

Jesus *integrated theory and practice*. He taught the disciples the secret of the kingdom and that they were to observe first and then act. He sent them out to preach, heal the sick, and cast out demons (Luke 9:1–5; Matt. 19:5–42; Luke 10:2–16). They had to learn through practical experiences and challenging situations. He developed their faith in turbulent circumstances (Mark 4:35–41). He did not want his followers to learn merely through mental ascent, but through practical applications.

Jesus *challenged people's assumptions and led them from intellectual knowledge to practical application*. His parable of the compassionate Samaritan was to challenge the assumption of the expert lawyer regarding the identity and role of one's neighbor. The statement of Jesus to the lawyer, "Go and do likewise" (Luke 10:37), shows that accumulation of knowledge and the intellectual ability to analyze and evaluate the content of teaching and learning must lead one to become a reflective practitioner and radical implementer of the truth.

Jesus taught his audience by *the use of questions*, either responding to the questions they asked him or asking them direct questions to elicit a response or make them silent. For example, Jesus's teaching on one's reward in heaven is an answer to Peter's question: "We have left everything and followed you. What then shall we have?" (Matt. 19:27). Jesus's interpretation of the parable of the sower is a response to the question of the disciples about the meaning of the parable (Mark 4:10; Luke 8:9). Jesus asked his hearers rhetorical questions, such as "But if the salt loses its saltiness, how can it be made salty again?" (Matt. 5:13) or "Which is lawful on the Sabbath: to do good or to do evil, to save life or to kill?" (Mark 3:4). The use of questions could change their perspectives or result in a "perspective transformation" (Mezirow 1991).

Jesus *interacted and associated with the poor, the marginalized, and the outcasts*. Therefore, he was called a friend of tax collectors and sinners (Matt. 11:19). The disciples were questioned by the Pharisees about the attitude and action of Jesus: "Why does he eat with tax collectors and sinners?" (Mark 2:14–16; Matt. 11:19; Luke 5:29–31). He made very clear his mission to the poor through his message of liberation in the Nazareth Manifesto passage (Luke 4:16–30). He also made it clear that he came not to call the righteous but sinners unto repentance (Luke 5:32). His acts of compassion in touching and healing the outcasts (Mark 1:40–45) and his positive portrayal of the Samaritans (Luke 9:51–55, 10:30–37, 17:11–19) and his interaction with women (Luke 7:36–38; John 4, 8:4–11) are some examples that communicate powerfully his heart for the poor, the marginalized, and the outcasts and the nature of the kingdom that he came to inaugurate.

These teaching methods of Jesus strongly suggest that there is a place for diversity of pedagogical methods in Christian education. The context and worldview of the learner is important in communicating the content of the teaching. The life and modeling of the teacher are also as important as the impartation of knowledge. Head knowledge should be translated into practical outworking as the learner analyzes and evaluates theories. In learning, one should be challenged to reevaluate assumptions and practices. Characteristics such as humility and servant leadership must be part of Christian education. The learner should also be a reflective practitioner, engaging in questioning and dialogue. In relating to others, the learner must reflect Jesus's association with the humble and the needy in society.

References and Resources

Dillon, J. T. 1995. *Jesus as Teacher: A Multi-disciplinary Case Study*. Bethesda, MD: International Scholars Press.

Mezirow, Jack. 1991. *Transformation Dimensions of Adult Learning*. San Francisco: Jossey-Bass.

Newell, Ted. 2009. "Worldviews in Collision: Jesus as Critical Educator." *Journal of Education and Christian Belief* 13 (2): 141–154.

Wanak, Lee. 2009. "Jesus' Questions." *Evangelical Review of Theology* 33 (2): 167–178.

Wilkey Collinson, Sylvia. 2004. *Making Disciples: The Significance of Jesus' Educational Methods for Today's Church.* Milton Keynes, UK: Paternoster.

—V. J. Samkutty

Teaching Ministries

The role of teaching throughout the early church represents a desire to both communicate the faith and also shape followers' piety and personal walk into a faithful expression of the Gospel of Jesus Christ.[23] Missiologist David Bosch notes that the church, throughout history, engaged its missionary role though numerous social/historical contexts. To accomplish its ministry, the church adapted its forms and methods, but also shifted "paradigms" or basic orientations, in light of historical forces.[24] Similarly, the teaching ministries of the church often adapted and changed emphasis in an attempt to communicate the Gospel throughout history.[25]

Historical Orientations
Early teaching ministries centered around primary tasks of shaping new Christians through dyadic teaching relationships. However, teaching also occurred through the home and family, preaching, the lives of the saints, and communal ritual.[26] The teaching ministry also contributed to establishing and communicating core doctrines within the church. Bishops, who presided over the service of Eucharist, also preached to local congregations and oversaw the catechesis of new converts. Scripture provided the primary content of the early teaching ministries. However, bishops such as Origen and Cyril of Jerusalem also taught doctrines, often formulated through creedal confessions like the Apostles' Creed.[27]

As the church adapted through historical changes, teaching ministries also changed. Christianity enjoyed greater acceptance and growth, first through Emperor Constantine, and later through the establishment of the church across Europe in the Middle Ages. As a result, teaching ministries adapted to serve a larger social role. During periods of church decline, the content and practice of teaching were preserved primarily through monastic orders. Church law, known as canon law, often provided the primary pattern of social order. Teaching ministries incorporated the preparation of public officials, primarily through the presence of cathedral schools and later universities. These ministries complemented the church's continued role of preparing converts via catechesis and creed, but also constituted the rise of the magisterium or teaching office of the church.[28] The ensuing rise of the Protestant Reformation resulted in a renewed interest in teaching scripture and doctrine as differing Christian traditions sought to communicate their own distinct heritage though specific confessions of the faith and popular publications for families and personal piety.[29]

With the rise of the Enlightenment and Christian humanism, teaching ministries began to incorporate the perspective of individuals, particularly based on age and ability. While early efforts by Comenius, Herbart, and Pestaozzi included developmental considerations; the rapid expansion of Sunday schools and graded curriculum promoted through the Uniform Lesson Series of the American Sunday School Union provided the key impetus for an age-sensitive Christian education. Today's emphasis on age-level education within many congregations rests on the accomplishments of previous developmental research and implementation.[30]

Contemporary Expressions
Christian educators might note that current efforts in teaching ministries still revolve around the key concerns of previous generations. Teaching ministries still seek to both teach the Gospel through scripture and doctrine, while also shaping and empowering Christians toward Christlikeness. Key considerations include teaching scripture, orienting believers to basic Christian doctrines and more distinctive theological traditions based on denominational or popular religious heritage, as well as guiding moral/ethical decision making from within a

23. John Westerhoff, "The Challenge: Understanding the Problem of Faithfulness," in *A Faithful Church: Issues in the History of Catechesis,* ed. John H. Westerhoff and O. C. Edwards Jr. (Wilton, CT: Morehouse-Barlow, 1981), 1–9.

24. David J. Bosch, *Transforming Mission: Paradigm Shifts in Theology of Mission* (Maryknoll, NY: Orbis, 1994), 181–189.

25. Marianne Sawicki, *The Gospel in History: Portrait of a Teaching Church; The Origins of Christian Education* (New York: Paulist Press, 1988).

26. Robert Louis Wilkin, "Christian Formation in the Early Church," in *Educating the People of Faith: Exploring the History of Jewish and Christian Communities,* ed. John Van Engen (Grand Rapids, MI: Eerdmans, 2004), 48–62, especially 60.

27. Maxwell E. Johnson, *The Rites of Christian Initiation* (Collegeville, MN: The Liturgical Press, 1999), 57–59; Leonel L. Mitchell, "The Development of Catechesis in the Third and Fourth Centuries: From Hippolytus to Augustine," in *A Faithful Church,* ed. Westerhoff and Edwards, 60–63.

28. Sawicki, *Gospel in History,* 110–229; Milton McC. Gatch, "Basic Christian Education from the Decline of Catechesis to the Rise of the Catechisms," in *The Teaching Church: Moving Christian Education to Center Stage,* ed. Eugene C. Roehlkepartain (Minneapolis, MN: Search Institute, 1993), 79–108.

29. Richard Robert Osmer, *A Teachable Spirit: Recovering the Teaching Office in the Church* (Louisville, KY: Westminster John Knox Press, 1990), 73–135; William P. Haugaard, "The Continental Reformation of the Sixteenth Century," in *The Teaching Church,* 109–173; Fredrica Harris Thompsett, "Godly Instruction in Reformation England: The Challenge of Religious Education in Tudor Commonwealth," in *The Teaching Church,* 174–203.

30. James E. Reed and Ronnie Prevost, *A History of Christian Education* (Nashville, TN: Broadman & Holman, 1993), 225–330.

theological imagination. In addition, teaching ministries seek to shape and empower believers through Christian practices and other forms of devotion and discipline associated with Christian spiritual formation.[31] Similarly, teaching ministries may also empower believers in practices of witness, evangelism, and compassion, on both on local and global scales. Such efforts include specific teaching ministries for peace and justice, diversity, and even civic engagement for the common good.[32]

Unfortunately, many teaching ministries find themselves radically divided by age-level concerns. Ministries to children, youth, young adults, adults, men, women, senior adults, and families often subdivide teaching efforts along socio-developmental needs and capabilities.[33] The rise of these teaching efforts underscores the readiness of learners, curriculum specialization, and biblical instruction. However, the segregated nature of the efforts can impede intergenerational engagement, particularly in Western, industrialized settings of Christian education. Global Christian educators may return to the formative as well as informative practices of teaching within their contextual settings, incorporating intergenerational efforts while also providing the means to teach for faith and form the faithful, empowering disciples to live Christian lives.

References and Resources

Bass, Dorothy C., ed. (1997) 2010. *Practicing Our Faith: A Way of Life for a Searching People*. 2nd ed. San Francisco: Jossey-Bass.

Bosch, David J. 1994. *Transforming Mission: Paradigm Shifts in Theology of Mission*. Maryknoll, NY: Orbis.

Boys, Mary C. 1989. *Educating in Faith: Maps and Visions*. San Francisco: Harper & Row.

Johnson, Maxwell E. 1999. *The Rites of Christian Initiation*. Collegeville, MN: The Liturgical Press.

Osmer, Richard Robert. 1990. *A Teachable Spirit: Recovering the Teaching Office in the Church*. Louisville, KY: Westminster John Knox Press.

Reed, James E., and Ronnie Prevost. 1993. *A History of Christian Education*. Nashville, TN: Broadman & Holman.

Sawicki, Marianne. 1988. *The Gospel in History: Portrait of a Teaching Church; The Origins of Christian Education*. New York: Paulist Press.

Westerhoff, John H., and O. C. Edwards Jr. 1981. *A Faithful Church: Issues in the History of Catechesis*. Wilton, CT: Morehouse-Barlow.

Wilkin, Robert Louis. 2004. "Christian Formation in the Early Church." In *Educating the People of Faith: Exploring the History of Jewish and Christian Communities*, edited by John Van Engen, 48–62. Grand Rapids, MI: Eerdmans.

Yount, William R., ed. 2008. *The Teaching Ministry of the Church*. 2nd ed. Nashville, TN: B & H Academic.

—Dean Blevins

Teaching Ministry of Jesus

Jesus was frequently addressed as "Teacher" in all four canonical Gospels (Matt. 19:16; Mark 12:32; Luke 21:7; John 8:4) and further identified as a "rabbi" in three of the canonical Gospels (Matt. 26:25, 49; Mark 9:5, 11:21; John 1:49); John explains that this word identifies him as a teacher (John 1:38; 3:2). Nevertheless, the term cannot be equated with the institutionalized title that became common two centuries later with the formation of rabbinic Judaism, nor can the teaching practice of Jesus be regarded as an example of a typical rabbi. The content of Jesus's teaching differs significantly from the teachings of rabbinic Judaism (as well as from his contemporaries), and these differences are at the root of the eventual division between emergent Christianity and rabbinic Judaism. It is often claimed, however, that "most of the sublime ethical sayings ascribed to him in fact are commonplaces in other versions of Judaism" (Neusner 1985, 13). Of course the similar themes are undeniable (monotheism, election, covenant), and parallels can easily be drawn, but the originality and authority of Jesus were overwhelming to His listeners (Matt. 13:54; Mark 1:22; Luke 4:32), who quickly elevated his status to that of a prophet (Mark 6:15). It is striking, for example, that Jesus teaches a broad audience, well beyond his small group of chosen disciples, including the uneducated common people, women, and outcasts (Luke 10:38–42, 6:17–26). The originality of Jesus is seen more clearly against the backdrop of the developed wisdom tradition. Jesus tends to subvert the common wisdom. Examples include "let the dead bury the dead" (Matt. 8:22), which is a shocking call to forsake the commandment to love one's parents, and "the kingdom of heaven is like leaven" (Matt. 13:33), which utilizes a well-known motif for evil (leaven) to illustrate God's Kingdom. Jesus's favorite teaching style was the parable, and although this was not unique to Him (many Jewish teachers, rabbis, used parables to make or illustrate a point), His distinctive teaching voice comes through clearly in at least two critical features. The content of Jesus's parabolic teaching revealed that the history of Israel as God's elect covenant people was now coming to its climax (the emergence of the Kingdom of God) and that irruption centered on Jesus Himself

31. Dorothy C. Bass, ed., *Practicing Our Faith: A Way of Life for a Searching People*, 2nd ed. (San Francisco: Jossey Bass, 1997/2010).

32. Mary C. Boys, *Educating in Faith: Maps and Visions* (San Francisco: Harper & Row, 1989).

33. William R. Yount, ed., *The Teaching Ministry of the Church*, 2nd ed. (Nashville, TN: B & H Academic, 2008).

(Luke 10:23–24). That distinctive voice is heard in the summary statement at the beginning of Jesus's public ministry: "The time has come, the kingdom of God has drawn near, repent and believe the good news" (Mark 1:15). And it is heard at the end of Jesus's public ministry in the parable of the evil tenants (Matt. 21:33–46). Thus, the essence of the uniqueness of Jesus as teacher is the way He draws attention to Himself as the fulfillment of Israel's hopes and the consequent demand He places on His hearers to identify themselves with Him in order to enter into the Kingdom of God. Such teaching ultimately led to the separation between the followers of Jesus and rabbinic Judaism.

References and Resources

Dodd, C. H. 1970. *The Founder of Christianity.* New York: Macmillan.

Horne, Herman. 1998. *Jesus the Teacher: Examining His Expertise in Education.* Rev. and updated ed. Grand Rapids, MI: Kregel.

Neusner, Jacob. 1985. *Major Trends in Formative Judaism.* Chico, CA: Scholars Press.

Perrin, Norman. 1967. *Rediscovering the Teaching of Jesus.* New York: Harper & Row.

Scott, Bernard Brandon. 1990. "Jesus as Sage." In *The Sage in Israel and the Ancient Near East,* edited by John G. Gammie and Leo G. Purdue, 399–415. Winona Lake, IN: Eisenbrauns.

Stein, Robert. 1994. *The Method and Message of Jesus' Teachings.* Rev. ed. Louisville, KY: Westminster John Knox Press.

Witherington, Ben. 2000. *Jesus the Sage.* Minneapolis, MN: Fortress Press.

Wright, N. T. 1997. *Jesus and the Victory of God.* Minneapolis, MN: Fortress Press.

Zuck, Roy B. 1995. *Teaching as Jesus Taught.* Grand Rapids, MI: Baker Book House.

—Robert Keay

TEACHING MINISTRY OF PAUL

The subject of Paul's teaching was centered firmly on the death and resurrection of Jesus Christ (1 Cor. 2:2, 15:1–4). Paul tells us almost nothing of the life of Jesus (Rom. 1:3; 1 Cor. 9:5; Gal. 4:4) and only occasionally refers to the teachings of Jesus (1 Cor. 7:10, 9:14, 11:23–25; cf. Rom. 12:14 [with Matt. 5:10, 44]; 1 Thess. 5:2 [with Matt. 24:43]). He regularly cites the Old Testament, but his interpretation is always Christological (e.g., 1 Cor. 10:4). Paul is emphatic that the source of his teachings about Jesus is primarily revelation (Gal. 1:15–17), initially and perhaps primarily the revelation of Jesus on the road to Damascus (Acts 9; 22, 26; see Kim 1981/1982), but also from continuing revelations (2 Cor. 12:1, 7), and only secondarily tradi-

tions handed on from others (Gal. 1:18–22; 1 Cor. 15:3–8). Paul's teaching ministry was conducted in two primary modes: by his personal presence and by sending letters. Letters might have been regarded by their recipients as an inferior substitute for his personal presence, but later generations regard them as a providential blessing from God, enabling them to hear the authentic voice of the apostle. Regarding his personal presence, Paul mediated his teaching in two ways: oral instruction and exemplary lifestyle. He instructed people orally in a variety of venues. For example, within the city of Ephesus alone we find Paul teaching in the synagogue (Acts 19:8), in the house-church of Aquila and Prisca (1 Cor. 16:19, written from Ephesus), on the job as a tent-maker (Acts 20:33–35; 1 Cor. 4:11f., 9:6), and in a public building (the Hall of Tyrannus: Acts 19:9). But Paul seems to have taught about Jesus wherever he was, including while on trial before the Sanhedrin in Jerusalem (Acts 23:1–11) or Roman governors in Caesarea (Acts 24–25) and proconsuls in Corinth (Acts 18:12–17) and while under arrest (Acts 28:17–31, 16:25–34), and at riverside prayer gatherings (Acts 16:13–15). Paul also taught by example. His lifestyle and teaching were one: "I urge you to imitate me. Therefore I am sending Timothy to you. . . . He will remind you of my way of life in Christ Jesus, which agrees with what I teach everywhere in every church" (1 Cor. 4:16–17, cf. 11:1; Phil. 3:17). Such imitation goes beyond ethics and godly living and also includes suffering persecution with endurance and faithfulness (2 Cor. 1:3–7; 2 Tim. 1:8; 3:12) and working diligently (2 Thess. 3:6–13). Paul's lifestyle was itself an imitation of Christ (1 Cor. 11:1), but not an imitation of Jesus's itinerant lifestyle (Paul never draws this parallel, although it is evident that he could have done so) as much as of his self-lessness and suffering (2 Cor. 11:23; Phil. 2:1–11).

Paul's letters provide his teaching to later generations of Jesus followers. These letters are not systematic or thematic presentations of Paul's beliefs. One cannot find a chapter on Paul's teaching on salvation, for example, as one might find in a book today; instead, Paul's teaching is motivated by real situations in the life of the believers to whom he writes. There is therefore a dramatic vibrancy and vitality to the teaching in Paul's letters (e.g., Gal. 1:6–10, 3:1; 2 Cor. 11:1–3). The content of his teaching, regardless of the specific occasion, always has the same intent: to exhort the believers to grow in their faith or trust in Jesus Christ so that on the Day of the Lord he can present them to Christ as mature and blameless (1 Cor. 1:8; 2 Cor. 11:2; Col. 1:28; Phil. 1:9–11).

References and Resources

Dungan, David. 1999. *A History of the Synoptic Problem: The Canon, the Text, the Composition, and the Interpretation of the Gospels.* New York: Random House.

Kim, Seyoom. (1981) 1982. *The Origin of Paul's Gospel.* WUNT. Grand Rapids, MI: Eerdmans.

Schnabel, Eckhard J. 2008. *Paul the Missionary: Realities, Strategies, Methods.* Downers Grove, IL: InterVarsity Press.

Zuck, Roy B. 1998. *Teaching as Paul Taught.* Grand Rapids, MI: Baker Book House.

—Robert Keay

Teaching Religion

What is the meaning of the verb *to teach?* Teaching involves engaging in an activity that is directed toward another. This act contains a certain degree of intentionality wherein the teacher is directly concerned with a person's learning and takes steps to ensure such an outcome. A great teacher shows how to name, describe, and state what disturbs, challenges, and beckons the learner. The teacher's task lies in providing a means of processing information in a way that invites the emergence of the total person.

A comprehensive understanding of teaching regards it as an activity in which every human person and some nonhumans engage. The human person learns almost everything he or she knows by being taught. Teaching, in the words of Gabriel Moran (1997), means "showing someone how to do something." It is an activity that may or may not embrace reasons, explanations, or information. Its most complete expression, *to teach*, Moran continues, is "to show someone how to live." In this regard, it can be said that teaching also includes a religious aspect, because showing someone how to live eventually comprises showing someone how to die.

Teaching religion is one of the two aims of religious education. The other aim focuses on forming someone in a religious way of life. Teaching religion is mostly a matter of the mind and involves the provision of an understanding of religion, including one's own religion. This activity necessitates a double conversation: the dialogue among the major world religions and the dialogue of religion(s) and contemporary culture. While such an understanding of religion can take place anywhere, the classrooms of the school and parish have been intentionally established as the ideal setting for this process. The teaching of religion is an essential component of the field of religious education. Mindful that teaching involves showing someone how to do something, the responsibility for showing someone how to employ words and concepts in order to understand religion lies with the academic institution. Through dialectical discussion and academic criticism, the student is enabled to ascertain a deeper level of inquiry than would be available outside the classroom. Thus, the recipients of teaching religion span the entire human life cycle, from young child to older adult, taking account of the fact that the capacity to understand religion develops gradually over many years.

Gabriel Moran (1997) offers a fourfold approach to teaching religion. First, the teacher must intelligibly present the available material. Second, the teacher must enable the religious text to act as mediator between the community of another era and the community of today. Third, in order to facilitate the understanding of religious meaning, the teacher must participate in the meaning to a certain degree. In other words, the teacher must step into the shoes of the writer and perceive the world from that perspective. Finally, the teacher must draw upon the experiences of students and teachers.

The specific act of teaching religion unavoidably entails design. For example, the classrooms of the school and parish teach by design. They teach unintentionally through the ways in which they are designed—that is, whether they are authoritarian in style or are designed in a community-like fashion. They also teach intentionally through the design employed in showing someone how to do something.

References and Resources

Brennan, O., ed. 2004. *Critical Issues in Religious Education.* Dublin: Veritas.

Cunnane, F. 2004. *New Directions in Religious Education.* Dublin: Veritas.

Moran, G. 1997. *Showing How: The Act of Teaching.* Valley Forge, PA: Trinity Press International.

Moran, G., and M. Harris. 1998. *Reshaping Religious Education.* Louisville, KY: Westminster John Knox Press.

Oakeshott, M. 1989. "Learning and Teaching." In *The Voice of Liberal Learning*, edited by T. Fuller, 37–61. New Haven, CT: Yale University Press.

Palmer P. J. 2007. *The Courage to Teach.* San Francisco: Jossey-Bass.

—Finola Cunnane

Teaching Religion in Public Schools

Congress shall make no law respecting an establishment of religion, or prohibiting the free exercise thereof; or abridging the freedom of speech, or of the press; or the right of the people peaceably to assemble, and to petition the Government for a redress of grievances. (U.S. Constitution, First Amendment; proposed 25 September 1789, ratified 15 December 1791).

In the early years of our nation, the debate about teaching religion in the public schools did not exist, because there was no unified schooling system that defined, nationally, how children and youth were to be educated. During the common school era, defined approximately as 1835–1900, a federally funded, compulsory system of public schooling was created to provide a method by which all children and youth would be educated in order to provide for a strong democracy and to inculcate discipline in the nation's youth. Horace Mann, known as the father of the common school, presented models of the system that were defined as nonsectarian; however, early schooling during the common school era welcomed the Bible as a central part of teaching and learning (Cremin 1980).

As our nation has grown into an increasingly religiously pluralistic country, tensions over how religion is taught in the public schools, and who funds it, have grown hostile. Some have argued for a ban on all religious teaching in the public schools, to protect students from being pressured to consider one religion as better than another, against the family culture. However, by removing religion from the schools, teaching of content such as history, philosophy, literature, music, art, and even to some extent mathematics and biology is incomplete. According to Alexis de Tocqueville in his famous *Democracy in America*: "Liberty cannot be established without morality, nor morality without faith" (1847).

In addition, the First Amendment does not state that the public schools cannot teach about religion, nor does it silence any public sphere on the subject of religion. It only claims that the government shall not *impose* any one religion upon its people. A question is whether the abolition of the teaching of religion is in direct conflict with the First Amendment by restricting the free exercise of religion by the people in the schools.

Current Impact of Teaching Religion in the Public Schools on Christian Education

In recent years, and because of numerous court cases, this issue has been brought to the forefront of several organizations. Twenty-three associations, including a diverse range of groups such as the American Federation of Teachers, the Anti-Defamation League, the Council on Islamic Education, and the Christian Coalition, have developed and approved a set of principles to serve as common ground for how religion will be presented and discussed in public schools. The following is quoted at length from *Finding Common Ground* (Haynes and Thomas 2001):

Statement of Principles

I.   Religious Liberty for All
     Religious liberty is an inalienable right of every person.
II. The Meaning of Citizenship
     Citizenship in a diverse society means living with our deepest differences and committing ourselves to work for public policies that are in the best interest of all individuals, families, communities and our nation.

III. Public Schools Belong to All Citizens
     Public schools must model the democratic process and constitutional principles in the development of policies and curricula. Policy decisions by officials or governing bodies should be made only after appropriate involvement of those affected by the decision and with due consideration for the rights of those holding dissenting views.
IV. Religious Liberty and Public Schools
     Public schools may not inculcate nor inhibit religion. They must be places where religion and religious conviction are treated with fairness and respect. Public schools uphold the First Amendment when they protect the religious liberty rights of students of all faiths or none. Schools demonstrate fairness when they ensure that the curriculum includes study *about* religion, where appropriate, as an important part of a complete education.
V.   The Relationship between Parents and Schools
     Parents are recognized as having the primary responsibility for the upbringing of their children, including education.
VI. Conduct of Public Disputes
     Civil debate, the cornerstone of a true democracy, is vital to the success of any effort to improve and reform America's public schools. Personal attacks, name-calling, ridicule and similar tactics destroy the fabric of our society and undermine the educational mission of our schools. Even when our differences are deep, all parties engaged in public disputes should treat one another with civility and respect, and should strive to be accurate and fair. Through constructive dialogue we have much to learn from one another.

The establishment of common ground might seem, on the surface, to be an excellent idea; however, as Christian educators seek to find common ground, they are giving up the very groundedness that defines our faith. A religiously pluralistic position rests on the substantive judgment that the public sphere must be insulated from viewpoints that owe their allegiance not to its procedures, but to the truths they work to establish (Fish 1996). The sacredness of the process is worth more than the actual truth itself. Having every opinion given its chance, as long as it does not adhere to a strict universal truth as a first premise, is the goal of the pluralistic table; the "regime of virtue" is therefore in opposition to the "regime of process" (Fish 1996). In seeking to find a way forward by being broad in enabling a greater conversation about "religion" in the public schools, Christian educators are in actuality diminishing their position. In this system, the Christian voice is no more "true" than the other voices at the table, and what is valued is not the discovery of the actual Truth, but the process of the open-ended conversation and sharing about the strengths and weaknesses of different positions. To claim to have found the Truth and to have the conviction that this Truth is exclusive is to excuse oneself from the pluralistic "table." However, another perspective that many Christian educators claim is that "religion is too important—with its transformative capacities for both good and evil—to be left to separate faith communities to tend in isolation from each other" (Gates 2006). These are the ends of the spectrum, with much room in the middle for Christian educators to consider as they make decisions on how they will teach and reach.

References and Resources

Cremin, Lawrence. 1980. *American Education: The National Experience, 1783-1876*. New York : Harper & Row Publishers.

De Tocqueville, A. (1847). *Democracy in America*. New York: Walker.

Fish, S. 1996. "Why We Can't All Just Get Along." *First Things: A Monthly Journal of Religion & Public Life* 60: 18–26.

Gates, B. E. 2006. "Religion as Cuckoo or Crucible: Beliefs and Believing as Vital for Citizenship and Citizenship Education." *Journal of Moral Education* 35 (4): 571–594.

Haynes, C. C., and O. Thomas. 2001. *Finding Common Ground: A Guide to Religious Liberty in Public Schools*. Nashville, TN: First Amendment Center.

—Laura Barwegen

Teaching the Bible to Adolescents

Teaching the Bible to adolescents in the 21st century needs to take into consideration the characteristics of the youth of today and of contemporary society; a persistent literalist interpretation[34] may become a barrier to an adult appreciation of the biblical message and adversely affect the young person's decision to remain within the Christian tradition. "Teaching for Transformation" in understanding the Bible is an approach intended to address the difficulties that have their source in a literalist interpretation.

A Contemporary Educational Issue

Classroom experience indicates that adolescents raise questions about *the truth of the Bible*, the *role of evidence*, and the *perceived conflict between the biblical and scientific explanations of reality*. In an Australian study of Generation Y, the most common reasons given by those

who had moved away from belief in God were "doing further study, especially science" (16 percent) and "no convincing evidence or proof" (13 percent) (Mason, Singleton, and Webber 2007, 221). The challenges that increasing scientific knowledge presents are illustrated in the following statement by a 14-year-old male: "*Just studying about it . . . the study of evolution helped make me change my mind*" (222).

These issues are not new. The young participants in Goldman's study expressed their sense of "betrayal" and "shock and anger that they had been allowed to continue literal and childish beliefs for so long" (1964, 115); the tone of the language used testifies to the depth of feeling involved.

Theoretical Foundations

The theoretical foundations of "Teaching for Transformation" derive from cognitive development theory. This suite of theories, deriving largely from a Piagetian framework, provides insights into the thinking capacities of children as they grow toward adolescence, the cognitive demands of different types of texts, and awareness of the related changes in epistemological understanding (e.g., Kitchener 1983; Kuhn 1991). How students perceive what constitutes knowledge—its source, how beliefs are justified, the certainty of knowledge and perception of truth—influences the interpretation of the biblical text. For example, the primary school child is typically a concrete thinker operating in the realist epistemological mode: knowledge is certain, objective, and verified by reference to authority; truth is absolute. In the transition to adolescence, there is a growing capacity for critical thinking. Typically operating in the subjectivist mode, the adolescent perceives knowledge to be subjective, justified by personal experience, and truth uncertain.

James Fowler's theory of faith development facilitates the application of developmental changes to the young person's understanding of the Bible. Fowler emphasized the imaginative qualities of the young child's engagement with story and symbol (1981, 130–134). Mystery is embraced with both wonder and curiosity. Scripture for the young child is a mosaic of vivid stories from the Bible. For the concrete thinker, Fowler's "young empiricist" (135), the Bible is taken quite literally. With emerging adolescence a "demythologization" (163) may occur for many young people, which presents a pedagogical challenge.

A successful pedagogy requires that in presenting the Bible to adolescents, teachers take into account the disillusionment that occurs as adolescents question their earlier reading of biblical stories. This includes directly addressing the variety of literary genres in the Bible and exploring the characteristics of metaphorical language. Students' devel-

---

34. A distinction is made between the "literal sense" of the Bible and a "literalist" interpretation. The literal sense can mean "what the author intended" and "the verbal and grammatical sense" (Soulen and Soulen 2001, 104–105, 19). On the other hand, a "literalist" interpretation, often referred to as "Biblicism" (21, 25), takes Genesis 1–2, for example, as scientifically factual.

oping cognitive capacities make possible an understanding of metaphorical language (McGrady 1987, 1994a, 1994b) and the capacity to see the apparent conflict between scientific and religious accounts of creation as *complementary* rather than contradictory (Reich 1989).

Ricoeur's three dialectical moments in interpretation encapsulate the key stages in the process of responding to the biblical text. The young child is in the stage of "'naïve' understanding" (1980, 43), Ricoeur's *first naïveté* (e.g., Mudge 1980, 6, 25). Responding to a demythologization of the text in adolescence, Ricoeur's second moment in the interpretative task is apposite, "objective explanation" (Ricoeur 1980, 43–44). The educational task is to guide the adolescent through the process of demythologizing the stories taken literally in childhood in order that the religious meaning becomes more readily accessible. Respectful exploration of the biblical text can reveal, for example, the capacity of *myth* to evoke that which can be expressed in no other way. Similarly, the exploration of metaphorical language, of symbol, and of religious imagery can reveal erstwhile hidden depths of religious meaning in the scriptures. By engaging students' critical faculties, the possibility of a *dialectical engagement with the biblical text* is enhanced, and the barriers raised by students' perception that critical thinking and appreciation of the Bible are antithetical are breached. Accordingly, the possibility of a move toward Ricoeur's third dialectical moment, a "willed" or "second naïveté" (e.g., Mudge 1980, 6), or personal "appropriation" of the text (Ricoeur 1980, 44), is enhanced, and scripture becomes "revelatory" (Schneiders 1991, 39).

A Pedagogical Approach

This suggested approach[35] to "Teaching for Transformation" is intended to foster reflective thinking: to encourage students to identify their present understanding, engage openly with the text, and provide a context in which the skills derived from biblical scholarship may be applied to teaching the Bible to adolescents. There are five steps:

1. *Identifying one's present* understanding of a text or of a particular passage. This is facilitated by appropriate questioning by the teacher.
2. *Reflecting on and critically appraising one's present understanding of the text.* For example, students are encouraged to consider why they see the passage in a particular way and where their present ideas may come from in order to become aware of their pres-

ent assumptions and presuppositions. Initially this process is facilitated by questions from the teacher.
3. *Critical engagement with the text.* This stage involves specific skill development. For example, the teacher establishes the context in which the text was written, considers genre and narrative structure, and identifies and explores figurative language. Initially teacher directed, with practice students may suggest ways in which the text may be critiqued.
4. *Dialogic engagement with others.* Students compare their understandings, defend a position, and consider a number of ways of taking meaning from the text. Further activities could include dramatic portrayal of a story and comparison of the written text with artistic portrayals of the passage.
5. *Dialectic between the reader and the text.* Students ask: What is the text saying? Do I see it differently from my first reading? How do I respond? Does it relate to my life? This may be followed by the opportunity for quiet reflection, for prayer or meditation, or for reflective or imaginative writing.

This approach engages young people's questioning and critical faculties in an exploration of the language of the Bible, so that its religious truths become revelatory.

References and Resources

Fowler, James W. 1981. *Stages of Faith: The Psychology of Human Development and the Quest for Meaning.* New York: Harper & Row.

Goldman, Ronald. 1964. *Religious Thinking from Childhood to Adolescence.* London: Routledge & Kegan Paul.

Groome, Thomas H. 1980. *Christian Religious Education: Sharing Our Story and Vision.* Melbourne, Australia: Dove Communications.

Kitchener, Karen S. 1983. "Cognition, Metacognition, and Epistemic Cognition: A Three-level Model of Cognitive Processing." *Human Development* 26: 222–232.

Kuhn, Deanna. 1991. *The Skills of Argument.* Cambridge, UK: Cambridge University Press.

Mason, Michael, Andrew Singleton, and Ruth Webber. 2007. *The Spirit of Generation Y: Young People's Spirituality in a Changing Australia.* Mulgrave, Victoria: John Garratt Publishing.

McGrady, Andrew G. 1987. "A Metaphor and Model Paradigm of Religious Thinking." *British Journal of Religious Education* 9(2): 84–94.

———. 1994a. "Metaphorical and Operational Aspects of Religious Thinking: Research with Irish Catholic Pupils (Part 1)." *British Journal of Religious Education* 16(3): 148–163.

———. 1994b. "Metaphorical and Operational Aspects of Religious Thinking: Research with Irish Catholic Pupils (Part 2)." *British Journal of Religious Education* 17(1): 56–62.

---

35. This approach is indebted in part to Thomas Groome's "shared praxis" approach to Christian religious education, especially in the structure (Groome 1980).

Mudge, Lewis S. 1980. "Paul Ricoeur on Biblical Interpretation." In *Essays on Biblical Interpretation*, edited by Lewis S. Mudge, 1–40. Philadelphia: Fortress Press.

Reich, Helmut. 1989. "Between Religion and Science: Complementarity in the Religious Thinking of Young People." *British Journal of Religious Education* 11(2): 62–69.

Ricoeur, Paul. 1980. "Reply to Lewis S. Mudge." In *Essays on Biblical Interpretation*, edited by Lewis S. Mudge, 41–45. Philadelphia: Fortress Press.

Schneiders, Sandra M. 1991. *The Revelatory Text: Interpreting the New Testament as Sacred Scripture.* New York: Harper-Collins.

Soulen, Richard N., and R. Kendall Soulen. 2001. *Handbook of Biblical Criticism.* 3rd ed. Louisville, KY: Westminster John Knox Press.

—MARGARET M. T. KELLEHER

TECHNOLOGY, EDUCATIONAL

There is no single definition for the term "educational technology" (ET). For the purposes of this article, it refers to the appropriation of electronic technologies to deliver, enhance, and facilitate learning and teaching at all levels, from early school years through high-level tertiary education and beyond. This breadth of utilization also indicates a corresponding breadth of technology, since learners' needs and approaches vary considerably; ETs are now understood to include ways of delivering and managing the delivery of content (e.g., podcasts, videocasts, virtual learning environments), of communicating at a distance (e.g., e-mails, cell phones, Internet-based calls), of simulating reality (including classrooms), and of facilitating collaboration and social networking. ETs are perceived as successors to distance education, as they permit study when teachers and learners are not in the same geographical place at the same time. This has sometimes been criticized on theological grounds by those offering Christian education who consider education should be personal (and therefore take place face to face), social (and therefore happen in peer cohorts), and formative (and therefore take place in a community). Increasingly, technological advances are providing ways in which each of these can be simulated or replaced by electronically mediated alternatives, many situated on the web or Cloud. Many objections are countered by positive student feedback, together with excellent learning and formational results. Challenges still remain for institutions of religious, Christian, or theological education in terms of resources: the economies of scale of education supported by ETs are very different from those of face to face education, and teaching staff as well as students may face a steep learning curve in acquiring and putting into practice relevant digital literacies (with corresponding time demands).

Despite the resource implications, ETs are understood to lie at the heart of developments within the education sector, particularly at the tertiary level. As the sector responds to calls for students to learn more flexibly, ETs play an important role in facilitating flexibility of the pace, place, and mode of delivery, with an increasing emphasis on mobility. This may well have an impact on where the locus of power is found, with a potential shift from learners going to an institution to the web, allowing them to bring relevant learning materials to themselves. Web-based and online learning hence reconceptualize the notion of "place" (White and Le Cornu 2011), and the web becomes a location where communities and social interaction are constructed in an electronic environment through a variety of social media. Those involved in Christian education may need to engage in significant theological reflection in order to consider systematically and practically how to understand and make best use of these developments. They are accompanied by a pedagogy that tends to favor a social constructionist understanding of knowledge; there is a growing body of literature that explores the issues this raises in relation to Christian education, even if it does not specifically focus on ETs (e.g., Hermans et al. 2002).

Rapid technological advances mean that although certain principles of good educational practice have been established, there is growing agreement that there are many ways of "getting it right." Ongoing research is important in both secular and Christian contexts, as is a dialogue between the two, in order to appropriate ETs that are fit for the purpose.

References and Resources

Hermans, C. A. M., G. Immink, A. de Jong, and J. van der Lans, eds. 2002. *Social Constructionism and Theology*, edited by Johannes van der Ven. Empirical Studies in Theology vol. 7. Leiden: Brill.

Hess, Mary. 2005. *Engaging Technology in Theological Education: All That We Can't Leave Behind.* Lanham, MD: Sheed & Ward.

Schweitzer, Friedrich. 2002. "Social Constructionism and Religious Education: Toward a New Dialogue." In *Social Constructionism and Theology*, edited by C. A. M. Hermans, G. Immink, A. de Jong, and J. van der Lans, 3–21. Empirical Studies in Theology vol. 7. Leiden: Brill.

White, David S., and Alison Le Cornu. 2011. "Visitors and Residents: A New Typology for Online Engagement." *First Monday* 16 (9): 11–18.

—ALISON LE CORNU

TESTIMONY AS CHRISTIAN PRACTICE

Since the era of the New Testament church, testimony has been an essential component of the Christian life. Beginning, perhaps, with Peter's confessional testimony, "You are the Messiah" (Mark 8:29), the narratives of life in the early church are replete with testimonies. Some were presented before official councils (e.g., Peter and John before the Temple rulers in Acts 4:1–12; Paul before Felix in Acts 24:10–21). Some were testimonies of things seen (e.g., the apostles as eyewitnesses of the crucifixion as reported in Acts 5:30–33; Stephen's vision of Christ standing at the right hand of God in Acts 7:55–56). Others were testimonies of things done (e.g., the healing of the lame beggar in Acts 3:1–12; Peter's deliverance from prison in Acts 12:5–17). Those earliest testimonies were the initial means by which the message of the Gospel was made known. They served as confessions of belief and as encouragement to persevere in the midst of persecution. They made obvious contributions to the life and growth of the church.

In one sense, testimonies are, quite simply, stories. The stories referenced above are stories of the redeeming and miraculous Gospel of Christ. Rooting testimonies in the genre of narrative stories provides insight into how these early church testimonies contributed to the numerical and spiritual growth of the church. Stories are appealing; they attract listeners. Stories are emotive depictions of particular events.[36] There is an implication that the one telling the story, or testifying, has either witnessed or experienced that which the testimony is about (much like the testimony offered in a legal proceeding). This, then, is not secondhand knowledge, but rather personal revelation of insight gained from a particular and specific experience. The story may be one of an experience resolved, or it may be one of hope for a resolution in the midst of the experience.[37] Both are necessary and effective. They acquaint the hearer with the storyteller's perspective on the experience and the insight revealed, and as a result, the hearer's perspective is changed.[38] Stories evoke personal examination: questions of belief, of value, of action.[39] Such questioning is the kind of critical reflection or personal introspection that leads to change or, in the case of testimonies, to spiritual growth. Within both the speaker and the hearer, the testimonies and resultant questions develop gratitude for the blessings of God, faith in the promises of God, expectancy about the actions of God, and virtues in response to the goodness of God.

The questioning serves as interpretation[40] of the revealed insight. Interpretation is performed on a personal level, as one listens to the testimony, but is also a corporate endeavor, an opportunity for critical reflection within the community of faith.[41] This corporate interpretation lends unity to the beliefs and practices of the gathered community. It serves to shape the theology of the community, because testimony is, in a sense, an act of theologizing, the voicing of theology that is not limited to the trained theologian, but is open to all who testify.[42] Those who may have been deemed unworthy to speak of the deep things of God are given voice in the act of testifying. Testimony can be offered by anyone, at any time, and in any place; therefore, the theologizing voice isn't limited to the confines of the church building or the assembled congregation.[43]

In summation, the sharing of our stories through testimony has immediate and long-lasting effects on the well-being of the church and the individuals who comprise it. Testimonies give to all believers the opportunity to speak. They provide a means of confession, an articulation of one's beliefs. Those beliefs, when evaluated in a particular community of faith, promote a common confession of faith. The voiced experiences of God's intervention in everyday human life attract the nonbeliever, encourage the believer, and challenge long-held perspectives and practices. Though not often considered a component of Christian education, they are a proven means of educating toward Christlikeness.[44]

References and Resources

Johns, Jackie David, and Cheryl Bridges Johns. 1992. "Yielding to the Spirit: A Pentecostal Approach to Group Bible Study." *Journal of Pentecostal Theology* 1 (1): 109–134.

Makau-Olwendo, Agnes. 2009. "Influencing the Laity's Theologizing for Spiritual Empowerment: An African Perspective." *Common Ground Journal* 7 (1): 113–126.

Miller, Donald E. 1987. *Story and Context: An Introduction to Christian Education*. Nashville, TN: Abingdon Press.

---

36. Donald E. Miller, *Story and Context: An Introduction to Christian Education* (Nashville, TN: Abingdon, 1987), 117.

37. James C. Wilhoit, *Spiritual Formation as If the Church Mattered: Growing in Christ through Community* (Grand Rapids, MI: Baker Academic, 2008), 132.

38. Miller, *Story and Context*, 118.

39. Ibid., 119.

40. See Paul Ricouer, "The Hermeneutics of Testimony," in *Essays on Biblical Interpretation*, ed. Lewis S. Mudge (Philadelphia: Fortress Press, 1980), 119–154.

41. Jackie David Johns and Cheryl Bridges Johns, "Yielding to the Spirit: A Pentecostal Approach to Group Bible Study," *Journal of Pentecostal Theology* 1, no. 1 (1992): 126.

42. Agnes Makau-Olwendo, "Influencing the Laity's Theologizing for Spiritual Empowerment: An African Perspective," *Common Ground Journal* 7, no. 1 (Fall 2009): 118.

43. Mark A. Shivers, "William James and Elastic Preaching: Testimony after Exiting the Houses of Authority," *Journal of Speculative Philosophy* 21, no. 3 (2007): 183.

44. For insight into developing effective testimonial skills, see "Guidelines for Coaching Testimonies," in Wilhoit, *Spiritual Formation as If the Church Mattered*, 133–134.

Ricouer, Paul. 1980. "The Hermeneutics of Testimony." In *Essays on Biblical Interpretation*, edited by Lewis S. Mudge, 59–94. Philadelphia: Fortress Press.

Shivers, Mark A. 2007. "William James and Elastic Preaching: Testimony after Exiting the Houses of Authority." *Journal of Speculative Philosophy* 21 (3): 181–200.

Wilhoit, James C. 2008. *Spiritual Formation as if the Church Mattered: Growing in Christ through Community*. Grand Rapids, MI: Baker Academic.

—LISA MILLIGAN LONG

THAILAND AND CHRISTIAN EDUCATION

The French Franciscan Bonferre first introduced Christianity to Thailand in the mid-16th century. Franciscan, Dominican, Jesuit, and Augustinian missionaries followed, initiating a relationship with Siamese rulers that fluctuated between congeniality and persecution. Protestant missionaries arrived in 1828, uniting in 1934 under the umbrella association Church of Christ in Thailand.

Despite early periods of persecution, religious freedom has been constitutionally supported since 1878. According to the 2000 Census, 94.6 percent of the Thai population adheres to Theravada Buddhism. Islam is the second-largest religion, with 4.6 percent of the population, followed by Christianity at 0.7 percent. Small groups of Hindu, Sikh, Taoist, Jewish, Confucian, and animist communities also exist (0.1 percent). The four recognized Protestant groups in the nation are the Church of Christ in Thailand, the Evangelical Foundation of Thailand, and the Baptist and Seventh-day Adventist churches. The Roman Catholic Church constitutes 25 percent of the Christian population.

Realizing the importance of Christian education, the Roman Catholic Church established its first theological seminary, General College, to train national clergy in 1665. Religious schools for boys and girls followed in 1671. Currently there are over 200 schools run by the Catholic Church. In the 19th century, Protestant missionaries joined these efforts, promoting equal educational opportunities for all levels of society and particularly for women. Today the largest denomination, the Church of Christ in Thailand, operates 2 universities, 2 theological seminaries, and 30 Christian schools.

References and Resources

Wells, K. E. 1928. "Educational Work." In *Historical Sketch of Protestant Missions in Siam, 1828–1928*, edited by G. B. McFarland, 209–219. Bangkok: Bangkok Times Press.

———. 1958. *History of Protestant Work in Thailand, 1828–1958*. Bangkok: Church of Christ in Thailand.

—SARITA D. GALLAGHER

THEOLOGICAL EDUCATION

At its core, theological education must adequately and fruitfully instruct students in the critical dimensions of knowledge of God and knowledge of self; enabling Christians to reflect upon, appreciate, and integrate broad issues of theological understanding and appreciation. This calls for an instructional practice that integrates reason and reflection, combining the intellectual, spiritual, and experiential aspects of biblical thought and Christian life. Theological education should rightly define and refine truths in terms of human life and experience, while formulating a framework of personal understanding and lived expression based on a biblical worldview.

One of the ongoing challenges of Christian theological education has always been a process of response and reform: response to the influences of the day and educational reform that maintains the integration of intellect, faith, and action within the contemporary context and culture. Secular educators are becoming increasingly interested in reintroducing moral and ethical themes into education. This recent shift toward reemphasizing moral and spiritual development is both greatly needed and very difficult in our relativistic and pluralistic society. Theological education provides an opportunity to develop moral and ethical standards that are clearly rooted in well-developed and articulated biblical understanding. As Christian educators, we need to look for opportunities to bring a positive and sensitive biblical voice to this discussion. This requires that we remain close enough for dialogue to take place.

Theological education directly addresses the core philosophical categories and major questions of human life and existence, including metaphysics (the nature of reality and humanity's place in that reality), epistemology (the nature of knowledge and knowing), and axiology (the nature of value, ethics, and aesthetics). Each of these categories relates to the *why, what,* and *how* of theological education: what can be known, how it can be known, and why it matters. From a Christian perspective, metaphysics must speak of God, creation, and man and woman as the image of God. Christian epistemology identifies a tangible reality that can be known, as well as a spiritual reality that can also be known. We are created to know, act, and interact according to intellect, emotion, and revelation. This describes a basic Christian worldview. This Christian perspective on metaphysics and epistemology in turn bears directly on our understanding and expression of values and ethics. Worldviews, Christian or otherwise, influence how we understand ourselves, others, and the world around us. Ultimately, theological education should provide a comprehensive understanding of biblical truth, concepts, and principles that establish a framework of Christian thought and cultivate a pattern of Christian life and action (Rom. 12:1–3; Col. 3:1–2).

Certain areas of student needs should remain central in providing instruction in theological education. Theological education should be perceived by students as a valuable investment of their time. The value of theological education increases as students perceive that it is developing a deeper spiritual life and faith commitment, that they are learning valuable principles that apply to their chosen field, and that they are engaging in educational activates and experiences that are relevant to their current ministry. As such, instruction in theological education must set the integration of theory, theology, and application as a high priority.

References and Resources

Agee, Bob R., and Douglas V. Henry, eds. 2003. *Faithful Learning and the Christian Scholarly Vocation*. Grand Rapids, MI: Eerdmans.

Clark, Robert E., Lin Johnson, and Allyn K Sloat, eds. 1991. *Christian Education: Foundations for the Future*. Chicago: Moody Publishers.

Groome, Thomas H. 1999. *Christian Religious Education: Sharing Our Story and Vision*. 1st Jossey-Bass ed. San Francisco: Jossey-Bass.

—Gino Pasquariello

Theological Education as Professional Education

The usual model for combining practical training with academic work in the recent history of theological education is the professional model. Theological education trains people to do a professional job in the churches by the teachers' being good theological education professionals themselves. The historical verdict, however, is that although there are advantages, there are also real problems associated with the use of the adjective "professional" in theological education.

Edward Farley outlines a number of periods in theological education, particularly in the United States; his third period, from the 1940s onward, is when the professional paradigm becomes dominant and the ministry bears the sociological marks of a profession.[45] The historical application of this model to the realm of theological education is usually seen in the work of Friederich Schleiermacher (1987). In the 1950s, H. Richard Niebuhr developed the model in two books, published in 1956 and 1957, and in

1969, an ATS Conference took as its theme "Theological Education as Professional Education."

Despite this continued enthusiasm for the model, criticism was building up. It seemed to neglect the more spiritual aspects of ministry and to exclude the laity from participating in ministry. For the Catholic, it seemed to ignore the work of the sacramental person, and for the evangelical the divine call to ministry and the gifts of the Holy Spirit.

A landmark in the development of the model occurred when Jackson Carroll was funded by the ATS and released on sabbatical by the Hartford Seminary in 1984 to research the status of the model. His paper was finally published in the spring of 1985.[46] He accepts that the professional is still the dominant model in our society for the delivery of important services and so should be used for ministry, yet it should not concentrate on technical competence and practical skills, but rather on developing reflective practitioners. And unlike those in other professions, a minister should relate to a group, not an individual in need, and so empower the group. It should see the minister's authority derive not from competence but from religious authenticity.

Traditionally, the characteristics of a professional are a specialist body of knowledge learned over some years; membership in a self-regulating group that controls entry by examination and disciplines members when necessary; competence in a field of service to the public; a sense of vocation in altruistic service; and a high status in society, because professionals alone possess the knowledge and skills necessary to do a particular job.

However, this definition of professional has been eroded over the years. First, after a number of scandals, professionals are not usually left to self-regulate any more. Second, the term *professional* is widening out, so that sometimes it comes to mean something less than described above—often no more than competence in a task. So a baker can do a professional job of baking, or someone can be called a professional just because he gets paid for the job, such as a professional football player.

Where "professional" indicates the ability to do a job of service to the high standard society expects, the term and the contents of the idea are welcome among theological colleges and seminaries. This needs to be stressed today, as counseling, youth ministry, mission studies, and other practical subjects require those with a professional competence, sometimes attested to by the state. However, in that the adjective "professional" implies a status in society, it does need to be questioned. It is possible to

---

45. E. Farley, *Theologia: The Fragmentation and Unity of Theological Education* (Philadelphia: Fortress, 1983).

46. J. Carroll, "The Professional Model of Ministry, Is It Worth Saving?" *Theological Education* 21, no. 2 (1985): 7–48.

distinguish between acknowledgment of competence by a society and the according of status by society.

The Christian church has frequently been extended and built up by people often regarded by societies as without special status, from the apostles to the Moravian missionaries in the 18th century and including those ordinary people trained by the early Bible colleges and serving in the faith missions at home and abroad. Furthermore, to the extent that *professionalism* means exclusivity, the membership of a closed group in an authoritative position in the church called the ministry, it is inappropriate from both biblical and practical standpoints.

References and Resources

Dearborn, T. 1995. "Preparing New Leaders for the Church of the Future." *Transformation* 12 (4): 7–12.

Foster, Charles, et al. 2006. *Educating Clergy: Teaching Practices and Pastoral Imagination*. San Francisco: Jossey-Bass.

Kelsey, D. H. 1993. *Between Athens and Berlin: The Theological Education Debate*. Grand Rapids, MI: Eerdmans.

Schleiermacher, Friedrich, Keith Clements, and John W. De Gruchy. 1987. *Friederich Schleiermacher: Pioneer of Modern Theology*. London: Collins.

—Graham Cheesman

Theological Education, Assessment in

Assessment is an essential component of the process of effective education.[47] It is a major challenge in theological education institutions if there is to be integrity between their theological values and educational methodology, and if the values and attitudes of seminary[48] life have significant impact on students as they move into ministry situations.[49]

The Scope of Educational Assessment

In general terms "assessment" (and the closely related term "evaluation") describes the judgments made about aspects of the curriculum. More specifically, it is the process of "weighing up the performance of the learner"[50] and has a range of forms:

- *Norm-Referenced versus Criterion-Referenced Assessment:* Norm-referenced assessment weighs up a student's performance in relation to the performance of other students; criterion-referenced assessment weighs up student performance against a set of predetermined criteria.
- *Formative versus Summative Assessment:* Formative assessment provides learners with suggestions about how to improve their performance; summative assessment takes place usually at the end of a unit or course of study and is an appraisal of what has been acquired by the learners, especially the extent to which course objectives/outcomes have been achieved.
- *Formal versus Informal Assessment:* Assessment strategies may be placed on a continuum between formal and informal: "Broadly speaking, formal methods may be utilised to extract cognitively-mediated information-based material (e.g. facts, procedures, and problem-solving ability); whereas informal methods may be used to determine more affectively-based data (e.g. feelings, dispositions, preferences, and likes)."[51]

There are three broad reasons for educational assessment:[52]

- For the benefit of the students (e.g., to reinforce correct learning and to correct error and/or misunderstanding, to estimate present achievement, and to predict future learning capacity).
- For the benefit of the teachers (to monitor the pace of teaching and to evaluate the curriculum process).
- For the benefit of the institution/society (to report present achievement, to estimate aptitude for new learning and potential for responsibility, and to provide a character reference).

Assessment Challenges for Theological Education

Outcomes-Oriented Assessment

Seminaries, like any educational institution, may use assessment in any or all of the scope summarized above. What is essential is that the assessment procedures used actually contribute valid and reliable measures for the stated purpose.

In seminary-based ministerial/pastoral formation, four major domains of educational intervention may be identified: the cognitive acquisition of appropriate

---

47. An overview of the range of assessment research is in Carolyn Jurkowitz, "What Is the Literature Saying about Learning and Assessment in Higher Education?" *Theological Education* 39, no. 1 (2003): 53–92.

48. In this entry "seminary" is used as a generic term for institutions providing formal theological studies, predominantly for pastoral/ministerial formation, and including theological colleges and Bible colleges/schools.

49. Reflected in the power of the "hidden curriculum"; cf. the explicit curriculum in educational intervention.

50. Following Brian V. Hill, "Is Assessment Compatible with Agape?" *Journal of Christian Education* Papers 96 (1989): 6.

51. Richard Berlach, "A Christian Approach to Evaluation," *Journal of Christian Education* 45, no. 2 (2002): 23–24.

52. Hill, "Is Assessment Compatible with Agape?," 6–10.

knowledge, competence in required ministerial skills, personal character development, and empathy and passion.[53] The developing integration of these "results in credible minister-leaders who are competent, confident and compassionate."[54]

Assessment will be required in all four domains if they are significant outcomes, but common assessment criteria cannot be applied equally across all the domains. Appropriate assessment strategies need to be carefully developed and implemented, especially if elements of spirituality and formation are being assessed[55] and deep (cf. surface) learning is encouraged.[56] The common but artificial distinction between "academic" and "practical" outcomes will be challenged and reflected in assessment strategies that go well beyond simply cognitively focused ones, as well as shifting the weight given to content ("regurgitating the facts") versus thought processes ("critical analytical ability").

Assessment and Institutional Theological Values
Educational enterprises with integrity will ensure clear congruence between their espoused and operant theory:[57] In seminaries this will be expressed, inter alia, in the integration of their stated theological perspectives and values with their educational practices. No assessment strategy is value-neutral or value-free, and seminaries do well to demonstrate awareness of this when assessment methods are selected in their courses.

A number of theological values underlie effective Christian ministry. Evaluating the assessment processes in the seminary curriculum against these values is likely to result in greater congruence between seminary education reflecting ministry values and the seminary's espoused theological values and to demonstrate that there is something qualitatively distinctive about assessment in seminaries by virtue of their foundational values.

Theological values that are significant in orthodox Protestant theology and have implications for appropriate assessment strategies in seminaries include the following:[58]

1. *God's creative variety*, seen in human uniqueness and diversity alongside similarity and uniformity. Seminary assessment strategies will avoid "one size fits all" approaches.

2. *The worth of individuals.* In assessment, "Christians should be foremost in respecting and strengthening the self-esteem of students through affirmation of their worth as persons."[59]

3. *The interplay between judgment and love.* Because God values humanity, He both loves and affirms, and judges and disciplines. Assessment strategies will be to both correct and encourage.

4. *Education for holistic transformation.* Course outcomes and associated assessment will recognize the possibility of acquiring appropriate knowledge along with changes in behavior, attitude, and values.

5. *Collaboration in community*, expressed in greater emphasis on community-oriented rather than individualistic learning and associated assessment strategies.

6. *Education with a missional focus*, providing forms of assessment that encourage integrating critical, analytical, factual content with insights and reflection that relate to spiritual development and ministry practice.

References and Resources

Argris, Chris, and Donald Schön. 1974. *Theory in Practice: Increasing Professional Effectiveness.* San Francisco: Jossey-Bass.

Banks, Robert. 1999. *Re-envisioning Theological Education: Exploring a Missional Alternative to Current Models.* Grand Rapids, MI: Eerdmans.

Berlach, Richard. 2002. "A Christian Approach to Evaluation." *Journal of Christian Education* 45 (2): 21–31.

Biggs, John. 1987. *Student Approaches to Learning and Studying.* Hawthorn, Australia: Australian Council for Educational Research.

———. 1999. *Teaching for Quality Learning at University.* Buckingham, UK: SRHE and Open University Press.

Harkness, Allan. 2008. "Assessment in Theological Education: Do Our Theological Values Matter?" *Journal of Adult Theological Education* 5 (2): 183–201.

---

53. Allan Harkness, "De-Schooling the Theological Seminary: An Appropriate Paradigm for Effective Ministerial Formation," in *Tending the Seedbeds: Educational Perspectives on Theological Education in Asia*, ed. Allan Harkness (Manila: Asia Theological Association, 2010), 104–105. This is an expansion of the common "know-be-do" formula.

54. Ibid., 105.

55. Commentators like Brian Hill in *Beyond the Transfer of Knowledge: Spirituality in Theological Education* (Auckland, NZ: Impetus Publications, 1998) have highlighted that assessing an assignment in a course is quite different from making value judgments on a person's formation.

56. See Paul Ramsden, *Learning to Teach in Higher Education*, 2nd ed. (London and New York: RoutledgeFalmer, 2003); John Biggs, *Student Approaches to Learning and Studying* (Hawthorn, Australia: Australian Council for Educational Research, 1987); John Biggs, *Teaching for Quality Learning at University* (Buckingham, UK: SRHE and Open University Press, 1999).

57. The rationale for this is in line with theories of action, seen in the classical work of Chris Argris and Donald Schön, *Theory in Practice: Increasing Professional Effectiveness* (San Francisco: Jossey Bass, 1974).

---

58. Allan Harkness, "Assessment in Theological Education: Do Our Theological Values Matter?" *Journal of Adult Theological Education* 5, no. 2 (2008): 183–201.

59. Hill, "Is Assessment Compatible with Agape?," 13.

——. 2010. "De-Schooling the Theological Seminary: An Appropriate Paradigm for Effective Ministerial Formation." In *Tending The Seedbeds: Educational Perspectives On Theological Education in Asia,* edited by Allan Harkness, 103–128. Manila: Asia Theological Association.

Hill, Brian V. 1989. "Is Assessment Compatible with Agape?" *Journal of Christian Education Papers* 96: 5–20.

——. 1994. "May We Assess Religious Development at School?" *Spectrum* 26 (2): 125–139.

——. 1997. "Evaluation and Assessment: The Tail That Wags the Dog?" In *Agenda for Educational Change*, edited by Trevor Cooling and John Shortt, 132–147. Leicester: Apollos.

——. 1998. *Beyond the Transfer of Knowledge: Spirituality in Theological Education.* Auckland, NZ: Impetus Publications.

Jurkowitz, Carolyn. 2003. "What Is the Literature Saying about Learning and Assessment in Higher Education?" *Theological Education* 39 (1): 53–92.

Ramsden, Paul. 2003. *Learning to Teach in Higher Education.* 2nd ed. London and New York: RoutledgeFalmer.

—ALLAN HARKNESS

THEOLOGICAL EDUCATION, ATHENS VERSUS BERLIN MODEL OF

Every institution must provide training for its future leaders, and the church is no different. The question becomes, how is this training best offered, and what should center that training? The period between 1960 and 1980 saw some of the most profound changes the world has ever experienced. Advances in communication have reduced the world to a global village with profound implications for the church and its systems of theological education. Calls to educate emerging leaders from the non-Western world for ministry proliferated during this period. Western theological training, largely based on Greek thought or German method, was not up to the task of training global leaders.[60] Western theological education began a period of profound soul-searching about its aims and purposes. One of the major voices in that debate was David H. Kelsey, who was at that time professor of theology at Yale Divinity School.

Kelsey's book, *Between Athens and Berlin*, was a defining reference point for the debate over what should center theological education.[61] Kelsey classifies the two most pronounced philosophies at work in Western theological education, based on their geographical and cultural location. The "Athens" model of theological education embodies the Greek ideal of enculturation of the soul through a formation process the Greeks called *paideia*.[62] The roots of this educational approach can be seen in Plato's *Republic*, in which he contended that education should prepare the soul through discipline and contemplation to know the virtues needed to attain excellence (*arête*) of character and soul. Greek influence in theological training is obvious in the early church, especially among the Greek Christians at Alexandria, who used the word *paideia* to describe their educational philosophy.[63] Greek influence held sway well past the Middle Ages in the European university system, with the university "chair" and "faculty" reflecting ancient Greek educational philosophy.[64]

With the advent of the Reformation and the Enlightenment, new emphasis was placed on scholarship and reason. Before the 18th century, theology was seen as the "queen of sciences" and used as the normative standard for judging truth.[65] After the Enlightenment, theology was no longer regarded as a normative standard, because God could not be directly seen or studied. In 1810, a committee of scholars was given the task of shaping the curriculum of the University of Berlin according to Enlightenment standards. The committee was ready to remove theology from the curriculum, because it clashed with the Enlightenment ideals of *Lernfreiheit* (freedom to learn) and *Lehrfreiheit* (freedom to teach).[66] Friedrich Schleiermacher, a theologian on the committee, argued that theology was a "socially necessary" discipline of "specialized knowledge" needed to shape the "professional skills" through specialized research.[67] With its acceptance into the University of Berlin, the "Berlin" model of theological training caused theological training to disintegrate into an increasingly small and disjointed number of specialties, in a phenomenon some have called "Schleiermacher's Ghost."

Kelsey pointed out the extremes of both the Athens and Berlin models and advocated a middle ground between the two that accentuates the strengths of both, held together in "dialectic" tension to train ministry leaders.[68]

—JAMES T. FLYNN

---

60. Robert Banks, *Reenvisioning Theological Education* (Grand Rapids, MI: Eerdmans, 1999), 11–12.

61. David H. Kelsey, *Between Athens and Berlin: The Theological Debate* (Grand Rapids, MI: Eerdmans, 1993).

62. Ibid., 6–7.

63. Werner Jaeger, *Early Christianity and Greek Paideia* (Cambridge, MA: Belknap Press of Harvard University, 1961), 25, 70–83.

64. Edwin Hatch, *The Influence of Greek Ideals on Early Christianity* (New York: Harper & Brothers, 1957), 43–44.

65. James T. Flynn, Wie L. Tjiong, and Russell W. West, *A Well-Furnished Heart: Restoring the Spirit's Place in the Leadership Classroom* (Fairfax: Xulon, 2002), 101.

66. Kelsey, *Between Athens and Berlin*, 15.

67. Ibid.

68. Thomas H. Kelsey, *To Understand God Truly: What's Theological about a Theological School* (Louisville, KY: Westminster/John Knox, 1992), 250–251.

Theological Education, Berlin as a Model of

The University of Berlin has had a profound effect on the shape of Western theological education since its inception. In the centuries before the founding of this German university, Europe had experienced several cultural earthquakes that reshaped society, its outlook on reality, and its institutions. In the 14th and 15th centuries, the Renaissance reshaped the minds of Western Europe with a new emphasis on humanism and the intellect. The Reformation of the 16th century reshaped the soul of Western Europe with spiritual renewal, an emphasis on the scripture, revealed truth, and the priesthood of each believer. What followed in the 17th and 18th centuries was a renewed emphasis on reason and intellect as the primary means of knowing truth. This period, called the age of reason or the Enlightenment, had a profound effect on culture that rippled through Europe's institutions, including the university and its churches.

The University of Berlin was born in the early 1800s as an Enlightenment university. Before the Enlightenment period, the predominant model for theological education was based on the Greek philosophy of character formation called *paideia*.[69] Thomas H. Kelsey, in *Between Athens and Berlin*, called this the "Athens" model of theological education, because it emphasizes the enculturation of the soul through discipline and contemplation as a major pathway for ministerial formation. With the Enlightenment came a more rational approach to education that emphasized reason and scholarship as a centering educational philosophy. The University of Berlin was established to specifically embody the ideals of the Enlightenment in its new curriculum.

Because of the centrality of reason, the intellect, and research, the committee forming the new university began to question whether theology had a place in its curriculum. Before that time, theology had enjoyed the role of "queen of sciences" as a normative standard for truth.[70] The curriculum at the University of Berlin was designed to emphasize *Wissenschaft*: the enlightenment ideal of orderly, disciplined, critical research method to uncover truth.[71] Wilhelm von Humboldt had empowered a three-person committee to design the curriculum for the new university in 1809 and 1810. On that committee was Friedrich Schleiermacher, a theologian. The committee was unsure that theology should be included in the curriculum, since the university would only be granting the highest research degree, a doctorate, and

it was impossible to directly conduct empirical research on God. The committee members were also concerned that because theology was traditionally used to norm the other sciences, it would interfere with Enlightenment philosophy's prized freedom to learn (*Lernfreiheit*) and freedom to teach (*Lehrfreiheit*). Schleiermacher successfully argued that theology should be included in the curriculum because it involved practical education for a socially necessary profession.[72] With theology's inclusion in the curriculum of the University of Berlin, Schleiermacher inadvertently created a new identity for theological education and ministry. Whereas up to this point the Athens model of theological education had emphasized formation of the soul and its character as a pathway for ministerial preparation, the Berlin model emphasized research, critical thought, and reason as the major pathway for training ministers.

Since its inclusion in the curriculum in Berlin, Christian theology has been strongly influenced by German Enlightenment thought and its research-based approach. An immediate result was the proliferation of theological specialties, much as had occurred in the sciences. Edward Farley notes that this growth of specialty knowledge has led to a fragmentation of theology into increasingly smaller, disjointed subjects, until in some places theological education has become disjointed and divorced from the church and its central role in preparing students for ministry.[73] The effects still ripple through Western theological education in its educational structures, in a manner often referred to as "Schleiermacher's Ghost." The curriculum of many Western theological schools retains a German division into four theological specialties: Bible, dogmatics (systematic theology), church history, and practical theology. The German "degree" system, most notably the German research doctor of philosophy (PhD) degree, became an accepted standard in American theological education in the early 19th century.

By the 1950s in America, serious debate was under way about how to revitalize theological education. In earlier times, an overemphasis on the Athens approach to theological education had resulted in a lack of intellectual rigor in the preparation of ministers for ministry. The Berlin model, while seeking to introduce academic rigor, had badly fragmented theology into academic specialties that in many cases no longer prepared students spiritually and practically for ministry in the local church. Throughout the 1980s and 1990s, a vigorous debate in the theological education community ensued over renewing theological education. One of the conclu-

69. Kelsey, *Between Athens and Berlin*, 6–7.
70. Flynn, Tjiong, and West, *A Well-Furnished Heart*, 101.
71. Kelsey, *Between Athens and Berlin*, 12.

72. Kelsey, *To Understand God Truly*, 250–251.
73. Edwin Farley, *Theologia: The Fragmentation and Unity of Theological Education* (Philadelphia: Fortress Press, 1983), 8–9.

sions drawn from this debate is that both Athens and Berlin have their strengths and weakness, and the middle ground, "between Athens and Berlin," represents the best hope for theological training.

—JAMES P. FLYNN

THEOLOGICAL EDUCATION BY EXTENSION

Theological education by extension (TEE) is a nonresidential form of theological education that arose first of all in Central America in the early 1960s and is now a worldwide phenomenon, present on every continent. It developed in parallel to the increasing popularity of "open education" and the notion of the "Open University," pioneered in the same period in Britain. Participants can be any lay congregants wanting to connect faith with everyday life (see, e.g., http://www.sewanee.edu/EFM/) and trainees in various forms of lay and ordained ministry (e.g., http://www.tee.co.za/).

Common to TEE programs across the world is a novel methodology. It is often explained by the picture of a two-rail fence[74] or railway track. One rail of the fence is the Christian tradition (Bible, creeds, etc.); the second is the lived experience of the participants. These are brought together in a face-to-face seminar with a trained facilitator who enables a group of students to learn together. The method therefore joins together study and experience in a praxis methodology that results in renewed actions carried out after the seminar by participants. Thus the "teacher" in the program is written material studied by the participants at home either daily or weekly. Seminars occur at regular intervals, assignments are given, and assessments can be made of students' progress. Keys to excellence in TEE programs are the quality of the written materials and the skills of the seminar facilitator, combined with the desire of the learners to learn.

The rationale for TEE programs is pragmatic, educational, and theological. First, they enable large numbers of students to study without the expense of a residential facility. Second, the methodology puts learners in their rightful place in charge of their own learning and takes their life experiences seriously. Students learn and take action as a result of study in their own context—they are not removed from that context into a liminal institution where immediate application of learning is suspended for a period. This returns theological education and ministry to the *laos* (Kinsler 1983) and incarnates it in the local congregation of the faithful.

TEE programs have been questioned about (a) the content of the study material—it has sometimes relied on what is known as *programmed* learning, focusing on technical and factual detail (for an example see Study by Extension for All Nations, http://www.sean.uk.net/), to the detriment of problematizing "why" questions of theological depth; (b) how connected the programs are to residential theological education and what benefits or drawbacks this may have (Mabuluki, 2010), especially for accreditation at higher education levels; and (c) whether this is really theological education "on the cheap," which does not match up to the formational experience on offer in a traditional residential institution.

Although TEE programs have not replaced residential models, they have proven their worth over several decades. There is extensive evidence for their fruitfulness and capacity to offer different and successive levels of study, often accredited. TEE programs complement other models and can be creatively integrated with them for the learning of the global church. How online learning and its increasing worldwide availability will affect TEE delivery is yet to be seen.

References and Resources

Kinsler, F. Ross. 1978. *The Extension Movement in Theological Education: A Call to the Renewal of the Ministry.* Pasadena, CA: William Carey Library.

———, ed. 1983. *Ministry by the People: Theological Education by Extension.* Maryknoll, NY: Orbis.

———, ed. 2008. *Diversified Theological Education: Equipping All God's People.* Pasadena, CA: William Carey Library.

Mabuluki, Kangwa. 2010. "Diversified Theological Education: Genesis, Development and Ecumenical Potential of Theological Education by Extension (TEE)." In *Handbook of Theological Education in World Christianity: Theological Perspectives—Regional Surveys—Ecumenical Trends,* edited by D. Werner, D. Esterline, N. Kang, and J. Raja, 251–262. Oxford: Regnum.

Winter, Ralph D. 1969. *Theological Education by Extension.* Pasadena, CA: William Carey Library.

http://www.teenet.net/

—NIGEL ROOMS

THEOLOGICAL EDUCATION BY EXTENSION COLLEGE IN SOUTHERN AFRICA

Located in Johannesburg, South Africa, the Theological Education by Extension College (TEEC) provides theological education to conciliar and nondenominational ministry, both lay and ordained, in Southern Africa. With an extensive network of churches and denomina-

---

74. For a particularly nuanced pictorial representation, see http://www.efmuk.org.uk/programme.html (accessed 30 October 2012).

tions, it currently educates over 3,400 students from five countries and 28 denominations, providing some 7,000 courses, fulfilling its mission of "equipping anyone, anywhere, for ministry."

The TEE College has a special historic significance within the educational and ecclesiastical scene of the region. The ecumenical church project was established in 1976 as an anti-apartheid institution to "provide Theological Education within a non-racist, non-sexist, ecumenical, and multilingual setting." The initiative came from the Joint Board for the Diploma in Theology and involved the South African Council for Theological Education, an arm of the South African Council of Churches, with John Thorne (United Congregational Church) as president and John Rees (Methodist Church of Southern Africa) as general secretary. The foundations of the college were laid by its first director, Father Louis Peters (1976–1984).

Various churches support the distance learning private institution of higher education, which provides theological training for students preparing for ordination and ministry. The current supporting churches are the Anglican Church of Southern Africa, Evangelical Lutheran Church in Southern Africa, Methodist Church of Southern Africa, Uniting Presbyterian Church in Southern Africa, Roman Catholic Church, United Congregational Church of Southern Africa, and Salvation Army in Southern Africa.

In 2008, TEE College received full registration with the Department of Higher Education and Training in South Africa, which means that its degrees, diplomas, and higher certificates are recognized nationally and internationally. Now managed from premises donated by the former Transvaal Education Department, TEEC offers a range of programs: bachelor of theology, diploma in theology, diploma in theology and ministry, higher certificate in theology, certificate of competence in theology, and award in theology. The students study course material supplied by the institution in the English language and gather in regional tutorial groups to discuss the academic work and how it relates to the practice of ministry in the church.

At Benoni, Cape Town, Port Elizabeth, Rosettenville, and Sophiatown in South Africa, tutorials are run by the local churches, not by the college. For instance, at Port Elizabeth in 2006 there were 21 groups tutored by representatives of four denominations, catering for over 150 learners. One of the groups met at the maximum security prison of St. Albans and was led by a female graduate of TEE College. The prison was known as "Little Beirut" because of the daily violence among the inmates, but TEE tutorials have helped to transform the lives of many of its prisoners incarcerated for murder

and rape. Also, the prisoners have organized a group called "Call Out Against Crime" to speak against the violence of gang activity.

In addition to the academic programs, the TEEC curriculum includes students' involvement in community projects, such as working with prisoners and those seeking rehabilitation from substance abuse, supporting victims of domestic violence, and helping disadvantaged youth and at-risk children, as well as organizing AIDS support groups, employment opportunities for women, classes on business skills, and assistance for the homeless.

—Robert L. Gallagher

THEOLOGICAL EDUCATION, CLASSICAL MODEL OF

Robert Banks, an Australian scholar, is known for the "classical model" of theological education. His contribution to the debate about the nature and the process of theological education is twofold. He has offered a comprehensive overview of the current proposals for reform, and in response to their limitations, he has proposed his own vision of the authoritative source, method, and goal of seminary training. Banks's analysis builds on David Kelsey's typology of the normative approaches to theological education: "Athens," the vision of education rooted in antiquity, which emphasizes the process of holistic formation of character (*paideia*), and "Berlin," the approach that originated under the Prussian reform in Europe, which emphasizes the scientific study of theology for the purposes of ministerial training (*Wissenschaft*).

Banks's "classical model" reflects his examination of the most significant reformulations of the "Athens" vision of theological education offered by Edward Farley and Richard Neuhaus (see Banks, 1999) on theological education and moral formation, and by the feminist theologians from the Mud Flower Collective and the Network Center for the Study of Ministry (Banks 1999, 17–33). This vision of theological education is characterized by three distinctive features. First, it advocates for a return to a less abstract, more intuitive, and practical theological wisdom (*theologia*) and an intentional cultivation of the students' disposition toward the intuitive and existential knowing of God (*habitus*). Second, it emphasizes the importance of restoring the notion of personal formation as an essential element and objective of theological education: by bringing to bear the classical Christian traditions of virtue upon its institutional culture and daily work of teaching and learning, the seminary sponsors the development of the distinctly Christian identity and commitment. Finally, it reveals that lasting reform of theological education requires not merely a change in the curriculum but also a conversion of the patterns of relationships within its community—especially as it is exemplified in its deliberate embracing of cultural diversity, orientation toward justice, and willingness to be transformed by the encounter with the traditionally marginalized minority groups.

Banks believes that the proponents of the classical model "pose a challenge which theological education cannot afford to ignore" (1999, 31). However, his main critique of their proposals is their insufficient emphasis on the role of scripture in revealing God and the resultant lack of clarity about the normative base by which to assess the content and dynamics of transformation. Without the normative base, the issues of fragmentation, morality, and domination in theological education cannot be adequately addressed.

See also Theological Education as Professional Education; Theological Education in the University

References and Resources

Banks, Robert J. 1999. *Reenvisioning Theological Education: Exploring a Missional Alternative to Current Models.* Grand Rapids, MI: Eerdmans.

Cannon, Katie G., and Mud Flower Collective. 1985. *God's Fierce Whimsy: Christian Feminism and Theological Education.* New York: Pilgrim Press.

Farley, Edward. 1983. *Theologia: The Fragmentation and Unity of Theological Education.* Philadelphia: Fortress Press.

———. 1988. *The Fragility of Knowledge: Theological Education in the Church and the University.* Philadelphia: Fortress Press.

Kelsey, David H. 1992. *To Understand God Truly: What's Theological About a Theological School.* 1st ed. Louisville, KY: Westminster John Knox Press.

———. 1993. *Between Athens and Berlin: The Theological Education Debate.* Grand Rapids, MI: Eerdmans.

Neuhaus, Richard John. 1992. *Theological Education and Moral Formation.* Encounter Series. Grand Rapids, MI: Eerdmans.

Rhodes, Lynn N., and Nancy Dale Richardson. 1991. *Mending Severed Connections.* San Francisco: San Francisco Network Ministries.

—NATALIA A. SHULGINA

THEOLOGICAL EDUCATION, DIVERSITY IN

Theological education has already experienced significant developments, with the process of rationalization in educational and ecclesiastical institutions, new accreditation standards, and the impact of globalization (Werner 2009, 260). This has resulted in a growing number of international students and multicultural student bodies. These new student constituencies reflect a wide spectrum of cultural backgrounds, personal histories, and theological commitments and represent diversity in terms of race, ethnicity, culture, class, gender, age, and sexual orientation. One of the most significant changes in theological education has been the increase in women students, resulting in political leverage for feminist theological education that continues to challenge traditional practices in seminaries. Diversity means resisting the homogenizing of racial, ethnic, cultural, and class differences into uniformity (Riebe-Estrella 2009, 20). It exists as a threat and promise, problem and possibility.

Theological institutions generally have treated diversity as a matter of accommodation (Foster 2002, 21). This approach no longer seems viable on either institutional or theological grounds. The 1996 accrediting standards of the Association of Theological Schools (ATS) in the United States emphasized that "attention to diversity is not simply a matter of inviting participating, but a lens in the theological school's essential task of learning, teaching, research and formation" (Gilligan 2002, 9). On the basis of the economics, seminaries cannot exist without recruiting students from other traditions. These students cannot be viewed as guests, but must be recognized as full participants in the life and ethos of the institution. In responding to changing student bodies, institutions are also called on to be transformed as well (Andraos 2012, 2). Despite the efforts to increase diversity in theological education during the last three decades (Lee, Shields, and Oh 2008), some but not enough progress has been made. In general, the lenses of race, ethnicity, class, gender, and sexuality have been used only as hermeneutical, pedagogical, and sometimes epistemic, critical perspectives on the production and function of knowledge in many disciplines (Andraos 2012, 2).

The issues of diversity are theologically complicated and contested as they are attached to religious dogma. The articulation of diversity and how people experience it is often highly charged (Mezirow and Associates 2000), simmering with all sorts of resentments and half-understandings and then emerging in explosive moments of crisis. In dealing with "otherness," educators cannot agree whether the goal is to "understand," or "convert," or bring them "into the fold," or explore their "interconnectedness" (Foster 2002, 21). Because handling diversity in education is so complex, educators need to recognize the validity of differences, which will require an appraisal of the educator's own personal and of institutional ideologies and perceptions, and a frank dedication to facilitate and manage learner diversity. Tisdell (2003, 372) suggests that student encounters with "otherness" provide a vehicle for an awareness and appreciation of identity differences, particularly around spiritual development. This encounter of "otherness" within one's immediate peer group provides lessons of multiculturalism in this rational context. Once the institutional culture begins to see its own situatedness, it can begin to shed its parochial and paternalistic tendencies (Foster 2002, 16). This is only possible when "whiteness" or "blackness," or heterosexuality, or being male is no longer conceived as the norm and is seen as one contextual position among many, albeit often carrying with it particular privileges and considerable power. Power relations based on social structures of race, class, gender, or sexual orientation are informed by critical pedagogy, feminist pedagogy, antiracist education, and critical multicultural literature (Tisdell 2003, 371). These theories focus on the analysis of power relations between dominant and oppressed groups and assume that structural social change will result when power relations are challenged (Brookfield 1995).

The aim of exploring diversity is to involve the theological community in looking at the ways in which difference is constructed, how its significance shifts, how it is operationalized in society, and most critically, why difference continues to matter. Within the institutional culture of theological communities, students are being shaped within diversity and socialized in how to respond to diversity. The way in which diversity is managed could create a source of division, or it could be used as a positive element in religious identity formation. The question at play here is how students might relate theology to their own context while also attempting to understand the other, such that their own presuppositions are challenged and their work in society becomes more effective. This can help students and faculty understand the formative means that institutional culture employs, so that together they might find a common theological discourse.

References and Resources

Andraos, M. E. 2012, January. "Engaging Diversity in Teaching Religion and Theology: An Intercultural, De-colonial Epistemic Perspective." *Teaching Theology & Religion*, v15 n1, 3-15.

Association of Theological Schools. 2003. Perspectives on Diversity in Theological Education. Workshop, March 2002.

Brookfield, S. 1995. *Becoming a Critically Reflective Teacher.* San Francisco: Jossey-Bass.

Foster, C. R. 2002. "Diversity in Theological Education." *Theological Education* 38 (2): 15-37.

Gilligan, M. 2002. "Diversity and Accreditation: A Measure of Quality." *Theological Education* 38 (2): v.

Lee, C., C. Shields, and Kristen Oh. 2008. "Theological Education in a Multicultural Environment: Empowerment or Disempowerment?" *Theological Education* 43 (2): 93-195.

Mezirow, J., and Associates, eds. 2000. *Learning as Transformation: Critical Perspectives on a Theory in Progress.* San Francisco: Jossey-Bass.

Parks, S. D. 2000. *Big Questions, Worthy Dreams: Mentoring Young Adults in Their Search for Meaning, Purpose and Faith.* San Francisco: Jossey-Bass.

Riebe-Estrella, G. 2009. "Engaging Borders: Lifting up Difference and Unmasking Divisions." *Theological Education* 45 (1): 19-25.

Tisdell, E. 2003. *Exploring Spirituality and Culture in Adult and Higher Education.* San Francisco: Jossey-Bass.

Volf, M. 1996. *Exclusion and Embrace: A Theological Exploration in Learning and Teaching.* New York: Oxford.

Warford, Malcolm, ed. 2007. *Practical Wisdom: On Theological Teaching and Learning.* New York: Peter Lang.

Werner, D. 2009. *Challenges and Opportunities in Theological Education in the 21st Century.* ETE/WCC. Geneva: Bossey Ecumenical Institute.

—MARILYN NAIDOO

THEOLOGICAL EDUCATION, FARLEY'S MODEL OF

Edward Farley is one of the most stimulating and critical voices in theological education. He has served nine different congregations as a part-time or full-time interim pastor, but his regular place of work has always been with a theological seminary or university. Farley is emeritus professor of theology for Vanderbilt Divinity School. His influence extends throughout Protestant mainline and evangelical theological education through books, journal articles, and consultations.

In his landmark work, *Theologia* (1983), Farley critiques theological education since the Enlightenment. He finds the dominant fourfold "theological encyclopedia" (i.e., Bible, systematic theology, church history, and practical theology) to be precariously fragmented. Farley contends that unity should be found in a disciplined way of thinking, called *theologia*, which can be used in all forms of ministry-related study. The essence of the training of a minister should be to treat theology as *habitus*, an orientation of the soul based in the knowledge of God and what God reveals.

Farley explores further the place of theology in the settings of university education, clergy education, and church education in *The Fragility of Knowledge* (1988). He deals with the Enlightenment conceptualization of knowledge and the compromise that happens when sciences become characterized by specialty fields rather than disciplined ways of thinking that bring unity to knowledge. Farley tries to bridge the gap between church education and theological education by showing how both clergy and laypeople can use *theologia* to do theology.

Practical theology, rather than being just one part of a fourfold theological encyclopedia, is the device that

Farley uses in *Practicing Gospel* (2003) to bring theology and ministry together. This moves theology outside the clerical paradigm and brings laypeople into the practice of theology.

References and Resources

Farley, Edward. 1983. *Theologia: The Fragmentation and Unity of Theological Education*. Philadelphia: Fortress Press.

——. 1988. *The Fragility of Knowledge: Theological Education in the Church and University*. Philadelphia: Fortress Press.

——. 2003. *Practicing Gospel: Unconventional Thoughts on the Church's Ministry*. Louisville, KY: Westminster John Knox Press.

—STEPHEN J. KEMP

THEOLOGICAL EDUCATION, FORMAL/NONFORMAL MODELS OF

Formal models of theological education are characterized by the schooling paradigm, whereas nonformal models are not. Rather, nonformal models are characterized by intentional learning in real-life contexts. The differences can be seen through the following categories.

Location. Formal theological education most often takes place on an academic campus. More specifically, it takes place primarily in classrooms according to academic structures. Even distance education programs largely attempt to replicate campus experiences. Nonformal theological education takes place primarily in churches and other ministry contexts, according to ministry structures.

Orientation. Recipients of formal theological education are generally called students and are expected to be able to function as scholars-in-training with a preservice orientation. Nonformal theological education recipients are generally called apprentices and are expected to be able to function as ministers-in-training with an in-service orientation.

Curriculum. Formal theological education is organized largely according to academic disciplines and the fourfold curriculum (Bible, theology, church history, and practical theology), expressed in an often fragmented array of courses. Nonformal theological education may vary greatly in terms of curricular structure, from mere observation and reflection on experiences to an intentionally designed set of integrated competencies that are carefully assessed.

Learning community. Formal theological education learning communities are composed of students enrolled in an academic institution being guided by faculty members. Even in distance education online courses, the discussion forums are composed of students from around the world in conversation with each other and a faculty member. Nonformal theological education learning communities are composed of apprentices in relationships in their churches, ministries, families, and other forms of community.

Assessment. Formal theological education assessment takes place primarily through examinations and research papers related to content acquisition and critical thinking. Nonformal theological education assessment takes place primarily through review of artifacts and attestations related to character and ministry skill development.

Certification. Formal theological education provides academic credentials that are often closely linked to ministry credentialing processes. In most cases, it is difficult to participate in formal theological education apart from an academic credential track. Nonformal theological education is usually linked to ministry credentialing processes, but not always linked to academic credentials, though it is becoming much more common, such as with the Antioch School of Church Planting and Leadership Development.

References and Resources

Kemp, Stephen. 2010. "Situated Learning: Optimizing Experiential Learning Through God-Given Learning Community." *Christian Education Journal*, Series 3, 7 (1): 118–143.

Reed, Jeff. 2013. "Church-Based Training That Is Truly Church-Based." Ames, Iowa: BILD International, 2001. Accessed 30 April 2013. http://bild.org/philosophy/ParadigmPapers.html.

Ward, Ted W. 2012. "Education That Makes a Difference." *Common Ground Journal* 10 (1): 22–25.

—STEPHEN J. KEMP

THEOLOGICAL EDUCATION, HISTORICAL OUTLINE OF

Beginnings

The intended purpose of theological education throughout history and in all cultures has been to train and develop leadership for the church. This function or basic principle is clearly rooted in scripture. But even in the scripture, this intended purpose or function is described in terms of a particular method or form that fits the needs and situation of a given context. Jesus chose to equip a select group of men with the knowledge and commitment necessary to lay the foundation for His church. This involved an intense, three-year program during which He was able to educate His followers concerning the essential matters of the kingdom. He taught them regularly and repeatedly concerning the Truths of the kingdom, accompanying this teaching with field learning experiences. Jesus taught his learners how to be the kind of leaders

His church would need by walking with and living as an example before them.

Jesus did not start a school, as this would not have met the needs the fledgling church had at that point in its history. Nor would a school have adequately addressed the contextual forces the church faced. First-century Palestine experienced a great deal of social upheaval and poverty, natural disasters, famines, epidemics, as well as commercial exploitation by the Romans. A school of any type would have been economically infeasible in Palestine. Although Jerusalem would have been the ideal location for a centralized school, the tension between the Jewish leaders in Jerusalem and the rural areas from which Jesus came would have prevented its success. Power struggles among the various Jewish groups, Herod, and the Roman procurator further complicated the situation for Jesus, who did not want to be perceived as a rival political figure. Theological factors shaping the nature of Jesus's "curriculum" included understanding the true character of the Kingdom of God as well as the nature and mission of God's Messiah. Educationally, Jesus could assume that these future leaders of His church could read, do basic arithmetic, and have a basic knowledge and understanding of the Old Testament through the synagogue schools.

Although Paul himself probably received a good Hellenistic education in Taurus and an advanced Jewish education "at the feet of Gamaliel," he, like Jesus, did not start a school to prepare church leaders. Following the method of Jesus, as well as the nomadic philosophers/teachers of his time, Paul trained a cadre of individuals who traveled with him. Selected during his journeys, these individuals were educated "on the job" in the truths of scripture as well as the basic functions and purposes of a church. Consequently, the training was done primarily in the context of the local assembly, with emphasis on lay leadership and the use of gifts within the church. Paul's sustainability plan for this approach was for his followers to pass on what they had learned from him to "reliable people who will also be qualified to teach others" (2 Tim. 2:2).

Paul's approach was effective because the necessary knowledge base was fairly simple and the number of leaders required by the church was relatively small. His students had received a basic education through secular schools and could read Greek as well as hear, retain, and repeat a body of oral tradition. Theological threats were mainly from within and included "Judaizing" as well as the dangers of incorporating pagan thought, culture, and beliefs. With his combined Hellenistic and Jewish education, Paul was able to handle these threats through his letters and visits. In addition, expectations for leadership roles were still rather uncomplicated.

The Early Church (AD 100–500)

The early church faced unique threats and cultural challenges. Theological threats included attacks from other circles of intellectuals and pagan philosophies. These, as well as contemporary cultural factors, contributed to heresies concerning the nature of the incarnation, the Trinity, and other matters, which the church leadership needed to confront. Other ministerial requirements at the time included the ability to effectively communicate the body of truth passed on from the apostles as well as to defend the faith from internal and external attacks. Leaders also had to provide guidance in the local assembly, properly administer the Eucharist and baptism, and show loyalty to the church's hierarchy as it was developing through the bishops.

As a result, formal theological education early in this era was minimal. Instruction was primarily provided through catechism and preaching during church services. Clergy did not go to a special school, but learned their theology and ministry skills through close contact with a bishop and/or older priests. General education was provided by secular education. By the middle of the second century, a few more-structured schools came into being, initiated by individuals who taught on their own and were not commissioned by the church. Mainly operating as apologists in opposition to the external attacks on Christianity, most of these functioned in the same way as pagan schools of philosophy and were not always intended for potential church leadership or even Christians. Because they were not deeply rooted in the church, most of these schools quickly faded.

The increased attacks by pagan philosophers and Jewish opponents, as well as the growing influence of the Gnostic heresy, eventually necessitated a more systematic educational experience for church leaders. Catechetical schools taught by the area bishop appeared by the mid-second century. As Christian doctrine became more stabilized and complex and as an increasingly established scriptural canon required authoritative interpretation, bishops began to delegate the teaching function to instructors who could provide the necessary theological teaching as well as the necessary components of general education. The Catechetical School of Alexandria is a classic example. Beginning at the end of the second century and continuing into the fifth, its masters included Clement, Origen, Didymus the Blind, and Phodon. Lebreton notes that a master was typically the only lecturer and that "the teaching was not exclusively religious" and "was no longer a mere apologetical preparation." Rather, it included "in the first place the whole series of profane sciences, and then rising to moral and religious philosophy, and finally to Christian theology, set forth in the form of a commentary on the sacred books" (Lebreton and Zeiller 1949, 893). Similar schools were also started in Caesarea, Antioch, Edessa, and Nisibis.

Dark Ages (AD 500–1000)

Barbarian invasion in the fourth and fifth centuries, as well as the advance of Islam in the sixth and seventh centuries, led to the collapse of the Roman Empire. The resulting deterioration of Western civilization in general resulted in the almost complete demise of education and other foundational components of Roman, Western civilization. The church responded to the crisis by founding the first purely Christian schools. These first appeared in the relative safety of monasteries, which were able to provide a safe haven for learning and Christian knowledge in the face of the barbarian invasions. Young boys were brought into the monasteries and prepared for the monkhood and/or priesthood. The monastic schools spread throughout Europe and provided general education as well as religious training for church leaders.

The monastic schools equipped priests to perform the Latin Mass, administer the sacraments, and display loyalty to the church hierarchy in areas where the church was securely established. However, during the early centuries of this period, the church also had to focus on overcoming the pagan cultural forces that had accompanied the barbarian invasions as well as winning back the groups it had lost to the barbarians. This involved preparing leaders who could carry the Christian message to the invaders, convert them, and then incorporate them into the church. The courage and commitment that such a task required was well served by an educational approach that allowed a young boy to grow up and be socialized in a cloistered community, the adult members of which demonstrated the necessary commitment on a daily basis.

Late Middle Ages (AD 1000–1500)

As the church reclaimed Europe and Western civilization became more stabilized, the need arose for more publicly accessible forms of education than were being provided by the monastic schools. In 1079, Pope Gregory issued a papal decree mandating that bishops create schools at their cathedrals for this purpose. These episcopal or cathedral schools performed the same educational functions as the monasteries, but the young male pupils were gathered around the local bishop, who still provided their general education as well. These "cathedral schools" spread throughout Europe and soon evolved into the continent's first universities. Although originally started for the education of clergy, the universities began to expand their offerings into "secular" fields such as law, mathematics, science, and medicine as Europe transitioned from the "Dark Ages" into the Renaissance.

The evolution of the cathedral schools into universities reflected contextual factors resulting from the decreasing distinctions between the secular and the sacred that began to occur during the latter half of the medieval period (AD 1000–1500). As European countries and their leaders were Christianized, the church and the state became more intertwined, with both the pope and kings claiming responsibility for the welfare of both entities. Although kings officially and publicly acknowledged the divine priority of the pope, in practice the lines were not always so clearly drawn. The impact on theological education was that it became increasingly "difficult to isolate ministerial training from that given in preparation for the service of God in the state" (Rowdon 1971, 78). As a result, the curricular scope of the cathedral schools expanded to include the broader range of subjects that came to characterize the multidisciplined universities.

Protestant Reformation (1500–1700)

The Protestant Reformation, with its emphasis on the ministry of the Word of God through preaching and teaching, brought a significant change in the content of ministerial education if not in the means by which it was provided. Reformation leaders emphasized leadership having an education that would be sufficient to enable them to independently interpret and preach the scriptures. In Reformation countries, the required education was a combination of theology along with the general, secular disciplines. Ministerial education thus began at childhood in grammar schools, which had been started to provide educated candidates some of whom had potential for ministry as they grew older. Although this general education focused on Latin and the classics, in Protestant settings it also revolved around the Bible. This combination continued on into the university level, where the students studied classical languages, philosophy, and the sciences together with theology.

A classic example of the Protestant approach is the Geneva Academy, founded by John Calvin in 1559. Calvin believed that upper level studies in theology would be unprofitable unless "first one is instructed in the languages and humanities," and so "a college should be instituted for instructing children to prepare them for the ministry as well as for civil government" (Reid 1954, 60). The Geneva Academy consisted of a *schola privata* at the lower level and a *schola publica* at the university level. During Calvin's lifetime, the latter focused mainly on ministerial preparation, although it later expanded to include other professional disciplines. In addition to Calvin, who taught theology, the academy opened with five other faculty members, who taught Greek, Hebrew, philosophy, and theology. Theodore Beza, one of the five, taught theology along with Calvin and was the first rector. The school, which started with 162 students, was an immediate success. In 1564, Beza reported that there were 1,200 students in the *schola privata* and 300 in the *schola publica*.

The diversity and complexity of the various Protestant Reformation movements preclude a detailed analysis of factors that shaped all theological education in the period. However, certain broad themes were common in all the movements. In the Calvinistic, Anglican, and Lutheran traditions, emphasis on the necessity of a certain body of knowledge concerning the distinctive theology of the Reformation reawakened interest in the classical era and its literature. This necessitated study in classical languages and philosophy. Intellectual attacks from Roman Catholic scholars, well versed in Hebrew and Greek, demanded mastery of these languages as well as the content of both testaments. In addition, this was the period of the Renaissance, when a great emphasis was put on scholarship at all levels of society.

Although the formal educational responses to these challenges were well suited to address them, only a small minority of ministers in the Reformation countries could take advantage of these educational opportunities, because of financial and/or geographic constraints. It is estimated that in 17th-century England, only one out of six ministers in the Church of England had sufficient education to be ordained or licensed. Some of the others were able to receive limited independent study provided by licensed ministers living in their area. Moreover, some groups (e.g., Free Church and Anabaptist) felt that there was no need for a fully trained ministry. Emphasizing the role of the laity, many of these groups felt that schooling was unnecessary. The need for a converted ministry meant that piety was given priority over formal education. Believing that God could do the equipping of those whom he called, these traditions felt that formal education in Hebrew, Greek, and philosophy was not needed. Economic factors also played a role, as many of these movements involved the lower, poorer classes, which often did not have access to or value formal education.

Roman Catholic Counter-Reformation (1500–1700)

Although often seen as a response to the protestant Reformation, the Catholic Counter-Reformation also resulted in many significant changes within the Roman Catholic Church. One involved the manner in which church leadership was educated and trained. By the 16th century, the cathedral schools, which had been instituted to provide more accessible educational opportunities for the preparation of priests, had evolved into universities throughout Europe. As they expanded, the more secular disciplines dominated the curriculum. Those who attended university and were preparing for the priesthood received little or no spiritual training. In addition, only a small percentage of Catholic clergy were able to attend the universities. As a result, the church found itself with leaders who were uneducated, or educated but not prepared for ministry in either character formation or practical preparation. Subsequent corruption and other abuses by church leadership at all levels had led to a serious divide between the clergy and laity. The growing Protestant Reformation, with its rejection of key church doctrines, was also of great concern.

These factors led the Catholic Church to initiate the Council of Trent, which began in 1545 and continued through 1563. In 1563, during its 23rd session, the council addressed the need for reformation of leadership development and mandated "the local creation and maintenance of an institution whose sole purpose was the intellectual and professional formation of clergy" (Comerford 1998, 999). These institutions were to be separate from the universities and under the church's complete control. The Council of Trent envisioned that the schools would be "perpetual seed-plots (*seminarium*) for the ministers of God" (Waterworth 1848, 189), giving rise to the designation "seminary" for such schools.

The council laid out the basic principles for these seminaries, which have largely shaped the educational preparation of Catholic Church leaders since that time. Students were to be at least 12 years old and possess basic reading and writing skills. In the seminary, they would "learn grammar, singing, ecclesiastical computation, and the other liberal arts." They would also "be instructed in sacred Scripture; ecclesiastical works; the homilies of the saints; the manner of administering the sacraments, especially those things which shall seem adapted to enable them to hear confessions; and the forms of the rites and ceremonies" (Waterworth 1848, 189). All expenses, including teachers' and staffs' salaries, along with the room and board of the students, were to be provided by the seminary's diocese. Although the council had earlier discussed requiring all candidates for the priesthood to attend a seminary, this requirement was dropped from the final written version. Rather, the model was put forth as an ideal, with the assumption that church leadership would be greatly improved if a significant percentage of future priests could go to seminary.

Comerford has pointed out that the introduction of the seminary model for the preparation of church leadership "represented a major change in thinking in the Reformation era," which "deepens our understanding of the Catholic Reformation" as well as the subsequent "practice of Catholicism and the organization of the Catholic Church" (Comerford 1998, 1010). The emphasis on practical training within a formal educational context represented a major shift in the curriculum design for the preparation of church leadership. This emphasis, coupled with the idea of an educational institution devoted solely to a select group preparing for a specific vocation, has significantly influenced the development of leaders for the church in all traditions from that time to the present.

Western Expansion (1600–2000)

The colonization of North America in the 17th and 18th centuries represented a significant step for the various Protestant denominations that greatly influenced the later worldwide spread of Protestantism. Theological education took on a wide diversity of forms, influenced by both the theological traditions of constituent churches as well as the sociological, economic, and cultural contexts of the groups associated with these traditions. While the specifics of these factors varied among the groups, all shared certain characteristics. This was a colonial society under the rule and dominion of European governments, which was seeking to establish that it was not culturally or socially inferior to its continental cousins. It was also a society that was moving toward unrest and ultimately revolution. Although major differences existed between individual denominations within the following two categories, one can distinguish two approaches to leadership development, represented by mainline Reformation denominations (e.g., Reformed and Lutheran) and the evangelical groups (e.g., Baptist and Methodist).

Reformed Theological Education

Expecting their ministers to be the intellectual elite of New England, many of these denominations placed an emphasis on educational qualifications for the ministry. This, and the desire to prove that they were not academically inferior to the European churches, led to the founding of Harvard (1636) and nine other colleges before the American Revolution in order to provide basic education for ministers. Since many of these denominational groups ministered to the upper classes in the colonies, financial resources were more available for these educational endeavors. Specific theological and ministerial training was provided through study under the tutelage of an established pastor. Because some churches were still controlled by a European denominational structure (e.g., Dutch Reformed), certain groups had some of their pastors trained in the universities or colleges located in their home countries in Europe. Both approaches proved difficult for those located in the frontier colonies because of distance and cost. Traveling abroad presented additional challenges, because there was no certainty that the student would return and, if he did, it was often difficult for him to fit into the local context.

By the time the American Revolution broke out, these churches had found that the expanding body of knowledge and the need for efficiency called for specialization in education that local church pastors/tutors could not totally fulfill. Furthermore, the educational missions of the colleges and universities, established for the general education of ministerial candidates, no longer adequately addressed the spiritual aspects of that need. Consequently, postgraduate seminaries such as Princeton Theological Seminary (1812), Harvard Divinity School (1816), and Yale Divinity School (1822) were established within each university to provide focused education for clergy. Independent, postgraduate seminaries also were established to meet denominational educational requirements. Presbyterians founded Union Theological Seminary in Virginia (1812) and Columbia Theological Seminary in South Carolina (1828). Episcopalians started Protestant Episcopal Theological Seminary in Virginia (1823), while Lutherans established Lutheran Theological Southern Seminary in South Carolina (1830) and Concordia Theological Seminary in Missouri (1839). With multiple faculty members representing the various theological disciplines, these schools were funded primarily by their respective denominations and charged minimal tuition. Many have built up significant endowments over the ensuing decades to supplement, and in some cases replace, earlier denominational support.

The educational expectations of these denominations were aptly illustrated in the 1815 version of the Dutch Reformed Church's constitution, which stated, "School masters, mechanics, or others who have not regularly studied shall not be admitted to the office of the ministry" (Forman 1815, 177). These strict educational mandates led to a shortage of qualified ministers, with the result that these denominations did not make significant headway into the frontier regions.

Evangelical Theological Education

Evangelical movements, such as the Baptists and the Methodists, enjoyed significant growth in the frontier regions following the Great Awakening and the Revolutionary War. Frontier society was characterized by a spirit of independence as well as great flux and unrest. Economic resources were limited, and there was little emphasis on or esteem for education. Churches focused more on evangelism than on theological grounding and were oriented more toward interpersonal dynamics than scholastic orthodoxy. By the mid-18th century, the rapid growth of new converts and churches resulting from the Great Awakening had created an overwhelming demand for pastors and other church leaders. Little was expected of these individuals other than the ability to preach the Gospel and "win souls." Pastors were expected to know the content of Scripture but not necessarily exegetical or systematic theology.

As a result of these contextual factors, churches and their leaders disdained the rigorous formal education practiced by their Reformed brothers. Their pastors tended to be farmers or skilled laborers rather than seminary or college graduates. However, many, especially Methodists, engaged extensively in self-directed learning. John Wesley had published a library of over 40 volumes for his preachers and demanded that they study at least five hours a day while they preached the Word. In some cases, aspiring church leaders would study literary theological books under the direction of a church elder and be examined about the content quarterly. Others strove to learn Hebrew and Greek while they rode to and from speaking engagements, under the tutelage of local pastors who had received some type of education. Although the absence of formal educational requirements produced more church leaders in a shorter time, it also led to a greater ignorance of the total scriptural message and subsequent teaching of heresy in some cases.

By the early 19th century, as the frontier became more civilized and education more valued, some evangelical groups increasingly articulated the need for an educated clergy. Church colleges were started to provide a general, undergraduate education for ministers that would be followed by focused ministerial training with an established pastor in a local church setting. However, these colleges taught little theology, and individual pastors were unable to efficiently provide the breadth of the necessary ministerial training. Thus, by the mid-19th century, like the Reformed denominations before them, some evangelicals began to establish specialized, theological seminaries to train ministers. Following their Reformed counterparts, these schools were also funded primarily by their respective denominations. However, moving into the 20th century, only a few maintained their denominational support, and even fewer were able to build a significant endowment base. Consequently, most of these schools are heavily dependent upon tuition rates, which soared in the latter part of the 20th century, diminishing their breadth of access.

In the late 19th century, nondenominational institutes were launched to provide basic Bible knowledge for both vocational and lay church leadership. Initiated by schools like the Missionary Training Institute in New York City (1882), Moody Bible Institute in Chicago (1886), and Toronto Bible School (1894), these schools did not initially grant degrees. However, through the first half of the 20th century, many of these institutions became Bible colleges, independent graduate seminaries, Christian liberal arts colleges, or Christian universities. Many of the liberal arts colleges and universities also created seminaries within the larger school for the training of church leadership. Other institutions remained in the Bible college movement, granting degrees focused on spiritual and ministry formation. Like the other evangelical schools mentioned above, these institutions are mostly tuition-dependent as well.

Moving Forward (AD 2000–Future)

The Protestant missionary movement of the 19th and 20th centuries, originating from Europe and the United States, produced a worldwide expansion of the church, with an accompanying need for developing its leaders in a wide variety of cultural, sociological, and economic contexts. To address that need, the Western church's initial response was to replicate its current models of theological education in the other cultures. Subsidized initially by Western funds, schools, colleges, and seminaries have been established for the sole purpose of educating and training indigenous church leadership. Although initially staffed by expatriate missionary personnel, by the late 20th and early 21st centuries, many of these institutions throughout the world were staffed by local personnel.

The new leadership finds itself addressing several significant challenges in order to make their educational programs more relevant to their particular contextual realities. One of the most significant has been to develop a financial model that is affordable for students and can survive in local economies. Often the students recognized as the gifted and called leaders of the church do not have access to the established educational program because of finances, prior educational level, or geographic location. Another challenge is the revision of largely Western curricula and theological resources that do not fully address the needs and realities of the host culture. Majority world churches have begun to address these and other challenges with a variety of educational responses that hold great potential for the future. Technology is being increasingly utilized to extend educational opportunities to church leaders with limited access. Asian, African, and Latin American approaches to theology and hermeneutics are being developed and published. Finally, nonformal educational approaches that are based on potential students' sociological, cultural, educational, and economic realities are being formulated and implemented.

References and Resources

Bruggink, D. J. 1966. "The Historical Background of Theological Education." *Reformed Review* 19 (4): 2–17.

Comerford, Kathleen. 1998. "Italian Tridentine Diocesan Seminaries: A Historiographical Study." *Sixteenth Century Journal* 29 (4): 999–1022.

Farley, Edward. 1988. *The Fragility of Knowledge: Theological Education in the Church and University*. Philadelphia: Fortress Press.

Forman, G. 1815. *The Constitution of the Reformed Dutch Church in the United-States of America*. Reformed Church of America. Google eBook. http://books.google.com/books?id=u_sTAAAAYAAJ.

Kelsey, D. H. 1993. *Between Athens and Berlin: The Theological Education Debate*. Grand Rapids, MI: Eerdmans.

Lebreton, Jules, and Jacques Zeiller. 1949. *The History of the Primitive Church*. Vol. II, Books III and IV. Translated by Ernest C. Messenegr. New York: Macmillan.

Noll, M. 1979. "The Founding of Princeton Seminary." *Westminster Theological Seminary* 42: 72–110.

Reid, J. K. S., ed. 1954. *Calvin: Theological Treatises*. Philadelphia: Westminster.

Rowdon, Harold. 1971. "Theological Education in Historical Perspective." *Vox Evangelica* 7: 75–87.

Vosloo, Robert. 2009. "Calvin, the Academy of Geneva and 150 Years of Theology at Stellenbosch: Historical-Theological Contributions to the Conversation on Theological Education." *Studia Historiae Ecclesiasticae* 35 (supp.): 17–33.

Waterworth, J., trans. 1848. *The Canons and Decrees of the Sacred and Oecumenical Council of Trent*. London: Dolman (XXIII Session, ch. XVIII).

Wills, Gregory. 2009. *Southern Baptist Theological Seminary, 1859-2009*. New York: Oxford University Press.

—John R. Lillis

Theological Education, History of

During the first centuries of the church, those Christian leaders who were educated were dependent on the training they received in the liberal arts, logic, grammar, and rhetoric in the schools of late antiquity. This kind of education was for the purpose of training young men for civic duty and responsibility. Much of this training centered around learning to read texts properly, to interpret and draw life-shaping wisdom from their message. Learning to compose clear, articulate discourse and to communicate convincingly and persuasively was deemed most important for carrying out one's civic duty. The best known early Christian leaders were beneficiaries of the ancient school system in its Roman and Greek forms. After their conversion and entry into pastoral leadership, they saw the necessity of "plundering the Egyptians" for the greater glory of God. During the early centuries of the medieval period, the monasteries carried forward the responsibility for theological education. The monks saw their calling as to love God completely, which included the intellect. An important part of their work was copying texts, scripture as well as Christian and ancient classics, to hand them on for the continued education and formation of fellow monks, priests, and competent laity.

Monastic learning prepared the way for cathedral schools, which emerged in the 12th century. These schools, typically founded and supported by a bishop, were attached to cathedrals that were centers of learning and culture. Theological education in these settings was primarily for priests who served in pastoral work, but an increasingly educated laity created a need for more formal and structured theological education for clergy. Universities were founded to meet this need in the 13th century under the patronage and direction of episcopal leadership. As universities continued to be established all over Europe, they provided a dramatic increase in educational opportunities for Christian leadership. At the same time, expanded educational and professional opportunities for the laity demanded that those in pastoral ministry be more thoroughly educated and formed for their calling. The rise of the universities marks the origins of modern academic life. It is important to note that the task of educating those set apart for the pastoral vocation continued to include the ascetical and practical disciplines established by the monasteries: daily prayer, liturgical participation, spiritual and moral apprenticeship, and corporate accountability. Theology and spirituality, knowledge and love, were still united.

The period of the Renaissance saw major changes in theological education, but also a renewed and even urgent commitment to its purpose of educating leaders to serve the intellectual, moral, and spiritual needs of the laity. Christian humanists such as Erasmus of Rotterdam led the way in recovering ancient Christian and classical sources of learning, which were hugely significant in prompting and leading the renewal of Christian education at all levels of the church's life. The reforms of the 16th century continued the significant leap forward in theological education, as university curricula were reformed and new academic institutions founded to prepare leaders for the task of establishing doctrinal and communal identity among newly formed state-supported churches in Europe. The early modern and modern period of theological education could be seen as an ongoing argument to resolve or move beyond the inherent tensions among confessional loyalties, standards of academic scholarship, and the requirements of the state.

From the period of the early church through the reforms of the 16th century, theological education was understood primarily as the history of biblical interpretation and practice. The modern division of the theological disciplines (Bible, church history, doctrine, practical theology) did not yet exist. The study of the Bible and theological reflection were closely tied to one another, just as the ties among scripture, doctrine, and Christian communities were closely aligned. Scripture was interpreted and theological wisdom imparted in a variety of contexts: liturgy, sacraments, catechesis, letters, apologetic treatises, sermons, homilies, hagiography, music, and art. The point is that while theological education has primarily to do with training leaders of the church, theological education understood as knowing God is a gift to the whole church and a calling of all Christians in their baptism. Perhaps the greatest challenge and opportunity of theological education in the 21st century will be recovering a vision for educating and forming the whole people of God in the knowledge of God.

References and Resources

D' Costa, Gavin. 2005. *Theology in the Public Square: Church, Academy, and Nation.* Oxford, UK: Blackwell Publishing.

Farley, Edward. 1983. *Theologia: The Fragmentation and Unity of Theological Education.* Philadelphia: Fortress Press.

Howard, Thomas Albert. 2009. *Protestant Theology and the Making of the Modern German University.* New York: Oxford University Press.

—MICHAEL PASQUARELLO III

THEOLOGICAL EDUCATION IN THE UNIVERSITY

Theological education is as old as universities themselves. Theology as an academic discipline emerged gradually, concomitant with the medieval universities. Modern universities stem from the monastic and cathedral schools of the Middle Ages. As such, Christian theological learning (including training for ecclesiastical offices and canon law) was the central focus of university study. Theology was considered to be *the queen of the sciences*, the capstone of the *trivium* (grammar, logic, and rhetoric) and the *quadrivium* (geometry, arithmetic, astronomy, and music). During this period, theological education constituted of the integration of revelatory, salvific knowledge and reason, that is, systematic, logical scrutiny of religious beliefs and practices. There was an assumption of the essential commensurability of revelation and reason. Further, theology reigned supreme as its principles, concepts, and methods were grounded in divine revelation; no other justification was necessary.

The centrality of theological education in the university gradually waned over time as nominalism, Renaissance humanism, science, the Enlightenment, historicism, and secularism arose and spread. Beginning in the 19th century, science dominated Western academic thinking because its knowledge claims seemed not only plausible, but also scarcely questionable. The Enlightenment and scientific revolution stressed rationality, empirical science, and skeptical secularism. Theology lost its position of privilege and faced an onslaught of attacks on its intellectual legitimacy, particularly its appeals to scriptural and ecclesial authority and lack of empirical justifications. Within the university, commitment to open inquiry became the central ethos. Specializations, such as law, medicine, and theology, were given ancillary status. Theology had a place in the university only as professional training for ministers.

American colleges had strongly religious moorings during the colonial period. Prior to 1870, religion influenced the fundamental structures of the college and university system. American colleges and universities were founded and supported by churches, and the faculties and administrations were mainly clergy. As the model of professional specialization emerged, universities began to adopt the German research method, jettisoning the traditional colonial college model of a broad liberal education. Post–Civil War America was characterized by a burgeoning technological interest, cultural transformation epitomized by pluralism, and the new positivist spirit. Eventually, the research model overshadowed the colonial college ideal along with its religious orientation. An emphasis on separation of church and state ousted theology from public colleges and universities, driving it into seminaries and divinity schools.

There was a gradual transformation from the implicit pervasiveness of theological education throughout subject matter (from mathematics and grammar to astronomy and philosophy). First, "divinity" became a distinct discipline within the university. Next, a graduate component was developed for the special education of the minister. Finally, seminaries were established, based on the German model of the fourfold division of the theological sciences (Bible, dogmatics, church history, and practical theology). Bible institutes and colleges had an immense influence on the face of education in the United States and Canada. The Bible school movement in America derived in large part from revivalism. Many of these schools developed into Christian colleges and universities in the 20th century. Theological education is constitutive of these institutions. Currently, Christian universities and colleges are influencing the agendas of "secular" institutions all over North America.

The 1963 Supreme Court ruling in *School District of Abington Township, Pennsylvania v. Schempp* has also affected theological education in the university. This ruling made a fundamental distinction between "religious instruction" and "instructions about religion." Such a distinction has led to the academic study of religion, that is, religious studies, distinguishing it from (and often opposing) theology. Religious studies was successful in justifying its existence in the modern secular university, though the so-called distinct agendas and purposes of theology and religious studies have come under scrutiny in recent years. Consequently, several theologians and religious scholars (such as Linell E. Cady, Delwin Brown, Linda Cannell, and Sheila Greeve Davaney) are seeking to redefine and redesign a 21st-century vision for theological education.

References and Resources

Apczynski, John, ed. 1990. *Theology and the University*. Lanham, MD: University Press of America.

Cady, Linell E., and Delwin Brown, eds. 2002. *Religious Studies, Theology, and the University: Conflicting Maps, Changing Terrain*. Albany: State University of New York Press.

Cannell, Linda. 2006. *Theological Education Matters: Leadership Education for the Church*. Newburgh, IN: EDCOT Press.

D'Costa, Gavin. 2006. *Theology in the Public Square: Church, Academy, and Nation*. Malden, MA: Blackwell Publishing.

Farley, Edward. 2001. *Theologia: The Fragmentation and Unity of Theological Education*. Eugene, OR: Wipf & Stock.

Sommerville, C. John. 2006. *The Decline of the Secular University: Why the Academy Needs Religion*. Oxford: Oxford University Press.

—Nathaniel Holmes Jr.

Theological Education, Missional Model of

Introduction: *Missio Dei* and Missional Church

The term "missional" serves as an orienting perspective that informs both theological reflection, particularly ecclesiology, and ministry practice. Missional theology's orientation is based on the belief that the primary attribute of God encompasses a desire to seek, engage, and reconcile God's creation to God-self and enjoin the church in this endeavor (2 Cor. 5:18–21). In short, the church exists to participate in the *Missio Dei* (the mission of God). Though the emphasis on the missional began in England, the movement primarily emerged through the Gospel in the Culture Network's seminal book, *Missional Church: A Vision for the Sending of the Church in North America*.[75] This movement also embraces the writings of earlier missiologists, particular the work of David Bosch and Leslie Newbigin.[76] Newbigin, in particular, serves as the exemplar both in his global missions ministry and through his later emphasis on engaging Western European culture as a missionary.[77] Newbigin may actually be the first person to articulate the idea of missional.[78]

The concept of missional includes the Western notion of the Triune God who sends the church (as the Father sends the Son, and the Father and Son send the Holy Spirit, so the Holy Spirit sends the church). Yet missional theology also embraces the Eastern church's Trinitarian idea of participation (as the Father, Son, and Holy Spirit relate dynamically in the Trinity, so the church finds God relating to the world in order to reconcile all creation). Informed by both perspectives, the missional movement understands that the church is shaped and sent by God into the world, only to discover places where God is already at work. The church's role includes not only witness, but also discernment and participation where God is already involved in reconciliation.[79]

Missional Christian Education

Christian educators seeking to embrace this approach to ecclesiology and ministry should note that many of the educational efforts begin in active ministry. Robert Banks asserts that learning in this model reflects a more immediate connection between action and reflection, revealing a praxis model (reflection in action) similar to that of educator Thomas Groome.[80] Banks also believes that scripture proves normative in missional Christian education, but it needs to retain a dynamic quality (more narrative than propositional) that allows it to interact with the "context of ongoing mission in the world."[81] Banks's observations are mirrored in other writings, like those of Alan Hirsch, who argues that discipleship is not following Jesus as "the way" but following Jesus "on the way" to mission and ministry.[82] Hirsch acknowledges a larger framework for discipleship, one that includes action, embodiment, and leadership training.[83] He also contrasts traditional ideas of focusing on knowledge transmission first in order to lead to action (he believes a Greek paradigm) with the idea of action-oriented learning that yields right thinking (his view of the Hebraic

---

75. Darrell L. Guder, ed. *Missional Church: A Vision for the Sending of the Church in North America* (Grand Rapids, MI: Eerdmans, 1998).

76. David Bosch, *Transforming Mission: Paradigm Shifts in Theology of Mission* (Maryknoll, NY: Orbis, 1994); Lesslie Newbigin, *The Gospel in a Pluralist Society* (Grand Rapid, MI: Eerdmans, 1989).

77. Paul Weston, "Introduction: A Biographical Sketch," in *Lesslie Newbigin, Missionary Theologian: A Reader*, comp. Paul Weston (Grand Rapids, MI: Eerdmans, 2006), 1–16.

78. John G. Flett, *The Witness of God: The Trinity*, Missio Dei, *Karl Bath, and the Nature of Christian Community* (Grand Rapids, MI: Eerdmans, 2010), 147–157.

79. Graig Van Gelder and Dwight J. Zscheile, *The Missional Church in Perspective: Mapping Trends and Shaping the Conversation* (Grand Rapids, MI: Baker Academic, 2011), 49–62, 102–123.

80. Robert Banks, *Reenvisioning Theological Education: Exploring a Missional Alternative to Current Models* (Grand Rapids, MI: Eerdmans, 1999), 159–160.

81. Ibid., 161.

82. Alan Hirsch, *The Forgotten Ways: Reactivating the Missional Church* (Grand Rapids, MI: Brazos Press, 2006), 103.

83. Ibid., 101–125.

paradign).[84] Learning in the midst of action serves as a beginning point for missional Christian education, one often associated with apprenticeship models or other action-oriented models of learning.[85]

Christian educators may also note that this learning includes various modes of discernment to recognize where and how God might already be at work within the world. This aspect of missional Christian education places an emphasis on people being present in gathering spaces other than work, home, and church; those "third places" where people gather.[86] In those spaces, missional leaders advocate practicing the "presence of Christ" through reflective listening to both truly sense the lives of people and also participate in efforts of peace, justice, and compassion that reflect the actions of God.[87] However, this engagement of listening also opens the opportunity for true hospitality and even reciprocity in how Christians learn from others in how God might be at work in the world.[88] Reflective discernment offers opportunities to both see God and receive from God fresh insights in the midst of the world the church is called to engage.

Christian educators may wonder if the emphasis on engagement leaves any room for the formative processes that often occur within the life of the community. Missional leaders would stress that there is indeed such a need, particularly to ensure authentic Christian engagement. Lois Barrett argues that missional disciples require a deeply formative experience based on the church as an alternative society, one that does not conform to the world.[89] This society remains deeply shaped by historic, communal, Christian practices that remain dynamic yet experiential in shaping Christian lives.[90] Even historically shaped educational processes, like catechesis, may serve missional end.[91] Overall, the emphasis on formation remains a key task to assist the identity of the church in the midst of engaging the world. Formative practices help create communities with a sense of *communitas*, a sense of being together for a purpose on the "edge" of engagement.[92]

Christian educators seeking to model a missional idea of education will need to take seriously the idea of the church

being "sent" by God to a world where it must model an alternative community. Yet the church will also need to listen carefully for God's ongoing work in and through that selfsame world. Naïve acceptance of a world either totally innocent or completely depraved fails in this model of education and engagement. Discipleship becomes the vocation of the Christians as they live out the life of Christianity by living into the world they inhabit. Preparing Christians not only "for" this engagement, but particularly "in the midst" of living and engaging the world, remains the key task of missional Christian education.

References and Resources

Banks, Robert. 1999. *Reenvisioning Theological Education: Exploring a Missional Alternative to Current Models.* Grand Rapids, MI: Eerdmans.

Blevins, Dean G. 2001. "A Missional Catechesis for Faithful Discipleship." *In Missio Dei: A Wesleyan Understanding,* edited by Keith Schwanz and Joseph Coleson, 141–148. Kansas City, MO: Beacon Hill of Kansas City.

Bosch, David. 1994. *Transforming Mission: Paradigm Shifts in Theology of Mission.* Maryknoll, NY: Orbis.

Flett, John G. 2010. *The Witness of God: The Trinity, Missio Dei, Karl Bath, and the Nature of Christian Community.* Grand Rapids, MI: Eerdmans.

Frost, Michael. 2006. *Exiles: Living Missionally in a Post-Christian Culture.* Peabody, MA: Hendrickson Publishers.

Guder, Darrell L., ed. 1998. *Missional Church: A Vision for the Sending of the Church in North America.* Grand Rapids, MI: Eerdmans.

Hirsch, Alan. 2006. *The Forgotten Ways: Reactivating the Missional Church.* Grand Rapids, MI: Brazos Press.

Newbigin, Lesslie. 1989. *The Gospel in a Pluralist Society.* Grand Rapids, MI: Eerdmans.

Van Gelder, Graig, and Dwight J. Zscheile. 2011. *The Missional Church in Perspective: Mapping Trends and Shaping the Conversation.* Grand Rapids, MI: Baker Academic.

Weston, Paul. 2006. "Introduction: A Biographical Sketch." In *Lesslie Newbigin, Missionary Theologian: A Reader,* compiled by Paul Weston, 1–16. Grand Rapids, MI: Eerdmans.

—Dean Blevins

THEOLOGICAL EDUCATION, OBJECTIVES IN

In theological colleges and seminaries, the importance of teaching objectives has increased as accreditation processes have shifted away from a static facilities approach to a more dynamic assessment of the formulation and achievement of objectives, and as teaching has become more student and learning result centered.

The almost ubiquitous model in use is that of the threefold classification of academic, ministerial, and

---

84. Ibid., 124

85. Banks, *Reenvisioning Theological Education,* 135–141.

86. Michael Frost, *Exiles: Living Missionally in a Post-Christian Culture* (Peabody, MA: Hendrickson Publishers, 2006), 62–63.

87. Ibid., 64–70.

88. Van Gelder and Zscheile, *Missional Church in Perspective,* 132–133.

89. Lois Y. Barrett, "The Church as Apostle to the World," in *Missional Church in Perspective,* 110–117.

90. Inagrace Dietterich, "Missional Community: Cultivating Communities of the Holy Spirit," in Van Gelder and Zscheile, *Missional Church,* 153–158.

91. Dean G. Blevins, "A Missional Catechesis for Faithful Discipleship," in *Missio Dei: A Wesleyan Understanding,* ed. Keith Schwanz and Joseph Coleson (Kansas City, MO: Beacon Hill of Kansas City, 2001), 141–148.

92. Hirsch, *Forgotten Ways,* 217–241.

spiritual formation of the student, reflecting Bloom's taxonomy of educational objectives. This is sometimes popularly referred to as preparing the head, the hands, and the heart. Two-category models are also in use, such as Pluddemann's two-bar fence, which is employed to describe the relationship between intellect and action. Fourfold models have traditionally been created by subdividing the spiritual formation objective into character or human development and spiritual development. This division can be driven by the recognition that students today often come into college or seminary at a crucial age for personal and social development. Alternatively, the shift in the Roman Catholic Church's set of objectives from a threefold model in the decree on the training of priests from Vatican II to the fourfold model of *Pastores Dabo Vobis*[93] almost 30 years later recognizes the struggle of ordinands with celibacy and other issues that have become sources of greater pressure in the contemporary world.

Following Farley's foundational critique of theological education as fragmented, much discussion has taken place, not so much on the nature of the objectives as on their interrelationship. Older approaches to this question have spoken of the need for balance, as Warfield talks of the need for both legs in a soldier—spiritual and academic formation[94]—and others have spoken of the need for a three-legged stool with all legs of equal length. It is difficult to see how balance today can (or should) be achieved in a crowded academic curriculum unless it be a balance of priority rather than of time spent on achieving each objective. A number of studies, however, have shown that people in congregations and ministry tend to believe that our recent past has demonstrated an imbalance toward academic achievement in the training of ministers.

More recent work has been done in the area of the integration of the objectives of theological education. After all, we do not address brains, hands, or hearts, but students—whole people. Nor will it be enough to cover the three areas in separate parts of the curriculum and leave the more difficult job of integration as a private task for each student. The literature is particularly united against the idea that we can "balance up" the historical emphasis on academic work by introducing extra lectures on spirituality. Increasingly, it is being understood that each objective needs to be actively pursued in each area of the college's work, and that each should permeate the expression of the other. So when in the classroom, the student needs to learn the meaning of the text or the

theological idea but also its application to him or her as a Christian and potentially a minister. Faith and the presence of God are issues for the teacher in class. Similarly, in chapel, careful academic exegesis needs to undergird the "spiritual" message and, on practical placement, the student needs to draw on all other things learned in class and chapel and be able to bring back questions from the practical situation into the classroom and library. As David Adams says, we are in the business of producing scholar-practitioner-saints.[95]

There have been a number of attempts to resolve the fragmentation of objectives by elevating one over the others as the unifying concept: for example, Banks's concept of "missional" theological education or Nouwen's use of the great commandments to love the Lord with all our heart, soul, mind, and strength and our neighbor as ourselves as an adequate summation of the objectives of theological education. Yet as we have come to see that academic formation is not satisfactory as an umbrella description of theological education, so we must question whether either of the other two objectives can function in this way. One of the most fruitful ways of talking about this integration is to use the specifically Christian ontology of the Trinitarian idea of *perichoresis*: the circulation of the divine life among the members of the Trinity. This will enable us to speak of each of the three main objectives as existing in a fundamental and close relationship with the other two, each helping to bring the others to life; when we encounter one, we encounter all three.

References and Resources

Banks, R. 1999. *Re-envisioning Theological Education*. Grand Rapids, MI: Eerdmans.

Farley, E. 1983. *Theologia: The Fragmentation and Unity of Theological Education*. Philadelphia: Fortress Press.

Nouwen, H. 1984. *Reaching Out: The Three Movements of the Spiritual Life*. Glasgow: Collins.

—GRAHAM CHEESMAN

THEOLOGICAL EDUCATION, PURPOSE OF

The idea of theological education, while deeply rooted in historical traditions and values, continues to be a practice refined and reformed over the course of time. During the Old Testament period, the Jewish family served as the educational center, with additional instruction provided through the priesthood and annual festivals. Following the period of the exile, Jewish education shifted notice-

---

93. *Pastores Dabo Vobis: Apostolic Exhortation of His Holiness John Paul II on the Formation of Priests* (London: Catholic Truth Society, 1992).

94. B. B. Warfield, *The Religious Life of Theological Students* (Phillipsburg, NJ: Presbyterian and Reformed, n.d.), 2.

95. David Adams, "Putting Heart and Soul into Research: Ad Inquiry into Becoming 'Scholar-Practitioner-Saint,'" *Transformation* 25, nos. 2 and 3 (2008): 144–157.

ably to a more formalized educational structure of Torah, Mishnah, rabbi, and synagogue. In the New Testament and early church period, theological education was primarily catechetical in nature, focusing on instructing new converts and passing on the accepted teachings of the Christian faith. Within the New Testament, there is a recognized body of teaching referred to as the *apostles teaching* (2 Thess. 2:15, 3:6–7). This commonly held teaching served as the source of authoritative instruction for Christian belief and living. The pastoral Epistles emphasize the need to pass on healthy and productive teaching (sound doctrine), as well as the need to avoid and refute unhealthy, unproductive teaching (1 Tim. 1:3–7, 4:6–16). Sound biblical knowledge was needed to instruct the church in right belief, refute wrong belief, correct wrong behavior, and encourage right behavior (2 Tim. 3:16). In this way, the church would be thoroughly equipped for Christian life and service (2 Tim. 3:17).

During the medieval and Renaissance periods, theological education focused on the development of professional priests and clergy, as well as on the traditionally accepted teachings, writings, and formal policies of the church. Along with this traditional emphasis came a desire to reengage with classic philosophical and rhetorical academic formulations. With the Reformation came the impetus to reestablish and articulate a Christian worldview centered on the biblical text and historical Christian beliefs. This would result in subsequent conflicts, as competing voices and ideologies would continue to emerge as a result of increasing enlightenment, scientific, and humanistic thinking. This gave rise to a more theoretical emphasis on critical and speculative theological studies.

Over the last few centuries, the emphasis on personal devotion, evangelism, and missions has shifted the focu of theological education toward Christian service and outreach and has moved practical pastoral ministry to the forefront. The formalized training of church leaders through Christian colleges and seminaries has become more marginalized in recent years, while local church Bible institutes, educational programs, age-specific programs, and support programs have become practically mandatory as centers of Christian education. As our society has changed, so has the shape of theological education. As such, the purpose of theological education exists in a continual dance between timeless values and changing times.

One of the challenges of contemporary theological education is the discovery of meaning and purpose within a vital and rigorous understanding of Christian faith and doctrine. Christian education should not simply offer a variety of biblical studies along with increased opportunity for social interaction, nor should it serve only for Christian vocational training; rather, its distinction should be to cultivate the creative and active integra-

tion of Christian faith, learning, and action. Theological education should prepare the people of God to adapt, to think, and to be effective in all of life's callings and circumstances. Theological education has a constructive task that employs a unifying Christian worldview large enough to give meaning to all the disciplines of biblical studies, theology, biblical languages, philosophy, sociology, and history.

Theological education, both formal and informal, should intentionally facilitate personal spiritual development as a primary goal. Three features are essential for our understanding of theological education as personal development: God has created us to be (1) reflective, thinking beings, (2) valuing beings, and (3) responsible beings. These are qualities that theological education seeks to cultivate, as well as the development of a breadth of doctrinal understanding. The purpose is to address the challenges of academic work and responsible action as Christians: exploring the mission of theological education in contemporary society as a transforming as well as informing practice. This vision helps give shape to what could be the most important facet of theological education:facilitating the emergence of God's unique expression and calling in the life of all students.

The ongoing challenge to theological education involves a process of reflection, response, and reform that maintains a vital integration of academics and action that is relevant to contemporary society while advancing the mission and purpose of the Christian faith. As we consider the purpose of theological education, we must begin by acknowledging the various contours of the past, recognizing the essential needs of the present, and anticipating the critical path for the future.

References and Resources

Anthony, Michael J., ed. 2001. *Introducing Christian Education: Foundations for the Twenty-First Century.* Grand Rapids, MI: Baker Academic.

Dockery, David S. 2008. *Renewing Minds: Serving Church and Society through Christian Higher Education.* Rev. and updated ed. Nashville, TN: B & H Academic.

Pazmiño, Robert W. 2008. *Foundational Issues in Christian Education: An Introduction in Evangelical Perspective.* 3rd ed. Grand Rapids, MI: Baker Academic.

Reed, James E., and Ronnie Prevost, eds. 1998. *A History of Christian Education.* Grand Rapids, MI: B & H Academic.

—Gino Pasquariello

THEOLOGICAL EDUCATION, RENEWAL IN

According to Edward Farley's *Theologia: The Fragmentation and Unity of Theological Education* (1983), *theolo-*

gia—sapiential knowledge, a *habitus* of practical wisdom, a matter of the heart and of practicing life, which represents a holistic understanding of theology—has been lost in theological education. In early Christian centuries, the unifying purpose of theology, *telos*, was to understand practical wisdom of God (*pronesis*) that attends to human life. However, this unifying concept of theology was displaced in the Middle Ages, and theology became a scientific discipline, an idea promoted by Thomas Aquinas (1225–1274). As a result, theological education was divided into theological scholarship and the practical training of ministers based on a clerical paradigm. This fragmentation of *theologia* resulted in the separation of theory and practice. The distance between the theological institutions and the church became greater, aided by the clericalization of theological education, primarily based on functionalism.

In the 19th century, the subject matter of theological study developed around the fourfold pattern of Bible (scripture), dogmatics (systematic theology), church history, and practical theology (pastoral care), based on German theological science.[96] This fourfold pattern was influenced by Schleiermacher (1768–1834), who provided cognitive and theoretical foundations for an indispensable practice in theology through the theological encyclopedia movement. However, according to Farley, the fourfold pattern, inherited by U.S. theological education, prevents the study of theology from obtaining *theologia*, which appeals to the disposition of the soul. Current theological education based on this fourfold pattern has fractured the material unity of theological studies and promoted a functionalist version of the clerical paradigm and a theory–practice mind-set. In other words, the fourfold pattern of theological study conceives of Bible, systematic theology, and church history as theoretical studies and practical theology as a ministerial responsibility. The interpretation of practice has been systematically eliminated from the structure of *theologia*. Farley argues that practice is built into theology by definition. He asserts that the challenge for theological education is the restoration of *theologia*.

Similarly, practical theologian Don S. Browning (1934–2010) argues that theology as a whole is fundamentally a practical theology. Browning adopted David Tracy's argument that all theology is inevitably correlational in nature. He developed a "revised critical correlation model," a dialectical method that seeks a critical dialogue between hermeneutics and practical wisdom (*pronesis*) through implicit or explicit questions and answers.[97] A

new understanding of theology as fundamentally practical includes descriptive, historical, systematic, and strategic approaches for theological education, which draws meaning and practice for transformative change from and through the Christian life.

A global context in the 21st century provides new challenges to theological education. The first challenge includes the influx of women students in theological education and the postcolonial context of the West, along with the male-oriented traditional pedagogy of theological education. The inclusion of postcolonial pedagogy in theological education—pedagogies of being a human, of restoration of self, of emancipation, and of agility—is urgent. Theological education in the 21st century should include the pedagogical practice of liberation, which facilitates change in the human condition of struggle related to race, gender, power domination, and sexual orientation. Second, the expansion of technology and online learning presents opportunities and challenges for theological education; one opportunity is the ability to provide theological education to a massive population through the Internet. A 21st-century challenge is to determine how to restore *theologia* and to keep theology relevant to online learners.

—HiRho Y. Park

Theological Education, Spiritual Formation in

The term "spiritual formation" has a long history within Roman Catholic circles but is a relative newcomer in Protestant writings. However, training in discipleship, growth in the Christian life, and godly living have always been prominent aims in Protestant ministry training.

The revival of interest in spirituality in the 1970s, 1980s, and 1990s in Western society, coupled with a growing realization that that the current emphasis on academic formation was insufficient in itself for training for ministry, stimulated widespread consultations and writings on spiritual formation in theological education during those decades.

The Association of Theological Schools (ATS) held a series of important consultations in North America, commencing with the Task Force on Spiritual Development, set up in 1972,[98] including the Denver Conference in 1980 and then the basic issues seminar on spiritual and moral formation in 1988, in which mainline theologians such as David Tracy and George Lindbeck took part. Strong messages about the need to reemphasize spiritual

---

96. Edward Farley, *Theologia: The Fragmentation and Unity of Theological Education* (Eugene OR: Wipf & Stock, 2001), 75.

97. Don S. Browning, *A Fundamental Practical Theology: Descriptive and Strategic Proposals* (Minneapolis, MN: Augsburg Fortress, 1991), 8.

98. "Report of the Task Force on Spiritual Direction," *Theological Education* 9, no. 2 (1972): 153–197.

formation in the North American seminary, the new situation created by a different type of student entering the seminaries, the need for meaningful integration of spiritual formation into the whole life and teaching of a seminary, and the fundamental role that must be played by the ordinary faculty member in this task all come out of these consultations.

On 24–28 April 1987, a small but very influential workshop took place on the Scottish island of Iona, initiated by Dr. Samuel Amirtham, under the auspices of the Programme for Theological Education of the World Council of Churches (WCC).[99] It began an extensive program of discussion about spiritual formation in theological education, which culminated in a large conference on the issue, held in Indonesia in 1989. It was a broad-ranging discussion, but often coalesced around the unnecessary tensions between internal and external spirituality, academic and spiritual formation, and private and community spirituality. Above all, it put the issue firmly back on the agenda for the many colleges related to the WCC across the world.

In the Roman Catholic Church, the synod of bishops that took place in 1990 resulted in the papal encyclical *Pastores Dabo Vobis* (I will give you shepherds) (PDV) in 1992, on the training of priests, and this document is still used extensively today in seminaries. The subtitle is "The formation of priests in the circumstances of today."[100] It built on the document arising from Vatican II on the training of priests and emphasizes the importance of communion and fellowship with Christ and the seeking of likeness to Him in both life and ministry. Changes were also taking place in the North American Catholic seminaries in the nature of spiritual formation, and these are chronicled by Katerina Schuth (1999, 2005) who recorded a movement away from a molding program, which, in its worst forms could push every student into a common mold, perhaps fashioned out of the life of a particular saint, to a more individualistic attitude of journeying with the student on his or her particular process of development.

Evangelical seminaries and colleges, with the growing self-assurance that has characterized the evangelical movement since World War II, have rediscovered their own roots for spiritual formation in the Reformation, Pietism, revivals, and the Bible college movement, and increasingly in the Pentecostal/charismatic movement. They have also become more willing to embrace and own the traditional Western spiritual formation tradition and read books by such authors as Merton and Nouwen, and the wider literature on the subject now being created. Mentoring of students and small tutor or fellowship groups not too different from the Methodist class meetings increasingly form part of the curriculum in evangelical schools worldwide.

Many are aware that, although there has been a great deal of talk and a plethora of new programs, often schools still resemble the theological departments of secular universities in the Enlightenment tradition. There is still much work to be done in creating for theological education a different concept of formation "space," in which academic aspirations sit comfortably with a central intention toward the spiritual formation of the student—and this is reflected in the curriculum.

References and Resources

Bonhoeffer, D. 1954. *Life Together (1949)*. Translated by John W. Doberstein. London: SCM.

Lindbeck, G. 1988. "Spiritual Formation and Theological Education." *Theological Education* supp. 1: 10–32.

Schuth, Katarina. 1999. *Seminaries, Theologates, and the Future of Church Ministry: An Analysis of Trends and Transitions.* Collegeville, MN: Liturgical Press.

———. 2005. *Educating Leaders for Ministry.* Collegeville, MN: Liturgical Press.

Smith, G. T. 1996. "Spiritual Formation in the Academy: A Unifying Model." *Theological Education* 33 (1): 83–91.

—Graham Cheesman

THEOLOGICAL EDUCATION, THE BOLOGNA PROCESS MODEL IN EUROPE AND

David Kelsey (1993) locates theological education (TE) symbolically "between Athens and Berlin," which represent two centers of philosophy and education that have greatly influenced Christian theology and TE. Up to the present time, TE has been shaped by the legacies of Greek philosophy and the modern university introduced in Berlin by W. von Humboldt. At the beginning of the 21st century, a new symbolic name of a city is needed: Bologna. Klaus Müller (2011) calls the Bologna process "the greatest reform in education since Humboldt." Introduced by the European ministers of education in 1999, the Bologna process has revolutionized higher education in Europe. Theological education is not excluded from this process. Some even speak of the "Bolognanization of theological education" (Bernhardt 2010).

The Bologna process aims at improving the global competitiveness of European higher education in the 21st century. The Bologna Declaration (Reinalda and Kulesz 2005, 8–10) states: "We engage in co-ordinating our policies to reach in the short term, and in any case within the

99. S. Amirtham and R. Prior, *Invitation to the Feast of Life* (Geneva: WCC, 1989).

100. *Pastores Dabo Vobis, Apostolic Exhortation of His Holiness John Paul II on the Formation of Priests* (London: Catholic Truth Society, 1992).

first decade of the third millennium, the following objectives, which we consider to be of primary relevance in order to establish the European area of higher education and to promote the European system of higher education world-wide." The key features at the structural level are (1) a system of easily readable and comparable degrees; (2) three main cycles of studies (bachelor's, master's, doctorate); (3) a unified credit system; (4) comparability and mobility; and (5) coordinated quality assurance at the European level. However, there is also an underlying educational philosophy, defined as "a change in perspective toward the learners and their development of competences" (Wintermantel 2008) in view of their employability and the development of the economy. This leads to a redefinition of educational quality, focusing on outcome assessment. Some of the key educational concepts are "fitness for purpose," "competences," and "learning outcomes." While this paradigmatic shift in education has been welcomed by the majority of universities, some critics say that these concepts are business-driven and that Bologna educationally buys into the agenda of a "governmental-economic" philosophy of education (Landshuter 2010, 43–61). Critics argue that Bologna is not just creating a European higher education area at the structural level, but that the legacy of classical education (*Bildung*) is being forsaken. They argue that the term "fitness *for* purpose" must be preceded by the phrase "fitness *of* purpose" (West-Burnham 2002). The issue is: Who defines the purpose? And what is the agenda behind that purpose?

It seems that TE is challenged once more to adjust to paradigmatic shifts in educational philosophy. The Bologna process can be evaluated positively as promoting greater emphasis on competencies, learning outcomes, and moving from teaching to learning. On the other hand, TE needs to look at the underlying philosophy of the Bologna reform and not subscribe to a one-sided, economy-driven model of education. The future of TE (at least in Europe) will be between Athens, Berlin, and Bologna.

References and Resources

Bernhardt, Reinhold. 2010. "Bolognanization of Theological Education in Germany and Switzerland." In *Handbook of Theological Education in World Christianity*, edited by Dietrich Werner et al., 584–593. Oxford: Regnum Books.

Dale, Roger, and Susan Robertson. 2009. *Globalisation and Europeanisation in Education*. Oxford: Symposium Books.

Grethlein, Christian, and Lisa J. Krengel. 2011. "Auswirkungen des Bologna-Prozesses auf die Evangelische Theologie." *Una Sancta: Zeitschrift für ökumenische Begegnung* 66 (2): 103–112.

Kelsey, David. 1993. *Between Athens and Berlin: The Theological Education Debate*. Grand Rapids, MI: Eerdmans.

Krengel, Lisa. J. 2011. *Die Evangelische Theologie und der Bologna-Prozess: Eine Rekonstruktion der ersten Dekade (1999–2009)*. Leipzig: Evangelische Verlagsanstalt.

Landshuter, Jürgen Hans-Werner. 2010. "Der dritte Zyklus des Bologna-Prozesses bei Masterabsolventen der Fachhochschulen—Eine kritische Studie zur Umsetzung eines europäischen Bildungsprogramms." PhD diss, University of Würzburg.

Müller, Klaus. 2011. "Die größte Studienreform seit Humboldt. Katholische Theologie im Bologna-Prozess." In *Katholische Theologie an der Universität. Situation und Zukunft*, edited by Joachim Schmiedl and Johann Hafner, 20–29. Ostfildern: Matthias Grünewald Verlag.

Ott, Bernhard. 2011. "Fit für die Welt? Neuere Entwicklungen in freikirchlicher theologischer Ausbildung." *Una Sancta: Zeitschrift für ökumenische Begegnung* 66 (2): 113–122.

Reinalda, Bob, and Ewa Kulesz. 2005. *The Bologna Process: Harmonizing Europe's Higher Education—Including the Essential Original Texts*. Opladen & Bloomfield Hills, Leverkusen, Germany: Barbara Budrich Publishers.

West-Burnham John. 2002. "Understanding Quality." In *The Principles and Practice of Educational Management*, edited by Tony Bush and Les Bell, 313–324. London: Paul Chapman Publishing.

Wintermantel, Margret. 2008. "Editorial." In *Educating for a Global World. Reforming German Universities toward the European Higher Education Area*, edited by German Rector's Conference, 3. Accessed 12 April 2013. http://www.hrk.de/resolutions-publications/publications.

Bologna Process. http://www.ehea.info

—Bernhard Ott

Theological Education, Teacher-Student Relationships in

In all the great variety of contemporary expressions of theological education, from the best-equipped Western seminary to the mud-walled college in some parts of the world, the great constant is that a teacher encounters students and enters into some form of relationship with them for the purposes of teaching and student development. Probably, the quality of that development depends on this relationship more than on any other single factor.

There have been a number of developments in the last 30 years or so in how the relationship has been perceived and practiced. In general, the effect of these developments has been to reduce the "distance" between teacher and student and to change the perception of the task of being a teacher to include more interactive attitudes. This has been driven partly by the shift in emphasis in higher education in general from teaching to learning;

the increasing use of concepts of reflective practice, which, as Brockbank and McGill point out, require a new, closer relationship between teacher and student;[101] and the growth in perceived importance of both spiritual and vocational elements in theological education. Living in a more egalitarian society and with an increasing preference for horizontal relationships rather than vertical power structures has also been influential, as have a number of studies showing that the greater the interaction between teacher and student in higher education, the more successful and pleasant is the learning.

This shift has become evident in an increasing use of different, more relational models to describe the role of the teacher in theological education. Older models—such as the delivery/reception idea of the task, in which the teacher provides the theology for the students to learn, understand, and remember, or even the motif of the teacher as an example—are all top-down models of theological education which, although of enduring value because they express essential elements of the role, are generally seen as not adequately describing the tutor-student relationship today.

Henri Nouwen can be regarded as the father of the new approach. As a result of disillusionment with current models and practice in the 1970s, he introduced the model of hospitality, which was picked up by many scholars,[102] such as Palmer (1993) and others, in both secular and theological higher education. He saw the teacher as the welcoming host, inviting the student into a safe place without too many preconditions, and so creating the opportunity for sharing in both directions. Others have used the model of the friend, echoing the words of Jesus to His disciples—"I have called you friends"—and this too is a useful model, providing that we define carefully the nature of the friendship envisaged and draw the boundaries carefully. Guenther, in speaking primarily of spiritual direction, follows Nouwen but also proposes the model of midwife to emphasize the teacher's role in helping students to bring forth their own development. Others, such as Vine and Unger (1996), have used the word "paraclete," someone who comes alongside to help, and Shepson (2012) has developed this model as the theme of "helper" running through the Old and New Testaments.

This selection is enough to illustrate that modern models tend to be more descriptive of a closer relationship between teacher and student than is envisaged when we think of theological teaching as an objective task. The de-velopment should be welcomed in general, although care must always be taken that only fully appropriate, transparent, and nonpreferential relationships are the goal.

It is sometimes said that this more relational approach has a problem of expression in the large classes of many colleges and seminaries today. It is true that these models can be well understood in one-to-one tutorials, small seminar situations, or extracurricular contact. However, advocates such as Nouwen have shown that they are also appropriate attitudes for the teacher in large class situations, where he or she can show humility, friendliness, and hospitality to the students' ideas and experiences and is always conscious of the need for a pastoral attitude of help toward students when they encounter difficult and faith-challenging concepts.

References and Resources

Collinson, S. W. 2004. *Making Disciples: The Significance of Jesus' Educational Methods for Today's Church*. Milton Keynes, UK: Paternoster.

Palmer, P. 1993. *To Know as We Are Known: Education as a Spiritual Journey*. New York: HarperCollins.

Shepson, D. 2012. "A Scriptural Model of Relational Christian Formation." *Christian Education Journal* 3 (9): supp.

Vine, W. E., and Merrill F. Unger. 1996. *Vine's Complete Expository Dictionary of Old and New Testament Words: With Topical Index*. Nashville: Thomas Nelson.

—Graham Cheesman

THEOLOGICAL EDUCATION, THEOLOGY OF

Theology of theological education (TTE) seeks to establish theological grounding for the purpose, the task, and the shape of theological education (TE). The concern for an explicit TTE has been on the agenda of theological educators in connection with the search for reform and renewal of TE since World War II. The call by H. Richard Niebuhr (1956, 3–5) to think about theological education theologically and not just methodologically, technically, or structurally set the agenda for that search. Niebuhr proposes an ecclesiological and ministerial foundation by shaping TE education according to the theological definition of *The Purpose of the Church and Its Ministry*.

Edward Farley (1981) calls for the reform of TE as a theological task. He argues that the fragmentation of the curriculum and the "disjunction between theory and practice" (1981, 93) can only be overcome by regaining *theologia* as the *ratio studiorum* (1984, 16), as the integrative and existential core of the study of theology, whereby *theologia* is defined as a "habitus of the Christian soul" (1984, 31) in the sense of "a personal knowledge of God and the things of God in the context of salvation" (1984, 7).

---

101. A. Brockbank and I. McGill, *Facilitating Reflective Learning in Higher Education*, 2nd ed. (Maidenhead, Berkshire, UK: Society for Research into Higher Education and OUP, 2007).

102. H. Nouwen, *Reaching Out: The Three Movements of the Spiritual Life* (Glasgow: Collins, 1984), ch. 2.

David Kelsey also asks, "What is theological about a theological school" (1992), and he depicts TE as a crossroads hamlet lying on the road of a particular Christian tradition, between two educational legacies: "Athens" and "Berlin," between the Greek *paideia* and modern science (1993). Kelsey claims that "persuasive theological arguments can be given for adopting each of these types," but he admits that neither of them "is theologically mandated by the very nature of Christianity" and that one "might suggest that, with its roots in 'Jerusalem,' Christianity in fact theologically mandates a third type of excellent schooling altogether" (1993, 5).

This discussion is taken up by Robert Banks (1999), who proposes a Jerusalem model by rooting TE directly in Jesus's ministry as reported in the Gospels. From that perspective, Banks criticizes traditional models of theological education. Thomas Schirrmacher (2000) suggests a similar approach, taking Jesus and Paul as models for TE.

The evangelical "Manifesto on the Renewal of Evangelical Theological Education" (1983) devotes an article to the "theological grounding" of TE, stating: "Evangelical theological education as a whole today needs earnestly to pursue and recover a thorough-going theology of theological education" (quoted in Ferris 1990, 142–143). The follow-up project by the International Council for Evangelical Theological Education culminated in a pamphlet by Dieuméme Noelliste suggesting three dimensions of a TTE: (1) theological education as education in the knowledge of God; (2) theological education as education of the whole people of God; and (3) theological education as education for the renewal and participation in the purpose of God.

"Theological Perspectives" also constitute the first part of *Theological Education in World Christianity* by Dietrich Werner (World Council of Churches). In accordance with the global and ecumenical agenda of WCC, issues of ecumenicity, contextuality, and globality form the core of this theological foundation. It is concisely summarized in the "Magna Charta on Ecumenical Formation in Theology" (Werner 2011, 34–41).

Andrew Kirk's (2005) "Reenvisioning the Theological Curriculum as If the Missio Dei Mattered" calls for a theologically defined conception of TE in missional perspective.

Despite the many contributions to TTE in recent years, a comprehensive articulation of biblical and theological foundations for TE remains a desideratum. Such a project will interact on biblical and theological grounds with the legacies of TE as well with recent paradigm shifts in global Christianity, education, economics, and worldviews. At the heart of the matter, however, is the relation of content and form. Is theology mainly concerned with content, which then can be delivered in various contexts and educational formats? Or is theology decisive even for the way TE is carried out? As Petros Vassiliadis aptly claims (for the Orthodox tradition): "The overall approach to theological education . . . is determined by its theology" (2010, 603).

References and Resources

Banks, Robert. 1999. *Reenvisioning Theological Education.* Grand Rapids, MI: Eerdmans.

Edgar, Brian. 2005. "The Theology of Theological Education." *Evangelical Review of Theology* 29 (3): 208–217.

Farley, Edward. 1981. "The Reform of Theological Education as a Theological Task." *Theological Education* 17 (2): 93–117.

———. 1984. *Theologia: The Fragmentation and Unity of Theological Education.* Philadelphia: Fortress Press.

Ferris, Robert W. 1990. *Renewal in Theological Education—Strategies for Changes.* Wheaton, IL: Billy Graham Centre.

Kelsey, David. 1992. *To Understand God Truly: What's Theological about a Theological School?* Louisville, KY: Westminster John Knox Press.

———. 1993. *Between Athens and Berlin: The Theological Education Debate.* Grand Rapids, MI: Eerdmans.

Kirk, J. Andrew. 1997. *The Mission of Theology and Theology as Mission.* Valley Forge, PA: Trinity Press International.

———. 2005. "Reenvisioning the Theological Curriculum as If the Missio Dei Mattered." In *Theological Education as Mission*, edited by Peter F. Penner, 15–38. Schwarzenfeld: Neufeld Verlag.

Niebuhr, H. Richard, et al. 1956. *The Purpose of the Church and Its Ministry: Reflections on the Aims of Theological Education.* New York: Harper & Row.

Noelliste, Dieuméme. 1993. *Toward a Theology of Theological Education.* Seoul: World Evangelical Fellowship.

Ott, Bernhard. 2007. *Handbuch Theologische Ausbildung.* Wuppertal: Brockhaus Verlag.

Schirrmacher, Thomas. 2000. "Ausbilden wie Jesus und Paulus." In *Ausbildung als missionarischer Auftrag*, edited by Klaus W. Müller and Thomas Schirrmacher, 7–45. Bonn: Verlag für Kultur u.Wissenschaft.

Vassiliadis, Petros. 2010. "Theological Education in the Orthodox World." In *Handbook of Theological Education in World Christianity*, edited by Dietrich Werner at al., 603–622. Oxford: Regnum Books.

Volf, Miroslav. 2005. "Dancing for God: Challenges Facing Theological Education Today." *Evangelical Review of Theology* 29 (3): 197–207.

Werner, Dietrich. 2011. *Theological Education in World Christianity.* Tainan, Taiwan: Programme for Theology and Cultures in Asia.

—BERNHARD OTT

THEOLOGICAL EDUCATION, TRADITIONS OF

This article deals with various current forms of theological education (TE) in different church traditions.

Orthodox Theological Education

Orthodox TE views itself as being in the tension between "academic" and "charismatic" theology (Vletsis 2011, 123). Petros Vassiliadis (2011, 603) states that "theological education in the Orthodox world is determined by its theology." It is shaped by three core convictions: "The *ecclesiological* awareness of the Orthodox Church, the *pneumatological* dimension of her understanding of the Holy Trinity, and her *anthropology*, i.e., her peculiar teaching of *theosis*." Orthodox theologians (Vassiliadis 2011, 604) are convinced that this "relational and synergetic theology has resulted in a much more inclusive understanding of theological education than the conventional exclusivist one that has developed in the West."

However, influenced by medieval scholasticism, the Enlightenment, and modernism, Orthodox TE became more rational and knowledge-centered, detached from its original community-centered and Eucharistic-liturgical core.

Similar to other church traditions, Orthodox TE has to find its way between the monastic model of church-related centers for theological training and the academic model of TE in the context of the modern university (Vletsis 2011).

In its structure, the curriculum of Orthodox TE generally follows the established disciplines: Bible, history, systematic, and practical theology. However, in light of the Orthodox core convictions, this division of the subject matter of theology has always been disputed. The results are a special emphasis on the study of the church fathers (patristics), as well as the "charismatic" dimension of theology (Vletsis 2011, 125).

Roman Catholic Theological Education

Catholic TE of the last 500 years can be divided into pre– and a post–Vatican II periods (Bevans 2010). In pre–Vatican II times (since the Council of Trent), Catholic theological training was provided mainly in ecclesiastical seminaries and served for the preparation of young men for priesthood. Over a period of normally six years, students received an all-encompassing mental and moral training. Intellectually, the main emphasis was on memorizing syllogisms in manuals. Such mental exercises aimed at uniformity and orthodoxy and served the stabilization of the church. This model of clerical training was dispersed among all parts of the world. Similar to other church traditions, Catholic TE was challenged by the rise of the modern university and had to define its place in the realm of modern academia. Generally speaking, Catholic TE was more reluctant to appropriate historical-critical methods than were Protestant theological schools.

Vatican II led Catholic theological training into a new era. TE was opened for everyone. According to Bevans (2010, 10–11), four movements have shaped more recent developments in Catholic TE: liberation theology, contextual theology, interreligious studies, and a missionary perspective. Equally important are growing ecumenical interactions (Rossi 2010) and a stronger emphasis on personal appropriation of the faith and spiritual formation.

More recently, Catholic theological institutions have had to deal with issues of quality assessment, accreditation, and integration into the schemes of national and continental higher education. Currently, Catholic TE education is provided in departments of state universities, in accredited seminaries, and in seminaries outside formal higher education structures.

Mainline Protestant Theological Education

Protestant TE is shaped by the legacy of the Reformation and the ethos of the modern university (Enlightenment) (Zumstein 1994). It owes its historic core convictions to the Reformation: Luther's definition of "the right way to study theology" through the practices of *oratio*, *meditatio*, and *tentatio*. However, over the last two centuries Protestant TE has been heavily shaped by the modern university and its ethos. In its philosophy and structure, it stands in the tradition of the "Schleiermacher model" (Farley 1983). In his *Theological Encyclopaedia*, Schleiermacher proposed a theory of TE that integrates ministerial preparation (training the leaders of the church) and academic studies in the context of the modern university. Edward Farley (1983) argued that this proposal actually produced two separate strands of TE, the academic model in the context of the university, often intentionally dissociated from confessional commitments and ministerial preparation, and the professional model of seminary education, with a confessional and ministerial intention. In addition, in many European countries, TE of mainline churches is still influenced by the historical alliance between states and churches. This gives mainline churches a privileged position in the context of state universities.

In the university model (European model), ministerial training comprises two phases, the first focusing on academic theological studies in the context of the university (normally five years), and the second on in-ministry preparation for the pastorate. In the seminary model (American model), academic theological studies and ministerial training are often more integrated into the curriculum of the seminary. In both models, the curriculum is generally shaped according to the "fourfold pattern" (Farley 1983), comprising biblical, historical, systematic, and practical studies.

Evangelical Theological Education

Evangelical TE represents the stream within Protestantism associated with Pietism, revivalism and the modern mission movement (Ott 2001, 45–53). It can be linked to the more conservative and mission-minded wings of mainline Protestant traditions as well as to free churches (believers' churches) and to mission movements. Theological schools of more Pentecostal-charismatic orientation can also be associated with the evangelical type of TE.

This diversity of church traditions and movements indicates that many models and forms of theological and ministerial training can be identified within evangelicalism: (1) Bible schools, Bible institutes, and Bible colleges; (2) theological colleges; (3) seminaries; (4) theology departments of evangelical universities; and (5) mission training centers.

Institutions of evangelical theological training may be formally affiliated with denominations, or they may be nondenominational. In terms of academic recognition, they may be accredited by an accrediting agency or affiliated with a university, or they may operate outside any accreditation system. Core values of evangelical TE are articulated in the "ICETE Manifesto on the Renewal of Theological Education" (Ferris 1990).

Global Networks and Common Challenges

A large number of theological schools of all traditions are linked through regional, continental, and global networks and associations. Institutions of ecumenical orientation are associated with the World Conference of Associations of Theological Institutions (WOCAT) and its regional and continental members. WOCATI closely cooperates with the Programme on Ecumenical Theological Education of the World Council of Churches (ETE/WCC). Evangelical institutions network through the International Council for Evangelical Theological Education (ICETE) and its regional and continental member associations.

Today all traditions of TE have to cope with major changes: (1) the growing emphasis on quality in education, including on outcome assessment and accreditation; (2) globalization at all levels: economic, information technology, and mobility; (3) the shift in world Christianity, including the decline of Western influence and the growth in and the dynamics of the churches in the global South; and (4) the emergence of a growing number of nontraditional, nonestablished, and nonformal Christian movements and training formats.

References and Resources

Bevans, Stepen. 2010. "From Roman Catholic Church to World Church: Roman Catholic Theological Education." In *Handbook of Theological Education in World Christianity*, edited by Dietrich Werner et al., 3–12. Oxford: Regnum Books.

Bollig, Michael. 2011. "Das überdiöszesane Seminar St. Lampert in Lantershofen. Modell einer ausseruniveritären Form der Priesterausbildung." *Una Sancta* 66 (2): 147–154.

Cheesman, Graham. 1993. "Competing Paradigms in Theological Education." *Evangelical Review of Theology* 14 (4): 484–499.

Faggioli, Massimo. 2011. "Die neuen geistlichen Bewegungen in der katholischen Kirche und die Prieserausbildungen in den Seminaren." *Una Sancta* 66 (2): 155–163.

Farley, Edward. 1983. *Theologia: The Fragmentation and Unity of Theological Education*. Philadelphia: Fortress Press.

Ferris, Robert W. 1990. *Renewal in Theological Education. Strategies for Change*. Wheaton, IL: Billy Graham Center.

Müller, Klaus. 2011. "Wissenschaftliche Theologie an staatlichen Universitäten." *Una Sancta* 66 (2): 90–102.

Ott, Bernhard. 2001. *Beyond Fragmentation: Integrating Mission and Theological Education: A Critical Assessment of Some Recent Developments in Evangelical Theological Education*. Oxford: Regnum Books.

Rossi, Theresa Francesca. 2010. "Theological Education in the Roman Catholic Church." In *Handbook of Theological Education in World Christianity*, edited by Dietrich Werner et al., 629–540. Oxford: Regnum Books.

Rowdon, Harold H. 1971. "Theological Education in Historical Perspective." *Vox Evangelica* 7: 75–87.

Vassiliadis, Petros. 2011. "Theological Education in the Orthodox World." In *Handbook of Theological Education in World Christianity*, edited by Dietrich Werner et al., 603–622. Oxford: Regnum Books.

Vletsis, Athanasios. 2011. "Charismatische oder akademische Theologie? Das Ringen der orthodoxen Theologie um ihren Platz an einer staatlichen Universität am Beispiel der griechisch-orthodoxen Kirche." *Una Sancta* 66 (2): 123–132.

Zumstein, Jean. 1994. "Theologische Fakultäten an staatlichen Hochschulen." In *Kirche und Staat. Bindung—Trennung—Partnerschaft*, edited by Alfred Schindler, 82–100. Zürich: TVZ.

—BERNHARD OTT

THEOLOGICAL EDUCATION, VOCATIONAL MODEL OF

Robert Banks's "vocational model" reflects his examination of the most significant reformulations of the "Berlin" vision of theological education offered by Joseph Hough and John Cobb, Max Stackhouse, and other contributors to the discussion of contextualization and globalization of theological education (Banks 1999, 34–45). In contrast to the classical emphasis on the holistic formation of students, the advocates of the vocational approach to theological education maintain that its overarching goal is to prepare students for the demands of their future ministry. Two avenues are identified for reaching such a goal: clarification of the meaning of church leadership and intentional response to the global and increasingly diverse context of ministry.

First, professional church leaders should be understood not as "pastoral managers" or "pastoral therapists," but as "practical theologians," whose distinctly Christian identity shapes their view of the world and their understanding of faithful living and service. To prepare its students for the vocation of a practical theologian, seminary training should be directed at the development of two complementary skills: an ability to think about practical realities of ministry from an explicitly theological perspective ("practical theological thinking") and a capacity for ongoing reflection throughout the practice of ministry ("reflective practice"). Second, ministers should be prepared to respond to the contemporary realities of cultural and religious pluralism with doctrinal integrity and enduring commitment to love and justice. To fulfill this goal, the process of intentional examination and articulation of the fundamental Christian convictions, carried out in genuine dialogue with surrounding cultures and religious traditions (*apologia*), must be placed at the center of seminary teaching and learning. Thus, the vocational approach to theological education is characterized by its emphasis on practical theology and contextualized apology.

Banks affirms the contributions of the current advocates of the vocational model of theological education, especially their attempt at recovery of scripture as the dominant point of appeal. However, their failure to provide a workable model for practical theological reflection and their neglect of the ministers' personal formation robs these proposals of their transformative power. Importantly, for Banks, the solution to the limitations of the "classical" and "vocational" models does not come from joining the two together. While he acknowledges the current attempts to develop a more "synthetic" model—most notably by Charles Wood, David Kelsey, and Rebecca Chopp (Banks 1999, 46–68)—he also finds them unsatisfactory. As an alternative, Banks proposes a biblically grounded and radically Judeo-Christian approach to ministerial training, which he describes as "missional."

References and Resources

Banks, Robert J. 1999. *Reenvisioning Theological Education: Exploring a Missional Alternative to Current Models.* Grand Rapids, MI: Eerdmans.

Browning, Don S., David Polk, and Ian S. Evison. 1989. *The Education of the Practical Theologian: Responses to J Hough & J Cobb's "Christian Identity & Theological Education."* Scholars Press Studies in Religious and Theological Scholarship. Atlanta, GA: Scholars Press.

Chopp, Rebecca S. 1995. *Saving Work: Feminist Practices of Theological Education.* 1st ed. Louisville, KY: Westminster John Knox Press.

Evans, Alice F., Robert A. Evans, and David A. Roozen. 1993. *The Globalization of Theological Education.* Maryknoll, NY: Orbis.

Hough, Joseph C., and John B. Cobb. 1985. *Christian Identity and Theological Education.* Scholars Press Studies in Religious and Theological Scholarship. Chico, CA: Scholars Press.

Kelsey, David H. 1992. *To Understand God Truly: What's Theological About a Theological School.* 1st ed. Louisville, KY: Westminster John Knox Press.

———. 1993. *Between Athens and Berlin: The Theological Education Debate.* Grand Rapids, MI: Eerdmans.

Stackhouse, Max L. 1988. *Apologia: Contextualization, Globalization, and Mission in Theological Education.* Grand Rapids, MI: Eerdmans.

Wheeler, Barbara G., and Edward Farley. 1991. *Shifting Boundaries: Contextual Approaches to the Structure of Theological Education.* 1st ed. Louisville, KY: Westminster John Knox Press.

Wood, Charles Monroe. 1985. *Vision and Discernment: An Orientation in Theological Study.* Scholars Press Studies in Religious and Theological Scholarship. Decatur, GA: Scholars Press.

—Natalia A. Shulgina

THEOLOGICAL REFLECTION

Theological reflection (TR) is a second-stage activity within the endeavor of Christian education, in that it assumes an existing but also developing familiarity with the Christian tradition and its sources, together with a commitment to living "faithfully" within the world. It seeks to draw together and make explicit connections among three contexts: that of the reflector with his beliefs, values, spirituality, personal experience, and worldview; the contemporary context that the reflector encounters; and the context and resources of the faith tradition (Cameron, Reader, and Slater 2012, 2). A key aspect of the process is discerning meaning that correlates these three contexts in a valid way, and which then results in the ongoing faith development of the participant(s), action based on the insights gained, and transformation (as "change toward greater justice, liberation, nurture, compassion, educational, and spiritual growth for the sake of the world"; Sharp 2012, 423). The latter is best evidenced through movements such as Latin American liberation theology and feminist theology, to which the origins and development of TR are sometimes attributed (Kinast 2000). Transformative action, whether small or large scale, has tended to be the most prized outcome of TR and has given it a central position within the branch of theology known as practical theology (PT). Over the past 20 years, responding to criticisms of poor focus, inadequate method, and weak outcomes, TR has most commonly formed part of a "pastoral cycle" based on Kolb's (1984) experiential learning cycle, the most basic version of which involves (a) the identification of a specific experience; (b) creating a "thick description" of that experience using as many perspectives as possible (including one's own); (c) reflecting critically on this description; (d) bringing the faith tradition into dialogue with the developing picture, allowing time and space for new understandings to emerge; and (e) using these insights to decide on consequent action. Recent systematic study has provided more robust understandings of both process and outcomes, with Kinast identifying five styles of TR that "correspond to a gradually widening range of experience and breadth of praxis" (2000, 5), and Graham, Walton, and Ward demonstrating seven different methods of TR (2005) drawn from biblical and historical sources.

Theological reflection is potentially a means of maintaining and reviving the relevance and vibrancy of Christianity in the 21st century. The skills involved in practicing it are an important dimension of Christian education, both as a corporate activity (which contributes to ensuring strong, wise conclusions) and an individual pursuit (linked to prayer, contemplation, and the development of a faithful *habitus*). Cameron, Reader, and Slater's contention that "the very process of engaging in theological reflection can be an experience of human flourishing" (2012, xi) and Ghiloni's (2012) understanding of theology as education put it firmly on the map of skills that every committed Christian should develop.

References and Resources

Ballard, Paul, and John Pritchard. 2006. *Practical Theology in Action: Christian Thinking in the Service of Church and Society*. 2nd ed. London: SPCK.

Cameron, Helen, John Reader, and Victoria Slater. 2012. *Theological Reflection for Human Flourishing*. London: SCM Press.

Ghiloni, Aaron. 2012. *John Dewey among the Theologians*. New York: Peter Lang.

Graham, Elaine, Heather Walton, and Frances Ward. 2005. *Theological Reflection: Methods*. London: SCM Press.

Kinast, Robert. 2000. *What Are They Saying about Theological Reflection?* Mahwah, NJ: Paulist Press.

Kolb, D. A. 1984. *Experiential Learning—Experience as the Source of Learning and Development*. Englewood Cliffs, NJ: Prentice Hall.

Sharp, Melina McGarrah. 2012. "Globalization, Colonialism, and Postcolonialism." In *The Wiley-Blackwell Companion to Practical Theology*, edited by Bonnie Miller-McLemore. 422–431. Chichester, UK: Wiley-Blackwell.

Thompson, Judith, Stephen Pattison, and Ross Thompson. 2008. *Theological Reflection*. SCM Studyguide. London: SCM Press.

—Alison Le Cornu

THEOLOGICAL RESEARCH

Honesty in research is imperative. In order to be honest, one must examine a broad range of literature in any field to assess any and all points of view. Researching theological perspectives necessitates reading these points of view to discover what one believes. Holding a theological position demands both a robust defense to substantiate one's own beliefs and a rigorous investigation to evaluate the beliefs of another.

Biblical Theology of Theological Research

All research begins with presuppositions. Christian theological research should begin with the presupposition that God is eternal. Everything temporal—reality, knowledge, ethics—comes from Him (Isa. 44:24, 45:7; John 1:3; Acts 7:5, 14:15, 17:24; Rom. 11:36; 1 Cor. 8:6). Since God is the Creator of all things (Prov. 16:4, 26:10; Eph. 3:9; Col. 1:16; Heb. 2:10; Rev. 4:11, 10:6), humans do not create but simply discover truth. All things are created through, by, and for God (Ps. 8:6; John 13:3; 1 Cor. 15:27, 28; Eph.1:22; Phil. 3:21; Heb. 2:8).

God's world is coherent; all things fit together in it (Col. 1:15–17). The complexity of all disciplines is under the jurisdiction of God (Heb. 1:3). Learning benefited from the fact that God created this world as stable, ordered, structured, and consistent (Ps. 111:2). The researcher depends on the "uni-verse." As such, the diversity of all things is understood within unity (Ps. 104).

The personal, eternal, Triune Creator, who has revealed Himself in His Word, His world, and His works, prompts the passion of the researcher to learn (Eph. 1:15–23; Phil. 1:9–11; Col. 1:9–10). As theological researchers, we ponder what God has done (Ps. 64:9), stand in awe of His wonders (Ps. 65:8), and benefit from all His works (Ps. 66:5), all of which cause a fear of Him to spread throughout the earth (Ps. 67:7). The Christian researcher acknowledges Truth wherever it is found, whomever discovers it, while pressing for the unity of all truth under the authority of God (1 Chron. 29:11–16; Neh. 9:6; Ps. 33:6–11, 50:9–12, 89:11). Truth for the people comes from common grace (Prov. 25.2; Acts 14).

The next presupposition of Christian research after God's eternality is the fallen nature of humanity that includes finitude. Any theological research must begin with an acknowledgment of limitation. The finite cannot define the infinite; the imperfect cannot understand the perfect. God can be known, but human knowledge of God and His work is necessarily incomplete (Job 26.14, 28).

Biblical Philosophy of Theological Research

1. God is the source and unity of His creation; therefore all truth is God's Truth wherever is found, by whomever it is stated (Ps. 119:152, 160; 1 Kings 3:1–15, 4:29–34, 10:1–9) in accordance with the previous presuppositions.

2. Multiple perspectives of peer review are essential. Experts in a field of study must evaluate the work of others for honesty, accuracy, and fairness. Research is better for the analysis and critique of others.

3. Qualitative, quantitative, and mixed research methods are necessary for theological study. Qualitative research acknowledges the various interpretations of individuals and their experiences. Quantitative research gathers data, substantiating points of view with numerical analysis. Mixed methods provide more complete analysis.

4. Listening to people (all ethnicities, all experiences) is imperative. Some Christians believe scripture is their sole source of authority in life. Other Christians believe that scripture is the final authority in life but also accept Christian tradition (writings of other believers in church history), human reason controlled by Revelation, and experience (prompted by the Holy Spirit or providential movements) as valuable adjuncts to biblical teaching.

5. Statistics can be useful within proper boundaries, but can also be made to substantiate any position. Multiple sources, multiple reviews can function as a frame within which numerical points of view can be validated. Mathematical precision is contained within the wisdom of creation. Properly mined, data can unearth jewels of truth (Prov. 8).

6. Verbal clarity is crucial. Words must be used carefully. Definitions need to be agreed upon to have a coherent dialogue (Col. 2.2–3; cf. 1.9, 2.4, 8).

7. Validity is vital in any research. Valid research means the study has worth, strength, value, truthfulness, and effectiveness. A standard of measurement for any endeavor that will be accepted by all people, in all places, at all times is the aim of valid research.

8. Humility is the essence of knowledge. The researcher remembers how much is unknown (Job 11:7; Isa. 55:9–11; Phil. 2:1–4).

9. Joy can be the result of both the opportunities and outcomes of research (Ps. 111:2; Ecc. 5:18–20).

10. Thankfulness should pervade the spirit of the researcher, who knows that it is the Spirit's work within the person and creation that allows any opportunity in this life. God has crowned the researcher with honor, who then reflects all glory back to God for His works and His work in the researcher (Deut. 8:11–20; Ps. 8:5, 115:1; Rom. 11:33–36; Eph. 5:20; 1 Thess. 5:18; 1 Tim. 6:17).

Christian Practice of Theological Research

Creational beneficence for all people, God's common grace, is the basis for all theological research (Gen. 39:5; Ps. 107:8, 15, 21, 31, 43, 145:9, 15–16; Matt. 5:44–45; Acts 14:16–17). God's generosity to nations through creation is the reason Christians can celebrate their research with others.

The Church fulfills Jesus's great commandment through research: loving God means loving others by sharing truth that is discovered (Mark 12:30–31). The research of creation is a direct response to loving God (Gen. 1:28). Vocational commitments because of the Spirit's gifts to God's people allow the practice of research. This shows love for others.

The church and its leaders bear the responsibility of defending those who cannot defend themselves via theological research that counteracts cultural error and deception (Prov. 2:1–6; Col. 2:8; 2 Tim. 2:24–26; Titus 1:9; Heb. 5:11–14; 1 John 4:1).

References and Resources

Barber, Cyril J., and Robert M. Krauss Jr. 2000. *An Introduction to Theological Research: A Guide for College and Seminary Students.* 2nd ed. Millburn, NJ: University Press of America.

Pazmino, Robert W. 2009. *Doing Theological Research: An Introductory Guide for Survival in Theological Education.* Eugene, OR: Wipf & Stock.

—Mark Eckel

THEOLOGY, CHRISTIAN SCHOLARSHIP IN

Christian scholarship in theology is diverse and expansive. The landscape of theological scholarship continues to grow and expand as it engages in the cultural influences of postmodernism, multiculturalism, and globalization. On the one hand, with these changes many traditional approaches to theology are being redefined by the influence of feminist theology, postcolonialist theology, open theism, and liberation theology. On the other hand, there is a renewed interest in more historical approaches to theology, such as kenosis theology, Trinitarian theology, and ecclesiology.

Kenosis Theology

The term *kenosis* comes from the Greek word *kenoo*, meaning "emptied," and is found in Philippians 2:6–7: "who, though he was in the form of God, did not regard equality with God as something to be exploited, but emptied himself, taking the form of a slave, being born in human likeness" (NRSV). Kenosis theology attempts to understand the incarnation of the second person of the Trinity based on Philippians 2:7. The aim is to solve the supposed paradox arising from Jesus having both a divine nature and a human nature. The challenge of the incarnation is that the second person of the Trinity took on human nature and gave up or lost some of His divine attributes, such that Jesus was not fully human. The *hypostatic union* is the doctrine of the two natures of Christ, and it maintains that Jesus possessed a full human nature and a full divine nature. Theologians are faced with addressing a variety of questions related to the understanding of what it means for Christ to "empty" Himself. Most theologians believe that when Jesus emptied Himself, that does not imply that He gave up His divine attributes. Kenosis theologians include Keith Ward, John Polkinghorne, and Jürgen Moltmann.

Trinitarian Theology

The doctrine of the Trinity has emerged as a central issue in theological scholarship. Current research and scholarship is reflected in the vast array of academic articles and books exploring the field. It is impacting the fields of ecclesiology, liturgical studies, systematic theology, and postmodern studies.

The doctrine of the Trinity is commonly expressed as the claim that one God exists as Father, Son, and Holy Spirit, or the claim that God exists in three persons (*hyposataseis*), in one "essence" or "being" (*essential*). Trinitarian doctrine was formulated in the fourth century and was challenged from the Reformation through the 19th century. Much of the 20th-century literature on the Trinity is derived from the influential work of theologians Karl Barth (1886–1968) and Karl Rahner (1904–1984). Since Barth and Rahner, there has been renewed interest in Trinitarian theology from the likes of Jürgen Moltmann and Wolfhart Pannenberg. Moltmann, in *The Trinity and the Kingdom* (1993), distinguishes between the immanent and the economic Trinity and views the Trinity as a concept that stands in the place of God as supreme substance or God as absolute Subject. Thus, the Trinity is the only concept needed to define the being of God. He adopts a social model of the Trinity. He stresses the *perichoresis* of the Father, Son, and Holy Spirit. He believes the three dwell in one another. The three persons are differentiated in their characteristics, but related in the original exchange.

In his systematic theology, Wolfhart Pannenberg (2010) has extended the development of Trinitarian thought into the realm of creation. While the tradition affirmed that the work of God in the creation was attributed to the work of God, the Father, Son, and Holy Spirit without distinction, Pannenberg argues for a distinctive role for each person of the Trinity. Thus the role of the Father is as the origin of creatures in their contingency, granting them existence, caring for them, and making possible their continued life and independence. The Son is identified as the principle of otherness and distinction and hence as the origin of the different creatures in their specific distinctiveness. This role of the Son is inextricably linked with that of the Holy Spirit, who is the life-giving principle to which all creatures owe life, movement, and activity.

Other significant scholarship in Trinitarian theology includes the works of Miroslav Volf, *After Our Likeness: The Church as the Image of The Trinity* (1998), and John Zizioulas, *Being as Communion: Studies in the Personhood and the Church* (1985).

Liberation Theology

Liberation theology is the belief that Christianity involves not only faith in the teachings of the church but also committing to changing social and political conditions from within societies that are considered exploitative and oppressive. Liberation theology is concerned about social justice, poverty, and human rights. It is to do theology "from below" based on the viewpoint of the poor and oppressed. Liberation theology asserts that God favors the poor and advocates for them.

Liberation theology, especially prevalent in the Roman Catholic Church in Latin America, is a response to the poverty and oppression of ordinary people. It stresses a gospel that frees people from political, social, and material oppression. Gustavo Gutierrez, a Roman Catholic priest, is referred to as the father of liberation theology. His book, *A Theology of Liberation* ([1971] 1998), speaks to the importance of liberation from oppression and a chance at a more fulfilled human life on earth. His theology views God as on the side of the poor and oppressed, and that God is involved in the injustices of humanity. Paulo Freire, in *The Pedagogy of the Oppressed* (1970), provides a critical pedagogy to liberate the uneducated of society. He is concerned that all people have an opportunity for learning. The goal of education is to raise the critical consciousness of the learner by means of experiential encounters with the realities of culture.

Liberation theology is not limited to Latin America, but includes African American theology, feministic theology, postcolonial biblical interpretation, and critical pedagogy.

Open Theism

Open theism became mainstream in evangelical theology through the book *The Openness of God: A Biblical Challenge to the Traditional Understanding of God* (1994), by David Basinger, William Hasker, Clark Pinnock, Richard Rise, and John Sanders. The work has caused an uproar in evangelical circles because it exposes the reality that many evangelical Christians are influenced more by the theology of John Calvin and Martin Luther. Most of these evangelicals do not identify themselves with a non-open, non-relational view of God.[103] However, evangelicals who find their theological roots in James Arminius and John Wesley, who reject divine predestination and support human freedom, resonate with open theism's approach to human agency.

Open theists have a variety of theological approaches, but hold to the following core values: (1) God's primary characteristic is love; (2) humans are genuinely free to make choices; (3) both creatures and God are relational beings: (4) God's experience changes, yet God's nature or essence is unchanging; (5) the future is open; it is not predetermined or fully known by God; and (6) expiation of Christ about the future are often partly dependent upon creaturely actions.[104]

The "openness of God" was first posited by Richard Rice in *The Openness of God* (1994). Open theism is the belief that God does not exercise control of the universe but leaves it "open" for humans to make choices that impact their relationship with God and others. Since humans have free will and have the capacity to impact the future by their choices, God does not know the future. The future is depending on human agency. If God is ultimately in control of all things, then humans cannot fully exercise free will. Because God desires relationship with humans, God has given humans the freedom to respond relationally.

Another motivation for open theism is the issue of theodicy. Since humans are free agents, and God is not ultimately in control, God is not the author of evil. Since God is a God of love, and is in relationship with creation, God could not will human suffering. Human suffering exists because of the Fall of humanity, and God is not the author of evil or human suffering.

References and Resources

Freire, Paulo. 1971. *The Pedagogy of the Oppressed*. New York: Herder and Herder.

Gutierrez, Gustavo. (1971) 1998. *A Theology of Liberation: History, Politics, and Salvation*. Maryknoll, NY: Orbis.

McGrath, Allister. 2011. *Christian Theology: An Introduction*. 5th ed. West Sussex, UK: Wiley-Blackwell.

Moltmann, Jürgen. 1993. *The Trinity and the Kingdom*. Minneapolis, MN: Fortress Press.

Oord, Thomas Jay, ed. 2009. *Creation Made Free: Open Theology Engaging Science*. Eugene, OR: Pickwick Publications.

Pannenberg, Wolfhart. 2010. *Systematic Theology* Vol. 1. Grand Rapids, MI: Eerdmans.

Pinnock, Clark H. 2001. *Most Moved Mover: A Theology of God's Openness*. Grand Rapids, MI: Baker Books.

Pinnock, Clark H., Richard Rice, John Sanders, William Hasker, and David Basinger. 1996. *The Openness of God: A Biblical Challenge to the Traditional Understanding of God*. Downers Grove, IL: InterVarsity Press.

Volf, Miroslav. 1998. *After Our Likeness: The Church as an Image of the Triune God*. Grand Rapids, MI: Eerdmans.

Zizioulas, John D. 1985. *Being as Communion: Studies in the Personhood and the Church*. Yonkers, NY: St. Vladimir's Seminary Press.

—Mark A. Maddix

THEOLOGY OF FATHERING

Theology of fathering includes (1) a normative discussion of God as the archetypal father and what God communicates to us regarding fathering and (2) practical application of this theology. Fathering, as God models it and communicates it, is integral in His kingdom. And because it is apparent in Western cultures, particularly the United States, that fathers are significantly absent (physically or relationally) from their children's lives, leaving deleterious effects in their wake (McLanahan and Booth 1989; Blankenhorn 1995), a theology of fathering is valuable in providing guidance in the local church and in training future leaders and Christian educators.

God as Father

So what is theologically normative as exemplified in God the Father, and what does He communicate regarding fathering? In emulating God the Father in view of His communicable attributes, we see that fathering is being intentional (Eph. 1:9; Rom. 8:29–30), holy (1 Pet. 1:16), righteous (Rev. 16:5), gracious, merciful (Ps. 86:15; James 5:11), nurturing (Ps. 91:4), rational (Isa. 1:18; Rom. 12:1–2), providing (Matt. 6:26; 1 Tim. 5:8), just (Rev. 16:7), forgiving, loving (John 3:16; Rom. 5:8), compassionate (Luke 15:20f.), and disciplining (Heb. 12:7–11; Rev. 3:19), to name a few characteristics (mothers are to emulate God in these areas as well).

What God Says about Fathering

A theology of fathering also necessitates theological discussion about children. Children, like all of humankind, are made in the image of God (Gen 1:26; James 3:9) and,

---

103. Ibid., 3.
104. Thomas Jay Oord, ed., *Creation Made Free: Open Theology Engaging Science* (Eugene, OR: Pickwick Publications, 2009), 3.

despite that image being marred in the Fall, share in that image (Hoekema 1986) having characteristics with God (intellect, volition, emotions, etc.; Grudem 1994), especially being spiritual relational beings (Moreland and Rae 2000). Being a relational spiritual being is to relate to and love God, thereby obeying Him and loving others on His behalf (Deut. 6; Matt. 22:37–38). Also, being in God's image functionally means man is representative of God's rule in the world, representing His virtues, values, and aims. Being in the image of God, then, children are, among other things, to emulate God (Eph. 5:1; 3 John 11), relate to, and love God as representatives of God's rule now, and parents are to nurture children to that end (Eph. 6:1; Prov. 22:6).

Fathers are specifically called by God to be the primary leaders within the family in the spiritual formation of their children (Eph. 5:23; 1 Cor. 11:3; 1 Tim. 2:13–14), though it cannot be overstated that fathers are not the sole leaders (mothers—Prov. 1:8, 6:20; the faith community—Deut. 6:1–15; 1 Tim. 5:19–20, etc.). And while this is discussed in greater detail elsewhere (e.g., Clark 2011; Hamilton 2010), both Old and New Testaments provide ample direction theologically for this aspect of fathering: God the Father has headship in the Triune Godhead (Gen. 1:1–2; John 1:1–3; 1 Cor. 8:6; Heb. 1:2; Grudem 1994); fathers' leadership is modeled in God's role for Adam (1 Tim. 2:13–14; 1 Cor. 11:3); and Abraham was specifically challenged to command his children and his household to keep the ways of the Lord (Gen. 18:19).

Further biblical insight comes from both testaments. Deuteronomy 6 places fathers in charge of their families, community, and nation, especially with respect to their relationship with God. Fathers are individually and specifically spoken to in leading their children. The "you" in Deuteronomy 6:7 is masculine singular (Hamilton 2010, 12), implying that Moses addressed individual fathers as accountable leaders, not the community, in training their children. In addition, a theological principle gleaned from Ephesians 5:21–6:4 is that fathers, as Christlike leaders, in contrast to cultural expectations, are to take responsibility in leadership in the home by sacrificially loving their wives and nourishing their children spiritually (Clark 2011, 152). Husbands are to lead the home, loving their wives sacrificially as Christ loved the church sacrificially (Eph. 5:25–30). And fathers are specifically singled out to lead in the discipline and instruction of their children in the Lord (Eph. 6:1–4), nourishing them in things of the Lord, being self-controlled, gentle, and patient educators, not exasperating or provoking their children.

Practical Prescription

Practical application of this theology follows from who God is as Father and what He says about fathering. It nec-

essarily transcends cultures, is normative for all situations, and yet is sensitively conveyed to the fatherless individuals and communities where a concept of father is minimal, or even nonexistent to the extent that it seems irrelevant. However, the individual or cultural fatherless plight does not justify shirking the responsibility or aspiration toward God's ideal. Fathers, like God (who is intentional and the initiator of all relationships), need to be intentional, particularly in the spiritual formation of their children and their leadership therein. Leaders within Christian education and the church need to employ means to disciple fathers and come along the fatherless. Effective fathering is a learned skill, with competencies that can improve. Fathers need to be encouraged and equipped to meet not only the physical needs of their children, but also their emotional, intellectual, and spiritual needs. Fathers need to be taught a proper theology of the spiritual nature of their children, how to accordingly better interact with them spiritually, and that father-mother, father-mother-God relationships significantly model relational spirituality to their children. Ministries to the fatherless (orphans, children with imprisoned fathers, foster children, single mothers, etc.) are ways to be fathers to the fatherless.

References and Resources

Blankenhorn, D. 1995. *Fatherless America: Confronting Our Most Urgent Social Problem*. New York: Harper Basic Books.

Canfield, K. 1992. *The 7 Secrets of Effective Fathers: Becoming the Father Your Children Need*. Wheaton, IL: Tyndale House.

———. 2005. *They Call Me Dad: The Practical Art of Effective Fathering*. West Monroe, LA: Howard.

Clark, C. 1998. *Daughters and Dads: Building a Lasting Relationship*. Carol Stream, IL: NavPress.

Clark, S. 2011. "Intentional fathering: Fathers' Positive Influence on the Relational Spiritual Formation of Their Children." *Dissertation Abstracts International: Section A* 72 (11).

Fowler, L. 2009. *Raising a Modern-day Joseph: A Timeless Strategy for Growing Great Kids*. Colorado Springs, CO: David C. Cook.

Grudem, Wayne. 1994. *Systematic Theology: An Introduction to Biblical Doctrine*. Downers Grove, IL: InterVarsity Press.

Hamilton, J. 2010. "That the Coming Generations Might Praise the Lord." *Journal of Family Ministry* 1 (1): 10–17.

Hoekema, A. 1986. *Created in God's Image*. Grand Rapids, MI: Eerdmans.

McLanahan, S., and K. Booth. 1989. "Mother-Only Families: Problems, Prospects, and Politics." *Journal of Marriage and the Family* 51 (3): 557–580.

Moreland, J. P., and S. Rae. 2000. *Body and Soul: Human Nature & the Crisis in Ethics*. Downers Grove, IL: InterVarsity Press.

Stonehouse, C., and S. May. 2010. *Listening to Children on the Spiritual Journey: Guidance for Those Who Teach and Nurture*. Grand Rapids, MI: Baker Academic.

Vitz, P. 1999. *Faith of the Fatherless: The Psychology of Atheism.* Dallas, TX: Spence.

—Steven R. Clark

Theosis as Christian Practice

Overview

In Christian theology, *theosis* is the process of divinization that takes place when people are united with Jesus Christ and indwelt by the Holy Spirit. It means becoming like God.

Though rooted in biblical concepts and verses (e.g., 2 Pet. 1:4), the term *theosis* was coined by Gregory of Nazianzus in the fourth century. Pseudo-Dionysius in the sixth century provided the first concise definition: "Divinization consists of being as much as possible like and in union with God."[105] His definition raises the question of just how much *is* possible. Here most Orthodox theologians have followed Gregory Palamas (1296–1359), stating that humanity can partake in God's energies, but not God's essence. This distinction between energy and essence safeguards against pantheism. Some earlier theologians such as Irenaeus did not make this distinction, but avoided pantheism by other means.

Theosis has always been a central motif in Orthodox theology. In the 20th century, it became a popular topic for ecumenical dialogue, with scholars finding support for the concept in the writings of Western theologians such as Augustine, Luther, and Calvin.

Theosis becomes pertinent to Christian education when people discuss either education's process or its ultimate purpose. Regarding process, the line of logic may run like this: the Holy Spirit is the Teacher and the anointing of the Spirit resides within people (John 16:13, 1 John 2:27), so the human activity of teaching becomes a subset of participation in the divine life, another name for which is *theosis*. So, too, if one believes that the ultimate purpose of education is imitating God's perfection (Matt. 5:48, Eph. 5:1), or becoming totally transformed (Rom. 12:2, Eph. 4:24), or being completely conformed to Christ (Rom. 8:29, 2 Cor. 3:18), then all these aims also point directly to the concept of *theosis*.

Biblical Basis

There have been charges that the concept owes too much to Platonic or Stoic ideas of divinization, or worse, to popular Hellenistic notions of emperors and heroes becoming gods. In response, theologians have argued for its grounding in the Old and New Testaments. In general, these arguments maintain that wherever there is real contact or relationship between God and humanity, there is the potential for human participation in the life of God, which opens the door to *theosis*.

The first striking example is in Genesis, the creation of humankind in God's image and likeness. Then, in the wake of human transgression, God draws people into covenants that are wrapped in language of adoption and of paternal-filial relationship. Meanwhile, Wisdom literature portrays true learning as proceeding from a reverence that opens the mind to divine instruction. Insofar as *theosis* entails being filled with wisdom and knowledge that come from God, this divinizing learning process can eventually take on cosmic proportions: "The earth will be filled with the knowledge of the glory of the Lord, as the waters cover the sea" (Hab. 2:14; cf. 1 Cor. 15:28, "When all things are subjected to him, then . . . God may be all in all").

The basis for *theosis* in the New Testament is the birth of Jesus. In answering the question of why God became human, many early theologians gave a similar answer, which was stated most succinctly and memorably by Athanasius: God became human in order that humans could become gods. Only the Son has the same substance (*homoousios*) as the Father, but people can become God's children, God's adopted offspring, and in this sense "gods" (Ps. 82:6, John 10:34). The Incarnation and language of adoption undergird *theosis*, but further biblical support is found in Pentecost and all language that speaks of people being indwelt by the Holy Spirit, as well as in baptism and all language that speaks of being united with Christ.

Practical and Ecumenical Implications

Theosis defines the goal of Orthodox education. For Catholic educators, it casts a vision of sacramental life as participation in the divine life, with Jesus Christ being the primordial sacrament. For Reformed educators, it puts sanctification into grander and more relational terms. Relationality is a critical dimension of *theosis* for Reformed theologians like T. F. Torrance, who stresses that *theosis* cannot mean a mixture of human and divine being; rather, it denotes a *koinonia* or fellowship between God and humanity. For Methodists and other Pietist or Holiness traditions, the concept of *theosis* converges with the goals of dying to sin and becoming perfected in love. For Pentecostals and others who emphasize the priority of the Holy Spirit in teaching, *theosis* could be a way to talk about the total transformation that education hopes to achieve. Finally, for those who want to put liberationist education into conversation with traditional theological

---

105. Stephen Finlan and Vladimir Kharlamov, eds., *Theosis: Deification in Christian Theology* (Eugene, OR: Pickwick Publications, 2006), 5.

categories, there is opportunity to think about Christian humanization and divinization as being complementary processes, even flip sides of the same coin.

References and Resources

Finlan, Stephen, and Vladimir Kharlamov, eds. 2006. *Theosis: Deification in Christian Theology*. Eugene, OR: Pickwick Publications.

George of Mount Athos. 2006. *Theosis: The True Purpose of Human Life*. Mount Athos, Greece: Holy Monastery of Saint Gregorios Mount Athos.

Kharlamov, Vladimir. 2011. *Theosis: Deification in Christian Theology*. Vol. 2. Princeton Theological Monograph. Eugene, OR: Pickwick Publications.

—RUSSELL HAITCH

THOMISM

Thomism refers to any system of theology or philosophy that draws insights from the writings of the medieval scholastic scholar Thomas Aquinas (1225–1274). Thomism is a form of early scholasticism (1200–1350), which was dominated by Aristotelian realism, as opposed to later scholasticism (1350–1500), which was dominated by nominalism. The basic premise of Thomism is that theology is rational, deducible, and verifiable by reason. Like many authorities of the early church, Aquinas affirmed that natural reason as advocated by the Greek philosopher Aristotle can lead to faith. This rational expression of the reason of the Christian faith is presented for both the Christian, in *Summa Theologica*, and the non-Christian, in *Summa contra Gentiles*. Hence, Thomism represents the integration of Aristotelian realism and the theological traditions of medieval Western Christianity, that is, Roman Catholicism. Thomism became a dominant theological and philosophical position within the Roman Catholic Church in 1879 when affirmed by Pope Leo XIII (Cessario 2005).

Aquinas's three principal contributions to medieval philosophy form a foundation for the fuller philosophical expression of his thoughts, known as Thomism. First is the principle of analogy, which affirms the value of natural theology, providing a theological foundation for knowing God through His creation. Second is his five arguments for the existence of God based on reason and nature:

- Motion—God is the unmoved Prime Mover
- Causality—God is the uncaused First Cause
- Possibility—God is the Necessary Self-Existent being
- Imperfection—God is the absolute standard for perfection

- Design—God is the Designer of the ordered/complex universe

Third, and perhaps most influential on Christian education, is the relation of faith and reason. Thomism's epistemology affirms that humans can know through reason and revelation. Truth can be discerned through their own intellectual pursuits and conclusions and being directly told by God. As such, Thomism is a combination of Aristotelian realism and the teaching of Augustine on Paul. It affirms the interaction between faith and reason (Olson 1999, 337).

Thomism affirmed the value of the revelation of nature and special revelation, the legitimacy of natural theology and dogmatics, and the integration of faith and reason as the means of discerning and appropriating God's truth.

Thomism and Education

Numerous approaches and divergent movements in both theology and education claim their roots are in classic 13th-century Thomism (cf. Kerr 2002). The teachings of Aquinas were appropriated by the Jesuits and the Dominicans in the 17th and 18th centuries, and even later by a movement called neo-Thomism (19th–20th centuries), which was advocated by Pope Pius X (1835–1914). However, later 20th- and early 21st-century reactions to the very conservative and narrow theological and educational agenda of neo-Thomism have led to its decline among later scholars, such as Karl Rahner, Bernard Lonergan, and Jacques Maritain, each of whom has an educational agenda rooted in the theologically informed philosophy of Thomas Aquinas.

Several core educational implications are readily deduced from Thomism. First, it affirms that human reason is a legitimate means of exploring God and His truth, and hence knowledge is principally found through human reason. Second, Thomism was concerned not only with the mastery of content and the development of reason, but also with how this in turn influenced the moral formation of students, emphasizing the whole student and not just the mind. Third, it provides a rationale and model for the integration of faith/spirituality (theology) and the physical world (realism), which is a fundamental issue in modern Christian education's integration of theology and the social sciences. Fourth, the content of Thomism was indeed the traditional teaching of the Roman Catholic Church, but his teaching methods, the means of appropriating that teaching, have varied according to the spectrum of his interpreters. On one side, the neo-Thomists maintain that through repetition, drill, and memorizations the content would be learned, being Thomistic in content mastery. On the other end of the spectrum, those theologians and educators who reject neo-Thomism focus more on the process of doing theology as Aquinas did it, being Thomistic by adhering to the pattern of Aquinas's theological method. Finally, the educational legacy of Thomism is perhaps seen best in that it is part of contemporary theological education, both in theory and educational practice.

References and Resources

Cessario, Ramanus. 2005. *A Short History of Thomism*. Washington, DC: Catholic University of America Press.

Kerr, Fergus. 2002. *After Aquinas: Versions of Thomism*. Malden, MA: Blackwell Publishing.

McInerny, Daniel. 1999. *The Common Things: Essay on Thomism and Education*. Washington, DC: Catholic University of America Press.

Olson, Roger E. 1999. *The Story of Christian Theology*. Downer's Grove, IL: IVP.

Spangler, Mary Michael. 1983. *Principles of Education: A Study of Aristotelian Thomism Contrasted with Other Philosophies*. New York: University Press of America.

—JAMES RILEY ESTEP JR.

THOMISTIC TRADITION

Thomism is a philosophical tradition deriving from the work and thought of St. Thomas Aquinas (1225–1274). A doctor of the church, his multivolume *Summa Theologica*, *Commentaries on Aristotle*, and *Summa Contra Gentiles* remain among the most influential philosophical tracts of the Western world. His works cover metaphysics, ethics, logic, politics, and theology, while his development of Aristotelian thought remains perhaps the most detailed, sustained, and historically authoritative. Both faith and reason have an essential place in Thomistic thought, and his work amplifying the natural law in the context of divine revelation; his metaphysics supporting his proofs for the existence of God; his analysis of action, mind, and ethics; and in particular his formulation of the principle of double effect, are all fundamental features of the Thomistic tradition.

Causation

In his *Metaphysics*, Aristotle recognizes four kinds of cause that became central to Thomistic thought: (a) material cause, the stuff of existent things; (b) formal cause, or essence of a thing; (c) efficient cause, the cause of a thing's alteration; and (d) final cause, the end or purpose of a thing.[106] One important feature of these categories is that both Aristotle and Aquinas see a thing's purpose

as irreducible. In modern terminology, final causation is not reducible to any Humean causation. David Hume's understanding of causation as constant conjunction between events may have some place in the catalog of necessary explanations, but it is by no means exhaustive. Aquinas's teleological analysis unites with his theory of act and potency. Potency explains the tendency or disposition of a thing to achieve its end. This is distinct from many modern versions of causation, in that a thing's end and purpose can never be explained away as the sum of its Humean or event-causal parts. There is still more, and a completely different form of, explanation necessary. To undertake this kind of explanation, it is necessary to be able conceptually to access such ideas as final, never mind, formal, and efficient agent-based causation.[107]

Five Proofs

Aquinas is famous for his view that reason allows us to know the existence of a first cause, pure act, and ultimate purpose (which may be called God but need not). His Five Ways are outlined simply in the *Summa Theologica*[108] and set out to demonstrate the existence of God via the arguments of (1) unmoved mover, (2) first efficient cause of the universe, (3) contingency, (4) degree, and (5) teleology. Aquinas allows for the intervention of miracles and angels in the natural order of the physical universe, so sacred mysteries such as the Trinity are knowable to man through miracles and divine revelation.

For Aquinas, the existence of God and other like truths about God, which can be known by natural reason, are not articles of faith, but are preambles to the articles: "[F]or faith presupposes natural knowledge, even as grace presupposes nature, and perfection supposes something that can be perfected." Nevertheless, "there is nothing to prevent a man, who cannot grasp a proof, accepting, as a matter of faith, something which in itself is capable of being scientifically known and demonstrated."[109]

The teleological argument holds that as all bodies act toward ends, and these objects are in themselves unintelligent, acting toward an end is a characteristic of intelligence, and there exists an intelligent being that guides all natural bodies toward their natural ends. Thomistic tradition regards the purpose or end of human existence as union and eternal fellowship with God.

Natural Law Tradition

The Thomistic tradition is also part of the natural law tradition. Aquinas regards law as "an ordinance of reason

106. Aristotle, *Metaphysics*, trans. John P. Rowan (Chicago: H. Regnery Company, 1961), para. 1013a.

107. Ibid.

108. Thomas Aquinas, *The Summa Theologica of St. Thomas Aquinas Literally Translated by Fathers of the English Dominican Province* (London: Burns Oates and Washbourne, 1920), II-I, Q. 2, art. 3.

109. Ibid., Summa II-I, Q. 2, art. 2.

for the common good, made by him who has care of the community, and promulgated:"[110]

1. Eternal law, or ultimate source of physical and moral laws (Summa, II-I, Q.93);
2. Natural law, which involves our consciousness of good and evil, which is the rational being's participation in the eternal law (Summa, II-I, Q.91, art. 2);
3. Human or temporal law, laws made by humans by necessity (Summa, II-I, Q.95, art. 1); and
4. Divine law, which are moral stipulations specifically given through revelation (Summa, II-I, Q.91, art. 4).

St. Thomas regards the natural law as written on the heart of man (Rom. 2:15) and the soul as the substantial form of living beings. Plants have "vegetative souls," animals have "sensitive souls," while human beings alone have intellectual, rational, and immortal souls. Addressing the theological question of revelation, he shows that the Old Law, which was given to the Jews before the coming of Christ, was fulfilled rather than made void by the coming of Christ and the establishment of the New Law, which in turn is meant for all human beings.

The Principle of Double Effect

The principle of double effect is a matter necessary to the proper comprehension of ethics and law. This is the principle outlined in Aquinas's *Summa Theologica*, II-II, Q.64, art. 7, which is a justification of homicide in self-defense: "Nothing hinders one act from having two effects, only one of which is intended, while the other is beside the intention. . . . Accordingly, the act of self-defense may have two effects: one, the saving of one's life; the other, the slaying of the aggressor."[111] Aquinas goes on to regard self-defense as justifiable: "Therefore, this act, since one's intention is to save one's own life, is not unlawful, seeing that it is natural to everything to keep itself in being as far as possible." He includes another condition so that (1) an act that is not intrinsically evil and (2) is intended and not merely foreseen, (3) is a side-effect and not intended, may still not be permissible unless it is (4) proportionate to the end sought. Thus he insists: "And yet, though proceeding from a good intention, an act may be rendered unlawful if it be out of proportion to the end. Wherefore, if a man in self-defense uses more than necessary violence, it will be unlawful, whereas, if he repel force with moderation, his defense will be lawful."[112]

---

110. Ibid., Summa II-I, Q. 90, art. 4.
111. Ibid., II-II, Q. 64, art. 7.
112. Ibid.

Contemporary Thomistic Tradition

Aquinas's first interest was truth, and he sought it not only in the thought of the Greeks and Romans, but also in Judaic and Islamic thought. He discussed the work of Plato, Aristotle, Cicero, Averroes, Avicenna, and Maimonides. There is no suggestion that he was a theological fundamentalist refusing rational discussion with those who might have genuine understanding.

Those writing in the scholastic Thomistic tradition are too numerous to mention, largely because his work became the very foundation of philosophical and theological learning in the greater Middle Ages and afterward. Francisco Suárez (1548–1617) and Francisco de Vitoria, OP (1483–1546), both of the school of Salamanca, are among some the more interesting Thomists, in part because of their concern that the *ius gentium* be properly understood, given the spread of Christianity for largely commercial concerns.

In the mid-20th century, Jacques Maritain and Etienne Gilson defended in new ways the view that the human soul is immortal and a unique subsistent form, that human knowledge is based on sensory experience as well as an internal reflective capacity, and that all creatures have a natural tendency toward God that can be perfected by grace. Both did so in a continental, postexistentialist rather than an analytical style.

In recent times, Thomism has enjoyed a revival. Such thinkers as Germaine Grisez, John Finnis, Joseph Boyle, Robert George, and Christopher Tollefsen have adopted what has come to be known as a "new natural law" theory. Critics include Ralph McInerny, Anthony Lisska, Henry Veatch, Alasdair MacIntyre, David Oderberg, and Russell Hittinger. Old natural lawyers regard the new as having more in common with what Elizabeth Anscombe (a Wittgensteinian Thomist) called the "modern moral philosophers." They evince this tendency by virtue of accepting central modern ideas like Hume's is-ought dichotomy and the separation of law from morality. There is also a propensity by the new natural lawyers to play down such metaphysical matters as the ontology of supra-human intelligences (like angels—or demigods for that matter) and miracles. This is perhaps with a view to speaking the same language as the modern moral philosophers. Although all parties to the debate agree on a teleological metaphysics, the debates are prone to become quite heated, to the astonishment of outsiders.

Thomistic tradition, entrenched as it is by the natural law tradition, provides a foundation for Christian education and rational discourse across dissimilar worldviews. It is comprehensive, well-argued, faithful, and rational. For the purposes of general education, it shows us a way of speaking to non-Christians and those of no faith. Its beauty, simplicity, transparency, and rationality are perennially significant.

References and Resources

Aquinas, Thomas. 1920. *The Summa Theologica of St. Thomas Aquinas Literally Translated by Fathers of the English Dominican Province.* London: Burns Oates and Washbourne.

Aristotle. 1955. *The Ethics of Aristotle: The Nichomacheann Ethics.* Rev. ed. Translated by J. K. Thomson. New York: Viking.

———. 1961. *Metaphysics.* Translated by John P. Rowan. Chicago: H. Regnery Company.

Augustine in City of God and On Free Will. 1887. Translated by Peter Holmes and Robert Ernest Wallis. Revised by Benjamin B. Warfield. *Nicene and Post-Nicene Fathers*, First Series, vol. 5. Edited by Philip Schaff. Buffalo, NY: Christian Literature Publishing.

Finnis, J. 1980. *Natural Law and Natural Rights.* Oxford: Clarendon Press.

George, Robert P. 1999. *In Defence of Natural Law.* Oxford: Clarendon Press.

Grisez, Germain. 1965. "The First Principle of Practical Reason: A Commentary on the Summa Theologiae, 1–2 Question 94, Article 2." *Natural Law Forum* 10: 168–201.

Hittinger R. A. 1989. *Critique of the New Natural Law Theory.* Notre Dame, IN: University of Notre Dame Press.

Laing, Jacqueline A., and Russell Wilcox. 2013. *The Natural Law Reader.* Oxford: Wiley Blackwell.

Lisska, Anthony. 1996. *Aquinas's Theory of Natural Law: An Analytic Reconstruction.* New York: Clarendon Press.

MacIntyre, Alasdair. 1985. *After Virtue.* 2nd ed. London: Duckworth.

———. 1999. *Dependent Rational Animals.* Chicago: Open Court.

McInerney, Ralph. 1980. "The Principles of Natural Law." *American Journal of Jurisprudence* 25: 1–15.

Oderberg David S. 2010. "The Metaphysical Foundations of Natural Law." In *Natural Moral Law in Contemporary Society*, edited by H. Zaborowski, 44–75. Washington, DC: Catholic University of America Press.

Tollefsen, Christopher. 2008. "The New Natural Law Theory." *Lyceum* 10: 1–19.

Veatch, Henry. 1990. "Natural Law and the 'Is-Ought' Question: Queries to Finnis and Grisez." In *Swimming Against the Current in Contemporary Philosophy*, edited by Henry Babcock Veatch, 293–311. Washington, DC: Catholic University of America Press.

—Jacqueline Laing

Tracts and American Tract Society

Tracts are booklets or pamphlets designed to educate a reader (educational) or to persuade a reader to consider a specific perspective (controversial). "Tract racks" are commonly located near the entry to a church building, and thus provide a variety of tracts to worshippers. Tracts may address a particular topic of interest, such as prayer or stewardship. Others may provide a general introduction to basic Christian doctrines and practices or explain the customs and history of a particular denomination. They are commonly used evangelistically. Gospel tracts (as literary evangelism) are an approach to transmitting the Gospel when geographical locations may prevent it. God has communicated to humanity in written form, and thus tracts are tremendously effective to proclaim the Gospel message by means of the written word. John's Gospel may, indeed, be the first evangelistic tract in human history (John 20:31). Historically, the purpose of tracts was to promote a particular viewpoint during a time of controversy. For example, "Tractarians" such as John Keble, John Henry Newman, and Edward B. Pusey, published tracts to recollect and sustain the Catholic tradition of the Church of England. Tracts are predominantly religious in content, but some can also be political. Probably the best-known political tract is *Common Sense*, which Thomas Paine published in 1776 to persuade readers to revolt against British rule. Political tracts were also used prior to the start of World War II (specifically to propagate Nazism).

During the time of the Second Great Awakening (1787–1843), foreign and home missions expanded tremendously. Considerable numbers of nondenominational voluntary societies were organized for Bible distribution, missions, and social outreach. To assist the home missions' efforts, the American Tract Society was founded in 1825 (a merger of the Boston-headquartered American Tract Society, which was formally known as the New England Religious Tract Society, and the New York Religious Tract Society). Early in the 19th century, innumerable denominations began publishing weekly religious papers for their congregations. In 2012, the American Tract Society and Good News Publishers began a mutual publishing arrangement to print and distribute Gospel tracts throughout North America. Many of the early tracts published by the American Tract Society were reprints from British tract societies, such as the Religious Tract Society of London (founded in 1799), which is characteristic of many evangelical institutions formed in the early 1800s, since the church in Europe normally preceded such efforts.

Beginning in the 1830s, the American Tract Society began publishing more original works. The authors were frequently British (and even German or Swiss) and lived at the time their works were published; the majority of anonymous tracts were printed in the 19th century. The most common subjects addressed by American Tract

Society publications were (1) conversion; (2) education (and conversion) of children, and family life; and (3) instruction in doctrine and the grace of God. Most of the publications were in the third grouping, which indicates the mission of the American Tract Society as not only edifying Christians, but also proclaiming the Gospel to the lost. Whereas modern religious tracts may be 6–8 miniature pages in length (e.g., Bill Bright's popular 1960 tract, *God's Plan for Your Life*, precursor of *The Four Spiritual Laws*), the average American Tract Society publication was 16 pages of narrowly printed type (and many were 32 pages long). The history of the American Tract Society demonstrates a commitment to evangelical faith, as evident in the emphasis upon personal salvation and Christian living.

References and Resources

Brown, Perry C. 1994. "God Uses Gospel Tracts." *Journal of the Grace Evangelical Society* 7 (Autumn): 25–36.

Buttigieg, Emanuel. 2007. "'Clash of Civilizations,' Crusades, Knights and Ottomans: An Analysis of Christian-Muslim Interaction in the Mediterranean." In *Religion and Power in Europe*, edited by Joaquim Carvalho, 203–219. Pisa: Pisa University Press.

Elegant Narratives. 1850. New York: American Tract Society.

Foster, Charles I. 1960. *An Errand of Mercy: The Evangelical United Front, 1790–1837*. Chapel Hill: University of North Carolina Press.

Hutson, Curtis. 1983. *Soul Winning with Tracts*. Murfreesboro, TN: Sword of the Lord.

Nord, David Paul. 2004. *Faith in Reading: Religious Publishing and the Birth of Mass Media in America*. New York: Oxford University Press.

Proceedings of the First Ten Years of the American Tract Society. 1824. Andover, MA: Flagg and Gould.

—RON J. BIGALKE JR.

TRADITION AND REFORM

Tradition and reform necessarily go together and are entwined. Without tradition, there would be nothing to reform, reform being one of the responses to a tradition. Furthermore, without tradition, there would be no guiding principles and standards that serve as yardsticks for deciding if reform is necessary. Tradition without reform runs the risk of loss of vitality, inner contradictions, accommodation to alien (conceptual and cultural) environments, and failure to maintain the originating vision. Reform may be needed either because something essential to the tradition has been neglected (and should be reinstated), or because something inappropriate has been added (and should be discarded).

Receiving a tradition requires us to adopt and apply it, to let it become part of us, so that we draw from and live out of it; it is not simply an inheritance to be kept safe "in the bank." Inevitably, as individuals and communities receive a tradition in this way, it undergoes change in the midst of continuity. A tradition resides in, belongs to, and draws its life from a community or network of communities. Its purpose is to put into operation a vision or ideal, to convey the message of the Gospel, and communicate the life of faith. However, the means adopted to enact the vision may over time obscure that vision; indeed, such means can actually betray the ends they were intended to serve, hence the constant need for reform to correct and reorient members of the tradition, so that they get closer to the original "stream" or source of life.

Tradition may be thought of in two complementary ways. First, it refers to the *content* of what is handed on, which for Christians is the heritage of faith; this is only encountered in the lived and developing experience of the church. Second, it refers to the *process* of receiving it and handing it on. With tradition, one is not simply passing on an inert object that has no effect on us, nor is what is passed on unaffected by those to whom it is given. The faith has to be practiced if the tradition that "carries" it is to be safeguarded.

For Yves Congar (1904–1995), a major exponent of both tradition and reform, tradition serves to link God's self-communication, given in revelation, to the corporate life of the people of God. It refers to what is sacred in what is handed on; this includes scripture, the liturgy, the sacraments, prayer, and the teaching of the church, especially that of the leading patristic theologians and those called doctors of the church. It is to be distinguished from traditions—the customs, local rites, devotions, and particular forms of discipline and observance of the faith that pertain to local areas but that are not normative universally. Accepting that the church is always in need of reform, Congar offers four principles to guide reform efforts: the primacy of charity, striving to remain within and to maintain communion with the whole church, patience in the face of delays, and return to the foundational principles of the faith (Congar 2011). Protestants might wish to press Congar on whether he attributes too readily to the Holy Spirit the church's self-expressions in the unfolding of tradition. They might also be concerned that his assimilation of scripture within tradition fails to do justice to the authority of apostolic testimony as normative for and as exercising judgment over the church. Congar identified a creative tension between the Protestant commitment to the purity of the apostolic witness and the Catholic commitment to the plenitude of the apostolic heritage.

Christian educators, depending on the cultural context; the particular setting; and the spiritual maturity, intellectual capacities, and pastoral needs of church members or students where they minister or teach, are responsible for a five tasks with regard to the living tradition of their faith: first, to transmit and mediate it; second, to question and critique it; third, to articulate, explain, and interpret it; fourth, to deepen and transform it; and fifth, to apply it to the world's needs. In any blend of these tasks at a particular moment, some will be more salient than others. However, if they are to provide a faithful representation of tradition and to offer a worthwhile contribution to it, Christian educators will need to display both a critical appreciation and a creative appropriation of it. Although their primary role within the school or the church is not to reform, they should, in the process of handing on the living tradition, induct students (and disciples more generally) into the criteria, competencies, and commitments necessary for identifying what needs to be reformed and the will to address these issues.

References and Resources

Congar, Yves. 2004. *The Meaning of Tradition*. San Francisco: Ignatius Press.

———. 2011. *True and False Reform in the Church*. Translated by Paul Philibert. Collegeville, MN: The Liturgical Press.

Ladner, Gerhart. 2004. *The Idea of Reform*. Eugene, OR: Wipf & Stock.

Pelikan, Jaroslav. 1984. *The Vindication of Tradition*. New Haven, CT: Yale University Press.

Pieper, Josef. 2008. *Tradition: Concept and Claim*. Translated by E. Christian Kopff. Wilmington, DE: ISI Books.

—John Sullivan

Training Christians for Ministry Institute International

The Training Christians for Ministry International Institute (TCMII) develops Christian leaders for significant service. It trains disciple makers through graduate Christian leadership education to make a global impact by more effectively influencing their churches, cultures, and countries for Christ.

TCMII's work and ministry in Europe began with Gene Dulin's first visit to Russia and Poland in 1963. Gene was the founder and first president of TCM International, Inc. Between 1963 and 1970, he visited Eastern Europe and the Soviet Union five times while living in Toronto, Canada.

In 1982, a new emphasis was added. TCM International, Inc. initiated "Summer Seminaries" at Haus Edelweiss, its European headquarters near Vienna, Austria. Eastern European pastors and church leaders were invited to come to Haus Edelweiss for two weeks of study under professors and preachers from the United States. There was little formal Christian education in Eastern Europe during the Soviet years, so these summer courses gave pastors and church leaders an opportunity to add to their education.

In 1991 Dr. Tony Twist, the second president of TCM International, Inc., established the Institute for Biblical Studies (now TCM International Institute) at the request of pastors and church leaders from Eastern Europe. Over the years, students from Central Asia began to attend TCMII. The churches in these countries grew in size and planted other congregations, thus requiring more pastors and church leaders. This increased the number of students enrolled, and gradually increased the number of countries from which students came.

The institute provides accredited (Higher Learning Commission of the North Central Association, Chicago, Illinois), graduate-level study for pastors and church leaders. When students complete the required classes they receive a master of arts degree or master of divinity degree. As a means of extending education to students throughout Russia, Europe, and Central Asia, TCMII is now approved to offer degrees through distance education.

TCMII is also a member of the Euro-Asian Accrediting Association and the European Evangelical Accrediting Association. It has joined a consortium of graduate schools, the Center for Global Studies, which offers a PhD program in leadership studies. The PhD is housed at Johnson University and is accredited through the Southern Association of Colleges and Schools in the United States.

Based in Heiligenkreuz, Austria, TCMII also offers classes in Europe and Central Asia. Students attend five-day sessions at Haus Edelweiss in Austria or in a city in one of the other countries where TCMII operates. Permanent faculty come from European countries and from the United States, with additional adjunct faculty members coming from various countries around the world. In addition to their academic credentials, the faculty members must also have significant practical experience in the church, so the students can see scholarship in practice.

TCMII operates on the core values of lifelong learning, Christian maturity, servant leadership, and world Christian vision. Its holistic approach to Christian education includes a graduate "field-based" learning environment for bivocational nationals with a practical focus, preparing men and women to serve their cultures, knowing they may face various struggles and difficulties.

The institute advocates nondenominational Christianity based solely on biblical authority. It does not promote any denomination in Europe or Central Asia, but rather works hand in hand with anyone who follows Jesus Christ as Lord in obedience to His Word. TCMII recognizes and values the diverse indigenous Christian churches, institutions, and agencies already in place throughout Europe and Central Asia.

Students completing their formal education at TCMII are involved in a variety of ministries, including serving as church planters, counselors, chaplains, directors of orphanages, medical doctors, mission organization staff and leaders, pastors, radio ministers, social workers, teachers, women's ministers, worship ministers, and youth ministers. Because most of these graduates are bivocational, they have many contacts and skills that assist them in their ministry areas and advance the Kingdom of God in a variety of ways.

TCMII is committed to preparing national workers in Russia, Europe, and Central Asia for effective ministry in their own cultures, through graduate Christian leadership education based on experiential, practical learning grounded in sound theological principles and doctrines found in the Bible. Graduates seek to influence and change their cultures so they align with the Kingdom of God by making disciples who make disciples.

—MYRON WILLIAMS

TRAINING OF THE TWELVE

Jesus's training of the 12 disciples is often regarded as typical of first-century rabbi-disciple relationships within Judaism and as a model for training Christian leaders today, but it is neither. His methods of training His disciples were unique within their original setting and were not meant to be imitated. In first-century Judaism, teachers did not "call" students to "follow" them as Jesus did the Twelve. In the Old Testament, it is God alone who calls people (Jer. 1:4–10; Amos 7:12–16), and in rabbinic Judaism, a student chooses his teacher, not the other way around. Furthermore, rabbis were not "followed," primarily because they didn't go anywhere. But apocalyptic prophets and zealot leaders did have followers, precisely because they were actually itinerant, heading into the desert or into battle (Acts 5:36–37, 21:38; 1 Macc. 2:27–28). Accordingly, Jesus's "call" to the Twelve to "follow" Him has a much greater note of urgency and demand than the typical rabbi-disciple relationship. This heightened quality is seen in Jesus's characteristic saying "Amen, amen, I say to you" as opposed to "Thus says the Lord"; in His claims that "one greater than Jonah is here" (Matt. 12:41) and "one greater than Solomon is here" (Luke 11:31); and in His demands for total allegiance: "He who loves father or mother more than me is not worthy of me" (Matt. 10:37; cf. Luke 14:26). Furthermore, whereas the purpose of the training in Judaism was that the disciple might become a teacher, Jesus's purpose with His disciples was broader, that they would carry on his

mission as servants revealing the love of God until the apocalyptic day. Hengel (1981) believes the closest parallel to Jesus's method with the Twelve is Elisha's "following" Elijah (1 Kings 19:19–21).

Jesus warned His disciples not to set themselves up as rabbis and thus to perpetuate His method of training disciples. Jesus said, "You are not to be called 'Rabbi,' for you have only one Master and you are all brothers. . . . Nor are you to be called 'Teacher' for you have one Teacher, the Messiah" (Matt. 23:8, 10). Likewise, in John Jesus says that He has more to teach the disciples, but they are not yet ready; He will send the Spirit of truth to teach them these things soon (John 16:12–15). Thus, Jesus will be the only rabbi in the church, and He will teach all His followers through the Spirit of God. This is the background for Paul's teaching about the fundamental importance of exercising spiritual gifts within the body of Christ and the reason for the complete absence of discipleship terminology in Paul's letters. After the resurrection and ascension, Jesus's earthly model of discipleship is no longer possible; instead, the manner of maturing followers of Jesus is by means of His Spirit indwelling His new body, the church, and enabling their maturity and growth through the exercise of each member's spiritual gifts (1 Cor. 12, 14; Rom. 12:4–8; Eph. 4:7–16).

References and Resources

Hengel, Martin. 1981. *The Charismatic Leader and His Followers*. Edinburgh: T&T Clark.

Longenecker, Richard N. 1996. *Patterns of Discipleship in the New Testament*. Grand Rapids, MI: Eerdmans.

Luter, A. Boyd. 1980. "Discipleship and the Church." *Bibliotheca Sacra* 137: 267–273.

———. 1983. "A Theological Evaluation of the 'Christ-Model' of Disciple-Making." *Journal of Pastoral Practice* 5: 46–71.

———. 1985. "A New Testament Theology of Discipling." ThD diss., Dallas Theological Seminary, TX.

Segovia, Fernando. 1985. *Discipleship in the New Testament*. Augsburg Minneapolis: Fortress Press.

Wilkins, Michael J. 1992. *Following the Master: A Biblical Theology of Discipleship*. Grand Rapids, MI: Zondervan.

———. 1995. *Discipleship in the Ancient World and Mathew's Gospel*. Grand Rapids, MI: Baker Book House.

—ROBERT KEAY

TRANSFORMATION

The New Testament word *metamorpho* reveals a faith-inspiring image of transformation exhibited in the transfiguration of Jesus, an active expression of and invitation to the transforming work that God intends for the lives of His people. Viewing transformation in the supernatural realm portrayed in scripture and present in the world through God's redemptive work suggests a transformation that "transports us out of the old atmosphere of this aeon" to the gateways of God's new world (Kang and Feldman 2013). Through the supernatural unfolding of God's redemptive drama, that present reality succumbs to the power of Christ and authentic soul transformation occurs. This Gospel-centered account of transformation challenges Christian educators to practice the experiential-spiritual vision and pedagogy demonstrated in the life of Christ (Johnson-Miller 2013).

The nature of Christian transformation is best understood through a personal experience of transformation, because it provides a realistic illustration of the various dimensions and dynamics of the Christian life, in the context of communal and personal experiences of formation. Transformation involves change in the forms or structures of one's being, a conversion that individuals or groups of individuals experience in their journey toward fullness of life in Christ. Transformation enables individuals and communities of faith to experience the heights and depths of God's love, presence, and power. Christian transformation involves a change or a complex series of changes that enable movement from one state of being to another, leading ever more fully into the depth and mystery of our human existence in relationship with God. Transformation for the sake of spiritual life and Christian growth means change, ongoing change toward a new and deeper, more authentic faith experience.

Several theological and psychological concepts speak to the meaning of Christian transformation. In Christ we are to become new creatures, letting go of the old and embracing the new. Christians are to move from carnal to spiritual, immature to mature, shallow to deep, superficial to genuine, sickness to health, impure to pure, unholy to holy, oppression to freedom, and estrangement to communion with God. These theological concepts coincide with developmental psychology research that identifies biological and social forces.

Transformation incorporates all dimensions of life and all dimensions of being: spiritual, emotional, physical, intellectual, relational, existential, and social. Ultimate transformation involves the supernatural permeation of all these dimensions of being with an ineffable realm of spiritual meaning and mystery. Transformation takes varied forms. Whatever the form, however, transformation always means becoming different by morphing from the old to new. It can involve some degree or combination of *internal* changes in belief, perspective, awareness, attitude, affection, ideas, ideals, values, character, and vision, as well as *external* shifts in behavior, practices, lifestyle, relationship, community engagement, and vo-

cation. Transformation may mean movement toward clarity and simplicity, or a turn in the direction of ambiguity and complexity. In either case, transformation is about expanding our capacity for spiritual life; movement toward depth, authenticity, and integrity of faith; and liberation from oppressive limitations.

There are religious aspects to Christian transformation, involving change that one experiences within or in relationship to one's tradition. This may require movement from one religious tradition to another or a new way of relating, or being within, one particular tradition. The spiritual experience of transformation finds life-giving form and expression through religious practice.

Transformation is rooted in formation, a process of leading one into a particular form of existence (a religious worldview such as Christianity) or way of life (religious culture/practices such as Episcopalian, Pentecostal, Catholic, Orthodox, Amish, or evangelical) that is informed by beliefs and confessions, systems of symbols and rules, and worship practices and rites. How one is formed in faith will directly influence the possibilities and path of change. Formation cannot be separated from transformation.

Formation is shaped by transformation, involving dynamic and ongoing interaction among the past, present, and future in dialectical and dialogical tension. The results of change become the forces for further change. Transformation does not nullify the formation experience, but it reshapes, reacts against, or adds a new dimension.

Human development does not equal Christian transformation, but any change in the way we understand and live our Christian faith cannot be separated from any aspects of our existence and growth as human beings. Being Christian entails lifelong growth that directly corresponds to our development as human beings. The process of Christian transformation involves an ever-maturing perspective, an unquenchable thirst for more, and a constant movement toward depth, integrity, and authenticity. To be Christian is to participate in an unending process permeated by and culminating in the supernatural realm of meaning and mystery in communion with the living God. This transfiguring experience of transformation culminates in the vision of God's redemptive work in Christ.

References and Resources

Johnson-Miller, Beverly. 2013. "Transfiguring Transformational Teaching." *Christian Education Journal* (Fall): 360–364.

Kang, S. Steve, and Michael Feldman. 2013. "Transformed by the Transfiguration: Reflections on a Biblical Understanding of Transformation and its Implications for Christian Education." *Christian Education Journal* (Fall): 365–377.

Lawrence, Bruce. 1998. "Transformation." In *Critical Terms for Religious Studies*, edited by Mark C. Taylor, 334–335. Chicago: University of Chicago Press.

—BEVERLY JOHNSON-MILLER

TRANSFORMATION AND SOCIALIZATION, INTERACTION OF

Socialization features in many educational models, as does transformation. The interaction of these two forces is a special focus of James Loder's educational theory. It is also germane to educational approaches aimed at critical consciousness (e.g., Paulo Freire, Thomas Groome) and to stage-developmental theories (e.g., James Fowler, Erik Erikson, Jean Piaget).

Loder identified transformation and socialization as the two main dynamic forces of education. In describing their interaction, he critiqued socialization-oriented models of Christian nurture and formation.

Process of Socialization
Sociologists often define socialization as the process by which a group or society inducts and inculcates new members. Primary socialization happens in the family and home environment. Secondary socialization is done largely through schools and other institutions.

In the 20th century, educators such as C. Ellis Nelson (1967) highlighted biblical descriptions of socialization happening in ancient Israel (e.g., "Keep these words . . . recite them to your children and talk about them. . . . Write them on the doorposts of your house"; Deut. 6: 6–9). These theorists proposed that contemporary educators could perform socialization as well or better than the ancient Israelites, by utilizing the expertise of modern psychology and sociology. The goal was to have church and family work together to effect Christian nurture.

Loder (1989) responded by pointing to forces of socialization in the wider society. These forces, which the church does not dictate, propel people to adopt lifestyles contrary to Christianity. The church may think it is using socialization, yet larger forces of socialization may be using the church's rituals and practices to nurture people into lifestyles marked by addiction to achievement, or compliance with oppression, or endless journeys of self-discovery. The problem, Loder said, is not that socialization lacks power, but that it is too powerful to control. Educational, legal, religious, and political institutions all work in tandem. These social institutions are in turn influenced by the core values that permeate culture, and these values are not necessarily Christian or life-giving.

For additional reasons, Loder (1989) advised against socialization models of education. Socialization tends toward equilibration through established patterns and reduced tension. However, in the context of a human life, the ultimate picture of equilibrium is a flat line on the heart monitor, and in the context of the universe, the drive to equilibrium is also called entropy. In developmental models, Loder argued, the most notable feature is not the equilibrium of a particular stage, but the dynamic movement from one stage to the next. This movement is evidence of transformation. He proposed that transformation is more intrinsic to the human spirit, and therefore it should be given conceptual priority in education.

Pattern of Transformation
Transformation—whether in the realm of scientific discovery, personal growth, or spiritual conversion—is the process by which new and hidden order emerges. Influenced by Michael Polanyi's writings on epistemology, Loder proposed that transformation is a fivefold process that includes (1) conflict in context, (2) interlude for scanning, (3) insight felt with intuitive force, (4) release of energy bound up in the conflict and openness to new ways of seeing things, and (5) verification or testing of the new knowledge. Loder pointed to biblical examples of transformational learning, including Christ's appearing to Paul and to the two travelers to Emmaus.

Redemptive Interaction
Transformation and socialization interact and even depend on each other. Socialization requires transformation to resolve continual conflicts between internal desires and external constrictions. Transformation requires socialization to provide the context or framework out of which new order can emerge. The goal in education is not to suppress socialization, but to give full play to transformation. This approach could mean, for example, seeing conflicts as learning opportunities, or valuing the hunches and intuitions (interludes for scanning) of students.

Just as socialization is not altogether bad, so too transformation is not automatically good. Individuals can use their creativity to do harm. In society as a whole, transformation can be co-opted by malignant forces of socialization, as fascist societies illustrate starkly. In his Christian apologetic (1989), Loder pointed to Kierkegaard's distinction between the genius and the apostle. Geniuses can transform their environment or medium, for good or ill. Apostles are themselves being transformed by the Spirit of Christ.

Thus in Loder's view, transformation and socialization interact, but the former is more central to the creativity of the human spirit. At the same time, transformations of the human spirit often stand in need of being in turn transformed by the Holy Spirit. In regard to education, the process calls to mind Paul's injunction, "Do not be conformed to this world, but be transformed by the renewing of your minds" (Rom. 12:2). This transformation takes place in the context of prayer and worship. It propels people outward to be agents of redemptive transformation in the world.

References and Resources

Loder, James. n.d. "Education in the Logic of the Spirit." Unpublished manuscript, Princeton Theological Seminary Archives and Special Collections.

———. 1989. *The Transforming Moment.* Colorado Springs, CO: Helmers & Howard.

Nelson, C. Ellis. 1967. *Where Faith Begins.* Louisville, KY: John Knox Press.

—RUSSELL HAITCH

TRANSFORMATIONAL CONGREGATIONAL LEARNING

Christian education is often framed as a cumulative, developmental activity; knowledge and skills are added as layers. This approach assumes that we can receive information,[113] and that this knowledge, with perhaps some commended activities, will lead to wiser living. When this framework is applied to a congregation, leaders assume that they know what needs to be learned (in knowledge and skills) and that strategies can be shaped to deliver the needed concepts and training to various individuals and groups to achieve particular ends. There are some areas of congregational life that are suitable for this developmental approach, but many facets of Christian/congregational life do not fit this mode of managed education and predictable change.[114] Rather, transformational learning is less predictable, more discontinuous, less manageable, and dependent on the voices of members and neighbors.

Several key theological affirmations are relevant to transformative education: God is the primary subject, continually initiating with church participants and their neighbors; the Trinity models otherness and unity; and in the Trinity's actions of sending, the church learns that it is sent. In addition, a church is called, gathered, and sent, and has the vocation of discerning God's initiatives and priorities and living into those initiatives; neighbors are subjects (not objects), whose presence and voices are necessary for a church's learning, reflection, and behaviors.

Education in the West, especially among Euro-American churches, has tended to focus on the individual as learner rather than on the group as learner.[115] In recent decades, authors have addressed how organizations learn, often using the term "learning community."[116] Christian education scholars have also engaged this important shift, although the emphasis is usually on church as a context to support and resource the individual,[117] rather than to see the church itself as a learning entity.[118] The locus of the group is essential if a congregation is to be transformed.

Transformation in organizations engages the complex matrix of beliefs and actions, or culture, of the organization.[119] While churches constantly face "technical" challenges that can be met by developmental approaches, transformational change addresses "adaptive" challenges in which the organization's *habits* of thinking, feeling, and acting must be addressed.[120] Organizational habits are formed over years; they are mutually reinforcing, linked with contextual factors, and often below the awareness of participants. An organization needs transformation when it faces challenges that, unless addressed, will prevent the organization from successfully engaging essential purposes and activities. For example, if a church's habits prevent it from knowing and participating in God's initiatives among a younger generation, or among its neighbors, then it will fail in important, essential church purposes. Such situations require transformational learning.

Transformational change engages core elements of both identity (Who are we?) and agency (What do we do?). The specific goals and consequences of the transformation cannot be known prior to participants' engagement with processes that will challenge their habits. The role of leadership is not to provide expert answers and

---

113. Paulo Freire calls this cumulative approach "banking"; Paulo Freire, *Pedagogy of the Oppressed,* trans. Myra Bergman Ramos (New York: Continuum, 2000), ch. 2.

114. On why strategic planning is often inappropriate, see Alan Roxburgh, *Missional Map-making* (San Francisco: Jossey-Bass, 2010), ch. 5.

115. This characteristic varies among ethnic groups, with some cultures that are more collectivist exhibiting traits of corporate learning.

116. See Peter Senge, *The Fifth Discipline: Strategies and Tools for Building a Learning Organization,* rev. ed. (New York: Currency/Doubleday, 2006); Lee Bolman and Terrence Deal, *Reframing Organizations* (San Francisco: Jossey-Bass, 2008); Etienne Wenger, Richard McDermott, and William Snyder, *Cultivating Communities of Practice* (Boston: Harvard Business School, 2002). This framework was foreshadowed as a "community of interpreters" by Josiah Royce, *The Problem of Christianity* (Chicago: University of Chicago, 1968), 314–316.

117. This essential symbiotic relationship is often called enculturation; see John Westerhoff, *Will Our Children Have Faith?* rev. ed. (Harrisburg, PA: Morehouse, 2000) and C. Ellis Nelson, *Where Faith Begins* (Atlanta, GA: John Knox, 1967).

118. See Charles Foster, *Educating Congregations* (Nashville, TN: Abingdon Press, 1994); and Norma Cook Everist, *The Church as Learning Community* (Nashville, TN: Abingdon Press, 2002).

119. See Edgar Schein, *Organizational Culture and Leadership,* 4th ed. (San Francisco: John Wiley & Sons, 2010); and Chris Argyris, *On Organizational Learning,* 2nd ed. (Malden, MA: Blackwell, 1999).

120. See Ronald Heifetz and Marty Linsky, *Leadership on the Line* (Boston: Harvard Business School, 2002); and Sharon Daloz Parks, *Leadership Can Be Taught* (Boston: Harvard Business School, 2005).

creative plans, but rather to shape the environment in which a widening number of participants are listening, learning, reflecting, innovating, leading, and acting in order to make it more likely that the church sees and acts and begins to understand its way into a future that is not immediately knowable.[121]

Even though transformational learning does not work with prescribed goals and instructional content, there are iterative processes that can form the needed new relationships, conversations, practices, and imaginary.[122] The intentional practices of the iterative process occur in several parallel groups that stay in communication with each other, including the church's officers and staff. Following are these steps. (1) When a church is to enter such a cultural change, it needs an *awareness* that its corporate life—its identity and its activities—is in some significant way not only inadequate but also incapable of making the needed changes with current knowledge and activities. There is a sense of being lost, of being disoriented. Educators can shape environments (experiences, conversations, engagement with texts, reflection) in which such awareness is named.[123] (2) *Understanding* must increase, which means that the church pursues voices and information about historical, contextual, organizational, and relational factors that contribute to its disorientation and lostness. (3) The church engages a deeper *evaluation* by reflecting on its habits of thinking, feeling, and acting in light of core biblical and theological matters that include loving God, neighbors, and each other.[124] (4) Groups are sanctioned to try experiments that address what they are learning. These action-reflection experiments bring increased understanding, additional voices, deeper reflection, and new capacities for risk and innovation. (5) Some experiments lead to new *commitments* that indicate that the church's culture is shifting—that transformation of the church's identity and agency is occurring.[125]

Unlike strategic planning, transformational learning is not a straight line; the outcomes are unpredictable; and major changes regarding the church's leadership, character, and imagination are to be expected. Innovations (and risk) are diffused throughout the church, and capacities for learning, worship, and mission are expanded.[126] If real transformation has occurred the church will not revert to earlier habits; its character, imagination, and behaviors have been transformed. However, any church needs to continually explore further cultural shifts.

—MARK LAU BRANSON

TRANSFORMATIONAL LEADERSHIP

Transformational leadership is rooted in theories of organizational behavior that approach leadership as a process of change, wherein a leader performs the primordial role as animator of adaptive and generative change. In his Pulitzer Prize–winning book *Leadership*, James MacGregor Burns (1978) examines how leaders negotiate power and distinguishes leaders from power wielders. He differentiates what he considers the two fundamental types of leaders: the transactional and the transforming.

Transactional leaders are those who lead in exchange for something to gain: for example, jobs for votes or subsidies for campaign contributions among political enclaves. On the other hand, transforming leaders recognize the ultimate purpose of followers as persons-in-relationship, who seek holistic integration and problematize the human or organizational situation through the lens of their core values, priorities, and practices.

Consequently, transforming leaders are morally uplifting and have a vision of creating more leaders among followers toward moral agency and change for a common good. As early as 1924, Mary Parker Follett emphasized that leadership is not so much about exercising power, but rather one's capacity to intensify the sense of power among followers.

The shift in nomenclature from "transforming" to "transformational" is attributed to Bernard Bass. Building on Burns's work, Bass (1985) designed assessment methods to measure follower motivation and performance, such as the level at which they inspire a shared vision or forge respect, trust, and loyalty. Bass identifies four constitutive components of transformational leadership:

1. Intellectual stimulation—leaders demonstrate how to say "no" to the world as it is by systemically challenging the status quo; promote creative innovation; model critical thinking and generative decision making; and explore multiple and new ways of

---

121. Heifetz and Linsky, *Leadership on the Line*, emphasize the need to "give the work to the people" (123–139); Alan Roxburgh and Fred Romanuk write, "leadership is about cultivating an environment that innovates and releases the missional imagination present among a community of God's people." Alan Roxburgh and Fred Romanuk, *The Missional Leader* (San Francisco: Jossey-Bass, 2006), 5.

122. There are a number of processes that can provide modes that foster transformation; I am following a process designed by Roxburgh and Romanuk (2006, 79–108).

123. See also Roxburgh, *Missional Map-making*; and Mark Lau Branson and Juan Martínez, *Churches, Cultures and Leadership* (Downers Grove, IL: InterVarsity Press, 2011), ch. 10.

124. Leaders often experience resistance in various ways, such as marginalization, diversion, and attack; see Heifetz and Linsky (2002, 9–50).

125. Concerning discernment and new actions, see Craig Van Gelder, *The Ministry of the Missional Church* (Grand Rapids, MI: Baker, 2007).

126. See Dwight Zscheile, ed., *Cultivating Sent Communities* (Grand Rapids, MI: Eerdmans, 2012), especially Dwight Zscheile, "A Missional Theology of Spiritual Formation," 1–28.

meaning-making that sustain a dynamic learning community.

2. Individualized consideration—leaders advance the holistic growth and integration of each person-agent through effective mentoring or coaching, practice empathetic ways of listening, and promote sound interpersonal relationships that support an inclusive sense of identity and belonging in the organization.

3. Inspirational motivation—leaders articulate a shared vision that inspires others to act intentionally, engaging both head and heart.

4. Idealized influence—leaders reveal the ethical principles and moral values in which their transformative practices are grounded, by embodying virtues such as respect, trust, charity, integrity, collaboration, and justice.

For Bass, both transactional and transformational practices of leadership can be carried out mutually and concurrently. Contemporary theories that either build on or complement early literature on transformational leadership include the works of the following educator-practitioners: Frank Barrett; Juana Bordas; Richard Boyatzis and Annie McKee; Laurent Parks Daloz, Cheryl Keen, James Keen, and Sharon Daloz; James Kouzes and Barry Posner; Harry Kraemer; and Donna Markham.

References and Resources

Avolio, Bruce J. 2010. "Pursuing Authentic Leadership Development." In *Handbook of Leadership Theory and Practice*, edited by Nitin Nohria and Rakesh Khurana, 739–768. Boston: Harvard Business Press.

Barrett, Frank. 2012. *Yes to the Mess: Surprising Leadership Lessons from Jazz*. Cambridge: Harvard Business Review Press.

Bass, Bernard. 1985. *Leadership Performance Beyond Expectations*. New York: The Free Press.

Bordas, Juana. 2007. *Salsa, Soul, and Spirit: Leadership for a Multicultural Age*. San Francisco: Berrett-Koehler Publishers.

Boyatzis, Richard E., and Annie McKee. 2005. *Resonant Leadership: Renewing Yourself and Connecting with Others through Mindfulness, Hope, and Compassion*. Boston: Harvard Business School Press.

Burns, James MacGregor. 1978. *Leadership*. New York: Harper & Row.

Ely, Robin J., and Deborah L. Rhode. 2010. "Women and Leadership: Defining the Challenges." In *Handbook of Leadership Theory and Practice*, edited by Nitin Nohria and Rakesh Khurana, 377–410. Boston: Harvard Business Press.

Follett, M. P. (1924). Creative experience. (Reprint 1951.) New York: Peter Smith.

Glynn, Mary Ann, and Rich DeJordy. 2010. "Leadership Through an Organization Behavior Lens: A Look at the Last Half-Century of Research." In *Handbook of Leadership Theory and Practice*, edited by Nitin Nohria and Rakesh Khurana, 119–157. Boston: Harvard Business Press.

Graham, Pauline, ed. 1995. *Mary Parker Follett: Prophet of Management: A Celebration of Writings from the 1920s*. Washington, DC: Beard Books.

Kouzes, James M., and Barry Z. Posner. 2012. *The Leadership Challenge*. 5th ed. San Francisco: Jossey-Bass.

Kraemer, Harry M. Jansen. 2011. *From Values to Action: The Four Principles of Values-Based Leadership*. San Francisco: Jossey-Bass.

Markham, Donna. 1999. *Spiritlinking Leadership: Working through Resistance to Achieve Organizational Change*. Mahwah, NJ: Paulist Press.

Parks Daloz, Laurent A., Cheryl H. Keen, James P. Keen, and Sharon Daloz Parks. 1996. *Common Fire: Leading Lives of Commitment in a Complex World*. Boston: Beacon Press.

—Faustino M. Cruz

Transformative Learning

A learning theory typically employed in adult learning environments, the aim of transformative learning is to deeply transform one's core life beliefs (O'Sullivan 1999). The ultimate goal of transformative learning is to create a better world by raising individuals' worldview awareness (i.e., social justice, personal actualization) and their awareness of their interpersonal relationships (see Dirkx 1997). Mezirow (1991) explains that when individuals raise their worldview awareness and the level of alignment of their own epistemologies about our world, they take true ownership and thus fully understand their level of personal development. This is defined by Mezirow (1991) as *self-authorship*.

Adding to Mezirow's (1991) explanation about transformative learning, Dirkx elaborates on how this approach to learning adds to the individual's whole being: "Our journey of self-knowledge also requires that we care for and nurture the presence of soul dimension in teaching and learning" (1997, 80). When individuals view their experiences through *soul*, Dirkx explains, it draws "attention to the quality of experiencing life and ourselves, to matters of depth, values, relatedness, and heart. Soul has to do with authenticity, connection between heart and mind, mind and emotion, the dark as well as the light" (ibid.). Thus, according to Dirkx, transformative learning helps us to seek the ultimate goal connected to Christian living: living each day with a deep connection to our soul's higher purpose. Dirkx further reminds us that "learning is not simply a preparation for life. It *is* life" (ibid.).

Transformative learning environments require that the learner feel *safe* with the learning process. Students must be willing to take risks to learn from each other and grow in spirit and mind. In conjunction with this, an outcome of the transformative learning classroom is to create a community of learners who are united as one as they try to make meaning from their life experiences (Mezirow 1991). Such an approach shares this goal with other well-known educational theories, such as constructivist learning and experiential learning.

Dirkx (1997) further contributes to our understanding of transformative learning by proposing terms to describe how a student would characterize his self-interpretations of his worldview. He refers to how those students who are cognitively aware of the personal transformations they have experienced actually move toward what he describes as a *lens of mythos*, as opposed to viewing their world through a *lens of images*. According to Dirkx, experiencing our transformations through a lens of mythos allows us to frame our experiences of the world through our unconscious soul rather than only through the conscious symbols that we use to interpret our worldview. These kinds of experiences help us to better understand Christ's teachings, as well as to promote our own understanding of how we can best abide by His Truths. Given the basic tenets of transformative learning, then, we would expect that the learning we experience through this teaching model would produce more authentic epistemologies about the issues that matter most to Christian teachers and learners.

References and Resources

Dirkx, J. 1997. "Nurturing Soul in Adult Learning." In *Transformative Learning in Action: Insights from Practice*, edited by Patricia Cranton, 74. San Francisco: Jossey-Bass.

Mezirow, J. 1991. *Transformative Dimensions of Adult Learning*. San Francisco: Jossey-Bass.

O'Sullivan, E. 1999. *Transformative Learning: Educational Vision for the 21st Century*. Toronto: University of Toronto Press.

—DIANA D. ABBOTT

TYNDALE HOUSE, CAMBRIDGE

Foundation

Tyndale House (not to be confused with the entirely separate American publishing company of the same name) is a residential library and study center in Cambridge, England. It was founded in 1944 by leading evangelical figures such as D. B. Knox, Douglas Johnson, Alan Stibbs, F. F. Bruce, D. Martyn Lloyd-Jones, and John Laing, and is related to the Universities and Colleges Christian Fellowship. The House itself, and the associated Tyndale Fellowship of evangelical scholars, began at a time when many conservative Christians were unpersuaded of the value to the church of high-level research in biblical studies. Academics were also skeptical about whether evangelicals could engage in such research with intellectual integrity. Tyndale House and Fellowship were designed to convince and serve both of these constituencies.

After some internal debates over several years, it was decided to concentrate the library's acquisitions on books and journals directly relevant to biblical studies, and thus to downgrade other theological disciplines such as dogmatics, church history, and pastoralia. As a result, Tyndale House now possesses one of the finest libraries for biblical research in the world (rivaled perhaps only by the preeminent Roman Catholic libraries at the Pontifical Institute in Rome and the École Biblique de Jérusalem), with specialist material on the language, culture, history, and meaning of the Bible. It enjoys close links with the University of Cambridge, and a number of postgraduates, church leaders, and visiting scholars study there or stay in dedicated accommodations on the site.

Influence

The scholars and publications that have come from Tyndale House since its founding have had a significant global impact. Leading evangelicals such as D. A. Carson, Wayne Grudem, J. I. Packer, John Wenham, and Donald Wiseman have all been involved with the House, and wardens have included Sir Norman Anderson, Leon Morris, Derek Kidner, R. T. France, and Bruce Winter. A number of research fellows and lecturers are also employed on the staff, who along with qualified readers there provide some teaching and supervision in Cambridge University faculties. As well as publishing a regular academic journal, *Tyndale Bulletin* (since 1956), and dozens of "Tyndale Lectures" and "Tyndale Monographs," scholars from Tyndale have been the driving force behind the long-running series Tyndale Commentaries, the New Bible Dictionary, and *The Lion Handbook of the Bible*. They also have had important input into the major modern English translations of the Bible, including the ESV and NIV.

Tyndale House is the center of a scholarly network, hosting annual study group conferences in various biblical disciplines, organizing a larger triennial conference attended by academics from around the world, and sponsoring various educational initiatives linking the academy with the church. It also plays host to the Kirby Laing Institute for Christian Ethics. The House website contains numerous resources for in-depth study of the Bible and associated backgrounds in the original languages and hosts ongoing projects to make available free Bible study tools for those in poorer parts of the world with low-spec computers and/or intermittent Internet access. Tyndale House by far outshines other institutional initiatives by British evangelicals in the 20th century, such as Whitefield House in Oxford and Rutherford House in Edinburgh, which have not achieved the same level of reach, impact, and longevity.

References and Resources

Noble, T. A. 2006. *Tyndale House and Fellowship: The First Sixty Years*. Leicester: IVP.

www.tyndale.cam.ac.uk
www.klice.co.uk

—LEE GATISS

U

UGANDA AND CHRISTIAN EDUCATION

Uganda is a landlocked country in East Africa with a population of 33 million (July 2012 estimates) and over 40 ethnic groups. The Christian population comprises 83.9 percent of the population (41.9 percent Roman Catholic; 42 percent Protestant).

In 1877, Henry Morton Stanley of the Christian Missionary Society (CMS) arrived in Uganda. Stanley's 1886 letter of appeal to Europe resulted in the arrival of many missionaries from both Protestant and Catholic mission agencies. The intervention of the British government after a civil war in 1892 eventually led to the declaration of Uganda as a British protectorate in 1894. Missionaries established schools and offered religious instruction and literacy. Thus, Christian education was primarily done through schools.

The Ugandan church was influenced by the East African Revival, which is believed to have originated in Rwanda in the 1930s (Ward 2002a, 2002b). Unfortunately, Uganda's postdependence era (after 1962) was characterized by unprecedented political instability, paralleled by religious conflicts (Korieh and Njoku 2007; Kasozi, Musisi, and Sejjengo 1994). During Idi Amin's rule (25 January 1971–11 April 1979), many Christian leaders and followers were killed or persecuted. Ugandan Christians were scattered throughout East Africa, and some became Christian leaders in diaspora. After stability was achieved in the 1980s, the young Ugandan church strengthened itself and has since grown to be a conspicuous government partner in providing Christian education in schools and social action projects (Stambach 2010). However, Christian education programs need to address historical animosities along denominational lines.

References and Resources

Kasozi, Abdu Basajabaka Kawalya, Nakanyike B. Musisi, and James Mukooza Sejjengo. 1994. *Social Origins of Violence in Uganda, 1964–1985*. Montreal, Quebec: McGill-Queen's University Press.

Korieh, Chima Jocob, and Raphael Chijioke Njoku, eds. 2007. *Missions, States and European Expansion in Africa*. New York: Routledge.

Stambach, Amy. 2010. *Faith in Schools, Religion, Education, and American Evangelicals in East Africa*. Stanford, CA: Stanford University Press.

Ward, Kevin. 2002a. *A History of Christianity in Uganda*. http://www.dacb.org.

——. 2002b. "'Tukutendereza Yesu': The Balokole Revival in Uganda." http://www.dacb.org.

—ROSEMARY WAHU MBOGO

UGANDA CHRISTIAN UNIVERSITY

The Christian Gospel came to Uganda in the years 1877–1879 with Anglican and Roman Catholic missionaries. Many of the first Ugandan converts, pages to the king of Buganda, were martyred in 1886. Subsequently, in fulfillment of Tertullian's comment that "the blood of the martyrs is the seed of the Church," Christianity took root and spread, and today more than 80 percent of the population is nominally Christian.

Bishop Alfred Tucker, the first Anglican bishop in Uganda (1890–1911), promoted indigenization of the church, which included building of schools like Gayaza High School for girls (1905) and Kings College Budo for boys (1906), both remaining prominent secondary schools to this day. In 1913, missionaries of the Church

Mission Society founded a seminary in Mukono, later named in Tucker's memory: Bishop Tucker Theological College. Bishop Tucker College educated clergy and teachers until 1997 and continues to this day as the Bishop Tucker School of Divinity and Theology of Uganda Christian University.

University education in Uganda was an elite preserve, sponsored by the colonial and later the national government until the 1990s, when pressure for wider access to education led the government to pass legislation for accrediting private universities in 2001. The three main religious bodies then founded universities: the Islamic University in Uganda (1998), Uganda Martyrs' University (Roman Catholic; 1993), and Uganda Christian University (Anglican; 1997).

In 1996, under the leadership of Archbishop Livingstone Nkoyoyo, the Anglican Church of Uganda authorized the formation of Uganda Christian University (UCU) on the site of Bishop Tucker Theological College in Mukono. Mukono proved a propitious location, because it is only 20 miles from the nation's capital, Kampala, yet it is outside the urban congestion. The theological college provided sufficient infrastructure to accommodate the first student bodies while the new university built up capacity for future growth.

In 1999, Rev. Prof. Stephen Noll was appointed the University's first vice-chancellor (president). Noll was an Episcopal priest who had served as academic dean of a start-up evangelical Anglican seminary in Pennsylvania in the United States. This experience equipped him to prepare UCU to receive the first charter (full accreditation) granted under the new government legislation. This chartering in turn made UCU the university of choice for many Ugandans and East Africans, and the number of students grew quickly, from 1,000 in 2000 to more than 10,000 in 2013.

Professor Noll introduced a model of the Christian liberal arts college from the United States, and UCU was the first African affiliate member of the Council for Christian Colleges and Universities in the United States and Canada (CCCU). Key elements of Christian identity included a statement of faith to be subscribed to by full-time faculty, core courses in Bible and theology for all students, and a dynamic chaplaincy.

Another feature of UCU's identity came from partner Christian institutions and ministries: a health administration program and a maternal health program from Canada; a radio programming ministry from the United States; and a semester abroad program for North American college students through the CCCU. Noll also founded a U.S. charity called Uganda Christian University Partners, which raised scholarships and capital funds for UCU.

In its first 15 years, UCU filled in its lovely hillside campus with 25 new buildings, capped by the $4 million Hamu Mukasa Library (2011). The university has constructed residence and dining halls on campus for about 1,500 students; many more students live nearby in off-campus hostels.

The original curriculum offered courses in theology, education, business, and social work. In 2000 an undergraduate law degree was offered, and that program has been popular and recognized as one of the two best in the country. Another popular course is mass communications. Beginning in the mid-2000s, UCU founded a faculty of science and technology, with courses in information technology, computer science, public health, nursing, environmental engineering, and agriculture with entrepreneurship. Most courses in the first years were offered at the diploma and bachelor's level. However, UCU now offers a variety of master's-level courses and a research PhD in theology.

As part of the original vision for UCU to become a "federal" university, regional campuses have been established in western Uganda (Bishop Barham University College in Kabale), in the north (Arua), and in the East (Mbale). UCU also has an inner-city Kampala campus for evening students. As UCU's reputation has grown, it has attracted "international" students from all neighboring countries, including a few from Western and Southern Africa.

In 2010, Rev. Canon Dr. John Senyonyi, a Ugandan educator and evangelist, became the second vice-chancellor. Dr. Senyonyi, who had served as university chaplain and deputy vice-chancellor since 2001, has continued the emphasis on holistic Christian higher education as "A Complete Education for a Complete Person."

Uganda Christian University has emerged over the past two decades as a forerunner and model of Christian higher education. In Uganda alone, there are more than 20 new private universities, half of these with religious affiliation. Several theological colleges in East Africa have converted to universities, in part out of economic necessity, but also with a vision of higher education as a mission opportunity to train up Christian leaders in Africa.

Resource

Noll, Stephen. 2013. "Higher Education as Mission: The Case of Uganda Christian University." In *Handbook of Theological Education in Africa*, edited by Isabel Apawo Phiri and Dietrich Werner, 912–917. World Council of Churches. Oxford: Regnum.

—Stephen Noll

UKRAINE AND CHRISTIAN EDUCATION

Ukraine was Christianized in 988 through the work of missionaries from Europe and Byzantium. Prince Vladimir the Saint and his son, Yaroslav the Wise (10th–early 11th centuries), supported the rise of church education, national teachers, and preachers. This led to a growth of culture both on the national level and ecclesiastically.

In the 21th century in Ukraine, there are 35,000 religious organizations representing 55 denominations of Christianity. The largest religious group is Orthodox Christianity, which includes the Ukrainian Orthodox Church Kyiv Patriarchate, the Ukrainian Orthodox Church Moscow Patriarchate, and the Ukrainian Autocephalous Orthodox Church. The largest non-Orthodox group is the Ukrainian Greek Catholic Church, followed by the Roman Catholic Church. Protestant groups, with the evangelical Baptists being the largest, also include Pentecostals, Seventh-day Adventists, Lutherans, Anglicans, Calvinists, Methodists, and Presbyterians. There are also the religious groups of Islam and Judaism. Other religious groups include Jehovah's Witnesses, the Church of Jesus Christ of Latter-day Saints (Mormons), Buddhists, Falun Gong, and adherents of Krishna consciousness.

Ukrainians can obtain theological education at Kiev Theological Academy and Seminary, Kyiv Orthodox Theological Academy, Ukrainian Catholic University, as well as at more than 60 various evangelical theological seminaries and colleges. Religious freedom in Ukraine is protected by the constitution and other laws and policies.

—Taras Dyatlik

Ukrainian Catholic University

Brief Historical Introduction, Including Christian Tradition

Ukrainian Catholic University (UCU) in Lviv is the first and only Catholic university on the territory of the former Soviet Union. It comes from the tradition of theological education of the Eastern/Byzantine rite Ukrainian Catholic Church, open to both Orthodox and Catholic theology. It trains priests and religious and lay leaders to serve the church and society in Ukraine and in the diaspora. It is run by the Ukrainian Catholic Church, which is the largest of the 22 distinct Eastern Catholic Churches in communion with the See of Rome. The establishment of the UCU in 2002 is the culmination of the hundred-year efforts of the Ukrainian Catholic Church to make its own contribution to ecclesial and cultural dialogue between the Byzantine East and Latin West.

With a few exceptions, most of the Eastern Catholic Churches historically emerged from an Eastern Orthodox tradition seeking communion with the Roman Catholic Church. Despite the fact that today the Eastern Catholic Churches sometimes are seen as an obstacle to unity between the Catholic and Orthodox Churches,

in the past some Orthodox Churches freely asked for reunion with Rome, retaining their distinctive theology; spirituality, liturgical, sacramental, and monastic practices; and canonical discipline. The Church of Kyiv, as the cradle of Slavic Christianity in Kyivan Rus', was a daughter church of the Patriarchate of Constantinople since the baptism of Kyivan Rus' in 988 by the Grand Duke Volodymyr. In 1596 the Orthodox Church, headed by the metropolitan in Kyiv, initiated the reunion with Rome at the Union of Brest and broke the communion with Constantinople. This event marked the establishment of the Uniate Church, which is nowadays referred to as "Greek-Catholic." In the wake of World War II, in 1946 Joseph Stalin ordered the forcible incorporation of the Ukrainian Greek-Catholic Church into the Patriarchate of Moscow, which found a modus vivendi with the Soviet atheistic regime. After the collapse of communism and Ukrainian independence in the 1990s, the underground Ukrainian Catholic Church, which was the largest outlawed ecclesial body in the world, began to revive its activity in Ukraine, including taking steps to reestablish higher educational institutions and seminaries.

Though formally established as a university in 2002, the UCU traces its history back to 1783 when, following the 10-year-long existence of the Greek Catholic General Seminary at the Church of St. Barbara in Vienna, the Greek Catholic Seminary in Lviv was established by Austrian emperor Joseph II. The seminary provided programs for the formation of priests from the lands of modern Ukraine, Hungary, and the former Yugoslavia. The next step was the establishment of the Greek Catholic Theological Academy in 1929 as a result of the efforts of Metropolitan Andrei Sheptytsky under the rectorship of Josyf Slipyj. Metropolitan Sheptytsky intended to create a single scholarly center, in which all seminarians, those intending to marry and those planning to be celibate, would have the same high level of theological formation. When the Soviet troops invaded Lviv in 1939, the Theological Academy was shut down, and the seminarians were repressed. During the second Soviet occupation in 1945, the academy was completely closed, and professors of the Academy—including its long-standing rector Josyf Slipyj, who after the death of Metropolitan Andrei Sheptytsky became head of the underground Ukrainian Greek Catholic Church—were exiled to Siberia. After Ukrainian independence in 1991, the Lviv Theological Academy was reestablished in 1994, and it received international accreditation in 1998. All Catholic and many non-Catholic educational institutions throughout the world recognized the bachelor of theology degree given to the first graduates of the LTA.

By learning, rethinking, and presenting the heritage of Eastern Slavic Christian tradition to the whole world, the

UCU strives to make its own contribution to dialogue between the Christian East and West. In 2006, the Ukrainian Catholic University in Lviv hosted a meeting of the Federation of European Catholic Universities (better known by its French acronym, FUCE). The federation unites all the Catholic universities of Europe and aims at coordination of various programs in these universities and cooperation between them. Meetings are conducted annually, but the 2006 meeting was the first to take place in a country that does not formally belong to the European Union. The Federation of Catholic Universities of Europe is a regional daughter organization of the International Federation of Catholic Universities established in 1924 and was canonically recognized by Pope Pius XII in 1949. At present the federation comprises more than 200 full and associated members from 1,300 Catholic universities around the world. The Ukrainian Catholic University has been a member of both organizations since 2003, representing not only Ukraine but also all of Eastern Europe.

Description of Most Notable Academic Programs

The university is open to representatives of all churches and denominations. Greek Catholics, Orthodox, Roman Catholics, Protestants, and Jews study and teach here. The UCU offers bachelor's and master's degrees in theology, history, social pedagogy, and journalism and graduate degrees in various subjects, with some 1,200 full- and part-time lay students and seminarians.

Faculty of Philosophy and Theology

The university has international and state accreditation of its bachelor's and master's degree programs. The study of the Bible, the writings of the church fathers, the liturgy, and the tradition of the church are at the center of a curriculum that begins with a thorough course in historical and systematic philosophy. The undergraduate curriculum provides students with a basic knowledge of the sources for philosophy and theology—from the ancient to the postmodern periods—while seeking to foster the students' capacity for critical reflection. There are requisite courses in systematic, moral, and pastoral theology; church history; and canon law.

The library of the Ukrainian Catholic University is a leading academic theological library in Ukraine, which is developing rapidly and has more than 140,000 volumes of academic literature, especially in theology and related disciplines.

Summary of Christian Philosophy and Mission of Education

The Ukrainian Catholic University is an open academic community living the Eastern Christian tradition and

forming leaders to serve with professional excellence in Ukraine and internationally—for the glory of God, the common good, and the dignity of the human person. The UCU sees its mission as a meeting point and a locus for dialogue between the church and society through academic investigation of and sharing in the spiritual riches of Kyivan Christianity.

—ROMAN ZAVIYSKYY

UKRAINIAN EVANGELICAL THEOLOGICAL SEMINARY

Ukraine was Christianized in 988 through the work of missionaries from Europe and Byzantium. Prince Vladimir the Saint and his son, Yaroslav the Wise (10th–early 11th centuries), supported the rise of church education, national teachers, and preachers. This led to a growth of culture both on the national level and ecclesiastically, lasting until the early 13th century, when Ukraine was conquered by the Mongols.

After the Mongol invasion, the church and national culture declined until the middle of 16th century, when many Protestant missionaries came to Ukraine. During this time several Jesuit missionaries arrived in Ukraine as well. The Jesuits placed a strong emphasis on education, planting schools where theology and secular subjects were taught. The Ukrainian Orthodox Church also founded its own Bible schools, such as the Academy at Ostrog Castle and the Kyiv-Mohilanska Academy, in 1631. The latter, enduring many decades of civil war in the 17th century, came to be known as the Kyivan Theological Academy in the 19th century. The same institution is known to have participated in the Russian translation of the Bible.

In the mid-19th century, Protestant missionaries again came to Ukraine. But they did not manage to found their own schools. Only after the collapse of the USSR in 1991 did evangelical churches begin to establish their Bible schools. Ukrainian Evangelical Theological Seminary (UETS) was one of these institutions.

The UETS was founded in Polyana (Western Ukraine) by the Union of Free Evangelical Churches of Ukraine in 1992 as a one-month training school. After its completion, it became clear that pastors, church planters, and other church leaders needed a more complete education. In response to that need, a one-year certificate-level program in Christian theology and ministry was started. In time, the school grew into a four-year bachelor of theology and Christian ministry program, which currently offers residential and modular forms of study. Later other programs emerged, providing training for other areas of church and mission activities. Key roles in the founding of the seminary were played by Bishop Vladimir

Gluhovskyi, Bishop Vasiliy Raitchinets', and Dr. Anatoliy Gluhovskyi, who was the first rector of the school.

The UETS campus is located in Pushcha-Vodytsya, in Kyiv (Ukraine's capital). The seminary also has five regional schools in various parts of Ukraine, together educating about 300 students a year. On the UETS campus, there is a special museum of the history of the evangelical movement in Eastern Europe, with a unique archive of periodicals published during the foundational years of the movement and during the time of Soviet persecution. The UETS library contains more than 20,000 Christian books in Russian, Ukrainian, English, and other languages. The seminary publishes its own theological magazine, *Christian Thought*. The UETS is actively involved in the Lausanne movement, diaspora ministry, mission work in Central Asia, the Caucasus and among Crimean Tatars.

Even though the seminary was founded to fulfill the needs of local churches and ministries in Ukraine, today its ministry has expanded to serve the needs of churches in approximately 15 countries of Eastern Europe, the Caucasus, and Central Asia. Seminary students and graduates serve in practically all of the countries of the former USSR and also in the United States, Canada, Iran, Iraq, Syria, and Turkey. The UETS is an evangelical, interdenominational school serving some 16 denominations and church unions. Presently, two UETS BTh programs are accredited by the European Evangelical Accrediting Association, with its MTL program being in the process of obtaining EEAA accreditation. In 2012, the UETS celebrated its 20th anniversary, with more than 1,000 graduates over its history. It offers seven academic programs, from certificate to master's level.

—Ivan Rusin

Uniform Lesson Series

Long after the popularity of the American Sunday School Union had faded, a small group of evangelical Protestant leaders, referred to as the Illinois Band, revitalized the Sunday school movement by developing, via a brilliantly organized volunteer network, a nationwide convention system (1869–1914), as well as the first International Sunday School Convention (1875). Two members of the Illinois Band, Chicago Methodist Episcopal pastor Rev. John Vincent and businessman and pioneer leader of the Illinois Baptist Mission Sunday School Benjamin Jacobs, provided fresh vision and strategy for widespread utilization of uniform Sunday school lessons. Uniform Sunday school lessons had been created in 1825 by the New York Association of Sunday School Teachers, but inattention from leaders of the first two National Sunday School Conventions (1832 and 1833) led to their demise.

John Vincent's regret about not attending college, along with a strong distaste for the excessive religious emotionalism of revivals, motivated him to devise various self-education strategies and shaped his preference for genuine, rational, and intelligent religious formation experiences. While he was a successful pastor of a prominent church, John Vincent's lectures, model lessons, and training institutes, aimed at professionalizing Sunday school teaching, provided substantial visionary leadership within the Chicago Sunday School Union.

During one of the teacher training institutes in 1865, Vincent raised the question: "Is it practical to introduce a uniform system of lessons into all our schools?" In that same year, he started a magazine that proposed, for the first time, a uniform lesson plan to potentially be followed by teachers in all evangelical denominations. In 1866, Vincent began a new system of Sunday school study, developing the Uniform Lesson Series, titled *Two Years with Jesus: A New System of Sunday School Study*. Another member of the Illinois Band, Edward Eggleston, completed the second year of this new course of uniform lessons. The uniform lessons were based on Vincent's belief that the entire Sunday school should study the same lesson for the sake of "concentration, repetition, definiteness, depth of impression and thoroughness" and a belief that uniform lessons would centralize the learning focus for the entire school. Vincent made this reasoning clear when he asked, "Would not all Christians hear God's voice speaking to them the same things if they were studying the same lesson?" (Lankard 1927, 206–207).

By 1900, more than three million Sunday school participants were using the lessons in several countries outside North America, including New Zealand, Australia, Japan, Korea, and China. Uniform lessons were translated into 40 languages and dialects for India. The popularity of the uniform lessons played a significant role in the widespread growth of the Sunday school under the leadership of the Illinois Band. Sunday school workers more than doubled during the 30 years following the 1875 convention.

Through the Uniform Lesson Series, adopted by the 1872 national Sunday school convention, potentially all children, regardless of denominational affiliation, would study the same scriptural lesson each week. It must be noted that the uniform lessons adopted at the 1872 convention bore great similarity to the uniform lessons promoted within the American Sunday School Union in the 1820s. The uniform lessons were written by an interdenominational international committee and promoted internationally by Benjamin F. Jacobs. Jacobs aimed at one lesson for all ages in all schools throughout the world by publication of the lessons in all religious and secular papers. Although Jacobs faced considerable criticism, he was successful in the international promotion of the uniform lessons. Among the critics, Europeans voiced concern that the uniform lessons failed to align with the liturgical church year, and the Chinese found the lessons unsuitable for the needs of the Chinese churches.

Although Vincent did not believe in having uniformity of the lesson text without age-appropriate adaptation of the material, the lessons were not child-centered, and the lesson material was more appropriate for adults than children. In addition to the age-appropriateness issue, critics voiced concerns that the lessons were almost entirely expository and exegetical, logical rather than psychological, and lesson-centered rather than learner-centered. Critics did acknowledge positive aspects, including opportunities for student expression via written response to lesson questions, and interesting Bible information (Lankard 1927).

These various concerns led to the development of the Improved Uniform Lessons. The Improved Uniform Lessons introduced topical lessons that attempted to begin with the life situation, yet they also failed to align with the learning needs of children. Dissatisfaction with the uniform lessons led to the introduction of the Graded Lessons around 1910. The essential foundational principle of the graded lessons was that the material of instruction must be determined by the needs and abilities of the students and relate progressively to the stages of their development. The Graded Lessons were based on a conviction that the religious life of childhood and youth is an unfolding process, and they offered biblical material that was better suited for children from a psychological standpoint. Graded lessons encouraged use of extra-biblical material and were more in touch with the needs, interests, and capacities of children.

The uniform-graded controversy was at the center of the debate between the "old timers"/conservative evangelical theology and the "progressives"/liberal theology. This controversy led to a decrease in participants in the international Sunday school, and denominations began to take control of the curriculum and management of the Sunday school. The "old timers" stuck to the Bible-centered approach, while the "progressives" embraced insights from social sciences.

The actual differences between uniform and graded lessons were, in reality, very modest, since Protestant Christian educational practice, especially since John Vincent, wanted the uniform lessons to be age-appropriate. Also, both the uniform lessons of Vincent and the graded lessons encouraged by the progressives had roots in a distaste for revivalism and a desire to promote a staged process of Christian growth. Vincent's approach was somewhat "progressive" for his time and context. His uniform lesson approach provided a means for more rational and more efficient Christian instruction, with its sacred value of scriptural authority.

At the root of these surface issues was the issue of the place of science in religion. Graded lessons were not just a means of more efficient instruction; they were a challenge to the Bible as a sufficient system of doctrine. They were viewed as an opening for modernism within the church. Graded lessons challenged the supremacy of the Bible and brought current events, biography, and historical studies into the church. They meant taking the Bible and beliefs apart to determine their value and that the traditional place of the Bible in Christian teaching was being challenged by the modern world of social science.

The deeper issues reflected in the uniform-graded controversy were central to the division between "old timers" and "progressives" regarding the purposes and practices of the Sunday school. These issues were at the heart of the modernist-fundamentalist debate, a controversy that involved the redefining of Christianity itself. Christian scholars throughout the 20th century, such as Clarence Benson, Lois LeBar, and Iris Cully, attempted to reconcile the theological, pedagogical, and philosophical differences between these distinct ideological streams, yet the deeper issues continue at the heart of many ongoing divisions within the 21st-century American Protestant church.

References and Resources

Boylan, Anne M. 1988. *Sunday School: The Formation of an American Institution, 1790–1880.* Westford, MA: Yale University, Murray Printing Company.

Boys, Mary. 1989. *Educating in Faith: Maps and Visions.* San Francisco: Harper & Row.

Lankard, Frank G. 1927. *A History of the American Sunday School Curriculum.* New York, Cincinnati, OH: Abingdon Press.

Lynn, Robert. 1980. *The Big Little School: Two Hundred Years of the Sunday School.* Birmingham, AL: Religious Education Press.

—BEVERLY JOHNSON-MILLER

UNITED KINGDOM THEOLOGICAL COLLEGES, COURSES, AND SEMINARIES

History

University education in the United Kingdom goes back to the 12th century, to a time when theology was foundational. The situation in England was paralleled in Scotland, though development within the two jurisdictions was separate. In the 19th century, London University was formed on a specifically secular basis, while in a separate move, around 40 Anglican teacher training colleges were formed to train staff for the large number of church schools that came into existence starting around 1840. By the mid-20th century, most universities had a theology department, and the theology studied was almost entirely Christian or biblical and dominated by Anglicans.

In a series of expansions of higher education in Britain from the 1970s onward, newer universities emphasizing technical and scientific subjects were founded. These ignored theology or, alternatively, rebranded the subject "religious studies." Religious studies (RS) were intended to be nonconfessional, and therefore nontheological, and to be largely descriptive of world religions. This development matched the changes taking place in schools, where the teaching of Christianity was beginning to be eclipsed by or mixed with Hinduism, Islam, Buddhism, and other faiths. Nevertheless, while new universities were being formed, many Anglican teacher training colleges were upgraded to university status, and most had a chapel on campus and were positive toward theology.

During the 1980s and 1990s, theology departments in the United Kingdom were under pressure from the government. The position of universities in the United Kingdom, as in most of Europe, is financially different from that of such institutions in the United States. Universities in the United Kingdom are funded by tax revenue, and this makes them susceptible to the imperatives of government policy. Where a combination of utilitarian philosophy and secularism is in force, theology departments have to justify their existence. Even departments that taught a mixture of theology and religious studies had to demonstrate their capacity to recruit students whose academic awards had currency on the job market. Moreover, many seminaries (Baptist, Methodist, Pentecostal, Jewish) preferred to retain control over the training of their students while at the same time securing validation from secular universities. This meant that a student wishing to study theology might choose either the secular environment of the university or the faith-based environment of the seminary and, at the end of the course, receive a BA or BTh of identical quality or value. By the end of the 1990s, about 50 percent of theology degrees were being earned on the campuses of validated seminaries or Bible colleges; this added to the vulnerability of university theology and RS departments, and many contracted or closed.

The result of these cultural changes was to force theology and religious studies departments to expand their postgraduate offerings. And then, by the first part of the 21st century, other pressures on theology were being caused by secularist presuppositions, so that, for instance, a theology department might find itself forced to combine with the law or philosophy department (with, for example, a philosopher heading the combined department) or shunted into "pastoral sciences" with

psychology. In Scotland, where traditional centers of excellence were found (e.g., St. Andrews or Edinburgh), theology was able to maintain its pure profile; in England, in ancient universities like Oxford, Cambridge, Durham, and King's London, there was a willingness to accept the discipline wholeheartedly. In universities that had grown out of Anglican training colleges (such as in Chester or Canterbury), there was a similar acceptance of theology's place on a modern campus; in such places, student numbers were healthy and graduates found their way into teaching, social work, the church, and a variety of other employments.

—WILLIAM K. KAY

UNITED STATES CHRISTIAN EDUCATION

The United States of America was formed because individuals were seeking freedom from religious persecution in other countries, such as England. This country was first settled by colonists who came to settle the new land because they wanted to freely practice their religious beliefs. When the first English colonists came to America, they brought with them their European customs. However, life in the colonies was very different from their lives in England, and as a result it was necessary for them to adapt to their surroundings. Some traditions were left behind or adapted to fit the new life in the new land. Before the United States was formally established, colonies were founded, beginning in 1607. The colonial period lasted through 1776, when the colonies banded together and revolted against England, subsequently forming the United States of America. There is evidence that before the revolution, the government was slightly involved in the education of the people. After the American Revolution and the establishment of a strong central government, there is evidence the government was very involved in making sure that individuals attending school would receive foundational religious education in Christianity.

The first religious groups who formed the northern colonies were the Pilgrims and the Puritans. It was not long before the Puritans' way of life became predominant. It also affected the educational system at that time. During the early years of establishing themselves in the new land, education was predominantly used to shape the standards by which people lived. Education was based on religious understanding. It was important that individuals learn how to read before learning other lessons, and because education at that time was centered on the Bible, the Bible was the first textbook used in training children to read. In the beginning, education was a means to teach obedience, reverence, and industry to young men. The teaching of girls was not totally neglected; however, it was not as extensive as education for boys. A Yale University graduate established the first all-girls school in 1780 in Middleton, Connecticut. Native Americans and African slaves were not considered eligible for education of any kind during this time.

Reading was taught systemically throughout the colonies. The family was the main social organization; therefore, homeschooling was the mode by which education was pursued. Children were taught by parents, siblings, peers, and other adults. The method most commonly used to teach reading was individual reading, responsive reading, in the home on a daily basis. This tradition was brought from England and carried over into the new land. When there was no one in the household able to teach the children, there would usually be an adult, a wife of a neighbor, nearby who could teach the children. This resulted in *dame schools* begin organized for the children to begin their education.

In the southern states, it the Anglican Church (Church of England) was predominant and dictated how education was administered to children. Since the Anglican Church regarded education as a private matter, it was a family matter, and the state was not involved. Children were educated at home, and those plantation owners who were financially able to do so hired private tutors for their households. Those who were not so well off would pay a fee for their children to be educated at private schools. All children learned spelling, writing, reading, and arithmetic. Girls were permitted to learn French, but were not permitted to learn Latin or Greek. Instruction for boys included Greek and Roman classics. When it was not possible to send children to private schools, plantation owners would pool their resources to buy a field not fit for planting, hire a teacher, and have a field school. Poor children did not receive instruction at this time and were more likely than not to seek apprenticeships to learn a trade.

When it became necessary for children to pursue higher education, schools were created for this purpose. However, though higher education was not neglected, it centered on preparing men for ministry. Universities and colleges were formed to teach and prepare men for ministry: Harvard was established as a primarily religious school in 1636 to train clergy; William and Mary was founded in 1693 to prepare students for ministry; Yale was founded in 1699 by 10 ministers to further Reformed Protestantism; Princeton was established in 1746 by Presbyterians; and the Baptists founded Brown University in 1764 during the religious revival known as the Great Awakening. The Catholics did not neglect establishing an institute for high learning as well: Georgetown University was formed in 1789 to train Roman Catholic clergymen. When slaves were permitted to be educated, institutes of higher education were founded to assist in their learning. Institutes such as Morehouse College and Howard University were established in 1867 to train ex-slaves to become teachers and preachers.

Early in the 17th century, the individual territories appeared to become involved in the education of the people. In 1624, the Virginia General Assembly passed a law to begin educating Native Americans. But it wasn't until 1717 that slaves and their offspring were legally allowed to be educated. The trend of the government being involved in the education of children becomes more evident after the Revolutionary War, when Congress approved the purchase of Bibles specifically for use in schools. A major milestone in teaching Christianity in schools was reached in 1844, when the U.S. Supreme Court ruled that American schools were to teach Christianity using the Bible. Another milestone occurred in 1890, when the Supreme Court ruled in the *Trinity* case that America was "a religious people. . . . [T]his is a Christian nation and their people would teach their children Christianity" (*Holy Trinity Church vs. United Stated States* 143 U.S. 457, 12 S. Ct. 511 36 L.Ed. 226).

At that time all textbooks had references in them to Christianity and the Bible. However, the Supreme Court began to reverse itself in 1948, ruling in *McCollum vs. Board of Education Dist. 71*, 333 U.S. 203 (1948), that setting aside time at school for prayer was unconstitutional. After this time the Supreme Court began to remove religious privileges in public schools, with, for example, the landmark ruling in 1963 in *Abington School District vs. Schempp*, 374 U.S. 203 (1963) and also *Murray vs. Curlett* 374 U.S. 203 (1963) stating that individual school prayer and Bible reading were not permissible in public schools. The education that children receive in the public school system today in no way resembles the education established by the forefathers of this nation.

References and Resources

Cremin, Lawrence, A. 1970. *American Education, The Colonial Experience, 1607–1783.* New York: Harper & Row.

Lascarides, V., Celia, and F. Hinity Blyth. 2000. *History of Early Childhood Education.* New York: Palmers Press.

Rudolph, Frederick. 1962. *The American College and University: A History.* New York: Alfred A. Knopf.

—Candace C. Shields

UNITED THEOLOGICAL COLLEGE OF THE WEST INDIES

Brief Historical Introduction Including Christian Tradition

United Theological College of the West Indies (UTCWI) was established in 1965 by the Anglican Church, Jamaica

Diocese, the Disciples of Christ in Jamaica, the Guyana Presbyterian Church, the Jamaica Baptist Union, the Methodist Church in the Caribbean and the Americas, the Moravian Church–Jamaica Province, the Presbyterian Church of Trinidad and Grenada, the United Church of Jamaica and the Cayman Islands,[1] and the Lutheran Church in Guyana. It was formally dedicated on 27 April 1966 and located in close proximity to the University of the West Indies (UWI), Mona Campus, Jamaica, West Indies, its main degree-granting institution. It continues to be an ecumenical seminary, with students attending primarily from various territories across the Caribbean and Americas. The role of the Theological Education Fund (TEF) of the World Council of Churches (WCC) in its formation is notable.

Antecedent institutions of UTCWI are Union Theological Seminary, formed by Methodists, Presbyterians (Jamaica), Moravians, Congregationalists, and Disciples of Christ; Calabar College, of the Jamaica Baptist Union; and St. Peter's College of the Anglican Church, Jamaica Diocese. Their leaders had a vision for ecumenism and made it a reality in a region of newly emerging nations that were seeking closer working relationships.

UTCWI sees itself as "the theology department within UWI,"[2] along with St. Michael's Theological College RC. In 1988, UTCWI began offering the doctor of ministry program cooperatively with Columbia Theological Seminary (CTS), Atlanta, Georgia, and it also confers degrees independently.

Description of Most Notable Academic Programs

UTCWI offers academic programs at the undergraduate, graduate, and postgraduate levels. With UWI, it offers a BATh in theology and in ministerial studies, an MA in theology, and the MPhil and PhD. It offers the DMin with CTS. Independently, UTCWI offers the certificate and diploma in ministerial studies, an associate's degree in ministerial studies, and an MDiv. UTCWI also has a Center for Continuing Education, focusing on lay leadership and offering certificate and diploma programs. Other significant programs are specialist training in HIV/AIDS counseling using the voluntary counseling and testing (VCT) method, CPE, and global exchanges with some North American seminaries.

The BATh is one of the foundational programs at UTCWI for anyone from any tradition for whom professional ministry will be a career. It is earned concurrently with the diploma in ministerial studies, which focuses on courses that offer more hands-on ministry experience.

Summary of Christian Philosophy and Mission of Education

UTCWI successfully combines various aspects of its identity: being Christian, being located in the Caribbean and the Americas, and having rigorous and outward looking ministerial preparation. It fosters an educational environment that allows for openness, multidirectional communication, and questioning. It also seeks to provide a biblically rooted moral compass and challenge for the Caribbean. Furthermore, UTCWI understands that to achieve excellence, priority must be given to engaging those who combine their commitment to teaching with research and outreach.[3]

This is the mission statement of UTCWI: "The United Theological College of the West Indies (UTCWI) as a Christian Institution, seeks to provide Theological Education in a student-centred [sic] environment that promotes spiritual, emotional and social development, and prepares men and women for mission and service."[4] Student leadership is especially seen in community outreach programs and meaningful participation in the governance of the institution.

UTCWI focuses on preparing people for ministry within their own traditions. This ecumenical institution educates people as they live, worship, serve together, and learn from each other. Its pedagogical processes facilitate inquiry and integrated learning. UTCWI's location in the Caribbean and Americas permeates all aspects of its life and educational strategies. It is a growing, dynamic seminary that constantly works to meet the ministry needs of a developing people in a developing region, exercising theological leadership therein, while ever extending its hand to a global world. It does this in harmony with its vision and mission.

References and Resources

Kuck, David, coordinator of graduate studies, United Theological College of the West Indies. 2013. E-mail message to author, 2 April.

Lewis, Marjorie, president, United Theological College of the West Indies. 2013. E-mail message to author, 9 March.

United Theological College of the West Indies. n.d.-a. "Bachelor of Arts in Theology." Accessed 1 April 2013. http://www.utcwi.edu.jm/Bachelor-of-Arts-Theology.

———. n.d.-b. "Our Mission, Vision and Aims." Accessed 1 April 2013. http://www.utcwi.edu.jm/our_mission_vision_aims.

---

1. The Disciples of Christ in Jamaica subsequently joined this denomination in 1992, which was then renamed The United Church in Jamaica and the Cayman Islands.

2. United Theological College of the West Indies, "Our Mission, Vision and Aims," http://www.utcwi.edu.jm/our_mission_vision_aims (accessed 1 April 2013).

3. Ibid

4. Ibid.

———. 2012. "The United Theological College of the West Indies: Who We Are." *The Tidings: Spiritual Sustainability and Academic Excellence* 3–4 (August–December): 7.
—CLAIRE ANNELISE SMITH

UNIVERSITY, MEDIEVAL DEVELOPMENT OF THE

The modern university is a wholly medieval creation—one of the most important and valuable contributions that the Middle Ages made to civilized life in Europe. Prior to the 12th century, universities had been preceded by monastic schools that provided a traditional literary education, generally for monks, and by cathedral schools, which originally were established to educate choirboys of cathedral churches and sometimes provided a free education to poor boys in cathedral cities. In many cases, it was the latter school that evolved into the university, by papal bull or charter.

Today the term "university" refers to the breadth of subjects taught (identified by "colleges"), but originally it referred to the international student population, particularly in the Italian universities, where students created an artificial citizenry that sometimes came into conflict with the city in which they were located.

At first there was no formalized or standardized program, and students in Italian universities basically ran the school as employers of the faculty; in universities outside of Italy, however, such as the University of Paris, the faculty were in control.

By the 13th century, universities in France, Italy, and Spain taught the liberal arts and three higher faculties (like graduate schools). The term "liberal arts" refers to those aptitudes or "skills" (Greek *artes*) that were taught in the ancient world to Greeks and Romans who were liberated or free (as opposed to those who learned trades or served as slaves). The curriculum was based on a twofold understanding of reality: the *trivium*—grammar, rhetoric, and dialectic or logic—dealt with transient signs that *point* to what is eternal; and the *quadrivium*—arithmetic, geometry, astronomy, and music—dealt with the eternal itself, which is unchangeable reality. One might spend up to five years studying for a bachelor's degree and an additional year or two for a master's degree, after which one could move on to the higher, more specialized subjects. Those subjects or higher faculties were civil and canon law (for which Bologna was famous), medicine (for which Salerno was famous), and theology (for which Paris was famous).

The typical teaching methods were lectures by the Master and disputations (debates) by students, who marshaled support for contrary positions from the Bible and early church fathers, all to be resolved by the response of the Master. The 12th-century theologian Abelard (1079–1142) typifies this approach in his book *Sic et Non* ("Yes and No"): a question or dilemma is posed (such as, "That God may do all things and that He may not"), followed by seemingly opposing views of biblical passages and church fathers (such as Chrysostom and Augustine, in this case), only to be resolved in such a way that one realizes the discrepancies were only apparent. This may reflect Plato's strategy of introducing seeming contradictions to motivate learning.

The liberal arts were the basis of all secular and sacred learning, and they undergirded biblical exegesis. As early as Augustine, Boethius, Cassiodorus, and Alcuin (fourth through ninth centuries), the goal of all education in the liberal arts was to learn for the sake of understanding scripture and the Latin fathers, and this held until the mid-13th century.

"Scholasticism" refers to the educational tradition of these medieval schools and universities. Among other things, it referred to the method of philosophical and theological speculation that aimed at a better understanding of revealed truth, especially by employing dialectic based on Aristotelian logic. Since the church was seen as the recipient and guardian of Truth, reason was employed for understanding the church's teaching. Before the cozy alliance of reason and faith began to break down in some circles during the mid-13th century, theologians were confident to use philosophy to explain and defend Christian truths (such as Anselm's logical explanation of why God had to become incarnate as a human being).

Following Augustine, belief preceded understanding. In fact, though he meant something slightly different from Augustine's notion of "understanding," in the 12th century, Anselm (1033–1109) said, "I believe in order that I may understand, and I believe that if I do not believe, I shall not understand." Even his argument for God's existence is couched in the context of a prayer.

In this same century, the word *theologia* was first used to describe the systematic statement of the Christian faith in the schools. The systematic arrangement of theological questions and their answers was called "Sentences." The most famous of these were written by Peter Lombard (1100–1160), and his *Four Books of Sentences* became *the* textbook in theological schools until the 16th century. Thomas Aquinas (1225–1274) produced the *Summa Theologica*, the crowning achievement of Scholastic theology. In the answers, biblical and patristic sources were relied on as the authorities to be investigated by reason and logic.

Among others, major theological issues that were discussed among the university Scholastic theologians had to do with the sacraments (such as penance and the Lord's Supper), the nature of Christ's atoning work, and whether society and the church are structured in ways that reflect eternal realities or are simply established according to somewhat arbitrary conventions (a debate under the rubric of "universals").

References and Resources

Dawson, Christopher. 1950. *Religion and the Rise of Western Culture*. New York: Doubleday.

Knowles, David. 1962. *The Evolution of Medieval Thought*. New York: Vintage Books.

Logan, F. Donald. 2002. *A History of the Church in the Middle Ages*. New York: Routledge.

—Dennis Okholm

University of Bologna

The University of Bologna was one of the earliest universities in Europe and is considered by some to be the very first. It originated in the High Middle Ages and served as one of the primary models for later universities. Its location in the northern city of Bolgona was important to the way the university began and developed.

Origins of the University

Some traditions hold that the University of Bologna was founded in 1088 as a guild of students. During the Middle Ages there were cathedral schools and monastic schools, most of which were controlled by bishops and abbots, and in which only clergy or orders taught and canon law and administration was the core subject.

However, scholars (secular as well as clergy) migrated to such large cities as Bologna. Students would move into the city and pay to attend scholars' lectures. Students were also responsible for securing and paying for their food and lodging. Students in Bologna comprised two groups: the "cismontanes" from south of the Alps and the "ultramontanes" from north of the Alps (many of whom were from Germany).

Students—and especially the ultramontanes—were vulnerable to real and perceived abuse by local authorities. In response, they began to organize into groups or guilds, as was common among medieval craftsmen. These guilds served as mutual aid societies that, typically, consisted of students of the same nationality. Hence, they were often referred to as "nations." Through these nations, students collectively negotiated with scholars from the city to teach them, set fees, etc. The agreed upon guidelines regulated the rights and the behavior of students and teachers alike. The student guilds also pressured the city for certain protections, fairer treatment, and equitable living costs. (The threat of a "migration" or mass exodus of students and faculty and the resulting economic impact was a major bargaining tool for the university.)

The Bolognan model of the university also included professors' being required to complete certain requirements to be allowed to teach. The model, then, was that of an independent and self-regulating institution, free from church and governmental control. Secular scholars taught there, and secular subjects (in addition to the liberal arts) were the core, with law becoming its most important area of study.

Development of the University

Teachers already approved to teach in the University of Bologna were so well-reputed that they were generally approved for teaching in other places of study, a practice known as *jus ubique docendi*, "the right of teaching everywhere." The university's graduates often enjoyed similar privileges.

In 1158, a panel of legal scholars from the University of Bologna affirmed certain rights of the Holy Roman emperor Frederick I, also known as Frederick Barbarossa, over some of those of the papacy. Though the school was already independent, Frederick responded by issuing a decree chartering the University of Bologna, formally granting it his imprimatur.

Soon after, the university added faculties of medicine and philosophy, which would bring added distinction to the university.

Contributions of the University

Scholars who studied and/or taught at the University of Bologna throughout its history represent a great range of clergy, theologians, artists, writers, and scientists, including Popes Innocent IX, Alexander VI, and Gregory XV, as well as Patriarch Heraclius of Jerusalem (12th century), Dante Alighieri, Nicolas Copernicus, Giovanni Cassini, and many others.

References and Resources

Janin, Hunt. 2008. *The University in Medieval life, 1179–1499*. Jefferson, NC: McFarland.

Jordan, William Chester. 2001. *Europe in the High Middle Ages*. New York: Penguin Books.

Reed, James E., and Ronnie Prevost. 1993. *A History of Christian Education*. Nashville, TN: Broadman & Holman.

—Ronnie Prevost

University of Cambridge

The University of Cambridge has long been an important center of Christian education. One only need survey the names of the old colleges (St. John's, Trinity,

Magdalene, Corpus Christi, Jesus, Emmanuel, Christ's) or view the magnificence of the many chapels to see the indelible imprint Christian tradition has left on the institution. Having come into being in 1209, the university received official papal recognition by 1233, and its earliest constituent college, Peterhouse (namesake St. Peter), was founded in 1284 by the bishop of Ely, Hugh Balsham. One of the oldest professorships in the world, and the oldest professorship of the university, is the Chair of Divinity, established in 1502 by Lady Margaret Beaufort, mother of King Henry VII. The figures associated with the University of Cambridge who have had some effect on the history of Christian education are almost too many to count. They include the "Oxford Martyrs"—Hugh Latimer, Nicholas Ridley, and Thomas Cranmer—who helped form and spread the English Reformation; John Harvard, who left an endowment in his will leading to the creation of Harvard College (later University), which was at first a center for training Congregationalists; and Isaac Newton, whose religious ideas had an influence on theism and natural theology.

Of particular note, members of Cambridge's Faculty of Divinity have played an important historical role in the production of critical Greek editions of early Christian literature. Christian humanist Desiderius Erasmus of Rotterdam (at Cambridge 1511–1515) initiated the process by collecting manuscripts to produce several critical editions of the Greek New Testament (1514–1535), each with its own corrections based on inclusion of newly found readings. Three and a half centuries later, B. F. Westcott and F. J. A. Hort published a modern critical edition of the New Testament (1881) that reflected a matured development in text-critical principles and access to a great breadth of manuscripts; it became the point of departure for subsequent critical editions. Westcott and Hort made up two-thirds of a group known as the "Cambridge Trio." The third member, J. B. Lightfoot, was responsible for producing a five-volume critical edition of the *Apostolic Fathers* (1885–1890). By demonstrating the authenticity and early dating of the Epistles of Ignatius and Clement, Lightfoot was able to disprove previous attempts to assign dates from the mid- to late second century to New Testament writings. This type of careful scholarship has remained a hallmark of biblical studies at the university, and the list of Cambridge professors renowned for this virtue is too long to include here.

Although the University of Cambridge was chartered in part by the Roman Catholic Church and later tied to the Church of England, it is now a public research institution independent of any single religious affiliation. There is no test of religious commitment required to complete a degree in any field, including religious studies and theology. The current Faculty of Divinity offers programs specializing in Hinduism, Buddhism, Islam, Judaism, and Christianity, with a number of subspecializations available. Nevertheless, the historical connection between Christianity and the university remains. The aforementioned Lady Margaret's Professorship is still held today, as are the Regius Professorship of Divinity (established by King Henry VIII in 1540) and the Norris-Hulse Professorship of Divinity (the product of a 1934 merger of two chairs that go back to 1777 and 1860, respectively). Because of the diversity of ideological viewpoints represented within the current Faculty of Divinity, it is difficult to attribute a particular ethos to Christian education at the university. Approaches to biblical studies range from use of historical-critical methods to application of identity construction theories and gender analysis. Approaches to theology range from investigation of traditional philosophical and systematic categories to utilization of game theory, evolutionary theory, and cognitive theories of religion. For those training for ordination, a number of theological training colleges, representing various Christian traditions (e.g., Roman Catholic, Church of England, Eastern, Methodist, Reformed), make up the Cambridge Theological Federation. Ordinands may be jointly enrolled in their respective colleges and the university as they prepare for ministry. In sum, Christian education at the University of Cambridge is best characterized by dialogue engendered by diversity.

References and Resources

Collinson, Patrick, Richard Rex, and Graham Stanton. 2003. *Lady Margaret Beaufort and her Professors of Divinity, 1502 to 1649.* Cambridge, UK: Cambridge University Press.

Leedham-Green, Elisabeth. 1996. *A Concise History of the University of Cambridge.* Cambridge, UK: Cambridge University Press.

McKim, Donald K. 1998. *Historical Handbook of Major Biblical Interpreters.* Downers Grove, IL; Leicester, UK: InterVarsity Press.

University of Cambridge, Faculty of Divinity. http://www.divinity.cam.ac.uk/

—S. BRIAN POUNDS

UNIVERSITY OF DIVINITY (MELBOURNE, AUSTRALIA)

Founded by a 1910 act of the Victorian State Parliament, with amendments in 1956, 1972, and 1990, MCD University of Divinity (previously known as the Melbourne College of Divinity) is the sixth oldest higher education organization in Australia and one of the oldest ecumenical institutions in the world.

The denominations involved in 1910 were Baptist, Church of England, Churches of Christ (by co-option), Congregational, Methodist, and Presbyterian. Currently the education provider comprises colleges in Adelaide, Melbourne, and Sydney of various ecclesial traditions: Baptist, Churches of Christ, Coptic Orthodox, Anglican (Episcopalian), Lutheran, Presbyterian Church of Australia, Roman Catholic, Salvation Army, and Uniting Church in Australia (a merger of Congregational, Methodist, and Presbyterian churches in 1977).

There are several affiliated colleges. Australian Lutheran College in North Adelaide, South Australia, is the postsecondary education provider of the Lutheran Church of Australia. The Catholic Theological College in East Melbourne, Victoria, is a federation of autonomous seminaries, and diocesan and religious orders of the archdioceses of Melbourne and Hobart, the dioceses of Ballarat, Sandhurst and Sale, the Oblates of Mary Immaculate, the Salesians of Don Bosco, and the Conventual Franciscan Friars. Morling College, a Baptist theological college in Macquarie Park, New South Wales, is the theological college of pastoral and related ministries for accreditation in the state of New South Wales and the Australian Capital Territory Baptist churches.

The Sentir Graduate College of Spiritual Formation coordinates MCD University of Divinity courses in Christian spirituality and spiritual direction. The institute collaborates with other centers of spiritual formation, particularly the WellSpring Spirituality Centre in Ashburton and the Campion Ignatian Spirituality Centre in Kew, Victoria, to offer specialist graduate certificate and diploma courses in addition to the master of arts in spirituality and spiritual direction. The Catherine Booth College of Ministry in Parkville, Victoria, focuses on the training of Salvation Army officers. St. Athanasius Coptic Orthodox Theological College was established in 2000 and is the tertiary education institution of the Coptic Orthodox Diocese of Melbourne. The college is named after the doctor of the church, St. Athanasius the Apostolic (20th pope of Alexandria), who stood in defense of the biblical doctrine of Christ. SACOTC is the first Coptic Orthodox Theological College in the world to receive accreditation.

Stirling Theological College (formerly the Churches of Christ Theological College) in Mulgrave, Victoria, is an agency of the National Conference of Churches of Christ in Australia and a partner department of the Victorian and Tasmanian Conference of Churches of Christ. The United Faculty of Theology in Parkville, Victoria, is a cooperative venture in theological education involving three independent theological institutions who share staff and teaching facilities: the Jesuit Theological College (Roman Catholic), Trinity Theological School (Anglican), and the Uniting Church of Australia (Synod of Victoria and Tasmania) Theological College.

Established in 1891, Whitley College in Parkville is the Baptist College of Victoria and a residential college of the University of Melbourne. A wide range of theological studies are possible at Whitley, whose mission is to equip women and men for leadership in church and society. Finally, Yarra Theological Union in Box Hill, Victoria, is a center of theological and ministerial education comprising the religious institutes of the Blessed Sacrament Congregation; Divine Word Missionaries; Discalced Carmelites; Dominicans; Franciscans (OFM); and Missionaries of the Sacred Heart, Pallottines, Passionists, and Redemptorists (Australia and New Zealand).

The ecumenical consortium has its headquarters in Kew, Victoria, and was affiliated with the University of Melbourne in 1993 while retaining its autonomy and degree-conferring status. Committed to ecumenical collaboration in theological education, faculty and students participate with the association through a college that follows its particular spiritual heritage, while contributing to the theologically diverse community of scholarship. "MCD University of Divinity therefore participates proudly in a collaborative effort that seeks to achieve collectively what member institutions could not accomplish individually." Accredited to teach courses in philosophy and religious studies, as well as housing a center for the study of Christian spirituality, the institution aims to fulfill its motto of *Qui est ex Deo verba Dei audit* (The one who is from God hears the words of God; John 8:47).

In 2001, the Australian government recognized the MCD as a Schedule 1 higher education institution, and it became eligible to receive federal funding for research and Australian and international postgraduate research scholarships. Further, the Higher Education Support Act of 2003 allowed MCD students to receive federally funded loans under the FEE-HELP scheme. Recognized as one of the leading research establishments in the nation by the Australian Research Council in 2010, MCD offers extensive library facilities, including the online Research Repository, which is used to store and publicize faculty and postgraduate research, in addition to publishing an academic journal, *Pacifica*.

The theological syndicate was one of three self-accrediting institutions in Australia issuing degrees while not being recognized as a university. Then in 2012 the organization became the first body of higher education in Australia to be granted "specialized university" status by the Victorian Regulations and Qualifications Authority. In that same year it became known as the "MCD University of Divinity," with Peter Sherlock appointed as its first vice-chancellor.

—Robert L. Gallagher

UNIVERSITY OF HALLE

History

The University of Halle was founded on 12 July 1694 in the city of Halle, Germany, located along the banks of the Saale River. Around 1817, the University of Wittenberg and Halle merged to form one institution, named United Frederick University, and all teaching ceased in Wittenberg. In 1933, the university changed its name again, to Martin Luther University Halle-Wittenberg. Under Nazi rule during World War II, the authorities forced the university to expel politically and racially undesirable persons.

Whereas Wittenberg was a stronghold of Lutheranism, with faculty members like Martin Luther and Philipp Melanchthon, from the beginning the University of Halle was open to all theological traditions and denominations. It closed its doors during World War II for about a year, but when it reopened in 1946, the university operated under communist ideology (Zumkeller 2001).

Educational Influence

The university had a powerful influence on education in Europe and the United States. The primary reason for this was the presence of August Hermann Franke (1663–1727) on the faculty. Franke's rationalism, combined with his warm-hearted Pietism, made him a unique blend of head and heart educationally. While he insisted on rigorous academic preparation for his brightest and most promising students, he also wanted to see knowledge and theology translated into life. John Amos Comenius (1592–1670) influenced many of his educational views, in particular the home and parents as the primary center and teachers of children. In Franke's view, the teacher was in loco parentis and therefore had to have the highest character and serve as an appropriate role model for students to imitate. This was extremely important, since Franke insisted that teachers and students live together at the school.

From Comenius, Franke and the university also learned the concept of sense realism and from Bacon (1561–1626) the importance of the scientific method and the role of observation of facts through the application of inductive reasoning. The educational approach of the university in all of its various manifestations was emphasis on the facts of nature and the appropriate use of teaching methods. One of the most unique way students were encouraged to investigate firsthand the universe God created was through the cabinet of artifacts and curiosities. The university acquired, built, or purchased a number of visual aids that enabled students to not only understand a concept or theory but actually see it operate. This collection became so prolific that it became necessary to house it in a separate room in the orphanage building on the campus. The university has maintained the collection, and it is available for visitors even today. The teaching aids included a human fetus, a human skull, stuffed animals, flora and fauna from around the world, a mineral and coin collection, and cult objects of world religions. They also included representative clothing from different nations, death masks, a weapons collection, various mechanical devices, a miniature solar system built on the Copernican model, models of Dutch frigate ships, and many oil paintings and artifacts brought back by missionaries serving around the world. The most prominent oil painting is that of the Brandenburg-Prussian ruling family, who provided financial support to help start the collection toward the end of the 17th century.

The university served as an incubator for a host of auxiliary enterprises that sprang up over the years to augment the primary educational endeavors: a trade school, a school for girls, a Bible publication enterprise called the Bible Institute, the Oriental Seminary, a common school, an orphanage, a teacher training academy, a high school, a bookstore, a widows' home, a laundry, a home for beggars, a Latin school, a chemical laboratory, and a drugstore (Brown 1996). These were all started in faith and continued by faith, trusting God to provide for their continuation through the gifts of God's people.

One of the least appreciated educational influences of the university was the creation, under the leadership of Franke, of the Oriental Seminary (*collegium orientale theologicum*) in 1702. Students enrolled in this course of study prepared for church ministry and received instruction in biblical languages, preaching, and pastoral theology in a curriculum that lasted between four and six years. Students had to read the Old Testament in Hebrew and the New Testament in Greek without the aid of translations, which Franke often found woefully inadequate. He even had the audacity to criticize Luther's translations from the original Hebrew and Greek, offering suggestions for improvement (Schroeder 1963). He was a competent theologian in his own right and often published his works in German, for which he was criticized because he was "casting pearls before swine."

Missionary Influence

In 1651, the faculty of the University of Wittenberg produced a white paper on the continuing validity of the Great Commission of Jesus. The opinion included three essential points: (1) Jesus only gave the Great Commission to His disciples, not to the church; (2) unbelievers are assumed to have rejected the Gospel and are not the concern of the church; and (3) rulers are responsible for propagating the Gospel in their own regions. When the university wanted to send missionaries to India in the early 1700s, the Lutheran church would not ordain them to missionary service because of the white paper produced by the Wittenberg faculty. About this same time, Frederick IV of Denmark, who was concerned about the continued expansion of Roman Catholic missionaries around the world, heard about the University of Halle through his royal chaplain, who was a graduate of the university (Mulholland 1999).

Upon the request of Frederick IV, the university sent out its first missionaries to India in 1706. From that time forward, the university was a hub for missionary enterprise and activity around the world. Today one may visit the museum located on the campus of the university and see the artifacts collected by Halle's missionaries from around the world.

Students were regularly recruited from the classroom to the mission field. When Halle sent out missionaries, it also provided support that made their work even more effective. Many of Halle's missionaries translated the Bible into the local vernacular, and then the university would print copies of those translations at its Bible Institute printing house. The missionaries sent out from Halle had to learn the language of the people with whom they worked, and they often sent very detailed reports back to the university describing the culture and customs of those people.

Pietistic Influence

The University of Halle was the center of Pietistic influence in Europe, Scandinavia, and America. The Pietistic influence emanated from Franke, who accepted a nonpaying teaching position at the university in 1691 due to the influence of Phillip Spener (1635–1705). Several years later, he assumed the chair of the Department of Theology, and he continued teaching at the university until his death. A saying current in the heyday of the university was that, "he who goes to Halle returns either a Pietist or a Rationalist" (Brown 1996).

While later Pietism, especially the American kind, could often be legalistic and antiworldly, early Pietism, although sincere and at times austere, was more tolerant than it is often portrayed. The university established a brewery at one point in its history and even allowed its missionaries to keep polygamous marriages in Africa and the Caribbean intact, believing that they had been ordained of God (Brown 1996).

References and Resources

Brown, D. 1996. *Understanding Pietism.* rev. ed. Nappanee, IN: Evangel Publishing House.

Mulholland, K. 1999. "From Luther to Carey: Pietism and the Modern Missionary Movement." *Bibliotheca Sacra* 156: 85–95.

Schroeder, P. 1963. "August Hermann Franke, 1663–1963." *Concordia Theology Monthly* 34: 664–668.

Zumkeller, W. 2001. "The University of Halle through the Centuries." *Molecular Pathology* 54: 36–37.

—Stephen D. Lowe

University of Notre Dame

Established in 1842, the University of Notre Dame du Lac is a Roman Catholic institution founded by a priest (Edward Sorin) of the Congregation of Holy Cross. Notre Dame is a research university located adjacent to the city of South Bend, Indiana. From the beginning of the university's history, collegiate instruction was provided only in the studies that were then regarded as equipping students with a liberal education. University admission is decidedly competitive, as evident in the fact that 70 percent of arriving freshmen were ranked in the upper 5 percent of their high school graduating classes. Nearly 80 percent of the student population is Caucasian and Roman Catholic, and although the university has continuously attempted outreach to minority students (the percentage of whom has tripled over the past couple of decades), nevertheless, this lack of diversity is the institution's greatest weakness. The university has lessened resistance to Roman Catholicism by yearly admitting a significant number of non-Catholic students, which has also encouraged religious sentiment among those characterized as indifferent. The Indiana General Assembly normally consults the university if proposed legislation would affect the Roman Catholic Church, and any remonstration is respectfully considered. Notre Dame is generally rather conservative; nevertheless, the Standing Committee on Gay and Lesbian Student Needs grants verbal expression to homosexuals, who are treated with respect by both faculty and students.

The mission of education at the University of Notre Dame has been consistently related to principles such as living in community and volunteering in community service. Residence hall life is a distinctive characteristic of the academic experience at Notre Dame and is the seminal basis of the university's abundant tradition. The Center for Social Concerns, which serves as the stimulus for student volunteerism, is one of the more recent dynamics of the university's tradition. Approximately 80 percent of students are engaged in some capacity of volunteer service—throughout their study programs at the university—and no less than 10 percent devote time after graduation to meeting the needs of the less fortunate both nationally and abroad. Notre Dame's distinctive influence on the church in the Midwest is evident from its foundation, which was during a time when Catholic missionaries were urgently needed, and being located within a focus of missionary activity, the university assisted the stalwart expansion of Roman Catholicism in the Northwest. Ave Maria Press was established in 1865, which published a weekly literary and religious magazine (the *Ave Maria*) for 105 years, and continues to publish significant Catholic authors, in addition to being recognized as a leader in publishing Catholic high school religion textbooks.

Undergraduate schools include the College of Arts and Letters, College of Engineering, College of Science, Mendoza College of Business, and School of Architecture. The most popular majors include accounting, business administration and management, finance (general), and political science and government (general). The quality of the university's undergraduate programs is evident in the achievement of its students in postbaccalaureate studies. Established in 1918, the Graduate School has four divisions: engineering, humanities, science, and social sciences. Founded in 1869, the Notre Dame Law School is the oldest Catholic school of law in the United States; it is consistently ranked in the highest tier in various rankings. Programs at the Law School include international human rights, which is sponsored by the School's Center for Civil and Human Rights. In 1968, the Law School began a study abroad program in London, and it currently offers a program in international and comparative law at the Notre Dame London Law Centre. The mission of international studies at the university is to facilitate global learning and make research experiences possible that will enhance the academic, intercultural, and spiritual formation of students, in addition to enriching their cultural and global awareness, thereby serving to develop citizens who are meaningfully engaged internationally and thus leaders in a global world. More than 40 international study programs are offered in 20 nations, in addition to a domestic program in Washington, D.C. The school competes in NCAA Division I-A athletics, and its mascot is the fighting Irish leprechaun. Notre Dame's distinctive buildings include the 14-story Hesburgh Library, the Basilica of the Sacred Heart, and the historic Main Building (wherein the famed golden dome resides). The foundation of the university's academic prowess is its faculty. Since 1999, faculty members have received 46 fellowships from the National Endowment for the Humanities, which is more than any university in the United States.

References and Resources

A Brief History of the University of Notre Dame du Lac, Indiana from 1842 to 1892. 1895. Chicago: Werner.

Hesburgh, Theodore M. 1990. *God, Country, Notre Dame.* New York: Doubleday.

Langford, Jim, and Jeremy Langford. 2005. *The Spirit of Notre Dame.* New York: Doubleday.

Moloney, William Alan. 1907–1912. "Notre Dame du Lac, University of." In *The Catholic Encyclopedia,* edited by Charles G. Herbermann, 11: 132–133. 15 vols. New York: Encyclopedia Press.

Schmuhl, Robert. 1986. *The University of Notre Dame.* Notre Dame, IN: University of Notre Dame Press.

—RON J. BIGALKE JR.

UNIVERSITY OF PARIS (SORBONNE)

Historical Introduction

One of the oldest universities in the world, the University of Paris dates back to the 13th century in the formal sense, but a longer formative period occurred prior to that, in which guilds of scholars came together to form collegiums in order to engage in intellectual dialogue. In the 12th and 13th centuries, a *stadium generale* was an institution of higher learning authorized by the pope or emperor (Verger 1992, 35). In the 12th century, master teachers such as Peter Abelard and Hugh of St. Victor attracted many students to Paris from all over Europe (Kibre 2003, 886). There was a desire for education in the Christian faith and heightened intellectual interest in religion. Due to the influx, some of the masters attached to the Cathedral School of Notre Dame began to teach outside the school in the left bank of Paris. This association of masters was formally chartered in 1200 by King Philip. Between 1208 and 1215, the university obtained papal sanction (Kibre 2003, 887). The "Sorbonne" is actually a misnomer that refers to the Faculty of Theology of the University of Paris. The Sorbonne was one of the colleges and residences of doctoral candidates, named for French theologian Robert de Sorbon. The school has an illustrious history, defining issues of academic freedom and relationships between schools and the church that remain relevant today. Early on, there was conflict with the Holy See over jurisdiction, but at the height of its influence the school had the support of various popes and kings of France. It contributed to the development of doctrine and moral teachings. Bitter tensions arose between secular masters and the mendicant religious orders (Dominicans and Franciscans) at the school over their autonomy and possible exemption from some of the obligations required of secular scholars. The revolutionary ideas of the friars came into conflict with the vested interests of the school, and the secular masters feared the growing power of the mendicants. Riots and violence resulted (Leff 1968, 2, 15). Throughout the 14th century, Paris and Oxford had the most prominent faculties of theology and they, plus Cambridge, were the only universities with the right to confer degrees in theology (Asztalos 1992, 414).

The University of Paris became a key site for theological debates leading up to the Reformation. The orthodox Faculty of Theology opposed humanism and led the censure of new biblical interpretation. The Parliament of Paris decreed that all books dealing with religion had to be submitted to the Faculty for approval. On 15 April 1521, the Faculty of Theology formally condemned Martin Luther. In 1527, they forbade the publication of vernacular translations and new translations of the Latin Bible. This was followed by the censure of Erasmus (Hillerbrand 1996, 88). The Faculty produced 26 Articles of Faith in 1543 and an Index of Prohibited Books to affirm Catholic doctrine that was being challenged by Protestant reformers. The French Parliament, in corporation with the Faculty, continued to prosecute dissenters in inquisitional court (Hillerbrand 1996, 89). The Western Schism of the Church in 1378, in which the university took sides, caused students and some faculty to depart. The Faculty was also consulted on the trial of Joan of Arc and in the matter of Henry VIII's divorce from Catherine of Aragon. The university was suppressed during the French Revolution but reopened by Napoleon in 1808.

Academic Programs

In the medieval period, the University of Paris consisted of four faculties: theology, canon law, medicine, and arts. The first three were considered "graduate" or higher faculties, and members had to hold a doctorate. The Faculty of Theology was considered the leading school in Western Europe and was influential in ecclesial and political affairs in the early 13th century. The first Parisian printing press was installed at the university in 1472, which allowed faculty to publish works of scholastic theology. By 1500, almost all teaching was carried out in one of the approximately 40 colleges of the university. Young boys studied with individual masters to prepare for examinations, and if they passed several levels of exams, they were granted the baccalaureate and might enter one of the graduate schools. After acquiring a master of arts, a man who wanted to pursue the doctorate in theology had to undergo 13 to 15 additional years of study. The Bible and the *Sentences* of Peter Lombard formed the core of the curriculum (Farge 1985, 4, 8, 11). The method of instruction was generally lecture and commentary and gloss on a specific text (Kibre 2003, 887). It was an arduous process, requiring not only intellectual stamina, but also socialization and character formation.

Summary of Philosophy and Mission

The philosophy of Scholasticism dominated the medieval European university, which employed dialectical reasoning to defend biblical truth, until the rise of humanism and modern empirical science.

At the height of its influence in the 13th and 14th centuries, the University of Paris attracted many renowned theologians and educators, including Thomas Aquinas, Bonaventure, and Duns Scotus. Jean de Gerson (1363–1429) served as chancellor and was known for his special interest in the education of the young. He wrote *The ABCs for Ordinary Folk*, which contained lists of Christian beliefs, and *On Drawing the Little Ones to Christ*.

The early mission of the school was to offer superior education to train doctors of theology in service to the church. The Faculty of Theology exemplifies the struggle over doctrine and the role of theologians in shaping the mission of the church. Today the University of Paris is a public research university with more than 20,000 students, 17 departments, and 1,300 teachers and research professors on 12 campuses. The chapel is the only building standing of the original structures (www.english.paris-sorbonne.fr).

References and Resources

Asztalos, M. 1992. "The Faculty of Theology." In *A History of the University in Europe*. Vol. 1, edited by W. Rüegg, 409–441. Cambridge, UK: Cambridge University Press.

Farge, J. K. 1985. *Orthodoxy and Reform in Early Reformation France: The Faculty of Theology of Paris, 1500–1543*. Leiden: E.J. Brill.

Hillerbrand, H. J., ed. 1996. *The Oxford Encyclopedia of the Reformation*. Vol. 2. New York: Oxford University Press.

Kibre, P. 2003. "Paris, University of." In *New Catholic Encyclopedia*. 2nd ed., 10:886–890. Detroit: Gale Virtual Reference Library.

Leff, G. 1968. *Paris and Oxford Universities in the Thirteenth and Fourteenth Centuries: An Institutional and Intellectual History*. New York: Wiley.

Thijssen, J. 1998. *Censure and Heresy at the University of Paris, 1200–1400*. Philadelphia: University of Pennsylvania Press.

Verger, J. 1992. "Patterns." In *A History of the University in Europe*, edited by W. Rüegg, 1:35–68. Cambridge, MA: Cambridge University Press.

—SUSAN WILLHAUCK

UNIVERSITY, THE

Christian education has been propelled down through the centuries by the institution known as the university. During the medieval period, cathedral schools and guilds were formed to provide focused training and build literacy among the clergy. As these entities grew, they developed into learning centers that brought together scholars and students. Many things have changed over the years, but the basic process of and passion for providing a solid Christian education to priests, pastors, missionaries, and lay leaders has not changed since the first university was founded in 1088.

Three factors marked the medieval university: its corporate character, its special privileges and immunities, and its protection. Corporations were uncommon in medieval times, which made these universities stand out. Privileges and immunities were granted to students and faculty as incentives to stay located in that city. Protection was developed for student and faculty against improperly priced housing and other necessities in the local communities. Universities enjoyed these benefits due to the power they had in granting licenses to teach anywhere in orthodox Christendom and to the prestige they gave the community.

The university was originally a society of teachers and scholars called *universitas societas magistrorum discipulorumque*, meaning the university, or society, of masters and students. The first universities had no buildings or equipment and were not bound to their cities. With their primary aim of professional training, they maintained a certain freedom and independence from any governing body or local authority. The corporate character of the medieval university could be seen in a guild of tradesmen or a guild of teachers and students. These people gathered as a unit and became a legal corporation. As they grew in size, these corporations organized themselves into specific guilds to maintain common interest; provide support; and develop communal understanding, partnership, and sentiment among them.

The medieval church wanted people to attend the university so that they could be prepared to serve as clergymen and leaders with a basic set of knowledge and experiences. The university provided the molding environment to allow the church to educate Christians and license them to go teach others. The standardized licensing for completing the university training provided the church a baseline for appointments anywhere in the church's realm.

The original universities had three higher professional faculties: theology, law, and medicine. A fourth, lower faculty, called the arts, developed for study in preparation for entering one of the upper three. Universities typically focused on one type of professional training, yet offered the other two. An example is the University of Paris, which was a theology school, whereas the University of Bologna was a law school. Christian universities provided and continue to provide a biblical worldview and integrate scripture into every facet of life. Christian education, scholarship, and research have been primary products of Christian universities, along with the development of countless well-trained priests, pastors, missionaries, and godly leaders.

Many modern universities were originally founded to train clergy based on Christian doctrine. Harvard, Yale, Oxford, Cambridge, Paris, and other universities were established to teach theology and train ministers of the church. Latin was the common language used at the early universities, and it fostered internationalism between students and faculty from many countries. Foundational to their success, using Latin as a common language created a unity among students and teachers from all nationalities. This common language drew people from all over Christendom and created a significant loyalty to the church and the Papal Curia. Currently, modern universities utilize technology to teach all nations over great distances in their own languages.

References and Resources

Duggan, Stephen. 1936. *A Student's Testbook in the History of Education*. New York: D. Appleton-Century.

Eby, Frederick. 1952. *The Development of Modern Education: In Theory, Organization, and Practice*. 2nd ed. Englewood Cliffs, NJ: Prentice-Hall.

Eby, Frederick, and Charles Arrowood. 1940. *The History and Philosophy of Education Ancient and Medival*. New York: Prentice-Hall.

Graves, Frank. 1915. *A History of Education During the Middle Ages and the Transition to Modern Times*. Vol. 2. New York: Macmillan.

Haskins, Charles. 1923. *The Rise of Universities*. New York: Henry Holt.

Holmes, Arthur. 1975. *The Idea of a Christian College*. Rev. ed. Grand Rapids, MI: Eerdmans.

Kennedy, James, and Jerry Newcomer. 1994. *What If Jesus Had Never Been Born?* Nashville, TN: Thomas Nelson.

Knight, Edgar. 1940. *Twenty Centuries of Education*. Boston: Ginn and Company.

Moore, Ernest. 1938. *The Story of Instruction: The Church, the Renaissances, and the Reformations*. New York: Macmillan.

Norton, Arthur. 1909. *Readings in the History of Education: Mediaeval Universities*. Cambridge, MA: Harvard University Press.

Payne, W. 1886. *History of Pedagogy*. Boston: J.S. Cushing & Co. Printers.

Rait, Robert. 1912. *Life in a Medieval University*. Cambridge, UK: Cambridge University Press.

Rashdall, Hastings. 1936. *The Universities of Europe in the Middle Ages*. New ed. Edited by F. M. Powiche and A. B. Emden. Oxford: Oxford University Press.

Ringenberg, William. 2006. *The Christian College: A History of Protestant Higher Education in America*. 2nd ed. Grand Rapids, MI: Baker Academic.

Sandys, John. 1936. *A History of Classical Scholarship*. Cambridge, UK: Cambridge University Press.

Schachner, Nathan. 1938. *The Medieval Universities*. London: George Allen and Unwin.

Ulich, Robert. 1965. *Three Thousand Years of Educational Wisdom: Selections of Great Documents*. Cambridge, MA: Harvard University Press.

Walden, John. 1912. *The Universities of Ancient Greece*. New York: Charles Scribner's Sons.

Wilds, Elmer, and Kenneth Lottich. 1970. *The Foundations of Modern Education*. 4th ed. New York: Holt, Rinehart and Winston.

—STEVE YATES

URBAN CONTEXTS, EDUCATING CHRISTIANS IN

While the urban environment presents many opportunities for sharing the Gospel, it also presents a number of challenges. Cities typically include areas of great wealth, often juxtaposed with areas of considerable deprivation and marginalization. They are composed of many tightly packed "mini-villages," small community units sometimes with fiercely separate and independent identities. These very different communities have very different needs in relation to Christian learning. The focus of both Christian mission and social action has tended to be on the areas of deprivation and marginalization, where the need is *perceived* to be greatest. Little attention has been given to the business and affluent residential areas where, in some places, the population might be characterized as materially wealthy and spiritually poor.

In some respects, the marginalized may seem to be particularly open to the Gospel message—"I come to bring Good News to the poor" (Luke 4:18), "Blessed are the poor" (Matt. 5:3), and so forth—particularly as they often exhibit a strong hospitality and community ethic. However, obstacles present themselves in the form of chaotic lifestyles, overwhelming pastoral and social needs, sometimes local conflict or violence, and often a vast cultural disconnect between those bringing the message (usually from more privileged backgrounds and cultures) and those receiving it. Traditional formal approaches to education are often fiercely resisted because they are culturally inappropriate.

Because there are challenges that are specific to urban contexts, some Christian mission agencies have specialized in developing Bible engagement in such areas. The primary principle is that the work is contextualized. In other words, it is essential that educators take the time to listen thoroughly first and come to know and understand the local culture within which they are working, then shape their approach to that culture appropriately.

Approaches that have been successful are strongly relational and rely on a considerable investment of time and effort in building trust. They engage the strengths of marginalized urban communities: their ability to be spontaneous, resourceful, and creative. They focus on working with people in small community groups, rather than individually or in larger church groups. They rely on storytelling, rather than printed texts.

The most productive starting point is people's own stories. Skilled facilitators are able to help people make connections between their own day-to-day lives and the scriptures. The use of active creative techniques—art, film, music, drama—with people working together in small groups to make or do things, has been found to be particularly effective. It creates an unforced space with creative energy in which further thinking and discussion can develop, leading to greater insights and sometimes to group actions within the wider community.

These approaches have been formulated by "Unlock"[5] into a learning cycle that has been applied and found to be effective in a range of different urban contexts.

The evidence indicates that beginning the process with experience rather than scripture is powerfully transformative. Anybody can tell their own story. Everybody's story is a part of the bigger story of how God relates to God's people. With appropriate facilitation, everyone is capable of making connections between their own stories and the stories in the Bible. Such connections bring the scriptures alive and make them relevant to ordinary people's everyday lives. This style of learning engages the heart as well as the head, and the connections that are made lead to insights and changes to attitudes and behavior, not just intellectual knowledge. Individuals and communities are empowered; indigenous leadership is nurtured. The Gospel is most authentically shared among people within their own local culture (see http://www.unlock-urban.org.uk/pdf/FW14unlockstorycollectionprintversion.pdf).

This is a liberal educational approach; it does not predetermine what the participants will learn and how they will be challenged and changed. The power rests primarily with the learners (and with the Holy Spirit).

The approach has been found to be effective not just in bringing people to faith, but also in the nurturing and development of faithful lifestyles. People working together in small local groups, sharing their own experience and making connections with scripture, is a powerful model for Christian growth even against the most deprived, marginalized, and chaotic backgrounds.

The radical truth we discover, if we are open to it, is that when we work in Christian education in urban contexts, the people we think we might be there to educate have an awful lot to teach us.

---

5. Unlock (www.unlock-urban.org.uk) has been engaged in urban mission in the United Kingdom since 1972.

References and Resources

Green, Laurie. 2002. *Let's Do Theology: A Pastoral Cycle Resource Book*. New York: Continuum.

Richardson, Mary Jennifer. 2001. "Educators with Attitude." MA diss. (pdf available from office@unlock-urban.org.uk).

—DAWN A. LONSDALE

URUGUAY AND CHRISTIAN EDUCATION

The Oriental Republic of Uruguay is perhaps the most dissimilar to any other South American country. It has the highest percentage of atheists and nonreligious people, and over 90 percent of its population is of European origin.

Introduction of Christianity

Franciscan and Jesuit missionaries arrived in 1616 and began to set up communal villages among the Indians. Following the expulsion of the Jesuits in 1767, these villages were destroyed. Nevertheless, the constitution of 1830 made Catholicism the religion of the state and subsidized missions to Indians. In 1878, Montevideo was elevated to a diocese and in 1897 to an archdiocese. Protestant work began in 1838 when North American Methodists entered the country. But ongoing civil strife caused the mission to close until 1878. The first Anglican Church was erected in 1844 by British traders and is considered a historical landmark. In 1856, Italian Waldensians arrived, followed by German Lutherans, the Salvation Army, and Seventh-day Adventists. In 1911, Southern Baptists entered Montevideo from Argentina.[6]

Modern Developments and Opportunities

Church and state were officially separated in 1916.[7] According to the most recent official survey (2010), 58 percent of Uruguayans define themselves as Christian (47 percent Roman Catholic, 11 percent Protestant), 41 percent profess no religion, and less than 1 percent are either followers of an African religion called Umbanda, Jewish, or other (e.g., Bahai, etc.). But the majority of Uruguayans do not actively practice a religion and are only nominal Catholics.[8]

In contrast with its earlier emphasis on evangelism, the Catholic Church in recent years has prioritized ministries to the urban poor. The church's progress in Uruguay has been hampered by the attitude of the local inhabitants, who are primarily of Spanish, French, or Italian background. Many demonstrate anticlericalism and an opposition to state-related Catholicism, a legacy their forefathers may have brought from Europe.

According to *Operation World* (*Operation World: The Definitive Prayer Guide to Every Nation* by Jason Mandryk, Downers Grove, IL: IVP Books), a new interest in the transcendent is slowing emerging amid the secularism and humanism that characterized Uruguayan society in the 20th century. Many have sought to fulfill this longing through false religious systems. The largest non-Catholic religious bodies are the Jehovah's Witnesses and New Apostolic Church. Brazilian Spiritists, long banned, are now becoming influential. More occult centers (1,200) are registered than Protestant churches. The agnostic middle class and intelligentsia are latching onto "New Age" thinking. On the other hand, some evangelical groups have been able to take advantage of the search for spiritual fulfillment and have found "unprecedented spiritual openness."

Current Religious Presence

Progress for Protestant missions is slow, but recently seven Pentecostal groups have made a significant impact in the country. The Assemblies of God and the Church of God (Cleveland) have seen the greatest growth. The Pentecostal movement is gaining steady growth in Uruguay even in face of its reputation as Latin America's most secular country, helping the number of evangelicals rise from 2 percent a decade ago to 6 percent of its current population of 3.3 million. The growth of evangelical churches is due in part to educational efforts through radio and television platforms and preaching in unconventional venues like plazas and movie theaters.

"While we don't have any specific studies or surveys, we do have approximately 1,600 Christian churches, 300 which are evangelical and 1,200 that are Pentecostal," says Jorge Taberna, president of the Representative Council of Evangelicals of Uruguay (CREU). A Uruguayan sociologist, Nestor Da Costa, says the Pentecostal movement has strategically played a role in helping individuals deal with practical life issues, because their belief system is based on supernatural occurrences like miracles, and many experience an individual connection when they are receptive to the Pentecostal doctrine.[9]

Uruguay's liberal and socialist government continues to pass laws that often do not align with the interests of families. So churches and mission agencies offer Christian educational opportunities through work with children, Bible studies, marriage encounters, providing programs and equipment for local Christian radio stations, promoting the sending of Latin missionaries, and providing tools for evangelism and discipleship.

—MARK A. LAMPORT

---

6. http://www.sim.org/index.php/country/UY.

7. The constitution provides for freedom of religion, and the government generally respects this right in practice. Foreign missionaries face no special requirements or restrictions. http://www.state.gov/j/drl/rls/irf/2007/90270.htm

8. http://en.wikipedia.org/wiki/World_Christian_Encyclopedia.

9. http://www.christianpost.com/news/pentecostal-churches-on-the-rise-in-predominantly-secular-uruguay-101466/.

V

VACATION BIBLE SCHOOLS

Vacation Bible school (VBS), also known as Vacation church school (VCS) in some denominations and geographical regions, is a beloved program for many from childhood to adulthood. No one group holds a monopoly on how a VBS or VCS program should be conducted. Programs can be generational or intergenerational, cultural or multicultural, and denominational or nondenominational. All can become a part of God's household through Jesus. Regardless of where you live, all who participate can share a sense of belonging to God's family.

History

There are countless things to do during vacations. A Sunday school teacher named D. T. Miles, who was also a public school teacher, felt that teaching the Bible to children was so important that more time was needed, so she started a daily Bible school during the summer, in Hopedale, Illinois, in 1894. She used a local school for classes and an adjoining park for playtime.

In 1898 Eliza Hawes, the director of the children's department at Epiphany Baptist Church in New York City, started an "everyday Bible school" for poor children during the summer that lasted for seven years. She structured her program around worship music, Bible stories, scripture memorization, games, crafts, drawing, and cooking. By the time she retired in 1901, she had presided over seven separate schools.

Learning about the success of the "everyday Bible school," Dr. Robert Boville of the Baptist Mission Society recommended it to other Baptist churches. By engaging students from Union Theological Seminary, he was able to start many summer schools, which reached hundreds of students. In 1922, he founded the World Association of Daily Vacation Bible Schools, and Vacation Bible Schools became a national association in 1922.

If history credits Boville with starting the movement for a world vacation Bible school, then Standard Publishing can be credited with making it popular. In 1923, a full-scale VBS program was offered, and shortly afterward it was divided into graded levels. A single themed concept was used, and churches were offered the tools to use the concept. The lessons, which were similar to Sunday morning church school lessons, included music, recreation, arts and crafts, drama, and storytelling.

In the 1970s, churches experienced a drop-off in youth attendance, which affected the summer program. However, one of two statistical analyses of black religious education programs was done by Scripture Press and published in 1970. Listed among the most popular education agencies in black churches was vacation bible school. Scripture Press research suggested that new types of resources and programs would be needed to meet the needs of black congregations in order to keep the program popular. Alternative summer activities, as well as changes in society, affected both the interest in and support of VBS in many denominations. Whether the ministry setting is suburban, urban, or rural, VBS is not that exciting to children and youth anymore.

In spite of competing programs that affected vacation Bible schools, they continued to exist. By the end of the 1970s, they started to change. Congregations offered alternative models to try to keep their programs popular. Today, this specialized Christian education program seems to be experiencing a resurgence of popularity.

Today

Like the earliest vacation Bible schools, the effectiveness of today's programs depends on trusted leadership, careful planning that is sensitive to other programs in the ministry setting, clear objectives and goals, publicity, and leader preparation. Planners must decide whether to purchase a commercial VBS program or create their own. A wide variety of programs are available on Google.com, with links for how to plan a program, and denominational publishers also offer excellent programs. Planners must also decide if VBS is to be an outreach program for the nonchurched or only for church members. The focus of this specialized religious education program is usually on children and youth, but it can include an adult learning companion Bible study. It is important that leaders be intentional about making the Bible a central focus of every lesson and program regardless of the age of participants.

Churches can offer the program in a variety of ways and at no cost to the participants if their budgets can support it. A small fee could be charged to help with the expenses. Often there is a mission project that the program supports, and while attending VBS, participants learn about it and how to support it. Today's programs are often a week long, and evening programs that begin with dinner and fellowship can be attractive. Since parents are often the volunteer teachers and leaders of the program, it is often possible to recruit new teachers and leaders who are most gifted for a shorter and less formal setting like VBS. The planners must decide what will work best for their specific program and congregation.

Updating VBS or making it innovative does not change its purpose. How the program is updated can make it more appealing to today's young people. Technology makes possible Broadway-style musicals with strobe lights and fog machines. The language used may reflect the use of computers, cell phones, and social media. Music and dancing reflect pop culture and hip-hop. The program may be more successful if churches repack the old-fashioned VBS program with contemporary notions of religious education and worship services. The fun is still directed, and while the performances are entertaining, the religious lessons teach faith development and spiritual formation.

The purpose of VBS for all ages is to help make strong disciples, to be able to articulate what it means to be a Christian and what that means for how we live in the world.

References and Resources

Birchette, Colleen. 1989. "A History of Religious Education in the Black Church." In *Urban Church Education*, edited by Donald Rogers, 80–81. Birmingham, AL: Religious Education Press.

Freedman, Samuel. 2012. "Giving Vacation Bible School An Update for the 21st Century." *New York Times*, 28 July.

Gardner, F. A. 1990. "Vacation Bible School." In *Harper's Encyclopedia of Religious Education*, edited by Iris V. Cully and Kendig B. Cully, 677–678. San Francisco: Harper & Row.

Gertz, Steven. 2003. "From Beer to Bibles to VBS." In *Christianity Today*, 4 July. http://en.wikipedia.org/wiki/Vacation_Bible_School.

—Jacqulyn Brown Thorpe

VALUES

Dictionaries define the *value* of something as the regard it is thought to deserve: its importance, worth, merit, or importance. *To value* is to have certain values, to hold certain things to be of value. It takes the form of a particular (positive) kind of appraisal, assessment, or evaluation: making judgments about something's value. *Values* are things that are highly esteemed; they are sometimes called goods and may be viewed as aspects of "the good life." The term *values* is particularly used for broad preferences concerning appropriate courses of action or how people ought to be. But scholars often list among our values nonmoral things and qualities that are considered worthwhile or desirable, including beauty, family, friendship, health, peace and quiet, truth, and so forth.

Many values are regarded as intrinsic: that is, as being good or of value in themselves, if they existed on their own. Other features of our life are valued only instrumentally, as means toward the production or enjoyment of these ends (the intrinsic values). Such means-values (e.g., status, wealth, or exercise) are sometimes called *extrinsic values*. Some regard values as essentially subjective, identifying them with human desires; others insist that they have an objective, real existence that is independent of us. Most Christians make some sort of identification between true values and God's mind, will, or desires.

Virtues, which are settled attitudes that dispose us to habitual right action, are species of values that are strongly emphasized in the Christian tradition. Paul's category the "fruit of the spirit" includes love, joy, peace, patience, kindness, generosity, faithfulness, gentleness, and self-control (Gal. 5:22–23). New Testament virtues also include considerateness, compassion, endurance, forgiveness, godliness, gravity, humility, impartiality, integrity, meekness, mercy, mutual affection, prudence, purity, reverence, righteousness, sincerity, temperance, thankfulness, and not being hypocritical (see Col. 3:12–15; 1 Tim. 6:11; Titus 2:1–10; James 3:17; 2 Pet. 1:5–7). Medieval moral theology promoted the *theological virtues* of faith, hope, and self-giving love, together with the classical *cardinal virtues* of prudence, justice, temperance, and fortitude, which were thought to be needed for their expression. Certain attitudes have been designated *ontic values*, "because they are the very structure of the spiritual subject . . . the actual constituents of a person's spiritual nature," as distinct from moral, intellectual, or other values.[1]

Education and Values

Going beyond values clarification, Christian education passes on (and educates learners about) the Christian values that define Christian morality and spirituality. It strives to engender a value commitment by persuading and prescribing a favorable attitude toward certain values, together with a value vision, understood either as an objective perception of moral value or as a way of seeing the world (e.g., seeing others *as* children of God). It also teaches knowledge of the character and will of God (celebrating this in worship) and of Christian exemplars who express and act on Christian values, so that "we learn to be as they are" (in Stanley Hauerwas's phrase). Fundamentally, its teachers should be people "who are themselves clearly committed to integrity, truth and justice and who have sought to transform the school and the classroom [or church] into the kinds of communities where a love of what is right, decent and good is exhibited as often as possible in the conduct of those into whose care they have been given"—as should be the case with all teachers.[2]

Our values make us what we are; they are the things in which we most strongly believe. Despite much educational debate, it is not the teaching of particular values that requires educational justification, but neglecting to teach them. If we do not wish to share our values, they are probably not really our values.

References and Resources

Astley, Jeff. 2000. *Choosing Life? Christianity and Moral Problems*, chs. 1, 9, and 10. London: Darton, Longman and Todd.
Carr, David. 1991. *Educating the Virtues: An Essay on the Philosophical Psychology of Moral Development and Education*. London and New York: Routledge.

—Jeff Astley

VALUES CLARIFICATION

The term "Christian values" historically refers to the values derived from the teachings of Jesus and taught by Christians throughout the history of the religion. The term has various applications and meanings, and specific definitions can vary widely among denominations, geographical locations, and different schools of thought.

Virtues or Values

Virtue is a pattern of thought and behavior based on high moral standards. Virtues can be placed in a broader context of *values*. Each *individual* has a core of underlying values that contributes to his or her system of beliefs, ideas, and opinions (Jackson 2000). Integrity in the application of a value ensures its continuity, which separates a value from beliefs, opinions, and ideas. In this context, a value (e.g., Truth or Equality or Creed) is the core from which we operate or react. Societies have values that are shared among many of the participants in that culture. An individual's values typically are largely, but not entirely, in agreement with the values of his or her culture.

Individual virtues can be grouped into one of four categories:

- ethical (virtue-vice, good-evil, moral-immoral-amoral, right-wrong)
- aesthetic (unbalanced, pleasing)
- doctrinal (political, ideological, religious, or social beliefs and values)
- innate/inborn

Seen in these terms, values refer to the faith worldview of a person, a group, or a society and will be invoked to describe core purpose.

In contemporary politics, it is not unusual for a politician to call on values to determine what is "right thinking" and perhaps to imply that there was a golden age in the past when those values were normative. For example, in American politics, "family values" are invoked to denote a stance that is concerned with censorship of sexual abstinence or to refer to a previous age when faith played a stronger role. Similarly, in British politics a call to "Christian values" evokes a return to a more biblically inspired tradition without moral ambiguity.

If an organization is endeavoring to clarify its purpose or to bring about a more focused way of working, values will have to be clarified. When those values are articulated, it becomes apparent what particular change is required to achieve the original vision.

For Anglican church schools in the United Kingdom, the Church of England has created a website offering 15 key values, theologically interpreted to enable a church school to be distinctively Christian (http://www.christianvalues4schools.co.uk/).

If an organization is to be involved in change management, it must first reflect on its values and then build its

1. Raymond Holley, *Religious Education and Religious Understanding: An Introduction to the Philosophy of Religious Education* (London: Routledge & Kegan Paul, 1978), 108. In addition to many already listed, Holly cites chastity, self-sacrifice, sympathy, and pity. *See also* Donald Evans's list in the entry Spiritual Learning.
2. David Carr, *Educating the Virtues: An Essay on the Philosophical Psychology of Moral Development and Education* (London and New York: Routledge, 1991), 269.

organizational structures around them. This is of particular importance to the church, in that it is based on the story and the teachings of Jesus Christ. Therefore, the values of the church are all linked to that primal narrative. Reflection on this reveals that values in themselves are not freestanding outside their context. For example, the value of "love" within a Christian context is likely to be different from the value of "love" within a commercial context. In the Christian context, love is primarily defined by a story of self-sacrifice and relates to community as well as to the individual. In the commercial context, love is understood to be more about mutual benefit. Another example is the value of honor, which is perceived as being tribal within some communities, whereas in a Christian context it is about honoring God.

Reference

Jackson, B. S. 2000. *Studies in the Semiotics of Biblical Law.* Sheffield, England: Sheffield Academic Press.

—HOWARD WORSLEY

VAN CASTER, MARCEL

Born 6 July 1907 in Antwerp, Belgium, Van Caster became known as "the artisan of the Catechetical Renewal of the 20th century" through 82 years of "intense" work (Partos 2000). He is linked to the Come to the Father catechetical series of the 1960s and 1970s, a curriculum developed at "a time when the whole of Catholic life and thought were experiencing a profound renewal" (Hurley 1997, xi). He is among the founders of the International Catechetical Center, *Lumen Vitae,* Brussels, Belgium, and is listed as a major theological influence, who helped shape the outcome of the renewal movement (Hurley 1997, 162–165). By 1959, his fame had spread abroad, as he taught courses and seminars and led conferences in "pastoral institutes" on five continents (Partos 2000). He died on 5 February 2000.

Van Caster's schooling was diverse. He attended the Onze-Lieve-Vrouwekathedraal school in Antwerp from 1919 to 1925. From primary source documents, Frank Newton concludes that "a milestone in Father van Caster's life occurred on September 23, 1925," when he joined the Society of Jesus (Newton). He was trained in philosophy and literature (1927–1929), and received additional training in philosophy at Nijmegen, Netherlands (1929–1932) and in theology at Leuven (1932–1939), while teaching courses in religion. During this time, he was ordained a deacon (on 21 August 1938) and four days later a priest. After serving in the military for the second time in 1939–1940, he completed his oral exams on two separate occasions: 9 September 1940 and 8 July

1941, being examined by Van de Vorst. His final vows were taken in Aalst, Belgium, on 2 February 1943.

The literature produced by van Caster is immense. Robert J. Hurley (1997) believes that van Caster identified the primary task of catechesis as "the proclamation and interpretation of the Word of God," achieved by teaching "facts and truths of an objective historical revelation," instilling "a Christian mentality based on the values found in the Gospel," and aiming "to initiate children into a relationship with Jesus Christ . . . into the mystery of God" (162–163).

The relational aspect is strongly perceived throughout van Caster's writings, as exemplified in *The Structure of Catechesis* (Van Caster 1965). In this work, van Caster offers his synthesis for the *kerygmatic* movement and his philosophy of Christian education. The ultimate aim of catechesis is for persons to hear God and have a genuine encounter with God, and the starting point is to take the word of God seriously. "Catechesis, then, must transmit the word of God, and because of this its first duty is to be faithful to that word." But fidelity transcends the written words to the "present action," thus leading persons into the mystery of God, who continues to speak through "Jesus Christ in his Church" (1965, 9). Ultimately, if there is doctrine and life but no encounter with God, the path is "unacceptable," just as is "doctrine cut off from life or a life cut off from doctrine. Instruction and formation cannot be separated from initiation" (1965, 10). Dialogue with God happens through the integrative sacredness of it all—that is, through the Bible, liturgy, witness, doctrine, psychology, anthropology, and sociology. For van Caster, balance and integration were necessary marks of spiritual formation. These themes are explored in detail. This volume sets the tone for his other works, also available in English: *God's Word Today: Principles, Methods and Examples of Catechesis* (1966), *Experiential Catechetics* (1966), *The Redemption: A Personalist View* (1965), *Themes of Catechesis* (1966), and *Values Catechetics* (1966).

Not everyone agreed that van Caster reached the proposed balance. Some criticized his intense theological bent. Hurley notes that James Michael Lee acknowledges van Caster's guiding inspiration from theology, but argues that his "theological anthropology" is just that: "theological" (Hurley 1997, 163). Nonetheless, the language he uses definitely exposes a docetic or a Gnostic appeal, so prevalent in Western Christianity. From a practical perspective, the "incarnate" Christ is the only "prophet" who can affirm that knowing Him one knows God, and loving Him one loves God, which translates into "Jesus-being-with-them, as the bread of life," making possible connections in the here and now (van Caster and Stuhlmueller 1973, 69–70).

References and Resources

Hurley, Robert J. 1997. Foreword by Gregory Baum. *Hermeneutics and Catechesis: Biblical Interpretation in the Come to the Father Catechetical Series*. New York: University Press of America.

Partos, Ladislas, SJ. 2000. *In Memoriam*. Translated by Frank Newton. Accessed 20 February 2013 (temporary link).

Van Caster, Marcel. n.d. "Complete Bibliography." http://limo .libis.be or http://bib.kuleuven.be/engligh/ub.

———. 1965. *The Structure of Catechetics*. New York: Herder and Herder.

Van Caster, Marcel, and Carroll Stuhlmueller. 1973. *Believing and Praying from Reality*. Pretoria, South Africa: Michel.

—Sophia R. G. Steibel

Van Kaam, Adrian

Adrian van Kaam was born on 9 April 1920 in The Hague, Netherlands. He was the oldest child of Charles and Anna van Kaam, who subsequently had three daughters. At the age of 12, he enrolled as a student at the preparatory academy of the Holy Ghost Fathers in Weert, where he studied for six years. In 1939, he moved to Gennep to study philosophy and theology, where he completed his novitiate, then professed vows on 29 August 1940, at Gemert.

With World War II under way, van Kaam devoted himself to aiding Jewish refugees, including enduring the infamous Hunger Winter of 1944–1945, when 22,000 people died as the Nazis made a last-ditch effort to hold out against advancing troops. It was during this time of intense suffering and death that he formulated many of the ideas he later wrote about.

Van Kaam was ordained as a Roman Catholic priest in the Order of the Holy Ghost Fathers on 21 July 1946. Shortly afterward, he began teaching philosophical anthropology at the seminary in Gemert. In 1947, he began ministry at the Dutch Life Schools of Formation for Young Adults, also serving as a counselor for Dutch juvenile delinquents. He also continued his formal study, earning a degree in pedagogy and andragogy in 1953.

In 1952, the Holy Ghost Fathers assigned Father Adrian to Paris to research and write the life of the order's founder, the Venerable Francis Libermann, which was published under the title *A Light to the Gentiles*. In 1954, Father Adrian accepted an invitation from Duquesne University in Pittsburgh, Pennsylvania, to found the Department of Psychology, with its special phenomenological-anthropological approach. Some of his most fruitful years (1955–1963) were spent teaching and writing at the university, including the publication of one of his best-known books, *Religion and Personality*.

In the midst of an acclaimed teaching ministry, he also completed a PhD in 1955.

In 1963, Duquesne asked Father Adrian to launch the Institute of Man, which would in 1979 be renamed the Institute of Formative Spirituality. This institute allowed him to synthesize all his thought and work and to give it a focus that his more generalized teaching and writing had not provided. Father Adrian was now able to formally develop what has come to be known as formation science—a unique blending of theology, psychology, and anthropology—which has caused some people to refer to him as the Thomas Aquinas of the 20th century. Under his supervision, students graduated from Duquesne with both master's and doctoral degrees in formation science.

Father Adrian was joined in 1966 by Susan Muto, a Roman Catholic laywoman who shared many of his interests. She completed her PhD in 1972, a study experience that gave her a specialty in post-Reformation spiritual writers. Together, Adrian and Susan cofounded the Epiphany Association in 1979, located in Pittsburgh—a ministry that applied their commitments and interests in spiritual formation to the larger Christian world, particularly to the formation of laypersons. In addition to granting master's and doctoral degrees, Duquesne began an epiphany certification program, which became a standard for non-degree formative education.

Father Adrian retired from Duquesne in 1993, devoting the next decade to teaching and writing through the auspices of the Epiphany Association. His productivity is evidenced by his four-volume series on formation theology and his six-volume series on formative spirituality. It is also reflected in professional journals (e.g., *Envoy, Humanitas, and Epiphany Inspirations*), which gave Adrian, Susan, and their students further outlets for their ideas.

In 2004, Father Adrian's health had declined to the point where he retired to Libermann Hall in Bethel Park. From 2005 until his death in 2007, he was under the care of the Little Sisters of the Poor on the north side of Pittsburgh.

The influence of Adrian van Kaam in Christian education has been primarily academic, through his teaching and writing, which extends beyond Roman Catholicism to embrace not only the entire Christian world, but also non-Christians. The ecclesial impact of Father Adrian in Christian education is evident through the students who graduated from Duquesne to become priests and active laypersons in their own right, and through his writings, which have been used in a variety of settings.

References and Resources

van Kaam, Adrian. 1968. *Religion and Personality*. New York: Doubleday Image Books.

——. 1983. *Fundamental Formation*. Formative Spirituality series no. 1. New York: Crossroad Publishing.

——, with Susan Muto. 2004. *Foundations of Christian Formation*. Formative Theology series no. 1. Pittsburgh: The Epiphany Association.

The best way to access all of Father Adrian's writings is via the internet at The Epiphany Association (www.epiphany association.org)

—Steve Harper

VATICAN II DECLARATION ON CHRISTIAN EDUCATION

The Declaration on Christian Education is a document issued by the Second Vatican Council of the Catholic Church on the subject of Catholic education and school systems.

The Origins of the Declaration

In the course of the debates at the Second Vatican Council, 1962–1965, the opinion was expressed that the issues of education did not require a comprehensive document, because Pope Pius XI had already issued an encyclical dedicated to this problem, *Divini Illius Magistri*, in 1929. Eventually, however, a document concerning the issue of Christian education and school systems was prepared by the commission called De seminariis, de studiis et de educatione religiosa, under the leadership of Cardinal Giuseppe Pizzardo. The first version of the document was passed in March 1962, but it was subsequently amended several times, taking the shape of the *Declaration on Christian Education* in November 1964 (Tarnowski 1967, 303–304). The final version of the declaration, bearing the Latin name *Gravissimum Educationis*, was proclaimed by Pope Paul IV on 28 October 1965.

The Content of the Declaration

The declaration comprises two parts. The first four sections are devoted to the problem of education, whereas the remaining eight (two-thirds of the whole document) discuss various aspects of school systems, with particular emphasis on Catholic education (Wenger 1966, 213–217). According to Janusz Tarnowski (1967, 305), the most important problems discussed in this document are natural and Christian education; coresponsibility of the church for education, and the presence of the church in the intellectual world.

Natural and Christian Education

The declaration calls for the integration of natural and supernatural education, for the saturation of natural education with the Christian spirit, emphasizing the following: "Therefore children and young people must be helped, with the aid of the latest advances in psychology and the arts and science of teaching, to develop harmoniously their physical, moral and intellectual endowments" (*Declaration* 1965, n. 1).

In the context of natural education, the *Declaration* also positively recognizes the problem of sex education, stating: "Let them be given also, as they advance in years, a positive and prudent sexual education" (*Declaration* 1965, n. 1).

Appreciating the importance of natural education, the Fathers of the Council emphasized, however, that the pinnacle of education to which a Christian is entitled is "to know and love God" (Vandermeersch 162), which should also "help in the Christian formation of the world that takes place when natural powers viewed in the full consideration of man redeemed by Christ contribute to the good of the whole society" (*Declaration* 1965, n. 2). The purpose of such a vision of education is to achieve salvation, and catechesis should most of all be the tool leading to it (*Declaration* 1965, n. 3).

Coresponsibility of the Church for Education

The declaration devotes significant space to those responsible for education, among whom parents, the whole society, and the church are enumerated. Interestingly, not only believers but also the whole of humanity are the recipients of this education: "The Church is bound as a mother to give to these children of hers an education by which their whole life can be imbued with the spirit of Christ and at the same time do all she can to promote for all peoples the complete perfection of the human person, the good of earthly society and the building of a world that is more human" (*Declaration* 1965, n. 3).

The Presence of the Church in the Modern World

The declaration also calls on Christian educators to "strive to excel in pedagogy and the pursuit of knowledge in such a way that they not merely advance the internal renewal of the Church but preserve and enhance its beneficent influence upon today's world, especially the intellectual world" (*Declaration* 1965, conclusion).

The document draws attention to the necessity for the church to establish and run all kinds of schools, but it also obliges not only those attending Catholic schools but all believers, regardless of where they acquire education. However, it also calls on Catholic schools to give special testimony: "So indeed the Catholic school, while it is open, as it must be, to the situation of the contemporary world, leads its students to promote efficaciously the good of the earthly city and also prepares them for service in the spread of the Kingdom of God, so that by leading an exemplary apostolic life they become, as it were, a saving leaven in the human community" (*Declaration* 1965, n. 8).

The declaration also addresses the issue of Catholic universities, calling on them to exercise theology but also to engage in ecumenical and interreligious dialogue (Tarnowski 1967, 312).

References and Resources

Augustyn, J. 2002. "Wprowadzenie do Deklaracji o wychowaniu chrześcijańskim." In *Sobór Watykański II: Konstytucje. Dekrety. Deklaracje*, 305–313. Poznań, Poland: Pallottinum.

Hahnenberg. E. P. 2007. *A Concise Guide to the Documents of Vatican II*. Cincinnati, OH: St. Anthony Messenger Press.

Paul VI. 1965. *Declaration on Christian Education [Gravissimum Educationis]*. Vatican II. Vatican.

Tarnowski, J. 1967. "Wprowadzenie do Deklaracji o wychowaniu chrześcijańskim." In *Sobór Watykański II: Konstytucje. Dekrety. Deklaracje*, 303–312. Poznań, Poland: Pallottinum.

United States Conference of Catholic Bishops. 2005. *Catholic Identity in Our Colleges and Universities: A Collection of Defining Documents*. Washington, DC: USCCB.

Vandermeersch, Edmond. 2008. *Ecole: Eglise et Laïcité, la rencontre des deux France: Souvenirs autour de la loi Debré (1960-1970)*. Paris: L'Harmattan.

Vatican II: Renewal Within Tradition. 2008. Edited by Matthew L. Lamb and Matthew Levering. New York: Oxford University Press.

Wenger, A. 1966. *Vatican II: Chronique de la troisième session*. Paris: Centurion.

—PAWEŁ MĄKOSA

VATICAN LIBRARY, THE

The Bibliotheca Apostolica Vaticana (Vatican Apostolic Library) was established in 1475. It serves the Holy See of the Roman Catholic Church. One of the oldest libraries in the world, it draws upon the private collections of the first Roman pontiffs. At present, the Vatican Library stands at just over one million books and roughly 75,000 manuscripts, including documents that date from the eighth century AD. (The Vatican Secret Archives, separated from the larger library in the 17th century, contain an additional 150,000 texts.) Internationally considered among the most significant repositories of historical documents, it functions as a research library for qualified scholars, who study history, law, philosophy, science, and, most important, theology. One particularly famous holding of the library is the *Codex Vaticanus Craecus* (1209), the oldest known nearly complete manuscript of the Bible.

The library's history began long before its official establishment in Rome in 1475; the church had already held a collection of texts for about a thousand years. It grew from the private holdings of the earliest pontiffs into a more formal library at the Lateran, then experienced a period of prodigious expansion when the papacy moved to Avignon and finally to its present-day home in Rome. Though Sixtus IV formally instituted the library in 1475, Pope Nicholas V has traditionally been regarded as the founder of the Vatican Library. A major proponent of humanism and the liberal arts, Nicholas directed his educational interests to organizing and making public his extensive collection of Greek, Latin, and Hebrew codices, which he compiled in 1448. Some notable acquisitions since then include manuscripts from the imperial library of Constantinople (1448), the Palatine Library of Heidelberg (1623), the manuscripts of the Dukes of Urbino (1657), and the library of Queen Christina of Sweden (1989).

From its inception, the Vatican Library was revered not only as a repository of Bibles and works of theology, but also for its extensive collection of secular works, particularly Greek and Latin classical texts. The latter attracted the attention of humanist scholars throughout Europe and established the Vatican Library's central role in the cultural revival of the Renaissance. However, the liberal vision that inspired the library's establishment soon came into conflict with Catholic tradition, as humanist scholars began to call for more critical scrutiny of the church and its privileges. With the further challenge of the Protestant Reformation in the 16th century, the Vatican Library shifted from a center of liberal-minded scholarship to one of systematic censorship and ideological suppression. As these tensions declined, particularly during the late 19th century, church authorities gradually eased many restrictions on access to the library, and it has become a renowned center for research, attracting scholars from around the world. In 2012, the Bodleian Library announced plans to partner with the Vatican Library in digitizing over one million pages of material, making possible even greater access to this extensive collection.

References and Resources

Battles, Matthew. 2003. *Library: An Unquiet History*. New York: W. W. Norton.

Baumgarten, Paul Maria. 2005. *The Vatican Library and Its Secret Archives*. Whitefish, MT: Kessinger Publishing.

Collins, Michael. 2011. *The Vatican*. New York: DK Publishing.

Fagiolo dell'Arco, Maurizio, and Angela Cipriani. 1983. *The Art of the Popes: From the Vatican Collection; How Pontiffs, Architects, Painters, and Sculptors Created the Vatican*. New York: Greenwich House.

Reese, Thomas J. 1996. *Inside the Vatican: The Politics and Organization of the Catholic Church.* Cambridge, MA: Harvard University Press.

Ruysschaert, José. 1982. *The Vatican: Spirit and Art of Christian Rome.* New York: Metropolitan Museum of Art.

—JEFFRY C. DAVIS

VENEZUELA AND CHRISTIAN EDUCATION

Christian History

Christianity was brought to the lands of modern-day Venezuela by Spanish missionaries. Religious education of the native peoples occurred within the *doctrinas* system, which bore some resemblance to the mission station settlement that became common in Africa during the 19th and 20th centuries. Although the extensive Archdiocese of Caracas has less than half the number of priests found within the major archdioceses of colonial Latin America, the rapid expansion of plantation agriculture and trade help account for why, in the early 18th century, it had the greatest income, as measured by the royal tithe, of any colonial see in Latin America.

A century later, however, the Catholic church in Venezuela had become among the most marginal in Latin America, due to nearly constant civil disturbances, economic disruption, and severe bouts of hostility to the church. In the 1824 Law of Patronage, for example, the Venezuelan state claimed the power to establish ecclesiastical divisions, appoint bishops, restrict activities of religious orders, and control migration of foreign priests. By the 1870s, the president of the republic, Antonio Guzmán Blanco, found the church to be the only independent source of opposition, however weak, to his personal authority. He thus continued the already established anticlerical program by taking away from the church the registry of births, celebration of marriages, and ownership of cemeteries. All religious orders were expelled and their property seized, and seminaries were closed. Attempts were made to foster rival belief systems, and there was even talk of creating a national Venezuelan church separated from allegiance to Rome. By the end of his rule, the Catholic church was for all practical purposes nonexistent as a force in the life of civil society.

By the last decade of the 19th century, the process of rebuilding the Catholic church in Venezuela had begun. Not surprisingly, the model followed was exclusively religious, conscious of limitations within an inhospitable political climate. During the series of dictatorial governments that followed, the church carefully avoided political entanglements. It kept a low political profile and neither excessively committed itself to nor explicitly opposed any government. All the while it sought loopholes and advantages where it could, attempting in the process to rebuild and expand its institutional space (Froehle 1994). Yet loyalty to the church and Catholicism remained, fostered in popular religious devotion and even potentially traceable in some way back to the original evangelization of the country. Some credit the Augustinian religious order's biblically based catechesis, particularly its emphasis on Bible stories in evangelization and teaching, for forming religiosity within those parts of the country where a religious commitment is strongest (Gonzalez Oropeza 1991).

The fluctuations in the number of priests in the country illustrate the dramatic changes that took place during this period. During the height of the colonial period, the number of priests increased dramatically, from 456 in 1784 to 547 in 1810 and 640 by 1820. In the aftermath of independence and civil wars, as well as under ensuing restrictive legislation, their number decreased to 440 by 1847. Those remaining were for the most part old or infirm, and only 273 were physically able to attend parishes, leaving 40 percent of the parishes unattended. A few years later, in 1855, only 154 priests were left, leaving almost seven in ten parishes without resident priests. By the time the census was taken in 1881, conditions had stabilized, the number of priests had increased to 255, and two in five parishes had resident priests.

Given that the boundaries of each parish were usually coterminous with those of the civil division in which it was situated, each unattended parish generally meant that inhabitants of a town of some size and its hinterland had considerably reduced contact with the institutional church. The population, however, did not stop being Catholic. These developments did leave most of the country without regular religious services (Watters 1971), and many of the traditions of popular religiosity and religious practice, including baptism by one's parents or grandparents, developed during this period (Pollak-Eltz 1994). Over time, many families replaced orthodox practice and formation formerly offered by the priest with religious practices and formation fostered within the family, chiefly passed on by mothers and grandmothers from generation to generation. As a result, Catholicism in Venezuela has been characterized more by popular religiosity and lay initiative and has been relatively less clerical in daily life and practice.

Christian Life

Christianity during the three centuries of colonization experienced a similar trajectory to that in the rest of Spanish America (Picon Salas 1966): a period of energetic mission work and settlement, followed by a period of maturity, and then a time of ecclesial difficulties as the church experienced more control by the crown and loss of resources during the mid- and late-18th-century so-called Bourbon reforms. After further reductions of the church's public presence and resources in the 19th century, religious orders were invited back into the country to provide social services and education. By the mid-20th century, the organizational life of the church grew among the urban middle sectors. Catholic institutions—parishes, schools, and hospitals—proliferated and made their presence felt, and democratization in the 1960s benefited the Catholic Church, even as it provided opportunities for other churches to grow.

Evangelicals and Pentecostals experienced dramatic growth during this period, with small house-churches appearing all over the country. Nonetheless, organized religion in any form remains relatively weak in Venezuela, especially in comparison to neighboring Colombia, though signs of flourishing Christian life are also evident (Levine 1981; Luciani 2009; Smilde 2007).

Christian Education

Christian education in Venezuela, as elsewhere, has always depended on the family, whether during the period of the dramatic disappearance of parish priests in the early 19th century or the rapid growth of evangelicals and Pentecostals in the 20th. The research center CISOR, founded as the Centro de Investigaciones Socio-religiosos in 1967, conducted a number of research projects on religious education as well as religion among young people, particularly in its first two decades.

Church-State Relations and Christian Education

Church-state relations have had a dramatic effect on Christian education at various points in the country's history. This is not only due to various political efforts to control the churches, such as limiting access to public schools for purposes of religious education, expelling religious personnel and controlling who may be admitted to the country, and confiscating church land and resources. It is also due to the use of wealth at the government's disposal. Since the early 1900s, Venezuela has been a major petroleum-producing country, and some of the wealth has been given by the government to various churches and church-related schools for building projects or other needs. It follows that having access to such funds—then losing access to such funds—dramatically affects church life. The modus vivendi between the Catholic Church and the Venezuelan government is another example of this sort of control (Levine 1973), as are church-state relations during the Chavez period (1999–2013).

Ordinary Methods of Religious Education

The ordinary methods of formal religious education in Venezuela are church-based, through materials provided by congregations and taught by volunteers, though there has also been some religious education in the public schools. Controversies have grown up around this issue, and there is an option provided for students to study ethics in place of religion. The situation is different in Catholic schools, of course, where religious education is more formal and in-depth than in other contexts. The largest network of Catholic schools in Venezuela is Fe y Alegria, which was founded by Jesuits in 1955 and includes about 160 schools and 290,000 students, including those in non-school-based programs.

Christian education is also supported by various religious bookstores and publishers. Catholics and some others make use of the Paulinas and Centro Gumilla. Other churches make use of flows of printed materials from their judicatories or the equivalent, such as the Assemblies of God and other transnational religious bodies. Materials provided by the Biblical Society are widely used (Ayerra 1980).

References and Resources

Ayerra, J. 1980. *Los Protestantes en Venezuela*. Caracas: Ediciones Tripode.

Fe y Alegria. n.d. http://old.feyalegria.org/?idSeccion=28.

Froehle, B. 1994. "Religious Competition, Community Building, and Democracy in Latin America: Grassroots Religious Organizations in Venezuela." *Sociology of Religion* 55 (2): 145–162.

Gonzalez Oropeza, H. 1991. "La iglesia en la Venezuela Hispanica." In *Los tres primeros siglos de Venezuela 1498–1810*. 231–256. Caracas: Fundacion Eugenio Menoza.

Levine, D. 1973. *Conflict and Political Change in Venezuela*. Princeton, NJ: Princeton University Press.

———. 1981. *Religion and Politics in Venezuela and Colombia*. Princeton, NJ: Princeton University Press.

Luciani, R. 2009. "Politics and Church in Venezuela: Perspectives and Horizons." *Theological Studies*, 192–195.

Picon Salas, M. 1966. *A Cultural History of Spanish America*. Berkeley: University of California Press.

Pollak-Eltz, A. 1994. *La religiosidad popular en Venezuela*. Caracas: San Pablo.

———. 2000. *Estudio Antropológico del Pentecostalismo en Venezuela*. Caracas: Universidad Santa Rosa.

———. 2005. "Venezuela." In *Worldmark Encyclopedia of Religious Practices*, edited by Thomas Riggs, 556–561. Farmington Hills, MI: Gale.

Shorack, J. 2012. *Nail Scarred Hands Made New: Making Sense of the Gospel in a Violent Latin American Slum*. Eugene, OR: Wipf & Stock.

Smilde, D. 2007. *Reason to Believe: Cultural Agency in Latin American Evangelicalism*. Berkeley: University of California Press.

Watters, M. 1971. *A History of the Church in Venezuela, 1810–1930*. New York: AMS Press.

—BRYAN T. FROEHLE

Victims of Abuse

Understanding the Meaning and Types of Abuse
By definition, victims of abuse include individuals who have experienced any form of abuse or a combination of various types of abuse, including verbal, emotional, physical, and sexual, or the experience of deprivation or neglect in regard to an insufficiency of necessary food, clothing, shelter, and other forms of essential human care needed to live and thrive. Deprivation, however, may be caused by other conditions not involving abuse, such as poverty, war, or natural disaster.

Abuse may be perpetrated upon individuals of any age, gender, or circumstance. Perpetrators of abuse include parents, siblings, relatives, neighbors, friends, or acquaintances; strangers; fellow students or fellow prisoners; authority figures in school, church, prisons, or community; medical personnel; counselors; and various types of in-home or institutionally related caregivers for the ill, disabled, or elderly. Individuals who are vulnerable due to age, physical or mental condition, and proximity to abusers or potential abusers are the populations that most often experience one or more kinds of abuse.

The Results of Abuse
The emotional and physical trauma resulting from the experience of abuse may have long-lasting effects on an individual's cognitive, emotional, and relational abilities, leading to various levels of impairment, including depression; inability to concentrate and to learn; feelings of worthlessness; withdrawal from interaction with others; desire for suicide and other self-destructive behaviors, such as anger, rage, use of addictive substances, and cutting of one's body; and abusive actions toward others. Without aftercare in the form of medical intervention, if needed; counseling; protection from the original abuser(s); and a stable, safe environment including supportive care, victims of abuse may never fully recover to lead emotionally stable, productive lives.

Considerations in Educating Victims of Abuse
Educators of abuse victims require an understanding of the various types and levels of damage from abuse resulting in impairment of a student's cognitive, emotional, and relational abilities. They need to be alert and sensitive to a student's attitudes and behaviors that may indicate he or she is a victim of abuse. Teachers and educational administrators also need knowledge of the means for evaluation and testing that are helpful in determining and addressing a student's need for counseling and other healing interventions. They also need to know how to facilitate effective academic learning based on a student's abilities and specific needs in order

to provide necessary and adequate care for the abuse victim's journey of recovery.

Providing Safe Environments in Schools, Churches, and Care Facilities
Most professionals and other employees providing leadership and service in Christian institutions are individuals with integrity, knowledge, ability, and trustworthiness in providing education, care, and other services for vulnerable persons. However, a continuing concern and challenge for Christian churches, schools, hospitals, residential communities for the disabled or elderly, nursing facilities, and other organizations is preventing opportunities for abusive situations and the abuse of individuals within those contexts. Christian institutions need to implement systemic security systems and other appropriate measures to prevent caregivers and other authority figures engaging in inappropriate private interactions with vulnerable persons. The careful investigation and vetting of those employed or volunteering in Christian faith-based institutions is also a necessary measure that has become more widespread in providing protection for vulnerable individuals.

The Expansion of Knowledge in Understanding Abuse
Beginning in the latter decades of the 20th century and continuing into the 21st, the subject of abuse has received increasing attention from psychologists, counselors, physicians, clergy, educators, and other leaders in both secular and Christian faith-based communities. Media attention has been instrumental in increasing society's level of awareness and knowledge about types of abuse, recognizing signs and symptoms of abuse, the treatment of abuse victims, and the legal issues surrounding crimes involving abuse. Public knowledge has increased public response and the willingness of secular authorities and organizations, as well as faith-based organizations, churches, and charities, to proactively provide information for the purpose of increasing the protection of vulnerable persons and addressing existing cases of abuse. Informing the public about abuse results in a movement toward the goals of a continual reduction in the incidence of abuse and providing effective avenues of treatment, including faith-based programs of recovery for victims.

References and Resources
Crosson-Tower, Cynthia. 2001. _When Children Are Abused: An Educator's Guide to Intervention._ Upper Saddle River, NJ: Pearson.

Cruise, Tracy K., and Connie Burrows Horton. 2001. _Child Abuse and Neglect: The School's Response._ New York: Guilford Press.

Heitritter, Lynn, and Jeanette Vought. 2006. *Helping Victims of Sexual Abuse: A Sensitive Biblical Guide for Counselors, Victims, and Families.* Grand Rapids, MI: Bethany House.

Horsman, Jenny. 2000. *Too Scared to Learn: Women, Violence and Education.* New York: Routledge.

Hunt, June. 2010. *How to Rise above Abuse: Victory for Victims of Five Types of Abuse.* Eugene, OR: Harvest House.

Lowenthal, Barbara. 2001. *Abuse and Neglect: The Educator's Guide to the Identification and Prevention of Child Maltreatment.* Baltimore, MD: Brookes Publishing.

Nason-Clark, Nancy, and Catherine Clark Kroeger. 2004. *Refuge from Abuse: Healing and Hope for Abused Christian Women.* Downers Grove, IL: InterVarsity Press.

Neal, Gerald W. 2008. *Quiet Desperation: The Effects of Competition in School on Abused and Neglected Children.* Lanham, MD: Hamilton Books.

Shoop, Robert J. 2004. *Sexual Exploitation in Schools: How to Spot It and Stop It.* Thousand Oaks, CA: Corwin Press.

Tracy, Steven R. 2005. *Mending the Soul: Understanding and Healing Abuse.* Grand Rapids, MI: Zondervan.

—MARA LIEF CRABTREE

VICTIMS OF NATURAL DISASTERS

In a speech presented in 2010, Elizabeth Ferris reported that "the frequency and severity of sudden-onset natural disasters is increasing. Presently there are about 400 natural disasters globally per year, affecting 200 million people."[3] According to Michael Evans of the *Earth Times*:

Natural disasters fall into three broad groups:

1. Those caused by movements of the Earth. These occur with the minimum amount of warning and include earthquakes, volcanic eruptions and tsunamis. They are difficult to predict and impossible to stop. . . .
2. Weather related disasters. These will include hurricanes, tornadoes, extreme heat and extreme cold weather. There will usually be some degree of advanced warning, but since weather is unpredictable, nothing can be done to stop these disasters from developing once the weather system develops. . . .
3. Floods, mudslides, landslides and famine. These are usually the consequence of extreme weather events, or are supplementary to other natural disasters. Often they are the result of extreme and unforeseen conditions.[4]

Material Impact

The effects of natural disasters can be felt at the community, city, and regional levels, and often in the entire country. At the individual level, the impact can often be felt physically, mentally, and emotionally. Natural disasters cause destruction of property, loss of financial resources, and personal injury or illness. The loss of resources, security, and access to shelter can lead to massive population migrations. Natural disasters also often leave behind many vulnerable children, such as orphans, refugees, and street children. If these children are not rescued, they risk being swept up by perpetrators of evil, who exploit them through various forms of child labor, including prostitution. How well the impact of a disaster is absorbed has much to do with its intensity and the level of preparedness and resilience of those affected.

It is almost always the poor and marginalized who are disproportionately affected by natural disasters.[5] They tend to live in less safe environments and shelters. Shoddily constructed slums are more vulnerable to earthquakes and flooding than the homes where the rich are more likely to live. These victims have the least resources for coping and rebuilding.

Spiritual Impact

While some call natural disasters "acts of God," others struggle to understand how a God who is all-powerful and all-knowing can also be considered good and loving. How do we reconcile so great a love shown to us at the cross with all the trouble and suffering in the world? Writer Mark Galli, in an article about the varied responses to Hurricane Sandy in 2012, reminds us that the Old Testament recounts many natural disasters that God used to teach, to judge, to punish, or to test one's faith. Scriptural accounts include the plagues God sent to the Egyptians, the flood in Noah's time, the storm God hurled into the sea in response to Jonah's disobedience, and the windstorm in which all of Job's 10 children died.[6] Those who survived these events must have asked similar questions.

Trust and faith are foundational to our spiritual growth and maturity. Disaster victims must remember that while God does not give us all the answers, He has given us Himself, and that is why we can have faith. Faith is believing God when one does not have all the answers. Disasters test that faith—some people draw closer to God, while some pull away.

---

3. Elizabeth Ferris, "Natural Disasters, Conflict, and Human Rights: Tracing the Connections," *The Brookings Institution*, 3 March 2010, http://www.brookings.edu/research/speeches/2010/03/03-natural-disasters -ferris.

4. Michael Evans, "Natural Disasters," *The Earth Times*, 14 May 2011, http://www.earthtimes.org/encyclopaedia/environmental-issues/natural -disasters/.

5. United Nations International Strategy for Disaster Reduction (UNISDR) Secretariat, *Global Assessment Report on Disaster Risk Reduction* (Geneva, 2009), http://www.unisdr.org/we/inform/publications/9413.

6. Mark Galli, "What Jesus Might Say about Sandy," *Christianity Today*, 30 October 2012, http://www.christianitytoday.com/ct/2012/october-web -only/what-jesus-might-say-about-sandy.html.

Transformation

Mark Galli also points out that with the coming of Jesus, everything was transformed, including how we understand natural calamities. That which was formerly a sign of God's judgment, intended to punish or prod toward repentance, is now the occasion to demonstrate God's power and holiness. That which was seen as merely destructive is now a symbol of eternal life: "The difference between the old way of thinking (Old Testament) and the new way of thinking (New Testament) is this: Fear not—that which seems horrible, destructive, and pointless is embraced by the holiness of God and redeemed by the storm of the Cross."[7] Christian educators have the task of helping the church delineate between "the old way of thinking and the new way of thinking" if they are to understand the power of transformation.

The Church's Response

If the church is to demonstrate the Gospel to victims of disasters, it must take seriously Jesus's exhortation to be both the salt of the earth and the light of the world (Matt. 5:13–14). This role requires the church to identify with and reach out to the affected and vulnerable populations in times of chaos. In responding to the many opportunities to offer practical help, counsel, and prayer and to lead people to a saving faith in Christ, the church can be a stable, familiar, and supportive oasis.

Jeremiah sums up the hope the church can offer to victims who have been impacted by natural disasters. Between his accounts of woe and tribulation and feelings that God must have deserted him, Jeremiah reminds us that even in the midst of terror, and even when it seems God Himself would be held responsible for that terror, we can trust in His goodness: "But this I call to mind, and therefore I have hope: The steadfast love of the LORD never ceases; his mercies never come to an end; they are new every morning; great is your faithfulness."[8]

—Phyllis Kilbourn

VICTIMS OF WAR AND TERROR

Most wars today are civil or "intrastate" wars, fueled as much by racial, ethnic, or religious animosities as by ideological fervor. Most victims are civilians, a feature that distinguishes modern conflicts. During World War I, civilians made up fewer than 5 percent of all casualties. Today, 75 percent or more of those killed or wounded in wars are noncombatants.[9]

War impacts not only nations but also families and communities. Apologetics, the branch of Christianity that defines issues concerning the defense and establishment of the Christian faith, has many issues to grapple with when it comes to war: Is war ever right? Is it biblical for a Christian to be a solider? What is the appropriate Christian attitude toward, and response to, the death, destruction, and devastation caused by war? When Christians ponder how to apply their faith to the realm of warfare, they realize that a person's Christian values have consequences.

Children: Primary Victims of War

According to the United Nations, children are the primary victims of armed conflict.[10] Hundreds of thousands serve as soldiers in armed conflicts around the world. Child soldiers are victims, whose participation in conflict bears serious implications for their physical and emotional well-being. They are commonly subjected to abuse, and most of them witness death, killing, and sexual violence. Many participate in killings, and most suffer serious long-term psychological consequences.

Caught up as victims of war, those who represent what is precious and of the highest value to the church are forced to set aside the innocence of childhood. Children are immersed in a sea of adult hatreds to learn to kill or be killed for causes they do not fully understand in a world increasingly hostile to their experiences.

Life Experiences of Victims

Understanding the experiences that victims of war encounter is basic to understanding their need for a holistic Gospel—a Gospel that presents both the demonstration as well as the proclamation of the Word. Too often, the church dichotomizes compassionate deeds, which demonstrate the truths of the Gospel, and the written Word. When this happens, war victims who are emotionally or physically sick or are hungry find it difficult to embrace spiritual truth. Compassionate deeds prepare hearts for proclamation. With victims of war, the church must seek to be the incarnation of the same Gospel that Christ so compassionately lived, demonstrated, and preached.

One example of a war victim who needed to be shown compassionate deeds before being able to embrace the proclamation of the Gospel is 12-year-old Junior, who had been captured by the opposing military forces in his country. One year after his capture, he confided to his former Sunday school teacher, "I have killed more people than I can remember. We are given drugs in the daytime to make us brave to fight. In the evenings we are given alcohol to

---

7. Ibid.

8. Lamentations 3:21–23 (English Standard Version).

9. "The World at War," GlobalSecurity.org, http://www.globalsecurity.org/military/world/war/index.html (accessed 7 June 2013).

10. UN Office for Disarmament Affairs, "International Day against the Use of Child Soldiers," UNODA, 13 February 2012, http://www.un.org/disarmament/content/news/day_against_use_\of_child_soldiers/.

make us forget what we did. But the memories keep coming back—I cannot forget." Girls serving as soldiers or wives of soldiers recount their own tales of horror and brokenness.

Spiritual Harm of War

Those who work with children caught up in war-related violence are witnesses to their psychological traumas. The experiences of these children destroy the basic building blocks of their spirituality, which results in fear; lack of trust, which leads to an inability to form relationships; and distorted ideas about God's character and how God works in the world. They also lose their sense of self-value and self-worth, describing themselves as damaged goods that no one would love or want. They are robbed of the sense of awe associated with having been created in the image of God.

Dr. Perry Downs points out that war victims also lose their moral compass: "Children who have been brutalized by the effects of war, and by the direct actions of warriors, find it especially difficult to understand the difference between right and wrong."[11] A major task for Christian educators is helping these victims—adults and children alike—to recover the ability to discern right from wrong and to make moral decisions based on what is just and right. The victims and their families also require support groups as they go through restoration processes.

Victims of War Need Truth

The need for truth that contradicts Satan's lies highlights a major task of Christian education when addressing the spiritual needs of all victims of war. Both children and adults need and want to be in a loving, caring relationship with a benevolent and forgiving God. To achieve this, they need to know that whatever their situation, God offers forgiveness and His continued presence. Victims of war also need help in resolving guilt about their part in any tragic event and dealing with anger they may feel toward a God who, in their view, did not help to change their situations. Most of all, they need the hope that comes from knowing that God has not abandoned them. The church must provide opportunities for all victims of war to experience, in community, spiritual healing, reconciliation, forgiveness, and hope.

—Phyllis Kilbourn

Victorian Era, Christianity and Naturalism during the

Naturalism is a philosophy based on the idea that all reality is basically natural reality—that the only true and

factual basis for any phenomenon comes from nature, or the laws of nature. As is the case with many important philosophies, the terms and ideas underlying naturalism are nebulous, diffused across many periods and philosophies, past and present. However, the heyday of naturalism as a philosophical movement was the Victorian era, when it influenced not only intellectual life, but also the arts and literature.

Naturalism dismissed the possibility of a divine or supernatural dimension of history and science. It therefore had significant ramifications for religion. During the Victorian era, it frequently clashed with the adherents of Christianity. The battles and debates it spawned remain some of the most famous intellectual clashes of the 19th century. And unlike some of the earlier great debates of the medieval or classical periods, whose factions and points of contention have arguably become less urgent and more academic, Victorian era debates remain quite close to the surface. Many present-day realities of modern academia can be directly traced to the struggles over naturalism that occurred during the Victorian era.

Naturalism as a Term

The term *naturalism* refers to multiple areas of focus and inquiry. Many seem very different in outlook and approach. Naturalism has appeared in art and literature, as well as in philosophy and science. Overall, it is a school of beliefs that share a common assumption that all matter, and all the patterns and properties of matter, exist solely within the framework of nature and the laws of nature. It is somewhat comparable to the idea of materialism: the idea that only physical things exist, and that there are no spiritual or supernatural forces. Even nonmaterials things such as love or hate are really just products of materialist forces, such as instinct, brain chemistry, or natural biological drives. Pushed to the extreme, naturalism dismisses the possibility of spiritual or supernatural forces playing a role in such areas as history or science.

Naturalism was also closely linked to the ascendancy of science in Western cultural and intellectual life. As applied to philosophy and science, it demanded the application of the scientific method to virtually all forms of inquiry. In this sense, naturalism was closely allied with the movements that predated it in the Renaissance and baroque periods.

In the mid-19th century, naturalism became especially equated with the writings of Charles Darwin and the theory of evolution, which provided a new, different, and scientifically plausible framework for studying humanity. This new view of human and biological development vaguely implied that there was no place for God, either as a causal force in natural events or as an observer. It was not so much that Darwin actively denied God or promoted "atheism"—though that seemed to be the

11. Perry Downs, "Moral Development," in *Healing the Children of War: A Handbook for Ministry to Children Who Have Suffered Deep Traumas*, ed. Phyllis Kilbourn (Monrovia, CA: MARC, 1995), 91.

way his writings were sometimes understood, both by his supporters and his detractors. It was that God now seemed irrelevant. For many after Darwin, religion was consigned to the ashtray of history: a mere relic of past superstitions, and just another in the long and melancholy list of erroneous human ideas that had eventually been exposed as bogus.

However, naturalism also entailed much more than theories about the evolution of human life or the origin of plant and animal species. It was a broad-based philosophical movement that also affected a wide range of other endeavors. Inasmuch as naturalism implied a range of beliefs about humans and animals, it also heavily influenced seemingly unrelated areas, including literature and the arts. Ultimately, naturalism played a hugely formative role in the history of modern education, especially in the formation of academic disciplines in the late 19th and early 20th centuries. Whole new disciplines such as anthropology and psychology emerged, especially in the newly conceived academic "social sciences." Hence, it is not an exaggeration to say that naturalism is one of modern academia's most important ancestors. While the universities as stewards of intellectual and educational life had existed since the High Middle Ages in Western Europe, in the Victorian era they were recast as more secular and with more highly specialized faculties. Science became arguably the most prestigious and coveted sector of the Western university. Scientific outlooks affected virtually all academic disciplines, including even the study of religion and the Bible, and other formerly humanistic disciplines such as history.

"Victorian" as a Term

Naturalist philosophy both predates and follows the reign of England's Queen Victoria (1837–1901). Nonetheless, its heyday was the later decades of the 19th century, placing it squarely in the period dominated by England's venerable and long-reigning monarch. Beyond the Victorian time frame, naturalism dominated much thinking through the fin de siècle and up to the outbreak of World War I. This era might also be called the "late modern" period, since it represents the intellectual conclusion of many of the assumptions and tendencies of modern thought, assumptions that had begun with the Enlightenment, or even the Renaissance.

Geographically, "Victorian" most properly references England and Great Britain. However, the term can also encompass virtually the entire English-speaking world of the 19th century, especially the imperial dominions like Canada, New Zealand, and Australia, and the former colony the United States of America. The term also sometimes has a global connotation, touching on themes of contact between Western and non-Western societies.

Indeed, inasmuch as Queen Victorian reigned over an empire spanning virtually all the world (one of her titles was Empress of India), "Victorian" is closely intertwined with larger geopolitical and social topics such as colonialism and racism. On occasion, English speakers may use the term "Victorian" when referencing European countries like France or Germany, especially when emphasizing traits or cultural themes that were common to Western Europe as a whole.

When Victoria died in 1901, she was replaced by her popular and very patient son, Edward VII (1901–1910). The term "Edwardian" also enjoys some widespread usage, usually referring to a still largely Victorian culture, but also characterized by emerging 20th-century elements, especially inventions such as the car and the telephone. Overall the term "Edwardian" is used less frequently and arguably exists primarily as a means of expressing a transition between the Victorian period and what came later.

As a stand-alone adjective, "Victorian" is perhaps especially equated with sexual morality and propriety. "Victorian morality" instinctively evokes images of sexual propriety—of excruciatingly reserved and formalized models of courtship, especially among the British upper class and, to a lesser extent, the bourgeoisie. Well-loved Victorian novels frequently draw on these attractive and fascinating social themes. Alongside social and moral connotations, however, the Victorian ideal was also expressed in numerous other areas, especially industry and science.

Antecedents to Victorian-Era Naturalism

The influence of naturalism on 19th-century thinking would be difficult to overstate. While not exactly the same thing, the ideas espoused by naturalist thinkers related to scientific ideals. Several of the most important "modern" thinkers are from the Victorian era and reflect the direct or indirect influence of naturalist thinking. At the same time, naturalist ideas were the result of many centuries of evolution in Western thought. Tensions pitting naturalistic or empirical approaches against traditional ideas (often religious) were well-established. In the Victorian era, however, many of these tensions crystallized into their most mature and sophisticated forms. Naturalism also moved into an even more mainstream and ascendant trajectory.

Naturalism derived from some of the most quintessential ideas of the Enlightenment. One of the most important in this regard was the oft-cited notion of "natural laws." The idea of natural law was borrowed from the ancient Stoic notion of *ius naturale*, which held that natural laws and principles governed the universe. Human laws should conform to these natural laws. For the Romans, these natural laws were closely linked to reason and the traditions of rationalism found in Greek and Hellenistic philosophers. During the heyday of the Roman Empire, stock ideals loosely influenced Roman legal codes, especially in the later period, when the universality of the law became a special concern. With the empire ruling over such a huge range of territory, peoples, and languages, universal ideals that transcended particular customs and traditions became an increasingly attractive basis for legal decision making.

Natural Law Ideas during the Enlightenment

During the height of the Enlightenment, many of Western Europe's most important thinkers had emphasized that nature and human experiences were determined by inviolable natural laws governing a whole range of activities and phenomena, from the movements of planets, to politics, to economics. Sir Isaac Newton's law of gravity was one of the most famous and influential of these ideas. Like other major and revolutionary ideas, Newton's ideas about gravity not only influenced thinking about actual gravity and planetary orbits; they also reinforced in a powerful and substantiated fashion the idea of physical laws governing the cosmos. They brought regularity, order, and functionality to the potential chaos of moving objects.

Newton's belief in natural laws also echoed comparable ideas in other areas. In politics, thinkers like Thomas Hobbes (1588–1679), Baron de Montesquieu (1689–1755), and John Locke (1632–1704) wrote about governments, freedom, and the historical development of social infrastructures in ways that portrayed human political endeavors as the products of natural principles. Borrowing heavily from classical political theorists like Aristotle and Polybius, they often cast human political behavior in almost organic terms. Stages of historical political development might be linked to population, urbanization, or the simple duration/maturity of a given culture. These political ideas reflected ideas about natural law, implying that liberty could only exist in certain situations and contexts. In 1651, Thomas Hobbes penned one of the most famous works arguing for natural laws and principles in the political arena, his widely read work *The Leviathan*. For Hobbes, basic human drives such as the need for food, shelter, and clothing, or sex, resulted in a continual state of struggle between human individuals and groups. This jungle-like, savage "state of nature" necessitated strong government to wrest human societies from a violent and self-destructive state of un-civilization.

The application of natural law reasoning to the political realm was not always quite so grim as Hobbes implied, however. For Hobbes, the state of nature connoted a dark image of warring, violent, anarchic states—an arguably more pessimistic view of human nature. But the same reasoning could also lead to more optimistic theories. "Freedom," which for Hobbes had seemed a dangerous state of anarchy, might also be embraced in a more positive fashion. Presaging the famous "nature versus nurture" debate of 20th-century sociologists and psychologists, Enlightenment political theorists often saw freedom as the human being's natural habitat. Humans were born free. This made freedom a universal birthright. Yet this same freedom was also inevitably imperiled and limited by artificial barriers to liberty created by humans: tyrannical government, economic or social oppression, and religion.

The idea of freedom as a "natural state," something that comes to humans as a birthright, was especially inherent in John Locke's emphasis on the tabula rasa: the "clean slate." In his famous *Two Treatises of Civil Government* (1689), Locke reasoned that humans were part of nature and born in a pristine, blank state without preconceived cultural, social, or intellectual beliefs. Nature, or nature's God, had endowed all humans with natural rights, which Locked famously described as life, liberty, and the pursuit of property. Government, he reasoned, existed solely to secure these basic human freedoms. Locke's writings in this regard proved enormously influential, obviously influencing later theoreticians like Thomas Jefferson, who all but plagiarized Locke when writing the American Declaration of Independence. More generally, Locke's notions of natural rights as being inherent in the human condition also informed more modern ideas and terminology, especially the late-20th-century's notion of "human rights." Locke's work was published in the immediate aftermath of England's Glorious Revolution (1688) and the expulsion of the absolutist Stuart line of monarchs. Its thoughtful advocacy of a blending of libertarian ideals with responsible government seemed to support the reformist, constitutional monarchy that England had established.

Another writer who saw freedom as the natural state of human beings was Jean Jacques Rousseau (1712–1778), the famous French philosopher. In the opening lines of *The Social Contract* (1762), Rousseau proclaimed that freedom was the natural birth-state of all human beings, which made accounting for all the oppression, tyranny, and slavery in the world even more urgent. "*L'homme est né libre, et partout il est dans les fers* [Man is born free, and everywhere he is in chains]." Like many of his Enlightenment contemporaries, Rousseau saw government as an artificial but useful human invention—as a compact—a social contract between the people and their rulers. Government should ensure the natural, organic will of the people.

Natural Law Ideas and Revolution

The great revolutions of the time—the English Glorious Revolution of 1688, the American Revolution of 1776, and the French Revolution of 1789—all reflected the influence of Enlightenment political thinking in various forms and fashions. The idea that freedom was a natural birthright—inherent in such documents as the American Declaration of Independence (1776) or the French Declaration of the Rights of Man and Citizen (1789)—emerged as one of the Enlightenment's most influential ideas, however imperfectly realized. Given the natural history of humanity, with its welter of different political climates and statuses, liberty seemed to require fertile ground to flourish. Eternal vigilance on the part of freedom lovers was required if such natural patterns of corruption and degradation were to be avoided.

Economic Ideas and Natural Law

Economics was one of the most telling areas in which ideas about natural laws and the inviolable patterns of human social behavior prevailed. By the end of the 18th century, perhaps no subject was more vigorous and influential than economics. In the 18th century, the term "economist" was not really used. The term "physiocrat" is probably the closest, borrowing from the great financial advisor to and minister to both Louis XV and Louis XVI, Turgot (1727–1781). Famous for allegedly coining the phrase "laissez-faire," Turgot was an early proponent of the notion that economic behavior was self-regulating, therefore obviating the need for the heavy mercantilist regulations that drove the policies of most of the great European powers of the day. In the English-speaking world, probably the most famous proponent of these ideas was the great Scottish writer Adam Smith. Smith's *The Wealth of Nations* (1776) is one of the most influential books of the modern age. It gave Western thinkers one of the most powerful versions of the notion that natural laws—as opposed to man-made laws—governed economic behavior.

For Smith, the most important and comprehensive of natural laws was the law of supply and demand, which dictated price fluctuations, in turn affecting such areas as the consumption and production of goods and services. Moreover, the law of supply and demand presupposed predictable patterns of human economic behavior. According to Smith, humans generally acted in their own self-interest. They bought more when prices declined and less when prices rose, for example. The natural extrapolation of these arguments was that markets were self-regulating. Put another way, natural laws such as the law of supply and demand drove price mechanisms in the market. State regulation of markets was redundant

at best, if not outright harmful. This was the core belief behind Smith's idea of "The Invisible Hand"—the idea that invisible natural forces kept prices and supply fluctuating eternally up and down, but always returning to affordable levels.

The law of supply and demand is a great example of Enlightenment ideas about natural law. It is on a par with other powerful, comprehensive principles around which whole subjects and disciplines developed: Newton's law of gravity, or Darwin's principle of natural selection, for example. Related theories followed. In 1789, Thomas Malthus's famous *Essay on Population* applied the law of supply and demand to population, food supply, and human reproduction. For Malthus, low prices and abundant supply tended to stimulate human procreation, resulting in population increases. Nonetheless, the fluctuation mechanisms espoused by economists like Smith would result, according to Malthus, in corrections, both in terms of prices and population. In other words, as population increases strained available food supplies, prices of food would rise, therefore reducing demand for food. Also, as food prices rose, farmers would naturally increase production to benefit from the better returns on their harvests. Increased food production would ultimately result in a greater supply, renewing downward pressure on the price of food. Unfortunately, according to Malthus, population always increased at a faster rate than agricultural production. In his famous thesis, land available for tillage could only grow arithmetically, whereas population grew geometrically. Put another way, steady population increases would inevitably outstrip the ability of the agricultural markets to feed people, resulting in famine and scarcity. The "correction" Malthus envisioned in this fluctuation between food and population growth was famine and death on a mass scale.

Malthus's ideas were shocking to many. They seemed to manifest a dark dimension of Adam Smith's "Invisible Hand." The "corrections" of price, or supply, that Smith had described in a somewhat prosaic manner when discussing pin factories, or trade in wine, seemed grotesque when applied to such topics as human population and reproduction. Malthus all but evoked the pale rider of death, right out of the Bible. Similarly, Malthus's implied argument that humans reproduced as thoughtlessly and as relentlessly as rabbits seemed unromantic, as did his call for more contraception and birth control. It is also often argued that Malthus's ideas about the inevitably of food scarcity were disproved in the 19th century by the improved food production techniques of the Industrial Revolution, as well as by the securing of imported food for England after the 1840s. Nonetheless, his ideas were enormously influential, however dystopian they might have seemed. His ideas about natural laws governing price fluctuations and food production also influenced the great early 19th-century economist David Ricardo (1772–1823), whose "iron law of wages" also argued for inevitable natural economic patterns resulting from human economic behavior.

From the list of economists and theoreticians of the 18th and 19th centuries, Malthus remains among the most noted, with his ideas of "Malthusian" corrections to the population still inspiring horrific images in the popular imagination still today. There was also a biological component to human sexual reproduction that made Malthus's ideas influential beyond mere economics. His relatively short *Essay on Population* (1798) is usually dismissed as flawed, or even "disproved." Nonetheless, Malthus is one of the most important of the late Enlightenment's proponents of natural law. He is also one of the best examples of the rising tide of realism and naturalism that emerged with such cultural, intellectual, and psychological vigor in the 19th century. His work heavily influenced later thinkers, including Charles Darwin.

"Isms" and Modernity

Though it had its roots in earlier periods, naturalism had seasoned and matured by the 19th century. It was then that it emerged as one of the most important and influential "isms" in Western thought. Its outlooks and assumptions helped shape the development of numerous modern academic disciplines that emerged in the university systems of the Victorian era. It also deeply affected those disciplines and subjects that had already existed for centuries.

In the 19th century, many important ideas that had been incubating since the early Enlightenment reached their fruition in the great "modern" schools of thought. Today, "modern" might merely imply contemporary to most casual speakers. But to students of history, "modern" has a very specific connotation. It refers specifically to the historical period that emerged roughly with the end of the Renaissance. The modern period is characterized by many important intellectual changes, including the rise of science and an intellectual emphasis on empiricism. Like other great Victorian-era schools of thought, naturalism draws on these earlier developments, but developed into its most coherently articulated and comprehensive forms during the heyday of 19th-century intellectual life. In particular, naturalism is one of the 19th century's most famous "isms."

An "ism" is a curious manifestation of the English language. "Ism" was a suffix that came from the Greek, where it was used to change nouns or verbs into abstract belief systems or religions (e.g., Judaism, Hellenism, etc.).

Similarly, in English the use of the suffix converts a word into a noun that connotes abstract belief or a system of beliefs. The Victorian era is characterized by most of the important modern schools of thought, which are often tagged with the "ism" suffix: capitalism, socialism, romanticism, Darwinism, etc. Collectively, these views constitute the heyday of modern thinking. Today, it is often argued that the tidy sureties of the various Victorian isms inadequately addressed such later horrors as Auschwitz, Hiroshima, or indeed, the seemingly inescapable folly of August 1914. Therefore, in terms of being a historical period, the "modern" age has already ended, leaving thinkers and artists in a limbo era known as "postmodern." Nonetheless, the legacy of the Victorian isms endures in contemporary intellectual life. Naturalism—with its emphasis on materialism and empiricism, and its myth-busting eschewal of romanticism—is arguably one of the most important of the surviving isms.

The Challenge of the Industrial Age

If it is true that the "isms" of modernity failed to account for the horrors of the 20th century, it is also true that many Enlightenment beliefs faltered in the face of 19th-century developments, especially the rise of industry. The Industrial Revolution, which has been compared to the Neolithic agricultural revolution in its historical significance and effects, changed the world very rapidly during the Victorian era. This development was something that no Enlightenment thinker fully envisioned. Industrializing societies underwent massive social change. Populations that had been relatively stable for centuries burst into exponential growth. Between 1750 and 1850, the population of England grew from roughly 4 million to 25 million. Other industrializing nations experienced similar population growth. Moreover, this growth was accompanied by various social and economic maladies, made known by period writers such as Charles Dickens (1812–1870) and Victor Hugo (1802–1885). Preindustrial Europe's most brilliant thinkers had not really anticipated the London of Dickens's *Oliver Twist*, or the indifferent and cruel Paris of Hugo's *Les Misérables* (1862).

In the wake of these enormous changes, older Enlightenment beliefs about freedom, progress, social equality, and political rights now seemed insufficient. In terms of both practical public policy and the philosophical debates of the times, something new seemed required. In particular, the Industrial Revolution challenged the old Enlightenment notions of natural law. It was not so much that the Industrial Revolution proved natural laws governing economics and social structures to be wrong per se. But for Adam Smith and his contemporaries, unregulated markets and the development of industry had seemed almost wholly beneficial. Similarly, the political rights advocated by Enlightenment thinkers ranging from Locke to Jefferson seemed to offer little to the new problems facing factory workers: minuscule wages, horrible and unsafe working conditions, and working-class slums.

By the early 19th century, Enlightenment-era ideas seemed heartless. In the 18th century, arguments about "invisible hands" and "laissez-faire" liberties had been equated with Jefferson, John Locke, and Adam Smith. By the middle of the 19th century, the very same arguments about freedom seem more akin to Ebenezer Scrooge. During England's industrialization, wages and working conditions—something Adam Smith had seemed to take for granted in his Invisible Hand formulae—were truly horrific by almost any measure. Conditions were not much better in other industrializing areas of Europe: the Rhine-Ruhr areas of Germany, northeast France, and Belgium. Given the new realities, older assumptions about economic progress and political rights could seem as quaint as a gilded baroque altar. If such natural laws truly existed, they might be as cruel and as indifferent as nature itself. The old Enlightenment emphasis on economic freedom seemed anachronistic in these new Dickensian conditions.

The great political revolutions that had swept across Europe, starting with France in 1789, had also achieved somewhat mixed results. Liberal politics of the 18th century had generally emphasized political rights. These were often expressed as negative rights—rights that limited state powers in a whole host of areas, including economics. These rights were also rooted in natural law ideas, such as man's natural state of freedom. Political rights were often expressed in the various bills of rights that were an important feature of constitutional and liberal politics of the day. By the middle of the 19th century, however, political outcomes often resulted in discouragement with 18th-century-style political rights and liberties. Many liberals began to emphasize a more activist state, one with greater powers to intervene in private matters, especially for the betterment of the poor and needy. As was the case for economic ideas, the Enlightenment's emphasis on natural rights felt unsuited to the times.

The Arts and Literature

Naturalism developed further in the 19th century, shaped by these new sensibilities wrought by industrialization. Arguably, it veered in two separate directions. On the one hand, naturalism as a philosophy was no longer so influential in the most prevalent political and economic arguments of the day. To the extent that it had been based on baroque-era assertions about natural law and a generalized belief in science, Victorian naturalism evolved into a philosophy more closely linked to scientific movements such as Darwinism or struggles with religion, especially Christianity. It remained equated with a disinterested, scrupulous search for truth, generally borrowing from the language and approaches of the scientific method. Curiously, the other stream naturalism followed was in the realm of the arts. Here, naturalism came to represent the *downside*, as it were, of the old beliefs in progress. As a movement in the arts and literature, naturalism depicted, and drew attention to, the many losers of Victorian progress: the working poor, women, slaves, and the sick.

Naturalism in the arts and literature intersects with yet another important movement of 19th-century culture: realism. Realism in the arts is generally depicted as a counterweight to the romantic movement, which often featured idyllic and even escapist visions of the past, or mythologized a Europe that no longer really existed. Idyllic images of rural England, found in the works of poets like Wordsworth (1770–1850) and painters like John Constable (1776–1837), are quintessential examples of this romanticized view of the English countryside—one that seems almost willfully divorced from the reality of the sooty industrial cities like Manchester or London's teeming East Side. The occasional escapism and antiquarianism of poets like John Keats (1795–1821), Percy Shelley (1792–1822), and Samuel Coleridge (1772–1834) also provided famous and wonderful examples of this sort of romanticism, so popular in the early 19th century.

While not particularly ecclesiastical or even orthodox, such iconic figures of the romantic period also eschewed naturalism, in that they embraced religion and mystery. They seemed to find in religious imagery and myth a fascinating beauty and deeper meaning that was not necessarily understood in purely rational terms. Indeed, they often consciously rejected the arrogant emphasis on "reason" that had characterized so much thinking during the Enlightenment. In terms of Christianity, this renewed intellectual affection for religion often expressed itself especially powerfully in a love of the medieval saints, pilgrimages, and sacred medieval architecture, including ruins.

This romantic fascination with the mystical and the sacred was not limited to Christianity, however. During the 19th century, the romantics manifested a revived interest in classical myths. Similarly, many romantics developed a deep affection for Islam, creating the so-called orientalist movement. An offshoot of romanticism, orientalism replenished the arts during the 19th century with new images, sounds, and perspectives. The movement especially flourished in France and Victorian England. In France, numerous fine artists like Ingres (1780–1867), Delacroix (1798–1863), and Jean Léon Gérôme experimented with orientalist themes in their painting. Their efforts frequently highlighted "oriental" religion (i.e., Islam), as well as the dazzling desert beauty they envisioned in the Middle East. In Victorian England, the exploits and activities of Sir Richard Francis Burton (1821–1890) similarly reflected this novel interest in Muslim civilization, especially his translation of *A Thousand and One Arabian Knights* (1885).

In reaction to romanticism's idealized scenes and motifs, however, naturalism in the arts produced scenes that seemed to accentuate reality to the point of pessimism. In art, literature, and music, naturalistic influences sought to depict the plight of the poor and downtrodden. If naturalism's roots were in the older ideas of natural laws governing such areas as the economy and political development, it now seemed intent on highlighting the failures of nature to provide for those unfortunates at the other end of the food chain. The French artist Édouard Manet (1832–1883) featured many such realistic themes in his art. His *Olympia* is one such work, featuring a classical nude posed in the ancient style of the reclining Venus. However, Olympia appears to be a prostitute, and it is often suggested that the faint dirt on her legs and arms indicates that she probably needs a bath.

In Victorian England, an even more telling specimen of realism and naturalism in the arts is the work of Joseph Turner (1775–1851). Turner is famous for his paintings of mythological scenes, including the iconic *The Golden Bough*, which would later inspire the masterwork of anthropologist Sir James George Frazer. But in addition to his scenes from the classical past, Turner gained fame as a painter who depicted nature—not nature in its charming and idyllic landscape forms, as the baroque and neoclassical painters had often emphasized—but nature in its most chaotic, destructive, and violent forms. One of Turner's most famous paintings in this regard is his 1840 work *The Slave Ship*, which shows a slave ship caught in a storm, struggling to stay afloat in the turbulent ocean waters. Horrifically, the slavers have thrown over some of their human cargo in the attempt to stay afloat. A shackled black leg juts out of the choppy water, while menacing ocean fish attack.

In terms of English literature, many Victorian novels highlighted the plight of the poor, women, or other disenfranchised members of society. Though arguably too much of a popularizer and commercial writer to fit comfortably into any one of the great literary and philosophical schools of his time, Charles Dickens's writings are among the most important with regard to sympathetic and/or "realistic" depictions of the poor. For students learning about this important and transitional period in European intellectual and social history, Dickens is probably one of the most instructive and helpful writers to reference. His acute moral concern for the plight of the poor—grounded in his humanity and his Christian faith—produced some of the most iconic images of London in the midst of the Industrial Revolution: chimney sweeps, orphanages, gangs of child pickpockets, and squalid, teeming streets reeking of gin and danger.

In late 19th-century America, writers like Stephen Crane (1871–1900) and Kate Chopin (1850–1904) showed people struggling against impersonal social or political forces. Even more closely equated with naturalist literature in America was the important writer Jack London (1876–1916). His works featured classic "man against nature" stories. They seemed to highlight the struggle inherent in all nature, casting man in the role of just another animal struggling like all the others.

Naturalism and the Rise of the Social Sciences

If an increasingly pessimistic interpretation of Enlightenment views on natural law loosely informed movements in the fine arts and literature, it was in philosophy that the evolution of natural law ideas had the largest and most clearly delineated outcomes. Naturalism as it continued to evolve from its earlier versions developed into some of the Victorian era's most famous philosophical schools. Perhaps even more important, several distinct academic disciplines emerged during the period, largely owing to the influence of naturalism. Chief among these were anthropology, sociology, and economics. Older "subjects," such as history, the Bible, and classical literature, were also deeply affected by the naturalist movement. Moreover, the entire category of disciplines grouped under the label "social sciences" emerged in the later 19th century, indebted to naturalist philosophy. Though usually included in the study of biology, Darwinism also emerged in this period and overlaps with many concerns of the social science disciplines.

In economics, naturalist thinking helped shape the emergence of scientific socialism. "Socialism" as a general term had emerged earlier in the 19th century, largely as a moral response to the inequities of capitalist, industrial Western Europe. However, many of the early socialists were utopian thinkers of various sorts, experimenting with different social models, but primarily basing their ideas on moral values. In many cases the "utopian socialists," as they came to be called, did not even really envision a general transformation of society along socialist lines. Instead, they often fantasized about fashioning various and often fantastical forms of communal living, set far apart from the mainstream of the capitalist world.

Socialism in its supposedly "scientific" mode was first propounded by Karl Marx (1818–1883), one of the most important thinkers in Western European history. Rejecting the romantic, utopian socialists of the early 19th century, Marx sought to formulate a theory of history and economics based on scientific principles. His *Communist Manifesto*, a kind of revolutionary tract more than a serious book, was published in 1848. While it contains the core of Marxist thinking, along with his most famous and appealing phrases, the more serious work Marx produced was *Capital*, published in 1867.

Marx based much of his social and economic theorizing on his notion of "dialectical materialism," borrowing from the German philosopher Georg Hegel (1770–1831). Hegel's idea of a "dialectic" process envisioned a perpetual struggle between a dominant spirit of the age (zeitgeist), the "thesis," and its opposing reaction, the antithesis. For Hegel, however, the zeitgeist of each age was essentially a cultural or intellectual entity. Marx turned Hegel on his head, arguing that nonmaterialist forces in history, such as religion and nationalism, were mere facades for deeper struggles between economic classes over the means of production.

Marx's revised version of Hegel's dialectic provided the foundation for his hugely influential class interpretation of history. For Marxists, class became the dominant historical focus. Older historical foci, such as monarchs, military campaigns, or elite cultural endeavors like art and music, were generally subordinated to class analysis, unless they could be shown to relate to the economic class struggle that was the invisible mover of all history. Marx reinforced his work with a thesis about the French Revolution, which became almost dogma in later years. In 1789, he argued, the bourgeois class had successfully overthrown the aristocracy, after centuries of class struggle dating back to the Renaissance. Now they owned and controlled the means of production. Some day, Marx argued, the proletariat—wage earners working for the bourgeoisie, who owned capital and the means of production—would similarly overthrow the bourgeoisie.

Marx's writings deeply shaped the development of social sciences in Western thought and academic disciplines. A synthesizer in his approach to philosophy and intellectual inquiry, Marx sought to apply scientific principles to diverse areas, ranging from history, to economics, to philosophy. While he was not necessarily the first to do this, he perhaps did it the most explicitly and the most successfully. The fact that his ideas seemed connected to social and political values enhanced his influence. In communist countries his work became de rigueur in the universities, replacing former canonical texts like the Bible or, in China, the Confucian classics. In Western nations, his work has also been enormously influential in academic circles, especially in the social sciences.

Darwinism and Naturalism

Charles Darwin (1809–1882) is probably an even more important figure in the diffuse history of naturalism. In

1859, he published *On the Origin of Species by Natural Selection*. The idea underlying Darwin's landmark book was natural selection. From the vast array of biological diversity evidenced in the plant and animal world, nature favored animals and plants with the most useful characteristics, especially those that could give an animal an advantage in terms of the struggle for survival. Sexual selection was an important subcomponent of Darwin's reasoning. Qualities favoring survival were genetically transmitted at a greater rate, eventually becoming dominant over less advantageous traits. Over time, new plants and animals evolved as a result of this process of selection. In 1871, Darwin published another book, *The Descent of Man*, which proved to be even more controversial. In it, he extrapolated on his earlier theories, suggesting that humankind had evolved from primates. Both Darwin's views—not only on the origin of species, but also on the evolution of human beings from apes—directly impinged on biblical understandings, and even humanist ones.

There were two important influences on one of Darwin's ideas. One was the social theorist and economist Thomas Malthus. From Malthus, Darwin absorbed the idea of selection, especially as it related to the struggle for resources. The other was the biologist Charles Lyell (1797–1875), who is best remembered today for his association with Darwin. However, in his time he was one of Europe's most important biologists. In *Principles of Geology* (1830–1833), Lyell probed fossil records, a still relatively novel endeavor for serious scientists in the early 19th century. Foreshadowing Darwin's *Origin of Species*, Lyell probed the fossil records to argue for the evolution of species across time.

In both his *Principles of Geology* and his later work *The Antiquity of Man* (1863), Lyell especially emphasized the virtually unfathomable millennia upon millennia of time that had passed before the dawn of recorded history—literally millions of years. Whether talking about the age of the earth itself, or about the relatively more recent history of human beings, Lyell showed that time went back much further than most had envisioned. Lyell's work not only challenged science with issues of dating and geological chronology; it also affected the popular imagination with not only its depictions of incredibly ancient fossil animals, but also its discussion of such topics as prehistoric cave paintings. In *The Antiquity of Man*, much of Lyell's work focused on prehistoric Denmark, referencing finds in the still new field of archaeology. *The Antiquity of Man* is one of the Victorian era's most important books, in that it further expanded the geographical and chronological boundaries that had defined "history" for many centuries.

Both directly and indirectly, Darwin's and Lyell's works challenged and revolutionized learning in a host of areas, not all of which were directly related to biology. Their writings helped to unravel the traditional chronological and geographical orientation of the history of civilization, which had typically begun in Mesopotamia. The emphasis on beginning history in Mesopotamia also more happily corresponded with the biblical narrative, which placed the first human societies in Eden, a mythical oasis-like place supposedly somewhere between the Euphrates and the Tigris Rivers. The Bible, so long held as sacred, gradually began to fit into a more historical framework. In the following years, scholars began to examine biblical texts more critically, weighing them carefully against other historical sources.

The theory of evolution that Darwin popularized proved explosive. The Victorian debates between "Darwinism" and the church, in particular, still loom large in popular thinking. Nonetheless, ecclesiastical responses to Darwin's challenge were considerably more sophisticated than they are often characterized. In 1860, only a few months after the appearance of Darwin's *On the Origin of Species*, six Anglican clergymen and a layman published *Essays and Reviews*, was a collection of writings penned by men representing the liberal wing of the Anglican Church, including Frederick Temple, the future archbishop of Canterbury (1821–1902). His was probably the most famous essay in the collection; it cautioned modern intellectuals against a world governed solely by rigid laws of cause and effect. Temple's greatest fear was a belief in determinism, as opposed to scientific principles or natural laws. Overall, *Essays and Reviews* sought to reconcile science, including evolution, with Christianity. The writings were controversial, with the authors of the essays actually being called to appear before clerical courts, where they were acquitted.

Darwin's writings raised debates across most of the Western intellectual world—not simply in English-speaking countries. The Catholic Church was arguably less charitable. Pope Pius IX's (r. 1846–1878) famous *Syllabus of Errors* denounced a host of modern developments as anathema to Christian and Catholic principles. Among other errors criticized by Pius, the document condemned the view that natural laws and principles were sufficient to explain all knowledge, including sacred and divine matters. His successor, Leo XIII (r. 1878–1903), tried to bridge the gap between naturalism and Christianity, emphasizing the traditional notion of a divinely conceived creation, one ultimately compatible with thoughtful scientific inquiry.

In subsequent years, most Christians tried to make their peace with science and evolution—though they continued to chafe at any naturalistic perspectives that denied God altogether, thereby promoting atheistic viewpoints. By the early 20th century, probably the most vociferous critics of Darwin remaining were in the more conservative denominations of Protestantism, especially in North America. The famous "Scopes monkey trial" in 1925 pitted a high school teacher who was teaching evolution against the laws of Tennessee (a Bible Belt state), which outlawed the teaching of evolution in the classroom. The colorful and witty attorneys employed in the trial—American politician and former presidential candidate Williams Jennings Bryan represented the state of Tennessee, while the famous attorney Clarence Darrow defended Scopes—added to the circus-like atmosphere of the proceedings. Though Scopes lost at trial, the decision was overturned on a technicality.

Darwin's Ideas Applied to History and Society

Darwin had many defenders. Especially notable in this regard was the prominent British physician Thomas Huxley, who declared himself "Darwin's Bulldog." Huxley defended Darwin not only generally on scientific grounds, but also on the grounds of freedom of inquiry. Huxley defended Darwin in a famous a debate at Oxford University in 1860. In other writings, Huxley further espoused agnostic beliefs, including his famous assertion that people living in a religious society—like medieval people surrounded by saints, relics, and belief in miracles—develop a "mythopoetic" orientation, almost like children. The image seemed to equate religion—and in particular Christianity—with unscientific backwardness. It came to shape intellectual attitudes very powerfully by the late Victorian period.

Another person heavily influenced by Darwin was Hebert Spencer (1820–1903). Spencer is often regarded as one of the founders of the modern academic discipline sociology. He was heavily influenced by the "positivist" French philosopher August Comte (1798–1857). Comte had argued that civilization moved through predictable stages under natural law. Moreover, through the careful consideration of evidence, and also logical rigor, it was possible to know and understand social phenomena "positively." Comte was one of the first to use statistics, graphs, and other measuring devices now common in the social sciences. Comte's *Positive Philosophy* (1851–1854) was a view of progress in which religion was equated with superstition and a less advanced stage of social development.

Borrowing heavily from both Comte and Darwin, Spencer developed a complex theory of social development, supposedly based on the positivist methods of Comte, plus the principles of selection espoused by Darwin. In his writings, Spencer coined the famous phrase "survival of the fittest," a phrase later used by Darwin. Spencer's ideas generally applied Darwin's ideas of selection and adaptability to human society, an approach later dubbed "social Darwinism."

Though often characterized in overly simplistic fashion, Spencer's ideas did seem to justify the notion that the poor were genetically or biologically inferior to the rich. Though generally discredited today, social Darwinism gained credence in the late 19th century. It dovetailed nicely with the older notion of the Protestant work ethic, which saw wealth as a sign of God's favor and the just reward of hard work and wise stewardship of resources. Social Darwinism became closely linked with the gospel of wealth, a prosperity approach to Christianity popular in the late Victorian era. More generally, Spencer's ideas gave a self-justifying theory to the gross economic and social inequities of the Gilded Age.

Early Anthropology

The area that naturalism probably influenced most heavily of all was the newly emerging discipline anthropology. Though like most areas of inquiry it had antecedents dating well into the ancient period, anthropology as it emerged in the Victorian era was a new and exciting discipline. It was destined to play an important role in 20th-century academic life. Borrowing heavily from methods like those espoused by Spencer or Comte, anthropologists probed the ancient past to find clues about human history that were missing from the written sources traditionally studied by historians and classicists. Victorian anthropology almost always reflected naturalist ideals, because it assumed that patterns of behavior or development in a given society pointed to larger principles governing human cultures. Another important point about anthropology is that it began to focus intently on many peoples and places left out of the traditional historical narratives: Africa, Asia, indigenous peoples in the Americas, and the Middle East.

With regard to Christianity, anthropology was often controversial. Religion was usually seen as primitive. The same ideas that formed precious doctrines in Christianity, for example, might be compared to those of primitive tribes or ancient pagan cults. Virtually all of the early anthropologists were naturalists. John Lubbock (1834–1913) and E. B. Tylor (1832–1917) are two of the most important early figures in anthropology. Both Tylor and Lubbock borrowed heavily from Darwin and Lyell. Their writings posited stages of development derived from naturalistic principles regarding stages of historical development, focusing on "progress," including intellectual and technological progress. They drew heavily on the evolutionary concepts of the day, but applied them to relatively contemporary indigenous peoples or to ancient cultures. Religion was invariably seen as an earlier stage of development, followed by science and reason.

The most famous of the late Victorian anthropologists was Sir James George Frazer (1854–1941). In 1890, he published the first volume of what would become one of the most significant landmark books of the modern age. Titled *The Golden Bough*, Frazer's work sought to explain an obscure Roman rite practiced in Rome in the ancient Italian town of Nemi. Purporting to examine the underlying theology of the rite, which he linked to agricultural cycles and the ancient notion of the "dying and reviving god," Frazer embarked on a massive study of ritual beliefs and practices across virtually all times and places. The most controversial sections of *The Golden Bough* seemed to imply that many aspects of Christian belief, ritual, and doctrine could be compared to similar practices found in undeveloped tribal areas or the classical pagan world.

Somewhat inadvertently, Frazer produced one of the seminal works of anthropology. He also helped forge related disciplines that were largely unknown to scholars prior to the late Victorian era. In particular, *The Golden Bough*'s vast compendium of detail regarding such things as Europe's peasant culture made Frazer relevant to his own time and place. He also helped shape the interest in folklore that characterized the late Victorian era. Today, *The Golden Bough* is largely discredited as an anthropological work, though it had a huge influence in the arts, literature, and even film. It influenced a wide variety of writers, most notably T. S. Eliot.

The Ongoing Importance of Naturalist Philosophy

Most of the Victorian-era works in the social sciences have been superseded by newer methods, perspectives, and approaches. Nevertheless, the naturalist ideals of earlier decades remain important considerations—not only in terms of the history of education, but also in terms of their important contributions to scholarly approaches. Today, an emphasis on thorough collecting of factual evidence remains, as well as the expectation that data will be examined with care and meticulous rigor. Naturalist approaches broadly influenced a wide swath of academic disciplines. Along with disciplines like anthropology and sociology, which emerged in the 19th century, naturalist principles deeply influenced a broad range of older subjects, including history and literature.

Vestigial elements of the old Victorian-era debates between religion and science persist. The unwillingness to include supernatural causal forces as elements in serious scholarship endures, arguably one of the most lasting legacies of Victorian naturalism. Similarly, though called a theory, evolution is generally regarded as fact. Challenges to it, or to its underlying naturalist ideals, are often dismissed out of hand. The noted British evolutionary biologist Richard Dawkins (b. 1941) is one of the most famous naturalists today. His books, like *The God Delusion* (2006), have helped popularize naturalist ideas with new generations, albeit in an often polemical fashion.

In other ways, however, naturalist ideals from the past are less important. The older ideas of "natural laws" that played such an important role in shaping naturalist philosophy in its early development are now often downplayed. Such ideals are more difficult to canvass given the narrower specializations of modern scholars. Modern social researchers are much more apt to restrict their focus to very closely defined and specified periods, places, or peoples. They tend to avoid grand theories and sweeping natural laws.

References and Resources

Barraclough, Geoffrey. 1978. *Main Trends in History.* New York: Holmes & Meier.

Chadwick, Owen. 1975. *The Secularization of the European Mind in the Nineteenth Century.* New York: Cambridge University Press.

Chandler, James, Arnold I. Davidson, and Harry Harootunian. 1991. *Questions of Evidence: Proof, Practice and Persuasion across the Disciplines.* Chicago, IL: Chicago University Press.

Dale, Peter Allan. 1989. *In Pursuit of a Scientific Culture: Science, Art, and Society in the Victorian Age.* Madison: University of Wisconsin Press.

Mullen, Shirley A. 1987. *Organized Freethought: The Religion of Unbelief in Victorian England.*

Stromberg, Roland N. 1966. *European Intellectual History since 1789.*

Turner, Frank Miller. 1974. *Between Science and Religion: The Reaction to Scientific Naturalism in Late Victorian England.*

—DAVID WALTER LEINWEBER

VIETNAM AND CHRISTIAN EDUCATION

The political situation and church tradition have profoundly shaped the typical attitudes and practices of Christian education in Vietnam. Protestantism entered Vietnam in 1911 through the American Christian and Missionary Alliance. The Evangelical Church of Vietnam (ECVN) is the largest officially recognized Protestant church in Vietnam. Because of their association with the colonial West, Christians have experienced political suspicion and religious restrictions in post-1975 Vietnam. The Vietnamese government has yet to register many other Protestant denominations.

Vietnamese Protestant clergy look within and outside of Vietnam for theological education. They access theological education through onsite, online, or underground means. Given restrictions on religious freedom, Vietnam has only one government-sanctioned Protestant Bible school, in Saigon. This school opened in February 2003 with almost 50 students and subsequently takes in new admissions every other year, up to a maximum of 100 students. This limitation has left Vietnamese Christians struggling to meet the greater need of preparing Christian educators for their churches.

Vietnamese Christians, those of the ECVN in particular, strongly focus on Bible reading and prayer as a means of spiritual growth. This practice takes place through daily devotion in an individual, family, or small group context. The goal is to cultivate a personal relationship with Christ, an experience of the Spirit, and loving relationship to others. This emphasis is rooted in the history of the evangelical tradition, which stresses the centrality of the Bible and personal piety. The responsibility of Christian education thus centers not only on the church but also on the family's ability to teach and pass on the values distinctive to the shaping of evangelical Christian identity in Vietnam.

References and Resources

Marsden, George M. 1991. *Understanding Fundamentalism and Evangelicalism.* Grand Rapids, MI: Eerdmans.

Reimer, Reg. 2011. *Vietnam's Christians: A Century of Growth and Adversity.* Pasadena, CA: William Carey Library.

Truong, Tu Thien Van. 2012. "Vietnam." *Ecumenical Review* 64 (2): 94–103.

—QUYNH-HOA LE NGUYEN

VINCENT, BISHOP JOHN HEYL

Bishop John Heyl Vincent is a primary developer of the Protestant Sunday school (SS) in the United States from the 1860s to the early 1900s. Initially, Vincent worked with other Chicago SS leaders, B. F. Jacobs and Edward Eggleston, to develop a regularized series of SS Bible lessons, which became the model for the Uniform Sunday School Lesson Series (1872). Elected to represent the Chicago SS Union to the General SS Convention in London in 1862, in 1864 he became a general agent of the Sunday School Union of the Methodist Episcopal Church and then its corresponding secretary from 1868, supervising Methodist SS work (northern United States) for 20 years.

In July 1866, he initiated the first comprehensive SS teacher periodical, containing a series of SS lessons as well as articles on teaching and biblical study, *The Sunday School Teacher.* In 1868, he edited the Methodist *The Sunday School Journal for Teachers and Young People.* Elected as a Methodist Episcopal bishop in 1888, he served in Kansas and then Europe until his retirement in 1904. During this time, he was a preacher at Harvard University from 1893 to 1896, receiving an honorary STD in 1896 (later also serving as a preacher at Yale, Cornell, Chicago, and Wellesley). During his retirement, he continued to teach and write, until his death in Chicago on 9 May 1920.

Early Background and Education

John H. Vincent was the fifth child born (and the first to survive) to John Himrod and Mary Raser Vincent, in Tuscaloosa, Alabama, on 23 February 1832. Consecrated at his birth to ministry, he taught school for a time before receiving his license to preach and becoming a Methodist circuit rider in Pennsylvania, New Jersey, and then Illinois (Joliet, Galena, and Rockford).

While he attended local academies as a child (before he was 14) and one year of theological school at the Wesleyan Institute in Newark, New Jersey (1852–1853), he was basically self-educated through reading and on the job experience, including a year of travel in Egypt and Palestine (1863) learning about the origins of Christian faith. A voracious reader of both classics and theology, he always regretted his limited formal education and sought to extend education to others through both SS and adult institutes.

Significant Contributions to Christian Education

Vincent was the key architect of a strategy for enhancing SS teacher training that included lessons on pedagogy, classroom management, and biblical history and geography. He revised the Methodist revival camp meeting practice into a summer teachers' institute for SS teacher training, the first being the Des Plaines Methodist Camp Ground in Illinois, purchased in 1865 (also the first site for training students in SS work, from Garrett Biblical Institute and Northwestern University).

Later, with Lewis Miller, he developed a more extensive program at Chautauqua, New York, which opened on 4 August 1874 and became the Chautauqua Institution. In addition to SS teacher training and biblical study, Vincent extended the Chautauqua curriculum to include the best of literature, political reflection, and the arts, even including classes for university credit.

From his model, "Chautauquas" were expanded into tent meetings serving the rural United States, church training campgrounds were founded, and the Chautauqua Literary and Scientific Circles were launched, extending education to persons who had few other opportunities. Vincent believed that Christian education was essential to the education of the nation. For him, education was the development of persons "to secure true character" and be prepared "for personal and social responsibilities" to the nation and the world as children of God (Vincent 1890, 13–14).

Notable Publications

Vincent wrote many books and articles for both the Sunday school and the public, including a world history. Among them are *The Chautauqua Movement* (Boston: Chautauqua Press, 1886); *The Modern Sunday School,* rev. ed. (New York: Eaton and Mains, 1900); *A Study in Pedagogy* (New York: W.B. Ketcham, 1890); and *Sunday-School Institutes and Normal Classes* (New York: Nelson and Phillips, 1872). Autobiographical essays are "The Autobiography of Bishop Vincent," *Northwestern Christian Advocate* 58 (6 April–2 November 1910) and "How I Was Educated," *FORUM* 1 (June 1886): 337–347. His complete papers are collected at Southern Methodist University.

References and Resources

Seymour, Jack L. 1982. *From Sunday School to Church School: Continuities in Protestant Church Education in the United States, 1860–1929.* Washington, DC: University Press of America.

Trimmer, Edward A. 1986. "John Heyl Vincent: An Evangelist for Education." EdD diss., Teachers College, Columbia University.

Vincent, John Heyl. 1890. *A Study in Pedagogy.* New York: W.B. Ketcham.

Vincent, Leon H. 1925. *John Heyl Vincent: A Biographical Sketch.* New York: Macmillan.

—JACK L. SEYMOUR

VIRGINIA THEOLOGICAL SEMINARY

Virginia Theological Seminary was founded in 1823 to educate men for the ordained ministry in the Episcopal Church. Nearly 200 years later, the mission has expanded to include women, laity, and continuing theological education for all ages. Though still a denominational seminary, its long commitment to Christian education has attracted a rich ecumenical following.

While there is evidence before 1980 of instruction in religious education, and to a lesser extent Christian education, as pastoral theology, Virginia Seminary's focus on Christian education began in 1983 with the installation of Dean Richard Reid. His inaugural address identified an urgent need for the Episcopal Church to renew its commitment to Christian education. That same year, Rev. Dr. Locke E. Bowman, then executive director of the National Teacher Education Project and editor of *Church Teacher,* was elected professor of Christian education and pastoral theology.

In January 1985, Dr. Bowman oversaw the creation of the Center for the Ministry of Teaching (CMT) "to train and equip the laity for effective teaching of the gospel," grounding it in the seminary's evangelical and missionary commitments. Believing there is no such thing as education without teaching, Locke argued for the investment of resources to equip teachers, who in turn would create optimal learning environments for their students. Beginning as a library of resources in Christian education with a centralized calendar of events for church teachers/educators, the CMT expanded to become a laboratory for congregational leaders and to offer new courses, before establishing a department of research and development. Amelia J. Gearey joined the VTS faculty in 1987. With a PhD in early childhood education, she became the CMT assistant director in 1990 and was the director from 1995 to 2008.

The CMT's publications program began in 1986 with the production of a tabloid newspaper, *Episcopal Teacher*. It was issued 10 times per year and distributed to 3,500 paying subscribers. Today it is a quarterly free e-publication. In 1987 the CMT published a confirmation program, *Encountering Christ in the Episcopal Church*. In 1988 the signature publication, *Episcopal Children's Curriculum*, was released (jointly with Morehouse Publishing) to be followed by the *Episcopal Youth Curriculum*. This extensively researched, developmentally appropriate curriculum was designed to assist individuals in living out the covenant made in holy baptism, while taking seriously the demands and opportunities of contemporary life.

In 1989, the VTS board approved a new degree program, the master of arts in Christian education (MACE), and the first students were enrolled in 1990. Patterned after the Presbyterian School of Christian Education, the two-year program combined foundational theological education with specialized courses in Christian education. Soon demand from working professionals led to the degree being offered as a four-year summer intensive. In 2011, the master of arts in Christian formation replaced the MACE, reflecting a growing church-wide emphasis on lifelong Christian education in formal and informal settings.

When Dr. Elisabeth M. (Lisa) Kimball joined the faculty as professor of Christian formation and congregational leadership and director of the CMT in August 2009, she was charged with transforming the strengths of the CMT for the future. Key Hall, the elegant heart of the CMT, now serves as both a physical Christian education resource center and a laboratory for digital content creation and curation. Embracing the motto, "Message, Method, then Media," the CMT is committed to equipping church leaders to serve at the vital intersection of evangelism, communication, and faith formation in a hyper-connected world. Reverend Kyle Oliver was hired July 2012 as the CMT's first digital missioner to maintain a dynamic, theologically astute web presence. From bricks and mortar, classrooms, and printed curricula, the CMT at VTS has grown into a virtual hub for Christian education in the 21st century.

—Elisabeth M. (Lisa) Kimball

VIRTUAL SCHOOLS

The increase in online learning hasn't been limited to higher education and corporate environments; K–12 schools have also embraced nonresidential models of education delivered over the Internet. In addition to teachers and schools using digital technology to enhance traditional courses or offer selected courses online, a relatively new type of school has developed in which all of the students attend online. When these fully online institutions first started in the late 1990s, they were typically high schools and so were labeled "virtual high schools"; however, "now that middle and elementary school students are also participating in online courses the term virtual school more accurately describes the phenomenon as a whole, with virtual schooling denoting all K–12 online courses."[12]

Virtual Charter Schools

Much of the impetus for virtual schools, beyond the cultural explosion of digital technology and online communication, was the charter school movement, which also emerged in the 1990s. A charter school is a public institution created with a contract or charter "specifying how it will operate and what it must do in order to receive public funds for a set period of time."[13] The charter identifies the parameters that are used to hold the school accountable for student performance and fulfillment of the school's mission. In contrast to private schools and homeschooling, charter schools are public schools and thus are tuition-free for qualified students.

The parallel emergence of charter schools and online learning resulted in entrepreneurial companies developing virtual charter schools. A virtual charter school is a free public institution guided by a charter that delivers the educational programs online. Since its unveiling in 2000, K12 Inc. has largely pursued a three-pronged online education strategy: virtual charter schools, supplemental online courses for public and private schools, and online programs for homeschoolers. These charter schools use tax dollars to fund a virtual public school using the K12 curriculum, thus providing K12 with a sizable opportunity for tuition revenue while offering qualified parents a free primary and secondary school.

Soon after its launch, K12 Inc. was able to partner with virtual charter schools in Colorado, Pennsylvania, Wisconsin, Alaska, and California. Currently K12 partners with virtual charter schools in 32 states and the District of

12. Julie Young, Foreword to *Virtual Schools: Planning for Success*, eds. Zane L. Berge and Tom Clark (New York: Teachers College Press, 2005).

13. U.S. Department of Education, "A Study of Charter Schools: First-Year Report" (1997), http://www.ed.gov/pubs/charter/index.html.

Columbia.[14] In 2003, there were approximately 50 virtual charter schools across the United States[15] from a variety of providers. Presently there are hundreds of virtual charter schools in over two-thirds of the states, along with numerous state-run online public schools. In addition to virtual charter schools, K12 offers individualized online learning to public and private schools and individual course or full grade programs directly to families.[16] With public and private schools facing budget challenges and digital technology becoming more ubiquitous, virtual schools should continue to grow in the years to come.

Virtual Christian Schools

Virtual schools haven't been limited to public and charter schools; Christian educators have also launched a variety of virtual schooling options. These take a variety of forms, ranging from online private Christian schools to online Christian homeschooling curriculum programs. Some are connected to Christian colleges, such as Liberty University Online Academy or The Academy of Home Education, affiliated with Bob Jones University. Others are independent private Christian schools, such as Eagle Christian School and The Morning Star Academy.[17] Still others license online curriculum for use by traditional private Christian schools. Sevenstar partners with more than 300 Christian schools to provide online curriculum and instruction and also runs Sevenstar Academy to provide online courses for individual homeschooling students.[18] Given the growth in online education in both the K–12 and higher education sectors, the future should see a continued increase in the number of virtual Christian schools as well.

—Jason D. Baker

Virtue

A virtue is a firm disposition, habit, or tendency to do the good. The virtues are habits that permit one to perform good acts. The virtuous person tends toward the good with all his appetitive and spiritual powers; he pursues the good and opts for it in specific actions.

In traditional Christian teaching, there are cardinal, intellectual, and theological virtues. The cardinal virtues are prudence, justice, fortitude, and temperance. The virtues are outlined by Aristotle in his *Nicomachean Ethics*, in which he sees many of the virtues as a mean between two extremes.[19]

Thomas Aquinas ranks the cardinal virtues thus: prudence, first; justice, second; fortitude, third; and temperance, fourth. He reasons that fortitude without justice is an occasion of injustice, since the more powerful a man is, the more prepared he is to oppress the weaker. Aquinas considers fortitude or courage as being primarily about endurance, not daring. Citing Aristotle, he says: "Fortitude is more concerned to allay fear, than to moderate daring."[20] Therefore, the principal act of fortitude is endurance, standing immovable in the midst of dangers rather than attacking them.

According to Aristotle and St. Thomas Aquinas, there are five intellectual virtues: three pertaining to the theoretical or speculative intellect concerned with the contemplation of the true, and two pertaining to the practical intellect, concerned with the two forms of action, making and doing. The three speculative intellectual virtues are understanding, science, and wisdom. The two practical intellectual virtues are art (know-how or *techne*) and prudence.

The three theological virtues, occasionally depicted in the art of the Western world, are faith, hope, and charity. Faith is the theological virtue by which we believe in God and believe all that He has revealed to us, for He is Truth itself. By faith, "man freely commits his entire self to God." For this reason the believer seeks to know and do God's will. "The righteous shall live by faith." A debate about whether faith necessarily encompasses works rages between Catholics and various denominations of Protestants. Whether the debate is largely terminological is also a moot point.

The disciple of Christ must not only have the virtue of faith, but also profess and bear witness to it: "So everyone who acknowledges me before men, I also will acknowledge before my Father who is in heaven; but whoever denies me before men, I also will deny before my Father who is in heaven" (Matt. 10:32). Hope is the theological virtue by which we desire the kingdom of heaven and eternal life as our happiness, placing our trust in Christ's promises and relying not on our own strength, but on the help of the grace of the Holy Ghost. Charity is the theological virtue by which we love God above all things for His own sake, and our neighbor as ourselves for the love of God.

St. Thomas Aquinas argues that the seven gifts of the Holy Ghost proceed from the seven capital virtues, and that four of these gifts (wisdom, understanding, knowledge, and counsel) direct the intellect, while the other

14. K12 Inc., "Online Public Schools" (2013), http://www.k12.com/schools-programs/online-public-schools.

15. Krista Kafer, "Progress on School Choice in the States," The Heritage Foundation, 10 July 2003, http://www.heritage.org/research/reports/2003/07/progress-on-school-choice-in-the-states.

16. K12 Inc., "About Us" (2013), http://www.k12.com/about-k12.

17. Jason D. Baker, "K12: Christian Online Degree Directory," *Baker's Guide to Christian Online Learning* (2013), http://www.bakersguide.com/directory/search-by/degree?value=K-12.

18. Sevenstar, "Solutions" (2013), http://www.sevenstar.org/solutions.php.

19. Aristotle, *The Ethics of Aristotle: The Nichomachean Ethics*, rev. ed., trans. J. K. Thomson (New York: Viking, 1955), 104.

20. Ibid., iii, 9.

three gifts (fortitude, piety, and fear of the Lord) direct the will toward God. Whereas the virtues operate under the impetus of human reason (triggered by grace), the gifts operate under the impetus of the Holy Ghost.

For Aquinas, virtue and practical wisdom are necessary but not sufficient for happiness. Human beings need the assistance and grace of God to achieve it. The theological virtues of faith, hope, and charity are necessary. The virtue of faith, "by means of a Divine light," permits a perfecting of the intellect. The virtue of charity brings the human being to God. The theological virtues, like the infused moral virtues, are habits that fully embody Augustine's definition of virtue.

Christian teaching on the virtues highlighting faith, hope, and charity and the seven gifts of the Holy Ghost (wisdom, understanding, knowledge, counsel, fortitude, piety, and fear of the Lord), in a world that regards human life as expendable, morality as a fiction and justice as socially constructed, is likely to be more essential even in a pluralist world.

See also Jurisprudence; Moral Philosophy; Natural Law; Thomistic Tradition.

References and Resources

Annas, Julia. 1993. *The Morality of Happiness.* New York: Oxford University Press.

———. 2004. "[Presidential Address:] Being Virtuous and Doing the Right Thing." *Proceedings of the American Philosophical Association* 78 (2): 61–75.

Anscombe, G. E. M. 1958. "Modern Moral Philosophy." *Philosophy* 33: 1–19.

Aquinas, Thomas. 1920. *The Summa Theologica of St. Thomas Aquinas Literally Translated by Fathers of the English Dominican Province.* London: Burns Oates and Washbourne.

Aristotle. 1955. *The Ethics of Aristotle: The Nichomachean Ethics.* Rev. ed. Translated by J. K. Thomson. New York: Viking.

Crisp, Roger, ed. 1996. *How Should One Live?* Oxford: Clarendon Press.

Foot, Philippa. 1978. *Virtues and Vices.* Oxford: Blackwell.

Geach, Peter. 1956. "Good and Evil." *Analysis* 17: 33–42.

———. 1977. *The Virtues.* Cambridge, UK: Cambridge University Press.

Laing, Jacqueline A., and Russell Wilcox. 2013. *The Natural Law Reader.* Oxford: Wiley Blackwell.

MacIntyre, Alasdair. 1985. *After Virtue.* 2nd ed. London: Duckworth.

———. 1999. *Dependent Rational Animals.* Chicago: Open Court.

Solomon, David. 1988. "Internal Objections to Virtue Ethics." *Midwest Studies in Philosophy* 13: 428–441.

Williams, Bernard. 1985. *Ethics and the Limits of Philosophy.* Cambridge, MA: Harvard University Press.

—Jacqueline Laing

Virtue Ethics as Christian Practice

Early Christian ethics took root in the soil of ancient moral philosophy; imitation, the virtues, interior dispositions, character, and transformation into the divine image and likeness. This tradition was not rejected; rather, its framework was maintained, adapted, and altered to fit God's self-revelation in Christ, bringing together the theological virtues—faith, hope, and love—and the moral virtues—prudence, justice, fortitude, and temperance—in the ministry of the Gospel. Moreover, the Sermon on the Mount provided the call to be holy, to be "perfect as your Father in heaven is perfect." Christians understood their life in light of this larger end, a teleological ordering of human life inherited from ancient wisdom that was reoriented by the eschatological fulfillment of God's good purposes in the ministry of Jesus Christ. Human actions were therefore assessed and judged when directed to the most praiseworthy of all ends, the Triune God who is the supreme good.

The aim of this vision was to lead people to living a happy life in God in accord with the truest and deepest aspirations of human creatures. It was significant that the Beatitudes begin with "blessed" or "happy," so that Jesus is heard as the Teacher of Wisdom who Himself is the Way to happiness, which is the goal of human life. The Beatitudes were therefore read as depicting both the character of true happiness and the way leading to that goal. God is the highest good, since nothing else is sufficient for human creatures made in God's image, so that the end hoped for was also present in the beginning. Communion with God, consisting of knowledge, love, and delight, brings fulfillment to human life; only our return to God by grace and for communion brings genuine human happiness. For the early Christians, holy and happiness were one.

The moral life and the religious life were complementary. Although thinking about the moral life moved within a conceptual framework received from Greek and Latin moralists, Christian thinkers redefined the good by making fellowship with the living God the end, revising the beginning by introducing the teaching that we are made in the image of God and complicating the middle with the inevitability and persistence of sin. Christian virtue and happiness were seen as the "more" human creatures desired and longed for, and which is known and received through the gracious activity of God. Moreover, because the Christian life is Trinitarian, Christian virtue and happiness are received in Christ and bestowed by the Holy Spirit.

To know and be conformed to this reality is dependent upon virtues that qualify the mind *and* heart for communion with God. The virtues function to energize, integrate, and direct our capacities so that everything about us is disposed to attain the happiness enjoyed in friendship with God and others. Rather than mere expressions of "works righteousness," the virtues assume that the intellect and will are ordered to understanding and loving an object external to the human person. This something comes to us and happens to us, calling, summoning, evoking, and provoking, and can be known, loved, and desired: the communication of God's truth and goodness revealed in the form of Jesus Christ.

Rather than focusing on rules, obligations, and duties, virtue ethics emphasizes the interior formation of the God-given strengths, or capacities, along with a correlative emphasis on desire, deliberation, and discernment, including the passions and intentionality, by which fully human acts, ordered by the gift of divine love, draw human creatures closer to God as the source and end of all things. Seen from this perspective, all existence is the overflow of God's goodness, all intelligible forms participate in God's wisdom, all causality is the effect of divine action, and all perfection is the work of God's guidance. Since the whole Trinity is the source and end of human salvation, knowing, loving, and delighting in God requires habits that are capable of elevating and transforming our intellectual and moral capacities to a measure fitting for their proper subject.

References and Resources

Cessario, Romanus, OP. 1996. *Christian Faith and the Theological Life*. Washington, DC: Catholic University of America Press.

Hauerwas, Stanley, and Charles Pinches. 1997. *Christians Among the Virtues: Theological Conversations with Ancient and Modern Ethics*. Notre Dame, IN: University of Notre Dame Press.

Pinckaers, Servais, OP. 1995. *The Sources of Christian Ethics*. Translated by Sr. Mary Thomas Nobel, OP. Washington, DC: Catholic University of America Press.

—Michael Pasquarello III

Vocation

Christians have long taught that God, through a variety of means, calls or invites individuals to a particular path in life. The term *vocation* comes from the Latin verb *voco*—to call or summon—and the noun *vocatus*—a calling or invitation. When understood as involving the voice of God, it bears a weightier meaning than the contemporary understanding of vocation as merely a career or the teaching of job skills.

In patristic and medieval theological discussions, the primary concern was the way in which a person could be called to ordained ecclesial offices. It was the duty of wise churchmen to help discern whether an individual was called to the serious commitment of lifelong service to the church. Thus, while it was important for an individual to internally sense a call to ordained ministry, the Roman Catholic Church and the magisterial Protestant tradition both insisted that an individual could not be self-appointed to church offices. Rather, ministers needed to have a call of God emanate through the means of the church itself. In Western Christian education, therefore, vocational discernment for professional church work has been a strong theme and a primary way to cultivate future leaders. Proponents of the Radical Reformation typically rejected the necessity of an official invitation to ordained roles; for this, they experienced periods of persecution and their preachers were often labeled "usurpers" or "renegades" by Roman Catholics and magisterial Protestants.

After the 16th century, Christian educators developed a broader application of the concept of vocation, expanding it to the variety of ways in which God invites an individual to a role of service. After the Catholic reformation, this took the form of Ignatian discernment practices, which followed Ignatius of Loyola's (1491–1556) devotional classic, *Spiritual Exercises* (1524). In this process, individuals seek to hear God's voice through reflection—often in the context of a retreat—on God's inward and outward calls. Through a variety of spiritual disciplines, including prayer and meditation, and with the help of a spiritual director, participants attempt to discern the presence and call of Jesus in their lives. This does not necessarily lead to a call to ordained ministry or a monastic order.

The Protestant reformers were even more active in extending the doctrine of vocation to the laity. Following the teaching of Martin Luther and John Calvin on the related doctrine of the priesthood of all believers, the early evangelicals taught that all legitimate callings—whether ecclesial or laical—were equally valuable before God and might rightly be considered acts of worship. In this, there was no hierarchy of dignity with respect to vocations. Thus, much of the discussion regarding vocation in the early Protestant churches took place in the context of a shortage of professionally trained clergy and the difference between the inner, subjective calling to church and the external, formal, and administrative criteria developed by churches to determine whether a potential pastor was qualified to receive a call. This latter issue influenced the nature of theological education, since such training needed to prepare students to meet such external criteria, such as a liberal arts background, knowledge of doctrine, biblical languages, practical ethics, and in some cases—such as Zurich—foundational knowledge of philosophy. Not surprisingly, Anabaptist churches found the rigorous external requirements for Reformed and Lutheran clergy dangerously close to the hierarchical and institutionalized approach to church vocations in the Roman Catholic tradition.

Despite the increased importance of attention to the doctrine of the office of the ministry in fledgling Protestant churches, a calling to this office was of no greater worth than that of a cobbler or a lawyer. Vocations were God's way, according to Luther, of loving neighbors and providing for the needs of creation as a whole. Accordingly, vocations in the earthly kingdom tend to operate in the realm of law and preservation of an orderly community for all neighbors. Vocations in the kingdom of grace involve proclaiming the gospel, mediating grace, and proclaiming salvation. The effects of this are apparent in the work of J. S. Bach, who famously indicated the worshipful quality of his secular music by signing his compositions with the phrase *Soli Deo Gloria*: to God alone be the glory.

This distinction between the earthly and heavenly kingdoms affects education in a unique way. Unlike traditions that seek to resolutely integrate faith and all disciplines, reformers insisted that there was value in serving God through scholarship itself, not just because it could prepare one for church careers. The reformers thought that people might have multiple, sometimes simultaneous, vocations in life. Thus, there are callings to be citizens, students, teachers, spouses, parents, workers, and pastors, often simultaneously. Moreover, an especially important vocation of parents in the home was to provide theological education to children and complement the catechetical work of the church.

In North American Protestant education, the concept of vocation arguably became a great theological motivation for curricular breadth and multiple secular tracks, especially in the foundational years of church-affiliated liberal arts colleges and universities. This theme remained a focal point of secularizing church-related institutions, even in cases where these same institutions abandoned commitments to their confessional identity and experienced declining attendance at campus worship. According to some observers, this particular conception of vocation in liberal Protestant colleges of North America likely contributed to secularizing trajectories in church-related institutions, since a critical approach to scholarship requires significant academic freedom and faculty members who are unhindered by the strictures of dogmatism and ecclesiastical authority. In such a milieu, educators see their primary role as defenders of secular space within democratic society.

In the 21st century, the academic conversation about vocation has intensified, due in large part to a 1999 initiative launched by the Lilly Endowment, which funded church-related institutions that agreed to conduct theological exploration of vocation. The initiative's purpose was to help students connect their faith to career and life choices, expose them to the possibility of callings to church ministry, and help faculty and staff become better guides in the discernment process. At least 88 institutions received grants for this purpose, and at least $218 million went to support this endeavor. In addition, the foundation supports programs for theological training of adolescents and programs that help people transition to theological vocations. It is likely that the participating institutions will continue to research, reflect on, and publish ideas about vocational theology and discernment for the foreseeable future.

References and Resources

Haughey, John, ed. 2004. *Revisiting the Idea of Vocation: Theological Explorations*. Washington, DC: Catholic University of America Press.

Maag, Karin. 2004. "Called to Be a Pastor: Issues of Vocation in the Early Modern Period." *The Sixteenth Century Journal* 35 (1): 65–78.

Placher, William. 2005. *Callings: Twenty Centuries of Christian Wisdom on Vocation*. Grand Rapids, MI: Eerdmans.

Veith, Gene. 2011. "Vocation in Education: Preparing for Our Callings in the Three Estates." In *Learning at the Foot of the Cross: A Lutheran Vision for Education*, edited by Joel Heck and Angus Menuge, 97–112. Austin, TX: Concordia University Press.

Wingren, Gustaf. 1957. *Luther on Vocation*. Translated by Carl Rasmussen. Philadelphia: Muhlenberg Press.

—Jeff Mallinson

Volunteer Satisfaction, Local Church

Not only do local church Christian education ministries depend on volunteers to accomplish God's ministry and mission, the satisfaction of those volunteers should also be a concern of those who oversee them. A tension may exist between volunteers' needs and the organization's needs. "Volunteers expect to feel good about themselves. In contrast, the organization expects volunteers to act as free agents who can independently manage feelings of pain and self-doubt" (Yanay and Yanay 2008, 65). Locke (1976) defines job satisfaction as a pleasurable or positive emotional state resulting from job expectations and job experiences.

Value of Volunteer Satisfaction and Retention to the Organization

The value of volunteer satisfaction to volunteer organizations cannot be overstated. Volunteers provide human labor and often leadership essential to an organization's mission fulfillment. Satisfied volunteers typically continue to serve and can assist in recruiting and training new volunteers.

Allen and Shaw note that "volunteer satisfaction is considered important because of an assumed association between satisfaction and retention. Volunteer motivation and satisfaction have been a focus of research aimed at developing an understanding of factors influencing volunteers' performance and retention" (2009, 80). Volunteer organizations must retain volunteers for practical as well as efficiency reasons. Meaningful human capital and investment of time are necessary to recruit and train volunteers. Losing volunteers requires additional recruitment and training in order to continue volunteer services and achieve mission fulfillment (McCurley and Lynch 2007).

Prior Research in Volunteer Satisfaction

In a review of volunteer satisfaction studies, Galindo-Kuhn and Guzley identified five elements of volunteer job satisfaction: communication quality, work assignment, participation efficacy (how one feels about the results of one's efforts), support, and integration (how volunteers build relationships with others in the organization) (2008, 51). These elements of satisfaction form the basis of satisfied volunteers in the non-faith-based volunteer sector. Little research has been conducted on local church volunteer satisfaction.

Newer Research in Local Church Volunteer Satisfaction

In a recent study, Garverick (2013) reports that local church volunteers may have a variety of motives for volunteering and a resulting variety of levels of satisfaction. Few volunteers begin with pristine motives, but those motives and resulting satisfaction can change as they continue to serve. Local church volunteer growth positively affected not only their level of satisfaction, but their motivation to volunteer as well.

Several elements in a local church affected local church volunteer satisfaction in Garverick's study: organizational leadership that provides liberty to volunteers to fulfill their role; leadership's openness to new ministries and new ministry ideas; building relationships in the local church, including with organizational leadership and among other volunteers; and participation efficacy (how a volunteer feels about the effects of her ministry). Volunteers also reported that liberty to do their ministry with measures of accountability and support not only validated their ministry, but provided a sense of validation of their person. Organizational leaders who were open to volunteers' ideas for new ministries or new ministry ideas sensed a great deal of satisfaction and felt affirmation

not only in the fact that God led them, but also that God worked in their lives.

Longer-term volunteers found new ways to articulate satisfaction beyond what prior research had shown (Garverick 2013), including four unique types of satisfaction that they termed residual, cumulative, contagious, and core. These volunteers reported feeling a kind of residual satisfaction as they saw teenagers continuing to grow beyond the time of their ministry with them. They understood that their influence in earlier years still positively affected those young people, and they derived satisfaction from their prior investment. Cumulative volunteer satisfaction resulted from an individual experiencing satisfaction not only in her ministry, but also when other ministries experienced growth or effectiveness in their local church. This appears to be a kind of corporate sense of volunteer satisfaction. A similar kind, called contagious satisfaction, also arose. The local church volunteer felt individual satisfaction, but also satisfaction beyond that, to what is happening in the larger church, in other ministries, and among other volunteers, in a kind of contagion.

Core satisfaction was the height of local church volunteer satisfaction in Garverick's study. This particular kind resulted from seeing one's ministry as an offering to the Lord that cannot be taken away. Whether these volunteers cleaned the basement of a mission building or preached in the mission, they derived deep satisfaction from knowing that God saw their service as worship, and that elicited core satisfaction in them.

These four kinds of local church volunteer satisfaction suggested a kind of quantum satisfaction. Most previous volunteer studies focused on individual satisfaction as it related to individual volunteer roles. In this research, Garverick (2013) suggested that a larger kind of satisfaction can exist in a local church beyond the person's satisfaction in individual service. The idea of quantum satisfaction needs further research to understand its essence and impact on individuals and a local church.

References and Resources

Boezeman, E. J., and N. Ellemers. 2009. "Intrinsic Need Satisfaction and the Job Attitudes of Volunteers versus Employees Working in a Charitable Volunteer Organization." *Journal of Occupational & Organizational Psychology* 82 (4): 897–914.

Galindo-Kuhn, R., and R. M. Guzley. 2008. "The Volunteer Satisfaction Index." *Journal of Social Service Research* 28 (1): 45–68. doi: 10.1300/J079v28n01_03.

Garverick, P. 2013. "How Volunteers Experience Ministry Satisfaction in the Context of a Local Church and Its Organizational Leadership: A Case Study." PhD diss., Indiana Wesleyan University, Marion.

Locke, E. A. 1976. "The Nature and Causes of Job Satisfaction." In *The Handbook of Industrial and Organizational Psychology*, edited by M. D. Dunnette, 87–129. Chicago: Rand McNally.

Yanay, G. V., and N. Yanay. 2008. "The Decline of Motivation? From Commitment to Dropping Out of Volunteering." *Nonprofit Management & Leadership* 19 (1): 65–78.

—PAUL E. GARVERICK

VOLUNTEER TEACHER TRAINING

Volunteer teacher training is the process of equipping God's people for the work of ministry and supporting those serving as volunteers.[21]

Equipping in the New Testament

In the early New Testament church, there were no ordained clergy working with teams of volunteers. However, under the direction of the Holy Spirit, the church appointed leaders, and others assisted them. In Ephesians chapter 4, the apostle Paul gives a description of how the church, the body of Christ, is to function:

God gives gifts for ministry to members of the body.

Leadership gifts are given to some: apostles, evangelists, pastors, teachers.

These leaders are to equip the saints for the work of ministry.

The God intended work of the church is accomplished as each member of Christ's body does his or her part. Every gift and every role is crucial. (4:8, 11–16)

Leaders in New Testament times used several means to train or equip the saints. First, the preaching and teaching of the apostles and then the New Testament writings provided the needed instruction. In the Acts of the apostles and the Gospels, the story of Jesus and the story of God at work from creation was the core content of Christian teaching. Leaders of the church realized that teachers must know God's story well.

Paul began equipping the saints at Ephesus by challenging them to live a life worthy of their calling and identified the resources that made possible the living of a worthy life: God's grace, their relationships with Jesus, and their relationship with the body of believers (Eph. 4:1, 7.15–16). The understanding of God—theology—was also important. The epistles provided instruction on how to live the Christian life and helped young Christians grow in their understanding of theology. Another New Testament means of equipping was mentoring. We see this in the relationships of Barnabas and Saul, Paul and Timothy.

Equipping in Church History

The young church first focused on instructing new believers prior to baptism, to be sure that they believed in the true Gospel (Reed and Prevost 1993, 71). As early as the second century, a catechetical school had been established in Alexandria for this purpose. In the 1500s, Martin Luther, John Calvin, Ignatius Loyola, and the order of priests he led, the Jesuits, provided basic and Christian instruction for children through the schools they established (Reed and Prevost 1993, 192–193, 197–198). The Jesuit educational system also stressed the preparation and dedication of teachers (Reed and Prevost 1993, 204–206). However, it was not until the mid- to late 1700s that faith communities began to give significant teaching ministries to lay volunteers.

Lay ministry became a vital part of the early Methodist movement. By 1741, John Wesley had developed a series of lay-led, small groups to support the formation of new and growing Christians. The equipping of those leaders began while they participated in the first group—the class meeting—learning, growing spiritually, and experiencing God's transforming grace. Their leadership skills developed in smaller groups—bands—that were led by the group members. Wesley next developed "Select Societies" for the instruction and ongoing growth of the lay leaders (Henderson 1997, 45, 79–80).

With the birth of the Sunday school, lay volunteers claimed their place in the teaching ministry of the church. Robert Raikes, a journalist and newspaper editor concerned about the hundreds of children receiving no education or moral formation, is credited with founding the Sunday school in 1781. The first few women teachers were paid, but the number of children needing the ministry of the Sunday school called for more than a few paid teachers. Encouraged by the Methodists and their experience with lay leaders/teachers, Sunday school teachers were soon volunteers, and the ministry expanded rapidly (Reed and Prevost 1993, 256–260).

Those leading this amazing volunteer movement soon realized there was a need to train the willing and passionate teachers if their teaching was to be effective. In 1785, the Sunday School Society was formed to provide materials that would guide the teachers. In 1803, the London Sunday School Union was established to bring teachers together for instruction, inspiration, and discussion of questions. It also provided printed resources (Benson 1943, 124, 126–127). In 1824, the American Sunday School Union was founded with objectives similar to those of the London Union. In national, international, and state conventions, teachers came together for inspi-

---

21. Some church leaders prefer to use the term "ministry partners" rather than volunteers, possibly implying greater significance to the role.

ration and instruction, and the development of resources to equip them for effective teaching was ongoing (Benson 1943, 154–156, 166, 190–194).

In the beginning, the Sunday school was what today would be called a parachurch movement. However, in the late 19th and early 20th centuries the Sunday school became a ministry of the church, and denominations began to take seriously the equipping of their volunteer teachers. At the beginning of the 20th century, as the training of public school teachers became more thorough, church and Sunday school leaders realized that volunteer teachers also needed to be well trained. The International Sunday School Association and the Southern Baptist Training Department both developed comprehensive courses of study for volunteers. In 1931, the Evangelical Teacher Training Association was founded, and it developed courses of study to be taught in local churches by instructors who had been trained through completing the course of study. These training programs included courses that focused on understanding the Bible, the pupil, and the teacher; as well as how to plan lessons, teach, and lead a Sunday school (Benson 1943, 236–257).

Focus on the importance of training volunteers continued into the mid-20th century. Churches offered regular training, in some cases weekly. Denominational leaders developed resources for training in the local church and offered regional training events. State Sunday school associations brought volunteers together for inspiration and instruction. However, the increasing number of families with both husband and wife working outside the home, the growing number of activities families engage in, and the accelerated pace of life at the turn of the century impacted the recruiting and training of volunteers. Leaders wanting to train volunteer teachers in the 21st century face major challenges.[22]

Equipping in the 21st Century

The preceding brief historical overview showed that certain elements were considered essential in the preparation of God's people for ministry. These elements continue to be important for equipping volunteer teachers. Volunteer training should provide

1. nurture of the teacher's spiritual life, leading to a life worthy of the calling;
2. opportunities to know God and God's story more fully;
3. growing understandings of the students and how to teach them;
4. resources to equip and guide the volunteer in the teaching task; and
5. inspiration, fellowship, and support.

But given the challenges of 21st-century societies, how can we hope to involve teachers in training? Effective training begins with the mind-set and values of church leaders and with the congregation. Pastors who realize that they are responsible for the equipping of the people under their care (Eph. 4: 11–12) and who, over time, lead the congregation to understand that each member has a part to play in the work of God's Kingdom, will find the number of volunteer partners in their ministry increasing. The discipling of volunteer teachers is most likely to occur in a church where discipleship is a core value, where equipping for ministry begins as children, youth, and adults learn what it means to be a committed follower of Jesus. Opportunities to know and love the Bible can also be woven into the life of the church. The pastor's preaching and the teaching of children, youth, and adults can introduce the Bible as the unified, exciting, continuing story of God at work in the world, a story in which each Christian can find his or her place of ministry (Bartholomew and Goheen 2004, 12). Volunteers and potential volunteers can be trained as they participate in the life of the church.

Church leaders seeking to train volunteer teachers find that training must be accessible and convenient. Through the Internet, leaders are able to support volunteers with notes of encouragement, post instructional presentations or articles, and encourage online discussions to enhance learning. Some ministry teams gather 15 minutes before their teaching responsibilities begin for inspiration and prayer together. Intentional mentoring can be built into ministries where teachers serve in teams, allowing new volunteers to learn through experience and from better-trained colleagues. Quality curriculum resources also provide ongoing equipping.

In spite of their busy lives, volunteers still value times when they can experience fellowship and learn together. Members of a ministry team may be assigned a book to read and then gather for discussion. One or two well-planned and -promoted training events a year could provide basic and continuing instruction. Large conferences that focus on teaching ministries offer opportunities for volunteers to be equipped and encouraged. One ministry leader has discovered that, in spite of the challenges, "when volunteers are given support and invited to be part of something that will impact communities and lives they show up in ways that surprise us." Involving and training volunteer teachers in the 21st century is not a lost cause.

---

22. Insights on the status of volunteer training in the 21st century and ideas for effective approaches come from personal e-mail conversations with the following people: Ty Brant, children's pastor, Perimeter Presbyterian Church; Dr. James Hampton, professor of youth ministry, Asbury Theological Seminary; Ken Lupton, regional sales/support representative, Lifeway; Dr. Kristi Williams, preschool minister, Johnson Ferry Baptist Church; and Sharon Yancey, founder and director of The Matthew Initiative.

References and Resources

Bartholomew, C. G., and M. W. Goheen. 2004. *The Drama of Scripture: Finding Our Place in the Biblical Story.* Grand Rapids, MI: Baker Academic.

Benson, C. H. 1943. *A Popular History of Christian Education.* Chicago: Moody Press.

Henderson, D. M. 1997. *John Wesley's Class Meeting: A Model for Making Disciples.* Nappanee, IN: Evangel Publishing House.

Reed, J. E., and R. Prevost. 1993. *A History of Christian Education.* Nashville, TN: Broadman & Holman.

—Catherine M. Stonehouse

VOLUNTEERISM, LOCAL CHURCH

Volunteer Definition

Local church Christian education ministries largely depend on volunteers to accomplish God's mission and ministry. The Bible does not utilize the term *volunteer* per se, but some definitions and qualities of volunteers help us understand them and their motives. Ellis and Campbell (2006) note that volunteers "choose to act in recognition of a need, with an attitude of social responsibility and without concern for monetary profit, going beyond one's basic obligations." Yanay and Yanay provide this definition: "Volunteerism is a service that one person provides to another or to the public out of his or her own free will and without any material reward" (2008, 66). These definitions flow from sociological and psychological frameworks recognizing volunteer values, attitudes, recognition of need, and volunteering without material or monetary reward. Hybels uses a biblical and Christ-centered approach to understanding local church volunteers' sense of call, motive, and purpose:

> We were created by God to join him on a mission. Some people think of God as hanging around beyond the edges of the universe somewhere, listening to really good worship music. The Bible sees it much differently. It teaches that God is at work 24/7, all over our world, filling his followers with grace and mercy and power to reclaim and redeem and fix this broken planet. (2004, 13)

Volunteer Motivation

Volunteers have a variety of motivations for their volunteer service. Black and DeNitto's (1994) study in a women's shelter reports that "altruistic motivation of helping others in need more strongly motivates" (1994, 92) volunteers than any other motivation. Drucker declared, "One of the great strengths of the non-profit organization is that people don't' work for a living, they work for a cause" (1990, 150). Becker and Dhingra (2001) note that volunteers in Catholic and liberal Protestant congregations tend to view their work as an obligation to help others, while evangelicals are more likely to focus on serving as a way of becoming more Christlike. While not every volunteer begins her ministry in the local church with pristine motives, God calls, empowers, and leads her in relation to His work. Most volunteer studies to date were done outside of the local church, and motives often exhibited varying levels of self-centeredness. Yanay and Yanay declare that "Volunteers expect to feel good about themselves" (2008, 65). Volunteer motives include the desire to build relationships (group integration) and feel good about their contribution (participation efficacy) (Galindo-Kuhn and Guzley, 2008; Boezeman and Ellemers 2009).

Local church volunteers may have some level of self-interest in their own satisfaction resulting from their volunteer ministry. Many local church leaders hope their volunteers' motives are characterized primarily by selfless, sacrificial love, or as some in the literature would describe it, a type of altruism. Yanay and Yanay identify two primary reasons for volunteering, other-directed motives and self-directed motives (2008, 66).

Kinlaw reminds us that "Jesus demonstrated that the ultimate authority in all creation is self-sacrificing. The center of absolute, ultimate, eternal authority is found in the broken, bleeding body of the Eternal Son of God. Power is not what we humanly think it is; power is the ability to sacrifice yourself for someone other than yourself. Most of us miss this point" (1998, 17). Many local church organizational leaders hope that volunteers will mature and sacrificially serve in the spirit of Jesus Christ. Some local church volunteers come to discover that a motivation of service as an act of worship brings incredible satisfaction (*see also* Volunteer Satisfaction, Local Church).

Volunteer Empowerment

Two elements of importance to volunteers' satisfaction and retention are empowerment and organizational support. Volunteers want to know the what and why of their service. They often want to do good work and need a rationale, orientation, and a sense of mission and vision. They also want to be heard when they have suggestions for more efficient or effective ways to accomplish their mission (empowerment). Boezeman and Ellemers (2009) identify volunteer need for autonomy, which includes choice in how they perform tasks and a measure of self-control. Volunteers want to successfully carry out tasks and meet performance standards. Even the need for secure and respectful relationships empowers volunteers. Garverick (2013) indicates that local church organizational leadership's openness to new ministries and providing volunteers liberty to accomplish their tasks or ministries both provides empowerment to local church volunteers and brings them great satisfaction. In addition, when local church organizational leadership provides vision for ministry, volunteers see the value of their work. Even in the general volunteer sector, the provision of vision empowers. Drucker posits: "In contrast to the work of businesses and the government, the non-profit's 'product' is a changed human being. The non-profit institutions are human-change agents. . . . Their 'product' is a cured patient, a child that learns, a young man or woman grown into a self-respecting adult; a changed human life" (1990, xiv).

Volunteer Value

Hybels summarizes the value of volunteers thus: "There's not enough money in the world to pay for all the good deeds desperately needing to be done in the name of God in my church and yours, in my community and yours, in my country and yours" (2004, 32). Volunteers accomplish the overwhelming majority of ministry in local churches. Ephesians 4:11–16 describes God's vision for building up the body of Christ unto maturity. God's pattern to accomplish that end equips the saints for the work of the ministry.

References and Resources

Becker, P. E., and P. H. Dhingra. 2001. "Religious Involvement and Volunteering: Implications for Civil Society." *Sociology of Religion* 62 (3): 315–335.

Black, B., and D. DiNitto. 1994. "Volunteers Who Work with Survivors of Rape and Battering: Motivations, Acceptance, Satisfaction, Length of Service, and Gender Differences." *Journal of Social Service Research* 20: 1–2.

Boezeman, E. J., and N. Ellemers. 2009. "Intrinsic Need Satisfaction and the Job Attitudes of Volunteers versus Employees Working in a Charitable Volunteer Organization." *Journal of Occupational & Organizational Psychology* 82 (4): 897–914.

Drucker, P. F. 1990. *Managing the Non-profit Organization.* New York: HarperCollins.

Ellis, S. J., and K. H. Campbell. 2006. *By the People: A History of Americans as Volunteers.* 3rd ed. (Kindle digital version). Philadelphia: Energize.

Galindo-Kuhn, R., and R. M. Guzley. 2008. "The Volunteer Satisfaction Index." *Journal of Social Service Research* 28 (1): 45–68. doi: 10.1300/J079v28n01_03.

Garverick, P. 2013. "How Volunteers Experience Ministry Satisfaction in the Context of a Local Church and Its Organizational Leadership: A Case Study." PhD diss., Indiana Wesleyan University, Marion.

Hybels, B. 2004. *The Volunteer Revolution: Unleashing the Power of Everybody.* Grand Rapids, MI: Zondervan.

Kinlaw, D. F. 1998. *How Every Christian Can Have the Mind of Christ.* Nappanee, IN: Partnership Press.

Yanay, G. V., and N. Yanay. 2008. "The Decline of Motivation? From Commitment to Dropping Out of Volunteering." *Nonprofit Management & Leadership* 19 (1): 65–78.

—Paul E. Garverick

Vygotsky, Lev

Lev Vygotsky was born in 1896 into a middle-class Jewish family in Orsha, a town in Byelorussia. He died at the age of 38 in Moscow. His father was a bank manager at the United Bank of Gomel, and his mother was a licensed teacher. He grew up in a family rooted in the Jewish tradition and in a social environment that stimulated intellectual development. A private tutor educated Vygotsky in his early years. He studied law at Moscow University and literature, philosophy, psychology, and art at Shanjavsky People's University. Vygotsky was proficient in eight languages: Russian, German, English, Hebrew, French, Latin, Greek, and Esperanto. This enabled him to develop his future interdisciplinary research and theories.

Vygotsky's early works reflected the turbulent environment of postrevolutionary Russia, which was marked by massive illiteracy, cultural differences, and lack of assistance to those who had become physically and mentally challenged. Differing from the prevalent educational philosophy of his epoch, Vygotsky sought to develop an approach to education that would improve the conditions of those excluded from formal educational settings. He stressed that the conditions of impairment not only alter the person's relationship with the world, but also disrupt a person's social connections. For this reason, he considered it essential to provide special attention to a person's strengths rather than to focus on her or his disabilities.

He believed that our relational life experiences influence our development and ways of being. Therefore, to understand the teaching-learning process, one needs to understand the social, cultural, and political contexts in which learning and development take place. According to Vygotsky, it is through interaction that human beings learn to use intellectual and cognitive "tools." Because of his emphasis on the social and cultural elements that influence the cognitive process, his educational theory became known as socio-constructivism.

Vygotsky acknowledged that human beings develop themselves mediated by symbols and in collaboration with others. He stressed the idea that knowledge is constructed through actions shared among all the individuals involved in a social learning process. Therefore, the cognitive development process presupposes learning how to use the tools of culture—inventions of society, such as language—through the assistance and guidance of adults and peers. In this dialogical process, the younger members of society acquire knowledge and skills to solve problems, first with assistance and later independently. For Vygotsky, the group plays a fundamental part in a child's development, as it is through this interaction that children learn to think and behave by way of cooperative dialogues that reflect a community's culture. He called attention to the teacher's role as a provocative partner, a co-constructor of knowledge who has the responsibility to create opportunities for learning according to the learner's emerging needs. He also emphasized the crucial role parents, peers, and community play in children's development.

One of his most central and widely mentioned theories is the concept of the zone of proximal development (ZPD), which comprises the hypothetical and dynamic locus in which learning and development may take place. This zone is "defined by the distance between what a child can accomplish during independent problem solving and what he or she can accomplish with the help of an adult or more competent member of culture" (Vygotsky 1978, 86). In other words, the first dimension refers to the individual's capacity for independent problem solving, and the second refers to the capacity of problem solving under the guidance of or in collaboration with more mature members of the culture. In his understanding, what a child is able to do with the help of an adult now, she will be able to do by herself tomorrow. Therefore, the ZPD is also a psychological area in constant transformation, in which learning and cognitive development occur. The idea of the potential zone characterizes not what the individual has accomplished, but rather what she will be able to achieve through the interference or help of other individuals. When the ZPD is operating, the process of development is moving. To Vygotsky, the team's result is more important than the individual achievement, for it is through *social* experience that children can construct knowledge within the limits of their potentiality.

Implications for Christian Education

Vygotsky's emphasis on the sociocultural dimension of the educational process can help illuminate our un-

derstanding of faith community as spaces to promote human development and advance faith formation. His ideas underscore the potential of forming and transforming education through collaborative efforts among those involved in the educational endeavor, noticing how individuals construct and acquire information, skills, attitudes, and values through the experiences and interactions shared within sociocultural contexts. In this regard, faith communities are fertile terrains for promoting and advancing individual potential, but also for discovering the collective potential that resides within the community as a whole to form and transform participants and their contexts. In addition, by engaging people from different ages, postures, and experiences, faith communities facilitate the interaction of multiple ZPDs, through which participants influence and support each other. In this context, religious educators, as provocative partners, challenge and support learners in advancing their faith journey. Through these engaging interactions, both educators and learners foster creative ways to become culturally educated, socially engaged, and theologically sound.

References and Resources

Berk, Laura E., and Adam Winsler. 1995. *Scaffolding Children's Learning: Vygotsky and Early Childhood Education.* Washington, DC: National Association for the Education of Young Children.

Daniels, Harry, ed. 1996. *An Introduction to Vygostsky.* New York: Routledge.

Newman, Fred, and Lois Holzman. 1993. *Lev Vygotsky: Revolutionary Scientist.* New York: Routledge.

Veer, René van der, and Jaan Valsiner. 1991. *Understanding Vygotsky: A Quest for Synthesis.* Oxford, Cambridge, MA: Blackwell.

———. 1994. *The Vygotsky Reader.* Edited by René van der Veer and Jaan Valsiner. Oxford, Cambridge, MA: Blackwell.

Vygotsky, L. S. 1978. *Mind in Society: The Development of Higher Psychological Processes.* Cambridge, MA: Harvard University Press.

Vygotsky, L. S., and Alex Kozulin. 1986. *Thought and Language.* Cambridge, MA MIT Press.

—Débora B. Agra Junker

W

WANAMAKER, JOHN

The world-famous American business pioneer, public servant, and educational entrepreneur John Wanamaker was born 11 July 1838 in Philadelphia, Pennsylvania, where he later established Wanamaker's, the store that would become America's largest and most successful retail business. He is commonly known as the originator of the department store, the father of modern advertising, and the creator of the money-back guarantee.

Wanamaker's notable career in public life included service as U.S. postmaster general. But his first love was the Bethany Presbyterian Sunday School (later Bethany Memorial Presbyterian Church), which he founded at age 20 in a small room over a cobbler's shop. The first meeting was broken up by rival gangs of rowdy young men brandishing clubs. Yet from this humble beginning in 1858, Bethany grew to become the largest Sunday school in the United States, with more than 5,000 pupils attending weekly. As superintendent, Wanamaker was actively involved in the school's instruction and administration for decades and nurtured personal, spiritually edifying relationships with many of the students. He taught them to pray: "We will make heart-room for Jesus, Thy Son, the name to sinners most dear. We live in the grace of His redeeming love and our only hope is in the finished salvation of Calvary" (Zulker 2009, 39).

Wanamaker's formal education did not begin until age nine, when he attended school at Landreth House, where his grandfather had been elected as the first president of the school board. Equally formative, if not more so, were the many hours that he spent at worship services and in Sunday school classes at his boyhood church, where he was frequently under the instruction of his father and grandfather. His conversion to personal faith in Jesus

Christ occurred at around age 15, when he was walking down Broad Street after work, heard congregational singing, and entered a midweek prayer service. There he heard an elderly man declare that as a follower of Christ, he felt well-prepared to die, as well as a younger man testify that following Christ was everything a young man could dream for. That night, Wanamaker gave his heart to God for Christian service.

In the same year that he founded the Bethany Sunday School, Wanamaker was hired as secretary of the Philadelphia Young Men's Christian Association (YMCA), which had been established by a local clergyman a few years earlier "to bring the young to faith in Jesus Christ" (Zulker 2009, 67). Under Wanamaker's leadership, membership increased from several dozen to more than 2,000. The Philadelphia YMCA sponsored Sunday evening Bible classes throughout the city and sought to strengthen the work of local Sunday schools. In three years as secretary Wanamaker recruited and trained scores of Bible teachers with the stated goal of reaching "the many thousands of neglected children and youth not likely to be brought under any moral influence by other means" (Zulker, 2009, 77). Wanamaker also partnered with black clergy to open a "colored branch" of the YMCA. After considering the possibility of a call to pastoral ministry, he left the ministry of the YMCA for a career in the clothing business. Yet he remained actively involved with the organization through generous financial support for constructing new facilities overseas (Calcutta, Kyoto, Peking, Seoul) and later by serving as president of the Philadelphia chapter.

Wanamaker was interested in evangelism as well as discipleship. Throughout his service as secretary of the YMCA, he organized evangelistic rallies throughout the city. When D. L. Moody and Ira Sankey came to Philadelphia in 1875, he covered all of their expenses and delayed opening his new department store in order to host the public meetings at which they preached the gospel to more than a million souls. "The new store can wait for a few months for its opening," he said; "the Lord's business comes first" (Zulker, 2009, 139). His commitment to evangelism also marked his service as YMCA president: during his first summer in office, the ministry conducted more than 300 open-air meetings across the city.

Wanamaker's other educational endeavors included establishing the John Wanamaker Commercial Institute (later the American University of Trade and Applied Commerce) and Camp Wanamaker on Barnegat Bay, New Jersey, as venues for the moral, physical, intellectual, and spiritual training of the young men and women who worked at his department store; founding the Bethany Brotherhood "to promote Christ's kingdom especially among men, and for their spiritual, social, and mental improvement" (Zulker 2009, 157); securing the approval of Abraham Lincoln during the Civil War to form the Christian Commission for the Army and Navy; founding the Bethany Home and Day Nursery to provide free kindergarten for more than 3,000 children; and rescuing the *Sunday School Times* from bankruptcy in 1871, then increasing its national circulation before eventually turning over the paper's ownership to its editors. To give one remarkable example of the man's personal care for his students and attention to detail, for several years he took time during vacations and business trips to write postcards of friendly encouragement to each of the more than 1,000 men who belonged to the Bethany Brotherhood.

Near the end of his life, in the last of his more than 5,000 newspaper editorials, John Wanamaker wistfully remarked, "The only wish I have is that I could have done all my work better" (Zulker 2009, 207). Yet he did his work more effectively than perhaps any other man of his generation, and when he died on 12 December 1922, flags across his native Philadelphia were lowered to half staff. On the day of his funeral, the city's public schools were ordered closed, City Council adjourned early, and more than 15,000 mourners—many of whose lives had been touched by his lifelong commitment to Christian education—braved extreme cold to pay the merchant and educator their last respects. In addition to mayors, governors, congressmen, and senators, notable pallbearers included the statesman William Jennings Bryan, Chief Justice William Taft, and inventor Thomas Alva Edison.

Reference

Zulker, William Allen. 2009. *John Wanamaker: King of Merchants*. 2nd ed. Richland, PA: Eaglecrest

—Philip Graham Ryken

WARD, TED

Early Life and Education

Ted Warren Ward was born in 1930 in Punxsutawney, Pennsylvania, during the Great Depression. In 1936, the Ward family moved to Avon Park, Florida, where Ted completed all of his public school education and became a promising young flutist and conductor. The Wards attended a Presbyterian church, and at 11 years of age, Ted made a formal faith commitment and joined the church. In 1948, Ward began a degree in music education at Wheaton College. There he met another flutist, Margaret Hockett, from Evanston, Illinois. Ward graduated with a bachelor's degree in music education in 1951, and in June he and Margaret were married. He earned a master of education (1954, music teacher education) and a doctor of education (1956, educational research and curriculum for professional development) from the University of Florida.

Ward then accepted an appointment as professor of education and curriculum research at Michigan State University (MSU), East Lansing, Michigan (1956–1986). In 1985, Ward started his final year at Michigan State and began working half time at Trinity Evangelical Divinity School (TEDS) in Illinois. Soon after, he was appointed professor of Christian education and mission and dean of international studies, mission, and education, and was named Aldeen Professor of Missions, Education, and International Studies. He retired in 1994, but continued an active teaching role until 1999, and served as a consultant to the PhD programs in educational studies and intercultural studies.

Significant Contributions to Christian Education

Ted Ward's professional interests have coalesced around three major areas of professional research:

- *The education of educators.* His influence on the development of educators spans the university, the seminary, and the Christian college. There is hardly an evangelical theological institution in North America, not to mention in many countries of the world, that does not have at least one faculty member who has been touched in some way by Ward's instruction.
- *Education in developing nations.* Over 100 mission professors, missionary executives, and Christian education leaders did their doctoral work under his tutelage. His contributions include scholarly works on Third World education, especially nonformal education, and involvement in the production of the *World Dictionary of Mission Related Educational Institutions* (1968). He was influential in the early

years of the theological education by extension movement (1967–1976).

- *Moral development.* During the 1970s, Ward established and directed the Michigan State University Values Education Research Center. His work in the area of moral development and the family led to involvement with the National Association of Evangelicals and the U.S. Congress on the Family (1976). For five years he chaired the Task Force on the Family (NAE) and in 1980 was research adviser and delegate-at-large to the White House Conference on Families, Washington and Los Angeles.

Ward had a passion to ensure that the field of Christian education be driven by sound theology and guided by careful research. He has challenged North American professors of Christian education as a body on several occasions, at one time arguing that "Christian Education is neither." Through his writing, speaking, and teaching, he has continually prodded Christian educators to be more Christian and better educators.

Over two-thirds of the students who completed doctoral programs under Ward at MSU were working in the field of Christian education when they came to study with him, and all the students at TEDS were in Christian education. Over 200 men and women have completed their graduate programs with Ward since 1956, and they presently serve around the world in Christian higher education, mission leadership, theological education, and Christian education.

Significant Publications

Ward is the author of more than 125 journal and encyclopedia articles; 50 popular articles; 20 major monographs; and 9 books, including *Living Overseas: A Book of Preparation* (Macmillan, 1984) and *Values Begin at Home* (Scripture Press, 1979/1989). He is the editor of two yearbooks of professional associations. He was founding editor of *Faculty Dialogue*.

Editorial note: We are grateful for the permission of the director of the *Christian Educators of the 20th Century Project* for unlimited use of a biography of Ted Ward written by Stephen T. Hoke and Linda Cannell. See http://www.talbot.edu/ce20/educators/protestant/ted_ward/

—MARK A. LAMPORT

WARREN, MICHAEL

Early Background and Education

Michal Warren (1935–), a Caucasian American writer, was educated at Catholic University, earning his BA in English literature and MA and PhD in religious educa-

tion. Prior to beginning his professorial career, he was a high school teacher and adult catechetical minister. Since 1975, he has taught exclusively at Saint John's University in Jamaica, New York, as professor of theology and religious studies. He has written more than a dozen books in the areas of marriage, youth ministry, and money and has lectured in Canada, New Zealand, Ireland, and the United States in such academic institutions as Princeton Theological Seminary. His book *Perspectives on Marriage* is often a foundation textbook for courses on marriage at Catholic universities.

Significant Contributions to Christian Education

We can derive at least four insights about Christian education from the study of Dr. Warren's life and work, although not all of these are insights that Warren himself set out to convey to future Christian educators.

First, he focuses primarily on the importance of traditional marriage. Because the definition of marriage within the United States is being challenged by gay, lesbian, and transgender groups, Warren continues to argue that not only is traditional marriage deeply embedded in the Jewish and Christian traditions, but it also provides societal benefits that nontraditional marriage cannot offer. For Warren, marriage is more than a contract or avenue to personal happiness; it is the means by which God makes a husband and wife holier, even Christlike. The issue of conflict and conflict resolution is a process of personal and matrimonial sanctification.

Second, Warren emphasizes money matters. With climbing divorce rates, bankruptcy, and financial scandals, Warren claims that financial choices are at the core of many societal ills. The Bible underscores Warren's concern by highlighting that the love of money is the root of all kinds of evil (2 Tim. 6:10), and that greed has led many individuals to make foolish and life-altering decisions that have had long-term consequences. Christian educators should not shy away from focusing on financial stewardship.

Third is Warren's critique of academic slothfulness. He notes that once professors develop their course syllabi and have fine-tuned their lectures/presentations, they can become complacent, avoiding critical analysis and additional revisions when needed. For Warren, this nonreflective teaching is a form of laziness that does not portray an aspect of the Gospel that challenges Christian professors to examine their motives to rise above the status quo.

Fourth, Warren is also concerned that educators can place a greater emphasis on teaching the right doctrine but can avoid expressing social concern. The Gospel is principally the justification of sinners by a Holy God through faith in the work of Jesus Christ; however, the

Gospel message should also result in works that display love for the orphans and widows—those in society who need additional support. Warren believes that followers of Jesus should not only *preach* the Gospel but should also *live* it, through actions that reflect what Jesus did by providing food for the hungry and healing for the sick. The Gospel not only reconciles the believer with God, but also produces good works that can transform a society.

Most Notable Publications

Scott, Kiernan, and Michael Warren. 2001. *Perspectives on Marriage: A Reader.* New York: Oxford University Press.

Warren, Michael. 1998. *Youth, Gospel, Liberation.* Dublin: Veritas.

——. 1999. *At This Time, in This Place: The Spirit Embodied in the Local Assembly.* Harrisburg, PA: Trinity Press International.

—David McGee

Wesley, John

An Anglican clergyman and founder of the Methodist movement, John Wesley was born in Epworth, Lincolnshire, England, on 28 June 1703. He was the 15th child and second surviving son of Samuel and Susanna Wesley. Raised in a home with deep piety and Puritan discipline, Wesley was educated at the Charterhouse School, London, and Christ Church, Oxford, where he received his baccalaureate degree in 1724. The following year, he was ordained an Anglican deacon; he was elected a fellow of Lincoln College, Oxford, in 1726, and became a priest in 1728.

In early 1729, while serving as an assistant to his father as curate in Wroot, a number of influences converged in Wesley's life, convincing him of the ultimate purpose of Christianity: holiness of heart and life. Initially, the means to this holiness remained elusive. However, two developments took place over the next decade that helped Wesley understand how God works to make people holy.

First, Wesley saw the necessity of group discipleship in the work of sanctification. After he returned to Lincoln College in 1729, he took over leadership of an existent "Holy Club" at Oxford. Called "Methodists" derisively, members dedicated themselves to spiritual disciplines and to service to marginalized groups in British society. Under Wesley's direction, through trial and error, the Holy Club became the foundational model for the Methodist class meeting, which in turn became the vehicle used to fuel the flames of the Methodist revival.

When fully developed, Wesley's class meeting became the centerpiece of three interconnected groups at the heart of Methodist discipleship. The largest group, called

a society, was comprised of 50–150 members and met once a week. Here members were educated in the major doctrines of Methodism through preaching and teaching.

To be a part of a Methodist society, participants were required to regularly attend class meetings, held once a week. These small groups had 10–12 members, with spiritual oversight provided by an appointed leader. Participants had Methodist teaching reinforced and were held accountable in three areas: to do as much good for as many people as possible; to avoid evil and do no harm; and to make a regular practice of individual and corporate spiritual disciplines. Wesley believed these practices were the means by which God's grace worked to make people holy. Here members who had been spiritually awakened through Methodist preaching often experienced conversion.

Once converted, they were encouraged to seek Christian perfection. For the most devoted Methodists seeking Christian perfection, "bands" were formed with 5–10 members. Although participation in bands was not required, it was encouraged. Here reflection on four questions directed the meeting: What known sins have you committed since our last meeting? What temptations have you met with? What have you thought, said, or done of which you doubt whether it was sin or not? Have you nothing you desire to keep secret?

Second, Wesley developed a theology of divine grace. On 24 May 1738 on Aldersgate Street in London, Wesley experienced salvation by divine grace through faith. If the class meeting became the medium of the Wesleyan revival, Wesley's conversion experience helped to solidify his message and theology. Holiness of heart and life is by divine grace through faith. Until Aldersgate, Wesley had viewed Christian faith primarily as a mental assent to Christian doctrine and salvation as a result of good works. Now Wesley saw that humanity is justified, regenerated, and sanctified by a grace-enabled trust and confidence in Christ's saving work.

Fully developed, Wesley believed Christian salvation in life entailed deliverance from the guilt, power, and nature of sin, liberating the heart to love God entirely and neighbor as self. In the experience of new birth, believers are absolved of the guilt of sin in justification and set free from the power of sin in regeneration. This enables Christians to walk in obedience to God, no longer slaves to sin. However, while Christians walk in victory over sin and mature in Christian discipleship, they continue to be confronted with the nature of sin that remains, causing them to fight against sinful desires and impulses. While Christians make progress in this struggle, Wesley believed that in a moment of divine grace, appropriated by grace-enabled faith, Christians could be freed from the nature of sin, restoring the moral image of God and enabling them to walk in the perfect love of God and neighbor in this life.

Encouraged by an account of the Great Awakening in New England by Jonathan Edwards, John Wesley accepted the invitation of George Whitefield to do "so vile a thing" as preach in the fields to the unchurched masses in Kingswood. On 1 April 1739, with fear and trepidation, Wesley began preaching the Gospel to large crowds neglected by the Anglican Church. Later Wesley declared "the World is my parish." The masses responded to Wesley's message, and the Methodist revival began, fueled by a theology of divine grace that could "save to the uttermost" and a method of discipleship that actively placed people in the means of God's saving and sanctifying grace. In the 50 years between the start of Wesley's field preaching and his death on 1 March 1791, approximately 80,000 people were brought to Christ and became active participants in Methodist class meetings.

References and Resources

Collins, Kenneth J. 2000. *A Real Christian: The Life of John Wesley.* Nashville, TN: Abingdon Press.

Henderson, D. Michael. 1997. *A Model for Making Disciples: John Wesley's Class Meeting.* Nappanee, IN: Evangel Publishing House.

Lindstrom, Harold. 1946. *Wesley and Sanctification: A Study in the Doctrine of Salvation.* London: Epworth Press.

Outler, Albert Cook, ed. 1964. *John Wesley.* New York: Oxford University Press.

Rack, Henry. 1989. *Reasonable Enthusiast: John Wesley and the Rise of Methodism.* London: Epworth Press.

—CHRISTOPHER T. BOUNDS

WESLEYAN CHURCH CHRISTIAN EDUCATION

History

Wesleyan education traces its roots to John Wesley and the Methodist movement he founded in England and the United States. While a student at Oxford, he met with his brother, Charles, and a few others to pursue Christian maturity though Bible study, prayer, good works, extensive self-examination, and accountability. The group earned the nicknames "Holy Club" and "Methodist."[1] After finding assurance of his own salvation (noted later in this article), Wesley shared his testimony and teaching with others, and a spiritual awakening spread across the British Isles.

The movement spread to America by the emigration of Methodists, who, beginning in 1766, began to organize Methodist societies and classes in the colonies. In 1784, the Methodist Episcopal Church was organized in Baltimore, Maryland.[2] The new church experienced rapid growth, especially on the frontier, and by the mid-1800s, the Methodist Church was the largest denomination in America. The Wesleyan Methodist Church (a branch of this movement) was organized in 1843 in opposition to the institution of slavery. John Wesley and other early Methodists had been uncompromising in their denunciation of slavery. However, as time went on, the Methodist Episcopal Church accepted many members (and ministers) who were slaveholders. When the Wesleyan Methodist Church merged with the Pilgrim Holiness Church in 1968, the name of the denomination was changed to the Wesleyan Church.

Notable Academic Programs

John Wesley placed a high value on education, beginning schools of various kinds and emphasizing education in his societies, which later became churches. During the 1800s, the Wesleyan Church started schools like Wheaton College (Illinois) and Adrian College (Michigan). While both of these schools later became independent, the church continued to organize Bible schools, colleges, and universities. Today, the Wesleyan Church operates five colleges and universities in North America: Indiana Wesleyan University, Oklahoma Wesleyan University, Southern Wesleyan University (South Carolina), Houghton College (New York), and Kingswood University (Canada). Indiana Wesleyan is the largest Wesleyan university, with 3,000 students attending classes at the main campus and 12,000 additional students studying online or at extension campuses. Indiana Wesleyan University is also the largest university in the Council of Christian Colleges and Universities (103 member schools) and has perhaps the largest number of ministry majors of any school belonging to this organization. The Wesleyan schools are fully accredited and offer a wide range of majors in both undergraduate and graduate programs. In 2009, Wesley Seminary was organized on the campus of Indiana Wesleyan University. It offers innovative programs in English and Spanish leading to the MA and MDiv degrees. Alternative routes to ordination are offered by the denomination through intensive classes ("FLAME") and correspondence courses. Bible colleges are also available in several of the 90 countries where the Wesleyans have organized (or mission) churches. In addition to these institutions of higher learning, local Wesleyan churches offer Sunday and/or midweek programs of education for all ages.

---

1. *Wesleyan Discipline* (Indianapolis, IN: Wesleyan Publishing House, 2000), 5.

2. Ibid.

Christian Philosophy and Mission of Education

1. Wesleyan education is biblical. John Wesley said, "I am a man of one book."[3] In Wesleyan churches, education classes are filled with people with open Bibles who search the scriptures to find what Wesley called "the only sufficient rule both of Christian faith and practice."[4]

2. Wesleyan education is evangelical. It wholeheartedly affirms the historic creeds of the Christian church and the doctrinal statement of the National Association of Evangelicals. Wesleyan education emphasizes the Great Commission and the Great Commandments.

3. Wesleyan education seeks to involve Christians in meeting the needs of hurting people. The Wesleyan Methodist Church was founded in opposition to slavery. John Wesley ministered to the poor, to orphans, and to those who were sick or in prison. Today, Wesleyans are involved in many compassionate ministries as well as social justice issues, including immigration reform, the rights of the unborn, human trafficking, and so forth.

4. Wesleyan education is inclusive. The great Pentecostal promise (Acts 2:17–21) affirms that (1) the Holy Spirit has been outpoured upon all classes of people, (2) anyone who calls on the name of the Lord will be saved, and (3) both men and women will prophesy (or proclaim God's message). Wesleyans emphasize the inclusive grace of God in providing salvation, empowering the church, and bestowing gifts for ministry.

5. Wesleyan education is ecumenical in the sense of welcoming and working together with Christians from a variety of backgrounds. One of the most frequently noted statements of John Wesley is: "If your heart is as my heart . . . give me your hand."[5]

6. Wesleyan education values experience. As an Anglican priest, John Wesley sought for assurance of his salvation, until one day at a meeting on Aldersgate Street (while listening to the leader read Luther's preface to the Epistle to Romans), he "felt his heart strangely warmed" and he knew that Christ had taken away his sins. In addition to the Anglican emphasis on scripture, reason, and tradition, Wesleyans add a fourth source of authority: experience. (These four are often referred to as "the Wesleyan quadrilateral.")

7. Wesleyan education is innovative. When Anglican pulpits were closed to him, John Wesley preached in the fields. When a church building was not available, he moved his society into a foundry. When not enough clergy were available, he appointed lay preachers. Wesley pioneered free schools for disadvantaged children, offered free medical care to the poor, and began a highly developed system of small group discipleship, which enrolled seekers and new converts in classes, societies, and bands. Today, Wesleyan education continues to be innovative, providing unconventional methods of ministerial training and extensive programs of adult education.

8. Wesleyan education emphasizes holiness. Wesley called people to live holy lives. The centerpiece of this emphasis is in Romans 6, where Christians are called to consecrate their lives to God and to live in victory over continual, willful sin. Wesleyans are optimistic about what God can do in the life of a consecrated believer. Wesleyan education challenges disciples to leave behind attitudes and actions of sin and to be filled with the Holy Spirit.

In addition to the general description of the philosophy and mission of Wesleyan education (given above), colleges and universities of the Wesleyan Church include the following ideas in a description of their philosophy and mission:

1. Wesleyan education believes that God is the source of all truth. Wesleyans believe that pursuing truth (in any field) "within the framework of God's will . . . is a sacred act."[6]

2. Wesleyan education shares opportunities "to study a broad range of interests in a community of faith" and "provides a Christian perspective from which a wide range of . . . occupations can be pursued."[7]

3. Wesleyan education is committed to the integration of faith and learning. Since truth is one and whole, "the truth that converts the soul does not conflict with truth that develops the mind or enhances quality of life."[8] The objective of such integration is "not only the redemption of individuals, but of human society and its institutions."[9]

4. Wesleyan education is committed to exploring new truth. While God's revelation in scripture does not change, our understanding of our world and of God's revelation is limited and therefore in need of continual refinement and change. Wesleyan education recognizes the need for academic

---

3. John Wesley, *Standard Sermons* (Salem, OH: H.E. Schmul, 1967), xx.
4. Ibid., 27.
5. Ibid., 385.
6. "General Board: Standards of the Wesleyan Church for Educational Institutions," May 2011, GB1138.
7. Ibid., GB1112.
8. Ibid., GB1144.
9. Ibid., GB1146.

freedom that earnestly searches for truth while respecting both Christian tradition and God's revelation in scripture.[10]

5. Wesleyan education gives high priority to training persons for professional church leadership.[11]

References and Resources

Black, Robert, and Keith Drury. 2012. *The Story of the Wesleyan Church*. Indianapolis, IN: Wesleyan Publishing House.

Caldwell, Wayne. 1992. *Reformers and Revivalists: The History of the Wesleyan Church*. Indianapolis, IN: Wesleyan Publishing House.

"General Board Standards of the Wesleyan Church for Educational Institutions." 2011. May. Marion, IN: General Secretary of the Wesleyan Church, R.R. Brannon, 1985.

McLeister, Ira Ford, and Roy S. Nicholson. 1976. *Conscience and Commitment: The History of the Wesleyan Methodist Church*. Marion, IN: Wesleyan Publishing House.

Thomas, Paul William. 1976. *The Days of Our Pilgrimage*. Marion, IN: Wesleyan Publishing House.

Wesley, John. 1967. *Standard Sermons*. Salem, OH: H.E. Schmul.

Wesleyan Discipline. 2000. Indianapolis, IN: Wesleyan Publishing House.

—KEITH SPRINGER

WESLEYAN QUADRILATERAL

The Wesleyan Quadrilateral is a model illustrating the sources of religious authority in theological method, as interpreted from the works of John Wesley. The quadrilateral indicates four sources of authority that are uniquely interdependent, with each shedding light on the other. These four sources are scripture, tradition, reason, and experience. It is meant as a helpful model as one reflects and attempts to conceptualize an understanding of theology. Each "side" of the quadrilateral has influence on our theological method and our understanding of various theological questions.[12]

In this model, *scripture* is the primary source and standard for Christian doctrine, namely the Holy Bible.[13] *Tradition* is the development and growth of the teachings of the church through the past centuries as seen in many nations and cultures. *Reason* is the discerning application of clear, logical thought brought to bear on the issue.

Experience is the individual's understanding and appropriating of the faith in the light of his or her own life.[14]

John Wesley did not use the term "Wesleyan Quadrilateral," nor does it appear in any of his works. It was first coined by Albert Outler (1964), who theorized that Wesley used four different sources in coming to a theological conclusion.[15] Wesley recognized that while scripture is the primary and foundational source for our theological methodology, many differ in their hermeneutical perspectives. Scripture is interpreted through the lens of tradition, reason, and experience.[16] Wesley built upon the Anglican tradition of scripture, tradition, and reason by allowing experience to serve as a legitimate source in theological reflection.[17] This addition, of experience as a source of religious authority, is regarded by some to be his greatest contribution to the development of Christian theology.[18]

Outler has said he regrets using the term "Wesleyan Quadrilateral," as he intended it to be a metaphor and not to be taken so literally or used so exactly. One misunderstanding has been that all four sides are equal (an equilateral), thus giving experience equal weight as scripture. This is not Outler's understanding of Wesley. Scripture is meant to be the center point from which the other sources are engaged. On the second tier, tradition offers a helpful expansion to the witness of scripture, providing the church's teachings where scripture has remained quiet and historical insight to "dark or intricate" passages.[19]

But scripture and tradition would not be enough without the analytical and discerning help of reason and experience. Outler notes that Wesley insisted on logical coherence, especially when differing opinions or arguments existed; yet the rational steadiness of reason was not enough. Wesley asserted that one's experience of God and salvation was necessary, even essential, to understanding and interpreting scripture.[20]

While Wesley may not have intended his theological method to take a geometric form, it has been helpful to many as they develop spiritually and theologically. It is a realistic description of the contextual way that Christians make decisions. The influence of tradition, reason, and particularly experience is not always recognized or acknowledged as part of the theological process. Some may find it helpful to reflect on how their theology has

---

10. Ibid., GB1148,1150,1152.

11. Ibid., GB1112.

12. Donald A. D. Thorsen, *The Wesleyan Quadrilateral: Scripture, Tradition, Reason & Experience as a Model of Evangelical Theology* (Nappanee, IN: Francis Asbury Press, 1997), 127.

13. Alan K. Waltz, "Wesleyan Quadrilateral," in *A Dictionary for United Methodists* (Nashville, TN: Abingdon Press, 1991).

14. Albert C. Outler, ed., *John Wesley* (Oxford: Oxford University Press, 1964), iv.

15. Albert Outler, "The Wesleyan Quadrilateral in Wesley," *Wesleyan Theological Journal* 20, no. 1 (1985): 16–17.

16. Ibid., 10.

17. Ibid.

18. Thorsen, *The Wesleyan Quadrilateral*, 201.

19. Ibid., 153.

20. Outler, "Wesleyan Quadrilateral in Wesley," 10.

been formed and affected by all four of these. Some communities may find that this intentionality in their method brings a renewal or reemphasis on scripture. Others may uncover a rich treasure through a deeper or broader examination of tradition. Still others may discover an exciting dynamic by exploring the relationship of reason and experience.

References and Resources

Gunther, W. Stephen, [et al.]. 1997. *Wesley and The Quadrilateral: Renewing the Conversation.* Nashville, TN: Abingdon Press.

Outler, Albert, ed. 1964. *John Wesley.* Oxford: Oxford University Press.

———. 1985. "The Wesleyan Quadrilateral in Wesley." *Wesleyan Theological Journal* 20 (1): 7–18.

Thorsen, Donald A. 1997. *The Wesleyan Quadrilateral: Scripture, Tradition, Reason & Experience as a Model of Evangelical Theology.* Nappanee, IN: Francis Asbury Press.

Waltz, Alan K. 1991. "Wesleyan Quadrilateral." In *A Dictionary for United Methodists.* Nashville, TN: Abingdon Press.

           —JAMES P. BOWERS AND MICHAEL MCMULLIN

WEST INDIES AND CHRISTIAN EDUCATION

The accidental and opportunistic "discovery" of the West Indies by European explorers in the late 15th century precipitated a frenzied power struggle for economic wealth and the domination of indigenous peoples that lasted into the 20th century. Despite a series of revolts and independence movements generated largely by counter-educational impulses, it may be argued that the struggle for self-determination is far from over.

The Spanish brought with them a Catholicizing impulse that catechized and baptized, teaching a doctrine of "protection" and subservience through the *encomienda* and *misión*. Few voices resisted; that of Bartolomé de las Casas (1484–1566), Dominican advocate of human rights for all, is outstanding in this regard.

Attitudes toward colonized and enslaved peoples were further bedeviled by mythic readings of "race," an approach to ethnicity that created hierarchies of human ability and educational worth. At one end of the spectrum, the "inferior races" were considered uneducable.

In all colonial systems, education for subjugation and control was the norm. The Catholic Church in the Spanish and French colonies privileged membership in the church as the primary social affiliation, suppressing local cultural expressions. The 17th century experienced limited experiments in a theology of enculturation, but these did not touch the West Indian context.

The Anglican Church taught obedience as a primary virtue and rarely challenged the status quo. In any case, the plantocracy was suspicious of all education for slaves, regarding it rightly as potentially subversive. Antislavery movements in Europe slowly filtered through to the West Indies, leading to slave uprisings (Maroons in 17th- and 18th-century Jamaica) and independence movements (Haiti in 1804). The French Revolution, from its inception, became the backdrop against which all political and religious philosophy was measured.

Causes célèbres fed into the popular consciousness and into key texts and manifestos. Notable were *The Interesting Narrative of the Life of Olaudah Equiano* (1789), the imprisonment and death in Demerara of the London Missionary Society missionary John Smith (1824), and the Jamaican Slave Revolt (1831–1832), fomented by black Baptists. Protestant nonconformity was thus the primary source of Christian education against slavery.

The rise of the principle of universal education in the 19th century led to the parallel establishment of national and denominational schools in British colonies, with access for Christian education in the state system. French colonies experienced the same oscillation between Catholic and secular impulses as the mother country, while Spanish colonies privileged the Catholic establishment.

Church institutions in the West Indies did not have a libertarian educational agenda. However, it can be argued that the mere provision of education, in which the churches and religious communities had the largest investment, facilitated formal and informal freedom movements. The early generations of local political leadership were almost without exception educated in Christian contexts.

Currently, liberation and black theologies inform many in the traditional denominations, vying with North American fundamentalism, Pentecostalism, and African independency for the minds of the people. The West Indies remain strongly religious, but formal Christian education in schools and in churches is now far less significant. Traditional and new media and the postcolonial search for cultural identity have replaced church and school as the prevailing influences in the region's ongoing religious and spiritual formation.

References and Resources

Blackburn, Robin. 1988. *The Overthrow of Colonial Slavery 1776–1848.* New York: Verso.

Edmonds, Ennis B., and Michelle A. Gonzalez. 2010. *Caribbean Religious History: An Introduction.* New York: New York University Press.

Kidd, Colin. 2006. *The Forging of Races: Race and Scripture in the Protestant Atlantic World, 1600–2000.* Cambridge, UK: Cambridge University Press.

Lampe, Armando. 2001. *Christianity in the Caribbean: Essays in Church History*. Mona, Kingston, Jamaica: University of the West Indies Press.

Newson, Linda. 1976. *Aboriginal and Spanish Colonial Trinidad: A Study in Culture Contact*. Maryland Heights, MO: Academic Press.

UNESCO General History of the Caribbean. 1997–2012. 6 vols. London, UK.

Walvin, James. 1992. *Black Ivory: A History of British Slavery*. New York: HarperCollins.

Williams, Eric. 1969. *Inward Hunger: The Education of a Prime Minister*. London: André Deutsch.

———. 1970. *From Columbus to Castro: The History of the Caribbean 1492–1969*. New York: Harper & Row.

—Adrian Chatfield

WESTERHOFF, JOHN HENRY, III

Early Background and Education

John Henry Westerhoff III was born in Paterson, New Jersey, in 1933 and baptized as "John Henry Christian" that same year at the First Presbyterian Church in Patterson.[21] His parents were of Dutch Reformed descent, but Westerhoff described them as having "only a surface relationship with the church."[22] Westerhoff looked back on his baptism as personally and vocationally formative and the beginning of a series of transformative experiences that have significantly shaped his life. His mother took him to Sunday school "out of duty," but it was a powerful visionary and mystical experience in a revival service at a small church he attended at the invitation of a neighbor that impacted Westerhoff and gained him the attention of the group's minister. Westerhoff described having a Pentecostal-like vision of Jesus—"who looked like a woman"—at the close of a sermon, which led to a pastoral visit and the suggestion to his mother that he was a "holy man."[23] His mother prevented him from returning to the church, but Westerhoff wandered into a Reformed Church in Glen Rock, New Jersey, where his family had moved, and the minister there also saw a ministerial future for him and had him assisting in worship services and teaching a Sunday school class.

When Westerhoff became a student at Ursinus College, from which he graduated with a baccalaureate degree (1955), he was immediately dubbed "Preach" by his fraternity despite his lessened spiritual passion and

increasingly relativistic perspective.[24] He argued against much of Christian doctrine and biblical fundamentalism, although he emerged from his early life with a "positive attitude toward conservative evangelical faith."[25] He considered his acceptance at Harvard Divinity School "somewhat of a fluke," but graduated with a master of divinity (1958) and completed a doctor of education at Columbia (1974) before being ordained in the United Church of Christ.

Westerhoff considered the influence of Harvard faculty members Father George Florovsky, Krister Stendahl, James Luther Adams, Amos Wilder, and Paul Tillich especially transformative for his life. Especially from Tillich, but also from the mentoring of Rev. Dr. Herbert Smith and his own pastoral experiences, Westerhoff became convinced of the singularly important formation of liturgy and of the larger community of faith and determined to focus on adult education as the most essential aspect of parish work. He would take these convictions into his work as professor of religion and education at Duke Divinity School and his role as editor of *Religious Education* for 10 years. Westerhoff was ordained an Episcopal priest in 1978.

Significant Contributions to Christian Education

From his early formative experiences with Christian liturgy and the communities of faith in which he participated, Westerhoff developed his pastoral and educational emphasis. He credits connections with anthropologists—especially Gwen Kennedy Neville, with whom he coauthored two books—for shaping his vision of the value of enculturation, and the work of C. Ellis Nelson for providing him with the theological foundations and insights into religious socialization that shaped his theory of Christian education.[26] Westerhoff's greatest contribution has been to present socialization as the model for the work of Christian formation. Through various publications, but especially in *Will Our Children Have Faith?*, he has argued for a catechetical—faith-initiating and forming-experience—process of participation in the life of the faith community, its liturgy, and the influence of its adult members as the central means of Christian formation.[27]

Westerhoff's understanding of the nature of Christian education as the pastoral activity of catechesis taking place in the dialogue, activities, and liturgical practices of the faith community stands out against "schooling" models and instructional approaches. He does not reject the role of instruction, but considers it only helpful for

---

21. John H. Westerhoff III, "A Journey into Self-Understanding," in *Modern Masters of Religious Education*, ed. Marlene Mayr (Birmingham, AL: Religious Education Press, 1983), 120–121.
22. Ibid.
23. Ibid., 121.

24. Ibid., 122.
25. Ibid.
26. Ibid., 129 and 131.
27. James E. Reed and Ronnie Prevost, *A History of Christian Education* (Nashville, TN: Broadman & Holman, 1993), 357.

facilitating mastery of propositional truth.[28] Harkening back to the original insights of Horace Bushnell concerning the organic nature of Christian education, Westerhoff has been the apostle of concern for how the quality of faith in the Christian community forms and shapes the faith of children and other initiates for spiritual health and faithfulness.

Most Important Publications

Westerhoff's most important publications in Christian education have all focused on the formational significance of the life, liturgy, and catechetical experience of the Christian community. His book, *Will Our Children Have Faith?*, has been the most widely recognized and read volume on his basic argument for a socialization approach to formation. Other notable works dealing with aspects of this same theme are *Learning through Liturgy* (with Gwen Kennedy Neville, 1978), *Liturgy and Learning through the Life Cycle* (with William H. Willimon, 1980), *Bringing Up Children in the Christian Faith* (1980), *The Spiritual Life: Learning East and West* (with John D. Eusden, 1982), and *Building God's People in a Materialistic Society* (1983).

References and Resources

Reed, James E., and Ronnie Prevost. 1993. *A History of Christian Education*. Nashville, TN: Broadman & Holman.

Westerhoff, John H., III. 1983. "A Journey in Self-Understanding." In *Modern Masters of Religious Education*, edited by Marlene Mayr, 115–134. Birmingham, AL: Religious Education Press.

—JAMES P. BOWERS

WESTMINSTER SHORTER CATECHISM

The *Westminster Shorter Catechism* (WSC) is one of the chief documents produced by the Westminster Assembly—a group of 30 laymen and 121 clergymen appointed by the Long Parliament to reform the Church of England. Many of the assembly's members were catechists, and several had published catechisms that were in wide circulation at the time (Warfield 1931, 62). The assembly met from 1643 to 1649 and was comprised of Episcopalians, Presbyterians, Congregationalists, and Erastians. As well as the WSC, the assembly produced the *Westminster Larger Catechism*, the *Westminster Confession of Faith*, and the *Directory of Public Worship*. These are considered to be the greatest documents produced in the English Reformation. The WSC was finished in 1647, was

presented to the Long Parliament on 14 April 1648, and was approved in late September of that year.

The content and general structure of the WSC resembles that of earlier Reformed catechisms (e.g., Calvin's catechisms and the *Heidelberg Catechism*). Like Calvin's catechisms, discussion of faith is followed by discussion of the Decalogue—unlike Luther's catechisms, which treat the Decalogue before faith. Unlike Calvin's catechisms, the WSC places discussion of the sacraments before discussion of the Lord's Prayer. Also, it begins with an exposition of the Apostles' Creed (faith), but faith in Christ is discussed after the Decalogue.

The WSC is in a simple question-and-answer format, conducive for memorization and recitation. It was designed as a short manual of religion for beginners. Though primarily a manual of doctrine and faith for children, it was also designed to be used by adult converts.

The WSC contains 107 questions, with no sections or subheadings. The dialogue moves organically—there are no firm stops between different discussions, and the transitions are remarkably fluid. Questions 1–12 discuss God as Creator; questions 13–20 deal with original sin and the fallen state of humanity; questions 21–38 discuss Christ the Redeemer and the benefits of salvation; questions 39–84 discuss the Decalogue; questions 85–87 discuss faith in Christ and repentance; questions 88–97 discuss the sacraments of baptism and communion; questions 98–107 discuss prayer and provide an exposition of the Lord's Prayer; and an "appendix" includes the Ten Commandments, the Lord's Prayer, and the Apostles' Creed.

The WSC is not polemical, though it largely reflects Reformed and Puritan distinctives, especially on discussions of God's providence, election, and Sabbath observance.

The most famous question is the first: "Question: What is the chief end of man? Answer: Man's chief end is to glorify God, and to enjoy him forever." It is remarkably similar to the opening question of Calvin's second catechism: "Master: What is the chief end of human life? Scholar: To know God by whom men were created." The first question of the WSC, therefore, reflects the seriousness of the Reformed faith—all things exist for God. The WSC is concerned with outlining true knowledge and worship of God, not an anthropocentric pragmatism.

The WSC gained immediate popularity in Nonconformist England and Scotland. It became a religion textbook in many schools, and it was quickly transmitted to America. Presbyterian missions diffused it throughout the world, and many Reformed, Presbyterian, and Baptist catechisms mimicked its form and content (Warfield 1931, 64). It remains significantly influential into the

---

28. Ibid.

21st century and is used by Reformed and Presbyterian churches worldwide. Even the *New City Catechism* (2012), developed by Gospel Coalition leaders, modeled its form and adapted its content. As B. B. Warfield once said of the WSC, "No other catechism can be compared with it in its concise, nervous, terse exactitude of definition, or in its severely logical elaboration; and it gains these admirable qualities at no expense to its freshness or fervor, though perhaps it can scarcely be spoken of as marked by childlike simplicity" (1931, 66).

References and Resources

Fisher, James. 2001. *The Westminster Assembly's Shorter Catechism: Explained by Way of Question and Answer.* Eugene, OR: Wipf & Stock.

Hall, Joseph H. 2004. "The Westminster Shorter and the Heidelberg Catechisms Compared." In *The Westminster Confession into the 21st Century.* Vol. 2, edited by Ligon Duncan, 54–81. Rossshire: Christian Focus Publications.

Mitchell, Alexander F. 1897. *The Westminster Assembly: Its History and Standards.* Philadelphia: Presbyterian Board of Publication.

Schaff, Philip. 1977. *Creeds of Christendom.* Grand Rapids, MI: Baker Book House.

Warfield, B. B. 1931. *The Westminster Assembly and Its Work.* New York: Oxford University Press.

—Kevin P. Emmert

WESTMINSTER THEOLOGICAL SEMINARY

Foundation

Westminster Theological Seminary was founded in 1929 by a group of men who were leaving the divided faculty of the newly reorganized Princeton Seminary, including Robert Dick Wilson, J. Gresham Machen, Oswald T. Allis, and Cornelius Van Til. Though not all the conservative professors left (Geerhardus Vos and C. W. Hodge, for example, remained at Princeton), Westminster was therefore founded by Old School, antimodernists who had become increasingly disenchanted by the toleration of more liberal views within the Presbyterian Church, U.S.A. The basis of the seminary was from the start a distinctive blend of American Reformed Presbyterianism, confessionally expressed in the *Westminster Confession and Catechisms*, and significant Dutch Calvinist influences, particularly in presuppositional apologetics. Although one of the things that Machen and others campaigned against at Princeton was the abolition of the bicameral nature of the seminary's governing bodies, Westminster is governed by a single self-perpetuating board of 15–30 members.

Development

The influence and prestige of Westminster has not been developed by a particularly high number of graduates or by connections to large denominations; Machen's Orthodox Presbyterian Church, for example, remains relatively small by comparison with the mainline Presbyterian Church, U.S.A. from which it separated in 1936. Rather, its influence has been the result of "the force of its ideas transmitted through the teaching and publications of its faculty, through its role in helping to educate a number of scholars and leaders in evangelical churches" (Godfrey 2004). The *Westminster Theological Journal* was founded in 1938, and the faculty was soon enhanced by the talents of E. J. Young, a notable Old Testament scholar, and John Murray, a Scottish systematician and New Testament commentator. Other well-known faculty members have also displayed an ability to integrate different theological disciplines, such as Meredith G. Kline and Richard B. Gaffin Jr., though with a strong commitment to "Biblical theology" as developed and championed by Vos, or redemptive-historical hermeneutics. New campuses were opened in Florida and California during the presidency of Ed Clowney, and Westminster Seminary California is now an independent institution. The Groves Center at Westminster has been a leading player in advancing the application of information technology to study of the biblical text and maintains the canonical version of the electronic representation of the Leningrad Codex of the Hebrew Bible and the significant Westminster Hebrew Morphology database.

Notable Academic Programs

The seminary offers a full range of degrees, from MAR, MDiv, and ThM to DMin and PhD, with a strong emphasis on original language study of the Bible. All MDiv, MAC, and MAUM students are required to be involved in "mentored ministry" as part of their pastoral ministry, counseling, or urban missions course, being guided in applying what they learn in the classroom to practical ministry settings. The seminary also offers a London (England)–based ThM in historical theology in association with the John Owen Centre for Theological Study.

References and Resources

Calhoun, D. B. 1996. *Princeton Seminary: The Majestic Testimony 1869–1929.* Edinburgh: Banner of Truth.

Gatiss, L. 2008. *Christianity and the Tolerance of Liberalism: J. Gresham Machen and the Presbyterian Controversy of 1922–1937.* London: Latimer Trust.

Godfrey, W. Robert. 2004. *An Unexpected Journey: Discovering Reformed Christianity.* Phillipsburg, NJ: Puritan and Reformed Publishing.

VanDrunen, D., ed. 2004. *The Pattern of Sound Doctrine: Systematic Theology at the Westminster Seminaries.* Phillipsburg, NJ.: Presbyterian and Reformed.

Wells, D. F., ed. 1985. *Reformed Theology in America: A History of Its Modern Development.* Grand Rapids, MI: Eerdmans.

                                       —LEE GATISS

WHEATON COLLEGE (ILLINOIS)

On a summer day in 1853, a small group of Wesleyan Methodists made their way to a tall prairie knoll on land owned by the first founders of Wheaton, Illinois, and prayerfully dedicated a 40-acre tract of land for Illinois Institute, a Wesleyan institution committed to reform principles that centered on abolition, anticaste, the abolishment of Masonry, and the education of African Americans and women.

Seven years later, the second president of Knox College, Jonathan Blanchard, arrived at Wheaton determined to save the college from extinction, since it was clear that the Wesleyan church and administration could not sustain it. Blanchard immediately affirmed the founding principles of the institution. By that time there were several collegiate institutions that were termed "radical reformatory," committed to abolition and broad-based civil rights for African Americans, Native Americans, and women. Hence, Blanchard brought the Illinois Institute into the radical orb of Oberlin, Grinnell, and Berea Colleges, all influenced or founded by New England Congregational abolitionists.

By the time of his death in 1892, the postmillennial vision of Blanchard and other radical presidents like Charles Finney at Oberlin was coming to an end. Under the influence of Moody Bible Institute's cofounder, Emma Dryer, Blanchard's son Charles (1882–1925), an early Wheaton graduate, reversed the social and political stances of his father and steadily brought the institution into the fundamentalist movement. Several scholars have speculated that Wheaton's refusal to seriously engage in the larger issues of the Progressive Era academies (e.g., Darwin, Marx, Freud, and biblical higher criticism) aligned the college with outside fundamentalist forces that influenced the college until the 20th-century evangelical movement.

However, under the third president, J. Oliver Buswell (1926–1940), a Presbyterian and intellectual, the college began to attract faculty and students who held to high academic standards. Because of the restrictive nature of its code of conduct and statement of belief, the institution has never applied for Phi Beta Kappa status and has always held a tenuous position among other secular collegiate institutions.

By the end of World War II and the advancement of Wheaton's arguably most famous alumnus, evangelist Billy Graham, the college began wrestling with its identity. Former English professor Kent Gramm has titled Wheaton during and after this period a *fundagelical* institution: one that has kept its identity in both religious fundamentalist and modern evangelical circles.

The ubiquitous battles over its idiosyncratic statement of faith and behavioral codes has kept the institution from the "slippery slope" of secularism by filtering the admission and retention of students and faculty. During the administrations of V. Raymond Edman (1940–1965) and Hudson Armerding (1982–1993), both of whom were committed to Protestant fundamentalism, the institution remained on a steady course of resistance to cultural forces that would compromise its stances.

It was during the Richard Chase (1982–1993) administration that the institution began to open its doors to historically underrepresented groups at Wheaton, like Episcopalians, Mennonites, Pentecostals, and ordained women, among the faculty. However, its historic stance against the hiring of Roman Catholics was retained, though severely challenged by alumni like Thomas Howard, who converted to Roman Catholicism while a professor of English at Wheaton's sister institution, Gordon College.

Also, the influence of church historian and alumnus Mark Noll, the author of the *Scandal of the Evangelical Mind*, and Wheaton trustee and alumnus Nathan Hatch, the current president of Wake Forest, quietly and forcefully challenged the board of trustees to reconsider the institution's stances. While there were some progressive changes made during Chase's administration, the board became alarmed at the rapid pace of change and appointed Duane Litfin (1993–2010), a graduate of two fundamentalist institutions, as the next president. Upon his arrival he initiated a reaffirmation of the statement of faith (by then literal Creation was under scrutiny), the code of behavior (restriction of alcohol and dancing), and the continued exclusion of Roman Catholic faculty.

Significantly, though, Wheaton has risen in the academic ranks of American colleges, with academically sound students and professors who publish on a regular basis with secular and religious presses and have engineered an academically rigorous environment. Also, their Division III sports teams are highly regarded and continually ranked on a national level. Add to that an endowment of over $300 million, and Wheaton is arguably termed the "Harvard of American evangelical schools," especially when examined through the lens of successful alumni, who are legislators, lawyers, doctors, teachers, and preachers. Wheaton is known for the overall strength and balance of its academic programs. However, the future of evangelical institutions, women's colleges, and historically black colleges and universities is imperiled in this new century. Though Wheaton's history and reputation seem secure for the immediate future, its long-term status as an exclusively evangelical institution remains questionable.

References and Resources

Barnard, John. 1969. *From Evangelicalism to Progressivism at Oberlin College, 1866–1917.* Columbus: Ohio State University Press.

Bechtel, Paul. 1984. *Wheaton College: A Heritage Remembered, 1860–1984.* Wheaton, IL: Shaw Publishers.

Hamilton, Mike. 1994. "The Fundamentalist Harvard: Wheaton College and the Enduring Vitality of American Evangelicalism." PhD diss., University of Notre Dame.

Noll, Mark. 1995. *The Scandal of the Evangelical Mind.* Grand Rapids, MI: Eerdmans.

Taylor, Richard. 1977. "Seeking the Kingdom: The Life and Ministry of Jonathan Blanchard." PhD diss., University of Northern Illinois.

—Louis B. Gallien Jr.

WILL

The scriptures view the human personality holistically. Consequently, the will is always seen as having both inner and outer components. In the Bible, knowledge, attitude, and action all play a significant role in the exercise of the will. Will is not the same as desire, and good intent without implementation is viewed in the Bible as reflective of weakness of character.

In the Gospels, the almost exclusive usage of the Greek term *thelēma* ("will") is to speak of *God's* will (rather than human will). The imperative is to know God's will and do it (Matt. 7:21, 12:50, 21:31, 26:42; Mark 3:35; Luke 12:47, 22:42; John 4:34, 6:38, 9:31), and that will is to see God's redemptive kingdom come (Matt. 6:10, 18:14; John 6:39–40). The apostolic letters provide specifics on the meaning of God's will, discovered through careful study of his Law (Rom. 2:18), and entailing such elements as a life of purity (Eph. 5:15), control over sinful impulses (1 Cor. 8:37; Eph. 2:3, 1 Thess. 4:3), generosity in giving and support to Christian ministry (2 Cor. 8:5; 1 Pet. 2:15), a community life characterized by reconciliation and the acceptance of all (Eph. 1:9), and an attitude of joyful thanksgiving in all circumstances (1 Thess. 5:18), especially in suffering for Christ (Heb. 10:36; 1 Pet. 4:19).

In Christian education, the term "dispositional learning" has been used to describe the process by which the will is disciplined to choose and act in accord with the will of God, to turn our natural tendencies away from self and toward God. When we do not move ahead in developing dispositions toward godliness, we endanger our relationship with God. Due to the habits and inclinations of our former life apart from God, at any time we can revert back to our old "self." We need to "put on the new self, created to be like God in true righteousness and holiness" (Eph. 4:22–24). In the end, dispositional learning is what Christian maturity is all about, but it is usually the most ignored aspect of Christian learning—possibly because it is the most difficult to evaluate.

Ultimately the formation of the will is a divine act in the individual. However, Christian educators can facilitate dispositional change through promoting a balance among cognitive, affective, and behavioral learning by (1) providing opportunities for the mind to be renewed (Rom. 12:2) through the reading of and meditation upon scripture; (2) encouraging right attitudes in submission to the values of the Kingdom of God, often through mentoring relationships with mature men and women; and (3) providing opportunities through which Christians can work out the will of God in doing what is right.

This holistic formational process is the basis of the classic spiritual disciplines (Foster 1978; Willard 1988). Reading and meditating on scripture shapes the mind and clarifies God's purposes. Prayer, fasting, solitude, and acts of submission discipline the heart and turn our desires toward the father-heart of God. Worship, acts of service, and the sacrificial giving of time and finances provide opportunities for action that is consistent with the kingdom values taught by Jesus, promoting the proclamation of his rule.

The cognitive, affective, and behavioral learning experiences found in the spiritual disciplines do not function in isolation; rather, each affects the other: positive attitudes motivate students to think more carefully and take risks in action, experience changes belief and attitude, and right thinking provides guidelines for evaluating both emotions and behavior. An imbalance between the learning dimensions creates distortions in the disposition: a focus on the affective domain can lead to ignorant and detached pietism, a focus on the behavioral domain can lead to uniformed activism, and a focus on the cognitive domain too often leads to pharisaic pride and divisiveness (Shaw 2006). Only through a holistic concert of the ABC of learning can the disposition come to know, desire, and act according to the will of God.

References and Resources

Blackaby, H., R. Blackaby, and C. King. 2008. *Experiencing God: Knowing and Doing the Will of God.* rev. ed. Nashville, TN: B & H Publishing.

Foster, R. J. 1978. *Celebration of Discipline.* New York: Harper & Row.

Nouwen, H. J. M. 1975. *Reaching Out: The Three Movements of the Spiritual Life.* New York: Doubleday.

Shaw, P. W. H. 2006. "Multi-dimensional Learning in Ministerial Training." *International Congregational Journal* 6 (1): 53–63.

Wilhoit, J. C. 2008. *Spiritual Formation as If the Church Mattered: Growing in Christ through Community.* Grand Rapids, MI: Baker.

Willard, D. 1988. *The Spirit of the Disciplines: Understanding How God Changes Lives.* San Francisco: HarperCollins.

———. 2002. *Renovation of the Heart: Putting on the Character of Christ.* Downers Grove, IL: InterVarsity Press.

—PERRY W. H. SHAW

WILLIAMS COLLEGE

Williams College holds a unique place in American higher education and in the world Christian movement. This institution began modestly in 1793 as a men's college in Williamstown, Massachusetts, with a simple motto in Latin meaning "through the generosity of E. Williams, Esquire." Durfee provides background about its benefactor, Ephraim Williams, a third-generation descendent of the Puritan Robert Williams and a colonel in the Massachusetts military, who died young and provided resources to start a free school (1860, 31–67).

Taking a closer look through the pages of history, Williams College's Christian educational influence can be seen inextricably interwoven with the Second Great Awakening and through its best representatives, who include missions-minded students, influential presidents, and a very spiritually minded professor. Whereas some schools are rightly noted for their academic programs and theoretical contributions, the history of Williams College reveals some extraordinary examples of investment in people and in Christian spiritual matters.

The Haystack Prayer Meeting

Shedd points out that just 5 of 93 graduates were Christians in the first seven years of Williams College (1934, 48). Hewitt records for 100 years later not the number of Christian graduates, but biographies of 127 Williams College missionaries from the classes of 1806 through 1908 (1914, 1–630). In between these reports, which trend in very different directions, something extraordinary happened. From about 1790 to 1830, the Second Great Awakening profoundly impacted the United States (Orr 1975). Yet before spiritual renewal came to Williams College, there was a preceding context of spiritual decline, even in the form of a mock celebration of holy communion (Rudolph 1962, 38).

However, Richards chronicles that in the class of 1804, three young men "brought with them the fervor of the revivals" and that "their devotion was not without its reward in the revival of 1805 and 1806 in the college" (1906, 15). In August 1806, a thunderstorm drove a group of five students (Samuel J. Mills, James Richards, Francis L. Robbins, Harvey Loomis, and Byram Green) to move their prayer efforts into a nearby haystack (16). Out of that "Haystack prayer meeting," a related string of efforts marked the beginning of the modern missionary movement. Howard unfolds these subsequent events as fruit of their prayers: the 1808 formation of the Society of Brethren, the 1810 institution of The American Board of Commissioners for Foreign Missions, and the 1816 establishment of the American Bible Society (1979, 76–78).

Samuel J. Mills and Other Missions-Minded Graduates

Samuel J. Mills participated in all of these breakthrough events, from the Haystack prayer meeting through formation of the American Bible Society. Spring recounted that even before reaching Williams College, Mills had benefited from the impact of the Second Great Awakening through the church where his father, Samuel John Mills, served as a Congregational minister, and from the influence of a mother who said, "I have consecrated this child to the service of God as a Missionary" (1829, 1–12). In his relatively short life, Mills primarily served as a mobilizer of people and resources for the work of Christian mission. For instance, he encouraged the sending out to Calcutta, India, of the first Protestant missionaries of The American Board of Commissioners for Foreign Missions. These contemporaries were Adoniram Judson from Brown, Samuel Newall from Harvard, Samuel Nott from Union College, and fellow Williams College alumni Gordon Hall and Luther Rice (Williams College Archives 2012b).

President Edward Dorr Griffin, President Mark Hopkins, and Professor Albert Hopkins

A related trio of two presidents and a professor together bridge the Second Great Awakening generation to the academic prestige known by the school today. Earlier in his career, Edward Dorr Griffin served in the midst of revival in New Salem, Massachusetts, New Hartford, Connecticut, and Newark, New Jersey before coming to Williams College in 1821 (Kling, 1993; Orr, 1975; Nash, 1842). Nash presents the positive and the negative that Dr. Edward Dorr Griffin quickly faced, "The revival saved the college. There were but two professors. One of them appeared to be sinking into the grave with the consumption, the other had made up his mind to leave . . ." (1842: 42). In the face of losing those two,

Griffin more than matched the need by the hiring of two brothers, Mark and Albert Hopkins (Williams College Archives, 2012a).

Mark Hopkins served first as a professor and then as Griffin's successor as president for the following 36 years. He came to embody not only Williams College but small American college education itself, to such a degree that in 1871 President James A. Garfield remarked at a New York gathering of Williams College alumni, "The ideal college is Mark Hopkins on one end of a log and a student on the other" (quoted in Rudolph 1957, vii). In 1940, the U.S. Postal Service affirmed Mark Hopkins's standing by choosing him as the face of the small liberal arts college in a stamp series that also honored Harvard's Charles William Eliot, Booker T. Washington, and Horace Mann (Rudolph 1957, vii).

From personal correspondence of their day, historian Frederick Rudolph reports that Albert Hopkins, though a professor of philosophy and astronomy, was highly commended by his brother Mark in 1851 for his spiritual influence, "that almost everything that had been done in the way of religion at Williams in recent years had been the work of Albert" (1957, 90), a reference that certainly would include the at least eight campus revivals that occurred throughout the years of the combined Hopkinses' influence on the campus (1957, 118). As to Albert's lasting impact, Sewall excerpts these words from the funeral sermon given by then Williams College president Dr. Chadbourne: "How many devoted missionaries have gone out quickened by his Christian life, and rendered more efficient in their work through his instruction, his precepts and example!" (1870, 24). While Williams College's legacy involves some significant episodes in American higher education and in Christian history, a graduate of the class of 1898 and later philosophy professor there from 1905 to 1943 (Williams College Archives 2012c), James Bissett Pratt expressed a general observation about generational levels of spiritual commitment. While not solely addressing one school, Pratt's thinking certainly would involve his Williams College experiences both as a student and as a professor. In a 1923 *Yale Review*, Pratt made this concise statement, in which he admittedly used exaggeration for effect: "Most important of all, they were not interested in the religious things that interested the older generation. Their grandfathers believed the Creed; their fathers a little doubted the Creed; they have never read it" (1923, 594).

In retrospect, Williams College has produced a range of exemplars from whom Christian education can learn. This school has literally trained world-changing graduates, been led by providential college presidents, and benefited from very insightful professors. Williams College offers great examples of the power of prayer, timely leadership, and nonformal education in the midst of a community. The challenge for those who learn from this college's story is simultaneously to build on the best of these lessons and not to lose the Christian faith and vision that have produced its greatest moments.

References and Resources

Durfee, C. 1860. *A History of Williams College.* Boston: A. Williams.

Hewitt, J. H. 1914. *Williams College and Foreign Missions: Biographical Sketches of Williams College Men Who Have Rendered Special Service to the Cause of Foreign Missions.* Boston: Pilgrim Press.

Howard, D. M. 1979. *Student Power in World Missions.* 2nd ed. Downers Grove, IL: InterVarsity Press.

Kling, D. W. 1993. *A Field of Divine Wonders: The New Divinity and Village Revivals in Northwestern Connecticut, 1792–1822.* University Park: The Pennsylvania State University Press.

Nash, A. 1842. *Memoir of Edward Dorr Griffin, President of Williams College.* New York: S.W. Benedict & Co.

Orr, J. E. 1975. *The Eager Feet: Evangelical Awakenings 1790–1830.* Chicago: Moody Press.

Pratt, J. B. 1923. "Religion and the Younger Generation." *Yale Review* 12 (3): 594–613.

Richards, T. C. 1906. *The Haystack Prayer Meeting: A Brief Account of Its Origin and Spirit, Together with a List of Missionaries Who Have Gone Out from Williams College and Williamstown.* Williamstown, MA: The Haystack Centennial.

Rudolph, F. 1957. *Mark Hopkins and the Log: Williams College, 1836–1872.* 2nd ed. New Haven, CT: Yale University Press.

———. 1962. *The American College and University.* New York: A. Knopf.

Sewall, A. C. 1870. *Life of Prof. Albert Hopkins.* New York: Anson D. F. Randolph & Company.

Shedd, C. P. 1934. *Two Centuries of Student Christian Movements.* New York: Association Press.

Spring, G. 1829. *Memoir of Samuel John Mills.* New York: Perkins and Marvin.

Spring, L. W. 1917. *A History of Williams College.* Boston: Houghton Mifflin.

Williams College Archives. 2012a. *America's First Protestant Missionaries.* Accessed 26 October. archives.williams.edu/buildinghistories/missionpark/missionaries.html.

———. 2012b. *Edward Dorr Griffin (1770–1837).* Accessed 2 December. archives.williams.edu/williamshistory/biographies/griffin-edward-dorr.php.

———. 2012c. *James Bissett Pratt (1875–1944).* Accessed 10 November. archives.williams.edu/williamshistory/biographies/pratt-james.php.

—RICHARD J. MCLAUGHLIN

WILSON, DOUGLAS

Douglas Wilson is an American pastor and educator who lives in Moscow, Idaho. He is a conservative Reformed and evangelical theologian and is known for numerous books and articles, as well as his debates with atheist Christopher Hitchens.

Early Background, Education, and Professional/Family Life

Douglas James Wilson was born 18 June 1953. After serving in the U.S. Navy in the submarine service, he completed a BA and an MA in philosophy and a BA in classical studies from the University of Idaho.

Wilson is the pastor of Christ Church in Moscow, Idaho. He is a founding board member of Logos School and a senior fellow of theology at New Saint Andrews College, and he serves as an instructor at Greyfriars Hall, a ministerial training program at Christ Church. He helped to establish the Communion of Reformed Evangelical Churches (CREC).

Douglas and his wife Nancy have been married more than 35 years and have coauthored a number of books together. They have three children and numerous grandchildren.

Significant Contributions to Christian Education

Wilson is widely noted in Christian school and home-school circles as the best-known proponent of the classical model of Christian education. This model is presented in his popular book, *Recovering the Lost Tools of Learning: An Approach to Distinctively Christian Education* (1991). Greatly influenced by an essay by Dorothy Sayers, "Recovering the Lost Tools of Learning" (1947), Wilson sets forth the importance of training children in the tools of learning as opposed to the memorization of facts in various disciplines. This model includes the *trivium*, a Greco-Roman approach that emphasizes grammar, rhetoric, and logic. Each of these stages is tied to developmental characteristics of students in elementary, middle, and high school grades and makes use of unique instructional techniques that respond to these developmental stages. Classical Christian schools also integrate biblical and theological truth into all subjects and grade levels. Students receive wide exposure to the liberal arts, including classical Western languages such as Latin and Greek. The Logos School in Moscow, Idaho, is patterned after this classical model.

Wilson is the publisher of and a contributor to the Reformed cultural and theological journal *Credenda/Agenda*.

Most Notable Publications

Wilson has authored books on marriage and family, including *Future Men, Reforming Marriage, Standing on the Promises: A Handbook of Biblical Childrearing*, and *Fidelity: What It Means to Be a One-Woman Man*. Wilson's books in the area of theology include *"Reformed" Is Not Enough, Mother Kirk: Essays and Forays in Practical Ecclesiology*, and *God Is. How Christianity Explains Everything*.

References and Resources

Wilson, D. 2009. "About the Proprietor." *Blog and Mablog*, 31 December. http://www.dougwils.com/Random-Topics/about-the-proprietor.html.

Wilson, Douglas. 1991. *Recovering the Lost Tools of Learning: An Approach to Distinctively Christian Education*. Wheaton, IL: Crossway Books.

—KENNETH S. COLEY

WIMBERLY, ANNE E. STREATY

Anne E. Streaty Wimberly is a renowned African American researcher, scholar, professor, advocate, and champion of black youth. A leading Christian educator, she has inspired students, colleagues, pastors, church leaders, and countless admirers to pursue education with a "zest to know." Indeed, her passion for learning has undergirded her educational ministry and lifelong vocation.

Early Background and Education

Wimberly was born in Anderson, Indiana, a small, predominantly white community. She attended the black Methodist church, where she received sustained guidance and encouragement from the "whole village." The church customarily called forth the children (at the age of 12) to participate in a laying-on of hands, wherein the congregation named each child's individual gifts. "I was told," she recalls, "my gifts were music and teaching."

Although Wimberly was "called to ministry early," she resisted the call because she did not have female role models in pastoral ministry. Nevertheless, she developed her gifts in music and teaching. She completed a bachelor of science in education with a major in music education from Ohio State University and a master of music from Boston University School of Fine and Applied Arts. At Boston, she also completed doctoral course work and was the first black American to become a doctoral teaching fellow. She completed a graduate certificate in gerontology and a PhD in educational leadership from Georgia State University. In addition, she completed postdoctoral studies at the Institute for Religion and Wholeness, now the Clinebell Institute, in Claremont, California. Over 20 years, Wimberly taught in several schools during her studies. But her call to ministry was undeniable, so she returned to the classroom to pursue a master of theological studies at Garrett-Evangelical Theological Seminary.

Wimberly began teaching at the Interdenominational Theological Center (ITC) in Atlanta in 1991and became professor emerita in 2007. She challenged students to explore two primary questions: "How do we make Christian education central to the life of the church?" and "How can we empower, excite, and tool pastors, Christian education directors, and leaders in the educational ministry of the church?" Today, these questions still guide her teaching, scholarship, and innovative approaches to the black church's educational ministry. While teaching in prestigious institutions, she has also served as organist, choir director, and director of Christian education in the church.

Significant Contributions to Christian Education

With her book *Soul Stories*, Wimberly introduced a new model of African American Christian education that reclaims the African practice of storytelling as a vital resource for Christian education. Her subsequent work also challenges churches to draw upon African American cultural themes while emphasizing the need for social activism, transformation, and liberation.

As the first African American president of the Association of Professors and Researchers in Religious Education and the second African American president of the historic Religious Education Association, Wimberly oversaw the successful merger of these two organizations. She is also a founding member of the Pan African Scholars in Religious Education and the Black Experience Task Force, which gather during the annual meetings. Wimberly has served as a keynote speaker, presenter, and editorial board member for the *Religious Education* journal and is an inspiring role model and mentor to students, colleagues, and friends.

Finally, Wimberly has pioneered the advancement of ministry with black youth. She founded the Youth and Family Convocation in 1994. The success of the convocation inspired the development, in 2002, of the Youth Hope-Builders Academy for black high school youth, of which Wimberly is executive director. In its 10th year, YHBA launched the "Bridges Initiative," which emphasizes communal support, mentoring, community service, leadership development, and instilling a strong sense of Christian identity, vocation, and pride in one's African American heritage. Wimberly's work on behalf of African American youth has refocused the church's attention on issues facing contemporary black youth and shaping effective models of youth ministry. Her work has touched churches throughout the United States, the West Indies, and Africa.

Most Notable Publications

Wimberly's most notable publications are *Soul Stories: African American Christian Education*, *Keep It Real:* *Working with Today's Black Youth*, *Nurturing Faith and Hope: Worship as a Model of Christian Education*, and *The Winds of Promise: Building and Maintaining Strong Clergy Families* (coauthored with Edward Wimberly).

References and Resources

Mulder, John M. n.d. "Building Hope with Real Faith: Anne Streaty Wimberly and African-American Youth Ministry." *Resources for American Christianity*. Accessed 27 March 2013. http://www.resourcingchristianity.org.

Wimberly, Anne S. 2013a. "Short Biographical Summary for Anne E. Streaty Wimberly, PhD." http://www.talbot.edu/ce20/educators/protestant/Anne_streaty_Wimberley/

———. 2013b. Telephone interview with Yolanda Y. Smith, 30 March.

—Yolanda Yvette Smith

WISDOM

Wisdom represents a broad idea, extolled in the Bible, and perhaps best summarized as *well-applied knowledge*. It is an attribute of God, and it originates with Him. As people are made in the image of God, human wisdom is a reflection of God's wisdom; therefore it begins with a healthy fear of God (Prov. 1:7, 9:10; Ps. 111:10). Human wisdom covers a range of knowledge applications, such as practical skills, metaphysics, theology, justice, faith, and political savvy. The Bible recognizes that there is wisdom in the world that does not point to God—such wisdom works against Christian development and spirituality (1 Cor. 1:18–25). Since the need for wisdom is at the heart of human beings, at the heart of God's work in Christ, and at the heart of biblical interpretation, it must also be at the heart of Christian education.[29]

Since the beginning of recorded history, wisdom has played a significant role in education. In the ancient Near East, wisdom was perhaps the largest component of basic education, occupying the greatest percentage of the curriculum.[30] In Greek society, it was much beloved (philosopher = lover of wisdom); to Socrates, it was what made virtues virtuous.[31] In Israelite society, it served to instruct moral lives.[32] This is best evidenced in that

---

29. Edward Farley, "Can Church Education Be Theological Education?" in *Theological Perspectives on Christian Formation: A Reader on Theology and Christian Education*, ed. Jeff Astley, Leslie J. Francis, and Colin Crowder (Grand Rapids, MI: Eerdmans, 1996), 33.

30. Paul-Alain Beaulieu, "The Social and Intellectual Setting of Babylonian Wisdom Literature," in *Wisdom Literature in Mesopotamia and Israel*, ed. Richard J. Clifford, SBL Symposium Series 36 (Atlanta, GA: Society of Biblical Literature, 2007), 3–4.

31. Plato, *Phaedrus* 69b1–3.

32. Joseph Blenkinsopp, *Wisdom and Law in the Old Testament: The Ordering of Life in Israel and Early Judaism*, rev ed., Oxford Bible Series (Oxford: Oxford University Press, 1995), 6.

part of Christian scripture that is devoted to wisdom—a whole section is labeled as wisdom literature (Prov. 1:2; see Prov., Job, Eccles., James). The book of Proverbs identifies its purpose as cultivating wisdom (Prov. 1:24). As a result of wisdom's importance, it often took on an institutionalized role in the ancient world (Gen. 41:8; 1 Kings 4:30; Jer. 18:18; Matt. 23:34).[33] During the Second Temple period, many texts such as the Wisdom of Solomon and Sirach contain a strong bent toward educating people in wisdom.

Wisdom has always held an integral position in the development of Christian education. As the basis of human education, wisdom remained extremely popular among the early church fathers—Augustine believed wisdom and eloquence were at the center of human development.[34] The same was very much true in the medieval era, as Thomas Aquinas argued that wisdom is the greatest science available to humanity (cf. Prov. 9:3).[35] Even up until the early modern period, wisdom was the primary means of study.[36] The desire to gain wisdom was at the heart of the first attempts at curriculum development in the earliest Western European universities.[37] However, in the 17th century, the concept of theology in Christian education began to move away from *well-applied knowledge* to *doctrinal system*.[38] By the modern era, wisdom was pushed to a minor role in Western Christian education; only recent work in the theory of Christian education and related areas has highlighted the need to return to the centrality of wisdom.[39] The exception to this is the Western homeschooling movement, which has adopted wisdom as one of its foundational planks.

References and Resources

Astley, Jeff, Leslie J. Francis, and Colin Crowder, eds. 1996. *Theological Perspectives on Christian Formation: A Reader on Theology and Christian Education*. Grand Rapids, MI: Eerdmans.

Blenkinsopp, Joseph. 1995. *Wisdom and Law in the Old Testament: The Ordering of Life in Israel and Early Judaism*. Rev ed. Oxford Bible Series. Oxford: Oxford University Press.

---

33. Ibid., 9.

34. Augustine, *On Christian Doctrine*.

35. Thomas Aquinas, *Summa Theologiæ*, 1, Q1.

36. Juan Luis Vives, *The Education of a Christian Woman: A Sixteenth-Century Manual*, ed. and trans. Charles Fantazzi, The Other Voice in Early Modern Europe (Chicago: University of Chicago Press, 2000), 71.

37. Christopher Dean Flesoras, "The Historical Place and Character of Mentoring in Higher Education: A Study of Christian Formation in the Byzantine East" (PhD diss., University of California, Davis, 2009), 2.

38. Edward Farley, "Can Church Education Be Theological Education?" in *Theological Perspectives on Christian Formation*, ed. Astley, Francis, and Crowder, 39; and cf. Francis Schüssler Fiorenza, "Thinking Theologically about Theological Education," in *Theological Perspectives on Christian Formation*, ed. Astley, Francis, and Crowder, 320.

39. Cf. David F. Ford, *Christian Wisdom: Desiring God and Learning in Love*, Cambridge Studies in Christian Doctrine no. 16 (Cambridge, UK: Cambridge University Press, 2007), 16.

Clifford, Richard J., ed. 2007. *Wisdom Literature in Mesopotamia and Israel*. SBL Symposium Series no. 36. Atlanta, GA: Society of Biblical Literature.

Flesoras, Christopher Dean. 2009. "The Historical Place and Character of Mentoring in Higher Education: A Study of Christian Formation in the Byzantine East." PhD diss., University of California, Davis.

Ford, David F. 2007. *Christian Wisdom: Desiring God and Learning in Love*. Cambridge Studies in Christian Doctrine no. 16. Cambridge, UK: Cambridge University Press.

Littlejohn, Robert, and Charles T. Evans. 2006. *Wisdom and Eloquence: A Christian Paradigm for Classical Learning*. Wheaton, IL: Crossway.

Mulligan, David. 1994. *Far Above Rubies: Wisdom in the Christian Community*. Marshfield, VT: Messenger.

—Douglas Estes

WISDOM LITERATURE

Wisdom literature (*see also* Proverbs) of the Hebrew Bible includes the books of Proverbs, Job, Ecclesiastes, and various Psalms. The deuterocanonical (apocryphal) works, Wisdom of Solomon and Sirach (or the Wisdom of Jesus ben Sirach), are also considered wisdom literature.

In Old Testament society, the wise man was one of the three most important voices of instruction. The priest (*kohen*) mainly taught and interpreted the ceremonial law; the prophet (*nabi*) mainly declared God's moral, ethical, and spiritual teachings. But the *hakham*, "sage" or "wise man" set forth words of *hokhmah* "wisdom," "skillful advice," or "good sense" to the learner. In addition to his role in providing practical counsel on personal problems and self-improvement, the sage also reflected upon the larger, more perplexing, and confusing issues of human existence (see Jer. 18:18).

The wise mainly looked at life through the lens of empirical reasoning, personal experience, and common sense. As such, they sometimes provided a "this-worldly" and more "secular" challenge to the seemingly more theologically rooted teachings of the priests and prophets. Wisdom literature reminds the reader that the Bible does not contain a "monochromatic" theology, but is made up of a complexity of colorful theological strands—including wisdom—each strand complementing and enhancing the other within the full fabric of revelation.

Several main features characterize wisdom literature. First, wisdom is international; it belongs to the world and thus is far more "universal" in its applicability. Wisdom that is useful and workable in one culture is apt to be sought after, borrowed, and adopted by another. For example, Proverbs 22:17–24:22 bears a striking resemblance to the Egyptian work, Wisdom of Amenemope. Second, wisdom literature concerns the skill and success of the individual person; it is not directed to the corporate community or to the nation as is often the focus of prophetic literature. A third distinctive is its general avoidance of traditional theological themes (e.g., election, covenant, faith, day of the LORD) or historical references, which are usually found in other parts of scripture. A fourth characteristic is the importance this literature gives to an ancient assumption that an individual's personal behavior would receive retribution or reward in this life. Thus, the wealthy were believed to be righteous or pious, and the destitute were thought to be unrighteous or ungodly. Psalm 1 is an example of a "wisdom" Psalm that reflects the teaching that the way of the righteous will prosper and the way of wicked will perish—in this life.

Further, biblical wisdom is associated with the "fear of God" (see Prov. 1:7; Job 1:1; Eccles. 12:13). One was to revere God and stand in awe of Him by submitting to His will and teachings in every aspect of life. Prudence and discernment were the handmaidens of morality and ethics. Wise actions were thought to lead to a mastering of life; they were vital to the well-being of society and also were essential to validate one's place among the wise.

The book of Job is an example of speculative or reflective wisdom; it questions the accepted teaching about individual retribution, namely that those who have suffered the most are those who have sinned the most. The book of Job deals with theodicy, the problem of the justice and goodness of God in light of the great suffering of a righteous man. Job, a man of impeccable moral character who experienced great tragedy and loss, challenges the standard orthodox position of his day. Indeed, sometimes the world's greatest sufferers are among the world's greatest saints.

In the end, the contemplative wisdom of the book of Job does not solve the mystery of why the righteous suffer. The denouement of the story occurs when God speaks out of a whirlwind, taking Job on a "cosmic mystery tour." God reveals His infinite wisdom and power in the creation of the universe and throughout the world of nature, not in answering the why of Job's suffering. The wisdom of the story seems to be that in the end, one must value relationship over reason.

In the book of Ecclesiastes, Qoheleth, the "Teacher," considers the puzzling question of the meaning of existence. His is a quest to find the significance, happiness, and highest good in life. By using a sort of dramatis personae, the author seems to look at life through the eyes of Solomon. In his search, he seeks to find ultimate meaning in various areas of life. He tries wealth, wisdom, fame, pleasure, work, and the beauty of nature.

The Teacher's conclusion is the same—namely, everything is *hebel,* which literally means mist, breath, vapor, that which appears transitory, fleeting, and hence futile or meaningless. Man is finite and his understanding limited. Life is short and often vexing, irrational, and sometimes absurd. Amid the mysteries, contradictions, and paradoxes of life, the Teacher advises his readers that "under the sun" they must seize the moment and take from life what fleeting enjoyments they can find. There is a time or season for everything, but in the end, there is no coherent pattern detectable in existence. Thus the Teacher's quest is left unresolved, for human wisdom has its limits.

Man cannot control God's mysterious ways and cannot impose order on human life. Humans must be faithful in keeping commandments and in fearing God, for they are accountable for their actions (12:13, 14). In life, humans may "get no (permanent) satisfaction" but rather may get some frustration that can lead to despair. So the wisest action is for humans not to resort to being jaundiced, cynical, or pessimistic by jumping to rash conclusions. Accordingly, "God is in heaven and you are on earth so let your words be few" (5:2). People must ultimately value relationship over rationality. In the larger canonical context of scripture, this means individuals must know their limitations and "keep the faith" by believing God is *shalom,* the great "Integrator" of life (2:24, 25).

References and Resources

Crenshaw, James L., ed. 1976. *Studies in Ancient Israelite Wisdom.* New York: Ktav Publishing House.

Day, John, Robert P. Gordon, and H. G. M. Williamson, eds. 1995. *Wisdom in Ancient Israel.* Cambridge, UK: Cambridge University Press.

Murphy, Roland E. 1996. *The Tree of Life: An Exploration of Biblical Wisdom Literature.* Anchor Bible Reference Library. 2nd ed. Grand Rapids, MI: Eerdmans. (1st ed. New York: Doubleday, 1990.)

Perdue, Leo G. 1994. *Wisdom and Creation: The Theology of Wisdom Literature.* Nashville, TN: Abingdon Press.

—MARVIN R. WILSON

WITNESS AS CHRISTIAN PRACTICE

The word "witness" plays an important role in both the Hebrew Old Testament and the Christian New Testament. The Hebrew word for witness is *mô'ēd,* while the Greek word is *marturía.* Whether in Hebrew or in Greek, the word carries a legal connotation with it regardless of contextual use by biblical authors (Trites 1977). Many may be surprised to learn that the phrase "you are my witnesses" did not originate with Jesus and the disciples in the New Testament. That important New Testament phrase originates in a dramatic courtroom scene in Isaiah

43 and 44, in which Yahweh issues a summons for the nations of the world to present witnesses to testify to the power and superiority of their gods. None appears in the dock. However, God declares to Israel "you are my witnesses" and thus God designates Israel to fulfill this role for God to the nations.

New Testament writers like Luke and Paul link Israel's mission to the nations with the church's mission (Luke 24:44–49; Acts 13:46–47, 15:14–18, 26:17–18). Both Luke (24:44–49) and Matthew (28:16–20), in their respective versions of the Great Commission, link the church's mission to Israel's mission to the nations by the use of the pregnant phrase *panta ta ethné* ("all the nations"). One finds the phrase in the covenant texts of Genesis (18:18, 22:38, 26:4) as well as Isaiah (2:2b, 25:6–7, 52:10, 56:7, 61:11, 66:18, 20). Given this connection, one should not be surprised to find Luke using the term "witnesses" to describe the followers of Jesus (Luke 24:48; Acts 1:8, 2:32, 5:32, 10:39). As Christ's witnesses, his disciples are to "make disciples of all the nations, baptizing them . . . teaching them to observe all that I commanded you" (Matt. 28:19–20).

The biblical concept of witness involves both a proclamation to those outside the faith community (Israel, Church) and instruction of the faithful. Guder refers to the latter as "the inward evangelization of the church" in which believers receive "equipping for our calling to be Christ's witnesses in the world" (1985, 151). Brueggemann refers to this "inward evangelization" as "saturation witness" (1993, 103) when faithful parents in the Old Testament repeat, reiterate, and recite to their children who God is and what God has done for Israel (Exod. 12:29, 13:8, 14; Deut. 6:21; Josh. 4:7, 21). Christian education in the local church organizes and arranges the opportunities and experiences of witness that involve both evangelism and edification. The gift of mission is the task of witness carried out through the empowerment of the Holy Spirit (Luke 24:49; Acts 1:8) under the command of Jesus (Matt. 28:16–20). The mission of Christian education is the mission of the church centering on teaching God's people how to be His faithful witnesses in the world.

References and Resources

Brueggemann, Walter. 1993. *Biblical Perspectives on Evangelism*. Nashville, TN: Abingdon Press.

Coenen, L. 1971. "Witness." In *Dictionary of New Testament Theology*. 3 vols. Grand Rapids, MI: Zondervan.

Guder, D. 1985. *Be My Witnesses*. Grand Rapids, MI: Eerdmans.

Keck, L. 1964. *Mandate to Witness*. Valley Forge, PA: Judson Press.

Kraus, C. 1979. *The Authentic Witness*. Grand Rapids, MI: Eerdmans.

Newbigin, J. 1978. "Church as Witness: A Meditation." *Reformed World* 35: 5–9.

Schmalenberger, J. 1993. *Called to Witness*. Lima, OH: C.S.S. Publishing.

Trites, A. 1977. *The New Testament Concept of Witness*. London: Cambridge University Press.

—STEPHEN D. LOWE

WITTGENSTEIN, LUDWIG

Ludwig Wittgenstein was born in Vienna in 1928, the youngest of eight children, and died in Cambridge, England, on 29 April 1951. Although originally a student of engineering, which he attended the University of Manchester to study, he increasingly became interested in the philosophical foundations of mathematics, and this led him to study with Bertrand Russell at Cambridge. Upon the outbreak of World War I, he returned to Austria and volunteered for military service. After the war, he worked in various jobs: schoolteacher, gardener, and house designer; at one stage he considered becoming a monk. In 1929 he returned to Cambridge, where he spent much of the remainder of his life. From 1939 to 1947, he was professor of philosophy at the University of Cambridge. He is regarded by many as the most influential philosopher of the 20th century.

Wittgenstein is associated with two contrasting philosophical movements, logical positivism and linguistic analysis. Both movements have a common focus on language and linguistic usage, but they are different in their orientation and conclusions. His early philosophy is embodied in a short book (some 80 pages), the *Tractatus Logico-Philosophicus* (1921, in German; 1922, English version). Its central idea is what is called "a picture theory of meaning," namely that there is a one-to-one correspondence between the objects and relationships of the world and the elements of language; basically, words mirror the state of affairs in the world ("the facts"). According to Wittgenstein's understanding at this point, propositions can state only what is in the world; hence silence is enjoined about ethics and that which is "transcendental." Wittgenstein's posthumously published *Philosophical Investigations* (1958) indicated the extent to which he believed his earlier understanding of language, sense, and meaning was mistaken. He presented a series of arguments to show that his earlier view misunderstood the nature of linguistic meaning and that language communicated sense and meaning in ways not appreciated and even rejected by his earlier philosophy. His later philosophy is often characterized by the slogan "meaning is use," which conveys the idea that words work in different ways in different contexts, and it is presumptuous to think that one theory can account for (and be used to determine) legitimate uses of language. Language occurs within "forms of life," and the different uses of language can be regarded as different "language games." This position constitutes a rejection of philosophical theorizing about language and meaning and instead invites the philosopher "to look and see" how language is used successfully to communicate in different human contexts.

The relevance of Wittgenstein's contrasting positions to religion has been variously assessed. Three different historically successive periods of influence can be identified. From the late 1920s until the late 1950s and early 1960s, when he was under the influence of logical positivism, many interpreted the *Tractatus* as lending support to the denial of meaning to religion, ethics, and metaphysics. The realm of cognitive meaning was tied to what can be described and evaluated in terms of sense experience; arguably, this was not the view of Wittgenstein. From the 1960s until the 1990s, a number of influential philosophers and theologians appealed to the later philosophy of Wittgenstein to contend that "a religious form of life" does not require philosophical or theoretical support, rather the fact that people engage in religion is sufficient of itself to justify religion for the people concerned. This apologetic strategy was welcomed and employed by some, such as D. Z. Phillips, and criticized by others, most notably the atheist philosopher Kai Nielsen. The last few decades have seen Wittgenstein's later philosophy being used constructively in a more piecemeal fashion to illuminate and clarify aspects of the religious life and theology, for example, the nature of the soul and the relationship of faith to reason.

The later thought of Wittgenstein is significant for Christian educators at a number of points. First, it draws attention to the way in which religious language is part of a broader "form of life" that involves prayer, worship, ritual, moral obedience, and religious commitment: religion is essentially practical. Second, it underlines the role of doctrines and beliefs in facilitating experience and the way in which religious rituals and practices give expression to beliefs. The meaning of religion is given in the believer's use of religious language, and use in turn (following Wittgenstein) depends on training (in German *Abrichtung*). Consequently, a focus on religious language and religious concepts facilitates an understanding of religion and creates the conditions for individuals to experience religion for themselves.

References and Resources

Wittgenstein, Ludwig. 1922. *Tractatus Logico-Philosophicus.* London: Routledge and Kegan Paul.

———. 1958. *Philosophical Investigation.* Oxford: Basil Blackwell.

—L. Philip Barnes

WOLTERSTORFF, NICHOLAS

Nicholas Wolterstorff (b. 1932) is an American philosopher who has written influentially on a broad range of subjects, including Christian education. He is Noah Porter Professor of Philosophical Theology Emeritus, Yale University, having previously taught for 30 years at Calvin College, where he studied as an undergraduate before earning his MA and PhD at Harvard. Raised in the Reformed tradition as the son of Dutch migrants in rural Minnesota, he acknowledges a lifelong debt to this upbringing, and particularly its Kuyperian accents. He has been an endowed lecturer on several occasions, including presenting the Gifford Lectures in 1995.

Whereas the 20th-century philosophical context has not been hospitable to overtly religious discourse beyond the confines of philosophy of religion, Wolterstorff's achievement in this respect is noteworthy. As a founder in 1978 of the Society of Christian Philosophers, now the largest affiliate of the American Philosophical Association, and past president of the latter's Central Division, he has done much to establish the legitimacy of scholarship reflecting faith-based and other particularist perspectives. Indeed, as we shall see, he goes so far as to claim that such particularity is inevitable in any academic work.

Wolterstorff describes Abraham Kuyper as "in many ways the spiritual eminence behind [Calvin] college" (1993, 6). One of the most important things he learned from Kuyper was that the Western ideal of generic theorizing, according to which one was to leave one's particularities at the door when entering on intellectual pursuits, was fundamentally flawed. These particularities include nationality, class, gender, political conviction, but above all, religion. Religion is "a fundamental determinant of [a] person's hermeneutic of reality"; Wolterstorff affirms this statement: "I believed it when I first learned of it in my college days; I believe it still" (6). This acknowledgment of an ineluctable pluralism is a postmodern, but also a premodern, insight. With Alvin Plantinga and William Alston, Wolterstorff initiated Reformed epistemology, which repudiates the foundationalist perspective that has dominated the modern Western theory of knowledge.

His influential but surprisingly brief book, *Reason within the Bounds of Religion* ([1976] 1984), provides a "theory of theorizing" that is respectful of the role of *authentic commitment* in theoretical investigation. It is thus an argument for construing faithful Christian scholarship—and indeed, all scholarship in a religiously plural world—as a process of weighing theoretical projects in the context of the whole complex of a person's beliefs. Of special importance are *data-background beliefs* and *control beliefs.* The former will include "an enormously complicated web of theory" (67) that is taken for granted in any instance of determining what will count as legitimate data. The latter are more significant, however, for Wolterstorff's project in this book, and comprise "certain beliefs as to what constitutes an acceptable *sort* of theory on the matter under consideration. . . . They include beliefs about the requisite logical or aesthetic structure of a theory, beliefs about the entities to whose existence a theory may correctly commit us, and the like." These beliefs will lead to the *rejection* of theories that are inconsistent or do not comport well with them; they will also guide the *devising* of theories. Wolterstorff's contention is that "the religious beliefs of the Christian scholar ought to function as *control* beliefs within his devising and weighing of theories" (67–71).

Although Wolterstorff has published only a few books directly on the topic of education, he has been a frequent contributor to conferences for Christian educators in North America and elsewhere. Many of these presentations, and other published articles, have been collected in two volumes, one on Christian teaching and learning (2002) and the other addressing issues in Christian higher education (2004). Virtually all of his writings, however, address issues bearing on the relation between faith and scholarship, insofar as they constitute consciously Christian reflection on a variety of topics (e.g., art, ethics, politics, and more esoteric philosophical concerns) that not only illuminates a particular theme in a way that is directly useful to the educator but also exemplifies an approach that may serve as a model for research and teaching in other areas.

Wolterstorff has engaged directly in educational planning, most notably as chair of the Curriculum Committee at Calvin College in the 1960s. The report of this committee set the framework for education at Calvin for more than a generation, but it is as a starting point from which he steadily departed that it is more interesting in outlining the contours of Wolterstorff's developing philosophy of education. Whereas that early document enshrined the liberal arts model that characterizes American higher education as the legitimate approach for explicitly *Christian* education, such that the pursuit of knowledge through the academic disciplines was to be about nothing but that knowledge itself, Wolterstorff came to believe that learning was to be about something quite different, namely, the world in which knowledge was situated. Specifically, it had to be about *shalom*, which itself must be grounded in justice. The second edition of *Reason within the Bounds of Religion* is noteworthy in this respect; published in 1984, it includes several additional chapters that reflect this significant shift, away from "pure theory" (theorizing for its own—and the scholar's—sake) to "praxis-oriented theory" in service of shalom (without

thereby denying that theory can be of intrinsic value). He concludes the book with these words:

> The person who turns one of his ears to the prophetic unmasking of the gospel and the other to the cries of those who suffer deprivation and oppression is not likely to suffer from the illusion that he is engaged in pure theory when in fact he is working to shore up his own position of privilege. ([1976] 1984, 146)

Though the connection is not explicit, the argument in *Educating for Responsible Action* (1980) that Christian education should be concerned with "tendency learning"—the formation of dispositions—is continuous with what later became a dominant theme, namely, that schooling had to be structured so that students learned not only to orient themselves toward justice and *shalom* but needed to learn to act in pursuit of these goals. Wolterstorff credits his deepening grasp of this to face-to-face encounters with Palestinians and Black South Africans—many of them Christian—and the agonies they experienced as a result of oppressive regimes. He thus comes to see empathy as a primary motivator for action. And his courageous meditations on the loss of his relatively young son in a climbing accident are powerful evidence of the significance of suffering as a shaper of human sensibilities (1987a).

Seeing the faces and hearing the voices of oppressed people is, Wolterstorff says, what changed him and led him to reflect deeply on justice; eventually, he came to see that "the Bible is a book about justice." But this is not the conception of justice taken for granted by many in Western societies, that "of no one invading one's right to determine one's life as one will." No, it is "a strange and haunting form of justice! . . . [T]he justice of the widow, the orphan and the alien. A society is just when all the little ones, all the defenseless ones, all the unprotected ones have been brought back into community, to enjoy a fair share in the community's goods, and a standing and voice in the affairs of the community" (1993, 8). Of his son's death, he writes:

> My whole tradition had taught me to love the world, to love the world as a gift, to love God through and in the world—wife, children, art, plants, learning. It had set me up for suffering. But it didn't tell me this: it didn't tell me that the invitation to love is the invitation to suffering. It let me find that out for myself, when it happened. Possibly it's best that way. (1987a)

Wolterstorff's 1981 Kuyper Lectures were published as *Until Justice and Peace Embrace* (1983). The title echoes Psalm 85:10, but characteristically corrects the common English translation of *sedeq* as "righteousness"; it may be regarded as Wolterstorff's hope for human life and Christian education, as long as the way to its attainment is seen to be a matter of empathetically taking up one's cross in solidarity with those who are suffering.

References and Resources

Wolterstorff, Nicholas. (1976) 1984. *Reason within the Bounds of Religion*. Grand Rapids, MI: Wm. B. Eerdmans.

———. 1980. *Educating for Responsible Action*. Grand Rapids, MI: CSI Publications/Eerdmans.

———. 1983. *Until Justice and Peace Embrace: The Kuyper Lectures for 1981 Delivered at the Free University of Amsterdam*. Grand Rapids, MI: Eerdmans.

———. 1987a. *Lament for a Son*. Grand Rapids, MI: Eerdmans.

———. 1987b. *Teaching for Justice*. St. Paul, MN/Grand Rapids, MI: Christian University Press.

———. 1993. "The Grace That Shaped My Life." In *Philosophers Who Believe: The Spiritual Journey of Eleven Leading Thinkers*, edited by Kelly James Clark. Downers Grove, IL: InterVarsity Press. http://www.calvin.edu/125th/wolterst/w_bio.pdf.

———. 2002. *Educating for Life: Reflections on Christian Teaching and Learning*. Edited by Gloria Goris Stronks and Clarence Joldersma. Grand Rapids, MI: Baker Academic.

———. 2004. *Educating for Shalom: Essays on Christian Higher Education*. Edited by Clarence Joldersma and Gloria Goris Stronks. Grand Rapids, MI: Eerdmans.

———. 2008. *Justice: Rights and Wrongs*. Princeton, NJ: Princeton University Press.

———. 2011. *Justice in Love*. Grand Rapids, MI/Cambridge, UK: Eerdmans.

—Doug Blomberg

WOMEN AND EARLY CHURCH CHRISTIAN EDUCATION

Introduction

The roles and activities of women in early Christianity are a complex issue, and scholars are divided on how women were involved in teaching in the Greco-Roman world. Some social historians depict the patriarchal society with the authority of the father over the household. Others find that Christianity evoked new attitudes about gender roles and argue that Jesus broke through cultural barriers in His treatment of women. Feminist scholarship has illuminated constructions of gender in the ancient world (Kraemer 2008). On the one hand, active participation of women in early Christian communities was less than equal due to the social realities of the time, but on the other hand, as biblical scholar Elisabeth Schüssler Fiorenza has claimed, women were clearly counted among those who were taught by and traveled with Jesus as disciples and had prominent roles as missionaries, teachers,

and leaders in the early Christian movement (1983, 186). She makes the point that sources of information about women in the early church were written and interpreted in patriarchal cultures, and we should not assume that the church was for men only, or that women could not serve as apostles, prophets, or teachers (MacHaffie 1986, 23). The fact that Jesus taught women is significant, considering that in Judaism women were not permitted to study scripture with a rabbi. In Luke 10:38–42, Mary sits at the feet of Jesus like a male student traditionally sat before a master (15). Mark and Matthew tell of a woman who taught Jesus that knowledge of God is not limited to particular groups and persons, but belongs to any person of faith (King 1998). Jewish feminist scholars, however, suggest that Christianity did not create the first "discipleship of equals," noting leadership among women in synagogues. Christianity may have coincided with a movement toward greater social freedom for women (Osiek and MacDonald 2006, 2). Education was an ideal in the rise of Hellenism.

House-Churches

Mothers of course instructed and had special influence over their children. There is evidence that sisters in faith in the house-churches also helped educate children in the Christian faith. Early Christian texts stress the communal responsibility for educating children (Osiek and Mac-Donald 2006, 70). It has been the practice to distinguish between the private and public domains and claim that women's influence was limited to the private and domestic, while the public domains of temple, market, and law courts belonged to men. This polarity, however, is treated with suspicion by some feminists. The house-church has been thought to fall into the category of the private domain, so therefore women could be leaders and teachers within them. Yet Osiek and MacDonald argue that the house-churches went beyond immediate family, and that women often owned the houses in which Christians met and participated in all activities of the house-church, including worship, providing hospitality, and education (2006, 4–6). It seems that house-churches had elements of both the private and public spheres. Women like Mary, mother of John Mark (Acts 12:12); Lydia (Acts 16: 14, 40); and Nympha (Col. 4:15) housed Christian assemblies in their homes.

Religious instruction probably occurred in gender-specific groups. Older women are encouraged to form the character of younger women (Titus 2:3–8). Older women are exhorted to be well-behaved and not excessive drinkers so that they may be *kalodidaskaloi*, or good teachers. The pastoral Epistles offer evidence of women's involvement in the socialization of the young. Timothy's faith was attributed to his grandmother Lois and his mother Eunice. Ironically, in other places in the pastoral Epistles, women are strictly prohibited from teaching (1 Tim. 2:12). These protests against the leadership of women do not describe the status of women in all churches, but may have been an attempt to impose the patriarchal standards of the culture on the Christian communities so as not to draw the attention or hostility of society (MacHaffie 1986, 26). By the fourth century, the church's ministry had become more institutionalized and hierarchical, with distinct offices that took over sacramental and teaching functions, with more power invested in the bishops and presbyters. The vehemence with which women's teaching was denounced suggests that it was going on in some places (28).

Female Deacons, Widows, Patrons

Early Christians, both male and female, were regarded as having received certain gifts from the Holy Spirit to be used in service to the community. Paul refers to women as coworkers in the evangelization of the Hellenistic world, commending Mary, Tryhana, Tryphosa, and Persis for their labors for the Lord. He mentions the missionary work of Prisca and others who worked alongside him (MacHaffie 1986, 24–25).

An important part of the wisdom passed from women to girls and other women in early Christianity would have been instruction and preparation for baptism. This role became institutionalized by the third century in the East in the office of female deacons. The fourth century *Apostolic Constitutions* described female deacons preparing women and assisting with the rite (Osiek and MacDonald 2006, 92). Phoebe was a prominent woman in the early church called both a *diakonos* (agent or go-between) and a *prostasis* (patron). While Phoebe likely acted as an emissary on behalf of her community, the precise nature of her leadership role in the church at Kenchreae is difficult to determine. A few centuries later, women deacons performed a variety of services, including the teaching of doctrine, visiting the sick, and providing for the poor (Campbell 2009, 50). Widows were sometimes listed with other offices of the church, and while they may not have been directly responsible for teaching, held an honored place and were given the duty of intercessory prayer. A little-known woman named Grapte in the second century relayed a teaching from Hermas to widows and their children. It is believed that her role was to gather widows and orphans not part of other households for instruction. A young aristocratic woman named Thecla was said to be commissioned by Paul to "go forth and teach the word of God." She renounced marriage and became a missionary, preacher, and teacher (Kraemer 2008).

Ignatius mentions Tavia and Alke, widows who were patrons, whose homes became important centers of education (Osiek and MacDonald 2006, 13). Early Christian female writers included Perpetua and Felicitas and Elgeria. Elgeria described a pilgrimage she took, revealing intellectual conversations she had with bishops. She also wrote in detail about the catechumenate in fourth-century Jerusalem.

Women's prominence as teachers and educators did not go unchallenged. Tertullian wrote about women being heretical because they were teaching and baptizing. Yet even by the late third century, women were commonly depicted in frescoes or sarcophagi holding scrolls or books (Tkacz 2008, 23–24). Augustine and Chrysostom provide details about their mothers' influence on their faith. In the early fifth century, St. Jerome wrote that parents should educate their daughters as well as their sons. As the monastic movement and schools developed, a group of women in Rome sought the teaching of St. Jerome and became the first women to adopt the monastic life. He corresponded with Marcella, whom he recognized as a teacher (*magistra*), not only of him, but of other clergy, and corresponded with St. Paula, commenting on her exegetical skills (20–22). Ute Eisen (2000) examined papyrus letters from Alexandria and found evidence of women teachers, noting the preserved sayings of the Desert Mothers Theodora and Synkletica.

In summary, while there were definite prohibitions against women's teaching and there is debate about how much women were allowed to teach, evidence demonstrates that women were models, mentors, and educators in the home and beyond in the early church.

References and Resources

Aquilina, M., and C. Bailey. 2012. *Mothers of the Church: The Witness of Early Christian Women.* Huntington, IN: Our Sunday Visitor.

Campbell, J. C. 2009. *Phoebe: Patron and Emissary.* Collegeville, MN: The Liturgical Press.

Clark, E. 1983. *Women in the Early Church.* Wilmington, DE: Michael Glazier, Inc.

Eisen, U. 2000. *Women Officeholders in Early Christianity.* Collegeville, MN: The Liturgical Press.

Gryson, R. 1976. *The Ministry of Women in the Early Church.* Translated by Jean Laporte and Mary Louise Hall. Collegeville, MN: The Liturgical Press.

King, K. 1998. *Women in Ancient Christianity: The New Discoveries.* http://www.pbs.org/wgbh/pages/frontline/shows/religion/first/women.html.

Kraemer, R. 2008. "Women and Gender." In *The Oxford Handbook of Christian Studies*, edited by Susan Ashbrook Harvey and David G Hunter, 465–492. New York: Oxford University Press.

MacHaffie, B. 1986. *Her Story: Women in Christian Tradition.* Philadelphia: Fortress Press.

Newson, C., et al., eds. 2012. *The Women's Bible Commentary*. Rev. and updated. Louisville, KY: Westminster John Knox Press.

Osiek, C., and M. MacDonald. 2006. *A Woman's Place: House Churches in Earliest Christianity*. Minneapolis, MN: Fortress Press.

Schüssler Fiorenza, E. 1983. *In Memory of Her: A Feminist Theological Reconstruction of Christian Origins*. New York: Crossroad.

Tkacz, C. 2008. "Is the Education of Women a Modern Idea?" *Catholic Answers* 19 (3):17–24.

—SUSAN WILLHAUCK

WOMEN, EDUCATION OF

Women's education is perhaps one of the areas in which disadvantages and lack of opportunities worldwide are the most evident.[40] In terms of pedagogy, are you teaching in a class where women and men are learning together? Or is your experience this: "Was I teaching women? Or was I just teaching and the people in the room happened to be women?" As teachers, it is very significant to know how to educate women, the way they process information, and how to present it. If you as a teacher want them to learn well, then you have to understand how the brain and body work when women learn.[41] It is important to understand the following.

Women's brains are different from men's. The left and right hemispheres of their brains are activated when they are exposed to new, concrete experiences in an emotional setting. Neuro-biological research has shown how women's brains actually work and how they can learn best. One researcher has commented: "When mental resonance imaging machines were hooked up to students taking SAT tests, it was noted that women actually process information differently than men."[42] She notes that women's brains have more connections in the corpus callous, the area between the two hemispheres,[43] which is larger and more developed. This permits the two parts to work together more easily. Women's cerebral cortex (responsible for memory, attention, thought, and language) is dedicated to verbal functions.

The limbic system controls emotions, and because of their more active limbic systems, women's thoughts and emotions may combine in their brain functions. "Women employ 'whole brain thinking.'"[44]

Women process information, listen, read, and experience emotion in different ways than men do. The emotionally charged learning environment, coupled with cooperative learning and multiple intelligences approach to instruction, is appropriate for making science and mathematics learning compatible. This has implications for the learning environment and teaching techniques for educating women. Since they use the language section of their brains to process their learning, they can learn math easily if the instructor uses practical applications and "story problems."[45]

Because of their superior language skills, women like context in their process of learning and learn through narrative. For example, they want to know why Beethoven composed a certain piece and where he was when he wrote it, instead of just playing or listening to the song.[46]

Women can understand complex human relationships and how they fit together in emotional context and psychological systems.

They hear better than men and are highly auditory.

They learn better when they work together in small groups and relate what they study to their lives. So it is especially important for these students to link their experiences to their education.

In the classroom settings, women work best in cooperative ways.

They have higher perceptiveness to concrete experiences and verbal, vocal, and body language aspects.

They respond to stress differently than men[47] and shy away from the competitive type of classroom activities. For them, competition is stress.

Women evaluate their self-performance very critically, which is why it is necessary to encourage them constantly. Show them that you have faith that they can do well.

Women look at their leaders from all angles—body language, experiences, and attitudes—to determine whether or not they want to listen to a person. Also, they want to be the center of their teacher's attention and know that their teacher cares deeply about them. Research shows

40. Eddy Coronado, "Educación, salud y empleo preocupan a las mujeres," *Periódico Siglo Veintiuno*, 3 October 2012, 11. According to the 2003 demographic calendar of the Association Pro, family welfare, education, and poverty are highly related. This report states: "The disparity in coverage levels of education, access and efficiency, affect in the presence of higher levels of poverty, mainly in rural areas and in indigenous communities."

41. Michael Gurian and Kathy Stevens, The *Minds of Boys: Saving our Sons from Falling Behind in School and Life* (San Francisco: Jossey-Bass, 2005).

42. Sharon Begley, "How Men and Women's Brains Differ," *Newsweek* 125, no. 3, 2007, 48.

43. Ibid.

44. Ibid.

45. Ibid.

46. Karin Derichs-Kunstmann, "Women Learn Differently," *Learning in Later Life: A European Network*, http://www.lill-online.net/5.0/E/5.3/women.html (accessed 16 July 2013).

47. Brenda Hayashi, "Do Women Learn Differently? A Conversation," *ELT NEWS: The Website for English Language Teachers* (September 2005), http://www.eltnews.com/columns/thinkank/2005/08/do_women_learn_differently_a_c.html (accessed 15 July 2013).

that women students are more concerned about pleasing adults, such as teachers and parents.[48]

Pease and Pease (2003) explain the differences between men and women as follows: "They think differently. They believe different things. They have different perceptions, priorities and behaviors. . . . Men and women should be equal in terms of their opportunities to exercise their full potential, but they are not identical in their innate abilities."[49] This is important to note when educating women.

In the 1990s, Dr. Carol Gilligan at Harvard University developed a theory that the female's more complex, emotional way of thinking is detrimental in coeducational classes. Her theory may explain why even smart girls feel stupid, incompetent, and inadequate in school. Girls may have to suppress their natural way of problem solving to fit into a male mold that is considered not only different but superior to their way of thinking.[50]

In light of what has been written on how women learn and how they should be educated, if you have a coeducational class, do not ignore how women are best taught. Accept the challenge to teach them in the way God created them, in the way that they learn, in order to transform their lives. You are teaching for eternity.

References and Resources

Begley, Sharon. 2007. "How Men and Women's Brains Differ." *Newsweek* 125 (3): 47–49.

Chira, Susana. 1992. "An Ohio College Says Women Learn Differently." *New York Times*, 13 May. Accessed 15 July 2013. http://www.nytimes.com/1992/05/13/education/an-ohio-college-says-women-learn-differently-so-it-teaches-that-way.html?pagewanted=all&src=pm.

Coronado, Eddy. 2012. "Educación, salud y empleo preocupan a las mujeres." *Periódico Siglo Veintiuno*, 3 October, 11.

Derichs-Kunstmann, Karin. n.d. "Women Learn Differently." *Learning in Later Life: A European Network*. Accessed 16 July 2013. http://www.lill-online.net/5.0/E/5.3/women.html.

Gurian, Michael, and Kathy Stevens. 2005. *The Minds of Boys: Saving our Sons from Falling Behind in School and Life*. San Francisco: Jossey-Bass.

Hayashi, Brenda. 2005. "Do Women Learn Differently? A Conversation." *ELT NEWS: The Website for English Language Teachers* (September). Accessed 15 July 2013. http://www.eltnews.com/columns/thinkank/2005/08/do_women_learn_differently_a_c.html.

---

48. Ibid.

49. Allan Pease and Barbara Pease, *Why Men Don't Listen & Women Can't Read Maps* (London: Pease International Pty, Limited, 2003), 22, 24.

50. Susana Chira, "An Ohio College Says Women Learn Differently," *New York Times*, 13 May 1992, http://www.nytimes.com/1992/05/13/education/an-ohio-college-says-women-learn-differently-so-it-teaches-that-way.html?pagewanted=all&src=pm (accessed 15 July 2013).

Pease, Allan, and Barbara Pease. 2003. *Why Men Don't Listen & Women Can't Read Maps*. London: Pease International Pty, Limited.

—ANA MARÍA E. CAMPOS

WOMEN IN CHRISTIAN EDUCATION, EMERGING ROLE OF

No consensus exists today on the usage of key terminology in faith education. Terms that are used include catechetics, religious education, Christian education (the term most frequently used by Protestant and Catholic theorists to describe the process of educating in faith), and Christian religious education.

Scholars in a variety of academic fields agree that Christian education (particularly in North America) has been stereotypically identified in the church as "woman's" work. This stereotype is rooted in what is identified as the "feminization" of American culture and society: a time in the 19th century when both women and Christianity were relegated to the margins of society and were defined by "feminine" virtues like passivity, dependency, vulnerability, and privatization. Educating others in religious faith became the work of women, whose domain was the private realm of the home, while men were otherwise preoccupied in more important ways in the public realm or the "real world." Given these limits, women worked as practitioners of Christian education within the contexts of their home, Sunday or church schools, vacation Bible schools, and missionary societies. Within the 19th-century American Roman Catholic Church, religious orders of women staffed large elementary and secondary schools, where they focused their service on the education of the immigrant masses, especially in faith education.

At the beginning of the 20th century, women's role in Christian education began to change due to two events: the emergence of religious education as a distinct professional field within the church and the establishment of Christian education as an academic discipline taught not only in mainline Protestant seminaries but also in denominational colleges and universities. The emergence of religious education as a professional field is traced to the first decade of the 20th century and to the advocacy of leaders in the Religious Education Association, founded in 1903. Fashioned by liberal Protestants to bring the findings of modern scholarship and secular education to bear on faith education in the churches, the REA envisioned developing a professional specialist who would shape educational activities in local congregations. Early on, the profession attracted both laywomen and laymen, so that by the end of the 1920s almost an equal number of women and men were working as directors of religious education (DREs). Women dominated the field during and after the Great Depression, but with the end of World War II, men returned to the profession. Protestant laywomen however, continued to complete degree programs in Christian education. As their activity and influence expanded as both practitioners and theorists, they joined national denominational staffs responsible for developing faith education programs for particular denominations. Women also worked within interdenominational networks as staff members and executives, as educational consultants, authors of children's books, and writers in the area of curriculum resources. Because Catholic schools in the United States were never able to enroll every Catholic student, parishes organized religious vacation schools for children and, at the beginning of the 20th century, established the Confraternity of Christian Doctrine (CCD) for the religious education of children and young people. The CCD's work was primarily done by laywomen and became by midcentury the most common ministry of Catholic women in the United States. The number of Catholic laywomen who entered the field of religious education increased exponentially in the years after Vatican Council II (1962–1965). As a result of the first flush of the ecumenical movement, Catholic women pursued academic degrees in both Catholic and non-Catholic institutions of higher learning. Many women became DREs in Catholic parishes in the 1970s and like their Protestant sisters developed as both practitioners and theorists in the field.

Throughout the 20th century, women's impact on the field of Christian education continued to deepen and expand. In both Protestantism and Roman Catholicism, women PhDs in Christian education have had long teaching careers as professors in theological seminaries, universities, and colleges throughout the United States. Their scholarship has instigated rethinking of questions foundational to faith education and has significantly shaped curriculum development and the praxis of teaching. Women have held leadership roles in professional organizations like the REA and the Association of Professors and Researcher in Religious Education. Since the 1960s, women Christian educators have engaged in an ongoing conversation with feminist and womanist educators, philosophers, and theologians. This dialogue has had a profound impact on the entire enterprise of Christian education as feminist and womanist Christian educators continue to focus their work on issues of power, gender, race, and class and to offer bold and broad visions for transforming the field as we move into the future.

References and Resources

Durka, Gloria. 1984. "Women, Power, and the Work of Religious Education." In *Changing Patterns of Religious Education*, edited by Marvin J. Taylor, 169–180. New York: Pantheon.

Furnish, Dorothy Jean. 1986. "Women in Religious Education Pioneers for Women in Professional Ministry." In *Women and Religion in America*. Vol. 3, *1900–1968*, general editors, Rosemary Radford Ruether and Rosemary Skinner Keller, 310–338. San Francisco: Harper & Row.

Geltner, Fern, ed. 1985. *Women's Issues in Religious Education*. Birmingham, AL: Religious Education Press.

Keely, Barbara Anne, ed. 1997. *Faith of Our Foremothers Women Changing Religious Education*. Louisville, KY: Westminster John Knox Press.

Thistlethwaite, Susan. 1981. "The Feminization of American Religious Education." *Journal of Religious Education* 76 (4): 391–402.

—CATE SIEJK

WOMEN IN EDUCATIONAL MINISTRY

The first woman we find involved in the teaching ministry of the church in New Testament times is Priscilla. She and her husband, Aquila, took aside the promising young preacher, Apollos, and gave him a "more accurate" understanding of the way of God (Acts 18:26). In effect, they offered Apollos a theological education. Lois and Eunice, Phillip's four prophesying daughters, and a number of other women from New Testament times would have been engaged in teaching ministries at home or in the church. Paul wrote to the congregation at Corinth, "You can all prophecy . . . so that all may learn" (1 Cor. 14:31), which allows us to assume there were women in that church who taught.

In the first millennium after Christ, monasticism was established, and many women found places of ministry in abbeys and convents, which gave them the possibility of both an intellectual life and opportunities to teach, write, and engage in other ministries.

Following the Protestant Reformation, women found additional ways to be involved in Christian education. George Fox (Quaker) and John Wesley (Anglican/Methodist) allowed some women to exhort, teach, and preach. In the 1800s, a number of women founded ministries, which gave them opportunities to teach and to lead. Isabella Graham was one of those women. In 1816, she and a group of friends founded the Female Union for the Promotion of Sabbath Schools in New York City.[51] This movement planted many Sunday schools and simultaneously became a way of empowering women. Other examples from this era include Mary McLeod Bethune,

---

51. Keith Drury, *Short History of Sunday School* (2012), 30 March 2012, http://www.drurywriting.com/keith/sunday.school.history.htm.

who founded a school for poor African American children; Emma Willard, who founded Troy Seminary for Women; and Frances Willard, who lectured on the Bible and preached for D. L. Moody[52] and served as the first female college president in the United States, accepting the leadership of Evanston Women's College in 1871.

The explosion of missionary efforts in the 19th and early 20th centuries opened additional doors for women, offering unparalleled opportunities for ministry. Women established and taught in schools, trained nationals, developed curriculum, and led ministries. Mary Anne Cook is an example of a missionary teacher from this era. In 1821, this 37-year-old English governess arrived in Calcutta as the first single female missionary to India. "Over the course of her career there, she became a teacher, school supervisor, advisor to benevolently inclined colonial elites, and headmistress and owner of an orphanage. She asserted authority over a large community of students, servants, assistant teachers, and potential converts and gave instruction to both missionary societies in Britain and Hindu and Muslim women in India."[53]

In contemporary society, women are involved in educational ministries in local churches, higher education, itinerant and freelance ministries, missionary institutions, and a variety of other avenues of service. One of the most prominent ministries in which women teach is ministry to children. No statistics have been collected for the percentage of women in vocational children's ministry, but that number would be quite high compared to other ministry positions. A prominent example of a woman serving in vocational children's ministry is Sue Miller, who led the Promiseland Children's Ministry for 17 years at Willow Creek Community Church in Chicago. Volunteer children's ministry is predominantly led by women and includes children's Sunday school, children's church, vacation Bible school, and a variety of other ministries. Women's inclusion in children's ministries is indicated by looking at the number of female leaders of breakout sessions at the 2013 Children's Pastors' Conference, one of the largest conferences of its kind. Over 36 percent of these sessions were led by women.[54]

Women also find opportunities to serve in youth and adult Christian education in local churches. Many women are discipleship pastors, youth pastors/ministry directors, and leaders of women's ministries. The best known Christian education director from the past century is Henrietta Mears. Her Sunday school grew from 400 to 6,500, she wrote and published curriculum, she founded Gospel Light Publishing, and she engaged in a number of other educational endeavors. She was influential in the discipleship of many evangelical leaders, including Bill Bright and Billy Graham.[55]

Leading Bible studies is another educational ministry in which women have served in large numbers. The highly structured Bible Study Fellowship was started by Audrey Wetherell Johnson in 1959. The impetus for starting this organization began in 1958, when Audrey accepted an invitation to help disciple converts from a Billy Graham Crusade and discovered how needed was a structured study of God's Word.[56]

Contemporary Bible study teachers include Anne Graham Lotz, Kay Arthur, and Beth Moore. These women minister mostly to other women, but men also attend their conferences and use their resources. In 2010, *Christianity Today* reported that over 658,000 women have attended Beth Moore's Living Proof Live conferences, and millions more have read her books, many of which are Bible studies.[57] Kay Arthur has written scores of inductive Bible study books, with over 11 million in print. Her resources are available in nearly 150 countries and in approximately 70 languages.[58] Ann Graham Lotz, who was named by the *New York Times* as one of the five most influential evangelists of her generation, started her ministry as a Bible study fellowship teacher. Like Arthur and Moore, she has spoken to hundreds of thousands and is a prolific author of Bible studies.[59]

In recent history, Christian higher education has also opened many doors to women. Of the 111 schools that were members of the Council for Christian Colleges and Universities (CCCU) in 2013, six have female presidents. Women also serve in large numbers as faculty members, board members, and administrators in these institutions.[60]

Curriculum publishing is another ministry to which women have made significant contributions. Marlene LaFevre, vice president of educational development for David C. Cook, is a well-known leader in this category. Her books, *Creative Teaching Methods* and *Learning Styles*; her teacher training conferences and speaking ministry; and her impact on company practices and decisions reflect her expertise in using educational research to enhance church curricula.

52. Fraces E. Willard, *Glimpses of Fifty Years* (Chicago: H.J. Smith, 1889), 356–359.

53. Smith, "Ladies and Females: Women's Missionary and Educational Work in Nineteenth-century India" (senior thesis, Columbia University, 2010), 1, http://history.columbia.edu/undergraduate/theses/Smith/thesis.pdf.

54. http://incm.org/cpc/orlando.

55. John Woodbridge, ed., *More Than Conquerors* (Chicago: Moody, 1992), 288–291.

56. http://en.wikipedia.org/wiki/biblestudyfellowship.

57. Sarah Pulliam Bailey, "Why Women Want Moore," *Christianity Today*, 18 August 2010, 42.

58. http://en.wikipedia.org/wiki/kayarthur.

59. Ibid.

60. Katelyn Beaty, "Wheaton Students Advocate for Woman President," *Christianity Today*, 2 November 2009, 27.

References and Resources

Bailey, Sarah Pulliam. 2010. "Why Women Want Moore." *Christianity Today*, 18 August.

Beaty, Katelyn. 2009. "Wheaton Students Advocate for Woman President." *Christianity Today*, 2 November.

Drury, Keith. 2012. "Short History of Sunday School." 30 March. http://www.drurywriting.com/keith/sunday.school.history.htm.

Reed, James A., and Ronnie Prevost. 1993. *A History of Christian Education*. Nashville, TN: Broadman & Holman.

Smith. 2010. "Ladies and Females: Women's Missionary and Educational Work in Nineteenth-century India." Senior thesis, Columbia University http://history.columbia.edu/undergraduate/theses/Smith_thesis.pdf.

Tucker, Ruth, and Walter Liefeld. 1987. *Daughters of the Church: Women and Ministry from New Testament Times to the Present*. Grand Rapids, MI: Zondervan.

Willard, Frances E. 1889. *Glimpses of Fifty Years*. Chicago: H.J. Smith.

Woodbridge, John, ed. 1992. *More Than Conquerors*. Chicago: Moody.

—KEITH SPRINGER

WOMEN IN HISTORICAL CHRISTIAN CONTEXT

Early Christianity

Early Christian communities seem to have favored the participation, and by extension, the education, of women. Early Christians met in private homes, a space where women played an important role and became influential in decision-making procedures and ministerial tasks. Christian literature of the first two centuries AD gives testimony to many female figures; some scholars today have been able to establish the practice of ordination of women in the early church, suggesting sometimes that the majority of early Christians may have been women. Aside from women mentioned in the New Testament as Jesus's followers, we possess several noncanonical texts that are either attributed to women or tell the story of Christian female disciples (e.g., the "Acts of Thecla" and the "Gospel of Mary"). In both cases, women are portrayed as playing an essential role in transmitting Jesus's teachings.

Perpetua, who died around AD 202 as a martyr in Carthage, left a prison diary that is the earliest extant Christian text written by a woman. Her testimony is representative of many women's voices in early Christianity. Perpetua was from the high Roman class, was educated and fully conversant with Christian beliefs as well as literary traditions, and was later held as a model of Christian faith.

When Christianity reached an official political status in the Roman Empire in the fourth century, the church became a public institution and quickly excluded women from its midst. Women were then confined to the private sphere of their homes, and their duty was limited to household tasks. The New Testament canon reflects this shift; Ephesians, the pastoral letters, and the later addition of 1 Corinthians 14: 34–35 in Paul's letter, prohibiting women to speak in churches, all contrast with the Gospel narratives and the role of women during Jesus's life.

Good and Virtuous Woman

As of the fourth century AD, the role of women in Christendom was limited to two options: marriage or nunnery. In this context, the education provided to women served those roles; the general purpose of women's education was to ensure that they become good wives, good mothers, and virtuous Christians. However, in the specific context of the convents, nuns were often highly educated and versed in literary, biblical, and theological writings. Women mystics in the Middle Ages are an interesting case, able to transform their confinement into a recognized spiritual experience. The French writer Christine de Pizan (c. 1364–c. 1430) is regarded as a unique feminine figure in the history of Western Christianity; she was a well-respected author in her time and wrote repeatedly against the mistreatment of women, holding the teachings of the church responsible for it. Scholars have now recognized Christine de Pizan as one of the forerunners of feminism; she spent her entire career defending women, pleading for respect for their moral strength, their skills, and their intellectual contributions.

Aside from a few exceptions (e.g., the Quakers, who encouraged the education of women in the 17th century), it was not until the 18th and 19th centuries that real changes occurred in the status of women; interestingly, the struggle for their political rights had a direct impact on the question of education and its relationship to Christianity. Two contributions at the end of the 18th century deserve to be mentioned: the publication of the *Vindication of the Rights of Women* (1792), by the British writer Mary Wollstonecraft (1759–1797) and of *The Declaration of the Rights of Woman and the Female Citizen* (1791), by the French writer Olympe de Gouges (1748–1793). In the United States, the project of the "Women's Bible," published in 1895 and 1898, marks a turning point in feminist biblical scholarship and was a unique voice pleading in favor of women's equality and right to speak in matters of religion and theology. Elizabeth Cady Stanton (1815–1902) was the main instigator of this project, seeing it as an integral part of a greater struggle for women's rights. The controversy that surrounded the publication of the "Women's Bible" hindered its dissemination, and it was only in the second half of the 20th century that feminist scholars shed light on this precursor of feminist biblical hermeneutics.

Today in the United States, many women's colleges have a Christian affiliation. They represent several denominations that have favored and supported women's education over the years. Significantly, the majority of them were founded in the 19th century, when the movement for women's rights was born. For example, Judson College was founded in 1838 by Baptists in Marion, Alabama; Mount Holyoke Seminary opened its doors in 1837 in South Hadley, Massachusetts; and Agnes Scott College in Decatur, Georgia, was founded by the Presbyterians in 1889. As a consequence of the growing number of institutions dedicated to the education of women, the 19th century also witnessed the development of the role of women as educators, especially in the realm of religious education.

References and Resources

Epp, Eldon J. 2005. *Junia—The First Woman Apostle*. Minneapolis, MN: Fortress Press.

Graham Brock, Ann. 2003. *Mary Magdalene, the First Apostle: The Struggle for Authority*. Cambridge, MA: Harvard Divinity Press.

Haines-Eitzen, Kim. 2011. *Gendered Palimpsest. Women, Writing, and Representation in Early Christianity*. Oxford: Oxford University Press.

King, Karen. 2003. *The Gospel of Mary of Magdala: Jesus and the First Woman Apostle*. Santa Rosa, CA: Polebridge Press.

Osiek, Carolyn, and Margaret Y. MacDonald. 2005. *A Women's Place. House Churches in Earliest Christianity*. Minneapolis, MN: Fortress Press.

Osiek, Carolyn, and Kevin Madigan, eds. 2005. *Ordained Women in the Early Church: A Documentary History*. Baltimore, MD: Johns Hopkins University Press.

Schüssler Fiorenza, Elisabeth. 2011. *Transforming Visions. Explorations in Feminist Theology*. Minneapolis, MN: Fortress Press.

Vives, Juan L. 2000. *The Education of a Christian Woman; A Sixteenth-Century Manual*. Chicago: University of Chicago Press.

Zink-Sawyer, Beverly. 2003. *From Preachers to Suffragists: Woman's Rights and Religious Conviction in the Lives of Three Nineteenth-Century American Clergywomen*. Louisville, KY: Westminster John Knox Press.

—Muriel Schmid

Women, Rights of

The Progression of Women's Rights

A definitive era of progression in acknowledging the human rights of women relative to Christian education can be traced to the four Gospels' accounts of the life and ministry of Jesus Christ. His interactions with women throughout the narrative accounts model Jesus's attitudes toward women of intellectual respect and affirmation of women's equality with men as human beings, as those created in *Imago Dei*: in God's image. Jesus emphasized the meaning and value of women's lives in recognizing their individual giftings and the vocational purposes signified by those giftings. His conversations with women indicate a willingness to confront stringent cultural and religious traditions and misapplied religious laws of that period, when those traditions and laws limited even appropriate, morally principled interactions among men and women and restricted women's educational opportunities.

Many of Jesus's interactions with women clearly indicate a departure from traditions of the period, designating the beginning of new opportunities for women. He often engaged women in theological discourse. His conversation with the Samaritan woman (John 4: 4–26) indicates an intellectual level of theological interchange that was also profoundly and deeply spiritual in its intent to transform her life. Jesus commended Mary of Bethany for her willingness to focus her attention on His teachings rather than attend to the traditional women's duties of preparation and serving in times of hospitality. Although women were proscribed from the intensive study of religion and spiritual life provided in the tradition of itinerant rabbis, Jesus, who taught in that tradition, invited both men and women to receive His teachings.

The apostle Paul encouraged the spiritual education and ministries of women, as evidenced by his commendation of Junia, an apostle (Rom. 16:7); of Priscilla, who with her husband Aquilla served as a coworker with Paul and was instrumental in providing instruction in the faith to Apollos, another apostle (Acts 18:26); and of Phoebe, apparently a patroness of Paul and a deaconess or servant-leader (Rom. 16: 1–2). In his first letter to Timothy, Paul instructed Timothy to "let the women learn" (1 Tim. 2:11), thereby aligning with Jesus's invitation to Mary of Bethany to live as a devoted disciple of His teaching.

Although the individual theologies of various denominations and groups concerning the rights of women in education differ throughout the postbiblical era, diverse movements of revival and renewal, beginning with the emergence of monastic communities, opened opportunities for women to receive education and to become educators. The emergence of church schools provided opportunities for girls to receive the teaching and mentoring of older women and eventually to undergo training as teachers. As monasteries and other Christian communities opened their doors to the ill, the indigent, the disabled, and the elderly, women's skills in nursing and teaching other women in medical and nursing skills were essential to many of these communities.

Women's roles in education expanded during the emergence of the Industrial Revolution from the 17th through the 19th centuries. Various Christian revival and renewal movements motivated women to embrace educational vocations as they worked to establish new schools and to further education for both genders. The Azusa Street Revival, beginning in Los Angeles, California, in 1906, and the subsequent 20th-century cross-denominational evangelistic and charismatic movements, contributed to the general advancement of education and to furthering new opportunities for women to receive education and to train for careers in teaching and other academic contexts. These various movements encouraged women's involvement in ecclesial ministry and mission, creating an increased need for theological education and ministry training for women.

Women's Rights in Education: New Opportunities

Although general acceptance of and support for the right of girls and women to receive education at several academic levels and in various fields developed as a widely accepted standard in Christianity, there remains a diversity of opinion about the rights of women in seminary education, especially those programs providing preparation for ministerial leadership. However, in the 20th century various denominations opened their Bible college and seminary doors to women and approved ministerial licensure and ordination for women.

Historically, the right of women to education has been supported more in Western countries, although various religion-affiliated and secular organizations are currently working to provide several levels of education for women in global contexts. The global movement for women's rights in education has been furthered by both women and men from various Christian denominations and groups, who have responded to a sense of missionary call to establish schools for children and adults in locations where educational opportunities are nonexistent or limited.

References and Resources

Cunningham, Loren, David Joel Hamilton, and Janice Rogers. 2000. *Why Not Women? A Biblical Study of Women in Missions, Ministry and Leadership.* Seattle, WA: YWAM Publishing.

Grogan, Margaret, and Carol Shakeshaft. 2011. *Women and Educational Leadership.* San Francisco: Jossey-Bass.

Levine, Robert A., Sarah Levine, Beatrice Schnell-Anzola, Meredith L. Rowe, and Emily Dexter. 2012. *Literacy and Mothering: How Women's Schooling Changes the Lives of the World's Children.* New York: Oxford University Press.

Nash, Margaret A. 2005. *Women's Education in the United States, 1780–1840.* New York: Palgrave Macmillan.

Oden, Amy. 1994. *In Her Words: Women's Writings in the History of Christian Thought.* Nashville, TN: Abingdon Press.

Solomon, Barbara Miller. 1986. *In the Company of Educated Women: A History of Women and Higher Education in America.* New Haven, CT: Yale University Press.

Tucker, Ruth A., and Walter Liefeld. 1987. *Daughters of the Church: Women and Ministry from New Testament Times to the Present.* Grand Rapids, MI: Zondervan.

Witherington, Ben. 1994. *Women in the Ministry of Jesus: A Study of Jesus Attitudes to Women and Their Roles as Reflected in His Earthly Life.* Cambridge, UK: Cambridge University Press.

Wrigley, Julia. 1992. *Education and Gender Equality.* New York and London, UK: RoutledgeFalmer.

—Mara Lief Crabtree

WORLD

The scriptures use the term *kosmos* ("world") in a highly ambivalent fashion. On the one hand, the whole world is loved by God (John 3:16; Ps. 50:12; Exod. 19:5). On the other hand, the world is a place full of sin (Isa. 13:11; John 15:19, 16:33; 1 Cor. 3:19). The key is to recognize that the world is the theater of God's salvific work in history.

The world belongs to God and is the context of His creative activity and therefore precious to Him. However, the beauty of God's created world has been distorted by sin, and consequently we see both good and evil at work in the world (Matt. 13:38; cf. Matt. 18:7). The redemptive work of Christ is not only for fallen humanity, but for the whole world as the precious created order of God (John 1:29, 3:17, 12:47; 2 Cor. 5:19; 1 Tim. 1:15; 1 John 2:2). The New Testament views God's rescue and re-creation of the entire *kosmos* as the object of eschatological expectation (Matt. 6:10; Rev. 21–22; Wright 2008, 184; Wright 2010, 26–28), and in the meantime the whole world longs for the completion of God's restorative work (Rom. 8:22).

That Christ's commissions to Peter (John 21) and to all disciples (Matt. 28:18–20) are intrinsically intertwined with His resurrection points to Jesus's resurrection as not focused on safety and rest in heaven, but as a summons to dangerous and difficult tasks in this world (Wright 2008, 241). Likewise, Paul saw the hope of the resurrection not as a reason for withdrawing from the world but as a motivation for working hard in the present for the good of the world (1 Cor. 15:58; Wright 2008).

As God's kingdom-people, Christians are called upon to be "the light of the world" (Matt. 5:14; cf. John 8:12). Consequently, the Christian's primary response to the world should be neither rejection nor uncritical embrace, but rather proclamation (Matt. 28:18–20; Luke

24:47–48; cf. Mark 16:15), holy living, and advocacy for a just world (Matt. 6:10).

At the heart of Jesus's teaching for His disciples are the Great Commandment and the Great Commission: to love God and neighbor, to live in obedience to Jesus's commandments, and to take the message of redeemed life to all the world. Educational ministry for lifelong discipleship to Jesus in this fallen but loved world therefore entails cognitive, affective, and behavioral dimensions; we must know the scriptures (cognitive) to live the life of faith in a growing heart relationship with God (affective) that works out in obedience through love and care for His world and those who live in it (behavioral).

A holistic understanding of the church's educational ministry emerges out of an understanding of God's missional-ecclesial call to His people. God's mission is the restoration of the world, and He has chosen His people, the church, as the primary agency for the accomplishment of this mission. However, local churches generally fall far short of this ideal due to the external societal challenges and internal dysfunctions that blur its vision and stifle its effectiveness. The educational mandate of local churches hence begins with the nurturing of an atmosphere of worship and fellowship that then enables the community of faith to engage in witness, service, and advocacy (Pazmiño 1992; Dykstra 1985).

References and Resources

Bramer, P. D. G. 2007. "Christian Formation: Tweaking the Paradigm." *Christian Education Journal*, Series 3, 4 (2): 352–363.

Dykstra, C. 1985. "No Longer Strangers." *Princeton Seminary Bulletin* 6 (3): 188–200.

Kang, S. S. 2011. "'Your Kingdom Come': Practical Theology as Living Out Three Great Pillars of Christianity." *Christian Education Journal*, Series 3, 8 (1): 114–129.

Pazmiño, R. W. 1992. *Principles and Practices of Christian Education*. Grand Rapids, MI: Baker.

Wright, C. J. H. 2010. *The Mission of God's People: A Biblical Theology of the Church's Mission*. Grand Rapids, MI: Zondervan.

Wright, N. T. 2008. *Surprised by Hope: Rethinking Heaven, the Resurrection, and the Mission of the Church*. New York: HarperOne.

—Perry W. H. Shaw

World Council of Churches

History and Mission

Following the 1910 Edinburgh World Missionary Conference and the 1920 Synod of Constantinople, the creation of the World Council of Churches (WCC) was initially envisioned in 1937 by leaders representing more than 100 churches. Its actual foundation, however, was delayed by the outbreak of World War II and took place shortly after the end of the war, during its first assembly, held in 1948 in Amsterdam, Netherlands; representatives from 147 churches were present. As the direct product of the broader ecumenical movement of the late 19th and early 20th centuries,[61] the WCC seeks to foster the global fellowship of Christian churches and communities to bear witness to the unity of Christian faith and service. The WCC has adopted the Greek term *oikoumene*[62] as a central element of its logo, thus reminding its members and readers that the etymology of the word "ecumenism" derives from the terminology that designated in the ancient world "the whole (known) inhabited earth"; the modern usage of the word, according to the WCC, "embraces the unity of God's whole creation and recognizes every human pursuit as subject to the healing ministry of Christ's Spirit."

Members

Currently, the WCC is the largest institution in the history of the ecumenical movement, bringing together

> 349 churches, denominations and church fellowships in more than 110 countries and territories throughout the world, representing over 560 million Christians and including most of the world's Orthodox churches, scores of Anglican, Baptist, Lutheran, Methodist and Reformed churches, as well as many United and Independent churches. While the bulk of the WCC's founding churches were European and North American, today most member churches are in Africa, Asia, the Caribbean, Latin America, the Middle East and the Pacific. (Briggs, John, Mercy A. Oduyoye, and George Tsetsis, eds. 2004, 128)

The assembly represents the legislative body of the WCC and meets every seven years only; the 10th and most recent assembly of the WCC took place in Busan, South Korea, 30 October–8 November 2013. Aside from regular full members, the WCC welcomes joint bodies, churches and denominations that are not members per se, but collaborate and work closely on various projects with the WCC's members and its executive branch, the Central Committee; the most important of those joint bodies is the Roman Catholic Church. The WCC's administrative center is located in Geneva, Switzerland.

---

61. The first formal gathering of representatives of Eastern and Western religions was held in Chicago in 1893.

62. We find 15 occurrences of the word *oikoumene* in the New Testament. Luke particularly favors this term; he uses it five times in the Book of Acts (Acts 11:28, 17:6, 17:31, 19:27, 24:5) and three times in his Gospel narrative (Luke 2:1, 4:5, 21:26).

Programs

The WCC has developed and sponsored numerous educational programs. Its current projects are

- the WCC and the ecumenical movement in the 21st century;
- unity, mission, evangelism, and spirituality;
- public witness: addressing power, affirming peace;
- justice, *diakonia*, and responsibility for the creation;
- education and ecumenical formation; and
- interreligious dialogue and cooperation.

The entire WCC's educational edifice rests on its strong commitment to disseminating knowledge, sharing experiences, and providing tools for Christians worldwide to help them live their faith and spirituality in a just and responsible way. The WCC's communication department publishes books and other printed material and maintains the WCC's website. Its staff prepares background notes on current events for the WCC general secretary, writes statements, and produces briefings.

The Ecumenical Institute of Bossey

The Ecumenical Institute of Bossey plays a central role in the educational mission of the WCC. Located in Geneva and attached to the University of Geneva and its Faculty of Theology since 1952, Bossey offers seminars and programs on ecumenism, organizes intercultural and interconfessional encounters, and trains church leaders as well as laypeople to be part of the ecumenical movement. The institute seeks to develop a culture of ecumenism throughout the world and offers a unique space for dialogue among Christians from various traditions. At the same time, it fosters research on current issues related to the ecumenical movement and facilitates debate on those issues. Its library is the home of an extensive and unique collection of documents, books, and archives of the WCC.

References and Resources

Briggs, John, Mercy A. Oduyoye, and George Tsetsis, eds. 2004. *A History of the Ecumenical Movement*. Vol. 3, *1968–2000*. Geneva: World Council of Churches.

Fey, Harold E., ed. 1970. *The Ecumenical Advance: A History of the Ecumenical Movement*. Vol. 2, *1948–1968*. London: SPCK.

Fitzgerald, Thomas E. 2004. *The Ecumenical Movement: An Introductory History*. Westport, CT: Praeger.

Kasper, Walter. 2004. *That They May All Be One: The Call to Unity Today*. London: Burns & Oates.

———. 2009. *Harvesting the Fruits: Aspects of Christian Faith in Ecumenical Dialogue*. New York: Continuum.

Lossky, Nicolas, José Míguez Bonino, and John Pobee, eds. 2002. *Dictionary of the Ecumenical Movement*. Geneva: World Council of Churches.

Mackay, John A. 1964. *Ecumenics: The Science of the Church Universal*. Englewood Cliffs, NJ: Prentice-Hall, Inc.

Internet Resources

WCC. http://www.oikoumene.org (access to declarations, documents, and educational material)

—MURIEL SCHMID

WORLD SUNDAY SCHOOL MOVEMENT

The World Sunday School Movement began in the 18th century with the efforts and support of English philanthropist Robert Raikes Jr. (1737–1811). Raikes inherited a newspaper, the *Gloucester Journal*, which he used to draw attention to the plight of persons who were imprisoned, impoverished, and in need of assistance. To achieve real progress, Raikes sought to address the issue of juvenile delinquency that occurred after working hours and on Sundays. He believed that providing literacy and spiritual training to children was the solution. Sunday was the only day off for these youth. Initially, the school was for children ages six to fourteen, and ran from 10:00 a.m. to 5:00 p.m.

The purpose of Sunday school was to instruct children in reading, writing, morals, and manners as well as to evangelize those considered in need of a spiritually renewed life. Since many of the students were illiterate, the first step was to instill basic reading and writing skills, using the Bible as the textbook. Sunday school was established with paid teachers and strict discipline. Later, most teachers were volunteers, with more than 160,000 volunteer teachers involved in Sunday school ministry by the early 19th century. Sunday school garnered an international reputation, gradually spreading throughout Europe and America. Four years after the publication of Raikes's original article, nearly 250,000 children were participating in Sunday school. Adults also recognized the benefit of Sunday school. It was an opportunity for improved education. By 1835, an estimated 1,500,000 people were attending Sunday school in England alone.

Although the Sunday school movement was met with steep opposition from the church (the archbishop of Canterbury formed a group to prevent the movement from growing in England), several organizations attempted to provide structure and support to the program, including the Society for the Support and Encouragement of Sunday School (commonly known as the Sunday School Society), the Sunday School Union, the Sunday School

Association, the Methodist Sunday School Union, the Sunday School Institute, and the Society of Friends First Day School Association. This helped the perpetuation and spread of the movement throughout Europe.

The Sunday school movement crossed the Atlantic to the United States and Canada between 1780 and 1830. The population in the United States and Canada grew exponentially during this period. By 1889, the population in the United States was around 60 million, and Sunday school enrollment accounted for one-sixth of the population.

Henry Clay Trumbull (1893) outlined three periods prior to 1900, and Jack L. Seymour (1993) outlined three periods after 1900, for the development of the Sunday school:

1780–1839	The Sunday School as missionary and philanthropic agency
1830–1860	From an extra-church agency to a church institution concerned with the evangelization and nurture of the young
1870–1900	Period of expansion, when the evangelical spirit of revival became rooted in the Sunday school as the primary agent of church growth
1903–1929	An allegiance to liberal Protestant thought and Progressive religious education
1929–mid 1960s	Rise of neoorthodox thought and the partial demise of liberal religious education
Mid-1960s–1990	Decline in mainline church schools; evangelicals remain stable and strong

Today, Sunday schools remain strong and plenteous. One of the most famous contemporary examples of Sunday school programs is the "Sidewalk Sunday School," implemented by Bill Wilson of Metro Ministries in Brooklyn, New York, in 1988. This program converted a 14-foot cube truck into a sound stage fit for outdoor teaching and service. Volunteers laid tarps on the sidewalks for children to sit on while listening to Bible lessons and have playtime. At present, more than 20,000 children participate in the Sidewalk Sunday School—the largest Sunday school in the world. Though not exactly the model of Raikes's intention, the Sidewalk Sunday School of Metro Ministries is an exemplar of the enduring relevance and strength of the World Sunday School Movement.

References and Resources

Anthony, Michael J., and Warren S. Benson. 2001. *Introducing Christian Education: Foundations for the Twenty-First Century*. Grand Rapids, MI: Baker Academic.

———. 2003. *Exploring the History and Philosophy of Christian Education: Principles for the 21st Century*. Grand Rapids, MI: Kregel.

Elias, John L. 2002. *A History of Christian Education: Protestant, Catholic, and Orthodox*. Grand Rapids, MI: Kregel.

Knoff, Gerald E. 1979. *The World Sunday School Movement: The Story of a Broadening Mission*. New York: Seabury Press.

Seymour, Jack L. 1993. *Mapping Christian Education: Approaches to Congregational Learning*. Nashville: Abingdon.

Trumbull, Henry Clay. 1893. *The Sunday School Yale Lectures*. Philadelphia: John D. Wattles.

—Nathaniel Holmes Jr.

WORLDVIEW, CHRISTIAN

A Christian worldview, in its most basic sense, is a set of assumptions about everything, derived from the Bible. The complexity arises in what is meant by "everything." While the origins of the term "worldview" can be traced to Immanuel Kant, and its use in evangelical Christianity may be traced to Abraham Kuyper or James Orr in recent years, it is the definition provided by James W. Sire that seems most influential: "a set of presuppositions (assumptions which may be true, partially true or entirely false) which we hold (consciously or subconsciously, consistently or inconsistently) about the basic make-up of our world" (1988, 17). Sire and others have since concluded, however, that this definition is inadequate, because it restricts worldview to a person's beliefs and knowledge. He has revised it as follows:

> A worldview is a commitment, a fundamental orientation of the heart, that can be expressed as a story or in a set of presuppositions (assumptions which may be true, partially true, or entirely false) which we hold (consciously or subconsciously, consistently or inconsistently) about the basic constitution of reality, and that provides the foundation on which we live and move and have our being. (2004, 122)

In large part due to a historical study of the term by David K. Naugle (2002), the concept of worldview has now been expanded to incorporate not only the propositional dimension of beliefs and knowledge, but also behavior and heart orientation (Schultz and Swezey 2011, 3).

Behavioral ideas of worldview stem from Colson and Pearcey (1999) and Barna (2003). The most significant addition to the concept of worldview, however, comes from writings that advocate for what Sire (2004) called the orientation of the heart. In addition to Sire, these authors include Dockery and Thornbury (2002), Naugle (2002), Brown et. al (2004), and Ryken (2006).

While the ideas of propositional and behavioral dimensions of worldview may be self-evident, the idea of heart orientation begs further clarification. According to Naugle:

> In Hebraic thought, the heart is comprehensive in its operations as the seat of the intellectual (e.g., Prov. 2:10z; 14:33; Dan. 10:12), affective (e.g., Exod. 4:14; Ps. 13:2; Jer. 15:16), volitional (e.g. Judg. 5:15; 1 Chron. 29:18; Prov. 16:1), and religious life of a human being (e.g., Deut. 6:5; 2 Chron. 16:9; Ezek. 6:9; 14:3). (2002, 268–269)

Naugle also notes that "the heart's perspective on reality has been altered radically by sin" (2002, 274). The importance of heart as a dimension of worldview is clear.

Within the propositional dimension, further subdivision has been proposed by various authors. Noebel proposes that "worldview" encompasses 10 divisions: "theology, philosophy, ethics, biology, psychology, sociology, law, politics, economics, and history" (1991, 319). Smithwick identifies politics, economics, education, religion, and social issues as representative of a larger body (Nehemiah Institute, Inc. 2003); Horner (2003) includes literature; and Hughes (2003) includes Christian education. Indeed, if a Christian worldview includes everything, then there is nothing about which it does not have something to say.

References and Resources

Barna, G. 2003. *Think Like Jesus: Make the Right Decision Every Time.* Nashville, TN: Integrity Publishers.

Brown, Dale, Steven Cowan, Ervin Duggan, Paul Cleveland, John Currid, and Craig Branch. 2004. "Building a Christian Worldview." *Radix: The Journal of the Apologetics Resource Center.* Volume 1, Number 2 (entire issue).

Colson, C., and N. Pearcey. 1999. *How Now Shall We Live?* Wheaton, IL: Tyndale House Publishers.

Dockery, D. S., and G. A. Thornbury, eds. 2002. *Shaping a Christian Worldview: The Foundations of Christian Higher Education.* Nashville, TN: Broadman & Holman.

Horner, G. 2003. "Glorifying God in Literary and Artistic Culture." In *Think Biblically! Recovering a Christian worldview,* edited by J. MacArthur, 315–334. Wheaton, IL: Crossway Books.

Hughes, J. A. 2003. "Why Christian Education and Not Secular Indoctrination?" In *Thinking Biblically! Recovering a Christian Worldview,* edited by J. MacArthur, 239–258. Wheaton, IL: Crossway Books.

Naugle, D. K. 2002. *Worldview: The History of a Concept.* Grand Rapids, MI: Eerdmans.

Noebel, D. A. 1991. *Understanding the Times: The Religious Worldviews of Our Day and the Search for Truth.* Eugene, OR: Harvest House Publishers.

———. 2003. Worldview. http://allaboutworldview.org/worldview.htm.

Ryken, P. G. 2006. *What Is the Christian Worldview?* Phillipsburg, NJ: P&R Publishing.

Schultz, K. G., and J. A. Swezey. 2011. "A 3-Dimensional Concept of Worldview." Paper presented at the 2011 annual meeting of the American Educational Research Association, New Orleans, April. Accessed 28 January 2013. AERA Online Paper Repository.

Sire, J. 1988. *Universe Next Door.* Downers Grove, IL: InterVarsity Press.

———. 2004. *Naming the Elephant: Worldview as a Concept.* Downers Grove, IL: InterVarsity Press.

—Katherine G. Schultz

Worship

Along with the "culture wars" coloring contemporary Christianity, the "worship wars" have disappointingly, but not unexpectedly, emerged. One might assume at least this one aspect of the church would not be divisive. Hermeneutical and historical-theological differences (intra- and interdenominational), however, make even worship an inevitable battleground.

Worship practices (prayers, praises, and propitiations) have been around since the earliest humans, as evidenced by the early chapters of Genesis and the written and ritual artifacts of archaeology. The nature of Old Testament (OT) and New Testament (NT) worship evolved with the progress of written revelation or scripture. Debate centers on finding agreement on what the Bible describes or prescribes as worship, per what the OT and/or NT demand or depict. The matter is complicated when conclusions are drawn based on translations, as opposed to the foundational Hebrew and Greek texts of the Bible, or on traditions as authoritative.

Adding to the confusion, the word "worship" in English may represent one of several different words in the Bible. In the OT it usually translates a Hebrew word for "serve, slave." At other times it represents a term meaning "bow down before some-thing/one" or "fear." NT Greek words rendered "worship," some of which are part of quotations from the Greek OT, have to do with "lying prostrate," "obeying," "being devoted," "fearing," or "serving." When contemporary believers hear the word "worship," however, their minds usually and immediately think of attending a worship service comprised of songs, a sermon, and supplications. In modern times, a separate meeting time was added for the purposes of Christian education, the sermon being viewed more as an evangelistic or edificatory event.

Today Christians argue over worship as either a lifestyle or liturgy. Within the weekly congregation, the differences are over formulated or free expressions, traditional or contemporary music, and simple or spectacular trappings or architecture. But scripture seems not to dictate particulars, only basic principles on this subject. Personal preference has to give way to community consensus in light of the clear Christian call to selflessness. In the OT there is an emphasis on "praise," but this word is not usually translated "worship." Yet the Hebrew word for "praise" and the English word "worship" (< "worth" + "scipe/ship") have the same basic meanings. Both have to do with giving vocal and public acknowledgment to the worth of someone's character or conduct. Fascinating is the fact that the OT word, often translated "give thanks," which more correctly is "give testimony," is often used as a poetic restatement for "praise" (cf. Ps. 100:1–4). And the word "praise" can sometimes also be rendered "bless" or "favor." Ways to demonstrate God's supreme worth are through bowing, respect, devotion, and pledging service or obedience (cf. Rom. 12:1).

King David at times (cf., e.g., Ps. 35:17–18) vowed to God that if he experienced extraordinary deliverance from his enemies, he would go to the Temple and give witness to God's greatness and goodness as a Savior. Whatever else is added to a worship service, essential worship is whatever draws attention to specific attributes and actions of God. Christian education connects to worship in that its focus is remembrance (rehearsal, repetition) of God's character and conduct in history.

For Christian education currently, this calling and controversy suggests that seminaries give renewed emphasis to the pastor's role as a worship leader and his or her necessary task of incorporating the testimony and talent of many members beyond a designated and superficially elevated team of professionals or preferential laypersons. The emphasis in the NT on the calling of local church members to serve "one another" in many ways (Rom. 12:10, 15:7, 14; Gal. 5:13; Eph. 4–5; Col. 3:16; 1 Thess. 5:11; et al.), especially speaking to one another with songs or psalms (Eph. 5:17), prescribes a gathering in which encouragement and even instruction (Rom. 15:14; Col. 3:16) come from more than a few in the congregation.

References and Resources

Crenshaw, James L. 1998. *Education in Ancient Israel*. New York: Doubleday.

Long, Thomas G. 2001. *Beyond the Worship Wars: Building Vital and Faithful Worship*. Washington, DC: Alban Institute.

Martin, Ralph P. 1975. *Worship in the Early Church*. rev. ed. Grand Rapids, MI: Eerdmans.

Wainwright, Geoffrey, and Karen B. Westerfield Tucker, eds. 2005. *The Oxford History of Christian Worship*. New York: Oxford University Press.

—W. Creighton Marlowe

Worship as Christian Practice

Worship is the central aspect of what makes a Christian community distinctive. It provides the fundamental ground for Christian unity and identity and also serves as an educational process for spiritual formation. In practice, it serves an important educational function, communicating what is central to a Christian community. Today, more Christian educators recognize the educational importance of worship for nurturing Christian identity, instructing central beliefs and doctrines, and transmitting the rich heritage of Christian faith.

Definition of Worship

In understanding the meanings of worship, there are two aspects that all who participate in worship ought to remember. One is that worship is not to be approached from a consumerist perspective that seeks to fill one's entertainment and personal needs. The second is that Christian worship requires that all participants approach it with genuine spiritual hunger and longing to be in the presence of Holy God. As Max Weber (1968) has warned, charisma in worship cannot be routinized into a dead ritual, but instead must be revived anew every time.

The biblical meanings of worship suggest both the importance of service—that is, *abad* or *asab* in Hebrew, which means *to serve*—and offering of oneself to God—that is, *latreia* in Greek, which means *to offer oneself* to God. The additional meaning of worship is *to exhibit an attitude of reverential fear* in the presence of Holy God. Both *shachac* in the Old Testament and *proskyneo* in the New Testament suggest this attitudinal quality and intention of the worshipper. These meanings suggest clearly what is required in the act of worship for those who practice. Worship, in general, is also understood as the encountering activity between God's self-revelation and our human response to God's self-revelation in and through Jesus Christ. Thus it is crucial to maintain a proper balance between these two dynamics—between God's self-revelation and the human response to it—as this balance is intrinsic to Christian worship.

Worship as Christian Practice

Christian worship as a form of faith practice incorporates a rich array of learning opportunity. Since worship is the response of grateful people to the living God, where submission, sacrificial service, praise, profession of faith, testimony, and gratitude are freely and joyfully expressed in innumerable ways, it provides many opportunities to form, shape, and educate God's people through its practice.

Worship, as a Christian practice, comprises the following educational efficacies (Osmer 2005):

1. As a socially shared activity, it builds up a common sense of identity.
2. The character-shaping nature of the practice points to the habits of thoughts, feelings, and actions of the participants that give shape, texture, and motivation to the collective sense of identity.
3. It embodies an interpretation of the ultimate context of existence, which gives a distinctive religious character to our faith practice.

Through worship, the members of a faith community strengthen their relational bonds and solidarity through performance and participation in the same ritual practice. Those who participate in Christian worship bring with them intentionality and the sense of purposefulness that enhance the communication of the core aspects of communal identity. Perhaps one of the greatest educational benefits of worship is its ability to tacitly communicate the central core values and theological conviction of a community to its members through collective performance.

Worship and Christian Education

In implementing worship as a collective formative practice, worship leaders need to be more intentional in preparing the worship to be the central aspect of a faith community through which people encounter the living presence of God. What would an educationally responsible worship experience be? Worship should

1. be relevant to the developmental needs and characteristics of all worshippers;
2. provide religious experience with a proper balance between God's revelatory act and human response;
3. be participatory and interactive, providing multisensory experiences to the participants;
4. subordinate human goals to God's goals by prioritizing service toward the Kingdom of God; and
5. be intentional in choosing religious language, liturgies, and prayers as well as other constitutive elements, so that the participants are able to learn the Christian faith tradition and heritage;

As one of the most vital aspects of faith practice, worship provides a tremendous array of educational opportunities for God's people. Through Christian worship, the community of faith experiences the redemptive power God has given to the Christian church; worship empowers participants to uphold and honor the faith precepts, rekindles the fire of commitment to live and serve others in Christ's name, and also compels people to witness the Gospel to those who are suffering under various forms of affliction, oppression, and injustice. To these ends, Christians are called to worship the living God educationally and educate God's people worshipfully in who they are and all that they do.

References and Resources

Dykstra, Craig. 1987. "Formative Power of Congregation." *Religious Education* 82 (Fall): 530–546.

———. 1999. *Growing in the Life of Faith: Education and Christian Practices.* Louisville, KY: Geneva Press.

Harris, Maria. 1987. *Teaching and Religious Imagination.* San Francisco: Harper & Row.

Labberton, Mark. 2007. *The Dangerous Act of Worship.* Downers Grove, IL: InterVarsity Press.

Langer, Suzanne K. 1942. *Philosophy in a New Key: A Study in the Symbolism of Reason, Rite, and Art.* Cambridge, MA: Harvard University Press.

Osmer, Richard Robert. 2005. *The Teaching Ministry of Congregations.* Louisville: KY: Westminster John Knox Press.

Son, Timothy D. 2014. *Educating Congregations through Rituals: Exploring Educational Efficacies of Ritual Practice for Congregational Identity Formation.* Lanham, MD: Lexington Books.

Weber, Max. 1968. *On Charisma and Institutional Building.* Chicago: The University of Chicago Press.

White, James F. 2001. *Introduction to Christian Worship.* Nashville, TN: Abingdon Press.

—TIMOTHY D. SON

WYCKOFF, DEWITTE CAMPBELL

Early Background and Education

D. Campbell Wyckoff (1918–2005), known to his friends as "Cam," was an influential professor, writer, and educational ministry activist in the mainline Protestant movement of the mid- to late 20th century in the United States. Born in Geneseo, New York, he was influenced by his parents' involvement in the church's educational and mission efforts, and by his own experiences within the church, to pursue ministry with the Presbyterian Board of National Missions and the Presbyterian Board of National Ministries (PCUSA) from 1937 through 1947. Among the roles he took on were director of youth work for the Greater New York Federation of Churches, and secretary of the Unit of Rural Church and Indian Work.

During his time of service with the Board of National Ministries, he pursued graduate studies at New York University, earning both master of arts and PhD degrees there. This simultaneous involvement in ministry and study developed his keen appreciation for the ways that theory and practice needed to inform each other. This attention to both theory and practice was an important thread throughout his work.

Wyckoff began teaching at New York University in the department of religious education in 1947 and chaired the department from 1950 until 1954, when he accepted a new position at Princeton Theological Seminary. He served there as the Thomas W. Synnott Chair in Christian Education, eventually serving as director of the school's doctoral studies program for seven years and director of the summer school. He retired in 1983, but remained involved in writing and consultation work in the field of Christian education for the next two decades.

Significant Contributions to Christian Education

Wyckoff's impact on Christian education was multifaceted. Through his teaching at New York University and Princeton Theological Seminary, he impacted a generation of educational ministry leaders. Through his continued involvement in ecumenical educational ministry efforts, he helped various denominations develop philosophies of education and curriculum to carry their visions forward to their congregations. Through his writing, he influenced the thinking and practice of many educational ministry leaders, both within his own theological tradition and in others. Among his many publications, a few major works stand out as worthy of note. In *The Task of Christian Education* (1955), he discussed the purpose of Christian education, striving to help churches aim for the transformation of persons through their educational efforts. In *The Gospel and Christian Education* (1959), Wyckoff discussed how the good news of the Gospel serves as a guiding framework for the purposes, principles, and practices of educational ministry design. In *Theory and Design of Christian Education Curriculum* (1961), Wyckoff had a major impact in helping curriculum developers and ministry leaders develop instructional materials that reflected sound educational theory that were sensitive to the educational goals and contexts of the church. In addition, from 1960 until 1987, Wyckoff annually compiled and disseminated annotated bibliographies on recent publications in the field for use by seminary and college libraries, greatly impacting their acquisitions and holdings.

Wyckoff received many honors during his lifetime, from New York University, the Association of Presbyterian Church Educators, and the North American Professors of Christian Education. After retirement, he and his wife, Mildred, moved first to Pennsylvania, and then to Albuquerque, New Mexico, where he was active in his local church until his death due to cancer in 2005.

Most Notable Publications

Wyckoff, D. C. 1955. *The Task of Christian Education*. Philadelphia: Westminster Press.

——. 1959. *The Gospel and Christian Education: A Theory of Christian Education for Our Times*. Philadelphia: Westminster Press.

——. 1961. *Theory and Design of Christian Education Curriculum*. Philadelphia: Westminster Press.

——. 1983. "From Practice to Theory—and Back Again." In *Modern Masters of Religious Education*, edited by M. Mayr, 87–114. Birmingham, AL: Religious Education.

——, and George Brown Jr., comps. 1995. *Religious Education, 1960–1993: An Annotated Bibliography*. Westport, CT: Greenwood Press.

References and Resources

Much of the content of this essay is adapted from material presented in G. Brown Jr., "Wyckoff, DeWitte Campbell," in *Christian Educators of the 20th Century* (n.d.; http://www.talbot.edu/ce20/educators/protestant/dewitte_wyckoff/).

—Kevin E. Lawson

Y

YALE UNIVERSITY

Founding and Early History

The Puritans founded Yale in 1701, under the banner of what is commonly called the Congregationalist denomination. It was established as a Christian college, primarily designed to educate ministers for the preaching of the Gospel. Over time, Yale College also became a place where other professionals, such as doctors, lawyers, and government leaders, could receive their educational training. Yale was the third college founded in what would become the United States, following Harvard in 1636 and William and Mary in 1693. The Puritans founded Yale largely because some of their leaders perceived that Harvard College was not adhering to conservative religious principles as steadfastly as it should be, and therefore a new college was needed. Cotton Mather was the primary Puritan leader who appealed to Elihu Yale to provide the financing to establish Yale (Urban and Wagoner 2000).

Higher education was a major Christian emphasis in the 1700s and 1800s, and therefore 121 of the first 122 U.S. colleges were private Christian colleges. Yale is a major part of this tradition, and its motto of "light and truth" reflects this fact. As is true of all the Ivy League universities founded in the 1600s and 1700s, for many years Yale's presidents were all ministers. And indeed, all seven original Ivy League colleges (the eighth, Cornell, was founded later) have definitively Christian mottoes (Jeynes 2007).

Yale's Place and Importance

Yale University is one of the "Big Three," that is, the finest universities in the United States. Throughout American history, academics have regarded Harvard University as chief among the Big Three. In the past, Yale has often ranked second, although in recent rankings, such as in *U.S. News & World Report*, Princeton has pulled ahead of Yale (no. 3), and the University of Chicago and Columbia have ranked just behind (tied for no. 4). In world rankings of universities, Yale is not far behind Harvard University and Cambridge University as being among the top three or six finest universities in the world. Yale also possesses the second largest endowment in the world, trailing only Harvard University.

Later History

As time went on, many Christian academics perceived that Yale, in similar fashion to Harvard, was beginning to become less true to its founding Christian convictions. This concern contributed greatly to the founding of Princeton, the nation's fourth college, in 1746. Ironically, even to this day, Princeton is considered the least liberal of the "Big Three," and Harvard is considered the most liberal of them. Even with the founding of Columbia in 1754, most New Yorkers preferred to send their college-age youth to Harvard, Princeton, or Yale.

Some of the nation's most prominent colleges were deeply affected by the revivals of the 1820s and 1830s and the revival of 1857 (Davis 1967). Yale University was among the institutions most affected by these tremendous moves of God. There are especially elaborate, detailed descriptions of the attitudinal changes that took place in a number of colleges, including Yale, Columbia, the University of Rochester, and Oberlin College. Many historians call the revival of 1857–1858 "The Event of the Century," because (1) two studies indicate it was the single greatest event that caused northerners to vote for the demonstrably antislavery Abraham Lincoln, and (2) it caused many of the nation's largest cities to close down for two hours at lunch each weekday in order for people to pray and study the Bible (Burns and Furbish 1901; Jeynes 2007; Orr 1989).

In the post–World War II era, in particular, concerns grew that Yale faculty were attempting to undermine students' belief in God, against the Christian traditions of Yale supporters. Conservative intellectual William F. Buckley highlighted this in his classic book, *God and Man at Yale*, published in 1951. These concerns continue to grow to this day.

References and Resources

Bailyn, B. 1960. *Education in the Forming of American Society.* Chapel Hill: University of North Carolina.

Burns, H. E., and E. B. Furbish. 1901. In *Two Centuries of Christian Activity at Yale, 1701–1901*, edited by J. B. Reynolds, S. H. Fisher, and H. B. Wright, 93–94. New York: G. P. Putnam.

Clarke, J. (1730) 1973. "John Clarke's Classical Program of Studies." In *Theories of Education in Early America*, edited by Wilson Smith, 38–45. Indianapolis: Bobbs-Merrill.

Davis, B. 1967. *Ante-bellum Reform.* New York: Harper & Row.

Jeynes, W. 2007. *American Educational History: School, Society & the Common Good.* Thousand Oaks, CA: SAGE Publications.

Orr, J. E. 1989. *The Event of the Century.* Wheaton, IL: International Awakening Press.

Urban, W., and J. Wagoner. 2000. *American Education: A History.* Boston: McGraw-Hill.

—William Jeynes

YMCA and YWCA

The Industrial Revolution brought with it migration of young adults to urban areas in search of work. As early as the 1600s, associations of urban workers formed to meet together for spiritual encouragement and prayer. In 1844, one such group in London, under the leadership of George Williams, sought to expand the holding of religious services for young men in work establishments. They formed the Young Men's Christian Association (YMCA), which grew and quickly expanded into France, Germany, and Switzerland. In 1851, the first YMCA groups were formed in the United States and Canada, and over time there was rapid growth and expansion into the various settings where young men gathered, including the armed services, colleges, urban work settings, on the railroad, and in the mines. In 1853, just two years after the YMCA came to the United States, the first YMCA for blacks was founded by Anthony Bowen, a former slave.

The primary efforts of the YMCA in its early years were gathering young men together for prayer, Bible study, and social gatherings. There was a strong evangelistic focus and emphasis on personal piety and training young men for involvement and leadership within the church's ministry and mission efforts. In the late 1800s and early 1900s, more emphasis was placed on character development; service; and a "muscular faith" that emphasized moral character, behavior, and action over beliefs. YMCAs also addressed the needs of new immigrants to the United States, teaching English and providing social services. From the 1890s, the YMCA logo emphasized the development of people in spirit, mind, and body. As the 20th century progressed, YMCAs developed greater emphasis on youth and family recreation, health, and fitness programs. The YMCA World Council took a stand against apartheid in 1985 and has since become more active in global issues, such as racism, globalization, sustainable development, and HIV/AIDS prevention.

The Young Women's Christian Association (YWCA) was founded in 1855 in England during the Crimean War. What began as a prayer meeting, led by Emma Roberts, developed under the leadership of Mary Jane Kinnaird to address the needs of women for housing, education, and spiritual and social support as they moved to urban areas during the war and in the years that followed. The first YWCA in the United States was formed in 1858 in New York City, and the first YWCA serving black women opened in Dayton, Ohio, in 1889. The World YWCA, formed in 1898, is based in Geneva, Switzerland. The YWCA has a long history of involvement in social issues impacting the well-being of women, including racism and fair employment practices. The YWCA currently is actively involved in providing programs for women and families addressing domestic violence, racism, economic development, leadership development, health and fitness, and child care. While in many national YWCA groups, the "Christian" emphasis has been changed to a focus on the broader social and economic needs of women, some regions still have a strong Christian focus. Over 25 million women and girls in 125 countries are impacted by the work of the YWCA today.

In both organizations, what began from explicit Christian religious concerns for the spiritual needs of young men and women eventually changed to a more expansive focus on physical, social, mental, and spiritual needs. Whereas early Ys required members to be Christians involved in local evangelical churches, contemporary Ys do not carry that kind of requirement. Some local Ys, due to their history and local leadership, may still emphasize Christian beliefs and spiritual growth concerns. As the leadership of other Ys has shifted away from an evangelical religious perspective, social needs have been emphasized more, with many Ys strongly engaged in community development and social change. Both organizations are examples of parachurch, nondenominational, lay mobilization to address the needs of society.

References and Resources

Hopkins, C. H. 1951. *History of the Y.M.C.A. in North America.* New York: Association Press.

Ninde, H. S., J. T. Bowne, and E. Uhl. 1891. *A Handbook of the History, Organization, and Methods of Work of Young Men's Christian Associations.* New York: The International Committee of Young Men's Christian Associations.

Setran, D. P. 2007. *The College Y: Student Religion in the Era of Secularization.* Hampshire, UK: Palgrave Macmillan.

Seymour-Jones, C. 1994. *Journey of Faith: The History of the World YWCA, 1945-1994.* London: Allison & Busby.

Sims, M. S. 1950. *The YWCA: An Unfolding Purpose.* New York: Woman's Press.

Wilson, E. 1916. *Fifty Years of Association Work among Young Women: 1866-1916.* New York: National Board of the Young Women's Christian Associations of the United States of America.

—Kevin E. Lawson

YOUTH AND FAMILY MINISTRY

Introduction

The concept of youth and family ministry acknowledges the specific role of parents and the familial context in Christian faith formation, as distinct from "youth ministry" (or "student ministry"), which generally focuses on developmental and spiritual needs of adolescents. The addition of "family" is not generally restricted to a particular biblical model or traditional family system, but viewed as inclusive of all adults within a household, extended family, or even a church community.[1] John Westerhoff has suggested that religious education has always been rooted in the home and that "other forms of education have been considered at best an extension or supplement to the training children receive from their parents."[2]

The parental role in faith formation was affirmed in the Search Institute's study of Christian education practices, which found family devotions, serving others, and discussing faith issues with parents paramount in adolescent faith development.[3] Similarly, the National Study

of Youth and Religion concluded that "the single most important social influence on the religious and spiritual lives of adolescents is their parents."[4]

Biblical Foundations

The familial responsibility for passing faith from one generation to the next is mentioned throughout scripture. The Hebrews were to teach children about their rescue from Egypt through celebration of the Passover (Exod. 13:8) in order to "tell to the coming generation the glorious deeds of the Lord" (Ps. 78:4, NRSV). Moses encouraged the Israelites to model God's commands in every aspect of daily living, underscoring the child-parent relationship as the context for speaking about and acting on faith: "Recite them [God's commands] to your children and talk about them when you are at home and when you are away, when you lie down and when you rise. Bind them as a sign on your hand, fix them as an emblem on your forehead, and write them on the doorposts of your house and on your gates" (Deut. 6:7-9, NRSV).[5]

Descriptions of Christian worship within the home (including baptism and the Eucharist) appear frequently in Acts (e.g., 2:46-47, 16:14-15, 32-33, 18:8, 20:20-21; cf. Rom. 16:5). Paul emphasizes a reciprocal relationship in which children are to honor parents (cf. Exod. 20:12), while parents in turn care for and educate their children (see Eph. 6:1-4; 2 Col. 3:20-21; cf. 1 Thess. 2:11-12).[6] Paul also suggests the impact of intergenerational relationships, noting Timothy's faith as a reflection of his mother and grandmother (2 Tim. 1:5-7).

Historical Perspectives

The *Didache*, a collection of the earliest apostles' teachings, includes the maxim that parents are not to "neglect your responsibility to your son or your daughter, but from their youth you shall teach them to revere God."[7] In the 4th century, St. John Chrysostom encouraged parents to raise their children "in the discipline and instruction of the Lord," likening parents to artists who shape and form children into the image of God.[8] Chrysostom believed the virtues of goodness, forgiveness, love, generosity, and hospitality should be modeled by parents for their children's sake.

---

1. David W. Anderson and Paul Hill, *Frogs without Legs Can't Hear: Nurturing Disciples in Home and Congregation* (Minneapolis, MN: Augsburg Fortress Publishers, 2003), 23-24; Diana R. Garland, *Family Ministry: A Comprehensive Guide* (Downers Grove, IL: InterVarsity Press, 1999), 22-24; Merton P. Strommen and Richard A. Hardel, *Passing on the Faith: A Radical New Model for Youth and Family Ministry* (Winona, MN: Saint Mary's Press, 2000), 17. For a brief sociological overview of "family," see "A Socioeconomic History of the American Family" in Garland, *Family Ministry*, 251-273.

2. John H. Westerhoff III, *Bringing Up Children in the Christian Faith* (Minneapolis, MN: Winston Press, 1980), 7.

3. Peter L. Benson and Carolyn H. Eklin, *Effective Christian Education: A National Study of Protestant Congregations* (Minneapolis, MN: Search Institute, 1990), 38.

4. Christian Smith and Melinda Lundquist Denton, *Soul Searching: The Religious and Spiritual Lives of Teenagers* (New York: Oxford University Press, 2005), 261.

5. Cf. Prov. 6:20-22.

6. For an interpretation of Paul's citations, see Judith M. Gundry-Volf, "The Least and the Greatest," in *The Child in Christian Thought*, ed. Marcia J. Bunge (Grand Rapids, MI: Eerdmans, 2001), 53-57.

7. *The Didache*, in *Early Christian Fathers*, trans. and ed. Cyril C. Richardson (New York: Touchstone, 1996), 173.

8. Vigen Guroian, "The Ecclesial Family," in *The Child in Christian Thought*, ed. Marcia J. Bunge (Grand Rapids, MI: Eerdmans, 2001), 66-69.

Martin Luther authored his *Small Catechism* in the 16th century as a tool for Christian instruction in the home, sensing a failure among bishops and priests to teach children in their midst the tenets of the Christian faith.[9] In their place, Luther called parents to the task: "Most certainly father and mother are apostles, bishops, and priests to their children, for it is they who make them acquainted with the gospel."[10]

As a response to the 19th-century revivalist movement, Horace Bushnell published *Christian Nurture* in 1847, a treatise describing the parental role in developing faith through the day-to-day activities of child rearing. Bushnell's thesis, that "the child is to grow up a Christian, and never know himself otherwise," was attainable through parental modeling, nurture, and discipline in the earliest years, dispensing with the need for a dramatic spiritual conversion.[11]

The Second Vatican Council's *Gaudium et Spes* describes parents' responsibility for religious education and modeling the Christian faith among their children.[12] Pope John Paul II frequently used "the domestic church" as a metaphor for family, and the National Conference of Catholic Bishops in 1988 described "the Christian family as the church of the home," a context for worship, evangelism, and service.[13]

Contemporary Models and Practices

Merton Strommen and Richard Hardel developed a conceptual model for youth and family ministry that proposed faith formation as involving all generations and integrated into a congregation's total life and mission. The model is built on the principles of (1) providing faith-focused Christian education, (2) strengthening family relationships, (3) understanding the congregation as family, and (4) creating a Christian youth subculture.[14]

In *Family-Based Youth Ministry*, Mark DeVries described age-segregated youth ministries as counterintuitive, as "there is no such thing as successful youth ministry that isolates teenagers from the community of faith."[15]

DeVries provided numerous suggestions for youth and family ministry programming, many elements traditionally found in congregational youth ministry (such as fellowship activities, Bible study, and service project), but with the added component of parental or church family involvement.[16]

Most youth and family ministry proponents suggest providing parenting classes, family life education, and support groups to assist parents in their role in raising children. Diana Garland proposes such elements within a comprehensive family ministry: (1) developing a congregational life that supports and nurtures all family relationships; (2) organizing and facilitating support groups and networks, to address specific issues in contemporary family life; (3) providing educational programs and resources; and (4) providing counseling services.[17] Adult Christian faith formation is also seen as essential in youth and family ministry.[18]

Despite rhetoric and research emphasizing the parental and familial role in faith formation, a frequent criticism of congregation-based ministry is the extent to which the roles of parents, households, and intergenerational connections are downplayed in faith development of children and youth. Instead, many congregations continue to segregate ministries by age and employ professional staff to provide religious education and youth programming.[19]

References and Resources

Anderson, David W., and Paul Hill. 2003. *Frogs Without Legs Can't Hear: Nurturing Disciples in Home and Congregation.* Minneapolis, MN: Augsburg Fortress Publishers.

Benson, Peter L., and Carolyn H. Eklin. 1990. *Effective Christian Education: A National Study of Protestant Congregations.* Minneapolis, MN: Search Institute.

Bunge, Marcia J., ed. 2001. *The Child in Christian Thought.* Grand Rapids, MI: Eerdmans.

Bushnell, Horace. 1861. *Christian Nurture.* New York: Charles Scribner's Sons.

DeVries, Mark. 2004. *Family-Based Youth Ministry.* 2nd ed. Downers Grove, IL: InterVarsity Press.

Didache, The. 1996. In *Early Christian Fathers,* translated and edited by Cyril C. Richardson, 161–182. New York: Touchstone.

Garland, Diana R. 1999. *Family Ministry: A Comprehensive Guide.* Downers Grove, IL: InterVarsity Press.

Luther, Martin. 1959. "Small Catechism." In *The Book of Concord,* translated and edited by Theodore G. Tappert, 337–356. Philadelphia: Fortress Press.

9. Martin Luther, "Small Catechism," in *The Book of Concord,* trans. and ed. Theodore G. Tappert (Philadelphia: Fortress Press, 1959), 338.

10. Martin Luther, "The Estate of Marriage, 1522," in *Luther's Works,* vol. 45, ed. Walther I. Brandt (Philadelphia: Muhlenberg Press, 1962), 46.

11. Horace Bushnell, *Christian Nurture* (New York: Charles Scribner, 1861), 10.

12. *Gaudium et Spes:* "Pastoral Constitution on the Church in the Modern World," in *Catholic Social Thought: The Documentary Heritage,* ed. David J. O'Brien and Thomas A. Shannon (Maryknoll, NY: Orbis, 1992), 196–197.

13. National Conference of Catholic Bishops Committee on Marriage and Family, *A Family Perspective in Church and Society: A Manual for All Pastoral Leaders* (Washington, DC: National Conference of Catholic Bishops, 1998), 20.

14. Strommen and Hardel, *Passing on the Faith.* The model was built on 30 years of Search Institute research on faith development and practices.

15. Mark DeVries, *Family-Based Youth Ministry,* 2nd ed. (Downers Grove, IL: InterVarsity Press, 2004), 103.

16. Ibid., 197–210.

17. Garland, *Family Ministry,* 378–380.

18. Anderson and Hill, *Frogs without Legs,* 83–95, 171–176.

19. Marjorie J. Thompson, *Family: The Forming Center* (Nashville, TN: Upper Room Books, 1989), 25; Roland D. Martinson, *Effective Youth Ministry: A Congregational Approach* (Minneapolis, MN: Augsburg Publishing House, 1988), 11–12.

——. 1962. "The Estate of Marriage, 1522." In *Luther's Works*, vol. 45, edited by Walther I. Brandt, 76–111. Philadelphia: Muhlenberg Press.

Martinson, Roland D. 1988. *Effective Youth Ministry: A Congregational Approach*. Minneapolis, MN: Augsburg Publishing House.

National Conference of Catholic Bishops Committee on Marriage and Family. 1998. *A Family Perspective in Church and Society: A Manual for All Pastoral Leaders*. Washington, DC: National Conference of Catholic Bishops.

O'Brien, David J., and Thomas A. Shannon. 1992. *Catholic Social Thought: The Documentary Heritage*. Maryknoll, NY: Orbis.

Olson, Richard P., and Joe H. Leonard Jr. 1996. *A New Day for Family Ministry*. Herndon, VA: Alban Institute.

Reed, James E., and Ronnie Prevost. 1993. *A History of Christian Education*. Nashville, TN: Broadman & Holman.

Smith, Christian, and Melinda Lundquist Denton. 2005. *Soul Searching: The Religious and Spiritual Lives of Teenagers*. New York: Oxford University Press.

Stonehouse, Catherine. 1998. *Joining Children on the Spiritual Journey*. Grand Rapids, MI: Baker Books.

Strommen, Merton P., and Richard A. Hardel. 2000. *Passing on the Faith: A Radical New Model for Youth and Family Ministry*. Winona, MN: Saint Mary's Press.

Thompson, Marjorie J. 1989. *Family: The Forming Center*. Nashville, TN: Upper Room Books.

Westerhoff, John H., III. 1980. *Bringing Up Children in the Christian Faith*. Minneapolis, MN: Winston Press.

—MARK J. JACKSON

YOUTH DEVOTIONAL LITERATURE

One way Christians try to cultivate a closer relationship with God is through the use of devotional literature, which is meant to transform the believer into the image of Christ (Dittmore 2010). It seems that devotional literature may have come to fruition as an outgrowth of the Pietist movement (Dittmore 2010), and children's literature of this kind emphasized the need for purity and living a devout Christian life (Donelson and Nilson 2005).

Dittmore (2010) explains that there is no established genre of writing for devotional literature to set the tone for the thousands of titles that exist for our worship, devotion, and prayerful contemplation of living out God's Word in our daily lives. Written with young children in mind, youth devotional literature dates back to the 18th century. This work includes William Mason's *Spiritual Treasury for the Children of God* (Mason 1800), which offered to children a collection of devotions for each day of the year. These were set in motion with Mason's introductory prayer to God's children:

May the Lord the Spirit witness to thy heart of Jesus whilst thou art reading them, and render them the means of glorifying Him in thy life and conversation, that thou mayest learn from every page to trust him more, to hope more in him, and to love Him more who is thy all; and if thou livest upon him *in all,* he will be thy heaven upon earth, and thy heaven of heavens in eternal glory. (Mason 1800, 5)

It seems, however, that youth devotional literature developed from the devotional hymnals and collections of prose written specifically for children. One pioneer of this kind of literature was the poet Anna Aikins-Barbauld. Raised in the Presbyterian Church, Anna Aikins-Barbauld was most known for her poetry and writings on social and political concerns (see Ockerbloom 1994). Author of many school texts for children, her 1797 children's book was her only documented publication of this kind. A collection of devotional prose and songs for children, this work was entitled *Hymns in Prose for Children* and was well-received in its time (see Ockerbloom 1994). In the preface of the book, Barbauld (1797) shared her reasons for penning a hymnal of prose, as well as why she was called to do so: "[T]he peculiar design of this publication is to impress devotional feelings as early as possible, on the infant mind . . . and that a child, to feel the full force of the idea of God, ought never to remember the time when he had no such idea" (A2–A3). Barbauld (1797) also credited Isaac Watts and his early 1700 children's hymnal for influencing her work. The son of a preacher, Watts sought to teach God's word in what he viewed as a more far-reaching and memorable way, through song (Hutcheson n.d.). It is important to note that Watts contributed much more to children than just songs of worship and praise to our Lord, and he later published prayer books for children; one well-known work is *A Plain and Easy Catechism for Children, 1811*.

Today's devotional literature for young people represents a range of genres and is written for a range of ages. Its primary purpose continues to be to instill values into our children, as well as to nurture their Christian behaviors (Peyton 1998). Presented through a myriad of media—picture books, trade books, and more recently as e-books, e-subscriptions, blogs, and through both android and iPad apps—these works focus on teaching our youth how to put their faith into practice through both word and example. Today's youth devotional literature also seems to be published for different age ranges: emerging (birth to age five), primary (ages five to nine), and young adult (age 10 and older). A well-known hardcover compilation of youth devotional literature is the *International Companion of Children's Literature*, published by Routledge Limited in 2004. The following are other modern works:

Sara Young's *Jesus Calling: 365 Devotions for Kids* (Nashville, TN: Tommy Nelson, Inc., 2010)

Malcolm Cox's *An Elephant's Swimming Pool* (DPI Books, 2007)

Lois Sink's *Cat in the Pulpit* (Xulon Press, 2003)

Jim Burns' *Addicted to God: 50 Days to a More Powerful Relationship with God* (Regal Books, 2007)

Jim Burns's *One Life: 50 Powerful Devotions for Students* (Regal Books, 2011)

Robert Ellsberg's *Blessed Among All Women* (Crossroad Publishers, 2007)

Magazine and digital works include the following:

Dave Strehler's *Devotions from the Bible*, http://www.truthforkids.com/kids-devotions-online/

M. S. Lowdnes's *Heaven's Inspirations*, http://childrensministry.com/bible-activities/devotions

Children's Ministry Magazine, Group Publishing, available online and through the app store.

Classic works include the following:

Isaac Watt's *Divine and Moral Songs for Children* (William Butler, 1805)

Isaac Watt's *Divine Songs for Children* (A. M. Maltby & Co., 1715)

W. Mason's *Spiritual Treasury for the Children of God: Consisting of a Meditation for Each Day in the Year* (American Tract Society, 1800)

Anna Aikin Barbauld's *Hymns in Prose for Children* (W. Spotswood, 1797)

S. Ashton-Goodrich's *Sabbath Talks with Little Children, on the Psalms of David* (J. E. Tilton, 1860)

References and Resources

Barbauld, A. 1797. *Children's Book Collection: Hymns in Prose for Children*. Boston, MA: W. Spotswood.

Dittmore, M. 2010. "Devotional Literature." In *The Encyclopedia of Christian Literature*. Vol. 1, edited by George Thomas Kurian and James D. Smith III, 57–60. Lanham, MD: Scarecrow Press.

Donelson, K., and A. P. Nisen. 2005. *Literature for Today's Young Adults*. 7th ed. Boston: Pearson Education.

Hutcheson, S. n.d. "Biography of Isaac Watts." In *Eclectic Ethereal Encyclopedia*. Grand Rapids, MI: Christian Classics Ethereal Library. http://www.ccel.org/browse/authorInfo?id=watts.

Mason, W. 1800. *A Spiritual Treasury for the Children of God: Consisting of a Meditation for Each Day in the Year, upon Select Texts of Scripture*. New York: American Tract Society.

Ockerbloom, M. M. 1994. *A Celebration of Women Writers: Anna Laetitia Aikin Barbauld (1743–1825)*. Philadelphia: University of Pennsylvania. http://digital.library.upenn.edu/women/barbauld/biography.html.

Peyton, M. A. 1998. "A List of Picture Books to Promote Religious Understanding." *Early Childhood Education Journal* 35: 387–389.

—DIANA D. ABBOTT

YOUTH MINISTERS

Youth ministry (and therefore, the role of youth minister/director) is a relatively recent ministry emphasis within the church and its desire to reach the world with the Gospel. As such, it often operates in a fluidity of roles and practices. This is often due to a lack of thinking theologically about the role, tending instead to focus on the skills desired in such a person or the tasks he or she should be doing as opposed to the rationale for such a role. For the purpose of this article, a youth minister/director is one called of God to minister to the lives of adolescents (and for many, the families of adolescents), both within and outside the church, in order to help the adolescent experience the saving power of Christ and consequently be transformed by God's redeeming power to become mature in a holy lifestyle and engage the church and world in ministry and service.

Rationale for the Youth Minister/Director

Biblical

While the role of the youth minister/director is not directly listed in scripture, one can look at the biblical story and see that there is a clear trajectory in which the narrative is fully aware of the importance of ministering to children (which included what we would term adolescents). In addition, there seems to be a clear focus on the importance of one's youth, recognizing the many critical decisions that are made during that time.

Some might argue that because the title of youth minister/director is not included in the various lists (e.g., apostles, prophets, evangelists, pastors, teachers, elder, deacon, etc.), it should not then be a legitimate role today. However, it is apparent that God did not list by name every single ministry in which the church was to participate. Rather, as Vukich and Vandegriff note:

> When specific and unique needs arose, men called of God would attempt to meet those needs. Just as God raises up individuals to specific tasks at certain periods of time, so also He raises individuals to minister to specific age groups. The youth pastor specializes in ministering to adolescents. His flock is the adolescents in the local congregation. As their pastor, the youth minister has the same responsibility of day-to-day building up of the ado-

lescent flock and their spiritual protection. . . .The youth minister's calling is equal to and just as important as the calling to be the senior pastor of a church.[20]

Historical

The development of youth ministry and the factors that made it necessary are dealt with in another article (*see* Youth Ministry). That development led to the need for more and better trained adults who could now minister effectively to this new and growing age group called adolescence. As mentioned previously, the role of youth minister/director is a relatively recent phenomenon within the church, because age-level specialization within the church is also relatively recent. For much of the early life of youth ministry, it was volunteer led. In fact, Francis E. Clark, the founder and first president of Christian Endeavor (one of the earliest groups to really focus on youth ministry), believed so strongly in the importance of volunteers running Christian Endeavor as the best way to reach the youth of his day that he made it a condition of his employment as president of the organization.[21]

There have been some who were modestly paid to work with adolescents in a spiritual context, including YMCA/YWCA workers and some denominational directors (both nationally and regionally), and there is at least one recorded episode of a Baptist church in St. Louis, Missouri, that in 1937 hired what is believed to be the first youth director in the Southern Baptist denomination.[22] However, until the rise of Young Life and Youth for Christ, most churches did not have a youth minister/director. Even then, it wasn't until the 1980s that local church youth pastors/directors become commonplace in the United States. Today most churches in the Western world recognize the importance of these people in helping adolescents within the church develop into lifelong Christians. In fact, the youth pastor/director is quite often the first staff position hired in a local church, as more pastors recognize the importance of ministering to this age group. And this is not solely limited to the Western world, as churches in many different areas of the world (including Central America, South America, Africa, Asia, and Australia) are now hiring professionals to work with the adolescents of their congregations.

Practical

The world is becoming increasingly complex. The adolescents in our midst deal with far more critical issues today than perhaps at any time in history. They also are dealing with the premise of lengthened adolescence, which suggests that adolescence today actually runs from approximately age ten to the mid- to late twenties. According to Erik Erickson, identity formation is still the major task of adolescence (even in lengthened adolescence). Recent research indicates that the adolescents of today have adopted a faith that would be charitably described as "moralistic, therapeutic deism,"[23] and that the majority of teenagers and young adults are leaving the church in droves.[24] Given these issues, it only makes sense that the church would begin to recognize the necessity for those trained specifically to minister to this particular age group.

Primary Roles

There are many different titles used by those who assume this role: youth minister, youth pastor, minister of youth and their families, youth director, director of student ministries, and so forth. While each title may indicate certain emphases, in general, the person taking on one of these titles assumes many different roles in ministry to adolescents. Following are three of the most important roles:

- Pastor/priest: There is a need to see oneself first and foremost as a minister. The flock is the adolescents in the local congregation. Jesus called pastors to "feed my sheep" (John 20). Therefore, we are called to mediate the presence of God to the congregation. This includes things like faithful proclamation of the Gospel (Luke 10) to both the converted and the unconverted, the administration of the sacraments, and faithful pastoral care. As one called to be a minister, the youth minister/director should see his or her position as being one called of God to a particular group and recognize that it is just as important as that of any other staff member, including the senior pastor. This includes an educational component focused on the nurturing of adolescents as they grow in faith and maturity and engage the world around them.
- Prophet: Recognizing that we live in a sinful culture, the youth pastor/director has to be willing to both name sin as well as offer an alternative reality and invite others to that new reality. Micah 6:8 reminds us that we should act justly, love tenderly, and walk humbly with God. As those who potentially have

20. Lee Vukich and Steve Vandegriff, *Timeless Youth Ministry* (Chicago: Moody Press, 2002), 234–235.

21. Mark H. Senter, *When God Shows Up: A History of Protestant Youth Ministry in America* (Grand Rapids, MI: Baker Academic, 2010), 292.

22. Richard Ross, *The Work of the Minister of Youth*, rev. ed. (Nashville, TN: Convention Press, 1989), 11.

23. Christian Smith and Melinda Lundquist Denton, *Soul Searching: The Religious and Spiritual Lives of American Teenagers* (Oxford: Oxford University Press, 2005), 162–170.

24. David Kinnaman, *You Lost Me: Why Young Christians Are Leaving the Church . . . and Rethinking Faith* (Grand Rapids, MI: Baker, 2011).

tremendous influence on the lives of the adolescents to whom we minister, we can speak into their lives in powerful ways as we point them toward the Kingdom of God. This includes a missiology that is focused squarely on contextualizing the Gospel so that adolescents can hear and appropriate it.

- Theologian-in-Residence: It is important to recognize that all of life is a theological endeavor, and therefore every decision that is made needs to have a theological basis. Our ministries reflect our theological thinking, and therefore we need to ensure that we know what we believe, as well as how those beliefs work themselves out in our ministries. This includes the necessity of the youth worker operating from a practical theology that enables her or him to bring together the biblical, theological, and social worlds to best minister to the adolescent. It also speaks to the importance of having theological education to prepare one for this role.

While the role of the youth minister/director may be a newer addition to the ministerial roles the church endorses, it is not any less important. In fact, given the issues raised earlier in this article, if the church did not seek ways to minister specifically to adolescents, not only would the church potentially lose the next generation, it would also lose the vitality and passion that adolescents bring to the church. Therefore, the role of youth minister/director is a vital one as the church moves forward into the 21st century and beyond.

References and Resources

Dettoni, John M. 1993. *Introduction to Youth Ministry.* Grand Rapids, MI: Zondervan (see especially chapter 3).

Lamport, Mark A. 1997. "What Is the Status of the Professional Youth Worker?" In *Reaching a Generation for Christ,* edited by Richard R. Dunn and Mark H. Senter, 239–260. Chicago: Moody Press.

Nash, Sally, ed. 2011. *Youth Ministry: A Multi-Faceted Approach.* London: SPCK.

Senter, Mark H. 2010. *When God Shows Up: A History of Protestant Youth Ministry in America.* Grand Rapids, MI: Baker Academic.

—James K. Hampton

Youth Ministry

A confluence of sociological and physiological factors sparked into existence the phase of life known as "adolescence." As the need for further education delayed marriage and independence and the onset of puberty arrived earlier, youth, as a distinct age category, evolved beginning in the 1800s and gathered steam as high schools, media, and specific marketing created a sharp divide between adolescence and both childhood and adulthood. Over time, as the church was somewhat slow to embrace innovative means of attracting and retaining youth within its fold, parachurch organizations stepped in to introduce a slew of new ideas. The attention focused on youth ministry over the last two generations, particularly in Western societies and most prominently in the United States, has seen unprecedented expansion.[25]

The Evolution of Youth Ministry

Youth ministry, then, is the church's attempt to socialize adolescents into the faith community through culturally relevant measures of Christian teaching and worship. The church's relationship with youth ministry has evolved over the last 50 years and can be observed in four phases:

- A *socialization* model, in which youth are associated with children and adults of the faith community and are seamlessly incorporated into the life of the church. This was the case for the entire history of the church until the mid-20th century.
- A *segmented* model, in which youth within a local church are grouped with other youth for programs, largely fragmented from other age groups.
- A *parachurch* model, which operates outside the purview of the local church (and frequently without collaboration) and gears its programs solely for the youth market.
- A *homogenous* model, which seeks to create fully functioning, self-contained churches exclusively for youth outside the traditional blending with children and adults.

Most of youth ministry is composed of what is described in the second and third models above, while the fourth model is unique, for example, to the United Kingdom, and the first model continues in small churches and some worldwide cultures that continue to embrace a narrow socialization stance.

The Goal of Youth Ministry

Simply put, youth ministry is the purposive quest by both natural and supernatural means to share with adolescents God's message of good news, which is central to the Christian faith. Its ultimate end is to cultivate a life transformation of youth by the power of the Holy Spirit, that they might be conformed to the revealed will

---

25. The sheer number of youth ministry professionals, resources, conferences, and camps verifies this phenomenon.

of God as expressed in scripture. Those from liturgical traditions use the term "youth catechesis" and define it as the process by which persons become incorporated into the community of believers. The goal of youth ministry, then, is to enable youth to respond to God in a community of love and acceptance, and to grow as individuals so they minister to one another, the larger church, and society.

With this in mind, several characteristics should give direction to effective youth ministry practice: The guiding universal principles for constructing such a ministry to, with, and for adolescents that nurtures this effectual calling toward God must consider these driving considerations: first, that youth ministry must be Gospel-centered, speaking truth in a cultural sea of shifting truths; second, that it must be culturally sensitive, faithfully and creatively communicating this Gospel in appropriate and contemporary vehicles; third, that youth ministry must be relationship-oriented, embodying the reconciliation demonstrated by God through Jesus; fourth, that it must be intentionally driven in its purpose and vision and not a slave to trends and programmatic drift; fifth, that youth ministry must be supernaturally guided, conscious that what it attempts is God's work and we lesser participants of this offering; sixth, that it must be developmentally aware, dedicated to be competent in not only speaking biblical truth and having appropriate facility in cultural awareness, but also to be students of research on adolescence; and seventh, that youth ministry must be team focused, careful to involve a coterie of adult mentors who possess various personalities, skill sets, and interests in order to more effectively relate to the diversity represented by a range of adolescents.

A Rationale for Youth Ministry

Some argue that the role of modern youth ministry should be reconsidered because it minimizes, even usurps, parental responsibility for faith formation of offspring. These proponents, and with some cogent reasoning, push for the first model above and prefer that children, youth, and adults intimately participate in worship, service, and mission together, and not be segmented into age groups.

Others propose several reasons why youth ministry, as described by the last three models above, is vital to the health of the church. First, never before have youth been more distinct from children or adults. Due to youth's unique needs, a specialized ministry is more effective in attracting and retaining this sizable contingent of God's people. Second, adolescents are ardently interested in spirituality. Unfortunately, even though religious belief is high, spiritual commitment is low. Ecclesiastes 12:1 charges us "to remember your Creator in the days of your youth." Some research indicates that three of five

people who become Christian do so before the age of 18.[26] Third, youth ministry can be invaluable in providing aid to parents in the spiritual nurture of their own teenagers. The best scenario is to engender communication between parents and youth. When churched youth were asked, "Do your parents ever sit down to discuss Bible, God or religious things with you?," 43 percent said never, yet two-thirds of these same parents said they would like to help their child grow spiritually.[27] Christian parents want (and need) help. Fourth, under the auspices of youth ministry, teenagers can be enabled to discover their spiritual gifts and the potential they possess to contribute to the church. Youth can be empowered to minister to their peers. The residual effect is self-discovery and a safe place where youth may develop a healthy self-esteem. Fifth, not only do youth need the church, but the church needs youth. Whereas adults bring wisdom and perspective and stability, youth bring energy and creativity and passion.

The Challenge of Youth Ministry

As adolescents seek to discover ways of making meaning in their lives, loud noises have sometimes prevented the Gospel from being heard and the Christian education of youth from being as powerful as it could. Three trends from postmodernity have effects on doing youth ministry today.[28]

First, until the advent of modernity, religious traditions provided the categories by which people constructed life's meaning and purpose. Typically, these categories played an integrative function in society, binding groups together with a shared vision and worldview. Religion no longer plays this integrative function. No overall system of moral meaning unites a defiantly pluralistic society. The overall effect is to relativize the values of the groups that carry out the individual's primary socialization.

Second, generational discontinuity is prevalent; that is to say, today there seems to be a diminished role of adults (teachers, parents, religious leaders) as moral exemplars for the younger generations. Today's generation tends to "think from scratch," unlike in past eras, which fed from the accumulated wells of wisdom. In some quarters, there has even been role-reversal, with the older looking to the younger for guidance.

Third, the revered status of science and technology in our society has in some measure conditioned youth to feel great dissonance with the supernatural dimensions

26. Mark A. Lamport, "Adolescent Spirituality: Age of Conversion and Factors of Development," *Christian Education Journal* (Spring 1990): 17–30.

27. Merton Strommen and Ram Gupta, *Five Cries of Youth: Issues that Trouble Young People Today*, rev. ed. (San Francisco: HarperCollins, 1993).

28. Some of these are adapted from Richard Osmer, *Confirmation: Presbyterian Practices in Ecumenical Perspective* (Louisville, KY: Geneva Press, 1996).

of the Christian faith. Some perceive it to be inferior or unreal compared to the verifiable boasts of hard science.

The Practice of Youth Ministry

Today's youth have been characterized as alienated, angry, depressed, despairing of hope, dark, lacking in civility, and unwilling (or perhaps unable) to readily admit to absolute truth. This generation looks through social and emotional lenses rather than intellectual lenses. The spirituality of this generation is transrational; they are looking for concrete expression.

Adolescents need an embodied apologetic, a flesh-and-blood, living and breathing argument for God. Christian adults who seek to reach youth are vital agents of transmitting faith. Hear the poetic elocution in which Michael Warren expresses this truth: "Faith can be elaborated, explained, and systematized in books, but it shouts, it dances, it lives and takes flesh in people."[29] Effective youth ministry can serve as an effective means for the church to bring its progeny into a sustained relationship with God and the church.

The practices of youth ministry, of course, must persistently point to nurturing faith and educating emerging members into the ongoing story of the Christian faith. In addition to the significance of *relationships*, primarily with parents, peers, and other significant adults, the *responsibilities* given adolescents to experience faith in community are also highly instructive to spiritual formation. Such responsibilities may include peer ministry (by teaching and serving other youth), service projects (in expressing care to those in need of justice or compassion), and cross-cultural experiences (a window beyond one's own culture to gain insight into how God works). Then, when exercises that call for *reflection* are introduced, further faith-stretching often eventuates in spiritual insight. When adolescents experience doubt (serious wrestling with faith and life), small group participation (a safe and dialogical context for truth-testing), and prayer (in earnest pleading with God for life direction, faith experiences, and world difficulty), the most critical factors for being educated in faith are at hand.

References and Resources

Browning, Donald. 2006. *American Religions and the Family: How Faith Traditions Cope with Modernization and Democracy.* New York: Columbia University Press.

Lamport, Mark A. 1996. "What Is Youth Ministry?" *Christian Education Journal* (Spring): 61–70.

Pahl, Jon. 2000. *Youth Ministry in Modern America: 1930–the Present.* Peabody, MA: Hendrickson Publishers.

Smith, Christian. 2005. *Soul Searching: The Religious and Spiritual Lives of American Teenagers.* New York: Oxford University Press.

Ward, Pete. 1999. *God at the Mall: Youth Ministry That Meets Kids Where They're At.* Peabody, MA: Hendrickson Publishers.

—Mark A. Lamport

Youth Ministry, Paul and

The apostle Paul is a key figure in the New Testament. Many of the Epistles were written by him, others were written in his name, and he is one of the subjects of the book of Acts. As long as there has been youth ministry, there have been youth ministry curricula that make use of Paul's passionate and poignant words concerning topics of interest to Christians such as grace, judgment, justification, works, sin, and love. Traditionally, Paul has been used in youth ministry in several ways, including to encourage good behavior; to explain the role of Christ's death in salvation; and to use images from Paul, such as the Body of Christ (1 Cor. 12) to teach youth about their role in the church. Paul also offers a significant and unique contribution to youth ministry in the strength of his worldview as a theological resource for helping youth understand the challenges and joys of their lives. This is a new frontier for the use of Paul in ministry with young people.

Traditional Uses of Paul in Youth Ministry

A survey of youth ministry curricula will show that Paul is often used to share with young people that Christians are expected to behave well. Many youth ministries have as one of their goals, usually along with Christian formation and acceptance of church or denominational doctrine, to help youth make decisions for sobriety, sexual abstinence, and kindness. In Paul's letter to the Galatians, for example, he writes of the fruits of the Spirit and the works of the flesh in a way that is easily translated to a list of dos and don'ts for Christian teenagers.

Paul has also been used in youth ministry to explain the role of Jesus's death in salvation. In traditional uses of Paul in youth ministry, humanity is interpreted as responsible for the presence of both sin and death, and forgiveness of human sins is contingent on acceptance of Christ's death for those sins. This theology places human agency in competition with divine agency, understands sin as only human action, sees Christ's death as substitutionary atonement, and views redemption as contingent on human decision.

The Body of Christ image in 1 Corinthians 12 is a description of Paul's hope for the community of believers in Corinth as Paul responds to reports of division. Youth

---

29. *Youth and the Future of the Church* (Minneapolis, MN: Seabury Press, 1990), 20.

ministry's target age group usually incorporates ages 12 to 18, and often includes education in the form of confirmation classes. Therefore, the Body of Christ is an image from within the Pauline corpus that is often used to help young people learn about and take responsibility for their role in the larger church.

New Possibilities with Paul

When Paul's worldview is taken into account, his writing can offer much more to youth ministry. Importantly, using Paul in this new way will help to complicate the ways that Christ's salvific actions have been taught to youth traditionally and to offer a new reading that is more helpful to those in this life stage. Paul writes vibrantly about the time in which he finds himself. Paul understood that the current time and space had been invaded by Jesus Christ, and that on the cross at crucifixion, Christ conquered the powers of sin and death. The language Paul uses to describe his reality of this time invaded and changed by Christ's crucifixion can be used in ministry with youth in ways that speak directly to their lived experience.

When Paul's theology is seen as a resource for helping youth think theologically about their own lives, the result can be both empowering and liberating for them. Scholars of youth ministry Kenda Creasy Dean and Andrew Root have written about the "theological turn in youth ministry."[30] They argue that church youth workers are looking for "something solid and deep on which to stand with young people, a way to move beyond the consumer habits and entertainment focus that too often consume youth ministry."[31] Reading Paul, while taking his worldview as primary and while taking seriously his theological anthropology, is consistent with the turn the field of youth ministry is making toward helping youth interpret their lives in light of the action of God.

Paul's worldview includes several specific elements: a concept of two aeons, the embattled sovereignty of God, cosmological language, an emphasis on suffering, and certainty of divine judgment of the present time. In terms of anthropology, Paul sees humanity as always under the influence of one power or another. New Testament scholar Ernst Käsemann explained it this way:

> Man for Paul is never just on his own. He is always a specific piece of world and therefore becomes what in the last resort he is by determination from outside, i.e. by the power which takes possession of him and the lordship to which he surrenders himself. His life is from the beginning a stake in the confrontation between God and

the principalities of this world. In other words, it mirrors the cosmic contention for the lordship of the world and is its concretion.[32]

The human agent is never autonomous, but rather under the power of sin and death or under the power of Christ. In Christ, the human agent is free; under sin, the human agent is captive. When in Christ, sin no longer has power over the human, and therefore the human can be expected to act in ways consistent with the fruits of the Spirit as expressed in Galatians 5. This free way of acting and being in the world is sustained by and possible through the community of fellow Christians. Actions, then, become not the basis for judgment, but the sign of freedom in Christ or captivity to sin. For youth ministry, this worldview offers an important connection to the lives of teenagers.

Youth experience pressures for success in school, social acceptance, and identity formation. Developmentally, they are differentiating themselves from their families of origin.[33] The marketing industry has targeted teenagers since the mid-20th century as a population with expendable income and the possibility of becoming lifelong consumers of products.[34] These realities, along with systemic oppressions (e.g., racism, sexism, classism, and hereterosexism), help youth to feel that they are living in a contested time. Youth may even feel as if their schools, homes, and neighborhoods are battle zones between their own desire for autonomy and individuality and these social, environmental, and familial pressures. Their social and developmental liminality adds to their feeling of powerlessness while people and forces with much more power are determining their current and future lives.

Examining the experiences of teenagers as the context for doing theology with them, Paul is an obvious and powerful biblical correlation. Helping youth interpret the oppressive systems and pressures of school, family, and society as part of the cosmic landscape, Paul reveals in his writing, can be a main task of youth ministry at this theological turn. Pressures of social acceptance, whether in the form of cliques or gangs, become part of the way the power of sin operates in this time between the advent of Christ and his return at the eschaton. Systemic oppressions hold society and the youth within it captive, as part of sin's action. The freedom Christ offers is not contingent upon acceptance of religious creeds by teenagers, but is rather the result of Christ's action on the cross,

---

30. Andrew Root and Kenda Creasy Dean, *The Theological Turn in Youth Ministry* (Downers Grove, IL: IVP Books, 2011), 16.

31. Ibid.

32. Ernst Käsemann, *New Testament Questions of Today* (Philadelphia: Fortress Press, 1969), 136.

33. James W. Fowler, *Stages of Faith: The Psychology of Human Development and the Quest for Meaning* (New York: HarperSanFrancisco, 1981), ch. 10.

34. Grace Palladino, *Teenagers: An American History* (New York: Basic-Books, 1996), ch. 7.

regardless of the human response to it. Human response, Paul's worldview, and its resulting anthropology offer youth a much more powerful way to interpret their lives theologically than how Paul has been used traditionally.

References and Resources

Eastman, Susan. 2007. *Recovering Paul's Mother Tongue: Language and Theology in Galatians*. Grand Rapids, MI: Eerdmans.

Fowler, James W. 1981. *Stages of Faith: The Psychology of Human Development and the Quest for Meaning*. New York: HarperSanFrancisco.

Gaventa, Beverly Roberts. 2007. *Our Mother Saint Paul*. Louisville, KY: Westminster John Knox Press.

Käsemann, Ernst. 1969. *New Testament Questions of Today*. Philadelphia: Fortress Press.

———. 1971. *Perspectives on Paul*. Philadelphia: Fortress Press.

Martyn, J. Louis. 1997. *Theological Issues in the Letters of Paul*. Nashville, TN: Abingdon Press.

Palladino, Grace. 1996. *Teenagers: An American History*. New York: Basic Books.

Root, Andrew, and Kenda Creasy Dean. 2011. *The Theological Turn in Youth Ministry*. Downers Grove, IL: IVP Books.

—EMILY A. PECK-MCCLAIN

YOUTH PROGRAMS, DENOMINATIONAL

Early Influences

Public High Schools and Adolescence
The rise of mainline Protestant youth organizations coincides with the American high school's increasing prevalence in the late 19th century. A combination of forces, including compulsory children's education, restrictions on childhood labor, an increase in the marriage age, and public funding of schools, led to greater numbers of children attending high school before assuming adult roles. The dramatic shift fostered the emergence of adolescence as a distinct post-child, pre-adult life stage, a social phenomenon first described in 1904.[35]

Society of Christian Endeavor

Local churches turned their attention toward teen spirituality as the number of adolescents in their midst escalated. Concerned about youth beyond an initial conversion experience, Rev. Dr. Francis Clark sought to reshape the church's functions of education, worship, stewardship, fellowship, and service into the language

of youth. Central to Clark's design was accountability, with participants pledging a commitment to Christian living. Finding immediate success, he founded the Young People's Society of Christian Endeavor in 1881, widely regarded as the first church-based ministry to "teenagers." The movement quickly spread, with 22,000 societies involving over a million youths by 1892.[36]

Emergence of Denominational Youth Programs

While Christian Endeavor emphasized spiritual growth, concerns emerged over a church's ability to promote denominational loyalty, ensure distinctions in belief and practice, and retain youth as members and future leaders.[37] Some saw a pledge or form of accountability as too strict a prerequisite for participation.[38] Many churches therefore created their own youth programs, often adapting Christian Endeavor's model.

The First Youth Auxiliaries

Most national youth programs developed as mergers of existing local and regional societies, as Mark Senter describes regarding the formation of the Baptist Young People's Union:

> The first stage was the spontaneous efforts of local churches to meet the needs of their youth. . . . The second stage began when manuals were developed in order to spread the ideas across a state or throughout the nation. . . . The third stage happened when the grassroots and regional ideas were formalized into a national program.[39]

The Epworth League was among the first major denominational youth organizations, created as a merger of five Methodist youth societies in 1889.[40] The Baptist Young People's Union followed in 1891, though a local group of the same name dates to 1884. Originally designed for those age 17 and older, the union was formed to "secure the increased spirituality of the Baptist young people," including "instruction in Baptist doctrine and history," a response to Christian Endeavor's failure to connect youth with the church.[41] The Walther League likewise formed in 1893 to "keep the young people with the Church of true Lutheran believers," gathering a

---

35. See G. Stanley Hall, *Adolescence: Its Psychology and Its Relations to Physiology, Anthropology, Sociology, Sex, Crime, Religion, and Education* (London: Appleton and Company, 1904).

36. Mark H. Senter III, *When God Shows Up: A History of Protestant Youth Ministry in America* (Grand Rapids, MI: Baker Academic, 2010), 159.

37. Mark H. Senter III, *The Coming Revolution in Youth Ministry* (Wheaton, IL: Victor Books, 1992), 102.

38. Senter, *When God Shows Up*, 62; Senter, *The Coming Revolution*, 101.

39. Senter, *The Coming Revolution*, 101.

40. Ibid., 100.

41. Strommen, "Recent Invention," 29; Clarence Peters, "Developments of the Youth Programs of the Lutheran Churches in America" (ThD thesis, Concordia Theological Seminary, 1951), 33.

dozen disparate societies mostly related to the Lutheran Church-Missouri Synod (some dating to the 1850s).[42]

Other denominational organizations emerged throughout the 1890s, including Westminster League (Presbyterian General Assembly, 1891), Young People's Christian Union (United Brethren, 1894), Young People's Christian Union (United Presbyterian Church, 1895), Keystone League (United Evangelical Church in America, 1895), and Luther League of America (multiple Lutheran synods, 1895).[43]

Programmatic Emphases

Local societies generally gathered participants on a frequent (if not weekly) basis for Bible study, leadership training, and social interaction. Leagues were often divided into age-specific groups to encourage peer support. The Epworth League, for example, was separated into juniors (ages 10–12), intermediates (13–17), and a senior league (18–34).[44] Local, domestic, and international missions emerged as early emphases, with the desire to engage youth in service activities.[45] Ambitious philanthropic projects (both domestic and global) were common, such as Walther League's construction of a sanitarium for young Lutherans with tuberculosis.[46] After the turn of the century, many auxiliaries sponsored summer Bible camp programs.

Local societies were generally led by young adults. The national organizations were initially volunteer led, often by seminarians or young pastors; paid national directors weren't common until the 1920s. Nearly all organizations produced resources to support local societies, including manuals for starting groups and training leaders; curricular guides, including outlines for Bible studies or fellowship gatherings; periodicals (the primary means of mass communication); and songbooks. National conventions, usually held every one to three years, gathered participants for theme-driven spiritual enrichment and social connection. Delegates conducted the organization's business, including election of national officers. District-level conventions were also common.

Youth Fellowships

Adolescent spirituality began to wane in the 1930s as Christian beliefs were increasingly challenged and the public high school continued to grow as the center of community life.[47] Many denominations responded by eliminating or restructuring youth auxiliaries in favor of creating "youth fellowships."[48] Examples include the Baptist Training Union (Southern Baptist, 1934), Pilgrim Fellowship (Congregational Christian, 1936), Methodist Youth Fellowship (1939), Baptist Youth Fellowship (American Baptist, 1941), Westminster Fellowship (Presbyterian, 1943), and Reformed Church Fellowship (1946).[49]

Local churches increasingly provided youth programming related to Christian education, discipleship, service, mission, stewardship, and worship. Programmatic support was largely delegated to denominational offices, which employed regional and national staff to produce curricular resources, provide leadership training, run summer programs, organize conventions, and provide for continuity in organizational leadership.[50]

Demise of Denominational Youth Programs

Two factors contributed to the decline of national youth programs beginning in the 1940s. First, the increasing pluralization of American society and the public high school's prominence as a social hub provided for a diversity of extracurricular activities and entertainment that competed for teens' time and attention.[51] Second, the relationship-based parachurch youth organizations that emerged after World War II (e.g., Young Life, Youth for Christ) were highly attractive, if not more relevant, to youth.

Responding to these challenges, most Protestant denominations in the 1960s and 1970s dismantled their youth ministry departments. In their place, local congregations were expected to assume responsibility for youth ministry programs and integrate youth into the whole of congregational life. The move, expected to increase retention, largely lacked trained staff and the resources necessary to sustain youth ministry at the local level.[52] As a result, most churches created relationship-based programs that imitated parachurch club models, led by lay youth workers with little training.

42. Cited in Gerald Jenny, *The Young People's Movement in the American Lutheran Church* (Minneapolis, MN: Augsburg Publishing House, 1928), 22; Jon Pahl, *Youth Ministry in Modern America, 1930 to the Present* (Peabody, MA: Hendrickson Publishers, 2000), 19.

43. Senter, *When God Shows Up*, 170.

44. Senter, *Coming Revolution*, 100.

45. Ibid.

46. Pahl, *Youth Ministry*, 30.

47. Senter describes the Scopes monkey trial as a "crisis point" for the Christian faith; see Senter, *When God Shows Up*, 186–187.

48. Not all denominations followed this trend; for example, Walther League and Luther League of America continued as youth auxiliaries, though they added paid national staff.

49. While this article concerns mainline Protestant bodies, it should be noted that in 1937 the National Catholic Welfare Conference initiated steps to form a National Council on Catholic Youth, and a youth department was established in 1940.

50. Strommen, "A Recent Invention," 30.

51. Andrew Root, *Revisiting Relational Youth Ministry: From a Strategy of Influence to a Theology of Incarnation* (Downers Grove, IL: IVP Books, 2007), 34–35, 39.

52. Thomas E. Bergler, "The Place of History in Youth Ministry Education," *Journal of Youth Ministry* 1, no. 1 (2002): 58.

It wasn't until the 1970s that youth ministry education and resource providers were widely available to support struggling programs and leaders; however, by this time congregations had lost significant numbers of youth, a phenomenon since labeled "an ecclesial crisis."[53] While many denominations retain offices for youth ministry or Christian education, most are led by a small staff and are limited in their ability to influence congregation-level youth ministry.

References and Resources

Bergler, Thomas E. 2002. "The Place of History in Youth Ministry Education." *Journal of Youth Ministry* 1 (1): 57–71.

———. 2012. *The Juvenilization of American Christianity.* Grand Rapids, MI: Eerdmans.

Dean, Kenda Creasy. 2004. *Practicing Passion: Youth and the Quest for a Passionate Church.* Grand Rapids, MI: Eerdmans.

Hall, G. Stanley. 1904. *Adolescence: Its Psychology and Its Relations to Physiology, Anthropology, Sociology, Sex, Crime, Religion, and Education.* London: Appleton and Company.

Jenny, Gerald. 1928. *The Young People's Movement in the American Lutheran Church.* Minneapolis, MN: Augsburg.

Kett, Joseph F. 1977. *Rites of Passage: Adolescence in America, 1790 to the Present.* New York: Basic Books.

Pahl, Jon. 2000. *Youth Ministry in Modern America, 1930 to the Present.* Peabody, MA: Hendrickson.

Peters, Clarence. 1951. "Developments of the Youth Programs of the Lutheran Churches in America." ThD thesis, Concordia Theological Seminary.

Root, Andrew. 2007. *Revisiting Relational Youth Ministry: From a Strategy of Influence to a Theology of Incarnation.* Downers Grove, IL: IVP Books.

Senter, Mark H., III. 1992. *The Coming Revolution in Youth Ministry.* Wheaton, IL: Victor Books.

———. 2010. *When God Shows Up: A History of Protestant Youth Ministry in America.* Grand Rapids, MI: Baker Academic.

—MARK J. JACKSON

---

53. Kenda Creasy Dean, *Practicing Passion: Youth and the Quest for a Passionate Church* (Grand Rapids, MI: Eerdmans, 2004), 7.

Z

ZAMBIA AND CHRISTIAN EDUCATION

In 1991, the president of Zambia declared his country to be a Christian nation, reflecting that over 90 percent of the population calls itself Christian. The education system of the country has largely grown out of Christian schools, now run by the government. Religious education continues to be a required part of the curriculum in state-run schools. Religious broadcasting can be heard 24/7 on both television and radio. Evangelical churches are increasing.

Nevertheless, nominalism and syncretism are problems. Biblical knowledge tends to be superficial, and the living out of one's faith leaves much to be desired in a country with a history of corruption, and with significant gaps between rich and poor.

Quality Christian education is needed at all levels to develop spiritual depth for the Zambian church. A growing number of Bible schools, church-based training institutes, and education by extension programs have been developed to respond to denominational needs. One important training institution is the Theological College of Central Africa in Ndola, cosponsored by the 200 denominations of the Evangelical Fellowship of Zambia. Two other key programs, both located in the capital city of Lusaka, are the Baptist Seminary and Justin Mwale Theological Seminary (Reformed). All three of these schools offer master's level training for church leadership in cooperation with programs elsewhere.

Contextually appropriate training literature is a major need. Few Zambian authors have written materials for the church, and little publishing is done within Zambia. Much of what exists is expensive imports.

—STEVE HARDY

ZIMBABWE AND CHRISTIAN EDUCATION

Zimbabwe, formerly known as Southern Rhodesia,[1] embraced Christianity through the missionary work of the London Missionary Society in 1859. Reverend Robert Moffat translated the Bible into the Tswana language that same year. The translation, conducted at Inyati, set the stage for Christian education in the country.[2] The country is now considered a Christian nation, with over 85 percent of the population believing in the Christian faith.[3]

Christian schools constitute one-third of the schools in the country.[4] The aim is to build schools in which Christ is central in all areas: educational theory, procedures, and methodologies. Well-known Christian schools in Zimbabwe are Inyati High School (1896), Hanke Adventist High School (1910) in Shurugwi, and Chaplin High School (1902) in Gweru, among others. Recent tertiary institutions are African University (1992) in Mutare, Catholic University (1998) in Zimbabwe, The Reformed Church University (2012) in Morgenster, and Solusi University (1994) in Bulawayo.

Global Family[5] in Matabeleland promotes girls' education and teacher training, in addition to resourcing and vocational training for young adults through community-

---

1. Named for Cecil Rhodes, and home of the Shona and Ndebele peoples; the name was changed to Zimbabwe in 1980. *History Today*, 20 February 2013, http://www.historytoday.com.

2. Robert Reese, "A History of Protestant Missions in Zimbabwe," http://www.wmausa.org.

3. "Zimbabwe, Africa," http://www.zimbabwe.cc/html/christianity-in-zimbabwe.html.

4. Bureau of Democracy, human rights, and Labor, "Zimbabwe: International Religious Freedom Report 2005," U.S. Department of State, http://www.state.gov/j/drl/rls/irf/2005/51503.htm

5. Global Family of Mennonite Central Committee, a worldwide ministry of Anabaptist churches, http://globalfamily.mcc.org/who

based education. Christian education in local churches is made possible through communal rituals. It is a paradigm for teaching and learning, the meanings of valuing people's worth and interdependency, hospitality, mentoring, and announcing God's hope.[6] In ensuring that individuals are better equipped for prayer, knowledge of God's Word and true witnessing to others, theological education in Zimbabwe is solidly founded on practical teachings. Notable schools are Chishawasha Seminary (1947) in Harare, United Theological College (1954) in Harare, and Murray Theological (1925) in Masvingo. The Crosby Scholarship Fund for Theological Education in Zimbabwe is an independent body responsible for funding theological education in certain parts of African countries.[7]

References and Resources

Bureau of Democracy, Human Rights, and Labor. 2005. "Zimbabwe: International Religious Freedom Report 2005." U.S. Department of State. http://www.state.gov/j/drl/rls/irf/2005/51503.htm.

Gondwe, Eric. 2007. "Zimbabwe, Africa." http://www.zimbabwe.cc/html/christianity-in-zimbabwe.html.

Moorcraft, P. 1990. "Rhodesia War of independence." *History Today* 40 (9). http://www.historytoday.com/paul-moorcraft/rhodesias-war-independence.

Streaty Wimberly, A. S. 2001. "Discovering Communal Vitality in African Rituals: Seeing and Hearing God through Zimbabwean Christians." *Religious Education*, 96, no. 3 (2001): 369–384.

Summers, C. 2002. *Colonial Lessons: Africans' Education in Southern Rhodesia 1918–1940*. Bloomington, IN: Heineman.

Crosby Scholarship Fund for Theological Education in Zimbabwe. http://globalministries.org/africa/projects/crosby-scholarship-fund.html

Global Family of Mennonite Central Committee: A Worldwide Ministry of Anabaptist Churches. http://globalfamily.mcc.org/who

Hanke Adventist Secondary School. http://www.adventistyearbook.org/default.aspx?page=ViewEntity&EntityID=13682

—Ogechukwu Kalu Ibem

ZINZENDORF, NICHOLAS LUDWIG VON

Lutheran Pietist, educator, and leader of the Moravian Church, Nicholas Zinzendorf was trained as a lawyer and also pursued theological studies. When he was 10,

he attended August Hermann Francke's school in Halle, but felt oppressed by the 11-hour days that robbed children of the normal activities of play, which he later emphasized as essential for the healthy development of children. Zinzendorf soon distanced himself from the strong conversion-centered approach of Francke. In 1722, he invited the persecuted exiles of the Bohemian Brethren to his estate, soon known as Herrnhut ("the Lord's Watch"), thus initiating the revitalization of the *Unitas Fratrum* or Moravian Church. While shaped by the writings of Bernard of Clairvaux (1090–1153), Martin Luther, Johann Arndt (1555–1621), Philipp Jakob Spener (1635–1705), and Francke, Zinzendorf was also influenced by Reformed and Roman Catholic theology. His ecumenical spirit, inspired by a deep appreciation of grace, created a persistent desire to encourage Christian unity through love in Jesus Christ. His theology of the heart was strongly Christocentric and emphasized resting in the wound of Christ's side as a token of the Savior's love and redemption and figured significantly in both his sermons and hymns. This was associated with his teaching on the mystical union between the crucified Christ and the believer, known as spiritual marriage, and envisioned Jesus as the husband of each Christian soul. Zinzendorf enthusiastically borrowed the erotic language of the Song of Songs, which over time become controversial. Critics asserted that his teachings on spiritual marriage would create a distorted understanding of sexuality and gender order. His deeply inward experiential spirituality was combined with a fervent zeal for evangelism and missionary efforts and influenced later evangelicals, in particular John Wesley, as well as Friedrich Schleiermacher and Karl Barth.

Zinzendorf was a prolific author, producing a vast collection of sermons, letters, and hymns and liturgical resources. Most significant for the study of education were his catechisms, hymns, and *Losungen* (i.e., watchwords or daily texts). When only age 22, he wrote his first children's catechism, *Pure Milk* (1722), consisting of 78 questions and answers, for mothers to instruct their children in the principles of the Christian faith. With time, the importance of catechisms diminished in Zinzendorf's philosophy of education. More important than the acquiring of knowledge was the child's experience of "walking with Christ." Zinzendorf wrote over 2,000 hymns and felt that they were the best means for communicating spiritual truths and stirring the heart for Christian growth. He himself referred to this as the "liturgical method" of Christian education. Among the many hymnals produced by Zinzendorf was one specifically crafted for children. Zinzendorf's educational efforts were also advanced through the *Losungen*, which consisted of a brief daily scripture verse and served as

---

6. A. S. Streaty Wimberly, "Discovering Communal Vitality in African Rituals: Seeing and Hearing God through Zimbabwean Christians" in *Religious Education*, 369.

7. Crosby Scholarship Fund for Theological Education in Zimbabwe, http://globalministries.org/africa/projects/crosby-scholarship-fund.html.

the primary focus for the day's conversation and worship. Zinzendorf wrote many talks specifically directed to children as well as challenging adults to recognize the importance of providing faithful examples for children. Throughout Zinzendorf's writings, the importance of the Holy Spirit is evident as the person who creates the proper context for the experience of Christ.

Zinzendorf consistently focused on the "Child Jesus" as a model for children. As children and youth grew, they were to imagine Jesus advancing at their same age. This developmental awareness was unique at this time and reinforced the freedom and individualism of each student. Zinzendorf further taught the importance of a personal spiritual awakening, which would often result from disequilibrium in the person's life. This, combined with Zinzendorf's organizational genius and formation of groups to enhance learning, later inspired John Wesley's own development of classes and bands for Christian nurture. Larger groups known as "choirs" were arranged according to age and gender, from the youngest child to the older adult, and focused on instruction and discipleship. Zinzendorf regularly circulated among all the groups to both observe and provide encouragement to the members. The choirs were further divided into "bands" of four to eight people and provided a more experiential focus on worship, fellowship, and accountability. Reflective of the importance of worship and hymn singing, Zinzendorf created special festival days and love feasts, or services of singing and prayers based on the New Testament agape meal, to further guide the group's experience of Christ.

References and Resources

Kinlock, T. F. 1975. "Nicholas Ludwig Zinzendorf." In *A History of Religious Educators*, edited by Elmer L. Towns, 200–208. Grand Rapids, MI: Baker.

Meyer, Henry H. 1928. *Child Nature and Nurture According to Nicholas Ludwig von Zinzendorf* (includes English translation of *Pure Milk* catechism and selected other educational writings). New York: Abingdon Press.

Vogt, Peter. 2005. "Nicholas Ludwig von Zinzendorf." In *Pietist Theologians*, edited by Carter Lindberg, 207–223. Malden, MA: Blackwell.

Vogt, Peter, and John R. Weinlick. 1984. *Count Zinzendorf.* Bethlehem, PA: Moravian Church in America.

—TOM SCHWANDA

ZWINGLI, HULDREICH

Introduction

Huldreich Zwingli (1484-1531) was a Swiss pastor, theologian, and scholar who initiated the Swiss Reformation. Educated in the humanist tradition, Zwingli's preaching ministry and commitment to the sole authority of scripture in church life led him to fight for ecclesial reform in Zurich, Switzerland. That same commitment to the authority of scripture was at the center of his approach to Christian education.

Early Life and Education

Zwingli was born in Saint Gall, Switzerland, on 1 January 1484. From 1500 to 1502, Zwingli attended the University of Vienna, where he studied under renowned classicist Conrad Celtis. From 1502 to 1506, Zwingli attended the University of Basel and earned both bachelor's and master's degrees under humanist Thomas Wyttenbach. It was under Wyttenbach that Zwingli came to believe in the sole authority of scripture in church life and Christ's death as the only means for salvation.

In 1506, Zwingli became a priest in the town of Glarus, a post he held until 1516. During his time in Glarus, Zwingli became fluent in biblical Greek, began studying biblical Hebrew, and voraciously consumed patristic literature. He also explored the writings of Desiderius Erasmus, a theologian to whom Zwingli owed much of his own thought. Due to political circumstances, Zwingli moved to Einsiedeln, where he gained a reputation as a Greek scholar and staunch opponent of indulgence sales.

In 1518, Zwingli's reputation as a fine scholar and humanist earned him election to serve as priest at the Grossmünster in Zurich. In Zurich, Zwingli preached through the entire New Testament in expository fashion. Throughout his preaching ministry, Zwingli attacked various aspects of Roman Catholic practice, including the veneration of saints, the power of infant baptism to save children from hellfire, and the assertion that tithing was a divine prerogative. Zwingli remained steadfast in criticizing the sale of indulgences for the building of St. Peter's Basilica in Rome, a criticism Martin Luther inculcated in 1517 by publishing the "95 Theses." At this time, Zwingli developed a theological system that was uniquely his own. In 1519, Zwingli was struck by the bubonic plague and almost died. However, he made a full recovery and persevered in his preaching ministry.

In 1522, controversies erupted over the necessity of fasting and celibacy, which brought about great tension between Zwingli and the bishop of Constance. In 1523, with tensions mounting between Zwingli and the bishop, the city council ordered a public disputation, wherein Zwingli could debate doctrine with John Faber, the bishop's vicar general. Zwingli outlined in 67 articles his belief in the sole authority of scripture in church life and the denial of the sacrificial nature of the Mass, the salvific power of good works, and prayers to saints, among other items. The council declared Zwingli the victor in the debate, as he derived his beliefs solely from scripture. The council called for a second disputation after Zwingli's confidante, Leo Jud, advocated the swift removal of statues and icons from the city. Zwingli's opponents sought to include the sacrificial nature of the Mass in the debate, and Anabaptists decided to join the discussion, advocating for adult baptism. The council eventually voted in favor of Zwingli, though the reforms took place gradually.

Between 1524 and 1525, Zurich slowly broke away from Rome; statues and icons were removed from churches, monasteries were dissolved, services were conducted in German instead of Latin, and the Mass was abolished in 1525. In 1525, Zwingli authored *The Commentary on True and False Religion*, which provided the theological rationale for the reforms taking place in Zurich. Zwingli enthusiastically sought to spread the revolutions of Zurich across other parts of Switzerland and Germany. He engaged in heated debate with the Anabaptists, who asserted that Zwingli made too many concessions to the Zurich council; these debates proved futile, as both sides failed to reach a compromise.

The cantons of Switzerland remained officially Catholic, except for Zurich. Though Zwingli sought peace between Zurich and the other cantons, war broke out, with the other cantons defeating Zurich decisively in battle at Kappel in 1531. Zwingli himself was severely injured in battle and succumbed to his wounds. He was cremated so that devoted followers could not claim his body as relics. Though Zwingli's reforms were initially defeated, John Calvin would later foster Zwingli's cause to great success in Geneva.

Contribution to Christian Education

At the heart of Zwingli's approach to Christian education was the centrality of scripture as the means of knowing Christ. Zwingli believed that the Bible, read in the power of the Spirit, was the sole means of faith transformation, and he sought to ensure that laypeople and children were educated properly in biblical doctrine. After the Swiss Reformation was underway, the city council of Zurich commissioned Zwingli to create a catechism and statement of faith that reflected the religious and educational reforms in the city. Zwingli authored *On the Christian Education of Youth* (1523), which outlines his educational philosophy. Zwingli argues that education, though valuable, cannot lead to a saving faith, as only God the Holy Spirit can change one's heart and mind. The Holy Spirit uses the Bible as a means of growth and transformation in one's spiritual walk. The value of biblical education is to point out the necessity of saving faith in Christ, and from there, learn what it means to follow and love God wholeheartedly. Zwingli argues that the outcome of biblical education is right conduct toward others, the formation of Christian character, and service to others.

Zwingli started a theological institute in Grossmünster called the Prophezei, where a community of scholars would come together to exchange ideas and educate clergy. It is likely that the Zurich Bible, a translation traditionally attributed to Zwingli, was the product of participation by the community of the Prophezei. While Zwingli's ministry in Zurich lasted a short time, he nonetheless remained devoted to the education of clergy and reform in Zurich, which paved the way for similar reforms by John Calvin in Geneva, Switzerland.

References and Resources

Aubigné, J. H., and Mark Sidwell. 2000. *For God and His People: Ulrich Zwingli and the Swiss Reformation*. Greenville, SC: BJU Press.

Chadwick, Owen. 2001. *The Early Reformation on the Continent*. Oxford: Oxford University Press.

Steinmetz, David Curtis. 2001. *Reformers in the Wings: From Geiler Von Kaysersberg to Theodore Beza*. Oxford: Oxford University Press.

Zwingli, Ulrich, Samuel Macauley Jackson, and Clarence Nevin Heller. 1981. *Commentary on True and False Religion*. Durham, NC: Labyrinth.

—Benjamin D. Espinoza

Lead-in Introductions

The 1200 entries found in these three volumes are arranged in an A to Z format; however they are also organized by unifying sections. Following are 19 essays composed by scholars that introduce the reader to each major section of the encyclopedia. Each of the relevant entries arranged by section are included at the end of each lead-in introduction.

Section	Author
1. Christian Education in the Early Church from A.D. 33 to the end of Roman Empire	John Westerhoff
2. Christian Education in the Middle Age and Early Modern Age	George T. Kurian
3. Christian Education in the Modern World: Continental Profiles & Select Countries	Steve Kang
4. Christian Education in the Modern World: Denominational Profiles in Christian Education	Don Tinder
5. Christian Education in the Modern World: Institutional/University/Seminary Profile	Bryan Froehle
6. Intellectual Traditions in Christian Education	Hal Poe
7. Biblical/Theological Frameworks for Christian Education	Robert Pazmiño
8. Missions & Christian Education	Robert Gallagher
9. Christian Curriculum	Thomas Groome
10. Christian Higher Education	Perry Glanzer
11. Education of Children and Adolescents	Mark A. Lamport
12. Theological Education	Jeff Astley
13. Christian Pedagogy	Larry Richards
14. Christian Practice & Christian Education	David Smith
15. Christian Education in Difficult Circumstances	Mara Crabtree
16. Literature & Christian Education	Wesley Nan Barker
17. Biographies of Influential Christian Educators	George Brown
18. Christian Educational Law and Policies	Mai-Anh Tran
19. Christian Libraries	George T. Kurian

CHRISTIAN EDUCATION IN THE EARLY CHURCH FROM AD 33 TO THE END OF THE ROMAN EMPIRE

John Westerhoff

The history of the world and the history of the church are interrelated. So are the history of the church and that of Christian education. Insofar as the historical context of the church is always changing, so are its strivings to form and transform, to nurture and nourish both converts and the faithful. What follows is a summary of Christian education from the birth of the church in the first century of the common era (CE) to the death of the Roman empire in the fifth century. During the reign of Tiberius (14–37 CE), one Jesus of Nazareth was born, lived, and died. During His life He proclaimed that the reign of God had come and formed a community of disciples who, after His death, experienced His resurrection and ascension, followed by another life-transforming experience, the coming of the Holy Spirit, which empowered them to witness to the Gospel this Jesus had proclaimed. It is this event that marks the birth of the Christian church. The history of this church begins as the story of a troublesome Jewish sect, which became an illegal religion under Roman persecution. In the fourth century, however, the emperor Constantine I (306–337) issued the Edict of Milan (313), establishing freedom for all religions in the empire including Christianity, which in 392, under the reign of Theodosius I, became the official religion of the empire. While stability in the church was achieved, new problems faced the church's educational ministry. Then the empire fell, in 476, and a new era in the church's history and Christian education began.

At the beginning of what we in the church know as the Christian era (AD), Rome was the dominant world power, and according to Roman policy, the Jews retained control of their own religious affairs. Into this historical, social, and cultural context one Jesus of Nazareth was born into a faithful Jewish family. While we know little about His education, we can assume that He participated in the observance of Jewish household rituals, life in a synagogue, and pilgrimages to the temple in Jerusalem. During His early adulthood, He left home, gathered 12 disciples, and went forth to preach and teach about both the coming of the reign of God and the nature of God's Kingdom. His preaching and teaching were one, and His teaching is best understood in terms of an apprenticeship. Jesus called His followers learners and invited them to identify with Him and His mission, to observe His way of life, and to imitate it. This new movement within Judaism advocated a communal way of life, founded on the faith that the long-awaited and hoped-for reign of God had begun.

While preaching that the reign of God had arrived was foundational to the emerging church, without teaching there would have been no Christian church to witness to the truth of that proclamation. For this reason, those with the charisma to teach became increasingly important to the survival of the Christian message and its implications for the spiritual and moral lives of those who had become convinced that the historical Jesus of history was truly the Christ (Messiah) of their faith.

From the beginning, Christianity was understood to be a personal and communal life of faith, faith being defined as a perception of reality that is true in spite of any evidence to the contrary. This revealed faith necessarily manifests itself as a way of life participated in and practiced, so that the faithful might act their way into these new ways of perceiving life and their lives. Christianity was not to be primarily about intellectual moral convictions or rational truths about God. Nor was it to be solely about believing intellectually that some particular propo-

sitions are true. Christian education was to be about a life of faith acquired by the telling of stories, of sharing spiritual experiences, of praying and singing hymns, and of practicing Christlike living under the established rule of God. Christianity was to be a household faith comprised of adults and their children, in which parents were primarily responsible for their nurture.

After the death, resurrection, and ascension of Jesus, the Holy Spirit gave birth to communities of Christian faith comprised of small groups of Jews, "God-fearers," and in time Gentiles. Men and women, rich and poor, wise and simple, were brought together by charismatic leaders and teachers to form small household communities. Nicknamed "Christians" by their detractors, with them a new religion was born. As communities of faith existing in an oral culture, they focused on nurturing the Christian life of faith. While preaching, addressing large crowds in public places, and performing acts of mercy attracted the attention of many, Christian teaching was personal and practiced in small group liturgical settings, in which stories of and about Jesus were repeated, Hebrew scripture was read and reinterpreted, apostolic letters were read, and a common meal (agape or love feast) was shared. This was followed by a Eucharistic meal that included prayers, the singing of psalms and spiritual hymns, experiences of the Holy Spirit (God present and active among them and within them), the speaking in tongues and their interpretation, and personal testimonies of faith in the presence of God's reign.

In time, Simon Peter and James the brother of Jesus emerged as leaders in these new Christian communities within Judaism. Opposition soon arose, especially among Jewish Sadducees and Temple authorities. Martyrdom at the hands of Jews resulted. One of the Jews who opposed the Christian movement was Saul of Tarsus (Paul), who early on became a convert to the Christian faith as well as its defender and advocate in expanding the movement to include Gentiles. Paul's early leadership and pastoral letters provide a theological foundation and an explanation of what it means to be a follower of Jesus.

By the second century, Christianity had moved from being a Jewish sect to being an established religion comprised of Jews, and increasingly Gentiles, from throughout the Roman world. There is good reason to believe that education in these earliest Christian communities was influenced by Jewish education, in which household rituals were the primary means used to nurture children and nourish adults. Besides weekly rituals held in the context of a family meal on the Sabbath, there were also special life-cycle rites and yearly festivals, such as Passover, Tabernacles, and Pentecost. There were also a few synagogues that existed for the purpose of worship and edification, for teaching, and for the prayerful reading of holy scripture and its interpretation by rabbis (teachers), which became models for the church. The Jews also had somewhat elaborate programs for the instruction of converts to Judaism in preparation for a spiritual bath, which incorporated them into the Jewish faith. Such practices provided models for baptismal preparation.

Among the church's earliest written documents on teaching and learning was the Didache, composed by the apostolic fathers in the late first century. This catechism is made up of a number of sections: the Gospel of the passion and the resurrection and the sayings of Jesus, Christian ethics, the rituals of baptism and Holy Communion, and church organization. It appears to be founded on the belief that humans are liturgical beings and that Christian education takes place within the context of and participation in communal rituals. The primary aims of Christian education are related to faith (perceptions of reality), character (habits of the heart and behavioral dispositions), and consciousness (awareness of the presence and action of the Holy Spirit). And these "teachings" were to be transmitted and acquired by participation in and the practice of the Christian life of faith, especially in the church's rituals, by critical reflection on experience, and by the acquisition of knowledge and skills fundament to this life of faith.

As the church slowly developed into an institution, an understanding of the relationship between pastoral leadership and the ministry of teaching emerged. The people began to call bishops (overseers) to be guardians of the faith and the church's primary teachers. Deacons were chosen by bishops to be the church's servant ministers. And as the church grew in numbers, the office of presbyter (elder) developed to provide assistance for bishops. By the second century, these bishops had begun to establish an authoritative canon of holy scripture along with their authority to be the interpreters of scripture.

Concerning Christian education, the early church father Tertullian explained, "Christians are made not born." The question was then "How?" and the answer was in the Greek "catechesis," literally to "echo the Word," the Word being a person, Jesus, or any formative processes that make Christlike persons. Preparing Jewish and Gentile converts for baptism, a rite of initiation into the Christian community of faith in the second century, expanded into an established catechetical system in the third century. Christian education increasingly focused its efforts on a "catechumenate," a process of moving converts from being hearers of the Word to being doers of the Word. The Gospel of Jesus announced the presence of God's reign within and among those who had faith that He was the Christ. These needed to be prepared to live in this present realm with an allegiance to another; that is, they were to learn how to abide in God's reign until it would, in God's good time, come in its fullness.

The growing number of persons attracted to the church necessitated more formal means of initiation into the Christian life of faith, so that by third century a catechetical system had evolved. Unbaptized adults were known as catechumens, and their preparation for baptism became the responsibility of the bishop. Catechetical method was predominantly a process of reflection on experience, comprised of a number of stages:

- Stage one was a precatechumenal period, a time of inquiry when those attracted to the Christian life of faith were aided in an examination of their readiness to pursue the implications of life within the Christian community of faith.
- Stage two was the catechumenate, initiated by a public liturgical act and lasting about three years. The amount of time this period lasted was judged by the community in terms of the transformation of the lives of those desiring baptism. During this period, catechumens participated in the church's worship, being dismissed after the sermon, before the creed, the prayers of the people, and the Eucharistic feast (the Lord's Supper). They were also aided by a baptized sponsor or catechist in practicing the Christian life of faith, in developing a spiritual discipline, and in making the Christian story their story.

When the community believed that they had been fully prepared, they became candidates for baptism and during the weeks before Easter participated in a series of liturgical actions to prepare them for this symbolic act of death and rebirth. They were then baptized at the Easter Vigil and for the first time were invited to affirm what was to become known as the Apostles' Creed and enter the "priesthood of all believers" by joining the congregation in a priestly act, namely praying the prayers of the people, prayers of intercession intended to bring the people to God and God to the people. This was followed by a liturgical action, the exchanging of "the Peace" and then participating in the Eucharistic prayer and communion.

Following their baptism, during the weeks following Easter and before Pentecost, the candidates entered the last stage of their initiation, known as the "mystagogy," in which having experienced the church's two great sacraments, baptism and Eucharist, they reflected upon and were informed of their meaning, significance, and implications for their lives. While bishops became the source for the church's oral tradition, in time catechetical schools, communities of higher education modeled after pagan philosophical schools, were created to provide an intellectual response to the growing diversity of understandings of the Christian life of faith. The Catechetical School at Alexandria, the first, became a Christian school for theologians to resolve theological conflicts in the church and provide an apologetic for the Christian faith as it confronted Greek philosophy.

As Christianity developed, it increasingly became a threat to the pagan Roman government, which responded with increased persecution. But the death of martyrs resulted in the growth of the church. The emperor Constantine concluded that legitimizing Christianity was a wiser way to deal with this new religion. And so, by the Edict of Milan in 313, he granted religious freedom to all Roman citizens, recognizing the church as a legitimate religion. When he became aware that there were divisions within Christianity that were a threat to the unity of the empire, he called a council of Christian bishops in Nicaea in 325, at which a creed was established to define the core of the apostolic faith. Importantly, the creed of the apostles, used at baptisms, and the creed of Nicaea began: "I (We) believe in," not "I (we) believe that."

In 380 a new emperor, Theodosius I, made Christianity the official religion of the empire. The consequences were significant. As Christianity became acceptable to the world, it became influenced by the world. No longer was death the price for being a Christian; death was the possible price of not being a Christian. In time the catechumenate's strict procedures for preparing adults whose lives had been transformed by the Gospel for baptism was replaced by focusing on baptism for infants. Being made "a" Christian immediately by baptism replaced a serious, lengthy process of becoming Christian. Christians might still be made and not born, but they were made Christians by participating in the sacrament of baptism and not by a process of "baptismal" catechesis before and after baptism in a lifelong educational process.

In time theological concerns replaced pedagogical ones, and Christian education faced a crisis. Faith was replaced by beliefs, intellectual propositions about truth. Character was replaced by rigid moral laws for behavior. And consciousness was transformed into particular religious experiences. As a consequence, Christian education moved from nurture for everyone within a community of faith to instruction, the transmission of beliefs, in a schooling context. But that part of the story is yet to be told.

References and Resources

Murphy Center Liturgical Resources. 1976. *Made, Not Born: New Perspectives on Christian Initiation and the Catechumenate.* Notre Dame, IN: University of Notre Dame Press.

Sawicki, Marianne. 1988. *The Gospel in History: Origins of Christian Education.* New York: Paulist Press.

Sherrill, Lewis J. 1944. *The Rise of Christian Education.* New York: Macmillan Company.

Ulich, Robert. 1968. *History of Religious Education.* New York: New York University Press.

Westerhoff, John, and O. C. Edwards, eds. 1981. *A Faithful Church: History of Catechetics.* Wilton, CT: Morehouse-Barlow Co.

Relevant Entries

Alexandria, School of

Alexandria, The Importance of

Ancient World, Christian Education in the

Antioch, Church of

Apologists

Art and Architecture, Early Church Instructional Use of

Augustine, Educational Contributions of

Baptism, Theology of

Basil the Great

Bishops, An Overview of the Teaching Role of

Bishops, New Testament Foundations of the Teaching Role of

Caesarea, School of

Catechesis in the Early Church

Catechetical Schools in the Early Church

Catechetical Sermons

Catechumenate

Chrysostom, John

Constantine's Influence on Education

Creeds

Desert Fathers and Mothers

Didache as Early Christian Education Strategy

Early Church Families and Education

Edessa, School of

Ephesus, School of

Heresy, Response to

Hymns as an Educational Tool

Jewish Catechetical Tradition

Libraries, Early Christian

Liturgical Calendar, Development of

Mystagogy

Nisibis, School of

Rome, School of

Spiritual Direction, Early Development of

St. Matthew, School of

Women in Christian Education, Emerging Role of

CHRISTIAN EDUCATION IN THE MIDDLE AGES AND EARLY MODERN AGE

George Thomas Kurian

The "Middle Ages" is a rather imprecise chronological term, defined by historians as the period beginning with the fall of the Roman Empire and ending with the Renaissance and Reformation in Western Europe. The key descriptor is "Middle," which indicates that it is an osculant period linking two other eras. The earlier medieval centuries are sometimes called the Dark Ages. However, the term "Dark Ages" is a misnomer, because the period was anything but dark. It was rather the early dawn of the modern world, when many formative institutions were taking shape, new value systems were being adopted, and the foundations were being laid for a new social order. First and foremost among these institutions was the school.

Christianity began as—and still remains—a noumenon, that is, a spiritual phenomenon, rather than a secular and temporal one. It regards human life not as acephalous or autonomous but as *sub species aeternatatis*, a subset of eternity. But in its engagement with the world, Christianity had to make inroads into and establish beachheads in secular systems such as law, education, health, and politics. In other words, Christians found that before they could reshape the world they had to create a whole new civilization. The key to such a new civilization would be education.

The rise of the Christian church coincided with the decline of the Roman Empire and its religious and social order. By the time Christianity had become the official religion of the empire after Constantine, the Roman school system was in disarray. However, Christians were suspicious of the old Roman educational legacies, including the classics. Classical education stood for a profligate culture, and many Christians, including the great Tertullian, welcomed its demise. "What," he asked, "has Athens to do with Jerusalem?" So the first questions confronting Christian educators were not merely pedagogy, but even more fundamental: What should be taught, and what is worth learning?

Meanwhile, more moderate Christian spokesmen, especially Tatian, Jerome, and Augustine, reached a compromise. Classics would be taught in public schools by Christian teachers, but religious instruction would be primarily limited to seminaries and catechetical schools. This dichotomy has remained to this day. As Christians were trained in public schools under non-Christian teachers, safeguards for the faith were essential, for even a superior conventional wisdom was too great a price to pay for a faith that was debilitated by pagan influences.

Hostility between classical and Christian education remained stronger in Western Christendom than in the East. There was little intussusception or cross-fertilization of ideas between paganism and Christianity in the East. Christian writers, however, were less proficient in the arts of persuasion, and as Christian doctrine matured, its exposition needed a literary refinement that only competent schooling could supply.

The midwives of Christian education were not educators but theologians, like Basil and Clement of Alexandria, Jerome, Origen Ambrose, and John Chrysostom. Clement was the first scholar to leave a written record of a discussion on education, and he advanced an audacious doctrine that championed learning as a means of advancing virtue and even perfection. Origen refused to acknowledge the independent worth of secular knowledge, but regarded it as a means of understanding Christian doctrine. Ambrose and Chrysostom refused to proscribe secular texts. Jerome held that elements of grammar and logic were essential to Christian learning and an understanding of Christian doctrine. Such an understanding, he held, could be gained only through religious literacy. The first great burst of Christian educational activity came after Emperor Julian tried to suppress Christian schools and revive classical learning. It was the last hurrah of paganism.

In 529 Emperor Justinian outlawed pagan schools, thus creating a vacuum in the system of institutionalized learning. Christian schools were not quite prepared to meet the new challenge of instructing the young and transmitting knowledge. Furthermore, they had no sympathy for the world of learning that was steeped in pagan traditions.

Sometime in the fourth century, monasticism began to flourish in the West, after migrating from the East, especially Greece and Egypt. Religious rule obligated nuns and monks to public and private prayer and required basic literacy for devotional reading and the care and education of minors. The novitiate was converted into a period of preparation in the rudiments of learning. Grammar and rhetoric were ignored, and the less literate were required to memorize by heart. The Bible and the rules of the order were required reading, and each monastery had an attached scriptorium, which served as a library. The "Rule" of St. Benedict called for a monastic school that prepared boys for monastic life. In addition, bishops trained priests in Episcopal schools. As Christianity spread to rural areas, the Episcopal school system was extended to parishes, where the parish priest was in charge of the instruction of young boys. Both the Council of Toledo in 527 and the Second Council of Vaison in 529 added teaching to the general responsibilities of the parish priest. These schools survived from the sixth to the eighth centuries and provided a test run for the educational systems that followed. Before the end of the millennium, these schools had assumed responsibility for the education of European Christian children and had completely displaced Roman schools.

The scholastic framework of Christian education was still threadbare. The monks were sure that they did not want to teach classics, but less sure about what should be taught. A number of Christian educators tried to formulate programs of studies suitable for Christians. Augustine's *On Christian Doctrine* encouraged Christian educators to be selective in deciding how profane scholarship could be used to edify Christians. Boethius was less influential than Augustine, but his *Consolation of Philosophy* tried to integrate classical legacies with Christian faith, with only modest success. By the fifth century, Martianus of Capella identified seven liberal arts needed for a complete education: grammar, rhetoric, dialectic, arithmetic, geometry, music, and astronomy. But liberal arts were alien to monastic culture. It was not until Cassiodorus (480–575) that the idea that it was possible to yoke scholarship and faith took root. When he failed to establish a school, he founded two monasteries and wrote two seminal works, *Definition of the Seven Liberal Arts* and *An Introduction to Divine and Human Readings*. Cassiodorus was convinced that the liberal arts were handmaidens of theology and doctrine. He was the first to introduce literary monasticism, which combined learning with a deep knowledge of and respect for all fields of knowledge, and the tradition whereby monasteries became embryonic universities and schools. Cassiodorus further Christianized Quintilian's educational philosophy and praxis by demoting rhetoric and oratory and emphasizing more practical subjects. Another architect of Western learning was Isidore of Seville, the encyclopedist. He was the first to reconstruct the tradition of erudition and scholarship that was dying out in the last days of the Roman Empire. Not only was knowledge being created, but it was being transmitted efficiently through institutionalized structures that acknowledged faith and doctrine. With libraries, schools, and monasteries, a new educational infrastructure was being created for a post-Roman world. The culmination of this period was the educational reform of Pope Gregory the Great at the end of the sixth century, which solidified and legitimized the work of Cassiodorus. In the ninth century, certain monastic schools achieved great distinction: Monte Cassino, Bobbio, Pomposa, and Classe in Italy; Fulda, Reichenau, Hirschau, Gandersheim, Wissenbourg, and Hersfeld in Germany; St. Gall in Switzerland; Fontenelles, Fleury, Ferieres, Corbie, Tours, Toulouse, Cluny, and Bec in France; and Canterbury, York, Wearmouth, Yarrow, Glastonbury, St. Albans, Croyland, and Malmesbury in England.

The canon of studies in medieval schools illustrates its evolution from Graeco-Roman days. It was based on Plato's division of liberal studies into higher and lower subjects, the lower consisting of gymnastics, music, and letters and the higher made up of arithmetic, geometry, and algebra. Eventually, the course of study settled down to seven subjects: grammar, rhetoric, and dialectic, making up the *trivium*, and arithmetic, geometry, music, and astronomy, making up the *quadrivium*. Later Varro added architecture and medicine. In addition, all students were taught the Lord's Prayer, the Apostles' Creed,

and the Psalms. Pedagogy was catechetical, based on a set of questions and answers.

Education of Women

Christian schools were the first in the Roman Empire to admit women, and the tradition continued well into the Middle Ages. This was a legacy that Christians passed on to the humanists. Although the role of women in society remained the same, the door of learning was open to them. Their curriculum was similar to that for men, except for rhetoric. Appropriately, the curriculum for a "Christian lady" included history and moral and religious studies.

Charlemagne and Christian Education

In the sixth century, the lamps of learning in Europe were still only dimly lit, until the arrival of Charlemagne and his extraordinary friendship with Alcuin. Charlemagne himself was reputed to be illiterate, but he had an immense love of learning and an even deeper love for his Christian faith. What led Charlemagne to become the founder of European education and the great ally of learning? The answer may be found in the Aachen palace school, which he set up as a model for his Frankish Empire. The king opened the palace schools to laymen and monks outside the aristocracy. To expand the school, Charlemagne recruited Alcuin, a master from York. In 787 and 802, Charlemagne issued his famous capitulary or law, asking all officers of the realm to "open a school in each bishopric and monastery." Any one able to teach was expected to do so, and all children, rich and poor alike, were to receive free education. This capitulary is the birth certificate of European education.

Alcuin recognized that all learning is acquired through reading and directed all elementary schools to emphasize the teaching of Latin. He does not seem to have been afraid of paganism or the liberal arts. Vocabulary and grammar were introduced in carefully written, graded readers. As early as the 10th century, all priests were required to engage teachers, who were required to teach without compensation The Council of Lateran (1179) formalized this arrangement. The decree was binding on every diocese. In addition to diocesan schools, there was a variety of schools under varying auspices, among them

1. private schools;
2. monastic schools, which were among the most advanced, some even offering study in law and medicine;
3. parish schools;
4. cathedral schools, headed by a chancellor, and collegiate schools, headed by a scholasticus;
5. municipal schools;

6. guild schools for training apprentices;
7. court schools;
8. chantry schools, funded by philanthropy in honor of a deceased person; and
9. Burgher schools, run by towns.

By the end of the 10th century, the educational reforms of Charlemagne and Alcuin had begun to bear fruit in Western Europe. The first condition permitting educational progress was peace. For the first time, Europe had respite from not merely the Arabs but also the Vikings and Magyars. Second, the magisterium of the church as the compass and conscience of the continent had become moribund. Scholars, rather than theologians, had the autonomy to determine what should be taught and how. As the control of education moved outside the church, its content expanded. The growth of curricular diversity was most visible in law, medicine, and philosophy. Law was divested of its feudal trappings and was no longer based on Christian morality alone, but on an empirical philosophy derived from prevailing social values. Medicine was no longer based on natural philosophy, magic, and alchemy, but on science. General literature was not sanitized, but reflected life with all its warts, pollution, and corruption. In addition, many schools taught older subjects, such as logic, rhetoric, and letter writing. New disciplines were introduced almost every decade, and all of them were welcomed as adding to the sum total of human knowledge. Nevertheless, subjects like biology, political science, economics, geography, and psychology lay far in the future.

Universities

From the middle of the 12th century to the end of the 14th, 79 universities (then called *studia generalia*) were established in Europe. (See appendix B.) The oldest university was that at Salerno near Naples, which specialized in medicine. The University of Bologna specialized in law. North of the Alps, the most famous university was that in Paris, which grew out of the cathedral school of Notre Dame, the home of Abelard. In England, Oxford began in the second half of the 12th century and Cambridge in the first half of the 13th. Naples was established by imperial decree in 1224. Padua and Arezzo were recognized in 1355. The universities of Palencia, Salamanca, and Valladolid in Spain and of Lisbon in Portugal were founded during the 13th century, followed by Toulouse and Montpellier in France. The first German university, in Prague, was founded in 1348, followed by Vienna, Erfurt, Heidelberg, and Cologne. All universities had some kind of ecclesiastical connection, but any one, whether Catholic or heterodox, could pursue studies there. Lectures were dictated from a master's notes, for which the students directly paid a fee, set by

the guild. From the beginning all institutions, masters, and students were granted a variety of privileges, exemptions, and immunities by the rulers. They were free of taxation and military service.

A university was organized in the same manner as a medieval guild. This is shown by the complete name: *Universitas Magistorum et Scholarium* (Body of Masters and Scholars). The term "university" was not originally an academic term and meant nothing more than a corporation. The academic body was divided into faculties based on disciplines. Law was the most important of the faculties, followed by arts, medicine, and theology. Each faculty elected a dean, who along with the councilors of the student bodies elected the rector. The content of the courses varied from university to university, but there were standard authorities, such as Peter Lombard's *Sentences* in theology and Hippocrates and Galen in medicine. Pedagogy was based solely on lectures, because before the invention of printing, books were scarce.

Education was an exchange transaction in which knowledge was transferred from the professor to the student for a fee. Lectures gave the master a platform to display intellectual acumen and academic prowess. The pedagogy was crude, but even with all its shortcomings, it had a good track record. The word "curriculum" was never used to describe the subjects taught. "Faculty" was the preferred term for the academic subjects and the professional faculties gave a university its special distinction. The language of instruction was Latin. Students who passed muster were called masters. In law and medicine, the degree was a doctorate, and all other graduates were simply bachelors. A "bachelor" was essentially an apprentice who also tutored students and worked toward a master's degree.

The universities were the engines of humanism. They were led by humanists, who turned on the church and tried to jettison large parts of the corpus of medieval learning and replace the City of God with a City of Man. In the world that emerged in the early modern age, faith was on the defensive, and the vision of a Christ-inspired education as developed by Augustine and Tertullian became dim.

Early Modern Age

The chronological markers of the early modern age are the discovery of the New World, the Reformation, and the decline of the threat of Islam. By the 15th century, the educational system had taken its modern form and had adopted the rubrics and protocols that characterize it today. Education had been divided permanently into its three stages: primary, secondary, and higher. As for the centuries-old conflict between Athens and Jerusalem, the latter had lost decisively. Even where institutional control rested with the Christian church, the contents of education had shifted, and schools as well as the state had adopted secular knowledge as the goal of all learning. Faith and learning maintained an uneasy and asymmetrical relationship thereafter, but the balance of power was with the secular teachers and institutions. The church had always been concerned with the purpose of knowledge rather than knowledge per se, but after the 15th century, knowledge was acquired for its own sake. The church became a tributary rather than the mainstream.

By the 15th century, the philosophical underpinnings of education were defined not by Augustine or Gregory the Great but by humanists like Desiderius Erasmus, Francesco Petrarch, Peter Paul Vergerius, and Manuel Chrysoloras. For the most part early humanists—unlike later ones—were religious persons dedicated to the truth of their profession and deeply committed to its preservation. Nevertheless, their focus was entirely on the temporal world and the self-fulfillment of human beings, and they were driven by the unassailable conviction that raw and unfiltered knowledge in itself would improve the human condition. No one expressed this belief better than Petrarch, who equated good literature with a good life. He subscribed to the Greek ideal of *kalos*, the *summum bonum* of physical and mental health. As a professor of logic at Padua, Vergerius issued the humanist manifesto *On Noble Character and Liberal Study*, which equated virtue and character with learning. These humanist ideals were put into practice in two schools: Guarino's school at Ferrara, founded in 1429, and Vittorino de Feltre's school at Mantua, founded in 1423.

References and Resources

Cabban, Alan B. 1975. *Medieval Universities*. London, UK: Methuen.

Cook, T. G. 1974. *History of Education in Europe*. London, UK: Methuen.

Gibbon, Edward. 1960. *Decline and Fall of the Roman Empire.* 7 vols. London, UK: Methuen.

Leach, Arthur F. 1915. *Schools of Medieval England*. London, UK: Methuen.

Pelikan, Jaroslav. 1967. *The Excellent Empire: The Fall of Rome and the Triumph of the Church*. San Francisco, CA: Harper.

List of Major Universities and Their Founding Dates

1088 Bologna	1229 Toulouse
1150 Paris	1246 Siena
1167 Oxford	1248 Piacenza
1204 Vicenza	1257 Sorbonne
1209 Cambridge	1290 Coimbra
1211 Palencia	1293 Alcala (Studium Generale)
1218 Salamanca	
1220 Montpellier	1303 La Sapienza, Rome
1222 Padua	1303 Avignon
1222 Naples	1306 Orleans

1308 Perugia	1502 Wittenberg
1332 Cahors	1512 Puerto Rico
1339 Grenoble	1527 Marburg
1343 Pisa	1531 Grenada
1348 Prague (Charles University)	1538 Santo Domingo
1349 Florence	1544 Konigsburg
1361 Pavia	1551 Pontifical Gregorian University, Rome
1364 Krakow	
1365 Vienna	1551 Lima
1379 Erfurt	1551 Mexico
1386 Heidelberg	1574 Leiden
1388 Cologne	1586 Graz
1391 Ferrara	1592 Trinity College, Dublin
1402 Wurzburg	
1405 Turin	1595 Cebu, Philippines
1409 Leipzig	1611 Manila
1413 St. Andrews	1636 Harvard
1419 Rostock	1655 Kiel
1425 Louvain	1693 College of William and Mary, Williamsburg
1431 Poitiers	
1432 Caen	1694 Halle
1441 Bordeaux	1701 Yale
1444 Catania	1746 Princeton
1450 Barcelona	1754 King's College (Columbia)
1451 Glasgow	
1456 Greifswald	1764 Rhode Island (Brown)
1457 Freiburg	
1459 Basle	1766 Queen's College, Rutgers
1471 Genoa	
1472 Munich	1769 Dartmouth
1477 Tubingen	1789 Georgetown
1477 Uppsala	1829 King's College, London
1479 Copenhagen	
1494 Aberdeen	1880 Amsterdam Free University
1495 Santiago de Compostela	
1499 Alcala Complutensian	1887 Catholic University of America, Washington, DC
1499 Valencia	

Relevant Entries

Amish Christian Education
Art and Architecture, Instructional Use of
Asceticism
Benedict, Educational Ideas of
Bible Conference Movement
Bible, Early Vernacular Translations of the
Blind, History of the Christian Education of the
Book of Kells
Brethren of the Common Life
Byzantine Medieval Church
Calvin, John

CHRISTIAN EDUCATION IN THE MODERN WORLD: CONTINENTAL PROFILES AND SELECT COUNTRIES

S. Steven Kang

Andrew Walls (2002), a prominent missiologist-theologian, observes that the Christian church has advanced serially throughout its 2,000-year history. Still retaining roots in their origins and having spread across much of the world, Christianity and Islam have been embraced quite differently by their adherents. While civilizations or countries that became Muslim have remained Muslim, many places once known as the heartlands of Christianity (centers of Christian devotion, scholarship, and missions, etc.) no longer make that same claim, perhaps lacking a certain fortitude that Islam possesses. Though Christianity may have faded in the heartlands, the Christian faith itself did not fade. Quite the contrary is true. Whenever these heartlands were pushed to the margins for various reasons, Christianity blossomed either at or beyond the margins. Christian advance in this sense is serial, taking root in one place and then in another, declining in one area, while spreading and blossoming anew in another. Walls asserts, "The great event in the religious history of the 20th century was the transformation of the demographic and cultural composition of Christianity brought about by the simultaneous processes of advance and recession" (quoted in Johnson and Ross 2009, 48).

Indeed, the great "Christian century" that the U.S. mainline churches had anticipated throughout the country at the beginning of the 20th century actually took place around the globe. While the number of Christian adherents in the U.S. mainline churches has declined dramatically over the past century, the number of Christian adherents worldwide has grown exponentially, to the point that not only half of all Christians in the entire history of the church have lived within the past century, but also close to half of all Christian adherents who have ever lived are currently living. It is not an overstatement to say that the representative Christians now belong to Africa, Asia, and Latin America, with intellectual and theological consequences—the reverberations of "the Christian heartland"—in this late-modern era still evident.

The prominence of Christianity in these regions, corollary to its serial nature, is clearly a direct result of the ways in which Christianity has constantly crossed cultural frontiers, for various reasons. From the inception of the church in Jerusalem in the first century, Christianity spread through persecution and the fall of the city. While Christianity barely lasted two generations with Jerusalem as the Christian heartland, the bicultural church at Antioch flourished, carrying Christianity's cross-cultural impetus to the Hellenistic world. Later, as Christianity faded in the eastern provinces of the empire due to the rise of Islam and in the western provinces due to devastating wars, "barbarians" inherited the empire, flourishing in its midst for many centuries. With the decline of Christianity in Europe, it flourished yet again in North America. The late-modern church has been witnessing the missionary impulse of Christianity spreading across cultural boundaries of ethnicity, language, and culture into Africa and Asia, South America, and the Pacific.

With the emergence of the plethora of valuable data on the global church in recent years, assessing the vitality of the church in specific regions of the world has become more sophisticated and nuanced. For instance, according to *Atlas of Global Christianity*, every United Nations region (Africa, Asia, Europe, Latin America, North America, and Oceania) has experienced numerical growth in terms of the raw number of Christian adherents, from 1910 to 2010. This is in step with population growth in these regions. Compared to general population growth during the same 100 years (1910–2010), however, only Christian growth rates in Africa and Asia regions outpaced general population growth rates (3.82 vs. 2.14 and 2.68 vs. 1.41, respectively) (Johnson and Ross 2009, 113, 137), whereas the reverse is the case for Europe, Latin America, and North America (.37 vs. .54; 2.02 vs. 2.05; and 1.14 vs. 1.31, respectively) (157, 177, 193) and the two rates paced evenly in Oceania (at 1.61) (195). On the one hand, the ratios of Christian growth rates in comparison to general population growth rates in Africa and Asia, as impressive as they may be, are even more staggering given that many of the Christians in these regions have been subjected to religious, and more broadly sociocultural, persecution as Christian minorities. On the other hand, the same ratios for Europe and North America should be a cause of a greater concern, when we factor in the fact that immigrant families who were already Christians in their former countries account for much of the population growth in these regions.

What is interesting about the Latin American region is that the percentage of Christian adherents in the population over the past century has actually decreased slightly (from 95.2 to 92.5 percent) (276). Whenever the expansion of the church in the global South is discussed, however, the church in Latin America is celebrated as a major success story, in which Protestant and evangelical growth rates outpaced the population growth rate by nearly 200 percent

(4.04 vs. 2.05 and 4.07 vs. 2.05, respectively) (91, 99). These are impressive statistics, especially as they represent 56 million Protestant and 48 million evangelical adherents. Even more astounding, though, is how the Pentecostal/charismatic growth rate far outpaced the population growth, by 470 percent (9.67 vs. 2.05), at 156 million adherents. What is noteworthy about the Pentecostal/charismatic growth rate in Latin America is that, while 25 million people attend Protestant, evangelical, and/or Pentecostal churches, a significant number (131 million) have remained within the Catholic church, living out their calling as renewalists within the church (102–103).

Although accounting for such a renewalist/missionary impulse *from within* requires a careful assessment of data, such an impulse is not limited to one branch of Christianity, but available for a country, as well as other regions of the world. For instance, recent decades have witnessed thousands of southern Indian Christians migrating to northern and northwestern parts of India, where Christian presence historically had been sparse. They have engaged in not only church planting efforts, but also holistic Christian outreach, as well as the establishment of schools to train pastors and other Christian reflective practitioners. This is in an attempt to sustain such ambitious projects with newly converted indigenous Christians. More broadly, many churches in the global South have been active in sending out cross-cultural missionaries within their regions and all over the world to evangelize the unreached groups and to re-evangelize so-called Christian adherents in Europe and North America.

While many have been bemoaning the unprecedented relative decline of Christian adherence in Europe in recent years, which has moved from Christian heartland to Christian wasteland, the *Atlas of Global Christianity* (Johnson and Ross, 2009) estimates that Christian adherents in Europe in 2010 made up more than 80 percent of its population, although this represents a decline of 14 percent from 1910 (156). Of course, the term "Christian adherents" is notoriously difficult to quantify. Christian adherents can be placed in at least four major categories: professing Christians (professing one's choice), affiliated Christians (affiliated to organized Christianity), practicing Christians (church attenders), and Great Commission Christians (those involved in the church's outreach) (343). Each subsequent category is a subset of the previous category. Seen in this light, the majority of Europeans do profess that they are Christians. Many are also counted as affiliated Christians by many state churches, most of whom willingly pay taxes that support state churches. There is no denying, however, that only a small number of Christian adherents attend church regularly. What is remarkable is that the salience of "Christian civilization" persists, and social institutions broadly maintain its structures in varying degrees across Europe and North America. One such institution is higher education, in which academic study of Christianity continues to exert its significant influence for the global church.

The question remains: How has Christianity been so effective in advancing serially, as well as across cultural frontiers? Lamin Sanneh, a noted scholar of African studies, asserts that it is Christianity's vernacular translation that "enabled the ethnic group concerned to grasp with immediate cogency the message of Scripture, and the accompanying orthography, grammars, dictionaries and studies of ethnic groups have contributed immensely to the recovery of the cultural identity that laid the basis for political parties, welfare societies, and particularly for the growth of self-governing, self-propagating and self-supporting churches and congregations" (Johnson and Ross 2009, 222). In other words, Bible translation into local vernaculars has had a profound impact on colonized and subjugated populations, helping them to rediscover their identity as people of God and to assess their own lives' limiting conditions and circumstances as well as the cultural potential of their own history and experience. During the era of colonial rule in Asia and Africa, schools promoted Western ideas and ideals. While Bible translation promoted indigenous customs and institutions, local languages were suppressed as impediments to modernization and administrative control. In these places, "the flag and the Bible served opposing interests" (Johnson and Ross 2009, 222). As new indigenous Christians became prominent, the Bible was read, studied, and preached in the vernacular, which resulted in a revival and renewal of Christianity. The new leaders defied denominational and other sociocultural boundaries to rearticulate Christianity as a religion of the open road.

In response to the question, "How has Christianity been so effective in advancing serially, as well as across cultural frontiers?" Mark Noll, a renowned church historian, observes: "Christianity in its American form has indeed become very important for the world. . . . How Americans have come to practice the Christian faith is just as important globally as what Americans have done" (2009). In other words, he asserts that the characteristics of the faith shared by American missionaries, which are "conversionist, voluntarist, entrepreneurial, and nondenominational," have had enormous influence in shaping the nature and function of the global church in the modern world, especially in the global South, where much advancement in Christianity has been made in recent years. In keeping pace with the economic development in these regions of the world, these forms of Christianity maintain an affinity with the ever-protean economic, demographic, social, and cultural character of the world itself.

The Christianity that is "made in the U.S.A." has moved the Christianity of the modern world in the direction of these preferences, as Noll astutely observes:

- Individual self-fashioning over communal identification
- A language of choice and personal freedom alongside a language of given boundaries and personal responsibility
- Comfortable employment of commerce as opposed to cautious skepticism about commerce
- A conception of religious organizations as voluntary bodies organized for action instead of inherited institutions organized for holding fast
- An optimistic hope expressed in the creation of new institutions instead of a pessimistic skepticism about innovation
- Personal appropriation of sacred writings over inherited or hierarchical interpretation of those scriptures
- A plastic, utilitarian attitude toward geography as oppose to a settled, geographically-determined sense of identity
- A ready willingness to mingle different ethnic groups (in at least public settings and despite America's wretched black-white history) as opposed to strong convictions about ethnic purity
- The innovations of the bourgeois middle classes instead of deference to traditional elites. (2009, 120–121)

The serial and cross-cultural spread of Christianity throughout history thus continues in this modern era. Indigenous self-governing, self-propagating, and self-supporting churches in Africa, Asia, and South America have even become a prominent part of the global church in late modernity, as a result of holistic missionary efforts and Bible translation into local vernaculars. The Christianity that is largely shaped in the United States—conversionist, voluntarist, entrepreneurial, and nondenominational—has even become a significant impetus for the "Next Christendom" of the global South in an effort to actively participate in the expansion of the global church in the 21st century.

As a crucial aspect of the church, Christian education, or the teaching ministry of the church, has directly followed the trajectory that Christianity has taken over the last two millennia. For example, the teaching ministry that the apostles handed down to the next generation of Christians was codified into the Didache and other documents. These documents became the seminal foundation of the ancient catechesis that developed over the centuries in the varying sociocultural contexts of the serially and cross-culturally migrating centers and margins of Christianity. The Protestant reformers in the 16th and 17th centuries, who had attempted to recover the teaching ministries of the early church, were able to do so in the peculiar sociohistorical context of their time. Furthermore, the Sunday school movement, which started in a particular sociohistorical context during the period of the Industrial Revolution in England, has developed over the past three centuries, spreading serially and cross-culturally as a direct result of the movement of Christianity across the globe. Christian education, also a loose modern Christian movement, has been an unequivocal outcome of the blend of modern developmental psychology with U.S.-made Christianity. Christian education, as a handmaiden of Christianity and the teaching ministry of the church, has again, in its modern form, spread almost unconsciously throughout many parts of the global church in the modern era. What remains to be seen is how the churches of the global South will indigenize the teaching ministries of the church so that the Gospel of Jesus Christ will be further authenticated, proclaimed, and obeyed as the global household of God in this late modern period.

References and Resources

Barrett, David, George Kurian, and Todd Johnson. 2001. *World Christian Encyclopedia*. 2nd ed. 2 vols. New York: Oxford University Press.

Jenkins, Philip. 1999. *The Next Christendom: The Coming of Global Christianity*. New York: Oxford University Press.

———. 2006. *The New Faces of Christianity: Believing the Bible in the Global South*. New York: Oxford University Press.

———. 2007. *God's Continent: Christianity, Islam, and Europe's Religious Crisis*. New York: Oxford University Press.

Johnson, Todd, and Kenneth Ross, eds. 2009. *Atlas of Global Christianity*. Edinburgh: Edinburgh University Press.

Lawson, Kevin, et al. 2013. "International Perspectives on Christian Education," special supplement, *Christian Educational Journal* 3 (10).

Martin, David. 2002. *Pentecostalism: The World Their Parish*. Oxford: Blackwell.

Noll, Mark. 2009. *The New Shape of World Christianity: How American Experience Reflects Global Faith*. Downers Grove, IL: InterVarsity Press.

Sanneh, Lamin. 1989. *Translating the Message: The Missionary Impact on Culture*. Maryknoll, NY: Orbis.

———. 2003. *Whose Religion Is Christianity? The Gospel Beyond the West*. Grand Rapids, MI: Eerdmans.

———. 2008. *Disciples of All Nations: Pillars of World Christianity*. New York: Oxford University Press.

Walls, Andrew. 1996. *The Missionary Movement in Christian History*. Maryknoll, NY: Orbis.

———. 2002. *The Cross-Cultural Process in Christian History*. Maryknoll, NY: Orbis.

Relevant Entries

Africa and Christian Education
Albania and Christian Education
Angola and Christian Education
Argentina and Christian Education
Armenia and Christian Education
Asia and Christian Education
Australasia and Christian Education
Australia and Christian Education
Austria and Christian Education
Belarus and Christian Education
Belgium and Christian Education
Bolivia and Christian Education
Bosnia/Herzegovina and Christian Education
Brazil and Christian Education
Bulgaria and Christian Education
Canada and Christian Education
Chile and Christian Education
China and Christian Education
Colombia and Christian Education
Congo and Christian Education
Costa Rica and Christian Education
Croatia and Christian Education
Cuba and Christian Education
Cyprus and Christian Education
Czech Republic and Christian Education
Denmark and Christian Education
Egypt and Christian Education
El Salvador and Christian Education
England/Wales and Christian Education
Estonia and Christian Education
Ethiopia and Christian Education
Europe and Christian Education
Finland and Christian Education
France and Christian Education
Georgia and Christian Education
Germany and Christian Education
Ghana and Christian Education
Greece and Christian Education
Guatemala and Christian Education
Honduras and Christian Education
Hong Kong and Christian Education
Hungary and Christian Education
Iceland and Christian Education
Ireland and Christian Education
India and Christian Education
Indonesia and Christian Education
Italy and Christian Education
Japan and Christian Education
Jordan and Christian Education
Kenya and Christian Education
Latin America and Christian Education
Latvia and Christian Education
Lebanon and Christian Education
Lithuania and Christian Education
Macedonia and Christian Education
Madagascar and Christian Education
Malawi and Christian Education
Malaysia and Christian Education
Malta and Christian Education

CHRISTIAN EDUCATION IN THE MODERN WORLD: DENOMINATIONAL PROFILES

Donald Tinder

It is surely noteworthy that three of the most significant institutional expressions of the Christian church—Constantinianism (the very close linkage with the civil state); monasticism (with its later modification of the more mobile religious orders); and since the 1500s, Protestant denominationalism—are nowhere anticipated in the New Testament. Moreover, each of these has had an especially significant role to play in Christian education. As the general introduction to this encyclopedia indicates, in the countries of the Western world as well as many outside it, what is now the secular educational system had its origins within the church during its Constantinian period. The church-state linkage is now politically vestigial where it exists at all. But for ethnic groups, the linkage persists wherever Christianity was once the state-supported religion. Indeed, it has often been the means of keeping a distinct ethnic identity despite the loss of political power. In differing ways, the selected Orthodox communions profiled in this encyclopedia illustrate this. Likewise, the huge size of the Roman Catholic Church compared to others owes a lot to the state support that it long received in southwestern (and some other parts of) Europe and the overseas empires four of those nations once controlled. Catholicism's religious orders not only served educationally, with state support where feasible, but were crucial in transmitting Catholicism to succeeding generations in lands where the state may have been indifferent or even hostile, not least in America.

Various expressions of Protestantism are usually called "denominations." This word is unusually interesting both as a term and as a concept. Denominations are important historically, sociologically, and theologically as the way that almost all Protestants, at least until recently, experience the one universal church. In view of this, it is surprising that the various textbooks on theology that schools use normally have very little to say about this phenomenon, as a check of their subject indexes readily confirms. It is now widely observed that many places are transitioning to what is often called "postdenominationalism." Papers from a conference of one of the largest denominations addressing the significant implications of this transition are now available in *Southern Baptists, Evangelicals, and the Future of Denominationalism* (Nashville, TN: Broadman and Holman Academic Press, 2011). We can expect more such studies to appear.

Certainly a forerunner to the development of postdenominationalism was the rise over the past 100–150 years of countless independent Christian organizations, many evangelistic, but just as many educational in purpose. These are often (and by some, derisively) referred to as "parachurch." That label is valid only in the sense of being alongside congregations (local churches), for their participants are just as much part of the one universal church as are the many Christians who function only within denominational boundaries. Moreover, parachurch participants are usually active in local churches as well, except for the few years they may be away in college, the military, professional sports, or prison. These nondenominational institutions have sought to communicate a more or less broadly Protestant understanding of Christianity while avoiding the traditional denominational distinctives. Even when they are identified with a specific Protestant viewpoint, such as Reformed or Baptist or Pentecostal, they still serve many denominations sharing those perspectives. "Protestant Interdenominational Church Christian Education" in volume II elaborates on this complex development. It is because of this that congregations that once were served educationally by denominational agencies—Sunday school curriculum publishers, colleges, seminaries, youth ministries, and sometimes elementary and secondary schools—can now make use of comparable independent institutions that may be more to their liking. Congregations can do this whether or not they retain some tie to their denominations, though inevitably it seems that the ties weaken, symbolized by dropping historic names from signboards in favor of some more attractive alternative. Instead, inclusive and welcoming designations such as "community" are featured in the congregation's name.

Before reflecting further on this developing trend, let us examine the term "denomination" itself. Derived from Latin, it simply means "something that is being named." Conceivably, English speakers could have referred to "denominations" of airlines or of food stores instead of "company" and "corporation" designating those kinds of organizations. Curiously, "denomination" seems to have become widely used only in two unrelated ways, for (1) certain kinds of Christian organizations and (2) certain numbered items. That is, besides Baptists or Lutherans, one also identifies bank notes or postage stamps belonging to "denominations" with the same number. Without the prefix "de-," "nomination" also means "naming," but more commonly refers to individuals rather than groups. Sometimes "denominations" in other religions are identified, such as Judaism or Hinduism. But care must be taken to include the idea of mutual tolerance. For example, in view of the level of violence often occurring between Sunni and Shia, it would be misleading to speak of them as denominations within Islam.

Knowing the basic meaning and breadth of the term helps to explain why "denomination" is used, even when just referring to religious organizations, in such varied and contested ways. I suggest that as a concept, denominationalism within Christianity only applies to Protestants and hence dates from the 15th or 16th centuries. The concept needs to be clearly distinguished from certain other widely used terms. Besides the Constantinian church, which evolved into Roman Catholicism and Eastern Orthodoxy, there were numerous "named" and distinct parts of the Christian movement from earliest times, such as Gnostics (of several varieties), Montanists, Novatians, Nestorians, Donatists, and Waldensians. But these were usually called "sects" and/or "heresies" by the Constantinians, even when their differences were not primarily doctrinal in nature. Indeed, in many countries even today, especially in Europe and Latin America, non-Catholic and non-Orthodox bodies are often referred to as "sects" or "cults," reserving the term "church" for themselves. This can also be true in northwestern Europe, where Anglicans, Lutherans, and Reformed once had significant state support.

In most Protestant lands, the terms "sect" and "cult" are used for professedly Christian bodies that do not agree with the Nicene Creed. Such groups are confessionally non-Trinitarian and proudly so, at least in the sense that the term "Trinity" has normally been understood. Since "sect" and "cult" are often used pejoratively, I suggest the term "non-Trinitarian" be used instead. As it happens, this encyclopedia has restricted itself to Trinitarian Christianity; hence you will not find entries on such large and global bodies as the Mormons or Jehovah's Witnesses. And although some may refer to such groups as "denominations," they in fact do not fit the concept as it is normally used within Protestantism. For that matter, neither do the Roman Catholic or Eastern Orthodox bodies, at least in their traditional homelands. However, as they evangelize and their members disperse globally, they tend to act in practice, if not in theory, as denominations.

There are both broad and narrow usages of "denomination." Broadly, it refers to the historic Protestant families, of which there are not many. The term "confession" can similarly be used, especially with respect to Lutherans and Reformed. For others, it seems more appropriate to speak of a Baptist or Mennonite denominational family. Narrowly, "denomination" refers to the specific subdivisions of one of these families. Such subdivisions are numerous even in countries where Christians, or even that particular family of them, are relatively few. The massive standard *World Christian Encyclopedia* and the *Atlas of Global Christianity* demonstrate this. Moreover, through divisions and occasional reunions, the exact count is ever changing. "Denomination" can also appropriately be used for distinguishable groups that are within the Protestant or Trinitarian spectrum but have few or no historical ties to one of the traditional families. These are increasingly common in the Western world, but especially globally. However, the term, though not the reality, appears to be falling out of favor, to be replaced by terms such as "network" or "fellowship."

Some profiles in this encyclopedia report on specific denominations, such as the Christian Reformed Church in North America and the global Seventh-day Adventist Church. But most of the profiles are of denominational families, from Anabaptist and Anglican through Pentecostal and Restorationist.

To add to the complexity, nondenominational organizations from sending countries often start what become denominations in receiving countries. This suggests that instead of regarding denominations as being expressions of the church, while other organizations are only "parachurch," it is preferable to see both denominations and specialized agencies (which includes schools, youth ministries, publishers, etc.) as diverse expressions of the one church. Both kinds of organization come alongside congregations to assist in their ministries. This encyclopedia has numerous entries on just such specialized institutions, both denominationally related and not. Since they are nowhere hinted at in scripture, one could argue that denominations are also "parachurch" entities. At least specialized agencies have the biblical example of "Paul and his companions," a missionary team that was sent out by and reported to congregations. Active fellowship in a congregation is expected for all Christians, whatever their age or social status. But Paul's team was restricted to those who were invited, even as schools have restrictions on who may teach or study in them. And Paul's team was not directed by the congregations or some higher authority other than the Holy Spirit, which is how nondenominational agencies generally function. But Paul did publicize his team's activities to the congregations. Today's independent agencies do that and also have formed associations to accredit and otherwise hold them accountable, as several entries in this encyclopedia attest.

Besides holding some expression of Protestant Christian doctrine, denominations always include congregations (local churches), in which Christians of various ages meet regularly. Historically they also included specialized educational agencies such as schools, camps, and conference centers, and publishers as well as agencies to facilitate expansion at home and abroad. The newer "networks" are less likely to have this same full range, for reasons that should be clear from the rise of nondenominational agencies that serve such purposes. It is important to recognize that it is *not* required that a denomination have a formal organizational structure. There are various ways that congregations can maintain close links without reporting to some headquarters.

The concept (as distinct from the term) of "denominationalism" means distinguishable groupings within Protestantism that do not identify themselves in any way as more than "branches" of the one universal church of Christ. The corollary to this is that they recognize at least some other equally legitimate branches. This is not to say that they may not contend that they are the most biblically or theologically faithful expression of the church.

However, in our postmodern climate, such tendencies are increasingly muted. And it decidedly does *not* mean that denominations recognize *all* other denominations. Indeed, many subdivisions have arisen because of a faction splitting away from an existing denomination that it thinks has compromised theologically too much. Other subdivisions have arisen because of organizational or other sociological factors.

By contrast, those Trinitarians who are not Protestant tend to see their organization as the only fully valid expression of the church either globally (the Roman Catholics) or ethnically (the various Orthodox bodies). They also claim to be led by bishops who are in historic descent from the apostles. The Anglicans make this claim as well and have many other "catholic" features, but in most ways seem to behave like Protestants, not least in their doctrinal variations. The Catholic and Orthodox bodies are willing to recognize nonmembers as Christians who meet in "ecclesial communities."

It is noteworthy that, generally speaking at least until recently, no group intends to start life as a new denomination. The original three denominational families from the 1500s—Lutheran, Reformed, and Anglican—certainly did not see themselves this way, but rather as "reforming" the existing Catholicism in certain doctrines (though not those addressed in the Nicene Creed) and practices (such as the papacy and the role of monasticism, but not the close link with the state). The fourth original Protestant movement, the so-called Anabaptists (subsequently represented mostly by the Mennonites), were violently persecuted by both Catholics and the Constantinian-minded Protestants (often called "magisterial," to indicate the level of state support). The Anabaptists were seen as subversive for denouncing the church-state linkage and insisting on personal commitment to accept Christ as Savior and to follow Him as Lord, symbolized by believer's baptism. This contrasted with being Christian, because one's society or extended family said so and baptized one as an infant. Though with very small numbers both in their beginnings and subsequently, the Anabaptist pattern has become by far the most widespread, commonly referred to now as "free churches" or "believers' churches." Outside their homelands, magisterial Protestants have to act like free churches as well, though usually retaining infant baptism.

In the 1600s, Baptists and Friends (informally known as Quakers) emerged, and the former have eventually become almost as large, without ever having state support, as the "magisterial" Protestants have done with it. This is also true of the Methodist movement, which arose in the 1700s and did not intend to become a separate denomination from the state-supported Church of England, but nevertheless did.

By the 1800s, with so many denominations on the scene, the biblical and theological insistence that there is only one church was being visibly contradicted. So it is not surprising that movements arose that denied they were denominations (and some adherents still make that claim) and tried to find ways to get all true Christians into one fellowship, as in the beginning. But like their predecessors, these movements only added to the diversity within Protestantism. The latter sought to renew Methodism, but also led to many new denominations splitting from other branches of Protestantism. In the 1900s, what has become the largest free church movement of all, Pentecostalism, emerged from within the Holiness movement, but was joined by individuals from other groups.

The reality of denominationalism would seem to—but does not—require Christians to stop repeatedly asserting that there is only one church. In some ways, this confession is similar to the equally asserted belief that Christ died for our sins. Such statements are made on the basis of faith, without which the Bible says it is impossible to please God. Even as the Bible is the record of God's faithfulness despite His people's repeated failures, so is the history of Christianity a similar record. Denominations are just one of many manifestations that Christians are not yet glorified. With the passage of time, within denominational families and the countless individual subdivisions, spectrums of belief and practice develop. The result is not only the rise of nondenominational agencies, but also that subdivisions from quite different families can be closer to each other than other subdivisions with which they have a historical connection. Another result is that influences both doctrinal and practical spread from one family to another. There are indeed differences within Christianity, both in teaching and in practice, but much fewer than the number of denominational families or subdivisions would suggest. And it is interesting to observe, as so many of the entries in this encyclopedia demonstrate, that educational techniques, concepts, influences, and the like rarely if ever come with denominational labels.

Relevant Entries

Adventist Church Christian Education
Anabaptist Christian Education
Anglican Church Christian Education
Armenian Orthodox Church Christian Education
Assemblies of God Church Christian Education
Assyrian Orthodox Church
Baptist Curricular Outcomes
Brethren Church Christian Education
Christian and Missionary Alliance and Christian Education Christian Camps
Christian Reformed Church Christian Education
Congregational Church Christian Education

Coptic Orthodox Church Christian Education
Eastern Orthodox Church Christian Education
Episcopal Church Christian Education
Friends/Quaker Church Christian Education
Greek Orthodox Church Christian Education
Lutheran Church Christian Education
Mennonite Church Christian Education
Methodist Church Christian Education
Pentecostal Movement
Presbyterian Church Christian Education
Protestant
Protestant Interdenominational Church Christian Education
Reformed Curricular Outcomes
Restorationist Church Christian Education
Roman Catholic Church Christian Education
Russian Orthodox Church Christian Education
Wesleyan Church Christian Education

INSTITUTIONAL, UNIVERSITY, AND SEMINARY PROFILES

Bryan T. Froehle

Christian Education and Higher Education

Christian education takes place in an institutional setting, whether a congregation or parish, an elementary or secondary school, a university or seminary, or some other context. The ongoing nature of education simply requires an institutional basis, sometimes at a congregational level, sometimes beyond it (Osmer 2005). This entails organizations with their own history, context, personality, mission, and capacity. Such a grounding is all the more critical for the preparation of Christian educators, ordained and lay. Thus, universities and seminaries have a critical role as seedbeds of Christian education. Organized preparation of Christian educators goes back to the beginning, in informal schools of the various leaders of the early church, following educational practices of the time. It can be traced through the monasteries and cathedral schools and became decisively formalized with the emergence of universities. Still later, seminaries specifically created for ministerial formation emerged. Today both seminary- and university-based theological education remains largely confessional in sponsorship, and therefore varied in doctrinal texture and organizational expectations.

Christian education is far more than the acquisition of simple technical knowledge. Rather than merely passing on skills and knowledge, Christian institutions seek to mold persons through practice within an educational community, so that they might mold others in turn, again as part of a community. Rooted in the ancient Christian practice of *marturia*, or witnessing (Groome 2011, 172; Osmer 2008), Christian education goes beyond practices of *kerygma* (proclamation) and *didache* (doctrine). This discipleship-based understanding of Christian education emphasizes *phronesis*, reflective praxis, or conation, wisdom-formation, practices that far exceed the demands of mere *techne*, or everyday artisanal skills (Cahalan 2010; Flyvberg 2001; Groome 1999). The ancient Greeks understood, as did other ancient sources of human wisdom around the world, that knowledge at its highest is an art that is dynamically generative (*poiesis*), not an end in itself: a character-builder, virtue-former, and person-shaper (Wright 2012). Such an understanding contrasts with Enlightenment-derived, historically bound, and specifically modernist claims that learning can be value-free and entirely neutral. In the 20th century, for example, the instrumental knowing of war and the conduct of war could not be compartmentalized, but rather inevitably and profoundly distorted whole societies in the heart of Christendom in spite of their beautiful cultural creations and ancient Christian heritage. Faith and practice, culture and everyday life, cannot be separated. Today, modernist claims of value-neutrality no longer dominate the discussion. The turn to various rival approaches, including virtue ethics (McIntyre 2007), means that leaders of educational institutions of all kinds have renewed an insistence on higher education as formative practice (Bass and Dykstra 2008). This is certainly the Christian understanding of education and educational institutions. In any case, the historical record clearly suggests that mere instrumental approaches lead to the extinguishing of the Christian institutional mission (Burtchaell 1998).

The wide range of institutions and related organizations tied to Christian education are part of the Christian engagement with the world and its work of transformation. These institutions cannot form educators if they are not themselves reflections of the transformation to which God calls the world in Christ. A Christian educational institution can never be an end in itself, but instead is only itself when it participates in the educational mission of Christ. For this reason, any specific individual instance of the global Christian educational institutional infrastructure is best understood when refracted by lenses that offer a wider vision. One such lens is the perspective gained by seeing these individual institutions within a single global reality of Christian education institutions. Considering such a profile as a whole allows one to better see the parts. Another lens builds from the deep origins shared by all Christian educational institutions, ones within the rich legacy of Christian life and practice over the millennia. Understanding the common origins of today's institutions offers a powerful perspective for understanding

Christian educational institutions today. Finally, the challenges and prospects that Christian education faces today are shared by Christian educational institutions, however much they might see their situation as unique and distinctive. Knowing the nature of these challenges and prospects leads to greater clarity for the future possibilities of each institution.

Nontertiary Educational Institutions around the World
Christian education includes institutions at a wide variety of levels, and nontertiary levels are critical in any consideration of the global profile of Christian educational institutions. Tertiary institutions provide educators for primary and secondary education, and such institutions themselves often grow into, or are part of, tertiary educational institutions themselves. Today, educational institutions initiated by Catholic missionary religious orders and other Christian groups outside of Europe now solidly outnumber those in countries once defined as the heart of "Christendom." Among Catholic religious orders, the Jesuits in particular are celebrated for their schools and their pedagogical system (Traub 2008); this reality of Christian extension around the world is as true for works of the Society of Jesus as it is for other groups. Christian mission is no longer a sending of missionaries from Christendom to elsewhere. Rather, mission is a constant and central aspect of Christianity in all places everywhere (Bevans 2010; Bevans and Schroeder 2004).

Within the global profile of Christian educational institutions today, Catholic institutions make up the largest component, at a level significantly higher than that of Catholics within the Christian population as a whole, which is about 50 percent (Johnson and Ross 2009, 71). This institutional impetus is a reflection of Catholic Christianity's ecclesial self-understanding, together with a variety of historical and structural factors. Of the estimated more than 300,000 Christian schools in the world (Kurian and Lamport 2012, 2), approximately 200,000 are Catholic. In 2010, the Catholic Church reported a total of 206,742 nontertiary schools and had such institutions within all but some 20 countries of the world. These include 43,351 secondary institutions with 17.8 million students, 92,847 elementary schools with 31.2 million students, and 70,544 kindergartens with 6.5 million students (ASE 2010, 290). The 10 countries with the largest numbers of Catholic secondary schools are India (6,236), Congo (4,299), France (2,555), Argentina (1,781), Spain (1,807), Mexico (1,735), Colombia (1,561), Kenya (1,429), Brazil (1,350), and the United States (1,229) (ASE 2010, 281–289). The Christian group with the next highest number of schools is the Seventh-day Adventists, which has 5,813 primary schools and 1,823 secondary schools and a total of 1 million primary school students and 494,000 secondary school students (General Conference of Seventh-day Adventists 2012). Taken together, however, the number of schools affiliated with evangelical Christianity around the world is much larger than that of any single denomination. The Colorado Springs–based Association of Christian Schools International, for example, counts a total of 23,000 member schools in approximately 100 countries, which enroll 5.5 million students from the preschool to the secondary school level (ACSI 2012). Beyond these figures, there are many more Christian schools not counted by these groups, representing a wide variety of denominations and traditions across the spectrum of Christianity. In addition, some Christian-majority countries fund religious education in public schools, making the overall size of the "Christian school" sector a matter of definition as well as of counting.

Tertiary Educational Institutions around the World

The global profile of Christian higher education is extensive. There are about 1,861 Catholic institutions of higher education worldwide. About 14 percent of these, 262, are in the United States (ACCU 2013; Snyder, Dillow, and Hoffman 2007), which accounts for about 6 percent of the world's Catholic population (Froehle and Gautier 2003). The next biggest number by confessional affiliation is Methodist institutions, which comprise some 700 colleges and universities around the world, of which 100 are in the United States (GBHEM 2013). Adventists count 111 tertiary institutions globally (General Conference of Seventh-day Adventists 2012). Among evangelicals in general, the Council for Christian Colleges and Universities, a Washington-based organization that serves evangelical institutions, reports 175 institutions in 21 countries, 119 of which are in the United States (CCCU 2013). In addition, the Association of Christian Schools International reports 120 member colleges and universities (ACSI 2012), and the Grand Rapids–based International Association for the Promotion of Christian Higher Education reports 73 institutions of higher education (IAPCHE 2013). These numbers alone reach 2,865, and the sector is a growing one (Joeckel and Chesnes 2011; Carpenter, Glanzer, and Lantinga 2014). Given the difficulty of counting institutions of higher education that may or may not be affiliated with one group or another, as well as controversies over what counts as a Christian university, the widest possible estimate likely exceeds 3,000 Christian colleges and universities worldwide. Such figures should be taken with caution, however, since these institutions vary so widely in size and complexity, as well as in programs and curricula (Lantinga 2008). Nonetheless, this broad global profile is suggestive of the overall global presence of Christian colleges and universities.

Seminaries around the World

Seminaries are a special case of Christian education. As primarily specialized schools of theological education and ministerial formation, they vary by the sponsoring Christian traditions from which they originate. Traditions that require seminary education for ordination naturally place particular importance on them, in distinction to others, particularly evangelicals and Pentecostals, who do not require a seminary degree for ordination. Many of these traditions, however, emphasize biblical literacy among members and especially those who serve congregations, resulting in the creation and support of the approximately 200 Bible institutes in the United States (ABHE 2011), and of course many more around the world, but the number cannot be known with certainty. Bible institutes are analogous in some ways to seminaries in that they train ministerial leadership and sometimes even function as graduate schools of theology. In other ways, however, they are analogous to institutions of higher education in general, particularly the initial years of study, and at times even to nontertiary institutions.

Globally, various organizations serve as accrediting agencies, or the functional equivalent, for seminaries, producing lists of affiliated institutions seen as providing acceptable levels of theological education. Thus, Catholic seminaries are listed by the Congregation for Christian Education of the Holy See, the central administration of the Catholic Church based in the Vatican City State. In general, seminaries of whatever Christian tradition are listed by one or more such organization, whether based within a single church or denomination or at a parachurch level.

As of 2010, a total of 1,184 Catholic institutions were counted worldwide for priestly formation at the level of philosophical or theological study (ASE 2010, 261). Within North America, accreditation by the Association of Theological Schools serves to recognize institutions of theological education. The ATS has a total of 273 member schools, all graduate schools of theology, in the United States and Canada. Of these, 177 are entirely independent of any larger educational institution, while the rest exist within a larger university (ATS 2013). Members include 55 Catholic institutions, but do not include most members of the Association for Biblical Higher Education. There is no equivalent of the ATS outside of North America, but the International Council for Evangelical Theological Education, which includes the Association for Biblical Higher Education and is part of the World Evangelical Alliance, counts 872 evangelical theological schools in 113 countries (ICETE 2012). Taken together, and without double counting, the institutions named number 2,274. When European Protestant and Orthodox faculties and schools of theology are considered, together with other uncounted institutions around the world, the total figure likely exceeds 2,500.

The cities with the largest numbers of seminaries or schools of theology are Chicago, with 11 members of the Association of Chicago Theological Schools (ACTS), all accredited by ATS, and an additional instance of an ordination-type degree (MDiv) offered by a 12th institution (Loyola University Chicago's Institute of Pastoral Studies), in turn sponsored by 10 different Christian traditions; Boston, with 10 members of an association similar to ACTS, the Boston Theological Institute (two of which are different entities within Boston College); Berkeley, with 9 member institutions of the Graduate Theological Union, sponsored by 7 different Christian traditions; and Rome, with 10 pontifical universities that grant theology degrees for ordination in the Catholic Church. In various other cities, such as Nairobi in East Africa, Manila in East Asia, and Delhi in South Asia, similar regional concentrations for theological study and ministerial formation are emerging for a variety of Christian traditions.

Ultimately, such a statistical profile as this is limited, not definitive. Institutions are not entirely comparable, and some dwarf many others. Nonetheless, such a profile can provide a sense of the global distribution of Christian seminaries and theological education in general.

Origins of Contemporary Christian Educational Institutions

In the first centuries of Christianity, bishop-theologians such as Athanasius, Augustine, and Gregory the Great explicated the truths of the Christian faith in light of practical realities, including widespread heterodox beliefs (such as Arianism), new practices (such as infant baptism), and changing cultural contexts (such as shifting groups within and beyond the old Roman Empire). Of course Christianity is a world movement, always found beyond the confines of the Mediterranean world (Irvin and Sunquist 2001). By the 11th century, however, the lands of the old western Roman Empire and its northern frontiers were increasingly isolated following the rise of Islam and the 1054 schism with the eastern Roman Empire. This reality, together with the emergence of the universities during the Middle Ages (Haskins 1957; Pedersen 2009), gave way to new codification and systematization, replacing the relative diversity of practice and theology that had characterized the patristic period and later monastic and cathedral schools (Jaeger 2000).

Theological thought and sacramental praxis became increasingly aligned into a more precise whole fabric through the twin systematizing tendencies of scholastic reason and canon law. The new consensus, with its notably systematic, speculative emphasis, was not universally accepted, however, and an alternative orthodoxy grew, though not as strongly as the emerging universities, in part due to the privileges they and their faculty enjoyed (Kivinen and Poikus 2006). The great Franciscan thinkers Alexander of Hales, Bonaventure, and Duns Scotus, through whom some of the reformers' theological stances may be traced, countered the analytic approach of the Dominicans by emphasizing the practical side of theology. This tradition understood the practice of awakening fear and love of God as the highest good, as opposed to the intellectual encounter with the knowledge of God (Pannenberg 1976, 213). Rooted in the tradition of theology as *sapientia*, wisdom, they sought to hold in union the theoretical and practical sides of life striving toward God, the ultimate good. As the growth of formal models in the intellectual life of the universities continued, however, increasing separation occurred between sapiential approaches based in practice and systematization of theological knowledge, with the latter, more deductive and abstract, approach prevailing in the academy.

The seminary movement that began in the 16th century marked a turn from the practice of systemization to the systematization of practice (Faus 2012, 136–139; Farley 2001, 49). The new ways of forming ecclesial leaders in the newly Protestant lands of northern Europe, together with changes in Catholicism related to the Council of Trent (1545–1563), stimulated the development of curricula and manuals ("handbooks") for seminary education. Theology, which had been configured by its university context in the medieval period, now became focused on the seminary, and "theological education" came to take on a new meaning over time. "Pastoral theology" emerged as a field in the work of Peter Canisius, SJ (1521–1597), who himself contributed to the catechisms and manuals of the immediate post-Tridentine period (Heitink 1999, 98). Among Catholics, pastoral practice was learned through the art of casuistry, the case-based application of church norms (canon law), designed to help determine the acceptable pastoral decision, typically in cases having to do with confession and pastoral care more generally (Duffy 2010). Among Protestants, the beginnings of the development of the fourfold curriculum emphasizing the Bible, systematics, church history, and practical theology can also be traced to this period (Farley 2001, 49). The manuals, compendia, and catechisms that emerged came through the early modern standardization made possible by the printing press and improved communications. The *Ratio Studiorum* of the Society of Jesus, issued in its definitive final form in 1599, represented the same trends, in this case for the humanist educational curriculum offered in Jesuit schools around the world then and over the next four centuries (Traub 2008).

The seminary itself was an embodiment of the "clerical paradigm" (Farley 2001, 87). That is, within both

Protestantism and Catholicism, theology was tied to the ordained and those to be ordained, making theological knowledge their possession. The cleric thus became a professional who linked theological theory to practice. Such a one-way exchange effectively took theological meaning out of practice itself, continuing the diminishment of the practical (Farley 2001, 163). The focus on the pastoral and practical that now emerged for the first time as a field of study thus was an application of theory from within the clerical paradigm. A professorship in pastoral theology was first established for seminarians at Vienna in 1774, well before similar moves within Protestantism in the early 19th century (Heitink 1999, 98). Though the models of theological education in Protestant institutions in the United States borrowed from British practices in the early days, by the late 19th century, the German model had become as dominant in seminaries as it was in university life (Ringenberg 2006; Farley 2001).

In the French context, 17th-century seminary life was renewed by the Society of St. Sulpice and the French School of Spirituality, which brought a common vision to the formation of the ordained. It was transferred to Catholic seminary life in the United States by priest émigrés during the era of the French Revolution (White 1990) and, over the following generations, by the Irish clergy in particular, as they especially tended to share this spirituality. By the 19th century, the struggle with the tectonic shifts of the French Revolution and the emergence of capitalism led to strenuous and mostly successful efforts to build a separate Catholic intellectual and social universe as a means of external resistance and internal rebuilding. As a result, Catholic educational institutions, including seminaries and higher education more broadly, began to expand rapidly around the world. The Jesuits were restored in 1814 after having been universally suppressed in 1773; the Dominicans were reborn from the ashes of the French Revolution under Lacordaire; and countless apostolic communities of women religious were founded (Hostie 1983). Catholic intellectual life became marked by a common intellectual agenda when in 1879 Leo XIII named Thomism the official philosophical and theological system of the Catholic Church. Neoscholasticism thus became the reigning form of Catholic intellectual understanding through the Second Vatican Council (1963–1965). These developments together nourished a creative energy that renewed Catholic practice decades before the Council, particularly in the liturgical movement and catechetical renewal, which became seen as the "pastoral mission" of the whole church rather than mere schooling for children (Hofinger 1957).

Such ferment decisively shaped developments in Catholic university life and in theological education. Within the United States, the more than 250 Catholic colleges and universities at the time of the Second Vatican Council gave their students a strong dose of Catholic intellectual life and often the equivalent of a second major in philosophy, the discipline seen as required for advanced study in theology. Nonetheless, few Catholic colleges and universities had courses in theology beyond a basic level. As theology in the Catholic context moved away from the "clerical paradigm," however, it took root throughout Catholic higher education, away from the seminaries, and undergraduate and graduate programs proliferated for those not seeking ordination. This is different from developments in other Christian traditions, where theological scholarship continued to be based within institutions preparing candidates for ordained ministry. In colleges and universities within these traditions, the tendency was toward required Bible and religion courses becoming religious studies courses. Thus, before 1964 the organization today known as the American Academy of Religion (AAR) was called the National Association of Biblical Instructors (NABI).

The single greatest expansion in theological education within the Catholic world took hold in universities and summer programs in the two decades after the Second Vatican Council, within lay ministry and academic formation rather than seminaries for priesthood formation. Initially geared primarily toward women religious, these university programs expanded even while diocesan programs in ministry training grew, often themselves in connection with such university-based resources (Froehle and Gautier 2000). Some Catholic universities around the world began graduate-level ministry education for religious and laypersons after the Second Vatican Council, but generally a new, separate school or department, with a separate mission outside a university-based department of theology, was charged with ministry training. The locus of Catholic theology in the United States thus fundamentally pivoted from the seminary to the university, and to some degree from the abstract to the practical. Fordham University's Graduate School of Religion and Religious Education (GSRRE) was founded in 1968, following on Loyola University Chicago's Institute of Pastoral Studies (IPS), founded in 1964. Boston College's Institute for Religious Education and Pastoral Ministry (IREPM) was founded in 1971 and today is within its School of Theology and Ministry, a former stand-alone school of theology until 2008. The IREPM developed its singular and distinctive interdisciplinary doctoral program in religious education, critical for any consideration of developments in Christian religious education, under the leadership of Tom Groome. Boston College's Department of Theology remains administratively separate from its School of Theology and Ministry. Four other institutes were founded at major Catholic universities, all of which were outside of their departments of theology or religious studies: Loyola New Orleans's Loyola Institute for Ministry (LIM), founded in 1968 at Notre Dame Seminary in New Orleans; Loyola University Maryland's Department of Pastoral Counseling and Spiritual Care, founded in 1976; and Seattle University's School of Theology and Ministry (STM), founded in 1969. In addition, the University of Santa Clara has both the Jesuit School of Theology in Berkeley, which joined the university in 2009 after having been a stand-alone school, and a long-existing master's program in pastoral ministries, which had always been a program within the university itself.

During this same time, events in northern Europe and then the United States, the largest Protestant country in the world, shaped developments in global Protestant theological education as it took on global dimensions. Changes within orthodox theology and theological education, as well as in other branches of the world Christian movement, began to intersect with these various developments as relationships and networks increased in the wake of globalization and other events. Even as seminaries developed increasing theological sophistication and specialization, they continued to reflect the wider denominational context and the modernist-fundamentalist debates of the mid-20th century. Over time, even as the religious divisions settled down into a mainline and evangelical split, a greater openness emerged across denominational lines. Thus seminaries and schools of theology frequently enroll students of a wide variety of ecclesial traditions, and this new collaboration reflects the increasing dominance of the mainline-evangelical split over the more historical, denominational ones. Similarly, the Protestant-Catholic divide became increasingly less salient, particularly for those seeking theological study or lay ministry. Much of this resulted from going beyond the clerical paradigm as theological studies continued to open to those who are not ordained or pursuing ordination.

These developments can be seen in the continued rise of "practical theology," which is also the disciplinary home of the field of religious education. Within Catholic circles in the United States, the 29 member institutions of the Association of Graduate Programs in Ministry (AGPIM 2013) have made the notion of "practical theology" central to their self-understanding and collective definition. These approaches build on the see-judge-act approach from Catholic social and pastoral engagement, typically by the religious orders (Whitehead and Whitehead 1995; Holland and Henriot 1983), but also in increasing dialogue and sharing across the Christian tradition. In all these developments, from the preuniversity roots of Christian educational life through the increasing use of Internet-based distance learning delivery systems, institutional context remains critical. Numerous specialized programs in these institutions and others, seminary

and university alike, have emerged over the past two generations for those wishing to study or serve as professional Christian religious educators as well as to work within Christian education more generally. Today the conversation has returned to core practices, including the ever-critical practice of teaching, within a Christian educational institution (Smith and Smith 2011).

Challenges and Prospects

Christian-founded institutions face issues of identity and perennial resource limitations. The focus on the Christian mission is a challenging one: far more universities in the world began as Christian institutions than are currently Christian in mission. Self-secularization is a far bigger threat than external secularization resulting from government takeover. The tendency toward isomorphism—institutions of like kind becoming more alike over time, in this case universities of different kinds and sponsorship becoming ever more similar to each other, with Christian universities slowly giving up their distinctiveness—is ever-present (Foster 1921). Funding challenges loom large, as the bulk of these institutions are tuition-dependent. Expenses are much harder to control in smaller institutions, so the pressure for seminaries and schools of theology to become part of larger Christian universities will continue. Growth in Christianity throughout the global South means that the demographic dividend of increasing students ready for university studies as well as seminary studies suggests strong growth prospects over the coming decades. At the same time, this points to considerable allocation problems. Simply put, there are many more universities and seminaries where they are less needed, relative to demand, and many fewer where they are needed. To some degree, Internet-based distance learning allows for a better response to the allocation problem than in the past, but it also reveals a problematically high investment in brick and mortar, as well as personnel, in various contexts.

The challenges that Christian universities faced under modernism—where religion had no place except behind a private, compartmentalized wall away from "authentic" intellectual life—is intellectually no longer sustainable as a result of globalization trends and powerful postmodern critiques. This opens new opportunities for Christianity, Christian intellectuals, and Christian educational institutions (Eaton 2011). However, these forces live on in structures and actors that assume the absence of a serious engagement with faith in intellectual and academic life. One can no longer justify the absence of faith any more than the presence of faith, and serious acknowledgment of faith and religion has clearly been increasing (Marsden 1994), but it will take time for Christian universities and intellectuals to see themselves as full citizens of academe rather than somehow special pleaders or second-class citizens. This is not simply the case within Christian institutions, but in the intellectual support and networking of those in Christian institutions with Christians throughout university and academic life (Dockery 2012; Hart 2002). Today, students and faculty alike bring spiritual questions to campus without any sense that they are illegitimate. The outlines of the relationship between religion and higher education are thus quite different (Jacobsen 2008), though many continue to operate as if this is not this case.

Christian universities will always grapple with questions of identity, but it has only become clear recently that there is a real diversity of ways in which they do so. Their strategy—whether intentional or not—typically depends on a mix of their internal institutional trajectory and external contextual pressures, sometimes predictable by their Christian tradition, but usually determined by a complex mix of factors (Gleason 1995; Marsden 1994; Burtchaell 1998). These distinct forms of embodying the Christian mission include an orthodox (Benne 2001) or purist (Simon 2003) or comprehensive (Kennedy and Simon 2005, 16–19) or immersion (Piderit and Morey 2006) approach, meaning that all within the institution, particularly faculty and leadership, share the same religious commitment, often to the point of committing to a common statement of faith, immersing those within the institution within that tradition. This is by no means the only such approach, however, to Christian identity of the institution. For many, a critical-mass (Benne 2001) or so-called persuasion type institution (Piderit and Morey 2006) will be the most appropriate, since it positions the institution clearly as Christian, though sometimes specifically in denominational terms and sometimes as a kind of Christianity, such as evangelical or ecumenical, and so forth (Kennedy and Simon 2005, 16–19). Thus some distinguished, for example, between a comprehensive denominational institution and a comprehensive evangelical institution or comprehensive ecumenical institution. In this formulation, others are welcomed, either within a broad band that will assure that a critical mass is present, or in such a way that others might be persuaded to be accompany the tradition to which the institution commits itself.

Beyond these forms are pluralistic approaches, both of which embrace diversity, but fundamentally in terms of the surrounding culture. The intentionally pluralistic (Benne 2001) grounds an embrace of pluralism in the mission as a strategic expression of the Christian understanding of the institution, providing space for specific expression of the Christian heart of the institution in particular, cohort (Piderit and Morey 2006) expressions where there can be a kind of small-scale expression of critical mass. Finally, the accidentally pluralist (Benne 2001) is an expression of what happens when the Christian educational institution is pulled away from its commitments by overriding external pressures poorly understood or otherwise ignored by institutional leadership, resulting in a significant deterioration of the Christian mission. This is often, but not always, the result of the institution's location or core market being far from those who live the tradition. In other words, it is a kind of model for an institution in a religious diaspora (Piderit and Morey 2006), though the actual situation may be far more complicated.

The most critical conversation today, however, might be not within the institution itself but within theology and theological education. It is from within theology and the nature of theological education—that is, understanding the meaning of the intellectual engagement with scripture, Christian tradition, and practice—that the intellectual disciplines in which the identity of the Christian educational institution is rooted (Piderit and Morey 2012). At the heart of this question is a critical claim: the Christian identity of the institution rests not so much in that theology is taught, but in that the institution and its leaders are committed to an understanding of theology as saving and sapiential (Hughes 2011, 290; Farley 2001). The implication is clear: institutional identity is not merely structural but personal, and must be constantly nourished. Institutions can move across categories—or a complex mix of categories—but this, too, depends on personal commitments no less than structural strategies and contexts (Glanzer, Beaty, and Lyon 2005).

A Final Word

The entries to follow in this section of the Encyclopedia include non-tertiary forms of Christian education, including distinguished Christian secondary schools and forms of congregational based religious education such as Sunday school. Primarily, however, the reader will encounter institutions of higher learning. This includes universities and stand-alone seminaries and schools of theology, some with ancient roots and others with innovative programs providing for distance learning in theological education, frequently but not always internet-based. In addition, umbrella groups supporting and sometimes accrediting Christian higher education, particularly theological education, are also listed.

In all of the entries in this encyclopedia on institutions of higher learning, a common theme may be seen. Christian education depends not only on a sound institutional-structural basis, but also a missional-theological understanding. At whatever level of study and in whatever context, these two dimensions continue to shape Christian education.

References and Resources

"Annuarium Statisticum Ecclesiae 2010" (ASE 2010). 2012. In *Statistical Yearbook of the Church*. Vatican City: Libreria Editrice Vaticana.

Association for Biblical Higher Education (ABHE). 2011. "About the Association." http://www.abhe.org/pages/NAV -aboutAssociation.html

Association of Catholic Colleges and Universities (ACCU). 2013. "Frequently Asked Questions." http://www.accunet .org/i4a/pages/index.cfm?pageid=3797

Association of Christian Schools International (ACSI). 2012. "Frequently Asked Questions." http://www.acsiglobal.org/ home-2/faq

Association of Graduate Programs in Ministry (AGPIM). 2013. "Member Institutions for 2013." https://sites.google.com/ site/agpiminfo/2012-member-institutions

Association of Theological Schools (ATS). 2013. "Annual Data Tables." http://www.ats.edu/uploads/resources/insti tutional-data/annual-data-tables/2012-2013-annual-data -tables.pdf

Bass, D., and C. Dykstra, eds. 2008. *For Life Abundant: Practical Theology, Theological Education, and Christian Ministry.* Grand Rapids, MI: Eerdmans.

Benne, R. 2001. *Quality with Soul: How Six Premier Colleges and Universities Keep Faith with Their Religious Traditions.* Grand Rapids, MI: Eerdmans.

Bevans, S., SVD. 2010. "The Mission Has a Church." Unpublished manuscript.

Bevans, S., SVD, and R. Schroeder, SVD. 2004. *Constants in Context: A Theology of Mission for Today's Church.* Maryknoll, NY: Orbis.

Burtchaell, J. 1998. *The Dying of the Light.* Grand Rapids, MI: Eerdmans.

Cahalan, K. 2010. *Introduction to the Practice of Ministry.* Collegeville, MN: The Liturgical Press.

Carpenter, J., P. Glanzer, and N. Lantinga, eds. 2014. *Christian Higher Education: A Global Reconnaissance.* Grand Rapids, MI: Eerdmans.

Council for Christian Colleges and Universities (CCCU). 2013. "Members and Affiliates." http://www.cccu.org/mem bers_and_affiliates

Dockery, D. 2012. *Faith and Learning: A Handbook for Christian Higher Education.* Nashville, TN: B & H Academic.

Duffy, R., OFM. 2010. *A Roman Catholic Theology of Pastoral Care.* Eugene, OR: Wipf & Stock.

Eaton, P. 2011. *Engaging the Culture, Changing the World: The Christian University in a Post-Christian World.* Downers Grove, IL: IVP Academic.

Farley, E. 2001. *Theologia: The Fragmentation and Unity of Theological Education.* Eugene, OR: Wipf & Stock.

Faus, J., SJ. 2012. *Builders of Community: Rethinking Ecclesiastical Ministry.* Miami, FL: Convivium.

Flyvbjerg, B. 2001. *Making Social Science Matter: Why Social Inquiry Fails and How It Can Succeed Again.* Cambridge, UK: Cambridge University Press.

Foster, O. 1921. "Religion in American Universities." *Christian Education* 4 (9): 3–69.

Froehle, B., and M. Gautier. 2000. *Catholicism USA.* Maryknoll, NY: Orbis.

———. 2003. *Global Catholicism.* Maryknoll, NY: Orbis.

General Board of Higher Education and Ministry (GBHEM). 2013. "World Methodist Institutions." http://www.gbhem .org/education/world-methodist-institutions.

General Conference of Seventh-day Adventists. 2012. "Seventh-day Adventist World Church Statistics." http://www .adventist.org/world-church/facts-and-figures/.

Glanzer, P., M. Beaty, and L. Lyon. 2005. "Moral Education at Religious Research Universities: Exploring Faculty Attitudes." *Religious Education* 100 (4): 386–403.

Gleason, P. 1995. *Contending with Modernity: Catholic Higher Education in the Twentieth Century.* New York: Oxford University Press.

Groome, T. 1999. *Christian Religion Education: Sharing Our Story and Vision.* San Francisco: Jossey-Bass.

———. 2011. *Will There Be Faith? A New Vision for Educating and Growing Disciples.* New York: HarperOne.

Hart, D. 2002. *The University Gets Religion: Religious Studies in American Higher Education.* Baltimore, MD: Johns Hopkins University Press.

Haskins, C. 1957. *The Rise of Universities.* Ithaca, NY: Cornell University Press.

Heitink, G. 1999. *Practical Theology: History, Theory, Action Domains.* Grand Rapids, MI: Eerdmans.

Hofinger, J., SJ. 1957. *The Art of Teaching Christian Doctrine: The Good News and Its Proclamation.* Notre Dame, IN: University of Notre Dame Press.

Holland, J., and P. Henriot, SJ. 1983. *Social Analysis: Linking Faith and Justice.* Rev. and enlarged ed. Maryknoll, NY: Orbis.

Hostie, R., SJ. 1983. *The Life and Death of Religious Orders.* Washington, DC: Center for Applied Research in the Apostolate.

Hughes, B. 2011. *Saving Wisdom: Theology in the Christian University.* Eugene, OR: Wipf & Stock.

International Association for the Promotion of Christian Higher Education (IAPCHE). 2013. "IAPCHE Members." http://iapche.org/wordpress/?page_id=26.

International Colleges and Universities (ICU). 2013. "Directory of Christian Protestant Colleges and Universities in the World." http://www.4icu.org/religious/Christian-Protestant .htm.

International Council for Evangelical Theological Education (ICETE). 2012. *Newsletter.* November.

Irvin, D., and S. Sunquist. 2001. *History of the World Christian Movement: Earliest Christianity to 1453.* Maryknoll, NY: Orbis.

Jacobsen, D., ed. 2008. *The American University in a Postsecular Age.* New York: Oxford.

Jaeger, C. 2000. *The Envy of Angels: Cathedral Schools and Social Ideals in Medieval Europe, 950–1200.* Philadelphia: University of Pennsylvania Press.

Joeckel, S., and T. Chesnes. 2011. *The Christian College Phenomenon: Inside America's Fastest Growing Institutions of Higher Learning.* Abilene, TX: Abilene Christian University Press.

Johnson, T. and K. Ross. 2009. *Atlas of Global Christianity.* Edinburgh: Edinburgh University Press.

Kennedy, J. and C. Simon. 2005. *Can Hope Endure? A Historical Case Study in Christian Higher Education.* Grand Rapids, MI: Eerdmans.

Kivinen, O., and P. Poikus. 2006. "Privileges of *Universitas Magistrorum et Scolarium* and Their Justification in Charters of Foundation from the 13th to the 21st centuries." *Higher Education* 52 (2): 185–213.

Lantinga, N. 2008. *Christian Higher Education in the Global Context: Implications for Curriculum, Pedagogy, and Administration.* IAPCHE (International Association for the Promotion of Christian Higher Education). Dordt, IA: Dordt College Press.

Marsden, G. 1994. "What Can Catholic Universities Learn from Protestant Examples?" In *The Challenge and Promise of a Catholic University,* edited by T. Hesburgh, CSC, 187–198. Notre Dame, IN: University of Notre Dame Press.

McIntyre, A. 2007. *After Virtue: A Study in Moral Theology.* 3rd ed. Notre Dame, IN: University of Notre Dame Press.

Osmer, R. 2005. *The Teaching Ministry of Congregations.* Louisville, KY: Westminster John Knox Press.

——. 2008. *Practical Theology: An Introduction.* Grand Rapids, MI: Eerdmans.

Pannenberg, W. 1976. *Theology and the Philosophy of Science.* Philadelphia: Westminster Press.

Pedersen, O. 2009. *The First Universities: Studium Generale and the Origins of University Education in Europe.* Cambridge, UK: Cambridge University Press.

Piderit, J., SJ, and M. Morey. 2006. *Catholic Higher Education: A Culture in Crisis.* Oxford: Oxford University Press.

——. 2012. *Teaching the Tradition: Catholic Themes in Academic Disciplines.* Oxford: Oxford University Press.

Ringenberg, W. 2006. *The Christian College: A History of Protestant Higher Education in America.* 2nd ed. Grand Rapids, MI: Baker Academic.

Simon, C. 2003. *Mentoring for Mission: Nurturing New Faculty at Church-related Colleges.* Grand Rapids, MI: Eerdmans.

Smith, D., and J. Smith. 2011. *Teaching and Christian Practices: Reshaping Faith and Learning.* Grand Rapids, MI: Eerdmans.

Snyder, T., S. Dillow, and C. Hoffman. 2007. *Digest of Education Statistics, 2006.* Washington, DC: U.S. Government Printing Office.

Traub, G. 2008. *A Jesuit Education Reader.* Chicago: Loyola Press.

White, J. 1990. *The Diocesan Seminary in the United States: A History from the 1780s to the Present.* Notre Dame, IN: University of Notre Dame Press.

Whitehead, J., and E. Whitehead. 1995. *Method in Ministry.* Rev. ed. Lanham, MD: Sheed & Ward.

Wright, N. 2012. *After You Believe: Why Christian Character Matters.* New York: HarperOne.

Relevant Entries

Asbury Theological Seminary
Asia Graduate School of Theology
Asia Theological Association
Association for Biblical Higher Education
Association for Hispanic Theological Education
Association of Christian Theological Education in Africa
Australian Catholic University
Azusa Pacific University
Bangui Evangelical School of Theology
Baylor University
Biola University
Boston College's Institute of Religious Education and Pastoral Ministry
Calvin College
Caribbean Evangelical Theological Association
Catholic University of America
Center for the Study of Global Christianity
Chongshin University
Columbia International University
Concordia University System
Dallas Theological Seminary
Emory University
Ethiopian Graduate School of Theology
Euro-Asian Accrediting Association
European Catholic Universities and Faculties
European Evangelical Accrediting Association
Evangelical Theological Seminary in Cairo, The
Evangelical Training Association
Evangelische Theologische Faculteit
Fordham University
Foundation University
Fuller Theological Seminary
Furman University
Geneva Academy
Georgetown University
Harvard University
Institute for Christian Studies
International Council for Evangelical Theological Education
International Council for Higher Education
John Paul II Catholic University
Kyiv Theological Academy and Seminary
Langham Partnership
Liberty University
London School of Theology
Loyola University, Chicago
Middle East Association for Theological Education
Moody Bible Institute
National Institute for Christian Education, Australia
Oak Hill Theological College

Oral Roberts University
Orthodox Christian Education Commission
Overseas Council International
Pontifical Universities
Portuguese Bible Institute
Princeton Theological Seminary
Regent University
Roxbury Latin School, The
South Asia Institute of Advanced Christian Studies
South Pacific Association of Evangelical Colleges
Southwestern Baptist Theological Seminary
St. Sergius Orthodox Institute, Paris
St. Vladimir's Orthodox Theological Seminary
Stony Brook School
Theological Education by Extension College in Southern Africa
Training Christians for Ministry Institute International
Uganda Christian University
Ukrainian Catholic University
Ukrainian Evangelical Theological Seminary
United Kingdom Theological Colleges, Courses, and Seminaries
United Theological College of the West Indies
University of Cambridge
University of Divinity (Melbourne, Australia)
University of Notre Dame
Virginia Theological Seminary
Westminster Theological Seminary
Wheaton College (Illinois)
Williams College
World Council of Churches
World Sunday School Movement
Yale University

CHRISTIAN INTELLECTUAL TRADITIONS

Harry Lee Poe

Faith in Jesus Christ has produced several major schools of thought over the last 2,000 years that might be called intellectual traditions. An intellectual tradition goes beyond the parameters of a worship tradition or an ecclesiological tradition, moving beyond the church to all spheres of life. A Christian intellectual tradition may explore the implications of faith in Jesus Christ for every area of human experience and for every realm of knowledge.[1]

In many ways, the Christian intellectual life can be seen springing from Jesus Christ Himself in the Gospels.

In the Sermon on the Mount, Jesus did not teach in the established tradition of the rabbis. He dared to break with the tradition of biblical interpretation to examine the scriptures directly without reliance on the traditional way of reading scripture.

New Testament scholars often speak of a Johannine school, a Petrine school, and a Pauline school within the early church to suggest the development of different theologies among the apostles. This differentiation can be misleading to those for whom it suggests different beliefs about Jesus Christ. The apostles addressed major questions that arose among the widely diverse cultures within the Roman Empire. Different peoples had different questions, and the apostles demonstrate how the Gospel of Jesus Christ addresses a wide-ranging mass of questions and issues in different cultures. We see this growth of intellectual life in how Paul drew out the connection between the Gospel and the poetic tradition of the Greeks in his sermon on Mars Hill (Acts 17). We see it in the way John used the Stoic philosophical concept of the *logos* in explaining the relationship between the Father and the Son (John 1). We may also see it in how the author of Hebrews uses language similar to that of the Platonists in comparing the earthly tabernacle with the perfect heavenly tabernacle (Hebrews 9).

What Christians Believe

Regardless of their different styles, different issues addressed, and different metaphors for explaining the implications of their faith, the apostolic writings of the New Testament all share a common faith that appears in paragraph after paragraph of their writings. They called this common faith the *Gospel*, or the good news. Twentieth-century New Testament scholarship devoted a great deal of energy to exploring the extent to which the apostles shared a common *keygma*, or message that they proclaimed about Jesus.[2] While they did not have a stock formula for how they talked about Jesus, they followed the Hebrew tradition of saying important things in as many and varied ways as possible. The good news they believed, however, involved several recurring elements, around which their ideas and teachings centered.

The Creator God

The foundational belief upon which all other aspects of the Christian faith rests is their faith in a Creator God. In contrast to all the other religions of the ancient world in which

---

1. I have explored this idea at great length in several other places. See *The Gospel and Its Meaning* (Grand Rapids, MI: Zondervan, 1996), *Christian Witness in a Postmodern World* (Nashville, TN: Abingdon Press, 2001), *Christianity in the Academy* (Grand Rapids, MI: Baker, 2004), and *God and the Cosmos* (Downers Grove, IL: InterVarsity Press, 2012).

2. C. H. Dodd began the custom of referring to the Gospel message as the *kerygma*, which is the *koine* Greek word for the content of proclamation. Dodd began the 20th-century debate over the message of the Gospel in his book *The Apostolic Preaching and Its Developments*, in which he argued for a rigid distinction between the message the apostles preached in their evangelism and the content of their teaching for the church. This essay argues that the apostolic teaching was always based on the message of the Gospel.

the faith of the ancient Hebrews emerged, the Children of Israel believed in the God who created the heavens and the earth. When the people of God encountered the cultures around them, they distinguished their God from all others by explaining what kind of God exists. They sang about their Creator throughout the Psalms. The Pentateuch, with the long story of where the Hebrews came from, begins with the explanation of who God is: "In the beginning, God created the heavens and the earth" (Gen. 1:1). We find Jonah explaining his God to the sailors in the same way. It is not surprising then, that when the apostles first ventured into Gentile culture, they began their message by explaining who God is, as Paul did in Lystra (Acts 14:15–17) and in Athens (Acts 17:22–31), and as John did at the beginning of his Gospel (John 1:1–3).

The Fulfillment of Scripture

Jesus explained throughout His earthly ministry that He had not come to start a new religion but to fulfill or complete all that God had been doing since the beginning (Matt. 5:17–18; Luke 24:25–27, 44–48). The apostles explained the uniqueness of the holy writings of the Hebrews in contrast to the holy writings of all other religions in terms of fulfillment of what God had revealed. The prophecies received from God were understood as promises made by the Creator, who had the power to fulfill them, but even more, the character to keep His promises. God had explained to Moses when he left Egypt that He would send prophets to Israel, and the sign of the prophets would be that their message came to pass (Deut. 18:18–22). For this reason, the Bible is understood as the word of God and revelation from God, the basis for faith and practice.

The Incarnation

Christians believe that in the fullness of time, the Creator God took on flesh and became fully human as Jesus of Nazareth. While God never ceased to be all powerful, all knowing, and all present, yet God also experienced the limitations of a true human life from conception to death. He hungered and thirsted. He could be injured. He became like us in every way, yet without sin in order to bring us to Himself (Heb. 2:14–18, 4:14–16).

The Death for Sins

Having lived a human life, Jesus also died a human death. In Jesus, God literally reconciled Himself and humanity (Eph. 2:14–16). In Jesus, the oft-told human story of one person sacrificing himself so that someone else might live finds fulfillment. On the cross, God takes our death, yet we must die with Him. In explaining to the Romans how God deals with sin and death on the cross, Paul said that everyone sins, and the payoff for sin is death (Rom. 6:23). By mystically being joined with Christ, however, we are crucified with Christ, and the consequences of sin are fulfilled in Christ (Rom. 6:3–7).

The Resurrection from Death

Jesus rose from the dead on the third day after His crucifixion, and Christians believe that Jesus will also raise them from the dead (Rom. 6:8–10). The substitutionary death of Jesus has a double dimension: He takes our death but we take His life; we die with Him, and He lives in us (Gal. 2:20).

The Exaltation

Forty days after the resurrection of Jesus, He ascended into heaven as the exalted Lord, in which capacity He rules the universe, hears our prayers, and heads the church (Phil. 2:5–11). In their letters, the apostles always refer to Jesus in the present tense with the term *Lord*, which was the term used by first-century Jews to refer to God. Their relationship to the Lord Jesus Christ is immediate and intimate, for in sentence after sentence they speak of being *in* Christ, *in* him, *in* the Lord, or some similar expression that evokes the mystical union that exists between Christ and those who believe in Him.

The Gift of the Holy Spirit

The promise of God throughout all the judgmental prophecies of the ancient prophets of Israel involved a *new covenant*. The new covenant involved the coming of the Holy Spirit and the dwelling of God in the midst of His people (Jer. 31:31–34; Joel 2:28–32). Rather than a stone temple, the people of God form a living temple in which God dwells (1 Cor. 6:19). Jesus spoke about the coming of the Holy Spirit to Nicodemus when He explained to him that He had to be born again, and to the woman at the well when He explained that when the Spirit came, He would bring the water of life (John 3–4). The Holy Spirit solves the problem of Moses, who wanted to see the glory of God, but God explained that Moses could not exist in the presence of God's holiness (Ex. 33:18–20). Full of the Holy Spirit, however, the dying martyr Stephen could behold the full glory of the Father and the Son (Acts 7:55–56).

The Second Coming

Paul explained at the opening of his letter to the Romans that just as God's identity as Creator is foundational to the good news of Jesus, so too is His return at the last day to judge the world (Rom 2:16). He had made the same point to the Athenians on Mars Hill (Acts 17:30–31). Just as God made the first judgment in the beginning, when He judged creation good, He would make the last judgment at the new creation when He sorted out the wheat from the tares, the sheep from the goats, the good from the bad.

Faith, Culture, and Worldview

Though the apostles shared a common faith, they faced a particular challenge when they took the Gospel message beyond the territory of Judea. Though the Roman Empire had one government, it had no unifying beliefs and values that would comprise an integrated culture. It was held together by the might of the Roman Army under a military dictatorship that sometimes passed from father to son, but just as often passed by assassination and civil war. Within the Roman Empire, the apostles faced many cultures with a variety of beliefs, values, customs, and traditions. The apostles discovered that different aspects of the Gospel created the bridge for presenting the Gospel faith in different cultures. The Jews in the synagogues scattered across the empire adhered to the Pharisaical branch of Judaism as opposed to the Sadducees. Unlike the Sadducees, the Jews of the synagogues accepted the Psalms and the Prophets as scripture, believed in the resurrection of the dead on the Day of Judgment, and expected the Messiah to come to establish the throne of David. Among the Jews of the dispersion who belonged to the synagogues, the apostles stressed the fulfillment of the scriptures in their preaching. To the Gentiles, who knew nothing of the Law and the Prophets and who tended to believe in a plurality of nature gods, the apostles began by explaining what kind of God exists: the God who made the heavens and the earth.

Until Constantine legalized the Christian religion in 311, the focus of the Christian intellectual tradition involved making the faith clear and understandable to peoples across the empire. In different places and at different times, different aspects of the Gospel had greater importance in the experience of the church. In times of violent persecution, the present reality of the Exalted Christ brought great comfort to those who died for their faith.[3] Dietrich Bonhoeffer was the heir to this tradition in the 20th century.[4] When peace finally came and Christianity became the religion of the empire, the present experience of the Exalted Christ became the basis for the development of the monastic movement with Anthony and the Desert Fathers in Egypt.

For others within the empire, other issues attracted them to faith in Christ. Justin Martyr was a gentile educated in Greek philosophy who found the prophets of ancient Israel greater philosophers than Plato or the Stoics. The Greek philosophers had reasoned their way up to their different understandings of the divine, but the prophets of Israel had received direct illumination from God, which was confirmed by the fulfillment of their prophecies concerning Israel and the Messiah.[5] For Justin and Tertullian, who focused on this element of the Gospel in his controversy with Marcion, the authority of the Bible formed the locus of their growing intellectual understanding of their faith.[6] In contrast to Justin and Tertullian, Origen of Alexandria reflected the centuries-old tradition among the Jews of Alexandria of understanding the scriptures in light of the teachings of the philosophers.[7] Philo of Alexandria remains the most significant of the early Alexandrian rabbis for his incorporation of Platonic thought into his theology. Origen would do the same thing with his school of thought as he paved the way for more speculative theology.

Christians recognized heresy before the adoption of the official creeds because of beliefs and ideas that conflicted with the commonly understood Gospel message recorded in the New Testament. The Gnostics were condemned by early teachers like Irenaeus and Tertullian because they denied the coming of God in the flesh, and thus the death for sins and the resurrection. With the end of the persecutions and the official status of Christianity within the empire under Constantine, more complex questions arose that needed answers, including: In what way is the Son related to the Father? From the gathering of the Council of Nicea in 325, Christians put their collective brains to the task of clarifying the implications of the Gospel for doctrines such as incarnation and Christology.

The Middle Ages

Though the Roman Empire might be said to have lasted until 1453, when the Turks finally captured Constantinople, the sack of Rome by Alaric in 410 signaled the end of life as it had been in the West. One might argue that Augustine provided the intellectual foundation for medieval culture for a thousand years and more. Augustine (d. 430) utilized the idealism of Platonic thought as well as Plato's emphasis on the hierarchy of planes between the lowest forms and the ideals.[8] Augustine's theology synthesizes the Gospel categories with a logical structure bequeathed from the Greeks. A man of his times and of his own previous experiences, Augustine was influenced in his view of sex by his sojourn among the Manicheans, who joined the Platonists in regarding procreation as an evil for trapping souls in fleshly prisons. This synthesis allowed Augustine to break with the Irenaen explanation for the problem of the universality of sin and to develop his new theory of Original Sin. His training as a rhetorician also equipped

---

3. *The Martyrdom of Ignatius*, 2; *The Martyrdom of Polycarp*, 2.2–3; *The Martyrdom of Perpetua and Felicitas*, 1.3, 2.3–4, 3.1–3.

4. Dietrich Bonhoeffer, *The Cost of Discipleship*, rev. ed. (New York: Collier, 1963), 37.

5. Justin, *Dialogue with Trypho the Jew*, 7.1.198; *First Apology*, 31.

6. Tertullian, *Against Marcion*, 4.4.

7. Origen, *Against Celsum*, trans. Henry Chadwick (Cambridge, UK: Cambridge University Press, 1953), 12.

8. Augustine discussed how Plato first helped him with his theological question in his *Confessions*, trans. Henry Chadwick (London: Oxford University Press, 1991), 126.

him to defend the doctrine of salvation by grace against the ideas of Pelagius, who taught that people could refrain from sin and thus attain salvation.

In terms of his impact on Western culture, however, Augustine's intellectual influence goes beyond church life. Augustine provided the intellectual cement that would hold the medieval world together in the absence of a single strong government and in spite of many tribes and languages. If we think of a worldview as the core beliefs and values of a culture, then Augustine provided that comprehensive core to Western Europe after 400. The Roman Empire lacked a commonly held philosophical understanding of the world, just as it lacked a unifying religion. Augustine enthroned Plato as the philosopher of the West, with Christianity as its religion. From this synthesis flowed the hierarchical understanding of society known as feudalism, which ordered both church and government in a way that the Byzantine Empire would never know. The understanding of the Platonic ideals, however, also affected art. The West did not forget how to paint and make statues in a realistic way as the ancient world had done. It changed its understanding of art. Art became symbolic and stylized to reflect the understanding that the world into which we are born is not the real world, but merely a shadow of the real world.

The Modern World

Just as the fall of Rome lasted from 410 until 1453, the modern world may be said to have begun long before the end of the medieval world, for ideas take a while to grow and blossom. If Augustine provided the intellectual foundation for the medieval world, then we may say that Thomas Aquinas (d. 1274) provided the intellectual foundation for the modern world. Like Augustine, he relied on the categories of the Gospel, but unlike Augustine, he switched philosophical allegiance from Plato to Aristotle. Whereas Plato's philosophy focused on the other world of universal ideals and perfection, Aristotle's philosophy focused on the world of experience and particular objects. After several centuries, the perspective of Thomas Aquinas began to have its effects on theology, science, politics, art, and every other facet of culture. The emerging culture retained the Gospel as its core religious belief, but as its philosophical orientation changed in the context of the working out of daily life, the worldview of the culture changed.[9]

With his emphasis on the particular, or the things we experience in the world, Thomas Aquinas influenced a change in art from symbolic, stiff painting and sculpture to an interest in representing the world as we experience it, giving birth to the renaissance in art. He also made way for a revolution in political theory that paid attention to the individual. With an emphasis on knowledge that comes through sensory experience of particular things, Thomas Aquinas prepared the way for the scientific revolution.

The scientific revolution of the 17th century could not have occurred without the intellectual revolution of the preceding centuries in theology, which challenged tradition as a reliable way toward truth. Beginning with John Wycliffe (d. 1384), a new school of thought among theologians stressed scripture as the only authoritative source for theological truth. Those who led the way in the scientific revolution adapted this method to the study of the world. Francis Bacon (d. 1626) argued that no new knowledge of the world had been discovered since the ancient Greeks because of the reliance on tradition. He argued that new scientific knowledge can only come by examining the particulars of creation, as he laid out the principles of the scientific method.[10]

One of the greatest achievements of the Christian church of the last thousand years is the creation of the university with its discrete disciplines. Each discipline in the academy relates in some way to the Gospel.[11] The areas of knowledge that the Western academy has explored contrast dramatically with the traditional approaches to education found in cultures influenced by other religious traditions. Many of the disciplines relate in some way to the idea of a Creator God, such as the physical sciences and the fine arts. Some disciplines relate to the incarnation of God, such as social work, nursing, and medicine. Christian thought begins with understanding how any realm of knowledge relates to the Gospel.

Conclusion

Christian thought, in contrast to Christian theology, involves any realm of thought informed by the Gospel. For this reason, we may speak of many Christian intellectual traditions, from Augustine to Galileo. In different cultures at different times, the Gospel provides insight and understanding to grapple with the great questions of the day.

Relevant Entries
Analytic Philosophy and Theology
Anthropology, Christian Contributions to

---

9. I have discussed this shift in thought in several other places; including *Christianity in the Academy* (Grand Rapids, MI: Baker, 2004), 104, 111, 168; *Christian Witness in a Postmodern World* (Nashville, TN: Abingdon Press, 2001), 22, 113–115; *The Gospel and Its Meaning* (Grand Rapids, MI: Zondervan, 1996), 66–72.

10. For an expanded discussion of how the reformation tradition within the Western church influenced the development of modern science, see Harry Lee Poe and Jimmy H. Davis, *God and the Cosmos* (Downers Grove, IL: InterVarsity Press, 2012), 77–89.

11. For an exploration of this idea, see Harry Lee Poe, *Christianity in the Academy* (Grand Rapids, MI: Baker, 2004), 93–154.

BIBLICAL AND THEOLOGICAL FRAMEWORKS FOR CHRISTIAN EDUCATION

Robert W. Pazmiño

The Bible is the essential sourcebook for all Christian education ministries, and theology, which draws upon biblical sources, remains the queen of faith-based studies. Understanding the breadth and depth of biblical revelation is the wellspring for all theory, practice, and spiritual imagination exercised by educational leaders, who can use critical and creative theological reflection to undergird and guide their ministries. Biblical frameworks enable leaders to rightly divide the Word of Truth (written in scripture, living in Jesus Christ, and created in the universe; 2 Tim. 2:15) and to connect truth to life in theologically faithful ways. Teaching that draws upon a variety of Hebrew models from the Old Testament (e.g., Ezra 7:10), and the exemplary models of both Jesus and Paul, among others, enables Christian educators to plan, implement, and evaluate education with spiritual discernment in learning with diverse persons in a host of educational settings. Biblical and theological frameworks provide the essential categories for developing a viable educational philosophy.

Appreciating and grasping the whole counsel or purpose of God disclosed in the scriptures fosters an understanding of the educational implications of biblical canons. Frameworks enable students to explore the connections within and across distinct biblical genres, with sensitivity to the world *behind*, *of*, and *before* biblical texts (Boys 1980) that can guide interpretation in contemporary contexts, recognizing the cross-cultural challenges of interpreting biblical texts in contemporary settings. Educators elaborate upon a common-sense reading of texts, making use of more extensive critical, canonical, and contextual studies to explore meanings related to education (Fackre 1987, 157–210). For example, the First or Old Testament provides a wide variety of historical and communal settings in which to explore the nature of teaching and learning within the faith community. The work of the Latin American educator Matías Preiswerk is particularly insightful in identifying the various agents who were engaged in education. They included prophets, priests and Levites, wise persons or sages, scribes, and rabbis, along with the people themselves as a nation. Each educational agent had distinct purposes, content, method, and institutional expression (Preiswerk 1987, 50–66). Beyond these distinct teaching roles, it is instructive to consider the particular emphases in major portions of the Hebrew scripture or Old Testament. For example, in the Book of Deuteronomy, the stress is on passing on the basic content and norms essential for the life of the faith community. Walter Brueggemann (1982), a biblical scholar, identifies this component of the Old Testament Canon as the *ethos* (Jer. 18:18) of the Torah, the disclosure of that which is binding upon the faith community. Instruction in the traditional and accepted ways or the heritage provides continuity across the generations, especially in times of transition and change. The transformation made possible by the recovery of this heritage is described in texts such as Psalm 78 and the Book of Nehemiah. New life and joy are experienced by the entire nation in returning to the source of their faith. The wisdom literature embodies how the norms of faith relate to particular questions and issues of the day. Wisdom is required to relate faith demands to particular contexts. The counsel of wise persons guides the connection of faith to life. Brueggemann (1982) identifies this component of the Old Testament Canon as *logos*, the discernment of practical wisdom for life that provides meaning and order. Finally, the words of the prophets serve to explore the social dimension of faith and to decry breaches in faithfulness both within and beyond the faith community. The prophets are the social educators of their times, and they disclose the passion of God with their timely words that confront and hopefully heal the nation and its leaders. Brueggemann names this portion of the Canon *pathos*, which brings disruption to the life of the faith community or nation in the service of justice and righteousness (Brueggemann 1982, 13, 108–109). One additional element, named but not emphasized by Brueggemann, but of significance for the formation of faith, is the place of doxology, the place of praise and joy that denotes the embrace of believers by God and their embrace of God (Brueggemann 1982, 117). Each of these portions of scripture and their frameworks are instructive for educational thought and practice in contemporary contexts that call for the complementarity of the canonical elements identified.

The Second or New Testament, as was the case with the First or Old Testament, provides a variety of insights regarding education. The Gospels and the Epistles set an agenda for the propagation of the Christian faith in what often was an alien or hostile setting. Jesus as a teacher had to contend with an unwelcome reception by many of what He was proclaiming. The facts of His incarnation, the threat to His life in Bethlehem, His rejection at Nazareth, and His crucifixion in Jerusalem all point to the risks and costs of teaching the truth in His time. Christians in the first two centuries faced similar challenges to their sharing the gospel.

Much can be learned regarding education from a careful study of several New Testament teaching patterns, many of which are discussed in entries in this encyclopedia. Kevin Giles (1989) points out, in relation to the New Testament, that every leader of the faith community was a teacher. Those leaders included apostles, prophets, bishops, deacons, elders, women, church members, and even children who were brought within Jesus's circle of teaching. The vision was for all to be teachers (1989, 114–118). This was particularly the case for Matthew's Gospel, which served in many ways as both a teaching manual and curriculum; it is positioned first as a catechetical Gospel in the New Testament. The exemplary teaching of both Jesus and Paul is described in various entries in this encyclopedia.

Theological frameworks serve to guide the study of our understanding of God, creation, and humanity and to ground Christian educators in their calling, which is to be practiced with informed and transformed minds (Rom. 12:2). Faith commitments and beliefs are subject to systematic review, recognizing that truth and light emerge from God's Word (written, living, and created), calling for Christian educators to love God with all of our minds and to learn from others within and beyond our preferred theological traditions. There are diverse theologies of Christian education worthy of study and comparison (Miller 1995; Thompson 1982). The theological foundations of educational ministry and the theological frameworks that emerge from these foundations support the tasks of Christian educators to read texts, contexts, and diverse people with the goals of Christian discipleship and spiritual formation in view. These tasks are undertaken with an understanding of the purposes of the Christian church over time, calling for the study of historical theology, and an appreciation of balancing both change and continuity that requires theological discernment and spiritual imagination applied to specific ministry contexts. Developments in the field of practical theology support this undertaking by Christian educators working in partnership with faith communities.

Theological frameworks provide an essential ground for relating biblical directives and principles to Christian education in the postmodern world. Church theologies (Reformed, Thomistic, evangelical, Orthodox, and Pentecostal), philosophical theologies (process, empirical, and existential), and special theologies (feminist, *kerygmatic*, narrative, liberation, black, and ecological) all propose alternative frameworks worthy of consideration (Miller 1995). In addition, Lutheran, Anglican, Pietist, Arminian or Wesleyan, charismatic, and other theological frameworks build upon a common Christian heritage and are equally supportive of educational thought and practice. It is essential that Christian educators explore and rediscover those theological sources that provide beacon lights in the stormy waters of educational thought and practice in the world and thus glorify Jesus Christ in all aspects of life. Beyond the insights of theology and biblical study, Christian educators are also called to consider those philosophies that further clarify the essentials undergirding their thought and practice. These essentials are the givens, the assumptions, the ideals, and the values with which persons function in their lives and therefore influence teaching and learning. A tendency exists for one's theological framework to parallel the particular philosophy of education espoused, but philosophical foundations of Christian education are important to explore on their own terms (Knott 1990).

The biblical and theological frameworks for Christian education are multiple, but can be woven together to provide an impressive tapestry of ministry in the service of Jesus Christ. The warp and woof of that tapestry is the efforts of the sovereign Triune God and those of God's adopted family who have been gifted and equipped for educational ministry. The perspective of scripture provides the essential basis for educational ministries in the Christian tradition. In their various efforts, Christian educators may well take to heart Peter's exhortation to first-century believers:

> Each one should use whatever spiritual gift he has received to serve others, faithfully administering God's grace in its various forms. If anyone speaks, he should do it as one speaking the very words of God. If anyone serves, he should do it with the strength God provides, so that in all things God may be praised through Jesus Christ. To him be the glory and the power for ever and ever. Amen. (1 Pet. 4:10–11)

The entries in this section explore in depth the biblical and theological concepts, frameworks and implications that emerge from the study of both testaments of the Scriptures and their theological correlates. They consider the role of the Triune God as revealed in and interpreted from the Bible for educational thought and practice honoring both the Jewish or Hebrew roots and the canonical structures of the testaments. God the Father/Creator, Jesus the Son and the Holy Spirit are considered and honored in their ministries of teaching and guiding faithful followers who are invited to love God with all of their minds in theological responses to revelation through the Bible, tradition, reason and experience. The distinct literary forms and exemplary practices of the Bible are explored and their implications for education in a variety of historical and contemporary settings. Generative themes from the biblical and theological frameworks are identified and analyzed with fruitful outcomes for all those who teach and learn.

References and Resources

Biblical Foundations

Barclay, William. 1974. *Educational Ideals in the Ancient World*. Grand Rapids, MI: Baker.

Boys, Mary C. 1980. *Biblical Interpretation in Religious Education*. Birmingham, AL: Religious Education Press.

Bruce, A. B. 1971. *The Training of the Twelve*. Grand Rapids, MI: Kregel.

Brueggemann, Walter. 1982. *The Creative Word: Canon as a Model for Biblical Education*. Philadelphia: Fortress Press.

Giles, Kevin. 1989. *Patterns of Ministry among the First Christians*. Melbourne, Australia: Collins Dove.

Grassi, Joseph A. 1982. *Teaching the Way: Jesus, the Early Church, and Today*. Washington, DC: University Press of America.

Heschel, Abraham J. 1959. *Between God and Man: An Interpretation of Judaism from the Writings of Abraham Heschel*. Edited by Fritz A. Rothschild. New York: Free Press.

Horne, Herman H. 1920. *The Teaching Techniques of Jesus*. Grand Rapids: Kregel.

LeBar, Lois E. 1981. *Education That Is Christian*. Old Tappan, NJ: Fleming H. Revell.

Marino, Joseph S. 1983. *Biblical Themes in Religious Education*. Birmingham, AL: Religious Education Press.

Pazmiño, Robert. 2008. *So What Makes Our Teaching Christian? Teaching in the Name, Spirit, and Power of Jesus*. Eugene, OR: Wipf & Stock.

Preiswerk, Matías. 1987. *Educating in the Living Word: A Theoretical Framework for Christian Education*. Maryknoll, NY: Orbis.

Sawicki, Marianne. 1988. *The Gospel in History: Portrait of a Teaching Church, The Origins of Christian Education*. New York: Paulist Press.

Stein, Robert H. 1978. *The Method and Message of Jesus' Teaching*. Philadelphia: Westminster.

Theological Foundations

Boys, Mary C. 2000. *Has God Only One Blessing?* New York: Paulist Press.

Browning, Robert L., and Roy A. Reed. 1985. *The Sacraments in Religious Education and Liturgy*. Birmingham, AL: Religious Education Press.

Bushnell, Horace. 1979. *Christian Nurture*. Grand Rapids, MI: Baker.

DeJong, Norman. 1969. *Education in the Truth*. Nutley, NJ: Presbyterian & Reformed.

Downs, Perry G. 1994. *Teaching for Spiritual Growth: An Introduction to Christian Education*. Grand Rapids, MI: Zondervan.

Estep, James R., Michael J. Anthony, and Gregg R. Allison. 2008. *A Theology for Christian Education*. Nashville, TN: B & H Academic.

Fackre, Gabriel. 1987. *The Christian Story: Authority: Scripture in the Church for the World.* Vol. 2, *A Pastoral Systematics.* Grand Rapids, MI: Eerdmans.

Ferré, Nels F. S. 1967. *A Theology for Christian Education.* Philadelphia: Westminster.

Foster, Charles R. 1982. *Teaching in the Community of Faith.* Nashville, TN: Abingdon Press.

Francis, Leslie J., and Adrian Thatcher, eds. 1990. *Christian Perspectives for Education: A Reader in the Theology of Education.* Leominister, UK: Fowler Wright.

Gaebelein, Frank E. 1954. *The Pattern of God's Truth: Problems of Integration in Christian Education.* New York: Oxford University Press.

———. 1985. *The Christian, the Arts, and the Truth: Regaining the Vision of Greatness.* Edited by D. Bruce Lockerbie. Portland, OR: Multnomah Press.

Groome, Thomas H. 1991. *Sharing Faith: A Comprehensive Approach to Religious Education and Pastoral Ministry.* San Francisco: Harper & Row.

Harris, Maria. 1987. *Teaching and Religious Imagination: An Essay in the Theology of Teaching.* San Francisco: Harper & Row.

Knott, Garland. 1990. "Undergraduate Teaching of Religious Education." *Religious Education* 85 (Winter): 105–118.

Little, Sara. 1983. *To Set One's Heart: Belief and Teaching in the Church.* Atlanta, GA: John Knox.

Marthaler, Berard. 1987. *The Creed.* Mystic, CT: Twenty-Third.

Moore, Mary Elizabeth Mullino. 1991. *Teaching from the Heart: Theology and Educational Method.* Minneapolis, MN: Fortress Press.

Miller, Randolph Crump, ed. 1995. *Theologies of Religious Education.* Birmingham, AL: Religious Education Press.

Pazmiño, Robert W. 1994. *By What Authority Do We Teach? Sources for Empowering Christian Educators.* Grand Rapids, MI: Baker.

———. 2001. *God Our Teacher: Theological Basics in Christian Education.* Grand Rapids, MI: Baker Academic.

Richards, Lawrence O. 1975. *A Theology of Christian Education.* Grand Rapids, MI: Zondervan.

Schipani, Daniel S. 1988. *Religious Education Encounters Liberation Theology.* Birmingham, AL: Religious Education Press.

Seymour, Jack L., and Donald E. Miller, eds. 1990. *Theological Approaches to Christian Education.* Nashville, TN: Abingdon Press.

Thompson, Norma H., ed. 1982. *Religious Education and Theology.* Birmingham, AL: Religious Education Press.

———, ed. 1988. *Religious Pluralism and Religious Education.* Birmingham, AL: Religious Education Press.

Van Til, Cornelius. 1977. *Essays on Christian Education.* Nutley, NJ: Presbyterian & Reformed.

Westerhoff, John H., III. 2000. *Will Our Children Have Faith?* Rev. ed. Toronto: Morehouse.

Relevant Entries

MISSIONS AND CHRISTIAN EDUCATION

Robert L. Gallagher

Essential to the Christian missionary enterprise is the understanding of what constitutes the missionary task. Empowered by the Holy Spirit, it is a crucial responsibility of Christ's church and intrinsically educational. The term "Great Commission" is used to denote Christ's command to His followers after His death and resurrection (Matt. 28:18–20) when He commissioned them to "make disciples" and "teach" the nations of the world, which were educational ventures. It was not until the period of the apostle Paul that the people of the Way began to take the gospel beyond Jewish society, with the church at Antioch of Syria acting as the mission base (Acts 13:1–3). Between the time of Paul and the Reformation of the early 1500s, missionary evangelists practiced the commission of Christ with halting success and in a variety of ways: by advising individuals, preaching to groups, conducting Bible studies in homes, and writing iconic manuscripts (Book of Kells and Lindisfarne Gospels) to witness and nurture the biblical truth that God sent His Son, Jesus Christ, to bring salvation to a separated humanity.

The Historical Development of Mission Education

After the Reformation, the Catholic Church dominated the expansion of Christian mission, with orders such as the Jesuits, Franciscans, Dominicans, Observants, Capuchins, Reformed Franciscans, Discalced Carmelites, and Recollects. The modern era of Protestant mission began in the17th and 18th centuries with movements such as the Puritans (John Eliot, David Brainerd, and Thomas Mayhew), Pietists (Hans Egede, Bartholomäus Ziegenbalg, and Christian Schwartz), Moravians (Count Nikolaus Ludwig von Zinzendorf, August Gottlieb Spangenberg, and David Zeisberger), and Methodists (John and Charles Wesley, Francis Asbury, and Thomas Coke).

Over the past 200 years, the Great Commission has become the foremost Protestant mission directive, providing the principal motivation and strategy of the missionary undertaking. The growth of mission education during this time paralleled the expansion of colonialism. In Asia and Africa, where the British Empire expanded its rule, the Protestant churches and mission societies of England and Scotland developed missionary activities. The Society for the Propagation of the Gospel in Foreign Parts, for example, was incorporated by royal charter in 1701 by King William III as an organization able to send priests and schoolteachers to America to help provide the Church's ministry to the colonists. The new society had two main aims: Christian education for British people abroad, and evangelization of the world's non-Christian nations. The society's first missionaries began working in North America in 1702 and in the West Indies in 1703.

The Rise of Mission Agencies

Yet the rise of mission societies did not occur until nearly 100 years later. In 1792, the English missionary William Carey was instrumental in encouraging the progress of the Protestant mission movement when he wrote his influential book, *An Enquiry into the Obligation of Christians to Use Means for the Conversion of the Heathens*. He helped start the Baptist Missionary Society and spent nearly 40 years in India. Carey's letters home educated a generation of British Christians about missionary service. Consequently, other European and North American Protestants served in missionary societies such as the London Missionary Society (1795), Netherlands Missionary Society (1797), Church Mission Society for Africa and the East (1799), Baptist and Foreign Bible Society (1804), American Board of Commissioners for Foreign Missions (the first American Christian missionary organization, 1810), American Baptist Missionary Union (1814), Basel Mission (1815), Berlin Missionary Society (1824), Rhenish Missionary Society (1828), Swedish Missionary Society (1835), Norwegian Missionary Society (1842), Hermannsburg Mission Society (1849), Woman's Foreign Missionary Society (Methodist Episcopal Church, 1869), Foreign Christian Missionary Society (Disciples of Christ, 1876), and the Evangelical Missionary Society for German East Africa (1886), which launched an unprecedented surge of educational information for the world church.

In modern times, the missionary societies pioneered educating Christians about mission by sending representatives to churches to recruit workers, raise finances, teach biblical mission, and communicate the needs of the foreign arenas, as well as distribute materials. For example, from 1813 to 1855, the Church Mission Society in England published the first missions' periodical, the *Missionary Register*, containing an abstract of the principal missionary and Bible societies throughout the world.

Mission Societies, Denominations, and Ecumenism

The 19th century, Kenneth Scott Latourette's "Great Century" of missions, saw the growth of mission societies and denominational mission organizations (John Wesley's Methodists) in educating the church. By the end of the century, nondenominational faith missions such as the China Inland Mission (Hudson and Maria Taylor, 1865), the Sudan Interior Mission (Walter Gowans, Rowland Bingham, and Thomas Kent, 1893), and the African Inland Mission (Peter Cameron Scott, 1895) dominated the promotion of world missions. Over the years, each of these groups was supported in its recruitment of volunteers and money by exemplar foreign workers, such as Amy Carmichael, Adoniram and Ann Judson, David Livingstone, Henry Martin, Robert Moffat, Lottie Charlotte Moon, Robert Morrison, John Livingstone Nevius, John Paton, Mary Slessor, C. T. Studd, Hudson Taylor, and Lilias Trotter, who produced educational materials (books, journals, letters, pamphlets, and reports) for the Protestant churches of the West.

In 1887, at a student conference in Massachusetts, for example, Dwight L. Moody founded the Student Volunteer Movement for Foreign Missions, with the aim: "The evangelization of the world in this generation." The First International Convention of the Student Volunteer Movement met in Cleveland, Ohio, in 1891, and thereafter gathered in various locations every four years to educate students about missions. In 50 years the movement sent 20,500 students to overseas missions. The recruited college students to take the Gospel to the world included John R. Mott, a Cornell University student, who became instrumental in establishing several ecumenical organizations, including the World Student Christian Federation, World Young Men's Christian Association (YMCA), and World Council of Churches. He received the Nobel Peace Prize in 1946 for his work in establishing international Protestant Christian student organizations that worked to promote peace.

The zeal of the Student Volunteer Movement gave rise to an effort on the part of North American Protestant churches to work together in missionary education. In 1900, the Central Committee for the Study of Foreign Missions was established by an amalgamation of five women's boards of different denominations. Then in 1903 the Young People's Missionary Movement became the Missionary Education Movement (MEM), in which congregations united in producing study materials and opportunities for leadership training for missionary education. In 1950, with the formation of the National Council of Churches in the United States, the MEM joined the ecumenical organization and continued preparing mission materials under the auspices of Friendship Press, with the purpose not to educate about mission, but to educate toward involvement in mission. The foundation of all such educational activity remained the Great Commission to make disciples of all nations.

Mission Education in the 20th Century

The 20th century saw an even greater emphasis on the missionary task, yet with the definition changing to incorporate social activism and justice-compassion ministries (HCJB Global, Samaritan's Purse, World Relief, and World Vision; medical missionaries in majority world countries, such as Mary Fulton and Fred Manget of China and Paul Brand and Ida Scudder of India), together with proclamation and church planting. Contemporary missionaries pursued the Great Commission through an even greater diversity of educational means (e.g., Campus Crusade [CRU], Church of the Nazarene, Navigators, Operation Mobilization International, Overseas Mission Fellowship [OMF], and Serving in Mission [SIM]). Within the churches of the various societies in which they labored, cross-cultural workers educated through catechism and baptismal classes, discipleship and Sunday school programs, and small group Bible studies and training seminars, all designed to supplement the Sunday service and educate followers of Jesus in Christian understanding and behavior. Furthermore, the approach of biblical education by extension using correspondence courses and other means explicitly educational in design was an effective missionary tool for many decades, especially in creative-access countries.

Creative Access of Mission Education

Two mission organizations that were successful in educating the church in resistant political situations were Biblical Education by Extension (BEE) and Theological Education by Extension College. The BEE was originally founded in 1979 by five mission agencies working in Eastern Europe to train church leaders where formal theological education was restricted. Due to the oppression by the communist governments, Protestant denominations were unable to provide adequate theological training of their clergy or initiate new institutions for theological leadership development. The BEE was a cooperative educational mission whose nonformal extension programs offered biblical education to ecclesiastical leaders behind the Iron Curtain. Theological Education by Extension College of Johannesburg, South Africa, provided theological education to ministry in Southern Africa. The ecumenical church project was established in 1976 as an anti-apartheid institution to provide biblical training within a nonracist and ecumenical setting as it fulfilled its mission of "equipping anyone, anywhere, for ministry."

Among resistant groups, educational services provided a vehicle of Gospel access that normally did not occur. The global prominence of the English language created a demand for English teachers, and since the 1970s a number of Christian organizations have sent professionals among Gospel resilient groups to teach English to speakers of other languages (TESOL). Agricultural, business, development, and relief workers also provided educational skills as a way of incarnating the Christian message. Likewise, mass media services such as literature (CLC International in Sheffield, England) and radio ministries (HCJB in Quito, Ecuador, and Trans World Radio in the Principality of Monaco) were explicitly educational methods of Christian instruction that have been used by missionaries for many years, although they are now becoming irrelevant in many regions of the world. With the advent of the Internet (web, blog, Twitter, and Facebook) and cable television, theological education through these new approaches is proving to be a more effective instrument of the Gospel in restricted-access countries.

Mission Education and Scholarship

Together with the popular education of the local churches is a scholarly field of mission education. In the work of missions, theological education through means such as Bible schools and institutes, Christian colleges and universities, seminaries and libraries (the Day Missions Library at Yale Divinity School, New Haven, Connecticut, and the Evangelism and Missions Collection at Wheaton College Library, Wheaton, Illinois), theological education by extension (TEE), and academic societies and journals, as well as mission leaders' conferences and schools for missionary children, had a prominent instructional role in Christian ministries. The remaining portion of this article focuses on a number of these educational means.

Bible Schools and Institutes

Bible schools and institutes developed curriculum to train students for foreign missionary service. Schools such as the Missionary Training Institute (A. B. Simpson, New York, 1882), Moody Bible Institute (D. L. Moody, Chicago, 1886), Prairie Bible Institute (L. E. Maxwell, Three Hills, Alberta, Canada, 1922), Columbia Bible College (Robert McQuilkin, Columbia, South Carolina, 1923), Peace River Bible Institute (Walter McNaughton, Sexsmith, Alberta, Canada, 1933), Lancaster School of the Bible (Henry J. Heydt, Lancaster, Pennsylvania, 1933), Briercrest Bible Institute (Henry Hildebrand, Briercrest, Saskatchewan, Canada, 1935), and Multnomah School of the Bible (John G. Mitchell, Portland, Oregon, 1936) shaped a generation of world missionaries for the Great Commission of Christ.

The following Bible schools and missionary training centers are representative of the important role in mission education played over the last 60 years by institutions with their central focus of preparing church leaders and missionaries: Chuck Smith's Calvary Chapel Bible Schools of Southern California; Ralph and Roberta Winter's US Center for World Mission in Pasadena, California, with its publishing arm of William Carey Library and Perspectives on the World Christian Movement (providing college-level missions courses to local congregations); Nick and Leona Venditti's Institute of Theology by Extension (INSTE) via Open Bible Churches; Ken Chant's Vision Christian College in Australia; Sydney Missionary and Training College in Croydon, NSW, Australia; Barry and Rosalie Silverback's CRC Churches International of Papua New Guinea (PNG) and the South Pacific; and Loren and Darlene Cunningham's worldwide Youth With A Mission (YWAM). For example, YWAM, formed in 1960, is an interdenominational missionary organization, which currently has over 18,000 full-time volunteers from 180 countries working in 1,000 ministry locations around the world, as well as annually training more than 25,000 short-term missions' volunteers.

Likewise, the Silverbacks founded the CRC Bible Schools in Port Moresby, Papua New Guinea, with the full-time Bible School (1979), Institute of Evangelism (1981), and World Mission Faith Training School (1996), firmly establishing the Christian Revival Crusade as an indigenous training organization. Within two decades, more than 80 national pastors were ordained, and CRC Bible Schools were established in the Central, East New Britain, Oro, Gulf, Western, Milne Bay, Western Highlands, North Solomon, Enga, and Madang provinces of PNG. In addition, CRC missionaries from PNG started Bible training schools in the Solomon Islands, Fiji, Vanuatu, Indonesia, and Philippines. By December 1996, a total of 105 overseas students from the Solomon Islands, Philippines, India, Pakistan, Sri Lanka, Fiji, Vanuatu, Australia, New Zealand, United States, and Cook Islands had attended Bethel Centre's Bible School in Port Moresby, making it a truly international educational operation.

Colleges and Universities

The Council for Christian Colleges and Universities (CCCU) is an international association of Christ-centered colleges and universities instituted in 1976, which has grown to 119 members in North America and 54 affiliated organizations in 20 countries. The purpose of the CCCU is to advance the cause of Christ-centered higher education and help Christian educational institutions transform lives by faithfully relating scholarship and service to biblical truth. The majority of the participating schools offer tertiary programs in missions and intercultural studies to train cross-cultural workers, such as the California institutions of Azusa Pacific University in Azusa, Fuller Theological Seminary in Pasadena, Point Loma Nazarene University in San Diego, and Westmont College in Santa Barbara.

Along these same lines is Wheaton College in Wheaton, Illinois. Founded in 1860, the college has produced a plethora of missionary educators of the ilk of Evvy Hay Campbell, Jim and Elisabeth Elliot, Billy and Ruth Graham, John Gration, David Howard, Charles and Marguerite Kraft, Sherwood and Judy Lingenfelter, A. Scott Moreau, and John Piper. Drawing 2,500 undergraduates and 500 graduates from all 50 states, 60 countries, and more than 55 church denominations, Wheaton College offers 40 undergraduate majors and 19 graduate programs that promote intercultural competence, and an Intercultural Studies Department in the Graduate School that offers programs in intercultural studies and TESOL, evangelism and leadership, missional church movements, and intercultural studies and missions to develop effective cross-cultural professionals who are proficient communicators of Christ, sensitive to other cultures, and effective servants.

In the work of missions, another effective form of scholarly education has been theological education by extension, which was started in 1963 by the Latin American missionaries Ralph Winter, Ross Kinsler, Kenneth Mulholland, and Sam Rowen at the Evangelical Presbyterian Seminary of Guatemala. There they started a program to answer the question of how a seminary could prepare ministers for a range of ministry needs without the students leaving their homes and employment. Instead of coming to the seminary to attend courses, the students studied course material supplied by the institution and gathered in regional tutorial groups to discuss the academic work. Today TEE programs are run in at least 32 countries, including nine in Africa.

Mission Educators, Programs, and Academic Societies

Other influential mission educators of the 20th century whose thinking has shaped the academic discipline and praxis were such missiologists as Alan Tippett of Australia, Rubem Azevedo Alves of Brazil, C. René Padilla of Colombia and Ecuador, Philip Potter of Dominica (West Indies), Karl Barth of Germany, Kwame Bediako of Ghana, Kosuke Koyama of Japan, J. Samuel Escobar of Peru, Orlando E. Costas of Puerto Rica, David J. Bosch of South Africa, D. T. Niles of Sri Lanka, Lesslie Newbigin and Andrew F. Walls of the United Kingdom, Emilio Castro of Uruguay, and Peter C. Phan of Vietnam; and from the United States, R. Pierce Beaver, Stephen Bevans, Anthony Gittens, Arthur F. Glasser, Paul G. Hiebert, Charles Kraft, Kenneth Scott Latourette, Donald A. McGavran, Dana L. Robert, Robert J. Schreiter, Wilbert R. Shenk, and Charles E. Van Engen.

The academic discipline of missiology also has a number of schools in the United States that offer doctoral programs: Asbury Theological Seminary (Wilmore, Kentucky), Assemblies of God Theological Seminary (Springfield, Missouri), Biola University (La Mirada, California), Boston University (Boston, Massachusetts), Catholic Theological Union (Chicago, Illinois), Fuller Theological Seminary (Pasadena, California), Luther Seminary (St. Paul, Minnesota), Princeton Theological Seminary (Princeton, New Jersey), Southwestern Baptist Theological Seminary (Fort Worth, Texas), and Trinity Evangelical Divinity School (Deerfield, Illinois).

In addition, missiological academic education is gaining momentum through societies such as the American Society of Missiology (ASM), American Society of Missiology Eastern Fellowship, Association of Professors of Missions, Evangelical Missiological Society (EMS), International Association for Mission Studies (IAMS), Midwest Mission Studies Fellowship, and the Society for Pentecostal Studies (SPS), together with centers of missiological education such as the Boston Theological Institute; Maryknoll Catholic Mission Movement in New York (with its publishing arm, Orbis Books); Orthodox Christian Mission Center in St. Augustine, Florida; Overseas Ministries Study Center (OMSC) in New Haven, Connecticut; Faculdade Teológica Sul Americana in Londrina, Paraná, Brasil (cofounded by Antonio Carlos and Priscilla Barro); and Tabor Adelaide (cofounded by Barry Chant and Dennis Slape) and MCD University of Divinity in Australia. It is also advancing through academic publications such as the *Australian Journal of Mission Studies* (Australian Association for Mission Studies), *Evangelical Missions Quarterly* (EMIS, Billy Graham Center), *International Bulletin of Missionary Research* (OMSC), *Mission Studies* (IAMS), *Missiology: An International Review* (ASM), *International Review of Mission* (World Council of Churches), *Missionalia* (South African Missiological Society), and *Pneuma* (SPS).

Mission Conferences and Conventions

During the latter half of the 19th century in the United States and England, prominent missionary conferences were held in New York (1854), Liverpool, England (1860), London (1878 and 1888), New York (1900), and Edinburgh (1910), with the main focus to educate people about missions; other important conventions were the China Centenary Missionary Conference in Shanghai, China (1907) and the annual Keswick Convention in Keswick, England (1875). The organizers of the 1860 Liverpool conference claimed, whoever desires to maintain the missionary spirit must seek to have an intelligent knowledge of the mission field.

Edinburgh 1910 was both the culmination of the previous century's Protestant missions and the formal beginning of the modern Christian ecumenical movement. Major Protestant denominations and missionary societies, predominantly from North America and Northern Europe, sent 1,200 representatives to Edinburgh, Scotland, where the watchword of the conference was, "The evangelization of the world in this generation," together with a call to unity among the missionaries. Under the direction of John Mott, the continuing work of the conference established the International Missionary Council in 1921, which later became the World Council of Churches in 1948.

From the second half of the 20th century to the present time, missionary conventions have maintained their fundamental position in missionary education, attracting a wide audience of students, church leaders, and missionaries. Following is a sample of the annual missionary conferences in the United States: Christian Churches' International Conference on Mission, Christian Reformed Churches' GO Missions, Global Missions

Health Conference, International Brethren Conference on Missions, Missio Nexus' Mission Leaders Conference, Southern Baptist Convention's International Mission Board, United Methodist Women, and InterVarsity Christian Fellowship's Urbana Mission Conference. Since 1946, Urbana has propagated missions' education among college and university students with a five-day conference every three years, which attract some 15,000 attendees. Over the years, the total attendance of the conference has been more than 200,000 students, all of whom were educated concerning God's heart for the nations and challenged about their commitment to the Messiah's Great Commission.

On an international level, there were also a myriad of evangelism conferences to help educate the global church about the goals, methods, and means of world missions. The 1966 World Congress on Evangelism in West Berlin, Germany, for example, was an important event in 20th-century Christianity. At this meeting, Protestant evangelical Christian leaders from around the world met and began to build relationships that led to a much closer cooperation. The Lausanne movement, which was a direct result of this ecumenical cooperation, had its first International Congress on World Evangelization in 1974 in Lausanne, Switzerland. Sponsored by the Billy Graham Evangelistic Association and *Christianity Today* magazine, the gathering involved 2,500 evangelists from over 150 countries. This was followed by another international congress in 1989 in Manila, Philippines, and Lausanne III in Cape Town, South Africa, in 2010, each drawing 4,000 Christian leaders representing 170 and 198 nations, respectively. Since 1974, the Lausanne movement has continued to focus on world evangelization, with its mission statement, *"The whole Church taking the whole Gospel to the whole world."* Over the past several decades, Lausanne has convened gatherings on a wide range of issues related to world evangelization, such as Chinese, Jewish, and Muslim evangelism, and the topics of creative arts, business, international researchers, and young leaders and missions.

Missionary Schools in India

Serving the mission community, missionary schools throughout Protestant church history provided for the educational needs of missionary children. Such schools exist all over the world to help Christian cross-cultural workers provide quality education for their families close to their place of ministry. Missionaries established schools not only for their children, but also for educating the indigenous people. Both types of schools played a primary role in the Protestant movement from the beginning. Because of the huge outlay of mission resources in schooling, it is important to review this key emphasis of missions' education. As a case study, let us briefly consider the educational impact of Protestant mission in India.

Under the patronage of Frederick IV of Denmark, Bartholomäus Ziegenbalg, along with his fellow German Lutheran student, Heinrich Plütschau, became the first Protestant missionaries to India. They arrived at the Danish colony of Tranquebar in 1706, believing that church and school were to go together, and the propagation of the Christian faith needed to be linked with education since children must be trained to read the Word of God. To this end, the two Pietists began day schools for the Portuguese and Danish coworkers a year after their arrival. Following the August Francke Pietist model, a revolutionary innovation was made in 1710 when they started a day school for girls (India's first). The Halle missionaries adapted Francke's pedagogical principles (e.g., dividing children by age) and taught in the vernacular, with the Bible and the Lutheran catechism as their core texts. They believed it was critical to teach children the scriptures before they grew hardened to spiritual truth. Their curriculum included astronomy, cooking, geography, mathematics, medicine, poetry, reading, rhetoric, and writing using European clocks, globes, and world maps.

Although the Tamil society had a rich history in the arts and sciences—astronomy, cosmology, mathematics, medicine, moral teaching, music, physics, poetry, surgery, and writing—education was restricted to the high-caste Brahmins. In 1715, a Tamil "free-charity" boarding school and an orphanage (where poor children were entrusted to the care of house parents) were founded. The next year, they started a seminary (with eight senior Tamil students) to train teachers, catechists, and pastors, looking forward to a time when Europeans would no longer be needed. The Lutheran missionaries were against westernizing the Indian Christians, and diligently taught the Tamil schoolchildren their own language and customs using free Tamil church members, as well as the European curriculum through European teachers.

One hundred years later, William Carey, Joshua Marshman, and William Ward worked together to translate the Bible into a number of Indian languages and provided education for their children and the children of native Indians (including females) with instruction in these languages. Known as the Serampore Trio, these three English missionaries founded Serampore College at West Bengal in 1818 to provide an education in arts and sciences to students of every "caste, color or country" and to train people for ministry in the growing church of India.

Another educational influencer in British colonialism was Alexander Duff, the first missionary of the Church of Scotland to India, who played a significant role in the development of higher education. In 1830 he founded the General Assembly's Institution in Calcutta, now known as the Scottish Church College, and played a part in establishing the University of Calcutta. Duff believed that Bengali schools were inadequate in educating students in a broad range of subjects, and that they needed instruction using English instead of the local dialects. He concluded that Christian missions in India had only been successful in converting a few low-caste groups from poor socioeconomic backgrounds, and that the upper-caste Hindu and Muslim communities had not been accessed by traditional evangelical methods. By offering a Western education, Duff surmised that he would bring the children of the affluent classes into his range of Christian influence, which would lead to a change of religious allegiance. The success of his work had the effect of spreading mission-founded English-language schools across the subcontinent and exposing high-caste Hindus to Christian ideas. Only a few students converted, since Hindus did not consider the two faiths to be mutually exclusive and adapted well to the Western worldview.

In particular, three educational strengths of Duff's mission solidified the immense personnel and financial commitment of the Western church to mission schooling: the importance of literacy in Christian mission as a religion based on the Bible; the subsequent development of indigenous church leadership; and the belief that the intersection of the Western Christian instructional system and national leadership engendered social transformation along the lines of constitutional government, egalitarian human rights, capitalistic economies, and scientific and technological progress.

During the 19th and early 20th centuries, mission schools multiplied rapidly, and they were similarly important in Asia (especially China and Japan) and the Middle East. In particular, missionary schools in sub-Saharan Africa remained the primary source of education well into the 1960s, with the result that nearly 85 percent of the schoolchildren were influenced by the Christian educational model. In retrospect, however, the evangelistic outcome of mission schools was negligible, although they did provide an entrée to inaccessible groups and shaped the non-Western worldview of Africa's future national leaders. Yet after World War II, the connection between mission schools and imperialism proved problematic, with rising nationalism in Asia and Africa. The English colonial government of India in 1859, for instance, decided to provide financial assistance to schools that met their standards, curriculum, and inspection. This caused an expansion of the mission schools, which, when coupled with an increase in British missionary teachers, allowed them to remain prevalently influential until 1947 and independence, when all schools became a part of the national education program.

Mission education could be viewed as being education *about* mission, which involves engaging in mission theology, an awareness of the strategic paradigms of mission history, and informing people of the structures and programs of mission agencies and denominations; education *for* mission, which entails the selection and instruction of people training for cross-cultural service locally or globally; and education *in* mission, the process of reflection and action of those on the field involved in crossing barriers with the good news of Christ, especially the communication, incentive, and way of missions.

Relevant Entries
Art and Mission
Bible Translation
Education for Mission
Education for Urban Mission
Great Commission, The
Mission Schools
Missional Environments, Creating
Missionary Task
Missions and Democracy
Missions and Globalization
Missions and Literacy
Missions and Modernization
Missions and the Education of Women
Missions and Theological Education
Schools for Missionary Children
Seeker Courses

CHRISTIAN CURRICULUM

Thomas H. Groome

Moving Along Together

The English word "curriculum" comes from the Latin *curriculere*, meaning "to move along together." Its etymology has deep resonance among the Christian people of God as they make their pilgrim's way through history, ever reaching into God's reign that is coming to meet us. It suggests that the church's whole way of "moving along together" is constitutive of its Christian education curriculum and that every aspect of the life of the church and its ministries must be reviewed for how it is educating in faith (or mis-educating).

There have been times and places where the local culture was sufficient to enculturate people into Christian identity (indeed, I grew up in such an Irish village). But this is true no longer, at least in our more secularized Western world. Now we must intentionally craft our whole way of being together as families and communities of faith so as inform, form, and transform (lifelong conversion) people in Christian identity and faith commitment.

Life of Congregation and Family as Primary Curriculum of Christian Faith

Everything about the life of the Christian family and of the church in the world has the capacity to educate in Christian faith. Maria Harris (1989) summarized many years ago, the church does not simply "have" a curriculum (as in the instructional series that a parish or congregation purchases); it "is" its own curriculum. I say the same is true of the Christian family.

This means that we must ask of every aspect of the life of the family and congregation/parish: "What is this teaching?" and "Is it teaching the Christian faith we profess?" This requires us to bring a Christian education consciousness to review every structure and arrangement, every practice and commitment, every symbol and sacrament, every value and perspective, every prayer and language pattern—everything about the church—for its effectiveness in educating in Christian faith.

Crafting the Communal Curriculum

To harness the whole life of the congregation and family to educate in faith, it can help to imagine the educational potential of *all* the traditional functions of Christian ministry. A common listing of the church's ministries is *koinonia, marturia, leitourgia, diakonia,* and *kerygma/didache*; correspondingly, I name them here ministries of *welcome, witness, worship, well-being,* and *word*. We typically think of Christian education as an instance of the church's ministry of *the word,* and of course, it is most obviously so. My central proposal here, however, is that we expand our consciousness—and curriculum planning—to craft all of the church's ministries to take advantage of their potential to educate in faith. Beyond this, of course, we still need a distinctive ministry of Christian religious education—though in partnership with all the other ministries.

Koinonia/Welcome

Every parish/congregation must strive to be a vibrant community of Christian faith, hope, and love. In a special way, its witness to the Gospel must be epitomized in its inclusion and hospitality toward all. It needs to be a community that welcomes all as full members and to use their gifts in the church's mission and life. As its welcome should be unconditional, the same should be true of its outreach, care, and concern. In sum, it should be a truly "catholic" community—without borders.

Likewise, Gospel values should permeate the whole ethos of the Christian family. Its faith must be lived in the day-to-day joys and tensions of family life, shaping the whole family narrative. In particular, the "domestic church" must strive to be a Christian home for all its members, a community in which all are equally cherished and cared for, and that has a welcoming outlook toward others and the world. An insular "nuclear" family will not be effective to nurture in Christian faith.

Marturia/Witness

The parish/congregation must not only live the Christian faith it professes within its own community, but must be a visible and credible witness of this faith to its surrounding context and culture. Its witness as a community of disciples to Jesus is its most effective means of evangelization and education in faith. It must seek out opportunities for public witness to its Christian values, striving to be a leaven for God's reign in the public realm.

Likewise for the Christian family, its members are called upon to bear witness to their faith. They do this first to each other, in the dailiness of family life. Then, while faith, hope, and love should begin at home, they certainly should not stay at home. Every Christian family needs to bear witness to its faith to its surrounding context; its modes of engagement with the "outside" world should explicitly reflect its Christian commitments and values.

Leitourgia/Worship

Likely nothing that the church does in the world is as educational as its "public work" (*leitourgia*) of worshipping God. Of course, the community's worship should not become a didactic event; the liturgy's primary purpose always is to worship God. However, precisely because it is so symbol laden and suffused with a sense of the sacred, worship can have a powerful formative effect on people's faith. Its educational power is most evident in a worship's "liturgy of the word," but remembering how symbols affect what they symbolize, the celebration of Eucharist/Holy Communion also has powerful educational potential. Well-crafted liturgy will not only worship God, but will also be effective to nurture people in faith. Conversely, poor worship is likely hazardous to people's faith.

Likewise, every Christian family needs it sacred rituals that nurture and sustain the faith of its members. For sure, its children are more likely to grow up Christian if they experience in the home regular patterns of prayer and faith sharing, and some sacred times, symbols, or events that express and celebrate the faith of the family.

Diakonia/Well-being

We typically think of the praxis of Christian faith as emerging from our knowledge and belief in its regard. In fact, the doing of faith, and especially of its works of compassion, justice, and peacemaking, is a source for knowing its truth more deeply, the kind of truth that sets free (see John 8: 32). Every Christian community must mount its works of service to human well-being—with special favor, as Jesus had, for the least, the lost, and the last—if it is to effectively educate in faith. Such praxis and reflection upon it is integral to its curriculum. Likewise, the Christian family should be marked by its works of compassion, justice, and peacemaking, first among its own members and then by outreach to others in need.

Kerygma/Didache/Word

So, every aspect of the church's life in the world and every function of its ministries—in both the local and "domestic" church—should be scrutinized and adjusted as needed to effectively educate in faith. This being said, the community and family also *need* to be educated. They are ever both agent and recipient of evangelization and catechesis. Every Christian family can have ample opportunities—whether prompted or in response to teachable moments—to explicitly share its faith together. However, every congregation and parish needs its formal programs of intentional education in faith. I now turn to the task of crafting an explicit and formal curriculum of Christian education.

Crafting the Curriculum of Formal Christian Education

Most congregations and parishes purchase or gain access (via websites) to a published curriculum of some kind, be this for their Sunday school or parish programs, Christian schools, youth programs, adult Bible study, faith sharing, and so forth. Though there was a concerted movement some years ago to create "home grown curriculum," most congregations/parishes do not have the resources to mount such an effort successfully. On the other hand, in this greatly expanded age of information and communication technology, we are abundantly blessed to have ready access to multiple choices for high-quality religious education curricula—for all ages.

This being said, the people who produce such curricula, as well as communities that choose and purchase them, need clear guidelines for their crafting and choosing. Typically, people's first thought regarding curriculum is about *what* to teach; however, and this is a central point, curriculum must also be evaluated for the *who, why, where,* and *how* that it reflects and promotes. I offer a brief word on each of these constitutive aspects of the formal curriculum.

The What of Christian Education Curriculum

Every denomination will teach its own understanding and perspective on Christian faith. Beyond this, however, as a Christian community, it has the obligation to teach the "shared story and vision" of Christian faith, not simply what serves its own identity. In particular, the content of its curriculum must be defined by the centrality of Jesus, the Christ. As the *Catechism of the Catholic Church* summarizes, the center of Christian faith is not the Bible, nor the church's doctrines and creeds, nor the commandments or sacraments, central and constitutive as all these are; instead: "At the heart . . . we find a Person, the Person of Jesus of Nazareth, the only Son from the Father" (CCC 426).

As the *Catechism* suggests, the Christology of Christian curriculum must reflect both the *Jesus of history* and the *Christ of faith.* Thus, a Christian curriculum should teach Christ as Lord and Savior and also what Jesus the carpenter taught as He walked the roads of Galilee. About the *historical Jesus*, scholars now agree (whatever number "quest" this may be) that He announced the in-breaking of God's reign of justice, peace, and fullness of life for all, that He included the marginalized, sided with the oppressed, fed the hungry, and showed special favor for the least, the lost, and the last. *What* we teach as Christian educators must reflect such a Jesus and the call to follow His *way* as disciples. Likewise, we must teach the Christ of faith, the Son of God, the Second Person of the Blessed Trinity, whose dying and rising catalyzed "an abundance of God's grace" (1 Tim. 1:14; Paul repeatedly) that can enable people to live as Jesus's disciples.

The Who of Christian Education Curriculum

Of course, the first response to the *who* question is *every* Christian person and community. Christian education has no point of arrival, short of when our hearts finally rest in God (Augustine). Everyone is in need of lifelong religious education; the growth into holiness of life for Christians is never-ending—this side of eternity. The deeper issue I focus on, however, is the understanding of the person that a Christian education curriculum should promote. For example, are we sinners in the hands of an angry God (à la Jonathan Edwards), or good people in the hands of a loving God (à la Karl Rahner)? Whichever side of those scales a curriculum favors—even if only by a slight tip—will make a significant difference in how the curriculum is crafted.

Transcending Reformation polemics, we need a paradoxical sense of both human goodness and our proneness to sin, that we have an innate capacity to be responsible for our choices and yet are ever in need of God's grace, even to mount our own best efforts. Christian education should reflect and promote a realistic optimism about people that balances (1) our innate goodness, (2) our capacity for sin, and (3) that Jesus died and rose on our behalf, mediating God's abundant grace in human history. Its anthropology, then, should reflect that God's grace in Jesus enhances our responsibility—or better, our "response-ability"—to live as disciples.

The Why of Christian Education Curriculum

Every instance of education must be crafted with great intentionality, precisely because it intends to have "learning outcomes" in the lives of participants. Even the etymology of the word—*educare*, to "lead out"—reminds us that educators should have a sense of the direction in which they hope to lead people "out." What, then, are the direction and the intended learning outcomes of Christian religious education?

Aristotle distinguished final, formal, and efficient ends of human action, corresponding, approximately, to the ultimate end, to the intended consequences for people's lives, and to the immediate product. I propose that Christian education has as its final purpose the realization of *God's reign* in Jesus Christ, its middle outcome is *lived faith* toward *liberating salvation*, and its efficient purpose is *knowledge* of Christian faith that forms people's identity and enables them to live its spiritual wisdom for life. A brief word about each level of purpose.

Our ultimate and guiding purpose must be the same as that of Jesus: the in-breaking of God's reign of compassion and justice, of love and peace. Our educating must ready people to not only pray "thy kingdom come" but also do God's will "on earth as in heaven." Jesus's purpose of God's reign, so clearly reflected in His public ministry, should be the "canon within the canon" as we interpret and represent Christian faith and its intent for the world.

The intended effect in and on people's lives should be to inform, form, and transform them in Christian faith that is lived, living, and life-giving for themselves and "for the life of the world" (John 6: 51). There are many ways to name the consequences of Christian faith for people's lives and human history, beginning with Paul's multiple metaphors of salvation (Rom. 1:16), justification (Gal. 2:16–21), liberation (Gal. 5:1), reconciliation (2 Cor. 3:16–18), becoming a new creation (Gal. 6:15), new life (1 Cor. 15:45), adoption (Gal. 4:4–6), sanctification (1 Cor. 1:30), redemption and forgiveness (Eph. 1:7), and more. In our time, however, there seems to be particular effectiveness in responding to Anselm's enduring question, "*cur Deus homo*" (Why did God become a person?) with such terms as liberation, humanization, and human flourishing. Combining the contemporary with the traditional, I favor "liberating salvation" to describe the outcome of Christian faith for people's lives and human history. Christian education should intend to promote as much.

The immediate intention of all education is to mediate knowledge of some kind; for Christian education, the intent surely is knowledge in Christian faith. However, our purpose must be more akin to the holistic sense of knowledge and knowing that we find in the Bible than the knowing *about* abstract ideas that triumphed with the Enlightenment notion of "pure reason." Our intention should be that Christians come to *know* their faith at the very depths of their being so that it forms their identity and shapes their lives. Thus, the most accurate way to state the epistemological purpose of Christian education is that people come to make their own and personally embrace the spiritual wisdom of Christian faith for their lives.

The Where of Christian Education Curriculum

Regarding people's engagement with their situatedness in the world, we must craft Christian education curricula so that people come to a critical consciousness of their sociocultural context. Beyond awareness, however, we must encourage and prompt a Freire-like conscientization, in other words an awareness that is disposed to act to help realize God's reign. Key here is to craft curriculum that enables people to "see" what is and to imagine what should be, and to nurture a commitment to the works of justice and peacemaking.

Regarding curriculum in relation to its ecclesial context, I refer to the opening part of this essay. In sum, the whole life of the faith community and family must be constantly reviewed for what it is teaching and recrafted as needed to intentionally educate for Christian faith.

The How of Christian Education Curriculum

Not only are we to teach Jesus and what Jesus taught, but we are also to learn from how He went about it. Though we're in very different times and places from Him, our pedagogy can well reflect the basic dynamics of His; we'll be all the more effective the more we teach as Jesus did. I recognize the dynamics of His pedagogy as leading people *from life to faith to life*.

Jesus most often initiated teaching/learning events by getting people to look at their own lives. The list of examples is myriad; He began with references to farming, fishing, homemaking, trading, parenting, winemaking, traveling, throwing a party, picking grapes, finding work, responding to the poor, sickness and health, weddings and wakes; indeed, I can think of no instance of His teaching in which He does not begin with people's real lives. Then, however, He often caused them to "see" their lives in a whole new way; that the Samaritan is the neighbor, the prodigal is welcomed home, the rich man goes to hades while Lazarus goes to the bosom of Abraham. Such reversals and twists surely caused people to reflect critically on their lives in the world.

Then, more than prompting attention to and reflection on everyday life, Jesus boldly proclaimed the in-breaking of God's reign, inviting people to "repent and believe in the gospel" (Mark 1:15). In other words, His intent in turning people to look at their lives was precisely in order to bring them to faith.

From the very beginning, the people recognized that "he taught them as one having authority" (Mark 1: 22). Yet Jesus granted people a deep freedom in their lived response to His Gospel; His call to discipleship was always by invitation, never by threat or duress. He wanted people to "see for themselves" the blessings of responding to God's reign and to embrace it by conviction. His constant intention was that people make a decision for God's reign in their lives, but to do so by choice.

Though this *life to faith to life* approach was evident throughout His public ministry, and especially in His use of parables, it is writ large in the pedagogy of the "Stranger" on the Road to Emmaus (see Luke 24: 13–35). Note how He engages their lives, hears their traumatic story and shattered vision, shares the Story and Vision of the faith community. Yet He never tells them what to see but waits for them to "see for themselves," whereupon they freely decide to return to Jerusalem and reengage their faith. The more we can approximate such pedagogy—*life to faith to life*—by God's grace, the more effective our Christian education will be.

References and Resources

Groome, Thomas. 2011. *Will There Be Faith: A New Vision for Growing and Educating Disciples*. San Francisco: HarperOne.

Harris, Maria. 1989. *Fashion Me a People: Curriculum in the Church*. Louisville, KY: John Knox Press.

Relevant Entries

Affections, Christian
Anabaptist Curriculum Outcomes
Anglican Curricular Outcomes
Apologetics
Apostles' Creed
Architecture
Art, Painting
Art, Sculpture
Atonement
Attitudes toward Christianity
Authority
Baltimore Catechism
Baptist Curricular Outcomes
Bible as Literature, The
Biblical Theology
Bibliodrama
Catechesis/Catechisms
Catechetical Directories (Post–Vatican II)
Character
Character Education
Children's Bibles
Christ and Culture
Christian Formation, A Biblical View of
Christian Formation, Approaches to

Christian Formation: An Overview
Christian History/Church History
Christian Year
Church Architecture
Conversion
Creation, Doctrine of
Culture
Curriculum
Curriculum Development
Curriculum Planning, Jane Vella and
Curriculum Theory
Didache as Early Christian Education Strategy
Didactics
Doctrines, Instruction in
Easter
Ecumenical Publishing
Evangelization
Evangelization, New
Experience
Freedom
Gaming
Heidelberg Catechism
Hidden Curriculum
Holy Spirit
Hope
Human Rights
Hymns as an Educational Tool
Icons
Jesus Christ
Jesus Prayer, The
Jurisprudence
Kingdom of God
Knowledge
Lectio Divina as Christian Practice
Lectionary
Lectionary-based Curriculum
Liturgy
Lordship Salvation
Luther's *Small Catechism*
Mass
McGuffey Readers
Methodist Curricular Outcomes
Music Education
Natural Law
New England Primer, The
New Testament
Nicene Creed
Nurture
Old Testament
Power in Christian Education
Prison Ministry, History of
Protestant Catechisms
Proverbs

CHRISTIAN HIGHER EDUCATION

Perry L. Glanzer

From the beginning of what today we call the university, Christianity and higher education were inextricably intertwined. In fact, the university arose in the Middle Ages in the 12th and 13th centuries with the help of Christian scholars, ideas, and institutions. Intellectually, a number of key developments proved particularly important. Christian thinkers developed, "the belief in a world order, created by God, rational, accessible to human reason, to be explained by human reason and to be mastered by it" (Rüegg 1992, 32–33). This way of thinking gave intellectual leaders the confidence to develop systems of rational thought by which to understand both God and universe He created. Scholars compiled these systems into what were called *didascalicon*, as they sought to introduce students to the various writings they should read to be educated. They were basically instruction manuals for building the substantive content of the academic house.

The oldest functioning universities, such as the University of Paris, Cambridge, and Oxford, also benefited from the institutional church. The Roman Catholic Church placed a high priority on teachers and scholars emerging from these institutions, with one writer calling them the "mirror of the church," since the church's leadership came from the academic world (Nardi 1992, 81–82). The early universities that received the church's blessing housed four faculties: the general or liberal arts faculty and three professional faculties (law, medicine, and theology). Theology was understood as the queen or highest of all the faculties. The church granted students and teachers certain "universal" rights and privileges, in the sense that they "transcended all local divisions (such as towns, dioceses, principalities and states)" (Verger, 1992; Nardi, 1992).

Teachers and students were also placed under the protection of papal authority and given legal protection by the church against local and regional political authorities, and the degrees conferred allowed graduates to teach not only in a local area but across the universe that was Christendom. In this way, the church actually served to expand the academic freedom of the faculty and students (Nardi 1992). This challenge by the church to political authority cannot be overstated. As Fareed Zakeria has noted, the church during this time "was the first major institution in history that was independent of temporal authority and was willing to challenge it. By doing this it cracked the edifice of state power, and in nooks and crannies individual liberty began to grow" (2004, 34). This liberty also allowed the Catholic Church to encourage the growth of universities throughout Europe and the establishment of the first university in the New World (Universidad Autonoma de Santo Domingo, 1538, Santo Domingo, Dominican Republic), as well as the first university in Asia (University of Santo Tomas in the Philippines in 1611).

Yet it should be noted that this expansion of universities in Europe did not include the whole church. The Eastern Orthodox Church would not start its own universities until the late 20th century (Glanzer and Petrenko 2007). Instead, they would start the practice that would be carried on by certain Protestant traditions of only sponsoring narrow forms of Christian higher education in the form of theological seminaries. Indeed, in certain Eastern Orthodox countries today, Christian higher education is associated primarily with such seminaries instead of university education.

In contrast to Eastern Orthodoxy, Protestantism began in and embraced the university. Three of the most well-known protesters against particular Roman Catholic Church doctrines and practices, John Wycliffe, John Hus, and Martin Luther, originally taught in universities. In fact, what many consider the start of the Reformation began at what eventually became the first Protestant university, Martin Luther's young Wittenberg University. By 1700, Lutherans claimed or created fourteen new European universities, the Calvinists nine, and the Anglicans three (Frijhoff 1996).

For the most part, Protestant universities merely adopted the Catholic model and structure of the university. Nonetheless, a number of radical new Protestant groups started something new in North America, what today we would call the liberal arts college. The liberal arts college is in many ways merely one part of the old universities, without the law, medical, or theology faculties. The first liberal arts colleges in America, particularly Harvard, Yale, and Princeton, had the important feature of being residential—similar to Oxford and Cambridge's various residential colleges. In this respect, the college leaders sought to provide a more holistic formation of students that would include not merely cognitive education but also training in Christian practices (Marsden 1994; Tweksbury 1932). Only later was professional theological training for clergy in America developed into a separate system of seminaries and not within the university.

Yet as these liberal arts colleges became more American and less Puritan, theology lost its curricular place in these colleges. Instead, what became important was moral philosophy—a kind of general moral teaching upon which all Christian Americans could agree. Throughout the 19th century, this course played a key role in the numerous Christian liberal arts colleges that sprouted up throughout the United States (Glanzer 2010).

Eventually, however, new developments in Europe and America would bring about a change to Christian higher education in America. Nationalistic and secular currents in Germany led to the founding of what is commonly considered the first research university, the University of Berlin. In this modern research university, theology became sequestered into its own area and dethroned from being queen of the sciences by what was broadly called the philosophy faculty (which included the liberal arts). Professors in the research university began focusing less on providing wisdom, a morally informed type of knowledge, and more extensively on producing plain knowledge (Glanzer 2012). Scientists believed that one must separate facts and values, with only facts being the scientific source of empirical knowledge. This trend was furthered by the tremendous growth of state-funded education around the world. Particularly in North America, state education gradually was required to be religiously neutral. Furthermore, although much of American higher education had been private, by the mid-20th century, the state began creating and enrolling more and more students.

In both private and public institutions, the spiritual and moral life of students became sequestered in the growing area of student life. The cocurricular dimension came to be considered the area where character education and spiritual growth took place. This allowed for a whole variety of Christian student groups and campus ministries to form (e.g., YMCA, YWCA) and in the present (Cru, Intervarsity, various denominationally affiliated campus groups, and chaplaincies). Today, one will also find a wide variety of religious and secular student groups on campus, since the cocurricular remains one of the most robust areas in secular higher education where one finds a Christian presence (Glanzer, Hill, and Ream 2014).

Christian higher education, however, changed as a result of the fragmented vision promulgated within the research university. Fearful of the secularization process overtaking historical liberal arts colleges and new research universities, fundamentalist Christians created Bible colleges, which focused solely on biblical education and moral formation and largely avoided the rest of the arts. The Christian liberal arts colleges and universities that survived tended to follow the research university model by marginalizing Christianity into the cocurricular dimension of college life. "Christian" meant providing a certain kind of moral atmosphere for learning. Student life personnel and campus chapels would help encourage piety and religious devotion, and Bible classes provided the necessary knowledge, but the other areas of the curriculum became largely shorn of faith. If faculty presented Christianity in the classroom, they did so largely through pietistic practices (e.g., prayer before class) and modeling (Ringenberg 2006).

In the latter part of the 20th century, however, a revitalized group of Christian liberal arts colleges in America sought to change this situation. Drawing on the concept of "integration of faith and learning," a number of Christian thinkers at these institutions began formulating a more robust understanding of how Christianity can and should influence all of learning. The earliest formulations of this approach addressed efforts to form a Christian worldview. The results of this effort can be seen in the large number of Christian journals and professional societies that formed to provide venues for this type of conversation. Catholic institutions during this time also grew and added their own distinctive interest in what they would call the integration of faith and reason (Ream and Glanzer 2007).

In the past decade, the conversation about the integration of faith and learning has taken two new approaches and directions. First, attention has shifted from using worldview language to discussing how the Christian narrative shapes one's scholarly outlook, life, and living. In this vein, some scholars have criticized the earlier integration paradigm as relying too heavily on Reformed theological commitments and not taking into account the broad range and influence of various theological traditions and diversity within Christian higher education (e.g., Jacobsen and Jacobsen 2004; Ream and Glanzer 2007).

Second, a new strand of thought has developed that focuses on the integration, not merely of Christian theological or philosophical perspectives into the curriculum, but also of Christian practices into one's pedagogy (Smith and Smith 2011). This form of integration, they claim, not only shapes the moral character of the educator; it transforms the moral culture of the classroom. This approach tends to be better received among professions interested in the practical outcome of Christianity for one's vocational practice.

In addition to its increasing intellectual development and sophistication, Christian higher education has also experienced globalization through tremendous growth around the world (Glanzer, Carpenter, and Lantinga 2011). Contrary to the assumptions of secularization theory, the story of Christian higher education is not one of worldwide decline. Instead, it involves periods of regional secularization, as in the case of Western Europe after 1850, as well as periods of rapid expansion and growth, such as China in the early 1900s and Latin America, parts of Asia, and Oceania in the 1950s and 1960s. More recently, since the breakup of the Soviet Union in 1989, Christian higher education has grown in Africa, Asia, and Eastern Europe. The fact that almost 600 avowedly Christian colleges and universities currently operate outside North America demonstrates the continued relevance and vitality of Christian higher education around the globe (Glanzer 2013).

The future of Christian higher education faces plenty of difficult challenges and opportunities. Technological innovation has opened up new online learning opportunities for Christian institutions, but the technology could also undermine the holistic approach to human formation that is seen as one of the distinctives of Christian higher education. Economic pressures continue to batter Christian higher education, since it seeks to invest in these kinds of holistic initiatives. The regulatory state also poses challenges to Christian higher education, since global patterns reveal that it tends to flourish where private innovation in higher education is permitted and promoted by the state. Finally, leadership and faculty development and transitions will continue to pose difficulties, especially when most leaders and faculty are educated and shaped in secular higher education (Glanzer 2013). The future Christian leadership of Christian higher education will have to address these mounting challenges if it is going to flourish in the 21st century.

References and Resources

Frijhoff, Willem. 1996. "Patterns." In *A History of the University in Europe*. Vol. 2, *Universities in Early Modern Europe (1500–1800)*. Edited by Hilde De Ridder-Symoens and Walter Rüegg, 43–110. Cambridge, UK: Cambridge University Press.

Glanzer, P. L. 2008. "Why We Should Discard the Integration of Faith and Learning: Rearticulating the Mission of the Christian Scholar." *Journal of Education and Christian Belief* 12 (1): 41–51.

———. 2010. "Moving Beyond Value or Virtue Added: Transforming Colleges and Universities for Redemptive Moral Development." *Christian Scholar's Review* 39 (4): 379–400.

———. 2012. "How to Save the Christian College." *Christianity Today* (March): 18–23.

———. 2013. "Dispersing the Light: The Status of Christian Higher Education around the Globe." *Christian Scholar's Review* 43: 321–343.

Glanzer, P. L., J. A. Carpenter, and N. Lantinga. 2011. "Looking for God in the University: Examining Trends in Global Christian Higher Education." *Higher Education* 61 (6): 721–755.

Glanzer, Perry L., Jonathan Hill, and Todd Ream. 2014. "Changing Souls: Higher Education's Influence upon the Religious Lives of Emerging Adults." In *Emerging Adults' Religiousness And Spirituality: Meaning-Making in an Age of Transition* (152–170), edited by Carolyn Berry and Mona Abo-Zena. New York: Oxford University Press.

Glanzer, P. L., and K. Petrenko. 2007. "Resurrecting the Russian University's Soul: The Emergence of Eastern Orthodox Universities and Their Distinctive Approaches to Keeping Faith with Their Religious Tradition." *Christian Scholar's Review* 36 (Spring): 263–284.

Jacobsen, D. G., and R. H. Jacobsen, eds. 2004. *Scholarship and Christian faith: Enlarging the Conversation*. New York: Oxford University Press.

Marsden, G. 1994. *The Soul of the American University*. New York: Oxford.

Nardi, P. 1992. "Relations with Authority." In *A History of the University in Europe*. Vol. I, edited by H. D. Ridder-Symeons, 77–107. New York: Cambridge University Press.

Ream, T. C., and P. L. Glanzer. 2007. *Christian Faith and Scholarship: An Exploration of Contemporary Developments*. ASHE-ERIC Higher Education Report. San Francisco: Jossey-Bass.

Ringenberg, W. 2006. *The Christian College: A History of Protestant Higher Education in America*. Grand Rapids, MI: Baker Academic.

Rüegg, W. 1992. "Themes." In *A History of the University in Europe*. Vol. I, edited by H. D. Ridder-Symeons, 3–34. New York: Cambridge University Press.

Smith, D. I., and J. K. A. Smith, eds. 2011. *Teaching and Christian Practices: Reshaping Faith & Learning*. Grand Rapids, MI: Eerdmans.

Tweksbury, D. 1932. *The Founding of American Colleges and Universities before the Civil War*. New York: Teachers College, Columbia University.

Verger, J. 1992. "Patterns." In *A History of the University in Europe*. Vol. I, edited by H. D. Ridder-Symeons, 35–76. New York: Cambridge University Press.

Zakeria, F. 2004. *The Future of Freedom: Illiberal Democracy at Home and Abroad*. New York: W.W. Norton.

Relevant Entries
Administration
Asia and Christian Education
Association for Biblical Higher Education
Bible College Movement, Evolution of the
Board Governance
Campus Ministry
Chaplaincies
Character Development
Christian Education Journals
Christian Higher Education in China
Christian Higher Education in the Secular University
Christian Higher Education, The Future of
Christian Liberal Arts Colleges and Universities
Christian Worldview Education in a Public University
College Chapel
Correspondence Christian Education
Educational Leadership
Educational Program Outcomes
Ethnic Diversity
Holistic Education
Institutional Effectiveness
Institutional Mergers
Integrating Christian Practices
Integration of Faith and Learning
Moral Philosophy as Capstone Course
Oxford University as a Model for Christian Education
Pastoral Education, Clinical
Presidential Transitions
Secularization of Christian Colleges
Student Services
Technology, Educational
Theological Education, Berlin as a Model of
Theological Education by Extension

CHRISTIAN EDUCATION OF CHILDREN AND ADOLESCENTS

Mark A. Lamport

Say to the Israelites, "The LORD, the God of your fathers—the God of Abraham, the God of Isaac and the

God of Jacob—has sent me to you." This is my name forever, the name you shall call me from generation to generation. (Exod. 3:15)

Half of the Christians who have ever lived are living now.[12] And about half the inhabitants of this planet are under 24 years old.[13] What an incredible opportunity for the church to inculcate the transcendent truth of the faith it claims in its youngest members. And what a substantial burden to do it well—with sustaining effect and with a sound understanding of perpetuating the mission of God in the world.

Regrettably, fewer international research projects detail the effective rate of faith transference between the generations than such investigations piloted in the United States. Happily, a significant percentage of Americans share the same religious identity as their parents. Three recent and substantial studies bear that out: the General Social Survey, Pew Religion and Public Life surveys,[14] and Faith Matters Survey.[15] More specifically, while more than half of evangelical Protestants remain observant members of their parents' faith, the same is true for fewer than half of "Anglo" Catholics and mainline Protestants.[16] Research demonstrates that not only is there a higher birth rate among evangelical parents, but they are more apt to keep their offspring within the family's religious tradition.[17]

Certainly, then, as a result of the sheer numbers as well as the future stake of all stripes of Christianity in the next generations, careful attention must be given to faithfully and vigorously educating children and adolescents in the Christian faith.

Foundational Insights on Educating Children and Adolescents in Faith

In a broad sense, "education" composes the sum total of those processes whereby society transmits from one generation to the next its accumulated social, intellectual, and religious experience and heritage. In part, these processes are *informal and incidental*, arising from

12. Mark A. Noll, *The New Shape of World Christianity: How American Experience Reflects Global Faith* (Downers Grove, IL: IVP Academic, 2009).

13. Philip Jenkins, *The New Faces of Christianity: Believing the Bible in the Global South* (New York: Oxford University Press, 2006).

14. See Pew Forum on Religion & Public Life, U.S. Religious Landscape Survey.

15. See Roper Center for Public Opinion Research Study, *Faith Matters Survey 2006* [computer file], USMISC2006-FAITH Version 2, Saguaro Seminar [producer], 2006 (Storrs, CT: The Roper Center for Public Opinion Research, University of Connecticut, distributor, 2011).

16. Robert D. Putnam and David E. Campbell, *American Grace: How Religion Divides Us and Unites Us* (New York: Simon & Schuster, 2010).

17. Michael Hout, Andrew Greeley, and Melissa Wilde, "The Demographic Imperative in Religious Change in the United States," *American Journal of Sociology* 107, no. 2 (2001): 110.

participation in certain forms of social life and activity.[18] In another sense, more *formal educative processes* are designed to provide the immature members of society with a mastery over the symbols and techniques of civilization, including language (reading, writing, and speaking), the arts, the sciences, and religion, and to enlarge the fund of individual and community knowledge beyond the measure furnished by the direct activities of the immediate environment.

This understanding takes into account the melding of the less structured *socialization* approach (a powerful communicator of values and social norms) with the more structured *schooling* model (which may be significant if the interests of the learner can be anticipated). The most judicious means of successfully accomplishing this mixture of strategies has long been the source of many instructive debates about Christian education.[19]

Christian education among ancient and modern peoples alike reveals this twofold aspect and is particularly relevant for a balanced and meaningful growth in faith with children and adolescents. On its informal side, it consists of the transmission of Christian ideas and experience by means of the reciprocal processes of *imitation and example*. Children and youth, by actually participating in the religious activities and ceremonies of the social group, imbibe the spirit and ideals of the preceding generations, and in turn these are modified by the particular economic and industrial conditions under which the entire process takes place.

Formal Christian education of children and adolescents begins with conscious and systematic effort on the part of the mature members of a social group to initiate the immature members by means of solemn *rites and ceremonies* into the mysteries and obligations of their own faith community.

How, then, shall we define the church's attempts to infuse Christian education within its children and adolescents? Simply stated, the education of children and youth in Christian faith is the purposive, determined, and persistent quest by both natural and supernatural means to expose, transmit, or otherwise share with adolescents God's message of good news, which is central to the Christian faith. Its ultimate end is to cultivate a life transformation of youth by the power of the Holy Spirit, that they might be conformed to the revealed will of God as expressed in scripture, and chiefly in the person of our Lord and Savior, Jesus Christ.[20]

Although Jesus commanded the apostles to teach, no concrete directives were offered about how this would be accomplished. The church is left to discern the specifics. With cultural cues, educational wherewithal, childhood and adolescent human development research, and biblical and theological instincts, a strategy for communicating and living faith with children and adolescents can be engaged.

The Christian Education of Children

Some critics question the validity of educating children in Christian faith and advocate for children making decisions to embrace or reject the parental faith when they are developmentally able to reason for themselves. This sentiment flies in the face of scriptural admonition. In fact, the Bible clearly teaches that Jesus calls children to Himself. The most favorable soil for sowing seed is the soft heart of children. Children have natural faith, trust, and dependency, which are outgrown. Numerous studies describe the lack of receptivity to the Gospel as people age. We ask, then, what helps children open up to God, and what prevents or closes down an awareness of God?

Perhaps the most formative Christian education of children is that which is the most subtle. This could be said for the typical ways humans become members of any community, including the faith community. This, of course, aptly describes the incremental, almost subliminal, process of socialization.

A fascinating study by renowned Princeton University sociologist Robert Wuthnow (1998) claims that adults interviewed did not remember the doctrinal instruction they received as youth. He adds, however, that does not mean that they learned nothing about religion from their parents. What they recalled fondly about religion—and what often drew them as adults back to the church—were the rituals and sacred objects that were at the center of their religious upbringing.[21] The truly memorable and lasting aspects of a religious upbringing happen in the home with one's family. Christian educators, whether parents or church teachers, should strive for religious infusion as much as for religious instruction. Training children in the right way may involve creating an environment in which spirituality is fully and deeply embedded, rather than merely drilling youth on the creeds and catechisms.

Clues to how this would be operative in a religious sense are found, among other places, in Deuteronomy 6:1–9. Succinctly summarized, the most favorable conditions for life-changing impact are experienced best within a family context, where loving, consistent, and

---

18. See H. H. Meyer, "Education," in *International Standard Bible Encyclopedia*, education.htm.

19. One of the most cogent discussions is presented in John Westerhoff, *Will Our Children Have Faith?*, rev. ed. (Toronto: Morehouse Publishing, 2000).

20. Adapted from Mark A. Lamport, "Youth Ministry,"in *Encyclopedia of Christian Civilization*, vol. 4 (Oxford: Blackwell Press, 2011).

21. Robert Wuthnow, *Growing Up Religious: Christians and Jews and Their Journeys of Faith* (Kansas City, MO: Beacon Press, 1998).

committed relationships with God and family members are exhibited. Three factors seem to effectually foster the absorption of faith from one generation to the next.

First is a teacher/parent who has experienced the reality he or she is teaching to the children. "These are the commands, decrees and laws the LORD your God directed me to teach you to observe in the land that you are crossing the Jordan to possess, so that you, your children and their children after them may fear the LORD your God as long as you live by keeping all his decrees and commands that I give you, and so that you may enjoy long life. These commandments that I give you today are to be on your hearts" (Deut. 1–2, 6). The most noted obstacle to gaining the Christian faith from parents, as reported in numerous research studies and anecdotal stories, is the dissonance between what a Christian parent claims is so and how that parent actually lives in the portals of lived reality in the home, in the community, and in the workplace.

Second is a teacher/parent who has intimate relationships with those being taught. "Hear, O Israel: The LORD our God, the LORD is one. Love the LORD your God with all your heart and with all your soul and with all your strength. Impress them on your children" (Deut. 4–5, 7a). Social science lists those factors that enhance teaching/learning as frequent, long-term contact; a warm, loving relationship; exposure to the inner states; being observed in variety of life settings; exhibiting consistency in behavior; correspondence between behavior and the beliefs of the community; and an explanation of lifestyle.[22] Naturally, as applied to Christian education settings, these factors have rich value for exposing the faith in a meaningful, mentoring way.

Third is teaching that springs from real-life issues and natural situations. "Talk about them when you sit at home and when you walk along the road, when you lie down and when you get up. Tie them as symbols on your hands and bind them on your foreheads. Write them on the door frames of your houses and on your gates" (Deut. 7b–9). Humans are most ready to learn when the subject matter arises out of personal interest and in response to in-the-moment life circumstances, crises, and development tasks. The "curriculum" of Jesus's teaching, for example, most often arose from spontaneous questions or events; it was rarely preplanned or structured and did not occur in a formal "classroom."

Practical Considerations in the Christian Education of Children

The Anglican Church has a "welcome service" for children within its parishes, and one of the prayers of that service expresses the beautiful intentions of our educational efforts with children in faith: "May he/she learn to love all that is true, grow in wisdom and strength and, we pray, come to faith and to know the joy of your presence in his/her life with the fullness of your grace; through Jesus Christ, our Lord. Amen."[23] What a succinct and wonderful sentiment of experiencing both children and one's interactions with knowing, loving, and following God in the context of the church and in culture. How might the intentions in this prayer be accomplished?

The key influences on faith formation of children are parents and family, the community of faith, and culture.[24] Therefore, parents and churches should consider intentional strategies for welcoming children into faith communities. Obviously, public commitments for supporting families in raising children, such as baptisms and/or dedication ceremonies, are significant teaching events. Also critical to the faith formation of children is their intentional inclusion in corporate worship and/or children's church as a meaningful place to express their emerging realizations about God and the spiritual life. In addition, events that regularly engage intergenerational experiences nurture trust and provide a forum for developing adult, mentoring relationships.[25]

In sum, spiritual formation for children largely occurs through relationships, symbols, rituals, and senses. The processes that influence growth of children's faith are communicating belonging and participation within a vital faith community, modeling faith by the members of the faith community, interpreting and living biblical instruction with the members of the faith community, and encouraging growing experiences of personal choice in the context of faith.

The Christian Education of Adolescents

The writer of Ecclesiastes entreats youth to be followers of God from early on because potentially a life full of service lies ahead: "Remember your Creator in the days of your youth" (Eccles. 12:1). Youth is a time when a positive pattern for life should be established (1 Kings 18:12). These youthful years are clearly formative years of commitment which may make long-lasting impact on the adult life to come. The Psalmist likewise offers advice to the novice liver of life. "How can a young man keep his way pure? By living according to your word" (119:9).

---

22. Lawrence Richards, *Christian Education: Seeking to Become Like Jesus* (Grand Rapids, MI: Zondervan, 1988).

23. "Welcome Service," Book of Common Prayer (The Archbishops' Council of the Church of England, 2000).

24. Sadly, we acknowledge that any of these three powerful socializing agents may foster as well as deter experiences of faith.

25. For sound research and practical ideas on this topic, see Jackson W. Carroll and Wade Clark Roof, *Bridging Divided Worlds: Generational Cultures in Congregations* (San Francisco: Jossey-Bass, 2002).

In the New Testament, Paul counsels the young to "flee the evil desires of youth, and pursue righteousness, faith, love and peace" (2 Tim. 2:22) and exhorts the young to maintain godly discipline and character. "Don't let anyone look down on you because you are young, but set an example for the believers in speech, in life, in love, in faith and in purity" (1 Tim. 4:12). "Similarly, encourage the young men to be self-controlled" (Titus 2:6). God wants His followers to love Him uninterrupted throughout their lives in order to echo the words of this devotee: "For you have been my hope, O Sovereign LORD, my confidence.... Since my youth, O God, you have taught me, and to this day I declare your marvelous deeds (Ps. 71:5, 17).[26]

Yet in spite of these admonitions for developing religious sensibilities, adolescence is the period when people are most likely to experience a crisis of faith. Common causes for adolescents to reevaluate the Christian faith are peer pressure (away from religion and toward cultural values), a tendency toward institutional alienation (represented by the church and organized religion), separation from parental values (such as religious commitments), a personal search for meaning (typical of most who have the luxury of personal freedom to discover their place in the world), personal difficulty (such as low self-image, lack of social status among peers, illness, or family turmoil), and the secularizing cultural environment.

Despite these potential developmental and cultural factors that sometimes obstruct growth in Christian faith among adolescents, both interest in religion and the influence of religion among youth remain significantly high. Not only does the church need youth—as an impetus to engage in creative ways of expressing the faith in community and in service to the world—but youth need the church—specifically, as a stabilizing mentor to navigate life and cultural interaction. The Christian faith best serves adolescents as a *compass*—a moral compass, a set of guiding directives for charting a life course; as a *community*—a group of individuals, youth interacting with adults, who share similar values and can nurture mission; and as a *coach*—to identify and develop a set of faith and life skills through practice and encouragement.[27]

Whereas children are primarily influenced in faith by their parents and the faith community, adolescents, as a result of developmental tasks and the inevitable process of individuation, look more toward peers and other significant adults for influence in their quest to incorporate the Christian faith. Christian parents and family members still have a tremendous impact on adolescent faith, and research confirms this notion, but the circle of influence expands as a function of the journey for independence.

The Impact of Religion on Adolescents

Compared to the religious lives of children and adults, relatively little is known about the religious life of adolescents—most research does not address it. Yet from what is known, it appears that the impact of religion may have positive correlational consequences:[28]

- Adolescent religious behavior—Three of four adolescents believe in a personal God and prayed at least occasionally; however, frequency of attendance declines through secondary school (from 44 to 31 percent).
- Religious influence—Parents constitute the strongest source in the religious development of youth. Mothers are generally thought to be more influential than fathers.[29] The more important religion is to a mother, the more likely her child is to report a higher quality of relationship with her.
- Physical and emotional health—More-religious youth consistently eat better, exercise more frequently, and get more sleep than less- or non-religious youth. Religious expressions and behavior during adolescence promote long-term physical well-being. Higher personal religiosity corresponds with significantly lower distress and higher social adjustment.[30]

---

26. Some of this material is adapted from Mark A. Lamport, "Youth, Young," in *Dictionary of Biblical Imagery*, ed. Tremper Longman, Leland Ryken, and James Wilhoit (Downers Grove, IL: InterVarsity Press, 1998).

27. A rather innovative and controversial approach has been adopted by some, primarily in the United Kingdom, that advances single-generation churches, obviously an alternate—and arguably less effective—view of cross-pollinating the generations. For research on this initiative, see Mark A. Lamport, "The Rise of English Youth Churches as Cultural Resistance to Western Christianity: What the Global Church Can Learn from This Latest British Invasion," *Evangelical Journal* (Spring 2008): 19–29; and Mark A. Lamport, "The Rise of Youth Churches: What the American Church Can Learn from This Latest British Invasion," *Evangelical Missions Quarterly* (January 2005): 12–21.

28. For further information, see Christian Smith, *Soul Searching: The Religious and Spiritual Lives of American Teenagers* (Oxford: Oxford University Press, 2005); Mark Regnerus, Christian Smith, and Melissa Fritsch, *Religion in the Lives of Adolescents: A Review of the Literature*, A Research Report of the National Study of Youth and Religion, Chapel Hill, NC (University of North Carolina at Chapel Hill, 2003).

29. In addition, mainline Protestant parents have a greater difficulty retaining their children within the mainline Protestant fold than do evangelical Protestant parents. Conservative Protestants are more likely to hug and praise their children than those from less theologically conservative traditions. Religious socialization is more likely to occur in families characterized by considerable warmth and closeness. "While one's religiosity is determined largely by the religiosity of one's parents, it also is fostered among families where parents enjoy marital happiness, display moderate strictness, support and show affection to their children, and in households where husbands are employed and the mother is not." S. Myers, Religion in American Youth, volume 61 *American Sociological Review* (1996): 858–866.

30. Religious communities promote favorable self-images by providing opportunities for positive reflected appraisals and cultivation of spiritual resources. Several studies have reported a positive relationship between religiosity and self-esteem.

- Educational aspirations and achievement—The influence of religious practices is found to be positively correlated with desirable educational outcomes. Religious organizations provide functional communities amid dysfunction and reinforce parental support networks. Religious involvement bridges family life and a wider set of intergenerational ties, providing a broader base of community structure and resources.[31]
- Risky behavior—As parent religiosity increases, youth delinquency generally falls. Religious youth are less likely to use either marijuana or alcohol. Adolescents involved in religion tend not to associate with peers who drink or do drugs. Regular attendance sharply reduces the risk of early first intercourse when youth report having friends who attend the same congregation.

Given these benefits, which so favorably impact adolescents, parents, churches, and parachurch organizations should continue with due diligence in reaching out to youth around the world. By what means are adolescents drawn to and retained by Christianity?

Practical Considerations in the Christian Education of Adolescents

What draws adolescents to Jesus first are *supernatural interactions*: the theological notion that God searches for humans. While adolescents experiment with various philosophies and searches of their own, it is the longing for one's creator that fulfills our deepest desires for wholeness and meaning. And the *love* as shown in acceptance and affirmation by those who are part of a believing community aids in this appeal toward the divine. Due to these *socially comfortable relationships*, adolescents are more apt to experience an *atmosphere that allows doubt and sorting out of beliefs*. This same community, permeated with support and grace, provides "positive peer pressure" as it offers *demonstration* of the Christian way. Certainly, a *clear verbal articulation* of the Gospel is paramount to adolescents ultimately being drawn to Jesus. Finally, the idealism of youth and the need to exercise their growth abilities drive them to accept the *challenge to join a monumental cause*: to join the legion of God's called in taking the Gospel to the world.

This *Encyclopedia of Christian Education* offers more than 50 articles on the Christian education of children and adolescents, written by some of the foremost scholars and practitioners in this area of inquiry. Included are descriptions of some of the most important parachurch organizations involved in ministry with children and youth, biblical and theological statements to guide these ministry initiatives, and theoretically sound strategies for teaching.

References and Resources

Christian Education of Children

Beckwith, Ivy. 2010. *Formational Children's Ministry: Shaping Children Using Story, Ritual, and Relationship*. Grand Rapids, MI: Baker Books.

Carroll, Jackson W., and Wade Clark Roof. 2002. *Bridging Divided Worlds: Generational Cultures in Congregations*. San Francisco, CA: Jossey-Bass.

Csinos, David M. 2011. *Children's Ministry That Fits: Beyond One-Size-Fits-All Approaches to Nurturing Children's Spirituality*. Eugene, OR: Wipf & Stock.

Fischer, Becky. 2005. *Redefining Children's Ministry in the 21st Century*. Mandan, ND: Kids in Ministry International.

Stonehouse, Catherine, and Scottie May. 2010. *Listening to Children on the Spiritual Journey: Guidance for Those Who Teach and Nurture*. Grand Rapids, MI: Baker Books.

Westerhoff, John. 2000. *Will Our Children Have Faith?* Rev. ed. Toronto: Morehouse Publishing.

Wuthnow, Robert. 1998. *Growing Up Religious: Christians and Jews and Their Journeys of Faith*. Kansas City, MO: Beacon Press.

Christian Education of Adolescents

Carotta, Michael. 2000. *Sometimes We Dance, Sometimes We Wrestle: Embracing the Spiritual Growth of Adolescents*. Orlando, FL: Harcourt Religion Publishing.

Dean, Kenda Creasy. 2010. *Almost Christian: What the Faith of Our Teenagers Is Telling the American Church*. New York: Oxford University Press.

Jacober, Amy E. 2011. *The Adolescent Journey: An Interdisciplinary Approach to Practical Youth Ministry*. Downers Grove, IL: IVP Books.

Lamport, Mark A. 2008. "The Rise of English Youth Churches as Cultural Resistance to Western Christianity: What the Global Church Can Learn From This Latest British Invasion." *Evangelical Journal* (Spring): 19–29.

Root, Andrew, and Kenda Creasy Dean. 2011. *The Theological Turn in Youth Ministry*. IVP.

Smith, Christian. 2005. *Soul Searching: The Religious and Spiritual Lives of American Teenagers*. New York: Oxford University Press.

Ziemann, G. Patrick, Roger L. Schwritz, and U.S. Catholic Bishops. 1997. *Renewing the Vision: A Framework for Catholic Youth Ministry*. Washington, DC: USCCB Publishing.

---

31. Both conservative Protestant youth and youth who are biblical inerrantists held lower educational aspirations and were less likely to take college prep courses. Having a fundamentalist parent reduced the odds of a young woman taking college-prep courses by 42 percent. Pentecostals, Baptists, and Lutherans fare worse in educational attainment than those with no religious affiliation, while Methodists, Presbyterians, Episcopalians, the "liberally" religious, and Jews fare better.

Relevant Entries

THEOLOGICAL EDUCATION

Jeff Astley

"Theological education" is a phrase that can be interpreted in a more general or a more specific fashion. The term may be used to designate those processes of teaching and learning whereby individuals or groups gain knowledge and understanding of Christian theology, and (normally) become skilled in *doing* theology for themselves. In principle, this understanding may embrace the informal learning that can lead to reflective God-talk, in any Christian believer, which expresses his or her personal, salvific, and relational knowledge of God (sometimes referred to as "ordinary theology"). In practice, however, the term tends to be restricted to more formal, intentional, and sustained educational experiences that result in the more conceptual and systematic forms of academic or ecclesiastical theology. In this latter case, the theological education is limited to a smaller number of students, who may or may not personally appropriate this theology as Christian believers (both of these comments also apply to their teachers, many of whom are also involved in some form of academic theological research).

The term "theological education" is more often used for the professional education of clergy and other Christian ministers or leaders, often within specific, church-related educational institutions, variously named theological colleges or schools; seminaries; Bible colleges, schools, or institutes; or divinity schools. In some countries, the "ministerial formation" and (largely contextual and practice-based) "ministerial training" that take place in the seminary are complemented by university-based courses in schools, faculties, or departments of academic theology, some of which may be within secular educational institutions. More often, though, the seminary itself provides both (a) the students' ministerial, spiritual, and practical formation and training, and (b) their academic theological study, in what is intended to be an integrated educational experience. The great majority of theological teachers in seminaries are committed Christians, and many of them will themselves be ordained; whether they engage in theological research as well as theological teaching will depend on the particular institution and their role within it.

Much of the recent literature on theological education has been influenced by the distinction articulated by David Kelsey (2011) between two normative Christian theological educational models—that of "Athens" and "Berlin." The original, first-century "classical" Athens type labels processes of enculturation and education (*paideia*) that lead to holistic outcomes of wisdom, character, and virtue formation, and processes of knowing God, that transform the life of individuals in community. The Enlightenment-derived, 19th-century "vocational" Berlin model, by contrast, favors rigorous academic, scholarly, and scientific study that foregrounds the employment of human reasoning in producing competent professionals to apply theological theory to Christian practice for the benefit of the church. While some scholars have defended qualified and nuanced versions of these models, others have espoused alternative conceptualizations—including the more biblical, "Jerusalem" or "missional" approach of Robert Banks (1999) and more doctrinal (especially Trinitarian) understandings.

Current debate often seeks to resolve, or at least to keep in tension, various competing emphases within both the theory and the practice of theological education, many of which are encompassed by the following perennial, overlapping concerns:

- the occupational (ministerial) rather than personal and Christian identity formation of the student;
- the tension between teaching intellectual and practical competence, on the one hand, and spiritual and ministerial character, on the other;
- issues of individuality, personal freedom, and diversity (including gender, class, and ethnic differences) in the context both of corporate, relational outcomes, and of formation into a fixed model or ideal of Christianity or of ministry;
- tradition-based formative and transformative aims, processes, and learning outcomes, rather than more critical (evaluative and liberating) ones—especially those that are more learner-centered and draw on the student's own beliefs and experiences;
- issues of status and leadership within a ministry, properly understood as a form of service;
- the nature and role of practical theology, in relationship to other forms of theology;
- the dangers of adopting a clerical paradigm in theological education that demeans or ignores the lay Christian experience and its variety of voices;
- the balance between education for doing theology and ministry and education for *being* a theologian and minister;
- the different concerns of more confessional and ecclesiastical, and more independent, academic, or "secular" forms of theology; and
- the challenges of managing the hermeneutical conversation between academic theology and the church's teachings, on the one hand, and the learner's own original but developing (and deeply contextualized) Christian beliefs and values, on the other.

References and Resources

Banks, Robert J. 1999. *Reenvisioning Theological Education: Exploring a Missional Alternative to Current Models*, Grand Rapids, MI: Eerdmans.

Kelsey, David H. 2011. *Between Athens and Berlin: The Theological Education Debate*. Eugene, OR: Wipf & Stock Publishers.

Relevant Entries

CHRISTIAN PEDAGOGY

Lawrence O. Richards

Jesus posed a challenge for Christian educators when He observed, "A student is not above his teacher, but everyone who is fully trained will be like his teacher" (Luke 6:40). Christ's observation would hardly have shocked His first-century audience. It was the goal of every rabbi's disciple not only to come to learn all his teacher knew, but also to model his life on that of his mentor.

This maxim is, however, less familiar to moderns. We are practiced in the communication of information. But how to teach a lifestyle rooted in the biblical revelation has not sufficiently engaged our attention. Yet this was a consistent emphasis of the apostle Paul, who urged his disciple Titus to "teach what is in accord with sound doctrine." Paul went on to specify that Titus was to teach a lifestyle marked by temperance, self-control, love, endurance, reverence, and purity (Titus 2). In urging Titus to "set them an example by doing what is good" (2:7), Paul, like Jesus, seems to view the teacher more as a mentor than as a conduit for "sound doctrine."

In stating this, it is not my desire to minimize the importance of sound doctrine. Nor do I criticize the dedicated Sunday school and other teachers who serve in local churches. Each of us is aware that such teachers have had life-transforming impacts on many students, often simply by loving them as they shared stories from God's Word. Nor is it my desire to criticize teachers and professors in formal educational settings. What I hope is that we will become more aware of the need to focus on transformation and will become more intentional in shaping our pedagogy to that end.

A Biblical Model
Possibly the earliest biblical educational model is found in Deuteronomy 6:4–9, and it is repeated in 11:18–20.

The teacher is the parent who loves God, who talks about the commandments that shape his or her daily life when sitting at home or walking along the road, and whose home is filled with symbolic reminders of God's presence. This same pattern is seen in Christ's many conversations with His disciples, stimulated by events observed as they traveled with Him. As the Bible's story transitions into the New Testament, subtle changes can be observed. Focus on "a" teacher shifts to a focus on the Holy Spirit as teacher (cf. John 14:26). And the Holy Spirit is observed teaching through gifts provided to members of the local community of faith (1 Cor. 12:7f.). This emphasis is supported by the Ephesians 4 reference to God's gift to the church of "pastor and teachers" (v. 11), whose specific ministry is to "prepare God's people for works of service," for the building up of the body of Christ (v. 12). This community setting, in which both life and teaching are shared by the members, is pictured in Colossians 3, where Paul first emphasizes the relational context of ministry and then says, "Let the word of Christ dwell in you richly as you teach and admonish one another with all wisdom" (v. 16).

From these and other passage we draw a number of pedagogical guidelines. A distinctively "Christian" education

- involves a process that includes a believer who is moved by a profound love for God;
- is conducted in a context marked by love and mutual concern;
- is focused on the interpretation of daily life experiences in the light of God's revelation;
- is an interactive process open to the active involvement of colearners, who are also gifted by the Spirit to function as coteachers; and
- is intended to produce a character and lifestyle that are in harmony with sound doctrine.

Limitations in Contemporary Christian Education
Too much of Christian education today is limited by unawareness of guidelines like those outlined above. In too many cases, the education is conducted in a classroom setting, which is formal and inhibits the development of loving, caring personal relationships. Too often the education is focused on the transmission of biblical material with an emphasis on shaping the learner's belief system, rather than on interpreting the learner's experiences in light of God's revelation. In too many cases, the process forgoes the active involvement of the learners in favor of instructor-dominated transmission of information. In too few cases are learners perceived as coteachers so gifted by the Spirit. And too often the education results primarily in a learner's ability to provide "right answers"

when questioned on what the Bible teaches. Unfortunately, education as characterized in this paragraph inhibits rather than encourages the kind of transformation envisioned in scripture.

Thankfully, the Holy Spirit is not limited by the church's failure to provide Christian education experiences rooted in the biblical model. God is still wooing the lost, touching hearts, and shaping lives—often through relationships outside the programs provided by our churches and educational institutions. Yet an awareness of divine ability is hardly an excuse for failing to design educational experiences that intentionally seek to follow principles we can draw from scripture.

Understanding Why

Our understanding of why the biblical guidelines suggested above are significant has grown in the past two or three decades. When I wrote *Children's Ministry* in 1983, Christian education tended to focus on locating Bible truths on an individual's cognitive map, over time adding new information that could be linked to information already possessed by the leaner. This often resulted in individuals whose belief systems were a more or less accurate reflection of what the Bible teaches. But the truths learned all too often failed to produce believers whose motives, attitudes, and way of life were "in accord with sound doctrine." Teaching and learning that focused on cognition simply did not infuse the character or even transfer to behavior. Like any learning that needs to be generalized across a variety of life situations, Christian education's cognitively focused Bible teaching simply did not produce the desired results.

In the 1983 book, I postulated the existence of an "emotional map" similar to a cognitive map. Paul's statement that all the *peirasmos* (trials, temptations, stressful situations) that seize us are "common to man" (1 Cor. 10:13) suggested to me that there is an emotional structure built into human beings that is similar to the cognitive structure that enables us to organize and evaluate ideas. I suggested that designing our teaching to help learners locate biblical truths on their emotional maps would be a more effective way to help persons of any age develop a lifestyle shaped by a distinctively biblical perception of the meaning of their life experiences. In that book, I argued that "it is in fact our emotional response to situations that trigger our thoughts and shape our perceptions," rather than our analyses of situations triggering our emotions (Richards 1983, 401–497). I concluded that "as long as our understanding of the Bible and its teachings are not linked to our emotions, it is unlikely that we will remember and appropriately apply Bible truths in life situations" (402).

In 1981 Roger W. Sperry received a Nobel Prize for research that led to the development of right brain/left brain theory, which has had an impact on teaching and learning in our culture. Unfortunately, even though expressing emotions and reading emotions has been recognized as a right brain function, and educators have come to realize the importance of communication between the brain hemispheres, the theory has been applied primarily to designing better ways to enhance cognitive processing. Yet the research reminds us that human beings are whole persons, not computers. To reach and equip persons as whole beings, the emotional functions of the right brain must be engaged.

Far more significant insights have grown out of neurobiology, and especially the work of Daniel J. Siegel. Siegel clearly defines not only the impact of early attachment on an individual but also the continuing impact of significant interpersonal relationships. He also explains that "research suggests that emotion serves as a central organizing process within the brain" (2012, 9). While his research is directly applicable to psychotherapy, it has important implications for Christian educators as well. In fact, the findings he reports underline the importance of the guidelines I laid out above.

In the ideal Christian education setting, the process will be guided by those who love and follow the Lord, both modeling the truths they teach and mentoring. The setting will be informal enough for teachers and learners to develop close personal relationships as they come to know and care about each other. There will be an emphasis on processing lived experiences, which necessarily include the emotions of the learners, in light of God's revelation in scripture. And the whole process will be interactive, open to the active participation of colearners who are also gifted by the Spirit to function as coteachers. In such settings, we truly will be focused on nurturing believers whose characters and lifestyles are in harmony with sound doctrine.

Strategic Areas for Development

It seems to me that as we move deeper into the 21st century, there are four areas of pedagogy on which we should focus: children's and youth ministry, family ministry, ministry to adults, and mentoring.

In children's ministry, we have tended to tell Bible stories and attach a moral. We need to develop curriculum to communicate core theological truths, translating them into concepts appropriate to the learner's ability to understand. For instance, even an abstract doctrine such as omniscience can be meaningful to a four-year-old if translated, "Jesus always sees me." A variety of learning activities might be developed around this theme that links the truth to the lived experiences and emotions of the child. In this approach, a Bible story can be used to illustrate the truth being taught rather than being viewed as itself the content of the teaching. Here Jesus seeing Nathaniel (John 1:44–49) would be an appropriate story. While the Bible remains central in the process, as both the source of truth and an illustration, we no longer should view the story as "the lesson" (Richards 1983, 385–396). As children move on into adolescence, the Bible can and should be used more, as it is with adults (see below).

As life in our culture becomes more frantic and the family more fragmented, it will be increasingly important to help parents to communicate faith to their children. This, it seems to me, calls for a two-pronged approach. First is to provide settings in which parents can share their struggles and their insights and find guidance through directed Bible study. Second is to provide intergenerational classes, in which parents and children learn and share together. Siegel's research emphasizes the importance of parent-child bonding for healthy development. A sharing of thoughts, experiences, and emotions around a biblical theme can have special relevance for the family's lived experience. As few adults in our culture have experienced sharing what we used to call "inner states" with our children (or others), guided intergenerational experiences can equip adults to nurture their children far more effectively than books and lectures on how to parent.

Small groups meeting in homes, and to a lesser extent in time-limited Sunday school classes, provide the setting for the best adult education. For too long the goal in such settings has been to produce biblically literate adults rather than committed disciples of Jesus. Whether group meetings are structured as discussions of a particular passage of scripture or as teacher-led Bible studies, careful attention needs to be given to ensuring that the biblical guidelines are understood and infuse the process. A fine example of a teacher-led process illustrating effective use of scripture by a teacher who models grace and respectfully engages adult learners can be found in Bob Ekblad's *Reading the Bible with the Damned* (2005).

Christian educators also need to take very seriously the potential of mentoring, whether this takes place in one-to-one relationships or in accountability groups ranging in size from three to five or six. Group mentoring (accountability groups) is currently more employed in missions than by the American church. But a good source of information and materials is available at www.mentor link.org, a ministry established by Dr. Stacey Rinehart.

Each of these four areas seems critical to me and is best addressed in the context of the local church.

Toward a Distinctively Christian Pedagogy

There is, of course, a vital role in Christian education for cognitive mastery of scripture's teachings. We need this as a context within which to read, interpret, and teach scripture. But given this, in the future we need a much greater focus on developing transformational educational processes, firmly rooted in scripture's own pedagogical guidelines. Christian education is, and should be, essentially a theological discipline. Too often we have chased fads rather than exploring better ways to implement guidelines found in scripture. Yet working within the framework provided by biblical guidelines, we can learn much from the behavioral sciences that will help us shape more effective methods for transformational communication of God's life-giving Word.

References and Resources

Ekblad, Bob. 2005. *Reading the Bible with the Damned*. Louisville, KY: Westminster John Knox Press.

Richards, Lawrence O. 1983. *Children's Ministry*. Grand Rapids, MI: Zondervan.

Siegel, Daniel J. 2012. *The Developing Mind*. 2nd ed. New York: The Guilford Press.

Relevant Entries

Adult Learning
Aesthetics (Beauty)
Affectivity
Aging
Alpha Course
Andragogy
Assessment/Evaluation in Education
Association of Christian Schools International
Association of Classical and Christian Schools
Behavior Management
Catechesis of the Good Shepherd
Censorship
Children's Sermon
Christian Education
Christian Education, Challenges to
Christian Education, Fundamental Questions of
Christian Education, Postmodern
Church as Learning Organization
Civil Religion, Challenge of
Cognitive Taxonomy, Bloom's
Communion of the Saints
Community
Cone of Learning
Conscience
Conscientization
Consciousness
Constructivism
Contemplation
Convergent and Divergent Thinking
Counseling
Creativity
Critical Thinking

CHRISTIAN PRACTICE AND CHRISTIAN EDUCATION

David I. Smith

The tensions and possibilities inherent in combining Christian practices and modern education are well illustrated by Dietrich Bonhoeffer's experiments in seminary education at Finkenwalde. In 1935, Bonhoeffer became head of a small underground seminary belonging to the Confessing Church in Germany. He had recently endured dispiriting experiences in the mainstream academy. At Finkenwalde, he pursued what he called "a sort of new monasticism which has in common with the old only the uncompromising attitude of a life lived according to the Sermon on the Mount in the following of Christ."[32] This

involved combining classroom lectures with intentional community practices, including structured communal and individual devotions, but also a broader focus on the pattern of the community's life together.

Eberhard Bethge later recalled Bonhoeffer's insistence on a rule that students were never to talk about another member of the community in that person's absence, or were to tell the other person about it afterward if they did so. Bethge commented that "the participants learned almost as much from their failures to observe this simple rule, and from their renewed resolution to keep it, as they did from the sermons and exegeses."[33] This brief comment invites a range of questions that reside at the intersection of learning and Christian practices. What is the relationship between educational practices and Christian practices? How is the learning that takes place through participation in social practice distinct from and related to the learning that occurs through verbal instruction? In what sense are Christian practices themselves educational?

Practices and Learning

There has in recent decades been a significant resurgence of interest in the formative role of social practices. Academic work on the topic spans various disciplines, particularly philosophy, sociology, educational theory, and practical theology. The concern in key discussions is not with "practice" as understood in the familiar modern opposition between "theory and practice." That dichotomy tends to separate out the thinking task, seen as developing and clarifying ideas and theories, from the doing task, seen as a matter of applying the ideas developed by theory. It pictures learning as first getting the ideas straight and then applying them. Discussions of social practices represent a move away from a picture of human action in which we first formulate a theory or know a proposition and then "put it into practice," with the practice counting only as a secondary, less reflective outworking of knowledge that has already been formulated. "Practices" are, rather, actions intrinsically shaped and coordinated by our basic visions and stories about the world—and they help generate and give shape to those visions.

Drawing upon an older Aristotelian tradition and more recent seminal work by scholars such as Alasdair MacIntyre (2007) and Pierre Bourdieu (1977), recent work on practices sees them as having a more primary role in shaping our sense of self. In important respects, we become who we are through participating in the social practices in which we are embedded. As embodied, social, habitual creatures, we learn and are formed by

32. Dietrich Bonhoeffer, "Letter to Karl-Friedrich Bonhoeffer (14 January 1935)," in *A Testament of Freedom: The Essential Writings of Dietrich Bonhoeffer*, rev. ed., ed. Geffrey B. Kelly and F. Burton Nelson (New York: HarperCollins, 1995), 424.

33. Ferdinand Schlingensiepen, *Dietrich Bonhoeffer 1906–1945: Martyr, Thinker, Man of Resistance* (Bloomsbury, UK: T&T Clark, 2010), 181.

taking part with others, over time, in structured ways of living that are informed and shaped by visions of the goods that we are pursuing. Worshipping, going to the mall, giving, going to school, eating together, participating in sports, developing theoretical ideas—social practices such as these provide a matrix within which our desires are formed, our virtues are strengthened or weakened, and our sense of who we are takes shape. We learn particular repertoires, particular ways of moving through the world, and these are not only informed by, but themselves help to shape, our vision of what should be. As Charles Taylor puts it:

> The relationship between practices and the background understanding behind them is therefore not one-sided. If the understanding makes the practice possible, it is also true that it is the practice that largely carries the understanding. At any given time, we can speak of the "repertory" of collective actions at the disposal of a given group in society.[34]

Given this more closely intertwined relationship between practice and understanding, we can begin to see practices not just as part of the bodily backdrop of learning, but as themselves embodying a means of learning and growing.

Christian Practices

This general account of human practices fosters and resonates with the recognition that Christianity is not simply a set of beliefs, but also a cluster of practices, an enacted way of being in the world that has a particular shape and purpose. Christians not only confess that Christ is Lord, but also participate in communal practices that include prayer, worship, giving, offering testimony, celebrating Sabbath, providing hospitality, serving, confession, mutual encouragement, justice-seeking, interpretation of scripture and the world, and many more surveyed in this encyclopedia. Again, these are not simply an optional application in practical terms of theological truths; these practices are themselves in part constitutive of what it means to live as a Christian, and they furnish a basic way in which one learns to be Christian.

Particularly in Reformation-oriented sectors of the Christian church, an emphasis on the constitutive importance of practices can evoke concerns regarding "works righteousness" and attempts to engineer our own salvation. Shared practices in a Christian context are, however, not primarily something that we do in the pursuit of self-perfection, but rather "arenas in which something is done to us, in us, and through us that we

could not of ourselves do, that is beyond what we do."[35] Christian practices are both a response to grace and a vessel through and in which grace operates, such as when the congregation comes together to worship in thankfulness for God's grace and in hope of receiving from God in and through worship. As Bethge noted above regarding Bonhoeffer's students' efforts to master their tongues, Christian practices commonly open up our awareness of our need to be remade rather than offering techniques for confident mastery. They are oriented toward sustaining vulnerability toward God and others and openness to mutual correction and spiritual growth. They are also not to be primarily understood as individual undertakings, but rather as communal patterns of engagement that give shape to the Christian community within which individuals engage and grow.

Educational Practices

Education comes with its own set of formative practices, particular to specific historical and cultural times and places. Educational practices are very clearly designed to be formative, to shape the self toward a particular set of goods, and to foster the desire to pursue those goods. They embody visions of how learners should grow and the kind of society for which they should be formed. Particular educational practices may strengthen passivity or agency, conformity or critical distance, equality or stratification and social division, individualism or an orientation to community, competitiveness or cooperation, a focus on achievement or on wisdom, and so forth. A regular educational practice in which, for instance, work is graded on the curve and students are ranked publicly and rewarded on the basis of their ranking may help to foster an enduring disposition of competitiveness and ambition in relation to academic achievement. Education is never simply passing on information; it is also a set of ritual practices providing one of the contexts within which a pattern is offered and fostered for our relationships to one another, to the world, and to God. Attending to this reality necessitates a recognition that the relationship between Christianity and education is not simply a relationship between theological beliefs or ideas and approaches to education, but also a relationship between mutually supportive, partially overlapping, or rival practices.

Christian Practices and Educational Practices

This returns us to the tensions and possibilities at the intersection of Christian and educational practices. This intersection may be approached in a variety of ways. At one end of the spectrum, education may itself be seen as

34. Charles Taylor, *Modern Social Imaginaries* (Durham, NC: Duke University Press, 2004), 25.

35. Craig Dykstra, *Growing in the Life of Faith: Education and Christian Practices*, 2nd ed. (Louisville, KY: Westminster John Knox Press, 2005), 56.

a Christian practice. Providing and reforming education, especially in the context of concerns for just provision, holistic learning, and meeting the needs of the excluded and disadvantaged, has often itself been a practice of the Christian church. At the opposite end of the spectrum, Christian and educational practices may be understood as belonging to conflicting or strictly separate spheres, such as, for instance, when prayer is excluded by law from certain educational settings or when open academic inquiry is regarded as inimical to growth in faith.

Between these two poles (each of which is problematic) lies a broad range of possible forms of interaction between Christian practices and educational practices, and it is in the overlaps that further interesting questions arise. Practices may be borrowed from one context into another, such as when, for instance, prayer or Bible reading takes place in a school or university classroom, or when the current practices of the school classroom are imported into the church's educational ministry. Such borrowing invites fresh consideration of the contours of the practice and its context: if the teacher, for instance, prays in class and is an authority figure, might the practice of prayer become a form of behavioral control (used, for instance, to get students quiet at the start of class) or an abusive assertion of privilege (implying a shared faith that may not be present) rather than a spiritual discipline? If the pedagogical practices of, for instance, the lecture hall are transferred into the church setting, might they work against the holistic kinds of growth sought in that setting?

As well as attending to the tensions, there is reason to consider the potential for generating fruitful approaches to Christian learning through exploration of Christian practices. How might the wisdom embodied in patterns of Christian practice offer fresh perspectives on learning? What if a philosophy class studying ethics decided to fast before discussing poverty in class: Would that change the nature of the discussion and the learning that took place?[36] What if students learning a foreign language approached their task as one of learning how to exercise hospitality to strangers?[37] How might a church community frame congregational learning about contentious issues with the practice of reconciliation? How do our reading practices shape what we learn in church and school? Such questions point to concrete possibilities for exploring the kinds of learning afforded by particular Christian practices and the ways in which those practices embody a particular vision of learner formation.

These questions also suggest the possibility of a more general examination of whether the repertoires that make up the particular educational practices adopted in church and school resonate with or are in tension with the broader formative paradigm implied by Christian practices. Consider the example of reading practices. Practices such as *lectio divina* and *lectio continua* (which, respectively, represent disciplines of reading contemplatively and prayerfully and reading continuously rather than in isolated chunks) presuppose a relationship between more contemplative, sustained forms of engagement with text and spiritually formative learning. In educational settings, the balance is often tilted more toward learning to locate and extract particular pieces of information in order to demonstrate mastery. A focus on practices would require that Christian education consider this tension, focusing not just on *what* is read but on the kinds of formation taking place through the way in which reading is practiced together. This in turn suggests the need to question the dominance of wider educational practice paradigms that focus mainly on the rapid extraction and accumulation of items of knowledge.

Although Christian practices have always been part of the history and identity of the Christian church, it has proved surprisingly easy in a modern world heavily influenced by more detached, intellectually oriented visions of learning to miss their educational significance. Dietrich Bonhoeffer's experiments with a consistent regime of practices in the seminary education he provided at Finkenwalde, mentioned earlier, gave rise to his famous book *Life Together*. One recent essay about Finkenwalde describes efforts to teach themes from *Life Together* in a church setting:

> As a church planter and pastor who struggled for years to facilitate community in the church, I attempted over and over again to inspire the vision for community by the big narrative of the gospel. This was a key first step. But it often fell on deaf ears. What I did not understand was that it needed to be reinforced with a new ritual, a counter liturgy that encompassed the entire community. In fact, if I had seen the importance of ritual, a daily liturgy of worship and life to go along with the weekly corporate liturgy of the gospel, I might have seen more transformation of individuals and more engagement with the world around us. It was an insight I just missed, though I had read *Life Together* dozens of times.[38]

---

36. Bradford S. Hadaway, "Preparing the Way for Justice: Strategic Dispositional Formation through the Spiritual Disciplines," in *Spirituality, Justice, and Pedagogy*, ed. David I. Smith, John Shortt, and John Sullivan (Nottingham, UK: The Stapleford Centre, 2006), 143–165.

37. David I. Smith and Barbara Carvill, *The Gift of the Stranger: Faith, Hospitality, and Foreign Language Learning* (Grand Rapids, MI: Eerdmans, 2000).

38. Jim Belcher, "The Secret of Finkenwalde: Liturgical Treason," in *Bonhoeffer, Christ, and Culture*, ed. Keith L. Johnson and Timothy Larsen (Downers Grove, IL: InterVarsity Press, 2013), 201.

Taking practices seriously suggests a need to move beyond a dichotomy between teaching Christian ideas and individual appropriation of spiritual disciplines for personal growth, toward a more holistic consideration of the nature of embodied Christian life together, how we learn through and within it, and how it may challenge our visions of education.

References and Resources

Bourdieu, Pierre. 1977. *Outline of a Theory of Practice.* Cambridge, UK: Cambridge University Press.

Dykstra, Craig. 2005. *Growing in the Life of Faith: Education and Christian Practices.* 2nd ed. Louisville, KY: Westminster John Knox Press.

Hauerwas, Stanley, and William Willimon. 1989. *Resident Aliens: Life in the Christian Colony.* Nashville, TN: Abingdon Press.

MacIntyre, Alasdair. 2007. *After Virtue.* 3rd ed. Notre Dame, IN: University of Notre Dame Press.

Smith, David I., and James K. A. Smith, eds. 2011. *Teaching and Christian Practices: Reshaping Faith and Learning.* Grand Rapids, MI: Eerdmans.

Volf, Miroslav, and Dorothy C. Bass. 2001. *Practicing Theology: Beliefs and Practices in Christian Life.* Grand Rapids, MI: Eerdmans.

Relevant Entries

Advocacy as Christian Practice
Art as Christian Practice
Bible Study as Christian Practice
Celebration as Christian Practice
Centering Prayer as Christian Practice
Communities of Practice
Community-Building as Christian Practice
Confession as Christian Practice
Contemplative Prayer as Christian Practice
Cursillo as Christian Practice
Dance as Christian Practice
Devotional Reading as Christian Practice
Discernment as Christian Practice
Discussion as Christian Practice
Encouragement as Christian Practice
Fasting as Christian Practice
Film as Christian Practice
Forgiveness
Giving as Christian Practice
Guidance as Christian Practice
Healing as Christian Practice
Hospitality as Christian Practice
Imagination as Christian Practice
Journaling as Christian Practice
Justice-seeking as Christian Practice
Listening as Christian Practice
Meditation as Christian Practice
Missions as Christian Practice
Monastic Practices of Formation as Christian Practice
Music as Christian Education
Pilgrimage as Christian Practice
Poetry as Christian Practice
Prayer as Christian Practice
Reading as Christian Practice
Reconciliation as Christian Practice
Restitution as Christian Practice
Retreats as Christian Practice
Sabbatarianism as Christian Practice
Sabbath as Christian Practice
Service Learning as Christian Practice
Silence as Christian Practice
Simplicity as Christian Practice
Social Action as Christian Practice
Social Practices as Christian Practice
Solitude as Christian Practice
Spiritual Friendship as Christian Practice
Storytelling as Christian Practice
Submission as Christian Practice
Suffering as Christian Practice
Testimony as Christian Practice
Theosis as Christian Practice
Virtue Ethics as Christian Practice
Worship as Christian Practice

CHRISTIAN EDUCATION IN DIFFICULT CIRCUMSTANCES

Mara Lief Crabtree

Defining Christian Education in Difficult Circumstances

Certain approaches to education throughout history have tended to impart an attitude that negatively categorizes the unique and diverse interests and abilities, as well as certain limitations and disabilities, of individuals or groups defined as living in difficult circumstances. These attitudes result in educational emphases and approaches that do not fully embrace the needs and abilities of persons whose lives are defined as existing in difficult circumstances.

How precisely does one define the idea of Christian education in difficult circumstances? Difficult circumstances encompass the lives of all those who, in some manner, are living on the margins of society. Persons living in difficult situations, for numerous reasons and as a result of various circumstances, are faced with challenges and obstacles in personal life and in the lives of their family members that make receiving an education, at any level of the learning process, including informal or formal education, fraught with various degrees of difficulty. These challenges may be very individual and personal, such as genetically rooted disabilities, illness, or disease; disabilities resulting from illness, disease, or accident; or related to systemic challenges in education depending on particular circumstances of cultural, social, political, geographical, financial, and other issues such as war and other human conditions. These globally prevalent conditions call for the Christian community to provide education for individuals and groups experiencing various and often profoundly difficult challenges in life. The ever-changing global conditions in many areas of human life emphasize the Christian community's need for continuing commitment in providing educational opportunities for all people in all places and conditions, whenever possible.

The Importance of Christian Education in Difficult Circumstances

Education underlines the religious and moral vision of the Christian message. The community of Christ, the church, is motivated by the Holy Spirit to love and serve people whose lives exist in difficult circumstances by providing the quality of religious and academic education and vocational training that respects each person's unique situation and needs.

The spiritual, religious, and moral vision of the Christian faith holds in high regard the dignity and worth of all persons as created in the image of God (*Imago Dei*), each with individual areas of giftedness and divinely ordained vocations. The Judeo-Christian scriptures clearly indicate the process and progression of human life as moving from immaturity to maturity throughout the course of one's earthly journey. This developing maturity encompasses the physical, intellectual, emotional, spiritual, relational, and vocational aspects of the human person, resulting in a life of purpose and meaning for the individual, a life lived to the glory of God (*soli Deo gloria*) and for the good of others. Therefore God's gift of education is understood, in the context of the Judeo-Christian faith, as not only important, but essential to the formation and continuing development of maturity and life purpose for the individual.

Education for the Whole Person

The Gospels witness to Jesus's obvious care for His own beloved Jewish people and for all people, no matter the circumstances of their lives. During the period of His incarnation, Jesus healed numerous and varied illnesses, diseases, emotional needs, and spiritual conditions. His care and restoration of the marginalized in society prove God's concern for the well-being of the whole person. The Gospels' accounts of Jesus's ministry open a door to understanding the Messiah's teaching, healing, and deliverance: His holistic restoration of persons, many in difficult and often dire circumstances, made way for their growth in the spiritual, intellectual, emotional, relational, and vocational areas of life. His teaching and active examples of ministry educated His followers for the purpose of living meaningful, fruitful lives to glorify God and to serve God's purposes through their lives and vocations.

The Great Commission and Christian Education in Difficult Circumstances

In the Judeo-Christian tradition, the value and purpose of each individual life emphasizes that person's equality of worth, independent of one's perceived or actual personal challenges, difficulties, obstacles, or disabilities. Therefore, providing education for those in difficult circumstances is a religious and moral value as well as a collective vocation for the Christian community, in alignment with Jesus Christ's commission to His original disciples. Often referred to as "the Great Commission," Jesus commanded those disciples and others who would follow after them through the millennia of the Christian Church to "'[g]o therefore and make disciples of all the nations, baptizing them in the name of the Father and the Son and the Holy Spirit, teaching them to observe all that I commanded you'" (Matt. 28: 19–20 NASB). Clearly, Jesus's imperative to His disciples had as its focus the preaching of the Gospel: the reality of salvation through Jesus Christ and learning to express a life of authentic faith as one follows His teachings. Jesus emphasized the need for the believer's catechesis and the ongoing pedagogy within the Christian community by teaching disciples "to observe all" He had commanded. Jesus's primary commission to His disciples to teach others begins the progressive unfolding of Christian education's history. This unfolding of Christ-centered education would expand through the centuries into every corner of the earth, to diverse individuals and groups, by both informal and formal means of education, with the same understanding maintained by St. Paul, that it is "Christ Himself in whom are hidden all the treasures of wisdom and knowledge" (Col. 2: 2–3 NASB). Therefore, the Gospel message would come first, followed by opportunities for learning in the sciences, natural sciences, humanities, social sciences, and every field of knowledge originating from God's gifts of knowledge and wisdom to teach, equip, and train individuals for the realization of their maximum vocation in life.

Educating in Challenging Times

Transformation by renewal of the mind (Rom. 12:2) became the foundational principle of Christian education for those inundated with the culture, belief, and values of secularism and paganism in the era of the early church, thereby combatting the competing forces of Greek and Roman cultures and other existing cultural, philosophical, religious, and political forces present in that era.

The nascent church experienced intense oppression from spiritual, political, and cultural forces. Despite significant and ongoing challenges, church leaders, including apostles, prophets, evangelists, pastors, and teachers (Eph. 4:11–14), moved forward in the ministries of evangelism, church planting, teaching, and training individuals and communities of Christian believers. St. Paul instructs the Ephesian Church that the ascension gifts (4:11) are for the purpose of "equipping of the saints for the work of service, to the building up of the body of Christ; until we all attain to the unity of the faith, and of the knowledge of the Son of God" (vv. 12, 13 NASB). Paul emphasizes the end result of maturity, which ensures that "we may no longer be children, tossed to and fro between chance gusts of teaching, and wavering with every changing wind of doctrine . . ." (v. 14, NIV).

Providing Educational Advances

Difficult circumstances that hinder and compromise education for individuals or groups often remained hidden or little known in previous generations. In the present age, the proliferation of knowledge about effective educational methods and technological advances are important factors that both encourage and impel churches and other Christian groups to proactively address the diverse needs associated with educating persons who live in difficult circumstances.

As the global population is influenced and motivated by various degrees of technological change, these transitions provide new and increasing levels of knowledge and communication, resulting in wider dissemination of information about the educational needs of individuals in difficult circumstances. Information about newer and more effective ways to provide education for individuals and groups in difficult circumstances continues to move to the forefront, emerging in both scholastic settings and media contexts, ultimately encouraging a greater sense of connection among individuals and groups active in providing Christian education.

Outcomes of Christian Education in Difficult Circumstances

Historically, the hallmarks of distinction that separated the believer and the collective Christian community from secular society were the attitudes and practices associated with choosing to honor one another. Honor was indicated by respect for an individual's humanity, worth, and innate God-given ability to live a life of meaning and pur-

pose in ways unique to each person's needs and situation. Conversely, a secularized understanding of human abilities places a false sense of limitation on an individual's capacity to live meaningfully and successfully due to real or perceived kinds of disabilities or particular personal difficulties. The scriptures include numerous examples of individuals educated in the midst of difficult life circumstances, who, empowered by God through various processes of learning, expressed their personhood, giftings, and vocations, resulting in meaningful outcomes, including positively influencing the lives of others as a result of their efforts.

Call to Responsible Action

The Gospel's call to the Christian community sounds the message of truth from God's heart of compassion, witnessing to God's caring love, as shown through the finished work of Jesus Christ; a salvation available, through faith, for all who believe, individually and collectively; a redemption meeting the diverse needs of humankind. The *kerygma* of the gospel confirms the call to honor the dignity, importance, and inestimable worth of every human being, no matter his or her particular circumstances.

The Gospel message confirms the reality of the Christian community's responsibility to provide appropriate levels of education for all people based on each individual's unique needs, giftings, and potential for vocation, with the understanding that, in educating those in difficult circumstances, both faith and knowledge are required by Christian educators. Faith affirms the potential of each student's ability, in his or her unique way, to live a purposeful and meaningful life. Sound knowledge of the curriculum and methods of teaching that best correspond to each student's specific needs in his or her difficult circumstances ensures that the learning and training received will equip students to express God-given endowments, capacities, and callings for significant participation and contributions in all of life.

Achieving a Moral Vision

Educating persons in difficult circumstances has the potential to improve society collectively and to improve and enrich individual lives, in specific and even exceptional ways. The moral and religious vision of the Christian faith, witnessing to the reality that each person is created in the image of God, gives proof that every individual has the ability, in his or her singular way, for meaningful achievement in life, often rising above the levels of attainment others may have thought impossible, due to the often dire life circumstances of individuals in certain situations. The moral vision of the Christian faith throughout history and continuing into the future, as empowered and impassioned by the Holy Spirit, steadily continues in accepting the challenge to move forward, no matter the obstacles, in providing education, with quality and compassion, for individuals and groups living in difficult circumstances.

References and Resources

Adeney, Frances S., and Arvind Sharma, eds. 2007. *Christianity and Human Rights: Influences and Issues.* Albany: State University of New York Press.

Amesbury, Richard, and George Newlands. 2008. *Faith and Human Rights: Christianity and the Global Struggle for Human Dignity.* Minneapolis, MN: Fortress Press.

Clark, Doris C. 2000. *Feed All My Sheep: A Guide and Curriculum for Adults with Developmental Disabilities.* Louisville, KY: Geneva Press.

Claude, Richard Pierre, and Burns H. Weston, eds. 2006. *Human Rights in the World Community: Issues and Action.* Philadelphia: University of Pennsylvania Press.

Crosson-Tower, Cynthia. 2001. *When Children Are Abused: An Educator's Guide to Intervention.* Upper Saddle River, NJ: Pearson.

Donnelly, Jack. 2013. *Universal Human Rights in Theory and Practice.* Ithaca, NY: Cornell University Press.

Heitritter, Lynn, and Jeanette Vought. 2006. *Helping Victims of Sexual Abuse: A Sensitive Biblical Guide for Counselors, Victims, and Families.* Grand Rapids, MI: Bethany House.

Hollenbach, David. 2003. *The Global Face of Public Faith: Politics, Human Rights and Christian Ethics.* Washington, DC: Georgetown University Press.

Horsman, Jenny. 2000. *Too Scared to Learn: Women, Violence and Education.* New York: Routledge.

Hughes, Emma. 2012. *Education in Prison: Studying through Distance Learning.* Farnham, Surrey, UK: Ashgate Publishing.

Hunt, Lynn. 2008. *Inventing Human Rights: A History.* New York: W. W. Norton.

Long, Adrian. 2009. *Paul and Human Rights: A Dialogue with the Father of the Corinthian Community.* Sheffield, UK: Sheffield Phoenix Press Ltd.

Maritain, Jacques. 2011. *Christianity and Democracy and the Rights of Man and Natural Law.* San Francisco: Ignatius Press.

Marshall, Christopher D. 2002. *Crowned with Glory and Honor: Human Rights in the Biblical Tradition.* Harrisonburg, VA: Herald Press.

Marshall, Paul, Lela Gilbert, and Nina Shea. 2013. *Persecuted: The Global Assault on Christians.* Nashville, TN: Thomas Nelson.

Nason-Clark, Nancy, and Catherine Clark Kroeger. 2004. *Refuge from Abuse: Healing and Hope for Abused Christian Women.* Downers Grove, IL: InterVarsity Press.

Neal, Gerald W. 2008. *Quiet Desperation: The Effects of Competition in School on Abused and Neglected Children.* Lanham, MD: Hamilton Books.

Panter-Brick, Catherine, and Malcolm T. Smith, eds. 2000. *Abandoned Children.* Cambridge, UK: Cambridge University Press.

Shepherd, Frederick M., ed. 2009. *Christianity and Human Rights: Christians and the Struggle for Global Justice.* Lanham, MD: Lexington Books.

Shoop, Robert J. 2004. *Sexual Exploitation in Schools: How to Spot It and Stop It.* Thousand Oaks, CA: Corwin Press.

Tracy, Steven R. 2005. *Mending the Soul: Understanding and Healing Abuse.* Grand Rapids, MI: Zondervan.

Witte, John, Jr., and Frank S. Alexander, eds. 2010. *Christianity and Human Rights: An Introduction.* New York: Cambridge University Press.

Zoukis, Christopher. 2012. *Education Behind Bars: A Win-Win Strategy for Maximum Security.* Camp Hill, PA: Sunbury Press.

Relevant Entries

Autism
Blind, Current Trends in the Education of the
Children of Unchurched Parents
Deaf, Education of the
Disability, Intellectual
Disability, Learning
Disability Ministry
Disabled, The
Disadvantaged, Education of the
Emotional Disabilities
Gang Members
Global Poverty
Global Underground Churches
Government Officials
Human Rights Violations
Human Trafficking
Illiterates in a Literate Culture
Immigrants
Institutionalized and Elderly, The
Integrated Education
Muslim Cultures
Nominal Christians
Oral Cultures, Christian Education in
Orphaned, The
Pluralism and Christian Education
Postmodernism
Secularism, The Challenge of
Single Parents
Spirituality, Secular
Street Children
Suffering, Educational Value of
Urban Contexts, Educating Christians in
Victims of Abuse
Victims of Natural Disasters
Victims of War and Terror

LITERATURE AND CHRISTIAN EDUCATION

Wesley Nan Barker

T. S. Eliot (1888–1965), a writer and critic associated with New Criticism, analyzed the formal elements of a literary text as inherently bound to its meaning. In his 1935 essay, "Religion and Literature," Eliot writes, "And if we, as readers, keep our religious and moral convictions in one compartment, and take our reading merely for entertainment, or on a higher plane, for aesthetic pleasure, I would point out that the author, whatever his conscious intentions in writing, in practice recognizes no such distinctions."[39] Eliot's words suggest that literature embodies an imagination and passion akin to religiosity. Religion and literature are intertwined as a matter not just of formal similarities or because they both concern a particular theme. Their interrelatedness, even when antagonistic or shunned as though literature can be autotelic, becomes the impetus for considering them together. From Eliot's use of poetics to reflect and critique the turmoil of religion and the modern individual poetic critiques, to Milton's 17th-century biblical allegory *Paradise Lost*, which elevated biblical narrative to its aesthetic heights, Christian educators and critics have used literature to probe the depths of theological reflection and employed the methods of literary analysis to discover new truths of the biblical texts.

Eliot's words make a gesture to an irreducible bond that unites literature with Christianity, but the absence of decisive limits and boundaries prevents "literature and religion" from demarcating a specific niche in the discipline of religious studies.[40]

In the face of the diversity of discourses and approaches to the question of literature and religion, this section focuses on major historical and intellectual trends in literary studies to broach fundamental questions about what constitutes literature. These entries include the long history of determining and analyzing the elements of literature and applying techniques of literary analysis to Christian Scripture ("The Bible as Literature"). In addition, these entries consider the tensions and implications of a history of using literary methods that locate their origins outside the field of Christian theology and interpretation to decidedly Christian ends. The entry on "Secular Literature and Christian Education" therefore suggests that literature is never entirely secular, and literary analysis of Christianity is never entirely free of its debt to its non-Christian sources. Finally, the entries turn to the diverse ways one can approach the relationship between literature and Christianity beginning by providing a brief overview of the modern developments in literary theory that have influenced theology ("Literary Theory and Theology"). Continuing the exploration of literary theory, "Phenomenology" provides an overview of the literary adaptation of phenomenological philosophy, and "Literature and Christian Education" considers monumental works associated with literary movements and their usefulness and use in Christian education. The term "literature" derives from the Latin *litteratura*, with the root *littera*, or letter. That literature at its base is a means of "writing with letters" carries the possibility of things written and the act of writing itself, including the study and critique of the relationship of letters to each other and to the whole of a text. The letters vary in their linguistic origins and in their contexts; however, the Bible uses letters to write everything from its genealogies and commandments to its lyricism and imagery. The Bible is in its most basic sense a form of literature, and the entry "The Bible as Literature" in this encyclopedia traces the history of practices of reading the Bible and examines transformations in biblical interpretation in relation to shifts in literary methods and theories. As the entry reveals, every development in interpreting the Bible as literature, from allegorical to grammaticological to postmodern linguistic approaches and interrogations of the reader-author relationship, has been used by both those who view innovations in interpretation as opportunities to strengthen their access to the meaning of the Bible as God's divine revelation as well as those who apply these methods as a means to probe the artistic, cultural, and historical depths of the text as a cultural artifact or as an enduring literary masterpiece. The Bible is literature, and, read with or without a singular authoritative interpretive tradition or with or without a consensus on what type of literature the Bible represents, the letters of the text become the fundamental source through which Christian educators and their students situate their faith and understanding in relation to the breadth of the Christian tradition.

Precisely because the Bible is a form of literature, it has been read in accordance with literary practices of textual analysis. Early church fathers applied their Greek and Roman education in letters to read, wrestle with, and ultimately interpret scripture. By design, the entry "Secular Literature and Christian Education" in this encyclopedia therefore does not catalog "secular" works useful for Christian instruction or allegories of biblical literature for non-Christian markets. Rather, it interrogates and problematizes the division of secular and religious education by narrating the reciprocal relationship among literary,

---

39. T. S. Eliot, "Religion and Literature," in *Selected Prose of T. S. Eliot*, ed. F. Kermode (London: Faber and Faber, 1975), 101.

40. Wesley A. Kort, "What, After All, Is 'Religion and Literature'?" *Religion and Literature* 41, no. 2 (2009): 105–123.

biblical, and theological analyses. Theologian Graham Ward (2014) has suggested that theology is inherently literary, just as literature is inherently theological. Concepts of transcendence appear in secular literature and inform literary interpretation of the biblical text. Similarly, literary readings of the figurative language and imagery of the Bible have inspired imaginative allegories of biblical narratives that critically engage theological themes in relation to a secular world wishing to free itself from religious tradition.

The entry "Literary Theory and Theology" offers a cursory analysis of some of the major developments in literary theory in the 20th century and their impacts on theological questions about the nature of the relationship between God and humans. The late 20th-century movement toward "postmodern" disruptions of modern assumptions about truth claims, whether scientific or religious, demands creative responses from Christian theologians, who must engage a pluralistic world thoughtfully and faithfully.

Regardless of whether one believes the text presents a universal Truth, biblical literature does not emerge in a sociopolitical vacuum. The Bible is not the oldest form of writing with letters, and by the time the earliest biblical texts emerged in written form, such literature already had a history. The letters of literature were letters of certain peoples, and subsequent interpretive translation work and redaction similarly belonged to particular communities with historical, geographical, and political realities. Over the last half century or more, biblical criticism's focus on historicizing the biblical text has been transformed by literary theory's interrogation of knowledge, including knowledge of history. Phenomenology has pushed this line of inquiry by emphasizing that the things that appear to us as true are deeply contextual and constantly changing, such that the only experience one knows is one's own.

The entry in this encyclopedia "Phenomenology" traces the 20th-century philosophical movement's transformations from an exacting philosophical science to a theory that prioritizes interpreting human experience in terms of one's concrete, embodied relationships with others as the source of continuously evolving, multiple truths. Despite its disruptions of absolute truth claims and its tendency to deconstruct metaphysical distinctions between immanence and transcendence, later 20th-century phenomenology intertwined the hermeneutical dimensions of literary theory in ways that engendered ideas about a transcendent God emerging in and through infinite contextual interpretations rather than through a singular mode of investigation. For Christian educators, this emphasis on the truth of experience as a contextually dependent, interpretive endeavor opened the way for constructively embracing the pluralism of the modern world as the complex and diverse manifestation of divine reality.

Literature has served as inspiration and it has presented cutting critiques, but it continues to push the religious imagination in ways that might strengthen faith. If we understand Christian education to encompass a process of intellectual formation in accordance with certain spiritual, theological, moral, ethical, and spiritual systems of belief, Christian education provides a foundation for evaluating literary works, criticisms, and theories, in terms of their value for the edification of Christian principles. And yet that system too, if it is to engage developments in literature and literary theory critically, must wrestle with the unraveling of the very dogmatics that justify Christian education as a system. In terms of its root, *educare*, to lead outward, or lead forth, Christian education suggests a benevolent response to these challenges. Indeed, at its root, Christian education is an opening to the possibility of new ways of knowing and seeing, and a leading forth into that possibility such that the unknown can be faced with hope and generosity rather than fear.

References and Resources

Eliot, T. S. 1975. "Religion and Literature." In *Selected Prose of T. S. Eliot*, edited by F. Kermode, 101. London: Faber and Faber.

Kort, Wesley A. 2009. "What, After All, Is 'Religion and Literature'?" *Religion and Literature* 41 (2): 105–123.

Ward, Graham. 2014. *Unbelievable: Why We Believe and Why We Don't*. London: I. B. Tauris.

Relevant Entries

Bible as Literature, The
Literary Theory and Theology
Phenomenology
Radical Orthodoxy
Secular Literature and Christian Education

BIOGRAPHIES OF INFLUENTIAL CHRISTIAN EDUCATORS

George Brown Jr.

As one surveys the more than 100 names found among the Christian educator biographies included in this volume, one may wonder why a particular name has been included while another was omitted. Readers would expect to find Christian educators who have made significant contributions to the field over the centuries. But what about those well-known Christians whose influence has been felt but who are not automatically recognized as Christian educators?

Editors are faced with some difficult questions, especially when the size and scope of the encyclopedia present logistical constraints. For example, consider Elliot Eisner, who was not a religious or Christian educator, but whose understanding of curriculum is a significant contribution to education and curriculum theory that has had considerable influence in the field of Christian education. And can a justifiable case be made for including other explicitly non-Christians, such as John Dewey, William James, Lev Vygostky, Socrates, or Erik Erikson? What about Dorothy Sayers, whose primary association and contribution is more literary than directly related to Christian education? Should she be included? And what warrants including other Christians who did not directly teach or write explicitly on Christian education, such as Dietrich Bonhoeffer, Irenaeus, Count Nicholas van Zinzendorf, or John Wannamaker? These are some of the challenges facing editors when they contemplate biographical entries in a resource like this.

Following are a few reflections on the process of how the editors of this reference work made these kinds of decisions.

Primary Sphere of Engagement versus Influence on the Field

Some historical and contemporary figures have been directly engaged in the field of Christian education in theory and/or practice. One thinks, for example, of those who taught Christian education in free-standing seminaries or divinity schools affiliated with colleges or universities: Warren Benson and Bernice L. Neugarten; Randolph Crump Miller and Maria Harris; Lois E. LeBar and D. Campbell Wyckoff; George Albert Coe and Maria Harris.

But there are others who have had a significant impact on the field, but were not directly engaged in the theory or practice of Christian education. Over the course of the history of Christian education, biblical scholars, theologians, philosophers, psychologists, and sociologists have left their mark in ways large and small. Aristotle or Karl Barth may come to mind; the former an ancient philosopher, the latter a 20th-century theologian. While Karl Barth may not be associated directly with Christian education, the theological movement known as "neoorthodoxy" was a strong influence in the Presbyterian Christian Faith and Life Curriculum developed by Presbyterians under the leadership of James D. Smart following World War II.[41]

---

41. George Brown Jr., "Twentieth Century Presbyterian-Reformed Curricula: A Very Brief Survey," *APCE Advocate* 24, no. 3 (1999): 10–11, 14–15.

Historical and Cultural Context

Editors also have to consider matters such as historical and cultural context when selecting whom to include and whom to exclude from such an important reference work as this. The names should reflect the historical periods covered in the 2,000-year history of Christian education—early church, Middle Ages to early modern age, and modern world—and the cultural/geographical locations represented—global, national, and regional—as well as religious tradition or affiliation—Anglican, Orthodox, Protestant, and Roman Catholic.

Consider two "test cases": Paulo Freire and Sara Little. Freire, whose Brazilian roots place him in the Southern hemisphere, was not a religious worker, although he stood within the Roman Catholic tradition. He was an educator and activist, whose activities threatened those in power and resulted in his being exiled. While Freire's *engagement* was in education, especially literacy education, his *influence* was felt in the field of Christian education. Although his cultural roots were in Latin America, Freire's time spent working with the World Council of Churches introduced his ideas about education to the Western world. In the 1970s, many Christian educators read his *Pedagogy of the Oppressed* (Herder and Herder, 1970) and were influenced by his philosophy of education.

On the other hand, Little's *engagement* was in the field of Christian education theory and practice. Her *influence* was also significant. She spent most of her professional career teaching at the Presbyterian School of Christian Education and Union Theological Seminary in Richmond, Virginia. While Sara Little represents the same historical period as Paulo Freire, her cultural roots are in North America. Freire's religious affiliation was Roman Catholic, while Little's religious affiliation was Protestant (Presbyterian).

These are some of the challenges involved in selecting entries for the Christian educator biographies found in this volume. They account for some of the difficult choices editors must make in bringing to publication a reference work like this. The editors, along with the editorial advisory board who participated in the decision making, acknowledge that some readers may not in all cases agree with either those who have been included or those who have been omitted.

Nevertheless, we contend that these more than 100 individuals—and certainly many more not named herein—and their contributions have established richer foundations for effectively educating Christians.

Relevant Entries
Abelard, Peter
Aelred of Riveaulx

Alcuin
Amalorpavadass, D. S.
Ambrose
Anselm
Aristotle
Augustine
Bacon, Roger
Barth, Karl
Baxter, Edna
Baxter, Richard
Bellarmine, Robert
Berryman, Jerome
Beza, Theodore
Bonhoeffer, Dietrich
Borromeo, Charles
Bounds, E. M.
Boys, Mary
Braille, Louis
Bugenhagen, Johannes
Burroughs, Nannie
Bushnell, Horace
Calvin, John
Cavalletti, Sofia
Chambers, Oswald
Chrysostom, John
Clark, Francis E.
Clement of Alexandria
Clerc, Laurent
Coe, George Albert
Comenius
Cully, Iris
Cully, Kendig
Cyril of Alexandria
Cyril of Jerusalem
Dawson, Christopher Henry
de Foucald, Charles Eugene
de Sales, Francis
Dewey, John
Dykstra, Craig
Edge, Findley
Eisner, Elliot
Erasmus
Erikson, Erik
Fahs, Sophia
Foster, Richard J.
Fowler, James
Francis, Leslie J.
Francke, August Hermann
Freire, Paulo
Gaebelein, Frank e.
Gallaudet, Thomas
Gangel, Kenneth O.
Gergen, Kenneth J.

Gerson, Jean
Gregory of Nazianzus
Gregory of Nyssa
Groome, Thomas
Groote, Gerard
Grosseteste, Robert
Grundtvig, Nikolaj Frederik Severin
Harris, Maria
Hauerwas, Stanley
Hendricks, Howard G.
Herbart, Johann Frederich
Hesburgh, Theodore
Hofinger, Johannes
Holmes, Arthur
Hugh of Saint Victor
Hull, John
Irenaeus of Lyons
James, William
Jerome
Jones, E. Stanley
Justin Martyr
Kennedy, William B.
Kienel, Paul A.
Kierkegaard, Søren
Knowles, Malcolm
Knox, John
Kohlberg, Lawrence
Kuyper, Abraham
Laubach, Frank C.
LeBar, Lois E.
Lee, James Michael
L'Epee, Abbe Charles Michel de
Lewis, C. S.
Little, Sara Pamela
Lloyd-Jones, D. M.
Loder, James
Lonergan, Bernard
Lowrie, Roy, Jr.
Loyola, Ignatius
Luther, Martin
Lynn, Robert W.
Maslow, Abraham
Mears, Henrietta
Melanchthon, Philip
Merton, Thomas
Michel, Virgil
Miller, Randolph Crump
Montessori, Maria
Moore, Allen J.
Moore, Mary Elizabeth Mullino
Moran, Gabriel
More, Hannah
Murray, Andrew

Nebreda, Alfonso M.
Nelson, C. Ellis
Neugarten, Bernice L
Newman, John Henry
Nipkow, Karl Ernst
Nouwen, Henri
Ockenga, Harold John
Origen
Oser, Fritz K.
Owen, John
Packard, Frederick
Palmer, Parker
Palmer, Phoebe Worrall
Payne, Daniel Alexander
Peckham, John
Pestalozzi, Johann H.
Piaget, Jean
Plato
Pope Innocent III
Porter, Noah
Price, John Milburn
Raikes, Robert
Rayburn, Jim
Richards, Lawrence O.
Rossiter, Graham
Rousseau, Jean-Jacques
Sayers, Dorothy L.
Schmemann, Alexander
Schweitzer, Friedrich
Sherrill, Lewis Joseph
Shockley, Grant
Smart, James D.
Smart, Ninian
Smith, H. Shelton
Socrates
Spurgeon, Charles
St. John of the Cross
Stokes, Olivia Pearl
Stott, John
Streib, Heinz
Sturm, Johann
Taylor, Gardner
Van Caster, Marcel
Van Kaam, Adrian
Vincent, Bishop John Heyl
Vygostky, Lev
Wanamaker, John
Ward, Ted
Warren, Michael
Wesley, John
Westerhoff, John Henry, III
Wilson, Douglas
Wimberly, Anne E. Streaty

Wittgenstein, Ludwig
Wolterstorff, Nicholas
Wyckoff, DeWitte Campbell
Zinzendorf, Nicholas Ludwig von
Zwingli, Huldreich

EDUCATIONAL LAW AND POLICIES

Mai-Anh Le Tran

Regnum–Sacerdotium–Studium: State, Church, and Education in Cooperation

"Congress shall make no law respecting an establishment of religion, nor prohibiting the free exercise thereof."[42] Thus reads the First Amendment of the Bill of Rights of the U.S. Constitution, an institutional assertion ratified in 1791 that frames the extent and limitations of government's interference in matters of religious beliefs and practices for the new nation-state.[43] Translated into two inseparable clauses—religious (dis)establishment and free exercise of religion—the amendment encapsulates what Thomas Jefferson had described as a *"wall of separation* between the garden of the church and the wilderness of the world" and has affected a history of federal and state laws, legal exemptions, and court decisions that sought to interpret and adjudicate inevitable entanglements among state, church, and education.[44]

"In Western civilization, the connection between religion and education is both intimate and of long duration," one historian of religion wrote.[45] The premise presents a worthwhile investigative challenge for contemporary Christian religious educators, for such a query would yield important ideological bearings for closer review of the social, cultural, and political negotiations that underlie juridical decisions concerning the function of religion and education in the construction and maintenance of democratic society. For instance, what difference would it make for our understanding of the intersections among the church, the church's teaching task, and the law, if they were guided by the contention that Western Christianity was forged by a fusion between the "Christian church" and the "Graeco-Roman state," the product of which was a "politico-ecclesiastical empire" throughout the ancient Mediterranean? Fast-forward to an expansive medieval Europe, and the no-

42. David M. O'Brien, *Constitutional Law and Politics: Civil Rights and Civil Liberties*, 2nd ed., vol. 2 (New York: W. W. Norton, 1995).
43. Ibid., 644.
44. Quoted in Leonard Levy, *The Establishment Clause: Religion and the First Amendment* (New York: Macmillan, 1986), 184. Cited in O'Brien, *Constitutional Law and Politics*, 2:646.
45. Edwin S. Gaustad, *Church and State in America*, 2nd ed. (New York: Oxford University Press, 1999), 87.

tion of a "Christian commonwealth" continues to be sustained by an evolving triadic cooperation among *regnum* (state), *sacerdotium* (church), and *studium* (education) in the regulation of public religious lives—more specifically, for the maintenance of a "Christian society," such that baptism into the church also meant admission into citizenship.[46] Needless to say, cooperation is never without friction. If church and state had been collapsed into imperial unity in the Middle Ages, that unity dissolved with the Renaissance's "think cosmopolitan, act provincial" attitude, as churches took on national and regional flavors throughout Europe, and states began to assert secular sovereignty and common law.[47] Within the ensuing age of Enlightenment, one finds foundational political philosophies articulated by such figures as John Locke in *Two Treatises of Government*, as well as zealous, separatist, fundamentalist, anti-establishment religious expressions from such groups as the English Puritans. European political consciousness was populated with the diction of natural law, sovereignty of the people, social contracts, and political trusteeship; its religious praxis was enlivened by affinities for individual will, election, austerity, and moral triumphalism; and its emerging logic concerning the relationship between civil and ecclesiastical authority is that of separatism.[48]

With a liberal imaginative leap, we can see the above amalgam of religio-political ideologies being transported by the early colonists (or colonialists) to America and detect their metamorphosis into contemporary accommodationist legislative and judicial interpretations of church-state relations in the United States.[49] The United States since its early beginnings has maintained equivocal positions concerning cooperation between church and state when deciding religion's place in the public arena and government's place in the religious arena. More specific to concerns of secular and sectarian (i.e., religious) education, government, and religion (church, mosques, synagogues, temples) negotiate jurisprudence over a broad spectrum of issues that crisscross religious and public spheres.

The themes of this section give evidence to such complex scope, with topics ranging from governmental regulation of religious teachings, practices, and organization; to educational reform through social policies;

to constitutional and legislative mandates for religion's intersection with public life. However, a thematic thread laced through these disparate subjects is this enduring co-operation between church and state in the making and reforming of (U.S.-American) civil society.

(Dis)Establishment and Free Exercise

Establishment churches existed in early colonial America—from the Anglican establishment in the Virginia colony, to the Puritan Congregational establishment in New England. With varying degrees of tolerance for religious varieties, this form of "establishment without free exercise" ensured "positive support of religion by public funds" and "legal enforcement of certain orthodox beliefs" of the publicly endorsed religious establishment.[50] However, with increasing colonial settlements, expanding sectarian options and dissentions, and growing populist religious revivalism, colonial Americans recognized the need to move beyond tolerance to "equal rights of conscience," for a principled embrace of "religious freedom with no single or multiple establishment of religion by law."[51] Against a backdrop of tour-de-force political arguments for and against public endorsement of the Christian religion (including Patrick Henry's "Bill for Establishing a Provision for Teachers of the Christian Religion," James Madison's *Memorial and Remonstrance*, and Thomas Jefferson's "Statute for Establishing Religious Freedom" for the State of Virginia[52]), the 13 original states eventually ratified a Constitution in which "religion" is mentioned only once in what is later known as the "no religious test" of Article 6, and in which the very first amendment of the Bill of Rights guarantees religious freedom.[53]

"[R]eligion without governmental sanction or support" paved the way for robust development of religious varieties in the midst of national identity construction for the young republic.[54] Volunteerism shaped 19th-century American civil society, with a burgeoning of new religious and social service organizations (e.g., the American Bible Society in 1816, and later the American Sunday School Union in 1924 and the American Tract Society in 1925) and the rise of new denominational heavyweights (Baptists and Methodists overtaking the Congregationalists and Episcopalians). The religious scene was spirited in public life, while the federal government remained modest in size, and the country's Supreme Court had little intervention in religious matters until the adoption

46. See Ernest Barker, *Church, State and Education*, 1st ed. (Ann Arbor: University of Michigan Press, 1957), preface, 20, 37, 66; R. Freeman Butts, *The American Tradition in Religion and Education* (Westport, CT: Greenwood Press, 1974), 12.

47. Barker, *Church, State and Education*, 69.

48. Butts, *American Tradition in Religion and Education*, 21; Barker, *Church, State and Education*, 98, 114–119.

49. Butts, *American Tradition in Religion and Education*, 21; citing Evarts B. Greene, *Religion and the State* (New York: New York University Press, 1941), 8.

50. Butts, *American Tradition in Religion and Education*, 19–20.

51. Ibid., 9, 37.

52. Gaustad, *Church and State in America*, 38–40.

53. Ibid., 41–45.

54. Ibid., 47.

of the Fourteenth Amendment in 1868.[55] As a result of this new limit on state powers with regard to civil liberties writ large, along with increasing religious pluralism beyond Judeo-Christian varieties, the expanding role of the federal government in civil society, and the founding of advocacy groups for religious liberties (e.g., the American Civil Liberties Union, the American Jewish Congress, and Americans United for Separation of Church and State), the U.S. Supreme Court became a busier adjudicator of church-state contentions through the 20th century.[56]

Religious (dis)establishment and free exercise are constitutional guarantees wrought with ambiguity and controversy. In deliberations over the disestablishment of religion, the Court has vacillated among three stances: (1) "strict separation"; (2) "strict neutrality"; and (3) "accommodationist," which "allows for governmental accommodation of religion in ways that further religious freedom without endorsing a particular religion."[57] As for free exercise, the clause insinuates "freedom to believe" and "freedom to act," the former considered "absolute," while the latter is "subject to the regulation of society," as decided by the Court in *Cantwell v. Connecticut* (1940).[58] Rarely with unanimity, the Court and the states have demonstrated the variegated ways in which these clauses can be interpreted in determining the rights, privileges, and liabilities related to the teaching and practice of religion.

Religion in Public Schools

In the American/U.S. historical context, public schooling emerged as a logical means by which government and religion could remain separate in the formation of citizens for a democratic civil society.[59] Educational reform in the 1800s was a movement from religious establishment to separation, from sectarian schooling to secular education. The progression occurred in stages. In the beginning, there were "sectarian religious public schools," an instantiation of cooperation between state and a single established church with little religious freedom. Then came the educational revivals of the 1820s to 1850s, led by such figures as Horace Mann, who advocated for "nonsectarian religious public schools" that taught "common elements" of moral formation for cultivation of democratic citizens. This was a model of cooperation with some religious freedom for multiple religious establishments and schools for dissenters. However, what was nonsectarian was still primarily Protestant in flavor, made problematic

by the influx of Catholic immigrants from Ireland and Germany in 1820–1860, which ushered in the phase of church-state separation in education.[60] (For comparison, see the entry on "Comprehensive Schools, The Impact of" in this encyclopedia for discussion of a movement of educational reform in Western Europe in the 20th century, the ideological goal of which was the elimination of the social stratification sustained by curricular tracking of students in secondary education.[61])

The progression from private, sectarian schooling to public, nonreligious education in 19th-century America was formalized by two main principles:

1. Public funds shall not be granted to religious schools.
2. Sectarian religious instruction shall not be given in the public schools.[62]

The limits of cooperation may have been dictated in principle, but questions ensued concerning the place of religion in public education—many of which pertained to debates over sectarian dogma in public curricula and to public funding of auxiliary services for students of religious schools, including transportation, textbooks, access to federal student aid, the use of facilities, the use of religious texts, the sharing of time, and the right to religious activities on public school grounds.[63]

Horace Mann, lawyer and legislator of Massachusetts and a reformer of public education in the early 1830s–1840s, successfully championed compulsory education through age 16. While Mann's curricular core excluded "all dogmatical theology and sectarianism," it was shaped by a distinctive "nondogmatic Protestantism," traces of which are detectable in the construct of American civil religion.[64] However, as far back as the 1860s, parents were suing for a pervasive Protestant flavor of morality and piety being inculcated in public schools,[65] and into the 2000s, the categories of public school cases heard by the Supreme Court included the teaching of religion in public and parochial schools, religious rituals and practices (including religious garb and insignia) in public schools, curricular questions in which subjects were deemed to be religious in nature, and free exercise of religion by students on school grounds.[66] A few pertinent Court decisions merit highlighting here.

---

55. Ibid.
56. Ibid.
57. O'Brien, *Constitutional Law and Politics*, 2:653.
58. Ibid., 644.
59. Butts, *American Tradition in Religion and Education*, 211.
60. Ibid., 116–117.
61. See Bregt Henkens, "The Rise and Decline of Comprehensive Education: Key Factors in the History of Reformed Secondary Education in Belgium, 1969–1989," *Paedagogica Historica: International Journal of the History of Education* 40, nos. 1–2 (2004): 193–209.
62. Butts, *American Tradition in Religion and Education*, 112.
63. Ibid., 147–197.
64. Robert N. Bellah, "Civil Religion in America," *Daedalus* 134, no. 4 (2005); Gaustad, *Church and State in America*, 87–88.
65. Gaustad, *Church and State in America*, 87.
66. Ibid., 89.

When secular and religious education competed for instructional time, the Court identified with a strict separationist stance in striking down the practice of "released time" for instruction in respective faith traditions in the case of *McCollum v. Board of Education* (1945), with Justice Felix Frankfurter's famous conclusion: "Good fences make good neighbors."[67] As for deliberations over the exercise of religion, the Court drew ire from conservative politicians and religious leaders for deciding against mandatory school prayer in *Engle v. Vitale* (1962).[68] Adjudicating the constitutionality of daily Bible devotions and recitation of the Lord's Prayer in public schools (*Abingdon v. Schempp* and *Murray v. Curlett*, 1963), the Court established a "secular purpose–secular effect" test to determine whether statutes have a secular purpose and neither advance nor inhibit religion in public school settings.[69] To the two-pronged *Schempp* test, the Court later added a third criterion in the landmark case *Lemon v. Kurtzman* (1971). Ruling unconstitutional any direct public aid to parochial schools, the Court under Chief Justice Warren Burger advanced the principle of no "excessive government entanglement with religion," thus creating a tripartite *Lemon* test.[70] With reliance on the above tests, and almost always with dissension, the Court continued to decide a number of cases pertaining to the limits of religious exercise in public schools. Upholding voluntary expression of religious viewpoints and practices and student-organized religious clubs or gatherings on public school grounds, the Court showed its support of the "Students' Bill of Rights" and the Equal Access Act passed by Congress in 1984.[71] Controversies abound over decisions involving religious or sectarian content in public school curricula. Most notable is the Court's 9–0 decision in *Epperson v. Arkansas* (1968) against Arkansas's "monkey law," which prohibited the teaching of evolutionary theory in public schools.[72]

Regulated Free Exercise of Religion

Whether or not they are unanimous, judicial opinions against sectarian dogma in public instruction remain more or less in keeping with the First Amendment's establishment clause. Matters are further complicated when interpreting the right to free exercise and its implications for government's intervention in the affairs of parochial schools and private sectarian colleges. The "Magna Carta" for the rights of parochial schools is found in *Pierce v. Society of Sisters* (1925), which challenged an Oregon law requiring public education between the ages of eight and sixteen.[73] Debates are difficult when considering students' rights to public aid: public transportation, loan of textbooks and other educational resources, and any form of tuition subsidy such as vouchers, grants, tax credits, or reimbursement for costs and services.[74]

If the establishment clause stipulates that government cannot "assist or advance" religion, then the twin free-exercise clauses imply that neither can government "penalize or inhibit" religion.[75] Opinions vary on which of the two carries the lead—that is, whether protection of free exercise dictates the function of disestablishment, or vice versa. What seems clear is that free exercise is most significant for religious minorities. Arbitrating government accommodation of an establishment of religion for the protection of free exercise, the Court has appealed to three tests:

> (a) whether the activity was motivated by and rooted in legitimate and sincerely held religious belief, (b) whether the activity was unduly and substantially burdened by the government's action, and (c) whether the government has a compelling interest in limiting the religious activity that cannot be accomplished by less restrictive means.[76]

For instance, the Court ruled in favor of Amish opposition against compulsory public education beyond the eighth grade (*Wisconsin v. Yoder*, 1972), and Jehovah's Witnesses' exemption from flag salutes in school.[77] However, the Court also ruled against the New York legislature when it drew a school district to accommodate special educational needs of Hasidic Jewish children.[78]

Laws, Policies, and Church Life

The constitutional and legislative balancing act is equally delicate in the regulation of ministerial practice and ecclesiastical activities. The Court's purview has ranged from prosecution of clergy for crimes such as tax evasion, fraud, and child abuse, to broadening the definition of "religious training and belief" for determination of "sincere and meaningful" conscientious objection to military service.[79] With some exceptions, civil courts have

67. Ibid., 89–90; O'Brien, *Constitutional Law and Politics*, 2:653.

68. Gaustad, *Church and State in America*, 93; O'Brien, *Constitutional Law and Politics*, 2:655.

69. Gaustad, *Church and State in America*, 95; O'Brien, *Constitutional Law and Politics*, 2:657, 60.

70. Gaustad, *Church and State in America*, 113; O'Brien, *Constitutional Law and Politics*, 2:660; Richard R. Hammar, *Pastor, Church & Law*, 3rd ed. (Matthews: Indianapolis, IN: Christian Ministry Resources, 2000), 955–958.

71. Gaustad, *Church and State in America*, 104–105; O'Brien, *Constitutional Law and Politics*, 2:654.

72. Gaustad, *Church and State in America*, 101–102; O'Brien, *Constitutional Law and Politics*, 2:657.

73. Gaustad, *Church and State in America*, 107.

74. Ibid., 109–123.

75. Ibid., 127.

76. Hammar, *Pastor, Church & Law*, 961.

77. Gaustad, *Church and State in America*, 137–139; O'Brien, *Constitutional Law and Politics*, 2:747.

78. Gaustad, *Church and State in America*, 138–140.

79. O'Brien, *Constitutional Law and Politics*, 2:749–750.

generally followed the "rule of nonintervention" in ecclesiastical disputes that involve religious beliefs, procedures, or law, deferring to "higher judicial tribunals within the church hierarchy."[80] However, governmental regulatory laws and legal liability extend to a wide range of matters—from ministerial status and exemptions; to employment and labor practices; to the management of funds and properties; to the organization and administration of church-related social, health, and educational services (e.g., soup kitchens, health facilities, camps, day-care programs). Clergy and other church employees face criminal and civil liability in a number of forms, including but not limited to "negligence, defamation, undue influence, malpractice, contracts, securities, failure to report child abuse, diversion of church funds, counseling, and sexual misconduct."[81] Most states have statutory protection of clergy-penitent privilege, and each state's child abuse laws determine whether or not church employees are obligated mandatory reporters.[82] Interestingly, on the principle of noninterference in religious freedom, religious organizations are exempt (with stipulations) from the constraints of some important antidiscrimination laws—for example, the Civil Rights Act of 1964, the Americans with Disabilities Act of 1990, and the Fair Labor Standards Act. Religious organizations *may* discriminate on the basis of religious beliefs and values and would be protected by law if they can demonstrate a clear *theological* rationale for idiosyncratic employment practices.[83]

Legal exemptions notwithstanding, it is religious creed that motivates churches to commit to the advancement of civil liberties and the common public good. Good-faith efforts are evident in denominational initiatives that respond to public policies concerning social justice issues, or in ecumenical advocacy organizations such as the National Council of Churches (NCC) and the Baptist Joint Committee on Public Affairs (BJC), known for collaborative First Amendment activism with such secular organizations as the American Civil Liberties Union (ACLU) and Americans United for the Separation of Church and State (AU).[84]

Religion and Education Is Political

Very few teachers of religion, or religious educators, are legal experts, but most might agree with Catholic educator Thomas Groome that "educational activity" is a "political activity," for it involves "deliberate and structured intervention in people's lives" in ways that

"influence how they live their lives in society."[85] Surveys of laws and policies offer pragmatic guides for deciphering complicated "cooperations" between church and state over the teaching and practice of religion in private and public spheres. However, such perusals may be a "series of trifles,"[86] if we lose sight of the larger questions concerning the contributions of religion and education in the continuous making of civil society.

References and Resources

Barker, Ernest. 1957. *Church, State and Education.* 1st ed. Ann Arbor: University of Michigan Press.

Bellah, Robert N. 2005. "Civil Religion in America." *Daedalus* 134 (4): 40–55.

Butts, R. Freeman. 1974. *The American Tradition in Religion and Education.* 2nd ed. Westport, CT: Greenwood Press.

Gaustad, Edwin S. 1999. *Church and State in America.* 2nd ed. New York: Oxford University Press.

Groome, Thomas H. 1980. *Christian Religious Education: Sharing Our Story and Vision.* San Francisco: HarperSanFrancisco.

Hammar, Richard R. 2000. *Pastor, Church & Law.* 3rd ed. Matthews. Indianapolis, IN: Christian Ministry Resources, 2000.

Henkens, Bregt. 2004. "The Rise and Decline of Comprehensive Education: Key Factors in the History of Reformed Secondary Education in Belgium, 1969–1989." *Paedagogica Historica: International Journal of the History of Education* 40 (1–2): 193–209.

Hill, Kenneth H. 2007. *Religious Education in the African American Tradition: A Comprehensive Introduction.* St. Louis, MO: Chalice.

Levy, Leonard. 1986. *The Establishment Clause: Religion and the First Amendment.* New York: Macmillan.

Mazur, Cynthia S., and Ronald K. Bullis. 1994. *Legal Guide for Day-to-Day Church Matters: A Handbook for Pastors and Church Members.* Cleveland, OH: United Church Press.

O'Brien, David M. 1995. *Constitutional Law and Politics: Civil Rights and Civil Liberties.* 2nd ed. Vol. 2. New York: W. W. Norton.

Richardson, Joe M. 1986. *Christian Reconstruction: The American Missionary Association and Southern Blacks, 1861–1890.* Athens: University of Georgia Press.

Wuthnow, Robert, and John H. Evans, eds. 2002. *The Quiet Hand of God: Faith-Based Activism and the Public Role of Mainline Protestantism.* Berkeley: University of California Press.

Relevant Entries

---

80. Hammar, *Pastor, Church & Law*, 46–49, 79.

81. Ibid., 143–213.

82. Ibid., 102–134, 87–93.

83. Cynthia S. Mazur and Ronald K. Bullis, *Legal Guide for Day-to-Day Church Matters: A Handbook for Pastors and Church Members* (Cleveland, OH: United Church Press, 1994), 24–26, 67–69.

84. Wuthnow and Evans, *The Quiet Hand of God.*

---

85. Thomas H. Groome, *Christian Religious Education: Sharing Our Story and Vision* (San Francisco: HarperSanFrancisco, 1980), 15.

86. An expression attributed to Michelangelo, cited in Gaustad, *Church and State in America*, 159.

CHRISTIAN LIBRARIES

George Thomas Kurian

Libraries are not exclusively Christian in origin. The great library of Alexandria is an example of a library that predates the rise of Christianity. But because of the emphasis on the written word in evangelization, early Christian catechetical schools had a library attached to every scriptorium where the monks spent time copying the Gospels. Those at Alexandria, Caesarea, and Jerusalem were large and contained works not only in Hebrew but also in Greek and Latin. The library of Jerusalem was founded by the bishop Alexander and was used by Eusebius in researching his *Ecclesiastical History*. In Gaul, St. Martin of Tours established a large library along with his monastery.

Among notable private libraries was that of Augustine, which was destroyed during the Vandal invasion. The Holy See library in Rome was destroyed at the time of the Diocletian persecution but was replaced soon thereafter by Pope Hilarus and located in the Cloister of St. Lorenzo at Verano. It was enlarged by Popes Gelasius, and Agapetus. The latter also created the library on the Coelian Hill in Rome. New libraries were established by Gregory the Great, who later united them in the Pontifical library of the Apostolic See, now the Vatican Library. From the seventh century, every monastery had a scriptorium, and libraries became more numerous. In Italy, Cassiodorus's foundation of a vivarium in Calabria was closely linked to Benedict. At Bobbio, Columbanus founded a large library with help from Longobard kings. In Spain, Isidore of Seville, the great encyclopedist, created a large library in the archiepiscopal palace. In England, the largest libraries were at Iona, Lindisfarne, Canterbury, and Jarrow; in Germany they were at Fulda and Mainz; and in Switzerland at St. Gall.

The "Rule" of Benedict deals with the organization of books and uses the term "library" for the first time. The books were first placed in the cloister but later placed in a special room. Cluniacs appointed a special monk to care for the books, and the Carthusians and Cistercians even allowed outsiders to borrow books. Each library had two sets of books, one for reference and the other for borrowing. The works were mostly religious and devotional. Most monastic libraries contained only a few hundred books, but a few like Fulda, St. Gall, and Croyland had a few thousand, and Novalese, according to Montalembert, had 6,500. The library became such an important feature of monasticism that in 1170 there was a popular saying that *Claustrum sine armario est quasi castrum sine armementario* (a monastery without a library is like a castle without an armory).

The Middle Ages marked the transition of what is called a book from papyrus scrolls to flat surfaces such as parchment serially arranged and paginated and bound together. Most of the "books" in monastic libraries were handwritten manuscripts, either bound as volumes or loose as codices. Christians were responsible for the transition from papyrus rolls (favored by pagans) to the bound book. The major type of permanent writing surface used in the Middle Ages was the animal skin. The parchment sheets came to be organized by Christians as a codex; they were modeled on wax tablets joined together with leather thongs.

Two unusual medieval Christian libraries deserve mention. The first is the library of the Monastery of St. Catherine in Mount Sinai. It was built by Emperor Justinian as a fortified monastery, dedicated to the Blessed Virgin Mary and rededicated to St. Catherine in 1000. It contained one of the largest collections of Greek, Arabic, Syriac, and Georgian manuscripts, including the famous *Codex Sinaiticus*, which was taken by the archaeologist Constantin Tischendorf in the 19th century and moved to Berlin. The other is the celebrated Armenian library of the Mektiarist Fathers in Venice, which includes rare sources on Armenian history.

The invention of printing in the 16th century sounded the death knell for monastic libraries. There are now few dedicated world-class Christian libraries, with the exception of the Vatican Library. Archival materials for the history of the Christian Church are scattered all over the world and have never been digitized or cataloged.

Resource

Edwards, E. 1885. *Libraries and Founders of Libraries.* New York: Cambridge University Press.

Relevant Entries

Billy Graham Center and Library

Day Missions Library, The (Yale University Divinity School Library)

Hill Museum and Manuscript Library
Near East School of Theology
Tyndale House, Cambridge
Vatican Library, The

REFERENCES AND RESOURCES

Kevin Lawson

Overview
Compiling a bibliography on the wide range of topics
addressed in this *Encyclopedia of Christian Education*
is a challenging task. The objective of this bibliography
is to recommend the best sources for Christian education from the last two decades.[87] While I believe we have
crafted a strong resource, a number of issues have unfortunately limited what is included:

1. Because this is representative of recent scholarship,
   not exhaustive, it inevitably has gaps in what is
   listed, and many readers may find that some of their
   favorite recent books are not included.
2. What is included is almost exclusively in English,
   representing a portion of the literature available,
   but not all of what is being published internationally on these topics.
3. Those who worked on this bibliography were
   all from the United States, so their awareness of
   publications and use of online search tools has
   resulted in an overrepresentation of North American publications.
4. In addition, those who worked on the project were
   all from within particular theological traditions,
   so the results of their work may be more extensive
   within the traditions they are familiar with and not
   represent other traditions as thoroughly.

With these limitations acknowledged, we are still
confident that the bibliography that follows will introduce you to many helpful recent publications on topics
addressed within this encyclopedia. In addition to this
bibliography, you will also find reference lists in many of
the entries in this volume. Pleasingly, many of the contributors to this encyclopedia are also authors of some
of the following resources. Be sure to search within those
entries you are interested in to see what else you may find
helpful for further reading.[88]

---

[87]. Please note we have chosen not to include bibliographic references
for Christian Education in the Modern World: Institutional/University/
Seminary Profile and Christian Libraries.

[88]. I want to acknowledge the help of the following who worked
on selected sections of this bibliography: Orbelina Eguizabal, Octavio

I hope that you will find this resource helpful for your
research, work, and ministry.

Christian Education in the Early Church from AD 33 to the End of the Roman Empire

Bakke, Odd Magne. 2006. "Upbringing of Children in the Early
   Church: The Responsibility of Parents, Goals and Methods."
   Studia Theologica 60:145–162.

Dujarier, Michel. 1979. *A History of the Catechumenate: The
   First Six Centuries.* New York: Sadlier.

El Souriany, Samuel. 2010. "Christian Education in the Early
   Coptic Church." *Coptic Church Review* 31: 36–46.

Elias, John L. 2002. *A History of Christian Education: Protestant, Catholic, and Orthodox Perspectives.* Malabar, FL:
   Krieger Publishing.

Georges, Tobias. 2012. "Justin's School in Roman: Reflections
   on Early Christian 'Schools.'" *Zeitschrift für antikes Christen-
   som* 16: 75–87.

Harmless, William. 1995. *Augustine and the Catechumenate.*
   Collegeville, MN: The Liturgical Press.

Henson, E. Glenn. 2002. "Christian Teaching in the Early
   Church." *Review and Expositor* 99: 379–392.

Kelly, Joseph F. 1997. *The World of the Early Christians.* Collegeville, MN: The Liturgical Press.

Lawson, K. E. 2011. "Baptismal Theology and Practices and
   the Spiritual Nurture of Children, Part I: Early and Medieval
   Church." *Christian Education Journal* 8: 130–145.

Markowski, Michael. 2008. "Teachers in Early Christianity."
   Journal of Research on Christian Education 17: 136–152.

Milavec, Aaron. 2003. *The Didache: Text, Translation, Analysis,
   and Commentary.* Collegeville, MN: The Liturgical Press.

Ng, Nathan K. 2004. "The Transformation of Catechetical
   Instruction: Early Church and Reformation." *Hill Road* 7:
   25–46.

Sandnes, Karl Olav. 2009. *The Challenge of Homer: School,
   Pagan Poets, and Early Christianity.* New York: T & T Clark.

Snyder, Gregory. 2000. *Teachers and Texts in the Ancient
   World: Philosophers, Jews, and Christians.* New York: Routledge.

Suriel, Bishop. 2002. *Christian Education in the Church of Alexandria in the First Five Centuries.* Melbourne, Australia: St.
   Athanasius Press.

Topping, Ryan. 2010. "Christ as *Disciplina Dei* in Augustine's
   Early Educational Thought." *Studia Patricstica* 49: 101–105.

Wilken, Robert L. 2004. "Christian Formation in the Early
   Church." In *Educating People of Faith*, edited by John Van
   Engen, 48–62. Grand Rapids, MI: Eerdmans.

Wyrwa, Dietmar. 2005. "Religiöses Lernen im zweiten Jahr-
   hundert und die Anfänge der alexandrinischen Katecheten-
   schule." In *Religiöses Lernen in der biblischen, frühjüdischen*

Esqueda, James W. Estep Jr., Mark Henze, Dave Keehn, Tom Kimber,
and Tamene Menna.

und frühchristlichen Überlieferung, 271–305. Tübingen, Germany: Mohr.

Young, Frances M. 2004. "Christian Teaching." In *The Cambridge History of Early Christian Literature*, edited by Frances young, Lewis Ayres, and Angrew Louth, 464–484. Cambridge, UK: Cambridge University Press.

Christian Education in the Middle Ages and Early Modern Age

Begley, R. B., and J. W. Koterski. 2005. *Medieval Education*. New York: Fordham University Press.

Black, Robert. 2001. *Humanism and Education in Medieval and Renaissance Italy: Tradition and Innovation in Latin Schools from the Twelfth to the Fifteenth Century*. Cambridge, UK: Cambridge University Press.

Boylan, Anne M. 1988. *Sunday School: The Formation of an American Institution, 1790–1880*. New Haven, CT: Yale University Press.

Carruthers, L. 1990. "Allegory and Bible Interpretation: The Narrative Structure of a Middle English Sermon Cycle." *Journal of Literature and Theology* 4: 1–14.

Cunningham, Mary. 2002. *Faith in the Byzantine World*. Downers Grove, IL: InterVarsity Press.

Duffy, Eamon. 2005. *The Stripping of the Altars*. 2nd ed. New Haven, CT: Yale University Press.

———. 2006. *Marking the Hours: English People & their Prayers, 1240–1570*. New Haven, CT: Yale University Press.

Duncan, Thomas G. 2000. *Late Medieval English Lyrics and Carols, 1400–1530*. New York: Penguin Classics.

Evans, G. R. 2002. *Faith in the Medieval World*. Downers Grove, IL: InterVarsity Press.

Gill, M., and J. Hawkes, eds. 2011. *Images of Salvation: The Story of the Bible through Medieval Art*. 3rd ed. York, UK: Christianity & Culture. (Interactive CD-ROM.)

Green, Ian. 1996. *The Christian's ABC: Catechisms and Catechizing in England c. 1530–1740*. Oxford: Clarendon Press.

Hyma, Albert. 2004. *The Brethren of the Common Life*. Eugene, OR: Wipf & Stock.

Johnson, M. E. 1999. *The Rites of Christian Initiation: Their Evolution and Interpretation*. Collegeville, MN: The Liturgical Press.

Jung, Joanne J. 2011. *Godly Conversation: Rediscovering the Puritan Practice of Conference*. Grand Rapids, MI: Reformation Heritage Books.

Keely, Barbara Anne. 1997. *Faith of Our Foremothers: Women Changing Religious Education*. Louisville, KY: Westminster John Knox Press.

Lacey, Paul A., and the Friends Council on Education. 1998. *Growing into Goodness: Essays on Quaker Education*. Wallingford, PA: Pendle Hill Publications.

Lynch, Joseph H. 1998. *Christianizing Kinship: Ritual Sponsorship in Anglo-Saxon England*. Ithaca, NY: Cornell University Press.

Marthaler, Berard L. 1995. *The Catechism Yesterday & Today: The Evolution of a Genre*. Collegeville, MN: The Liturgical Press.

Muir, L. R. 1995. *The Biblical Drama of Medieval Europe*. Cambridge, UK: Cambridge University Press.

Orme, Nicholas. 2001. *Medieval Children*. New Haven, CT: Yale University Press.

———. 2006. *Medieval Schools*. New Haven, CT: Yale University Press.

Osmer, Richard. 1996. *Confirmation: Presbyterian Practices in Ecumenical Perspective*. Louisville, KY: Geneva Press.

Pedersen, Olaf. 2009. *The First Universities: Studium Generale and the Origins of University Education in Europe*. Translated by Richard North. Cambridge, UK: Cambridge University Press.

Rieser, Andrew Chamberlin. 2003. *The Chautauqua Moment: Protestants, Progressives, and the Culture of Modern Liberalism, 1874–1920*. New York: Columbia University Press.

Roest, Bert. 2004. *Franciscan Literature of Religious Instruction before the Council of Trent*. Studies in the History of Christian Traditions. Leiden: Brill Academic Publishers.

Setran, David P. 2007. *The College Y: Student Religion in the Era of Secularization*. Hampshire, UK: Palgrave MacMillan.

Shinners, J., ed. 1999. *Medieval Popular Religion, 1000–1500: A Reader*. Orchard Park, NY: Broadview Press.

Stansbury, Ronald J. 2010. *A Companion to Pastoral Care in the Late Middle Ages (1200–1500)*. Brill's Companions to the Christian Tradition, no. 22. Boston: Brill Publishing.

Sullivan, Richard E. 1995. *"The Gentle Voices of Teachers": Aspects of Learning in the Carolingian Age*. Columbus: Ohio State University Press.

Swanson, R. N. 1995. *Religion and Devotion in Europe, c. 1215—c. 1515*. Cambridge, UK: Cambridge University Press.

Turner, P. 2000a. *Ages of Initiation: The First Two Christian Millennia*. Collegeville, MN: The Liturgical Press.

———. 2000b. *The Hallelujah Highway: A History of the Catechumenate*. Chicago: Liturgy Training Publications.

Van Engen, J. 2004. *Educating People of Faith: Exploring the History of Jewish and Christian Communities*. Grand Rapids, MI: Eerdmans.

Watson, David Lowes. 2002. *The Early Methodist Class Meeting: Its Origins and Significance*. Eugene, OR: Wipf & Stock.

Wengert, Timothy J. 2009. *Martin Luther's Catechisms: Forming the Faith*. Minneapolis, MN: Fortress Press.

Woods, M. C., and R. Copeland. 1999. "Classroom and Confession." In *The Cambridge History of Medieval English Literature*, edited by D. Wallace, 376–406. Cambridge, UK: Cambridge University Press.

Christian Education in the Modern World: Continental Profiles and Select Countries

Ogbonnaya, A. Okechukwu. 2001. *African Ways: A Christian Education Philosophy*. Chicago: Urban Ministries.

Stambach, Amy. 2009. *Faith in Schools: Religion, Education, and American Evangelicals in East Africa*. Stanford, CA: Stanford University Press.

Egypt
Sedra, Paul. 2011. *From Mission to Modernity Evangelicals, Reformers and Education in Nineteenth Century Egypt*. London, New York: I.B. Tauris. http://site.ebrary.com/id/10480606.

Ethiopia
Abebe, Endale A. 2012. *The Holy Trinity Theological College: A Comparative Analysis of the Holy Trinity Theological College Academic and Extra/Co-Curricular Activities in the Pre 1977 and Post 1994*. CreateSpace Independent Publishing Platform, Amazon.

Ghana
Naaeke, Anthony Y. 2006. *Kaleidoscope Catechesis: Missionary Catechesis in Africa, Particularly in the Diocese of Wa in Ghana*. New York: Peter Lang.

Wiafe, Eric Oduro. 2010. *Faith Communication in Africa: The Ghanaian Experience*. CreateSpace Independent Publishing Platform, Amazon.

Kenya
Gachahi, Michael, and Lucy Njagi. 2012. *Implementation of Christian Religious Education Curriculum: In Secondary Schools in Murang'a South District, Central Province, Kenya*. Saarbrücken, Germany: LAP Lambert Academic Publishing.

Malawi
Matemba, Yonah. 2011. *Religious Education in Comparative Perspectives: Curriculum Developments in the Secondary School Sectors of Scotland and Malawi, 1970–2010*. Saarbrücken, Germany: LAP Lambert Academic Publishing.

Nigeria
Abba, JoeBarth C. 2009. *Special Pastoral Formation for Youths in Africa in the 21st Century: The Nigerian Perspective*. Frankfurt am Main; New York: Peter Lang.

Okoh, Michael. 2012. *Fostering Christian Faith in Schools and Christian Communities through Igbo Traditional Values: Towards a Holistic Approach to Christian Religious Education and Catechesis in Igboland (Nigeria)*. Wien: LIT Verlag.

Taylor, William H. 1996. *Mission to Educate: A History of the Educational Work of the Scottish Presbyterian Mission in East Nigeria 1846–1960*. Leiden: E. J. Brill.

Tanzania
Bahendwa, L. Festo. 1990. *Christian Religious Education in the Lutheran Dioceses of North-Western Tanzania*. Helsinki: Finnish Society for Missiology and Ecumenics.

Uganda
Sheldon, Mwesigwa Fred. 2012. *Religious Pluralism, Conflict as Issues in Ugandan Religious Education: An Investigation of the Complications Raised in Teaching a Confessional Religious Education in a Multi-religious Context*. Saarbrücken, Germany: LAP Lambert Academic Publishing.

Zambia
Carmody, Brendan Patrick. 1992. *Conversion and Jesuit Schooling in Zambia*. Leiden, New York: E.J. Brill.

———. 1999. *Education in Zambia: Catholic Perspectives*. Lusaka, Zambia: Bookworld Publishers.

Evans, Rob, and Tosh Arai, eds. 1980. *The Church and Education in Asia*. Singapore: Christian Conference of Asia.

Ragsdale, John P. 1986. *Protestant Mission Education in Zambia, 1880–1954*. London: Associated University Press.

Simpson, Anthony. 2003. *"Half London" in Zambia: Contested Identities in a Catholic Mission School*. Edinburgh: Edinburgh University Press for the International African Institute.

Shipton W., E. Coetzee, and R. Takeuchi. 2013. *Worldviews and Christian Education: Appreciating the Cultural Outlook of Asia-pacific People*. Bloomington, IN: Trafford on Demand Pub.

China
China Educational Commission. 2007. "Christian Education in China: A Study Made by an Educational Commission Representing the Mission Boards and Societies Conducting Work in China." Nabu Press, Amazon. (Original report published in 1922.)

India
Nugée, George Francis, and John Rivington. 2010. *The Necessity for Christian Education to Elevate the Native Character in India*. Bel Air, CA: BiblioLife.

Korea
Amos, N. Scott, Andrew Pettegree, and Henk F. K. Van Nierop. 1999. *The Education of a Christian Society: Humanism and Reformation in Britain and Netherlands: Papers Delivered to the 13th Anglo-Dutch Historical Conference, 1997*. London: Ashgate.

Bråten, Oddrun M. H. 2013. *Towards a Methodology for Comparative Studies in Religious Education: A Study of England and Norway*. New York: Waxmann Verlag GmbH.

Jongeneel, Jan A. B., Peter Tze Ming Ng, Chong Ku Paek, and Scott W. Sunquist. 2009. *Christian Mission and Education in Modern China, Japan, and Korea: Historical Studies*. New York: Peter Lang.

More, Hannah. 2010. *Considerations on Religion and Public Education, with Remarks on the Speech of M. Dupont, Deliv-*

ered in the National Convention of France. Farmington Hills, MI: Gale ECCO Print Editions.

Osmer, Richard Robert, and Friedrich Schwitzer. 2003. *Religious Education between Modernization and Globalization: New Perspectives on the United States and Germany.* Grand Rapids, MI: Eerdmans.

Proshak, Vitaliy. V. 2012. *Juridical Foundation to Religious Education in the Post-Soviet Eastern European State: Three Models Theory of the RED Co Research Project in Application to Ukraine.* Nijmegen, Netherlands: Wolf Legal Publishers.

Shin, Hyoung Seop. 2013. *Building a Eucharistic Pedagogy for the Presbyterian Church of Korea.* Eugene, OR: Wipf & Stock.

Finland

Kuusisto, Amiika. 2011. *Growing up in Affiliation with a Religious Community: A Case Study of Seventh-day Adventist Youth in Finland.* Berlin: Waxmann

Hungary

Talaber, Janos, and Péter Antaloczy. 2012. *The Liberty of Religious Rights and Religious Education in the Frame of the State Legislation in Hungary: A Comparative Legal Study.* Santa Cruz, CA: GRIN Verlag GmbH.

Greece

Adam, James. 2012. *The Religious Teachers of Greece: Being Gifford Lectures on Natural Religion Delivered at Aberdeen.* Indianola, OK: Ulan Press.

Italy

Malizia, Guglielmo, and Serqio Cicatelli. 2011. *The Catholic School Under Scrutiny: Ten Years of Research in Italy (1998–2008).* New York: Peter Lang.

France

Carter, Karen E. 2011. *Creating Catholics: Catechism and Primary Education in Early Modern France.* Notre Dame, IN: University of Notre Dame Press.

Curtis, Sara A. 2000. *Educating the Faithful: Religion, Schooling, and Society in Nineteenth-century France.* DeKalb: Northern Illinois University Press.

Great Britain

Green, I. M. 1996. *The Christian's ABC: Catechisms and Catechizing in England C. 1530–1740.* Oxford, New York: Clarendon Press.

Ireland

O'Donoghue, Thomas A. 1999. *The Catholic Church and the Secondary School Curriculum in Ireland, 1922–1962.* New York: P. Lang.

Woulfe, E. and J. Cassin, eds. 2007. *From Present to Future: Catholic Education in Ireland for the New Century.* Dublin: Veritas.

Russia

Edwards, Lisa M. 2012. *Roman Virtues: The Education of Latin American Clergy in Rome, 1858–1962.* New York: Peter Lang Publishing.

Glanzer, Perry L. 2002. *The Quest for Russia's Soul: Evangelicals and Moral Education in Post-Communist Russia.* Waco, TX: Markham Press Fund Pub. from Baylor University Press.

Maria, Joaquim P. 2003. *Moral Catechesis and Catholic Social Teaching: A Latin American Approach.* Lanham, MD: University Press of America.

Pazmiño, Robert W. 2002. *Latin American Journey: Insights for Christian Education in North America.* Eugene, OR: Wipf & Stock.

Wirtschafter, Elise. 2013. *Religion and Enlightenment in Catherinian Russia: The Teachings of Metropolitan Platon.* DeKalb: Northern Illinois University Press.

United States

Parrett, Gary A., and S. Steve Kang. 2009. *Teaching the Faith, Forming the Faithful: A Biblical Vision for Education in the Church.* Downers Grove, IL: IVP Academic.

Cuba

Esqueda, Octavio. 2009. *Cuban Christian Theological Higher Education: The History of the Eastern Cuba Baptist Theological Seminary.* Saarbrücken, Germany: LAP Lambert Academic Publishing.

Christian Education in the Modern World: Denominational Profiles

Aukerman, John H. 2011. *Discipleship That Transforms: An Introduction to Christian Education from a Wesleyan Holiness Perspective.* Anderson, IN: Warner Press.

Beddome, Benjamin. 2006. *A Scriptural Exposition of the Baptist Catechism: [By Way of Question and Answer].* Birmingham, AL: Solid Ground Christian Books.

Bernstine, Alvin C. 1995. *How to Develop a Department of Christian Education within the Local Baptist Church: A Congregational-enablement Model.* Nashville, TN: Townsend Press, Sunday School Pub. Board, National Baptist Convention, USA.

Boojamra, John L. 1989. *Foundations for Orthodox Christian Education.* Crestwood, NY: St. Vladimir's Seminary Press.

Hein, Steven A., Paul J. Cain, Cheryle Swope, and Tom Strickland. 2013. *A Handbook for Classical Lutheran Education: The Best of the Consortium for Classical and Lutheran Education's Journals.* CreateSpace Independent Publishing Platform.

Kitch, Anne E. 2004. *What We Do in Church: An Anglican Child's Activity Book.* Harrisburg PA: Morehouse.

Kitch, Anne E., and Dorothy T. Perez. 2006. *What We Do in Advent: An Anglican Kids' Activity Book.* Harrisburg, PA: Morehouse.

Michaels, Elaine, and Mary Hallick. 1990. *Sowing Seeds for Christ: A Practical Guide for Church School Teachers of All Grade Levels*. Brookline, MA: Greek Orthodox Archdiocese, Department of Religious Education.

Pearson, Sharon E. 2013. *The Episcopal Christian Educator's Handbook*. New York: Morehouse.

Price, Elizabeth Box, and Charles R. Foster. 1991. *By What Authority: A Conversation on Teaching among United Methodists*. Nashville, TN: Abingdon Press.

Rivers, Joshua W. 2012. *Founded Upon a Rock: Philosophy of Education from a Distinctively Baptist Perspective*. Lansing, MI: Calvary Publishing.

Shmeman, Aleksandr. 1991. *The Celebration of Faith: Sermons*. Crestwood, NY: St. Vladimir's Seminary Press.

Skvortsova, E. Artemyeva. 2010. *The Law of God: Orthodox Christian Religious Education in 5 Volumes Zakon Bozhiy v 5 Tomakh (in Russian Language)*. Mishawaka, IN: Knizhny Klub Knigovek (part of Open Library).

Vrame, Anton C. 1999. *The Educating Icon: Teaching Wisdom and Holiness in the Orthodox Way*. Brookline, MA: Holy Cross Orthodox Press.

White, Elizabeth. 2004. *Walking in Wonder: Nurturing Orthodox Christian Values in Your Children*. Ben Lomond, CA: Conciliar Press.

Roman Catholic

Elias, John L. 2002. *A History of Christian Education: Protestant, Catholic, and Orthodox Perspectives*. Malabar, FL: Krieger.

Hahn, Kimberly. 2013. *Catholic Education: Homeward Bound*. San Francisco: Ignatius Press.

McKinney, Stephen J., and John Sullivan. 2013. *Education in Catholic Perspective*. London: Ashgate.

Singer-Towns, Brian. 2013. *The Catholic Faith Handbook for Youth*. 3rd ed. Winona, MN: Saint Mary's Press.

Ziemann, G. Patrick. 2002. *Renewing the Vision: A Framework for Catholic Youth Ministry*. Washington, DC: USCCB Publishing.

Christian Intellectual Traditions

Abraham, William J. 2012. *Analytic Theology: A Bibliography*. Dallas, TX: Highland Loch Press.

Astley, Jeff, Leslie Francis, John Sullivan, and Andrew Walker. 2004. *The Idea of a Christian University: Essays on Theology and Higher Education*. London: Paternoster.

Bartholomew, Craig G., and Michael W. Goheen. 2013. *Christian Philosophy: A Systematic and Narrative Introduction*. Grand Rapids, MI: Baker Academic.

Bauer, Susan Wise. 2013. *The History of the Renaissance World: From the Rediscovery of Aristotle to the Conquest of Constantinople*. New York: W. W. Norton.

Cassirer, Ernst. 2009. *The Philosophy of the Enlightenment, Updated*. Princeton, NJ: Princeton University Press.

Chretien, Jean-Louis, and Anne A. Davenport, trans. 2004. *The Call and the Response: Perspectives in Continental Philosophy*. New York: Fordham University Press.

Coffey, John, and Paul C. H. Lim. 2008. *The Cambridge Companion to Puritanism*. Cambridge, UK: Cambridge University Press.

Dunham, Jeremy, Iain Hamilton Grant, and Sean Watson. 2011. *Idealism: The History of a Philosophy*. Montreal: McGill-Queen's University Press.

Duminuco, Vincent J., SJ. 2000. *The Jesuit Ratio Studiorum: 400th Anniversary Perspectives*. New York: Fordham University Press.

Englehardt, H. Tristram, Jr. 2000. *The Foundations of Christian Bioethics*. Beverly, MA: M & M Scrivener Press.

Feldmeier, Peter. 2007. *The Developing Christian: Spiritual Growth through the Life Cycle*. Mahwah, NJ: Paulist Press.

Ferber, Michael. 2010. *Romanticism: A Very Short Introduction*. Oxford: Oxford University Press.

Ghiloni, Aaron J. 2012. *John Dewey among the Theologians*. New York: Peter Lang.

Grunland, Stephen A., and Milton Reimer. 2001. *Christian Perspectives on Sociology*. Eugene OR: Wipf & Stock.

Gushurst-Moore, Andre. 2013. *The Common Mind: Politics, Society and Christian Humanism from Thomas More to Russell Kirk*. Tacoma, WA: Angelico Press.

Hahn, Scott W., and Benjamin Wiker. 2013. *Politicizing the Bible: The Roots of Historical Criticism and the Secularization of Scripture 1300–1700*. New York: Crossroad Publishing.

Hancock, Curtis L. 2005. *Recovering a Catholic Philosophy of Elementary Education*. Pine Beach, NJ: Newman House Press.

Harrison, Nonna Verna. 2012. *God's Many-Splendored Image: Theological Anthropology for Christian Formation*. Grand Rapids, MI: Baker Academic.

Hicks, Stephen R. C. 2011. *Explaining Postmodernism: Skepticism and Socialism from Rousseau to Foucault, Expanded ed.* Roscoe, IL: Ockham's Razor.

Holden, Joseph M., and Norman Geisler. 2013. *The Popular Handbook of Archaeology and the Bible: Discoveries That Confirm the Reliability of Scripture*. Eugene, OR: Harvest House Publishers.

Holmes, Arthur F. 2007. *Ethics: Approaching Moral Decisions*. Downers Grove, IL: IVP Academic.

Howard, Thomas Albert. 2011. *Imago Dei: Human Dignity in Ecumenical Perspective*. Washington, DC: Catholic University of America Press.

Howell, Brian H., and Jenell Williams Paris. 2012. *Introducing Cultural Anthropology: A Christian Perspective*. Grand Rapids, MI: Baker Academic.

Jacobsen, Douglas, and Rhonda Hustedt Jacobsen. 2004. *Scholarship and Christian Faith: Enlarging the Conversation*. New York: Oxford University Press.

Johnson, Eric L. 2010. *Psychology and Christianity: Five Views*. Downers Grove, IL: IVP Academic.

Knight, George R. 2006. *Philosophy & Education: An Introduction in Christian Perspective.* 4th ed. Berrien Springs, MI: Andrews University Press.

Litfin, Duane. 2004. *Conceiving the Christian College.* Grand Rapids, MI: Eerdmans.

Loomis, Steven R., and Jacob P. Rodriguez. 2009. *C. S. Lewis: A Philosophy of Education.* New York: Palgrave Macmillan.

Martinich, A. P., and David Sosa. 2011. *Analytic Philosophy: An Anthology.* 2nd ed. Oxford: Wiley-Blackwell.

Mesle, C. Robert. 2008. *Process-Relational Philosophy: An Introduction to Alfred North Whitehead.* West Conshohocken, PA: Templeton Press.

Morris, Christopher W. 1998. *The Social Contract Theorists: Critical Essays on Hobbes, Locke, and Rousseau.* Lanham, MD: Rowman & Littlefield.

Newberg, Andrew, MD, and Mark Robert Waldman. 2010. *How God Changes Your Brain: Breakthrough Findings from a Leading Neuroscientist.* New York: Ballantine Books.

Sadler, John Edward. 2007. *J. A. Comenius and the Concept of Universal Education.* History of Education, vol. 32. Oxford: Routledge.

Sheldrake, Philip. 2013. *Spirituality: A Brief History.* 2nd ed. Oxford: Wiley-Blackwell.

Smith, James K. A. 2004. *Introducing Radical Orthodoxy: Mapping a Post-secular Theology.* Grand Rapids, MI: Baker Academic.

Spears, Paul D., and Steven R. Loomis. 2009. *Education for Human Flourishing: A Christian Perspective.* Downers Grove, IL: IVP Academic.

Stasiak, Kurt. 2001. *Sacramental Theology: Means of Grace, Way of Life.* Chicago: Loyola Press.

Sullivan, Francis A., SJ. 2002. *Magisterium: Teaching Authority in the Catholic Church.* Eugene, OR: Wipf & Stock.

Van Asselt, Willem J., Maarten Wisse, T. Theo J. Pleizier, and Pieter L. Rouwendal. 2011. *Introduction to Reformed Scholasticism.* Grand Rapids, MI: Reformed Heritage Books.

Wood, W. Jay. 1998. *Epistemology: Becoming Intellectually Virtuous.* Downers Grove, IL: IVP Academic.

Yount, William. 2008. *The Teaching Ministry of the Church.* 2nd ed. Nashville, TN: B&H Academic.

Biblical and Theological Frameworks for Christian Education

Anderson, David. 2004. *Multicultural Ministry: Finding Your Church's Unique Rhythm.* Grand Rapids, MI: Zondervan.

Aukerman, John. 2011. *Discipleship That Transforms: An Introduction to Christian Education from a Wesleyan Holiness Perspective.* Anderson, IN: Warner Press.

Botticini, Maristella, and Zvi Eckstein. 2012. *The Chosen Few: How Education Shaped Jewish History, 70–1492.* Princeton, NJ: Princeton University Press.

Boys, Mary C. 2000. *Has God Only One Blessing?* New York: Paulist Press.

Bruce, A. B. 2000. *The Training of the Twelve.* Grand Rapids, MI: Kregel.

Carson, D. A. 2007. *A Model of Christian Maturity: An Exposition of 2 Corinthians 10–13.* Grand Rapids, MI: Baker Books.

Conner, Benjamin T. 2011. *Practicing Witness: A Missional Vision of Christian Practices.* Grand Rapids, MI: Eerdmans.

Cully, Iris V. 1995. *The Bible in Christian Education.* Minneapolis, MN: Augsburg Fortress.

Culver, Mary. 2008. *Applying Servant Leadership in Today's Schools.* Abingdon, UK: Routledge.

De La Torre, Miguel A. 2013. *Liberation Theology for Armchair Theologians.* Louisville, KY: Westminster John Knox Press.

Estep, James R., Michael J. Anthony, and Gregg R. Allison. 2008. *A Theology for Christian Education.* Nashville, TN: B & H Academic.

Everist, Norma Cook. 2002. *The Church as Learning Community: A Comprehensive Guide to Christian Education.* Nashville, TN: Abingdon Press.

———. 2007. *Christian Education as Evangelism.* Minneapolis, MN: Fortress Press.

McKinney, Lora-Ellen. 2003. *Christian Education in the African American Church: A Guide for Teaching Truth.* Philadelphia: Judson Press

Miller, Randolph Crump. 1995. *Theologies of Religious Education.* Birmingham, AL: Religious Education Press.

Moberly, R. W. L. 2013. *Old Testament Theology: Reading the Hebrew Bible as Christian Scripture.* Grand Rapids, MI: Baker Academic.

Osmer, Richard R. 2005. *The Teaching Ministry of Congregations.* Louisville, KY: Westminster John Knox Press.

Pazmiño, Robert W. 2001. *God Our Teacher: Theological Basics in Christian Education.* Grand Rapids, MI: Baker Academic.

Pazmiño, Robert E. 2008. *So What Makes Our Teaching Christian? Teaching in the Name, Spirit, and Power of Jesus.* Eugene, OR: Wipf and Stock.

Van Gelder, Craig. 2007. *The Ministry of the Missional Church: A Community Led by the Spirit.* Grand Rapids, MI: Baker Books.

Weed, Ronald, and John Von Heyking. 2010. *Civil Religion in Political Thought: Its Perennial Questions and Enduring Relevance in North America.* Washington, DC: Catholic University of America Press.

Westerhoff, John H., III. 2000. *Will Our Children Have Faith?* Rev. ed. Toronto: Morehouse.

Wheeler, Daniel W. 2012. *Servant Leadership for Higher Education: Principles and Practices.* San Francisco: Jossey-Bass.

Wilhoit, James. 2008. *Spiritual Formation as If the Church Mattered: Growing in Christ through Community.* Grand Rapids, MI: Baker Academic.

Wilson, Douglas. 1999. *The Paideia of God.* Moscow, ID: Canon Press.

Wright, N. T. 2012. *After You Believe: Why Christian Character Matters.* New York: HarperOne.

Yarnell, Walcolm B., III. 2007. *The Formation of Christian Doctrine*. Nashville, TN: B & H Academic.

Young, Brad H. 2007. *Meet the Rabbis: Rabbinic Thought and the Teachings of Jesus*. Grand Rapids, MI: Baker Academic.

Zuck, Roy B. 2002. *Teaching as Jesus Taught*. Eugene, OR: Wipf & Stock.

——. 2003. *Teaching as Paul Taught*. Eugene, OR: Wipf & Stock.

Missions and Christian Education

Barnett, Mike, and Robin Martin. 2012. *Discovering the Mission of God: Best Missional Practices for the 21st Century*. Downers Grove, IL: IVP Academic.

Borthwick, Paul. 2012. *Western Christians in Global Missions: What's the Role of the North American Church?* Downers Grove, IL: IVP Books.

Calderisi, Robert. 2013. *Earthly Mission: The Catholic Church and World Development*. New Haven, CT: Yale University Press.

Colson, Charles, and Richard J. Neuhaus. 1995. *Evangelicals and Catholics Together: Toward a Common Mission*. Nashville, TN: Thomas Nelson.

Escobar, Samuel. 2003. *The New Global Mission: The Gospel from Everywhere to Everyone*. Downers Grove, IL: IVP Academic.

Glasser, Arthur. F. 2003. *Announcing the Kingdom: The Story of God's Mission in the Bible*. Grand Rapids, MI: Baker Academic.

Goheen, Michael W. 2011. *A Light to the Nations: The Missional Church and the Biblical Story*. Grand Rapids, MI: Baker Academic.

Guthrie, Stan. 2002. *Missions in the Third Millennium: 21 Key Trends for the 21st Century*. Milton Keynes, UK: Paternoster.

Hastings, Ross. 2012. *Missional God, Missional Church: Hope for Re-evangelizing the West*. Downers Grove, IL: IVP Academic.

Hiebert, Paul G. 2008. *Transforming Worldviews: An Anthropological Understanding of How People Change*. Grand Rapids, MI: Baker Academic.

——. 2009. *The Gospel in Human Contexts: Anthropological Explorations for Contemporary Missions*. Grand Rapids, MI: Baker Academic.

Johnstone, Patrick. 2011. *The Future of the Global Church: History, Trends and Possibilities*. Downers Grove, IL: IVP Books.

Kendzia, Mary Carol. 2013. *Catholic Update Guide to the New Evangelization*. Cincinnati, OH: Franciscan Media.

Lingenfelter, Sherwood, and Judith Lingenfelter. 2003. *Teaching Cross-Culturally: An Incarnational Model for Learning and Teaching*. Grand Rapids, MI: Baker Academic.

Moreau, A. Scott, Gary R. Corwin, and Gary B. McGee. 2004. *Introducing World Missions: A Biblical, Historical and Practical Survey*. Grand Rapids, MI: Baker Academic.

Ott, Craig, Stephen J. Strauss, and Timothy C. Tennent. 2010. *Encountering Theology of Mission: Biblical Foundations, Historical Developments and Contemporary Issues*. Grand Rapids, MI: Baker Academic.

Payne, J. D. 2012. *Missional House Churches: Reaching Our Communities with the Gospel*. Downers Grove, IL: IVP Books.

Perspectives on the World Christian Movement: A Reader. 4th ed. 2008. Pasadena, CA: William Carey Library.

Piper, John. 1993. *Let the Nations Be Glad: The Supremacy of God in Missions*. Grand Rapids, MI: Baker Academic.

Plueddemann, James E. 2009. *Leading Across Cultures: Effective Ministry and Mission in the Global Church*. Downers Grove, IL: IVP Academic.

Schroeder, Roger P. 2008. *What Is the Mission of the Church? A Guide for Catholics*. Maryknoll, NY: Orbis Books.

Snow, Donald B. 2001. *English Teaching as Christian Mission: An Applied Theology*. Scottdale, PA: Herald Press.

Sunquist, Scott. 2013. *Understanding Christian Mission: Participating in Suffering and Glory*. Grand Rapids, MI: Baker Academic.

Taylor, William. 2013. *Sorrow and Blood: Christian Mission in Contexts of Suffering, Persecution and Martyrdom*. Pasadena, CA: William Carey Library.

Tennent, Timothy C. 2010. *Invitation to World Missions: A Trinitarian Missiology for the Twenty-first Century*. Grand Rapids, MI: Kregel.

Tucker, Ruth A. 2004. *From Jerusalem to Irian Jaya: A Biographical History of Christian Missions*. Grand Rapids, MI: Zondervan.

Winter, Ralph D. 1969. *Theological Education by Extension*. Pasadena, CA: William Carey Library.

Woodward, J. R. 2012. *Creating a Missional Culture: Equipping the Church for the Sake of the World*. Downers Grove, IL: IVP Books.

Wright, Christopher J. H. 2006. *The Mission of God: Unlocking the Bible's Grand Narrative*. Downers Grove, IL: IVP Academic.

Christian Curriculum

Allen, Holly Catterton, and Christine Lawton. 2012. *Intergenerational Christian Formation: Bringing the Whole Church Together in Ministry, Community and Worship*. Downers Grove, IL: IVP Academic.

Barnes, M. Craig. 2012. *Body & Soul: Reclaiming the Heidelberg Catechism*. Grand Rapids, MI: Faith Alive Christian Resources.

Calhoun, Adele Ahlberg. 2005. *Spiritual Disciplines Handbook: Practices That Transform Us*. Downers Grove, IL: InterVarsity Press.

Chittister, Joan. 2010. *The Rule of Benedict: A Spirituality for the 21st Century*. 2nd ed. New York: Crossroad Publishing.

Conde-Frazier, Elizabeth, S. Steve Kang, and Gary A. Parrett. 2004. *A Many Colored Kingdom: Multicultural Dynamics for Spiritual Formation*. Grand Rapids, MI: Baker Academic.

Congregation for the Clergy. 1998. *General Directory for Catechesis*. Washington, DC: USCCB Publishing.

Cranton, Patricia. 2006. *Understanding and Promoting Transformative Learning: A Guide for Educators of Adults*. 2nd ed. San Francisco: Jossey-Bass.

De Cointet, Pierre, Barbara Morgan, and Petroc Willey. 2008. *Catechism of the Catholic Church and the Craft of Catechesis*. San Francisco: Ignatius Press.

de Villers, Sylvia. 1994. *Lectionary Based Catechesis for Children: A Catechist's Guide*. Mahwah, NJ: Paulist Press.

Estep, James R., and Jonathan H. Kim. 2010. *Christian Formation: Integrating Theology and Human Development*. Nashville, TN: Broadman & Holman.

Ford, Paul Leicester. 2012. *The New-England Primer: A History of Its Origin and Development; with a Reprint of the Unique Copy of the Earliest Known Edition and Many Facsimile Illustrations and Reproductions*. Amazon Digital Services.

Gardner, Howard. 2011. *Truth, Beauty, and Goodness Reframed: Educating for the Virtues in the Age of Truthiness and Twitter*. New York: Basic Books.

Gooren, Henri. 2010. *Religious Conversion and Disaffiliation: Tracing Patterns of Change in Faith Practices*. New York: Palgrave Macmillan.

Gross, Bobby. 2009. *Living the Christian Year: Time to Inhabit the Story of God*. Downers Grove, IL: InterVarsity Press.

Leckey, Dolores R. 2003. *The Laity and Christian Education: Apostolicam Actuositatem, Gravissimum Educationis (Rediscovering Vatican II)*. Mahwah, NJ: Paulist Press.

Leganger-Krogstad, Heid. 2011. *The Religious Dimension of Intercultural Education: Contributions to a Contextual Understanding*. International Practical Theology Series. Berlin: LIT Verlag.

Lillig, Tina. 2007. *The Catechesis of the Good Shepherd in a Parish Setting*. Chicago: Liturgy Training Publications.

Luther, Martin, and Timothy J. Wengert. 2008. *A Contemporary Translation of Luther's Small Catechism*. Study ed. Minneapolis, MN: Augsburg Fortress.

Noddings, Nel. 2002. *Educating Moral People: A Caring Alternative to Character Education*. New York: Teachers College Press.

Null, Wesley. 2012. *Curriculum: From Theory to Practice*. Lanham, MD: Rowman & Littlefield.

O'Loughlin, Thomas. 2010. *The Didache: A Window on the Earliest Christians*. Grand Rapids, MI: Baker Academic.

Plaiss, Mark. 2006. *The Inner Room: A Journey into Lay Monasticism*. Los Angeles: St. Anthony Messenger Press.

Reid, Alvin. 2009. *Evangelism Handbook: Biblical, Spiritual, Intentional, Missional*. Nashville, TN: B & H Books.

Tada, Joni Eareckson. 2005. *A Place of Healing: Wrestling with the Mysteries of Suffering, Pain, and God's Sovereignty*. Colorado Springs, CO: David C. Cook.

Taylor, Edward W., and Patricia Cranton. 2012. *The Handbook of Transformative Learning: Theory, Research, and Practice*. San Francisco: Jossey-Bass.

Third Plenary Council of Baltimore. 2006. *Baltimore Catechism No. 1, No. 2, No. 3*. Charlotte, NC: Saint Benedict Press Classics.

Tradigo, Alfredo. 2006. *Icons and Saints of the Eastern Orthodox Church*. Los Angeles: J. Paul Getty Museum.

USCCB Department of Education. 2005. *National Directory for Catechesis*. Baltimore, MD: Port City Press.

Valters Painter, Christine. 2011. *Lectio Divina—The Sacred Art: Transforming Words and Images into Heart-centered Prayer*. Woodstock, VT: Skylight Paths Publishing.

Williamson, G. I. 2003. *The Westminster Shorter Catechism: For Study Classes*. 2nd ed. Phillipsburg, NJ: Presbyterian & Reformed Publishing Co.

Wuerl, Donald W. 2012. *New Evangelization: Passing on the Catholic Faith Today*. Huntington, IN: Our Sunday Visitor.

Christian Higher Education

Arthur, James. 2006. *Faith and Secularisation in Religious Colleges and Universities*. London: Routledge.

Benne, Robert. 2001. *Quality with Soul: How Six Premier Colleges and Universities Keep Faith with Their Religious Traditions*. Grand Rapids, MI: Eerdmans.

Dockery, David S. 2008. *Renewing Minds Serving Church and Society through Christian Higher Education*. Nashville, TN: B & H Publishing.

———. 2012. *Faith and Learning: A Handbook for Christian Higher Education*. Nashville, TN: B & H Publishing.

Eaton, Philip W. 2011. *Engaging the Culture, Changing the World: The Christian University in a Post-Christian World*. Downers Grove, IL: InterVarsity Press.

Esqueda, Octavio J. 2009. *Cuban Christian Theological Higher Education: The History of the Eastern Cuba Baptist Theological Seminary*. Saarbrücken, Germany: Lap Lambert Academic Publishing.

Glanzer, Perry L., and Konstantin Petrenko. 2007. "Resurrecting the Russian University's Soul: The Emergence of Eastern Orthodox Universities and Their Distinctive Approaches to Keeping Faith with Their Religious Tradition." *Christian Scholars Review* 36: 263–284.

Griffioen, Sander. 2002. "Christian Higher Education in Europe: A Catholic View." *Christian Higher Education* 1: 281–302.

Hittenberger, Jeffrey S. 2004. "Globalization, Marketization, and the Mission of Pentecostal Higher Education in Africa." *Pneuma: The Journal of the Society for Pentecostal Studies* 26: 182–215.

Hughes, Richard T., and William B. Adrian. 1997. *Models for Christian Higher Education: Strategies for Success in the Twenty-First Century*. Grand Rapids, MI: Eerdmans.

Hulst, J. B., P. Balla, and M. W. Goheen. 2003. *The Word of God for the Academy in Contemporary Culture(s): Proceedings of the Regional Conference for Europe of the International As-*

sociation for the Promotion of Christian Higher Education. Sioux Center, IA: Dordt College Press.

Jones, Gregory L., and Stephanie Paulsell. 2002. *The Scope of Our Art: The Vocation of the Theological Teacher.* Grand Rapids, MI: Eerdmans.

Lamport, Mark A. 1994. "Student-Faculty Informal Interaction and Its Relation to Christian College Settings: Research and Implications." *Research on Christian Higher Education* (Fall): 66–78.

Litfin, Duane. 2004. *Conceiving the Christian College.* Grand Rapids, MI: Eerdmans.

Maddix, Mark A., John Estep, and Mary E. Lowe. 2012. *Best Practices of Online Education: A Guide for Christian Higher Education.* Charlotte, NC: Information Age Publishing.

Marsden, George M. 1996. *The Soul of the American University from Protestant Establishment to Established Nonbelief.* Oxford: Oxford University Press.

———. 1998. *The Outrageous Idea of Christian Scholarship.* New York: Oxford University Press.

Mejía, José Ramón Alcántara. 2002. "Latin American Higher Education at the Crossroads: The Christian Challenge of Being Transformed through the Renewal of Understanding." *Christian Higher Education* 1: 235–251.

Ng, Peter Tze Ming Ng. 2009. "Globalization, Nationalism, and Christian Higher Education in Northeast Asia." *Christian Higher Education* 8:54–67.

Ng, Peter Tze Ming Ng, and Y. S. P. Leung. 2007. *Christian Responses to Asian Challenges: A Glocalization View on Christian Higher Education in East Asia.* Hong Kong: Centre for the Study of Religion and Chinese Society, Chung Chi College, the Chinese University of Hong Kong.

Noll, Mark A. 1995. *The Scandal of the Evangelical Mind.* Grand Rapids, MI: Eerdmans.

———. 2011. *Jesus Christ and the Life of the Mind.* Grand Rapids, MI: Eerdmans.

Ringenberg, William C. 2006. *The Christian College: A History of Protestant Higher Education in America.* Grand Rapids, MI: Baker Academic.

Romanowski, Michael H., and Teri McCarthy. 2009. *Teaching in a Distant Classroom: Crossing Borders for Global Transformation.* Downers Grove, IL: InterVarsity Press.

Van Der Walt, Bennie J. 2002a. "The Challenge of Christian Higher Education on the African Continent in the Twenty-first Century." *Christian Higher Education* 1:195–228.

———. 2002b. "Our Past Heritage, Present Opportunity, and Future Challenges: Reflections on the 25th Anniversary of the International Association for the Promotion of Christian Higher Education." *Christian Higher Education* 1: 123–137.

Vanzanten, Susan. 2011. *Joining the Mission: A Guide for (Mainly) New College Faculty.* Grand Rapids, MI: Eerdmans.

Vikner, David W. 2003. "Challenges to Christian Higher Education in Asia." *Christian Higher Education* 2: 1–13.

Wolterstorff, Nicholas, Clarence W. Joldersma, and Gloria Goris Stronks. 2002. *Educating for Shalom: Essays on Christian Higher Education.* Grand Rapids, MI: Eerdmans.

Xue, F. R. D. 1999. *International Conference on 21st Century Christian Higher Education in Multi-Cultural Asian Societies.* Taiwan: Fu Jen Catholic University.

Christian Education of Children and Adolescents

Christian Education of Children

Beckwith, Ivy. 2010. *Formational Children's Ministry: Shaping Children Using Story, Ritual, and Relationship.* Grand Rapids, MI: Baker Books.

Berryman, Jerome W. 2009. *Teaching Godly Play: How to Mentor the Spiritual Development of Children.* New York: Morehouse Education Resources.

Connors, Tracy D. 2011. *The Volunteer Management Handbook: Leadership Strategies for Success.* 2nd ed. Hoboken, NJ: John Wiley & Sons.

Denton, Ashley. 2011. *Christian Outdoor Leadership: Theology, Theory, and Practice.* Fort Collins, CO: Smooth Stone Publishing.

Drexler, James L. 2007. *Schools as Communities: Educational Leadership, Relationships, and the Eternal Value of Christian Schooling.* Colorado Springs, CO: ACSI & Purposeful Design Publications.

Fleming Drane, Olive M. 2004. *Clowns, Storytellers, Disciples: Spirituality and Creativity for Today's Church.* Minneapolis, MN: Augsburg Fortress Publishers.

Garland, Diana R. 2012. *Family Ministry: A Comprehensive Guide.* 2nd ed. Downers Grove, IL: IVP Academic.

Halverson, Delia. 2010. *Ready, Set, Teach! Training and Supporting Volunteers in Christian Education.* Nashville, TN: Abingdon Press.

Haywood, Janice. 2007. *Enduring Connections: Creating a Preschool and Children's Ministry.* New York: Chalice Press.

Hunt, Gladys. 2002. *Honey for a Child's Heart: The Imaginative use of Books in Family Life.* 4th ed. Grand Rapids, MI: Zondervan.

Joiner, Reggie. 2009. *Think Orange: Imagine the Impact When Church and Family Collide.* Colorado Springs, CO: David C. Cook.

Jutila, Craig. 2009. *Children's Ministry That Works! The Basics and Beyond.* Loveland, CO: Group Publishing.

Keeley, Robert J. 2010. *Shaped by God: Twelve Essentials for Nurturing Faith in Children, Youth, and Adults.* Grand Rapids, MI: Faith Alive Christian Resources.

Lawson, Kevin E. 2012. *Understanding Children's Spirituality: Theology, Research, and Practice.* Eugene, OR: Cascade.

Martineau, Mariette, Joan Weber, and Leif Kehrwald. 2008. *Intergenerational Faith Formation: Learning the Way We Live.* New London, CT: Twenty-Third Publications.

Moore, Mary Elizabeth, and Almeda M. Wright. 2008. *Children, Youth, and Spirituality in a Troubling World*. St. Louis, MO: Chalice Press.

Nye, Rebecca. 2009. *Children's Spirituality: What It Is and Why It Matters*. Norwich, UK: Church House Publishing.

Parr, Steve. 2010. *Sunday School That Really Works: A Strategy for Connecting Congregations and Communities*. Grand Rapids, MI: Kregel Academic & Professional.

Peters, Michael. 2008. *Robert Raikes: The Founder of Sunday School 1780; The Story of How the Sunday School Began*. Enumclaw, WA: Pleasant Word.

Ratcliff, Donald. 2004. *Children's Spirituality: Christian Perspectives, Research and Applications*. Eugene, OR: Cascade.

Stonehouse, Catherine, and Scottie May. 2010. *Listening to Children on the Spiritual Journey: Guidance for Those Who Teach and Nurture*. Grand Rapids, MI: Baker Academic.

Taylor, Allan. *Sunday School in HD: Sharpening the Focus on What Makes Your Church Healthy*. Nashville, TN: B & H Books.

Tolbert, La Verne. 2013. *Exploring and Engaging Children's Spirituality: A Holistic Approach*. Eugene, OR: Wipf & Stock.

Weldon, Laura Grace. 2010. *Free Range Learning: How Homeschooling Changes Everything*. Chino Valley, AZ: Hohm Press.

Wideman, Jim. 2003. *Children's Ministry Leadership: The You-Can-Do-It Guide*. Loveland, CO: Group Publishing.

———. 2004. *Children's Ministry Volunteers That Stick*. Loveland, CO: Group Publishing.

Will, Julianne M. 2004. *Catholic Prayer Book for Children*. Huntington, IN: Our Sunday Visitor.

Christian Education of Adolescents

Berard, John, James Penner, and Rick Bartlett. 2010. *Consuming Youth: Leading Teens through Consumer Culture*. Grand Rapids, MI: Zondervan.

Bosher, Bo. 2006. *The Be-with Factor: Mentoring Students in Everyday Life*. Grand Rapids, MI: Zondervan.

Brierley, Danny. 2003. *What Every Volunteer Youth Worker Should Know*. Cumbria, UK: Authentic Lifestyle.

Christerson, Brad, Korie L. Edwards, and Richard Flory. 2010. *Growing up in America: The Power of Race in the Lives of Teens*. Stanford, CA: Stanford University Press.

Crabtree, Jack. 2008. *Better Safe Than Sued: Keeping Your Students and Ministry Alive*. Grand Rapids, MI: Zondervan.

DeVries, Mark. 2008. *Sustainable Youth Ministry: Why Most Youth Ministry Doesn't Last and What Your Church Can Do About It*. Downers Grove, IL: InterVarsity Press.

Dunn, R. Richard. 2001. *Shaping the Spiritual Life of Students: A Guide for Youth Workers, Pastors, Teachers, and Campus Ministers*. Downers Grove, IL: InterVarsity Press.

Fields, Doug. 2002. *Your First Two Years in Youth Ministry*. Grand Rapids, MI: Zondervan.

Kinnaman, David. 2011. *You Lost Me: Why Young Christians are Leaving Church . . . and Rethinking Faith*. Grand Rapids, MI: Baker Books.

Lamport, Mark A. 1996. "What Is Youth Ministry?" *Christian Education Journal* (Spring): 61–70.

———. 2005. "The Rise of Youth Churches: What the American Church Can Learn From This Latest British Invasion." *Evangelical Missions Quarterly* (January): 12–21.

Linhart, Terry, and David Livermore, eds. 2011. *Global Youth Ministry: Reaching Adolescents Around the World*. Grand Rapids, MI: Zondervan.

Martinson, Roland, Wes Black, and John Roberto. 2010. *The Spirit and Culture of Youth Ministry*. St. Paul, MN: EYM publishing.

Oh, Kyungseokm, and Sungso Kim. 2008. *Youth Ministry Manual*. Seoul, South Korea: Bread of Life Press.

Root, Andrew, and Kenda Creasy Dean. 2011. *The Theological Turn in Youth Ministry*. Downers Grove: IL: InterVarsity Press.

Smith, Christian, and Melina Lunquist Denton. 2005. *Soul Searching: The Religious and Spiritual Lives of American Teenagers*. Oxford: Oxford University Press.

Websites

National Federation for Catholic Youth Ministry. 2007. "Understanding Catholic Youth Ministry." Accessed 21 October 2013. http://www.nfcym.org/catholicym/.

National Network of Youth Ministries. 2013. "Reaching Youth . . . Together." http://www.youthworkers.net.

Princeton Theological Seminary. 2012. "The Institute for Youth Ministry." http://www.ptsem.edu/iym/.

Youth Specialties. 2013. "Resources." http://youthspecialties.com/.

Videos

Smith, Christian. 2010. *Soul Searching* (DVD). Revelation Studios.

Theological Education

Aleshire, Daniel O. 2008. *Earthen Vessels: Hopeful Reflections on the Work and Future of Theological Schools*. Grand Rapids, MI: Eerdmans.

Astley, Jeff, and Leslie J. Francis. 2013. *Exploring Ordinary Theology: Everyday Christian Believing and the Church*. Rev. ed. London: Ashgate.

Banks, Robert. 1999. *Reenvisioning Theological Education: Exploring Missional Alternative to Current Models*. Grand Rapids, MI: Eerdmans.

Barker, Lance R., and B. Edmon Martin. 2004. *Multiple Paths to Ministry: New Models for Theological Education*. Cleveland, OH: Pilgrim Press.

Barrett, Lois Y. 2004. *Treasure in Clay Jars: Patterns in Missional Faithfulness*. Gospel & Our Culture. Grand Rapids, MI: Eerdmans.

Bass, Dorothy C., and Craig Dykstra. 2007. *For Life Abundant: Practical Theology, Theological Education, and Christian Ministry*. Grand Rapids, MI: Eerdmans.

Bosch, David J. 2005. *Misión en Transformación: Cambios de Paradigma en la Teología de la Misión*. Grand Rapids, MI: Libros Desafío.

Brazier, P. H. 2008. *Revelation and Reason: Prolegomena to Systematic Theology*. T&T Clark Theology. New York: T & T Clark.

Calian, Camegie Samuel. 2002. *The Ideal Seminary: Pursuing Excellence in Theological Education*. Louisville, KY: John Knox Press.

Cannell, Linda. 2006. *Theological Education Matters: Leadership Education for the Church*. Newburgh, IN: EDCOT Press.

Carey, Patrick W. 1997. *Theological Education in the Catholic Tradition: Contemporary Challenges*. New York: Crossroad.

Cetuk, Virginia S. 1998. *What to Expect in Seminary: Theological Education as Spiritual Formation*. Nashville, TN: Abingdon Press.

Cook, Matthew, Rob Haskell, Ruth Julian, and Natee Tanchanpongs. 2010. *Local Theology for the Global Church: Principles for Evangelical Approach to Contextualization*. Pasadena, CA: William Carey Library.

Duarte, de Oliveira, and Paulo Cesar. 2011. *Educação Teológica Intercultural: Uma Abordagem Latino-Americana a partir da Pedagogia Freireana e da Missão Integral*. Portuguese ed. Kennesaw, GA: Coram Deo Publishing.

Enns, Paul. 2011. *Compendio Portavoz de Teología*. Grand Rapids, MI: Portavoz.

Erickson, Millard. 2009. *Teología Sistemática*. Barcelona, España: Editorial CLIE.

Esterline, David V., and Ogbu U. Kalu. 2006. *Shaping Beloved Community: Multicultural Theological Education*. Louisville, KY: Westminster John Knox Press.

Ferreira, Franklin, and Alan Myatt. 2007. *Teologia Sistemática: Uma Análise História, Bíblica e Apologética para o Contexto Atual*. São Paulo, Brasil: Vida Nova.

Filho, Carlos Ribeiro Caldas. 2007. *Fundamentos da Teologia da Igreja*. São Paulo, Brasil: Mundo Cristão.

Flett, John G. 2010. *The Witness of God: The Trinity, Missio Dei, Karl Barth, and the Nature of Christian Community*. Grand Rapids, MI: Eerdmans.

Floding, Matthew. 2010. *Welcome to Theological Field Education*. Herndon, VA: Alban Institute.

Fowler, Mark A. 2006. *Mentoring into Vocation: Touchstones for the Journey*. Nashville, TN: United Methodist General Board of Higher Education.

González, Justo. 2004. *Retorno a la Historia del Pensamiento Cristiano: Tres tipos de Teología*. Buenos Aires, Argentina: Ediciones Kairós.

———. 2010. *Diccionario Manual Teológico*. Barcelona, España: Editorial CLIE.

Hardy, Steven A. 2006. *Excellence in Theological Education: Effective Training for Church Leaders*. Green Point, South Africa: Modern Printers.

Harkness, Allan. 2010. *Tending the Seedbeds: Educational Perspectives on Theological Education in Asia*. Quezon City, Philippines: Asia Theological Association.

Hillman, George M. 2008. *Preparing for Ministry: A Practical Guide to Theological Field Education*. Grand Rapids, MI: Kregel Academic and Professional.

Horrell, J. Scott. 2004. *A Essência da Igreja: Fundamentos do Novo Testamento para a Igreja Contemporânea*. Trad. Lena Aranha. São Paulo, Brasil: Hagnos.

Jenkins, Philip. 2007. *The Next Christendom: The Coming of Global Christianity*. Rev. ed. New York: Oxford University Press.

King, Stephen. 2007. *Trust the Process: A History of Clinical Pastoral Education as Theological Education*. Lanham, MD: University Press of America.

Kinsler, Ross. 2011. *Diversified Theological Education: Equipping All God's People*. Pasadena, CA: William Carey International University Press.

Kohl, Manfred Waldemar, and Antonio Carlos Barro. 2004. *Educação Teológica Transformadora*. Londrina, PR, Brasil: Editora Descoberta.

Lamport, Mark A. 2010. "The Most Indispensable Habits of Effective Theological Educators: Recalibrating Educational Philosophy, Psychology, and Practice." *The Asbury Journal* (Fall): 36–54.

Langmead, Ross. 2004. *The Word Made Flesh: Towards an Incarnational Missiology*. Lanham, MD: University Press of America.

Marks, Darren C. 2002. *Shaping a Theological Mind: Theological Context and Methodology*. Burlington, VT: Ashgate Publishing Company.

Marsden, George M. 2006. *Fundamentalism and American Culture*. Rev. ed. New York: Oxford University Press.

Moreau, A. Scott. 2011. *Contextualization in World Missions: Mapping and Assessing Evangelical Models*. Grand Rapids, MI: Kregel Academic & Professional.

Osmer, Richard R. 2008. *Practical Theology: An Introduction*. Grand Rapids, MI: Eerdmans.

Ott, Bernhard. 2011. *Beyond Fragmentation: Integrating Mission and Theological Education: A Critical Assessment of Some Recent Developments in Evangelical Education*. Regnum Studies in Mission. Eugene, OR: Wipf & Stock.

Penner, Peter. 2005. *Theological Education as Mission*. Schwarzenfeld, Germany: Neufeld Verlag.

Souza, Maruilson, and Rinaldo César. 2008. *A Educação Teológica em Perspectivas*. Recife, Brasil: Editora Êxodus.

Tennent, Timothy C. 2007. *Theology in the Context of World Christianity: How the Global Church Is Influencing the Way*

We Think about and Discuss Theology. Grand Rapids, MI: Zondervan.

Tizon, Al. 2008. *Transformation after Lausanne: Radical Evangelical Mission in Global-Local Perspective.* Regnum Studies in Mission. Eugene, OR: Wipf & Stock.

Trull, Joe E., and James E. Carter. 2004. *Ministerial Ethics: Moral Formation for Church Leaders.* Grand Rapids, MI: Baker Academic.

Warford, Malcolm L. 2005. *Practical Wisdom on Theological Teaching and Learning.* New York: Peter Lang Publishing.

Werner, Dietrich, David Esterline, Kangs Namsoon, and Joshva Raja. 2010. *Handbook of Theological Education in World Christianity.* Eugene, OR: Wipf & Stock.

Zaldívar, Raúl. 2006. *Teología Sistemática: Desde una Perspectiva Latinoamericana.* Barcelona, Espana: Editoril CLIE.

Christian Pedagogy

Alpha International. 2004. *The Alpha Course Manual.* 2nd ed. London: Alpha International.

Andrews, Alan. 2010. *The Kingdom Life: A Practical Theology of Discipleship and Spiritual Formation.* Colorado Springs, CO: NavPress.

Barnier, Carol. 2009. *The Big WHAT NOW Book of Learning Styles: A Fresh and Demystifying Approach.* Bingley, UK: Emerald Books.

Baucham, Voddie, Jr. 2011. *Family Driven Faith: Doing What It Takes to Raise Sons and Daughters Who Walk with God.* Wheaton, IL: Crossway.

Beates, Michael S. 2012. *Disability and the Gospel: How God Uses Our Brokenness to Display His Grace.* Wheaton, IL: Crossway.

Beckwith, Ivy. 2004. *Postmodern Children's Ministry: Ministry to Children in 21st Century Church.* Grand Rapids, MI: Zondervan/Youth Specialties.

Breeding, MaLesa, Dana Kennamer Hood, and Jerry E. Whitworth. 2006. *Let All the Children Come to Me: A Practical Guide Including Children with Disabilities in Your Church Ministries.* Colorado Springs, CO: David C. Cook.

Copeland, Matt. 2005. *Socratic Circles: Fostering Critical and Creative Thinking in Middle and High School.* Portland, ME: Stenhouse Publishers.

Copley, Terence. 2005. *Indoctrination, Education and God: The Struggle for the Mind.* London: SPCK Publishing.

Dykstra, Craig. 2005. *Growing in the Life of Faith: Education and Christian Practices.* 2nd ed. Louisville, KY: Westminster John Knox Press.

Folmsbee, Chris. 2010. *Story, Signs, and Sacred Rhythms: A Narrative Approach to Youth Ministry.* Grand Rapids, MI: Zondervan/Youth Specialties.

Fowler, James W. 1999. *Becoming Adult, Becoming Christian: Adult Development and Christian Faith.* rev. ed. San Francisco: Jossey-Bass.

Garland, Diana R. 2012. *Family Ministry: A Comprehensive Guide.* Downers Grove, IL: IVP Academic.

Gardner, Howard E. 2006. *Multiple Intelligences: New Horizons in Theory and Practice.* Rev. New York: Basic Books.

Graham, Elaine, Heather Walton, and Frankie Ward. 2005. *Theological Reflection: Methods.* Norwich, UK: SCM Press.

———. 2007. *Theological Reflection: Sources.* Norwich, UK: SCM Press.

Heflin, Houston. 2012. *Teaching Eutychus: Engaging Today's Learners with Passion and Creativity.* Amazon Digital Services (e-book).

Hegeman, Johan, Margaret Edgell, and Henk Jochemsen. 2011. *Practice and Profile: Christian Formation for Vocation.* Eugene, OR: Wipf & Stock.

Herrington, Jim, Mike Bonem, and James H. Furr. 2000. *Leading Congregational Change: A Practical Guide for the Transformational Journey.* San Francisco: Jossey-Bass.

Hoffman, Mary Byrne. 2012. *Catechesis in a Multimedia World: Connecting to Today's Students.* Mahwah, NJ: Paulist Press.

Jensen, Robin M. 2004. *The Substance of Things Seen: Art, Faith, and the Christian Community.* Grand Rapids, MI: Eerdmans.

Jones, Tony. 2001. *Postmodern Youth Ministry.* Grand Rapids, MI: Zondervan/Youth Specialties.

Keely, Barbara Anne. 1997. *Faith of Our Foremothers: Women Changing Religious Education.* Louisville, KY: Westminster John Knox Press.

Kelcourse, Felicity Brock. 2004. *Human Development and Faith: Life-cycle Stages of Body, Mind, and Soul.* St. Louis, MO: Chalice Press.

Killen, Melanie, and Judith G. Smetana. 2013. *Handbook of Moral Development.* New York: Psychology Press.

Knight, George R. 2006. *Philosophy & Education: An Introduction in Christian Perspective.* 4th ed. Berien Springs, MI: Andrews University Press.

Krauss, Jane I., and Suzanne K. Boss. 2013. *Thinking through Project-Based Learning: Guiding Deeper Inquiry.* Thousand Oaks, CA: Corwin Press.

Lamport, Mark A. 2008a. "Unintended Outcomes, Curious Inventions, and Misshapen Creatures: Juxtapositions of Religious Belief and Faith-Formed Practice and the Renewed Case of the Educational Mission of the Church." *Asbury Theological Journal* (April): 95–113.

———. 2008b. "Stealing Sacraments: What Protestant Educators Can Learn from Other Religious Traditions." *Christian Perspectives in Education* (Fall): 1–24.

Lamport, Mark A., and Darrell Yoder. 2006. "Faithful Gestures: Rebooting the Educational Mission of the Church." *Christian Education Journal* (Spring): 58–78.

Martineau, Mariette, Joan Weber, and Leif Kehrwald. 2008. *Intergenerational Faith Formation: Learning the Way We Live.* Mystic, CT: Twenty-Third Publications.

Murphy, Deborah Dean. 2004. *Teaching That Transforms: Worship as the Heart of Christian Education.* Grand Rapids, MI: Brazos Press.

Muthiah, Robert A. 2009. *The Priesthood of All Believers in the Twenty-First Century.* Eugene, OR: Wipf & Stock.

Nouwen, Henri J. M., Michael J. Christensen, and Rebecca J. Laird. 2006. *Spiritual Direction: Wisdom for the Long Walk of Faith.* New York: HarperCollins.

Ogden, Greg. 2003. *Transforming Discipleship: Making Disciples a Few at a Time.* Downers Grove, IL: IVP Books.

Qualters, Donna M. 2011. *Experiential Education: Making the Most of Learning Outside the Classroom.* New Directions for Teaching and Learning, no. 124. San Francisco: Jossey-Bass.

Payne, Charles M., and Carol Sills Strickland. 2008. *Teach Freedom: Education for Liberation in the African-American Tradition.* New York: Teachers College Press.

Pennock, Michael. 2000. *Catholic Social Teaching: Learning and Living Justice.* Notre Dame, IN: Ave Maria Press.

Riesen, Richard. 2002. *Piety and Philosophy: A Primer for Christian Schools.* Ozark, AL: ACW Press.

Ruppell, Gert, and Peter Schreiner. 2003. *Shared Learning in a Plural World: Ecumenical Approaches to Inter-Religious Education.* Berlin: LIT Verlag.

Rynsburger, Mary, and Mark A. Lamport. 2008–2009. "All the Rage: How Small Groups Are Really Educating Christian Adults—Part 1: Assessing Small Group Ministry Practice: A Review of the Literature." *Christian Education Journal* (Spring): 116–137; "Part 2: Augmenting Small Group Ministry Practice: Developing Small Group Leadership Skills through Insights from Cognate Theoretical Disciplines." *Christian Education Journal* (Fall): 391–414; "Part 3: Anchoring Small Group Ministry Practice: Biblical Insights and Leadership Development." *Christian Education Journal* (Spring): 112–130.

Schnase, Robert. 2008. *Five Practices—Intentional Faith Development.* Nashville, TN: Abingdon Press.

Stronge, James H. 2007. *Qualities of Effective Teachers.* 2nd ed. Alexandria, VA: Association for Supervision & Curriculum Development.

Thomas, Adam. 2011. *Digital Disciple: Real Christianity in a Virtual World.* Nashville, TN: Abingdon Press.

Thorsen, Don, 2005. *The Wesleyan Quadrilateral: Scripture, Tradition, Reason, & Experience as a Model of Evangelical Theology.* Lexington, KY: Emeth Press.

Willis, Avery, and Steve Evans. 2007. *Making Disciples of Oral Learners.* Woodford Green, Essex, UK: ION/LCWE (Lausanne Conference for World Evangelization).

Yaconelli, Mark. 2006. *Contemplative Youth Ministry: Practicing the Presence of Jesus.* Grand Rapids, MI: Zondervan/Youth Specialties.

Yount, William. 2010. *Created to Learn: A Christian Teacher's Introduction to Educational Psychology.* 2nd ed. Nashville, TN: B & H Academic.

Zachary, Lois J. 2011. *The Mentor's Guide: Facilitating Effective Learning Relationships.* 2nd ed. San Francisco: Jossey-Bass.

Ziolkowski, Peter. 2007. *Discipleship for Catholic Men: Embracing God's Plan for Our Life.* Minneapolis, MN: Parish Life Press.

Christian Practice and Christian Education

Allender, Dan B. 2009. *Sabbath.* Nashville, TN: Thomas Nelson.

Amerson, Melvin, and James Amerson. 2007. *Celebrating the Offering.* Nashville, TN: Discipleship Resources.

Bass, Alice S. 2001. *The Creative Life: A Workbook for Unearthing the Christian Imagination.* Print-on-demand ed. Downers Grove, IL: IVP Academic.

Belisle, Peter-Damian. 2003. *The Language of Silence: The Changing Face of Monastic Solitude.* Maryknoll, NY: Orbis.

Berghuis, Kent D. 2007. *Christian Fasting: A Theological Approach.* Richardson, TX: Biblical Studies Press.

Blogg, Martin. 2011. *Dance and the Christian Faith: A Form of Knowing.* Cambridge, UK: Lutterworth Press.

Brush, Sarah, Phil Greig, and Sarah Brush. 2011. *Moving Images, Changing Lives: Exploring the Christian Life and Confirmation with Young People through Film.* London: Church House Pub.

Cannon, Mae Elise. 2013. *Just Spirituality.* Downers Grove, IL: IVP Books.

Cepero, Helen. 2008. *Journaling as a Spiritual Practice: Encountering God through Attentive Writing.* Downers Grove, IL: IVP Books.

Chinnici, Joseph P., and Angelyn Dries. 2000. *Prayer and Practice in the American Catholic Community.* Maryknoll, NY: Orbis.

Clark, Freddy James. 2007. *Hospitality: An Ecclesiological Practice of Ministry.* Falls Village, CT: Hamilton Books.

Clark, R. Scott. 2008. *Recovering the Reformed Confession: Our Theology, Piety, and Practice.* Phillipsburg, NY: P&R Publishing.

Crossin, John W. 1997. *Friendship: The Key to Spiritual Growth.* New York: Paulist Press.

Davis, Jeffry C., Philip Graham Ryken, and Leland Ryken. 2012. *Liberal Arts for the Christian Life.* Wheaton, IL: Crossway.

Devine, Richard J., J. Favazza, and M. McLain. 2002. *From Cloister to Commons: Concepts and Models for Service-learning in Religious Studies.* Washington, DC: American Association for Higher Education.

Fee, Gordon D. 2000. *Listening to the Spirit in the Text.* Grand Rapids, MI: Eerdmans.

Flancher, Arlene. 2002. *Storytelling, Kids, and Christian Education.* Minneapolis, MN: Augsburg Fortress.

Foster, Richard J. 2010. *Freedom of Simplicity: Finding Harmony in a Complex World.* New York: HarperCollins e-books.

Galindo, Israel, and Marty Canaday. 2010. *Planning for Christian Education Formation: A Community of Faith Approach.* St. Louis, MO: Chalice Press.

George, Christian, and Calvin Miller. 2006. *Sacred Travels: Recovering the Ancient Practice of Pilgrimage.* Downers Grove, IL: IVP Books.

Gonzalo, Julio A. 2008. *Cursillos in Christianity Origins & First Expansion.* Madrid: Science & Culture.

Heffner, Gail Gunst, and Claudia DeVries Beversluis. 2002. *Commitment and Connection: Service-Learning and Christian Higher Education.* Lanham, MD: University Press of America.

Hirst, Anthony. 2004. *God and the Poetic Ego: The Appropriation of Biblical and Liturgical Language in the Poetry of Palamas, Sikelianos, and Elytis.* New York: Peter Lang.

Johnson, Jan. 2003. *Simplicity & Fasting: Spiritual Disciplines Bible Studies.* Downers Grove, IL: IVP Books.

Lawrence, Roy. 1996. *The Practice of Christian Healing: A Guide for Beginners.* Downers Grove, IL: IVP Books.

Leverich, Hall Edward. 2011. *Vocational Guidance and Employment Practice in the North American Young Men's Christian Associations.* Charleston, SC: Nabu Press.

Marder, John. 2009. *You're God's Gift to Teachers: Passages of Biblical Encouragement for Teachers.* Parker, CO: Outskirts Press.

Martin, Jim. 2012. *The Just Church: Becoming a Risk-taking, Justice-seeking, Disciple-making Congregation.* Carol Stream, IL: Tyndale Momentum.

Matthiesen, Michon M. 2012. *Sacrifice as Gift: Eucharist, Grace, and Contemplative Prayer in Maurice de La Taille.* Washington, DC: Catholic University of America Press.

McElvaney, William K. 2009. *Becoming a Justice Seeking Congregation: Responding to God's Justice Initiative.* New York: Bloomington: iUniverse, Inc.

Murphy, Charles M. 2010. *The Spirituality of Fasting: Rediscovering a Christian Practice.* Notre Dame, IN: Ave Maria Press.

Nabhan-Warren, Kristy. 2013. *The Cursillo Movement in America: Catholics, Protestants, and Fourth-day Spirituality.* Chapel Hill: University of North Carolina Press.

Nord, David Paul. 2004. *Faith in Reading: Religious Publishing and the Birth of Mass Media in America.* New York: Oxford University Press.

O'Connell, Jim. 2009. *Going the Heart's Way: Silence, Space, and Stillness in Our Day.* Blackrock, Ireland: Columba Press.

O'Flaherty, Edward, Rodney L. Petersen, and Timothy A. Norton. Ed. 2010. *Sunday, Sabbath, and the Weekend: Managing Time in a Global Culture.* Grand Rapids, MI: Eerdmans.

Pennington, M. Basil, OCSO. 2013. *A Place Apart: Monastic Prayer and Practice for Everyone.* Liguori, MO: Liguori Publications.

Phillips, Gene, and Jean Phillips. 2005. *Gleanings from God's Word.* Garland, TX: Hannibal Books.

Pope, Robert. 2007. *Salvation in Celluloid: Theology, Imagination and Film.* New York: T&T Clark.

Reininger, Gustave, and Thomas Keating. 1998. *Centering Prayer in Daily Life and Ministry.* New York: Continuum International Publishing.

Rohr, Richard. 2012. A *Lever and a Place to Stand: The Contemplative Stance, the Active Prayer.* New York: Paulist Press.

Sabin, Ardys Koskovich. 2001. *Art, Kids, and Christian Education: How to Use Art in Your Christian Education Program.* Minneapolis, MN: Augsburg Fortress.

Scales, T. Laine, and Michael S. Kelly, eds. 2012. *Christianity and Social Work: Readings on the Integration of Christian Faith and Social Work Practice.* Botsford, CT: North American Association of Christians in Social Work.

Strauch, Alexander. 2011. *Hospitality Commands.* Colorado Springs, CO: Lewis and Roth Publishers.

Tyre, Travis. 1995. *Introduction to Drama: A Theatre Study Curriculum for Christian Education; Curriculum Guide and Teacher's Edition.* Glen Rose, TX: Promise Productions.

White, R. E. O. 2000. *Listening Carefully to Jesus.* Grand Rapids, MI: Eerdmans.

Woodley, Matt. 2009. *The Folly of Prayer: Practicing the Presence and Absence of God.* Downers Grove, IL: IVP Books.

Worthington Jr., Everett L. 2003. *Forgiving and Reconciling: Bridges to Wholeness and Hope.* Rev. ed. Downers Grove, IL: IVP Books.

Yake, John C. 2005. *The Theory of Religious Ministry to Youth: Faith Development and the "Christ in Others" Retreat.* Lewiston, NY: Edwin Mellen Press.

Christian Education in Difficult Circumstances

Blomberg, Doug. 2007. *Wisdom and Curriculum: Christian Schooling after Postmodernity.* Sioux Center, IA: Dordt College Press.

Butler, Noah. 2012. *A 21st Century Deaf Ministry From a Biblical Perspective.* Birmingham, AL: International Institute of Deaf Services.

Byun, Eddie. 2014. *Justice Awakening: How You and Your Church Can Help End Human Trafficking.* Downers Grove, IL: IVP Books.

Caine, Christine. 2012. *Undaunted: Daring to Do What God Calls You to Do.* Grand Rapids, MI: Zondervan.

Carroll, R., and M. Daniel. 2008. *Christians at the Border: Immigration, the Church, and the Bible.* Grand Rapids, MI: Baker Academic.

Clark, Doris C. 2000. *Feed All My Sheep: A Guide and Curriculum for Adults with Developmental Disabilities.* Louisville, KY: Geneva Press.

Evans, James S. 1998. *Uncommon Gifts: Transforming Learning Disabilities into Blessing.* Wheaton, IL: Shaw.

Holder, Rich, Cynthia, and Martha Ross-Mockaitis. 2006. *Learning Disabilities and the Church: Including All God's Kids in Your Education and Worship.* Grand Rapids, MI: Faith Alive Christian Resources.

Hunt, Thomas C., and James C. Carper, eds. 2013. *Religion and Schooling in Contemporary America: Confronting Our Cultural Pluralism*. New York: Routledge.

Kazanjian, Victor H., and Laurence Kazanjian. 2000. *Education as Transformation: Religious Pluralism, Spirituality, and a New Vision for Higher Education in America*. New York: Peter Lang.

Koehler, Paul F. 2010. *Telling God's Stories with Power: Biblical Storytelling in Oral Cultures*. Pasadena, CA: William Carey Library Publishers.

Labosh, Kathy. 2011. *The Child with Autism Learns about Faith: 15 Ready-to-use Scripture Lessons, from the Garden of Eden to the Parting of the Red Sea*. Arlington, TX: Future Horizons.

Leach, Tom. 2010. *Compel Them to Come In: Reaching People with Disabilities through the Local Church*. Bloomington, IN: AuthorHouse.

McGann, Karen M., and Grace Harding. *My Church: A Young Girl Shares Her Catholic Deaf Community*. Pittsburgh, PA: Diocese of Pittsburgh.

Ordonia, Arturo Garcia. 2010. *Theological Education in the Context of Poverty and Injustice: What Do Theological Educators Think about Its Role*. Saarbrücken, Germany: LAP Lambert Academic Publishing.

Pierson, Jim. 2002. *Exceptional Teaching: A Comprehensive Guide for Including Students with Disabilities*. Cincinnati, OH: Standard Publishing.

Rapada, Amy. 2007. *The Special Needs Ministry Handbook: A Church's Guide to Reaching Children with Disabilities and Their Families*. Charleston, SC: BookSurge Publishing.

Roberts, Carlos C. 2009. *Christian Education Teaching Methods from Modern to Postmodern: Teaching the Faith to Postmoderns*. Bloomington, IN: AuthorHouse.

Sutton, Lawrence R. 2013. *How to Welcome, Include, and Catechize Children with Autism and Other Special Needs: A Parish-Based Approach*. Chicago: Loyola Press.

Swierenga, Robert P. 2005. *Elim: A Chicago Christian School and Life-training Center for the Disabled*. Grand Rapids, MI: Eerdmans.

Talbert, Charles H. 1991. *Learning through Suffering: The Educational Value of Suffering in the New Testament and in Its Milieu*. Collegeville, MN: The Liturgical Press.

Weber, Jason, and Paul Pennington. 2006. *Launching an Orphans Ministry in Your Church*. Little Rock, AR: FamilyLife Publishing.

Literature and Christian Education

Adu-Gyamfi, Yaw, and Mark Ray Schmidt. 2010. *Literature and Spirituality*. The Essential Literature Series. London: Longman.

Carruthers, Jo, Mark Knight, and Andrew Tate. 2013. *Literature and the Bible: A Reader*. New York: Routledge.

Crain, Jeanie C. 2010. *Reading the Bible as Literature*. Cambridge, UK: Polity.

Dawson, David. 1995. *Literary Theory*. Guides to Theological Inquiry Series. Minneapolis, MN: Fortress Press.

Detmer, David. 2013. *Phenomenology Explained: From Experience to Insight*. Chicago: Open Court.

Detweiler, Robert, and David Jasper. 2000. *Religion and Literature: A Reader*. Louisville, KY: Westminster John Knox Press.

Feduccia, Robert. 2006. *Great Catholic Writings: Thought, Literature, Spirituality, Social Action*. Winona, MN: Saint Mary's Press.

Fessenden, Tracy. 2006. *Culture and Redemption: Religion, the Secular, and American Literature*. Princeton, NJ: Princeton University Press.

Gabel, John B., Charles B. Wheeler, Anthony D. York, and David Citino. 2005. *The Bible as Literature: An Introduction*. 5th ed. New York: Oxford University Press.

Jasper, David, and Stephen Prickett. 2007. *The Bible and Literature: A Reader*. Malden, MA: Wiley-Blackwell.

Merleau-Ponty, Maurice. 2013. *Phenomenology of Perception*. New York: Routledge.

Milbank, John, Catherine Pickstock, and Graham Ward. 1998. *Radical Orthodoxy: A New Theology*. New York: Routledge.

Nickelsburg, George W. E. 2011. *Jewish Literature between the Bible and the Mishnah: A Historical and Literary Introduction*. 2nd ed. Minneapolis, MN: Fortress Press.

Quash, Ben. 2008. *Theology and the Drama of History*. Cambridge Studies in Christian Doctrine Series. Cambridge, UK: Cambridge University Press.

Roncace, Mark, and Patrick Gray. 2007. *Teaching the Bible through Popular Culture and the Arts*. Atlanta, GA: Society of Biblical Literature.

Ryken, Leland, and Philip Graham Ryken. 2007. *The Literary Study Bible: English Standard Version*. Wheaton, IL: Crossway.

Segal, Benjamin. 2013. *A New Psalm: A Guide to Psalms as Literature*. New York: Gefen Publishing House.

Smith, James K. A. 2004. *Introducing Radical Orthodoxy: Mapping a Post-secular Theology*. Grand Rapids, MI: Baker Academic.

Smith, James K. A., and James Olthuis. 2005. *Radical Orthodoxy and the Reformed Tradition: Creation, Covenant, and Participation*. Grand Rapids, MI: Baker Academic.

Thomas, Virginia. 1985. *Children's Literature for All God's Children*. Louisville, KY: Westminster John Knox Press.

Wesley, Addison, James S. Ackerman, Thayer S. Warshaw, and John Sweet. 1997. *The Bible As/In Literature: Anthology*. 2nd ed. Boston: Addison Wesley.

Biographies of Influential Christian Educators

Allen, Pauline, and Wendy Mayer. 1999. *John Chrysostom*. Oxford: Routledge.

Anderson, Phil. 2007. *Lord of the Ring: In Search of Count von Zinzendorf*. Ventura, CA: Regal.

Baird, Henry Martyn. 2001. *Theodore Beza: The Counselor of the French Reformation, 1519–1605*. Boston: Adamant Media Corporation.

Biber, Edward, and Johann H. Pestalozzi. 2007. *Henry Pestalozzi and His Plan of Education: Being an Account of His Life and Writings*. Whitefish, MN: Kessinger Publishing.

Birzer, Bradley J. 2007. *Sanctifying the World: The Augustinian Life and Mind of Christopher Dawson*. Front Royal, VA: Christendom Press.

Bradley, S. A. J. 2008. *N. F. S. Grundtvig, a Life Recalled: An Anthology of Biographical Source-Texts*. Aarhus, Denmark: Aarhus University Press.

Bratt, James D. 2013. *Abraham Kuyper: Modern Calvinist, Christian Democrat*. Grand Rapids, MI: Eerdmans.

Brotherton, Marcus. 2006. *Teacher: The Henrietta Mears Story*. Ventura, CA: Regal Press.

Chadwick, Henry. 2009. *Augustine of Hippo: A Life*. Oxford: Oxford University Press.

Choy, Leona. 2004. *Andrew Murray: The Authorized Biography*. Fort Washington, PA: Christian Literature Crusade.

Clanchy, M. T. 1999. *Abelard: A Medieval Life*. Oxford: Wiley-Blackwell.

D'Aubigne, Jean Henri Merle, and Mark Sidwell. 2000. *For God and His People: Ulrich Zwingli and the Swiss Reformation*. Translated by Henry White. Greenville, SC: BJU Press.

Dales, Douglas. 2012. *Alcuin: His Life and Legacy*. Cambridge, UK: James Clark & Co.

Daley, Brian. 2006. *Gregory of Nazianzus*. Oxford: Routledge.

Damrosch, Leo. 2007. *Jean-Jacques Rousseau: Restless Genius*. New York: Mariner Books.

Dunn, Geoffrey D. 2004. *Tertullian*. Oxford: Routledge.

Forest, Jim. 2008. *Living with Wisdom: A Life of Thomas Merton*. Maryknoll, NY: Orbis.

Garff, Joakim. 2007. *Søren Kierkegaard: A Biography*. Princeton, NJ: Princeton University Press.

Gordon, F. Bruce. 2011. *Calvin*. New Haven, CT: Yale University Press.

Henry, George William. 2011. *Malcolm Shepherd Knowles: A History of His Thought*. Hauppauge, NY: Nova Science Publishing.

Higgins, Michael W., and Kevin Burns. 2012. *Genius Born of Anguish: The Life and Legacy of Henri Nouwen*. Mahwah, NJ: Paulist Press.

Hoffman, Edward. 1999. *The Right to Be Human: A Biography of Abraham Maslow*. Rev. ed. New York: McGraw-Hill.

Huizinga, Johan. 2011. *Erasmus and the Age of Reformation*. Mineola, NY: Dover Publications.

Kelly, J. N. D. 1998. *Jerome: His Life, Writings, and Controversies*. Peabody, MA: Hendrickson Publishers.

Ker, Ian. 2009. *John Henry Newman: A Biography*. Oxford: Oxford University Press.

King, Darrel D. 1998. *E. M. Bounds: The Man Whose Life of Prayer Inspired Millions*. Ada, MI: Bethany House Publishers.

Kirylo, James D. 2011. *Paulo Freire: The Man from Recife*. New York: Peter Lang.

Malcom, Norman, and G. H. von Wright. 2001. *Ludwig Wittgenstein: A Memoir*. Oxford: Oxford University Press.

Mangina, Joseph L. 2004. *Karl Barth: Theologian of Christian Witness*. Louisville, KY: Westminster.

Marshall, Rosalind K. 2008. *John Knox*. Edinburgh: Birlinn Ltd.

Martin, Jay. 2003. *The Education of John Dewey*. New York: Columbia University Press.

Marty, Martin E. 2008. *Martin Luther: A Life*. New York: Penguin Books.

McCasland, David. 1998. *Oswald Chambers: Abandoned to God, the Life Story of the Author of My Utmost for His Highest*. Grand Rapids, MI: Discovery House Publishers.

McEvoy, James. 2000. *Robert Grosseteste*. Oxford: Oxford University Press.

McGuire, Brian Patrick. 2005. *Jean Gerson and the Last Medieval Reformation*. University Park: Pennsylvania State University Press.

McLynn, Neil B. 1994. *Ambrose of Milan: Church and Court in a Christian Capital*. Berkeley: University of California Press.

Meredith, Anthony. 1999. *Gregory of Nyssa*. Oxford: Routledge.

Metaxas, Eric. 2010. *Bonhoeffer: Pastor, Martyr, Prophet, Spy*. Nashville, TN: Thomas Nelson.

Moore, John C. 2009. *Pope Innocent III (1160/61–1216): To Root Up and to Plant*. Notre Dame, IN: University of Notre Dame Press.

Mullin, Robert Bruce. 2002. *The Puritan as Yankee: A Life of Horace Bushnell*. Grand Rapids, MI: Eerdmans.

Murphy, Daniel. 1995. *Comenius*. Dublin: Irish Academic Press.

Murray, Iain H. 2009. *The Forgotten Spurgeon*. Carlisle, PA: Banner of Truth.

———. 2013. *Life of Martyn Lloyd-Jones: 1899–1981*. Carlisle, PA: Banner of Truth.

Navia, Luis A. 2007. *Socrates: A Life Examined*. Amherst, NY: Prometheus Books.

O'Brien, Michael. 1998. *Hesburgh: A Biography*. Washington, DC: Catholic University of America Press.

Osborn, Eric. 2005. *Irenaeus of Lyons*. Cambridge, UK: Cambridge University Press.

———. 2008. *Clement of Alexandria*. Cambridge, UK: Cambridge University Press.

Pennington, M. Basil. 2002. *Aelred of Rievaulx: The Way of Friendship*. Hyde Park, NY: New City Press.

Perret-Clermont, Anne-Nelly, and Jean-Marc Barrelet. 2008. *Jean Piaget and Neuchâtel: The Learner and the Scholar*. New York: Psychology Press.

Peters, Michael. 2008. *Robert Raikes: The Founder of Sunday School 1780*. Enumclaw, WA: Pleasant Word.

Ratisbonne, Abbé Theodore. 2009. *St. Bernard of Clairvaux*. Rockford, IL: TAN Books and Publishers.

Rayburn, Jim, III. 2000. *From Bondage to Liberty: Dance, Children, Dance*. Houston, TX: Morningstar Press.

Richardson, Robert D. 2007. *William James: In the Maelstrom of American Modernism*. New York: Mariner Books.

Roper, Hohn Herbert, Sr. 2012. *The Magnificent Mays: A Biography of Benjamin Elijah Mays*. Columbia: University of South Carolina Press.

Russell, Norman. 2000. *Cyril of Alexandria*. Oxford: Routledge.

Schmemann, Matushka Juliana. 2007. *My Journey with Father Alexander*. Montreal: Alexander Press.

Stacpoole-Kenny, Louise. 2009. *St. Francis De Sales: A Biography of the Gentle Saint*. Rockford, IL: TAN Books and Publishers.

Standing, E. M. 1998. *Maria Montessori: Her Life and Work*. New York: Plume.

Steer, Roger, and David Neff. 2010. *Basic Christian: The Inside Story of John Stott*. Downers Grove, IL: IVP Books.

Strobert, Nelson T. 2012. *Daniel Alexander Payne: The Venerable Preceptor of the African Methodist Episcopal Church*. Lanham, MD: University Press of America.

Taylor, A. E. 2011. *Plato: The Man and His Work*. Mineola, NY: Dover Publications.

———. 2012. *Aristotle*. Mineola, NY: Dover Publications.

Tomkins, Stephen. 2003. *John Wesley: A Biography*. Grand Rapids, MI: Eerdmans.

Trigg, Joseph W. 1998. *Origen*. Oxford: Routledge.

Trueman, Carl R. 2007. *John Owen: Reformed Catholic, Renaissance Man*. Surrey, UK: Ashgate.

Turner, Denys. 2013. *Thomas Aquinas: A Portrait*. New Haven, CT: Yale University.

Tyler, Peter. 2010. *St. John of the Cross*. New York: Continuum.

Van Kaam, Adrian L., and Susan Muto. 2010. *The Life Journey of a Joyful Man of God*. Eugene, OR: Wipf & Stock.

Ward, Benedicta. 2009. *Anselm of Canterbury: His Life and Legacy*. London: SPCK.

Washington, Sondra. 2006. *The Story of Nannie Helen Burroughs*. Nashville, TN: Woman's Missionary Union, SBC.

Weigold, Isabel. 2007. *Hannah Moore: A Biography of a Nineteenth Century Missionary and Teacher*. Bloomington, IN: iUniverse.

Welchman, Kit. 2000. *Erik Erikson: His Life, Work and Significance*. Berkshire, UK: Open University Press.

Wengert, Timothy J. 2010. *Philip Melanchton, Speaker of the Reformation: Wittenberg's Other Reformer*. Surrey, UK: Ashgate Variorum.

White, Charles Edward. 2008. *The Beauty of Holiness: Phoebe Palmer as Theologian, Revivalist, Feminist, and Humanitarian*. Eugene, OR: Wipf & Stock.

Wilson, A. N. 2002. *C. S. Lewis: A Biography*. New York: W.W. Norton.

Yarnold, E. J. 2000. *Cyril of Jerusalem*. Oxford: Routledge.

Educational Law and Policies

Aguiar, Ron. 2008. *Keeping Your Church Safe*. Maitland, FL: Xulon Press.

Berg, Thomas C. 2007. *The First Amendment: The Free Exercise of Religion Clause*. Bill of Rights Series. Amherst, NY: Prometheus Books.

Betts, Julian R., and Tom Loveless. 2005. *Getting Choice Right: Ensuring Equity and Efficiency in Education Policy*. Washington, DC: Brookings Institution Press.

Bolick, Clint. 2003. *Voucher Wars: Waging the Legal Battle over School Choice*. Washington, DC: Cato Institute.

Bradley, Leo H. 2005. *School Law for Public, Private, and Parochial Educators*. Lanham, MD: Rowman & Littlefield.

Brighouse, Harry. 2003. *School Choice and Social Justice*. New York: Oxford University Press.

Budde, Michael L., and John Wright. 2004. *Conflicting Allegiances: The Church-Based University in a Liberal Democratic Society*. Grand Rapids, MI: Brazos Press.

Carl, Jim. 2011. *Freedom of Choice: Vouchers in American Education*. Praeger Series on American Political Culture. Santa Barbara, CA: Praeger.

Cirtin, Robert M. 2005. *Church Safety and Security: A Practical Guide*. Lima, OH: CSS Publishing Company.

Cobble, James F., Jr., Richard R. Hammar, and Steven W. Klipowicz. 2004. *Reducing the Risk II: Making Your Church Safe from Child Sexual Abuse*. Indianapolis, IN: Christian Ministry Resources.

Cookson, Catherine. 2001. *Regulating Religion: The Courts and the Free Exercise Clause*. New York: Oxford University Press.

Couser, Richard. 1993. *Ministry and the American Legal System*. Minneapolis, MN: Augsburg Fortress Publishers.

Crabtree, Jack. 2008. *Better Safe Than Sued: Keeping Your Students and Ministry Alive*. Grand Rapids, MI: Zondervan/ Youth Specialties.

Dayton, John. 2012. *Education Law: Principles, Policies & Practice*. CreateSpace Independent Publishing Platform.

Duncan, Ann W., and Steven L. Jones. 2008. *Church State Issues in America Today*. Westport, CT: Praeger Publishers.

Dunklee, Dennis R., and Robert J. Shoop. 2006. *The Principal's Quick-Reference Guide to School Law: Reducing Liability, Litigation, and Other Potential Legal Tangles*. Thousand Oaks, CA: Corwin Press.

Garry, Patrick M. 2007. *Wrestling with God: The Courts' Tortuous Treatment of Religion*. Washington, DC: Catholic University of America Press.

Gaustad, Edwin S. 2003. *Proclaim Liberty throughout All the Land: A History of Church and State in America*. Religion in American Life Series. New York: Oxford University Press.

Gill, Brian P., Michael Timpane, Karen E. Ross, Dominic J. Brewer, and Kevin Booker. 2007. *Rhetoric Versus Reality: What We Know and What We Need to Know about Vouchers and Charter Schools*. Santa Monica, CA: Rand Publishing.

Glover, Voyle A. 2005. *Protecting Your Church against Sexual Predators: Legal FAQs for Church Leaders*. Grand Rapids, MI: Kregel Academic & Professional.

Graham, Donovan L. 2011. *Making a Difference: Christian Educators in Public Schools*. Colorado Springs, CO: Purposeful Design Publications.

Green, Steven K. 2012. *The Bible, the School, and the Constitution: The Clash That Shaped Modern Church-State Doctrine*. New York: Oxford University Press.

Greene, Jay P. 2006. *Education Myths: What Special Interest Groups Want You to Believe about Our Schools and Why It Isn't So.* Lanham, MD: Rowman & Littlefield.

Grenz, Stanley J., and Roy D. Bell. 2011. *Betrayal of Trust: Confronting and Preventing Clergy Sexual Misconduct.* Grand Rapids, MI: Baker Books.

Griffin, Leslie C. 2010. *Law and Religion: Cases in Context.* Law & Business Series. New York: Wolters & Kluwer—Aspen Publishers.

Hammar, Richard R. 2007. *Pastor, Church & Law.* 4th ed. Indianapolis, IN: Christian Ministry Resources.

———. 2010. *Essential Guide to Copyright Law for Churches.* Carol Stream, IL: Your Church Resources/Christia.

Harder, Jeanette. 2010. *Let the Children Come: Preparing Faith Communities to End Child Abuse and Neglect.* Scottdale, PA: Herald Press.

Henze, Mark E. 2012. *Foundations & Cornerstones.* Denver: Aletheian Press.

Hopkins, Bruce R., and David Middlebrook. 2008. *Nonprofit Law for Religious Organizations: Essential Questions & Answers.* Hoboken, NJ: John Wiley & Sons.

House, H. Wayne. 1999. *Christian Ministries and the Law: What Church and Para-Church Leaders Should Know.* Grand Rapids, MI: Kregel Academic & Professional.

Imber, Michael, and Till Van Geel. 2010. *Education Law.* 4th ed. New York: Routledge.

Klicka, Christopher J. 2001. *Home Schooling: The Right Choice; An Academic, Historical, Practical, and Legal Perspective.* Nashville, TN: B & H Publishing.

Lantz, Charles Craig. 2012. *Church Law: A Concise Legal Handbook for Ministers, Pastors, and Church Leaders.* Vol. 1. CreateSpace Independent Publishing Platform.

MacMullen, Ian. 2007. *Faith in Schools? Autonomy, Citizenship, and Religious Education in the Liberal State.* Princeton, NJ: Princeton University Press.

Marshall, Paul, Lela Gilbert, and Nina Shea. 2013. *Persecuted: The Global Assault on Christians.* Nashville,TN: Thomas Nelson.

Melton, Joy Thornburg. 2003. *Safe Sanctuaries: Reducing the Risk of Abuse in the Church for Children and Youth.* Nashville, TN: Abingdon Press.

Parker, Dalene Vickery. 2012. *Christian Teachers in Public Schools: 13 Essentials for the Classroom.* Kansas City, MO: Beacon Hill Press.

Paul, Ron. 2013. *The School Revolution: A New Answer for Our Broken Education System.* New York: Grand Central Publishing.

Poe, Harry Lee. 2004. *Christianity in the Academy: Teaching at the Intersection of Faith and Learning.* RenewedMinds. Grand Rapids, MI: Baker Academic.

Progressive Business Publications. 2004. *Private School Law in America.* Malvern, PA: Center for Education & Employment.

Radan, Peter, Denise Meyerson, and Rosalinda F. Croucher. 2005. *Law and Religion.* Routledge Studies in Religion Series. New York: Routledge.

Robinson, David A. 2012. *Some Tips to Prevent Employment Discrimination Lawsuits: A Faith-Based Legal Guide for Managers.* Bloomington, IN: WestBow Press.

Russo, Charles J. 2008. *Encyclopedia of Education Law.* Thousand Oaks, CA: Sage Publications.

———. 2012. *Religion in Schools.* Debating Issues in American Education: A SAGE Reference Set. Thousand Oaks, CA: Sage Publications.

Russo, Charles J., Allan G. Osborne Jr., Joseph D. Massucci, and Gerald M. Cattaro. 2009. *The Law of Special Education and Non-Public Schools: Major Challenges in Meeting the Needs of Youth with Disabilities.* Lanham, MD: Rowman &Littlefield Education.

Schimmel, David, Louis Fischer, and Leslie R. Stellman. 2008. *School Law: What Every Educator Should Know, a User-Friendly Guide.* Boston: Allyn & Bacon.

Schneider, Frank, Jr. 2007. *The Establishment Clause and the City on a Hill.* Bloomington IN: Xlibris Corp.

Shaughnessy, Mary Angela. 1998. *Ministry and the Law: What You Need to Know.* Mahwah, NJ: Paulist Press.

Strasser, Mark. 2011. *Religion, Education and the State—An Unprincipled Doctrine in Search of Moorings.* Burlington, VT: Ashgate Publishing.

Swagman, Beth. 2009. *Preventing Child Abuse: Creating a Safe Place.* Discover Your Bible. Grand Rapids, MI: Faith Alive Christian Resources.

Swope, Cheryl. 2013. *Simply Classical: A Beautiful Education for Any Child.* Louisville, KY: Memoria Press.

Thoburn, John, and Rob Baker. 2011. *Clergy Sexual Misconduct: A Systems Approach to Prevention, Intervention, and Oversight.* Carefree, AZ: Gentle Path Press.

Tienken, Christopher H., and Donald C. Orlich. 2013. *The School Reform Landscape: Fraud, Myth, and Lies.* Lanham, MD: Rowan & Littlefield Education.

Toma, J. Douglas, and Richard L. Palm. 1998. *The Academic Administrator and the Law: What Every Dean and Department Chair Needs to Know.* New York: John Wiley & Sons.

Viteritti, Joseph P. 2001. *Choosing Equality: School Choice, the Constitution, and Civil Society.* Washington, DC: Brookings Institution Press.

———. 2007. *The Last Freedom: Religion from the Public School to the Public Square.* Princeton, NJ: Princeton University Press.

Walberg, Herbert J. 2007. *School Choice: The Findings.* Washington, DC: Cato Institute.

Weinberg, Lawrence D. 2007. *Religious Charter Schools: Legalities and Practicalities.* New Developments in the Politics of Education Series. Charlotte, NC: Information Age Publishing.

Wilson, Douglas. 2003. *The Case for Classical Christian Education.* Wheaton, IL: Crossway.

Wolfe, Alan. 2003. *School Choice: The Moral Debate.* Princeton, NJ: Princeton University Press.

Appendix A: World Statistics on Christian Populations

*Todd Johnson, associate professor of Global Christianity
and the director of the Center for the Study of Global Christianity*

World Populations and Educational Statistics

Country	UN Region	Population 2010	Education				
			Enrollment %	Schools	Universities	Literacy %	Internet %
Afghanistan	South-central Asia	31,412,000	43	2,600	5	28	2
Albania	Southern Europe	3,204,000	69	2,300	8	99	15
Algeria	Northern Africa	35,468,000	74	17,400	40	70	7
American Samoa	Polynesia	68,400	99	38	2	99	22
Andorra	Southern Europe	84,900	63	18	0	100	56
Angola	Middle Africa	19,082,000	26	6,300	1	68	1
Anguilla	Caribbean	15,400	90	7	0	90	32
Antigua & Barbuda	Caribbean	88,700	90	56	1	90	64
Argentina	South America	40,412,000	90	31,700	1,500	97	21
Armenia	Western Asia	3,092,000	71	1,400	14	99	6
Aruba	Caribbean	107,000	97	56	1	97	24
Australia	Australia/New Zealand	22,268,000	113	9,900	95	100	52
Austria	Western Europe	8,394,000	92	6,300	44	100	51
Azerbaijan	Western Asia	9,188,000	67	4,600	23	99	10
Bahamas	Caribbean	343,000	71	230	1	95	34
Bahrain	Western Asia	1,262,000	86	120	4	87	28
Bangladesh	South-central Asia	148,692,000	56	62,400	1,000	47	0
Barbados	Caribbean	273,000	89	140	1	100	93
Belarus	Eastern Europe	9,595,000	89	5,000	38	100	56
Belgium	Western Europe	10,712,000	96	6,700	21	100	47
Belize	Central America	312,000	82	270	4	93	11
Benin	Western Africa	8,850,000	51	3,000	13	35	1
Bermuda	Northern America	64,900	98	36	1	98	70
Bhutan	South-central Asia	726,000	42	190	2	43	4
Bolivia	South America	9,930,000	87	10,500	10	87	6
Bosnia-Herzegovina	Southern Europe	3,760,000	87	2,400	44	97	24
Botswana	Southern Africa	2,007,000	70	1,000	1	81	5
Brazil	South America	194,946,000	88	208,000	870	89	23
British Virgin Islands	Caribbean	23,200	95	18	1	93	35
Brunei	Southeastern Asia	399,000	78	190	4	93	42
Bulgaria	Eastern Europe	7,494,000	82	3,900	88	98	47
Burkina Faso	Western Africa	16,469,000	29	2,900	9	22	1
Burundi	Eastern Africa	8,383,000	38	1,500	8	60	1
Cambodia	Southeastern Asia	14,138,000	60	5,000	9	74	0

(continued)

World Populations and Educational Statistics (*continued*)

Country	UN Region	Population 2010	Education Enrollment %	Schools	Universities	Literacy %	Internet %
Cameroon	Middle Africa	19,599,000	63	6,800	5	68	2
Canada	Northern America	34,017,000	100	16,200	270	100	77
Cape Verde	Western Africa	496,000	67	370	3	82	6
Cayman Islands	Caribbean	56,200	95	20	1	93	46
Central African Republic	Middle Africa	4,401,000	30	980	1	49	0
Chad	Middle Africa	11,227,000	38	2,600	4	27	1
Channel Islands	Northern Europe	153,000	95	50	2	98	22
Chile	South America	17,114,000	83	8,600	200	96	25
China	Eastern Asia	1,341,335,000	70	954,000	1,100	91	10
Colombia	South America	46,295,000	76	44,700	240	93	14
Comoros	Eastern Africa	735,000	46	280	2	56	3
Congo	Middle Africa	4,043,000	51	1,600	120	85	2
Congo DR	Middle Africa	65,966,000	34	13,000	0	67	0
Cook Islands	Polynesia	20,300	90	35	0	92	27
Costa Rica	Central America	4,659,000	73	3,700	6	95	28
Cote d'Ivoire	Western Africa	19,738,000	40	7,200	1	50	2
Croatia	Southern Europe	4,403,000	74	2,400	54	98	37
Cuba	Caribbean	11,258,000	88	12,200	35	100	2
Cyprus	Western Asia	1,104,000	78	580	32	97	42
Czech Republic	Eastern Europe	10,493,000	83	5,300	23	100	35
Denmark	Northern Europe	5,550,000	103	3,000	240	100	58
Djibouti	Eastern Africa	889,000	26	82	1	67	1
Dominica	Caribbean	67,800	81	77	2	94	37
Dominican Republic	Caribbean	9,927,000	74	6,200	7	87	16
Ecuador	South America	14,465,000	91	18,400	21	91	12
Egypt	Northern Africa	81,121,000	55	19,200	12	71	8
El Salvador	Central America	6,193,000	70	3,800	6	81	10
Equatorial Guinea	Middle Africa	700,000	58	710	4	87	2
Eritrea	Eastern Africa	5,254,000	35	580	1	58	2
Estonia	Northern Europe	1,341,000	93	820	22	100	55
Ethiopia	Eastern Africa	82,950,000	42	8,100	11	36	0
Faeroe Islands	Northern Europe	48,700	99	77	1	100	72
Falkland Islands	South America	3,000	90	2	0	98	84
Fiji	Melanesia	861,000	75	690	5	93	9
Finland	Northern Europe	5,365,000	102	5,500	20	100	56
France	Western Europe	62,787,000	97	53,000	1,100	100	50
French Guiana	South America	231,000	91	110	1	83	21
French Polynesia	Polynesia	271,000	95	320	4	100	25
Gabon	Middle Africa	1,505,000	70	1,000	1	84	6
Gambia	Western Africa	1,728,000	50	280	9	40	5
Georgia	Western Asia	4,352,000	76	3,800	19	100	7
Germany	Western Europe	82,302,000	88	18,900	310	100	47
Ghana	Western Africa	24,392,000	51	16,700	16	58	3
Gibraltar	Southern Europe	29,200	95	22	1	99	22
Greece	Southern Europe	11,359,000	99	11,300	17	96	18
Greenland	Northern America	57,300	100	88	2	100	91
Grenada	Caribbean	104,000	73	76	1	85	21
Guadeloupe	Caribbean	461,000	90	420	1	90	18
Guam	Micronesia	180,000	99	63	1	100	38
Guatemala	Central America	14,389,000	67	12,700	5	69	10
Guinea	Western Africa	9,982,000	45	2,800	10	30	1
Guinea-Bissau	Western Africa	1,515,000	37	650	4	42	2
Guyana	South America	754,000	86	520	1	99	23
Haiti	Caribbean	9,993,000	52	6,700	2	52	8
Holy See	Southern Europe	460	100	1	1	100	90
Honduras	Central America	7,601,000	71	8,800	10	80	5

Country	UN Region	Population 2010	Education Enrollment %	Schools	Universities	Literacy %	Internet %
Hong Kong	Eastern Asia	7,053,000	76	860	9	92	53
Hungary	Eastern Europe	9,984,000	90	5,100	91	99	35
Iceland	Northern Europe	320,000	96	80	5	100	65
India	South-central Asia	1,224,614,000	64	813,000	8,000	61	11
Indonesia	Southeastern Asia	239,871,000	69	181,000	1,000	90	5
Iran	South-central Asia	73,974,000	73	81,100	0	77	26
Iraq	Western Asia	31,672,000	59	11,000	20	74	0
Ireland	Northern Europe	4,470,000	100	4,100	26	100	34
Isle of Man	Northern Europe	82,900	95	40	1	96	63
Israel	Western Asia	7,418,000	90	3,100	7	97	28
Italy	Southern Europe	60,551,000	91	38,500	50	98	53
Jamaica	Caribbean	2,741,000	78	930	15	80	49
Japan	Eastern Asia	126,536,000	86	48,000	1,200	100	68
Jordan	Western Asia	6,187,000	78	3,300	55	90	14
Kazakhstan	South-central Asia	16,026,000	94	12,000	61	100	9
Kenya	Eastern Africa	40,513,000	61	18,500	14	74	8
Kiribati	Micronesia	99,500	75	110	0	90	2
Kosovo	Southern Europe	2,084,000	65	1,000	30	93	13
Kuwait	Western Asia	2,737,000	75	670	1	93	29
Kyrgyzstan	South-central Asia	5,334,000	78	3,400	12	99	12
Laos	Southeastern Asia	6,201,000	62	9,200	9	69	1
Latvia	Northern Europe	2,252,000	90	980	14	100	47
Lebanon	Western Asia	4,228,000	85	2,100	20	88	26
Lesotho	Southern Africa	2,171,000	66	1,400	1	82	3
Liberia	Western Africa	3,994,000	57	2,100	3	52	0
Libya	Northern Africa	6,355,000	94	4,500	10	84	4
Liechtenstein	Western Europe	36,000	86	23	0	100	64
Lithuania	Northern Europe	3,324,000	92	2,500	14	100	32
Luxembourg	Western Europe	507,000	85	100	1	100	72
Macau	Eastern Asia	544,000	76	61	4	91	47
Macedonia	Southern Europe	2,061,000	70	1,100	27	96	13
Madagascar	Eastern Africa	20,714,000	60	14,800	5	71	1
Malawi	Eastern Africa	14,901,000	63	3,200	4	64	0
Malaysia	Southeastern Asia	28,401,000	75	8,400	54	89	54
Maldives	South-central Asia	316,000	66	260	0	96	9
Mali	Western Africa	15,370,000	37	1,800	7	19	1
Malta	Southern Europe	417,000	81	190	1	88	34
Marshall Islands	Micronesia	54,000	71	120	0	91	4
Martinique	Caribbean	406,000	98	360	1	97	27
Mauritania	Western Africa	3,460,000	46	1,700	4	52	1
Mauritius	Eastern Africa	1,299,000	76	420	2	84	25
Mayotte	Eastern Africa	204,000	40	95	1	86	3
Mexico	Central America	113,423,000	76	113,000	13,000	91	19
Micronesia	Micronesia	111,000	92	190	1	92	14
Moldova	Eastern Europe	3,573,000	70	1,700	18	98	17
Monaco	Western Europe	35,400	99	6	0	100	56
Mongolia	Eastern Asia	2,756,000	78	710	9	98	12
Montenegro	Southern Europe	631,000	75	290	10	96	44
Montserrat	Caribbean	5,900	90	15	1	82	25
Morocco	Northern Africa	31,951,000	59	6,500	50	52	20
Mozambique	Eastern Africa	23,391,000	53	4,000	2	40	1
Myanmar	Southeastern Asia	47,963,000	50	38,800	40	90	0
Namibia	Southern Africa	2,283,000	65	1,100	7	85	4
Nauru	Micronesia	10,300	51	6	1	99	5
Nepal	Southcentral Asia	29,959,000	58	26,800	3	49	1
Netherlands	Western Europe	16,613,000	99	10,900	210	100	86
Netherlands Antilles	Caribbean	201,000	97	140	1	97	5

(continued)

World Populations and Educational Statistics (*continued*)

Country	UN Region	Population 2010	Education				
			Enrollment %	Schools	Universities	Literacy %	Internet %
New Caledonia	Melanesia	251,000	96	340	6	96	33
New Zealand	Australia/New Zealand	4,368,000	109	2,800	7	100	79
Nicaragua	Central America	5,788,000	71	7,500	4	77	3
Niger	Western Africa	15,512,000	23	2,800	3	29	0
Nigeria	Western Africa	158,423,000	56	44,700	31	69	6
Niue	Polynesia	1,500	70	2	0	96	50
North Korea	Eastern Asia	24,346,000	80	6,100	280	95	0
N. Mariana Islands	Micronesia	60,900	96	27	1	99	22
Norway	Northern Europe	4,883,000	99	4,100	200	100	82
Oman	Western Asia	2,782,000	67	570	5	81	11
Pakistan	South-central Asia	173,593,000	40	156,000	800	50	8
Palau	Micronesia	20,500	87	32	1	100	4
Palestine	Western Asia	4,039,000	83	500	1	92	7
Panama	Central America	3,517,000	80	3,100	8	92	15
Papua New Guinea	Melanesia	6,858,000	41	3,200	2	57	2
Paraguay	South America	6,455,000	70	6,300	2	94	4
Peru	South America	29,077,000	86	63,600	660	88	23
Philippines	Southeastern Asia	93,261,000	81	42,200	810	93	6
Poland	Eastern Europe	38,277,000	88	31,800	140	100	37
Portugal	Southern Europe	10,676,000	90	14,100	250	94	30
Puerto Rico	Caribbean	3,749,000	94	2,000	45	94	25
Qatar	Western Asia	1,759,000	78	200	1	89	35
Reunion	Eastern Africa	846,000	88	440	1	88	26
Romania	Eastern Europe	21,486,000	77	16,800	63	97	52
Russia	Eastern Europe	142,958,000	89	72,600	570	99	18
Rwanda	Eastern Africa	10,624,000	51	1,700	3	65	1
Saint Helena	Western Africa	4,100	75	8	0	98	26
Saint Kitts & Nevis	Caribbean	52,400	73	5	0	90	32
Saint Lucia	Caribbean	174,000	75	84	0	90	62
Saint Pierre & Miquelon	Northern America	6,000	80	9	0	99	22
Saint Vincent	Caribbean	109,000	69	60	0	96	29
Samoa	Polynesia	183,000	74	210	6	99	4
San Marino	Southern Europe	31,500	99	17	0	99	57
Sao Tome & Principe	Middle Africa	165,000	65	64	2	85	14
Saudi Arabia	Western Asia	27,448,000	76	17,300	72	79	19
Senegal	Western Africa	12,434,000	40	2,800	18	40	5
Serbia	Southern Europe	7,772,000	75	3,700	110	96	13
Seychelles	Eastern Africa	86,500	83	45	1	92	36
Sierra Leone	Western Africa	5,868,000	45	2,000	2	35	0
Singapore	Southeastern Asia	5,086,000	93	390	7	93	59
Slovakia	Eastern Europe	5,462,000	79	3,400	14	100	42
Slovenia	Southern Europe	2,030,000	95	1,100	28	100	64
Solomon Islands	Melanesia	538,000	48	540	1	76	2
Somalia	Eastern Africa	9,331,000	10	1,300	1	25	1
South Africa	Southern Africa	50,133,000	77	22,400	32	82	8
South Korea	Eastern Asia	48,184,000	96	10,300	640	98	71
South Sudan	Northern Africa	10,798,000	37	2,700	6	62	9
Spain	Southern Europe	46,077,000	98	42,300	1,400	98	43
Sri Lanka	South-central Asia	20,860,000	64	18,700	8	91	2
Sudan	Northern Africa	32,754,000	37	8,000	18	62	9
Suriname	South America	525,000	77	450	1	90	8
Swaziland	Southern Africa	1,186,000	60	700	1	80	4
Sweden	Northern Europe	9,380,000	96	5,400	100	100	77
Switzerland	Western Europe	7,664,000	86	3,000	12	100	58

Country	UN Region	Population 2010	Education				
			Enrollment %	Schools	Universities	Literacy %	Internet %
Syria	Western Asia	20,411,000	65	10,200	47	80	8
Taiwan	Eastern Asia	23,216,000	100	3,700	120	97	59
Tajikistan	South-central Asia	6,879,000	71	3,400	22	99	0
Tanzania	Eastern Africa	44,841,000	51	10,900	4	70	1
Thailand	Southeastern Asia	69,122,000	72	37,400	84	93	13
Timor-Leste	Southeastern Asia	1,124,000	72	750	5	48	0
Togo	Western Africa	6,028,000	55	2,600	1	53	5
Tokelau Islands	Polynesia	1,100	70	1	0	99	8
Tonga	Polynesia	104,000	80	160	1	99	3
Trinidad & Tobago	Caribbean	1,341,000	65	580	1	98	22
Tunisia	Northern Africa	10,481,000	77	5,000	0	74	13
Turkey	Western Asia	72,752,000	69	50,700	420	87	18
Turkmenistan	South-central Asia	5,042,000	98	1,800	9	99	1
Turks & Caicos Islands	Caribbean	38,400	90	20	0	93	4
Tuvalu	Polynesia	9,800	70	11	0	95	19
Uganda	Eastern Africa	33,425,000	63	8,800	9	67	5
Ukraine	Eastern Europe	45,448,000	87	22,400	160	99	20
United Arab Emirates	Western Asia	7,512,000	61	360	1	89	37
United Kingdom	Northern Europe	62,036,000	93	28,200	820	100	63
United States	Northern America	310,384,000	94	85,400	5,800	100	70
U.S. Virgin Islands	Caribbean	109,000	95	20	1	95	27
Uruguay	South America	3,369,000	89	2,900	2	97	24
Uzbekistan	South-central Asia	27,445,000	74	9,300	52	99	4
Vanuatu	Melanesia	240,000	64	270	1	74	3
Venezuela	South America	28,980,000	75	17,400	100	93	15
Vietnam	Southeastern Asia	87,848,000	64	19,800	100	90	17
Wallis & Futuna Islands	Polynesia	13,600	85	20	0	95	4
Western Sahara	Northern Africa	530,000	45	45	1	10	0
Yemen	Western Asia	24,053,000	55	7,300	1	54	1
Zambia	Eastern Africa	13,089,000	61	4,000	2	68	4
Zimbabwe	Eastern Africa	12,571,000	53	6,200	28	89	9
Africa	*Africa*	*1,022,234,000*	*51*	*303,000*	*560*	*62*	*5*
Asia	*Asia*	*4,164,252,000*	*67*	*2,675,000*	*16,100*	*79*	*13*
Europe	*Europe*	*738,199,000*	*90*	*443,000*	*6,400*	*99*	*41*
Latin America	*Latin America*	*590,082,000*	*81*	*596,000*	*16,800*	*90*	*19*
Northern America	*Northern America*	*344,529,000*	*94*	*102,000*	*6,000*	*100*	*71*
Oceania	*Oceania*	*36,593,000*	*96*	*19,000*	*140*	*93*	*42*
Global Total	**Globe**	**6,895,889,000**	**70**	**4,138,000**	**46,000**	**82**	**18**

Christian Populations and Distribution of Scripture

Country	Christians		Scripture Distribution					
			Portions		New Testaments		Bibles	
	2010	%	Goal	% Met	Goal	% Met	Goal	% Met
Afghanistan	32,400	0.1	4,777,000	0.3	4,200	289.5	1,300	374.6
Albania	1,011,000	31.6	2,446,000	10.4	772,000	46.5	212,000	124.9
Algeria	61,800	0.2	18,091,000	0.5	31,500	391.5	6,200	975.0
American Samoa	67,300	98.4	42,300	35.1	41,000	65.5	9,400	244.3
Andorra	78,300	92.3	69,300	4.2	61,500	6.2	25,100	12.5
Angola	17,799,000	93.3	6,975,000	14.1	6,091,000	31.3	2,375,000	59.7
Anguilla	14,000	91.2	10,700	13.2	9,100	28.6	2,900	62.3
Antigua & Barbuda	82,500	93.0	61,900	12.9	49,300	30.2	18,200	57.8

(continued)

Christian Populations and Distribution of Scripture (*continued*)

| | Christians | | Scripture Distribution | | | | | |
| | | | Portions | | New Testaments | | Bibles | |
Country	2010	%	Goal	% Met	Goal	% Met	Goal	% Met
Argentina	36,430,000	90.2	29,509,000	40.0	26,490,000	77.2	11,018,000	132.5
Armenia	2,891,000	93.5	2,453,000	72.6	2,291,000	76.8	611,000	130.7
Aruba	104,000	96.8	84,500	62.5	78,300	101.8	26,900	295.9
Australia	16,204,000	72.8	18,040,000	81.1	10,856,000	118.4	4,467,000	144.8
Austria	6,508,000	77.5	7,158,000	13.1	5,217,000	34.7	2,353,000	56.9
Azerbaijan	304,000	3.3	7,182,000	4.9	237,000	76.2	62,500	70.8
Bahamas	320,000	93.3	252,000	112.7	220,000	253.8	74,700	740.8
Bahrain	94,300	7.5	875,000	56.2	65,300	1,486.0	12,600	7,132.2
Bangladesh	739,000	0.5	48,454,000	6.4	240,000	1,216.5	65,900	712.0
Barbados	260,000	95.1	225,000	11.2	162,000	29.0	53,100	60.1
Belarus	7,082,000	73.8	8,123,000	3.3	5,600,000	7.6	2,059,000	19.4
Belgium	7,661,000	71.5	8,905,000	13.7	6,343,000	30.3	2,826,000	39.2
Belize	284,000	91.1	188,000	52.3	164,000	115.3	51,500	363.5
Benin	3,874,000	43.8	1,765,000	35.9	771,000	133.8	254,000	337.0
Bermuda	58,000	89.3	49,300	39.7	39,600	80.6	19,600	96.5
Bhutan	6,700	0.9	220,000	2.5	2,000	419.9	540	829.0
Bolivia	9,181,000	92.5	5,512,000	172.2	5,080,000	304.6	2,091,000	158.8
Bosnia-Herzegovina	1,817,000	48.3	3,086,000	0.2	1,486,000	0.7	486,000	1.1
Botswana	1,378,000	68.7	1,098,000	24.4	630,000	53.4	164,000	186.6
Brazil	177,304,000	91.0	128,782,000	417.2	117,006,000	749.1	37,369,000	1,183.2
British Virgin Islands	19,600	84.3	15,300	25.8	10,500	72.0	3,700	144.2
Brunei	54,800	13.7	273,000	21.6	36,700	171.4	8,600	686.2
Bulgaria	6,216,000	82.9	6,351,000	7.8	5,262,000	16.5	1,848,000	42.6
Burkina Faso	3,691,000	22.4	2,001,000	21.1	448,000	168.6	132,000	493.1
Burundi	7,725,000	92.2	3,106,000	42.6	2,641,000	61.2	924,000	116.3
Cambodia	343,000	2.4	7,139,000	5.3	173,000	299.7	45,400	690.2
Cameroon	11,381,000	58.1	7,964,000	10.8	4,052,000	37.8	1,311,000	109.4
Canada	23,515,000	69.1	28,431,000	72.3	16,869,000	202.5	7,475,000	259.8
Cape Verde	471,000	95.0	276,000	21.1	262,000	40.7	75,400	139.7
Cayman Islands	45,600	81.1	37,100	33.0	22,200	105.8	7,800	297.2
Central African Republic	3,139,000	71.3	1,283,000	8.7	711,000	29.6	254,000	59.7
Chad	3,905,000	34.8	1,638,000	10.2	482,000	61.6	227,000	99.5
Channel Islands	131,000	85.4	128,000	14.1	83,900	18.2	49,300	27.8
Chile	15,168,000	88.6	12,758,000	45.1	11,146,000	68.0	3,491,000	195.9
China	106,485,000	7.9	983,141,000	6.2	78,038,000	123.8	23,631,000	365.6
Colombia	44,305,000	95.7	30,616,000	97.4	28,944,000	105.1	7,522,000	325.3
Comoros	3,500	0.5	238,000	0.2	1,100	87.2	340	220.8
Congo	3,629,000	89.8	2,036,000	72.4	1,560,000	188.3	559,000	496.0
Congo DR	62,673,000	95.0	23,891,000	7.4	21,707,000	15.7	6,735,000	48.5
Cook Islands	19,600	96.6	11,600	46.1	10,700	95.6	3,400	254.7
Costa Rica	4,464,000	95.8	3,319,000	73.7	3,167,000	125.7	1,004,000	369.8
Cote d'Ivoire	6,772,000	34.3	5,822,000	18.2	1,903,000	103.9	597,000	328.4
Croatia	4,117,000	93.5	3,675,000	17.6	3,259,000	35.3	1,236,000	80.6
Cuba	6,667,000	59.2	9,290,000	64.3	5,368,000	118.4	1,755,000	125.4
Cyprus	793,000	71.9	879,000	80.3	609,000	230.7	211,000	45.8
Czech Republic	5,810,000	55.4	9,004,000	11.2	3,286,000	44.5	1,415,000	45.0
Denmark	4,646,000	83.7	4,551,000	25.9	3,712,000	63.1	2,058,000	54.1
Djibouti	15,500	1.7	383,000	0.3	6,500	30.2	1,800	103.5
Dominica	64,000	94.5	49,400	14.5	46,400	28.6	13,900	68.2
Dominican Republic	9,429,000	95.0	5,957,000	61.2	5,613,000	76.1	1,596,000	208.9
Ecuador	14,042,000	97.1	9,172,000	43.9	8,880,000	50.0	3,109,000	114.7
Egypt	8,183,000	10.1	39,567,000	21.8	3,987,000	248.9	1,189,000	390.3
El Salvador	5,977,000	96.5	3,394,000	139.1	3,262,000	191.8	979,000	488.4
Equatorial Guinea	621,000	88.7	370,000	14.3	324,000	29.3	118,000	74.7

	Christians		Scripture Distribution					
			Portions		New Testaments		Bibles	
Country	2010	%	Goal	% Met	Goal	% Met	Goal	% Met
Eritrea	2,517,000	47.9	1,774,000	7.2	849,000	29.6	363,000	62.9
Estonia	589,000	43.9	1,133,000	7.3	348,000	38.1	133,000	83.1
Ethiopia	49,671,000	59.9	17,641,000	15.4	10,535,000	47.3	4,000,000	117.9
Faeroe Islands	47,800	98.1	39,900	30.5	38,800	62.5	15,800	59.6
Falkland Islands	2,500	82.9	2,400	6.9	1,600	14.6	660	34.1
Fiji	550,000	63.9	570,000	21.2	361,000	63.5	84,800	229.7
Finland	4,336,000	80.8	4,477,000	16.3	3,430,000	38.7	1,787,000	70.5
France	41,275,000	65.7	51,257,000	23.5	33,099,000	61.0	15,594,000	111.5
French Guiana	195,000	84.4	128,000	74.3	108,000	70.5	47,500	134.0
French Polynesia	254,000	93.8	203,000	26.4	184,000	55.0	52,500	166.0
Gabon	1,272,000	84.5	817,000	36.4	656,000	73.6	254,000	185.2
Gambia	75,200	4.4	384,000	4.5	16,000	208.6	3,400	927.9
Georgia	3,703,000	85.1	3,615,000	2.3	3,073,000	3.2	898,000	4.3
Germany	57,617,000	70.0	71,210,000	42.9	45,837,000	78.1	23,034,000	92.2
Ghana	15,601,000	64.0	8,721,000	72.2	5,079,000	242.9	1,688,000	710.1
Gibraltar	25,800	88.2	23,900	6.5	20,600	9.2	7,800	21.5
Greece	10,430,000	91.8	9,317,000	97.5	8,534,000	208.9	3,027,000	17.3
Greenland	55,100	96.2	47,000	30.1	31,700	88.7	21,500	53.2
Grenada	101,000	96.7	64,400	22.2	61,700	43.4	23,000	83.7
Guadeloupe	442,000	96.0	322,000	85.2	308,000	159.2	117,000	273.8
Guam	169,000	93.9	131,000	31.3	120,000	64.6	41,400	113.5
Guatemala	14,010,000	97.4	5,828,000	172.1	5,400,000	311.8	1,709,000	944.6
Guinea	365,000	3.7	1,736,000	6.8	61,200	224.7	22,800	568.9
Guinea-Bissau	185,000	12.2	370,000	6.5	44,800	98.8	18,600	234.4
Guyana	413,000	54.7	494,000	44.2	269,000	61.8	79,300	172.9
Haiti	9,429,000	94.4	3,336,000	105.7	3,052,000	111.6	1,083,000	251.1
Holy See	460	100.4	390	0.0	390	0.0	220	0.0
Honduras	7,278,000	95.8	3,846,000	101.7	3,546,000	132.1	984,000	343.3
Hong Kong	957,000	13.6	5,760,000	39.8	761,000	374.7	210,000	847.6
Hungary	8,653,000	86.7	8,459,000	6.1	7,305,000	12.3	2,953,000	27.0
Iceland	303,000	94.7	254,000	31.6	233,000	68.8	101,000	83.9
India	57,265,000	4.7	518,921,000	21.8	24,205,000	679.1	6,227,000	866.0
Indonesia	29,089,000	12.1	158,234,000	20.8	18,901,000	322.5	5,757,000	554.0
Iran	270,000	0.4	43,919,000	0.4	150,000	115.4	38,200	174.1
Iraq	489,000	1.5	13,351,000	8.5	200,000	257.1	39,500	535.8
Ireland	4,207,000	94.1	3,522,000	8.0	2,870,000	13.2	934,000	22.4
Isle of Man	69,700	84.1	65,700	19.7	43,800	38.1	26,500	56.6
Israel	180,000	2.4	5,245,000	27.8	123,000	1,417.7	45,800	1,229.1
Italy	48,853,000	80.7	51,214,000	11.8	41,239,000	28.7	17,138,000	43.7
Jamaica	2,318,000	84.6	1,558,000	23.6	673,000	103.7	226,000	305.8
Japan	2,601,000	2.1	109,633,000	5.2	1,920,000	583.5	739,000	445.3
Jordan	171,000	2.8	3,481,000	5.2	95,300	321.7	25,400	668.6
Kazakhstan	4,249,000	26.5	12,043,000	2.2	3,147,000	5.9	1,042,000	15.2
Kenya	32,923,000	81.3	17,236,000	33.9	13,660,000	76.8	3,829,000	267.8
Kiribati	96,500	96.9	65,100	31.4	63,000	61.4	13,100	252.1
Kosovo	122,000	5.9	1,605,000	0.8	93,700	24.7	37,900	47.9
Kuwait	241,000	8.8	1,867,000	12.4	162,000	284.8	29,900	870.5
Kyrgyzstan	412,000	7.7	3,683,000	1.0	273,000	9.0	92,800	22.0
Laos	181,000	2.9	2,800,000	7.5	81,800	448.4	20,800	847.4
Latvia	1,552,000	68.9	1,935,000	8.6	1,332,000	20.4	499,000	42.0
Lebanon	1,503,000	35.6	2,791,000	164.4	989,000	599.7	248,000	646.5
Lesotho	1,992,000	91.7	1,117,000	30.9	862,000	33.1	287,000	97.1
Liberia	1,619,000	40.5	1,174,000	58.4	365,000	296.7	129,000	746.5
Libya	172,000	2.7	3,711,000	76.3	99,000	3,692.9	26,300	2,502.2
Liechtenstein	32,200	89.4	30,500	39.9	25,200	81.8	9,900	189.4

(continued)

Christian Populations and Distribution of Scripture (*continued*)

Country	Christians 2010	%	Scripture Distribution Portions Goal	% Met	New Testaments Goal	% Met	Bibles Goal	% Met
Lithuania	2,950,000	88.8	2,819,000	12.0	2,378,000	16.8	873,000	17.9
Luxembourg	418,000	82.4	418,000	9.2	342,000	16.3	148,000	21.7
Macau	39,300	7.2	432,000	22.6	31,000	390.3	8,700	865.7
Macedonia	1,311,000	63.6	1,632,000	4.8	1,038,000	11.3	286,000	20.8
Madagascar	11,789,000	56.9	8,354,000	15.6	4,632,000	45.2	1,732,000	94.3
Malawi	11,885,000	79.8	5,204,000	49.0	3,693,000	76.3	1,585,000	141.0
Malaysia	2,528,000	8.9	17,551,000	6.7	1,528,000	78.7	448,000	218.4
Maldives	1,400	0.4	223,000	0.5	960	186.9	180	526.2
Mali	498,000	3.2	1,568,000	10.7	50,700	580.6	17,100	1,426.9
Malta	408,000	98.0	311,000	145.7	292,000	123.3	95,400	96.0
Marshall Islands	51,600	95.5	35,800	34.7	33,700	69.6	5,300	281.7
Martinique	391,000	96.4	319,000	69.2	299,000	132.6	113,000	243.5
Mauritania	9,100	0.3	1,072,000	1.3	2,700	663.3	900	364.9
Mauritius	431,000	33.2	856,000	59.4	282,000	52.5	68,000	197.3
Mayotte	1,400	0.7	94,700	0.3	630	65.9	240	135.1
Mexico	108,721,000	95.9	73,195,000	32.9	69,343,000	49.7	19,178,000	126.8
Micronesia	105,000	94.5	65,100	38.6	60,400	78.8	13,600	217.5
Moldova	3,426,000	95.9	2,929,000	17.7	2,804,000	29.4	990,000	72.0
Monaco	30,500	86.1	28,900	23.1	24,500	53.2	13,600	92.5
Mongolia	46,000	1.7	1,951,000	0.6	32,200	59.5	9,300	180.9
Montenegro	488,000	77.3	492,000	8.3	380,000	20.7	157,000	40.3
Montserrat	5,500	92.7	3,800	16.5	3,500	33.1	1,100	73.5
Morocco	31,600	0.1	12,056,000	0.7	11,500	1,218.5	2,800	4,150.0
Mozambique	12,269,000	52.5	5,166,000	9.5	2,531,000	26.7	1,029,000	48.7
Myanmar	3,786,000	7.9	32,121,000	2.9	2,521,000	58.1	652,000	138.1
Namibia	2,082,000	91.2	1,236,000	40.0	1,012,000	84.5	332,000	256.5
Nauru	7,700	75.1	7,400	25.3	5,300	67.0	910	338.8
Nepal	908,000	3.0	9,304,000	43.0	282,000	2,597.0	80,200	1,194.5
Netherlands	10,517,000	63.3	13,672,000	26.2	6,591,000	99.5	3,337,000	196.4
Netherlands Antilles	188,000	93.7	153,000	87.0	132,000	159.4	44,900	466.8
New Caledonia	214,000	85.3	180,000	26.1	135,000	66.5	44,000	177.4
New Zealand	2,666,000	61.0	3,473,000	55.4	1,751,000	189.3	759,000	237.4
Nicaragua	5,510,000	95.2	2,909,000	71.2	2,751,000	110.1	608,000	293.9
Niger	54,700	0.4	2,302,000	1.6	8,100	665.7	2,500	1,560.7
Nigeria	73,588,000	46.5	62,749,000	27.2	29,093,000	114.4	10,175,000	324.8
Niue	1,400	95.4	880	34.1	810	69.7	260	186.1
North Korea	204,000	0.8	17,836,000	3.4	149,000	769.7	40,300	1,423.1
N. Mariana Islands	49,500	81.3	43,700	32.4	35,300	75.3	10,600	174.4
Norway	4,379,000	89.7	3,969,000	32.8	3,484,000	74.0	1,949,000	90.3
Oman	120,000	4.3	1,649,000	11.5	69,500	147.9	25,800	353.0
Pakistan	3,784,000	2.2	55,800,000	10.7	1,210,000	827.1	297,000	2,966.4
Palau	19,000	92.8	14,900	40.0	13,500	84.6	3,100	263.7
Palestine	75,100	1.9	2,147,000	24.2	38,000	2,461.5	11,000	6,555.5
Panama	3,182,000	90.5	2,296,000	31.1	2,020,000	70.6	646,000	177.1
Papua New Guinea	6,502,000	94.8	2,395,000	26.5	1,983,000	40.2	707,000	103.0
Paraguay	6,159,000	95.4	4,011,000	235.5	3,748,000	46.9	1,200,000	110.7
Peru	28,045,000	96.5	17,873,000	79.6	17,142,000	99.1	4,799,000	275.8
Philippines	84,742,000	90.9	55,751,000	422.4	49,542,000	521.7	13,463,000	519.3
Poland	36,513,000	95.4	32,519,000	12.5	30,164,000	25.4	9,833,000	4.8
Portugal	9,729,000	91.1	8,504,000	12.0	7,715,000	19.4	2,392,000	38.9
Puerto Rico	3,591,000	95.8	2,779,000	51.3	2,584,000	75.6	909,000	155.4
Qatar	168,000	9.6	1,354,000	6.8	123,000	147.9	22,300	359.5
Reunion	741,000	87.6	551,000	193.5	477,000	60.1	169,000	150.1
Romania	21,161,000	98.5	17,731,000	10.3	17,454,000	19.5	6,639,000	47.7
Russia	116,147,000	81.3	120,781,000	14.4	97,976,000	16.5	36,037,000	40.3

| Country | Christians | | Scripture Distribution | | | | | |
| | | | Portions | | New Testaments | | Bibles | |
	2010	%	Goal	% Met	Goal	% Met	Goal	% Met
Rwanda	9,722,000	91.5	3,991,000	27.8	3,347,000	57.4	1,242,000	147.6
Saint Helena	3,900	94.7	3,300	46.1	2,800	97.1	1,100	222.7
Saint Kitts & Nevis	49,600	94.7	36,600	15.3	33,400	31.0	10,800	66.0
Saint Lucia	167,000	95.8	117,000	19.0	109,000	38.4	36,600	84.9
Saint Pierre & Miquelon	5,700	94.3	4,900	32.9	4,600	60.4	1,900	82.3
Saint Vincent	97,000	88.7	77,200	11.1	52,800	30.2	17,900	62.5
Samoa	181,000	98.9	112,000	36.2	110,000	70.0	22,700	290.6
San Marino	29,000	92.0	26,900	0.9	24,000	1.1	10,300	1.4
Sao Tome & Principe	159,000	96.1	83,900	20.0	75,800	39.8	31,700	88.7
Saudi Arabia	1,201,000	4.4	15,127,000	2.7	653,000	96.3	142,000	137.6
Senegal	683,000	5.5	2,805,000	12.5	154,000	96.7	31,000	424.6
Serbia	6,933,000	89.2	6,178,000	8.6	5,255,000	19.5	2,126,000	39.0
Seychelles	82,000	94.8	62,100	166.1	56,200	70.3	15,000	171.6
Sierra Leone	778,000	13.3	1,185,000	56.8	153,000	594.6	57,100	836.5
Singapore	964,000	19.0	3,892,000	30.6	695,000	150.2	216,000	387.5
Slovakia	4,675,000	85.6	4,636,000	1.8	3,892,000	2.9	1,528,000	6.1
Slovenia	1,779,000	87.7	1,741,000	10.5	1,448,000	23.0	543,000	56.7
Solomon Islands	513,000	95.3	246,000	43.8	223,000	91.8	66,000	267.8
Somalia	4,300	0.1	1,280,000	0.1	580	295.8	220	783.0
South Africa	41,106,000	82.0	28,893,000	39.2	20,626,000	94.3	6,418,000	272.7
South Korea	16,105,000	33.4	39,358,000	76.0	12,804,000	444.1	4,032,000	571.7
South Sudan	6,529,000	60.5	3,981,000	12.0	2,393,000	29.8	754,000	40.2
Spain	40,685,000	88.3	38,258,000	145.1	33,631,000	324.9	11,299,000	840.7
Sri Lanka	1,841,000	8.8	14,211,000	10.0	1,248,000	158.3	320,000	439.9
Sudan	1,761,000	5.4	12,074,000	1.4	638,000	35.8	201,000	46.5
Suriname	268,000	51.1	336,000	38.0	153,000	62.3	54,800	142.7
Swaziland	1,039,000	87.6	582,000	32.0	365,000	83.1	104,000	268.8
Sweden	5,963,000	63.6	7,829,000	45.9	4,924,000	145.6	2,681,000	47.1
Switzerland	6,316,000	82.4	6,496,000	49.4	5,277,000	77.2	2,830,000	138.5
Syria	1,061,000	5.2	10,291,000	12.6	532,000	345.7	136,000	291.1
Taiwan	1,394,000	6.0	18,197,000	65.3	893,000	2,074.6	292,000	700.3
Tajikistan	98,300	1.4	4,310,000	1.4	61,200	130.1	15,900	68.4
Tanzania	24,555,000	54.8	17,312,000	23.5	8,895,000	84.6	3,155,000	222.2
Thailand	845,000	1.2	50,903,000	23.5	604,000	405.8	143,000	892.0
Timor-Leste	961,000	85.5	290,000	329.0	248,000	686.4	115,000	813.7
Togo	2,831,000	47.0	1,944,000	28.6	779,000	132.8	231,000	428.5
Tokelau Islands	1,100	96.9	700	43.9	630	92.3	200	255.0
Tonga	99,700	95.8	64,400	38.8	61,300	77.6	16,100	257.5
Trinidad & Tobago	851,000	63.4	1,047,000	9.5	631,000	29.4	194,000	69.8
Tunisia	23,200	0.2	5,966,000	0.7	12,900	431.4	3,300	375.0
Turkey	195,000	0.3	46,824,000	1.2	119,000	790.0	36,000	393.8
Turkmenistan	77,400	1.5	3,525,000	0.1	52,100	14.8	13,100	58.7
Turks & Caicos Islands	35,300	92.0	27,600	41.9	18,800	117.0	8,100	269.6
Tuvalu	9,300	94.6	5,800	45.7	5,300	94.7	1,300	325.2
Uganda	28,223,000	84.4	11,592,000	23.6	9,602,000	49.3	3,880,000	110.0
Ukraine	37,864,000	83.3	38,774,000	38.6	32,295,000	29.4	11,762,000	67.2
United Arab Emirates	944,000	12.6	5,524,000	9.1	668,000	113.7	118,000	491.6
United Kingdom	45,044,000	72.6	51,263,000	79.7	32,431,000	98.6	14,535,000	199.7
United States	248,544,000	80.1	248,068,000	188.2	162,206,000	358.0	78,059,000	446.7
U.S. Virgin Islands	103,000	94.5	82,600	55.2	67,400	127.2	27,200	221.2
Uruguay	2,151,000	63.9	2,526,000	109.9	1,607,000	139.2	629,000	91.6
Uzbekistan	344,000	1.3	19,230,000	0.6	239,000	33.7	61,500	96.8
Vanuatu	224,000	93.5	110,000	44.7	97,800	95.0	31,100	256.5
Venezuela	26,822,000	92.6	19,011,000	33.1	17,459,000	61.8	4,670,000	187.5

(continued)

Christian Populations and Distribution of Scripture (*continued*)

| | Christians | | Scripture Distribution | | | | | |
| | | | Portions | | New Testaments | | Bibles | |
Country	2010	%	Goal	% Met	Goal	% Met	Goal	% Met
Vietnam	7,430,000	8.5	60,659,000	7.6	5,120,000	148.5	1,396,000	121.3
Wallis & Futuna Islands	13,200	97.3	8,000	59.7	7,800	117.8	2,500	318.9
Western Sahara	820	0.2	39,000	5.2	60	5,461.5	17	15,451.5
Yemen	41,400	0.2	7,247,000	0.3	11,700	362.0	3,700	1,052.2
Zambia	11,187,000	85.5	4,776,000	52.4	3,843,000	54.0	1,629,000	89.1
Zimbabwe	10,265,000	81.7	6,871,000	24.0	5,037,000	43.8	1,717,000	122.6
Africa	*494,046,000*	*48.3*	*375,829,000*	*23.1*	*175,613,000*	*80.9*	*60,124,000*	*206.8*
Asia	*342,958,000*	*8.2*	*2,436,444,000*	*22.4*	*215,253,000*	*338.7*	*62,161,000*	*481.0*
Europe	*579,959,000*	*78.6*	*619,046,000*	*34.8*	*469,349,000*	*64.4*	*189,931,000*	*117.4*
Latin America	*544,685,000*	*92.3*	*381,610,000*	*182.3*	*347,289,000*	*310.0*	*107,601,000*	*545.3*
Northern America	*272,178,000*	*79.0*	*276,600,000*	*176.3*	*179,150,000*	*343.2*	*85,577,000*	*430.2*
Oceania	*28,018,000*	*76.6*	*25,826,000*	*68.8*	*16,160,000*	*111.9*	*6,356,000*	*156.1*
Global Total	**2,261,844,000**	**32.8**	**4,115,355,000**	**49.8**	**1,402,813,000**	**205.5**	**511,750,000**	**314.8**

Christian Populations, Libraries, and Literature

| | Christians | | Christian Libraries | | Christian Literature | | | | |
| | | | | | Books on Country's Christians | | | Periodicals | |
Country	2010	%	Libraries	per Million	Total	1970–1999	per Year	Periodicals	per Million
Afghanistan	32,400	0.1	0	0.0	74	8	0	0	0
Albania	1,011,000	31.6	0	0.0	143	64	3	5	2
Algeria	61,800	0.2	10	0.3	612	230	9	10	0
American Samoa	67,300	98.4	0	0.0	15	0	0	8	117
Andorra	78,300	92.3	1	11.8	19	9	0	1	12
Angola	17,799,000	93.3	12	0.6	237	49	2	40	2
Anguilla	14,000	91.2	1	65.1	6	0	0	4	260
Antigua & Barbuda	82,500	93.0	0	0.0	15	0	0	7	79
Argentina	36,430,000	90.2	90	2.2	1,882	591	24	200	5
Armenia	2,891,000	93.5	0	0.0	947	260	10	10	3
Aruba	104,000	96.8	0	0.0	9	4	0	1	9
Australia	16,204,000	72.8	113	5.1	5,126	2,459	98	400	18
Austria	6,508,000	77.5	190	22.6	3,304	1,093	44	550	66
Azerbaijan	304,000	3.3	0	0.0	62	15	1	1	0
Bahamas	320,000	93.3	2	5.8	102	32	1	12	35
Bahrain	94,300	7.5	0	0.0	21	7	0	4	3
Bangladesh	739,000	0.5	20	0.1	184	58	2	40	0
Barbados	260,000	95.1	5	18.3	144	40	2	15	55
Belarus	7,082,000	73.8	0	0.0	139	66	3	20	2
Belgium	7,661,000	71.5	260	24.3	2,575	721	29	300	28
Belize	284,000	91.1	0	0.0	69	23	1	10	32
Benin	3,874,000	43.8	13	1.5	208	38	2	25	3
Bermuda	58,000	89.3	0	0.0	100	14	1	40	616
Bhutan	6,700	0.9	0	0.0	32	15	1	0	0
Bolivia	9,181,000	92.5	62	6.2	819	242	10	100	10
Bosnia-Herzegovina	1,817,000	48.3	0	0.0	69	3	0	20	5
Botswana	1,378,000	68.7	5	2.5	86	43	2	40	20
Brazil	177,304,000	91.0	450	2.3	5,330	2,351	94	500	3
British Virgin Islands	19,600	84.3	0	0.0	15	5	0	2	86
Brunei	54,800	13.7	0	0.0	16	2	0	4	10
Bulgaria	6,216,000	82.9	135	18.0	1,143	380	15	20	3
Burkina Faso	3,691,000	22.4	14	0.9	109	25	1	10	1
Burundi	7,725,000	92.2	17	2.0	101	28	1	20	2

Country	Christians 2010	%	Christian Libraries Libraries	Christian Libraries per Million	Christian Literature Books on Country's Christians Total	Christian Literature Books on Country's Christians 1970–1999	Christian Literature Books on Country's Christians per Year	Christian Literature Periodicals Periodicals	Christian Literature Periodicals per Million
Cambodia	343,000	2.4	0	0.0	74	22	1	5	0
Cameroon	11,381,000	58.1	21	1.1	513	228	9	40	2
Canada	23,515,000	69.1	250	7.4	14,197	2,578	103	800	24
Cape Verde	471,000	95.0	3	6.1	44	15	1	5	10
Cayman Islands	45,600	81.1	0	0.0	8	3	0	4	71
Central African Republic	3,139,000	71.3	8	1.8	69	33	1	20	5
Chad	3,905,000	34.8	8	0.7	192	23	1	15	1
Channel Islands	131,000	85.4	5	32.6	53	9	0	10	65
Chile	15,168,000	88.6	50	2.9	2,010	779	31	200	12
China	106,485,000	7.9	2	0.0	7,700	1,400	56	25	0
Colombia	44,305,000	95.7	120	2.6	1,624	460	18	150	3
Comoros	3,500	0.5	0	0.0	14	8	0	0	0
Congo	3,629,000	89.8	7	1.7	76	15	1	20	5
Congo DR	62,673,000	95.0	130	2.0	1,389	600	24	150	2
Cook Islands	19,600	96.6	2	98.6	20	7	0	5	246
Costa Rica	4,464,000	95.8	20	4.3	448	169	7	50	11
Cote d'Ivoire	6,772,000	34.3	13	0.7	57	20	1	40	2
Croatia	4,117,000	93.5	0	0.0	781	376	15	30	7
Cuba	6,667,000	59.2	11	1.0	1,033	254	10	20	2
Cyprus	793,000	71.9	16	14.5	391	149	6	12	11
Czech Republic	5,810,000	55.4	14	1.3	1,187	291	12	30	3
Denmark	4,646,000	83.7	30	5.4	2,698	681	27	250	45
Djibouti	15,500	1.7	0	0.0	14	1	0	0	0
Dominica	64,000	94.5	1	14.8	33	12	0	10	148
Dominican Republic	9,429,000	95.0	12	1.2	385	191	8	25	3
Ecuador	14,042,000	97.1	45	3.1	1,568	348	14	100	7
Egypt	8,183,000	10.1	52	0.6	4,532	674	27	50	1
El Salvador	5,977,000	96.5	12	1.9	699	381	15	40	6
Equatorial Guinea	621,000	88.7	6	8.6	27	13	1	15	21
Eritrea	2,517,000	47.9	0	0.0	30	9	0	10	2
Estonia	589,000	43.9	0	0.0	197	53	2	40	30
Ethiopia	49,671,000	59.9	60	0.7	977	316	13	40	0
Faeroe Islands	47,800	98.1	0	0.0	28	10	0	7	144
Falkland Islands	2,500	82.9	1	331.5	25	0	0	0	0
Fiji	550,000	63.9	8	9.3	196	46	2	25	29
Finland	4,336,000	80.8	60	11.2	1,084	394	16	150	28
France	41,275,000	65.7	670	10.7	31,852	6,662	266	1,800	29
French Guiana	195,000	84.4	0	0.0	19	5	0	4	17
French Polynesia	254,000	93.8	2	7.4	54	16	1	20	74
Gabon	1,272,000	84.5	4	2.7	85	24	1	10	7
Gambia	75,200	4.4	0	0.0	40	11	0	4	2
Georgia	3,703,000	85.1	0	0.0	19	8	0	10	2
Germany	57,617,000	70.0	0	0.0	32,087	9,677	387	3,600	44
Ghana	15,601,000	64.0	35	1.4	728	288	12	150	6
Gibraltar	25,800	88.2	0	0.0	49	3	0	5	171
Greece	10,430,000	91.8	500	44.0	6,960	1,115	45	110	10
Greenland	55,100	96.2	1	17.5	211	20	1	2	35
Grenada	101,000	96.7	0	0.0	37	16	1	15	144
Guadeloupe	442,000	96.0	4	8.7	47	18	1	15	33
Guam	169,000	93.9	2	11.1	38	10	0	18	100
Guatemala	14,010,000	97.4	60	4.2	1,716	346	14	80	6
Guinea	365,000	3.7	0	0.0	1,097	304	12	4	0
Guinea-Bissau	185,000	12.2	4	2.6	57	25	1	5	3

(continued)

Christian Populations, Libraries, and Literature (*continued*)

Country	Christians 2010	%	Christian Libraries Libraries	per Million	Christian Literature Books on Country's Christians Total	1970–1999	per Year	Periodicals Periodicals	per Million
Guyana	413,000	54.7	7	9.3	150	31	1	30	40
Haiti	9,429,000	94.4	20	2.0	662	222	9	50	5
Holy See	460	100.4	60	131,004.4	44,187	0	0	150	327,511
Honduras	7,278,000	95.8	19	2.5	326	140	6	40	5
Hong Kong	957,000	13.6	7	1.0	2,244	456	18	20	3
Hungary	8,653,000	86.7	45	4.5	2,312	573	23	50	5
Iceland	303,000	94.7	2	6.3	270	64	3	30	94
India	57,265,000	4.7	580	0.5	13,084	2,003	80	1,200	1
Indonesia	29,089,000	12.1	150	0.6	3,330	764	31	400	2
Iran	270,000	0.4	5	0.1	941	90	4	30	0
Iraq	489,000	1.5	8	0.3	353	23	1	25	1
Ireland	4,207,000	94.1	60	13.4	11,579	2,017	81	200	45
Isle of Man	69,700	84.1	0	0.0	93	5	0	15	181
Israel	180,000	2.4	32	4.3	6,565	793	32	150	20
Italy	48,853,000	80.7	850	14.0	25,034	9,672	387	2,000	33
Jamaica	2,318,000	84.6	15	5.5	732	140	6	80	29
Japan	2,601,000	2.1	120	1.0	7,765	1,467	59	400	3
Jordan	171,000	2.8	0	0.0	828	93	4	20	3
Kazakhstan	4,249,000	26.5	0	0.0	54	10	0	5	0
Kenya	32,923,000	81.3	28	0.7	1,204	578	23	200	5
Kiribati	96,500	96.9	3	30.1	21	9	0	10	100
Kosovo	122,000	5.9	50	24.0	318	100	4	30	14
Kuwait	241,000	8.8	0	0.0	29	4	0	5	2
Kyrgyzstan	412,000	7.7	0	0.0	14	8	0	1	0
Laos	181,000	2.9	0	0.0	115	22	1	4	1
Latvia	1,552,000	68.9	0	0.0	250	62	2	25	11
Lebanon	1,503,000	35.6	55	13.0	1,156	321	13	60	14
Lesotho	1,992,000	91.7	14	6.5	128	53	2	40	18
Liberia	1,619,000	40.5	16	4.0	415	132	5	50	13
Libya	172,000	2.7	0	0.0	35	8	0	2	0
Liechtenstein	32,200	89.4	0	0.0	35	4	0	5	139
Lithuania	2,950,000	88.8	0	0.0	602	210	8	25	8
Luxembourg	418,000	82.4	10	19.7	226	31	1	30	59
Macau	39,300	7.2	1	1.8	100	100	4	5	9
Macedonia	1,311,000	63.6	0	0.0	432	147	6	10	5
Madagascar	11,789,000	56.9	23	1.1	460	93	4	45	2
Malawi	11,885,000	79.8	22	1.5	323	146	6	50	3
Malaysia	2,528,000	8.9	10	0.4	520	143	6	50	2
Maldives	1,400	0.4	0	0.0	11	6	0	0	0
Mali	498,000	3.2	6	0.4	119	12	0	10	1
Malta	408,000	98.0	8	19.2	287	69	3	80	192
Marshall Islands	51,600	95.5	0	0.0	44	3	0	5	93
Martinique	391,000	96.4	2	4.9	34	10	0	5	12
Mauritania	9,100	0.3	0	0.0	23	13	1	1	0
Mauritius	431,000	33.2	2	1.5	120	48	2	5	4
Mayotte	1,400	0.7	0	0.0	9	5	0	0	0
Mexico	108,721,000	95.9	180	1.6	13,396	2,554	102	900	8
Micronesia	105,000	94.5	0	0.0	73	15	1	20	180
Moldova	3,426,000	95.9	0	0.0	74	23	1	25	7
Monaco	30,500	86.1	1	28.2	62	8	0	8	226
Mongolia	46,000	1.7	0	0.0	116	8	0	1	0
Montenegro	488,000	77.3	20	31.7	100	30	1	10	16
Montserrat	5,500	92.7	0	0.0	69	6	0	4	674
Morocco	31,600	0.1	4	0.1	346	9	0	20	1

Country	Christians 2010	%	Christian Libraries Libraries	per Million	Christian Literature Books on Country's Christians Total	1970–1999	per Year	Periodicals Periodicals	per Million
Mozambique	12,269,000	52.5	13	0.6	249	99	4	40	2
Myanmar	3,786,000	7.9	33	0.7	605	17	1	20	0
Namibia	2,082,000	91.2	5	2.2	309	155	6	40	18
Nauru	7,700	75.1	0	0.0	4	2	0	2	195
Nepal	908,000	3.0	2	0.1	216	30	1	15	1
Netherlands	10,517,000	63.3	300	18.1	7,572	1,673	67	700	42
Netherlands Antilles	188,000	93.7	4	19.9	29	9	0	20	100
New Caledonia	214,000	85.3	4	15.9	49	18	1	10	40
New Zealand	2,666,000	61.0	30	6.9	1,433	331	13	250	57
Nicaragua	5,510,000	95.2	16	2.8	848	501	20	40	7
Niger	54,700	0.4	0	0.0	119	20	1	5	0
Nigeria	73,588,000	46.5	80	0.5	2,955	1,158	46	300	2
Niue	1,400	95.4	1	681.2	15	0	0	2	1,362
North Korea	204,000	0.8	0	0.0	202	29	1	0	0
N. Mariana Islands	49,500	81.3	0	0.0	4	2	0	5	82
Norway	4,379,000	89.7	32	6.6	1,926	481	19	140	29
Oman	120,000	4.3	0	0.0	66	13	1	5	2
Pakistan	3,784,000	2.2	15	0.1	561	127	5	50	0
Palau	19,000	92.8	0	0.0	32	16	1	2	98
Palestine	75,100	1.9	30	7.4	3,661	1,023	41	40	10
Panama	3,182,000	90.5	20	5.7	321	65	3	40	11
Papua New Guinea	6,502,000	94.8	34	5.0	649	257	10	60	9
Paraguay	6,159,000	95.4	16	2.5	409	143	6	40	6
Peru	28,045,000	96.5	65	2.2	2,477	594	24	100	3
Philippines	84,742,000	90.9	195	2.1	2,822	992	40	300	3
Poland	36,513,000	95.4	76	2.0	5,531	2,305	92	200	5
Portugal	9,729,000	91.1	35	3.3	1,972	563	23	300	28
Puerto Rico	3,591,000	95.8	25	6.7	720	252	10	50	13
Qatar	168,000	9.6	0	0.0	14	6	0	0	0
Reunion	741,000	87.6	2	2.4	32	11	0	2	2
Romania	21,161,000	98.5	200	9.3	2,272	388	16	70	3
Russia	116,147,000	81.3	72	0.5	7,334	1,693	68	150	1
Rwanda	9,722,000	91.5	17	1.6	227	80	3	20	2
Saint Helena	3,900	94.7	1	242.8	33	0	0	3	729
Saint Kitts & Nevis	49,600	94.7	0	0.0	23	10	0	7	134
Saint Lucia	167,000	95.8	0	0.0	19	5	0	8	46
Saint Pierre & Miquelon	5,700	94.3	1	165.4	3	0	0	2	331
Saint Vincent	97,000	88.7	1	9.2	14	6	0	5	46
Samoa	181,000	98.9	3	16.4	139	42	2	20	109
San Marino	29,000	92.0	0	0.0	90	10	0	3	95
Sao Tome & Principe	159,000	96.1	0	0.0	15	5	0	2	12
Saudi Arabia	1,201,000	4.4	0	0.0	86	14	1	0	0
Senegal	683,000	5.5	8	0.6	109	29	1	20	2
Serbia	6,933,000	89.2	210	27.0	1,018	345	14	110	14
Seychelles	82,000	94.8	2	23.1	16	8	0	4	46
Sierra Leone	778,000	13.3	8	1.4	250	60	2	25	4
Singapore	964,000	19.0	10	2.0	432	144	6	50	10
Slovakia	4,675,000	85.6	0	0.0	380	139	6	20	4
Slovenia	1,779,000	87.7	0	0.0	379	195	8	20	10
Solomon Islands	513,000	95.3	5	9.3	172	60	2	10	19
Somalia	4,300	0.1	0	0.0	48	15	1	0	0
South Africa	41,106,000	82.0	150	3.0	3,958	1,644	66	400	8

(continued)

Christian Populations, Libraries, and Literature (*continued*)

Country	Christians 2010	%	Christian Libraries Libraries	per Million	Christian Literature Books on Country's Christians Total	1970–1999	per Year	Periodicals Periodicals	per Million
South Korea	16,105,000	33.4	160	3.3	1,389	758	30	200	4
South Sudan	6,529,000	60.5	3	0.3	292	90	4	12	1
Spain	40,685,000	88.3	300	6.5	12,043	4,581	183	1,500	33
Sri Lanka	1,841,000	8.8	25	1.2	588	129	5	100	5
Sudan	1,761,000	5.4	2	0.1	195	60	2	8	0
Suriname	268,000	51.1	2	3.8	143	13	1	10	19
Swaziland	1,039,000	87.6	3	2.5	90	41	2	40	34
Sweden	5,963,000	63.6	40	4.3	3,160	713	29	450	48
Switzerland	6,316,000	82.4	150	19.6	5,864	1,200	48	400	52
Syria	1,061,000	5.2	0	0.0	808	163	7	40	2
Taiwan	1,394,000	6.0	60	2.6	970	283	11	20	1
Tajikistan	98,300	1.4	0	0.0	13	5	0	1	0
Tanzania	24,555,000	54.8	60	1.3	658	253	10	100	2
Thailand	845,000	1.2	15	0.2	660	202	8	30	0
Timor-Leste	961,000	85.5	0	0.0	69	16	1	5	4
Togo	2,831,000	47.0	5	0.8	131	24	1	20	3
Tokelau Islands	1,100	96.9	1	881.1	11	0	0	1	881
Tonga	99,700	95.8	2	19.2	179	87	3	15	144
Trinidad & Tobago	851,000	63.4	10	7.5	122	43	2	30	22
Tunisia	23,200	0.2	2	0.2	119	46	2	1	0
Turkey	195,000	0.3	7	0.1	2,409	702	28	15	0
Turkmenistan	77,400	1.5	0	0.0	27	11	0	1	0
Turks & Caicos Islands	35,300	92.0	0	0.0	4	2	0	2	52
Tuvalu	9,300	94.6	0	0.0	14	6	0	2	204
Uganda	28,223,000	84.4	28	0.8	596	211	8	40	1
Ukraine	37,864,000	83.3	0	0.0	2,170	749	30	70	2
United Arab Emirates	944,000	12.6	0	0.0	38	12	0	5	1
United Kingdom	45,044,000	72.6	481	7.8	30,071	4,662	186	2,000	32
United States	248,544,000	80.1	2,700	8.7	76,856	21,067	843	8,000	26
U.S. Virgin Islands	103,000	94.5	0	0.0	25	10	0	15	138
Uruguay	2,151,000	63.9	20	5.9	399	141	6	70	21
Uzbekistan	344,000	1.3	0	0.0	37	10	0	5	0
Vanuatu	224,000	93.5	2	8.4	144	51	2	10	42
Venezuela	26,822,000	92.6	44	1.5	867	264	11	70	2
Vietnam	7,430,000	8.5	65	0.7	164	50	2	50	1
Wallis & Futuna Islands	13,200	97.3	0	0.0	11	5	0	2	147
Western Sahara	820	0.2	0	0.0	72	5	0	0	0
Yemen	41,400	0.2	0	0.0	34	17	1	0	0
Zambia	11,187,000	85.5	33	2.5	347	153	6	70	5
Zimbabwe	10,265,000	81.7	25	2.0	593	237	9	60	5
Africa	*494,046,000*	*48.3*	*984*	*1.0*	*25,889*	*8,521*	*341*	*2,358*	*2*
Asia	*342,958,000*	*8.2*	*1,623*	*0.4*	*62,616*	*13,008*	*520*	*3,439*	*1*
Europe	*579,959,000*	*78.6*	*4,867*	*6.6*	*252,011*	*54,319*	*2,173*	*15,774*	*21*
Latin America	*544,685,000*	*92.3*	*1,412*	*2.4*	*39,832*	*11,431*	*457*	*3,180*	*5*
Northern America	*272,178,000*	*79.0*	*2,952*	*8.6*	*91,367*	*23,679*	*947*	*8,844*	*26*
Oceania	*28,018,000*	*76.6*	*212*	*5.8*	*8,443*	*3,442*	*138*	*902*	*25*
Global Total	**2,261,844,000**	**32.8**	**12,050**	**1.8**	**480,158**	**114,400**	**4,576**	**34,497**	**5**

Christian Populations and Broadcasting

| Country | Christians | | Broadcasting | | |
| | | | Listener Population % | | |
	2010	%	Total	Christian	Secular
Afghanistan	32,400	0.1	0.3	0.3	0.0
Albania	1,011,000	31.6	20.0	10.0	15.0
Algeria	61,800	0.2	5.0	5.0	0.0
American Samoa	67,300	98.4	80.0	15.0	75.0
Andorra	78,300	92.3	75.0	10.0	70.0
Angola	17,799,000	93.3	9.0	3.0	7.0
Anguilla	14,000	91.2	52.0	5.0	50.0
Antigua & Barbuda	82,500	93.0	62.0	4.0	60.0
Argentina	36,430,000	90.2	70.0	10.0	65.0
Armenia	2,891,000	93.5	12.0	3.0	10.0
Aruba	104,000	96.8	75.0	20.0	60.0
Australia	16,204,000	72.8	62.0	15.0	50.0
Austria	6,508,000	77.5	77.0	3.0	75.0
Azerbaijan	304,000	3.3	0.8	0.8	0.0
Bahamas	320,000	93.3	77.0	2.5	75.0
Bahrain	94,300	7.5	15.5	15.5	0.0
Bangladesh	739,000	0.5	0.8	0.8	0.0
Barbados	260,000	95.1	72.0	3.0	70.0
Belarus	7,082,000	73.8	19.0	10.0	10.0
Belgium	7,661,000	71.5	68.0	4.0	65.0
Belize	284,000	91.1	84.0	15.0	75.0
Benin	3,874,000	43.8	7.5	3.0	5.0
Bermuda	58,000	89.3	78.0	5.0	75.0
Bhutan	6,700	0.9	3.0	3.0	0.0
Bolivia	9,181,000	92.5	55.0	8.0	50.0
Bosnia-Herzegovina	1,817,000	48.3	10.0	7.0	5.0
Botswana	1,378,000	68.7	20.0	8.0	15.0
Brazil	177,304,000	91.0	70.0	25.0	50.0
British Virgin Islands	19,600	84.3	75.0	7.0	70.0
Brunei	54,800	13.7	3.0	3.0	0.0
Bulgaria	6,216,000	82.9	6.0	3.0	3.0
Burkina Faso	3,691,000	22.4	8.7	1.0	8.0
Burundi	7,725,000	92.2	12.0	3.0	10.0
Cambodia	343,000	2.4	6.5	5.5	1.0
Cameroon	11,381,000	58.1	22.0	3.0	20.0
Canada	23,515,000	69.1	80.0	20.0	65.0
Cape Verde	471,000	95.0	7.0	3.0	5.0
Cayman Islands	45,600	81.1	28.0	25.0	5.0
Central African Republic	3,139,000	71.3	25.0	8.0	20.0
Chad	3,905,000	34.8	9.5	2.0	8.0
Channel Islands	131,000	85.4	77.0	10.0	70.0
Chile	15,168,000	88.6	60.0	6.0	55.0
China	106,485,000	7.9	15.0	15.0	0.0
Colombia	44,305,000	95.7	68.0	15.0	60.0
Comoros	3,500	0.5	2.0	2.0	0.0
Congo	3,629,000	89.8	7.0	3.0	5.0
Congo DR	62,673,000	95.0	21.0	8.0	15.0
Cook Islands	19,600	96.6	45.0	10.0	40.0
Costa Rica	4,464,000	95.8	63.0	10.0	55.0
Cote d'Ivoire	6,772,000	34.3	22.0	16.0	8.0
Croatia	4,117,000	93.5	18.0	4.0	15.0
Cuba	6,667,000	59.2	10.0	10.0	0.0
Cyprus	793,000	71.9	42.0	3.0	40.0
Czech Republic	5,810,000	55.4	9.0	5.0	5.0

(continued)

Christian Populations and Broadcasting (*continued*)

Country	Christians 2010	%	Broadcasting Listener Population % Total	Christian	Secular
Denmark	4,646,000	83.7	62.0	5.0	60.0
Djibouti	15,500	1.7	2.5	0.5	2.0
Dominica	64,000	94.5	45.0	6.0	40.0
Dominican Republic	9,429,000	95.0	48.0	20.0	40.0
Ecuador	14,042,000	97.1	85.0	45.0	60.0
Egypt	8,183,000	10.1	11.0	4.0	8.0
El Salvador	5,977,000	96.5	43.0	5.0	40.0
Equatorial Guinea	621,000	88.7	24.0	20.0	5.0
Eritrea	2,517,000	47.9	22.0	16.0	10.0
Estonia	589,000	43.9	30.0	15.0	20.0
Ethiopia	49,671,000	59.9	30.0	25.0	10.0
Faeroe Islands	47,800	98.1	44.0	6.0	40.0
Falkland Islands	2,500	82.9	44.0	6.0	40.0
Fiji	550,000	63.9	43.0	5.0	40.0
Finland	4,336,000	80.8	57.0	3.0	55.0
France	41,275,000	65.7	64.0	5.0	60.0
French Guiana	195,000	84.4	45.5	1.0	45.0
French Polynesia	254,000	93.8	62.0	3.0	60.0
Gabon	1,272,000	84.5	26.5	2.0	25.0
Gambia	75,200	4.4	20.5	1.0	20.0
Georgia	3,703,000	85.1	23.0	5.0	20.0
Germany	57,617,000	70.0	58.0	10.0	50.0
Ghana	15,601,000	64.0	36.0	8.0	30.0
Gibraltar	25,800	88.2	33.0	4.0	30.0
Greece	10,430,000	91.8	62.0	3.0	60.0
Greenland	55,100	96.2	21.5	2.0	20.0
Grenada	101,000	96.7	61.5	2.0	60.0
Guadeloupe	442,000	96.0	41.5	2.0	40.0
Guam	169,000	93.9	86.0	7.0	80.0
Guatemala	14,010,000	97.4	60.0	20.0	50.0
Guinea	365,000	3.7	0.7	0.2	0.5
Guinea-Bissau	185,000	12.2	6.0	2.0	5.0
Guyana	413,000	54.7	36.5	2.0	35.0
Haiti	9,429,000	94.4	21.0	4.0	18.0
Holy See	460	100.4	80.0	80.0	80.0
Honduras	7,278,000	95.8	40.0	6.0	36.0
Hong Kong	957,000	13.6	15.0	15.0	0.0
Hungary	8,653,000	86.7	64.0	5.0	60.0
Iceland	303,000	94.7	72.0	3.0	70.0
India	57,265,000	4.7	24.0	5.0	20.0
Indonesia	29,089,000	12.1	23.0	6.0	18.0
Iran	270,000	0.4	2.0	1.0	1.0
Iraq	489,000	1.5	4.0	4.0	0.0
Ireland	4,207,000	94.1	82.0	3.0	80.0
Isle of Man	69,700	84.1	78.0	4.0	75.0
Israel	180,000	2.4	9.5	2.0	8.0
Italy	48,853,000	80.7	67.0	3.0	65.0
Jamaica	2,318,000	84.6	41.0	8.0	35.0
Japan	2,601,000	2.1	37.0	10.0	30.0
Jordan	171,000	2.8	9.5	7.0	3.0
Kazakhstan	4,249,000	26.5	6.5	2.0	5.0
Kenya	32,923,000	81.3	45.0	8.0	40.0
Kiribati	96,500	96.9	66.0	2.0	65.0
Kosovo	122,000	5.9	44.0	6.0	40.0
Kuwait	241,000	8.8	15.0	15.0	0.0

Country	Christians 2010	%	Broadcasting Listener Population % Total	Christian	Secular
Kyrgyzstan	412,000	7.7	3.0	3.0	0.0
Laos	181,000	2.9	3.0	3.0	0.0
Latvia	1,552,000	68.9	33.0	4.0	30.0
Lebanon	1,503,000	35.6	70.0	17.0	60.0
Lesotho	1,992,000	91.7	13.0	4.0	10.0
Liberia	1,619,000	40.5	35.0	10.0	30.0
Libya	172,000	2.7	1.0	1.0	0.0
Liechtenstein	32,200	89.4	63.0	4.0	60.0
Lithuania	2,950,000	88.8	27.0	3.0	25.0
Luxembourg	418,000	82.4	74.0	5.0	70.0
Macau	39,300	7.2	15.0	15.0	0.0
Macedonia	1,311,000	63.6	21.5	2.0	20.0
Madagascar	11,789,000	56.9	38.0	10.0	30.0
Malawi	11,885,000	79.8	19.0	5.0	15.0
Malaysia	2,528,000	8.9	9.0	9.0	0.0
Maldives	1,400	0.4	2.0	2.0	0.0
Mali	498,000	3.2	7.5	2.0	6.0
Malta	408,000	98.0	73.0	7.0	70.0
Marshall Islands	51,600	95.5	91.0	8.0	90.0
Martinique	391,000	96.4	36.5	2.0	35.0
Mauritania	9,100	0.3	3.0	3.0	0.0
Mauritius	431,000	33.2	16.5	2.0	15.0
Mayotte	1,400	0.7	2.0	2.0	0.0
Mexico	108,721,000	95.9	84.0	5.0	80.0
Micronesia	105,000	94.5	91.0	8.0	90.0
Moldova	3,426,000	95.9	19.0	10.0	10.0
Monaco	30,500	86.1	83.0	6.0	80.0
Mongolia	46,000	1.7	3.0	3.0	0.0
Montenegro	488,000	77.3	44.0	6.0	40.0
Montserrat	5,500	92.7	64.0	6.0	60.0
Morocco	31,600	0.1	10.0	10.0	0.0
Mozambique	12,269,000	52.5	3.5	2.0	2.0
Myanmar	3,786,000	7.9	3.0	3.0	0.0
Namibia	2,082,000	91.2	33.0	4.0	30.0
Nauru	7,700	75.1	57.0	3.0	55.0
Nepal	908,000	3.0	4.5	2.0	3.0
Netherlands	10,517,000	63.3	52.0	4.0	50.0
Netherlands Antilles	188,000	93.7	75.0	20.0	60.0
New Caledonia	214,000	85.3	56.5	2.0	55.0
New Zealand	2,666,000	61.0	66.0	12.0	60.0
Nicaragua	5,510,000	95.2	45.0	6.0	40.0
Niger	54,700	0.4	5.5	2.0	4.0
Nigeria	73,588,000	46.5	45.0	20.0	30.0
Niue	1,400	95.4	53.0	5.0	50.0
North Korea	204,000	0.8	4.0	4.0	0.0
N. Mariana Islands	49,500	81.3	83.0	8.0	80.0
Norway	4,379,000	89.7	75.0	7.0	70.0
Oman	120,000	4.3	4.0	4.0	0.0
Pakistan	3,784,000	2.2	1.0	1.0	0.0
Palau	19,000	92.8	92.0	3.0	90.0
Palestine	75,100	1.9	6.5	2.0	5.0
Panama	3,182,000	90.5	69.0	5.0	65.0
Papua New Guinea	6,502,000	94.8	44.0	5.0	40.0
Paraguay	6,159,000	95.4	36.0	8.0	30.0
Peru	28,045,000	96.5	44.0	6.0	40.0

(continued)

Christian Populations and Broadcasting (*continued*)

Country	Christians 2010	%	Broadcasting Listener Population % Total	Christian	Secular
Philippines	84,742,000	90.9	55.0	10.0	50.0
Poland	36,513,000	95.4	76.0	12.0	70.0
Portugal	9,729,000	91.1	52.0	5.0	50.0
Puerto Rico	3,591,000	95.8	84.0	7.0	80.0
Qatar	168,000	9.6	3.0	3.0	0.0
Reunion	741,000	87.6	38.0	4.0	35.0
Romania	21,161,000	98.5	23.0	15.0	10.0
Russia	116,147,000	81.3	30.0	20.0	15.0
Rwanda	9,722,000	91.5	12.0	3.0	10.0
Saint Helena	3,900	94.7	55.0	6.0	50.0
Saint Kitts & Nevis	49,600	94.7	57.5	3.0	55.0
Saint Lucia	167,000	95.8	71.5	2.0	70.0
Saint Pierre & Miquelon	5,700	94.3	67.0	3.0	65.0
Saint Vincent	97,000	88.7	61.5	2.0	60.0
Samoa	181,000	98.9	73.0	5.0	70.0
San Marino	29,000	92.0	72.0	3.0	70.0
Sao Tome & Principe	159,000	96.1	27.0	3.0	25.0
Saudi Arabia	1,201,000	4.4	7.0	7.0	0.0
Senegal	683,000	5.5	12.5	1.0	12.0
Serbia	6,933,000	89.2	44.0	6.0	40.0
Seychelles	82,000	94.8	49.0	5.0	45.0
Sierra Leone	778,000	13.3	13.0	4.0	10.0
Singapore	964,000	19.0	22.0	12.0	15.0
Slovakia	4,675,000	85.6	9.0	5.0	5.0
Slovenia	1,779,000	87.7	21.5	2.0	20.0
Solomon Islands	513,000	95.3	43.0	5.0	40.0
Somalia	4,300	0.1	0.5	0.5	0.0
South Africa	41,106,000	82.0	55.0	8.0	50.0
South Korea	16,105,000	33.4	44.0	15.0	35.0
South Sudan	6,529,000	60.5	12.0	4.0	9.0
Spain	40,685,000	88.3	62.0	3.0	60.0
Sri Lanka	1,841,000	8.8	10.0	5.0	7.0
Sudan	1,761,000	5.4	12.0	4.0	9.0
Suriname	268,000	51.1	66.5	2.0	65.0
Swaziland	1,039,000	87.6	42.0	10.0	35.0
Sweden	5,963,000	63.6	63.0	5.0	60.0
Switzerland	6,316,000	82.4	68.0	5.0	65.0
Syria	1,061,000	5.2	5.0	5.0	0.0
Taiwan	1,394,000	6.0	52.0	15.0	40.0
Tajikistan	98,300	1.4	0.5	0.5	0.0
Tanzania	24,555,000	54.8	17.0	3.0	15.0
Thailand	845,000	1.2	13.5	4.0	10.0
Timor-Leste	961,000	85.5	23.0	4.0	20.0
Togo	2,831,000	47.0	18.0	3.0	16.0
Tokelau Islands	1,100	96.9	63.0	5.0	60.0
Tonga	99,700	95.8	54.0	6.0	50.0
Trinidad & Tobago	851,000	63.4	63.0	4.0	60.0
Tunisia	23,200	0.2	4.0	4.0	0.0
Turkey	195,000	0.3	1.5	1.5	0.0
Turkmenistan	77,400	1.5	0.5	0.5	0.0
Turks & Caicos Islands	35,300	92.0	70.0	15.0	60.0
Tuvalu	9,300	94.6	68.0	5.0	65.0
Uganda	28,223,000	84.4	40.0	15.0	30.0
Ukraine	37,864,000	83.3	40.0	20.0	25.0
United Arab Emirates	944,000	12.6	3.0	3.0	0.0

| Country | Christians | | Broadcasting | | |
| | 2010 | % | Listener Population % | | |
			Total	Christian	Secular
United Kingdom	45,044,000	72.6	65.0	15.0	55.0
United States	248,544,000	80.1	82.0	60.0	75.0
U.S. Virgin Islands	103,000	94.5	79.0	5.0	75.0
Uruguay	2,151,000	63.9	57.0	3.0	55.0
Uzbekistan	344,000	1.3	3.5	2.0	2.0
Vanuatu	224,000	93.5	23.0	4.0	20.0
Venezuela	26,822,000	92.6	70.0	15.0	60.0
Vietnam	7,430,000	8.5	5.0	5.0	0.0
Wallis & Futuna Islands	13,200	97.3	78.0	5.0	75.0
Western Sahara	820	0.2	0.5	0.5	0.0
Yemen	41,400	0.2	1.0	1.0	0.0
Zambia	11,187,000	85.5	28.0	4.0	25.0
Zimbabwe	10,265,000	81.7	38.5	5.0	35.0
Africa	*494,046,000*	*48.3*	*24.9*	*9.5*	*17.6*
Asia	*342,958,000*	*8.2*	*17.5*	*8.2*	*10.0*
Europe	*579,959,000*	*78.6*	*50.6*	*10.6*	*42.9*
Latin America	*544,685,000*	*92.3*	*66.9*	*15.1*	*56.0*
Northern America	*272,178,000*	*79.0*	*81.8*	*56.0*	*74.0*
Oceania	*28,018,000*	*76.6*	*58.5*	*11.9*	*49.5*
Global Total	**2,261,844,000**	**32.8**	**29.8**	**11.6**	**22.0**

Appendix B: World Listing of Christian Universities by Continent

Note: North America is not included in this list.

Country	Institution Name	URL
Africa		
Angola	Methodist University of Angola	
	(Universidade Metodista de Angola)	http://www.uma.co.ao/
	Catholic University of Angola	
	(Universidade Católica de Angola)	http://www.ucan.edu
Cameroon	Adventist University Cosendai	http://www.uacosendai.net/
	Catholic University of Central Africa	
	(Université Catholique d'Afrique Centrale)	http://www.fiuc.org/asunicam/ucac.html
DRC (Democratic Republic of Congo)	Adventist University of Lukanga Wallace	
	(Université Adventist University Lukanga Wallace)	
	Catholic University of Bukavu	
	(Université Catholique de Bukavu)	http://www.fiuc.org/asunicam/ucb.html
	Catholic University of Graben	
	(Université Catholique du Graben)	http://www.ucg-rdc.org/
	Christian University of Kinshasa	
	(Universite chretienne de Kinshasa)	
	Evangelical University in Africa	
	(Université évangéliue en Afrique)	http://ueafrique.org/
	Protestant University of Congo	
	(Université Protestante au Congo)	http://www.upc-rdc.cd/
	Shalom University of Bunia	http://www.unishabunia.org/home.php?l=en
	University of Notre Dame of the Kasayi	
	(Université Notre-Dame du Kasayi)	http://www.ukardc.org/
Ghana	All Nations University College	http://www.allnationsuniversity.org/
	Catholic University College of Ghana	http://www.cug.edu.gh/
	Central University College	http://www.centraluniversity.org/
	Christian Service University College	http://www.csuc.edu.gh/
	Ghana Christian University College	http://www.ghanacu.org/
	Maranatha University College	http://www.muc.edu.gh/
	Methodist University College	http://www.mucg.edu.gh/
	Pentecost University College	http://www.pentvars.edu.gh/
	Presbyterian University College, Ghana	http://www.presbyuniversity.edu.gh
	Regent University College of Science and Technology	http://www.regentghana.net/
	Valley View University	http://www.vvu.edu.gh/
Ivory Coast	Catholic University of West Africa	
	(Université Catholique d'Afrique de l'Ouest)	http://www.fiuc.org/asunicam/

(continued)

Country	Institution Name	URL
Kenya	Africa International University	http://puea.ac.ke/
	Africa Nazarene University	http://www.anu.ac.ke/
	Catholic University of Eastern Africa	http://www.cuea.edu/
	Daystar University (A)	http://www.daystar.ac.ke
	Kabarak University	http://www.kabarak.ac.ke/
	Kenya Highlands Evangelical University	http://www.khbc.ac.ke/
	Kenya Methodist University	http://www.kemu.ac.ke
	Pan Africa Christian University	http://www.pacuniversity.ac.ke/
	Presbyterian University of East Africa	http://puea.ac.ke/
	St. Paul's University	http://www.stpaulslimuru.ac.ke/index.php?Cat_Id=home
	Tangaza College—The Catholic University of Eastern Africa	http://www.tangaza.org/
	University of Eastern Africa, Baraton (UEAB)	http://www.ueab.ac.ke/
Liberia	African Methodist Episcopal University	
	Cuttington University College	http://cuttington.org/
Malawi	Catholic University of Malawi	
	University of Livingstonia	http://www.ulivingstonia.org/
Mozambique	Universidade Católica de Mocambique	http://www.ucm.ac.mz/cms/index.php
Nigeria	Ajayi Crowther University	http://www.acu.edu.ng/
	Babcock University	http://www.babcockuni.edu.ng/
	Benson Idahosa University	http://www.idahosauniversity.com/
	Bingham University	http://ecwang.org
	Bowen University	http://www.bowenuniversity-edu.org/
	Caritas University	http://www.caritasuni.edu.ng/
	Covenant University	http://www.covenantuniversity.com/
	Crawford University	www.crawforduniversity.edu
	Madonna University	http://madonnau.edu.ng/
	Crawford University	http://www.crawforduniportal.com/
	Obong University	http://www.obonguniversity.net/default.aspx
	Redeemer's University	http://www.run.edu.ng/
	Salem University	http://www.salemuniversity.org/
	University of Mkar	http://unimkar.edu.ng/
	Wesley University of Science and Technology	http://www.wusto.com/portal/
	Veritas University	http://www.veritas.edu.ng
Rwanda	Adventist University of Central Africa	http://www.auca.ac.rw/
	Kabgayi Catholic University (Université Catholique de Kabgayi)	http://www.uck.ac.rw/
South Africa	Helderberg College	http://www.hbc.ac.za/
	St Augustine College of South Africa	http://www.staugustine.ac.za/
Tanzania	Mount Meru University	http://www.mmu.ac.tz/
	Saint Augustine University of Tanzania	http://www.saut.ac.tz/
	St John's University of Tanzania	http://www.sjut.ac.tz
	Tumaini University	http://tumaini.ac.tz/index.html
	University of Arusha	http://www.universityofarusha.ac.tz/
Uganda	Bugema University	http://www.bugemauniv.ac.ug/
	Busoga University	http://www.busogauniversity.ac.ug/
	Central Buganda University	http://www.centralbugandauniversity.info/Home/Home_1.html
	Ndejje University	http://www.ndejjeuniversity.ac.ug/
	Uganda Christian University	http://www.ucu.ac.ug
	Uganda Martyrs University	http://www.umu.ac.ug
Zambia	Zambia Adventist University	http://www.zauniversity.com/
Zimbabwe	Africa University	http://www.africau.edu/
	Catholic University in Zimbabwe	http://www.cuz.ac.zw/
	Solusi University	http://www.solusi.ac.zw/

Country	Institution Name	URL
Asia—Middle East		
Israel	Bethlehem University	http://www.bethlehem.edu/
Lebanon	Haigazian University	http://www.haigazian.edu.lb/Default.aspx
	Holy Spirit University of Kasilik (USEK)	http://www.usek.edu.lb/usek08/content/homepage_nod2766/pge2767/en/index.asp?langmode=pass
	Middle East University	http://meu.edu.lb/
	Notre Dame University—Louaize	http://www.ndu.edu.lb
	Université Antonine	http://www.upa.edu.lb
	Université La Sagesse	http://www.uls.edu.lb/
	Université Saint Joseph de Beyrouth	http://www.usj.edu.lb/en/index.html
Asia—Northeast		
Hong Kong	Chung Chi College University of Hong Kong	http://www.cuhk.edu.hk/ccc/eng/
	Hong Kong Baptist University	http://www.hkbu.edu.hk/the_u/the_u.htm
Japan	Aoyama Gakuin University	http://www.aoyama.ac.jp/en/
	Doshisha University	http://www.doshisha.ac.jp/english/
	Heian Jogakuin (Saint Agnes') University	http://www.heian.ac.jp/
	Ibaraki Christian University	http://www.icc.ac.jp/
	International Christian University	http://www.icu.ac.jp
	Japan Lutheran College	http://www.luther.ac.jp/
	J.F. Oberlin University	http://www.obirin.ac.jp/en/index.html
	Keiwa College	http://www.keiwa-c.ac.jp/foreign/
	Kwansei Gakuin University	http://www.kwansei.ac.jp/english/
	Kyoto Notre Dame University	http://www.notredame.ac.jp/
	Kyushu Lutheran College	http://www.klc.ac.jp/etc/outline-english.html
	Meiji Gakuin University	http://www.meijigakuin.ac.jp/index_en.html
	Nagaski Wesleyan University	http://www.wesleyan.ac.jp/
	Nanzan University	http://www.nanzan-u.ac.jp/English/
	Notre Dame Seishin University	http://www.ndsu.ac.jp/6000_engl/6000_engl.html
	Osaka Christian College	http://www.occ.ac.jp/
	Poole Gaukuin University	http://www.poole.ac.jp/eng/index_e.html
	Rikkyo (Saint Paul's) University	http://english.rikkyo.ac.jp/
	Saint Andrew's University	http://www.andrew.ac.jp/english/
	Saint Catherine University	http://www.catherine.ac.jp/english/
	Saint Thomas University	http://www.st.thomas.ac.jp/english/
	Saniku Gakuin College	http://www.saniku.ac.jp/hp/index.html
	Seigakuin University	http://www.seigakuin.jp/english/ab.html
	Shikoku Christian College	http://www.sg-u.ac.jp/
	Sophia University	http://www.sophia.ac.jp/e/e_toppage.nsf
	Tohoku Gakuin University	http://www.tohoku-gakuin.ac.jp/en/
	Tokyo Christian University	http://www.tci.ac.jp/
	University of the Sacred Heart	http://www.u-sacred-heart.ac.jp/english/
South Korea	Baekseok University	http://www.bu.ac.kr/english/
	Catholic University of Daegu	http://www.cataegu.ac.kr/english/main/main.htm
	Catholic University of Korea	http://www.cuk.ac.kr/
	Catholic University of Pusan	http://www.cup.ac.kr/
	Chongshin University	http://www.chongshin.ac.kr/eng/main.asp
	Daeshin University	http://www.daeshin.ac.kr/
	Ewha Womans University	http://www.ewha.ac.kr/english/
	Handong Global University	http://www.handong.edu/
	Hannam University	http://www.hannam.ac.kr/eng_new/
	Hansei University	http://www.hansei.ac.kr/
	Hoseo University	http://eng.hoseo.ac.kr/
	Incheon Catholic University	http://www.iccu.ac.kr/
	Jeonju University	http://www.jj.ac.kr/
	Kangnam University	http://builder.kangnam.ac.kr/user/knueng/index.html
	Keimyung University	http://www.kmu.ac.kr/english/
	Korea Baptist Theological University	http://www.kbtus.ac.kr/

(continued)

Country	Institution Name	URL
	Korea Nazarene University	http://www.kornu.ac.kr
	Korean Bible University	http://www.bible.ac.kr/template/Temp_english.aspx
	Korea Christian University	http://www.kcu.ac.kr/
	Kosin University	http://www.kosin.edu
	Myongji University	http://www.mju.ac.kr/ENG/index.jsp
	Sahmyook Nursing and Health College	http://www.syhc.ac.kr/english
	Sahmyook University	http://www.syu.ac.kr/
	Seoul Christan University	http://www.scu.ac.kr/
	Seoul Jangsin University	http://www.sjs.ac.kr/
	Seoul Theological University	http://www.stu.ac.kr/homepage/en/main_en.jsp
	Seoul Women's University	http://www.swu.ac.kr/english/
	Sogang University	http://www.sogang.ac.kr
	Soongsil University	http://eng.ssu.ac.kr/index.jsp
	Sung Kong Hoe University	http://www.skhu.ac.kr/Main/Homepage/Eng/main.aspx
	SungKyul Christian University	http://en.sungkyul.ac.kr/Pages/default.aspx
	Sungkyul University	http://sky.sungkyul.ac.kr/english
	Yonsei University	http://www.yonsei.ac.kr/eng/
Taiwan	Chang Jung Christian University	http://www.cjcu.edu.tw/english/
	Christ's College	http://www.christc.org.tw/
	Chung Yuan Christian University	http://www.cycu.edu.tw/cycu_e/cycuwebsite/index.htm
	Fu Jen Catholic University	http://140.136.240.107/english_fju/
	Providence University	http://www.pu.edu.tw/english/
	Saint John's University	http://www.sju.edu.tw
	Soochow University	http://www.scu.edu.tw/eng/index_style_eng.html
	Taiwan Adventist College	http://www.sdatac.org.tw/
	Tunghai University	http://www.thu.edu.tw/english/enindex.htm

Asia—Southeast

Country	Institution Name	URL
Indonesia	Adventist University of Indonesia (Universitas Advent Indonesia)	http://www.unai.edu/
	Artha Wacana Christian University Kupang (Universitas Kristen Artha Wacana Kupang)	http://www.recweb.org/index.php?section=78
	Atma Jaya Catholic University of Indonesia (Universitas Katolik Atma Jaya Indonesia)	http://www.atmajaya.ac.id
	Atma Jaya Yogyakarta University (Universitas Atma Yaya Yogyakarta)	http://www.uajy.ac.id/
	Catholic University St. Thomas (Universitas Katolik Widya Mandira)	www.ust.ac.id
	Catholic University Widy Mandira Kupang (Universitas Katolik Widya Mandala)	http://www.wima.ac.id/
	Christian University of Indonesia Jakarta (Universitas Kristen Indonesia)	http://www.uki.ac.id/
	Christian University of Krida Wacana (Universitas Kristen Krida Wacana)	http://www.ukrida.ac.id
	Cipta Wacana Christian University (Universitas Kristen Cipta Wacana)	http://www.ukdw.ac.id/2009/id/
	Darma Cendika Surabaya Catholic University (Universitas Katolik Darma Cendika Surabaya)	http://www.ukdc.ac.id/
	De La Sale Manado Catholic University	http://www.delasalle.ac.id/
	Duta Wacana Christian University (Universitas Kristen Duta Wacana)	http://www.ukdw.ac.id/
	Kablat University (Universitas Klabat)	http://www.unklab.ac.id/home/
	Krida Wacana Christian University	http://www.ukrida.ac.id/en/
	Maranatha Christian University	http://www.maranatha.edu/
	Parahyangan Catholic University (Universitas Katolik Parahyangan)	http://www.unpar.ac.id/
	Pelita Harapan University (Universitas Pelita Harapan)	http://www.uph.edu
	Petra Christian University	http://www.petra.ac.id/

Country	Institution Name	URL
	Satya Wacana Christian University (Universitas Kristen Satya Wacana)	http://www.uksw.edu/id/
	Soegijapranata Catholic University Semarang (Universitas Katolk Soegijapranata)	http://www.unika.ac.id/
Philippines	Adventist International Institute of Advanced Studies	http://www.aiias.edu/
	Adventist University of the Philippines	http://www.aup.edu.ph/3/
	Aldersgate College	http://www.aldersgate-college.com/
	Angeles University Foundation	http://www.auf.edu.ph/
	Aquinas University	http://www.aq.edu.ph/
	Asbury College	http://www.asburycollege-anda.org/
	Assumption College-San Lorenzo	http://www.assumption.edu.ph/
	Ateneo de Davao University	http://www.addu.edu.ph/
	Ateneo de Manila University	http://www.ateneo.edu/
	Ateneo de Naga University	http://www.adnu.edu.ph/
	Ateneo de Zamboanga University	http://www.adzu.edu.ph/
	Central Philippine Adventist College	http://www.cpac.edu.ph/
	Central Philippine University	http://www.cpu.edu.ph/
	Colegio de San Juan de Letran	http://www.letran.edu/
	De la Salle College of Saint Benilde	http://www.dls-csb.edu.ph/
	De la Salle Lippa	http://www.dlsl.edu.ph/
	De La Salle University	http://www.dlsu.edu.ph/
	Filamer Christian College	http://www.filamer.edu.ph
	Harris Memorial College	http://www.harris.edu.ph/
	Holy Angel University	http://www.hau.edu.ph/
	Holy Cross of Davao College	http://www.hcdc.edu.ph/
	Lorma College	http://lorma.org/index.php
	Miriam College	http://www.mc.edu.ph/
	Mountain View College	http://www.mvc.edu.ph/
	Our Lady of Fatima University	http://www.fatima.edu.ph/
	Philippine Christian University	http://www.pcu.edu.ph/
	Philippine Women's University	http://www.pwu.edu.ph/
	Saint Louis University	http://www.slu.edu.ph/
	Saint Mary's University of Bayombong	http://www.smu.edu.ph/
	Saint Paul University	http://www.spup.edu.ph/
	Saint Scholastica's College	http://www.ssc.edu.ph/
	Silliman University	http://www.su.edu.ph
	South Philippine Adventist College	http://spaconline.org//index.php?option=com_frontpage&Itemid=1
	Trinity University of Asia	http://www.tua.edu.ph
	Union Christian College	http://www.ucc.edu.ph/
	University of Regina Carmeli	http://www.urc.edu.ph/
	University of Saint La Salle	http://www.usls.edu.ph/
	University of San Agustin	http://www.usa.edu.ph/
	University of San Carlos	http://www.usc.edu.ph/
	University of Santo Tomas	http://www.ust.edu.ph/
	University of the Assumption	http://www.ua.edu.ph/main/
	University of the Immaculate Conception	http://www.uic.edu.ph/
	Wesleyan University	http://www.wesleyan.edu.ph/
	Xavier University Ateneo de Cagayan	http://www.xu.edu.ph/
Thailand	Asia-Pacific International University	http://www.apiu.edu/
	Assumption University	http://www.au.edu/
	Christian University of Thailand	http://www.christian.ac.th/
	Payap University	http://www.payap.ac.th/english/
Asia—South		
India	Ahmednagar College	http://www.aca.edu.in/
	All Saints College	http://www.keralauniversity.edu/allsaints.htm
	Alphonsa College	http://www.alphonsacollege.in/
	Andhra Christian College	http://www.accollegeguntur.com/

(continued)

Country	Institution Name	URL
	Andhra Loyola College	http://www.andhraloyolacollege.ac.in/
	Annai Velankanni College	http://www.annaicollege.org/
	Arul Anandar College	http://www.arulanandarcollege.edu.in
	Assumption College	http://www.assumptioncollege.in/
	Auxilium College	http://www.auxiliumcollege.edu.in/
	B.C.M. College	http://www.bcmcollege.org/
	Baldwin Women's Methodist College	http://www.baldwinwomensmethodistcollege.com/
	Bankura Christian College	http://www.bankurachristiancollege.in
	Baring Union Christian College	http://www.buccbatala.org
	Bharata Mata College	http://www.bmc.ac.in/
	Bishop Appasamy College of Arts and Sciences	http://www.csibacas.org/
	Bishop Cotton Women's College	http://www.bcwclc.com/
	Bishop Heber College	http://www.bhc.ac.in/
	Bishop Kurialacherry College for Women	http://www.bkcollege.org/
	Bishop Moore College	http://www.bishopmoorecollege.in/
	C.M.S. College	http://www.cmscollege.ac.in/
	Carmel College	http://www.carmelcollegemala.org/
	Carmel College for Women	http://www.carmelcollegegoa.org/
	Catholicate College	http://www.catholicatecollege.co.in/
	Christ Church College	http://www.christchurchcollegekanpur.com/
	Christ College, Irinjalakuda	http://www.christcollegeijk.edu.in/
	Christ College, Rajkot	http://www.christcollegerajkot.edu.in/index.html
	Christ University, Bangalore	http://www.christuniversity.in
	Christian College	http://www.keralauniversity.edu/christian/index.htm
	Crossland College	http://www.crosslandcollege.org/
	CSI Ewart Women's Christian College	http://csiewartcollege.org
	Deva Matha College	http://www.devamathacollege.ac.in/
	Fatima College	http://fatimacollegemdu.org/
	Fatima Mata National College	http://www.fatimacollege.net/
	Flaiz Adventist College	http://www.flaiz.net/
	Fr. Agnel College of Arts and Commerce	http://fragnelcollege.com
	Gossner College	http://www.gcran.org/home.php
	Holy Cross College, Nagercoil	http://www.holycrossngl.in/
	Holy Cross College, Tiruchirappalli	http://www.holycrossindia.ac.in/
	Indore Christian College	http://www.indorechristiancollege.com/
	Isabella Thoburn College	http://www.itcollege.ac.in/
	JMJ College for Women	http://www.jmjcollege.ac.in/
	Jayaraj Annapackiam College for Women	http://www.annejac.com/
	Jesus and Mary College	http://www.jmcdelhi.com/
	Jesus Mary Joseph (JMJ) Degree College for Women	http://jmjcolleges.org/index.html
	Jyoti Nivas College	http://www.jyotinivas.org/
	Karunya University	http://www.karunya.edu
	Kittel Arts College	http://kittel.collinfo.com/
	Kittel Science College	http://kittelsciencecollege.com/
	Kuriakose Elias College	http://www.kecollege.in/
	Kuriakose Gregorios College	http://www.kgcollege.ac.in/
	Lady Doak College	http://www.ladydoak.org/
	Loreto College	http://www.loretocollege.org/
	Loyola Academy, Secunderabad	http://www.loyolaacademy.ac.in/
	Loyola College	http://loyolacollege.edu/
	Lucknow Christian Degree College	http://www.lcdc.edu.in/
	Madras Christian College	http://www.mcc.edu.in/
	Mar Gregorios College	http://www.margregorioscollege.net/
	Mar Ivanios College	http://www.mic.ac.in
	Mar Thoma College	http://www.marthomacollege.org
	Marian College Kuttikkanam	http://www.mariancollege.org/
	Maris Stella College	http://www.marisstella.ac.in/
	Mary Matha Arts and Science College	http://www.marymathacollege.org/
	Mercy College	http://xavierboard.com/view_col_info.asp?ccode=Mercy_Palakkad

Country	Institution Name	URL
	Morning Star Home Science College	http://www.morningstarhomescience.org/
	Mount Carmel College	http://www.mountcarmelcollegeblr.co.in/
	Nazareth Margoschis College	
	Newman College	http://www.newmancollege.org/
	Nirmala College	http://www.nirmalacollege.ac.in/
	Nirmala College for Women	http://www.nirmalacollegeonline.com/
	Nirmalagiri College	http://nirmalagiricollege.org/
	Noble College	http://www.apsira.com/colleges/index.php?instituteId=5100
	Patkai Christian College	http://patkaicollege.com/
	Patna Women's College	http://www.patnawomenscollege.in/
	Pavanatma College	http://pavanatmacollege.org/
	Pope's College	http://popescollege.com/
	Prajyoti Niketan College	http://prajyotiniketan.edu.in/
	Providence College	http://www.providencecoonoor.com/
	Providence Women's College	http://providencecollegecalicut.com/
	Rajagiri College of Social Sciences	http://www.rajagiri.edu/
	Rev. Jacob Memorial College of Arts and Science	http://www.tamilnaducolleges.com/Arts_Science/jacob_arts.htm#profile
	Rosary College of Commerce and Arts	http://www.rosarycollege.org/
	STBC Degree College	
	Sacred Heart College, Arcot	
	Sacred Heart College, Kochi	http://www.shcollege.ac.in/
	Sacred Heart College, Madanthyar	http://www.sacredheartcollege.net/
	Sacred Heart College, Thrissur District	http://www.shcollege.org/
	Sacred Heart College, Tirupattur	http://www.shctpt.edu/
	Saint Agnes College (Autonomous)	http://www.stagnescollege.org/
	Saint Aloysius College, Edathua	http://www.aloysiuscollege.org/
	Saint Aloysius College, Jabalpur	http://www.staloysiuscollege.ac.in/
	Saint Aloysius College, Mangalore	http://www.staloysius.ac.in/
	Saint Andrew's College of Arts, Science and Commerce	http://www.standrewscollege.ac.in/
	Saint Andrew's P.G. College, Gorakhpur	http://www.st-andrews-college.org
	Saint Ann's College for Women	http://www.stannspgmallapur.com/
	Saint Augustine's College	
	Saint Bede's College	http://stbedescollege.in/
	Saint Berchman's College	http://www.sbcollege.org/
	Saint Cyril's College	http://www.keralauniversity.edu/stcyril.htm
	Saint Dominic's College	http://www.stdominicscollege.org/
	Saint Edmund's College	http://sec.edu.in/
	Saint Francis College for Women	http://stfranciscollege.ac.in/
	Saint Francis De Sales College	http://www.sfscollege.org.in/
	Saint Gregorios College	http://www.keralauniversity.edu/grgorious.htm
	Saint John's College, Kollam	http://www.keralauniversity.edu/anchal.htm
	Saint John's College, Tirunelveli	http://www.stjohnscsi.org
	Saint Joseph's College, Bangalore	http://www.sjc.ac.in/
	Saint Joseph's College, Darjeeling	http://stjosephsdarjeeling.org.in/
	Saint Joseph's College, Jakhama	http://www.stjosephjakhama.ac.in
	Saint Joseph's College, Ranchi	
	Saint Joseph's College, Thrissur	http://stjosephs.edu.in
	Saint Joseph's College, Tiruchirappalli	http://www.sjctni.edu/
	Saint Joseph's College for Women, Alappuzha	http://www.keralauniversity.edu/stjoseph.htm
	Saint Joseph's College for Women, Visakhapatnam	http://stjoseph-vizag.com/
	Saint Joseph's Evening College	http://www.sjec.edu.in/
	Saint Jude's College	
	Saint Mary's College, Manarcadu	http://www.stmaryscollege.net.in/
	Saint Mary's College, Shillong	http://smcs.ac.in/
	Saint Mary's College, Sulthan Bathery	http://stmaryssby.org/

(continued)

Country	Institution Name	URL
	Saint Mary's College, Thrissur	http://www.stmaryscollegethrissur.edu.in/
	Saint Mary's Syrian College (affiliated with Mangalore University)	http://smscollege.org
	Saint Paul's Cathedral Mission College	http://www.stpaulscmcollege.org/
	Saint Peter's College	http://www.stpeterscollege.ac.in/
	Saint Philomena's College, Mysore	http://www.stphilos.ac.in
	Saint Philomena's College, Puttur	
	Saint Stephen's College, Delhi	http://www.ststephens.edu/
	Saint Stephen's College, Uzhavoor	http://ststephens.net.in/
	Saint Teresa's College, Ernakulam	http://www.teresas.ac.in/
	Saint Theresa's College for Women, Eluru	
	Saint Thomas College, Bhilai	http://www.stthomascollege.net/
	Saint Thomas College, Kozhencherry	http://www.stthomascollege.info/
	Saint Thomas College, Pala	http://www.stcp.ac.in/
	Saint Thomas College, Ranni	
	Saint Thomas College, Thrissur	http://www.stthomas.ac.in/
	Saint Xavier's College, Kolkata	http://www.sxccal.edu/
	Saint Xavier's College, Mapusa-Goa	http://www.xavierscollege-goa.com
	Saint Xavier's College, Mumbai	http://www.xaviers.edu
	Saint Xavier's College, Ranchi	http://www.sxcran.org/sxc/
	Saint Xavier's College, Thiruvananthapuram	http://www.stxaviersthumba.org/
	Saint Xavier's College, Tirunelveli	http://stxavierstn.edu.in/
	Saint Xavier's College for Women, Aluva	http://www.stxaviersaluva.ac.in/
	Salesian College	http://www.salesiancollege.net/
	Sam Higginbottom Institute of Agriculture, Technology and Sciences	http://www.aaidu.org/
	Sarah Tucker College	http://www.csitirunelveli.org/ministry/ministry.htm
	Scottish Church College	http://www.scottishchurch.ac.in/
	Sophia College for Women, Mumbai	http://www.sophiacollegemumbai.com
	Sophia Girls' College, Ajmer	http://sophiacollegeajmer.edu.in/
	Spicer Memorial College	http://www.spicermemorialcollege.org/
	Stella Maris College	http://www.stellamariscollege.org/
	Stewart Science College	http://stewartsciencecollege.org/index.php
	Synod College	http://www.synod-college.com/
	Teresian College	http://www.teresiancollege.org/
	The American College	http://www.americancollege.edu
	Tranquebar Bishop Manikam Lutheran College	http://www.tbmlcollege.com/
	Union Christian College, Aluva	http://www.uccollege.edu.in/
	Union Christian College, Umiam	http://www.unionchristiancollege.com/index.htm
	United Mission Degree College	http://www.umdcblr.org/
	Vidya Jyothi Degree & PG College	http://vjdpgc.org/
	Vimala College	http://vimalacollege.edu.in/
	Voorhees College	http://www.voorheescollege.in/
	Wesley Degree College Co-Ed	http://www.wesleydegreecollege.com
	William Holland University College	
	Women's Christian College	http://www.wcc.edu.in/
	Women's Christian College	http://womenschristiancollege.net/
Nepal	Saint Xavier's College, Kathmandu	http://www.sxc.edu.np/index-1.html
Pakistan	Pakistan Adventist Seminary and College	http://www.pasc.edu.pk/
Europe		
Austria	International University of Vienna	http://www.iuvienna.edu/
Belgium	Katholieke Universiteit Leuven	http://www.kuleuven.ac.be/english/
	Université Catholique de Louvain	http://www.uclouvain.be/en-index.html
Finland	Diaconia University of Applied Sciences	http://english.diak.fi/
France	Lille Catholic University	http://www.univ-catholille.fr/
	Université Catholique de l'Ouest	http://www.uco.fr/
	Université Catholique de Lyon	http://www.univ-catholyon.fr/

Country	Institution Name	URL
Germany	Protestant University of Berlin	
	(Evangelische Hochschule Berlin)	http://www.eh-berlin.de/
	Catholic University Eichstatt-Ingolstadt	http://www.ku-eichstaett.de/en
	Catholic University for Applied Sciences Berlin	
	(Katholische Hochschule für Sozialwesen Berlin)	www.khsb-berlin.de
	Catholic University of Applied Sciences Freiburg	http://english.kh-freiburg.de/
	Darmstadt Protestant University	
	(Evangelische Hochschule Darmstadt)	www.efh-darmstadt.de
	Evangelical Ludwigsburg University	www.efh-reutlingen-ludwigsburg.de
	Evangelical University of Applied Sciences for	
	Social Work, Education, and Care	http://www.ehs-dresden.de/
	Mainz Catholic University of Applied Sciences	http://www.kfh-mainz.de/
	Munich Catholic University of Applied Sciences	http://www.ksfh.de/
	Nuremberg Protestant University of	
	Applied Sciences	www.evfh-nuernberg.de
Hungary	Károli Gáspár University	http://www.kre.hu/
	Pázmány Péter Catholic University	http://www.ppke.hu/index_eng.html
Italy	LUMSA University	http://www.lumsa.it/LUMSA/site/878/home.aspx
	Pontificia Studiorum Universitas a S. Thoma	
	Aquinate in Urbe	http://www.angelicum.org/
	Pontificia Universita della Santa Croce	http://www.pusc.it/eng/
	Pontificia Università Gregoriana	http://www.unigre.it/
	Pontificia Università Lateranense	http://cms.pul.it/index
	Pontificia Universitas "Antonianum"	http://www.antonianum.ofm.org/
	Università Cattolica del Sacro Cuore	http://www.unicatt.it/
	Università Pontificia Salesiana	
	(Pontificial Salesian University)	http://www.ups.urbe.it/
Lithuania	LCC International University	http://www.lcc.lt
Netherlands	Christelijke Hogeschool Ede, Christian University	
	of Applied Sciences	http://www.che.nl/
	Gereformeerde Hogeschool	
	(Reformed University of Applied Sciences)	http://www.gh-gpc.nl/
	Radboud University Nijmegen	http://www.ru.nl/english
	Tilburg University	http://www.tilburguniversity.nl/
Norway	Ansgar College and Theological Seminary	http://ansgarskolen.ekanal.no/sider/tekst.asp?side=6
	Diakonhjemmet University College	http://www.diakonhjemmeths.no/web/english/
Poland	The John Paul II Catholic University of Lublin	http://www.kul.pl
Portugal	Universidade Católica Portuguesa	http://www.ucp.pt
Romania	Emmanuel University	http://www.emanuel.ro/
	Partium Christian University (PCU)	http://www.partium.ro/
Russia	Russian Christian Humanities Academy	http://rchgi.spb.ru/Engl/index.php`
	Saint John University	http://www.rpiofficial.ru/
	Saint Tikhon University	http://pstgu.ru/
	Zaoksky Adventist University	http://www.zau.ru/
Slovakia	Catholic University in Ružomberok	http://www.ku.sk/en/
Spain	Universidad Cardenal Herrera CEU	http://www.uch.ceu.es/
	Universidad Católica de Valencia "San Vicente Mártir"	https://www.ucv.es/index_ing.asp
	Universidad de Deusto	http://www.deusto.es
	Universidad de Navarra	http://www.unav.es/english/
	Universidad Pontificia Comillas	http://www.upcomillas.es/eng/
	Universidad Pontificia de Salamanca	http://www.upsa.es/
	Universidad San Pablo CEU	http://www.ceu.es/pages/ingles/eng_introduction.htm
	Universitat Ramón LLULL	http://www.url.edu/en/index.php
Switzerland	Université de Fribourg	http://www.unifr.ch/
United Kingdom	Canterbury Christ Church University	http://www.canterbury.ac.uk/
Ukraine	Ukrainian Catholic University	http://www.ucu.edu.ua/eng/
Vatican	Pontificia Università Lateranense	http://cms.pul.it/
	Pontificia Università Urbaniana	http://www.urbaniana.edu/it/

(continued)

Country	Institution Name	URL
Latin America		
Argentina	Pontificia Universidad Católica Argentina	http://www.uca.edu.ar
	Universidad Adventista del Plata	http://www.uapar.edu/es/
	Universidad Austral	http://web.austral.edu.ar/
	Universidad Católica de Cordoba	http://www.ucc.edu.ar/
	Universidad Católica de Cuyo	http://www.uccuyo.edu.ar
	Universidad Católica de la Plata	http://www.ucalp.edu.ar/
	Universidad Católica de Salta	http://www.ucasal.net/
	Universidad Católica de Santa Fe	http://www.ucsf.edu.ar/
	Universidad Católica de Santiago de Estero	http://www.ucse.edu.ar/
	Universidad del Norte Santo Tomas de Aquino	http://www.unsta.edu.ar/
	Universidad del Salvador	http://www.salvador.edu.ar/
	Universidad FASTA	http://www.ufasta.edu.ar/
Bolivia	Adventist University of Bolivia (Universidad Adventista de Bolivia)	http://www.uab.edu.bo/
	Bolivian Catholic University San Pablo (Universidad Católica Boliviana San Pablo)	http://www.ucb.edu.bo/
	Bolivian Catholic University Cochabamba (Universidad Católica Boliviana San Pablo Cochabamba)	http://www.ucbcba.edu.bo/
	Bolivian Catholic University Santa Cruz (Universidad Católica Boliviana San Pablo Santa Cruz)	http://www.ucbscz.edu.bo/
	Bolivian Catholic University Tarija (Universidad Católica Boliviana San Pablo Tarija)	http://www.ucbtja.edu.bo/
	Bolivian Evangelical University (Universidad Evangelica Boliviana)	http://www.ueb.edu.bo/
	Christian University of Bolivia (Universidad Cristiana de Bolivia)	http://www.ucebol.edu.bo/
Brazil	Adventist University Centre of São Paulo (Centro Universitário Adventista de São Paulo)	http://www.colegiounasp.com.br/site/
	Centro Universitario Sao Camilo	http://www.saocamilo-es.br/centrouniversitario/a_instituicao.php
	Adventist College UNASP (Colegio Adventista UNASP)	http://www.iae-sp.br/
	Catholic University Dom Brosco	http://www.fsdb.com.br
	Catholic University of Brasílla (Universidade Católica de Brasília)	http://www.ucb.br/
	Catholic University of Goiás (Universidade Católica de Goiás)	http://www.ucg.br/
	Catholic University of Pelotas (Universidade Católica de Pelotas)	http://www.ucpel.tche.br
	Catholic University of Pernambuco (Universidade Católica de Pernambuco)	http://www.unicap.br/
	Catholic University of Petrópolis (Universidade Católica de Petrópolis)	http://www.ucp.br/
	Catholic University of Salvador (Universidade Católica do Salvador)	http://www.ucsal.br/
	Catholic University of Santos (Universidade Católica do Santos)	http://www.unisantos.br/web/guest/principal
	Izabela Hendrix Methodist University Centre (Centro Universitário Metodista Izabela Hendrix)	http://www.metodistademinas.edu.br/
	Lutheran University of Brazil (Universidade Luterana do Brasil)	http://www.ulbra.br/
	Lutheran University Center of Mnaus (Centro Universitário Luterano de Manaus)	http://www.ulbra-mao.br/
	Lutheran University Center of Palmas (Centro Universitário Luterano de Palmas)	http://www.ulbra-to.br/
	Lutheran University Center of Santarem (Centro Universitário Luterano de Santarém)	http://www.iles.edu.br/

Country	Institution Name	URL
	Methodist University of São Paulo (Universidade Metodista de São Paulo)	http://www.metodista.br/
	Pontifical Catholic University of Campinas (Pontificia Universidad Católica de Campinas)	http://www.puc-campinas.edu.br
	Pontifical Catholic University of Paraná (Pontificia Universidad Católica de Paraná)	http://www.pucpr.br
	Pontifical Catholic University of São Paulo (Pontificia Universidad Católica de São Paulo)	http://www.pucsp.br
	Pontifical Catholic University of Rio Grande do Sul (Pontificia Universidad Católica do Rio Grande do Sul)	http://www3.pucrs.br/portal/page/portal/pucrs/Capa/
	Pontifical Catholic University of Minas Gerais (Pontificia Universidade Catolica de Minas Berais)	http://www.pucminas.br/
	Pontifical Catholic University of Rio de Janerio (Pontificia Universidade Catolica do Rio de Janeiro)	http://www.puc-rio.br/
	Presbyterian University Mackenzie (Universidade Presbiteriana Mackkenzie)	http://www.mackenzie.br/
	Saint Francis University (Universidade Sao Francisco)	http://www.saofrancisco.edu.br/
	Saint Úrsala University (Universidade Santa Úrsala)	http://www.usu.br/
	Vale do Rio Doce University (Universidade do Vale do Rio dos Sinos)	http://www.unisinos.br/english/
Chile	Alberto Hurtado University (Universidad Alberto Hurtado)	http://www.uahurtado.cl/
	Catholic University of Cardenal Raùl Silva Henriquez (Universidad Católica Cardenal Raùl Silva Henriquez)	http://www.ucsh.cl/
	Catholic University of the Holy Conception (Universidad Católica de la Santisima Concepción)	http://www.ucsc.cl
	Catholic University of Temuco (Universidad Católica de Temuco)	http://www.uctemuco.cl/
	Catholic University of Maule (Universidad Católica del Maule)	http://www.ucm.cl/
	Catholic University of the North (Universidad Católica del Norte)	http://www.ucn.cl/
	Chile Adventist University (Universidad Adventista de Chile)	http://www.unach.cl/
	Pontifical Catholic University of Chile (Pontificia Universidad Católica de Chile)	http://www.uc.cl
	Pontifical Catholic University of Valparaiso (Pontificia Universidad Católica de Valparaiso)	http://www.ucv.cl/
	Santo Tomás University	http://www.ust.cl
	University of the Andes (Universidad de los Andes)	http://www.uandes.cl/
Colombia	Adventist University Corporation	www.unac.edu.co
	Catholic University Foundation of the North (Fundación Universitaria Católica del Norte)	www.ucn.edu.co
	Catholic University of Columbia (Universidad Católica de Colombia)	http://www.ucatolica.edu.co/easyWeb/
	Catholic University of Manizales (Universidad Católica de Manizales)	http://www.ucm.edu.co/
	Catholic University of Risaralda (Universidad Católica Popular de Risaralda)	http://www.ucpr.edu.co/
	Catholic University of the East (Universidad Católica de Oriente)	http://www.uco.edu.co
	Instituto Universitario CESMAG	http://www.iucesmag.edu.co/

(continued)

Country	Institution Name	URL
	La Gran Colombia University (Universidad La Gran Colombia)	http://www.ulagrancolombia.edu.co/
	Luis Amigo University Foundation (Fundación Universitaria Luis Amigó)	http://www.funlam.edu.co
	Mariana University (Universidad Mariana)	http://www.umariana.edu.co/
	Pontifical Bolivariana University (Universidad Pontificia Boliviriana)	http://www.upb.edu.co/
	Pontifical Xavier University (Pontificia Universidad Javeriana)	www.javeriana.edu.co
	Reformed University of Colombia (Universidad Reformada Colombia)	http://www.unireformada.edu.co/
	Rosary University (Universidad del Rosario)	http://www.urosario.edu.co/
	Santo Tomàs University (Universidad Santo Tomàs)	http://www.usta.edu.co
	Temuco Catholic University (Univsersidad Católica de Temuco)	http://www.uctemuco.cl/
	University of La Sabana (Universidad de la Sabana)	http://www.unisabana.edu.co/inicio.htm
	University of la Salle (Universidad de la Salle)	http://unisalle.lasalle.edu.co/
	University of San Buenaventura, Bogota (Universidad de San Buenaventura-Bogotà)	http://www.usbbog.edu.co/
Costa Rica	Catholic University of Costa Rica (Universidad Católica de Costa Rica)	http://www.ucatolica.ac.cr/
	Evangelical University of the Americas (Universidad Evangelica de las Americas)	http://www.unela.net/
Dominican Republic	Catholic University Nordestana (Universidad Catolica Nordestana)	http://www.ucne.edu/ucne/
	Catholic University of Santo Domingo (Universidad Católica de Santo Domingo)	http://www.ucsd.edu.do/
	Dominican Adventist University (Universidad Adventista Dominicana)	http://universidadadventistadominicana.blogspot. com/2009/04/nuestras-ofertas-son.html
	National Evangelical University (Universidad Nacional Evangelica)	http://www.unev.edu.do
	Pontifical Catholic University Madre y Maestra (Pontificia Universidad Católica Madre y Maestra)	http://www.pucmm.edu.do/
Ecuador	Catholic University of Azogues (Universidad Católica de Azogues)	http://sitio.ucaazo.edu.ec/
	Catholic University of Cuenca (Universidad Católica de Cuenca)	http://www.ucacue.edu.ec/
	Catholic University of Santiago de Guayaquil (Universidad Católica Santiago de Guayaquil)	http://www2.ucsg.edu.ec/
	Christian Latin American University (Universidad Cristiana Latinoamericana)	http://www.ucl.edu.ec/
	Pontifical Catholic University of Ecuador (Pontificia Universidad Católica del Ecuador)	http://www.puce.edu.ec/
	Pontifical Catholic University of Ecuador Ambato Branch (Pontifica Universidad Catolica del Ecuador Sede Ambato)	http://www.pucesa.edu.ec/
	Pontifical Catholic University of Ecuador Ibarra Branch (Pontifica Universidad Catolica del Ecuador Sede Ibarra)	http://www.pucei.edu.ec/
	Pontifical Catholic University of Ecuador Santa Domingo Branch (Pontifica Universidad Catolica de Ecuador Sede Santo Domingo)	http://www.pucesd.edu.ec/

Country	Institution Name	URL
	Salesian Polytechnical University (Universidad Politècnica Salesiana)	http://www.ups.edu.ec/
El Salvador	Catholic University of El Salvador (La Universidad Católica de El Salvador)	http://www.catolica.edu.sv/
	Christian University of the Assemblies of God (Universidad Cristiana de las Asambleas de Dios)	http://www.ucad.edu.sv/index.htm
	Evangelical University of El Salvador (Universidad Evangelica de El Salvador)	http://www.uees.edu.sv/
	Lutheran Salvadorean University (Universidad Luterana Salvadorena)	http://www.uls.edu.sv/
Guatemala	Rafael Landívar University (Universidad Rafael Landívar)	http://www.url.edu.gt/Portalurl/
Haiti	Queensland University	http://www.uqstegnetwork.org
	Adventist University of Haiti (Universite Adventiste d'Haiti)	http://www.unah.edu.ht/
	University Notre Dame of Haiti	http://www.undh.org/
Honduras	Catholic University of Honduras "Nuestra Señora Reina de la Paz" (Universidad Católica de Honduras "Nuestra Señora Reina de la Paz")	http://www.unicah.edu/
Jamaica	Northern Caribbean University	http://www.ncu.edu.jm
Mexico	Anáhuac University of Mexico City (Universidad Anáhuac-Cdad. Mèxico)	http://www.anahuac.mx/
	Anáhuac University of Puebla (Universidad Anáhuac-Puebla)	http://www.anahuacpuebla.org
	Anáhuac University of Sur (Universidad Anáhuac-Sur)	www.uas.mx
	Panamerican University (Universidad de Panamericana)	http://www.up.edu.mx/
	Intercontinental University (Universidad Intercontinental)	http://www.univa.mx
	Pontifical University of Mexico (Universidad Pontificia de Mexico)	http://www.pontificia.edu.mx
	Universidad Vasco de Quiroga	http://www.uvaq.edu.mx/
Nicaragua	Ave Maria University	http://www.avemaria.edu/ni
	Catholic University of Stockbreeding of the Dry Tropics (Universidad Católica Agropecuaria del Tropico Seco)	http://www.ucatse.edu.ni/
	Central American University	www.uca.edu.ni
	Christian Autonomous University of Nicaragua (Universidad Cristiana Autónoma de Nicaragua)	http://www.ucan.edu.ni/
	Martin Luther King Nicaraguan Protestant University (Universidad Evangélica Nicaragüense, Martin Luther King)	http://www.uenicmlk.edu.ni/
	Polytechnic University of Nicaragua (Universidad Politecnica of Nicaragua)	http://upoli.edu.ni/
	Redemptoris Mater Catholic University (Universidad Católoca Redemptoris Mater)	http://www.unica.edu.ni/
Panama	Santa María la Antigua Catholic University (Universidad Católica Santa María la Antigua)	http://www.usmapanama.com/
Paraguay	Catholic University Our Lady of the Assumption (Universidad Católica "Nuestra Senora de la Asunción")	http://www.uc.edu.py/
	Evangelical University of Paraguay (Universidad Evangelica de Paraguay)	http://www.uep.edu.py/
Peru	Antonio Ruiz de Montoya University (Universidad Antonio Ruiz de Montoya)	http://www.uarm.edu.pe/
	Catholic University of San Pablo (Universidad Católica San Pablo)	http://www.ucsp.edu.pe/

(continued)

Country	Institution Name	URL
	Catholic University of Trujillo (Universidad Católica de Trujillo)	http://www.uct.edu.pe/
	Pontifical Catholic University of Peru (Pontoficia Universidad Católica de Perú)	http://www.pucp.edu.pe/
	Santa Maria Catholic University (Universidad Católica de Santa Marìa)	http://www.ucsm.edu.pe/
	Santo Toribio de Morgrovejo Catholic University (Universidad Católica Santo Toribio de Mogrovejo)	http://www.usat.edu.pe/
	Sedes Sapientiae Catholic University (Universidad Católica Sedes Sapientiae)	http://www.ucss.edu.pe/
	University of Piura	http://www.udep.edu.pe/
Puerto Rico	Pontifical Catholic University of Puerto Rico (Pontificia Universidad Católica de Puerto Rico)	http://www.pucpr.edu/
	Antillean Adventist University (Universidad Adventista de las Antillas)	http://www.uaa.edu/
	University of the Sacred Heart (Universidad del Sagrado Corazón)	http://www.sagrado.edu/
Trinidad & Tobago	University of the Southern Carribean	http://www.usc.edu.tt/
Uruguay	Catholic University of Uruguay Dámaso Antonio Larrañaga (Universidad Católica de Uruguay del Dámaso Antonio Larrañaga)	http://www.ucu.edu.uy/
	University of Montevideo (Universidad de Montevideo)	http://www.um.edu.uy/universidad/
Venezuela	Andès Bello Catholic University (Universidad Católica Andès Bello)	http://www.ucab.edu.ve/
	Catholic University Cecilio Acosta (Universidad Católica Cecilio Acosta)	http://www.unica.edu.ve/
	Catholic University of Táchira (Universidad Católica de Táchira)	http://www.ucat.edu.ve/
	Santa Rosa Catholic University (Universidad Católica Santa Rosa)	http://www.santarosa.edu.ve/default.htm
Oceania		
Australia	Australian Catholic University	http://www.acu.edu.au
	Avondale College	http://www.avondale.edu.au/
	Christian Heritage College	http://www.chc.edu.au
	The University of Notre Dame Australia	http://www.nd.edu.au/
	Wesley Institute	http://www.wesleyinstitute.edu.au
Papua New Guinea	Divine Word University	http://www.dwu.ac.pg/

Appendix C: Entries Listed by Author

Diana D. Abbott
Special Education as Christian Education
Teacher Education
Transformative Learning
Youth Devotional Literature

Marilyn Abplanalp
Assemblies of God Church Christian Education (authored with Stacie Reck)

John A. Adams
Fruit of the Spirit (authored with Benjamin Espinoza)

W. Gregory Aikins
Iceland and Christian Education

Risto Aikonen
Finland and Christian Education

Daniel O. Aleshire
Seminaries, Freestanding
Seminaries in University-based Schools, Current Status of
Seminaries, Theological Schools, and Divinity Schools

Michael Armstrong
Congregational Church Christian Education (authored with Janet Wootton)

Alan A. Arroyo
Behavior Management (authored with George Selig)
Character Development (authored with George Selig)
Kingdom Education (authored with George Selig)
Motivation for Learning (authored with George Selig)

Jeff Astley
Affections, Christian
Darwin and Evolutionary Theory
Freedom
Nurture as Metaphor
Spiritual Learning
Theological Education—Lead-in Introduction
Values

Harley T. Atkinson
Bacon, Roger
Bible, Early Vernacular Translations of the
Byzantine Medieval Church

Caesarea, School of
Christian Humanism
Continental Reformation, Educational Principles of the
Edessa, School of
Jesuits, The

Karri Backer
Forgiveness
Listening as Christian Practice
Smart, Ninian

Dan W. Bacon
Guidance as Christian Practice (authored with Shelley Trebesch)

Ken Badley
Canada and Christian Education

Jason D. Baker
Bible Study Software
Online Education, Growth of
Software, Educational
Virtual Schools

Péter Balla
Hungary and Christian Education

Jack Barentsen
Church as Learning Organization
Power in Christian Education
Practical Theology in Academic Contexts
Seeker Courses
Spiritual Growth Research

Wesley Nan Barker
Bible as Literary Genre, Roots of the
Literary Criticism
Literary Theory and Theology
Literature and Christian Education—Lead-in Introduction
Phenomenology
Secular Literature and Christian Education

L. Philip Barnes
Analytic Philosophy and Theology
Conversion

Calvin Chong
Singapore and Christian Education
Theodore Michael Christou
Constantine's Influence on Education
Julian the Apostate, The Edict of
Lily K. Chua
Taiwan and Christian Education
Norris J. Chumley
Jesus Prayer, The
Steven R. Clark
Confession as Christian Practice
Homeschooling, Impact of Legal Issues on
Theology of Fathering
Kenneth S. Coley
Gangel, Kenneth O.
Leadership Development in the United States (19th
Century to the Present)
Lowrie, Roy
School Finances
Wilson, Douglas
Steven Collins
Archaeology, Christian Contributions to
Peter Cotterell
Ethiopia and Christian Education
Ethiopian Graduate School of Theology
Suffering as Christian Practice
William F. Cox Jr.
Kingdom Education
Mara Lief Crabtree
Academics, Biblical Theology of Christian
Art, Painting
Art, Sculpture
Christian Education in Difficult Circumstances—Lead-in
Introduction
Human Rights Violations
Institutionalized and Elderly, The
Online Education for Theological Schools
Spiritual Formation
Spirituality in Christian Education
Victims of Abuse
Women, Rights of
Leslie J. Crawford
Pacific Islands and Christian Education
South Pacific Association of Evangelical Colleges
Faustino M. Cruz
Dialogue Education and Jane Vella
Nebreda, Alfonso M.
Transformational Leadership
Scott Culpepper
Baylor University
Christian Reformed Church Christian Education
English Puritanism and Separatism
Enlightenment Philosophy and Theology
Knox, John
Owen, John
Southern Baptist Convention Christian Education

Finola Cunnane
God, Images of
Religious Education
Teaching Religion
Eileen M. Daily
Art and Mission
Counter-Reformation, Educational Principles of the
Neil C. Damgaard
Dallas Theological Seminary
Faith Development
Music Education
Valerie Davidson
Children at Church, Protecting (authored with J. Gregory
Lawson)
Jeffry C. Davis
Censorship
Latin
Vatican Library, The
Marian de Souza
Adolescents, Spiritual Dimensions of
Learning, Spiritual Dimensions of
Pluralism and Christian Education
Olive Fleming Drane
Clowning/Clown Ministry
Mario O. D'Souza
Philosophy and Theology of Education
Philosophy of Education, Catholic
Randall Dunn
Christian Higher Education, Technology in (authored with
Benjamin Forrest)
Taras N. Dyatlik
Euro-Asian Accrediting Association
Ukraine and Christian Education
Kent Eby
Russia and Christian Education
Mark Eckel
Administration
Aesthetics (Beauty)
Attitudes
Authority
Didactics
Hebrew Bible and Old Testament
Hebrew Bible Interpretation
Heresy, Response to
Jewish Catechetical Tradition
Learning, Project-Based
Loyola University, Chicago
Meditation as Christian Practice
Pastor as Teacher
Poetry as Christian Practice
Simulation and Discussion
Submission as Christian Practice
Theological Research
Jonathan Eckert
Comprehensive Schools, The Impact of
Establishment Clause

Free Exercise Clause
Instrumentalism and John Dewey

Fred P. Edie
Baptism, Theology of
Imagination as Christian Practice
Narrative, Philosophical Foundations of
Sacraments

Martín H. Eitzen
Paraguay and Christian Education

Kevin P. Emmert
Baxter, Richard
Conscience
Doubt
Evangelism
Luther's *Small Catechism*
Westminster Shorter Catechism

Leona M. English
Curriculum Planning, Jane Vella and
Experiential Learning

Ralph E. Enlow Jr.
Association for Biblical Higher Education
Bible College Movement, Impetus for the
Columbia International University
Global Associates for Transformational Education

Gerald C. Ericson
Europe and Christian Education

Benjamin D. Espinoza
Asbury Theological Seminary
Bugenhagen, Johannes
Calvin College
Chrysostom, John
Cyril of Alexandria
Fruit of the Spirit (authored with John Adams)
Hendricks, Howard
Human Trafficking (authored with Gina Shaner Farcas)
Justin Martyr
Little, Sara
Shema (authored with J. Chase Franklin)
Zwingli, Huldreich

Octavio Javier Esqueda
Cuba and Christian Education
Mexico and Christian Education

James Estep
Christian Education, Greek Precursors to and Influences on
Christian Education, Roman Precursors to and Influences on
Jewish Model of Education
Neo-Thomism
Oser, Fritz K.
Philosophy, Educational
Pietists, The
Ratio Studiorum
Teaching in Acts
Thomism

Karen L. Estep
Billy Graham Center and Library
Gaebelein, Frank

Kindergarten
Teacher Character

Douglas Estes
Didache as Early Christian Education Strategy
Greek
Wisdom

Gina Shaner Farcas
Human Trafficking (authored with Benjamin Espinoza)

Silvia Regina Alves Fernandes
Brazil and Christian Education

Allan Fisher
Publishing, Christian Academic

James Flynn
Early Church, Christian Education in the
Printing Press
Theological Education, Athens versus Berlin Model of
Theological Education, Berlin as a Model of

Benjamin K. Forrest
Biblical Models of Education (authored with Michael Mitchell)
Christian Christian Education, Technology in (authored with Randall Dunn)
Liberty University (authored with David W. Hirschman)
Online Education, Instructional Design for (authored with Kenneth Law)
Paideia (authored with Michael Mitchell)
Praxis (authored with Michael Mitchell)

Charles Foster
Christian Education Movement
Church Education Movement
Packard, Frederick
Religious Education Movement
Sunday School Movement

Stavros S. Fotiou
Cyprus and Christian Education
Maximus the Confessor

Mark A. Fowler
Field Experiences/Practicums
Mentoring into Ministry

Rachel A. Fox
Prayer as Christian Practice

Leslie J. Francis
Attitudes toward Christianity
Empirical Theology and Christian Education
Psychological Type Theory and Christian Education

J. Chase Franklin
Shema (authored with Benjamin Espinoza)

Bryan T. Froehle
Catholic Reformation, Educational Principles of the
Georgetown University
Institutional, University, and Seminary Profiles—Lead-in Introduction
Pastoral Institutes (Catholic Universities)
Sociology, Christian Contributions to
Venezuela and Christian Education

Mary Froehle
Consciousness

Robert L. Gallagher
Biblical Education by Extension
Book of Kells
Day Missions Library, The (Yale Divinity School)
de Foucald, Charles Eugene
Great Commission, The
Lindisfarne Gospels
Missionary Schools
Missionary Task, The
Missions and Christian Education—Lead-in Introduction
Theological Education by Extension College South Africa
University of Divinity (Melbourne, Australia)

Sarita D. Gallagher
Armenia and Christian Education
Australasia and Christian Education
Cross-cultural Storytelling
Georgia and Christian Education
Global Poverty
Global Underground Churches
Immigrants
Missions and the Education of Women
Papua New Guinea and Christian Education
Schools for Missionary Children
Thailand and Christian Education

Louis B. Gallien Jr.
Integration of Faith and Learning
Wheaton College (Illinois)

Paul E. Garverick
Servant Leadership
Volunteer Satisfaction, Local Church
Volunteerism, Local Church

Lee Gatiss
Christian History/Church History
Oak Hill Theological College
Princeton Theological Seminary
Protestant Catechisms
Puritan Education
Scholasticism, Reformed
Teaching in Hebrews
Tyndale House (Cambridge)
Westminster Theological Seminary

Laima Geikina
Latvia and Christian Education

Shaké Diran Geotcherian
Armenian Orthodox Church Christian Education

Aaron J. Ghiloni
Holistic Education
Interreligious Education
Pragmatism and Christian Education

Elizabeth L. Glanville
Spirituality, Women's

Perry L. Glanzer
Christian Higher Education—Lead-in Introduction

Beth Faulk Glover
Pastoral Education, Clinical (authored with R. Kevin
    Johnson)

Wil Goodheer
International Council of Higher Education

Virginia Gray
Amish Christian Education
Curriculum Development
God, Children's Views of

Jeffrey P. Greenman
Christian Liberal Arts Colleges and Universities
Hauerwas, Stanley
Langham Partnership
Luther's Catechisms
Moral Philosophy as Capstone Course

Thomas H. Groome
Boston College Institute for Religious Education and
    Pastoral Ministry
Christian Curriculum—Lead-in Introduction

David Gyertson
Board Governance
Christian Higher Education, The Future of
Educational Leadership
Institutional Mergers
Presidential Transitions

Jan Hábl
Comenius

Russell Haitch
Schmemann, Alexander
Theosis as Christian Practice
Transformation and Socialization, Interaction of

James K. Hampton
Narrative Theology, Biblical Foundations of
Professional Academic Societies
Retreats as Christian Practice
Rousseau and Locke
Youth Ministers

Bryce Hantla
Dykstra, Craig

Steve Hardy
Angola and Christian Education
Bangui Evangelical School of Theology
Malawi and Christian Education
Mozambique and Christian Education
Overseas Council International
Zambia and Christian Education

Allan Harkness
Assessment/Evaluation in Education
Christian Education Journals
Early Christian Education, Jewish Influence on
Education, Paul's Concept of
Indoctrination

Steve Harper
Chambers, Oswald
Foster, Richard
Jones, E. Stanley
Merton, Thomas
Nouwen, Henri
Van Kaam, Adrian

Richard Kenneth Hart
Jordan and Christian Education
Middle East Association for Theological Education
Muslim Cultures

Sara M. Reichard
Academic Giftedness (authored with Joshua Reichard)
Patrick Bruner Reyes
Brothers of the Christian School
Critical Thinking
Justice-seeking as Christian Practice
Social Action as Christian Practice
Adam J. Richards
Disability, Learning (authored with Joshua Reichard)
Lawrence O. Richards
Christian Pedagogy—Lead-in Introduction
Jennifer Riley
Disability, Emotional (authored with Carol Anne Jantzen)
Disability, Intellectual (authored with Carol Anne Jantzen)
Amanda J. Rockinson-Szapkiw/Amanda Szapkiw
Christian Higher Education and Globalization
Freud, Sigmund
Online Education
Theresa Roco-Lua
Asia Graduate School of Theology
Asia Theological Association
Nigel Rooms
Alpha Course
Christian Formation, A Biblical View of
Cognitive Dissonance, Jesus's Use of
Enculturation
Epistemology, Praxis
Knowles, Malcolm
Missions and Theological Education
Ordinary Theology
Ordinary Theology, Implications of for Adult Christian Education
Theological Education by Extension
Viktor J. Rózsa
Campus Ministry (authored with Chris Kiesling)
Ivan Rusin
Ukrainian Evangelical Theological Seminary
Philip Graham Ryken
Wannamaker, John
George F. Sabra
Near East School of Theology Library
Martha Saint-Berberian
Guatemala and Christian Education
V. J. Samkutty
Sermon on the Mount, The Meaning of the
Teaching Methods of Jesus
Paul R. Sanders
International Council for Evangelical Theological Education (authored with Riad A. Kassis)
Olga Schihalejev
Estonia and Christian Education
Muriel Schmid
Existential Philosophy and Theology
Friends/Quaker Church Christian Education
Kierkegaard, Søren
Prison Ministry, History of

Women in Historical Christian Context
World Council of Churches
Alvin J. Schmidt
Catechism
Didache as Early Christian Education Strategy
Easter
Faith
Francis Schmidt
El Salvador and Christian Education
Laura Schmidt
Peter Schreiner
Germany and Christian Education
Schweitzer, Friedrich
Bernd Schröder
Nipkow, Karl-Ernst (authored with L. Philip Barnes)
Roger Schroeder
Pontifical Universities
Katherine G. Schultz
Association of Classical Christians Schools
Christian Worldview
Released Time Education, Status of
Tom Schwanda
Francke, August Hermann
Fuller Theological Seminary
Gerson, Jean
Laubach, Frank
More, Hannah
Mystery
Spurgeon, Charles
Zinzendorf, Count Nicholas von
Halee Gray Scott
Celebration as Christian Practice
Suffering, Educational Value of
W. George Selig
Behavior Management (authored with Alan Arroyo)
Character Development (authored with Alan Arroyo)
Kingdom Education (authored with Alan Arroyo)
Motivation for Learning (authored with Alan Arroyo)
David Setran
Coe, George Albert
Dewey, John
McGuffey Readers
New England Primer
Released Time Education, Origins of
Jack L. Seymour
Vincent, Bishop John Heyl
Perry W. H. Shaw
Culture and Learning
Greek Orthodox Church Christian Education
Will
World
Donald R. Shepson III
Christian and Missionary Alliance and Christian Education
Educational Ministry of Jesus
Leadership Development in the First Century: Jesus
Candace C. Shields
Children of Unchurched Parents

Index of Names

Aaron, 981
Abate, Eshetu, 480
Abbe Henri Huvelin, 390
Abbot Hadrian, 383
Abbot Mellitus, 382
Abbot Suger, 72
Abbot, John S., 918
Abelard, Peter, 2, 1048, 1105
Abraham, 628, 683, 922
Abraham of Bet Rabban, 880
Adam, 623, 626, 627, 652, 749
Adamantius, Leonides, 904
Adamantius, Origen, 904, 905
Adeodatus, 99
Adeyemo, Tokunboh, 90
Adomnán, Abbot of Iona, 651, 742
Adrian, William, 291
Aelfric, 384
Aelia Eudoxia, 281
Aelred of Rievaulx, 18–19, 1192
Aesop, 231
Afanassieff, Nicolas, 1208
Agapetus, Pope, 740
Aguiló, Eduardo Bonnín, 369
Aidan, 650
Alaric, 1453
Alberti, 284
Albertus Magnus, 59
Albright, William Foxwell, 61
Alcott, Louisa May, 231
Alcuin of York, 27–28, 189, 205, 222, 384, 1432
Alda, Alan, 510
Aldred, 741
Alexander the Great, 29, 42, 690, 711, 874, 919
Alexander, Archibald, 991
Alexander, Bishop, 740
Alexander, Cecil Frances, 617
Alighieri, Dante, 354
Allan, Edgar, 510

Allen, Leslie, 759
Allis, Oswald T., 1381
Allport, Gordon, 885
Alter, Robert, 130
Althizer, Thomas, 459
Alves, Rubem Azevedo, 1462
Alypius, 99
Amalek, 580
Amalorpavadass, Duraisamy Simon, 31–33
Amandus, 123
Ambrose of Milan, 33–34, 190, 241, 379, 618, 701, 856, 865, 941
Ames, William, 1014
Amirtham, Samuel, 1288
Anastasia of Sirmium, 826
Anatolius, bishop of Laodicea, 195
Anderson, Bernard W., 165, 1009
Anderson, Lorin, 306
Ando, Tadao, 285
Andrew of Saint Victor, 607
Andrew, Saint, 753, 1075
Andrews, James, 458
Andrews, Lancelot, 397
Andringa, Robert, 158, 159, 988
Anicetus of Rome, 431
Anna, 826
Anne, Saint, 767
Anscombe, Elizabeth, 842
Anselm of Canterbury, 51–52, 56, 952, 1029, 1324
Antoniy (Pakanych), 691
Antony of Egypt, 905
Apollinaris of Hierapolis, 57
Apollinaris of Laodicea, 657
Apollos, 648
Appenzeller, H. G., 1178
Aquinas, Thomas, 56, 59, 68, 109, 137, 205, 275, 460, 608, 610, 668, 716, 760, 778, 844, 864, 869, 870, 912, 952, 953, 955, 956, 962, 1107, 1246, 1301–1304, 1324, 1454
Arbuckle, Gerald, 501

Index of Entries

Contributing Authors

Diana D. Abbott (PhD, Syracuse University) is associate professor of education at Roberts Wesleyan College, Rochester, New York. She teaches her students how to design effective inclusive education for students with disabilities and serves as an advocate to ensure that students with disabilities receive responsive educational programs.

Marilyn Abplanalp (EdD, University of San Francisco) serves as president of the Alliance for Assemblies of God Higher Education (Springfield, Missouri). Prior to beginning her current post, she served for 18 years at Bethany University (California) as the associate dean for the School of Professional Studies and the director of the master of arts in education.

John A. Adams graduated from Portland Bible College with a BA in theology and earned an MA in biblical studies from Asbury Theological Seminary. He is an instructor in biblical studies at l'Institut Biblique Alliance de Grâce (Grace Covenant Bible Institute) in Cap-Haitien, Haiti.

W. Gregory Aikins (DMin, Biblical Seminary, Pennsylvania; MDiv, Trinity Evangelical Divinity School, Illinois) has served with Greater Europe Mission since 1983 and is that organization's field leader in Iceland, where he and his wife have been missionaries for 17 years. Greg's doctoral research focused on discipleship in Iceland.

Risto Aikonen has a licentiate in education and master of arts from Ptyhiouhos Theologias (Greece) and is senior lecturer in Orthodox Christian religion education pedagogy in the School of Applied Educational Science and Teacher Education at the University of Eastern Finland. Aikonen has researched religious education pedagogy by incorporating information and communication technology.

Daniel O. Aleshire (PhD) is executive director of the Association of Theological Schools in the United States and Canada (ATS). Prior to joining the ATS staff in 1990, he served as professor of psychology and Christian education at Southern Baptist Theological Seminary. He has written in the areas of Christian education and theological education.

Michael Armstrong (DThM, Durham University) is a congregational minister in England and tutor for the Congregational Federation degree program in practical theology. His doctoral research focused on the theology of his own congregation concerning life after death. Armstrong is currently developing a final year honors' degree project for congregational students to investigate the theology of their own congregations.

Alan A. Arroyo (PhD) is currently professor in the School of Education at Regent University, where he has served in a number of administrative and teaching positions since 1986. Before that, Arroyo was a teacher and administrator in public schools. His degrees are from Northern Illinois University and National College of Education.

Harley T. Atkinson (PhD, Talbot School of Theology) is professor of ministry and leadership at Toccoa Falls College (Georgia). He is a regular contributor to the *Christian Education Journal* and has published books in the areas of youth ministry, small groups, and young adult religious education. He is a contributor to the *Evangelical Dictionary of Christian Education* and the online *Christian Educators of the 20th Century Project*.

Karri Backer (MDiv, MA in clinical psychology) is a doctoral student in practical theology and spiritual formation at Claremont School of Theology and an Episcopal priest. She is interested in the integration of spirituality and psychology and in exploring contemplative practices that encourage healing and restoration.

Dan W. Bacon (DMiss) is a career missionary with OMF International. In this capacity, he served as a church planter in Japan and in a variety of roles including national director (USA), international director for personnel, and director for member development. Currently Dr. Bacon serves as a leadership consultant.

Ken Badley (PhD) teaches ethics in the doctoral program in education at George Fox University in Newberg, Oregon. He also serves as book review editor for the *Journal of Education and Christian Belief*, published by the Association of Christian Teachers (UK) and the Kuyers Center at Calvin College (USA).

Jason D. Baker (PhD) is a professor of education at Regent University, where he chairs the education doctoral programs. He teaches courses in educational technology, communication, research and statistics, and Christian worldview. His research and writing has focused on online learning, with a particular interest in Christian distance education.

Péter Balla (PhD) is chair of New Testament studies, Faculty of Theology, Károli Gáspár University of the Reformed Church in Hungary, and rector of the university since 2011. He has a PhD in 1994 from the University of Edinburgh, and habilitation in 2001 at the Evangelical Lutheran Theological University in Budapest.

Jack Barentsen (PhD, Evangelische Theologische Faculteit, Belgium) is associate professor of practical theology at the ETF in Leuven. He publishes in the fields of church leadership, notably his comprehensive study *Emerging Leadership in the Pauline Mission*; church development; and Christian education.

Wesley Nan Barker teaches at Mercer University in Atlanta. She received a PhD in comparative literature and religion from Emory University, an MTS from Duke Divinity School, and graduate certificates in women's studies from Duke and Emory. Her research engages Luce Irigaray's feminist interpretations of continental philosophy and phenomenology to construct a Christian ethic of intersubjectivity.

L. Philip Barnes (MA, MTh, PhD, Dublin) is reader in religious and theological education, King's College, London. He has published widely in the areas of theol-

ogy, religious studies, and the philosophy of religious education, and has recently completed a book, *Education, Religion and Diversity: Developing a New Model of Religious Education*.

Laura Barwegen (EdD, Northern Illinois University) is an associate professor of Christian formation and ministry at Wheaton College (Illinois), where she teaches courses in human development, research methodology, and spiritual formation and the brain. Her research, speaking engagements, and writing explore the correlations between neuropsychology and spiritual formation.

Andrea P. Beam (EdD) is associate professor of special education and education leadership at Liberty University (Virginia). She has worked as a teacher and administrator at both the elementary and secondary levels. Beam has authored or coauthored *Leadership Bloopers and Blunders* and *Standards-Based Differentiation*.

Lisa M. Beardsley-Hardy (PhD in educational psychology, University of Hawai'i at Mānoa; MPH, Loma Linda University; MBA, Claremont Graduate University) is director of education for the Seventh-day Adventist Church World Headquarters in Silver Spring, Maryland. She chairs the Board of the Accrediting Association of Seventh-day Adventist Schools, Colleges, and Universities.

Christa Buse Bearivo was born in Germany and trained there as a nurse. She served in a mission hospital in Botswana and as a midwife in South Africa. She received a licentiate of theology from the Baptist Theological College in Cape Town and an MA in theology from the University of South Africa. Bearivo has been involved with theological education by extension in Madagascar since 1997.

Andreas J. Beck (PhD, Utrecht University) is professor of historical theology and academic dean at the Evangelical Theological Faculty in Leuven, Belgium. He is also director of the Institute of Post-Reformation Studies and codirector of the Jonathan Edwards Center Benelux. He has authored or coedited five books and published numerous articles in the fields of late medieval and early modern theology and philosophy.

Ivy Beckwith holds a master's degree and a PhD in religious education. She has served in church educational ministry in the Midwest and on the East Coast. Beckwith has worked in the curriculum publishing industry and has authored several books on the spiritual formation of children.

John Behr is the dean of St. Vladimir's Orthodox Theological Seminary (New York). He has published numerous monographs with SVS Press and Oxford University Press, most recently an edition and translation of the fragments of Diodore of Tarsus and Theodore of Mopuestia and a monograph on Irenaeus.

David M. Bell (PhD, Emory University; MDiv Princeton Seminary) is senior lecturer in religion and social sciences at Georgia State University (Atlanta). His recent publications include works on religious identity, faith development, and narrative psychology. Bell conducts research in traumatic experiences of moral injury grounded in concepts of moral identity.

Robert Benne is Jordan-Trexler Professor of Religion Emeritus and founding director of the Benne Center for Religion and Society at Roanoke College, Salem, Virginia. He is author of *Quality with Soul—How Six Premier Colleges and Universities Keep Faith with Their Christian Traditions*.

Byard Bennett (PhD, University of Toronto; MDiv, Duke Divinity School; BA, Duke University) is professor of historical and philosophical theology at Grand Rapids Theological Seminary (Michigan). He has published on early Christian approaches to evil and suffering. Bennett's research examines the connection between education, spiritual formation, and self-transcendence in Christian and non-Christian writers in the Alexandrian Neoplatonic tradition.

Daniel Bennett (PhD, Clemson University) is the associate dean of students at Montreat College (North Carolina). With an MA in educational ministries and an MA in theology from Wheaton College, Daniel enjoys the opportunities to integrate theory and practice through the curricular and cocurricular ministry setting with college students. His research interests include Christian education, assessment, and organizational culture.

Jerome W. Berryman was educated at Princeton Theological Seminary (MDiv, DMin), University of Tulsa College of Law (JD), Centro Internazionale Studi Montessoriani in Bergamo, Italy (Montessori certificate), and three clinical residencies in medical ethics (Institute of Religion, Texas Medical Center). Granted honorary degrees from General Theological Seminary and Virginia Theological Seminary, he is an Episcopal priest and founder of Godly Play.

John A. Bertone has a PhD in New Testament from the University of St. Michael's College and is currently a psychosocial spiritual clinician for the Niagara North Palliative Care Team. He has previously published *The Law of the Spirit: Experience of the Spirit and Displacement of the Law in Romans 8:1–16* (Peter Lang, 2005) and other book chapters, journal articles, and book reviews. He has taught in universities and seminaries in Canada and the United States.

Jonathan L. Best is a PhD student in practical theology at St. Thomas University. He is currently the serials coordinator at the main library of St. Thomas University. Jonathan is also an ordained minister of the Convention of Original Free Will Baptist. He resides in Miami, Florida.

Ron J. Bigalke Jr. (BS, MApol, MDiv, MTS, PhD) is the Georgia state director for Capitol Commission and also a missionary with Biblical Ministries Worldwide. He has served for many years in numerous discipleship, educational, and evangelistic ministries. Bigalke is an ordained minister and a member of several Christian professional societies.

Doug Blomberg (MEdSt, PhD, EdD, FACE) is professor of philosophy of education and academic dean at the Institute for Christian Studies, Toronto. His vocation has been in Christian schooling, exercised as a student, teacher, and administrator. A major theme in his scholarship is how a biblical perspective on wisdom as an alternative to the theory-into-practice paradigm plays out in pedagogy (as problem-posing) and curriculum (as integral).

Benjamin B. Blosser is associate professor of theology at Benedictine College in Atchison, Kansas, where he teaches church history, New Testament, and systematic theology. He received his PhD in historical theology from The Catholic University of America.

Horst Born is professor of New Testament and biblical Greek at the Theological Seminary in Basel (Switzerland) and received his university training in theology and philosophy at Tübingen and Basel. He has an MTh in theology and an MA in languages and history from Staatsexamen. Born is president of his local free church and has responsibility with the European Evangelical Accreditation Association.

Michael Borowski has studied public law and theology in Germany, the United States, and Belgium. He currently teaches history of the church and history of theology at the Martin Bucer Seminary and works for the International Institute for Religious Freedom (Germany).

Christopher T. Bounds (PhD, Drew University) is professor of theology at Indiana Wesleyan University, where he has taught since 2002. He is an ordained elder in The Arkansas Conference of the United Methodist Church. Prior to coming to Indiana Wesleyan, Bounds served as a pastor for eight years.

Mark Bowdidge (MM, DMA in choral conducting) is the director of music at Central Christian Church in Springfield, Missouri. He has served on the music faculties of a small liberal arts college in Georgia and at Bethany College in Lindsborg, Kansas.

James P. Bowers (PhD, Southern Baptist Seminary) is visiting professor of spiritual formation and practical theology at Regent University and vice president for institutional development for William Seymour Theological College (launched fall 2013 in Washington, DC). He has written on the prosperity Gospel and pastoral wellness, and coauthored *So Much Better* (2013) and *What Women Want: Pentecostal Women Ministers Speak for Themselves* (in press).

Mark Lau Branson (EdD) is the Homer L. Goddard Professor of the Ministry of the Laity at Fuller Theological Seminary (California), where he teaches congregational leadership and community engagement. He has coauthored, with Juan Martínez, *Churches, Cultures and Leadership* (InterVarsity, 2011). Branson has served on church leadership teams and with Christian agencies in education, community development, and community organizing.

Oliver Brennan is a lecturer and pastor of a Roman Catholic parish church in Ireland. He held the position of professor of pastoral theology at the Pontifical University (Ireland) and adjunct professor of religious education at Fordham University (New York). He holds undergraduate degrees in arts and theology, an MA in religious education, and a PhD in education and church leadership.

George Brown Jr. (PhD) is G. W. and Eddie Haworth Professor of Christian Education Emeritus, Western Theological Seminary, Holland, Michigan. An ordained minister in the Reformed Church in America, he served as a pastor and then as a minister of Christian education before joining Western's faculty in 1988.

Michael T. Buchanan (PhD) is a senior lecturer and member of the Faculty of Education at Australian Catholic University. His research interests include leadership in Catholic schools and religious education.

Vladimir Bugera is from the Ukraine. He is a graduate of Sumy State Pedagogical University, Moscow Theological Seminary, and Moscow Theological Academy. Bugera serves as professor and prorector of Kyiv Theological Academy in the field of scientific research in theology. His areas of professional interest are the history of national Orthodox churches and theological education in Ukraine.

Bernard Bull (PhD) serves as an associate professor of education and assistant vice president of academics at Concordia University, Wisconsin. His scholarship focuses on emerging models of education, social and spiritual implications of digital culture, learning experience design, online learning communities, and educational entrepreneurship.

Hrisanti Bulugea (Doctor in educational sciences) is an experienced religious education teacher and school headmaster in Bucharest, Romania. Bulugea has collaborated as a lecturer with the Faculty of Orthodox Theology and the Catholic Institute in Bucharest with interests in Orthodox theology and educational sciences, comparative studies of teaching religious education in different international education systems, and the dialogue between science and religion.

Andrew Burggraff (EdD candidate, Southeastern Baptist Theological Seminary, North Carolina) is the pastor of discipleship and assimilation at Colonial Baptist Church in Cary, North Carolina. He is an also adjunct professor of Christian education at Shepherds Theological Seminary. He has served in pastoral positions and missionary for over 13 years.

Philip Bustrum (PhD, Talbot School of Theology) is professor of Christian education and former chair of the Bible, Religion, and Ministry division of Cornerstone University. He served for 14 years in Kenya, as a missionary doing theological education. His interests are intercultural studies and spiritual formation.

Emmanuel Buteau is a doctoral student in practical theology at St. Thomas University (Florida). His research focuses on a theology for grace as it relates to Haitian religious life. His scholarly interests include revelation, epistemology, and semiotics, as imagined through the lens of a postcolonial theory.

Philip D. Byers is an educator with a background in college student development, a scholarly interest in the history of American religion, and professional experience working for several American Christian colleges and universities. He has authored articles in journals including *Christian Scholar's Review*, *Christian Higher Education*, *Intégrité*, and *Growth*.

Thyra Cameron began her teaching career in higher education at Regent University (Virginia) where she taught spiritual formation to masters' students for seven years. At present she teaches leadership and character formation at Cornerstone Institute (Claremont, South Africa). Her research interests include the role of the Holy Spirit in Christian education, Christ-like character formation, and the development of a conceptual framework based on the principles of the Christian worldview.

Gary Philip Camlin is professor of New Testament and practical theology at Portuguese Bible Institute, where he has been since 1993. He earned a BS in Bible from Philadelphia College of Bible and a ThM in New Testament studies from Dallas Theological Seminary. Camlin served as pastor of Northwood Hills Bible Church in Dallas, Texas, from 1980 to 1993.

Michael W. Campbell (PhD, Andrews University) is assistant professor of historical/theological studies at the Adventist International Institute of Advanced Studies (Philippines). He is an ordained minister of the Seventh-day Adventist Church.

Carlos Campo is a higher education professional, professor, and leadership consultant. The former president of Regent University, he was the first Latino president of the Council for Christian Colleges & Universities. Campo is the chair of the Alliance for Hispanic Christian Education and was recently recognized by the National Hispanic Leadership Conference with its Excellence in Leadership Award.

Ana María E. Campos (DMin) was born in Lima, Perú. She teaches at Central American Theological Seminary (Guatemala), specializing in Christian education. Campos attended Dallas Theological Seminary, where she received the Howard Hendricks' award in Christian education and is an adjunct professor. She writes and offers conferences internationally.

Erik C. Carter, a dual citizen of the United States and Norway, received degrees in theology and religion from Southern Adventist University and Andrews University, as well as a DMin from Louisville Presbyterian Theological Seminary. He is currently a PhD candidate in practical theology at Claremont School of Theology.

Stephen G. Carter is a research affiliate at the University of New Brunswick (Fredericton, Canada) and adjunct lecturer of modern history at Crandall University (Moncton, New Brunswick, Canada). He received his PhD from the Department of Theology and Religion at the University of Durham.

Karina A. Casanova is Argentinian and has served in youth ministries there. She is practical ministry supervisor and Bible professor at Seminario Teológico Centroamericano (Ciudad de Guatemala, Guatemala) and serves in her local church. She came to Guatemala in 2005 to do her theological studies, earning a BA in theology, and is currently finishing a ThM in Bible at the Central American Theological Seminary.

Fernando A. Cascante Gómez (PhD) was born in San José, Costa Rica, and studied at the University of Costa Rica and Latin American Biblical Seminary. For 10 years he was professor of Christian education at Union Theological Seminary and Presbyterian School of Christian Education in Richmond, Virginia. Presently he works as director of pastoral formation and leadership development for the Association for Hispanic Theological Education (AETH) and director of the Justo González Center for Latino/a Ministries in Orlando, Florida.

Radoslaw Chałupniak is a Roman Catholic priest and professor in religious education at the Faculty of Theology, University of Opole (Poland). He teaches catechetics and pedagogics and is the author of scientific articles and books on religious education in Europe. Among Chałupniak's published books are *Contemporary Catechesis: Crises and Hope* (2010) and *Anticlericalism and Contemporary Catechesis* (2008).

Diane J. Chandler (PhD) serves as an associate professor of Christian spiritual and holistic formation, discipleship, and leadership development in the Regent University School of Divinity (Virginia). She holds a PhD in organizational leadership, an MDiv in practical theology, and an MS in education.

Adrian Chatfield is from Trinidad. He is an Anglican minister of 40 years and has worked in theological education in Trinidad, England, and South Africa. Chatfield is currently on the staff of Ridley Hall Cambridge, teaching Anglicanism, worship and spirituality, Christianity and the arts, and some biblical theology.

Graham Cheesman (PhD, Queens University, Northern Ireland) was the principal of Belfast Bible College, a constituent college of the Queens University Belfast, and director of the Centre for Theological Education. He works for the European Evangelical Accrediting Association and is an honorary lecturer of Queens University supervising doctoral students. Cheesman is the author of three books and a number of articles. His blog is www.teachingtheology.org.

Eun Sik Cho graduated from St. John's University (BA), Princeton Theological Seminary (MDiv), New York University (MA), and United Theological Seminary in Ohio (DMiss). As a mission coworker of the Presbyterian Church (USA), he taught at Silliman University in the Philippines. Presently, he is a chaplain and professor at Soongsil University in Korea. He has published *Christian Mission toward Reunification of Korea* (2007) and *Christian Mission in Our Life* (2009).

Calvin Chong (MTh, OT studies, King's College, London; PhD, educational studies, Trinity Evangelical Divinity School) is associate professor in educational studies at Singapore Bible College, where he has served since 1995. His teaching and research interests include orality studies, educational technologies, designing learning experiences, and contemporary urban mission issues.

Theodore Michael Christou is an assistant professor at Queen's University, Canada. He is the author of two books published in 2012. The first, *Progressive Education: Revisioning and Reframing Ontario's Public Schools, 1919–1942* (University of Toronto Press), is a historical study. The second, *An Overbearing Eye* (Hidden Brook Press), is a book of verse.

Lily K. Chua (PhD, Trinity Evangelical Divinity School) is assistant professor of Christian education and dean of spiritual Formation at China Evangelical Seminary in Taipei, Taiwan. She teaches on ministries to children and older adults, oversees field education program, and engages deeply in local church ministries.

Norris J. Chumley (PhD) is an author, professor, and executive producer of many books, films, and radio series on religion and history. He is executive producer/host for Columbia University's *Rethinking Religion*, instructor at New York University's Kanbar Institute of Film and Television, columnist for the *Huffington Post*, and chairman of Manhattan Neighborhood Networks.

Steven R. Clark (PhD, Talbot School of Theology; MA Christian apologetics, Biola University; MA education, Chapman University) is a speaker/writer on fathering issues; an adjunct professor in philosophy, apologetics,

and spiritual formation; a professional tennis coach; and a motivational speaker/consultant for collegiate athletes, with an extensive collegiate coaching background in the NCAA.

Kenneth S. Coley (EdD, University of Maryland) is the director of EdD studies at Southeastern Seminary (North Carolina). He finished a BA at Wake Forest University and an MA at the College of William and Mary. Coley's publications include *The Helmsman* (2006) and *Navigating the Storms* (2010).

Steven Collins (PhD, Trinity Theological Seminary, Indiana) is dean of the College of Archaeology, Trinity Southwest University, and director of the Tall el-Hammam Excavation Project in Jordan. His latest book, *Discovering the City of Sodom* (Simon & Schuster/Howard Books), recounts the past decade of his archaeological work at this important biblical site.

Peter Cotterell received the BD, BSc, and PhD (University of London) and an honorary DUniv (Brunel), and is a fellow of the Royal Society for the Advancement of Science. He was a missionary in Ethiopia from 1957 to 1976; principal, London School of Theology; and founding director, Ethiopian Graduate School of Theology.

William F. Cox Jr. is professor and director of Christian/kingdom education programs in the School of Education at Regent University, Virginia Beach, Virginia. His particular interests are to enable educational choice without government mandates and to promote the development of kingdom citizenship. His book *Tyranny through Public Education* addresses the inappropriateness of civil government involvement in education.

Mara Lief Crabtree (DMin) is associate professor of Christian spirituality and women's studies at the Regent University School of Divinity (Virginia). Ordained with the Communion of Evangelical Episcopal Churches, she also serves as a chapter chaplain and U.S. Region 2 representative for Virginia in the International Order of St. Luke.

Leslie J. Crawford (EdD) has been serving as academic dean at Adelaide College of Ministries for over 30 years and is involved in theological education internationally through the International Council for Evangelical Theological Education (ICETE) as a representative of the South Pacific Association of Evangelical Colleges (SPAEC).

Faustino M. Cruz is associate dean of academic affairs at Seattle University. He earned an interdisciplinary PhD in theology and education from Boston College. Born and raised in the Philippines, his academic, research, and pastoral commitments are deeply rooted in US immigrant life.

Scott Culpepper (PhD, Baylor University) serves as associate professor of history at Dordt College (Iowa). He received an MA at Northwestern State University, an MDiv at New Orleans Baptist Theological Seminary, and BA degrees at Louisiana College. Culpepper's teaching and research interests are British and European history, particularly early modern Europe, and the history of Christianity.

Finola Cunnane (MA, PhD, Fordham University, New York) has lectured extensively in religion and religious education throughout Ireland, Europe, the United States, West Africa, and New Zealand. She is the author of *New Directions in Religious Education* as well as over 100 articles.

Eileen M. Daily (JD, PhD, Boston College) is graduate program director of religious education programs at the Institute of Pastoral Studies at Loyola University, Chicago, and studies the integration of visual art and Christian education. She created the *art/y/fact.Xn* app for iPhone, iPad, and Android devices.

Neil C. Damgaard is senior pastor of Dartmouth Bible Church and Protestant chaplain at the University of Massachusetts at Dartmouth. He is an industrial engineering graduate of Virginia Tech, a former management engineering consultant for the U.S. Navy, and a graduate of Dallas Theological Seminary (ThM/DMin).

Valerie Davidson is the minister to preschool and children at Oak Valley Baptist Church, where she and her husband Louis live, in Franklin, Tennessee. With over 20 years of experience in children's ministry and Christian education, Davidson is currently working on her EdD at Southeastern Baptist Theological Seminary (North Carolina).

Jeffry C. Davis (PhD, University of Illinois at Chicago) is associate professor of English at Wheaton College, where he directs the Writing Center and the program for interdisciplinary studies. His scholarship focuses on ancient rhetorical connections to composition, instruction, and Christian liberal arts learning.

Marian de Souza (PhD) is a senior lecturer at Australian Catholic University. Marian has published extensively on the spirituality of young people and its implications for education in a globalized, pluralistic world. She was the

coordinating editor of the *International Handbook of the Religious, Moral and Spiritual Dimensions of Education* and the *International Handbook of Education for Spirituality, Care and Wellbeing* (Springer).

Olive Fleming Drane is Chaplain at International Christian College in Glasgow (Scotland); a fellow of St. John's college, University of Durham (England); and affiliate professor at Fuller Seminary, California. Her clown characters Valentine and Barni have been welcomed by churches of many different traditions throughout Europe, Australasia, the United States, and the Caribbean.

Mario O. D'Souza (CSB) is a Canadian. He has degrees from University College, Dublin, University of Calgary, University of Toronto, University of St. Michael College, and Boston College. He is a Roman Catholic priest of the Congregation of St. Basil. He is dean of theology at the University of St. Michael's College and holds the Basilian Fathers chair in religion and education.

Randall Dunn (EdD, University of Bath) is an assistant professor of education and director of educational technology at Liberty University's School of Education (Virginia).

Taras N. Dyatlik was born into a Baptist family in Ukraine. Raised during the Soviet period, he helped his father with an underground Christian publishing ministry as a child. Currently he is pursuing a PhD (ABD) at Evangelical Theological Faculty in Leuven, Belgium, and serves as educational development coordinator at the Euro-Asian Accrediting Association and as the regional director for Eurasia at the Overseas Council International.

Kent Eby (BBA, James Madison University; MMin, Bethel University; PhD, Trinity International University) is assistant professor of mission and director of the Intercultural Studies Program at Bethel College (Indiana). He and his family served in Christian education in Russia from 1994 to 2007, primarily with St. Petersburg Christian University.

Mark Eckel (PhD, Southern Baptist Theological Seminary, Kentucky; ThM, Grace Theological Seminary, Indiana) is vice president of academic affairs, director of interdisciplinary studies, and professor of Old Testament at Crossroads Bible College, Indianapolis, Indiana. Eckel speaks and writes on education, leadership, culture, and interdisciplinarity. Over 300 essays appear on Eckel's website at www.warpandwoof.org.

Jonathan Eckert is associate professor of education at Wheaton College (Illinois). From 2008 to 2009, he served at the U.S. Department of Education, where he worked in both the Bush and Obama administrations on teacher quality issues. Prior to that, he was a public school teacher outside of Chicago and Nashville for 12 years. He earned a doctorate in education leadership, policy, and organizations from Vanderbilt University, Peabody College (Tennessee).

Fred P. Edie (PhD, Emory University; MDiv, Vanderbilt University) is professor for the practice of Christian education at Duke Divinity School. He was founding director of Duke's Youth Academy for Christian Formation and remains its faculty advisor. Edie's research interests include the relationship of worship and faith formation, ministry with youth, theological anthropology, and epistemology.

Martin H. Eitzen (PhD, Trinity International University, Illinois) has been professor in missiology and intercultural studies at the Instituto Bíblico Asunción, School of Theology, at Evangelical University of Paraguay for 15 years. He is founder and director of the Instituto Aquila y Priscila, a mobile pastors training program.

Kevin P. Emmert (MA, Wheaton College) is assistant editor for *Christianity Today*, where he develops theological content for the Global Gospel Project. He is author of numerous articles on theology, church history, faith and culture, and preaching.

Leona M. English (PhD) is professor of adult education at St. Francis Xavier University, Nova Scotia, Canada. Her recent publications include *Learning with Adults: A Critical Pedagogical Introduction* and *International Encyclopedia of Adult Education*. She is interested in spirituality, poststructuralism, and gender in learning.

Gerald C. Ericson (DMin) has served on the governing boards of six theological schools in Europe during his 39 years of teaching in Portugal with Greater Europe Mission. He was director of Instituto Bíblico Português and European director of training/equipping. Ericson has authored two books and 19 articles. He is chair of the Board of Tyndale Theological Seminary (Netherlands) and adjunct professor, Lancaster Bible College, Pennsylvania.

Benjamin D. Espinoza is a graduate of Cedarville University and Asbury Theological Seminary and has contributed to *Christian Education Journal* and *Religious Education*. His research interests include theological approaches to Christian education, history and philosophy of Christian education, teaching ministry of congregations, and Christian practices among evangelicals.

Octavio Javier Esqueda (PhD) holds a licenciatura in Latin American literature from the University of Guadalajara, an MA in Christian education from Dallas Theological Seminary, and a PhD in higher education from the University of North Texas. He teaches in the doctoral programs in education at Talbot School of Theology as well as in several countries at different academic levels.

Karen L. Estep (PhD) currently serves as a professor of education, the associate dean for Christian education ministries field, and director of professional education at Lincoln Christian University (Illinois).

Douglas Estes (PhD, University of Nottingham; Post-Doc, Dominican Biblical Institute) is lead pastor, Trinity Church, Mesa, Arizona, and adjunct professor, Phoenix Seminary. He is the author of several books, including *The Questions of Jesus in John* (Brill, 2013) and *SimChurch* (Zondervan, 2009).

Gina Shaner Farcas is a graduate of Asbury Theological Seminary (Kentucky) with an MA in intercultural studies. She has served across the globe and worked alongside victims of human trafficking at many levels and currently works with a nonprofit fair trade ministry.

Silvia Regina Alves Fernandes (PhD) is professor of the graduate program of the Federal Rural University of Rio de Janeiro—UFRRJ (Brazil) and CAPES Foundation senior researcher at the University of Florida. She has been analyzing the Brazilian religious field and has published several articles on religion, with special interest in comparative research on youth in Brazil and the United States.

Allan Fisher served three companies during his 39-year career in publishing, finishing as senior vice president and publisher for books and Bible resources at Crossway. He earned a BA from Kalamazoo College and MDiv from Trinity Evangelical Divinity School, after which he entered publishing at Baker Book House.

James T. Flynn (PhD) is entering his fourth decade in pastoral ministry, specializing in teaching and leadership development. He is associate professor of practical theology and director of the DMin Program in the School of Divinity at Regent University (Virginia).

Benjamin K. Forrest (EdD, Liberty University) is the chair of practical studies at Liberty University Baptist Theological Seminary.

Stavos S. Fotiou (PhD, University of Athens) studied education and theology at Nicosia, Cyprus and Athens,

Greece. He is associate professor of theology and religious education in the Department of Education of the University of Cyprus. Fotiou is the author of 12 books and editor of 35.

Mark A. Fowler (DMin) holds the Murray H. Leiffer Associate Professorship in Congregational Leadership at Garrett-Evangelical Theological Seminary. He was director of field education and vice president of vocation-in-ministry. Fowler is an elder in full connection in the New England Conference of The United Methodist Church, serving churches in Williamstown, Framingham, Needham, and Lynn.

Rachel A. Fox (MA) is a PhD student in the practical theology degree program at Claremont School of Theology (California), with a concentration in spiritual formation and interested in the role of the Holy Spirit in the faith development of the Christian believer, especially within Pentecostal/charismatic spirituality.

Leslie J. Francis is professor of religions and education at the University of Warwick (England) and canon treasurer and canon theologian at Bangor Cathedral (Wales). He holds doctorates from Cambridge University (PhD, ScD), Oxford University (DD) and University of Wales (DLitt). He publishes on the psychology of religion, empirical theology, practical theology, and religious education.

J. Chase Franklin is currently a staff member at Asbury Theological Seminary, where he also earned an MA in biblical studies. He is a licensed minister with the Assemblies of God. His research interests include biblical Hebrew grammar, the history of Israel, and the book of Ruth.

Mary Froehle (PhD, sociology, The University of Michigan; MA, pastoral counseling, Institute of Pastoral Studies, Loyola University, Chicago) teaches intercultural counseling, social context, and field education in the Institute of Pastoral Studies, Loyola University Chicago. Her recent work has explored theological diversity in the context of field education.

Robert L. Gallagher (PhD, Fuller Theological Seminary) is the department chair, director of the MA program in intercultural studies, and associate professor of intercultural studies at Wheaton College Graduate School in Chicago, where he has taught since 1998. He previously served as the president of the American Society of Missiology (2010–2011) and as an executive pastor in Australia (1979–1990), as well as being involved in theological education in Papua New Guinea and the South Pacific since 1984.

Sarita D. Gallagher (PhD, Fuller Theological Seminary) joined the Department of Religious Studies at George Fox University (Oregon) in 2010. She taught courses in missiology and biblical studies at Azusa Pacific University, World Missions Faith Training School (Papua New Guinea), and Tabor College (Australia). Gallagher's dissertation, "Abrahamic Blessing: A Missiological Narrative of Revival in Papua New Guinea," is being published by Wipf & Stock (2014).

Louis B. Gallien Jr. is dean and professor of education at Oakland University (Michigan). He previously won Regent University's award as outstanding faculty member and has completed postgraduate studies at University of Michigan, University of Georgia, Oxford-Brookes University, Virginia Theological Seminary, Haverford College, Wye Institute, and Schloss Leopoldschron (Austria). Gallien has coedited two books on the achievement patterns of African American college students.

Paul E. Garverick (EdD, MA, MDiv) serves as director for religion programs, College of Adult and Professional Studies at Indiana Wesleyan University, after 17 years in pastoral ministry. His dissertation is "Local Church Volunteer Satisfaction in the Contexts of a Local Church and Its Organizational Leadership."

Lee Gatiss is the director of Church Society, an adjunct lecturer in church history at Wales Evangelical School of Theology, and editor of *Theologian* (www.theologian.org.uk). He is the author/editor of many books and articles on theology, biblical interpretation, and church history and has ministered in several Anglican churches.

Laima Geikina (DrPaed) has been a professor in the Faculty of Theology at the University of Latvia since 2001. Previously she taught for 12 years in primary and secondary schools. Geikina's dissertation is "Life-loving Attitudes and Christian Education in the Primary School."

Shaké Diran Geotcherian (Koujryan) (STM) is instructor in Christian education and director of the Christian Education Resource Center in the Near East School of Theology, Beirut, Lebanon.

Aaron J. Ghiloni (PhD, University of Queensland) is director of studies in ministry, mission and leadership at Trinity Theological College in Brisbane, Australia. He is also an affiliate lecturer in the School of Theology at the

Australian Catholic University. Ghiloni is the author of *John Dewey among the Theologians*.

Elizabeth L. Glanville (PhD, Fuller Theological Seminary) is assistant professor of leadership, formerly director of doctoral studies, and now core faculty for the DMiss program in the School of Intercultural Studies at Fuller Theological Seminary. Her areas of research include women in Christian leadership and biblical theology of leadership.

Beth Faulk Glover is an Association of Clinical Pastoral Education supervisor and the corporate director of the Pastoral Care & Education Department at New York Presbyterian, The Teaching Hospital of Columbia and Cornell, in New York City. She is ordained as an Episcopal priest.

Wil Goodheer has worked in Christian higher education in Europe most of his adult life. He received his undergraduate degree from Lipscomb University, master's degree from Eastern Seminary, and doctorate from American University in Europe. The recipient of six honorary doctorates, Goodheer is chancellor of International Council for Higher Education, past president of International University (Vienna), and founder of International Christian University (Kiev).

Virginia Gray is in the EdD program at Southeastern Baptist Theological Seminary (North Carolina). She has an MA in Christian education from Mid-America Baptist Theological Seminary and a BA in political science from Arkansas State University.

Jeffrey P. Greenman (PhD, University of Virginia) is academic dean at Regent College in Vancouver, British Columbia. He previously served as associate dean of biblical and theological studies at Wheaton College, Illinois, and as academic dean at Tyndale Seminary in Toronto, Ontario.

David Gyertson (PhD) is headmaster of Maranatha High School in Pasadena, California. Most recently he served as distinguished professor at Regent University. Gyertson was president of Regent University, Asbury University, and Taylor University. He holds the PhD from Michigan State University, with a concentration in higher education administration and management.

Jan Hábl (PhD) is professor of pedagogy at University J. E. Purkyne (Czech Republic) and pastor in Církev bratrská (Brethren Free Evangelical Church). He studied education at J. E. Purkyne University, theology at EMF School of Biblical Studies in England, and philosophy at University of Wales. He has taught systematic theology at Evangelical Theological Seminary in Prague and philosophy of education at University Hradec Králové.

Russell Haitch (PhD, Princeton Theological Seminary) is professor in practical theology and Christian education at Bethany Theological Seminary (Indiana). His published writings focus on the relationship among theology, popular culture, and Christian ministry. He is also author of *From Exorcism to Ecstasy: Eight Views of Baptism* (Westminster John Knox Press).

James K. Hampton (PhD) has been a local church youth pastor, denominational youth leader, cofounder of a youth ministry publishing company, author, and speaker, and is now professor of youth ministry at Asbury Theological Seminary. He is married to Carolyn, and they have two children, Alyssa and Nathan.

Bryce Hantla (Ed.D., Christian Education, Southeastern Baptist Theological Seminary, M.A., in English, North Carolina State University), is an Associate Professor of Christian Education and English for the College of Biblical Studies—Houston. He is interested in the integration of technology in Christian Higher Educational settings and critical thinking.

Steve Hardy (DMiss, Trinity International University) is based in the United States as SIM's advocate for theological education and a senior consultant for the International Council for Evangelical Theological Education. He has been involved in theological education while living in Brazil, Mozambique, and South Africa. Hardy directed Overseas Council's Institute for Excellence and for three years oversaw the scholar program for Langham Partnership.

Allan Harkness (PhD, Murdoch University, Western Australia) heads up Asia Graduate School of Theology Alliance, a postgraduate theological education institution in southeast Asia. From New Zealand, he specializes in Christian education and pedagogical issues in theological education. He serves on the editorial boards of several Christian and theological education journals.

Steve Harper (PhD) is professor emeritus of spiritual formation and Wesley studies at Asbury Theological Seminary, Florida-Dunnam campus in Orlando. He is also a retired elder in the United Methodist Church. He has been married to Jeannie since 1970. They have two children and two grandchildren.

Richard Kenneth Hart (BA, Houghton College; MAT, Oakland University; MDiv, Denver Seminary; PhD, Trinity International University) serves as the executive director of the Program for Theological Education by Extension and helped establish the Middle East Association for Theological Education, where he has served as executive director and accrediting commission chairperson. Hart has lived in Amman, Jordan, since 1979.

Robin Hart lives in Amman, Jordan, and is a missionary with World Venture. She serves as the principal of Whitman Academy, a school for missionary kids through grade twelve, that she and her husband Richard helped to found.

Stephen Heap (PhD) is the Church of England's national higher education adviser. His previous roles in education include senior Baptist chaplain to the Universities of London, ecumenical coordinating chaplain at the University of Bedfordshire in Bedford, and director of Bedford Ecumenical Lay Institute for Education and Faith.

Mark Chung Hearn is an adjunct instructor in the Practical Theology Department at Azusa Pacific University. He holds a PhD in practical theology, with an emphasis in religious education and spiritual formation from Claremont School of Theology.

Joel D. Heck (ThD, Concordia Seminary, Missouri) teaches courses in Old Testament, New Testament, Reformation history, and the life and writings of C. S. Lewis at Concordia University Texas. He is the author or editor of 13 books, most recently a reprint of the *Socratic Digest*, a reprint of *The Personal Heresy*, and a C. S. Lewis calendar.

Claudia H. Herrera, a native of Bogotá, Colombia, holds a BA in international relations, government, and political sciences from Universidad del Rosario (Colombia). She is pursuing a PhD in practical theology from St. Thomas University. Her research interests include popular religion among Latino/as in the United States. She works for the Archdiocese of Miami.

Mary E. Hess (PhD) is associate professor of educational leadership at Luther Seminary (Minnesota). Her books include *Teaching Reflectively in Theological Contexts: Promises and Contradictions* and *Engaging Technology in Theological Education*. A past president of the Religious Education Association, she has worked with both the Wabash Center and the Lexington Seminar.

Lorene Heuvelman-Hutchinson (EdD, Liberty University) is on the faculty at Liberty University in the Center for Counseling and Family Studies and is a certified school psychologist. Her research interests include personality assessment, family systems, adolescence, and building community in online education.

Christine Marie Hill (PhD, MA Talbot School of Theology) is associate professor of spiritual formation at Grace College and Seminary (Indiana). She is the director of the Women's Leadership Program in partnership with Grace Seminary and Women of Grace, USA. She teaches in the area of spiritual formation, interpersonal communication, and leadership.

David W. Hirschman (DMin, Liberty Baptist Theological Seminary) is the associate dean of Liberty University Baptist Theological Seminary.

Nathaniel Holmes Jr. is assistant professor of religion and philosophy at Florida Memorial University, Miami. He received his PhD from St. Thomas University, and his research areas include systematic and practical theology, American pragmatism, and the problem of evil.

Mariana Hwang received a PhD in educational studies from Talbot Theological Seminary (California) and is assistant professor and the program director of children and family studies and education and discipleship at Lincoln Christian University (Illinois).

Brendan Hyde (PhD) is a senior lecturer in religious education on the Melbourne campus of the Australian Catholic University. He has research interests in children's spirituality and in how the Godly Play approach to religious education nurtures spirituality in young children. He is the author of *Children and Spirituality: Searching for Meaning and Connectedness* (London/Philadelphia: Jessica Kingsley Publishers).

Ogechukwu Ibem (BA, MDiv, PGD theology) is in the PhD program at the School of Intercultural Studies at Biola University (California). He is an ordained pastor of the Presbyterian Church of Nigeria and a church planter in Togo, Benin, and Nigeria. Ibem is the author of *Stones for Pillows*.

Agametochukwu Iheanyi-Igwe (BEng, MA) is a PhD candidate in educational and leadership studies at Biola University's Talbot School of Theology (California), where he also serves on the faculty. He is an ordained pastor from Nigeria and has also served churches in North America. Iheanyi-Igwe is married with children.

Clement Iorliam (BST Urbaniana Rome; PGDE and MA, Makurdi, Nigeria) is a Roman Catholic priest of the diocese of Makudi, Nigeria, and currently a PhD student in practical theology at St. Thomas University, Miami, Florida. His research interests include youth, culture, and religion.

Klaus Issler (PhD, Michigan State University) is professor of Christian education and theology, Talbot School of Theology, Biola University. He specializes in sanctification and character formation, Christology with a focus on the humanity and example of Jesus, theological and philosophical foundations of education/formation, and the theology of vocation.

Mark J. Jackson is professor and department chair for children, youth and family studies at Trinity Lutheran College (Washington). His teaching interests include youth and family ministry, faith formation, service learning, history of youth movements, and program administration. He holds graduate degrees from Gonzaga University and Regis University.

Jennifer Jagerson is a doctoral candidate at Talbot School of Theology. She has an MA in education and an MA in biblical and theological studies diversified. Jennifer has served as a church-planting missionary in Southeast Asia, as a public school teacher, and as a developer of Bible curriculum.

Martin Jäggle was born in Vienna, Austria. He studied philosophy, physics, mathematics, and theology at the University of Vienna and University of Innsbruck and earned a DrTheol. Since 2003 he has been university professor of religious education and catechetics at the Faculty of Catholic Theology, University of Vienna, and has been dean since 2008.

Christopher B. James is a PhD candidate in practical theology at Boston University School of Theology with training from Fuller Theological Seminary, Wheaton College, and the Renovaré Institute. His research and teaching center on ecclesiology, mission, and spirituality. He can be found online at www.jesusdust.com and @chrisbjames.

Carol Anne Janzen (PhD, University of Alberta) is assistant professor of practical theology and dean of students at Acadia Divinity College, Acadia University (Nova Scotia, Canada). Her eclectic research interests include children's spiritual formation, sacred place and space, peace and justice education, and the spiritual care of people in continuing care and correctional institutions.

Nathan R. Jastram received a PhD in Near Eastern languages and civilizations from Harvard University.

He is professor of theology and chair of the department of theology and philosophy at Concordia University, Wisconsin.

Robert Jennings (BA, MTh, MA, DPhil, MBE) is Northern Irish, born in Enniskillen, County Fermanagh, married to Jennifer, and father to two adult children. He is an elder in his local church. Jennings was the founding principal of an integrated secondary school—an attempt to bring together children from both sides of the primary religious divide in Northern Ireland.

William Jeynes (PhD) is a senior fellow at the Witherspoon Institute in Princeton, New Jersey, and a professor of education at California State University in Long Beach. He has graduate degrees from Harvard University and the University of Chicago. Jeynes has spoken and written for the White House, as well as for governments overseas. He is a prolific academic writer.

Adam J. Johnson (PhD, Trinity Evangelical Divinity School) is an assistant professor of theology at Cedarville University. He is the author of *God's Being in Reconciliation* and *Atonement: A Guide for the Perplexed* (both with T&T Clark).

R. Kevin Johnson is administrator, worship coordinator, and CPE registrar for the Department of Pastoral Care and Education at New York Presbyterian/Columbia University Medical Center in New York City.

Todd M. Johnson (PhD, William Carey International University, California) is Associate Professor of Global Christianity at Gordon-Conwell Theological Seminary (Boston) and Visiting Research Fellow at the Institute on Culture, Religion, and World Affairs at Boston University. He is the author of several books including *The World's Religions in Figures: An Introduction to International Religious Demography* (Wiley-Blackwell, 2013).

Derek Jones received a MDiv from Duke Divinity School (North Carolina) and a BA in philosophy and religious studies from Westmont College (California). He has mentored high school and junior high aged youth for over a decade, specializing in curriculum addressing gender and sexuality. He currently lives and works in Durham, North Carolina.

Errol E. Joseph (PhD, Regent University, Virginia) is vice president for academic affairs at the West Indies School of Theology and lecturer at Open Bible Institute of Theology, Trinidad. He was the secretary/treasurer of the Caribbean Evangelical Theological Association

(1991–2012) and has been the association's accrediting coordinator since 1997.

Débora B. Agra Junker is assistant professor of Christian education and director of MA in multicultural Christian education at Christian Theological Seminary in Indianapolis, Indiana. Prior to joining CTS, Junker taught at the Methodist School of Theology in São Paulo, Brazil. Her scholarship is informed by her studies in Brazil, Argentina, and the United States.

Samjung Kang-Hamilton (EdD, Columbia University) is adjunct professor of Christian education at Abilene Christian University and book review editor of *Restoration Quarterly*. A native of South Korea, Kang-Hamilton teaches and researches in religious education and the spiritual formation of children, youth, and adults. She also lectures on issues in cross-cultural ministry.

Riad A. Kassis lives in Lebanon. He studied in Syria, Philippines, Canada, the United Kingdom, and the United States. He holds a PhD from the University of Nottingham. Kassis has been engaged in global theological education with Overseas Council International and currently is ICETE international director and director of Langham scholars.

William K. Kay completed a BA and MA at Trinity College, Oxford University, an MEd and a PhD in education at Reading University, and a PhD in theology at the University of Nottingham, where he was later awarded a DD. He was senior lecturer at King's College, London; Rrader at Bangor University; professor of theology at Glyndŵr University; and later professor of Pentecostal studies at the University of Chester.

Robert Keay (ThM, Gordon Conwell; PhD, St. Andrews) served as teaching fellow in New Testament at University of St. Andrews, honorary lecturer in New Testament and Hellenistic Greek at Queen's University Belfast, and lecturer in New Testament and theology at Belfast Bible College, and is currently pastor of First Baptist Church Wolfeboro, New Hampshire.

Scott Leonard Keith (PhD, Graduate Theological Foundation, Foundation House, Oxford) is the Director of Residential Education and Adjunct Professor of Theology at Concordia University, Irvine (California). He has published several articles on the theology of Philip Melanchthon, Christian education and theological ethics.

Margaret M. T. Kelleher (PhD, MCD University of Divinity, Melbourne, Australia). Margaret Kelleher is an experienced secondary school teacher of English, religious education, and the humanities, and is currently teaching at Avila College, Mount Waverley, Melbourne. Her doctoral thesis, "From Biblical Story to Biblical Interpretation—A Critical Transition," combined her interests in cognitive development, theology, and religious education.

Michael A. Kelly (CSsR, BTheol, STM, MEd, PhD) is a Catholic priest who teaches at Yarra Theological Union, a college of MCD University of Divinity (Australia). His field of expertise is pastoral theology and religious education. He is postgraduate coordinator at YTU and chair of the Academic Board of the University.

Stephen J. Kemp (PhD, Loyola University, Chicago) is academic dean of Antioch School of Church Planting and Leadership Development, part of BILD International, a leader in church-based theological education, and associate pastor of CityChurch (Ames/Des Moines, Iowa). He is former vice president of distance education, Moody Bible Institute.

Emerson K. Keung has an EdD in educational leadership and taught university students internationally for 10 years before moving to Hong Kong, where his current research continues in the areas of cultural intelligence, educational leadership, and intercultural schools.

Andrzej Kiciński (ThD, habilitation) is a professor of The John Paul II Catholic University of Lublin (Poland), director of the Institute for Pastoral Theology and head of the Chair of Special Catechetics, and vice president of the Polish Association of Catechists. Kiciński is an expert on the assessment of religious teaching programs and catechetical textbooks at the Commission of Catholic Education of the Conference of the Polish Episcopate.

Chris Kiesling (PhD, human development and family studies, Texas Tech University) is professor of human development and Christian discipleship in the School of Practical Theology at Asbury Theological Seminary. His areas of research and writing focus on spiritual formation in young and middle adulthood, family discipleship, marriage, college ministry, and catechesis.

Phyllis Kilbourn (PhD, Trinity International University) is founder of Rainbows of Hope and Crisis Care Training International, both global ministries of Worldwide Evangelization for Christ International, serving children in crisis. She is a child advocate, trauma trainer, and author/editor of eight handbooks focused on interventions for children in crisis. Killbourn has served in Liberia and Kenya with WEC International.

Hyun-Sook Kim is associate professor of Christian education at Yonsei University, Seoul, Korea. She is on the editorial board of *Religious Education* and is the author of *Christian Education for Postconventionality* (2002), as well as several articles, including "Multicultural Religious Education in a Trinitarian Perspective" and "The Hermeneutical-Praxis Paradigm and Practical Theology" (both in *Religious Education*).

Elisabeth M. (Lisa) Kimball (PhD) is the director of the Center for the Ministry of Teaching and professor of Christian Formation and Congregational Leadership at Virginia Theological Seminary. Passionate about contextual Christian education across the life span, her work has focused on the role of faith mentoring in intergenerational and nonformal settings.

Thomas Kimber (PhD, Talbot School of Theology) is adjunct professor of biblical and theological studies, and Christian ministry and leadership at Talbot School of Theology. He is a former missionary with the Evangelical Free Church of America.

Sheryl A. Kujawa-Holbrook (PhD) is professor of practical theology and religious education at Claremont School of Theology and professor of Anglican studies, Bloy House, the Episcopal Theological School at Claremont. Before her academic career, Kujawa-Holbrook worked worldwide for the Episcopal Church in Christian education ministries with young people.

Peter Kuzmič (ThD) is distinguished professor of missions and European studies at Gordon-Conwell Theological Seminary. A native of Slovenia and a citizen of Croatia, he is the foremost evangelical scholar in postcommunist contexts. Kuzmič has ministered in more than 80 nations on every continent and has served as an advisor on reconciliation for national leaders in the Balkans and for the United Nations and U.S. State Department as a member of the Helsinki Committee for Human Rights in Croatia. Kuzmič is an award-winning author of several books and a columnist for a secular newspaper.

Mariusz Kuźniar was born in Nysa, Poland. He has an undergraduate degree from Charles University in Prague (Czech Republic), a licentiate in catechetics at Opole University (Poland), and a PhD in catechetics from Università Pontificia Salesiana (Rome, Italy). Father Kuźniar was ordained in the Roman Catholic Church in 1995, since 2011 has been director of the Department for Catechesis at Czech Bishops´ Conference, and serves the parishes of Prague.

Eric J. Kyle is assistant professor of theology and director of the Service-Learning Program at the College of Saint Mary in Omaha, Nebraska. His research focuses on the systematic study and practice of spiritual formation. Kyle is also an Ignatian associate with the Omaha Community.

Jacqueline Laing (PhD) lectures in jurisprudence, criminal law, and law and religion at London Metropolitan University. She completed her doctorate in jurisprudence at Brasenose College, Oxford, after taking degrees in philosophy and law at the Australian National University. Her publications include books and articles on jurisprudence, criminal law, medical ethics, and human rights.

Jeffrey S. Lamp (PhD, Trinity Evangelical Divinity School) is professor of New Testament at Oral Roberts University (Oklahoma). He is the author of *First Corinthians 1–4 in Light of Jewish Wisdom Traditions* (Edwin Mellen Press) and *The Greening of Hebrews?* (Pickwick Press). He is an elder in the Free Methodist Church of North America.

Marlene Lang is in the doctor of philosophy program of practical theology at St. Thomas University (Florida). Formerly a journalist reporting on government, an editor, and a political columnist, she is now a high school teacher of religion and theology. She holds an MA in spirituality.

Kelly Langdoc (BS, early childhood education, Greenville College; MA, Christian education, Asbury Theological Seminary) is family minister at St. Andrew's Anglican Church in Versailles, Kentucky. She formerly served as missionary for 10 years with World Gospel Mission in Bolivia.

Michael D. Langford is assistant professor of theology, discipleship, and ministry at Seattle Pacific University and Seattle Pacific Seminary (Washington), where he teaches and writes on the interrelationship between theology and practice in fields such as Christian formation, disability, mission, pneumatology, spiritual disciplines, and youth ministry. He is also an ordained pastor in the Presbyterian Church (USA).

Jason Lanker (PhD, Talbot Theological Seminary) is the director of the Youth and Outdoor Leadership Ministry Programs at John Brown University (Arkansas). His teaching, speaking, and writing center around the spiritual formation of youth and on the role of mentoring. Lanker has published articles in the *Christian Education Journal* and *Journal of Youth Ministry*.

Kenneth C. Law (MBA, Regent University) is an instructional designer for Liberty University.

J. Gregory Lawson serves as professor of Christian education at Southeastern Baptist Theological Seminary and pastor of Union Chapel Baptist Church. He has a BA from Carson Newman College, an MA Tennessee Tech University, a JD from Campbell University, an MA and MDiv from Southwestern Baptist Theological Seminary, and an MEd and EdD at the University of North Texas.

Alison Le Cornu is the academic lead for flexible learning with the Higher Education Academy in the United Kingdom, and visiting scholar with the Oxford Centre for Ecclesiology and Practical Theology (OxCEPT) at Ripon College in Oxford, United Kingdom. She publishes in adult education, adult theological (religious) education, and online learning, as well as supervising postgraduate students in practical theology.

Samuel C. Lee is president of Foundation University, the Netherlands. He is a sociologist, specializing in sociology of religion and culture.

David Walter Leinweber (PhD, Michigan State University) is associate professor of history at Oxford College of Emory University (Georgia). He has won numerous awards for his popular classes and teaching style. His articles and essays have appeared in many journals and reference works. A lifelong pianist, Leinweber has also served area churches as a staff musician.

Bill J. Leonard is James and Marilyn Dunn Professor of Baptist Studies, and professor of church history, School of Divinity, Wake Forest University. He holds the PhD from Boston University and is author or editor of 21 books, including *Baptist Ways: A History* and *A Sense of the Heart: A History of Christian Religious Experience in the U.S.* (Abingdon).

George Levesque (PhD, Columbia University, New York) is assistant dean of academic affairs and lecturer in the Department of History at Yale University. His teaching and research interests focus on 18th- and 19th-century intellectual and cultural history in the United States and the history of education.

Stephen G. Lewis (MDiv, Southeastern Baptist Theological Seminary) works at Wingshadow Ministries, a Christian retreat center in West Michigan. With a great interest in missions and culture, he has served around the world, including at Cornerstone University, Mekong Evangelical Seminary in Thailand, and churches in South Africa.

Rosalind Lim-Tan (PhD) is director of the Holistic Child Development Institute at Malaysian Biblical Theological School. She also serves as an education consultant in Southeast Asia. Her interest is in developing contextual training for children's workers and her areas of study include education, human developmental theories, curriculum development, and instructional theories. Her dissertation is on Vygotsky and childhood faith formation.

Larry H. Lindquist (EdD, Northern Illinois University) is an associate professor and director of the MA in leadership development at Denver Seminary. He also taught public school in the suburbs of Chicago and served as adjunct professor at Moody Bible Institute and Trinity International University and continues to speak at churches, national conferences, summer camps, and retreats. Larry and his wife Cindy live in Littleton, Colorado.

Randy G. Litchfield is academic dean and Browning Professor of Christian Education at Methodist Theological School (Ohio). His PhD is from Claremont School of Theology and he is a former executive secretary of the Association of Professors and Researchers in Religious Education.

D. Bruce Lockerbie is chairman, PAIDEIA, a consulting firm serving schools, colleges, seminaries, and other Christian institutions. He served on the faculty and administration of the Stony Brook School (New York) from 1957 to 1991 and is author or editor of more than 40 books.

Annie A. Lockhart-Gilroy is a PhD candidate in Christian education at Garrett-Evangelical Seminary (Illinois). She received an MDiv from Princeton Theological Seminary with a focus on youth ministry, and a BA in English from Dickinson College. Lockhart-Gilroy has worked with adolescents as a youth minister, high school educator, and coach.

Lisa Milligan Long (PhD, educational studies, Talbot School of Theology) is associate professor of Christian formation and the director of graduate studies in Christian ministries at Lee University (Tennessee). Her educational experience is combined with a lengthy history of ministry, having served as a youth pastor, Christian education pastor, and children's pastor.

Dawn A. Lonsdale has been chief officer at Unlock (Sheffield, England) since 2004. Unlock has been working to enable Bible engagement within deprived urban communities in the United Kingdom since 1972. Previously she was laity development advisor for Derby Diocese and chair of the National Executive Committee of the Anglican Adult Education Network. Lonsdale has been a mentor within the Education for Ministry Program since 1997. She has a degree in archaeology from Durham University.

Mary Lowe (PhD) is the associate dean of the Virtual Campus at Erskine Seminary and also serves as the executive director of ACCESS, the Association for Christian Distance Education. Mary has published articles and coedited a book concerning online theological education. She codirected the National Consultation on Spiritual Formation in Theological Distance Education.

Stephen D. Lowe (PhD, Michigan State University) is professor of Christian education at Erskine Seminary (South Carolina). He has published in the field of Christian education on Christian camping, youth ministry, adult education, online education, and spiritual formation. He and his wife codirected the National Consultation on Theological Distance Education.

Wendy K. Lundberg (EdD, Liberty University, Virginia) has participated in Christian education for 20 years and is currently administrator at Fond du Lac Christian School (Wisconsin). Her doctoral research explored moral identity development of Christian college students and is pursuing research on narrative identity development within Christian education.

Joshua Lunde-Whitler received an MDiv from Fuller Theological Seminary and is pursuing a PhD in theology and education at Boston College. He copastors Christian Union Church (United Church of Christ) in West Groton, Massachusetts, with his spouse Amy. Lunde-Whitler is a licensed minister in the Reformed Church in America.

Kevin J. Mahaffy Sr. is director of operations and production for Moody Bible Institute's Distance Learning school. He has 20 years of experience in distance learning as a student, a course developer, an instructor, and an administrator. He is passionate about connecting with students in resident and online educational settings.

Paweł Mąkosa is assistant professor at John Paul II Catholic University of Lublin (Poland), chief of the Chair of Psychological and Pedagogical Catechetics. He specializes in religious education and catechetics. He has collaborated with the Sacro Cuore University in Milan (Italy), University of Oxford (UK), University of Malta,

and Theological Institute in Lviv (Ukraine). He has authored numerous books and articles.

Jeffrey Mallinson (DPhil, University of Oxford) serves as associate professor of theology at Concordia University, Irvine. His teaching and research focus on the intersections between the history of philosophy and the development of Christian thought. His previous experience in Christian education includes professional youth ministry, dean of theology at Colorado Christian University, and academic dean at Trinity Lutheran College (Washington).

W. Creighton Marlowe (PhD) is a professor of Old Testament studies at the Evangelical Theological Faculty in Leuven, Belgium. Originally from the United States, he has lived in Europe since 1989, where has served as an Old Testament professor, academic dean, and visiting lecturer at various schools in Western and Eastern Europe.

Ellen L. Marmon serves as associate professor of Christian discipleship at Asbury Theological Seminary in Wilmore, Kentucky, and resources oral communities through Voice for Humanity. She has a PhD in educational psychology from the University of Kentucky, an MA in Christian education from Asbury Theological Seminary, an MA in English from the UK, and a BS in education from Miami University (Ohio). She served a local church from 1988 to 2004.

Timothy H. Maschke (DMin, PhD) is professor of theology at Concordia University, Wisconsin. Since 1982, he has served as preseminary director and teaches Christian doctrine and worship. Maschke earned degrees from Concordia Seminary, St. Louis (MDiv, STM); Trinity Evangelical Divinity School (DMin); and Marquette University (PhD). He resides in Grafton, Wisconsin, with his wife.

Laurie Matthias is associate professor and coordinator of graduate programs in education at Trinity International University (Illinois). She spent 23 years teaching middle and high school English in Christian schools. Research interests include the integration of faith and learning, faculty professional development, and Christian higher education initiatives in the global South.

Scottie May (PhD, Trinity Evangelical Divinity School, Illinois) is associate professor of Christian formation and ministry at Wheaton College (Illinois). She publishes in the area of children's ministry and spirituality. May's most recent book, coauthored with Catherine Stonehouse, is *Listening to Children on the Spiritual Journey* (Baker, 2010).

Rosemary Wahu Mbogo (PhD, Talbot School of Theology, Biola University) is a lecturer in the Education Department of Africa International University in Nairobi, Kenya. She is a cofounder of two Christian schools in Kenya and has authored *How to Manage Househelps*, a booklet to educate Kenyan women on domestic matters.

Timothy M. McAlhaney is a graduate of North Greenville College and Furman University. He has an earned MA(Th) and a PhD in church history from Southwestern Baptist Theological Seminary (Texas). He is currently an adjunct for Liberty Baptist Theological Seminary and an appointed missionary to Egbe, Nigeria with SIM.

Carl McColman is an independent scholar and contemplative practitioner. He is a professed Lay Cistercian of Our Lady of the Holy Spirit Monastery in Conyers, Georgia. He is the author of *Answering the Contemplative Call* and *The Big Book of Christian Mysticism*. He blogs about Christian spirituality at www.carlmccolman.com.

Stephen K. McCord served for nearly three decades overseas as a Christian educator, administrator, publisher, and team leader in Asia, northern Africa, and the Middle East. He leads analysis services at International Mission Board (Southern Baptist Convention) and teaches cross-cultural leadership and communications at Southeastern Seminary and Dallas Baptist University.

Silas L. McCormick is director of institutional effectiveness and assistant university counsel at Lincoln Christian University (Illinois). He holds a BA in Christian education from Lincoln Christian University, a JD from The Ohio State University's Moritz College of Law, and a PhD in higher education from the University of Illinois at Urbana-Champaign.

Donald R. McCrabb (DMin) is the president of the Catholic Youth Foundation USA, a subsidiary of the National Federation for Catholic Youth Ministry. A pastoral theologian, Don is a nationally recognized leader in leadership, pastoral formation, strategic planning, campus ministry, and young adult ministry.

Sylvia McGeary (PhD, Fordham University School of Religion and Religious Education, New York) is assistant professor of religious studies at Felician College, Lodi, New Jersey. She was a parish religious educator for 25 years.

David McGee (Ed.D., Christian Education, Southeastern Baptist Theological Seminary) is an assistant professor for the School of Religion Online at Liberty University and is employed as an instructor of religion and adjunct professor of Bible and theology. He is interested in the history, philosophy, and theology of education.

Richard J. McLaughlin serves at Trinity College/Trinity Graduate School as the online programs academic coordinator and as a Christian ministries adjunct faculty member. He has studied at the University of Notre Dame, Moody Theological Seminary, Trinity Evangelical Divinity School, and Talbot School of Theology. His dissertation focuses on transformative learning and spiritual renewal.

Michael McMullin is a part-time instructor at Lee University (Cleveland, Tennessee) and a PhD student at Biola University, studying in the area of teaching and spiritual formation. His research interests include the intersection of worship, calling, and theological education.

Jennifer Powell McNutt (PhD, University of St. Andrews) is associate professor of theology and history of Christianity at Wheaton College. She specializes in the history of the Reformed tradition from Reformation Geneva through the 18th century, as reflected in her book, *Calvin Meets Voltaire: The Clergy in the Age of Enlightenment, 1685–1798* (Ashgate, 2013).

Marjorie Lamp Mead is associate director of the Marion E. Wade Center, Wheaton College (Illinois). She has published on Dorothy L. Sayers and C. S. Lewis, including on Sayers and education: "The Lost Tools of Learning and the Habits of a Scholarly Mind" in *Liberal Arts for the Christian Life* (Crossway, 2012). Mead serves as managing editor of *SEVEN: An Anglo-American Literary Review*, an annual journal that focuses on the seven authors of the Wade Center.

Alemayehu Mekonnen joined the Denver Seminary faculty in 2008 as associate professor of missions. He holds a PhD in intercultural studies, an MA in missions, and an MA in theology from Fuller Theological Seminary, as well as an MA in cross-cultural communication from Assemblies of God Graduate School of Theology and a BTh from East Africa School of Theology.

Angus Menuge was raised in England and became an American citizen in 2005. He holds a BA in philosophy from Warwick University, a PhD in philosophy from the University of Wisconsin–Madison, and a diploma in Christian apologetics from the International Academy of

Apologetics, Evangelism and Human Rights, Strasbourg. He is editor or author of nine books. Menuge's technical work focuses on the philosophy of mind and the philosophy of science. He serves as president of the Evangelical Philosophical Society.

Sadrac E. Meza (PhD, Trinity International University) is president of ESEPA Seminary (San José, Costa Rica) and also professor of systematic theology. He is author of the *Commentary on Ezra* in the forthcoming *Comentario Bíblico Contemporáneo* (C. René Padilla, gen. ed.).

Ronald T. Michener (DrTheol, Faculté Universitaire de Théologie Protestante de Bruxelles; MA, Western Seminary, Oregon) is professor and chair of the Department of Systematic Theology at the Evangelische Theologische Faculteit (Belgium). Michener has previous experience teaching theology and Bible in various local church settings and is a regular preacher on rotation at an international church in Leuven.

Mariet Mikalelian was raised in the Presbyterian church of Iran. She achieved an MDiv from the Near East School of Theology in Lebanon and is a PhD student in the Christian education program at Biola University (California). Mikalelian has been involved in the educational ministry of the church for more than 25 years.

Leonid Mikhovich received an MDiv from Moscow Theological Seminary in 1997 and an MA in practical ministry from TCMI Institute in Austria in 2005. Currently, he is working on his doctoral dissertation. He serves as rector of Minsk Theological Seminary and senior pastor of the Association of Churches in Minsk region (Belarus).

Veronice Miles (PhD, Emory University; MDiv, Candler School of Theology) is assistant professor of homiletics and Christian education at Wake Forest University School of Divinity. She has published in the fields of religious education and preaching. Miles's current project explores hope as a pedagogical construct and theological praxis.

Patrick Mitchel (PhD) is director of studies and lecturer in theology at Irish Bible Institute, Dublin. He is author of *Evangelicalism and National Identity in Ulster 1921– 1998* (Oxford University Press, 2003) and has edited and contributed chapters to various other books as well as articles published in the Irish press.

Michael R. Mitchell (EdD, Southern Baptist Theological Seminary) is an associate professor of Christian leadership at Liberty University Baptist Theological Seminary (Virginia).

Angelique Montgomery-Goodnough (PhD, practical theology, St. Thomas University, Florida) is an adjunct professor of religious studies at St. Edward's University. Her research focus is on the religious identity of students in higher education and the theology of the university as church.

Mary Elizabeth Moore (PhD, Claremont School of Theology; doctor honoris causa, University of Judaism) is dean and professor of theology and education, Boston University School of Theology. She has published eight books in theology and education, including *Teaching from the Heart* and *Teaching as a Sacramental Act*, and numerous articles.

Cesar Morales is a Peruvian pastor. He currently works as academic dean of the Evangelical Seminary of Lima (SEL) and youth pastor at Biblical Christian Church in Lima. He holds an MTh (QUB) and is pursuing a PhD at Talbot School of Theology.

Nelson R. Morales Fredes was born in Chile. He did his studies in Chile (BA, chemical engineering), Guatemala (BA, ThM Bible), and the United States (PhD, New Testament). Since 1996, he has been professor of biblical languages and New Testament and is the graduate programs director at Central American Theological Seminary, Guatemala.

Ariel Moreno is Panamanian. He is a theological student and collaborator with the Gospel Missionary Union of Panama in the areas of Christian education and youth ministry.

Andrew B. Morris has retired after 40 years' involvement in Catholic education as director of the National Centre for Christian Education at Liverpool Hope University. He is an associate member of the National Institute for Christian Education Research at Canterbury Christ Church University and the Maryvale Higher Institute of Religious Sciences, Birmingham.

Debra Dean Murphy is assistant professor of religious studies at West Virginia Wesleyan College and the author of *Teaching That Transforms: Worship as the Heart of Christian Education*. Her articles and essays have appeared in *Liturgy*, *The Christian Century*, *Theology Today*, *The Journal of Religious Education*, and other publications. She blogs at "Intersections: Thoughts on Religion, Culture, and Politics."

Marilyn Naidoo is associate professor in the Department of Practical Theology at the University of South Africa.

Her teaching specialization is religious education in the discipline of practical theology, with a research focus on theological education and ministerial formation of clergy. Her most recent publication is *Between the Real and the Ideal: Ministerial Formation in South African Churches* (Unisa Press 2012).

David Nemitz (EdD, Liberty University) is associate professor at Liberty Baptist Theological Seminary (Virginia), teaching biblical foundations of leadership and team leadership and conflict resolution. He also serves the university as the director of The Center of Curriculum Development. Nemitz and his wife Debbie have three children: Lydia, Luke, and Naomi.

Ted Newell (EdD, Columbia University) is associate professor in education at Crandall University, New Brunswick, Canada. He published a study of James Michael Lee's theology, *Education Has Nothing to Do with Theology* (Princeton Theological Monograph Series, 2006) and continues to research comparative and historical links of educational practice to worldview. He can be found at linkd.in/lnbfti.

Peter Tze Ming Ng (PhD, London; MA in religious education, University of London Institute of Education; MDiv, BA, Chinese University of Hong Kong) is now a professor and chair of Chinese Christianity at the China Victory Theological Seminary of Hong Kong. His most recent book is *Chinese Christianity: An Interplay between Global and Local Perspectives* (Brill, 2012).

Quynh-Hoa Le Nguyen (PhD, religion, Claremont Graduate University). Nguyen is interested in scriptures and peoples, evangelical Vietnamese Christian identities, and evangelical Vietnamese Christianity and society.

Rodger Y. Nishioka (PhD) holds the Benton Family Chair in Christian Education at Columbia Theological Seminary (Georgia). Ordained in the Presbyterian Church (U.S.A.) and a graduate of McCormick Theological Seminary and Georgia State University, his primary research interest is in congregational ministry with youth and young adults.

Stephen Noll (PhD, University of Manchester; DD, Nashotah House Theological School) is an Anglican priest, professor emeritus at Trinity School for Ministry (Pennsylvania), and founding vice chancellor of Uganda Christian University, Mukono (2000–2010). He has published books and articles in biblical studies, theology, and international higher education, the latest being *Higher Education as Mission* (2013).

Faustin Ntamushobora (PhD, Biola University) is Rwandan and president of Transformational Leadership in Africa (TLAfrica, Inc.), which empowers African Christian leaders to bring change in their communities. He is author of *From Trials to Triumphs* and *Transformation through the Different Other*. Ntamushobora's passion is leadership development and reconciliation.

Dennis Okholm (PhD, Princeton Theological Seminary) is a professor of theology at Azusa Pacific University (California) and an adjunct professor of Fuller Theological Seminary. His most recent book is *Monk Habits for Everyday People* (Brazos). He is an ordained priest in the Anglican Church in North America.

Trevecca Okholm is an adjunct instructor at Azusa Pacific University. She has served as a professional Christian educator for nearly 25 years and is certified in the Presbyterian Church (U.S.A.). Okholm received her MA in educational ministries from Wheaton Graduate School. She is author of *Kingdom Family: Re-Envisioning God's Plan for Marriage and Family* (Cascade, 2012).

Carol G. Olsen (PhD, Southern Baptist Theological Seminary; JD, University of Denver) serves as director/editor of The Volunteer Project, a resource for churches. She was a Bible teacher/church planter in Bosnia and Herzegovina and practiced law in Colorado. She earned a BA at Colorado State University and an MABS at Dallas Theological Seminary.

André Ong (PhD, Claremont School of Theology) is a faculty associate at Bethel Seminary San Diego and associate lecturer at the Academy for Christian Thought in New York. He is the founding and senior pastor of International Christian Church of San Diego. He is also the author of John Paul II's *Philosophy of the Acting Person*.

Peter G. Osborn (PhD, Michigan State University) is the associate professor of educational ministries at Grand Rapids Theological Seminary (Michigan). Osborn has served for over a decade in higher education and for over two decades in positions in the local church.

Bernhard Ott (DPhil, Oxford Centre for Mission Studies/Open University, United Kingdom) serves as the academic dean of the European School of Culture and Theology (German Campus of Columbia International University) and is the accreditation director of the European Evangelical Accrediting Association. He is the second chairman of the Syndicate for Biblically Renewed Theology, as well as a member of the Theological Workgroup of the Syndicate for Evangelical Missions (AEM) in Switzerland.

Stephen E. Overton (PhD in educational studies, Talbot School of Theology) is a Foursquare senior pastor in Moreno Valley, California, and has worked bivocationally as a manager for the City of Los Angeles. He has served as adjunct Christian education professor at LIFE Bible College.

Marvin Oxenham (PhD) leads the postgraduate program in theological education at London School of Theology and previously worked for 25 years in theological education among Italians. Since 2004, he has served the European Evangelical Accrediting Association, the International Council for Evangelical Theological Education, and Overseas Council. His dissertation is titled "Higher Education in Liquid Modernity."

Philip Ozinga (MDiv, Grace Theological Seminary) is a missionary with 30 years' experience in Central America, who has served as a professor, mentor, and advisor with Instituto Biblico Centroamericano and Seminario Biblico Centroamericano de Honduras to help churches develop a Christian philosophy and practice of education. He has designed numerous courses, conferences, seminars, and self-study courses.

Adam D. Paape (PhD) is assistant professor of education at Concordia University, Wisconsin. He teaches courses in mathematics education and educational technology. His areas of interest and research include the role of Christians in public education and the intersection of faith and learning.

Dylan Pahman is assistant editor of the *Journal of Markets & Morality* and a research associate for the Acton Institute. He is also a contributing editor to *Ethika Politika*, the journal of the Center for Morality in the Public Life. He has a master's of theological studies from Calvin Theological Seminary in historical theology with a concentration on the early church.

Wendell H. Paris Jr. is university chaplain and instructor of religion in society at Florida Memorial University. He is ordained by American Baptist Churches and National Baptist Convention. Paris studied at Tuskegee University, Colgate-Rochester Divinity School, and Christian Theological Seminary. He is a PhD candidate in practical theology at St. Thomas University (Florida).

HiRho Y. Park (PhD, Boston University; DMin, Wesley Theological Seminary) is director of clergy lifelong learning for the General Board of Higher Education and Ministry of the United Methodist Church. She is a coeditor of *Breaking through the Stained Glass Ceiling*. Park is the innovator of the online continuing education consortium and the UMC Cyber Campus.

Robert J. Parmach (PhD) is academic dean of freshmen and faculty director of the Manresa scholars program and teaches philosophy and theology at Fordham University (New York). His teaching and scholarship include philosophical and religious hermeneutics, philosophical theology, ethics for young adults, and Jesuit pedagogy.

Boris Paschke (DrTheol, Evangelische Theologische Faculteit, Belgium) is originally from Germany and a postdoctoral fellow of the Research Foundation–Flanders (FWO). He conducts research in the New Testament department of Evangelische Theologische Faculteit and is the author of *Particularism and Universalism in the Sermon on the Mount* (2012).

Michael Pasquarello III (PhD/MA, University of North Carolina; MDiv, Duke Divinity School) is the Granger E. and Anna Fisher Professor of Preaching at Asbury Theological Seminary (Kentucky), where he teaches homiletics, liturgical theology, historical theology, and pastoral theology. He has published five books on the theology and history of preaching and the formation of preachers. Pasquarello is an ordained elder in the United Methodist Church.

Gino Pasquariello (MA, theological studies, Bethel Theological Seminary; EdD, higher education leadership, Azusa Pacific University) is the vice president of student services and institutional research at Southern California Seminary. He teaches Christian education, organizational leadership, and research methodologies, and is a contributing author to Zondervan's *Dictionary of Christian Spirituality*.

Ian W. Payne (PhD, University of Aberdeen) is principal and head of theology at the South Asia Institute of Advanced Christian Studies (SAIACS), Bangalore, India. Originally from New Zealand, and with research interests in Karl Barth, he is the author of *Wouldn't You Love to Know? Trinitarian Epistemology and Pedagogy* (Wipf & Stock, forthcoming).

Sharon Ely Pearson is the Christian formation specialist for Church Publishing Incorporated, with experience in Christian formation on the local, judicatory, and church-wide level. The author of *The Prayer Book Guide to Christian Education*, 3rd ed. (Morehouse, 2009) and *Call on Me: A Prayer Book for Young People* (Morehouse, 2012), she is a graduate of Virginia Theological Seminary and a lifelong Episcopalian.

Larry Peck serves in Europe with Global Outreach International as a distance education and instructional design consultant with the Evangelical Theological Faculty (Belgium). Larry earned an MDiv from Columbia International University and has completed the coursework in the PhD instructional design and technology program at Old Dominion University in Norfolk, Virginia. Larry has also been a missionary educator in Germany and Italy.

Emily A. Peck-McClain is an ordained elder in the United Methodist Church. She is currently working on her doctorate at Duke Divinity School, focusing on Christian education and the New Testament. Her dissertation is on Pauline theology as a resource for liberative ministry with adolescent girls. She lives in New York with her husband and daughter.

Robert Pennington is a doctoral student of practical theology and ministry at St. Thomas University in Miami, Florida. He earned a master's degree in theology from Xavier University in Cincinnati, Ohio, and a BA in political science from Wheeling Jesuit University. Pennington has also previously served as a mission worker in the Dominican Republican.

Emmanuel P. Perselis (BD, Athens; MA in religious education and PhD, Lancaster University, UK) is professor of theory and practice of Christian religious education at the School of Theology University of Athens (Greece). His research interests focus on the history, philosophy, and theology of Christian religious education and human and religious development of young people.

Nativity A. Petallar (ThD in Christian education) is program director of Holistic Child Development at Asia-Pacific Nazarene Theological Seminary (APNTS). She coordinates the children's ministries at APNTS and also serves as director of Christian education at the First Free Methodist Church of Manila, where Mark Gil, her husband, pastors.

Ryan S. Peterson (PhD, Wheaton College, Illinois) is an assistant professor of theology at Cedarville University (Ohio). His doctoral dissertation, "The Imago Dei as Human Identity: A Theological Interpretation" (2010), was awarded the 2011 Dissertation Prize by the Center for Catholic-Evangelical Dialogue. Peterson is coauthoring a book titled *God-talk: A Guide for the Perplexed* (T&T Clark).

Harry Lee Poe (PhD) serves as Charles Colson Professor of Faith and Culture at Union University and as president of the Poe Museum of Richmond. He has written numerous books and articles on how the Gospel intersects with culture, including *Christianity in the Academy*, *The Gospel and Its Meaning*, and *God and the Cosmos*.

Jorge A. Ponce holds a DMin from Dallas Theological Seminary. He is professor of management and leadership in the Central American Theological Seminary (Guatemala) and also an adjunct professor and offers lectures in several universities. Having worked for Compassion International, Ponce has many years of experience in social development.

Anca Popescu is a lecturer in the Faculty of Orthodox Theology at Bucharest University (Romania) and has a doctoral degree in English literature. Having studied in Oxford and Paris, Popescu teaches theological terminology in English and is a translator of English books of theology and sacred art.

S. Brian Pounds (PhD candidate, University of Cambridge) is a guest instructor in the Department of Religion at the University of Georgia. He specializes in the quest for the historical Jesus and has published in the field of New Testament studies.

Ronnie Prevost (PhD, New Orleans Baptist Theological Seminary) is professor of church ministry at the Logsdon Seminary of Hardin-Simmons University. Past president of the Religious Education Association, he coauthored *A History of Christian Education* (Broadman, 1993), *Evangelical Protestant Gifts to Religious Education* (Smyth & Helwys, 2000), and *A Distinctively Baptist Church* (Smyth & Helwys, 2008).

Ian Randall is a senior research fellow at Spurgeon's College, London, and at the International Baptist Theological Seminary, Prague. He is the author of a number of books and many articles about evangelical movements. He lives in Cambridge, United Kingdom.

Todd C. Ream (PhD, Penn State University) is an associate professor of humanities and the senior scholar for faith and scholarship in the John Wesley Honors College at Indiana Wesleyan University. His most recent book (coauthored with Perry L. Glanzer) is *The Idea of a Christian College: A Reexamination for Today's University*.

Stacie Reck (PhD, University of Alberta) is assistant professor of education at Crandall University (Moncton, New Brunswick). She teaches undergraduate and graduate level courses in education. Reck's research interests include Christian education curriculum, issues of diversity, science, and social studies pedagogy.

Joshua D. Reichard (PhD, EdS) is the academic dean at Youngstown Christian School (Ohio), an urban, multicultural, K–12 Christian school serving more than 500 students.

Sara M. Reichard (EdS, RN) is the director of gifted education at Youngstown Christian School (Ohio), an urban, multicultural, K–12 Christian school serving more than 500 students.

Patrick Bruner Reyes is completing his PhD in practical theology/religious education at Claremont School of Theology. As a social activist and religious educator, his research consists of constructing a decolonial Latino/a and Hispanic practical theology and investigating theological responses to trauma and violence.

Adam J. Richards (MSEd, LPCC) is a licensed professional clinical counselor and a special education consultant for Christian schools, having served as the chief special education officer of the Summit Academy charter school system in Ohio.

Lawrence O. Richards (PhD) is an educator and author of over 200 books, including textbooks on Christian education, commentaries, and study Bibles. His works include *Theology of Christian Education, Creative Bible Teaching*, and the best-selling *Teen Study Bible* (Zondervan), of which more than four million copies have been sold.

Jennifer Riley (MA, Acadia Divinity College) is a pastor and educator in the African Canadian community in Nova Scotia, Canada. She is presently developing culturally sensitive curricula for Christian formation and exploring the pedagogical role of culturally specific ritual in the African United Baptist tradition.

Amanda J. Rockinson-Szapkiw (EdD, distance education, Regent University) has worked in higher education for more than five years and previously served as a teacher and counselor. She has published more than 30 peer-reviewed articles and paper presentations. Her research interests include distance education, quantitative research methods, and third culture kids.

Theresa Roco Lua (PhD) is dean and professor for the Asia Graduate School of Theology, based in the Philippines, a consortium of seminaries offering post-MDiv programs. She has recently been appointed secretary for accreditation and educational development for the Asia Theological Association, which has 270 member schools from 32 nations.

Nigel Rooms is director of ministry and mission for the Anglican Diocese of Southwell and Nottingham, England, and associate priest at Bestwood Park with Rise Park Anglican-Methodist Churches. He holds a master's degree from Nottingham University and a ThD from Birmingham University. He has worked as a priest and Christian adult educator in Tanzania and the United Kingdom. Since 2010, he has edited the *Journal of Adult Theological Education*.

Viktor J. Rózsa (MDiv, Asbury Theological Seminary) is a missionary with One Mission Society. His areas of ministry are Christian education, youth, young adult, and campus ministries.

Ivan Rusin serves as a rector of Ukrainian Evangelical Theological Seminary and holds an MTh from Wales University. He is actively involved in mission work to Muslims in Central Asia and Crimea. Rusin is also a head of Euro-Asian Diaspora Study Center and New Horizons Mission Organization.

George F. Sabra is Lebanese and professor of systematic theology and president of the Near East School of Theology. He holds a BA in philosophy from American University in Beirut; an MDiv from Princeton Theological Seminary; an MA in medieval studies from the Pontifical Institute of Medieval Studies, Toronto University; and a DrTheol from the Faculty of Theology in the University of Tübingen, Germany.

Martha Saint-Berberian is a multifaceted person, with experience in Sunday school and university teaching, as well as publishing a dozen books. She was born in New Jersey and raised in Argentina, and she and her husband train leaders in Guatemala. She has a BA in theology and a master's in pastoral theology.

V. J. Samkutty (BSc, Kerala University; BD, Union Biblical Seminary, Pune; MTh, United Theological College, Bangalore; PCHE and PhD, The University of Sheffield) is the undergraduate program leader and tutor in New Testament and Greek at All Nations Christian College (England). He is the author of *The Samaritan Mission in Acts*, LNTS 328 (Continuum: T&T Clark, 2006).

Paul R. Sanders served at the Nogent Bible Institute near Paris and the Arab Baptist Theological Seminary in Beirut. He led the European (EEAA), Middle Eastern (MEATE), and international (ICETE) networks of evangelical theological institutions. He holds the *doctorat* in modern history from the Sorbonne and lives in Nantes, France.

Olga Schihalejev is a senior lecturer and a researcher at Tartu University, Faculty of Theology, Estonia. She has worked as an educator in church and schools and has written teaching-learning resources. Her research focuses on how religion and religious diversity are perceived by young people, contextuality of attitudes to religion, and religious education didactics.

Muriel Schmid is assistant professor of comparative literary and cultural studies and director of religious studies at the University of Utah. Prior to this, she taught systematic and practical theology at the University of Neuchâtel (Switzerland). Her research interests include French literature and biblical themes, history of punishment and Christian roots of the penitentiary, secularism in 18th-century France, and religious peacemaking and interfaith dialogue. Schmid is an ordained minister in the Swiss Reformed Church.

Alvin J. Schmidt, born and reared in Canada, is a former member of the Royal Canadian Mounted Police. He has an MDiv from Concordia Seminary and a PhD from the University of Nebraska. Schmidt is the author of numerous journal and encyclopedia articles, plus eight books, including *How Christianity Changed the World* (2004) and *The American Muhammad: Joseph Smith, Founder of Mormonism* (2013).

Francis Schmidt is a missionary with Camino Global. He served in El Salvador from 1993 to 2006, working in church planting, theological education, and missions mobilization among Salvadoran evangelical churches. Since 2006, Schmidt and his family have lived in Guatemala, where he teaches at the Central American Theological Seminary. He is a graduate of Dallas Theological Seminary (MTh).

Laura Schmidt has been archivist at the Marion E. Wade Center, Wheaton College (Illinois) since 2005. She is knowledgeable about all seven of the Wade authors, with a particular concentration on Tolkien. She has published "Using Archives: A Guide to Effective Research" (2011).

Peter Schreiner (PhD, VU University of Amsterdam and Friedrich-Alexander University Erlangen-Nurenberg) is senior researcher at the Comenius-Institut in Münster (Germany), Protestant Centre for Research and Development in Education. He is president of the Intereuropean Commission on Church and School and an expert at the Council of Europe in the field of intercultural education. Schreiner's latest book is *Religion im Kontext einer Europäisierung von Bildung* (Münster, 2012).

Bernd Schröder (PhD, Free University Berlin; habilitation thesis, Münster) is professor in practical theology and religious education at Georg-August-University Göttingen (Germany). He has published in the field of comparative and historical religious education. Schröder's latest book is a comprehensive textbook, *Religionspädagogik* (Tübingen, 2012).

Roger Schroeder (DMiss, Gregorian Pontifical University, Rome) is professor of intercultural studies and ministry at Catholic Theological Union of Chicago and a Roman Catholic priest of the Society of the Divine Word (SVD). He has authored several books on mission theology and history and served for six years as a missionary in Papua New Guinea.

Katherine G. Schultz is an adjunct professor of graduate education at Indiana Wesleyan University, where she teaches courses in curriculum development and education leadership. She also serves as associate headmaster at a K–12 classical Christian school in Minnesota. Her research interests include student worldview development and Christian K–12 education.

Tom Schwanda (PhD, Durham University) is associate professor of Christian formation and ministry at Wheaton College. Before teaching full time, he was a pastor for 18 years. He is the author of *Soul Recreation: The Contemplative–Mystical Piety of Puritanism* (Pickwick, 2012) and is completing a volume on 18th-century evangelical spirituality for Paulist Press's Classics of Western Spirituality series (2014).

Halee Gray Scott (PhD) is an author and global leadership researcher who focuses on issues related to leadership and spiritual formation. Her book, *Dare Mighty Things: Mapping the Challenges of Leadership for Christian Women*, reveals her decade-long research on female Christian leaders. She teaches seminary courses in spiritual formation, theology, and leadership.

W. George Selig (EdD) received his BA and MA degrees from Central Washington State College and his doctorate from the University of Massachusetts. He is currently the distinguished professor of educational leadership at Regent University. He has served as dean of the School of Education and provost of the university. He has written on parenting, relationships, and individual differences.

Perry W. H. Shaw (EdD) is professor of Christian education at the Arab Baptist Theological Seminary in Beirut, Lebanon, and serves as a curriculum and faculty development consultant to regional theological schools and local church ministries throughout Asia, Africa, Europe, and the Middle East.

Donald R. Shepson III (PhD) is associate professor of ministry, leadership, and spiritual formation, Toccoa Falls College (Georgia). He enjoys training people for ministry and encouraging healthy spiritual growth throughout the church. Shepson is an Anglican priest of the Province de l'Eglise Anglicane au Rwanda, a subjurisdiction of the Anglican Church in North America.

Candace C. Shields holds a PhD in practical theology from Fuller Theological Seminary in Pasadena, California, and serves as the bishop of education for the Churches of Faith in Christ Fellowship in Indio, California. She also pastors Twice Called Christian Center in San Bernardino with her husband, Bishop Henry C. Shields.

Ivanas Shkulis has been the president of Vilnius Theological College (Lithuania) since 1995 and is the first deputy bishop of the Union of Pentecostal Churches of Lithuania. He graduated from Vilnius Electromechanical College as an engineer-electrician, and in 1982 he started his theological education at Moscow Theological Seminary. Shkulis has a DMin and is married to Olga, with whom he has three sons and four grandchildren.

John Shortt (PhD) is a professorial fellow in Christian education at Liverpool Hope University. He was until recently coeditor of *Journal of Education & Christian Belief*, traveling secretary for the European Educators' Christian Association, and adjunct professor at Calvin College (Michigan).

Natalia A. Shulgina (MDiv, ThM) is an ordained elder in the Russian United Methodist Church and a PhD candidate in The Person, Community, and Religious Life Program at Emory University (Georgia). Her primary areas of scholarship include practical theology, pastoral care, and religious education, with a special interest in the issues of spiritual formation and contemplative monastic spirituality.

Binsen Samuel Sidjabat (EdD, Asia Graduate School of Theology, Manila, Philippines) is lecturer of Christian education at Tyranus Bible College, Bandung, Indonesia. He has authored several books on Christian education in Indonesia and is interested in character formation in religious education.

Cate Siejk (PhD, theology and education, Boston College) has been a professor in the Religious Studies De-

partment and the Women's and Gender Studies Program at Gonzaga University since 1991. Her scholarly interests include foundational issues in religious education and feminist theory and theologies. Several of her articles have been published in the *Journal of Religious Education*.

Jeremy P. Sienkiewicz is assistant professor of theology at Benedictine College in Atchison, Kansas, where he teaches liturgical theology, missiology, and systematics. He received his PhD in systematic theology from The Catholic University of America.

Claire Annelise Smith (PhD, Union Presbyterian Seminary) is director of theology and youth ministry specialist-in-residence at Saint Paul School of Theology (Missouri). She is a member of the Religious Education Association and serves on the Board of the Association of Youth Ministry Educators. She coedited *Youth Ministry in a Technological Age*.

Yolanda Yvette Smith (PhD) serves as associate professor, research scholar, and lecturer of Christian education at Yale Divinity School. She is the author of *Reclaiming the Spirituals: New Possibilities for African American Christian Education*. Her forthcoming book is titled *Women's Spirituality and Education in the Black Church*.

Brenda A. Snailum is associate faculty at Denver Seminary in Littleton, Colorado, and has over 20 years' experience in family ministry. She received an EdD in educational studies from Talbot School of Theology, an MA in youth and family ministry from Denver Seminary, and a BS in organizational management and Christian leadership from Colorado Christian University.

Joanna Feliciano-Soberano (PhD, educational studies, Trinity International University, Illinois) is professor and chair of the Christian Education Department at Asian Theological Seminary (Manila, the Philippines). Her doctoral thesis explored the epistemological frameworks of Filipino students at ATS and their contextual and pedagogical implications. She also serves as an associate with Global Associates for Transformational Education.

Timothy D. Son (EdD) has been assistant professor of Christian education and youth ministry at Pittsburgh Theological Seminary since 2005. He served 14 years as a pastor in Presbyterian churches. Son received a bachelor's from Cornell University, MDiv/ThM from Princeton Theological Seminary, and a doctorate at Teachers College, Columbia University (New York).

Lucinda S. Spaulding earned her PhD in special education and educational psychology, MEd in special education, and BS in elementary education. She has taught general and special education in the United States and English as a Second Language in Japan. She teaches at Liberty University and resides in Lynchburg, Virginia, with her husband and three children.

Keith Springer received an MDiv from Nazarene Theological Seminary (Missouri) and a DMin from Northern Baptist Seminary (Illinois). For the past 23 years, he has served as a professor at Indiana Wesleyan University, teaching Christian education and Bible and directing the Christian education and children's ministry majors. Before that he served as a pastor and minister of Christian education for 17 years.

Tadej Stegu is an assistant professor at Faculty of Theology, University of Ljubljana, and secretary general of catechetical office in the Archdiocese of Ljubljana, Slovenia. His research explores religious education, especially adult religious education and adult catechesis in the context of new evangelization.

Sophia R. G. Steibel (PhD) has been professor of Christian education at the Gardner-Webb University School of Divinity (North Carolina) since 2001. Before that she taught at Baptist theological schools in Rio de Janeiro (south Brazil) and was director of Campinas Baptist Theological School (Campinas, SP, Brazil).

John Stewart (MTS, EdD, University of Toronto) is a professor emeritus from the Faculty of Education in the University of New Brunswick, Canada. As an educator and academic, he has 42 years of teaching experience and has authored 31 refereed journal articles, five book chapters, and two books. His interests lie in Christian spiritual formation.

Gary D. Stratton (BA, Wheaton College, Minzu University China, Shanghai Normal University; MA, PhD, Talbot Theological Seminary) is chair of the Christian Ministries Department, Bethel University (Minnesota). He is a senior fellow, The Association for Biblical Higher Education, and senior editor, TwoHandedWarriors.com. His dissertation is "The Holy Spirit and the Liberal Arts: Jonathan Edwards' Spirituality and American Higher Education Leadership."

Nelson T. Strobert (PhD, University of Akron; MA, John Carroll University; MDiv, Lutheran Theological Seminary at Gettysburg; BA, Hunter College, CUNY) is professor emeritus of religious education at the Lutheran Theological Seminary at Gettysburg. He has published in various areas of religious education. Strobert is the au-

thor of *Daniel Alexander Payne: The Venerable Preceptor of the African Methodist Episcopal Church*.

John Sullivan is professor of Christian education at Liverpool Hope University (United Kingdom) and has taught in secondary schools, universities, and parishes. Author or editor of seven books and 70 chapters on religion and education, his special interest is exploring factors that contribute to the effective communication of Christian faith.

Agneta Sutton (PhD) lectures in bioethics at Heythrop College, University of London. She is a fellow at the Center for Bioethics and Human Dignity attached to Trinity International University, Deerfield, Illinois. Sutton is also a member of the Editorial Consultancy Board of *Ethics and Medicine*. She served on the Executive Committee of the European Association of Centres of Medical Ethics between 1997 and 2002.

Marit Hallset Svare is assistant professor teaching religious education for students of early childhood education at Queen Maud University College, Trondheim, Norway. Her main interest is religious education for the very young in a diverse society.

James A. Swezey (EdD) is an associate professor of graduate education at Liberty University (Virginia), where he teaches courses in the history and philosophy of education and education leadership. His research interests include school culture, student worldview development, and Christian higher education.

Pablo Sywulka, son of missionary parents to Guatemala, is a graduate of Columbia International University and Dallas Theological Seminary. He has served since 1967 at the Central American Theological Seminary/SETECA in Guatemala. Pablo is president emeritus of SETECA and general secretary of AETAL, the Latin American Association of Evangelical Theological Schools.

Charles Taliaferro (PhD) is professor of philosophy, St. Olaf College (Minnesota) and the author, coauthor, or editor of 20 books, including *The Image in Mind* (Continuum) coauthored with Jil Evans, and *Turning Images* (Oxford University Press), coedited with Jil Evans. He has given lectures at Oxford, Cambridge, Princeton, and Yale.

Pieter F. Theron (PhD, University of Pretoria, South Africa) is a South African serving in Mongolia as the director of the Christian Leadership Training Center in Darhan. Previously he served in Zambia and the Philippines. Theron has many years of intercultural experience in theological education and leadership development.

Yvonne Thigpen is president of Evangelical Training Association. She earned her MA in educational ministries from Wheaton College (Illinois). She is a 40-year veteran in teaching ministries for evangelical churches. Her skills include curriculum development, administration, and collaborative projects that further God's Kingdom.

Jacqulyn Brown Thorpe received a BA in English literature from Fisk University and a master's of religious education from Wesley Theological Seminary. She has served as adjunct faculty at Howard University School of Divinity and Wesley Theological Seminary. Thorpe is an author and is ordained in the United Methodist Church.

Jeffrey Tirrell is an adjunct instructor at Azusa Pacific University (California) and a PhD candidate at the Claremont School of Theology. He holds an MA in biblical studies and theology from Fuller Theological Seminary and has extensive experience studying, working, and performing in live theater. He and his wife live in the Los Angeles area.

Shelley Trebesch (MDiv, PhD, Fuller Theological Seminary) is assistant professor of leadership and organization development at Fuller Theological Seminary (California). Her research and writing topics include organizational leadership, leadership and culture, and multinational capacity development.

Katherine Turpin (PhD, Emory University, Georgia) is associate professor of religious education at the Iliff School of Theology (Colorado). She is the author of *Branded: Adolescents Converting from Consumer Culture* (Pilgrim Press, 2006) and several publications in the fields of youth ministry and practical theology.

Samuel Twumasi-Ankrah (EdD, Biola University) is president and senior lecturer in practical theology of Heritage Christian College (Ghana). He has pastored and planted churches in various countries throughout West Africa for the past 29 years.

John Valk (PhD) is professor of worldview studies at Renaissance College, University of New Brunswick, Canada. He has presented papers at various national and international conferences and published in various academic journals and books. He is a visiting professor at the Protestant University Darmstadt (Germany) and a distinguished fellow at the University of South Africa (Pretoria).

Kirk A. VanGilder (PhD, Boston University) is assistant professor of religion at Gallaudet University in Washington, D.C. His book *Making Sadza with Deaf Zimbabwean Women* seeks to reorient practical theological methodology by bringing it into dialogue with deaf studies.

Gene Edward Veith (PhD) is provost and professor of literature at Patrick Henry College (Virginia). He is the author of 18 books on Christianity and culture, classical education, literature, and the arts. He previously served as culture editor of *World Magazine* and as dean of the School of Arts and Sciences at Concordia University, Wisconsin.

Hugo Verkest is senior lecturer at the University College VIVES campus Torhout (Flanders, Belgium). He is co-author and editor of several religious education manuals for primary and secondary education and has published articles in scholarly European journals. Since 2004 he has been an executive board member of the European Forum for Teachers of Religious Education (www.eftre.net).

Wolfgang Vondey is associate professor of systematic theology at Regent University School of Divinity. His research focuses on the work of the Holy Spirit in the church and in the world, and his publications cover topics such as Pentecostalism, ecumenical theology, the theology and science conversation, and the pneumatological orientation of contemporary theology.

Kevin E. Voss practiced veterinary medicine in Wisconsin for 14 years, then earned his MDiv from Concordia Seminary, Saint Louis. He has also received a PhD in health care ethics from Saint Louis University. Voss is director of the Concordia Center for Bioethics at Concordia University, Wisconsin, where he teaches bioethics, medical ethics, and philosophy courses.

Anton C. Vrame (PhD) is director of the Department of Religious Education of the Greek Orthodox Archdiocese of America, under the Ecumenical Patriarchate of Constantinople. He is also adjunct associate professor of religious education at Holy Cross Greek Orthodox School of Theology, Brookline, Massachusetts.

Tharwat Wahba earned a PhD from the London School of Theology. His dissertation was on the history of Presbyterian mission in Egypt and Sudan. Wahba is professor of mission and evangelism and the chair of the mission department at Evangelical Theological Seminary, Cairo.

Steve Walton professorial research fellow in New Testament, St. Mary's University, Twickenham (London), UK; Hon Research Fellow, Tyndale House, Cambridge, UK

Lee Wanak went to the Philippines in 1978, where he trained rural lay church leaders in Mindanao and directed church planting efforts. Later he served as dean of Asian Theological Seminary and Asia Graduate School of Theology. He has written several articles on Philippine theological education. While at ATS and AGST, he directed the MA in transformational urban leadership and the EdD programs.

David C. Ward (DPhil, ThM) teaches faith-learning integration and Christian interdisciplinary studies at Oxford Graduate School and serves on the faculty of Bryan College (both in Dayton, Tennessee).

Mary Carter Waren (DMin, Barry University; dissertation, marriage annulment) is associate professor in practical theology at St. Thomas University in Miami, Florida. She is a recognized religious educator at the local, university, and national levels and has worked extensively and published in the area of Catholic Identity.

Angela L. Watson is a graduate professor in the School of Education at Oklahoma Wesleyan University. She earned her BSE in English from Arkansas State University, her MA in public school administration from Oral Roberts University, and her PhD in educational psychology from Oklahoma State University.

Edward W. Watson currently serves as professor of biblical literature and practical theology in the Graduate College of Theology and Ministry at Oral Roberts University. Edward attained his MA in biblical literature from ORU, his ThM in New Testament from Duke University, and his PhD in biblical literature from Baylor University.

Theodore James Whapham (PhD) is assistant professor of historical and systematic theology and director of master's degree programs at St. Thomas University's School of Theology and Ministry (Florida). He has published in the areas of Trinitarian theology and fundamental theology. He is the author of "Person" in the *Trinitarian Theology of Wolfhart Pannenberg* and a forthcoming volume, *The Unity of Theology.*

Michael W. Wheeler (BA, ThM, PhD) is a professor of New Testament at the Seminario Bíblico de al UCE in Cochabamba, Bolivia, where has taught for over 20 years. He serves as a missionary with SIM.

Wendy Widder has a PhD in Near Eastern studies from the University of the Free State (South Africa), an MA from the University of Wisconsin–Madison, and an MDiv in educational ministries from Grand Rapids Theological Seminary. She is coauthor of *The Forest and the Trees: Helping Teachers Integrate a Biblical Worldview across the Curriculum.*

Timothy P. Wiens is an assistant professor of education at Wheaton College. He has served as an educator in public and independent K–12 schools and higher education. Wiens currently cochairs Vanderbilt University's Peabody Professional Institute for Independent School Leadership and is the executive director of the Council on Educational Standards and Accountability.

Metta M. Wierenga teaches at the Evangelisch College in Zwijndrecht (The Netherlands) and is also attached to other parachurch organizations, teaching in churches and interchurch groups. She studied for her master's of theology and religious studies (church and pastoral ministries) in Ede (The Netherlands) and Leuven (Belgium).

Susan Willhauck (PhD, The Catholic University of America) is an associate professor of pastoral theology at the Atlantic School of Theology (Halifax, Nova Scotia). She has published in *Religious Education, Teaching Theology and Religion*, and the *International Journal of Practical Theology*, among other periodicals. She is the author of *The Web of Women's Leadership, Backtalk! Women Leaders Changing the Church, Ministry Unplugged*, and *Women Pastoring Large Churches.*

Myron Williams (PhD, curriculum and instruction, Michigan State University), as part of his work as global outreach development pastor at Southland Christian Church in Lexington, Kentucky, teaches at TCMI, a graduate theological school based in Heiligenkreuz, Austria, and also in Meulaboh, Indonesia, in the Penyang District.

Marvin R. Wilson is the Ockenga Professor of Biblical Studies at Gordon College, Wenham, Massachusetts. He holds the BA from Wheaton (Illinois), MDiv from Gordon-Conwell Theological Seminary, and MA and PhD from Brandeis University. Wilson's teaching career spans more than 50 years. He is the author of *Our Father Abraham* (Eerdmans), a widely used textbook on the Jewish roots of Christianity.

Elizabeth Leggett Windsor (MDiv/DMin, Episcopal Divinity School) is director of Christian education at Sudbury United Methodist Church (Massachusetts) and Christian education consultant to the bishop, New England Conference of the United Methodist Church. She is an instructional designer/online facilitator for United Methodist Communications.

Stephen L. Woodworth (DMin) is the director of spiritual formation at Toccoa Falls College (Georgia) as well as the associate coordinator of the International Theological Education Network (ITEN). His academic interests and research have focused on homiletics, pastoral identity, ministerial metaphors, and faith development.

Janet Wootton (PhD) has been director of learning and development for the Congregational Federation since 2003. Having ministered in rural and urban churches for nearly 25 years, she cochairs the International Congregational Theological Commission and is involved in editing the *International Congregational Journal*. Wootton is also the editor and author of resources in feminist theology, hymnology, worship, and mission.

Howard Worsley is senior lecturer in Christian education at Canterbury Christchurch University. His ongoing research interest considers how children access faith and children's insights into the Bible. He also researches and writes about church schools in the United Kingdom and recently edited the book *Anglican Church School Education* (2012).

Marcin Wysocki (PhD, theology; MA, classics, John Paul II Catholic University of Lublin), is assistant professor in patrology at the John Paul II Catholic University of Lublin (Poland). He has published in the field of patristics and patrology, especially in eschatology and persecutions.

Steve Yates lives in Lancaster, Pennsylvania, with his wife Lisa, and his children, James, Raymond, and Lauren. He enjoys running, reading, new technology, and playing with his chocolate lab. He serves as pastor of community life at Calvary Church. He completed his PhD at The Southern Baptist Theological Seminary, studying leadership and Christian higher education.

Darrell Yoder (MDiv, Grand Rapids Theological Seminary) is adjunct professor and Kern Scholars Program director at Grand Rapids Theological Seminary (Michigan). While also serving as a nonstaff pastor at his local church, he works to train future pastors who are faithful to scripture, passionate about Christ's mission, and equipped to serve with humility and authenticity.

Habil Yousif (ThM, Jordan Evangelical Theological Seminary) is a former academic dean and professor of New Testament at JETS and is currently associate pastor to the Shadow Mountain Community Church/Arabic Ministry in El Cajon, San Diego, California. He is in the PhD program at Evangelical Theological Faculty (Leuven, Belgium).

Valerie G. Zahirsky is chair of the Department of Christian Education of the Orthodox Church in America. She is a graduate of the Claremont Graduate School in California (MA) and of St. Vladimir's Orthodox Seminary (MDiv). She has represented the Orthodox Church at several international meetings and writes curriculum for Orthodox schools in the United States, Middle East, and Eastern Europe.

Marian Zając is a professor at John Paul II University of Lublin (Poland) and head of the Department of Fundamental Catechetics. His research interests include the history of religious education and catechetics. Zając cooperates with the University of Trnava, the Faculty of Humanities, the University in Ružomberok (Slovakia), and the Theological Institute in Lviv (Ukraine). He is the author of scientific articles and books.

Roman Zaviyskyy is the dean of the Faculty of Philosophy and Theology at Ukrainian Catholic University and holds a doctorate in theology from the University of Oxford. His interests lie in systematic theology, including modern Eastern Orthodox theology; patristics; ecumenism; and the engagement between theology and modernity.

Daniella Zsupan-Jerome (PhD) is assistant professor of liturgy, catechesis, and evangelization at Loyola Institute for Ministry at Loyola University (New Orleans). She holds a bachelor's in theology from the University of Notre Dame, a master's in liturgy from St. John's University, a master's in religion and arts from Yale Divinity School, and a PhD in theology and education from Boston College. Her research explores media and ministry and its potential for catechetical formation.